# DISTRICT OF COLUMBIA MARRIAGE LICENSES

## Register 2: 1858–1870

*Wesley E. Pippenger*

HERITAGE BOOKS
2012

# HERITAGE BOOKS
*AN IMPRINT OF HERITAGE BOOKS, INC.*

### Books, CDs, and more—Worldwide

For our listing of thousands of titles see our website at
www.HeritageBooks.com

Published 2012 by
HERITAGE BOOKS, INC.
Publishing Division
100 Railroad Ave. #104
Westminster, Maryland 21157

Copyright © 1996 Wesley E. Pippenger

All rights reserved. No part of this book may be reproduced or transmitted in any form or by any means, electronic or mechanical, including photocopying, recording or by any information storage and retrieval system without written permission from the author, except for the inclusion of brief quotations in a review.

International Standard Book Numbers
Paperbound: 978-1-888265-17-0
Clothbound: 978-0-7884-9218-4

**DEDICATED**

TO

DOROTHY S. PROVINE

# INTRODUCTION

The provision for keeping a public record of marriages is not widely documented during the 1790's while the District of Columbia was being developed. Basic powers which were exercised by similar courts in Maryland were used as the basis for establishing a system in the District of Columbia. In 1812, the terms of an act to amend the charter for the City of Washington outlined that the duties of the court were to provide for recording births, deaths and marriages.

In March 1993, the earliest extant marriage records were moved from the Marriage Bureau of the District of Columbia's Superior Court to the Archives. In effect, the transfer rescued the surviving documents from further destruction by careless users. Some of the older pages are brittle, and others are now without portions which once contained information.

This volume contains about 18,259 marriage records which were kept in the District of Columbia from September 1858 through mid-June 1870. What is presented here is all information found in "Marriage Register 2" that covers the same period: name of groom, name of bride, date. It was not until 1870 that the format of information found in marriage records here was changed, and 1874 when additional information about the parties was documented. Marriage Register 2 is of particular value to local historians because it represents a jurisdiction, contrary to others in the area, which issued licenses continuously throughout the Civil War era. The number of records seems staggering; for example, 2,072 licenses were issued for 1864 alone. This seemingly large quantity makes one wonder if the issuing office had a revolving door. A summary of the number of licenses issued is as follows:

| | | | | | |
|---|---|---|---|---|---|
| 1858 (part) | 358 | 1863 | 1,833 | 1868 | 1,715 |
| 1859 | 918 | 1864 | 2,072 | 1869 | 1,575 |
| 1860 | 826 | 1865 | 2,065 | 1870 (part) | 643 |
| 1861 | 933 | 1866 | 2,012 | | |
| 1862 | 1,396 | 1867 | 1,913 | TOTAL: | 18,259 |

Some uncertainty may exist as to how and for what purpose the extant register was created. It occasionally contains records of seemingly duplicate events but with dates which differ from several days to many months. A few notations are found to indicate that an earlier license was not used and a new one was issued. After studying church records and newspaper announcements, we know that the register is comprised of entries of when a marriage license was issued. Overall, one can expect that the actual date of marriage occurred at least a few days after the license date given here. Several notations indicate particular licenses as recorded were not issued at all. Clues found in the National Archives confirm that marriage licenses were issued in the District of Columbia during this period. Just what happened to most of these licenses cannot be determined, as only a few are known to exist today. The register is noted on the page which begins June 1870: *By Act of Congress, approved June 1, 1870, terms of issuing Licenses changed-- see New Record of Licenses, Clk.*

In addition to the register, the only other public record of marriages which can now be found to cover this period is an index. The index completely duplicates the register, and it is sorted alphabetically by the name of both the groom and bride. Nearly all of it appears in the same handwriting, and contains about 890 pages that cross-reference all marriages. This compiler created the present work by typing directly from the register. The result was compared and noted to local church records, then it was sorted alphabetically and compared to the index.

One might characterize the register as being a jumble of phonetic puzzles. It contains many names which are seemingly impossible or poorly spelled, e.g. Washington Front Royal, Cotiglia Ratta, or Anabile Samuele. To preserve the integrity of the original record, the spelling presented in this volume is as close to the original as can be interpreted by the compiler. Therefore, users are cautioned to consider and search for any and every possible spelling of a surname. It would be worthwhile for researchers to consult the *National Intelligencer* newspaper, as it often contains valuable genealogical information.

Some notations have been made in brackets "[ ]" by the compiler, and these typically involve personal titles of the bride or groom, e.g., Capt., Col., Dr., Hon., Lt., Maj., Mrs., Sen., or insertion of missing information. Where damage to the register has occurred, the term [torn out] is used in this volume as it impacts a record entry. No explanation is made in the register for marriage records where the name of the groom or bride is either incomplete or missing. The lack of this type of information is noted by the term [blank]. Questionable characters are underscored in the text. The register's references to black persons (blk) or colored persons (col'd) have been preserved here.

Several extraneous notes in the register are of interest:
March 4, 1865: "Inauguration Day"
April 14, 1865: "Assassination of Abraham Lincoln, President of the United States, at Ford's Theater, at 10:30 p.m."
April 19, 1865: "Funeral of the late Abraham Lincoln, President of the United States!!!"

An unusual number of marriage licenses are recorded for March 3, 1863. Immediately following this sequence is a note for March 22: "This day R.J. Meigs, new appointed Clerk of the Supreme Court of the District of Columbia assumed duty of the office, R.J.M., Jr." Licenses resume on March 23, 1863.

An asterisk (*) after the groom entry indicates the original license is found at the National Archives, Washington, D.C., Record Group 21, "District of Columbia Marriage Records," Marriage Licenses, September 1836-October 1838, and May 1840-December 1862.

I am indebted to archivist Dorothy S. Provine whose generosity in providing photocopies of the register and index has literally made this work possible.

Wesley E. Pippenger
Arlington, Virginia

## ALTERNATE RECORD SOURCES

Abstracts of marriage records exist for a number of area churches. Many of these are found at the library of the Daughters of the American Revolution, in Washington, D.C. Entries in this transcription of Register 2 have been annotated with a number in brackets to signify at which church or by which minister the marriage is determined to have occurred. Explanation of these is given below.

[1]  Dumbarton Avenue Methodist Episcopal Church, Georgetown, D.C. [1c] by William H. Chapman (1862-1864), and [1e] by William B. Edwards.
[2]  Grace Protestant Episcopal Church, Georgetown, D.C., 1864-1870.
[3]  St. John's Episcopal Church, Georgetown, D.C., 1858-1867.
[4]  St. John's Church, St. John's Parish, Washington, D.C., 1858-1870.
[5]  St. Paul's Lutheran Church, Washington, D.C., 1866-1870.
[6]  Trinity Methodist Church, Washington, D.C., 1858-1870. [6c] by William H. Chapman; [6cl] W.T.D. Clemm; [6h] W.H. Holliday; [6le] Geo. V. Leech; [6r] by W.M.D. Ryan; [6l] by John Lanahan; [6m] by T.H.W. Monroe; H.N. Sipes [6s]
[7]  Wesley Methodist Church, Washington, D.C., 1866-1870. [7a] by A.H. Ames; [7b] B. Peyton Brown.
[8]  Westminster Church, 7th Street near E, S.W., Washington, D.C., 1868-1870.
[9]  Foundry Methodist Episcopal Church. [9n] by B.H. Nadal; [9e] by Wm. G. Edwards.
[10] Christ Church, Washington Parish, 1858-1870.
[11] Church of the Epiphany, 1869-1870. [11s] by T.A. Starkey; [11j] by Curtis P. Jones; and [11h] by C.H. Hall.
[12] First Presbyterian Church, John Marshall Place, N.W. [12s] by Dr. Sunderland; and [12n] by J.P. Newman.
[13] Fifteenth Street Presbyterian Church (colored). Sessional minutes published by the Columbian Harmony Society. [13g] by Rev. Henry H. Garnet; [13t] by Benj. T. Tanner; and [13c] by William T. Catto.

## ADDITIONAL RECORDS

Marriages which were noted in church records and were not linked to a marriage license in Register 2 are listed below

| | | |
|---|---|---|
| AMBROSE, Michael [4] | RAGAN, Mary | 06 JUN 1862 |
| COOKE, John B. [6c] | WOOLFORD, Emily | 16 SEP 1858 |
| PIERCE, Godurn [6l] | GORRELL, Mary | 28 MAY 1861 |
| SIMONDS, John R. [6c] | ASH, Sarah C. | 27 OCT 1858 |
| STAUGHAN, John [12s] | OATES, Sarah | 14 MAY 1860 |
| TALBERT, George W. [6r] | NOKES, Mary E. | 14 FEB 1861 |
| YOUNG, Amazi B. [4] | MARSTON, Mary S. | 15 NOV 1860 |

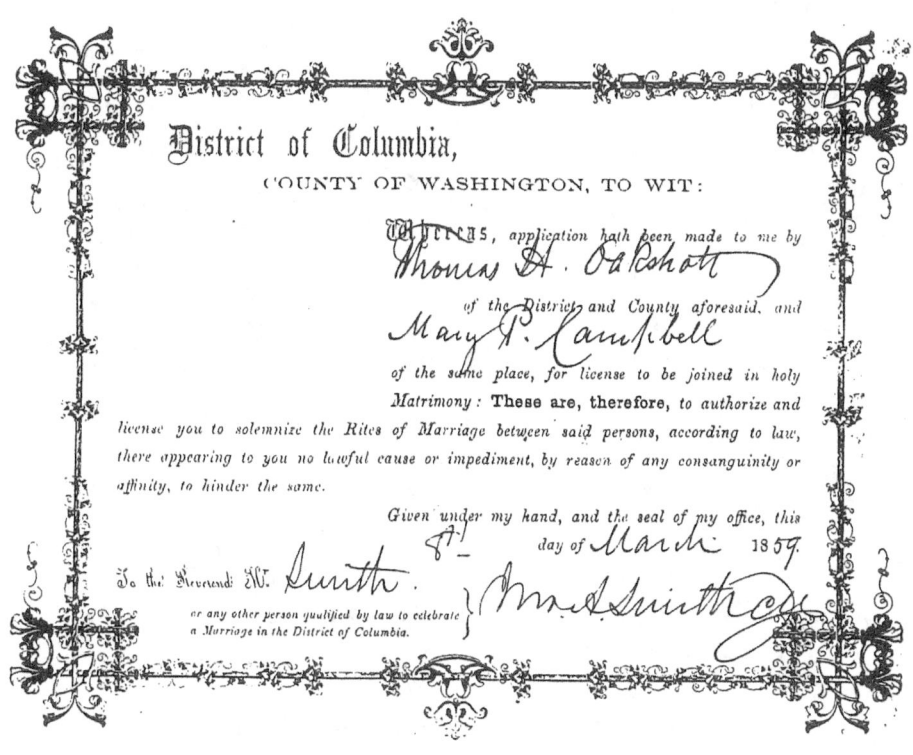

Figure 1 - Sample Marriage License

1860

| | | |
|---|---|---|
| Nov 14 | Patrick McHaggarty | Mary Ann Dwyer |
| " | 15 Lewis B. Place | Mary L. O'Brien |
| " | " Michael Butler | Marie Fitzgerald |
| " | " James King | Martha Reynolds (Blk) |
| " | " Richard E. Sinclair | Mary Jane Tidts |
| " | 16 James T. Sheckels | Elizabeth King |
| " | 17 Robert T. Mays | Martha V. Hogan |
| " | " Theodore Klahring | Emma Maria Rau |
| " | " John Getz Hoofnagle | Eleanor C. Mitchell |
| " | " Henry H. Shaw | Caroline V. Brummell |
| " | 19th William H. Myers | Salvadore Thompson (Blk) |
| " | " John H. Leiffert | Sarah J. Patch |
| " | 21 Thomas M. Cook | Lucretia A. Garner |
| " | " Augustus Lefreux | Anne C. Tait |
| " | " William B. Anderson | Margaret Ousley |
| " | 21 Charles C. Gregory | Alice W. Maury |
| " | " John S. Prather | Sarah Ann Brown (Blk) |
| " | " Thomas Styles | Annie Seabower |
| " | " Chas. F. Walson | Laura V. Boteler |
| " | 22 Abel Enslin | Mary A. Springer |
| " | " Daniel Buchanan | Lucy A. Mercury (Blk) |
| " | " Joseph Neumeyer | Ellen A. Hyatt |
| " | " Samuel Perkins | Martha A. Suit |
| " | 23 Owen McMahon | Elizabeth A. Skilly |
| " | 24 Nelson Edwards | Mary S. Brown |
| " | " Charles Hageman | Elanora Bumhoff |
| " | " Patrick Daley | Joanna Babbington |
| " | " Hanibal G. Wyman | Malvina F. Wyman |
| " | 26 Charles E. Tretter | Sallie V. Robinson |
| " | " Anthony Keuchel | Henrietta Born |
| " | " James C. Nelly | Sarah Ann Meads |
| " | " John Matthews | Mary Hawkins (Blk) |
| " | " Benjamin F. Larned | Maria H. Wilson |
| " | " S. Calvert Ford Jr. | Anna C. LeCompter |
| " | 27 Carson Kane | Henrietta Treakle |

Figure 2 - Sample Page From Marriage Register

District of Columbia Marriage Licenses, 1858-1870

# A

| | | |
|---|---|---|
| ABBOTT, Asa T. | CROSS, Fannie V. | 11 DEC 1865 |
| ABBOTT, George A. | WITHERS, Rosa Lee | 03 MAR 1863 |
| ABBOTT, James | CONLON, Catharine | 17 OCT 1864 |
| ABBOTT, James | JACKSON, Maria | 21 NOV 1868 |
| ABBOTT, Thos. | ELLIN, Sallie Ann | 07 AUG 1868 |
| ABEL, Christian | PAGENKOFF, Albertine | 01 AUG 1866 |
| ABELL, John B. | WILLIAMS, Violet A. | 03 OCT 1859 |
| ABENDSCHEIN, John | KHARN, Christine | 08 APR 1859 |
| ABIGAL, John N. | COUNTESS, Oceana | 04 NOV 1862 |
| ABINGTON, Edward | COOK, Catharine (blk) | 14 FEB 1866 |
| ABLE, John | DUMMEL, Cecilia | 16 APR 1866 |
| ABLE, Samuel | JOHNSON, Maria (blk) | 05 FEB 1868 |
| ABRAHAMS, James | BOYLE, Elizabeth, Mrs. | 31 MAR 1864 |
| ABRAM, Abraham | BACKUS, Gracie (blk) | 17 APR 1866 |
| ACERTON, B.M. [2] | BENTON, Martha Ann | 17 AUG 1869 |
| ACKEN, Samuel I. | BARTLETT, Kate F. | 07 JUN 1870 |
| ACKER, Charles A. [5] | SANDERSON, Saddie P. | 22 JUN 1868 |
| ACKER, Jacob N. | ST. CLAIR, Maggie L. | 29 SEP 1868 |
| ACKERMAN, Charles C. | JONES, Anna L. | 25 MAY 1868 |
| ACKERMANN, Curtis | WINSTANDLEY, Rebecca | 28 NOV 1864 |
| ACKERMANN, Paul | HARSCH, Catharine | 29 DEC 1862 |
| ACKERSON, Morris L. [11] | HOAGLAND, Annie M. | 25 NOV 1867 |
| ACTON, George | LEWIS, Caroline | 17 DEC 1860 |
| ACTON, George Thomas | HEALY, Elizabeth | 03 JAN 1870 |
| ACTON, Henry T. | DeNEAL, Mary E. | 22 FEB 1868 |
| ACTON, James | RIGSBY, Mary | 15 SEP 1863 |
| ACTON, Joseph | ENTWISTLE, Elizabeth E. | 11 OCT 1866 |
| ACTON, Theodore M. [12s] | GREENWOOD, Eliza V. | 06 MAR 1861 |
| ACTON, William | JONES, Ann | 30 JUL 1859 |
| ADAMS, Asbury | MITCHELL, Mary Ella (blk) | 20 NOV 1861 |
| ADAMS, Austin L. [10] | HATTON, Phebe E. | 12 JAN 1864 |
| ADAMS, Calup C. | HALL, Catharine (blk) | 29 NOV 1859 |
| ADAMS, Edward | GRAY, Mary E. (blk) | 15 MAR 1859 |
| ADAMS, Elmon A. [6l] | DIXON, Cornelia | 07 JAN 1862 |
| ADAMS, Frederick | BUTLER, Martha (blk) | 13 AUG 1864 |
| ADAMS, George A. | GONSALES, Martha J. | 25 JUL 1867 |
| ADAMS, George E. | CONNELLY, Sally | 03 NOV 1863 |
| ADAMS, George H. [6s] | WESTERFIELD, Ida E.M. | 23 FEB 1865 |
| ADAMS, George W. | BARCLAY, Jane L. | 18 DEC 1868 |
| ADAMS, J. Cookman [4] | HARKNESS, Mary V. | 26 DEC 1860 |
| ADAMS, Jacob H. | SKINNER, Sarah F. | 23 SEP 1869 |
| ADAMS, James | SELDEN, Laura | 13 DEC 1862 |
| ADAMS, James L. | DONALDSON, Roberta | 16 APR 1863 |
| ADAMS, Jesse G. | BERLIN, Emma C. | 26 JAN 1869 |
| ADAMS, John | UNDERWOOD, Ella | 13 DEC 1867 |
| ADAMS, John Henry | JACKSON, Julia (blk) | 21 AUG 1866 |
| ADAMS, John Q. | MOORE, Margaret L. | 08 OCT 1861 |
| ADAMS, John Q. | MOORE, Elizabeth J. | 27 FEB 1866 |
| ADAMS, John Quincy [6le] | NEWMAN, Louisa | 10 OCT 1866 |
| ADAMS, John R. | BOARMAN, Annie | 03 NOV 1869 |
| ADAMS, Jon B. | CLEMENTS, Harriet K. | 24 DEC 1864 |
| ADAMS, Marshall [13] | WALKER, Mahalia (blk) | 01 JUN 1859 |
| ADAMS, Nelson K. | GRAYSON, Sarah C. | 21 MAY 1860 |
| ADAMS, Paul | PEYTON, Rachel (blk) | 27 DEC 1866 |
| ADAMS, Robert | MADDOX, Jane (blk) | 28 JUL 1860 |

District of Columbia Marriage Licenses, 1858-1870

| | | |
|---|---|---|
| ADAMS, Robert | LUCAS, Mary Ann (blk) | 14 MAR 1861 |
| ADAMS, Robert [6le] | PINCKNEY, Harriet | 23 OCT 1867 |
| ADAMS, Robert D. [12s] | BAILEY, Lucy C. | 16 FEB 1859 |
| ADAMS, Samuel A. | JOHNSON, Madora Ellen | 10 DEC 1868 |
| ADAMS, Samuel, Dr. | CLAGETT, Ruth | 11 JUN 1866 |
| ADAMS, Thomas | BRODHEAD, Eliza, Mrs. | 10 OCT 1865 |
| ADAMS, Wesley | VOSS, Martha Ann (blk) | 24 DEC 1863 |
| ADAMS, William | FARRELL, Catherine | 20 OCT 1862 |
| ADAMS, William | STONE, Alice | 29 JUL 1863 |
| ADAMS, William | MAACK, Mary | 04 AUG 1863 |
| ADAMS, William C. | PURKS, Anna F. | 30 NOV 1867 |
| ADAMS, William H. [10] | EDELIN, Frances H. | 21 JUN 1866 |
| ADAMSON, Robert Lloyd | ADAMSON, Ellen | 07 SEP 1858 |
| ADDISON, Alfred | CRAWFORD, Louisa (blk) | 05 MAR 1867 |
| ADDISON, Anthony | WEEKS, Ann Rebecca (blk) | 17 DEC 1867 |
| ADDISON, Charles | BERRY, Mary Ellen (blk) | 24 DEC 1867 |
| ADDISON, David | PRATER, Jane (blk) | 11 NOV 1868 |
| ADDISON, Dennis | JACKSON, Lucy (blk) | 20 APR 1869 |
| ADDISON, Edward | LEE, Emily (blk) | 04 SEP 1865 |
| ADDISON, George | FORREST, Alethea (blk) | 20 SEP 1867 |
| ADDISON, Hannibal C. | CALLAN, Alice M.A. | 03 SEP 1863 |
| ADDISON, Henry | CHASE, Mary (blk) | 22 JUN 1867 |
| ADDISON, James H. | DOVE, Caroline A. | 28 NOV 1864 |
| ADDISON, James M. | DOVE, Caroline A. (blk) | 14 AUG 1862 |
| ADDISON, Nathan | SHAW, Annie (blk) | 19 OCT 1863 |
| ADDISON, William | LANE, Margaret (blk) | 21 DEC 1865 |
| ADGERLY, John | GREEN, Anna (blk) | 12 SEP 1867 |
| ADLEY, Peter | MALONEY, Mary | 29 JUL 1859 |
| ADLOW, Joshua | WEST, Martha (blk) | 05 JUN 1863 |
| ADMANSON, William Winsworth | SALBIER, Emma | 30 AUG 1869 |
| ADOLF, Gustav | SCHWERKE, Louisa | 10 NOV 1863 |
| ADOLPH, Julius | GIBBS, Mary Ann | 14 JUL 1866 |
| ADREON, George W. | GARDNER, Ruth Ann | 12 NOV 1867 |
| ADSON, George | WOOD, Margy (blk) | 11 APR 1870 |
| ADVENA, Joseph | VEAK, Emma | 25 DEC 1861 |
| AEDLER, Bertold | ERCKMAN, Eva | 04 FEB 1864 |
| AGAR, John W. | KEELY, Hellen | 07 MAY 1861 |
| AGER, Charles H. | PAYNE, Margaret | 12 MAY 1870 |
| AGER, E.C. | BAKER, Elisa H. | 01 AUG 1868 |
| AGER, George [4] | BRIAN, Jane | 26 OCT 1864 |
| AGNEW, John D. | BYRNE, Lizzie C. | 18 FEB 1867 |
| AGRION, Nicholas | OFERMAN, Eliza | 20 SEP 1862 |
| AHERN, John | BROWDER, Ellen | 19 SEP 1866 |
| AHERN, Thomas | CUSHAN, Ellen | 10 DEC 1869 |
| AHRENS, J.B.A. | PICKEN, Eliza | 08 OCT 1866 |
| AHUES, Nicholas L. | ALLOWAY, Jennie | 16 MAY 1863 |
| AILER, George | SEITZ, Sophia A. | 29 AUG 1860 |
| AIRES, Daniel | LEE, Louisa (blk) | 23 DEC 1864 |
| AKERS, Robert I. | CURTIN, Mary | 31 DEC 1867 |
| ALAZENBY, Amos | THOMPSON, Sarah E. | 31 OCT 1860 |
| ALBERS, John H. | HEITMILLER, Lizzie | 24 JUL 1868 |
| ALBERT, Augustus J. [11] | DOUGHTY, Julia | 03 JUL 1867 |
| ALBERT, Charles | HARTONSTEIN, Mary | 20 SEP 1866 |
| ALBERT, Henry | FRIK, Mary | 28 SEP 1863 |
| ALBERTUS, John | BAMPF, Catharina | 31 JUL 1866 |
| ALBRECHT, John Henry | HICKHOCK, Louisa | 29 FEB 1860 |

| | | |
|---|---|---|
| ALBRO, Joseph P. | WOOLLS, Anna Maria | 09 FEB 1863 |
| ALCORN, James | WORLING, Julia | 29 JUL 1864 |
| ALCOTT, William | O'NEIL, Mary Elizabeth | 05 OCT 1863 |
| ALDEN, James M. | BOWIE, Lotte E. | 09 JUL 1867 |
| ALDERSLADE, George E. | LLOYD, Jane Maria | 21 OCT 1859 |
| ALDRIDGE, John W. | JOHNSON, Huldah P. | 27 MAR 1866 |
| ALES, Adam | TILGHMAN, Frances (blk) | 22 OCT 1869 |
| ALEXANDER, Charles [11] | CURRAN, Julia A. | 05 JAN 1863 |
| ALEXANDER, Charles | PIPER, Matilda (blk) | 28 NOV 1863 |
| ALEXANDER, Charles A. | GRAY, Jane E. | 22 MAR 1866 |
| ALEXANDER, Charles D. | WOOLS, Lizzie | 25 OCT 1864 |
| ALEXANDER, Columbus O. | KELEHER, Sarah | 22 FEB 1865 |
| ALEXANDER, Edward | PARRIS, Susan (blk) | 02 SEP 1868 |
| ALEXANDER, Edward F. | WILSON, Virginia | 15 MAY 1861 |
| ALEXANDER, Henry H. | NEALE, Elizabeth A. | 26 JAN 1869 |
| ALEXANDER, Isaac | COLE, Josephine (blk) | 23 MAY 1860 |
| ALEXANDER, James | TAYLOR, Margaret Elizabeth | 11 NOV 1863 |
| ALEXANDER, John | DORSEY, Deborah (blk) | 18 DEC 1865 |
| ALEXANDER, John | OVER, Caroline | 21 NOV 1867 |
| ALEXANDER, John Henry | FEDRICK, Emma (blk) | 11 JUL 1867 |
| ALEXANDER, Joseph | CALVERT, Martin (blk) [sic] | 19 JAN 1863 |
| ALEXANDER, Joseph Bell [11] | LITTLE, Finnella Maury | 01 MAY 1866 |
| ALEXANDER, Lewis | SCOTT, Cecilia | 15 JUN 1866 |
| ALEXANDER, Moses | YOUNG, Virginia (blk) | 27 SEP 1866 |
| ALEXANDER, Moses | YOUNG, Virginia (blk) | 11 MAY 1867 |
| ALEXANDER, Sandy | SMITH, Elia | 05 JAN 1864 |
| ALEXANDER, Thomas R. | SALE, Sarah A. | 27 AUG 1859 |
| ALEXANDER, Thomson H. | DOW, Belle | 05 NOV 1861 |
| ALEXANDER, William | SANDERS, Louisa (blk) | 08 NOV 1867 |
| ALEXANDER, William F. [12s] | SHERMAN, Mary C. | 07 MAY 1861 |
| ALEXANDER, William P. [12s] | NORTON, Catharine | 19 JUL 1861 |
| ALEXANDRÉ, Parvarini | ROSA, Dolcini | 07 MAR 1865 |
| ALLAN, Wm. P. [10] | MURPHY, Julia Ann | 07 NOV 1867 |
| ALLAWAYS, Thomas B. | SANFORD, Mary Ella | 23 APR 1860 |
| ALLCONE, John | COHILL, Mary E. | 06 MAR 1862 |
| ALLEGRETTI, Ignatius | FONTANA, Josephine | 03 APR 1862 |
| ALLEN, Alfred | CLARKE, Adeline (blk) | 07 NOV 1861 |
| ALLEN, Aquilla R. | JOHNSON, Annie E. | 12 JUL 1865 |
| ALLEN, Aretus H. | DAVIS, Abigal E. | 08 APR 1862 |
| ALLEN, Aurelius | NICKENS, Jane (blk) | 23 JAN 1869 |
| ALLEN, Barney | BURNARD, Milley (blk) | 18 APR 1870 |
| ALLEN, Bernard McIntyre | BARRIS, Elizabeth | 09 SEP 1865 |
| ALLEN, C.W. | STOVER, Sarah M. | 13 AUG 1859 |
| ALLEN, Charles | RICE, Mary E. | 05 NOV 1866 |
| ALLEN, Charles H. | RUSSELL, Celia A. | 29 APR 1865 |
| ALLEN, David | DANGERFIELD, Caroline | 23 JUN 1864 |
| ALLEN, David J. | WALL, Mary Ann | 09 JUL 1863 |
| ALLEN, E.M. | AKERS, Elizabeth | 30 SEP 1865 |
| ALLEN, Edward B. | CROWN, Margaret S. | 30 NOV 1863 |
| ALLEN, Ethan | CLAGETT, Eliza | 19 AUG 1861 |
| ALLEN, Francis L. [6le] | BIGGS, Simphronia | 24 OCT 1867 |
| ALLEN, Frank H. | STEVENS, Emma F. | 06 APR 1868 |
| ALLEN, Frederick A. | DEVAUGHN, Landonia | 08 APR 1861 |
| ALLEN, George | CARTER, Lizzie (blk) | 05 DEC 1866 |
| ALLEN, George Columbus | JONES, Caroline (blk) | 18 SEP 1867 |
| ALLEN, George, Jr. [3] | HEPBURN, Maria A. | 26 JUL 1862 |

| | | |
|---|---|---|
| ALLEN, George W. [11] | BLAKENEY, Mary Elizabeth | 30 OCT 1862 |
| ALLEN, Henry | HARRIS, Eliza (blk) | 24 MAR 1864 |
| ALLEN, James | RYAN, Anne | 29 AUG 1864 |
| ALLEN, James F. | DOW, Julia A. | 23 OCT 1866 |
| ALLEN, James M. [7b] | BARTHOLOW, Mattie E. | 15 SEP 1869 |
| ALLEN, Joel | GARRET, Georgietta | 05 JUL 1865 |
| ALLEN, John | CLARK, Ellen (blk) | 22 DEC 1865 |
| ALLEN, John R. | POOLE, Lydia A. | 13 JUL 1868 |
| ALLEN, Joseph | WILLIAMS, Rose (blk) | 25 SEP 1866 |
| ALLEN, Joseph | SMILER, Margaret | 28 NOV 1866 |
| ALLEN, Joseph | FORSYTH, Margaret C. | 11 FEB 1867 |
| ALLEN, Robert | JORDAN, Delilah | 04 NOV 1864 |
| ALLEN, Robert | GALLOWAY, Henrietta (blk) | 24 OCT 1867 |
| ALLEN, Robert W. | ZIMMERMAN, Dora E. | 26 MAY 1870 |
| ALLEN, Samuel | READ, Mary Jane | 09 DEC 1858 |
| ALLEN, Samuel H. | TYLER, Mary (blk) | 15 OCT 1866 |
| ALLEN, Stephen W. | HANDY, Sciota C. | 13 AUG 1862 |
| ALLEN, Theodore Dwight | DUKE, Annie M. | 08 JUL 1863 |
| ALLEN, Thomas | CRONIKEN, Mary | 07 OCT 1861 |
| ALLEN, Thomas G. | PRITCHARD, Bertha E. | 01 APR 1867 |
| ALLEN, William | PAYNE, Martha | 28 DEC 1858 |
| ALLEN, William | BARNES, Eliza (blk) | 05 MAY 1864 |
| ALLEN, William | HARRIS, Catharine | 18 MAR 1865 |
| ALLEN, William | GREEN, Elizabeth (blk) | 15 FEB 1870 |
| ALLISON, Charles N. | BOTTLEMY, Kate | 18 AUG 1864 |
| ALLISON, Charles N. | BLACKMAN, Frances | 11 DEC 1866 |
| ALLISON, James W. | SMITH, Annie Virginia | 14 MAR 1870 |
| ALLISON, John W. | NEWHOUSE, Virginia M. | 16 JUN 1859 |
| ALLISON, William L. | SYPHERD, Molly | 07 JUL 1868 |
| ALLMAN, Alfred | JONES, Maria | 13 DEC 1865 |
| ALLWOOD, John | MURPHY, Johanna | 20 MAY 1868 |
| ALLYN, Lucius B. | BURRITT, Mary J. | 25 OCT 1867 |
| ALMANN, Joseph V. | KARPP, Mary L. | 04 JAN 1869 |
| ALSO, James H.R. | DIGGS, Cathe[r]ine (blk) | 10 APR 1866 |
| ALSOP, Benj. H. | WILSON, Margaret McAndrew | 13 MAY 1867 |
| ALSTON, James P. | TURNER, Christina | 05 OCT 1859 |
| ALTEMUS, A. Forest [5] | STEVER, Elizabeth A. | 20 APR 1868 |
| ALTEMUS, Frank S. | ELLIS, Hannah A. | 12 FEB 1866 |
| ALTEMUS, Thomas [10] | OSMUN, Elsie B. | 16 SEP 1867 |
| ALTMANNSPERGER, Chas. F.T. | KROUSE, Margaret R. | 30 JUL 1859 |
| ALTNER, Gustav | FRIEDE, Sophia | 17 APR 1868 |
| ALTON, Jacob | WEAVER, Sarah Jane | 03 DEC 1863 |
| ALTPETER, George | SCHUCKLER, Mary C. | 17 JAN 1863 |
| ALTSCHUH, Martin | ALTSCHU, Elizabeth E. | 26 JAN 1860 |
| ALWORTH, Daniel | SHANAHAN, Catherine | 02 JUL 1862 |
| AMAN, Sebastian | KOLB, Emma | 17 SEP 1863 |
| AMBER, Ezra | TAYLOR, Martha A. | 26 AUG 1865 |
| AMBLER, John | TURNER, Mary L. (blk) | 15 MAY 1860 |
| AMBROSE, William H. | BROOKS, Hannah (blk) | 30 SEP 1865 |
| AMBUSH, James | GREEN, Eliza (blk) | 26 SEP 1865 |
| AMBUSH, Joseph | JACKSON, Amelia (blk) | 05 JUL 1866 |
| AMBUSH, Stephen | ROBINSON, Celia (blk) | 21 JAN 1865 |
| AMERY, Robert L. | BOYD, Emma D. | 24 JAN 1865 |
| AMES, Nicholas | MYERS, Amelia | 23 APR 1864 |
| AMESBERRY, James | LYNCH, Mary Ann | 04 MAR 1862 |
| AMIDON, Hollis | MILBURN, Margt. A. | 24 DEC 1862 |

District of Columbia Marriage Licenses, 1858-1870

| Groom | Bride | Date |
|---|---|---|
| AMIDON, Jacob J. | ABELL, Virginia | 23 NOV 1867 |
| AMISS, Tazwell B. | WHEELER, Mary E. | 22 MAR 1865 |
| AMMEN, Daniel | ATOCHA, Zoe | 10 APR 1866 |
| AMOS, Joseph F. | BRUCE, Maria Louisa (blk) | 16 JUN 1868 |
| AMOS, [Sylvannus] Y. | COX, Mary E. | 08 JAN 1867 |
| AMREIN, John | WILLNER, Margaret A.H. | 06 OCT 1862 |
| ANDERMAN, Philip | NEWN, Barbara | 14 NOV 1864 |
| ANDERSON, Alexander | SIGH, Betsy (blk) | 01 JUN 1864 |
| ANDERSON, Ben | SMITH, Julia (blk) | 24 DEC 1864 |
| ANDERSON, Benjamin | WARNZER, Mary | 12 OCT 1864 |
| ANDERSON, Benjamin | BROWN, Sallie (blk) | 25 NOV 1867 |
| ANDERSON, Benjamin F. | ECKTON, Mary E. | 25 NOV 1869 |
| ANDERSON, Charles | DeMARQUE, Mary | 29 MAY 1862 |
| ANDERSON, Charles | LEE, Caroline (blk) | 12 MAR 1868 |
| ANDERSON, Daniel | DIGNAN, Bridget | 04 JUN 1863 |
| ANDERSON, E.J. | DAY, Caroline E. | 03 OCT 1868 |
| ANDERSON, Edward E. | EVANS, Sarah M. | 07 DEC 1858 |
| ANDERSON, Edward E. | PHILLIPS, Elizabeth | 16 DEC 1862 |
| ANDERSON, Edward H. | FERGUSON, Emily D. | 25 NOV 1864 |
| ANDERSON, Franklin S. | WINTERS, Emma | 25 NOV 1865 |
| ANDERSON, George | BERCHARD, Mary A. | 30 APR 1868 |
| ANDERSON, George F. [1l] | DAVISON, Sarah Ann | 23 FEB 1863 |
| ANDERSON, Henry | MULLIGAN, Margaret | 23 NOV 1865 |
| ANDERSON, Henry | TAYLOR, Maria (blk) | 11 NOV 1867 |
| ANDERSON, James | JACKSON, Catherine | 09 OCT 1863 |
| ANDERSON, James | JONES, Mary Ellen (blk) | 23 SEP 1863 |
| ANDERSON, James | BELL, Ann Maria (blk) | 02 FEB 1865 |
| ANDERSON, James | PERRY, Elizabeth | 16 OCT 1866 |
| ANDERSON, James G. | FORD, Elizth. Ward | 02 JUL 1862 |
| ANDERSON, James W. | NEALE, Glorvina A. | 06 OCT 1863 |
| ANDERSON, James W. | JONES, Marion H. | 27 AUG 1868 |
| ANDERSON, John | GUNNEL, Paulina (blk) | 14 JAN 1867 |
| ANDERSON, John | COLEMAN, Laura (blk) | 14 JUN 1869 |
| ANDERSON, John H. [6l] | DENNISON, Elmonia [Virginia] | 09 OCT 1861 |
| ANDERSON, John H. [6le] | GRIMES, Lizzie S. | 15 FEB 1866 |
| ANDERSON, John S. | LADAMEIL, Mary Lucinda | 29 FEB 1860 |
| ANDERSON, Joseph C. | BAILEY, Jane Elizabeth | 27 AUG 1867 |
| ANDERSON, Lewis | BUTLER, Henrietta (blk) | 26 DEC 1868 |
| ANDERSON, Mason | YOUNG, Amanda | 11 OCT 1860 |
| ANDERSON, Notley | LOUIS, Mary Emeline | 04 JUN 1870 |
| ANDERSON, Oliver P. [6m] | FRENCH, Olivia | 26 JAN 1863 |
| ANDERSON, Richard Barnard | BOND, Mary Eliza | 05 OCT 1863 |
| ANDERSON, Rich'd. M. | VERMILLION, Dorcas A.C. | 10 NOV 1859 |
| ANDERSON, Robert | CREAMER, Margaret | 22 SEP 1863 |
| ANDERSON, Samuel | JOHNSON, Lavinia (blk) | 24 DEC 1867 |
| ANDERSON, Samuel D. | BOYLE, Laura A. | 24 AUG 1861 |
| ANDERSON, William | WARNER, Ellenora (blk) | 28 JUN 1864 |
| ANDERSON, William | CHERRAY, Elizabeth | 23 JAN 1866 |
| ANDERSON, William | ADDISON, Jennie (blk) | 03 AUG 1866 |
| ANDERSON, William | SPEAKE, Susanna Virginia | 18 JUN 1867 |
| ANDERSON, William B. | OUSLEY, Margaret | 20 NOV 1860 |
| ANDERSON, Wm. J. | BARGER, Mary Ann | 04 SEP 1865 |
| ANDERSON, William Lee | REYNOLDS, Charlotte (blk) | 26 MAY 1866 |
| ANDIROT, Paul | LASALLE, Louisa P. | 06 SEP 1867 |
| ANDREWS, Daniel H. | NAYLOR, Sarah E. | 24 SEP 1863 |
| ANDREWS, Englebert | CULLINAN, Jane | 11 MAY 1870 |

District of Columbia Marriage Licenses, 1858-1870

| | | |
|---|---|---|
| ANDREWS, George L. | JONES, Mary | 26 JUL 1866 |
| ANDREWS, William [10] | BEAN, Mary J. | 14 JAN 1864 |
| ANDREWS, William H. [11] | JONES, Elizabeth Frances | 11 JAN 1868 |
| ANDREWS, William S. | CRACKNELL, Coralie A. | 28 MAR 1865 |
| ANGEL, Nicholas | HAMMELL, Margaret | 03 JAN 1859 |
| ANGELL, Nicholas | HAMILTON, Margaret | 26 JUL 1859 |
| ANGELL, William C. | SCHERRY, Julia A. | 23 APR 1868 |
| ANGERMAN, Philip | KRONISE, Catharine | 04 JUN 1865 |
| ANGERMAN, Theodore | COOK, Mary Ann | 17 MAY 1869 |
| ANGEVINE, Andrew F. | PARKER, Rebecca J. | 12 MAY 1864 |
| ANGEVINE, Edward G. | BARR, Margaret E., Mrs. | 24 OCT 1863 |
| ANSELINE, John Louis | CRUTCHER, Maria Louise Josephine | 15 OCT 1860 |
| ANTHONY, Henry | KILDUFF, Mary | 30 APR 1862 |
| ANTHONY, John | McDONNEL, Maria | 16 SEP 1865 |
| ANTHONY, John | LANDES, Susan (blk) | 21 DEC 1865 |
| APP, Caspar | O'NIEL, Mary | 08 MAR 1862 |
| APPELSTIEL, F. Augustus | HIRBITZ, Sophie | 18 DEC 1861 |
| APPICH, Jacob D. | MOHLER, Christina | 30 JAN 1863 |
| APPLEBY, Horatio G. [6m] | JARBOE, Mary H. | 29 OCT 1863 |
| APPLEBY, William | MILES, Frances | 13 JUN 1859 |
| APPLEGATE, Robert | CARTER, Rosina (blk) | 01 DEC 1865 |
| APPLER, Jesse H. | DEMENT, Virginia | 16 APR 1863 |
| APPLETON, William H. | STRANG, Mollie J. | 17 MAY 1866 |
| APPOLD, Samuel Andrew | PIGGOTT, Isabella Marcy | 12 DEC 1859 |
| ARBUCKLE, Frederick J. | LYNCH, Bridget Catherine | 29 JAN 1864 |
| ARCES, Don J.M. Celestino Y. | NAYLOR, Rachel Elizabeth | 11 SEP 1864 |
| ARCHER, John | KOONS, Agnes | 18 OCT 1860 |
| ARCHER, John | PORTER, Mary (blk) | 11 JUL 1867 |
| ARCHER, William | HARPER, Julia | 20 SEP 1866 |
| ARDEESER, Stephen | BERNHARD, Catherine | 26 DEC 1868 |
| ARDEISER, John | SPIGNALL, Mary | 12 FEB 1867 |
| ARDIESER, Christian | PREDAGAM, Catharine | 26 SEP 1864 |
| ARDIESER, Christian | NOLEN, Ann Rachel | 23 DEC 1868 |
| ARENZ, Martin | EIFERT, Elizabeth | 06 DEC 1861 |
| ARETZ, Heinrich Julius | SCHUHKNECHT, Selma Hermine | 28 FEB 1867 |
| ARLE, Joseph | BEHRENS, Emma | 07 JUL 1866 |
| ARLOW, Robert T. | BURROUGHS, Catharine H. | 30 NOV 1865 |
| ARMBRIGHT, Charles | BERGMANN, Minna | 28 MAR 1864 |
| ARMISTEAD, Addison | JONES, Harriet Ann | 03 JUL 1865 |
| ARMISTEAD, Alexander | COLEMAN, Betty (blk) | 03 JAN 1867 |
| ARMISTEAD, John | WHITE, Hester (blk) | 14 MAY 1870 |
| ARMOUR, Charles | KLOPFER, Rachel A. | 01 NOV 1864 |
| ARMOUR, Robert [4] | COHOE, Sarah Elizabeth | 18 JAN 1866 |
| ARMS, Simon | CARTER, Sophia (blk) | 13 SEP 1867 |
| ARMSTRONG, Charles Henry | JOHNSON, Hannah (blk) | 21 MAR 1868 |
| ARMSTRONG, G.L. | MISCROL, Cary | 02 JAN 1865 |
| ARMSTRONG, Isaac[1] | DIXON, Elizabeth | 22 AUG 1863 |
| ARMSTRONG, John | WALKER, Jettie | 07 SEP 1868 |
| ARMSTRONG, John N. | MIDDLETON, Susan R. | 26 MAR 1864 |
| ARMSTRONG, William | FRANKLIN, Sarah P. | 21 JAN 1861 |
| ARMSTRONG, William | SHEPHERD, Caroline (blk) | 24 MAY 1870 |
| ARNESTER, J.F. | TURNER, Jane (blk) | 08 DEC 1868 |
| ARNETH, William H. | WINTERS, Carrie S. | 26 MAR 1867 |
| ARNETT, Dorsey | MORTON, Mary (blk) | 14 SEP 1865 |

[1] Note: Chaplain, W.W. Winchester, Finley Hospital

District of Columbia Marriage Licenses, 1858-1870

| | | |
|---|---|---|
| ARNETT, Joseph | LENOIR, Louisa | 31 JAN 1866 |
| ARNOLD, Edmund C. | SEWALL, Jane A. | 01 SEP 1863 |
| ARNOLD, Francis B. | FOOTE, Augusta | 05 MAR 1869 |
| ARNOLD, Henry | SMITH, Annie Elizabeth | 03 NOV 1864 |
| ARNOLD, Henry A. [12s] | DAVIS, Fannie | 08 AUG 1861 |
| ARNOLD, Henry W. | BUTLER, Isabella | 22 JAN 1867 |
| ARNOLD, Jacob L. | MITCHELL, Mary E. | 19 MAR 1867 |
| ARNOLD, Richard | MARTIN, Harriet (blk) | 22 SEP 1869 |
| ARNOLD, Richard A. | PADGETT, Elizabeth A. | 14 MAY 1860 |
| ARNOLD, Richard A. | PADGETT, Elizabeth A. | 27 MAR 1861 |
| ARNOLD, Thomas G. | HILL, Elizabeth | 03 JUL 1866 |
| ARNOLD, Thomas O. [6r] | EVANS, Sarah R. | 18 APR 1860 |
| ARRENDS, Henry | KRAUS, Lizzie | 13 MAY 1870 |
| ARRINGTON, Andrew J. | BREWER, Mary B. | 01 SEP 1862 |
| ARRINGTON, William | PROCTOR, Mary R. (blk) | 20 JUL 1867 |
| ARRINGTON, William H. [7a] | PULLING, Sarah H. | 29 OCT 1868 |
| ARRISON, John R. | HOLLISTER, Mary D. | 05 AUG 1865 |
| ARTES, Henry | SIEBOLD, Jane | 17 FEB 1866 |
| ARTH, Christopher | ADAM, Catharine | 22 NOV 1865 |
| ARTH, Daniel | BAUER, Wilhelmina | 11 JUL 1867 |
| ARTHUR, Henry H. | TAIT, Mary Ann (blk) | 24 OCT 1864 |
| ARTHUR, James | DOCKET, Julia | 24 NOV 1865 |
| ARTHUR, John H. | WILLIAMS, Harriet A. | 24 SEP 1864 |
| ARTHUR, Patrick H. | FLOOD, Mary Jane (blk) | 16 NOV 1866 |
| ARTHUR, William | WINSLEY, Mary (blk) | 01 JAN 1867 |
| ARTÜSER, Mathias | REIDY, Barbara | 03 SEP 1858 |
| ARUNDEL, Philip J. | BLADEN, Adaline V. | 10 FEB 1870 |
| ASCHENBACK, Valentine | BRENDEL, Pauline | 17 MAY 1869 |
| ASH, Albert | GRINDALL, Juliana (blk) | 22 OCT 1860 |
| ASH, Charles J. | BRUCE, Margaret A. | 16 OCT 1862 |
| ASH, Frank L. | SIPES, Philippine | 03 OCT 1859 |
| ASH, John, Jr. | SOLDSBERRY, Ellen | 22 MAY 1865 |
| ASHBY, John A. [7b] | BURROUGHS, Martha E. | 23 NOV 1869 |
| ASHBY, John L. | ABBOTT, Rebecca Jane | 04 AUG 1869 |
| ASHDOWN, John | THURSTIN, Harriet | 22 NOV 1864 |
| ASHDOWN, William | REILLEY, Margaret | 09 FEB 1863 |
| ASHE, Moses | LEE, Eliza (blk) | 03 OCT 1863 |
| ASHFIELD, John M. | MILLER, Annie | 18 JAN 1870 |
| ASHFORD, Mahlon | BELL, Sidney L. | 17 MAY 1864 |
| ASHLEY, James A. | SCRIVENER, Anna | 27 SEP 1865 |
| ASHLEY, Jerome | QUEEN, Sarah E. | 04 APR 1864 |
| ASHMAN, William Neilson | HAHN, Mary Elizabeth | 29 MAY 1866 |
| ASHTON, James G. | STONE, Martha H. (blk) | 20 JUN 1867 |
| ASHTON, Joseph | WELSH, Catherine | 08 NOV 1860 |
| ASHTON, William Lucas | FAIRFAX, Sarah Ann (blk) | 16 AUG 1862 |
| ASHTON, William P. | WASHINGTON, Maria Ann | 06 DEC 1865 |
| ASKINS, David D. | BROWN, Cornelia | 11 JAN 1865 |
| ASTON, Albert [11] | WASHINGTON, Rose (blk) | 31 JAN 1867 |
| ATCHISON, Harris L. | BEAN, Eliza | 27 MAR 1862 |
| ATCHISON, Julius | EDWARDS, Jennett | 09 OCT 1867 |
| ATCHISON, William H.D. | JOCKEL, Catherine | 26 MAR 1860 |
| ATHEY, James | CHANEY, Ellen A. | 27 AUG 1863 |
| ATKINS, David | BROOKS, Susan (blk) | 07 JUL 1864 |
| ATKINS, George B. | SLUSHER, Elizabeth C. | 11 JAN 1859 |
| ATKINS, Henry G. | FITZGERALD, Reine (blk) | 02 AUG 1864 |
| ATKINSON, Charles O. | TREFETHERN, Sarah J.S. | 18 OCT 1864 |

District of Columbia Marriage Licenses, 1858-1870

| | | |
|---|---|---|
| ATKINSON, Edward S. | OVER, Mary E. (blk) | 18 SEP 1867 |
| ATKINSON, Frank F. | CROSS, Elizabeth | 06 MAY 1867 |
| ATKINSON, Frederick | SYBOTT, Eliza (blk) | 27 MAY 1863 |
| ATKINSON, Henry | SAVAGE, Sarah E. | 17 NOV 1864 |
| ATKINSON, Henry L. | FAGAN, Annie | 12 DEC 1867 |
| ATKINSON, M.B. | STONE, Elizabeth | 10 DEC 1860 |
| ATKINSON, Mahalm B. [1c] | TARMAN, Laura V. | 11 AUG 1863 |
| ATLEY, Matthew D. | TUCKER, Ellen B. | 01 DEC 1864 |
| ATLIE, Goodwin Y. | CROSSON, Mollie E. | 11 MAY 1861 |
| ATRUZ, Hypolite | FAY, Louisa | 13 OCT 1869 |
| ATTRIDGE, Alexander J.M. | JOYCE, Josephine A. | 19 APR 1864 |
| ATWELL, James W. | WARTHEN, Mary H. | 13 FEB 1862 |
| AUBINOE, Samuel N. | SWAIN, Mary E. | 02 JUN 1865 |
| AUDALE, John | CONNOR, Ellen | 27 OCT 1865 |
| AUER, Michael | UMBRIDGE, Regina V. | 21 OCT 1863 |
| AUFFORT, Charles F. | WHEATLEY, Sarah | 20 APR 1865 |
| AUGHERTON, James K. | FORSYTH, Elizabeth | 01 FEB 1866 |
| AUGHINSBAUGH, William L. | O'NEILL, Ann M. | 02 OCT 1868 |
| AUGUSTUS, Wm. Henry | CAMPBELL, Hannah (blk) | 28 DEC 1869 |
| AUKWARD, Horatio F. | SMITH, Julia A. | 07 AUG 1867 |
| AULD, David | FREY, Emma L. | 23 NOV 1863 |
| AULD, John G. | JACKSON, Alice | 29 APR 1867 |
| AULDRIDGE, Thomas | ENNIS, Catharine | 14 NOV 1865 |
| AUSBOURN, John W. | BELT, Catharine A. | 15 JUL 1862 |
| AUSTIN, Benjamin | JOHNSON, America J. | 07 APR 1866 |
| AUSTIN, Charles A. | FLATTERMAN, Berthina | 22 OCT 1861 |
| AUSTIN, James | RODD, Sarah | 19 NOV 1863 |
| AUSTIN, James | AYER, Julia | 21 AUG 1865 |
| AUSTIN, James B. | HANDY, Shepherd H. | 16 MAY 1870 |
| AUSTIN, Joseph | ADAMS, Henrietta | 28 DEC 1865 |
| AUSTIN, Manvil A. [6m] | RENNEY, Julia Olivia | 23 FEB 1863 |
| AUSTIN, Thomas | SMITH, Mary E. (blk) | 20 JUN 1867 |
| AUSTIN, Vallorous G. | RENNER, Cornelia | 04 OCT 1864 |
| AUTH, Cristantus | KLÜH, Gertruth | 16 APR 1864 |
| AVERY, Charles | TAYLOR, Mary | 24 JAN 1866 |
| AVERY, George W. | CHURCH, Frances | 28 MAY 1862 |
| AVERY, James | GATEWOOD, Frances | 20 JUL 1868 |
| AVERY, William O. | REYNOLDS, Hattie C. | 28 MAY 1867 |
| AWKWARD, Elijah | LINCOLN, Elizabeth (blk) | 13 MAY 1869 |
| AXTELL, Enos Ayres | TAYLOR, Catherine J. | 06 MAY 1867 |
| AYER, Henry G. | SHIELDS, Sarah E. | 02 NOV 1864 |
| AYER, Oliver P. | DAVIS, Margaret Ann | 18 JAN 1868 |
| AYRES, Ira | JAMES, Jennie | 21 DEC 1863 |
| AYRES, Lewis | GOINGS, Adda (blk) | 26 SEP 1867 |
| AYRES, William | SPARROW, Maria | 09 JAN 1869 |

# B

| | | |
|---|---|---|
| BAARAEM, Edgar J. | RABBITT, Beckie | 26 APR 1866 |
| BABBINGTON, Pierce | COSTELLO, Ellen | 21 FEB 1859 |
| BABBITT, Henry W. | HARLAN, Josephine | 29 JAN 1869 |
| BABCOCK, Daniel | SMILY, Susan, Mrs. | 16 JAN 1864 |
| BABCOCK, Elisha | MORAN, Mary M. | 03 JUN 1870 |
| BABCOCK, Heman P. | HARWOOD, Sally A. | 25 NOV 1863 |
| BABCOCK, Henry G. | VanBUSKIRK, Mary | 29 OCT 1861 |
| BABCOCK, Jeremiah | STALER, Jennie | 07 MAY 1864 |

| | | |
|---|---|---|
| BABCOCK, Sidney S. | KENDALL, Marian | 27 MAY 1864 |
| BABER, Horace | BANTLIN, Louisa (blk) | 19 FEB 1867 |
| BABTISTA, Antonio Joseph | COLLINS, Margaret | 05 JUL 1862 |
| BACON, Edward | LYLES, Laura (blk) | 01 APR 1862 |
| BACON, Newton W. | DAVINE, Maggie T. | 26 OCT 1868 |
| BACON, Samuel | SHEAHAN, Mary | 21 JUN 1859 |
| BADEN, Basil [10] | BELL, Amelia A. | 07 JUN 1860 |
| BADEN, James T. | YATES, Annie M. | 01 JUL 1863 |
| BADEN, John | O'BRIAN, Ellen | 11 JUL 1859 |
| BADEN, Joseph N. | ROBEY, Edwardina | 12 SEP 1868 |
| BADGLEY, H. | FRANZONI, B. | 27 NOV 1869 |
| BADY, James | PAINE, Mary D. | 07 MAY 1862 |
| BAECK, Christian | KEALIN, Catharine | 26 DEC 1861 |
| BAEDDING, John | HEIGGINS, Mary | 31 MAY 1860 |
| BAER, George H. | RISON, Mary Ann | 18 NOV 1864 |
| BAGGETT, Hugh | RUCKER, Cornelia (blk) | 10 DEC 1866 |
| BAGGETT, James | WHITE, Sarah A. | 26 JAN 1864 |
| BAGGETT, Stephen | McMAHON, Mary | 23 MAY 1863 |
| BAGGETT, William | CATON, Julia Ann | 05 MAY 1863 |
| BAGGOTT, Alexander [6m] | BROADBACK, Mary Ann | 08 DEC 1862 |
| BAGGOTT, Townsend | BEACH, Susanna | 04 AUG 1862 |
| BAGLY, Aaron | WASHINGTON, Alice (blk) | 01 MAR 1870 |
| BAHLEBER, David | RECKER, Frederica Louisa | 03 NOV 1859 |
| BAILEY, Albert W. | VonKAMECKE, Elizabeth | 21 JUN 1867 |
| BAILEY, Alfred W. | TRUSTY, Annie | 06 APR 1870 |
| BAILEY, Carroll | JOHNSON, Miranda (blk) | 17 NOV 1859 |
| BAILEY, Daniel P. [12s] | BERKER, Clarinda | 04 JAN 1860 |
| BAILEY, Francis | BRIGGS, Margaret (blk) | 07 JUN 1866 |
| BAILEY, Frederick W. [11] | ATLEE, Fanny Yorke | 05 DEC 1865 |
| BAILEY, George | KNOWLAND, Catherine | 14 AUG 1863 |
| BAILEY, George L. | ROBINSON, Caroline (blk) | 13 APR 1867 |
| BAILEY, Henry | DAVIS, Frances (blk) | 03 MAY 1866 |
| BAILEY, John | HANNEN, Catherine | 01 NOV 1864 |
| BAILEY, John | KANE, Mary | 26 OCT 1868 |
| BAILEY, John | SPENCER, Maria (blk) | 04 NOV 1869 |
| BAILEY, John A. [10] | BURROUGHS, Sallie R. | 11 MAY 1869 |
| BAILEY, John T. | GRIMES, Ada | 30 NOV 1865 |
| BAILEY, John W. | SHORTER, Annie M. (blk) | 08 MAY 1865 |
| BAILEY, Josiah E. | HURDLE, Lavinia E. | 12 NOV 1861 |
| BAILEY, Leonard | HOOE, Mary F. | 22 NOV 1864 |
| BAILEY, Lewis C. [Capt.] [11] | LINDSAY, Emma | 21 SEP 1863 |
| BAILEY, Marcellus | PAGE, Emmelyn Webster | 06 MAR 1867 |
| BAILEY, Milton J. | BURRIKER, Martha | 20 SEP 1858 |
| BAILEY, Robert | BELT, Nellie (blk) | 05 APR 1870 |
| BAILEY, Robert J. | SEDDEN, Eliza | 14 NOV 1861 |
| BAILEY, Samuel H. [6le] | McDANIELS, Annie | 15 FEB 1866 |
| BAILEY, Stephen A. | MURPHY, Catherine | 31 JAN 1866 |
| BAILEY, William | HUTCHINSON, Mary J. | 14 JUN 1861 |
| BAILEY, William | WOOD, Elizabeth (blk) | 03 MAR 1863 |
| BAILEY, William D. | BARRY, Rosina | 01 MAY 1860 |
| BAILEY, Wm. H. | BIERS, Margaretta A. | 28 DEC 1858 |
| BAILEY, William W. | VERNON, Julia E. | 12 DEC 1865 |
| BAILLEUL, George | VanTYNE, Mary A. | 10 MAY 1861 |
| BAILLIEUX, Louis | FLEURY, Seraphine | 02 APR 1859 |
| BAILOR, Henry | BAILOR, Martha Ellen (blk) | 06 JUL 1866 |
| BAILY, John | FORBES, Mary E. (blk) | 21 NOV 1867 |

District of Columbia Marriage Licenses, 1858-1870

| | | |
|---|---|---|
| BAINES, Martin | COATES, Lizzie (blk) | 19 OCT 1869 |
| BAIRD, James B. | MURRAY, Margaret A. | 15 NOV 1862 |
| BAIRD, William | NELSON, Amanda (blk) | 28 MAR 1867 |
| BAITMAN, John | CRIER, Sarah V. | 22 FEB 1865 |
| BAKEOVEN, William T. | ADAMS, Mary Emma | 11 MAY 1868 |
| BAKER, Andrew | SHOTROW, Mahala Jane | 24 OCT 1862 |
| BAKER, Benjamin | WILLS, Mary | 14 FEB 1865 |
| BAKER, Charles | GROVE, Just | 10 OCT 1863 |
| BAKER, Charles P. | LOND, Fannie L.W. | 22 AUG 1866 |
| BAKER, Clarence B. | McINTYRE, Laura E. | 16 FEB 1863 |
| BAKER, Edmund | GIBSON, Cornelia (blk) | 14 NOV 1863 |
| BAKER, Edmund | HORTON, Mary | 07 JAN 1870 |
| BAKER, Henry | LYLES, Amelia (blk) | 04 JAN 1865 |
| BAKER, Henry C. | LEDWITH, Catherine | 08 JAN 1864 |
| BAKER, Jacob H. | HARDING, Henrietta | 08 MAR 1870 |
| BAKER, John | CARTER, Annie (blk) | 18 FEB 1862 |
| BAKER, John | WHITING, Mary E. (blk) | 21 DEC 1869 |
| BAKER, John A. | BACON, Elizabeth C. | 10 JAN 1868 |
| BAKER, John R. [2] | JONES, Mary Ann | 18 DEC 1867 |
| BAKER, Lewis H. | AGER, Josepha H. | 01 JUN 1870 |
| BAKER, Michael | BROWN, Jane | 02 APR 1869 |
| BAKER, Thomas | SULLIVAN, Ida | 13 MAR 1867 |
| BAKER, Thomas T. | TISDALE, Charlotte L. | 31 JAN 1868 |
| BAKER, William C. | ELLIOTT, Mary R. | 05 MAR 1870 |
| BAKER, Wm. Robt. | WHEAT, Charlotte | 17 JAN 1865 |
| BAKER, William Whitfield | SPENCER, Harriet V. | 01 OCT 1861 |
| BAKERSMITH, Rudolph | GERNHART, Catherine | 14 MAR 1866 |
| BALDIES, Joseph | GREEN, Rebecca | 25 JUL 1866 |
| BALDIN, Andrew | CAMPBELL, Bridget | 02 OCT 1861 |
| BALDWIN, C.W. | BURKE, Catherine | 19 SEP 1866 |
| BALDWIN, Edgar [6s] | LINTHICUM, Maria E. | 26 MAY 1864 |
| BALDWIN, Henry | BROWN, Ellen (blk) | 17 MAR 1869 |
| BALDWIN, Henry, Jr. [11] | DAYTON, Kate [Irving] | 04 NOV 1861 |
| BALDWIN, Levi Ja. | HODGSON, Christiana A. | 23 DEC 1861 |
| BALDWIN, Perry C. | JACOBS, Sarah V. | 09 MAY 1865 |
| BALDWIN, Rignal W. | HALL, Rosa E. | 08 FEB 1869 |
| BALDWIN, William Dickson [11] | MAYNADIER, Margaret Fitzhugh | 03 SEP 1866 |
| BALDWIN, Wm. J. | WALKER, Mary E. | 29 JUL 1863 |
| BALDWIN, Wm. O. [11] | LITTLE, Sarah F. | 02 DEC 1863 |
| BALES, Henry A. | WHITE, Amelia F. | 01 NOV 1869 |
| BALL, Albert | CONWAY, Amelia E. (blk) | 18 AUG 1863 |
| BALL, Alexander | CARRIE, Cecilia Ardell | 11 MAR 1870 |
| BALL, Charles H. | BROWN, Lillie V. | 04 NOV 1861 |
| BALL, Daniel O. | POOLE, Julia E. | 07 OCT 1868 |
| BALL, Edgar | WINGFIELD, Elizabeth (blk) | 15 MAR 1865 |
| BALL, Edward N. | CATHALL, Emma R. | 07 SEP 1864 |
| BALL, James N. | BROWN, Jemima P. | 23 APR 1861 |
| BALL, John | DAVIS, Lucy | 25 OCT 1859 |
| BALL, John [Riggs] [2] | COX, Susanna | 23 MAY 1866 |
| BALL, John Thos. | BARNES, Sarah | 17 DEC 1859 |
| BALL, John W. [6le] | BARNSLEY, Annie F. | 04 OCT 1865 |
| BALL, Richard E. [6s] | THORN, Mary Elizabeth | 20 APR 1865 |
| BALL, William D. | BOSTON, Martha (blk) | 20 MAR 1866 |
| BALLANGER, George F. | DEANE, Mary A. | 03 NOV 1863 |
| BALLANTYNE, Thomas | SMITH, Jessy, Mrs. | 02 NOV 1863 |
| BALLARD, Gabriel R. | MARSH, Marilla M. | 12 FEB 1863 |

| | | |
|---|---|---|
| BALLARD, George C. | ENNES, Estelle M. | 12 AUG 1865 |
| BALLAUF, Louis | GREEN, Adolphina | 24 DEC 1859 |
| BALLENGER, George W. | JACK, Ella G. | 08 DEC 1869 |
| BALLENGER, William | TAYLOR, Mary E. | 25 MAR 1862 |
| BALLINGER, Frank M. | FATIO, Florence A. | 02 OCT 1865 |
| BALLINGER, Hamilton W. | ELLIS, Laura V. | 30 JAN 1866 |
| BALLINGER, John T. | THOMPSON, Annie E. | 09 OCT 1868 |
| BALLINGER, Richard | WADE, Sarah F. | 13 FEB 1862 |
| BALLINGER, Theophilus | PRICE, Mary | 15 JUN 1864 |
| BALLINGER, Wesley | STEVENS, Mary R. | 03 MAR 1863 |
| BALLUFF, Charles A. | WATSON, Maria L. | 28 DEC 1858 |
| BALOR, John | PITTS, Caroline (blk) | 17 NOV 1869 |
| BALTZELL, William D. | SAVAGE, Mary E. | 30 MAR 1863 |
| BALTZER, Adam | KNOPF, Amelia | 15 DEC 1865 |
| BALTZER, John T. | LARMAN, Elizabeth | 29 JUL 1861 |
| BALTZER, Kuhnrod | FOLTZ, Amelia | 19 OCT 1866 |
| BANAN, William | BRENNAN, Honora | 22 AUG 1861 |
| BANANDORF, Henry | BALL, Josephine C. | 13 OCT 1866 |
| BANCKMAN, George W. | MORAN, Mary C. | 13 DEC 1869 |
| BANCROFT, Thomas D. | ARCHER, Susanna | 07 MAY 1861 |
| BANCROFT, William F. | MUNDELL, Margaret R. | 23 OCT 1867 |
| BANGERT, Frederick A. | HUMPHRIES, Annie | 28 MAR 1870 |
| BANGS, Edward | THOMAS, Ellen E. | 06 NOV 1858 |
| BANK, James Winston | NELSON, Margaret Ann (blk) | 19 MAY 1868 |
| BANKERT, Thomas S. | TAYLOR, Eliza J., Mrs. | 05 OCT 1863 |
| BANKET, Addison | WHITE, Lizzie (blk) | 05 SEP 1863 |
| BANKET, Brice | OLIVER, Martha | 29 MAR 1866 |
| BANKHAGES, Frederick E. | APPLEBY, Sallie M. | 14 AUG 1865 |
| BANKHEAD, Armstead | BROWN, Betsey | 23 DEC 1865 |
| BANKHEAD, Dunmore | BAKER, Patience (blk) | 28 SEP 1865 |
| BANKS, Alexander [11] | RILEY, Susan | 21 DEC 1866 |
| BANKS, Anthony | CAMPBELL, Mary (blk) | 06 FEB 1869 |
| BANKS, Benjamin | SNOWDEN, Jane (blk) | 18 APR 1867 |
| BANKS, Daniel | STEVENSON, Matilda (blk) | 06 APR 1865 |
| BANKS, Daniel | WHITE, Matilda | 22 MAY 1866 |
| BANKS, David | WHEATLEY, Georgiana | 07 SEP 1858 |
| BANKS, Edgar | BANKS, Melvina (blk) | 09 NOV 1867 |
| BANKS, Essex | LEWIS, Cassy (blk) | 20 SEP 1865 |
| BANKS, George Washington | WILLIAMS, Cordelia (blk) | 14 MAR 1868 |
| BANKS, Harrison | BANKS, Susan (blk) | 04 JUN 1868 |
| BANKS, Jacob | OWENS, Elizabeth (blk) | 12 MAY 1866 |
| BANKS, James | BOONE, Lizzie | 05 SEP 1866 |
| BANKS, Jerry | MOCKABEE, Harriet (blk) | 26 DEC 1867 |
| BANKS, Marion | JANNEY, Eliza Ann | 03 AUG 1865 |
| BANKS, Moses | WHITE, Jane (blk) | 29 JUN 1867 |
| BANKS, Robert | BANKS, Henritta (blk) | 14 APR 1862 |
| BANKS, Washington | CARROLL, Nancy (blk) | 28 SEP 1867 |
| BANKS, William H. | BARKER, Mary V. | 09 AUG 1862 |
| BANNISTER, William | SMOOT, Charity (blk) | 18 APR 1868 |
| BANSMITH, William T. | NASH, Sally | 17 JUL 1861 |
| BANTER, Peter | MECKES, Louisa | 23 AUG 1866 |
| BANYION, George | ALEXANDER, Julia (blk) | 20 APR 1866 |
| BAPTIST, Jacob | LEWIS, Ellen (blk) | 25 JAN 1864 |
| BAPTIST, John | SHIPLEY, Mary (blk) | 31 MAR 1866 |
| BARBARIN, Francis Sinclair [2] | HOLLINGSWORTH, Hester Frances | 16 JAN 1865 |
| BARBER, C.G. [7b] | WILLIAMS, Nannie | 02 MAY 1870 |

| | | |
|---|---|---|
| BARBER, Jerry | HILL, Isabella (blk) | 06 OCT 1865 |
| BARBER, O.N. [11] | ROSE, Nettie F. | 28 AUG 1867 |
| BARBOUR, John | TAYLOR, Hannah (blk) | 21 DEC 1864 |
| BARBOUR, John | LEE, Betsey (blk) | 30 AUG 1867 |
| BARBOUR, Mercer | BURKE, Lucy J. | 13 JUN 1870 |
| BARBOUR, Simon | WILSON, Lucinda | 19 NOV 1863 |
| BARCHFELD, Ernst | WETTEMANN, Josephine | 30 AUG 1862 |
| BARCLAY, Thomas J. | JACKSON, Sophie D. | 08 SEP 1868 |
| BARCLAY, Wm. H.H. | RIDGELY, Katie | 12 DEC 1859 |
| BARDEN, James W. | JACKSON, Mary R. | 17 APR 1861 |
| BARDEN, James W. | JACKSON, Mary R. | 04 MAR 1867 |
| BAREGARD, Louis | BROCKWAY, Louisa A. | 04 MAR 1867 |
| BARGERSON, Richard | LEE, Ellin (blk) | 12 FEB 1867 |
| BARKER, Abram H. | RUSHMOND, Fanny | 01 JUL 1865 |
| BARKER, Andrew T. | BARKER, Catherine W. | 04 FEB 1869 |
| BARKER, Benjamin F. | PALMER, Balinda | 07 JUN 1859 |
| BARKER, Irwin S. | HEINACKE, Sarah E. | 12 MAY 1859 |
| BARKER, James Hook | REYNOLDS, Elizabeth Belt | 31 MAY 1867 |
| BARKER, James W. | BREWER, Amanda V. | 22 NOV 1865 |
| BARKER, John M. | BYRNE, Marion H. | 04 JUN 1868 |
| BARKER, Richard W. | TOMLINSON, M. Jane | 17 DEC 1860 |
| BARKER, Thomas | ALLEN, Ophelia | 30 JUL 1866 |
| BARKER, William H. | BRISCOE, Martha A. | 12 NOV 1862 |
| BARKMAN, George W. | GLADDEN, Alice | 20 FEB 1869 |
| BARKSCHMIDT, Charles | EFFRINGER, Anna | 07 SEP 1864 |
| BARLOW, Benj. F. | WRYNN, Bridget | 28 MAR 1866 |
| BARLOW, Harry N. | HASTUP, Kate B. | 01 JUL 1867 |
| BARLOW, John W. [11] | BIRNIE, Hessie H.N. | 24 DEC 1861 |
| BARNARD, Frank | FRANTUM, Barbara Ellen | 15 JAN 1863 |
| BARNARD, George A. | FRIES, Barbara A. | 01 SEP 1866 |
| BARNARD, Hanson F. | MILLER, Margaret R. | 29 APR 1865 |
| BARNARD, Samuel | OYSTER, Mary C. | 20 DEC 1858 |
| BARNARD, William T. | THOMAS, Emma J. | 04 MAY 1866 |
| BARNES, Andrew J. [6m] | BURGESS, Salina M. | 15 FEB 1864 |
| BARNES, Anson | TAYLOR, Jane Louisa (blk) | 16 SEP 1865 |
| BARNES, Charles W. | COLLINS, Mary E. | 19 OCT 1858 |
| BARNES, Clem | QUEEN, Lucinda J. (blk) | 03 NOV 1864 |
| BARNES, David | AMBUSH, Eliza (blk) | 23 SEP 1865 |
| BARNES, Edward L. | WILLIAMS, Catharine B. | 10 MAY 1862 |
| BARNES, George | CARROLL, Hannah M. | 26 APR 1867 |
| BARNES, George W. [9e] | DELAY, Martha E. | 02 SEP 1861 |
| BARNES, Henry | GRAYSON, Eliza Ann (blk) | 27 NOV 1868 |
| BARNES, Henry S. | WISE, Mary A. | 08 DEC 1863 |
| BARNES, James F. | DAVIS, Mary E. | 03 JUN 1862 |
| BARNES, James H. | ADAMS, Margaret | 25 MAR 1865 |
| BARNES, James T. | PORTER, Laura A. | 14 NOV 1861 |
| BARNES, James W. | COOPER, Maggie | 26 AUG 1867 |
| BARNES, John F. | SIMMAKA, Mary | 05 DEC 1866 |
| BARNES, John T.[2] | WRIGHT, Elizabeth A.F. | 27 JUL 1864 |
| BARNES, John Thomas | HAGGISON, Caroline (blk) | 28 AUG 1866 |
| BARNES, Joseph | JONES, Mary | 04 OCT 1865 |
| BARNES, Perry | JACKSON, Margaret (blk) | 04 OCT 1865 |
| BARNES, Stephen | MAHONEY, Ellen | 22 JAN 1870 |
| BARNES, Thomas | HOWISON, Lucretia | 06 JAN 1865 |

[2] Note: ret'd. Aug. 30 not used...

| | | |
|---|---|---|
| BARNES, Thomas | LEWIS, Ann (blk) | 04 OCT 1866 |
| BARNES, William | PARKER, Susan Ann (blk) | 29 OCT 1864 |
| BARNES, William | GLASGOW, Birdie (blk) | 28 JAN 1869 |
| BARNES, William A. | CHISM, Susanna | 09 APR 1860 |
| BARNES, William H. | RALEY, Mary Jane | 26 NOV 1862 |
| BARNES, William J. | SANGER, Fannie | 20 JAN 1865 |
| BARNES, William T. | SIMMS, Martha | 16 MAY 1865 |
| BARNETT, Frank | JONES, Susan (blk) | 20 MAY 1864 |
| BARNETT, James | MURRAY, Mary | 15 OCT 1861 |
| BARNETT, John | McCUEN, Julia | 27 JUL 1865 |
| BARNETT, William [11] | MOSS, Nancy | 25 JAN 1862 |
| BARNHART, Michael | [blank], Mary | 29 NOV 1862 |
| BARNSLEY, Columbus | BOYER, Christiana | 12 MAR 1866 |
| BARR, Charles | HOWARD, Henrietta | 08 AUG 1864 |
| BARR, George A. | HICKEY, Margaret | 30 DEC 1861 |
| BARR, J.F. | WALKER, Belle | 28 NOV 1868 |
| BARR, John A. | STEVENS, Lizzie M. | 16 FEB 1864 |
| BARR, John D. | DILLON, Kate J. | 24 OCT 1868 |
| BARR, Levi | BEHREND, Caroline | 14 MAY 1862 |
| BARR, William E. | SWEENEY, Bettie | 06 APR 1868 |
| BARRETT, Aaron | DOVER, Sallie (blk) | 10 SEP 1866 |
| BARRETT, Addison | HARRISON, Marion | 28 AUG 1866 |
| BARRETT, Carey | AYRES, Caroline (blk) | 05 SEP 1865 |
| BARRETT, Charles T.H. | LETTON, Laura D. | 16 MAR 1864 |
| BARRETT, Franklin | SMITH, Julia A. | 13 MAY 1865 |
| BARRETT, Henry | BROADBENT, Jane | 27 JUN 1862 |
| BARRETT, James | CONNOR, Ellen | 01 FEB 1864 |
| BARRETT, James W. | McDONALD, Isabel | 27 JUL 1865 |
| BARRETT, John F. | SHULTZ, Eliza | 24 FEB 1864 |
| BARRETT, Michael | WELSH, Ann | 27 FEB 1864 |
| BARRETT, Nicholas | MARTIN, Bridget | 05 DEC 1864 |
| BARRETT, Patrick | MURROONEY, Margaret | 23 SEP 1863 |
| BARRETT, Standish H. | COLEHOUSE, Virginia Ann | 28 DEC 1868 |
| BARRETT, Thomas | O'DAY, Catharine | 03 OCT 1863 |
| BARRETT, William [7a] | RHEA, Harriet Virginia | 24 MAR 1868 |
| BARRIER, George | RUSSEL, Kate | 04 OCT 1866 |
| BARRIERE, Isidore | FRANCIS, Mary | 29 OCT 1863 |
| BARRINGER, John B. | MALONEY, Mary Ellen | 08 JUL 1859 |
| BARRITT, Thomas | DILLON, Margaret | 17 JAN 1861 |
| BARROLL, Franklin H. | HUNTINGTON, Susan | 27 JUN 1865 |
| BARRON, Alfred D. | SMITH, Kathrine R. | 20 JUL 1863 |
| BARRON, Daniel S.H. | GODFREY, Margaret | 07 OCT 1858 |
| BARRON, Francis | SUIT, Mary Amanda | 21 DEC 1868 |
| BARRON, James | CURTIN, Ann | 30 MAR 1861 |
| BARRON, Leonard | BURNS, Hanna | 07 JAN 1864 |
| BARRON, Wallace C. | THOMPSON, Elizabeth | 05 JUN 1867 |
| BARRY, Daniel | GILL, Rachel Ann | 12 FEB 1863 |
| BARRY, Edward B. | TATSAPAUGH, Julia | 02 MAY 1865 |
| BARRY, James | DONNELLY, Leddy | 12 FEB 1862 |
| BARRY, James | NALLY, Mary Catherine | 06 OCT 1863 |
| BARRY, James | HOLLORAN, Bridget | 02 NOV 1864 |
| BARRY, John | SULLIVAN, Johanna | 24 MAY 1862 |
| BARRY, John | NALIGAN, Mary | 16 DEC 1862 |
| BARRY, John | LEARY, Mary | 16 OCT 1863 |
| BARRY, John N. | PALMER, Sarah Jane | 03 FEB 1859 |
| BARRY, Mahlon P. | WILKINSON, Mary L. | 17 FEB 1862 |

# District of Columbia Marriage Licenses, 1858-1870

| | | |
|---|---|---|
| BARRY, Patrick | CLARKE, Ann | 01 NOV 1865 |
| BARRY, Patrick C. | BARRY, Lucinda | 09 AUG 1859 |
| BARRY, Thomas | ROCHE, Hannah | 11 OCT 1858 |
| BARRY, Thomas | VINSON, Martha Jane | 11 NOV 1864 |
| BARSON, Charles | JACKSON, Elizabeth (blk) | 07 DEC 1864 |
| BART, Paul | BARNEY, Julia | 31 MAY 1860 |
| BARTELS, Henry | O'SHEA, Abbey | 29 JUN 1865 |
| BARTHEL, John | DIETENCH, Gottdilde Catharina | 22 JUN 1863 |
| BARTHOLMIA, Anton | KELLER, Elizabeth | 11 SEP 1861 |
| BARTHOLOW, F.M. | STOTT, Jennie | 28 SEP 1867 |
| BARTHOLOW, Presley | McDONNELL, Sallie V. | 09 MAR 1864 |
| BARTLE, Rudolph F. | ROBEY, Sianna | 09 NOV 1863 |
| BARTLETT, Frank | RIDDLE, Florence | 26 JAN 1866 |
| BARTLETT, George H. [11] | SEIBERT, Malvina E. | 19 MAR 1866 |
| BARTLETT, George W. | MATLOCK, Emma | 28 JAN 1868 |
| BARTLETT, John D. | MANKIN, Mary E. | 13 MAY 1862 |
| BARTLETT, John D. | BENJAMIN, A.A. | 28 JUN 1869 |
| BARTLETT, Joseph | PRENOT, Rose | 17 FEB 1866 |
| BARTLEY, Edward | SCOTT, Mary Jane | 25 AUG 1869 |
| BARTON, Aquilla | HAMMONDS, Susan (blk) | 25 NOV 1862 |
| BARTON, Charles | QUIGLEY, Bridget | 04 NOV 1859 |
| BARTON, Clarence M. | BOHLAYER, Catharine Virginia | 11 APR 1864 |
| BARTON, Isaac | BROWN, Harriet Ann | 29 MAY 1862 |
| BARTON, Lewis | STEVENSON, Luvenia | 03 MAR 1869 |
| BARTON, Perry | SETTLES, Caroline (blk) | 27 MAR 1868 |
| BARTON, Thomas | MARSHALL, Mary | 18 JUN 1866 |
| BARTON, William | PROCTOR, Carrie (blk) | 17 DEC 1868 |
| BASCH, Saul | JACKSON, Esther | 20 AUG 1869 |
| BASHFORD, Philip F. | MARKEY, Annie | 12 OCT 1869 |
| BASKER, John | SIDNEY, Catharine | 17 OCT 1866 |
| BASSETT, George A. [6s] | HOPKINS, Abbie Louise | 01 APR 1865 |
| BASSETT, George T. | TREADWAY, Ella A. | 03 DEC 1861 |
| BASSETT, John | PALMER, Priscilla | 05 JUN 1869 |
| BASSETT, Wesley E. [12s] | SMALLWOOD, Anna | 06 MAR 1861 |
| BASSLER, John | STRONG, Amanda | 19 MAR 1870 |
| BASSY, Shadrick | BASSY, Fanny (blk) | 11 MAY 1868 |
| BASTEN, John Ludeweig Hubert | WIEGMANN, Caroline Antoinette | 06 FEB 1868 |
| BATCHEN, James | PAULINE, Eleanor | 25 OCT 1858 |
| BATEMAN, Samuel | POSKER, Cora (blk) | 27 DEC 1866 |
| BATEMAN, Thomas J. | RODIE, Annie E. | 10 NOV 1863 |
| BATES, Charles A. | LOHNESS, Alice A. | 15 AUG 1868 |
| BATES, Charles S. | STRATTON, Sarah | 17 APR 1866 |
| BATES, George W. [4] | BOTTS, Rosalie | 15 NOV 1865 |
| BATES, Henry | STROSSNER, Mary | 22 NOV 1866 |
| BATES, Hiram G. | AVERY, Arabell E. | 19 FEB 1867 |
| BATES, Horatio | DIGGS, Sophia | 09 APR 1866 |
| BATES, John | HARKINS, Margaret | 17 JAN 1859 |
| BATES, John L. | WILKINSON, Sarah A. | 11 MAR 1867 |
| BATES, Lawson | WILLIAMS, Leathy (blk) | 15 JUN 1870 |
| BATES, William H. [7b] | PURDY, Susan | 21 OCT 1869 |
| BATES, William H.H. [4] | SHIRLEY, Virginia | 25 APR 1867 |
| BATH, Henry | RAHM, Vorona | 04 APR 1863 |
| BATSON, Daniel | JEFFERSON, Chloe (blk) | 18 JUN 1867 |
| BATSON, Thomas | SIMMS, Rebecca | 21 DEC 1861 |
| BATSON, Thomas Henry | GREEN, Jane (blk) | 11 MAY 1866 |
| BATT, John E. [2] | SKIDMORE, Henrietta | 13 JUN 1866 |

| | | |
|---|---|---|
| BATTEN, John | LENDON, Kate | 16 AUG 1866 |
| BATTENFIELD, Frederick | SALZMAN, Barbara | 11 JUN 1868 |
| BATTERY, Wm. H. | WEAKLEY, Sarah | 10 FEB 1864 |
| BATTRELL, John M. | HUNTER, Maria | 24 MAR 1859 |
| BATTS, George M. | CLUBB, Sarah Ann | 17 DEC 1861 |
| BATTY, Henry | DORSEY, Mary I. | 26 NOV 1861 |
| BAUER, George | GRILLBORTZER, Christiana | 03 MAR 1863 |
| BAUER, Sebastian | BAUER, Amelia | 23 JAN 1869 |
| BAUM, Edwin C. | LOMAX, Martha S. | 12 APR 1869 |
| BAUM, Lawrence G. | SCHMITT, Barbara | 03 AUG 1869 |
| BAUMAN, Conrad | HALL, Catharine | 04 JAN 1865 |
| BAUMAN, John M. | WALZ, Catherine | 15 NOV 1862 |
| BAUMANN, John L.F. | WASHEMUTH, Caroline L. | 26 MAR 1862 |
| BAUMANN, John T.L. | WIMMERSBERGER, Johanna B. | 29 NOV 1860 |
| BAUMGARTEN, Julius | HEXTER, Elizabeth | 09 FEB 1859 |
| BAUMLER, Herman | MELHORN, Joanne | 24 OCT 1864 |
| BAURGARD, Edward | LAWLER, Margaret | 29 JUN 1865 |
| BAUVAIS, Dolphis | CHARETTE, Rosalie | 24 NOV 1862 |
| BAWSEL, Minor | LINDSAY, Helen | 14 NOV 1859 |
| BAXTER, Francis H. | PARKER, Ann V. | 27 APR 1868 |
| BAXTER, James W. | WRIGHT, Elizabeth A.F. | 04 JUN 1865 |
| BAXTER, Samuel | McDANIEL, Sarah | 09 MAR 1864 |
| BAXTER, Samuel | CHAMBERS, Agnes | 25 MAR 1869 |
| BAXTON, John | COLEMAN, Betty (blk) | 30 MAY 1868 |
| BAYARD, Theodore W. [4] | SEYMOUR, Florence | 01 DEC 1862 |
| BAYLESS, Henry M. | KILLBRIGHT, Sarah E. | 31 MAY 1860 |
| BAYLEY, Frederick | HURST, Mary | 16 SEP 1863 |
| BAYLIS, George W. | BUSHBY, Mary E. | 22 MAR 1859 |
| BAYLISS, Henry M. | ALOWAY, Mary Ellen | 19 DEC 1864 |
| BAYLISS, John | WILSON, Marion | 18 FEB 1868 |
| BAYLISS, John E. | KUHNS, Susana | 14 JAN 1861 |
| BAYLISS, Peter | MITCHELL, Martha | 21 DEC 1865 |
| BAYLISS, Samuel B. | WINDSOR, Catherine | 24 DEC 1868 |
| BAYLISS, William | ADAMS, Cecelia A. | 09 AUG 1864 |
| BAYLISS, William | BARRETT, Ellen | 13 FEB 1866 |
| BAYLOR, Anderson | PAYNE, Lucy (blk) | 23 MAY 1863 |
| BAYLOR, Daniel | MILLER, Charlotte (blk) | 29 JUN 1867 |
| BAYLOR, John | BAYLOR, Octavia (blk) | 11 JUL 1866 |
| BAYLOR, Robert Allen | ROAN, Nellie (blk) | 24 DEC 1869 |
| BAYLY, Charles B. | HOWARD, Mary V. | 12 MAY 1868 |
| BAYLY, Cornelius | GROVE, Maria (blk) | 10 JUN 1867 |
| BAYLY, James F. [12s] | POLKINHORN, Caroline | 19 JUN 1860 |
| BAYLY, John A. [12s] | MIDDLETON, Mary T. | 24 MAY 1862 |
| BAYLY, Wm. H.C. | ZACHARY, E.G. | 17 JUN 1863 |
| BAYNARD, James S. | RIORDAN, Jennie C. | 12 FEB 1867 |
| BAYNE, John | CRANWELL, Harriet | 05 JAN 1865 |
| BAYNE, John D. | DAVIS, Jane V. | 31 MAY 1866 |
| BAYNE, William H. | NEALE, Mary Adelia T. | 29 JAN 1869 |
| BEACH, Edgar W. | DYSON, Emeline | 10 JAN 1867 |
| BEACH, Eli | CRAWFORD, Eliza Susanna | 03 AUG 1869 |
| BEACH, Horatio F. | HAMMERSLY, Catharine | 14 JUN 1864 |
| BEACH, Horatio F. | POSEY, Mary M. | 11 JAN 1868 |
| BEACH, John | HARDING, Eliza | 09 NOV 1869 |
| BEACH, Samuel | MILLS, Mary F. | 23 JUN 1866 |
| BEACH, Samuel C. | HICKS, Martha | 15 JUN 1867 |
| BEACH, William T. | ELD, Julia A. | 22 JAN 1868 |

# District of Columbia Marriage Licenses, 1858-1870

| | | |
|---|---|---|
| BEACHAM, Elisha James | CLEMENTS, Mary Jane | 02 JUL 1860 |
| BEACHAM, William | JOHNSON, Airy (blk) | 05 JUN 1869 |
| BEACHEM, Peter | TAYLOR, Mary (blk) | 11 AUG 1866 |
| BEADLE, Amos P. | JAMES, Cecelia M. | 22 NOV 1864 |
| BEALE, Aurelius M. | WOOD, Mary Porter | 12 JAN 1864 |
| BEALE, Henry | DORSEY, Ariana | 18 DEC 1862 |
| BEALE, John | CONWAY, Susan (blk) | 18 AUG 1863 |
| BEALE, John Henry | BURTON, Narcissus H. (blk) | 05 NOV 1868 |
| BEALL, Charles B. | RICKETTS, Addie | 11 JAN 1870 |
| BEALL, George A. | RUDD, Sarah | 30 DEC 1869 |
| BEALL, George W. | DORSEY, Fannie E. | 27 MAY 1865 |
| BEALL, Israel [10] | JONES, Cornelia E. | 22 JAN 1863 |
| BEALL, James E. | TRUNNELL, Ellen G. | 21 JUN 1860 |
| BEALL, John I. | DODGE, Elizabeth | 13 JUN 1862 |
| BEALL, John W. | ISAACS, Rebecca | 05 JUL 1864 |
| BEALL, Joseph | RICH, Mary Frances | 07 JUL 1866 |
| BEALL, Larkin A. | SESSFORD, Jeannie E. | 15 DEC 1862 |
| BEALL, N.E. | TUCKER, M.J. | 24 MAY 1869 |
| BEALL, Rich'd. J.P. | LITTLE, Annie E. | 31 MAR 1859 |
| BEALL, Rufus | PUMPHREY, Catherine S. | 22 DEC 1859 |
| BEALL, William | SCHUH, Minnie | 09 JUN 1870 |
| BEAMER, George | FAGAN, Fanny | 07 APR 1869 |
| BEAN, Benjamin F. | FOWLER, Mary Frances | 05 NOV 1861 |
| BEAN, Benjamin F. | HARRISON, Martha | 19 NOV 1867 |
| BEAN, Charles H. | BARBER, Mary A. | 13 DEC 1859 |
| BEAN, Edward D.E.R. | TURNER, Sarah Rebecca | 17 DEC 1860 |
| BEAN, Joseph | CUMMINGS, Mary Frances (blk) | 29 SEP 1869 |
| BEAN, Robert | JOHNSON, Levian (blk) | 01 AUG 1865 |
| BEAN, Thadius | MILLER, Mary Ann | 31 MAY 1870 |
| BEAN, Thomas J. | KIDWELL, Frances C. | 18 APR 1861 |
| BEAN, Washington | PRIOR, Julia (blk) | 20 MAR 1865 |
| BEAN, William H. | KING, Amanda L. | 12 SEP 1861 |
| BEANDER, Francis | WILLIAMS, Clara (blk) | 14 SEP 1864 |
| BEANDER, John | EASTER, Harriet (blk) | 06 JUL 1869 |
| BEANDER, Thomas | BROWN, Catharine (blk) | 01 AUG 1860 |
| BEANS, Asbury | BARNES, Margaret | 04 NOV 1861 |
| BEANS, Washington | BEANS, Kitty | 15 JUL 1868 |
| BEARD, Henry | WOODWARD, Elizabeth (blk) | 17 AUG 1864 |
| BEARD, Joseph S. | SMITH, Mary Ann | 28 DEC 1869 |
| BEARDSLEY, Paul F. | YOUNG, C. Alice | 10 SEP 1867 |
| BEARE, William Seaman [4] | STEPHENS, Eliza Jane | 27 NOV 1861 |
| BEARMAN, Armstead | GRAY, Eliza (blk) | 06 JAN 1866 |
| BEASLER, John | ORSSCESER, Kate | 22 JAN 1863 |
| BEASON, John [Indian] | TOWERS, Bettie G. | 19 FEB 1867 |
| BEATTY, Francis G. | KING, Julia Ann | 27 SEP 1859 |
| BEATTY, William G. | SHANK, Viola Jane | 13 APR 1870 |
| BEATTY, William W. | PAINE, Ann M. | 15 JAN 1867 |
| BEAUDOIN, Jean | BERNARD, Laura | 16 NOV 1861 |
| BEAUMONT, Myron H. [12s] | RANDOLPH, Mary G. | 30 JUN 1862 |
| BEAVERS, Thomas W. | KILLMAN, Annie S. | 06 OCT 1869 |
| BECHLER, Edward | DONOVAN, Catharine | 20 SEP 1865 |
| BECK, August | MILLER, Pauline | 07 MAY 1860 |
| BECK, William | BREWER, Louisa E. | 23 SEP 1858 |
| BECKER, Anthony | TANWEL, Mary | 14 JAN 1861 |
| BECKER, Charles Louis | BRANEMAN, Mary | 18 FEB 1862 |
| BECKER, James Francis | McCARTY, Mary | 19 JUL 1864 |

District of Columbia Marriage Licenses, 1858-1870

| | | |
|---|---|---|
| BECKER, John | SCHAEFER, Martha | 16 MAR 1859 |
| BECKER, William M. | YOST, Mary D. | 27 JAN 1869 |
| BECKERSCHMIDT, John | KORNER, Rosa | 02 FEB 1860 |
| BECKERT, Francis A. | BOCK, Mary Ann | 04 JUN 1862 |
| BECKET, Daniel | TYLER, Mary | 07 APR 1868 |
| BECKET, Isaiah | DELANEY, Frances (blk) | 10 DEC 1868 |
| BECKET, James | BROOKS, Elizabeth (blk) | 09 JUN 1866 |
| BECKET, Lemuel | CRAWFORD, Fannie (blk) | 03 MAY 1866 |
| BECKET, William | BROWN, Caroline (blk) | 03 MAY 1866 |
| BECKET, William | LEE, Elizabeth (blk) | 01 JUN 1869 |
| BECKETT, Andrew | JACKSON, Margaret (blk) | 07 JUL 1869 |
| BECKETT, Columbus | NORRIS, Anne (blk) | 14 JUN 1859 |
| BECKETT, Daniel | GASSAWAY, Catherine Lavinia (blk) | 22 FEB 1870 |
| BECKETT, Eli | LEE, Adele (blk) | 03 MAR 1863 |
| BECKETT, George | JENIFER, Martha (blk) | 30 NOV 1869 |
| BECKETT, Henry | PLUMMER, Elizabeth (blk) | 27 MAY 1865 |
| BECKETT, Robert | PUMPHREY, Elizabeth | 16 MAY 1861 |
| BECKETT, Robert | HUNTER, Hariett A. | 11 JUL 1863 |
| BECKETT, William | LANCASTER, Frances (blk) | 20 SEP 1858 |
| BECKETT, William | BROWN, Mary (blk) | 19 JUN 1866 |
| BECKETT, William | DENT, Susana (blk) | 25 MAR 1868 |
| BECKFORD, James | CROSS, Jane (blk) | 17 JAN 1865 |
| BECKHAM, Thomas E. | FAULCONER, Annie Letitia | 18 SEP 1869 |
| BECKLEY, John | WISE, Loucinda (blk) | 29 OCT 1863 |
| BECKLEY, John W. | WINFIELD, Susan V. (blk) | 04 DEC 1861 |
| BECKLEY, William S. | GIBSON, Rebecca | 30 MAY 1864 |
| BECKLEY, William S. | JONES, Emma A. | 25 AUG 1866 |
| BECKSTEDT, Henry | DREIER, Eliza | 08 JUN 1870 |
| BECKSTINE, William | MURLOCK, Emma | 02 SEP 1868 |
| BECKWITH, John H. | COLLINS, Mary J. (blk) | 13 OCT 1859 |
| BEDDOE, George | JACKSON, Eliza (blk) | 24 AUG 1865 |
| BEDFORD, John | NELSON, Mary (blk) | 31 DEC 1862 |
| BEECHAM, Henry | COLEMAN, Julia A. (blk) | 18 SEP 1865 |
| BEEDY, Seth Ela | HAMLIN, Amanda M. | 07 NOV 1861 |
| BEEK, Wm. [1c] | BROWN, Sarah A.L.V. | 15 DEC 1863 |
| BEELMYER, Andrew J. | HARPER, Martha | 31 DEC 1862 |
| BEEN, Jacob | ANGEL, Martha E. | 22 DEC 1864 |
| BEENDER, Thomas | JOHNSON, Anna (blk) | 09 SEP 1861 |
| BEGAN, Jeremiah | POWER, Mary | 11 JAN 1868 |
| BEGUIN, Maurice | O'CONNER, Catherine | 09 AUG 1866 |
| BEHRENDS, August | HART, Caroline | 25 JUN 1866 |
| BEHRENS, Charles F. | MEADER, Adelaide | 27 APR 1864 |
| BEHRENS, Charles Ferderick | BECK, Henrietta | 07 MAY 1865 |
| BEHRENS, Henri | STEIRERNAGEL, Mari | 27 APR 1868 |
| BEHRNE, August | BUCKLEY, Ellen | 15 JUN 1861 |
| BEITZELL, Josiah | WESER, Mary | 16 NOV 1859 |
| BELFORD, Henry | WILKINSON, Amanda (blk) | 04 FEB 1864 |
| BELL, Alfred | THOMAS, Eliza (blk) | 23 SEP 1858 |
| BELL, Alonzo | LEMON, Mary V. | 30 OCT 1868 |
| BELL, Anderson K. | GARNER, Eliza R. | 23 MAR 1868 |
| BELL, Anthony | BROWN, Martha (blk) | 16 APR 1869 |
| BELL, Asbury | GARDNER, Rachel Ann | 11 MAR 1867 |
| BELL, Baltimore | ROBINSON, Matilda (blk) | 14 DEC 1864 |
| BELL, Basil | HERBY, Louisa (blk) | 26 SEP 1865 |
| BELL, Benjamin [12s] | SPEAKS, Winnie Ann | 26 JUN 1862 |
| BELL, Charles | SCOTT, Sarah Elizabeth (blk) | 01 OCT 1868 |

17

District of Columbia Marriage Licenses, 1858-1870

| | | |
|---|---|---|
| BELL, Charles | BURROWES, Sarah (blk) | 07 JUN 1870 |
| BELL, Charles A. [11] | EVANS, Evanina F. | 04 DEC 1866 |
| BELL, Christopher | DIGGES, Fanny (blk) | 11 FEB 1869 |
| BELL, Daniel [12s] | BETTER, Mary J. (blk) | 11 APR 1861 |
| BELL, Daniel | WILLIAMS, Christy A. (blk) | 17 DEC 1860 |
| BELL, Edward | WILLIAMS, Sarah (col'd) | 23 JAN 1864 |
| BELL, Emanuel | MITCHELL, Catherine (blk) | 01 SEP 1863 |
| BELL, Francis | PROCTOR, Jane (blk) | 22 MAR 1859 |
| BELL, Frederick | KELLY, Mary E. | 05 DEC 1864 |
| BELL, George W. | WILLIAMS, Virginia E. | 17 FEB 1869 |
| BELL, Gilbert | HALL, Rebecca (blk) | 30 APR 1866 |
| BELL, Henry | HEVERN, Mary Jane (blk) | 18 JUL 1867 |
| BELL, Henry | MAGRUDER, Hester Ann | 29 AUG 1868 |
| BELL, Henry [1e] | BROWN, Caroline | 02 JUN 1866 |
| BELL, Jacob T. | HOLMES, Bettie (blk) | 25 JAN 1867 |
| BELL, John | WARD, Amanda (blk) | 24 DEC 1863 |
| BELL, John | WILSON, Jane | 25 FEB 1864 |
| BELL, John | OSBORN, Jane (blk) | 04 AUG 1864 |
| BELL, John | BROWN, Drusilla (blk) | 13 FEB 1865 |
| BELL, John | COLE, Margaret (blk) | 08 MAR 1866 |
| BELL, John | YOUNG, Bettie (blk) | 03 SEP 1866 |
| BELL, John | CHASE, Harriet (blk) | 13 FEB 1868 |
| BELL, John | COSBY, Maria (blk) | 19 MAY 1868 |
| BELL, John S. | WEAVER, Amelia | 05 JAN 1859 |
| BELL, John W. | ZIRKLE, Jennie M. | 13 JAN 1869 |
| BELL, Landon | TAYLOR, Ellen (blk) | 04 NOV 1868 |
| BELL, Lloyd C. | BURKE, Mary J. | 05 MAY 1859 |
| BELL, Mark B. | CARTER, Louisa (blk) | 25 SEP 1867 |
| BELL, Miles | DOUGLASS, Ann (blk) | 03 JUL 1869 |
| BELL, Peter | THOMAS, Martha (blk) | 16 JUN 1864 |
| BELL, Peter | LOCKINS, Maria | 21 NOV 1864 |
| BELL, Thomas | JACKSON, Eliza Ann (blk) | 13 JUN 1867 |
| BELL, William H. | SHELTON, Rebecca (blk) | 06 NOV 1869 |
| BELL, William Henry | RODES, Lucy (blk) | 03 DEC 1867 |
| BELLAW, Robert | KOUGH, Sarah | 14 SEP 1861 |
| BELLFIELD, Jesse | BAILY, Margaret (blk) | 03 MAY 1864 |
| BELLI, Bartolomeo | CUNIO, Maria | 24 APR 1865 |
| BELLMORE, Peter | LEE, Fanny (blk) | 12 NOV 1868 |
| BELLOWS, Josiah | BROWN, Helen A. | 19 DEC 1867 |
| BELT, George | MARS, Adaline (blk) | 20 JUL 1869 |
| BELT, Harvey C. | KRETZER, Anna | 16 FEB 1870 |
| BELT, John W. | NALLE, Mary D. | 29 JUN 1868 |
| BELT, Thomas | QUEEN, Mary (blk) | 05 OCT 1860 |
| BELT, Trueman, Jr. | TYLER, Annie Catherine | 08 NOV 1869 |
| BELT, William | GROSS, Eliza (blk) | 29 DEC 1868 |
| BELT, William M. | BOND, Eleanor E. | 15 OCT 1862 |
| BEMENT, Ernest M. | POLLARD, Mary L. | 06 APR 1861 |
| BEMIS, Isaac A. [11] | DAVIS, Annie M. | 10 JAN 1868 |
| BENCH, John T. | HEFFEL, Mary A. | 25 SEP 1867 |
| BENDER, Geo. W. | FAULKNER, Maria L. | 21 DEC 1865 |
| BENDER, Henry | McGUIRE, Mary A. | 28 APR 1862 |
| BENDZ, Waldeman E. | CLAUSON, Anna M. | 29 APR 1867 |
| BENF, John | RHEINHARDT, Lizzie | 11 MAY 1865 |
| BENHAM, Isaac [10] | HILL, Mary [Ann] | 20 AUG 1867 |
| BENHART, Henry Edward | THOMPSON, Addie Cecelia | 21 DEC 1869 |
| BENHEIM, Henry | WIERE, Sarah | 24 AUG 1869 |

| | | |
|---|---|---|
| BENISCH, Joseph | SOLOMON, Rosa | 23 OCT 1869 |
| BENJAMIN, Chas. F. | JAY, Virginia | 08 FEB 1869 |
| BENJAMIN, William T. | SMITH, Mary T. (blk) | 01 AUG 1866 |
| BENKENGER, Frederick H. | KREGER, Christiana | 02 NOV 1868 |
| BENNER, Allain R. [11] * | HARRISON, Ella | 01 JAN 1859 |
| BENNET, Charles N. | SHEDD, Alice J. | 13 JUN 1866 |
| BENNETT, Arthur J. | ESCHHOLTZ, Fannie G. | 27 JAN 1870 |
| BENNETT, Benjamin C. | BURKE, Mary Ann (blk) | 26 NOV 1862 |
| BENNETT, Charles M. | JACKSON, Eliza (blk) | 02 OCT 1869 |
| BENNETT, David J. | STAPLES, Sarah (blk) | 03 NOV 1865 |
| BENNETT, Edward | WOODS, Ellen | 31 OCT 1865 |
| BENNETT, George W. | WARD, Mary | 12 FEB 1862 |
| BENNETT, Harrison M. | KINCH, Angella H. | 21 FEB 1868 |
| BENNETT, Henry B. | SELEE, Mary L. | 27 JUN 1867 |
| BENNETT, James | MADDEN, Mary | 06 JAN 1863 |
| BENNETT, John | ROBISON, Ellen (blk) | 17 AUG 1869 |
| BENNETT, John E. | DAVIS, Ann | 15 MAY 1862 |
| BENNETT, John Matthias | TIBBLES, Mary Lucinda (blk) | 18 OCT 1864 |
| BENNETT, Richard A. [10] | DENNIS, Henrietta B. | 14 APR 1870 |
| BENNETT, Roger | KLINTENCE, Mary S. | 08 JAN 1863 |
| BENNETT, Rufus | WILLIAM, Bell (blk) | 21 JUL 1868 |
| BENNETT, William | FRINDE, Mary Jane | 25 DEC 1861 |
| BENNETT, William H. [1c] | TUCKER, Drusie M. | 15 FEB 1864 |
| BENNETT, William H. | WRIGHT, Laura C. | 17 MAR 1870 |
| BENNYX, Robert | BALL, Ann E. | 12 NOV 1862 |
| BENSER, George W. | DOVER, Marion | 23 NOV 1859 |
| BENSON, Geo. W.S. | HUTCHINSON, Emma | 29 JUN 1866 |
| BENSON, James | COBURN, Catharine | 12 DEC 1866 |
| BENSON, Thomas J. | WILCOXEN, Martha Ann | 09 OCT 1862 |
| BENSON, Wm. H. | COOVER, Elizth. V. | 28 JUL 1862 |
| BENTLEY, E., Dr., USA | WILLIAMS, Margaret E. | 02 SEP 1868 |
| BENTLEY, George A. | PLANT, Georgie A. | 04 MAR 1867 |
| BENTLEY, Henry | COUNTEE, Ellen (blk) | 09 FEB 1870 |
| BENTON, Edward T. | SHAW, Emma V. | 20 MAR 1862 |
| BENTON, John W. [11] | STEHLE, Lina | 15 JUL 1865 |
| BENTON, Theodore S. | WOLF, Mary Dorcas | 30 MAR 1869 |
| BENTON, Thomas [2] | DUNDA, Emma | 19 NOV 1868 |
| BENTON, Warren C. | HEPBURN, Mary M. | 13 JUN 1866 |
| BENTZ, Charles | WELLS, Susana | 11 NOV 1861 |
| BENTZLER, John | BURCH, Adaline | 27 NOV 1860 |
| BENTZLER, John L. [4] | CLEMENTS, Annie [R.] | 01 AUG 1867 |
| BENZ, Theodore | VOGELESANG, Anna E. | 13 MAR 1861 |
| BENZE, Henry | SIRLY, Sarah Louisa | 13 NOV 1862 |
| BEODICK, Conrad | LINTNER, Mary | 23 DEC 1863 |
| BERBERICH, Robert R. | WALTER, Magdalina M. | 26 OCT 1869 |
| BERGA, John | GERBER, Elizabeth | 18 APR 1867 |
| BERGER, Heinrich | MENZE, Lotte | 01 AUG 1859 |
| BERGER, Jacob | SPAIT, Annie | 12 MAY 1863 |
| BERGMAN, Henry E. | BAUMAN, Elizabeth Caroline | 09 FEB 1867 |
| BERKLEY, Charles T. [6c] | MEECHAN, Emma | 16 NOV 1858 |
| BERKLEY, David L. | WORTHINGTON, Frances Ann | 31 JAN 1862 |
| BERKLEY, James | SMITH, Mary E. | 29 MAY 1862 |
| BERKLEY, John W. | MASON, Sally M. | 30 OCT 1862 |
| BERKLEY, Joseph M. | BUCKLEY, Josephine | 28 MAY 1863 |
| BERKLEY, Joseph M. [10] | HOUGHTILLING, Ida | 10 AUG 1866 |
| BERKLEY, Thomas [10] | ALLEN, Amanda | 16 DEC 1869 |

District of Columbia Marriage Licenses, 1858-1870

| | | |
|---|---|---|
| BERKLEY, William E. | DUVALL, Mary Jane | 30 DEC 1859 |
| BERLINE, James M. | HENDERSON, Roberta | 04 JUN 1860 |
| BERLY, Griffith | JOHNSON, Lucy Ann | 04 MAY 1869 |
| BERNARD, R.F. | FRANK, Alice V. | 04 DEC 1866 |
| BERNARD, Richard | DUVALL, Lucy A. | 24 NOV 1863 |
| BERNARD, William H. | MARTIN, Margaret B. | 27 SEP 1862 |
| BERNHARD, Andrew | STOFFEL, Mary U. | 14 JUN 1861 |
| BERNHARD, Andrew | CASPER, Mary Rose | 12 MAY 1870 |
| BERNHARD, Caspar | RITLEY, Ellen F. | 10 DEC 1860 |
| BERRER, George | NANZ, Frederika | 01 AUG 1860 |
| BERRES, Joseph | GENSLER, Mary | 03 OCT 1864 |
| BERRIAN, Hobart, Jr. | GRENDLE, Mary E. | 25 JAN 1870 |
| BERRY, Benjamin C. | McGWINN, Hanora | 08 NOV 1869 |
| BERRY, Caleb | JOHNSON, Eliza | 14 DEC 1867 |
| BERRY, Charles H. | FOSSETT, Harriet | 10 OCT 1862 |
| BERRY, Dennis | BERRY, Lucy (blk) | 05 DEC 1865 |
| BERRY, Edward Payson, Lt. USA [12s] | FISHER, Mary E. | 14 JAN 1863 |
| BERRY, Gabriel | BARKER, Lucinda (blk) | 24 JAN 1868 |
| BERRY, George M. [1e] | MYERS, Emma J. | 03 AUG 1865 |
| BERRY, Jeremiah | BOGGS, Catherine Stewart | 31 MAR 1866 |
| BERRY, John | NICHOLSON, Sarah F. | 07 NOV 1859 |
| BERRY, John | HERBERT, Mary C. (blk) | 18 APR 1861 |
| BERRY, John | LOCKER, Martha (blk) | 16 MAY 1865 |
| BERRY, John | FREELAND, Jane | 05 DEC 1865 |
| BERRY, John | SUMBY, Mary A. (blk) | 27 DEC 1866 |
| BERRY, John | WHEELER, Sarah (blk) | 14 MAY 1870 |
| BERRY, John H. | SMALL, Grace | 29 MAR 1870 |
| BERRY, Lucien | BERRY, Amelia O. | 23 JUL 1860 |
| BERRY, Thomas | COOMBS, Mary | 02 OCT 1858 |
| BERRY, Thomas H. | CHAPMAN, Ann | 29 JUN 1868 |
| BERRY, William F. | BATEMAN, Sallie L. | 08 JAN 1868 |
| BERRY, William H. | FRY, Magdalena | 14 AUG 1861 |
| BERTHRONG, Henry W. | THOMPSON, Annie L. | 19 DEC 1864 |
| BERTHRONG, Henry W. | THOMPSON, Annie L. | 23 OCT 1865 |
| BESLEY, Bartholomew [1e] | WILSON, Sarah E. | 24 APR 1866 |
| BESSER, Joseph | EBERLING, Madeline | 29 AUG 1859 |
| BEST, Frank | ELZY, Sarah | 25 NOV 1868 |
| BEST, Samuel | TURNER, Margaret | 06 JAN 1863 |
| BESTER, Owen R. | CROMWELL, Hattie A. | 06 MAY 1867 |
| BETTER, William H. | NICHOLS, Georgianna (blk) | 22 JUN 1868 |
| BETTERTON, John | HARRISON, Cynthia A. | 27 OCT 1863 |
| BETTIS, F.A. | MITCHELL, Margaret | 31 OCT 1867 |
| BETTON, Joel W. | GRIFFIN, Jeannie | 25 MAY 1864 |
| BETTS, Barzilla [Chase] [6m] | JACOBS, Harriet [Cromwell] | 10 JUL 1862 |
| BETTS, Edward E. | ROBERTS, Caroline J. | 28 APR 1864 |
| BETTS, Royston M. | ROBINSON, Kate | 03 JUL 1861 |
| BETTS, William | NALLY, Elizabeth R. | 11 JAN 1861 |
| BETZ, Frank | MYER, Mary | 19 SEP 1864 |
| BETZ, John M. | HOLMES, Susan C. | 31 MAY 1860 |
| BEUCHERT, Edward | FUCHS, Josaphona | 08 SEP 1869 |
| BEUCHERT, William | REHBERGER, Agnes | 18 OCT 1867 |
| BEVAN, Thomas Walter | SERGEANT, Catharine Elizabeth | 30 MAY 1864 |
| BEVANS, James | DAVIES, Mary Virginia | 17 OCT 1864 |
| BEVANS, Thomas H. | AUSTIN, Adeline | 11 MAR 1861 |
| BEVENS, James | GARDNER, Caroline | 03 APR 1860 |
| BEVENS, William | FLASHMAN, Barbara | 19 DEC 1862 |

District of Columbia Marriage Licenses, 1858-1870

| | | |
|---|---|---|
| BEVERIDGE, M. William [9e] | CAMMACK, Elphine | 05 AUG 1861 |
| BEVERIDGE, M. William | McKELDEN, Susan J. | 12 SEP 1865 |
| BEVERLY, Horace | CARTER, Nancy (blk) | 11 DEC 1862 |
| BEVERLY, Jackson | BLACK, Jenny (blk) | 16 DEC 1867 |
| BEVERLY, John | BABER, Charlotte (blk) | 19 JUL 1864 |
| BEVERLY, John | PANGSLEY, Lizzie | 01 DEC 1869 |
| BEVERLY, Presley | CORBIN, Louisa (blk) | 18 AUG 1864 |
| BEVERLY, Robinson | BUCKNER, Delphia (blk) | 17 JUN 1867 |
| BEVERLY, Tucker | BROWN, Rosey (blk) | 06 JAN 1864 |
| BIAS, Henry | PRIMAS, Sophia (blk) | 06 AUG 1866 |
| BIBB, Caleb | FORTUNE, Susan | 06 SEP 1864 |
| BICKARD, Henry | HAAS, Louisa | 30 JUL 1859 |
| BICKELER, Martin V. | TAYLOR, Barbara A. | 14 MAY 1866 |
| BICKFORD, Warren C. | HARNER, Sarah R. | 12 APR 1866 |
| BICKLEHAUPT, John | BEVANS, Belinda | 30 AUG 1864 |
| BICKNELL, James | WESTON, Laura, Mrs. | 18 FEB 1865 |
| BICKSLER, Henry F. | BARKER, Sarah J. | 01 MAR 1866 |
| BICKSLER, John W. | MITCHELL, Susan R. | 04 APR 1866 |
| BIDWELL, Eli | BOTTS, Mary (blk) | 22 FEB 1864 |
| BIDWELL, John | KENNEDY, Annie E. | 10 APR 1868 |
| BIEGER, Philip | BARTHOLMAI, Julia | 19 OCT 1864 |
| BIEGLER, Philip | OSTHAUS, Mary M. | 24 JAN 1861 |
| BIERI, John | ANDERSON, Ella | 09 FEB 1864 |
| BIERLEIN, George | BEKERSCHMIDT, Anna | 13 SEP 1862 |
| BIGELOW, Benjamin F. | BURR, Maria L. | 02 SEP 1869 |
| BIGELOW, Jacob | OGDEN, Rebecca M. | 25 JUL 1859 |
| BIGELOW, Lendall H. | HARRIS, Bettie | 22 SEP 1865 |
| BIGGER, J.D. | SHOWELL, L.M. | 04 FEB 1868 |
| BIGGS, Dallas | LEAKE, Aurelia | 10 SEP 1866 |
| BIGGS, Daniel | DICK, Rutha | 28 AUG 1862 |
| BIGGS, Henry R. | SLAVEN, Martha C. | 02 JUL 1866 |
| BIGGS, John H. | JOHNSON, Isabella | 13 SEP 1858 |
| BIGGS, William | KERSHAW, Alice | 17 MAR 1868 |
| BIGGS, William [Henry] [10] | GUY, Sarah | 09 JUL 1861 |
| BIGGS, William T. | CRESHAW, Alice | 21 OCT 1858 |
| BIGGS, William T. | MARTIN, Hannah M. | 31 AUG 1863 |
| BIGLEY, D.R.P. | MOORE, Alice | 08 NOV 1864 |
| BILLING, Andrew | SCHNEIDER, Auguste | 11 OCT 1859 |
| BILLINGS, John S., Dr. [3] | STEVENS, Kate M. | 03 SEP 1862 |
| BILLS, Daniel W. | RUNDLE, Annie | 09 MAY 1864 |
| BILLS, Daniel W. | KENNEDY, Bridget | 02 NOV 1864 |
| BILYEN, Sanford | BROWN, Mary Ann | 28 MAY 1863 |
| BIMFORD, James M. | BERNARD, Jane | 23 JAN 1869 |
| BINCKLEY, John M. | MICHEL, Mary Louisa | 14 SEP 1859 |
| BINGHAM, John | BUTLER, Susan (blk) | 10 MAY 1864 |
| BINGHAM, L.W. | BANGS, Lucy A. | 13 MAY 1867 |
| BINGHAM, Lafayette | McKINSTRY, Calista A. | 12 JUL 1862 |
| BINGHAN, George | WASHINGTON, Sarah (blk) | 18 NOV 1862 |
| BINNEY, John | MILLER, Mary L. | 01 MAY 1862 |
| BIRCH, Charles W. [7a] | MYERS, Tacy Virginia | 18 SEP 1867 |
| BIRCH, Ealbeck W. | DAVIS, Frances | 17 MAR 1866 |
| BIRCH, James E.H. | GLASSGOW, Mary Caroline | 24 DEC 1861 |
| BIRCH, James Henry | PYLES, Sarah Ellen | 31 JAN 1860 |
| BIRCH, John | COLISON, Mary Jane | 24 FEB 1862 |
| BIRCH, Joseph R. | MURRAY, Mildred | 21 FEB 1860 |
| BIRCKLEY, Archie | SHERRIER, Emile Elizabeth | 15 JAN 1859 |

# District of Columbia Marriage Licenses, 1858-1870

| | | |
|---|---|---|
| BIRD, Alexander | SMITH, Lizzie (blk) | 26 APR 1867 |
| BIRD, Andrew N. [2] | JONES, Robina W. | 21 DEC 1864 |
| BIRD, Barny | BAYLOR, Evelina (blk) | 08 JUL 1867 |
| BIRD, Henry | JOHNSON, Lucinda (blk) | 13 JUN 1867 |
| BIRD, Samuel | CASEY, Caroline (blk) | 15 AUG 1867 |
| BIRD, Thomas R. | BRODEN, Mary | 11 JAN 1868 |
| BIRKIGT, Louis A. | ENGLE, Mary | 06 JUN 1862 |
| BIRKLEY, Richard | GARNET, Biddy (blk) | 04 NOV 1862 |
| BIRNEY, Sylvester | JOHNSON, Mary (blk) | 07 JUN 1869 |
| BIRTWELL, Daniel | BEMIS, Sylvia S. | 19 MAY 1870 |
| BISBEE, Fred W. | CARROLL, Sarah A. | 25 APR 1870 |
| BISCHOF, Andreas | SCHLEGEL, Maria | 09 APR 1864 |
| BISCOE, William | SASSER, Mary C. | 22 DEC 1858 |
| BISHOP, Augustus A. | DICE, Dora | 19 NOV 1866 |
| BISHOP, Charles C. | COUGHLAN, Anna Stacia | 02 SEP 1863 |
| BISHOP, Charles Eugene | WIMSATT, Mary Lodaisca | 03 MAY 1864 |
| BISHOP, Charles R. | BIRD, Elizabeth | 07 NOV 1860 |
| BISHOP, George W. | STINSON, Mary | 21 DEC 1863 |
| BISHOP, Henry | POOL, Annie E. | 04 JAN 1862 |
| BISHOP, Henry H. | REINHARD, Minnie | 24 NOV 1868 |
| BISHOP, Joseph B. | LACY, Lizzie | 23 APR 1861 |
| BISHOP, Leroy C. | WILLIAMS, Eliza E. | 09 MAY 1860 |
| BISHOP, Varden R. | CARR, Emma F. | 04 DEC 1860 |
| BISHOP, William | CLEMENTS, E.C. Mills | 13 JAN 1869 |
| BIVANS, James P. [6h] | CHILDS, Almina | 16 MAY 1868 |
| BIVINS, Charles | WHITAKER, Sarah | 21 DEC 1869 |
| BIXLER, John A. | SCHLOUGH, Sabina C. | 10 JAN 1865 |
| BLACK, Daniel | CAMPBELL, Laura A. (blk) | 16 SEP 1861 |
| BLACK, James H. | BROWN, Sydney Ann (blk) | 09 JAN 1862 |
| BLACK, John | THOMPSON, Ann Eliza | 08 APR 1862 |
| BLACK, Robert | WELCH, Susan T. | 09 AUG 1865 |
| BLACK, William James | MURPHY, Mary | 26 MAY 1865 |
| BLACKBURN, Isaac | SELBY, Mary | 25 MAY 1865 |
| BLACKBURN, Isaac | WASHINGTON, Emily (blk) | 23 DEC 1868 |
| BLACKBURN, James | WILLIAMS, Mary Ann (blk) | 31 JUL 1867 |
| BLACKBURN, Joseph | FORTNER, Lavinia | 03 JUL 1861 |
| BLACKBURN, Richard | YOUNG, Harriet (blk) | 09 NOV 1865 |
| BLACKFORD, Charles H. | WILLIAMS, Mary | 21 AUG 1865 |
| BLACKFORD, John S., Jr. | RITTER, Mary Fannie | 12 DEC 1859 |
| BLACKFORD, William D. | PILLSBURY, Frances T. | 08 OCT 1868 |
| BLACKLEY, Lamberth | GORDON, Caroline (blk) | 31 AUG 1864 |
| BLACKLOCK, F. Sydney | SWANN, Julia | 18 JUN 1859 |
| BLACKMAN, Andrew J. | HOLT, Henrietta J. | 27 AUG 1863 |
| BLACKSIN, Charles | BROOKS, Sarah Ann (blk) | 22 NOV 1866 |
| BLACKSON, George | JOHNSON, Eliza (blk) | 04 JUN 1866 |
| BLACKSTON, Henry | BROOKS, Margaret (blk) | 19 OCT 1869 |
| BLACKSTONE, James | MARSHALL, Josephine (blk) | 03 AUG 1865 |
| BLACKWELL, Eli | TYLER, Mary (blk) | 04 OCT 1869 |
| BLACKWELL, John | FOX, Fanny | 10 JUN 1864 |
| BLACKWELL, Joseph A. | BUTLER, Frances E. | 25 JUL 1867 |
| BLACKWELL, Solomon | JONES, Winney | 20 JUL 1865 |
| BLACKWELL, Solomon | JOHNSON, Patsey (blk) | 14 APR 1869 |
| BLACKWELL, Thornton | FOX, Annie | 30 MAY 1864 |
| BLACKWOOD, Hayward | THOMAS, Lucinda (blk) | 03 MAR 1863 |
| BLADE, George W. | WARD, Elizabeth | 14 NOV 1866 |
| BLADEN, Charles | WELDON, Mary | 15 JAN 1864 |

District of Columbia Marriage Licenses, 1858-1870

| | | |
|---|---|---|
| BLADEN, George | DAVIS, Anna | 10 JAN 1870 |
| BLADEN, John T. | KEIN, Alcyndia Ann | 23 FEB 1860 |
| BLAGBAY, Gibson | WILSON, Rachel (blk) | 30 MAY 1866 |
| BLAGUE, Theodore | WILLIAMSON, Lizzie R. | 07 OCT 1861 |
| BLAIN, Joseph A. | STONE, Emma C. | 18 AUG 1868 |
| BLAINE, Robert G. | HICKS, Rebecca A. | 11 FEB 1867 |
| BLAIR, Alonzo F. | GAVIT, Josephine O. | 19 MAY 1863 |
| BLAIR, David | EBERLE, Sarah | 04 DEC 1866 |
| BLAIR, James D. | LUDEKE, Annie | 06 SEP 1865 |
| BLAIR, Jeremiah [6] | MATTINGLY, Julia Francis | 23 NOV 1868 |
| BLAIR, John | GRAY, Charlotte (blk) | 07 MAR 1866 |
| BLAIR, John | BROWN, Eliza (blk) | 06 JUL 1868 |
| BLAIR, John M. | MILLER, Maggie D. | 26 JAN 1867 |
| BLAIR, Robert | WILKINS, Martha Lavinia (blk) | 12 AUG 1869 |
| BLAKE, Caleb | DEAN, Julia | 09 APR 1864 |
| BLAKE, Dennis | CONNOLLY, Margaret | 01 MAR 1862 |
| BLAKE, Francis | BROWN, Henrietta Ann | 18 MAR 1862 |
| BLAKE, Francis O. | HAMMOND, Amelia | 07 NOV 1862 |
| BLAKE, George W. | GREEN, Eliza (blk) | 03 DEC 1864 |
| BLAKE, George W. [7a] | HILL, Sarah A. | 22 NOV 1866 |
| BLAKE, James | LEE, Eliza | 11 APR 1867 |
| BLAKE, John | PAYNE, Catharine | 01 DEC 1862 |
| BLAKE, John F. | BUTLER, Helen M. | 17 DEC 1861 |
| BLAKE, Nicholas | CONNELL, Julia | 15 FEB 1862 |
| BLAKE, Temple | JOHNSON, Jennie (blk) | 29 JUL 1865 |
| BLAKELY, Thomas M. | HAWKINS, Catherine | 02 OCT 1869 |
| BLAKENEY, George W. | HOTTENFELLER, Ellen | 19 JUL 1864 |
| BLAKENEY, James T. | MANN, Hannah F. | 24 JAN 1859 |
| BLANCHARD, Charles B. | SCOTT, Lucy A. | 26 JUL 1867 |
| BLANCHARD, Job [6s] | BUTTERBALL, Emily A., Mrs. | 20 FEB 1865 |
| BLANCHFIELD, James | COLLINS, Ellen | 04 AUG 1862 |
| BLAND, Emanuel | ROBINSON, Agnes (blk) | 04 FEB 1870 |
| BLAND, Hiram Urbiff | SIMPSON, Margaret A. | 27 SEP 1869 |
| BLAND, James | FAIRFAX, Mary (blk) | 22 SEP 1868 |
| BLAND, James H. | FOWLER, Maria L. | 24 AUG 1865 |
| BLAND, James W. | BOYCE, Emma | 29 DEC 1864 |
| BLAND, Parker | BROOKS, Gracey (blk) | 01 DEC 1865 |
| BLAND, Parker | SWANIGAN, Martha (blk) | 01 OCT 1866 |
| BLANEY, William | KELLY, Ellen | 24 FEB 1868 |
| BLANHAM, Joseph | GRAY, Charlotte | 23 OCT 1865 |
| BLASTELLO, George | EMMERSON, Emma D. | 22 FEB 1865 |
| BLATTLER, Joseph | SUISKIND, Mary Ann | 10 JUL 1866 |
| BLEACH, Dennis | GUYNON, Julia | 31 JAN 1863 |
| BLEEKER, Stephen | LEWIS, Mary Etta | 25 DEC 1858 |
| BLEIDT, Peter | FRANZ, Frederika | 14 JAN 1864 |
| BLEIFUS, Adolph | BEICHERT, Kathe | 14 MAY 1867 |
| BLEW, Larcum | McKINNEY, Sarah (blk) | 15 OCT 1867 |
| BLEW, Samuel | MAFFIS, Ellen (blk) | 07 SEP 1868 |
| BLEWITT, Edward [6m] | McFARLAND, Catharine | 25 MAY 1863 |
| BLIGH, James | CONNOR, Mary | 13 AUG 1867 |
| BLIGH, John | CATON, Margaret | 31 MAY 1866 |
| BLINKHORN, T.A. | KELLIGAN, Ellen | 09 MAY 1868 |
| BLINKOE, Charles | WESEN, Susan | 03 NOV 1860 |
| BLISS, Dwight H. | MULLIKEN, Mary F. | 03 OCT 1864 |
| BLISS, James E. | KING, Sylvia L. | 25 APR 1863 |
| BLOOMER, Antone | FUGAL, Jane | 15 NOV 1862 |

## District of Columbia Marriage Licenses, 1858-1870

| Groom | Bride | Date |
|---|---|---|
| BLOOMER, William | CRAWFORD, Emma J. | 26 OCT 1859 |
| BLOOR, John D. | ALEXANDER, Catherine Mariamne | 29 FEB 1860 |
| BLOSS, Charles H. [12s] | SEABURY, Eliza M. | 24 DEC 1861 |
| BLOSS, John B. | GILBERT, Sarah R. | 11 OCT 1858 |
| BLOSSOM, Solomo | POOL, Mary James | 10 JUN 1859 |
| BLÖTTNER, William | MEYERS, Margaret | 10 NOV 1863 |
| BLOW, Peter B. | ADAIR, Maggie | 18 OCT 1865 |
| BLOW, Peter B. | ADAIR, Maggie | 18 OCT 1865 |
| BLOXTON, Allen H. | SCHAFFER, Christina Barbara | 04 MAY 1865 |
| BLÜCHER, Adam | KÖRNER, Louise | 23 JAN 1864 |
| BLUECKER, George Frederick | HUHN, Rosina | 26 JUL 1865 |
| BLUM, Gerhardt | SANDERS, Elizabeth | 16 JUN 1864 |
| BLUMER, Frederick E. [10] | BAKER, Elizabeth [Emmeline] | 05 FEB 1867 |
| BLUMER, John | BAKER, Christiann | 07 OCT 1863 |
| BLUMLEY, John A. | SHYROCK, Maggie | 04 FEB 1865 |
| BLUNDON, John F. | NOLAND, Fannie F. | 08 JUN 1866 |
| BLUSH, Edwin H. | KEENAN, Mary Jane | 27 JUN 1868 |
| BOARDLEY, Albert | WILLIAMS, Sarah (blk) | 23 JAN 1867 |
| BOARDMAN, George W. [11] | WIDDECOMB, [Catherine M.] | 14 JUL 1863 |
| BOARDMAN, Myron | HUESTIS, Almira L. | 04 APR 1868 |
| BOARMAN, William J. | DOVE, Mary A. | 04 AUG 1869 |
| BOAZ, Edward Thomas | DEWEES, Mary Amelia | 01 JUL 1868 |
| BOCKING, Richard C. | SHEDD, Susie L. | 24 NOV 1865 |
| BODDIE, John Henry | HUMPHREYS, Caroline | 06 DEC 1865 |
| BODELL, W.J. | YEATMAN, Anna R. | 11 MAR 1867 |
| BODEMER, Alfred | BERGMANN, Mary | 03 NOV 1866 |
| BOEGEHOLZ, Henry | BERGMAN, Charlotte | 26 AUG 1865 |
| BOEHME, F. William | SACK, C. Sophie | 28 NOV 1863 |
| BOEHME, Michael | RUPPERT, Lizzie | 04 SEP 1868 |
| BOER, Richard J.A. | ELRICKS, Eliza | 04 AUG 1865 |
| BOETTCHER, Frederick | ENGLE, Mary | 14 JAN 1869 |
| BOGAN, Charles J. | HAPP, Catherine E. | 16 MAY 1868 |
| BOGAN, Samuel W. | KLINKER, Mary E. | 20 SEP 1864 |
| BOGGS, Wm. M. | BLACK, Mary | 01 NOV 1866 |
| BOGIA, Charles | SMITH, Florida | 05 SEP 1864 |
| BOGLE, James | HIGGINS, Ellen | 18 MAY 1863 |
| BOGLEY, Reuben A. | FOWLER, Rutha A. | 20 JUN 1860 |
| BOHAN, Joseph | JOHNSON, Amanda (blk) | 17 NOV 1868 |
| BOHANAN, Thomas | YOUNGER, Pauline (blk) | 14 APR 1869 |
| BOHANNON, William Henry | DEMENT, Jane Elizabeth | 15 NOV 1862 |
| BOHANNUN, Christ. Columbus | OLIVER, Catherine | 10 SEP 1863 |
| BOHLAYER, David C. | NALLY, Mary E. | 30 APR 1866 |
| BOHLAYER, James H. | PULLING, Susannah M. | 02 SEP 1867 |
| BOHLMANN, Henry H. | RICKERS, Mary | 24 MAY 1869 |
| BOHRER, Benjamin R. | GAUBERT, Sarah A. | 02 DEC 1862 |
| BOHRER, George P. | HANCOCK, Eva Drusilla | 26 OCT 1867 |
| BOISEAU, Richard | DAVIS, Ellen Seville | 18 OCT 1864 |
| BOLAND, Anthony | O'CONNER, Catherine | 20 JAN 1860 |
| BOLAND, Peter | JENKINS, Lydia | 06 JUN 1870 |
| BOLDEN, Edward | DUGAN, Margaret | 17 AUG 1868 |
| BOLDEN, Thomas | WOODBON, Frances | 28 MAR 1870 |
| BOLDING, John | MULLIN, Mary (blk) | 01 JUL 1869 |
| BOLES, Andrew | KENNEDY, Mary Jane | 14 FEB 1859 |
| BOLIN, George | JOHNSON, Jennie (blk) | 31 MAR 1864 |
| BOLING, John W. | RAGAN, Victoria | 04 JAN 1865 |
| BOLSTER, Horatio | BUSH, Anna | 16 OCT 1868 |

| | | |
|---|---|---|
| BOLSTER, Horatio [5] | BUSH, Annie | 11 SEP 1869 |
| BOLSTER, John | TYSER, Laura Virginia | 20 OCT 1869 |
| BOLTON, Patrick | KENNEDY, Ellen | 18 SEP 1861 |
| BOLWAY, Joseph S. | RODBIRD, Ruth A. | 05 NOV 1866 |
| BOMBRAY, John | THOMPSON, Amelia (blk) | 31 JUL 1869 |
| BOMBRAY, William | STEWART, Nancy (blk) | 25 JAN 1866 |
| BOMBREY, Andrew | CAMPBELL, Mary (blk) | 20 JUL 1868 |
| BOND, Charles | LYNCH, Kate | 15 AUG 1868 |
| BOND, Charles T. | WHITLY, Susan (blk) | 12 SEP 1867 |
| BOND, George | BUSTER, Mildred | 28 MAY 1870 |
| BOND, Joseph | WELDEN, Lizzie (blk) | 07 NOV 1867 |
| BOND, Joseph D. | GREENWELL, Sarah | 19 DEC 1866 |
| BOND, Richard | GRUBB, Louisa | 08 OCT 1862 |
| BOND, Robert V. | MARSHALL, Anna | 23 JUL 1869 |
| BOND, Samuel | LEWIS, Ella (blk) | 30 DEC 1869 |
| BOND, Samuel | WARD, Cornelia (blk) | 07 MAY 1870 |
| BOND, Thomas | DELANY, Catherine (blk) | 09 JAN 1868 |
| BOND, Thomas | SCOTT, Mary (blk) | 12 JUN 1868 |
| BOND, William | JOHNSON, Maria Jane (blk) | 30 OCT 1869 |
| BONDY, Henry | LOEWEL, Ottilie | 03 DEC 1861 |
| BONEVERAS, Paul | GATTO, Maggie | 18 OCT 1869 |
| BONHAM, William D. | GILBERT, Sarah M. | 22 JAN 1864 |
| BONITZ, George H.W. | STEGNER, Elmira | 30 MAR 1860 |
| BONNELL, George W. [4] | DEGGES, Mollie V. | 11 JUN 1868 |
| BONNER, Frederick | BROOKS, Margaret (blk) | 01 SEP 1864 |
| BONNER, Philander J. | ROSSON, Mary | 03 FEB 1866 |
| BONSALL, Henry L. | ENGLAND, Lydia C. | 20 NOV 1865 |
| BONTZ, Jacob D. | HUNT, Joanna | 31 DEC 1862 |
| BOOKER, Albin | ROSS, Mary (blk) | 29 JUN 1866 |
| BOOKER, George | PATTIENT, Eliza | 15 FEB 1866 |
| BOOKER, L.J. | REESE, Caroline | 18 OCT 1867 |
| BOOKER, Samuel | PENDLETON, Elizabeth | 22 NOV 1866 |
| BOOL, Jacob | FLACK, Mary | 17 DEC 1866 |
| BOONE, Adam | BRYDEE, Josephine (blk) | 31 MAR 1870 |
| BOONE, George | SMALLWOOD, Annie (blk) | 10 SEP 1864 |
| BOONE, Isaac | ROSS, Sophia (blk) | 19 MAY 1868 |
| BOONE, Tobias | ADAMS, Julia (blk) | 07 MAY 1864 |
| BOORAEM, Henry | ESSEX, Hattie | 27 JAN 1865 |
| BOOTES, Samuel | BLOUNT, Mary B. | 24 JUN 1865 |
| BOOTH, John | McPHERSON, Ann M. (blk) | 26 DEC 1861 |
| BOOTH, William H. [1c] | JONES, Elizabeth | 26 MAR 1863 |
| BOOTHE, Benjamin | SORRELL, Mary (blk) | 28 JUN 1865 |
| BOOTHE, Frederick | CALVERT, Alice | 23 SEP 1865 |
| BOOTHE, William | CONNOR, Bridget | 24 AUG 1867 |
| BOPP, Charles [10] | McKENNA, Susan | 29 MAR 1860 |
| BORDEN, Douglas E. | ORMSBEE, Delphine | 11 JUN 1868 |
| BORDEN, Robert J. | MONSHOWER, Fannie | 22 AUG 1865 |
| BORLAND, George | MAHER, Winifred | 03 DEC 1858 |
| BORLAND, Zachariah F. | LANGE, Martha E. | 07 MAY 1864 |
| BORNEMANN, Conrad | WIELAND, Dorothea | 15 SEP 1865 |
| BORST, Henry A. | HOWELL, Emily | 06 MAR 1862 |
| BOSCHKE, Albert August | GILLETT, Mary Louise | 20 DEC 1859 |
| BOSLEY, George W. | QUINN, Isabella | 12 JUL 1869 |
| BOSLEY, Nelson J. | LANE, Anna | 15 MAY 1865 |
| BOSNER, Daniel | MARSHALL, Eliza (blk) | 02 DEC 1858 |
| BOSSIE, Hyson Isour | HALL, Augusta (blk) | 17 DEC 1863 |

# District of Columbia Marriage Licenses, 1858-1870

| | | |
|---|---|---|
| BOSSIE, William | KEENT, Lucy (blk) | 02 APR 1870 |
| BOSSIOUX, Louis J. | TAYLOR, Alvira V. | 27 FEB 1860 |
| BOSTON, Daniel | RHEA, Mary (blk) | 01 AUG 1863 |
| BOSTON, George | GIBSON, Julia | 03 JUL 1869 |
| BOSTON, Moses | DENMARK, Rachel Ann | 17 FEB 1864 |
| BOSTON, Nathaniel | NAILOR, Malvinia | 16 MAR 1868 |
| BOSTON, Robert | WILLIAMS, Charity (blk) | 24 AUG 1865 |
| BOSTON, Sawney | HICKS, Mary (blk) | 27 AUG 1869 |
| BOSTON, Thomas S. | WILSON, Anna (blk) | 12 OCT 1869 |
| BOSWELL, Aeneas | CURTIS, Rachel Ann (blk) | 07 JUL 1866 |
| BOSWELL, Allen T. | BEAN, Sarah E. | 15 FEB 1866 |
| BOSWELL, Alphonso M. | JOHNSON, Mary E. | 12 MAY 1870 |
| BOSWELL, Benjamin F. | BRADY, Ellen | 08 APR 1863 |
| BOSWELL, Bernard S. | RATCLIFFE, Roberta L. | 30 NOV 1866 |
| BOSWELL, Eugene A. | TROOK, Amanda S. | 29 JUL 1868 |
| BOSWELL, Frederick A. | FERNEY, Mary E. | 25 MAR 1870 |
| BOSWELL, George H. | DOVE, Eliza J. | 14 OCT 1865 |
| BOSWELL, James W. [6h] | WEAVER, Ida Elizabeth | 14 MAR 1868 |
| BOSWELL, John H. | COLLINS, Mary | 23 AUG 1860 |
| BOSWELL, John L.W. | JENNINGS, Willie Ann | 23 DEC 1863 |
| BOSWELL, Richard Henry | KEMAN, Sarah Jane | 16 FEB 1861 |
| BOSWELL, Rufus K. | O'NEAL, Ann Maria | 30 JUN 1869 |
| BOSWELL, Thomas | PARKER, Sophronia | 17 JUN 1867 |
| BOSWELL, Thomas Jefferson | COLLINS, Mary Ann, Mrs. | 06 JUL 1863 |
| BOSWELL, William H. | BOSWELL, Louisa | 24 JAN 1859 |
| BOSWORTH, H.P.A. | SMITH, Sarah V. | 28 JUN 1865 |
| BOSWORTH, Lewis | MILLER, Mary J. | 14 AUG 1868 |
| BOTELER, Edward M. | PRATHER, Susan E. | 24 NOV 1865 |
| BOTELER, Philip | TAYLOR, Isabella | 02 OCT 1858 |
| BOTELER, Zachary T. | TANNER, Esther | 01 SEP 1868 |
| BOTSCH, Leonart | FLINT, Rosina | 29 MAY 1862 |
| BOTSH, George Leonhardt | HIRT, Regina Barbara | 20 NOV 1858 |
| BOTT, John | HENKE, Karolina | 31 JAN 1870 |
| BOTTS, John M. | THOMPSON, Julia P. | 23 DEC 1869 |
| BOTTS, John Minor | BUTLER, Jane (blk) | 17 MAR 1869 |
| BOTTS, Thomas M. | HAISLIP, Catharine S. | 21 SEP 1865 |
| BOTTS, William | HARRIS, Maisie Ann (blk) | 04 JUN 1867 |
| BOUCHER, Henry | FORRELL, Annie | 18 JUL 1868 |
| BOUCHER, John E. | QUICK, Matilda C. | 19 FEB 1868 |
| BOULDEN, Isaiah | HALL, Jane C. | 22 NOV 1864 |
| BOULDEN, Robert | LUMSDEN, Sarah (blk) | 10 JAN 1867 |
| BOULDIN, Alfred | CARTER, Rosa Ann (blk) | 22 DEC 1868 |
| BOULIGNY, John Edward | PARKER, Mary Elizabeth | 25 APR 1860 |
| BOULTER, Edward | MARCELLUS, Emily | 27 JUL 1865 |
| BOURE, Jack | KENNEDY, Anna (blk) | 02 MAY 1866 |
| BOUVET, Napoleon | HENRY, Mary S. | 12 MAY 1859 |
| BOWBEER, Isaac [6s] | BADEN, Eliza Elizabeth | 21 JUL 1864 |
| BOWEN, Albert | JOHNSON, Polly | 02 APR 1864 |
| BOWEN, Amos E. | RICHARDSON, Matilda B. | 26 MAR 1863 |
| BOWEN, Amos M. | PERES, Caroline M. | 04 NOV 1863 |
| BOWEN, Charles H. | ROBINSON, Sidney A.G. | 22 AUG 1865 |
| BOWEN, Columbus | SMITH, Caroline | 05 FEB 1863 |
| BOWEN, Cornelius T. | RANDALL, Mary | 18 AUG 1862 |
| BOWEN, Daniel R. | SELDEN, Eliza (blk) | 18 APR 1861 |
| BOWEN, David | BUTLER, Louisa (blk) | 24 MAR 1870 |
| BOWEN, Ervin W. [5] | EVERTS, Eloise M. | 01 OCT 1868 |

| | | |
|---|---|---|
| BOWEN, George | CONOWAY, Margaret (blk) | 18 JUN 1868 |
| BOWEN, George D. | PUMPHREY, Mary E.S. | 14 NOV 1868 |
| BOWEN, Harrison S. | PRETTYMAN, Mary Julia | 23 APR 1860 |
| BOWEN, Henry B. | KETCHENS, Sarah | 09 JAN 1869 |
| BOWEN, James | FITZCHEW, Mary (blk) | 16 MAY 1861 |
| BOWEN, John | HARRINGTON, Catherine | 19 APR 1860 |
| BOWEN, John | PROCTOR, Maria (blk) | 09 MAR 1868 |
| BOWEN, Samuel | GATERS, Sinah (blk) | 30 OCT 1866 |
| BOWEN, William | YOUNG, Mary (blk) | 25 NOV 1865 |
| BOWEN, William | BELL, Louisa (blk) | 27 FEB 1869 |
| BOWEN, William P. | OYSTER, Ann Louisa | 19 DEC 1859 |
| BOWER, Charles | KING, Anna | 13 APR 1860 |
| BOWER, John | SCHOCHT, Dorah | 19 MAR 1870 |
| BOWERS, Jacob | CARR, Martha A. | 17 NOV 1859 |
| BOWES, M.F. | GOOD, Mary J. | 04 DEC 1863 |
| BOWIE, Frank | SPENCER, Sarah (blk) | 22 SEP 1866 |
| BOWIE, George F. | MAGRUDER, Nelie | 26 APR 1859 |
| BOWIE, J. Orlando | BARNES, Martha E. | 07 NOV 1859 |
| BOWIE, John J. | WEST, Rebecca (blk) | 23 DEC 1869 |
| BOWIE, Leonard O. | DREW, Willie B. | 14 OCT 1868 |
| BOWIE, Nathaniel | CHURCH, Victoria | 02 JAN 1866 |
| BOWIE, Thomas H. | SIMPSON, Carrie (blk) | 30 SEP 1867 |
| BOWIE, Walter | HARRIS, Eliza (blk) | 14 NOV 1867 |
| BOWIE, William | TASCOE, Ellen (blk) | 02 MAY 1870 |
| BOWIE, William F. | COOK, Mary Jane | 08 SEP 1859 |
| BOWIE, William W. | BUTLER, Jane (blk) | 06 JUN 1862 |
| BOWLES, Henry | TURNER, Marceline (blk) | 16 OCT 1867 |
| BOWLES, James | JURIX, Georgiana (blk) | 07 FEB 1870 |
| BOWLES, John B. | DEAGLE, Sarah | 04 APR 1859 |
| BOWLES, William A. [10] | McKINLEY, Mollie | 17 MAR 1868 |
| BOWLING, Charles C. | DIGGES, Mary S. | 18 NOV 1865 |
| BOWLING, Thomas | LEMON, Frances (blk) | 13 JAN 1869 |
| BOWMAN, Alexander | TRUAX, Margaret (blk) | 05 APR 1870 |
| BOWMAN, Augustus | HARRIS, Lizzie (blk) | 23 APR 1867 |
| BOWMAN, Charles F. | STEELE, Georgiana | 13 OCT 1864 |
| BOWMAN, Charles H. | MATHEWS, Martha | 06 MAY 1870 |
| BOWMAN, George K. [4] | PIERCE, Martha O. | 21 JAN 1862 |
| BOWMAN, James Henry | WILKINSON, Lucinda A.H. (blk) | 26 JAN 1864 |
| BOWMAN, Joseph | JACKSON, Rose (blk) | 10 AUG 1866 |
| BOWMAN, William | STROHL, Catharine | 13 FEB 1864 |
| BOWMAN, William | HAINES, Ellen (blk) | 01 NOV 1866 |
| BOWMAN, William H. | BUMERY, Henrietta | 13 APR 1867 |
| BOWMANN, Charles | KRAFFT, Ann Maria | 15 JAN 1866 |
| BOXALL, Wm. Frederick | RITCHIE, Liberta E. | 27 AUG 1866 |
| BOYCE, Charles H. | DRISCOLL, Mary C. | 03 JUL 1866 |
| BOYCE, Edward [4] | WOOD, Blandina D. | 19 JAN 1859 |
| BOYCE, James M. | WALINGSFORD, Alice | 07 JAN 1868 |
| BOYCE, Samuel E. | PRATHER, Adda L. | 09 JUN 1870 |
| BOYCE, William | BROWN, Rhoda | 13 MAY 1868 |
| BOYD, Cornelius [12s] | MILLER, Margaret | 04 JAN 1859 |
| BOYD, George | O'CONNOR, Margaret | 16 JUL 1867 |
| BOYD, Gusty | SCOTLAND, Margaret (blk) | 07 SEP 1863 |
| BOYD, Henry | BROWN, Jane (blk) | 13 DEC 1864 |
| BOYD, Henry | SWALES, Nancy | 30 SEP 1869 |
| BOYD, Joseph [4] | DALLAHUNT, Margaret | 30 APR 1859 |
| BOYD, Thomas A. [11] | JAMES, Laura | 16 SEP 1862 |

| | | |
|---|---|---|
| BOYD, William | JACKSON, Annie (blk) | 21 AUG 1867 |
| BOYD, William H. | PETERS, Annie (blk) | 16 SEP 1864 |
| BOYD, William J. | SELBY, Martha J. | 08 JUN 1864 |
| BOYD, William J. | ALTEMUS, Charlotte P. | 17 SEP 1869 |
| BOYES, Thomas A. | HUDSON, Elizabeth | 13 AUG 1867 |
| BOYKIN, Levi | SAUNDERS, Rachel (blk) | 02 MAY 1865 |
| BOYLAN, Andrew A. | VAUX, Sylvia | 31 AUG 1866 |
| BOYLE, James | CAMPBELL, Caroline | 01 DEC 1862 |
| BOYLE, James | RILEY, Catharine | 24 NOV 1862 |
| BOYLE, James | SHERRY, Catharine | 17 MAR 1865 |
| BOYLE, [James] H. [1c] | JONES, Caroline V. | 21 AUG 1863 |
| BOYLE, John | COLLINS, Ann | 14 MAY 1859 |
| BOYLE, John F. | GOODYEAR, Mary Virginia | 24 APR 1862 |
| BOYLE, John F. | BALL, Joann Ellen | 15 JAN 1866 |
| BOYLE, Junius I. | PULLEN, Martha A. | 24 NOV 1866 |
| BOYLE, Patrick | McNERHY, Catherine | 19 SEP 1868 |
| BOYLE, Richard B. | DRUMMON, Sarah C. | 06 OCT 1869 |
| BOYLE, Thomas | WILSON, Ann | 10 JUL 1865 |
| BOYLEN, Michl. | WALLACE, Ann | 17 JUN 1861 |
| BOZEL, Charles | LEE, Susan (blk) | 16 NOV 1866 |
| BRACHMAN, Bernard H. | RILEY, Mary Ann | 22 SEP 1863 |
| BRACKETT, Frederick | SHRYOCK, Narcissa A. | 28 MAY 1866 |
| BRACKETT, Reuben | COUNTEE, Fanny (blk) | 22 MAY 1867 |
| BRACKETT, Wm. J. | JACOBUS, Sarah L. | 02 SEP 1862 |
| BRADBURN, Thomas | BUTLER, Virginia | 03 JUL 1865 |
| BRADENGEYER, Charles | SEMTER, Catherine | 05 MAR 1866 |
| BRADFORD, Charles A. | BETTS, Harriet C. | 16 NOV 1867 |
| BRADFORD, Frank | HEDDEN, Charlotte R. | 11 NOV 1867 |
| BRADFORD, Frederick G. | GUNNELL, May | 10 NOV 1863 |
| BRADFORD, John S., Capt. | LLOYD, Rosalie | 28 FEB 1865 |
| BRADFORD, Morgan | SHIED, Mary C. | 05 SEP 1861 |
| BRADFORD, Thomas | BROWN, Louisa (blk) | 28 FEB 1865 |
| BRADFORD, Weedon | GALES, Matilda (blk) | 12 DEC 1866 |
| BRADIGAN, Christopher | MOORE, Ellen | 20 DEC 1862 |
| BRADISH, Joseph [4] | CREIGHTON, Emilie | 28 FEB 1859 |
| BRADLEE, James | RIGNEY, Catherine | 05 FEB 1859 |
| BRADLEY, Andrew J. | BAILEY, Ellen F. | 02 SEP 1869 |
| BRADLEY, Anon H. | GATES, Salie M. | 05 NOV 1864 |
| BRADLEY, Anon H. | VanDOREN, Jane Elizabeth | 10 JAN 1867 |
| BRADLEY, Charles T. | THOMPSON, Laura J.C. | 02 JUL 1868 |
| BRADLEY, Clayton | BRADLEY, Lucinda (blk) | 02 DEC 1869 |
| BRADLEY, Daniel | HEPBURN, Eliza (blk) | 09 MAR 1870 |
| BRADLEY, Francis M. | HAZARD, Helen H. | 24 DEC 1860 |
| BRADLEY, J. Davis | DAVIDSON, Maria L. | 31 MAY 1864 |
| BRADLEY, James | BUTLER, Eliza (blk) | 24 DEC 1864 |
| BRADLEY, John J. | ENGLEBRIGHT, Amanda E. | 28 JUN 1860 |
| BRADLEY, John T. | TALBERT, Jane | 19 OCT 1863 |
| BRADLEY, Joseph | WALSH, Jane | 22 JUN 1860 |
| BRADLEY, Joseph H., Junr. | DUNCAN, Mary P. | 04 JUN 1863 |
| BRADLEY, Patrick | JONES, Catharine | 06 SEP 1865 |
| BRADLY, George W. | DUCKETT, Alice | 17 FEB 1869 |
| BRADY, Franklin T. | HACKLEY, Susan F. | 26 MAY 1859 |
| BRADY, Isaac Thomas [3] | PARSONS, Sarah [Louisa] | 18 SEP 1865 |
| BRADY, James | McQUE, Mary | 08 NOV 1859 |
| BRADY, James | MOCLEAR, Kate | 13 FEB 1867 |
| BRADY, John | RYAN, Ellen | 14 MAY 1864 |

## District of Columbia Marriage Licenses, 1858-1870

| | | |
|---|---|---|
| BRADY, John E. | GOLDMAN, Amanda | 06 DEC 1867 |
| BRADY, Matthew | MONOQUE, Mary | 29 JAN 1859 |
| BRADY, Matthew | McNAMARA, Margaret | 06 JUN 1864 |
| BRADY, Michael [5] | TONNET, Louise | 19 APR 1869 |
| BRADY, Peter | McCARTY, Hanora | 05 MAY 1860 |
| BRADY, Silas | ETCHISON, Alice | 25 NOV 1865 |
| BRADY, Thomas | WELSH, Ann | 24 MAY 1862 |
| BRADY, Thomas | SHERIDAN, Rose | 10 OCT 1863 |
| BRADY, Thomas | CROKE, Margaret | 01 AUG 1864 |
| BRADY, Wm. M. [10] | ACTON, Elizabeth | 13 APR 1864 |
| BRAGARZIA, Antonia | CROWLY, Louisa | 08 AUG 1863 |
| BRAGG, Henry R. [7b] | GARTH, Sarah C. | 29 SEP 1869 |
| BRAHLER, Frantz | LEIMBACH, Mary L. | 07 JAN 1869 |
| BRAISTED, Garret V. | TUCKER, Dorcas A. | 31 OCT 1862 |
| BRALEY, Leonard H. | BAKER, Anna C.C. | 14 SEP 1866 |
| BRAMHALL, Bartlett M. | CUMMINGS, Laura C. | 19 MAR 1864 |
| BRAMHILL, Wm. Clarke | ESSELBURGGE, Wilhelmina | 23 DEC 1863 |
| BRAMILL, William | FRANKLIN, Ada | 08 JAN 1863 |
| BRAND, John | HANADY, Mary (blk) | 25 SEP 1866 |
| BRANDE, George Philip | STINGEL, Lena | 02 OCT 1867 |
| BRANDENBERG, Frederick W. | SEIBEL, Gertrude E. | 03 JUN 1864 |
| BRANDON, William | SMITH, Mary Ellen (blk) | 17 FEB 1870 |
| BRANDSON, John F. [10] | MURPHY, Mary M. | 03 SEP 1861 |
| BRANDT, Charles | HESSEMER, Abbie J. | 25 JUN 1869 |
| BRANDT, G.A. | BARNARD, S.L. | 02 MAY 1867 |
| BRANDT, George | KAHL, Margaret E. | 03 OCT 1866 |
| BRANDT, George W. | CASSADY, Louisa | 25 JAN 1865 |
| BRANER, William H. | EZEKIAL, Josephine G. | 20 DEC 1865 |
| BRANINGIN, Nelson | PUMPHREY, Frances | 31 JUL 1860 |
| BRANNER, James H. | ELLIOTT, Mary E. | 16 JUL 1860 |
| BRANNON, John | NORTON, Mary | 14 SEP 1861 |
| BRANNON, Samuel | WELSH, Ellen | 09 NOV 1861 |
| BRANSOM, Horace | FATELY, Catherine C. (blk) | 29 DEC 1869 |
| BRANSON, George | MARSHALL, Eliza (blk) | 05 NOV 1867 |
| BRANSON, James | BLACKWELL, Laura (blk) | 22 SEP 1869 |
| BRANSON, James A. | WALTHAN, Martha A. | 03 MAR 1863 |
| BRANSON, William | PAYNE, Matilda (blk) | 03 APR 1869 |
| BRANT, Charles F. | WOODBECK, Maria | 23 SEP 1863 |
| BRANT, John | KAYWOOD, Elizabeth | 23 MAR 1865 |
| BRANZELL, Isaac | CARR, Mary Jane | 14 JUN 1865 |
| BRASCHI, Pierri | McAULIFFE, Margaret | 05 NOV 1869 |
| BRASHEARS, Benjamin A. [10] | KEESE, Charlotte D. | 07 FEB 1870 |
| BRASHEARS, Thomas J. | PREUSS, Emma | 26 JUL 1860 |
| BRASHEARS, William H. | GRANT, Susan | 17 MAR 1868 |
| BRASHEARS, William H. | MAGBYRN, Mary | 31 JAN 1870 |
| BRASNAN, Timothy | RYAN, Penelope | 07 JUN 1866 |
| BRASSELL, Patrick | MURPHY, Margaret | 22 OCT 1860 |
| BRASSELL, Patrick | BROWN, Joanna | 04 APR 1863 |
| BRAUER, Frederick C. | ZEKIEL, Adaline | 01 NOV 1860 |
| BRAUM, Michael | KUNATH, Caroline | 06 NOV 1861 |
| BRAUMANN, John | SAUDER, Johanna | 15 JAN 1866 |
| BRAUN, Charles | DEITZ, Gertrude | 13 FEB 1862 |
| BRAWNER, Charles | GANNON, Catharine C. | 15 MAY 1862 |
| BRAWNER, J. Campbell | OULD, Carrie S. | 27 JUL 1859 |
| BRAWNER, Washington | BROWN, Jane | 27 NOV 1858 |
| BRAXTON, Alfred | BROOKS, Maria (blk) | 08 DEC 1868 |

District of Columbia Marriage Licenses, 1858-1870

| | | |
|---|---|---|
| BRAXTON, Frank | JOHNSTON, Emeline (blk) | 23 AUG 1864 |
| BRAXTON, George | TOLLIVER, Nancy | 21 JUN 1869 |
| BRAXTON, James H. | WILLIAMS, Josephine (blk) | 22 NOV 1865 |
| BRAXTON, Nelson | RICH, Eliza (blk) | 29 JUL 1865 |
| BRAY, Major | WASHINGTON, Rose (blk) | 04 NOV 1868 |
| BRAYDON, Dudley | UPSHER, Ellen (blk) | 15 NOV 1866 |
| BRAZE, Joseph H. | MORGAN, Mary | 12 JUN 1862 |
| BRAZEROL, John | ROTH, Catherine | 01 JUL 1862 |
| BREADY, Isaiah [1e] | WALTERS, Catharine | 05 SEP 1864 |
| BREAST, James S. | VanHORN, Martha W. | 01 SEP 1863 |
| BRECHT, T.C. [10] | DUVALL, Mollie | 13 JAN 1870 |
| BRECHT, Theodore C. [11] | VOSS, Louisa A. | 11 JUN 1862 |
| BRECKENRIDGE, E. (blk) | COOPER, W. | 24 DEC 1867 |
| BRECKENRIDGE, J. Cabell | JOHNSON, Sallie F. | 01 DEC 1869 |
| BREDE, Laurence M. | BUTLER, M. | 14 FEB 1860 |
| BREDERNITZ, Franz | ROSENTHALL, Bertha | 22 APR 1862 |
| BREEDEN, William N. | CRAWFORD, Emily | 13 DEC 1858 |
| BREEN, John | HEALY, Mary | 24 MAY 1859 |
| BREEN, John T. | BELFILS, Virginia | 30 JAN 1866 |
| BREEN, Michael | CROWLEY, Bridget | 24 JAN 1866 |
| BREEN, Patrick A. | COLMUS, Mary A. | 13 NOV 1865 |
| BREITHAUPT, George | SHANE, Agnes | 03 APR 1860 |
| BRELSFORD, Hiram W. | DELL, Elizabeth S. | 04 JAN 1870 |
| BRELSFORD, William H. | JONES, Mary Jane | 25 MAR 1863 |
| BREMAN, Edward | TWOOMY, Catharine | 21 JUN 1865 |
| BREMMERMAN, Thomas H. | REAVER, Carrie | 23 FEB 1869 |
| BRENEMAN, Edward deW., Dr. USA | WILSON, Marion [Virginia] [4] | 24 SEP 1866 |
| BRENEN, John | BARICKMAN, Mary Ann | 01 APR 1863 |
| BRENNAN, Bernard A. | RUTHERFORD, Jane | 26 MAR 1864 |
| BRENNAN, James | WHYTE, Laura A. | 16 JAN 1870 |
| BRENNAN, Patrick | HOLORAN, Mary Ann | 18 JUN 1861 |
| BRENNAN, Patrick | HINDS, Catharine | 22 MAY 1863 |
| BRENNAN, Peter | WELSH, Ellen | 09 SEP 1867 |
| BRENNAN, Robert | MUNGAN, Maggie | 18 FEB 1868 |
| BRENNAN, William | HERLIHY, Mary | 01 NOV 1862 |
| BRENNAN, William | GANLY, Mary | 27 APR 1865 |
| BRENT, James W. [7b] | TAYLOR, Amanda J. | 06 JAN 1870 |
| BRENT, John | McNAULTY, Margaret | 26 JAN 1863 |
| BRENT, John H. | JONES, Mary Ellen (blk) | 02 JUN 1863 |
| BRENT, Joseph | JACKSON, Mary (blk) | 30 DEC 1869 |
| BRENTON, William [7a] | RICHARDSON, Emma | 30 MAR 1867 |
| BRERETON, Edward | CARTER, Margaret | 24 FEB 1862 |
| BRESFORD, G.S.L. | CONNOR, Mary | 16 FEB 1870 |
| BRESNAHAN, John | ARCHER, Maria | 30 NOV 1865 |
| BREWER, Albert | BEVANS, Margaret Virginia | 21 FEB 1860 |
| BREWER, Cyrus A. | HANSON, W. Maria | 24 MAR 1866 |
| BREWER, Julian | HAYS, Maria T. | 12 MAY 1869 |
| BREWER, Kinsey [11] | SMITH, Sallie A. | 03 DEC 1862 |
| BRICE, Wilson | ADAMS, Mary | 22 JUN 1869 |
| BRICK, Patrick | SMITH, Margaret | 05 FEB 1866 |
| BRICKLEY, Isaac H. | SNYDER, Lucinda | 14 APR 1866 |
| BRICKLY, Patrick | BRILY, Bridget | 13 JUL 1861 |
| BRICKNER, Charles | SEIDLER, Wilhelmina | 20 FEB 1867 |
| BRIDWELL, John Henry | LLOYD, Mary Elizabeth | 02 MAR 1866 |
| BRIEK, Maurice | DONAHO, Ella | 24 JUN 1867 |
| BRIEN, Daniel | GAINEY, Honora | 12 JUL 1861 |

| Groom | Bride | Date |
|---|---|---|
| BRIEN, James F. | GATLEY, Sarah | 04 FEB 1869 |
| BRIEN, Patrick | MACHAMARA, Mary | 28 JUN 1859 |
| BRIEN, Patrick | KING, Catherine | 20 FEB 1867 |
| BRIGGS, Charles | HARRISON, Elizabeth (blk) | 12 MAY 1868 |
| BRIGGS, Emanuel | BRIGGS, Cecilia (blk) | 08 JAN 1866 |
| BRIGGS, Marvin | FOSSETT, Emma F. | 07 JUN 1864 |
| BRIGHAM, Chas. T. | DRAPER, Fannie | 12 OCT 1866 |
| BRIGHAM, Lucien B. | JONES, Laura J. | 21 DEC 1865 |
| BRIGHT, Carey S. | BROWN, Matilda (blk) | 26 MAR 1864 |
| BRIGHT, Francis C. | DORSEY, Annie (blk) | 21 NOV 1863 |
| BRIGHT, George S. | FITZPATRICK, Joanna F. | 13 SEP 1864 |
| BRIGHT, Henry J. [6r] | CARROLL, Mary Ellen | 02 JUN 1859 |
| BRIGHT, Jacob L. | FARRAR, Anne E. | 02 OCT 1863 |
| BRIGHT, James E. | HUTCHESON, Mary E. | 07 OCT 1869 |
| BRIGHT, John F. | DEMAIN, Mary H. | 30 NOV 1869 |
| BRIGHT, John G. | SEIFFERT, Margaret J. | 18 APR 1863 |
| BRIGHT, William H. | STEWART, Julia A. | 22 SEP 1862 |
| BRIGHT, William T. [6le] | HOLROYD, Sarah E. | 18 OCT 1865 |
| BRIGHTMAN, Henry W. | BROSNAN, Bettie J. | 12 APR 1869 |
| BRIGHTWELL, James W. [6r] | LYNCH, Elizabeth | 29 DEC 1859 |
| BRIGHTWELL, O. Hall | NAYLOR, Henrietta M. | 02 DEC 1862 |
| BRIM, William | GREENFIELD, Catherine | 30 APR 1866 |
| BRINKLEY, George Henry | MARSHALL, Christiana (blk) | 31 MAY 1865 |
| BRINKMAN, William D. | BUDD, Mary | 22 SEP 1864 |
| BRISCO, Chapman | ROBINSON, Anna | 31 JUL 1867 |
| BRISCO, John | DeCOSTA, Catherine (blk) | 11 MAY 1866 |
| BRISCOE, Abraham | SMALLWOOD, Treecy | 22 FEB 1868 |
| BRISCOE, Columbus | MYERS, Martha (blk) | 15 MAR 1864 |
| BRISCOE, Henry | DAY, Celia (blk) | 23 DEC 1862 |
| BRISCOE, Henry | CARROLL, Ellen | 09 NOV 1865 |
| BRISCOE, John | ALLEN, Margaret (blk) | 20 JUN 1863 |
| BRISCOE, Levi | LOCKWOOD, Emily (blk) | 13 APR 1869 |
| BRISCOE, Palmer | JONES, Charlotte (blk) | 28 APR 1859 |
| BRISCOE, Walter C. | EDELIN, Eleanor C. | 29 MAR 1870 |
| BRISSEY, Benjamin T. | HASLETT, Annie B. | 28 AUG 1866 |
| BRITT, John | BURKE, Johanna | 12 SEP 1868 |
| BRITT, Robert | GILLAM, Sarah | 01 JUL 1862 |
| BRITTAIN, William B. | PAYNE, Catherine J. | 08 OCT 1863 |
| BRITTON, Alexander T. | MARTIN, Mary A. | 27 SEP 1869 |
| BRITTON, John | PARKER, Harriet (blk) | 11 JAN 1869 |
| BROADUS, John | TURNER, Eliza (blk) | 23 NOV 1868 |
| BROADUS, John Henry | JACKSON, Eliza (blk) | 12 MAY 1866 |
| BROADWELL, Edward C. | ALTER, Mary L. | 09 JAN 1866 |
| BROAKER, Levi | THOMAS, Ann (blk) | 07 DEC 1864 |
| BROCK, Benjamin R. | GOODRICH, Jane R. | 19 NOV 1867 |
| BROCK, Towles | RED, Betsey (blk) | 07 NOV 1867 |
| BROCK, Walker | WARREN, Minerva Ann (blk) | 23 SEP 1864 |
| BROCKENBURY, Albert | JENNINGS, Florence (blk) | 03 SEP 1868 |
| BROD, Herman | DAVID, Mena | 12 AUG 1868 |
| BRODDUS, Samuel | MERRITT, Mary Jane (blk) | 16 JUL 1868 |
| BRODERICK, Edward | DRISCOLL, Margaret | 04 SEP 1866 |
| BRODERICK, Thomas | ROCHE, Ellen | 06 SEP 1861 |
| BRODERS, John | WOODYWARD, Virginia | 07 NOV 1865 |
| BRODIE, James | MAGIRR, Margaret | 11 JUL 1868 |
| BRODRECHT, Philip | HASSEL, Anna M. | 03 JUL 1862 |
| BRODUS, Moses | THOMAS, Catherine (blk) | 09 FEB 1870 |

District of Columbia Marriage Licenses, 1858-1870

| | | |
|---|---|---|
| BROGAN, William | FOWLER, Mary | 02 OCT 1867 |
| BROGDAN, Basil | DUCKETT, Sarah (blk) | 29 SEP 1864 |
| BROGDEN, Francis | FLEET, Annette (blk) | 05 OCT 1863 |
| BROGDEN, John F. | ASHTON, Mary Elizth. (blk) | 07 NOV 1861 |
| BROILS, Daniel | MACK, Elizabeth (blk) | 24 JUL 1865 |
| BRONAUGH, John C. | TAYLOR, Sallie C. | 24 APR 1861 |
| BRONELL, Charles H. | HARRIS, Mary Ann | 19 JAN 1867 |
| BRONSBERG, Ferdinand | NOLTEN, Mary | 10 MAY 1861 |
| BROOKBANK, John B., Capt. [12s] | SPATES, Mollie R. | 14 NOV 1861 |
| BROOKE, Albert A. | MYERS, Virginia C. | 23 JAN 1865 |
| BROOKE, Clement H. | JENKINS, Margaret E. | 02 DEC 1868 |
| BROOKE, Edgar S. | BARNACLE, Emma E. | 27 APR 1865 |
| BROOKE, Edmund H. | JUGH, Frances | 19 APR 1864 |
| BROOKE, Edward | SHANKLIN, Susan | 14 AUG 1862 |
| BROOKE, John | AMBROSUS, Elizabeth | 09 AUG 1865 |
| BROOKE, John B. | HILL, Helen | 25 APR 1859 |
| BROOKE, John M. | YERBY, Fannie J. | 02 MAR 1863 |
| BROOKE, Zach B. | MANKIN, Deborah C. | 25 JUL 1864 |
| BROOKER, George | BROWN, Eliza (blk) | 31 DEC 1866 |
| BROOKER, William H. | MULLIN, Sallie E. | 29 JAN 1863 |
| BROOKES, Charles Benkes | BEST, Ellen S. | 28 APR 1870 |
| BROOKHEIMER, Moses | FUCHS, Harriet | 15 MAR 1862 |
| BROOKS, Aaron | SHOOTER, Sally (blk) | 19 SEP 1864 |
| BROOKS, Adam | LEE, Jane (blk) | 07 JUL 1866 |
| BROOKS, Albert | GARNET, Sarah | 17 APR 1868 |
| BROOKS, Alexander | ADAMS, Mary (blk) | 10 DEC 1863 |
| BROOKS, Charles | RUSSELL, Sarah | 06 NOV 1862 |
| BROOKS, Charles Edward | GRANT, Ellen (blk) | 04 NOV 1868 |
| BROOKS, Edward P. | LEWIS, Georgiana | 16 JAN 1863 |
| BROOKS, George | BROKAW, Frances | 12 NOV 1862 |
| BROOKS, George | CLARKE, Louisa (blk) | 02 FEB 1865 |
| BROOKS, George | COLE, Mary (blk) | 21 SEP 1868 |
| BROOKS, Hanson | MARTIN, Millie (blk) | 06 JUN 1865 |
| BROOKS, Hanson | HOLLIDAY, Emiline (blk) | 17 MAR 1866 |
| BROOKS, Harrison | HILL, Fanny (blk) | 02 JAN 1868 |
| BROOKS, Henry | JACKSON, Phidelia (blk) | 13 NOV 1866 |
| BROOKS, Henry | QUALLS, Annie E. | 01 OCT 1867 |
| BROOKS, Horace H. | SMITH, Mary E. (blk) | 26 SEP 1868 |
| BROOKS, James | THOMPSON, Margaret E. | 29 MAR 1864 |
| BROOKS, James | GRAYSON, Lavinia (blk) | 12 MAY 1866 |
| BROOKS, James | SELMAN, Anna (blk) | 05 AUG 1869 |
| BROOKS, James J. | TURNER, Adeline | 28 MAY 1868 |
| BROOKS, James T. | SWANN, Georgiana (blk) | 21 DEC 1868 |
| BROOKS, John | COLLINS, Tamar | 16 DEC 1865 |
| BROOKS, John | EWELL, Annie (blk) | 10 FEB 1869 |
| BROOKS, John | WILLIKIN, Clarissa (blk) | 16 OCT 1869 |
| BROOKS, John H. | CAMBRIL, Edie (blk) | 23 JUN 1866 |
| BROOKS, John H. | DUNN, Ann (blk) | 16 MAR 1867 |
| BROOKS, John H. | TURNER, Mary (blk) | 02 NOV 1869 |
| BROOKS, John H. | BROOM, Laura (blk) | 19 NOV 1866 |
| BROOKS, Joseph | LEE, Eliza (blk) | 26 OCT 1864 |
| BROOKS, Joshua | ROBINSON, Ann (blk) | 29 JAN 1863 |
| BROOKS, Joshua | WILKINSON, Sophia (blk) | 12 OCT 1861 |
| BROOKS, Lewis | JONES, Catherine S. | 01 SEP 1860 |
| BROOKS, Madison | PRYOR, Sarah Ann | 18 FEB 1870 |
| BROOKS, Milton | SPURLOCK, Mahala (blk) | 17 SEP 1866 |

| | | |
|---|---|---|
| BROOKS, Oliver | CROW, Rachel (blk) | 25 SEP 1862 |
| BROOKS, Peter | ADAMS, Caroline (blk) | 09 JUL 1868 |
| BROOKS, Peter [not taken] | JACKSON, Hannah (blk) | 07 JUN 1866 |
| BROOKS, Robert | HAMILTON, Maria (blk) | 24 FEB 1865 |
| BROOKS, Robert | CAMERON, Lucy (blk) | 21 AUG 1865 |
| BROOKS, Silas | EVANS, Emily E. | 17 MAR 1859 |
| BROOKS, Thadeus | WRIGHT, Marthetta (blk) | 01 AUG 1868 |
| BROOKS, Thomas | KIMBLE, Adeline | 03 APR 1861 |
| BROOKS, Thomas | MARTIN, Carrie L. | 14 JUN 1864 |
| BROOKS, Tilghman | BERRY, Sarah M. | 14 JAN 1868 |
| BROOKS, Walter | SMITH, Sarah (blk) | 21 DEC 1867 |
| BROOKS, William | GAINES, Louisa (blk) | 27 FEB 1868 |
| BROOKS, William H. | WEBSTER, Minnie | 27 JUN 1865 |
| BROOKS, William H. | SHECKELLS, Martha | 11 AUG 1865 |
| BROOKS, William H. | SIMMONS, Mary E. | 04 NOV 1867 |
| BROOKS, William H. | DUST, Rachel Ann | 09 MAY 1870 |
| BROOKS, William Orange | MORRIS, Julia (blk) | 08 FEB 1865 |
| BROOKS, William S. | DUNN, Mary | 20 JAN 1869 |
| BROOKS, William W. | LUSBY, Cordelia | 26 SEP 1859 |
| BROOM, Andrew J. | BROWN, Charotte Ann (blk) | 22 AUG 1859 |
| BROSNAHAN, John | FALVEY, Lizzie | 07 MAY 1869 |
| BROSNEHAM, Michael | FITZGERALD, Honora | 19 OCT 1861 |
| BROSNIHIN, Cornelius | QUILL, Joanna | 16 JUL 1865 |
| BROUGH, John H., Lt., V.R.C. | SMITH, Annie A. | 20 AUG 1864 |
| BROUZE, William | MEISCH, Rosina | 14 OCT 1861 |
| BROWER, Horace H. | DECKER, Mary E. | 31 JAN 1866 |
| BROWN, Abraham | FOX, Rebecca (blk) | 13 MAR 1866 |
| BROWN, Abram | MATTHEWS, Margaret (blk) | 08 SEP 1866 |
| BROWN, Addison, Jr. | STARR, Florida L. | 07 FEB 1863 |
| BROWN, Albert | SAVAGE, Alice (col'd) | 21 MAY 1867 |
| BROWN, Albert L. | GARRETT, Caroline E. (blk) | 01 AUG 1861 |
| BROWN, Albert Lee | THOMPSON, Ellen Ann | 28 MAY 1868 |
| BROWN, Albert O. | MOCK, Eliza D. | 18 SEP 1866 |
| BROWN, Alexander M. | SPRINGER, Martha | 02 AUG 1865 |
| BROWN, Alonzo | LOBER, Ellen (col'd) | 03 FEB 1866 |
| BROWN, Alpheus | PROCTOR, Rose V. | 01 AUG 1859 |
| BROWN, Americus V. | SHEAHAN, Catherine | 17 AUG 1861 |
| BROWN, Archibald | MILLS, Lucinda | 01 NOV 1869 |
| BROWN, Arthur T. | WILSON, Georgiana (blk) | 21 DEC 1863 |
| BROWN, Augustus | HARRIS, Mary E. (blk) | 20 MAY 1863 |
| BROWN, Augustus | WEBB, Julia (blk) | 27 DEC 1864 |
| BROWN, B. Peyton | DICKSON, Harriett A. | 19 APR 1869 |
| BROWN, Barney | ROBINSON, Louisa (blk) | 02 JAN 1867 |
| BROWN, Basil | JONES, Laurelia (blk) | 01 JUN 1864 |
| BROWN, Basil | BROWN, Ellen (blk) | 22 NOV 1866 |
| BROWN, Benjamin | THOMAS, Ann (blk) | 22 JAN 1866 |
| BROWN, Benjamin | BARON, Ella (blk) | 27 MAY 1867 |
| BROWN, Benjamin | BACON, Lizzie | 25 APR 1870 |
| BROWN, Calfus | DUCKETT, Margarett Ann (blk) | 23 SEP 1867 |
| BROWN, Charles | CHAMBERS, Ann | 15 NOV 1862 |
| BROWN, Charles | DOUGHADAY, Sarah Jane | 21 JUL 1864 |
| BROWN, Charles | BELL, Anne (blk) | 03 APR 1865 |
| BROWN, Charles | RHUMSEIR, Louisa | 14 MAR 1865 |
| BROWN, Charles | WISE, Mary Ann | 06 MAR 1865 |
| BROWN, Charles | GREEN, Mary Ann | 12 APR 1866 |
| BROWN, Charles | ANDERSON, Betty (blk) | 10 JUN 1867 |

# District of Columbia Marriage Licenses, 1858-1870

| | | |
|---|---|---|
| BROWN, Charles | COLLINS, Laura V. | 20 JAN 1869 |
| BROWN, Charles A. | CONNER, Elizabeth A. | 20 FEB 1864 |
| BROWN, Charles B. | BURROWS, Mary V. | 27 OCT 1863 |
| BROWN, Charles F. | PRICE, Ida | 03 FEB 1863 |
| BROWN, Charles H. | SHEAD, Mary Ann (blk) | 12 OCT 1863 |
| BROWN, Charles H. | YEAGER, Catherine E. | 17 OCT 1867 |
| BROWN, Charles McD. | MYERS, Julia F. | 31 AUG 1864 |
| BROWN, Charles O. | WOLLARD, Lizzie | 14 JUN 1866 |
| BROWN, Charles Thomas | KING, Mary (col'd) | 16 JUN 1864 |
| BROWN, Charles W. | SNYDER, Sophia C. | 11 JUL 1867 |
| BROWN, Columbus | DAVIS, Mary E.A. | 04 DEC 1862 |
| BROWN, Daniel | ANDERSON, Jane (blk) | 20 NOV 1866 |
| BROWN, David | TUCKER, Laura Virginia | 22 NOV 1862 |
| BROWN, Edward | NORTON, Cornelia | 26 MAR 1864 |
| BROWN, Edward | JACKSON, Cecilia (blk) | 05 JUN 1867 |
| BROWN, Edward | BUTLER, Eliza | 12 JUL 1867 |
| BROWN, Edward | BUTLER, Eliza (blk) | 13 AUG 1867 |
| BROWN, Edward | HAMILTON, Emeline (blk) | 25 MAY 1869 |
| BROWN, Edward S. [7b] | DUVALL, Annie E. | 20 APR 1870 |
| BROWN, Edward W. | STAFFEL, Catarina | 13 OCT 1863 |
| BROWN, Eleazer R. | LePATCH, Lizzie | 02 MAY 1861 |
| BROWN, Emory | SAUNDERS, Ann Eliza (blk) | 11 NOV 1869 |
| BROWN, Ezra | WILEY, Martha | 02 FEB 1867 |
| BROWN, Francis | MERCER, Julia | 27 JUL 1865 |
| BROWN, Francis F. | WATERS, Mary E. (blk) | 05 MAR 1859 |
| BROWN, Francis F. | ADAMS, Mary (blk) | 14 SEP 1868 |
| BROWN, Frank | JOHNSON, Fanny (blk) | 21 MAY 1866 |
| BROWN, George | MULLOY, Elizabeth | 04 DEC 1861 |
| BROWN, George | COX, Sarah (blk) | 13 FEB 1865 |
| BROWN, George | HUGHES, Cordelia | 05 DEC 1865 |
| BROWN, George | BROWN, Lucy (blk) | 19 JAN 1866 |
| BROWN, George | SURMIHL, Jane | 04 MAY 1867 |
| BROWN, George E. | WARNER, Annie M. (blk) | 12 AUG 1869 |
| BROWN, George G. | REESE, Mary E. | 11 JUN 1868 |
| BROWN, George Henry | BROOKS, Mary Agnes (blk) | 10 AUG 1866 |
| BROWN, Gilbert [8] | WILEY, Susan | 27 AUG 1868 |
| BROWN, Greenberry | REMINGTON, Anne | 19 SEP 1863 |
| BROWN, Gustavus | YOUNG, Nelly (blk) | 04 AUG 1860 |
| BROWN, Hanson | CLARK, Anna | 13 JUL 1867 |
| BROWN, Harrison | HESS, Caroline | 24 APR 1865 |
| BROWN, Henry | OLLIVER, Annie | 02 JUN 1859 |
| BROWN, Henry | WALDEN, Ann | 01 FEB 1861 |
| BROWN, Henry | NEALE, Lucinda (blk) | 22 SEP 1862 |
| BROWN, Henry | HARRIS, Julia (blk) | 16 JUN 1863 |
| BROWN, Henry C. | HATHAWAY, Mary | 15 NOV 1868 |
| BROWN, Horace | SEDGWICK, Virginia (blk) | 02 JAN 1866 |
| BROWN, Ignatius [6le] | BAILEY, Mary | 24 FEB 1868 |
| BROWN, Isaac | HERBERT, Rebecca (blk) | 08 FEB 1859 |
| BROWN, J. Byron | GODFREY, Mary Annie | 31 MAY 1864 |
| BROWN, James | GOSZLER, Sarah | 14 MAY 1859 |
| BROWN, James | GRIFFIN, Mary | 22 JAN 1864 |
| BROWN, James | GRAHAM, Mary | 04 NOV 1864 |
| BROWN, James | WHIGGINS, Sarah (blk) | 29 DEC 1864 |
| BROWN, James | HONESTY, Maria Louisa (blk) | 20 APR 1867 |
| BROWN, James | WARREN, Susan (blk) | 13 FEB 1868 |
| BROWN, James | HILLER, Louisa | 19 OCT 1868 |

| | | |
|---|---|---|
| BROWN, James F. | BENJAMIN, Rebecca L. | 18 AUG 1868 |
| BROWN, James O. | BREASHEAR, Sarah | 29 JUL 1868 |
| BROWN, James Robert | MATHEWS, Emily (blk) | 23 OCT 1867 |
| BROWN, Jas. T. | JONES, Caroline | 21 OCT 1868 |
| BROWN, James T. [12s] | BROWNLEE, Lizzie | 09 FEB 1863 |
| BROWN, James Truett | SELECMAN, Virginia | 08 JUL 1863 |
| BROWN, John | LYONS, Anna | 27 DEC 1858 |
| BROWN, John | JOHNSON, Annie (blk) | 10 APR 1862 |
| BROWN, John | BROWN, Admonia (blk) | 04 APR 1863 |
| BROWN, John | ADAMS, Sarah (blk) | 28 NOV 1863 |
| BROWN, John | CONNER, Susan (blk) | 27 APR 1864 |
| BROWN, John | LAMPKINS, Sina | 05 AUG 1864 |
| BROWN, John | MANLY, Ellen | 19 SEP 1864 |
| BROWN, John | BROWN, Jane (blk) | 10 JUN 1865 |
| BROWN, John | FITZGERALD, Mary | 01 AUG 1865 |
| BROWN, John | MURRAY, Mary Ann | 28 FEB 1866 |
| BROWN, John | LANEY, Louisa (blk) | 01 JUN 1867 |
| BROWN, John | BROWN, Laura (blk) | 23 DEC 1867 |
| BROWN, John | THOMPSON, Annie (blk) | 17 MAY 1869 |
| BROWN, John | MORGAN, Anna | 22 MAY 1869 |
| BROWN, John | FARMER, Rebecca (blk) | 09 NOV 1869 |
| BROWN, John | CONNER, Sarah | 28 DEC 1869 |
| BROWN, John [6s] | ANDERSON, Elizabeth (blk) | 13 OCT 1864 |
| BROWN, John D. | COOK, Julia | 04 APR 1868 |
| BROWN, John F. | TRUNNELL, Anna M. | 28 SEP 1867 |
| BROWN, John H. | BROOKS, Sarah (blk) | 27 DEC 1866 |
| BROWN, John Henry | BERRY, Mary Catharine (blk) | 27 OCT 1864 |
| BROWN, John Henry | WRIGHT, Kate (blk) | 27 OCT 1866 |
| BROWN, John M. | FISHER, Annie | 25 MAY 1859 |
| BROWN, John Marshall [4] | CARROLL, Alida [C.] | 17 DEC 1866 |
| BROWN, John T. | PARKER, Ann V. | 08 NOV 1859 |
| BROWN, John V. [6s] | MOSS, Susan | 31 MAR 1865 |
| BROWN, John W. | O'NEALE, Anna E. | 26 JUL 1860 |
| BROWN, John W. | SPILLMAN, Frances M. | 18 OCT 1865 |
| BROWN, John W. | ROSS, Maria (blk) | 14 SEP 1868 |
| BROWN, John W. | SPILLMAN, Frances M. | 18 OCT 1865 |
| BROWN, John William | FERGUSON, Mary Frances | 07 JUL 1866 |
| BROWN, Joseph T. | BUCKEY, Jane C. | 01 DEC 1866 |
| BROWN, Joshua | FRISBIL, Henrietta (blk) | 13 JUN 1867 |
| BROWN, Lawrence E. | CASEY, Bridget A. | 27 APR 1867 |
| BROWN, Lee | BROWN, Elvira (blk) | 22 APR 1869 |
| BROWN, Levi | SPRIGGS, Rachel | 14 APR 1868 |
| BROWN, Lewis | SIMAKER, Barbara | 08 APR 1861 |
| BROWN, Lewis | BELL, Eliza | 10 AUG 1867 |
| BROWN, Lucius | ALEXANDER, Sarah (blk) | 26 DEC 1865 |
| BROWN, Matthias | GASSAWAY, Nancy (blk) | 29 JUL 1867 |
| BROWN, Michael | HOLLAND, Bridget | 15 JUL 1865 |
| BROWN, Michael | McGARVEY, Catherine | 21 SEP 1868 |
| BROWN, Nathaniel | GROSS, Maria (blk) | 06 APR 1869 |
| BROWN, Nelson | CURTIS, Elizabeth Ann (blk) | 15 AUG 1867 |
| BROWN, Nelson | DIXON, Mary (blk) | 28 NOV 1868 |
| BROWN, Patterson | HARPER, Ellen (blk) | 27 MAY 1867 |
| BROWN, Perry | CARTWRIGHT, Mahala (blk) | 05 FEB 1867 |
| BROWN, Peter | MASON, Kitty (blk) | 26 JAN 1860 |
| BROWN, Philip | LEE, Cornelia (blk) | 02 AUG 1865 |
| BROWN, Philip | HOWARD, Jane (blk) | 12 JUL 1866 |

## District of Columbia Marriage Licenses, 1858-1870

| | | |
|---|---|---|
| BROWN, Randall | FAUNCE, Mary Ellen | 21 DEC 1869 |
| BROWN, Richard | CLARK, Minty | 14 SEP 1863 |
| BROWN, Richard | GASSAWAY, Lethea (blk) | 11 NOV 1863 |
| BROWN, Richard | RYAN, Bridget | 24 JUL 1868 |
| BROWN, Richard F. | STANSBURY, Eliza | 06 DEC 1862 |
| BROWN, Richard H. | LUNAHER, Barbar L. | 21 NOV 1867 |
| BROWN, Richard T. | WHITE, Sarah | 05 NOV 1867 |
| BROWN, Robert | SHAW, Mary (blk) | 25 OCT 1864 |
| BROWN, Robert | SCOTT, Ellen | 25 OCT 1864 |
| BROWN, Robert | BELL, Nancy (blk) | 07 MAY 1867 |
| BROWN, Robert A. | MARSHALL, Delia Ann (blk) | 11 JUN 1870 |
| BROWN, Robert Randolph | BROWN, Diana (blk) | 30 JUN 1866 |
| BROWN, Robt. M. | HALL, Josephine S. | 04 JUN 1863 |
| BROWN, Sam | SESTER, Sophia (blk) | 20 SEP 1864 |
| BROWN, Samuel | POWELL, Rebecca (blk) | 23 DEC 1865 |
| BROWN, Samuel | WATSON, Alice (blk) | 16 JAN 1869 |
| BROWN, Samuel | DOMLESS, Emma | 01 MAY 1869 |
| BROWN, Samuel H. | PATTERSON, Bettie C. | 30 OCT 1858 |
| BROWN, Sligh | CHEW, Louisa (blk) | 01 MAR 1869 |
| BROWN, Theodore L. | THOMPSON, Mary E. | 05 APR 1866 |
| BROWN, Thomas | NALLEY, Harriet Louisa | 11 NOV 1858 |
| BROWN, Thomas [11] | FLETCHER, Eliza Jane | 12 MAY 1865 |
| BROWN, Thomas | LEE, Lucinda E. (blk) | 03 AUG 1865 |
| BROWN, Thomas D. | LEACH, Margaret H. | 09 NOV 1867 |
| BROWN, Thomas [6s] | DIGGES, Matilda (blk) | 01 OCT 1864 |
| BROWN, W.P. | CARPENTER, Mary | 07 JUN 1869 |
| BROWN, Washington | RUSTIN, Sarah Ann (blk) | 30 SEP 1861 |
| BROWN, William | ALLEN, Mary (blk) | 12 NOV 1863 |
| BROWN, William | EMMEL, Rachel L. | 10 MAR 1864 |
| BROWN, William | BROWN, Mary A. (blk) | 14 FEB 1865 |
| BROWN, William | TYLER, Hester (blk) | 17 MAY 1865 |
| BROWN, William | WILSON, Penelope | 31 MAR 1866 |
| BROWN, William | HEDGEMAN, Lucy (blk) | 08 JUN 1867 |
| BROWN, William | DYSON, Lucinda (blk) | 16 DEC 1867 |
| BROWN, William H. | ELKINS, Edinborough | 15 SEP 1860 |
| BROWN, William H. | GARNER, Caroline (blk) | 12 JUL 1867 |
| BROWN, William Henry | CROWDY, Mary Ann (blk) | 30 MAR 1866 |
| BROWN, William Henry | ANDERSON, Hetty | 02 JUN 1866 |
| BROWN, William J.* | RUPP, Caroline E. | 28 OCT 1859 |
| BROWN, Willis Young | DAVIS, Elizabeth Emma | 01 JUL 1867 |
| BROWNE, Charles L. | SHERWOOD, Kate A. | 29 SEP 1864 |
| BROWNE, Lewis K. | MALONE, Sarah E. | 13 OCT 1868 |
| BROWNER, J.B. | LEE, Sarah E. | 24 OCT 1859 |
| BROWNER, Richard R. | DRAYTON, Annie R. | 03 SEP 1866 |
| BROWNING, Edward | SWAIN, Mary Louisa | 22 OCT 1863 |
| BROWNING, Ezra C. | NORRIS, Louisa M. | 08 MAY 1865 |
| BROWNING, Henry | MURPHY, Ellen | 24 FEB 1868 |
| BROWNING, John W. [6m] | MATTHEWS, Mary W. | 08 APR 1862 |
| BROWNING, John W. | RICHARDSON, Virginia A. | 03 DEC 1863 |
| BROWNING, Lewis | GIBSON, Mary E. | 15 JUN 1865 |
| BROWNING, Silas | WYNN, Caroline | 20 APR 1869 |
| BROWNING, Thomas | GILBERT, Lizzie | 08 FEB 1867 |
| BROWNING, Washington Jackson [10] | WEBSTER, Sarah Frances | 28 JUN 1869 |
| BRUCE, Francis | GILES, Ellen (blk) | 08 APR 1869 |
| BRUCE, John | THOMAS, Ann Amelia (col'd) | 08 AUG 1864 |
| BRUCE, Philip | YOUNG, Emma Jane (blk) | 01 DEC 1866 |

| | | |
|---|---|---|
| BRUCE, Richard | HENSON, Susan (blk) | 28 NOV 1860 |
| BRUCE, Richard | MOSELEY, Mollie A. | 21 OCT 1869 |
| BRUCE, Thomas | ROY, Maria (blk) | 26 MAY 1866 |
| BRUCE, Thomas | THORNTON, Mary (blk) | 03 SEP 1868 |
| BRUCE, William H. | SILENCE, Regenda | 21 OCT 1863 |
| BRUCENA, Concepcion dela S. | HARRIS, Matilda | 27 MAY 1859 |
| BRUCHHOUSER, Jacob | SCHWORZ, Helen | 27 NOV 1865 |
| BRUFFY, James A. | CROUCH, Jane S. | 13 APR 1869 |
| BRUGGEMAN, Herman | MAGRUDER, Ellen | 10 MAR 1868 |
| BRUMET, Joseph | ENTWISLE, Alina | 21 JAN 1870 |
| BRUMLEY, William | HARMON, Catherine | 25 FEB 1862 |
| BRUNDAGES, Maston | WARD, Isabella | 15 OCT 1867 |
| BRUNER, Benjamin F. | LOW, Phoebe Ann | 23 OCT 1867 |
| BRUNICK, Michael | McGUIRE, Catharine | 01 FEB 1865 |
| BRUNSWICK, Samuel | CECIL, Dora | 08 FEB 1867 |
| BRUSH, George J. | TRUMBULL, Harriet S. | 21 DEC 1864 |
| BRUSNAN, John | FITZGERALD, Ellen | 25 AUG 1860 |
| BRUSSEAU, Peter | CLARKE, Leonora | 24 JAN 1865 |
| BRUTCHE, Julius | KLOCKE, Ann | 01 NOV 1862 |
| BRYAM, Francis M. | BEEDLE, Emma | 29 JUN 1868 |
| BRYAN, Augustus S. [10] | KEELING, Fannie | 02 DEC 1867 |
| BRYAN, Benjamin Henry | ERB, Caroline Josephine | 17 NOV 1862 |
| BRYAN, James Henry | RICHARDSON, Alice (blk) | 30 DEC 1869 |
| BRYAN, John | WILKERSON, Mary Jane (blk) | 21 JAN 1868 |
| BRYAN, John T. | CRAIG, Catharine E. | 20 DEC 1861 |
| BRYAN, John T. | COLLINS, Sealeaner | 09 JUN 1868 |
| BRYAN, John V. [6m] | KNIGHT, Virginia E. | 10 SEP 1863 |
| BRYAN, W. Page | SCOTT, Jennie C. | 04 SEP 1865 |
| BRYANT, James B. | REYNOLDS, Louisa Ann | 01 MAY 1862 |
| BRYANT, Lewis | SPOTSWOOD, Fanny (blk) | 09 MAY 1866 |
| BRYANT, Raphael | LAWLER, Anna | 23 AUG 1869 |
| BRYANT, William | JACKSON, Mary | 19 AUG 1868 |
| BRYANT, William | EVANS, Jane | 22 OCT 1868 |
| BRYANT, William C. | MARLOW, Sarah (blk) | 05 JUN 1866 |
| BRYANT, William F. | PARDEE, Lavina | 14 MAR 1867 |
| BRYANT, William H. | LUCAS, Josephine (blk) | 06 APR 1859 |
| BRYANT, William Henry | REYNOLDS, Jane P. | 03 OCT 1860 |
| BRYCE, Oliver | JOHNSON, Alice (blk) | 13 NOV 1866 |
| BRYON, John | NOSAY, Mary | 24 DEC 1863 |
| BRYSON, James | KANE, Eliza | 24 DEC 1868 |
| BRYSON, Martin | LITTLE, Araminta | 03 JUN 1868 |
| BUB, Casper | KORFF, Virginia | 04 NOV 1863 |
| BUB, Christopher | STAHL, Josephine | 02 NOV 1864 |
| BUBB, John W. | STEELE, Fannie H. | 18 NOV 1867 |
| BUCHANAN, Daniel | MERCURY, Lucy A. (blk) | 22 NOV 1860 |
| BUCHANAN, Henry | CONTEE, Elizabeth | 21 DEC 1864 |
| BUCHANAN, Henry | SIMMS, Charlotte (blk) | 07 APR 1869 |
| BUCHANAN, J. Milton | ELDRED, Emma L. | 28 AUG 1868 |
| BUCHANAN, John H. | CONNOR, Annie (blk) | 01 OCT 1867 |
| BUCHANAN, Robert | PEARSON, Mary (blk) | 22 JAN 1867 |
| BUCHIGNANI, Antonio | EATON, Margaret L. | 07 JUN 1859 |
| BUCHLER, John | WARMBOLD, Mary | 11 JUN 1867 |
| BUCK, Alonzo M. | DOUGLAS, Marion P. | 10 JUN 1867 |
| BUCK, Edward | HOLMAN, Margaret | 17 MAR 1864 |
| BUCKINGHAM, Samuel C. | RYAN, Emma L. | 24 JUN 1867 |
| BUCKLER, Samuel | HINSON, Lucinda | 30 MAY 1864 |

District of Columbia Marriage Licenses, 1858-1870

| | | |
|---|---|---|
| BUCKLEY, John D. | CLARE, Jane | 10 OCT 1865 |
| BUCKLEY, John O. | PAYNE, Laura | 30 APR 1870 |
| BUCKLEY, Michael | CONNORS, Mary | 19 JUL 1864 |
| BUCKLEY, Michael | HARTNETT, Margaret | 31 OCT 1864 |
| BUCKLEY, Michael Benjamin | KEATING, Annorah Rosilla | 27 MAR 1869 |
| BUCKLEY, Thomas | HINE, Mary | 21 JUL 1865 |
| BUCKLEY, Thomas E. | SUMMERS, Elizth. F. | 15 JUL 1861 |
| BUCKLEY, Thomas J. | WOLFE, Eliza H. | 25 JUN 1868 |
| BUCKLEY, Wm. C., Dr. | EVANS, Sallie P. | 26 AUG 1862 |
| BUCKLEY, William F. | PORTS, Frances D.M. | 07 FEB 1861 |
| BUCKMAN, Edward H. | DANA, Jennie | 07 JUN 1870 |
| BUCKMAN, Frederick | COOK, Margaret (blk) | 07 DEC 1867 |
| BUCKMAN, William M. | BRETT, Martha | 24 OCT 1863 |
| BUCKNER, Arthur | BRASHEARS, Susan (blk) | 08 APR 1868 |
| BUCKNER, Benjamin | LEE, Julia (blk) | 21 DEC 1869 |
| BUCKNER, Henry | GORDON, Mary Ann (blk) | 21 APR 1864 |
| BUCKNER, John | ROSS, Marcellina | 14 MAY 1867 |
| BUCKNER, Richard | NEWMAN, Mary (blk) | 14 OCT 1869 |
| BUCKNER, S. Ariss | FITZHUGH, Helen S. | 02 MAR 1868 |
| BUCKSBAUM, John | HEILMAN, Bauliene | 18 MAY 1864 |
| BUDD, Dennis | JACKSON, Martha (blk) | 26 MAR 1866 |
| BUDD, Joseph W. | DODENHOFF, Nannie J. | 23 JAN 1866 |
| BUELL, Martin | ENRIGHT, Margaret | 28 JAN 1870 |
| BUHLER, Francis | KRAUTER, Caroline | 14 NOV 1861 |
| BUHLER, Gustav Adolph | STRONG, Regina | 25 SEP 1865 |
| BUIE, David James | GARNER, Elizabeth F. | 24 JAN 1866 |
| BULKLEY, John W., Dr. | JOHNSTON, Virginia | 12 NOV 1861 |
| BULL, David M. | CLAXTON, Sarah L. | 29 JUN 1864 |
| BULL, Wakeley T. | MILLER, Helen A. | 15 DEC 1862 |
| BULL, William | OFFUTT, Eugenia E. | 02 DEC 1868 |
| BULLIS, John | GUNNELL, Gertrude | 03 MAY 1865 |
| BUMBREY, William | BUMBREY, Lucy (blk) | 11 JAN 1868 |
| BUNDICK, Carles P. | BRUMFIELD, Mary L. | 26 MAR 1864 |
| BUNDY, L.E. | GREEN, Mary A. | 15 MAY 1865 |
| BUNDY, Samuel | BEVEL, Eliza (blk) | 04 MAY 1870 |
| BUNKER, George W. | STRATTON, Calista G. | 26 SEP 1862 |
| BUNNELL, Caleb | IRVING, Elizabeth | 23 JUL 1868 |
| BUNNLEY, William | HERMOND, Catherine | 25 FEB 1862 |
| BUNTON, David A. | GIBSON, Catherine A. | 06 MAY 1861 |
| BURCH, George D. | BUSHBY, Emina | 13 SEP 1858 |
| BURCH, George D. [6m] | HARROD, Mary G. | 04 MAY 1863 |
| BURCH, George D. | CONSTABLE, Margaret | 09 APR 1868 |
| BURCH, Henry C. | THOMPSON, M. Eliza | 14 MAR 1866 |
| BURCH, John J. | SMITH, Mary C. | 07 SEP 1869 |
| BURCH, Thomas E. | LUXEN, Sarah D. | 03 AUG 1868 |
| BURCH, William J. | STANLEY, Sarah H. | 02 SEP 1868 |
| BURCHARD, William | KOCH, Augusta | 23 DEC 1868 |
| BURCHELL, John B. | BRYAN, Ann Elizabeth | 23 MAR 1861 |
| BURDETTE, Oliver P. [7b] | HYATT, Emma S. | 08 NOV 1869 |
| BURDETTE, Walter W. [11] | HELMICK, Susie E. | 22 NOV 1865 |
| BURDICK, William H. | O'HARE, Eliza | 29 APR 1865 |
| BURDINE, Alfred [6c] | GHEEN, Margaret | 10 FEB 1859 |
| BUREL, Henry | PAGE, Evelin (blk) | 15 DEC 1869 |
| BURFORD, Robert P. | ROBEY, Annie | 21 AUG 1862 |
| BURGDORF, Augustus | ESPEY, Maggie | 08 JUN 1868 |
| BURGEE, John | MILLER, Maggie | 14 SEP 1860 |

| | | |
|---|---|---|
| BURGER, Henry | BRECHT, Sophia | 05 JUL 1869 |
| BURGER, Joshisious | FOSTER, Mary G. (blk) | 02 OCT 1860 |
| BURGESS, Adam S. [6le] | GRIFFIN, Eliza E. | 17 FEB 1868 |
| BURGESS, Archibald [7a] | TURPIN, Sarah A. | 29 MAY 1868 |
| BURGESS, Caleb [W.], Jr. [6s] | CADLE, Mary A. | 26 APR 1865 |
| BURGESS, Charles | DORSEY, Kate (blk) | 21 JUN 1866 |
| BURGESS, Charles | CHAUNCEY, Margaret Ann | 23 SEP 1869 |
| BURGESS, Charles H. | ASHBY, Wilhelmina | 05 JUN 1867 |
| BURGESS, Clarke | TUCKER, Maria E. | 31 OCT 1865 |
| BURGESS, Dawson | CLOWSER, Margaret | 10 MAR 1859 |
| BURGESS, John | MATHISON, Sarah A. | 24 MAR 1866 |
| BURGESS, John R. | MILES, Sarah J. | 06 OCT 1859 |
| BURGESS, Judson | SMITH, Mary | 18 JUL 1865 |
| BURGESS, Silas | JACKSON, Susan (blk) | 15 NOV 1866 |
| BURGESS, William G. | MILLER, Almyra | 22 FEB 1870 |
| BURGISS, Abner | PEGG, Mary E. | 16 APR 1863 |
| BURGMAN, Frederick | WALKER, Mary | 24 SEP 1868 |
| BURGMAN, James A. | MILLER, Lucinda C. | 12 OCT 1864 |
| BURK, Andrew | MECHAN, Mary | 09 JAN 1865 |
| BURK, Charles Edward | JOHNSON, Martha Virginia (blk) | 28 JAN 1869 |
| BURK, Edward | BALL, Margaret (blk) | 07 JAN 1869 |
| BURK, James | SLATTERY, Ellen | 09 JAN 1860 |
| BURK, John | DOWNELY, Mary | 05 OCT 1866 |
| BURK, John | MYERS, Rosa | 30 MAR 1867 |
| BURK, Robert | DADE, Cornelia (blk) | 21 APR 1869 |
| BURK, Wesley | BETTS, Nancy (blk) | 30 JAN 1865 |
| BURK, William | DICK, Lavinia (blk) | 14 OCT 1863 |
| BURKE, Adam | MAJOR, Sarah (blk) | 23 DEC 1862 |
| BURKE, Alfred | ORR, Rebecca (blk) | 09 NOV 1864 |
| BURKE, Daniel | McBRIDE, Sarah Jane | 17 NOV 1862 |
| BURKE, Daniel M. | PESTRIDGE, Selena (blk) | 27 JUN 1861 |
| BURKE, DeWitt C. | WALSH, Annie | 06 MAY 1864 |
| BURKE, Edmund | TOWERS, Ellie | 16 JUL 1869 |
| BURKE, Edward | GREAVES, Margaret | 05 AUG 1859 |
| BURKE, Francis X. | WILLIAMS, Frances C. | 03 JAN 1867 |
| BURKE, James | MALONEY, Eliza | 09 JUL 1859 |
| BURKE, James | COFFEE, Catharine | 07 JUN 1862 |
| BURKE, James | OWENS, Mary E. (blk) | 13 SEP 1866 |
| BURKE, James | THOMAS, Lizzie | 20 FEB 1867 |
| BURKE, James D. | SMITH, Mary | 31 MAY 1869 |
| BURKE, James F. | GRADY, Mary Ann | 12 JAN 1859 |
| BURKE, John | SHERMAN, Mary | 12 SEP 1863 |
| BURKE, John | MADIGAN, Ann | 11 MAY 1865 |
| BURKE, John B. | SHANNON, Margaret | 26 NOV 1866 |
| BURKE, John H. | HARDEN, Catharine A. | 02 APR 1864 |
| BURKE, Joseph | McCOY, Anna | 02 FEB 1864 |
| BURKE, Michael | MURRONEY, Mary | 18 FEB 1865 |
| BURKE, Michael | HOLDEN, Bridget | 25 APR 1865 |
| BURKE, Patrick | QUINLAN, Mary | 16 JUL 1863 |
| BURKE, Paul | STIEFLER, Margaret | 02 NOV 1869 |
| BURKE, Robert | CHINN, Hannah (blk) | 29 MAY 1865 |
| BURKE, Thomas | PENDERGAST, Bridget | 29 JAN 1863 |
| BURKE, William E. | McLAUGHLIN, Rebecca C. | 28 OCT 1864 |
| BURKET, Neander K. | HERBERT, Lizzie G. | 13 JUN 1870 |
| BURKHARDT, Charles | FROEDE, Emilie | 19 NOV 1862 |
| BURKLEY, Augustus E. | HARSTKAMP, Mary E. | 03 MAY 1866 |

District of Columbia Marriage Licenses, 1858-1870

| | | |
|---|---|---|
| BURLEIGH, Lewis | RICHARDSON, Clarissa Ann (blk) | 31 AUG 1865 |
| BURLEY, Charles St. Clair | AUGUSTA, Elizabeth (blk) | 24 ARR 1865 |
| BURLEY, Fletcher W. | WEBSTER, Elizabeth (blk) | 27 APR 1868 |
| BURLEY, George | THORNTON, Hagar (blk) | 28 JUN 1866 |
| BURLEY, James | WEST, Ella | 31 JAN 1870 |
| BURLEY, Lewis B. | ARMSTRONG, Frances (blk) | 09 FEB 1870 |
| BURLEY, Richard | WEEDON, Martha | 23 DEC 1867 |
| BURLEY, Wesley | POWER, Cassie (blk) | 19 APR 1870 |
| BURLHOLD, Fredrick | KENNEY, Ane | 26 MAR 1859 |
| BURLINGAME, A. | DOWNS, Mary Elizabeth | 08 MAY 1867 |
| BURLY, James Henry | LOW, Harriet Ann (blk) | 18 OCT 1862 |
| BURN, James N. [6r] | DANFORD, Martha M. | 15 OCT 1859 |
| BURNELL, William | LITTLE, Julia A. | 01 DEC 1868 |
| BURNES, Alfred W. | DRANE, Kate | 29 FEB 1864 |
| BURNES, Benjamin F. | BASSETT, Mary A. | 04 OCT 1858 |
| BURNES, Millard F. | THOMA, Josephine | 04 APR 1868 |
| BURNES, William H. | NEWMAN, Elizabeth | 31 MAY 1864 |
| BURNETT, Addison | HERBERT, Caroline (col'd) | 01 JUL 1865 |
| BURNETT, Edward | GRAHAM, Martha (blk) | 18 AUG 1863 |
| BURNETT, Ephraim | RACKS, Elizabeth | 23 NOV 1863 |
| BURNETT, James T. | EDWARDS, Margaret S. | 05 JAN 1864 |
| BURNETT, Philip | WILLIAMS, Sarah Virginia | 16 NOV 1867 |
| BURNHAM, Nathan | SAGE, Caroline | 02 MAY 1863 |
| BURNS, David | SHANAHAN, Margaret | 07 MAY 1859 |
| BURNS, George W. | JACKSON, Elizabeth (blk) | 26 DEC 1867 |
| BURNS, James | MORGAN, Anna C. | 30 MAR 1870 |
| BURNS, John | McCANN, Annie | 06 DEC 1864 |
| BURNS, John | LAFFERTY, Sarah Ann | 24 DEC 1866 |
| BURNS, John Caldwell | TREAKLE, Mary Jane | 16 MAY 1864 |
| BURNS, Millard Fillmore | TOMA, Josephine Mary | 13 APR 1868 |
| BURNS, Patrick | CULLAN, Mary | 13 NOV 1858 |
| BURNS, Patrick | BOGLE, Mary | 03 FEB 1865 |
| BURNS, Robert | BOLAND, Mary | 30 OCT 1863 |
| BURNS, Theodore L. | GREENWELL, Kate A. | 03 JAN 1860 |
| BURNS, Timothy | BROWN, Susan A. | 08 NOV 1867 |
| BURNS, Washington C. | BARNS, Winnie Foot (blk) | 05 MAR 1866 |
| BURNSIDE, John | RAYNOR, Josephine, Mrs. | 23 MAR 1869 |
| BURR, Ben | JACKSON, Sylvia | 24 MAR 1866 |
| BURR, Benjamin B. | OFFUTT, Sarah R. | 19 NOV 1861 |
| BURR, Charles C. | PERRY, M.J.M. | 29 AUG 1867 |
| BURR, David A. [7a] | MOTHERSHEAD, Julia M. | 08 OCT 1868 |
| BURR, Howard C. | McLEOD, Mary Helen | 14 NOV 1866 |
| BURR, John | WRIGHT, Mary (blk) | 07 FEB 1866 |
| BURR, Richard H. | FENWICK, Maria M. | 03 MAY 1866 |
| BURR, Thomas | BURR, Rebecca (blk) | 15 JUL 1865 |
| BURR, William Henry | OSBORN, Victoria A. | 03 MAY 1869 |
| BURREL, George W. | FERGUSON, Louisa M. (blk) | 27 OCT 1858 |
| BURRELL, Albert | PETERS, Mary A. (blk) | 10 OCT 1864 |
| BURRELL, Charles H. | WHITING, Mary E. | 27 JUN 1867 |
| BURRELL, Marshall | STEWART, Cary Ann | 06 JUL 1863 |
| BURRELL, Robert | JOHNSON, Maria (blk) | 04 FEB 1867 |
| BURRELL, Thomas J. | ELLISS, Elizabeth | 09 SEP 1867 |
| BURRITT, Ira Nichols | NICHOLSON, Elizabeth | 02 JUN 1868 |
| BURROUGHS, Amos | CLOUGH, Catherine | 18 JUL 1860 |
| BURROUGHS, George | STALCUP, Jane A. | 18 JUN 1866 |
| BURROUGHS, George W. | BECKWITH, Malinda Ann America | 11 MAY 1864 |

| | | |
|---|---|---|
| BURROUGHS, Robert | HOWARD, Kattie (blk) | 15 SEP 1868 |
| BURROUGHS, Thomas | DOWNING, Mary Ann | 08 APR 1864 |
| BURROW, Brooks | WILLIAMS, Susanna (blk) | 22 AUG 1864 |
| BURROWS, Francis | COOK, Margt. H. | 05 MAR 1862 |
| BURROWS, Hezekiah | FRAZIER, Jane Ann | 27 DEC 1865 |
| BURROWS, James | KIEBER, Frances | 20 JAN 1868 |
| BURROWS, James W. | BEAN, Winnie (blk) | 24 DEC 1866 |
| BURROWS, John J. [1c] | KNODE, Amanda H. | 10 JAN 1863 |
| BURROWS, Joseph | JOSSLYN, Sarah | 03 JAN 1863 |
| BURROWS, Lewis | REED, Jennie (col'd) | 29 DEC 1865 |
| BURROWS, Richard | ARMSTRONG, Margaret (blk) | 25 AUG 1864 |
| BURROWS, William E. | FRIZZELL, Mary Alice | 28 APR 1868 |
| BURROWS, Wm. H. [6] | TEACHUM, Susie | 24 NOV 1868 |
| BURRUS, Hezekiah | SCOTT, Catherine | 18 MAY 1869 |
| BURSLEY, Lemuel [7a] | DODGE, Mary Elizabeth | 23 MAR 1867 |
| BURT, George | CROME, Henritta | 29 JAN 1861 |
| BURTELL, Henry C. | JOSEPH, Hannah T. | 07 MAY 1865 |
| BURTON, Darius E. | EDMONSTON, Mary E. | 22 APR 1861 |
| BURTON, Edward H. | BURTON, Katie | 31 DEC 1868 |
| BURTON, Fielding [6le] | WEBB, Jennie [Eunice] | 13 OCT 1865 |
| BURTON, Richard A. | SCAGGS, Caroline V. | 26 SEP 1868 |
| BURTON, Samuel C. | SHECKELLS, Elizabeth | 06 APR 1864 |
| BURTON, William | DEVLIN, Sarah Ann | 15 AUG 1866 |
| BUSCHER, John Henry | MAY, Elizabeth | 14 MAY 1869 |
| BUSE, Ferdinand | FRIES, Regena | 01 DEC 1858 |
| BUSEY, Albert | JENIFER, Charlotte (blk) | 26 AUG 1869 |
| BUSEY, Albert W. | CRAWFORD, Isabel | 05 NOV 1866 |
| BUSEY, Charles J. | PRATHER, Marion | 19 NOV 1866 |
| BUSEY, Henry | HILLEARY, Sarah Ann | 13 JAN 1863 |
| BUSH, Francis | KELLEHER, Mary | 07 OCT 1858 |
| BUSH, James | SMITH, Mary Elizabeth | 02 SEP 1869 |
| BUSH, James H. | CLEMENTS, Elizabeth Ann | 03 JUL 1863 |
| BUSH, Wesley | JOHNSON, Malvina | 25 NOV 1864 |
| BUSH, William H. | ANDERSON, Henrietta (blk) | 05 AUG 1869 |
| BUSHER, Charles | BREDECAMP, Sarah | 13 JAN 1862 |
| BUSHER, John | BENKHERT, Julia | 22 APR 1865 |
| BUSKIRK, Alexander | BRYAN, Sarah Jeannette | 31 JUL 1869 |
| BUSSIUS, John [7a] | HAGARTY, Anna E. | 05 FEB 1867 |
| BUTCHER, Harry | HALL, Caroline (blk) | 22 DEC 1864 |
| BUTCHER, John | DOUGLASS, Zelia | 31 JUL 1861 |
| BUTLER, Charles | HALL, Sarah E. (blk) | 05 FEB 1861 |
| BUTLER, Charles | HUDGINS, Susan | 24 MAY 1861 |
| BUTLER, Columbus C. | HENSON, Susan (blk) | 18 AUG 1864 |
| BUTLER, David S. | BEAVERS, Martha R. | 05 APR 1869 |
| BUTLER, Edward | WOOD, Harriet (blk) | 23 DEC 1865 |
| BUTLER, Elisha J. | BARNES, Ann M. | 08 MAR 1869 |
| BUTLER, Emanuel | TYLER, Nancy (blk) | 27 JUL 1865 |
| BUTLER, Frank | LUTZENBERG, Caroline | 06 MAY 1862 |
| BUTLER, Frederick | PARKER, Mary E. (blk) | 01 DEC 1859 |
| BUTLER, George | HANLIN, Ella | 22 OCT 1862 |
| BUTLER, George | COLLINS, Maria (blk) | 11 FEB 1869 |
| BUTLER, Henry | FLETCHER, Emily (blk) | 06 JAN 1864 |
| BUTLER, Henry | YOUNG, Sarah E. (blk) | 07 DEC 1864 |
| BUTLER, Henry | BROWN, Harriet Ellen (blk) | 12 MAR 1867 |
| BUTLER, Hezekiah | BROWN, Caroline (blk) | 22 JAN 1863 |
| BUTLER, Isaac N. | JOHNSON, Mary G. (blk) | 30 OCT 1866 |

# District of Columbia Marriage Licenses, 1858-1870

| | | |
|---|---|---|
| BUTLER, J.H., Maj. | FATIO, Ida deM. | 29 MAY 1867 |
| BUTLER, James | DONN, Rosa A. | 19 DEC 1864 |
| BUTLER, James | McPHERSON, Julia (blk) | 22 OCT 1868 |
| BUTLER, James | ELLS, Frances (blk) | 15 DEC 1869 |
| BUTLER, James H. | LEWIS, Elizebeth (blk) | 29 OCT 1868 |
| BUTLER, James J. [7a] | GROVER, Sarah E. | 04 NOV 1868 |
| BUTLER, James L. | WATERS, Sallie (blk) | 03 OCT 1860 |
| BUTLER, James S. | MATHEWS, Cordelia | 25 JUL 1867 |
| BUTLER, John | ROPER, Octavia | 20 MAY 1863 |
| BUTLER, John | FITZGERALD, Alice | 29 DEC 1863 |
| BUTLER, John | CLEARY, Mary | 22 DEC 1868 |
| BUTLER, John | WILLIAMS, Jane (blk) | 18 FEB 1869 |
| BUTLER, John A. | BROWN, Sarah A. (blk) | 05 SEP 1860 |
| BUTLER, John A. | McDERMOTT, Mary Francis | 09 OCT 1867 |
| BUTLER, John E. | WASHINGTON, Maria (blk) | 09 JUL 1868 |
| BUTLER, John H. [10] | DANT, Nora [Cecilia] | 05 JUN 1862 |
| BUTLER, John H. | CRAWFORD, Louisa C.C. (blk) | 16 MAY 1867 |
| BUTLER, John Henry | EMMERSON, Martha (blk) | 28 JUN 1865 |
| BUTLER, John S. | MATTHEWS, Ann Virginia (blk) | 13 OCT 1868 |
| BUTLER, John Sam'l. | LANCASTER, Elizabeth Anna (blk) | 02 FEB 1869 |
| BUTLER, John William | MINER, Mary Margaret (blk) | 19 DEC 1867 |
| BUTLER, Joseph | WILLIAMS, Roberta (blk) | 06 OCT 1864 |
| BUTLER, Joseph | RIGGS, Maria (blk) | 27 JUL 1865 |
| BUTLER, Joseph | HODGE, Mary Louise | 27 MAY 1868 |
| BUTLER, Lemuel J. | MOORE, Mary V. | 10 DEC 1863 |
| BUTLER, Levi | WASHINGTON, Ruthie (blk) | 16 FEB 1870 |
| BUTLER, Madison | FORD, Sophia (blk) | 06 JAN 1870 |
| BUTLER, Matthew | ALEXANDER, Annie (blk) | 21 APR 1866 |
| BUTLER, Michael | FITZGERALD, Maria | 15 NOV 1860 |
| BUTLER, Overton C. | BOYER, Kitty | 03 JAN 1869 |
| BUTLER, Robert | JASPER, Henrietta (blk) | 24 DEC 1861 |
| BUTLER, Robert | MONROE, Louisa (blk) | 04 MAY 1863 |
| BUTLER, Samuel | TEWS, Elizabeth (blk) | 28 JUN 1866 |
| BUTLER, Stephen | CURTIS, Sarah (blk) | 04 DEC 1867 |
| BUTLER, Strother | CURTIS, Mary | 29 JUL 1868 |
| BUTLER, Thomas | GRAY, Mary (blk) | 28 JAN 1860 |
| BUTLER, Thomas | GROGAN, Bridget | 01 OCT 1861 |
| BUTLER, Thomas | WOOD, Agnes (blk) | 29 JUL 1868 |
| BUTLER, Thomas William | ROY, Rebecca (blk) | 17 SEP 1868 |
| BUTLER, VanBuren | DAWSON, Maria (blk) | 02 NOV 1868 |
| BUTLER, Walter | SLOAN, Mary | 01 APR 1869 |
| BUTLER, Walter A. | STEWART, Anna H. | 07 JUN 1870 |
| BUTLER, Washington | ENNIS, Ann (blk) | 14 NOV 1867 |
| BUTLER, William | LEE, Nannie (blk) | 21 DEC 1865 |
| BUTLER, William | HAGAN, Elizabeth (blk) | 29 JAN 1867 |
| BUTLER, William B. | HALL, Elizabeth | 10 FEB 1869 |
| BUTLER, William H.B.* | WRIGHT, Sarah E. | 10 MAR 1859 |
| BUTLER, William J. | O'SULLIVAN, Margaret | 06 MAY 1863 |
| BUTT, Charles | SCHRIER, Annie | 29 JUL 1867 |
| BUTT, William B. [11] | ALLYN, Maggie | 07 MAY 1862 |
| BUTTERS, William M. | PEASE, Ellen W. | 28 OCT 1864 |
| BUTTRILL, William | MILLER, Mary Ann | 21 FEB 1865 |
| BUXBAUM, Aaron | SCHESINGER, Leana | 25 JUN 1864 |
| BUXTON, Otis S. | SIMPSON, Ann Jane | 31 MAY 1869 |
| BUYER, Victor [10] | ATCHINSON, Mary | 19 MAR 1860 |
| BUYNITZKY, Stephen N. | PETSCH, Caroline H. | 15 NOV 1869 |

District of Columbia Marriage Licenses, 1858-1870

| | | |
|---|---|---|
| BUZZARD, Orlando | ORRISON, Jennie | 05 FEB 1868 |
| BYAS, Job | DAVIS, Catherine | 06 APR 1870 |
| BYERS, Benjamin | KING, Ann E. | 16 NOV 1865 |
| BYERS, Noah | TATE, Ann (blk) | 24 NOV 1858 |
| BYERS, Noah | WILLIAMS, Alice (blk) | 29 MAY 1861 |
| BYERS, William H. | HOPKINS, Mary E. | 15 AUG 1867 |
| BYNG, George T. | WESTON, Sarah A. | 03 FEB 1868 |
| BYRNE, Francis X. | JOHNSON, Mattie | 29 MAR 1869 |
| BYRNE, George F. | BEACH, Jane C. | 12 JUN 1867 |
| BYRNE, Patrick | BRYSON, Elizabeth | 19 SEP 1861 |
| BYRNES, George W. | BENSON, Harriet | 15 DEC 1866 |
| BYRNES, James | MILLER, Bridget | 04 APR 1866 |
| BYRNES, James | LYNCH, Bridget | 13 APR 1866 |
| BYRNES, John J. | TYLER, Sarah E. | 14 SEP 1865 |
| BYRNES, Thos. R. | OWENS, Rose E. | 19 JUN 1862 |

## C

| | | |
|---|---|---|
| CABEL, Beverly | BARNES, Martha (blk) | 20 DEC 1864 |
| CABOT, John F. [4] | HAWLEY, A.S. | 27 APR 1859 |
| CADDIN, David | O'NEIL, Bridget | 15 JUL 1864 |
| CADEN, James | HOFFMAN, Mary | 02 SEP 1864 |
| CADEY, Matthias | GRIFFIN, Ann | 08 OCT 1858 |
| CADEY, Patrick | CLANSY, Margaret | 07 NOV 1861 |
| CADMAN, Walter | BUTHMANN, Adeline E. | 04 NOV 1861 |
| CADY, Martin | McDERMOTT, Cecelia | 27 JUL 1859 |
| CADY, Martin | DRURY, Annie | 19 JUL 1865 |
| CAESAR, Henry | DRISCOLL, Johannah | 10 FEB 1864 |
| CAESER, Julius | [blank], Sarah (blk) | 18 SEP 1862 |
| CAFFREY, James | MURPHY, Johanna | 22 JUL 1863 |
| CAHELL, William | DEMOND, Harriet | 03 MAR 1870 |
| CAHILL, James | MADDEN, Margaret | 03 MAR 1863 |
| CAHILL, Nicholas | CULL, Sarah | 05 OCT 1866 |
| CAHLAN, Martin | CAIN, Bridget | 08 JUL 1862 |
| CAHN, Felix | NEWMYER, Jenny | 09 JUL 1864 |
| CAHO, John T.I. | COST, Sarah E. | 28 DEC 1861 |
| CAIN, Jeremiah | PRYOR, Jeremiah P. (blk) | 30 JUL 1863 |
| CAIN, Jonathan F. | HAMILTON, Edwardanna | 09 FEB 1860 |
| CAIN, Thomas | LAWRENCE, Cecilia (blk) | 25 AUG 1864 |
| CAINE, Solomon | O'NEILL, Catherine | 13 JAN 1868 |
| CAIRN, Joseph | LENEHEN, Margaret | 08 AUG 1866 |
| CAKE, David | HICKS, Martha | 07 AUG 1867 |
| CALDER, Thomas | CARTER, Mary Ann (col'd) | 18 MAY 1870 |
| CALDWELL, Charles W. | McINTYRE, Margaret | 10 DEC 1868 |
| CALDWELL, Eugene S. | JOY, Jane E. | 09 MAY 1867 |
| CALDWELL, John | ROSE, Jane E. | 06 MAR 1865 |
| CALDWELL, John H. | LUCHESSI, Josephine | 09 DEC 1868 |
| CALDWELL, John L. | WILLIAMSON, Harriet E. | 10 DEC 1868 |
| CALDWELL, John S. | BEARD, Mary E. | 22 MAR 1870 |
| CALDWELL, William | HURLEY, Jane | 29 DEC 1864 |
| CALEF, Rufus | PAGE, Sarah | 17 JUL 1865 |
| CALEF, W.H.H. [7a] | FROST, Lizzie A. | 10 DEC 1868 |
| CALHOUN, Charles B. | MAHORNEY, Sarah C. | 14 FEB 1860 |
| CALHOUN, James A. | FRYE, Amanda M. | 22 NOV 1858 |
| CALHOUN, Robert H. | PAYNE, Mary Emma | 05 MAY 1864 |
| CALLAGHAN, Donald | CONNOR, Joanna | 05 APR 1867 |

| Groom | Bride | Date |
|---|---|---|
| CALLAGHAN, Edward O. | SUIT, Mary | 03 OCT 1868 |
| CALLAGHAN, Patrick | MARTIN, Mary | 20 AUG 1864 |
| CALLAGHAN, Richard | O'LEARY, Ellen | 10 OCT 1865 |
| CALLAHAN, Eugene | SWEENY, Mary | 25 NOV 1859 |
| CALLAHAN, Jerome | SAGE, Fannie W. | 31 DEC 1867 |
| CALLAHAN, John | COLLINS, Catharine | 22 SEP 1858 |
| CALLAHAN, John | ROACH, Elizabeth | 07 SEP 1861 |
| CALLAHAN, John | BRODERICK, Margaret | 22 MAY 1863 |
| CALLAHAN, John | NOTHEY, Eliza | 27 OCT 1866 |
| CALLAHAN, John | CASCORRO, Mary | 17 SEP 1867 |
| CALLAHAN, Thomas | HOWLETT, Mary | 25 MAY 1869 |
| CALLAHAN, Timothy | ROURKE, Julia | 13 DEC 1862 |
| CALLAN, Bartholomew | HORRIGAN, Margaret | 12 OCT 1866 |
| CALLAN, Charles C. | BENSON, Ida A. | 20 APR 1868 |
| CALLAN, John | MANGHAR, Bridget | 16 OCT 1868 |
| CALLAN, Lawrence F. | McSWEENY, Margaret E. | 10 JAN 1865 |
| CALLAN, Nicholas, Jr. | FORSYTH, Mary R. | 17 JAN 1867 |
| CALLAN, Patrick | KEEFE, Kate | 21 OCT 1861 |
| CALLNAN, James | MALONE, Margaret | 06 MAR 1862 |
| CALUNAN, Walter | ROSS, Rose (blk) | 03 DEC 1867 |
| CALVERT, Frederick G. | PERKINS, Fannie M. | 09 MAY 1862 |
| CALVERT, James | JOHNSON, Martha (blk) | 16 APR 1864 |
| CALVERT, John J. | PARKHURST, Annie T. | 11 JAN 1860 |
| CALVERT, Leonard | JACKSON, Elizabeth (blk) | 14 FEB 1863 |
| CALVERT, Richard | CALVERT, Mary Ann (blk) | 07 DEC 1861 |
| CALVERT, Richard | BRENT, Mary L. (blk) | 10 AUG 1869 |
| CALVERT, Washington Custis [11] | RANDOLPH, Bettie Gibbon | 27 OCT 1862 |
| CALVIN, Jere. | HONESTY, Mary (blk) | 23 JAN 1868 |
| CALVIN, Thomas | O'CONNER, Margaret | 20 SEP 1866 |
| CAMERON, Alexander [12s] | ELLMORE, Juli | 14 OCT 1862 |
| CAMERON, Anderson C. | HENSHAW, Ella P. | 16 FEB 1869 |
| CAMERON, John Arno | GREEN, Elizabeth | 25 JUL 1863 |
| CAMMACK, Alfred [5] | SIOUSSA, Lottie R. | 16 MAY 1870 |
| CAMMACK, Edmund | NEWCOMB, C. Virginia | 16 JUN 1863 |
| CAMMACK, George C. | DOLAN, Kate | 01 NOV 1862 |
| CAMMACK, John J. | BOWMAN, Susan E. | 05 OCT 1867 |
| CAMMACK, William H.H.D. | HINTON, Jennie | 15 OCT 1867 |
| CAMP, Elisha E. [Capt.] [11] | KELLER, Louisa | 15 FEB 1862 |
| CAMPBELL, Alexander | COTTER, Alice | 03 OCT 1861 |
| CAMPBELL, Alexander | CUNNINGHAM, Agnes L. | 17 APR 1862 |
| CAMPBELL, Andrew | COSGROVE, Jane | 21 JUL 1863 |
| CAMPBELL, Archy | CALLAGHAN, Joahanna | 22 JUN 1863 |
| CAMPBELL, C.C. | ALLEN, Alma L. | 18 MAY 1868 |
| CAMPBELL, Carter W. | BOWIE, Henrietta (blk) | 27 DEC 1869 |
| CAMPBELL, Charles | JACKSON, Rachel (blk) | 14 MAY 1864 |
| CAMPBELL, Chas. A. | JOHNSON, Louisa | 07 AUG 1860 |
| CAMPBELL, Charles R. | REEVES, Sallie | 30 OCT 1869 |
| CAMPBELL, Edwin | SAGE, Agnes Virginia | 30 OCT 1869 |
| CAMPBELL, George [6l] | ANDERSON, Emma | 12 NOV 1861 |
| CAMPBELL, Henry | JOYCE, Catharine | 18 APR 1862 |
| CAMPBELL, Henry | DONOGHUE, Sarah A. | 11 FEB 1865 |
| CAMPBELL, Henry C. | AYTON, Ginnie | 28 FEB 1863 |
| CAMPBELL, John | ANGEL, Margaret | 03 JAN 1859 |
| CAMPBELL, John | PARKER, Jane (blk) | 26 DEC 1862 |
| CAMPBELL, John | DAY, Bettie (blk) | 27 DEC 1866 |
| CAMPBELL, John | CONLAY, Margaret | 14 APR 1869 |

District of Columbia Marriage Licenses, 1858-1870

| | | |
|---|---|---|
| CAMPBELL, John | PARKER, Sarah (blk) | 01 SEP 1869 |
| CAMPBELL, John T. | GRIFFITH, Alice C. | 24 APR 1869 |
| CAMPBELL, King | ANDERSON, Eliza (blk) | 28 MAY 1868 |
| CAMPBELL, Patrick | ZEFONT, Elizabeth | 25 FEB 1859 |
| CAMPBELL, Peter | WEST, Frances | 23 MAR 1869 |
| CAMPBELL, Robert [10] | FOWLER, Elizabeth | 12 JUN 1865 |
| CAMPBELL, Robert | ASHTON, Fanny (blk) | 11 AUG 1866 |
| CAMPBELL, Robert Gray | McDEVITT, Hannah | 16 NOV 1866 |
| CAMPBELL, Robert Tolmie | CLARKE, Julia | 23 MAY 1860 |
| CAMPBELL, Spencer | HENRY, Mary (blk) | 15 JUN 1869 |
| CAMPBELL, Thos. B. [11] | CHRISTIE, Sarah C. | 12 NOV 1867 |
| CAMPBELL, William | EPPERSON, Mary (blk) | 26 MAR 1866 |
| CAMPBELL, William C. | HAYES, Matilda Ann (blk) | 09 JAN 1868 |
| CAMPBELL, William John | MARSHALL, Mary Jamison | 26 DEC 1866 |
| CAMPBELL, William W. | CHANDLER, Caroline | 28 MAY 1861 |
| CAMPMIRE, C.W. | CRANAGE, Rosina | 04 SEP 1866 |
| CAMPMIRE, Charles W. | HOFFMAN, Mary Jane | 06 APR 1864 |
| CANADA, Archa | BROOKS, Millie (blk) | 21 OCT 1867 |
| CANADY, Adolphus A. | ROACH, Virginia H. | 13 DEC 1869 |
| CANALY, Patrick | HUNT, Sarah | 14 JUL 1863 |
| CANAVAN, John | MADDEN, Catharine | 14 MAR 1868 |
| CANDLER, Thomas J. | JONES, Hester E. | 30 DEC 1868 |
| CANDLER, Wm. Montgomery | EFFUTTS, Elizabeth Ellen | 08 NOV 1862 |
| CANN, David C. | GIBBONS, Lizzie | 20 MAY 1867 |
| CANN, John | MOORE, Catherine Frances | 09 JUL 1863 |
| CANNON, Alfred D. | SKILLEN, Mary | 09 NOV 1861 |
| CANNON, John A. | BARNS, Helen M. | 23 MAR 1868 |
| CANNON, Martin E. | MAROONEY, Bridget R. | 31 MAR 1862 |
| CANNON, Owen | McMUN, Jane | 07 MAY 1863 |
| CANNON, William | MATTHEWS, Laura | 09 MAY 1865 |
| CANOWAY, John C. | JACKSON, Laura (blk) | 15 NOV 1862 |
| CANTER, Charles | SMITH, Judy (blk) | 13 DEC 1860 |
| CANTLER, Abraham T. | DENHAM, Caroline A. | 04 OCT 1865 |
| CANTON, Richard | BOWIE, Clarissa (blk) | 16 MAY 1864 |
| CANTWELL, Enoch J. | HAGAN, Sarah Ann | 18 AUG 1859 |
| CANTY, Patrick | MURT, Catharine | 05 FEB 1864 |
| CAPEHART, Charles E. | SAWYER, Louie | 23 JUL 1866 |
| CAPLE, James Edward | BRAMLEE, Helen | 16 OCT 1866 |
| CAR, Henry | MAGRAW, Margaret | 31 DEC 1860 |
| CARD, Benjamin C. [11] | HUNTER, Isabel L. | 26 MAY 1866 |
| CARDOW, William H. | STEWART, Martha Ann | 25 AUG 1860 |
| CAREW, Albert J. | HILL, Johanna | 10 FEB 1866 |
| CAREY, Asa B. [11] | COLBY, Laura M. | 23 JUL 1867 |
| CAREY, Edward | SWEENY, Mary Ann | 13 OCT 1864 |
| CAREY, Edward | SMITH, Lizzie (blk) | 05 JUN 1867 |
| CAREY, James | CAVANAGH, Maria | 17 JAN 1863 |
| CAREY, John | KEHOE, Georgiana | 28 JUL 1866 |
| CAREY, John | DAVIS, Annie (blk) | 25 JAN 1869 |
| CAREY, Morgan | MYERS, Nannie | 22 DEC 1869 |
| CARF, John | JOACHIM, Anna M. | 24 MAY 1860 |
| CARLIN, George C. | GRIMES, Ann A. Needen | 23 NOV 1859 |
| CARLIN, George W. | SHACKLEFORD, Sucillia | 18 FEB 1864 |
| CARLIN, John A. | MULANY, Hannah | 04 JUL 1862 |
| CARLIN, Wm. H.F. | BOUCHER, Margaretta | 22 FEB 1866 |
| CARLISLE, James C. | CONNOLL, Kathleen | 23 MAY 1863 |
| CARMAN, Peter | WILLIS, Martha | 28 MAY 1866 |

District of Columbia Marriage Licenses, 1858-1870

| | | |
|---|---|---|
| CARMAN, William C. | CATEN, Alice | 15 SEP 1864 |
| CARMICHAEL, Benjamin | McGARITY, Catherine | 13 OCT 1862 |
| CARMON, John L. | NORRIS, Lidia | 09 MAY 1859 |
| CARN, John | KENNEDY, Eliza | 26 MAR 1867 |
| CARNAY, Luke | MULLARNY, Bridget | 21 FEB 1859 |
| CARNELL, William | RHODES, Mary E. (blk) | 05 FEB 1861 |
| CARNEY, Luke | HAGERTY, Mary | 18 OCT 1861 |
| CAROLAN, Thomas E. | HANDLEY, Ellen | 06 JUN 1862 |
| CARON, Charles L. | WOLFF, Bertha | 08 AUG 1866 |
| CARPENTER, Churchwell | TAYLOR, Martha | 22 JUL 1869 |
| CARPENTER, David A. | CAREY, Mary | 24 JUL 1865 |
| CARPENTER, George W. | BAILY, Louisa H. (blk) | 10 APR 1866 |
| CARPENTER, George W. | HAUPTMAN, Helen C. | 10 NOV 1868 |
| CARPENTER, Henry | DAVIS, Hester (blk) | 04 FEB 1867 |
| CARPENTER, John R. | BALL, Kate | 02 DEC 1867 |
| CARPENTER, John R.P. | JOHNSON, Sarah Ann | 12 JUN 1860 |
| CARPENTER, Madison | HONESTY, Harriet E. (blk) | 04 APR 1866 |
| CARPENTER, Patrick | COLEMAN, Margaret | 03 MAY 1862 |
| CARPENTIER, Jules Michel Gustave Le | DeJARDINS, Marie Anastasie | 23 JUL 1867 |
| CARR, Andrew H. [6s] | BURGESS, Emma | 26 APR 1864 |
| CARR, Bernard | CROSS, Joanna | 04 MAY 1866 |
| CARR, Charles L. | BRANSOM, Susan H., Mrs. | 15 JUN 1870 |
| CARR, Francis | ENRIGHT, Margaret | 30 OCT 1865 |
| CARR, Henry | CUSTIS, Rose (blk) | 26 SEP 1865 |
| CARR, John | WILLIAMS, Jane | 06 APR 1863 |
| CARR, John H. | SWANN, Anna | 08 MAR 1870 |
| CARR, Patrick | SUMMERS, Winifred | 03 NOV 1864 |
| CARR, Richard Levi | GODDARD, Sarah E. | 30 NOV 1858 |
| CARR, William | WESTWOOD, Eliza C. | 29 FEB 1860 |
| CARRICK, Andrew | ALLEN, Mary (blk) | 13 FEB 1868 |
| CARRICK, Frederick | CARRICK, Eliza | 09 MAR 1867 |
| CARRICK, Michael | DOYLE, Bridget | 01 FEB 1864 |
| CARRICO, James | SULLIVAN, Ellen | 16 AUG 1869 |
| CARRICO, Wm. H. | MASTERS, Emma | 23 DEC 1863 |
| CARRIER, Arthur I. [11] | BRUCE, Mary C. | 13 MAR 1866 |
| CARRIER, John H. | O'BRIEN, Johana | 27 APR 1864 |
| CARRIERE, Charles | SICKEL, Caroline | 01 JUN 1864 |
| CARRIGAN, Daniel [6l] | SMITH, Sarah J. | 09 AUG 1861 |
| CARRINGTON, Eugene [10] | DIMMOCK, Cora * | 12 APR 1859 |
| CARRINGTON, Henry | DAVIS, Sally | 14 JAN 1870 |
| CARROLL, Andrew J. [6s] | SNIFFIN, Susan A. | 05 JAN 1865 |
| CARROLL, Bryan | ZELL, Mary | 04 FEB 1868 |
| CARROLL, Charles | CARROLL, Anne (blk) | 15 MAR 1866 |
| CARROLL, Daniel | O'CONNOR, Johanna | 02 NOV 1858 |
| CARROLL, Daniel | MINNEX, Margaret | 22 NOV 1861 |
| CARROLL, Daniel | BOWEN, Joanna | 02 DEC 1863 |
| CARROLL, Daniel | BUMBRAY, Fanny (blk) | 25 OCT 1865 |
| CARROLL, Daniel | OGLE, Rachel (blk) | 05 MAR 1867 |
| CARROLL, Daniel | CONTEE, Martha | 08 JAN 1868 |
| CARROLL, David | HUMPHREYS, Mary A.E. (blk) | 19 DEC 1861 |
| CARROLL, Emanuel | TURNER, Harriet (blk) | 22 MAY 1866 |
| CARROLL, George | TAYLOR, Jane (blk) | 09 NOV 1866 |
| CARROLL, George W. | DYER, Ann O. | 23 FEB 1870 |
| CARROLL, Hercules | PORT, Josephine M. | 29 JUL 1863 |
| CARROLL, John | WILLIAMS, Mary Ann (blk) | 13 JAN 1863 |
| CARROLL, John | SHERWOOD, Rosa A. | 12 APR 1864 |

| | | |
|---|---|---|
| CARROLL, John | HILTON, Martha A. | 11 MAY 1866 |
| CARROLL, John Thomas | KING, Mary Catherine | 18 APR 1866 |
| CARROLL, Joseph H. | LOVELESS, Eliza J. | 25 JUN 1860 |
| CARROLL, Laurence | PROPELTON, Catharine | 15 JUN 1863 |
| CARROLL, Michael | DANIEL, Mary Maack | 15 SEP 1862 |
| CARROLL, Morton | JONES, Elizabeth (blk) | 21 MAY 1866 |
| CARROLL, Oratio G. | DUVALL, Margaret B. | 16 AUG 1862 |
| CARROLL, P. Burgess | KELLEY, Cecilia (blk) | 22 NOV 1869 |
| CARROLL, Patrick | LYNCH, Mary | 16 JUN 1863 |
| CARROLL, Patrick | HOOKER, Anna Eliza | 17 APR 1866 |
| CARROLL, Robert A. | LEWIS, Katherine C. | 22 JAN 1870 |
| CARROLL, Samuel | NEALE, Flora (blk) | 02 MAY 1867 |
| CARROLL, Thomas | BEAN, Ann (blk) | 04 SEP 1867 |
| CARROLL, Walter T. | ALLISON, Elizabeth D. | 29 JAN 1862 |
| CARROLL, William Henry [6m] | HOWARD, Julia [Elizabeth] | 12 MAY 1863 |
| CARROLL, William Henry | MARTIN, Josephine Rebecca | 13 JUL 1869 |
| CARSON, Edward | FISHER, Anna | 28 JUL 1863 |
| CARSON, Edward T. | CRAWFORD, Mary Eliza | 06 DEC 1869 |
| CARTER, Abram | SMITH, Lucy (blk) | 11 APR 1867 |
| CARTER, Addison | CARTER, Delphi (blk) | 29 JUL 1865 |
| CARTER, Alfred | NORTON, Mary (blk) | 12 MAY 1863 |
| CARTER, Archey | MARLOW, Lydia (blk) | 03 JUL 1867 |
| CARTER, Archy | COFFEE, Sally | 05 AUG 1863 |
| CARTER, Arthur | MASON, Mary Nicholas, Mrs. (blk) | 27 NOV 1867 |
| CARTER, Benjamin | JOHNSON, Nancy (blk) | 18 OCT 1866 |
| CARTER, Beverly | JUNIPER, Caroline (blk) | 04 JUN 1868 |
| CARTER, Cary [11] | JONES, Emily | 23 FEB 1859 |
| CARTER, Charles M. | ARCHER, Mary H. | 26 MAR 1862 |
| CARTER, Daniel | COMMENS, Mary Frances (blk) | 25 AUG 1868 |
| CARTER, Dennis | CARTER, Laura V. | 24 APR 1867 |
| CARTER, Edmund | FREEMAN, Elizabeth (blk) | 19 SEP 1864 |
| CARTER, Edward | MITCHELL, Louisa (blk) | 01 MAR 1869 |
| CARTER, Edward L. | HEDGEMAN, Catherine (blk) | 14 JUN 1867 |
| CARTER, Fielding | RUSTIN, Annie (blk) | 16 APR 1867 |
| CARTER, Fitzhugh | FIELDS, Mary (blk) | 22 DEC 1868 |
| CARTER, Founty | CAMPBELL, Louisa (blk) | 03 SEP 1866 |
| CARTER, Garret | JONES, Rosa (blk) | 09 MAR 1867 |
| CARTER, George | JENIFER, Elizabeth (blk) | 13 SEP 1866 |
| CARTER, George | WILMORE, Delia (blk) | 01 NOV 1866 |
| CARTER, George | SHEPHERD, Ann (blk) | 06 SEP 1867 |
| CARTER, George | CLARK, Fannie (blk) | 26 JUN 1868 |
| CARTER, Harrison P. | PETTY, Mary E. | 03 MAY 1859 |
| CARTER, Henry | SHORTER, Lizzie (blk) | 04 JAN 1865 |
| CARTER, Henry | STEWART, Ellen S. (blk) | 09 MAR 1866 |
| CARTER, Henry E. | GOLDEN, Catherine A. | 16 MAR 1866 |
| CARTER, Henry H. | ROBERTSON, Margaret Ann | 26 JAN 1864 |
| CARTER, Horace | HIGGINS, Mary (blk) | 18 SEP 1862 |
| CARTER, Israel E. | SHERMAN, Eunice R. | 25 JUN 1863 |
| CARTER, James | MONTGOMERY, Margaret (blk) | 20 NOV 1866 |
| CARTER, James | FORD, Mary Ann | 01 APR 1867 |
| CARTER, James B. [3] | THOMAS, Ann (blk) | 12 AUG 1863 |
| CARTER, James B. | COMBS, Mary E. | 01 DEC 1864 |
| CARTER, Jeremiah | LEE, Chloe (blk) | 23 NOV 1867 |
| CARTER, Jerry | HARRISON, Lucy Ann (blk) | 16 MAR 1868 |
| CARTER, Jerry | HARRISON, Patience A. | 08 OCT 1868 |
| CARTER, John | HERBERT, Martha (blk) | 16 OCT 1862 |

District of Columbia Marriage Licenses, 1858-1870

| | | |
|---|---|---|
| CARTER, John | O'CONNER, Catharine | 11 SEP 1864 |
| CARTER, John | WILLIAMS, Annie (blk) | 06 JAN 1870 |
| CARTER, John Calvin | RATCLIFFE, Emma Irene | 28 OCT 1858 |
| CARTER, John S. | FOUNTAIN, Mary Jane | 25 OCT 1859 |
| CARTER, John Wesley | HENSON, Elizabeth (blk) | 28 JAN 1869 |
| CARTER, Joseph | SCOTT, Adelaide V. | 30 JAN 1862 |
| CARTER, Lewis [12s] | MILES, Maria (blk) | 25 MAY 1859 |
| CARTER, Lewis | JACKSON, Mary (blk) | 14 JAN 1864 |
| CARTER, Luke | TURNER, Hannah (blk) | 27 JUL 1867 |
| CARTER, Luther | WORTHINGTON, Margaret Anna | 12 AUG 1863 |
| CARTER, Malachi | FLINT, Isabella (blk) | 12 APR 1870 |
| CARTER, Pascar | COLLINS, Margaret (blk) | 16 MAY 1867 |
| CARTER, Richard | JONES, Ann Maria | 20 APR 1859 |
| CARTER, Richard | BARNES, Henrietta | 08 MAR 1865 |
| CARTER, Robert | JORDAN, Maria | 29 APR 1869 |
| CARTER, Spencer | LUCAS, Margaret (blk) | 03 DEC 1868 |
| CARTER, Stephen | BROWN, Lydia (blk) | 03 JUL 1865 |
| CARTER, Theodore | JOHNSON, Hannah (blk) | 30 MAY 1866 |
| CARTER, Thomas | NELSON, Mary (blk) | 23 OCT 1868 |
| CARTER, Thomas | HOWARD, Susannah (blk) | 25 NOV 1869 |
| CARTER, Washington | HARPER, Eliza (blk) | 29 SEP 1864 |
| CARTER, William | VENABLE, Mary | 24 MAY 1859 |
| CARTER, William | CARR, Lucinda | 03 JAN 1866 |
| CARTER, William | FREELAND, Dorcas (blk) | 11 DEC 1867 |
| CARTER, William | HAWKINS, Lizzie | 21 APR 1870 |
| CARTER, William | CARTER, Rachel (blk) | 29 APR 1870 |
| CARTER, William H. | BLACKSTONE, Julia Adaline | 19 OCT 1868 |
| CARTER, Wm. Hy. | SANLEY, Jane (blk) | 26 JAN 1865 |
| CARTLITT, Philip | SMITH, Mary (blk) | 01 MAR 1867 |
| CARTTER, Henry | BROWN, Elizabeth (blk) | 25 MAY 1864 |
| CARTWRIGHT, Charles | MARCY, Mary | 01 SEP 1864 |
| CARTWRIGHT, Hamilton L. | WILLIAMS, Maria (blk) | 17 DEC 1863 |
| CARTWRIGHT, Philip | GREENFIELD, Elizabeth (blk) | 29 JUL 1864 |
| CARUSI, Eugene | STANDFORD, Fanny | 16 APR 1860 |
| CARUSI, John McLean | HURLEY, Susan | 05 NOV 1861 |
| CARVER, J.P. [7b] | JONES, E.M.F. | 06 APR 1870 |
| CARY, Thomas | RYAN, Mary | 03 MAY 1862 |
| CASE, George W. | CALLENDER, Catherine | 29 MAR 1860 |
| CASE, John W. | HOUSE, Annie S. | 09 JUN 1870 |
| CASEY, Edward [F.] [6le] | GRACE, Mary | 13 MAY 1865 |
| CASEY, George [1c] | ADKINSON, Mary | 24 DEC 1862 |
| CASEY, John | RAGAN, Mary | 05 FEB 1859 |
| CASEY, John | FINN, Kate | 13 SEP 1859 |
| CASEY, John | CALLAN, Florence E. | 01 OCT 1867 |
| CASEY, Martin | FITZGERALD, Kate | 06 FEB 1864 |
| CASEY, Martin | RYAN, Catharine | 09 MAY 1865 |
| CASEY, Michael | OWEN, Mary Jane | 26 MAY 1862 |
| CASEY, Peter | DADEY, Mary | 08 OCT 1861 |
| CASEY, Silas (Gent.) [4] | GORDON, Florida | 12 JUL 1864 |
| CASEY, Stephen | DACEY, Honora | 24 NOV 1858 |
| CASHEN, Michael | DELANEY, Mary Anne | 27 MAY 1864 |
| CASHIER, David | FRAULY, Mary | 10 APR 1867 |
| CASHWELL, Charles | CLARK, Rittle E. | 05 JAN 1864 |
| CASLOW, Timothy | LAWLER, Mary | 01 DEC 1863 |
| CASON, Edward E. [6le] | MURPHY, Sarah | 17 MAR 1866 |
| CASS, James M. [6s] | CONNOR, Kate | 21 MAR 1865 |

| | | |
|---|---|---|
| CASSALL, Thomas M. | WETZELL, Henrietta | 06 JAN 1863 |
| CASSEDY, James T. | MANN, Sarah | 05 SEP 1863 |
| CASSEL, Alfred C. | DAVIS, Mary V. | 03 FEB 1864 |
| CASSEL, George W. | PAXON, Ann E. | 21 NOV 1864 |
| CASSELL, George T. | DAVIS, Lizzie A. | 14 OCT 1861 |
| CASSELL, Thomas M. | ROBINSON, Sarah B.E. | 26 MAY 1859 |
| CASSIDAY, Charles | McDONALD, Elichea | 29 JUL 1865 |
| CASSIDAY, Thomas A. [9e] | PATTERSON, Mary E. | 10 AUG 1861 |
| CASSIDY, Henry | KEARNS, Bridget | 21 MAY 1860 |
| CASSIDY, Henry | HILBRUSH, Mary E. | 23 DEC 1867 |
| CASSIDY, Henry H. | GARTRELL, Mary Kate | 17 MAY 1869 |
| CASSIDY, Marquis W. | GETHEN, Clara V. | 30 AUG 1864 |
| CASSIDY, Peter | MURRAY, Margaret | 27 OCT 1858 |
| CASSIDY, Richard | DOREMUS, Mary E. | 13 SEP 1861 |
| CASSIN, Joseph R. | WILLIAM, Annie Elizabeth | 03 OCT 1867 |
| CASSIN, William D. | TYLER, Mary A. | 27 DEC 1858 |
| CASTEEL, Edward | STEWART, Mary C. | 27 NOV 1867 |
| CASTEN, Alexander | ANDERSON, Mary (blk) | 30 APR 1866 |
| CASTLE, Davis E. | BISHOP, Annie | 02 JUL 1866 |
| CASTLEMAN, Stephen D. | PETTIT, Lucinda V. | 16 SEP 1861 |
| CASTON, John | CUNNINGHAM, Sarah J. | 11 OCT 1858 |
| CASWELL, William F. [10] | WATSON, Martha Rebecca | 01 JUL 1865 |
| CATON, Emanuel D. | ROSE, Susannah | 25 JUL 1859 |
| CATON, James O. | HARRISON, Margaret E. | 31 DEC 1861 |
| CATON, Patrick A. | CARTER, Catherine | 25 OCT 1867 |
| CATON, William | ROWAN, Margaret | 20 FEB 1860 |
| CATOR, Thomas | LUSBY, Elizabeth | 05 FEB 1861 |
| CATTIN, B.E. | BROWN, Mattie L. | 08 MAR 1869 |
| CATTS, Rosier D. | BROWN, Fanny A. | 20 JAN 1860 |
| CAUGHLAN, Daniel | FITZGERALD, Margaret | 16 FEB 1863 |
| CAUSTEN, Manuel C. [6l] | HOMILLER, Isadora | 02 MAY 1861 |
| CAVALLO, Carlos, Dr. | BAYLISS, Emma | 27 FEB 1867 |
| CAVANAUGH, John | CONNELLY, Catherine | 30 DEC 1859 |
| CAVANAUGH, John | MULROY, Bridget | 06 SEP 1861 |
| CAVANAUGH, John | IGO, Margaret | 04 APR 1866 |
| CAVANAUGH, John | SIMMONS, Louisa | 02 SEP 1867 |
| CAVANAUGH, Timothy | MURPHY, Ellen | 25 FEB 1865 |
| CAVE, Benjamin | HILL, Emma G. | 17 APR 1869 |
| CAVE, Frederick A. | WARING, Celestia | 23 JUL 1862 |
| CAVENAGH, James | McCARTHY, Mary | 28 MAY 1862 |
| CAVENDER, L.L. | BRADY, Mollie | 02 MAR 1869 |
| CAWOOD, Philip A. [6c] | GREEN, Sarah E. | 14 OCT 1858 |
| CAWOOD, Samuel H. | WELLS, Mary F. | 19 NOV 1862 |
| CECIL, Joseph B. | GAUBERT, Mary | 09 NOV 1869 |
| CECIL, Richard | KERR, L.M. | 25 APR 1861 |
| CECIL, Thomas F. | McFARLIN, Jane VanDelia | 29 SEP 1858 |
| CENEY, James | PINKNEY, Mary (blk) | 07 APR 1866 |
| CERIGHO, Joseph | MONTOVERDE, Mary | 21 MAY 1862 |
| CESSEEN, Frederick | HOSKINS, Susan | 07 JUL 1864 |
| CHAMBER, Caleb | CHICK, Georgia | 24 AUG 1867 |
| CHAMBERLAIN, D.H. | INGERSOLL, Alice C. | 15 DEC 1869 |
| CHAMBERLAIN, James Henry | AGER, Clarence Louisa | 09 MAY 1868 |
| CHAMBERLAIN, John W.H. [4] | WORTHINGTON, Rebecca M. | 16 JUN 1866 |
| CHAMBERLAIN, Joseph G. | MYERS, Eliza V. | 31 OCT 1864 |
| CHAMBERLAIN, Julius | JONES, Ann (blk) | 26 OCT 1867 |
| CHAMBERLAIN, William S. | SAGE, Clara A. | 18 FEB 1864 |

District of Columbia Marriage Licenses, 1858-1870

| | | |
|---|---|---|
| CHAMBERLIN, Alfred H. | GLASCOW, Elizabeth | 21 MAY 1863 |
| CHAMBERLIN, David H. | NOLAN, Harriet L. | 20 DEC 1862 |
| CHAMBERLIN, Josiah Adams | CHAMBERLIN, Georgette Averina | 12 AUG 1862 |
| CHAMBERS, Benjamin, Jr. | TYLER, Rachel | 18 MAR 1865 |
| CHAMBERS, Boon | BOHLE, Eliza Anne | 21 DEC 1869 |
| CHAMBERS, William | McDONALD, Rosanna | 31 OCT 1863 |
| CHAMBERS, William | HIGDON, Mary Ann | 19 NOV 1867 |
| CHAMP, Alfred | AUGUSTA, Mary M. (blk) | 15 DEC 1863 |
| CHAMP, Luke | BERRYMAN, Berny (blk) | 19 MAR 1868 |
| CHAMP, Robert | KING, Teresa (blk) | 10 JAN 1867 |
| CHAMPAYNE, Henry R. | WIRT, Airey E. | 30 MAY 1859 |
| CHAMPION, Charles | HYDE, Catharine E. | 01 MAY 1863 |
| CHAMPION, William H. [11] | IRVING, Sarah | 14 OCT 1867 |
| CHANDLER, George F. | AMERICA, Jane Elizabeth | 13 MAY 1867 |
| CHANDLER, Henry | JOHNSON, Mary (blk) | 07 JUL 1869 |
| CHANDLER, James H. | SHEETS, Elizabeth A. | 31 OCT 1859 |
| CHANDLER, James P. | GOULD, Mary F. | 09 JUN 1863 |
| CHANDLER, John | THOMPSON, Clara (blk) | 30 JUN 1864 |
| CHANDLER, William | HILL, Francis (blk) | 06 JAN 1866 |
| CHANDONE, Victor A. | LEVEQUE, Margarite A. | 25 JUL 1861 |
| CHANDONÉ, Victor A. | WOLPHE, Cécile Augustine | 30 OCT 1869 |
| CHANEY, Frank | LEE, Louisa (col'd) | 29 DEC 1865 |
| CHANEY, James | KING, Mary Jane | 20 OCT 1866 |
| CHANEY, Richard | CROUDEN, Martha (blk) | 30 DEC 1862 |
| CHANEY, Thomas | JACKSON, Anna (blk) | 14 APR 1869 |
| CHAPIN, Elisha | BYRNE, Annie | 15 APR 1867 |
| CHAPLIN, John | JOHNSON, Hannah | 24 JUL 1867 |
| CHAPMAN, Charles H. | ADAMS, Martha C. | 02 AUG 1869 |
| CHAPMAN, Charles L. | EDWARDS, Johnana P. | 02 AUG 1864 |
| CHAPMAN, Elijah | STANBURY, Emeline (blk) | 08 DEC 1868 |
| CHAPMAN, George T. | BULL, Anna | 15 SEP 1869 |
| CHAPMAN, John | JOHNSON, Nellie (blk) | 04 DEC 1863 |
| CHAPMAN, John | STROEBEL, Elizabeth D. | 21 JUL 1864 |
| CHAPMAN, John | McCAULEY, Mary Ann | 14 MAY 1866 |
| CHAPMAN, John B. | DEMENTT, Susan A. | 19 JAN 1859 |
| CHAPMAN, John G. [10] | JONES, Fannie L. | 29 DEC 1863 |
| CHAPMAN, Samuel | WILSON, Josephine | 08 DEC 1868 |
| CHAPMAN, Walter S. | VOLANDT, Augusta F. | 01 DEC 1866 |
| CHAPPELEAR, George | MONTGOMERY, Emily | 02 NOV 1865 |
| CHAPPELEAR, William Henry | JOHNSON, Sarah Elizabeth | 26 JAN 1869 |
| CHARLES, Albert E. | FENNESY, Mary Jane | 16 NOV 1858 |
| CHARLES, William | SWIFT, Sarah (blk) | 03 MAR 1868 |
| CHARLOCK, James C. | McGEORGE, Sarah A. | 10 SEP 1867 |
| CHARLTON, Benjamin | HAVENER, Sarah A.S. | 27 MAY 1862 |
| CHASE, Basil | STEVENSON, Ann | 13 FEB 1867 |
| CHASE, Benedict | TOODLE, Nancy (blk) | 09 NOV 1864 |
| CHASE, Buel B. | PFISTER, Maria | 02 APR 1866 |
| CHASE, Charles Henry | HOBBS, Margaret Ann (blk) | 21 DEC 1863 |
| CHASE, Daniel | WHITE, Susan (blk) | 10 NOV 1864 |
| CHASE, Daniel Thomas | BROWN, Josephine (blk) | 02 OCT 1862 |
| CHASE, David | DORSEY, Sophia | 09 JUL 1869 |
| CHASE, David | BRADLY, Polly (blk) | 27 DEC 1869 |
| CHASE, Edward | WARD, Louisa (blk) | 10 DEC 1859 |
| CHASE, Francis | PEPPER, Henrietta | 27 FEB 1869 |
| CHASE, George Alfred | TINNEY, Sarah (col'd) | 19 JUN 1862 |
| CHASE, George H. | SEXTON, Annie | 02 SEP 1865 |

District of Columbia Marriage Licenses, 1858-1870

| | | |
|---|---|---|
| CHASE, George N. [12s] | McCONNELL, Mary C. | 07 JAN 1861 |
| CHASE, Henry | HOWARD, Ellen | 13 MAY 1867 |
| CHASE, John | GANTT, Eliza (blk) | 24 DEC 1862 |
| CHASE, John | GREEN, Sarah (blk) | 26 FEB 1867 |
| CHASE, John | PHOENIX, Annie (blk) | 17 MAY 1869 |
| CHASE, Joseph H. | BROWN, Mary Jane (blk) | 30 APR 1867 |
| CHASE, Newton | BOYD, Georgiana (blk) | 12 SEP 1867 |
| CHASE, Paul | POLK, Patsy (blk) | 06 AUG 1868 |
| CHASE, Robert H. | BROWN, Mary E. (blk) | 04 DEC 1862 |
| CHASE, Samuel N. | HAWKINS, Ann C. (blk) | 08 DEC 1859 |
| CHASE, Thomas | MURRAY, Anna (blk) | 21 NOV 1867 |
| CHASE, William | CARRIER, Amanda D. | 02 NOV 1858 |
| CHASE, William | AMBUSH, Elizabeth (blk) | 09 JUL 1862 |
| CHASMORE, John | HYDE, Virginia | 24 NOV 1863 |
| CHASS, John | BRASHEARS, Flowilly (blk) | 31 MAY 1866 |
| CHAUNCEY, John H. | JOHNSON, Margaret Ann | 11 AUG 1864 |
| CHAUNCEY, William A. | PRATHER, Laura V. | 03 FEB 1864 |
| CHEATHAM, Frederick | JOHNSON, Elia (blk) | 06 OCT 1864 |
| CHEEK, James H. [10] | ENNESS, Cornelia | 04 JUN 1863 |
| CHEEK, Richard | CISSON, Lucretia | 13 JUL 1865 |
| CHEEKS, Morton | YATES, Ellen (blk) | 20 DEC 1869 |
| CHELLA, Antone | FOCACHY, Theresia | 04 OCT 1862 |
| CHESHIRE, John R. [12s] | BOWDEN, Ann Maria | 02 FEB 1860 |
| CHESSER, Elihu | LEE, Matilda Jane | 08 SEP 1864 |
| CHESSER, Ephraim | TAYLOR, Mary | 23 OCT 1858 |
| CHESSON, Wilson | SCHWINN, Maria | 05 APR 1869 |
| CHESTER, Eliphalet N. | DODGE, Elizabeth | 15 APR 1868 |
| CHESTNEY, Theodore O. | MURPHY, Kate P. | 11 FEB 1867 |
| CHEW, Christopher C. | MILES, Mary J. | 16 SEP 1858 |
| CHEW, Daniel | LEWIS, Emma C. | 18 OCT 1866 |
| CHEW, George B. | ESSEX, Alice V. | 20 NOV 1866 |
| CHEW, John C. | VanBUSSUM, Hannah | 25 OCT 1858 |
| CHEW, John H. | HAWKINS, Mary Catherine (blk) | 29 MAY 1866 |
| CHEW, John W. | FLETCHER, Mary (blk) | 19 OCT 1858 |
| CHEW, John W. | DAY, Frances V. (blk) | 10 APR 1860 |
| CHEW, Philip R. | HILLERY, Emmeline (blk) | 03 SEP 1868 |
| CHEW, Robert F. | CROSS, Mary C. | 10 JUL 1861 |
| CHEW, William [12s] | DORSEY, Phoebe (blk) | 07 FEB 1863 |
| CHICHESTER, William | FORD, Mary E. | 03 FEB 1864 |
| CHICK, Edmund | CAMERON, Mary (blk) | 18 JUL 1866 |
| CHICK, Jesse [6le] | CROSS, Sarah | 24 APR 1867 |
| CHICK, Joseph C. [1c] | SILENA, Martha V. | 08 OCT 1863 |
| CHICK, Richard T. | HURLY, Margaret G. | 14 NOV 1863 |
| CHILDRESS, Edward G. | GATEWOOD, Mary J. | 24 JAN 1866 |
| CHILDS, Edmund | CHILDS, Adeline (blk) | 18 JUL 1867 |
| CHILDS, Hiram | HICKS, Charlotte (blk) | 09 JAN 1867 |
| CHILDS, James E. [10] | JENNEY, Sophia S. | 16 AUG 1864 |
| CHILDS, John Levin | ADAMS, Lucinda (blk) | 04 MAY 1866 |
| CHILDS, John W. | BRICE, Anna R. | 06 SEP 1869 |
| CHILDS, Lindsay | GLASTER, Elizabeth (blk) | 27 DEC 1864 |
| CHILDS, Nathaniel, Jr. | CHILDS, Margaret A. | 11 MAY 1865 |
| CHILDS, Zachariah W. | PAYNE, Mary Catharine | 05 MAY 1863 |
| CHINN, John | SMITH, Mary E. (blk) | 08 OCT 1858 |
| CHINN, John F. | TYLER, Kitty | 11 NOV 1868 |
| CHIPMAN, M.J. | PARR, Ades C. | 17 NOV 1868 |
| CHIPPA, Luigi | NIECA, Louisa | 02 JUL 1860 |

District of Columbia Marriage Licenses, 1858-1870

| | | |
|---|---|---|
| CHISLEY, Louis | LEE, Elizabeth (blk) | 27 OCT 1868 |
| CHISMAN, Samuel Reade | WHITING, Mattie Kennon | 20 FEB 1861 |
| CHITTAMS, Stephen | KENT, Lucy (blk) | 12 DEC 1867 |
| CHOATE, Warren | RAGAN, Kate M. | 29 NOV 1864 |
| CHONE, Michael | MILLER, Elizabeth | 10 JUN 1868 |
| CHORPEUNING, George | MacLELLAN, Carrie V. | 27 DEC 1864 |
| CHRISMAN, George W. | FRY, Sophia | 02 SEP 1869 |
| CHRIST, Charles | ARTH, Margaret | 03 SEP 1864 |
| CHRIST, Henry | BUB, Susanne Ann | 29 MAR 1864 |
| CHRISTENSEN, Niel | TURKENTON, Ann Jane | 17 APR 1865 |
| CHRISTIAN, Jordan | FLETCHER, Sophia (blk) | 15 OCT 1867 |
| CHRISTIAN, Mike | CARPENTER, Charlotte (blk) | 26 DEC 1863 |
| CHRISTIAN, Oliver | JACKSON, Sarah (blk) | 01 AUG 1866 |
| CHRISTIAN, Solomon | PARKER, Margaret (blk) | 13 MAY 1868 |
| CHRISTIAN, Walter | WOODWARD, Fannie | 08 JAN 1870 |
| CHRISTMAN, Horace C. | SCHWARTZE, Emma G. | 09 OCT 1862 |
| CHRISTMAN, Philip | PORTELLO, Flora | 05 AUG 1863 |
| CHRISTOPHER, Francis A. | BAIRD, Margaret P. | 06 FEB 1865 |
| CHUBB, Samuel | GANTT, Airy (blk) | 14 OCT 1861 |
| CHUBBUCK, Hollis L. | DORMAN, Lottie | 12 JAN 1864 |
| CHUCK, Allen | GARDNER, Ellen (blk) | 07 AUG 1866 |
| CHUN, William | JENIFER, Sarah (blk) | 19 OCT 1869 |
| CHURCH, James | BARNES, George Ann (blk) | 05 MAY 1862 |
| CHURCH, John | WILSON, Harriet (blk) | 14 APR 1869 |
| CHURCHMAN, Edward | FORWARD, Laura P. | 22 DEC 1863 |
| CHURCHWELL, George | CARRINGTON, Jane (blk) | 16 JAN 1865 |
| CHURN, Charles H. | SHILES, Maria (blk) | 06 SEP 1869 |
| CISSEL, Charles A. [4] | WHITNEY, Susan E. | 08 JUN 1863 |
| CISSEL, Charles H. | TILMON, Rosetta (blk) | 10 SEP 1867 |
| CISSEL, Richard S.T. | RITTENHOUSE, Clementina C. | 25 MAY 1868 |
| CISSEL, William C. | KAISER, Caroline Virginia | 01 FEB 1869 |
| CISSEL, William H.H. | RIGGLES, M.C. | 24 OCT 1864 |
| CISSELL, William H. | LATHAM, Alice | 03 APR 1862 |
| CLABORNE, George | WATERS, Polly (blk) | 23 MAY 1868 |
| CLAGETT, Cornelius H. | McCARTIN, Mary Ann | 04 FEB 1869 |
| CLAGETT, John H. | KINCHLOE, Mary A.L. | 03 FEB 1870 |
| CLAMPITT, John W. | GOODRICK, Mary A. | 22 NOV 1865 |
| CLAMPITT, William H. | MOYER, Amanda | 07 SEP 1866 |
| CLANCY, Daniel A. | CLEMENTS, Mary Ellen | 26 DEC 1863 |
| CLANCY, John B. | WAGNER, Margaret | 22 JUL 1862 |
| CLANCY, Martin | DONOGHUE, Mary | 10 APR 1868 |
| CLANSEY, John | RYAN, Ellen | 01 MAY 1863 |
| CLANSY, James | SHEEHAN, Mary | 18 FEB 1867 |
| CLANSY, Patrick | DORSY, Bridget | 21 MAY 1859 |
| CLANSY, Peter | HINDS, Anna | 13 OCT 1859 |
| CLANSY, Thomas | NOLAN, Sarah | 12 JUN 1867 |
| CLAPP, E. Dwight | EDMONSTON, Emma | 27 FEB 1860 |
| CLARE, Robert L. | BRADLEY, Rose A. | 30 JAN 1864 |
| CLARK, A.B. | HARRISON, Alice | 16 FEB 1870 |
| CLARK, Albert | GASSAWAY, Charlotte (blk) | 07 JAN 1869 |
| CLARK, Ambrose F. | STEPHENSON, Mary G. | 10 JUL 1865 |
| CLARK, Andrew W. | BOWMAN, Rachel A. (blk) | 20 JUN 1863 |
| CLARK, Augustus A. | LEIB, Emma J. | 17 NOV 1866 |
| CLARK, Caleb C. | DANCE, Mary | 24 FEB 1868 |
| CLARK, Charles | BROWN, Nancy | 29 JUL 1864 |
| CLARK, Charles Henry | WHEELER, Mary A. | 05 SEP 1859 |

| | | |
|---|---|---|
| CLARK, Charles L. | BROWN, Mary E. | 08 MAY 1866 |
| CLARK, Cornelius P. | JAGER, Emily | 21 APR 1870 |
| CLARK, Corns. | McCOY, Emily (blk) | 23 NOV 1858 |
| CLARK, Dennis | EASTON, Sophie | 18 DEC 1865 |
| CLARK, Frank B. | KING, Olivia J. | 11 MAR 1867 |
| CLARK, George | NELSON, Caroline (blk) | 13 SEP 1866 |
| CLARK, H.P. | HERRICK, M.E. | 22 APR 1869 |
| CLARK, Henry | CURTIS, Josephine (blk) | 03 MAR 1863 |
| CLARK, Henry | BERKLEY, Mary Jane (blk) | 11 DEC 1868 |
| CLARK, James | ARMSTRONG, Jane | 14 FEB 1859 |
| CLARK, James | POTTER, Hannah | 12 DEC 1865 |
| CLARK, James | MIDDLETON, Catherine (blk) | 21 MAY 1868 |
| CLARK, James | MULLOY, Elizabeth (blk) | 14 SEP 1868 |
| CLARK, James C. | VanHOLT, Mary Cordelia | 11 NOV 1863 |
| CLARK, James F. | LEE, Mary E. | 24 OCT 1868 |
| CLARK, John | WASHINGTON, Martha (blk) | 22 MAY 1867 |
| CLARK, John | CONNORS, Hanora | 06 AUG 1869 |
| CLARK, John DeGustis | ALLEN, Virginia Elizabeth (blk) | 15 FEB 1867 |
| CLARK, John F. | ROBEY, Harriet | 18 FEB 1869 |
| CLARK, John Henry Theodore | STEWART, America (blk) | 14 JUN 1869 |
| CLARK, John Thomas | MATTINGLY, Julia Jane | 12 OCT 1863 |
| CLARK, Joseph F. | VERMILLION, Sarah | 05 MAY 1870 |
| CLARK, Levin | BARNES, Frances Virginia | 21 APR 1870 |
| CLARK, Martin J. | REALS, Anna | 02 FEB 1865 |
| CLARK, N. Stanley [6] | EDWARDS, Rosa C. | 01 JUN 1869 |
| CLARK, Nelson | FRAZIER, Sarah | 21 DEC 1865 |
| CLARK, Patrick | CARNEY, Margaret | 25 AUG 1868 |
| CLARK, Perry | JACOBS, Sidney (blk) | 23 DEC 1869 |
| CLARK, Randolph E. | COYLE, Mary Ann | 07 APR 1862 |
| CLARK, Richard | MARTIN, Phebe (blk) | 19 JUL 1869 |
| CLARK, Richard | LEMMONS, Martha (blk) | 29 JUN 1869 |
| CLARK, Samuel | HOWARD, Miranda (blk) | 31 AUG 1869 |
| CLARK, Seth W. | HALL, Nellie Maud | 19 DEC 1866 |
| CLARK, Thomas E. | HODGSON, Martha E. | 05 DEC 1865 |
| CLARK, Tobias | SHORTER, Laura Jane | 17 SEP 1863 |
| CLARK, William | ELLIOT, Sarah A. | 18 JUN 1866 |
| CLARK, William H. | WARE, Julia (blk) | 19 JUL 1866 |
| CLARK, William H. | JONES, Nancy E. | 27 SEP 1869 |
| CLARK, William J. | WINN, Christina W. | 03 AUG 1868 |
| CLARKE, Albert S. | SWANSBERRY, Amelia | 26 JUN 1866 |
| CLARKE, Calhoun | HURDLE, Martha D. | 06 DEC 1860 |
| CLARKE, Charles H. | SHEARER, Amanda C. | 24 SEP 1858 |
| CLARKE, Daniel | CLARKE, Ann Rebecca | 11 APR 1867 |
| CLARKE, Fred M. | GONZALES, Ettie A. | 04 JAN 1867 |
| CLARKE, Gabe | PAYNE, Mary (blk) | 18 JUN 1864 |
| CLARKE, George | REED, Mary Ann | 11 JUL 1862 |
| CLARKE, George | ROBINSON, Mary (blk) | 03 NOV 1864 |
| CLARKE, Geo. L. [11] | HURDLE, Marian M. | 03 FEB 1866 |
| CLARKE, George W. | SUTTON, Annie R. | 03 MAR 1863 |
| CLARKE, Henry | WILLIAMS, Catherine (blk) | 01 OCT 1863 |
| CLARKE, Henry F., Maj. USA [11] | TAYLER, Belle | 21 SEP 1861 |
| CLARKE, Isaac | HARROD, Martha Ellen (blk) | 08 JAN 1863 |
| CLARKE, James H. | BOGLE, Ottaway (blk) | 10 AUG 1865 |
| CLARKE, James W. | COLKIN, Laura S. | 15 MAY 1863 |
| CLARKE, James Wright | NAILOR, Marion F. | 04 JUN 1867 |
| CLARKE, John | BEALL, Josephine A. | 30 JAN 1867 |

District of Columbia Marriage Licenses, 1858-1870

| Groom | Bride | Date |
|---|---|---|
| CLARKE, John | CRAWLEY, Jane (blk) | 10 FEB 1869 |
| CLARKE, John E. | CORNELL, Maria | 03 AUG 1864 |
| CLARKE, John L. | FORD, Josephine (blk) | 21 NOV 1865 |
| CLARKE, John R. | GRIFFITH, Alice | 08 SEP 1864 |
| CLARKE, Michael | BYRNE, Catherine | 13 OCT 1866 |
| CLARKE, Owen | McGARVEY, Mary | 24 APR 1863 |
| CLARKE, Peter G. [7b] | HANFORD, Mary A. | 19 OCT 1869 |
| CLARKE, R.C. | YATES, Julia E. (blk) | 11 AUG 1866 |
| CLARKE, Richard H. | SEMMES, Ada | 06 OCT 1858 |
| CLARKE, Richard N. | FORD, Sarah E. (blk) | 12 MAR 1867 |
| CLARKE, Robert | BUTLER, Virginia (blk) | 01 DEC 1864 |
| CLARKE, Thomas | FITZHUGH, Sarah (blk) | 09 OCT 1862 |
| CLARKE, Thomas W. | TAYLOR, Caroline M. | 09 SEP 1865 |
| CLARKE, W.J.P. | RADCLIFFE, Ada B. | 21 DEC 1868 |
| CLARKE, Walter | LEDNER, Ellen | 12 APR 1864 |
| CLARKE, William | BURKE, Mary | 08 JAN 1859 |
| CLARKE, William H. | PRINTER, Mary | 20 AUG 1863 |
| CLARKE, William S. | REEVES, Carrie E. | 17 JAN 1870 |
| CLARKE, Wilson | MORAN, Emma J. | 14 MAY 1864 |
| CLARKE, Wilson | MORAN, Emma J. | 25 MAY 1864 |
| CLARKE, Wm. H. | MORRIS, Martha (blk) | 23 SEP 1861 |
| CLARKSON, Edward H. | HOWARD, Louisa | 01 JUN 1862 |
| CLARKSON, Thomas | SHEAHAN, Margaret | 05 AUG 1862 |
| CLARKSON, William F. | WALKER, Anna | 13 SEP 1869 |
| CLARVOE, Napoleon B. | BECKET, Jane Bayliss | 21 SEP 1865 |
| CLARY, John | McCARTHY, Julia | 12 AUG 1862 |
| CLARY, John C. [12s] | GRIFFITH, Sarah E. | 31 DEC 1861 |
| CLARY, Robert E., Junr. [4] | UPHAM, Abby G. | 03 JUL 1863 |
| CLAUS, Henry | RIMBEL, Ernestine | 20 DEC 1864 |
| CLAXTON, R.W. | DAVIS, Elizabeth, Mrs. | 28 SEP 1867 |
| CLAY, Henry | MALLON, Ann | 15 JAN 1863 |
| CLAY, Henry | SCOTT, Mary (blk) | 02 APR 1867 |
| CLAY, Henry | SMALLWOOD, Elizabeth (blk) | 13 JUL 1867 |
| CLAY, Henry | LEWIS, Georgiana (blk) | 15 APR 1868 |
| CLAYBROOK, John W. | ROSS, Emma (blk) | 22 OCT 1866 |
| CLAYTON, Addison | BROWN, Ann (blk) | 10 MAR 1864 |
| CLAYTON, Alfred | WILKERSON, Maria | 08 JUL 1869 |
| CLAYTON, Enoch M. | SEWELL, Ruth Anna | 14 AUG 1869 |
| CLAYTON, Henry | KENNER, Julia Ann (blk) | 16 MAY 1867 |
| CLAYTON, James S. | TREADWAY, Frances A. | 27 APR 1870 |
| CLAYTON, William | RIGGINS, Betsey (blk) | 07 JUL 1866 |
| CLAYTON, William Henry | JOHNSON, Lethe (blk) | 24 APR 1869 |
| CLEAR, Alpheus W. | RANDALL, Malvina | 01 NOV 1867 |
| CLEARY, James | SEABURN, Mary | 20 AUG 1869 |
| CLEARY, James K. | NOBLE, Alice | 04 OCT 1869 |
| CLEAVELAND, James | HARP, Margaret | 28 MAR 1864 |
| CLEEVES, Arnold | MALLEY, Alice | 19 MAR 1867 |
| CLEFFIN, Richard | [blank], Eliza (blk) | 12 JUN 1865 |
| CLEMENSON, William | PAYNE, Anna | 25 JAN 1869 |
| CLEMENT, Joseph | CONNELL, Annie | 25 APR 1863 |
| CLEMENTS, Alexander H. [11] | HARRY, Kate | 06 JAN 1863 |
| CLEMENTS, Algernon S. | DEMPSTER, Eunice A. | 16 NOV 1868 |
| CLEMENTS, Arthur | ROLLINS, Fannie | 17 MAY 1862 |
| CLEMENTS, Edward | PORTER, Sarah | 22 JUN 1864 |
| CLEMENTS, Francis | COOMBS, Annie | 06 JAN 1864 |
| CLEMENTS, John | EASTON, Matilda (blk) | 09 APR 1864 |

| | | |
|---|---|---|
| CLEMENTS, John | MEACHEN, Sylla (blk) | 30 JUN 1866 |
| CLEMENTS, John T. | WARNER, Fannie E. | 23 APR 1859 |
| CLEMENTS, John T. | LOCKE, Florella E. | 15 JUN 1870 |
| CLEMENTS, John Thomas | CLEMENTS, Emily (blk) | 27 APR 1868 |
| CLEMENTS, Louis F. | HENDERSON, Martha J. | 06 APR 1868 |
| CLEMENTS, Samuel B. | COLCLASER, Barbara C. | 28 SEP 1863 |
| CLEMENTS, Samuel T. | STEWART, Alexina | 18 FEB 1862 |
| CLEMENTS, W. DeLes | O'DONOGHUE, Eleanor | 04 OCT 1864 |
| CLEMENTS, William [12s] | DOVER, Wealthy Ann | 02 AUG 1860 |
| CLEMENTS, William [5] | MEINIKLEIM, Barbara | 24 JUN 1869 |
| CLEMONS, Frederick W. | MEURER, Laura W. | 26 MAR 1869 |
| CLENDENIN, Richard H. | SCOTT, Anna E. | 08 APR 1870 |
| CLENDENING, William | CAMPBELL, Alice G. | 16 NOV 1861 |
| CLEVELAND, Erastus L. | VERMILLION, Louisa J. | 11 DEC 1861 |
| CLEVELAND, William B. | HAMILTON, Julia N. | 30 SEP 1858 |
| CLEVER, William | WHITE, Hildah | 15 DEC 1863 |
| CLIFFORD, James A. | BARGY, Hannah Johnson [expunged] | 24 JUL 1869 |
| CLIFFORD, William G. | RIDGWAY, Emma | 29 NOV 1869 |
| CLINE, Joseph C. | MASON, Ann Rebecca | 02 FEB 1870 |
| CLINE, Lawrence | FOLEY, Catharine | 08 DEC 1864 |
| CLINGAN, G. Frank | CUMBERLAND, Emma I. | 08 MAY 1867 |
| CLINKENS, Edward | BROOKS, Mary (blk) | 13 JUN 1867 |
| CLINKINS, Edward | ANDERSON, Martha Ann (blk) | 13 NOV 1866 |
| CLINTON, Clay C. | FRIES, Henrietta | 09 MAR 1869 |
| CLINTON, Edward | McDONALD, Julia J. | 08 NOV 1860 |
| CLINTON, James | DALEY, Mary | 31 OCT 1864 |
| CLINTON, John | TYLER, Susan (blk) | 08 DEC 1863 |
| CLOSSON, John | KING, Mary Elizabeth | 08 SEP 1863 |
| CLOUD, Harry B. | PARKER, Harriet | 03 JUL 1868 |
| CLOUGHLEY, Alfred [11] | BRYAN, [Edna] | 22 SEP 1865 |
| CLOVER, Francis A. | GERMAN, Lula Virginia | 21 SEP 1863 |
| CLUBB, John W. | PURCELL, Mary F. | 11 FEB 1862 |
| CLUBB, William H. | DOVE, Sarah E. | 25 JUL 1861 |
| CLUBB, William H. | HODGES, Virginia | 06 FEB 1869 |
| CLUCHEY, Lewis | TEEBOW, Mary Ann | 23 JAN 1866 |
| CLYMER, John D. | HOLTER, Kate A. | 14 MAR 1864 |
| COALE, John H. | CARTER, Emily | 25 OCT 1867 |
| COATES, Addison | WILLIAMS, Lucy (blk) | 09 FEB 1866 |
| COATES, Anthony | ROBINSON, Elizabeth (blk) | 15 NOV 1866 |
| COATES, Delitha | GIBBONS, Anna | 05 JUN 1862 |
| COATES, Elias | BRADSHAW, Mary (blk) | 17 AUG 1863 |
| COATES, Henry | WILLIAMS, Mary (blk) | 19 MAR 1868 |
| COATES, Lewis | JACKSON, Susan (blk) | 26 DEC 1868 |
| COATES, Lloyd | DIGGS, Maria (blk) | 19 JAN 1869 |
| COATES, Mathew | TOULSON, Sarah Jane (blk) | 03 NOV 1866 |
| COATES, Nathan | WETZEL, Maria (blk) | 08 JUL 1869 |
| COATES, Robert | SOLOMON, Sarah (blk) | 04 OCT 1869 |
| COATS, Edward | BOWEN, Josephine (blk) | 14 APR 1870 |
| COBAUGH, William D. | TAYLOR, Helen J.W. | 03 MAR 1869 |
| COBB, Clarence F. | REED, Emma L. | 01 APR 1870 |
| COBBS, Tobias | HOOE, Catherine (blk) | 31 DEC 1863 |
| COBER, Thomas | CLARK, Mary (blk) | 25 SEP 1867 |
| COBOURN, Caleb | ESLIN, Harriet E. | 30 JUN 1864 |
| COBURN, J.B. | PADGETT, Sarah A. (blk) | 08 AUG 1868 |
| COBURN, Royal L. | McCAFFRY, Mary | 17 SEP 1866 |
| COCHRAN, George | SPELMAN, Ann Maria | 05 SEP 1859 |

District of Columbia Marriage Licenses, 1858-1870

| | | |
|---|---|---|
| COCKER, Travis [4] | BRAMMELL, Mary Maria | 28 DEC 1868 |
| COCKER, William H. | O'DAY, Mary | 28 SEP 1869 |
| COCKERILLE, Samuel J. | DUFOUR, Hevila R. | 13 FEB 1860 |
| COCKRELL, John H. | NEALE, Henrietta | 25 OCT 1864 |
| COCKRILL, Samuel T. | GRIMES, Rebecca | 31 DEC 1863 |
| CODRICK, John [9n] | UPTON, Sarah | 06 NOV 1858 |
| CODRICK, William F. | CUMBERLAND, Marian E. | 05 JUL 1866 |
| CODY, Michael | McCORRIGAN, Mary | 18 SEP 1858 |
| COE, William H. | TRUNNELL, Mary A. | 19 APR 1870 |
| COFFEE, Francis | WASHINGTON, Nancy (blk) | 26 JUL 1860 |
| COFFEY, Albert | DINAWOOD, Louisa (blk) | 11 AUG 1866 |
| COFFEY, Alfred | COLE, Barbara (blk) | 11 JAN 1868 |
| COFFREN, Stanley [6r] | JENKINS, Margaret | 27 DEC 1859 |
| COGAL, John | McKANAN, Catherine | 28 DEC 1868 |
| COGAN, John | LEARY, Mary C. | 19 OCT 1858 |
| COGAR, Charles | TWINE, Ann | 22 JAN 1862 |
| COGER, Francis | BUTLER, Agnes (blk) | 08 NOV 1864 |
| COGER, William | CARTRIGHT, Mary E. (blk) | 24 MAR 1859 |
| COGSWELL, Stacy W. | MITCHELL, Maggie | 09 NOV 1864 |
| COGY, Tarlton | COOK, Mary | 26 OCT 1865 |
| COHAGAN, William T. | MUMENTHALER, Louisa | 01 APR 1865 |
| COHEL, James | COHAN, Margaret | 12 NOV 1862 |
| COHEN, Mendal | LOEWENTHAL, Betsy | 09 SEP 1865 |
| COHEN, Moses | LÖB, Yette | 16 AUG 1862 |
| COHEN, Robert H. | STALLINGS, Mary E. | 13 SEP 1858 |
| COHIL, John P. | MATTHIESON, Mary E. | 15 DEC 1860 |
| COHLER, John C. | RITZ, Stephana | 08 OCT 1864 |
| COHN, Solomon | LINZ, Anna | 11 APR 1864 |
| COIT, Levi Howland [11] | HARTLEY, Martha F. | 30 DEC 1867 |
| COKE, Benj. F. | HUGHES, Mary E. (blk) | 21 MAY 1866 |
| COKELY, Benjamin | WILLIAMS, Lydia (blk) | 28 NOV 1865 |
| COLBERT, James | HARMON, Mary (blk) | 12 JAN 1869 |
| COLBERT, James William | YOUNG, Isabella (blk) | 03 JUN 1865 |
| COLBERT, John | LACEY, Amelia (blk) | 05 JUN 1867 |
| COLBERT, Joseph W. | STUART, Bettie A. | 01 NOV 1860 |
| COLBERT, Thomas | CROWLEY, Catherine | 26 DEC 1863 |
| COLBERT, William B. | WILSON, Mary E. | 20 JAN 1869 |
| COLBURN, Royal L. | WALDEN, Helen | 05 MAY 1868 |
| COLBURN, William B. [4] | GREGG, Laura V. | 09 DEC 1867 |
| COLBY, John E. | BRUCE, Ella A. | 02 MAR 1865 |
| COLCLASER, Frederick L. | GLASGO, Margaret | 03 SEP 1859 |
| COLCORD, Austin N. | SPEAR, Sarah E. | 13 JUN 1864 |
| COLDEN, James | BUNDY, July (blk) | 13 AUG 1864 |
| COLE, Albert F. | TURNER, Cecilia A. (blk) | 21 JUN 1866 |
| COLE, Alfred | ANDERSON, Anna Dora (blk) | 30 NOV 1865 |
| COLE, Baker | RANDOLPH, Jane (blk) | 25 NOV 1867 |
| COLE, Benjamin | DODSON, Georgiana (blk) | 30 APR 1864 |
| COLE, Charles N. | PERRY, Emma | 29 JUN 1868 |
| COLE, Charles N. | PERRY, M. Fannie | 29 JUN 1868 |
| COLE, Daniel | WILLIAMS, Seldra (blk) | 09 FEB 1865 |
| COLE, George Henry | WILLIAMS, Anna Maria (blk) | 11 NOV 1868 |
| COLE, Isaac | [blank], Mary Susan (blk) | 29 DEC 1864 |
| COLE, Jackson | MILLS, Maria, Mrs. | 15 AUG 1866 |
| COLE, James | TATTERSON, Malissa | 04 JAN 1859 |
| COLE, Jeremiah | BOND, Jane (blk) | 02 MAY 1867 |
| COLE, John | WILSON, Laura (blk) | 01 DEC 1858 |

| | | |
|---|---|---|
| COLE, John E. | RATCLIFFE, Elizabeth | 17 APR 1860 |
| COLE, Lucien | SHARESWOOD, Mary E. | 26 APR 1866 |
| COLE, Rosalvo F. | COQUILLARD, Helen | 12 JUL 1864 |
| COLE, Scott | BONDS, Mary (blk) | 09 JUL 1863 |
| COLE, Thomas S.H. | ROBBINS, Julia | 09 MAY 1867 |
| COLE, Washington | JACKSON, Anna (blk) | 27 AUG 1867 |
| COLE, William | BEAN, Margaret Ellen | 07 JUN 1860 |
| COLELL, Robert | RIESSNER, Margaretha | 14 OCT 1858 |
| COLEMAN, Aaron S. | HUNTER, M. Alice | 18 DEC 1862 |
| COLEMAN, Alanson | BROWN, Mary Ann (blk) | 11 AUG 1866 |
| COLEMAN, Alfred | BOTTS, Lucinda (blk) | 27 AUG 1867 |
| COLEMAN, Charles | LARRIMOUR, Polly (blk) | 03 APR 1867 |
| COLEMAN, Daniel | MARTIN, Mary (blk) | 14 NOV 1868 |
| COLEMAN, Frank | JACKSON, Matilda | 29 OCT 1868 |
| COLEMAN, George | LOMAX, Lucy (blk) | 30 DEC 1864 |
| COLEMAN, George G. | JACKSON, Olivia | 04 MAR 1868 |
| COLEMAN, George W. | RICHEY, Jane Elizabeth | 10 JUN 1867 |
| COLEMAN, Harry | BISHOP, Ada E. | 26 JAN 1864 |
| COLEMAN, Henry | BUSH, Cecilia Ann (blk) | 02 JAN 1867 |
| COLEMAN, Henry | QUEEN, Mary Elizabeth (blk) | 18 APR 1867 |
| COLEMAN, Henry | CAMARON, Susan (blk) | 03 SEP 1867 |
| COLEMAN, Henry | JOHNSON, Isabell (blk) | 13 APR 1868 |
| COLEMAN, James | MURPHY, Mary | 02 JUL 1859 |
| COLEMAN, James | SMOOT, Ann Virginia | 12 JUN 1860 |
| COLEMAN, James | SMITH, Lizzie (blk) | 28 APR 1864 |
| COLEMAN, James | TAYLOR, Sallie Ann (blk) | 09 JUN 1866 |
| COLEMAN, James | BURGESS, Laura (blk) | 25 FEB 1869 |
| COLEMAN, Jeremiah | HURLEY, Margaret | 26 FEB 1862 |
| COLEMAN, John H. | SHAWS, Elizabeth (blk) | 30 JUN 1864 |
| COLEMAN, John J., Jr. | RODES, J. Cyntha V. | 30 JUN 1860 |
| COLEMAN, Joseph | DIGGES, Henrietta (blk) | 24 DEC 1869 |
| COLEMAN, Lindsay | JACKSON, Rosetta (blk) | 22 SEP 1866 |
| COLEMAN, Patrick | KELLY, Bridget | 01 JUN 1859 |
| COLEMAN, Patrick | CONNOR, Mary | 08 APR 1863 |
| COLEMAN, Patrick | MATTHEWS, Elizabeth | 01 JUL 1865 |
| COLEMAN, Patrick | MALONEY, Mary | 25 AUG 1865 |
| COLEMAN, Paul | FANTROY, Elizabeth | 17 DEC 1866 |
| COLEMAN, R.T. | ANDERSON, Martha E. (blk) | 21 APR 1868 |
| COLEMAN, Richard | MURPHY, Catharine | 08 NOV 1862 |
| COLEMAN, Robert | MEIGS, Maria (blk) | 15 DEC 1864 |
| COLEMAN, Robert | COLEMAN, Betsey (blk) | 18 SEP 1868 |
| COLEMAN, Robert | BELL, Louisa (blk) | 15 OCT 1868 |
| COLEMAN, Samuel | TOLOVER, Mary (blk) | 21 FEB 1863 |
| COLEMAN, Samuel E. [12s] | HUGHES, Mollie J. | 29 OCT 1859 |
| COLEMAN, Spencer | PAYNE, Martha (blk) | 16 APR 1863 |
| COLEMAN, Tony | REED, Cilia (blk) | 19 MAR 1870 |
| COLEMAN, William | BROWN, Sarah (blk) | 19 JUL 1864 |
| COLEMAN, William | WATSON, Catharine | 15 AUG 1864 |
| COLEMAN, William | COLEMAN, Lucinda | 11 JUN 1866 |
| COLEMAN, William | CRAWFORD, Henrietta (blk) | 18 MAY 1868 |
| COLEMAN, William | MOORE, Jane Margaret | 11 MAY 1868 |
| COLEMAN, William E. | SANDERS, Susan A. | 16 NOV 1868 |
| COLES, Norman H. | RONEY, Elizabeth R. | 17 JUN 1862 |
| COLES, Sharper | JACKSON, Lucy Ann (blk) | 05 JAN 1867 |
| COLES, William H., Jr. [11] | STELLE, Adelaide H. | 09 OCT 1865 |
| COLF, Hughey | McEVOY, Rose | 14 JUL 1865 |

District of Columbia Marriage Licenses, 1858-1870

| | | |
|---|---|---|
| COLFER, William H. [10] | EVERETT, Mary H. | 23 SEP 1865 |
| COLGROVE, Patrick | KING, Mary | 01 SEP 1866 |
| COLISON, Charles C. | BURCH, Amanda E. | 20 JUL 1859 |
| COLLARD, George | WHITNEY, Eliza S. | 04 NOV 1863 |
| COLLEDGE, Chas. B.R. | COGSWELL, Annie | 31 OCT 1867 |
| COLLEY, John | KELLY, Margaret | 05 NOV 1859 |
| COLLIER, Champaign | WILSON, Jane | 12 NOV 1861 |
| COLLIGAN, James A. | MURPHY, Mary Ellen | 20 OCT 1866 |
| COLLIN, Alfred | BOYCE, Elizabeth | 03 JUN 1865 |
| COLLINS, Christopher | McKEE, Bridget | 20 MAY 1862 |
| COLLINS, Edward Jenne | ANTHONY, Frances Ida | 06 AUG 1868 |
| COLLINS, Frank | FRAZIER, Sarah Jane (blk) | 09 NOV 1868 |
| COLLINS, Henry | BURNS, Eveline | 08 AUG 1861 |
| COLLINS, Henry | McGRAW, Annie | 14 MAY 1869 |
| COLLINS, James | MINT, Ann | 15 MAY 1863 |
| COLLINS, James | MERRITT, Eliza | 10 JUL 1865 |
| COLLINS, James | LITTLE, Mary Jane (blk) | 13 OCT 1866 |
| COLLINS, James | HICKS, Elizabeth E. (blk) | 13 FEB 1867 |
| COLLINS, James | MARTIN, Mary | 15 APR 1868 |
| COLLINS, James | HAYS, Mary | 25 FEB 1868 |
| COLLINS, James E. | BARNES, Mary V. | 01 APR 1864 |
| COLLINS, James Edward | RICARD, Sarah Elizabeth | 24 DEC 1869 |
| COLLINS, James L. | KETTLER, Mary E. | 05 JAN 1864 |
| COLLINS, James V. | STONE, Frances | 23 NOV 1858 |
| COLLINS, John | BROSNAHAN, Mary A. | 03 JUN 1865 |
| COLLINS, John | BROWN, Maria | 01 MAY 1866 |
| COLLINS, John [6s] | BURROUGHS, Catharine R.A.W. | 15 NOV 1864 |
| COLLINS, John F. | BENJAMIN, Rachel I. | 19 MAR 1862 |
| COLLINS, John W. | BAKER, Catharine C. | 13 JUN 1863 |
| COLLINS, John W. | HURDLE, Mary E. | 18 JUN 1864 |
| COLLINS, John W. | BURRUS, Maggie A. | 18 SEP 1868 |
| COLLINS, John [4] | McNAMARA, Bridget | 31 JAN 1867 |
| COLLINS, Joseph | DEAN, Sarah | 11 AUG 1869 |
| COLLINS, Lewis | CARTER, Mary (blk) | 01 MAR 1870 |
| COLLINS, Lewis [1c] | GOODMAN, Sarah L. | 27 FEB 1864 |
| COLLINS, Michael | MORIARTY, Mary | 26 NOV 1862 |
| COLLINS, Michael | HARTNET, Annie | 28 FEB 1865 |
| COLLINS, Patrick | MALIGAN, Mary | 08 JUL 1867 |
| COLLINS, Patrick | DAILY, Mary | 14 SEP 1867 |
| COLLINS, Samuel | NEALE, Mary (blk) | 26 MAY 1864 |
| COLLINS, Samuel H. | GOODYER, Augusta S. | 19 OCT 1864 |
| COLLINS, Stephen | CAUSINE, Margaret | 11 SEP 1863 |
| COLLINS, Thomas | FLINN, Margaret | 26 FEB 1859 |
| COLLINS, Thomas | CONLON, Catherine | 15 JAN 1859 |
| COLLINS, Thomas | FLYNN, Hannah | 03 OCT 1863 |
| COLLINS, Thomas | GASTING, Elizabeth (blk) | 29 OCT 1868 |
| COLLINS, Thomas | SULLIVAN, Ellen | 07 OCT 1869 |
| COLLINS, Thomas | McNAMARA, Mary | 17 NOV 1869 |
| COLLINS, Thomas J. | MINN, Genevive M. | 22 APR 1867 |
| COLLINS, W.R. | HUTCHINS, Laura V. | 15 JAN 1867 |
| COLLINS, William [13t] | ADAMS, Mary (blk) | 16 MAY 1861 |
| COLLINS, William | BURGESS, Mary | 31 AUG 1869 |
| COLLINS, William H. | THOMAS, Mary Lucinda | 23 JUL 1866 |
| COLLINS, William Hy. | NETTER, Ellen (blk) | 30 DEC 1858 |
| COLLINS, William P. | McDERMOTT, Ellen | 08 SEP 1866 |
| COLLINS, William R. | CLEMENTS, C.A. Lavina | 06 OCT 1858 |

| | | |
|---|---|---|
| COLLINS, William T. | MOORE, Annie A. | 04 APR 1864 |
| COLLINS, Zachariah T. | SNOW, Jane | 25 JUL 1868 |
| COLLINSER, Andrew | RAGAN, Ellen | 19 OCT 1860 |
| COLLISON, George Z. | FERGURSON, Caroline | 26 MAY 1859 |
| COLLISON, John A. | BURCH, Polina | 02 MAY 1868 |
| COLLISON, John M. | DUKES, Margaret A. | 17 JUN 1867 |
| COLLISS, Levi | BROWN, Amanda (blk) | 28 NOV 1863 |
| COLLY, James | BERRY, Rose (blk) | 26 MAY 1866 |
| COLMAN, Christopher | PRYOR, Barbary (blk) | 18 JUL 1867 |
| COLMAN, Moses | MARX, Caroline | 17 DEC 1864 |
| COLSTON, Richard | PAINE, Cecelia (blk) | 21 NOV 1867 |
| COLT, William D. | GIDEON, Susie | 09 OCT 1866 |
| COLTMAN, Robert | CLEMENTS, Mary Jane | 30 APR 1861 |
| COLTMAN, Robert | WORMLEY, Maria Louisa | 05 JUN 1868 |
| COLTON, Harvey V. | CRIPPEN, Victoria | 24 JAN 1867 |
| COLTS, Rosier A. | BALDERSON, Frances A. | 14 AUG 1868 |
| COLVIN, Alpheus B. | COLVIN, Pfelenia C.C. | 07 MAR 1859 |
| COLVIN, Robert W. | HURT, Louisa | 08 AUG 1864 |
| COMBER, Thomas F. | KERVIN, Mary | 09 DEC 1862 |
| COMBS, Ignatius George | CLEMENTS, Annie E. | 23 JAN 1868 |
| COMBS, William N. | WALSH, Kate J. | 11 MAY 1863 |
| COMINGS, Samuel L. | SWITZER, Elvira | 01 MAR 1862 |
| COMMAGERE, Frank Y. | O'FLYNN, Mary V. | 25 JAN 1869 |
| COMMINS, Majenor V. | MORELAND, Anna | 30 DEC 1864 |
| COMMODORE, Lucius Henry | BROOKER, Mildred Ann (blk) | 14 JUN 1867 |
| COMMODORE, Thomas | SWALIES, Anna (blk) | 16 JUN 1868 |
| COMPTON, Charles E. | LITTLE, Emily F. | 16 MAY 1864 |
| COMSTOCK, Cyrus B. | BLAIR, Elizabeth | 25 JAN 1869 |
| CONARDUS, Henry | NOTBAUM, Emma | 10 AUG 1860 |
| CONAWAY, Rias | DOREY, Annie (blk) | 03 JUN 1870 |
| CONAWAY, Spencer | CRAWLEY, Clara (blk) | 14 OCT 1869 |
| CONBOYE, J.C. | TAITE, Jane | 08 MAR 1860 |
| CONCH, Alfred T. | THOMPSON, Ellen A. | 28 JUN 1864 |
| CONDON, Patrick | COY, Bridget | 04 JAN 1868 |
| CONDON, Robert | SULLIVAN, Mary | 01 OCT 1869 |
| CONDON, William A. | ANGEL, Laura V. | 10 JUL 1865 |
| CONE, August E. | HARRIS, Ann C. | 06 AUG 1866 |
| CONE, David D. | GRONARD, Ellen C. | 04 APR 1863 |
| CONELY, Josiah | GLEASON, Annie | 24 MAR 1864 |
| CONEVARO, Antonio | RYAN, Mary | 11 FEB 1861 |
| CONKLING, Edgar | COOK, Elizabeth | 12 DEC 1863 |
| CONLAN, Francis | SMITH, Catherine | 05 MAR 1859 |
| CONLAN, James | McCAULY, Kate | 06 OCT 1864 |
| CONLAN, Patrick | GARVIN, Mary | 03 NOV 1858 |
| CONLAN, Patrick | LYNCH, Bridget | 02 FEB 1861 |
| CONLEY, James H. | COLE, Margaret Ann | 16 AUG 1864 |
| CONLEY, John | McGUIRE, Ann | 12 SEP 1863 |
| CONLIN, John | LAZIER, Ellen | 09 JUN 1864 |
| CONLON, Peter | CONNELL, Mary | 09 DEC 1861 |
| CONLY, Henry | WELSH, Mary | 10 MAY 1865 |
| CONLY, James | SULLIVAN, Mary | 20 AUG 1864 |
| CONLY, Thomas | WHITE, Alice | 02 MAY 1864 |
| CONN, George W. | DOUGLASS, Margaret Ann | 04 MAY 1859 |
| CONNAWAY, Lewis | HOWARD, Susan (blk) | 23 OCT 1866 |
| CONNELL, Dennis | ROVER, Catherine | 24 AUG 1860 |
| CONNELL, Jeremiah | FITZGERALD, Johanna | 25 JAN 1862 |

District of Columbia Marriage Licenses, 1858-1870

| | | |
|---|---|---|
| CONNELL, Jeremiah | MULLOWNEY, Mary | 16 OCT 1863 |
| CONNELL, Jeremiah | CONNELL, Margaret | 30 SEP 1865 |
| CONNELL, Jeremiah | QUILL, Ellen | 24 MAY 1859 |
| CONNELL, John | MARONEY, Catherine | 11 JAN 1870 |
| CONNELL, John | QUILL, Mary | 18 JUN 1860 |
| CONNELL, John F. | MARTIN, Mary E. | 16 JAN 1865 |
| CONNELL, Mathew | DIGGINS, Margaret | 06 JUN 1868 |
| CONNELL, Owen | RYAN, Margaret | 28 AUG 1861 |
| CONNELL, P.A.J. | JOHNSON, Jeannette | 22 NOV 1862 |
| CONNELL, Thomas | KENNALLY, Mary | 08 MAR 1864 |
| CONNELL, Tim | McMEEKIN, Jane | 07 APR 1868 |
| CONNELLY, Francis | HARPER, Mary | 27 JUL 1868 |
| CONNELY, Jerry | BRADY, Mary | 05 APR 1861 |
| CONNER, Cain [6le] | FLYNN, Eliza | 25 APR 1866 |
| CONNER, George | GLASCO, Ellen | 01 OCT 1864 |
| CONNER, George W. [10] | THOMPSON, Sarah E.M. | 07 OCT 1862 |
| CONNER, George W. | JONES, Mary A. | 26 JAN 1859 |
| CONNER, James W. | DIVINE, Louisa A. | 24 OCT 1864 |
| CONNER, John | SHEA, Margaret | 12 JUN 1860 |
| CONNER, John | HUNTER, Lucinder | 16 NOV 1862 |
| CONNER, John | READY, Catharine | 14 OCT 1863 |
| CONNER, John Henry | SLATER, Margaert E. (blk) | 27 MAY 1863 |
| CONNER, Lawrence | READY, Ellen | 07 JUL 1864 |
| CONNER, Lawrence | RILEY, Sarah | 22 JAN 1867 |
| CONNER, Luke | DORSEY, Catherine | 09 NOV 1860 |
| CONNERS, Michael | HINES, Mary | 27 JUL 1866 |
| CONNERS, Richard | SADLER, Ann Elizabeth | 30 DEC 1864 |
| CONNOLLY, Burns | DOWNS, Alice | 05 FEB 1866 |
| CONNOLLY, Charles Cashel | McNICKLE, Selecia | 08 AUG 1864 |
| CONNOLLY, Daniel A. | ESLIN, Cornelia A. | 14 FEB 1860 |
| CONNOLLY, James | DAVIS, Sarah E. | 04 MAY 1864 |
| CONNOLLY, James | McFEE, Annie | 27 NOV 1867 |
| CONNOLLY, John | DONNOGHUE, Mary | 21 NOV 1862 |
| CONNOLLY, John | JOYCE, Hannah | 14 JUN 1864 |
| CONNOLLY, John F. | REAURA, Lavinia G. | 10 OCT 1860 |
| CONNOLLY, Matthew | LEYDEN, Bridget | 08 SEP 1865 |
| CONNOLLY, Nicholas | HOLLAND, Kate | 15 JAN 1867 |
| CONNOLY, John | RAINGER, Sarah Elizabeth | 08 DEC 1869 |
| CONNOR, Daniel | HURLEY, Julia | 20 FEB 1860 |
| CONNOR, Daniel | FLEMING, Mary | 14 JUN 1862 |
| CONNOR, Daniel | QUEEN, Harriet (blk) | 25 FEB 1864 |
| CONNOR, Edward [11] | ALLEN, Margaret | 23 OCT 1862 |
| CONNOR, James Wesley | CHASE, Sarah Ann (blk) | 01 DEC 1868 |
| CONNOR, Jeremiah | SULLIVAN, Margaret | 14 MAR 1864 |
| CONNOR, John | DOYLE, Mary | 22 JAN 1859 |
| CONNOR, John | KELCHER, Hanoragh | 01 MAR 1862 |
| CONNOR, John | RYAN, Ellen | 05 JAN 1863 |
| CONNOR, John | O'ROURKE, Catherine | 06 FEB 1864 |
| CONNOR, John | SLATTERY, Johana | 22 NOV 1864 |
| CONNOR, Lewis | COWGY, Henny (blk) | 22 DEC 1866 |
| CONNOR, Patrick | HURNEY, Ann | 23 OCT 1863 |
| CONNOR, Patrick | MARANVILL, Ellen | 23 MAY 1864 |
| CONNOR, Patrick | BURKE, Mary | 27 APR 1870 |
| CONNOR, Selden | BIALEY, Henrietta W. | 18 OCT 1869 |
| CONNOR, Thomas | FLANIGAN, Catharine | 05 JUL 1862 |
| CONNOR, Thomas | HARKINS, Ellen | 03 MAR 1865 |

District of Columbia Marriage Licenses, 1858-1870

| | | |
|---|---|---|
| CONNOR, Timothy | CURTIN, Ellin | 16 OCT 1865 |
| CONNOR, Valentine | COOK, Ann E. | 21 SEP 1858 |
| CONNOR, William Jerome | ADAMS, Hester A. | 06 DEC 1860 |
| CONNORS, John | CROWLEY, Margaret | 25 JUL 1861 |
| CONNORS, Michael | HALLORAN, Mary | 07 APR 1863 |
| CONNORTON, Patrick H. | CHAMICK, Matilda P. | 12 MAY 1864 |
| CONRAD, Charles E. | PARKER, Rebecca W. | 13 DEC 1860 |
| CONRAD, Charles E. | PARKER, Mary A. | 02 JUN 1868 |
| CONRAD, Frederick | GIDDINGS, Mary Ellen | 26 APR 1864 |
| CONRAD, Michael St. | CHAMBERLIN, Mary E. | 09 AUG 1861 |
| CONRON, Isaac | RICHARDSON, Margaret K. | 10 SEP 1866 |
| CONROY, Patrick | CUMINSKY, Hannah | 09 JUN 1866 |
| CONROY, Thomas | GOULEY, Anna | 29 AUG 1863 |
| CONROY, William H. | CONNOR, Catherine E. | 29 MAY 1867 |
| CONSTABLE, William M. [11] | WILLS, Sarah A.T. | 03 JAN 1867 |
| CONTEE, Frederick | QUEEN, Martha (blk) | 26 DEC 1863 |
| CONTEE, John | TADLE, Harriet (blk) | 26 DEC 1864 |
| CONTEE, Orpheus | BROWN, Susan (blk) | 28 OCT 1863 |
| CONWAY, Albert G. | ROBERTS, Sue B. | 17 OCT 1867 |
| CONWAY, Albert V. | COLE, Virginia | 15 NOV 1864 |
| CONWAY, Charles | JACKSON, Mary Ella (blk) | 25 JUN 1863 |
| CONWAY, George | SPOTSWOOD, Hannah (blk) | 16 APR 1868 |
| CONWAY, James C. | GATCHEL, Melissa C. | 26 JUN 1865 |
| CONWAY, John B. | SMITH, Mary | 20 AUG 1863 |
| CONWAY, Joseph | TASKER, Martha | 30 MAR 1863 |
| CONWAY, Patrick | SWEENY, Margaret | 04 OCT 1867 |
| CONWAY, Patrick | MAROONEY, Catherine | 22 APR 1868 |
| CONWAY, Robert | NEALE, Frances (blk) | 16 AUG 1864 |
| COOK, A.J. | COPELAIN, Emma | 05 MAR 1869 |
| COOK, Albert J.W. | GAINES, Ellen (blk) | 09 APR 1870 |
| COOK, Albert M. | FOX, Mary (blk) | 19 SEP 1863 |
| COOK, Alexander J. | DOLAN, Annie F. | 09 APR 1866 |
| COOK, Amaziah | HAMILTON, Sarah (blk) | 09 APR 1862 |
| COOK, Andrew J. | WEADERMAN, Martha | 06 FEB 1864 |
| COOK, Benjamin | MATHEWS, Maggie (blk) | 16 MAY 1868 |
| COOK, Charles | McCAULEY, Elizabeth | 08 APR 1863 |
| COOK, Charles | SILK, Caroline | 07 MAY 1869 |
| COOK, Elbert P. | MYERS, Emma S. | 10 JUN 1869 |
| COOK, Fenton | FERGUSON, Mary E. (blk) | 27 NOV 1867 |
| COOK, Frederick | TALBERT, Jennie | 05 DEC 1868 |
| COOK, Frederick H. | MITCHELL, Annie | 03 JAN 1865 |
| COOK, George | KING, Jane Eliza | 30 NOV 1864 |
| COOK, George R. [6m] | CREIGHTON, Annie E. | 14 OCT 1862 |
| COOK, Hamilton | PARSLEY, Sarah | 21 NOV 1863 |
| COOK, Henry | SHAFER, Johanna | 15 AUG 1860 |
| COOK, James | WASHINGTON, Martha (blk) | 22 JUN 1868 |
| COOK, James F. [10] | HENRY, Lucy C. | 01 SEP 1865 |
| COOK, James R. [6r] | HUNTER, Margaret | 19 SEP 1860 |
| COOK, James R. | ATCHISON, Mary H. | 22 MAY 1862 |
| COOK, John | PUMPHREY, Dorcas Ann (blk) | 17 MAR 1869 |
| COOK, John Aug.Geo.Wash.Scott Alex. | LAWRENCE, Rebecca (blk) | 20 JAN 1864 |
| COOK, John Francis | COOK, Sarah (blk) | 04 OCT 1866 |
| COOK, John Richard | HAYS, Annie (blk) | 08 DEC 1865 |
| COOK, Joseph M. | CALLAN, Mary A. | 12 JAN 1860 |
| COOK, Joseph T. | JACKSON, Mary A. (blk) | 30 NOV 1868 |
| COOK, Lewis G. [10] | O'DONNELL, Mary | 02 MAR 1864 |

District of Columbia Marriage Licenses, 1858-1870

| | | |
|---|---|---|
| COOK, Morris | LUNDY, Susan (blk) | 31 MAY 1866 |
| COOK, Richard R. | BRYAN, Sluday | 29 AUG 1861 |
| COOK, Robert | COLEMAN, Sally | 08 SEP 1864 |
| COOK, Salma | BARRY, Cynthia | 03 DEC 1866 |
| COOK, Squire | TUDEN, Eliza (blk) | 26 OCT 1863 |
| COOK, Thomas M. | GARNER, Lucretia A. | 20 NOV 1860 |
| COOK, Trueman A. | SCRIVENER, Mary V. | 13 SEP 1862 |
| COOK, William | GREENWELL, Alice | 10 FEB 1869 |
| COOK, William | SMALLWOOD, Henrietta | 05 APR 1869 |
| COOK, William E. | FOWLER, Willie E. | 29 DEC 1864 |
| COOK, William H. [6s] | CROSS, Hannah E. | 28 JAN 1865 |
| COOK, Wm. J. | LEWIS, Lizzie S. [not used] | 13 AUG 1868 |
| COOK, William Thos. | HODGE, Elizabaeth | 19 JAN 1865 |
| COOKE, Charles L. | LEWIS, Lucinda | 25 APR 1863 |
| COOKE, John T. [6c] | HUNTER, Anna R. | 13 NOV 1858 |
| COOKSEY, John A. | GREEN, Mary J. | 18 APR 1870 |
| COOKSEY, Joshua D. | TIPPETT, Lizzie J. | 14 NOV 1867 |
| COOKSEY, Joshua J. | KING, Mary Ellender | 10 DEC 1868 |
| COOLEDGE, Henry [12s] | MULLIN, Catherine | 22 JAN 1863 |
| COOLEY, Joseph W. | PARTELLO, Kate | 17 AUG 1864 |
| COOMBES, Thomas | MUDD, Issabella | 21 DEC 1858 |
| COOMES, George H. | COCKRELL, Sarah E. | 31 OCT 1861 |
| COONEY, John | FOLEY, Bridget | 20 AUG 1867 |
| COONEY, Michael | AHERN, Catherine | 01 SEP 1863 |
| COONEY, Patrick | MURPHY, Ellen | 26 OCT 1868 |
| COONS, Walter | HALL, Mercy | 27 JUL 1865 |
| COOPER, Bishop [9n] | BABB, Sarah E. | 25 OCT 1858 |
| COOPER, Charles H. | CONNELL, Sarah E. | 31 OCT 1865 |
| COOPER, David T. | DOWNES, Elizabeth | 20 FEB 1865 |
| COOPER, E. Mason [11] | BALDWIN, Mary Flora | 01 OCT 1866 |
| COOPER, G.R. | TALIAFERRO, Beattie | 12 JUL 1866 |
| COOPER, George F. | MONTGOMERY, Sarah A. | 26 SEP 1865 |
| COOPER, George H. | JOHNSON, Josephine | 18 JUL 1864 |
| COOPER, Granville P. | HODGES, Mary E. | 04 MAY 1869 |
| COOPER, James | SAMMONS, Elizabeth (blk) | 22 SEP 1869 |
| COOPER, James R. | DIGNO, Sarah | 16 OCT 1866 |
| COOPER, John | WILLIAMS, Mary (blk) | 07 FEB 1867 |
| COOPER, John S. | BUTLER, Francis (blk) | 25 JUL 1867 |
| COOPER, Joseph | STEEL, Susan V. | 31 DEC 1866 |
| COOPER, Richard L. | GIDDINGS, Elizabeth O. | 24 DEC 1869 |
| COOPER, Samuel C. | LUCK, Eliza | 31 OCT 1864 |
| COOPER, Thomas | MORAN, Margaret | 31 MAY 1862 |
| COOPER, Thomas [11] | CRAWFORD, Charlotte | 17 AUG 1865 |
| COOPER, W. | BRECKENRIDGE, E. (blk) | 24 DEC 1867 |
| COOPER, William A. | WARNER, Sarah Jane | 07 FEB 1866 |
| COOPER, William Ringgold | MOTHERSHEAD, Julia Mary | 01 AUG 1866 |
| COOTE, Isaac | BRESTE, Mary F. | 30 JAN 1860 |
| COPELAND, Hilliary | DOMLISS, Anna (blk) | 04 MAR 1870 |
| COPELAND, Martin G. | CAMPBELL, Mary J. | 02 MAY 1866 |
| COPELAND, William P. | PARISH, Sarah H. | 28 JUL 1868 |
| COPPERSMITH, Wm. B. | SPENCER, Emma | 14 FEB 1867 |
| COPPES, Augustus | FOLEY, Mary A. | 07 APR 1864 |
| COPRARI, Pepo | CONIA, Johanna | 14 APR 1859 |
| COPRELL, Dennis | JOHNSON, Ellen (blk) | 08 NOV 1864 |
| CORBET, James | KERR, Mary | 24 OCT 1868 |
| CORBIN, Andrew | COLEMAN, Amy (blk) | 26 SEP 1863 |

District of Columbia Marriage Licenses, 1858-1870

| | | |
|---|---|---|
| CORBIN, Armistead | CARTER, Caroline (blk) | 29 OCT 1867 |
| CORBIN, E. Lyon | CREIGHTON, Emily R. | 27 APR 1859 |
| CORBIN, Frederick | FIELDS, Nellie (blk) | 06 JUN 1866 |
| CORBIN, Joseph B. | CHAMBERS, Hannah M. | 01 SEP 1863 |
| CORBIN, Robert | BARNES, Louisa | 05 JAN 1869 |
| CORBITT, William | GARVIN, Mary | 19 DEC 1867 |
| CORCORAN, Patrick T. | FRAYNE, Julia | 02 MAY 1862 |
| CORDETT, John Martin | BRAUMEN, Adelaide | 02 DEC 1864 |
| COREMANS, Francis | SMITH, Emily | 27 MAR 1865 |
| COREY, James W. | CAYWOOD, Charlotte E. | 14 DEC 1864 |
| CORIDON, Philip | BROSNAHAN, Mary | 06 DEC 1862 |
| CORKINS, George B. | TONNETT, Louisa | 21 OCT 1861 |
| CORLISS, Hiram C. | TURNER, Lucretia | 02 NOV 1865 |
| CORMER, John | WOODMAN, Creecy (blk) | 12 AUG 1865 |
| CORNELIUS, Evert H. [6le] | HOWARD, Charity | 15 SEP 1866 |
| CORNELIUS, James | EVANS, Laura B. | 07 AUG 1869 |
| CORNELL, Richard | BROWN, Martha M. (blk) | 29 DEC 1862 |
| CORNICE, George | REYNOLDS, Mary (blk) | 18 NOV 1865 |
| CORNVAY, Thomas | MALONE, Ellen | 01 MAY 1868 |
| CORNWALL, George W. | BEACHAM, Josephine M. | 13 OCT 1864 |
| CORNWALL, John P. | TRAMMELL, Jane A. | 07 MAR 1865 |
| CORNWELL, James A. | KING, Mary E. | 29 JAN 1870 |
| CORNWELL, John B. | OWENS, Susan Ann | 20 DEC 1860 |
| CORODON, Patrick | EGAN, Margaret | 30 APR 1860 |
| CORREY, Edward J.R. | ADAMS, Sarah E. | 02 OCT 1865 |
| CORREY, Vincent | WILSON, Mary (blk) | 14 NOV 1867 |
| CORRIDON, John | CONLON, Ellen | 24 SEP 1859 |
| CORRIDON, Philip | O'CONNOR, Catharine | 13 JUN 1862 |
| CORRIGAN, Thomas | PARKER, Jane | 27 JUN 1864 |
| CORTS, George P. | BATEMAN, Harriet A. | 27 OCT 1864 |
| COSNELL, Ambrose | BROWN, Martha V. | 24 SEP 1860 |
| COSNELL, Ambrose | BROWN, Martha Virginia | 16 OCT 1860 |
| COSSLEY, H. Worthington | WILSON, Olivia Harrison (blk) | 07 MAY 1867 |
| COSTELLO, Jeremiah | LAWTON, Catharine | 01 SEP 1860 |
| COSTELLO, John | NALLEY, Eliza Jane | 10 AUG 1868 |
| COSTELLO, John | CONNOLLY, Mary E. | 01 MAR 1870 |
| COSTELLO, Joseph | POWERS, Ellen | 18 JAN 1865 |
| COSTELLO, Michael | JOYCE, Mary | 27 NOV 1865 |
| COSTELLO, Michael | GALLOWAY, Jamima L. | 08 AUG 1867 |
| COSTELLO, Patrick | MORAN, Mary | 29 JAN 1867 |
| COSTELLO, Thomas | VENABLE, Margaret | 16 FEB 1863 |
| COSTELLO, Timothy | QUILL, Ellen | 10 JAN 1862 |
| COSTER, John | SMITHSON, Mary Ellen | 28 FEB 1861 |
| COSTER, Samuel | GILES, Margaret (blk) | 28 MAY 1868 |
| COSTOLOW, Christopher | RYON, Elizabeth M. | 25 AUG 1864 |
| COTTERILL, Edmond | FALVEY, Ellen | 01 NOV 1864 |
| COTTON, Charles T. | STEWART, Ella R. | 20 FEB 1866 |
| COTTON, James | CURRY, Anna | 10 OCT 1867 |
| COTTON, William H. | MULLEN, Mary E. | 02 JUL 1864 |
| COTTON, William H. | BARROWS, Elizabeth R. | 24 JUL 1866 |
| COTTRELL, Jeremiah | WILKINS, Mary E. | 15 OCT 1864 |
| COTTRELL, Robert | BOYLE, Ellen | 28 MAY 1862 |
| COUCH, Alfred T. | THOMPSON, Ellen A. | 28 JUN 1864 |
| COUGHLAN, John | O'CONNOR, Johanna | 28 OCT 1865 |
| COUGHLIN, Charles | COSTELLO, Ellen | 12 FEB 1868 |
| COUGHLIN, Daniel | FITZGERALD, Mary | 05 SEP 1860 |

District of Columbia Marriage Licenses, 1858-1870

| | | |
|---|---|---|
| COULINAN, Benjamin | SCHOENHOF, Sarah | 31 DEC 1858 |
| COUNTEE, John | DAVIS, Jane (blk) | 25 SEP 1866 |
| COUNTI, Grafton | BROWN, Mary (blk) | 02 OCT 1866 |
| COURAND, Orlando E. | HARVEY, Fannie M. | 16 FEB 1865 |
| COURIER, John F. | CUMMINGS, Amanda | 31 DEC 1861 |
| COURTIN, Cornelius | COURBY, Mary | 26 JAN 1859 |
| COURTNEY, Balor | PAYNE, Jane (blk) | 03 JUL 1869 |
| COURTNEY, Francis | FINN, Lizzie | 26 JUN 1863 |
| COURTNEY, George | CONLAN, Maggie | 25 APR 1866 |
| COURTNEY, William H. | BRANSON, Sallie A. | 22 APR 1869 |
| COURTNEY, William L. | HARROVER, Georgianna | 06 APR 1866 |
| COUSINS, Frederick | WATTS, Lena (blk) | 03 APR 1862 |
| COVINGTON, James E. | SIMPSON, Mary F. | 16 MAR 1865 |
| COWAN, John F. | STEWART, Josephine B. | 24 APR 1861 |
| COWAN, William L. [6m] | POPE, Jane E. | 13 AUG 1862 |
| COWAN, William L. | CROSS, Mary E. | 22 MAR 1866 |
| COWHIG, Richard | COLEMAN, Mary | 02 AUG 1862 |
| COWL, Dewitt P. [6le] | GUY, Alto V. | 06 OCT 1866 |
| COWLING, Edward | KENNARD, Agnes M. | 22 APR 1868 |
| COWLING, Edward, Jr. [7a] | SOTHORON, Roberta | 30 AUG 1866 |
| COWLING, Thomas | PLANT, Indiana | 21 JUN 1865 |
| COX, Daniel | NALLY, Eliza A. | 16 APR 1862 |
| COX, David B. | PARTELLO, Eliza A. | 16 MAY 1859 |
| COX, David B. | PARTELLO, Eliza A. | 26 DEC 1866 |
| COX, Frank [12s] | OWENS, Seleah | 05 NOV 1861 |
| COX, Glanville | COX, Arabella | 18 NOV 1863 |
| COX, James | MALONEY, Johana | 14 FEB 1862 |
| COX, James | BURK, Mary T. | 31 MAR 1869 |
| COX, John | HAWKINS, Virginia (blk) | 15 SEP 1863 |
| COX, John | WEATHERELL, Augusta | 14 NOV 1865 |
| COX, John William Francis | SIMPSON, Caroline Roberta | 18 JAN 1870 |
| COX, Joseph B. | HOLLAND, Sarah | 12 DEC 1864 |
| COX, Kennard | WILLIAMS, Rhoda O'Neal | 31 OCT 1864 |
| COX, Morris | BROSNEHAN, Bridget | 22 NOV 1861 |
| COX, Robert | FLETCHER, Mary E. (blk) | 01 APR 1861 |
| COX, Robert | ENGLAND, Emily (blk) | 03 DEC 1868 |
| COX, Thomas | HARRIS, Annie (blk) | 09 NOV 1864 |
| COX, Thomas C. | ROBINSON, Margaret | 03 SEP 1861 |
| COX, Walter S. | DUNLOP, Margaret L. | 30 OCT 1866 |
| COX, William | ENRIGHT, Hanora | 21 MAY 1867 |
| COX, William | PORTER, Julia Ann | 25 SEP 1868 |
| COX, William E. | CROGGON, Mary | 29 NOV 1859 |
| COXALL, John | SOLOMON, Nannie | 12 MAY 1868 |
| COXE, Benjamin [10] | DEAN, Louisa | 17 NOV 1858 |
| COXEN, George [6] | STEELE, Lizzie [Mrs.] | 20 APR 1869 |
| COYLE, Andrew | McNAIR, Annie Stuart | 14 OCT 1862 |
| COYLE, Francis | COLLINS, Kate | 27 DEC 1862 |
| COYLE, Francis | CAHILL, Margaret | 26 SEP 1868 |
| COYLE, Francis | McCARTHY, Hannah | 03 FEB 1870 |
| COYLE, John [10] | CARROLL, Jane A. | 04 OCT 1864 |
| COYLE, John | REIDY, Ellen | 06 JUN 1867 |
| COYLE, Martin | O'TOOLE, Fanny | 13 JUL 1863 |
| COYLE, Peter | GARACTY, Margaret | 12 SEP 1859 |
| COYLE, Thomas | HANRIHAN, Mary Ann | 31 MAY 1861 |
| COYNE, John | TIGHE, Margaret | 10 JUL 1863 |
| COZINNO, Joseph | SIMPSON, Roberta | 07 MAR 1862 |

| Groom | Bride | Date |
|---|---|---|
| CRABBE, Robert B. | SELDEN, Emily M. (blk) | 21 DEC 1867 |
| CRAFT, Richard | PALMER, Elizabeth Ella | 18 FEB 1863 |
| CRAIG, John W. | MALLOY, Mary M. | 14 OCT 1865 |
| CRAIG, Samuel | LOWRY, Sarah | 26 NOV 1866 |
| CRAIG, Samuel [Jersey City] [5] | WOLFE, Mary Emma | 19 FEB 1868 |
| CRAIG, William | SMOOT, Winnie (blk) | 04 SEP 1865 |
| CRAIG, William Henry | RUNNELLS, Catharine (blk) | 13 MAR 1862 |
| CRAIGEN, William J. | PUE, Rebecca D. | 12 OCT 1864 |
| CRAMER, Henry | MILLER, Lizzie | 26 NOV 1866 |
| CRAMER, Joseph | MITCHELL, Julia | 30 JUN 1866 |
| CRAMPTON, Charles | BUTLER, Rebecca (blk) | 25 AUG 1869 |
| CRAMPTON, James | HENSON, Eveline (blk) | 03 MAR 1863 |
| CRAMPTON, William Henry | WHINUM, Maria Louisa (blk) | 27 JUL 1863 |
| CRAMWELL, Charles | COOK, Rebecca (blk) | 10 AUG 1869 |
| CRANE, Adolphus P. | ROCKFELLER, Eve Ann | 15 MAY 1865 |
| CRANE, George L. | DOW, Helen M. | 04 NOV 1865 |
| CRANE, Ira M.D. | BURROUGHS, A.E.G. | 02 JUL 1864 |
| CRANGLA, Francis | CAREY, Mary | 27 DEC 1860 |
| CRANKUM, William H. | JACKSON, Mary (blk) | 13 SEP 1866 |
| CRANSTON, Arthur | BACON, Mary | 11 OCT 1869 |
| CRANY, John | JONES, Winney (blk) | 25 MAY 1865 |
| CRAPSTER, William T. | WARFIELD, Ellen A. | 05 MAY 1864 |
| CRATHY, Daniel | WHITE, Mary | 20 NOV 1867 |
| CRATHY, James | RAGAN, Johanna | 25 MAR 1862 |
| CRAULY, P.W. [1e] | TENNANT, Caroline | 20 SEP 1865 |
| CRAUSE, Henry | YOCHON, Margaret | 13 OCT 1863 |
| CRAVEN, George | NIGHTENGALE, Arminta | 17 SEP 1864 |
| CRAVEN, John | NALLS, Mary E. | 27 DEC 1864 |
| CRAVEN, Timothy | NOLAN, Mary | 03 JUN 1865 |
| CRAWFORD, George | CURTIS, Sallie (blk) | 25 JUN 1863 |
| CRAWFORD, George | MASON, Catharine (blk) | 04 NOV 1864 |
| CRAWFORD, George | SMITH, Louise (blk) | 21 SEP 1869 |
| CRAWFORD, Jack | CAMPBELL, Eliza (blk) | 28 MAY 1868 |
| CRAWFORD, James | HENLY, Mary Ellen | 10 DEC 1867 |
| CRAWFORD, John | JOHNSON, Emily (blk) | 04 OCT 1865 |
| CRAWFORD, John A. [12s] | YOUNG, B. Addie | 20 APR 1859 |
| CRAWFORD, Oliver | SMITH, Sarah (blk) | 24 DEC 1864 |
| CRAWFORD, Robert | WALL, Helen | 28 AUG 1863 |
| CRAWFORD, Samuel | PERKINS, Hallie B. | 08 JUN 1870 |
| CRAWFORD, Thomas | ARCHER, Sarah | 19 JUL 1865 |
| CRAWFORD, W. Sidney, Jr. [11] | COLE, Fannie T. | 22 MAR 1859 |
| CRAWFORD, William B. [of Chicago] | SWOARD, George Emma [10] | 22 SEP 1864 |
| CRAWFORD, William G. | LEE, Maria Louise (blk) | 16 OCT 1866 |
| CRAWFORD, William H. | WILLETT, Sallie | 27 MAY 1869 |
| CRAWFORD, William W. | SIBLEY, Elizabeth | 09 DEC 1869 |
| CRAWFORD, Wm. | SIMONDS, Georgiana (blk) | 17 MAY 1864 |
| CREAGHAN, Patrick | GALVIN, Johanna | 24 FEB 1859 |
| CREAGHAN, Thomas | HINDS, Bridget | 28 JAN 1860 |
| CREAHAN, Martin | MYERS, Mary | 19 JUL 1865 |
| CREAHAN, William | DUMPHY, Catharine | 18 JAN 1865 |
| CREAMER, Thomas E. | KIBBLE, Henrietta | 15 MAY 1865 |
| CREAMER, William | HAVRESS, Mary | 27 NOV 1863 |
| CREARY, Wm. E. | CLARK, Annie E. | 03 JUL 1866 |
| CREECY, Charles Eaton | FENWICK, Sarah C. | 21 OCT 1867 |
| CREED, Jeremiah | FAEYNE, Catherine | 17 JUL 1863 |
| CREEGAN, John | JOY, Ann | 05 JUL 1862 |

| | | |
|---|---|---|
| CREEK, William | MODOCK, Lizzie (blk) | 04 NOV 1869 |
| CREIGHTON, William F. [11] | VOWELL, Hattie N. | 07 MAY 1862 |
| CREW, William S. | O'BRIEN, Endora | 24 AUG 1869 |
| CRIDER, Joseph H. | MANUETT, Mary V. | 15 JUL 1867 |
| CRIMMIN, Eugene | HARTIGAN, Ellen | 23 SEP 1864 |
| CRIMMIN, William | NEVILLE, Ellen | 06 OCT 1869 |
| CRIPPS, George H. | McKIN, Kate | 10 JAN 1863 |
| CRIPPS, George S. | DICKENSON, Ellen | 23 FEB 1870 |
| CRISMAN, Lewis | DAVIS, Louisa (blk) | 15 OCT 1868 |
| CRITTENDEN, John | GRAHAM, Ann (blk) | 07 OCT 1869 |
| CRITTENDEN, Sandy | MILLER, Mary E. (blk) | 20 DEC 1865 |
| CROCKER, James H. | DOUGLAS, Margaretta M. (blk) | 23 MAY 1867 |
| CROCKER, James J. | ALLENBAUGH, Mary Jane | 15 AUG 1860 |
| CROCKER, John S., Jr. [5] | CARPENTER, E. Virginia | 27 SEP 1869 |
| CROCKET, Henry | CROCKET, Eliza | 10 MAY 1862 |
| CROGAN, John G. | O'MERA, Annie | 06 JUN 1868 |
| CROGAN, Patrick | ACTON, Isabella | 18 JUL 1864 |
| CROGGINS, Edward | BROOKS, Millie (blk) | 26 JUN 1868 |
| CROGGON, Henry | HOGE, Roberta V. | 08 SEP 1859 |
| CROGGON, William J. | FLYNN, Ellen H. | 15 AUG 1865 |
| CROGHAN, Patrick A.M., Dr. | BACON, Cornelia M.A.V. | 07 NOV 1866 |
| CROMPTON, Alexander | LEE, Harriett Anne (blk) | 27 JUL 1863 |
| CROMWELL, Daniel | HALL, Caroline V. | 23 NOV 1859 |
| CROMWELL, Joseph W. | WHITE, Caroline | 20 OCT 1859 |
| CROMWELL, Thomas | LAUCK, E. Serena | 26 JAN 1859 |
| CROMWELL, Zachariah W. | DUNBAR, Isabella K. | 06 NOV 1867 |
| CRONIN, James | MURTHY, Annie | 07 MAY 1862 |
| CRONIN, Jeremiah | NASH, Ellen | 19 SEP 1863 |
| CRONIN, John | SULLIVAN, Ellen | 23 JAN 1864 |
| CRONIN, John | MURPHY, Mary Jane | 14 SEP 1868 |
| CRONN, William Samuel | WHITZELL, Mary | 28 MAY 1866 |
| CROOK, John | STARWIGHT, Elizabeth | 06 OCT 1866 |
| CROOK, Walter | KREAMER, Alice | 26 APR 1870 |
| CROOK, William | RODBIRD, Jane Catharine | 09 FEB 1863 |
| CROOKS, Jetson | CROOKS, Emeline | 17 SEP 1863 |
| CROP, Payton | CAMPBELL, Susan (blk) | 04 SEP 1869 |
| CROPLEY, Richard L. | JONES, Rebecca | 01 OCT 1862 |
| CROPLEY, Thomas L. | JONES, Alice J. | 23 MAR 1870 |
| CROSBY, Harry T. [4] | KAUFMAN, Amelia R. | 02 MAR 1867 |
| CROSBY, William | JUNIPER, Margaret (blk) | 13 MAR 1867 |
| CROSEN, John H. | MELHORN, Cornelia | 13 NOV 1866 |
| CROSS, Amos | BROOKS, Henrietta (blk) | 17 SEP 1868 |
| CROSS, Charles | SMOTHERS, Annie Frances (blk) | 25 JUN 1867 |
| CROSS, Charles | HINSON, Anna (blk) | 23 APR 1868 |
| CROSS, George B. | CLEMENTS, Mary E. | 04 SEP 1867 |
| CROSS, Israel | CHAMPION, Elizth. | 01 NOV 1860 |
| CROSS, James C. | NORTON, Laura V. | 15 AUG 1861 |
| CROSS, Jno. F. | OSBORN, Alice M. | 21 MAY 1861 |
| CROSS, Joseph | McNAMARA, Johana | 25 AUG 1862 |
| CROSS, Joseph | TURNER, Celia (blk) | 24 DEC 1862 |
| CROSS, Richard | WALKER, Anna (blk) | 24 JAN 1867 |
| CROSS, Robert | TIBBS, Albert (blk) | 05 JAN 1867 |
| CROSS, Robert R. | PROSPERA, Annie Maria | 22 JUN 1861 |
| CROSS, Samuel [6m] | GETZENDANER, Catherine | 23 JUL 1863 |
| CROSS, Samuel G. | SIMS, Rosa (blk) | 16 OCT 1862 |
| CROSS, T.H. | LEWIS, Mary E. (blk) | 14 JUN 1866 |

District of Columbia Marriage Licenses, 1858-1870

| | | |
|---|---|---|
| CROSS, Thomas B., Jr. | TALTAVULL, Catherine | 20 JUN 1866 |
| CROSS, Thomas H. | FLETCHER, Ellenora (blk) | 20 OCT 1864 |
| CROSS, William | JONES, Sarah Jane (blk) | 01 APR 1867 |
| CROSS, William H. | McGRAW, Mary A. | 03 JUN 1869 |
| CROSSET, Wilson | HOFLER, Virginia A. | 20 SEP 1858 |
| CROUCH, Edwin D. | MURPHY, Lizzie A. | 16 OCT 1862 |
| CROUCH, Elias | SPITTLE, Landonia C. | 31 JAN 1866 |
| CROUNSE, Amos | CAMERON, Bella | 17 APR 1866 |
| CROVER, Francis | HUBBARD, Mary | 06 MAY 1862 |
| CROW, Francis | MURPHY, Mary | 15 NOV 1866 |
| CROW, Theodore Boucher | RODIER, Alice Virginia | 12 OCT 1867 |
| CROWLEY, Daniel | McMAHAN, Mary | 26 FEB 1859 |
| CROWLEY, James | MURPHY, Mary | 28 JUN 1862 |
| CROWLEY, Jeremiah | DAILEY, Catherine | 25 JUN 1860 |
| CROWLEY, John | O'BRIEN, Elizabeth Ann | 03 JUN 1864 |
| CROWLEY, Joseph A. | WESTEN, Emma L. | 24 MAR 1862 |
| CROWLEY, Nicholas | SULLIVAN, Anna | 11 SEP 1863 |
| CROWLEY, Thomas | JONES, Margaret | 19 DEC 1863 |
| CROWLEY, Thomas | NILAND, Bridget | 07 NOV 1864 |
| CROWLEY, William H. | FINK, Lizzie S. | 31 JAN 1865 |
| CROWN, Charles | KING, Caroline | 25 NOV 1869 |
| CROWN, James T. | COLE, Mary F. | 30 APR 1864 |
| CROWN, John F. | PARKER, Martha | 29 APR 1863 |
| CROWN, Joseph H. | MAHORNEY, Mary E. | 20 DEC 1861 |
| CROWN, William H. | REEDER, Sarah C. | 29 SEP 1863 |
| CROWN, William S. | HOWSE, Sarah S. | 21 SEP 1866 |
| CROWNAN, Michael | KENNEDY, Ellen | 18 APR 1867 |
| CROWNER, George | BOWEN, Hester (blk) | 22 APR 1867 |
| CROWNER, George | MITCHELL, Jane | 02 DEC 1867 |
| CROWNER, John | LEWIS, Emma (blk) | 01 OCT 1864 |
| CROWNER, William | SMITH, Frances (blk) | 14 APR 1859 |
| CRUIKSHANK, John | ANTISELL, Margaret Euphrasia | 17 OCT 1866 |
| CRUIT, Edwin D. | FOWLER, Mary E. | 20 SEP 1859 |
| CRUIT, Richard, Jr. | PAXTON, Mary | 19 JUL 1859 |
| CRUMP, Edward | CLARK, Mary | 14 FEB 1865 |
| CRUMP, Emory S. [12s] | SHREEVE, Susan S. | 09 JAN 1860 |
| CRUMP, George W. | STUDDS, Emma | 15 DEC 1868 |
| CRUMP, Henry A. | TAYLOR, Mary A. | 10 JUN 1868 |
| CRUMP, James E. | COX, Addie S. | 01 JUL 1863 |
| CRUMP, Jas. P. | BRADFORD, Elmira | 23 DEC 1862 |
| CRUMP, Shedrack | PETERSON, Elizabeth (col'd) | 10 NOV 1863 |
| CRUMREY, Eli | NASH, Amelia (blk) | 19 AUG 1867 |
| CRUPPER, John | CAWOOD, Elizabeth J. | 29 JUN 1864 |
| CRUPPER, John Q.A. | GREEN, Frances A. | 01 APR 1862 |
| CRUSER, William | GUTHRIDGE, Mary V. (blk) | 05 JAN 1870 |
| CRUTCHETT, Francis S. | HALLEY, Sarah E. | 15 SEP 1864 |
| CRUTCHFIELD, Alfred | FOX, Lucind (blk) | 26 APR 1864 |
| CRUTCHFIELD, Reuben | LEE, Louise (blk) | 20 MAY 1869 |
| CRUTCHLEY, George W. | KIDWELL, Sarah E. | 16 FEB 1863 |
| CRUTCHLEY, John W. [6m] | GARNER, Annie D. | 27 OCT 1862 |
| CRUX, William | BURRISS, Mary Ellen | 24 DEC 1860 |
| CRYER, Robert | MOORE, Lucinda (blk) | 03 DEC 1863 |
| CUDDY, John Michael | DONNELLY, Catherine | 01 MAR 1869 |
| CUDDY, Thomas | GARDINER, Annie M. | 27 APR 1859 |
| CUDDY, Thomas | DEMOLLE, Charlotte | 14 APR 1860 |
| CUDDYER, Patrick | CLANCY, Margaret | 06 JAN 1864 |

District of Columbia Marriage Licenses, 1858-1870

| | | |
|---|---|---|
| CUDLIP, George D. | LLOYD, Nellie E. | 14 FEB 1865 |
| CUDLIPP, William B. | GALLAGHER, Sarah Jane | 10 OCT 1868 |
| CUDMORE, Michael | KEALY, Bridget | 21 NOV 1863 |
| CUFF, Thomas | DUFFY, Catherine | 25 OCT 1862 |
| CULBERTSON, Cyrus J. | BENNET, Sarah A. | 21 AUG 1861 |
| CULBERTSON, Joseph | BURK, Eliza (blk) | 26 DEC 1864 |
| CULL, James | HATEWILL, Margaret | 01 NOV 1869 |
| CULL, John | LYNCH, Mary | 19 DEC 1863 |
| CULL, Patrick | GRACE, Catharine | 12 JAN 1866 |
| CULLAN, James | HUNTT, Mary | 21 DEC 1861 |
| CULLEN, James | WILLIAMS, Carrie A. | 28 APR 1865 |
| CULLEN, John | GREGORY, Eliza A. | 29 NOV 1864 |
| CULLEN, Matthew | TOBIAS, Mary Ann | 04 MAY 1863 |
| CULLIGAN, John | McNAMARA, Mary | 01 NOV 1866 |
| CULLIN, Thomas | NOLAND, Catherine | 15 AUG 1859 |
| CULLINAN, Edward | GIBSON, Elizabeth | 21 FEB 1868 |
| CULLINAN, Lot | CULLINAN, Mary | 07 JAN 1867 |
| CULLMAN, Daniel A. | HOLSTEIN, Bettie T. | 18 JUL 1865 |
| CULLMAN, Jacob [4] | DIXON, Emily | 13 MAR 1866 |
| CULLNAN, Michael | SHEA, Bridget | 19 AUG 1862 |
| CULVER, Elias [6m] | BELL, Rachel Ann | 08 SEP 1863 |
| CULVERWELL, John G. | SCRIVENER, Martha | 16 DEC 1867 |
| CULVERWELL, Samuel E. | JOHNSON, Mary | 26 SEP 1865 |
| CUMBERLAND, Albert | KILEY, Margaret | 04 NOV 1863 |
| CUMBERLAND, Charles T. | HAMILTON, Ann Rebecca | 17 APR 1860 |
| CUMBERLAND, David H. | POWER, Mary C. | 16 FEB 1860 |
| CUMBERLAND, George T. | NORRIS, Mary | 20 SEP 1859 |
| CUMBERLAND, John | BANNISTER, Mary E. | 21 MAY 1870 |
| CUMING, Valentine H. | McLEAN, Mary Louisa | 29 JAN 1867 |
| CUMMING, John C. | SMITH, Mary E. | 12 MAR 1864 |
| CUMMING, William A. | VIERS, Kate | 28 OCT 1862 |
| CUMMINGS, James | WALL, Mary | 05 MAR 1859 |
| CUMMINGS, William T. | HOLDSWORTH, Sarah E. | 05 NOV 1860 |
| CUMMINS, Charles F. | DYER, Josephine | 22 JUL 1867 |
| CUMOR, John T. | GRUBB, Eliza A. | 18 SEP 1865 |
| CUNAN, John | SULLIVAN, Mary | 27 NOV 1865 |
| CUNDIFF, Alfonso | CUNDIFF, Virginia | 23 NOV 1859 |
| CUNNINGHAM, David J. | CLINE, Annie Rebecca | 16 SEP 1862 |
| CUNNINGHAM, Dennis | CASSEDY, Mary | 07 SEP 1863 |
| CUNNINGHAM, Frederick S. [12s] | TAYLOR, Annie E. | 03 MAR 1862 |
| CUNNINGHAM, George [6h] | PARKER, Zora | 12 AUG 1868 |
| CUNNINGHAM, George E. | BOGAN, Leanna | 07 JUL 1868 |
| CUNNINGHAM, George Law | McCAFFRY, Mary Louisa Susan | 12 OCT 1863 |
| CUNNINGHAM, James | McGUIRE, Ann | 07 MAR 1859 |
| CUNNINGHAM, James G. | CROWN, Ann Amelia | 08 SEP 1862 |
| CUNNINGHAM, John | O'BRIEN, Catharine | 15 FEB 1864 |
| CUNNINGHAM, John W. | NEILL, Sue E. | 08 JUN 1869 |
| CUNNINGHAM, Patrick | DORAN, Bridget | 07 DEC 1867 |
| CUNNINGHAM, Theodore Hill | LITTON, Harriet Josephine | 30 NOV 1863 |
| CUNNINGHAM, Thomas | MURPHY, Mary | 09 MAY 1865 |
| CUNNINGHAM, William A. | CUNNINGHAM, T.R. | 01 MAR 1865 |
| CUNNINGHAM, William E. | STEWART, Marietta | 03 SEP 1866 |
| CUNNINGTON, G.S.R. | BEACH, Mary E. | 07 SEP 1869 |
| CUNNUMHAND, Richard | GOINGS, Jane E. | 28 APR 1862 |
| CUPLER, Perry | RYLAND, Mary | 09 MAY 1865 |
| CURRAID, Zachariah | JOHNSON, Mary C. (col'd) | 14 SEP 1865 |

District of Columbia Marriage Licenses, 1858-1870

| | | |
|---|---|---|
| CURRAN, Francis | CROEKEN, Kate Virginia | 14 JUN 1859 |
| CURRAN, Patrick | CONREY, Mary | 10 JUL 1860 |
| CURRHEY, J.B. | CHAMBERLAIN, Virginia | 24 DEC 1868 |
| CURRIER, George W. | BATCHING, Anna | 13 NOV 1865 |
| CURRY, Alfred | RICH, Frances (blk) | 13 FEB 1868 |
| CURRY, John | MALONY, Margaret | 18 FEB 1867 |
| CURRY, John W. | GARRETT, Elizabeth F. (blk) | 27 MAR 1861 |
| CURRY, John W. | SIMON, Kate | 20 DEC 1865 |
| CURRY, Levi | DUVALL, Dora E. | 02 MAR 1867 |
| CURRY, Spencer | BAYLOR, Maria (blk) | 12 NOV 1866 |
| CURSEEN, William | MARLOW, Margaret (col'd) | 01 FEB 1866 |
| CURTAIN, Charles | O'CONNELL, Mary | 28 JUL 1865 |
| CURTH, Weigand | GEIG, Elizabeth | 06 JUL 1863 |
| CURTIN, Cornelius | CROWLEY, Julia | 01 FEB 1868 |
| CURTIN, Daniel | GRIFFIN, Mary | 01 FEB 1865 |
| CURTIN, David | BOOTH, Mary Ann | 19 JUN 1867 |
| CURTIN, Patrick | BARRETT, Mary | 21 MAY 1861 |
| CURTIN, Richard | LYONS, Margaret | 14 JAN 1868 |
| CURTIN, William | HALL, Mary | 07 NOV 1860 |
| CURTIS, Amos | HAWKINS, Susan (blk) | 29 JAN 1868 |
| CURTIS, George | WATKINS, Euphemia | 16 JUN 1865 |
| CURTIS, George D. | CROWELL, Maria B. | 08 JUN 1870 |
| CURTIS, Isaiah | SIMPSON, Winnie (blk) | 05 NOV 1868 |
| CURTIS, James | STEWART, Eliza | 09 MAY 1870 |
| CURTIS, Jno. F. | SIMPSON, Lavinia C. | 24 DEC 1866 |
| CURTIS, John | KEARNEY, Margaret | 24 AUG 1864 |
| CURTIS, John H. | BARNES, Julia (blk) | 11 DEC 1867 |
| CURTIS, John M. | HOWARD, Jane, Mrs. | 21 JAN 1867 |
| CURTIS, T. Alden [12s] | HALL, Ellen E. | 15 NOV 1861 |
| CURTIS, Thomas | ROBESON, Jane (blk) | 30 SEP 1869 |
| CURTIS, William | MATTHEWS, Sarah (blk) | 21 APR 1862 |
| CURTIS, William | HALLIGER, Louisa (blk) | 14 MAY 1863 |
| CURTIS, Wm. H. | WARE, Isabella (blk) | 14 JAN 1861 |
| CURTISS, Wright [11] | FARNHAM, Carrie | 14 OCT 1867 |
| CUSHING, George J. | WILLIAMS, Fannie | 15 MAR 1864 |
| CUSSAN, Maurice | O'CALLAGHAN, Catherine | 20 OCT 1866 |
| CUSTIS, George [4] | CORCORAN, Louise Morris | 04 APR 1859 |
| CUSTIS, Henry | JOHNSON, Matilda (blk) | 16 SEP 1865 |
| CUSTIS, Henry | SHARPE, Abby Jane (blk) | 25 MAY 1867 |
| CUTHBERTSON, Thomas | DRAKE, Jane | 15 JUN 1865 |
| CUTLER, Edward R. | ROGERS, Millie A. | 26 APR 1864 |
| CUTLER, John K. | ROSS, Elizabeth (blk) | 29 NOV 1864 |
| CUTSHAW, George B. [1c] | BANGS, Irene M. | 15 OCT 1862 |
| CUTTER, Benjamin P. | GAUGHAN, Jennie | 06 NOV 1865 |
| CUTTING, Bruckholst | RAMSAY, Marion | 18 SEP 1860 |

# D

| | | |
|---|---|---|
| d'AUCHAMP, Oscar Robert | DEGILE, Louise Marie | 19 MAY 1863 |
| d'ORVORST, Arthur dePelgrou | deSAVAGNE, Sophie Favaiger | 24 NOV 1863 |
| DAAR, August | MARTIN, Louisa | 07 MAR 1859 |
| DABBS, James | SWANAGIN, Laura (blk) | 25 SEP 1866 |
| DABNEY, Benjamin | JOHNSON, Lizzie (blk) | 16 FEB 1865 |
| DABNEY, Thomas S. | CROZIER, Virginia H. | 10 SEP 1861 |
| DACEY, James | CRAHEN, Bridget | 05 JAN 1861 |
| DACEY, John | COURTNEY, Catherine | 08 JAN 1859 |

District of Columbia Marriage Licenses, 1858-1870

| | | |
|---|---|---|
| DACHENHAUSEN, Adolphus von | HUNTER, Elizabeth | 10 JUN 1863 |
| DADE, Caleb | WALLACE, Susan (blk) | 05 SEP 1867 |
| DADE, Peter | BOWLES, Caroline (blk) | 14 AUG 1862 |
| DADE, Travers H. | GREEN, Sadie A. (blk) | 31 MAY 1870 |
| DADE, Washington | BUTLER, Cornelia (blk) | 05 FEB 1868 |
| DADE, William | GRIFFIN, Catharine (blk) | 04 APR 1863 |
| DAFFNEY, William | NEALE, Margaret (blk) | 19 MAY 1864 |
| DAGGS, Nathaniel | FARMAN, Delia (blk) | 30 OCT 1868 |
| DAGGS, Robert | SMITH, Fannie (blk) | 12 OCT 1864 |
| DAGNAY, Daniel | KENNAWAY, Agnes | 21 NOV 1863 |
| DAHLER, A. Gustav | WAHL, Anna E. | 12 MAY 1860 |
| DAILEY, Jacob | DOBSON, Winnie (blk) | 06 OCT 1868 |
| DAILEY, John | McCORMICK, Ann | 18 FEB 1859 |
| DAILEY, John | ALBRITTON, Jane | 14 MAY 1866 |
| DAILEY, Samuel | McCULLOUGH, Hester G. | 04 JUN 1863 |
| DAILEY, William | SULLIVAN, Johanna | 28 JUL 1860 |
| DAILY, Benjamin F. | MATHEWS, Victoria | 18 APR 1866 |
| DAILY, John | BOWDEN, Ellen | 29 JAN 1863 |
| DAILY, Patrick | MURPHEY, Mary | 27 NOV 1858 |
| DAINGERFIELD, William H. | HOWLE, Mary E. | 13 SEP 1858 |
| DAIREY, Patrick | BABBINGTON, Joanna | 24 NOV 1860 |
| DAKE, Frederick E. | MASON, Catherine | 23 OCT 1866 |
| DAKIN, Reuben B. | BOSWELL, Mary S. | 15 DEC 1863 |
| DALANEY, James H. | DELEVI, Julia | 01 SEP 1868 |
| DALAY, Thomas | DEVINE, Margaret | 30 APR 1866 |
| DALE, William | STEWART, Emma | 08 SEP 1864 |
| DALEY, Carroll | HURLEY, Mary | 27 OCT 1858 |
| DALEY, James | MORGAN, Mary | 02 DEC 1861 |
| DALEY, John | DASEY, Ellen | 08 OCT 1859 |
| DALEY, John | HAYDEN, Mary Ann | 17 NOV 1864 |
| DALLAS, Andrew | PETERS, Louisa (blk) | 13 MAY 1863 |
| DALTON, Gardner E. | COHEN, Sallie E. | 29 OCT 1866 |
| DALTON, Henry F. | CONNER, Mary | 30 SEP 1862 |
| DALTON, John | HORAN, Kate | 17 FEB 1865 |
| DALTON, John | GRADY, Hanora | 31 DEC 1868 |
| DALTON, Thomas F. | McNEILL, Marion W. | 25 JAN 1869 |
| DALTON, Thomas W. | SESSFORD, Caroline K. | 14 APR 1868 |
| DALTON, William | HUME, Ella A. | 03 NOV 1864 |
| DALTON, William N. | WILLIAMS, Olivia A. | 02 NOV 1868 |
| DALWATHER, Conrad H. | POWELL, Susan | 04 APR 1864 |
| DALY, Carroll | KANE, Margaret | 01 NOV 1865 |
| DALY, Cornelius | CLEMENTS, Alice Virginia | 30 JUL 1864 |
| DALY, Edward | McDONALD, Mary | 25 MAR 1869 |
| DALY, Francis | LEONARD, Ann | 07 NOV 1859 |
| DALY, H.J. | McHUNE, Anna | 18 JAN 1870 |
| DALY, James | JOYCE, Margaret I. | 21 APR 1868 |
| DALY, Jeremiah | GRIFFIN, Mary | 06 AUG 1859 |
| DALY, John | McMANN, Margaret | 17 OCT 1860 |
| DALY, John | DONOGHUE, Mary | 07 MAY 1869 |
| DALY, John L. | SHAUNESSY, Mary | 30 JUL 1864 |
| DALY, Michael | BRASNAHAN, Margaret | 18 SEP 1858 |
| DALY, Michael | DRISCOLL, Joanna | 28 FEB 1867 |
| DALY, Timothy D. | DONOVEN, Johanna | 25 SEP 1858 |
| DALY, Walter H. | VICKERS, Mary E. | 08 MAY 1868 |
| DALY, William | GRAY, Abby | 26 JAN 1863 |
| DAME, John W. | HOPKINS, Annie Sophia | 18 JAN 1869 |

District of Columbia Marriage Licenses, 1858-1870

| | | |
|---|---|---|
| DAMIESON, James | WEAVER, Elizabeth | 16 APR 1861 |
| DANAHY, John | BUCKLEY, Hannah | 01 SEP 1858 |
| DANDRIDGE, Luther | WALTER, Rosanna (blk) | 22 JAN 1866 |
| DANGERFIELD, John | JOHNSON, Mary (blk) | 08 OCT 1863 |
| DANGERFIELD, John | HARRIS, Eliza (blk) | 21 DEC 1864 |
| DANGERFIELD, William | DYSON, Margaret (blk) | 09 NOV 1868 |
| DANGERFIELD, Willis | CARTER, Sarah | 13 JUN 1866 |
| DANGLER, Curtis | REED, Margaret E. | 23 FEB 1864 |
| DANIEL, Charles | RICHARDSON, Maria (blk) | 24 JUL 1865 |
| DANIEL, Frederick | GAA, Louisa | 22 MAY 1868 |
| DANIEL, Joseph | DOVE, Amand | 05 JAN 1869 |
| DANIEL, Joseph H. | WERDEN, Emily R. | 26 SEP 1859 |
| DANIEL, W.H. | BROWN, Mary | 20 JUL 1869 |
| DANIEL, Walter | HUNTINGTON, Elizabeth A. | 04 FEB 1864 |
| DANIELL, Robert R. | SHAW, Jane Susan | 08 FEB 1862 |
| DANIELS, Edward F. | RICARDE, Clara | 25 JUL 1864 |
| DANIELS, Frank G. | FULLER, Mary | 19 NOV 1867 |
| DANIELS, George L. | BAYLISS, Trace C. | 09 DEC 1859 |
| DANIELS, Joseph | BURKHARDT, Elizabeth | 08 JAN 1867 |
| DANIELS, Naham W. | SCOTT, Cora L.V. | 08 DEC 1865 |
| DANIELS, Walter | DAVIS, Amelia | 30 JUN 1868 |
| DANIELS, William H. | DOBBS, Alice J. | 06 JUN 1864 |
| DANIELS, William H. | BOSS, Edna J. | 03 SEP 1868 |
| DANIELS, William H. | BOSS, Edna J. | 15 SEP 1868 |
| DANLEY, Asher | MILLER, Mary Ann | 25 SEP 1867 |
| DANN, William | ROBINSON, Mary Elizabeth | 14 DEC 1865 |
| DANNAHY, Jeremiah | CONNOLLY, Margaret | 19 FEB 1859 |
| DANNISON, Thomas R. [6r] | STANSBURY, Mary Jane | 02 APR 1860 |
| DANT, Charles W. | GRAY, Kate M. | 28 AUG 1863 |
| DANT, John Marcellus | MOCKABEE, Mary W. | 21 OCT 1867 |
| DANT, Joseph M. | HOWARD, Emma | 27 DEC 1860 |
| DANT, Richard A. | YOUNG, Mary P. | 27 NOV 1867 |
| DANT, Thomas C. | ELLIOTT, Mary E. | 28 JAN 1862 |
| DANT, William T. [12s] | McLAUGHLIN, Mary | 19 AUG 1861 |
| DARBY, George W. | NELSON, Mary Frances | 18 FEB 1864 |
| DARBY, Harrie D. | JONES, Maggie R. | 06 DEC 1869 |
| DARBY, John E. | BREMMERMAN, Lottie A. | 24 DEC 1869 |
| DARCY, John | MURTH, Kate | 18 JUN 1864 |
| DARDEN, Joseph | HARKNESS, Emma E. | 31 JAN 1859 |
| DARING, Jonas | WAGNER, Helen V. | 30 DEC 1861 |
| DARLING, George A. | COCKRELL, Julia F. | 30 AUG 1862 |
| DARMSTADT, C.C. | SOUDER, Tenie | 21 NOV 1868 |
| DARN, Fayette | DAVIDSON, Susanna | 14 OCT 1862 |
| DARNALL, Martin | KEARNEY, Jane | 24 NOV 1862 |
| DARNE, Alexander C.H. | HALL, Thirza Virginia | 25 JAN 1865 |
| DARNE, John Robert | SCOTT, America V. | 30 JAN 1863 |
| DARNEILLE, Philip A. | HARRY, Emily M. | 13 JUN 1867 |
| DARR, Thomas E. | McCARTON, Ann | 14 APR 1866 |
| DARRELL, Armistead M. | BROOKE, Nannie E. | 13 FEB 1866 |
| DARRELL, John H. | PENDLETON, Rose B. | 19 AUG 1862 |
| DARRELL, Maxmilian | WINDSOR, Frances Ann | 07 MAR 1870 |
| DASHIELDS, James Hy. | WARNER, Jane Elizth. (blk) | 07 JAN 1860 |
| DASHIELL, Columbus W. | SUTTON, Virginia | 26 NOV 1861 |
| DASHIELL, James | GREENE, Mary (blk) | 30 NOV 1866 |
| DATCHER, Samuel J. | COOK, Mary V. | 19 APR 1866 |
| DAUBERT, August | HERTZING, Magadelana | 26 NOV 1866 |

District of Columbia Marriage Licenses, 1858-1870

| | | |
|---|---|---|
| DAUGHERTY, Charles S. | DARCEY, Margaret | 21 JUN 1864 |
| DAUGHTON, Burly [10] | WARNER, Margaret A.E. | 26 APR 1867 |
| DAUGHTON, Darius | SMART, Emma | 16 NOV 1863 |
| DAUGHTON, John | HUNTER, Martha | 23 APR 1866 |
| DAVENPORT, Charles E. | HUGHES, Rebecca | 14 DEC 1868 |
| DAVENPORT, Francis | DAVENPORT, Eliza (blk) | 11 JUL 1867 |
| DAVENPORT, Isaac | HAWKINS, Eliza (blk) | 24 JUN 1864 |
| DAVENPORT, Jesse | SHEAHAN, Bridget | 20 JUN 1865 |
| DAVENPORT, Simeon J. | MYERS, Mary | 28 JAN 1862 |
| DAVERN, James | KIRBY, Hanorah | 18 AUG 1866 |
| DAVIDGE, Sandy | HERBERT, Lena (blk) | 09 FEB 1870 |
| DAVIDGE, Walter D. [11] | WASHINGTON, Anna L. | 08 JAN 1862 |
| DAVIDSON, Alexander | FOWLER, Ella C. | 19 APR 1866 |
| DAVIDSON, Delozier | TAYLOR, S.V. | 02 NOV 1864 |
| DAVIDSON, James G. | CUNNINGHAM, Esther A. | 04 APR 1866 |
| DAVIDSON, John H. | REEVES, Martha J. | 15 APR 1861 |
| DAVIDSON, Thomas H. | REYNOLDS, Sophronia E. | 14 OCT 1862 |
| DAVIDSON, William M. | BURNES, Martha E. | 01 MAR 1866 |
| DAVIES, Francis Asbury, USA | YOUNG, Mary Cecilia | 15 NOV 1862 |
| DAVIS, Albert P. | GRAYSON, Emma J. (blk) | 06 APR 1869 |
| DAVIS, Alvin | SMITH, Adaline (blk) | 06 NOV 1868 |
| DAVIS, Arthur E. | PAGGETT, Sarah E. | 28 MAR 1861 |
| DAVIS, Benj. F. | KIRVAN, Cordelia | 22 OCT 1862 |
| DAVIS, Benj. F. | BURGESS, Laura | 03 SEP 1863 |
| DAVIS, Benjamin A. | SAYRE, Josephine | 25 FEB 1862 |
| DAVIS, Beverly | PAYNE, Susan (blk) | 25 NOV 1863 |
| DAVIS, Beverly | JACKSON, Louisa (blk) | 01 DEC 1863 |
| DAVIS, Charles | REED, Eliza | 05 NOV 1860 |
| DAVIS, Charles | QUEEN, Treacy | 09 AUG 1865 |
| DAVIS, Charles A. | PAGE, Martha B. | 20 MAR 1862 |
| DAVIS, Charles W. | MOELER, Eliza | 21 JUN 1862 |
| DAVIS, Charles W.S. | TROXELL, Julia S. | 12 APR 1870 |
| DAVIS, Cornelius | MAHONEY, Elizabeth (blk) | 08 FEB 1865 |
| DAVIS, Cornelius W. | ALEXANDER, Maria | 24 FEB 1864 |
| DAVIS, Curtis | KELLY, Caroline T. | 18 DEC 1861 |
| DAVIS, David | LYNN, Mary | 01 MAY 1861 |
| DAVIS, Edward | BALL, Ann Maria (blk) | 08 AUG 1866 |
| DAVIS, Edward | ECK, Annie | 26 OCT 1867 |
| DAVIS, Edward, USA | DAVIS, Mardie | 16 SEP 1867 |
| DAVIS, Edward W. | WEBSTER, Martha | 06 SEP 1865 |
| DAVIS, Ephraim | WYLAND, Mary | 21 JUL 1868 |
| DAVIS, Francis | O'HEARN, Margaret | 21 MAY 1864 |
| DAVIS, Francis | COKELEY, Magline | 30 APR 1868 |
| DAVIS, G.M. | GILL, Ellen | 05 DEC 1863 |
| DAVIS, George C. | PETTY, Sallie M. | 23 FEB 1870 |
| DAVIS, George F. | SEWALL, Elizabeth | 16 MAY 1868 |
| DAVIS, George W. | NEALE, Indiana | 23 OCT 1861 |
| DAVIS, George W., Capt., USA | ATOCHA, Carmen | 30 APR 1870 |
| DAVIS, Henry | BOWSER, Margaret (blk) | 30 OCT 1858 |
| DAVIS, Henry | AMBUSH, Charity (blk) | 15 OCT 1863 |
| DAVIS, Henry | NORRIS, Rachel Ann | 16 APR 1867 |
| DAVIS, Henry R. | ANDREWS, Eugenia N. | 11 DEC 1868 |
| DAVIS, J. Thomas | MARBURY, Anna | 13 JUN 1862 |
| DAVIS, Jacob | KANE, Treacy | 08 FEB 1864 |
| DAVIS, James | WAUGH, Helen (blk) | 17 FEB 1863 |
| DAVIS, James | SMITH, Hellen | 18 MAY 1866 |

District of Columbia Marriage Licenses, 1858-1870

| | | |
|---|---|---|
| DAVIS, James H. | NIE, Rachael K. | 22 DEC 1862 |
| DAVIS, James Henry | MORRIS, Harriet Elizabeth (blk) | 18 DEC 1869 |
| DAVIS, James N.W. | CRAIG, Martha E. | 14 DEC 1858 |
| DAVIS, James W. | APPERSON, Ann E. | 19 JUL 1865 |
| DAVIS, James W. | HORNER, Anna M. | 07 JUL 1868 |
| DAVIS, Jerome M. | KING, Virginia | 13 JUN 1870 |
| DAVIS, Jno. | JOHNSON, Kate | 13 OCT 1863 |
| DAVIS, John | GRAY, Anne ~~Emma~~ | 20 AUG 1863 |
| DAVIS, John | SMALLWOOD, Rosetta | 13 DEC 1867 |
| DAVIS, John | PATTERSON, Harriet (blk) | 29 MAR 1869 |
| DAVIS, John A. | HENDERSON, Fanny | 11 SEP 1858 |
| DAVIS, John A. | GOLDEN, Mary A. | 03 OCT 1868 |
| DAVIS, John C. | BROWNLEE, Dianah | 13 MAY 1870 |
| DAVIS, John E. | RALPH, Sena | 17 FEB 1864 |
| DAVIS, John F. | STEWART, Elizabeth | 28 FEB 1860 |
| DAVIS, John H. | MADDOCKS, Josephine | 19 NOV 1867 |
| DAVIS, John Henry | DAILY, Eliza | 24 MAY 1870 |
| DAVIS, John T. [11] | QUIGLEY, Mary E. | 15 OCT 1861 |
| DAVIS, John T. | BARNES, Sarah Jane | 21 APR 1862 |
| DAVIS, John T. | MOORE, Laurinda (blk) | 01 MAR 1865 |
| DAVIS, Joseph | COUNTEE, Celia (blk) | 10 JUN 1867 |
| DAVIS, Josiah [12s] | REEVE, Sarah E. | 25 MAR 1859 |
| DAVIS, Josiah | LOVELESS, Jane C. | 12 SEP 1859 |
| DAVIS, Kent D. | WOODRUFF, C. Elise | 24 OCT 1864 |
| DAVIS, Lindsay | JONES, Hannah (blk) | 25 OCT 1866 |
| DAVIS, Lorenzo | ROBINSON, Ann Maria (blk) | 03 MAR 1863 |
| DAVIS, Madison [6cl] | RUFF, Virginia M. | 17 MAY 1870 |
| DAVIS, Marshall | RIGNER, Hester | 21 DEC 1863 |
| DAVIS, Martin | SHAW, Frances Cornelia | 27 JUL 1869 |
| DAVIS, Martin H. | KEYS, Nancy | 11 NOV 1862 |
| DAVIS, Moses | LANE, Fanny (blk) | 15 AUG 1866 |
| DAVIS, Nelson (soldier) | PARKER, Annie (blk) | 09 JUL 1863 |
| DAVIS, Nimrod [2] | ELMS, Susan | 04 JUN 1870 |
| DAVIS, Peter | PETTIT, Mary Frances | 17 JUN 1864 |
| DAVIS, Philip | KOLB, Sarah | 16 NOV 1868 |
| DAVIS, Primus | BULLOCKS, Mary (blk) | 24 NOV 1866 |
| DAVIS, Richard | THOMAS, Sophia (blk) | 26 FEB 1866 |
| DAVIS, Robert H. | DAVIS, Mary E. | 02 JAN 1867 |
| DAVIS, Samuel | WISEBECKER, Elizabeth | 19 JUL 1864 |
| DAVIS, Samuel | PARKER, Caroline (blk) | 12 NOV 1866 |
| DAVIS, Samuel J. | CORBIN, Ann Eliza (blk) | 09 MAY 1866 |
| DAVIS, St. Clair | QUEEN, Adeline (blk) | 15 APR 1861 |
| DAVIS, Summers | HENSON, Eliza (blk) | 23 FEB 1865 |
| DAVIS, Thomas | MINNICE, Jennie | 15 MAR 1867 |
| DAVIS, Thomas | HALL, Sallie | 07 SEP 1868 |
| DAVIS, Thomas | WHITELY, Anna J. (blk) | 12 APR 1869 |
| DAVIS, Thomas E. | WESTERN, Sarah | 26 DEC 1862 |
| DAVIS, Thos. George | STEWART, Mary C. | 24 MAY 1860 |
| DAVIS, Thomas K. | PLUMMER, Josephine A. | 02 NOV 1859 |
| DAVIS, Thos. L. | HENRY, Sallie C. | 02 JUL 1868 |
| DAVIS, Thomas M. | HENNING, Alice C. | 14 OCT 1863 |
| DAVIS, Warren | LUNKIN, Mary Jane (blk) | 11 NOV 1868 |
| DAVIS, William | DUNN, Johanna | 04 JUN 1859 |
| DAVIS, William | DONOHO, Catharine | 13 DEC 1862 |
| DAVIS, William | BUTLER, Frances | 11 APR 1867 |
| DAVIS, Wm. | CALDWELL, Catharine | 12 FEB 1861 |

District of Columbia Marriage Licenses, 1858-1870

| | | |
|---|---|---|
| DAVIS, William A. | MILLER, Julia A. | 02 DEC 1863 |
| DAVIS, William A. | SPENCER, Mary | 14 SEP 1865 |
| DAVIS, William B. | CRYER, Mary A. (blk) | 09 JUL 1868 |
| DAVIS, William B. | SKILES, Fannie | 25 JUN 1869 |
| DAVIS, William F. | BRAIN, Amanda | 04 MAY 1861 |
| DAVIS, William F. | HAYS, Frances M. | 23 NOV 1861 |
| DAVIS, William H. | MARTIN, Mary Alice | 13 OCT 1864 |
| DAVIS, William H. | RAYNOR, Anne L. | 11 OCT 1869 |
| DAVIS, William Henry | BLADEN, Sarah E. | 06 FEB 1867 |
| DAVIS, William J. [1c] | EDWARDS, Emma | 24 AUG 1863 |
| DAVIS, William J. | MURPHY, Mary A. | 11 NOV 1867 |
| DAVIS, William L. | MITCHELL, Annie (blk) | 06 JAN 1864 |
| DAVIS, William M. | HENNING, Elizth. Virginia | 18 APR 1861 |
| DAVIS, William [M.] [10] | DIGGS, Susan | 02 JUL 1868 |
| DAVIS, William N. | CORNEY, Martha | 17 MAY 1866 |
| DAVIS, William R. | CARR, Mary Ann | 23 FEB 1869 |
| DAVIS, William T. | SCOTT, Mary A. (blk) | 10 DEC 1861 |
| DAVISON, Henry L. | HUNT, Mary E. | 17 AUG 1867 |
| DAVISON, John | THOMSON, Lucinda | 07 MAY 1862 |
| DAVY, Henry [11] | PIE, Mary | 15 JAN 1861 |
| DAW, William Henry | HARVEY, Agatha Elizth. | 21 NOV 1861 |
| DAWES, Richard M. | JOHNSON, Josephine Arnice Charlotte | 13 JUL 1867 |
| DAWSON, Edward L. | CLARK, Maggie A. | 05 MAY 1866 |
| DAWSON, James | ROMAN, Sarah (blk) | 17 NOV 1858 |
| DAWSON, James | MORGAN, Bridget | 25 JAN 1868 |
| DAWSON, John E. | ROSS, Lucretia (blk) | 08 MAY 1862 |
| DAWSON, John M. | BURBON, Rachel | 18 DEC 1865 |
| DAWSON, John Randolph | VOLLAND, Caroline | 16 MAY 1866 |
| DAWSON, R. Joseph | WISE, Mary L. | 13 MAY 1867 |
| DAWSON, Rezin | CAMPBELL, Chlora Ann | 03 OCT 1868 |
| DAWTRY, John | HARRIS, Ellen (blk) | 22 AUG 1864 |
| DAY, Addison | BUCHANAN, Alice (blk) | 22 OCT 1868 |
| DAY, Alfred | BELL, Maria | 19 JUN 1862 |
| DAY, Andrew | JOHNSON, Julia | 12 FEB 1869 |
| DAY, Benjamin F. | BALDWIN, Flora J. | 21 SEP 1869 |
| DAY, Emanuel | SMITH, Milly (blk) | 21 MAY 1864 |
| DAY, George T. | WHITE, Ann E. | 17 DEC 1861 |
| DAY, Isaac (blk) | EDWARDS, Sarah M. | 04 JUN 1863 |
| DAY, John F. | SULLIVAN, Mary | 26 JUL 1862 |
| DAY, John F. | BROWN, Mattie (blk) | 10 DEC 1869 |
| DAY, Nathan | BEACHAM, Mary (blk) | 14 DEC 1868 |
| DAY, Richard T. | GRAY, Eliza (blk) | 10 OCT 1867 |
| DAY, Samuel E. | MARTIN, Valinda F. | 09 SEP 1858 |
| DAY, Washington | JOHNSON, Anna (blk) | 27 JUL 1868 |
| DAY, William | JONES, Ann (blk) | 03 MAR 1863 |
| DAY, William Henry | DUVALL, Elizabeth Catherine | 13 MAY 1869 |
| DAYSPRING, George | KELLY, Mary E. | 18 MAY 1866 |
| DAYTON, William | BEARDSLEY, Martha E. | 03 NOV 1864 |
| DEABLE, Samuel | ROBERTS, Elizabeth | 24 AUG 1863 |
| DEACON, Harry B. | WILLIAMS, Emma T. | 03 MAR 1869 |
| DEAGAN, Michael | FORD, Catharine | 06 FEB 1864 |
| DEAKINS, Dennis E. | STEELE, Emma E. | 07 APR 1863 |
| DEALE, James W. | BRUMBACK, Barbara Ann | 13 DEC 1858 |
| DeALMA, Henry Chas. | MUSGRIFF, Augusta | 18 AUG 1862 |
| DEAN, Augustus | BEACH, Lucinda | 09 FEB 1864 |
| DEAN, George | REYNOLDS, Ellen | 24 JUL 1863 |

| | | |
|---|---|---|
| DEAN, James R. | BROWN, Betty. | 14 SEP 1863 |
| DEAN, John [6] | LITZ, Frances P. | 17 NOV 1868 |
| DEAN, Joshua [10] | HANCOCK, Martha A. | 08 AUG 1865 |
| DEAN, William | YOUNGER, Mary | 04 APR 1859 |
| deANTALFA, Louis Solyom | GOOD, Sallie Jane | 21 AUG 1866 |
| DEARBORN, Charles [6cl] | SWAINE, Minnie A. | 23 APR 1870 |
| DeATLEY, John H. | BUTLER, Fanny | 28 APR 1869 |
| DeBENST, William | PATTISON, Margaret | 06 SEP 1865 |
| deBODISCO, Constantine [3] | BARTON, Charlotte E. | 08 JUL 1867 |
| DEBOW, Christian | PASTORFIELD, Martha A. | 12 DEC 1865 |
| DEBOY, John Adam | KIEFER, Christiana Katharina | 04 DEC 1866 |
| DeCAMP, H. | EVERITT, Elizabeth | 10 JUL 1863 |
| DECK, William [11] | FLYNN, Margaret | 02 OCT 1862 |
| DECKER, James [2] | STALLINS, Martha | 03 JUL 1866 |
| DECKER, Levi H. | DAKER, Mary Rosannah | 13 AUG 1869 |
| DECKER, Levi W. [2] | DUTROW, Sarah Catherine | 23 JAN 1867 |
| DECKMANN, William | HARTMANN, Louisa | 06 FEB 1865 |
| DeCOONS, Richard | HUSER, Celia | 29 MAR 1870 |
| DECOSTER, Horace Bridge | SNYDER, Margaret Ann | 11 MAY 1864 |
| DeCOVER, Francis M. | STALLINGS, Martha E. | 01 APR 1862 |
| deCROY, Jules F.L. | HARRY, Sarah I. | 30 NOV 1863 |
| DEDRICK, Charles M. | BAKER, Evea Anna | 27 OCT 1863 |
| DEE, John | CULLEN, Elizabeth | 20 APR 1865 |
| DEEBLE, James W. [1e] | MEEM, Ann America | 06 JAN 1866 |
| DEELY, James | MADDEN, Mary | 03 MAR 1863 |
| DEERING, John, Jr. [11] | CHASE, Lizzie H. | 13 AUG 1866 |
| DEERY, Thomas P. | COYLE, Ellen | 28 APR 1865 |
| DEETH, Edward W. | COMPTON, Jeannette D. | 07 SEP 1863 |
| DEETON, Albertus | SIPPLE, Mary A. | 09 JUN 1862 |
| DEEVERS, Silas [12s] | HALL, Rebecca | 08 MAY 1862 |
| DEEVERS, William | LYLES, Biney Smith | 21 DEC 1863 |
| DEEVERS, William | JAMES, Sarah E. | 14 FEB 1870 |
| DEFFER, Frederick | BLAND, Denizar Ann | 16 FEB 1865 |
| deFRONDAT, Charles | MASI, Caroline R. | 05 MAY 1862 |
| DEGGER, Richard | WINGFIELD, Henrietta C. | 09 NOV 1858 |
| DEGGES, John F. | BACON, Louisa H. | 09 JUN 1870 |
| DEGGES, William A. | SWEENY, Rosetta | 09 FEB 1861 |
| DEGGES, William H. | COX, Ann Elizabeth | 14 SEP 1867 |
| DEGGS, John | ADELLA, Rosanna | 05 NOV 1861 |
| DEGGS, Michael | HENRY, Ellen (blk) | 30 NOV 1869 |
| DeGRAFF, John T. | KEYS, Mary A. | 12 NOV 1864 |
| DeGRAFF, Lewis | PHELPS, Mariam | 22 DEC 1862 |
| DeHART, H.M. | KAUFMAN, S.C. | 15 JUN 1866 |
| DEHNE, August | HEIDER, Mary | 14 JAN 1865 |
| DEIBEL, Charles | MILLER, Mary | 18 JAN 1859 |
| DEITZ, Henry Louis | BLÜCHER, Louisa | 06 SEP 1865 |
| DEITZ, Louisa H. | ATCHISON, Elizabeth | 17 OCT 1864 |
| DEKINS, Richard F. | GRIMES, Mary Ellen | 15 MAY 1866 |
| DeKNIGHT, William T. | PETTIBONE, Rosalia H. | 08 APR 1863 |
| DeKRAFFT, John W. | SCRIVENER, Elizabeth Ann | 22 SEP 1859 |
| DeLACEY, Richard | O'BRIEN, Ann | 26 APR 1862 |
| DeLACY, Michael | SULLIVAN, Julia | 09 JAN 1864 |
| DeLAINE, Edward | McGINNIS, Catherine | 30 SEP 1858 |
| DELANE, M. | WELSH, Mary | 09 JAN 1869 |
| DELANEY, Alfred F. | BOWDEN, Mary E. (blk) | 24 NOV 1858 |
| DELANEY, John | SULLIVAN, Joanna | 02 JAN 1863 |

District of Columbia Marriage Licenses, 1858-1870

| | | |
|---|---|---|
| DELANEY, John | STEWART, Ann Elizabeth (blk) | 07 FEB 1870 |
| DELANEY, Richard | JONES, Elizabeth (blk) | 18 APR 1867 |
| DELANEY, Robert | MACKALL, Isabella (blk) | 02 AUG 1866 |
| DELANEY, Shadrack | SOLOMON, Ellen (blk) | 27 JUN 1866 |
| DELANO, Philip A. | HOWARD, Ann O. | 17 NOV 1862 |
| DELANY, Francis | MORFIT, Ann | 03 JAN 1865 |
| DELANY, Henry | TAYLOR, Annie | 20 JUL 1866 |
| DELAP, Cyrus N. | MILLER, Louisa | 28 NOV 1862 |
| DELAP, George R. | DAVIS, Mary S. | 23 JUN 1862 |
| DELAPLANE, James B. | BEALL, Annetta Josephine | 08 FEB 1869 |
| DELAUGHDER, John | FRIDLY, Jane Ann | 23 MAY 1859 |
| DELAVAR, Thomas | MUSE, Lucind (blk) | 21 AUG 1865 |
| deLaVERGNE, C.B. | WORTH, Josephine | 12 JAN 1870 |
| DelaVERGNE, Henry H. | DURKIN, Maria | 13 MAR 1869 |
| DELAY, James | WALLACE, Mary | 05 SEP 1868 |
| DELL, John E. | SHEKELL, Margaret E. | 20 JUL 1868 |
| DELOOHAN, Louis B. | GRANT, Alice H. | 08 JUN 1868 |
| DELPHEY, J.A. | HANNY, A.E. | 08 SEP 1865 |
| DELPHY, John A. | PEYTON, Laura M. | 01 SEP 1859 |
| DELPHY, Orlando R. | FLOWERS, Jane L. | 29 AUG 1859 |
| DeMAIN, John W. | WHITE, Martha E. | 22 AUG 1866 |
| DEMAIN, John W. | WHITE, Martha E. | 19 AUG 1864 |
| DEMAR, Charles H. | HURDLE, Fannie E. | 23 MAY 1860 |
| DEMENT, Hezekiah R. | MANGUM, Martha N. | 10 JUN 1862 |
| DEMENT, James E. [6m] | MORICE, Sarah E. | 14 OCT 1862 |
| DEMENT, John D. | RICHARDS, Fannie R. | 18 JUL 1865 |
| DEMING, Andrew J. | GRAHAM, Catherine L. | 16 FEB 1869 |
| DEMING, Israel | COMPTON, Linda | 25 APR 1865 |
| DeMODENA, Domenico | FONTANA, Charrisia Maria | 26 AUG 1862 |
| DEMOND, Charles | CAMPBELL, Ada B. | 17 NOV 1858 |
| DEMONGCOT, Marcissa | GIRAND, Maria | 24 JUL 1862 |
| DeMORTIE, Mark R. | DOWNING, Cordelia | 14 MAY 1870 |
| DEMPSEY, William H. | FETLER, Margaret | 11 SEP 1865 |
| DENEAL, William Nelson | BARR, Laura Virginia | 17 JUL 1867 |
| DENEL, S.T. | WELLS, Sarah H. | 25 SEP 1867 |
| DENGEL, Philip H. | BRESNAHAN, Catharine | 02 APR 1863 |
| DENHAM, Charles S. | EDWARDS, Susan E. | 24 OCT 1861 |
| DENHAM, John L. [7b] | MARTIN, Sallie A. | 26 JAN 1870 |
| DENHAM, Oliver B. | BARTLETT, Elizabeth J. | 20 SEP 1858 |
| DENISON, Urbane A. | INGERSOLL, Georgie | 28 OCT 1864 |
| DENMAN, Hampton B. | YOUNG, Mary B. | 29 OCT 1866 |
| DENMEAD, George W. | WARDEN, Margaret Elizth. | 09 AUG 1859 |
| DENNIS, James T. [5] | DENNO, Josephine | 13 FEB 1869 |
| DENNISON, Alfred M. | DANSEY, Sarah Ellen | 12 OCT 1867 |
| DENNISON, C.A. | McNAUGHTON, M.E. | 04 FEB 1864 |
| DENNISON, Harrison | GATES, Mary Ellen | 01 MAR 1865 |
| DENNY, Philander | DENNY, Catharine | 26 JUL 1865 |
| DENNY, Washington | HARRIS, Anna (blk) | 13 AUG 1868 |
| DENS, George C. | REDDICK, Maude A. | 07 JUL 1869 |
| DENT, Bruce | JACKSON, Harrison (blk) | 04 OCT 1866 |
| DENT, Charles A. | MORELAND, Alice (blk) | 21 OCT 1865 |
| DENT, F.T.C. | MOXLEY, Mary T. | 05 FEB 1866 |
| DENT, Joseph | DENT, Elizabeth (blk) | 30 JUL 1866 |
| DENT, Josiah | LINTHICUM, Mary Kate | 16 OCT 1860 |
| DENT, Matthew | ROLLET, Mary F. | 17 NOV 1864 |
| DENT, Robert | DOYLE, Hannah (blk) | 17 JUL 1867 |

District of Columbia Marriage Licenses, 1858-1870

| | | |
|---|---|---|
| DENT, Robert [4] | EASTON, Nellie (blk) | 02 DEC 1869 |
| DENT, William | DORSEY, Lucretia (blk) | 18 OCT 1867 |
| DENTINGER, Joseph | HEIMHOFER, Walburger | 01 OCT 1858 |
| DENTON, Henry | GANTT, Jane (blk) | 13 MAR 1865 |
| DENTON, Philip | DIGGS, Mary (blk) | 14 NOV 1865 |
| DENTY, Elisha [12s] | LISLE, Josephine | 16 JUN 1859 |
| DEPONAI, M.J. | RHULE, Mary A. | 26 NOV 1869 |
| DERGERS, Joseph | LEWIS, Harriet | 28 APR 1863 |
| DERMODY, John | McDEVITT, Emma | 14 JAN 1868 |
| DERR, Jeremiah | MORRISON, Anna | 22 OCT 1864 |
| DERRICKSON, William | ERNEST, Alice Virginia | 25 OCT 1866 |
| DERWAN, George | DONAHUE, Joanna | 11 SEP 1864 |
| DESCH, C.S. | HAGAN, L.A. | 31 AUG 1863 |
| DESMOND, Cornelius | VERNON, Madeline | 02 APR 1859 |
| DESMOND, Jerry | DEMSEY, Annie | 26 FEB 1870 |
| DESMOND, Michael P. | CULLIN, Margaret T. | 01 NOV 1860 |
| DESONTER, Joseph | FORD, Catharine E. | 15 AUG 1862 |
| DESOUTER, Joseph | FORD, Catherine E. | 07 APR 1862 |
| DESPAR, James | DESPAR, Fanny (blk) | 20 JAN 1866 |
| DESPREZ, Louis | SELLA, Elizabeth | 06 OCT 1865 |
| DESUE, Joseph | MILLER, Catherine | 31 DEC 1859 |
| DETCH, Otho | WOOD, Anna (blk) | 08 OCT 1868 |
| DETER, Charles | HOWARD, Mary (blk) | 14 JUN 1866 |
| DETRICK, Reuben Baxter | WRIGHT, Susanna Emily | 13 MAR 1866 |
| DETTER, Elias | NASH, Maria (blk) | 04 MAR 1867 |
| DETTOR, Artemus | HALL, Nancy (blk) | 01 SEP 1868 |
| DEUBIL, Adam | BRÖND, Christina | 06 APR 1864 |
| DEVAN, James M. | MANGUM, Mary A. | 21 OCT 1858 |
| DEVANTIER, Jean Charles | HOFFMANN, Eliza | 13 NOV 1861 |
| DeVAUGHAN, John H. | DeVAUGHAN, Emma R. | 10 AUG 1863 |
| DeVAUGHN, David | DEAN, Elizabeth | 06 FEB 1869 |
| DEVAUGHN, William | CARTER, Rose | 01 FEB 1865 |
| DEVAUGHN, Charles J. | COOK, Martha E. | 06 NOV 1862 |
| DEVAUGHN, Levin | GRINDELL, Racheal R. | 14 JUN 1859 |
| DEVAUGHN, Marshall | WHITMORE, Rachel | 08 FEB 1860 |
| DEVEAL, Jackson | PARKER, Caroline | 19 AUG 1865 |
| DEVEAUX, Robert F. | GATES, Mary C. | 06 AUG 1860 |
| DEVELLE, Isaac | GANT, Maria (blk) | 25 MAR 1865 |
| DEVEREUX, John | DONOHO, Catherine | 02 JUN 1862 |
| DEVERS, George | PAYNE, Henrietta | 04 JAN 1862 |
| DEVIER, Hiram K. | PENNYBACHER, Mary V. | 27 APR 1866 |
| DEVINE, Eugene | MURPHEY, Margaret | 12 FEB 1861 |
| DEVINE, James | KANE, Catharine | 14 FEB 1863 |
| DeVINNE, James | SPROUT, Celestia (col'd) | 29 DEC 1863 |
| DEVLIN, Edward | VOGELSBERGER, Amelia | 30 MAY 1864 |
| DEVOTE, Anthony | QUIGLEY, Anna Maria | 10 APR 1860 |
| DEWER, Robert | HUGHES, Ellen | 25 SEP 1867 |
| DEYO, Peter K. | WILLIAMS, Roberta V. | 28 DEC 1861 |
| DIBBLE, Seymour H. [6le] | JENKINS, Mary J. | 03 SEP 1867 |
| DICE, George D. [6m] | EMERSON, Hester A. | 30 DEC 1863 |
| DICK, John | BAYLUM, Mary (blk) | 29 APR 1869 |
| DICK, William | BROWN, Elizabeth (blk) | 12 JUL 1861 |
| DICKAS, Christopher | FRAILER, Catherine | 26 NOV 1858 |
| DICKENS, James | WOLFORD, Elizabeth | 02 FEB 1860 |
| DICKERSON, Charles | CAREY, Martha | 06 OCT 1863 |
| DICKERSON, Edward | BAYLOR, Lydia (blk) | 09 DEC 1868 |

District of Columbia Marriage Licenses, 1858-1870

| | | |
|---|---|---|
| DICKERSON, John | COOK, Harriet Ann | 14 JUL 1862 |
| DICKERSON, John | COOMBS, Elizabeth | 25 SEP 1862 |
| DICKERSON, Randall | LIVERPOOL, Sophia (blk) | 19 AUG 1863 |
| DICKEY, J.T. | FISHER, E.E. | 09 FEB 1860 |
| DICKEY, James T. | FISHER, Elizth. E. | 16 DEC 1859 |
| DICKEY, William T. [1c] | HOUGH, Elmira | 12 AUG 1862 |
| DICKINSON, Daniel | WASHINGTON, Sarah (blk) | 17 MAY 1866 |
| DICKINSON, Hallowell | BUCKLEY, Julia A. | 28 AUG 1862 |
| DICKINSON, John S. | CLARKE, Ellen M. | 26 APR 1864 |
| DICKINSON, Julian E. | MORRIS, Amanda W. | 17 SEP 1868 |
| DICKINSON, Nelson | JOHNSON, Almira (blk) | 11 AUG 1868 |
| DICKINSON, R.H. | SMITH, Mary E. (blk) | 20 AUG 1867 |
| DICKINSON, Samuel | DAVIS, Hassie | 19 MAY 1868 |
| DICKSON, Charles H. | TAYLOR, Jennie | 20 AUG 1867 |
| DICKSON, Frank | DEE, Cado | 28 NOV 1862 |
| DICKSON, John | ORME, Anna | 24 JAN 1859 |
| DICKSON, John R. | ADAMS, Margaret A. | 01 AUG 1865 |
| DIEBITSCH, Herman | ZANDER, Magdalena | 29 APR 1861 |
| DIEBOLD, John A. | HAUSTINE, Sophie | 15 FEB 1864 |
| DIEDZ, William | BACHING, Laura | 04 JUN 1869 |
| DIEHL, John | FREMIN, Mary L. | 11 SEP 1866 |
| DIEMER, Jacob | McENERY, Mary | 02 JUN 1870 |
| DIESCHER, Charles | STEINBRENNER, Eva Mary | 22 SEP 1860 |
| DIETERICK, Henry | HOHLSCHUH, Katherine | 10 OCT 1863 |
| DIETRICK, Bertram | DÖLL, Eliza | 28 FEB 1868 |
| DIETRICK, Charles W.O. | WULFORT, Maria | 04 MAY 1864 |
| DIETZ, Frederick | HOCH, Katherina Jacobina | 21 DEC 1861 |
| DIFFENBACH, John | FUNK, Annie | 15 FEB 1869 |
| DIGENY, Thomas | WELSH, Margaret | 27 SEP 1860 |
| DIGGES, Cornelius | MOORE, Eveline | 22 APR 1868 |
| DIGGIN, Morris | SHEA, Julia | 08 NOV 1862 |
| DIGGINS, Bartholomew [7b] | WALLACE, Mary H. | 21 FEB 1870 |
| DIGGINS, Thomas | BOYLE, Julia | 13 MAY 1865 |
| DIGGLE, Alfred | JACOBS, Caroline E. | 12 OCT 1861 |
| DIGGLE, Samuel | MANGUM, Mary Ann | 03 MAR 1864 |
| DIGGS, Alexander | COPELAND, Maggie (blk) | 28 DEC 1869 |
| DIGGS, Charles | MARTIN, Lucinda (blk) | 18 JUL 1865 |
| DIGGS, Dennis | CONTEE, Catherine (blk) | 31 OCT 1864 |
| DIGGS, Ewell | COLBERT, Ophelia (blk) | 03 OCT 1867 |
| DIGGS, Franklin M. | CARR, Amanda Jane (blk) | 04 SEP 1867 |
| DIGGS, Franklin Michael | JOHNSON, Priscilla Ann (blk) | 23 SEP 1863 |
| DIGGS, George W. | HOLLAND, Harriet Ann (blk) | 28 JUN 1866 |
| DIGGS, George W. | PROCTOR, Sarah Catherine (blk) | 18 NOV 1868 |
| DIGGS, Henry | MARTIN, Mary C. (blk) | 29 MAY 1862 |
| DIGGS, Herbert | TOWNSEND, Sophia (blk) | 14 NOV 1867 |
| DIGGS, Horace | WILLIAMS, Martha (blk) | 24 OCT 1867 |
| DIGGS, Isaac | WHITON, Sarah (blk) | 10 APR 1867 |
| DIGGS, John Henry | MEEKINS, Rachel Ann (blk) | 11 AUG 1868 |
| DIGGS, John P. [11] * | ANDERSON, Anna (blk) | 17 AUG 1868 |
| DIGGS, John Wesley | JACKSON, Ann (blk) | 06 NOV 1862 |
| DIGGS, Philip | COX, Lizzie (blk) | 12 MAR 1867 |
| DIGGS, William | LOWNDES, Nancy (blk) | 10 DEC 1863 |
| DIGNAN, Dennis | COHEN, Mary | 21 APR 1863 |
| DILL, Frederick | SPRINGER, Mary | 27 MAR 1869 |
| DILLARD, Noah | LOMAX, Martha | 15 MAY 1863 |
| DILLARD, Robert | WRIGHT, Josephine | 28 FEB 1867 |

| | | |
|---|---|---|
| DILLER, J.P. | BARBOUR, Isabella | 27 MAR 1865 |
| DILLEY, Monroe [6h] | MARKS, Josie R. | 02 JUN 1868 |
| DILLEY, Thomas L. | YOUNG, Carrie H. | 16 FEB 1867 |
| DILLON, Andrew | MAHONEY, Bridget | 28 SEP 1867 |
| DILLON, Edward | GALLAGHER, Johanna | 26 MAY 1870 |
| DILLON, Robert | SLATER, Mary | 26 OCT 1866 |
| DILLON, William | MONROE, Jane | 19 SEP 1868 |
| DIMMICK, Joseph F. | KELLY, Mary A.V. | 31 OCT 1859 |
| DINES, Philip | HENSON, Mary Ann (blk) | 11 OCT 1862 |
| DININN, John | HOLLAND, Johanna | 27 MAY 1867 |
| DINOELZIA, Joh. Bap. | CASALEGE, Maria Julia | 15 DEC 1866 |
| DIRKOPH, Franz | REITER, Louise | 06 JUL 1869 |
| DISHMAN, Benjamin | JACKSON, Lucy | 17 JUL 1865 |
| DISNEY, Joseph A. | GOODRICKS, Laura | 30 MAR 1869 |
| DISNEY, William H. [9e] | McREA, Sarah V. | 08 OCT 1860 |
| DISPREY, James Henry | TALLEY, Ann Eliza | 15 JAN 1869 |
| DITCHER, Henry | JOHNSON, Myra (blk) | 07 OCT 1863 |
| DITSCH, Matthew | McCARDDEN, Maggie F. | 15 JUN 1863 |
| DITTMAN, Charles W. [12s] | LAMB, Martha | 04 FEB 1863 |
| DITTON, Jacob | SULLIVAN, Mary | 22 JAN 1862 |
| DIVINE, William | CUNNINGHAM, Mary | 29 OCT 1864 |
| DIX, John Thomas | PENN, Amelia (blk) | 15 DEC 1864 |
| DIXON, Aaron | GOINGS, Malinda (blk) | 23 APR 1863 |
| DIXON, Alfred | CHASE, Mary | 31 JAN 1867 |
| DIXON, Carter | WILLIAMS, Rachel (blk) | 11 NOV 1869 |
| DIXON, Charles | LYLES, Elizabeth (blk) | 09 MAY 1863 |
| DIXON, Charles | TAYLOR, Mary (blk) | 26 DEC 1863 |
| DIXON, D.G. | CARVER, Alice | 24 OCT 1868 |
| DIXON, Dennis | SIMS, Matilda (blk) | 18 JAN 1866 |
| DIXON, Edward | BUTLER, Cassy (blk) | 07 AUG 1863 |
| DIXON, Edward | FREEMAN, Rebecca (blk) | 08 OCT 1866 |
| DIXON, Frank | BELFOUR, Caroline (col'd) | 31 DEC 1863 |
| DIXON, George | BOWEN, Henrietta (blk) | 25 JUN 1864 |
| DIXON, George | MURPHY, Mary (blk) | 23 MAR 1869 |
| DIXON, George L. | ARMSTEAD, Mary (blk) | 17 NOV 1865 |
| DIXON, Gustavus | PAYNE, Ada | 04 SEP 1866 |
| DIXON, Gustavus R. [2] | RHODES, Mary H. | 21 SEP 1864 |
| DIXON, James | BAKER, Nellie (blk) | 30 APR 1864 |
| DIXON, James | MAGRUDER, Julia (blk) | 27 JUN 1867 |
| DIXON, John | COFFEE, Lizzie | 08 NOV 1864 |
| DIXON, John | GIBSON, Eliza (blk) | 04 SEP 1867 |
| DIXON, Laban B. | SMITH, Ella B. | 08 SEP 1862 |
| DIXON, Marion G. | RAWLINGS, Malvina | 25 JAN 1870 |
| DIXON, Moses | IGNORANT, Mary (blk) | 31 OCT 1863 |
| DIXON, Robert | BAYNERD, Lydea | 05 JUN 1862 |
| DIXON, S. Henry | DIXON, Ann [50 yrs. together] (blk) | 11 JUN 1866 |
| DIXON, Walter | RAWLINGS, Malina | 25 JAN 1870 |
| DIXON, Washington | SHARP, Sophia (blk) | 01 MAY 1869 |
| DIXON, William | TAYLOR, Nellie (blk) | 19 OCT 1864 |
| DIXON, William Edward | NUTWELL, Sophia Fannie | 15 MAY 1865 |
| DIXON, William T. | FRASHER, Angella C. (blk) | 29 OCT 1867 |
| DIXON, Wm. T. | KATTENER, Rachel | 23 FEB 1860 |
| DIZE, William H.B. | MARSHALL, Mary V. (blk) | 20 MAY 1865 |
| DLOURA, James A. | NAMRELLE, Blanche | 16 OCT 1869 |
| DOBBIN, Joseph R. | JENKINS, Sarah M. | 23 DEC 1862 |
| DOBBINS, Richard J. | EMMERT, Wilhelmina | 26 FEB 1861 |

# District of Columbia Marriage Licenses, 1858-1870

| | | |
|---|---|---|
| DOBBYN, James R. | STILLINGS, [blank] | 14 SEP 1858 |
| DOBBYNS, Thomas | HOST, Ann Madora | 24 AUG 1860 |
| DOBIE, Thomas W. | GOVER, Eliza A. | 01 OCT 1860 |
| DOCHRER, August | VOEHL, Elise | 04 MAY 1870 |
| DODD, James A. | WRIGHT, Louisa, Mrs. | 18 JUL 1863 |
| DODD, James A. | WRIGHT, Maria Louisa | 05 JUL 1864 |
| DODGE, Don A. | MOORE, Alabama J. | 15 JAN 1867 |
| DODGE, Frederick | THOMPSON, Emily | 06 FEB 1861 |
| DODGE, James | BLAKENEY, Sarah E. | 03 DEC 1863 |
| DODGE, Joseph [Spencer] [6l] | MARTIN, Mary J. | 26 FEB 1862 |
| DODGE, Orestes B. [7a] | GILMORE, Nellie J. | 31 JAN 1868 |
| DODGE, Richard E. | NOURSE, Annie W. | 02 JUL 1866 |
| DODGE, William | PEYTON, Mary (blk) | 12 DEC 1865 |
| DODGE, William Alexander | THOMAS, Sarah Elizabeth | 15 MAR 1869 |
| DODGE, William C. | SCRIVENER, Elizabeth A. | 05 MAR 1861 |
| DODSON, Albert | WALKER, Martha (blk) | 21 MAY 1869 |
| DODSON, David | JOHNSON, Emeline (blk) | 13 NOV 1866 |
| DODSON, Edward | DODSON, Julia | 16 SEP 1869 |
| DODSON, Elias B. | BROOKE, Mary A. | 06 JUL 1864 |
| DODSON, George | WATSON, Sarah (blk) | 02 AUG 1864 |
| DODSON, Henry | GASKIN, Lucinda (blk) | 27 AUG 1869 |
| DODSON, Jacob | WASHINGTON, Catherine (blk) | 08 OCT 1861 |
| DODSON, James | DODSON, Harriet Ann (blk) | 23 OCT 1865 |
| DODSON, John W. | WOODRIDGE, Sarah Jane (blk) | 03 APR 1863 |
| DODSON, Thomas | SHELTER, Mildred (blk) | 17 FEB 1859 |
| DOETERLEIN, August | FRANK, Louisa | 06 OCT 1864 |
| DOGAN, Henry | TAYLOR, Lucinda (blk) | 17 SEP 1866 |
| DOLAN, John | KERR, Sarah Ann | 02 SEP 1858 |
| DOLAN, John | READY, Margaret | 21 FEB 1862 |
| DOLAN, Patrick | SHENNESSY, Margaret | 06 MAY 1865 |
| DOLAN, Thomas F. | O'BRIEN, Rebecca | 11 SEP 1866 |
| DOLAND, James | LAFFERTY, Alice | 02 JAN 1867 |
| DOLBY, James | ZEIR, Mary Catherine | 07 SEP 1868 |
| DOLIN, Isaac | LUCAS, Francis (blk) | 11 AUG 1866 |
| DOLLOUGHAN, Henry | McVARRY, Bridget | 01 NOV 1866 |
| DOLPHUS, Robert | HILL, Elizabeth (blk) | 21 APR 1870 |
| DOLSEN, William | MYERS, Mary E. | 13 JUN 1865 |
| DOLSEN, William | MYERS, Mary | 03 FEB 1866 |
| DOMINIKO, Vendeline | COSTELLO, Louisa Brenta | 04 NOV 1865 |
| DOMINIS, Samuel | LEWIS, Mary (blk) | 26 JAN 1870 |
| DONAGAN, Henry V. | McGILL, Julia | 06 JUL 1865 |
| DONAHUE, John | KELLY, Mary | 23 DEC 1867 |
| DONALDSON, Benjamin S. | WEBSTER, Lucy F. | 17 MAY 1859 |
| DONALDSON, Charles | STATEN, Sarah | 01 MAY 1863 |
| DONALDSON, Charles W. | MARTIN, Mary E. | 16 DEC 1868 |
| DONALDSON, Franklin A. | SUMMERS, Martha E. | 25 OCT 1858 |
| DONALDSON, George S. | BARNES, Elizabeth | 07 SEP 1867 |
| DONALDSON, George W. | WHITEMORE, Mary E. | 31 JUL 1869 |
| DONALDSON, James | KNOX, Elizabeth | 14 AUG 1866 |
| DONALDSON, James N. | WOODS, Annie | 06 JUL 1869 |
| DONALDSON, John W. | PATTERSON, Mary Jane | 30 MAY 1863 |
| DONALDSON, Joseph Thomas | BOWMAN, Louisa | 23 MAR 1866 |
| DONALDSON, Mack L. | SIMMS, Sarah (blk) | 10 AUG 1864 |
| DONALDSON, Montgomery | ROBBINS, Sarah | 05 NOV 1862 |
| DONALDSON, Thomas G. | BRANNER, Frances C. | 27 DEC 1866 |
| DONALDSON, William A. | JENKINS, Mary F. | 26 MAR 1859 |

District of Columbia Marriage Licenses, 1858-1870

| | | |
|---|---|---|
| DONATH, Augustus | LEWIS, Emily | 19 NOV 1866 |
| DONEGAN, Patrick H. | CRONIN, Mary | 29 JAN 1862 |
| DONEHUE, Thomas H. | RYAN, Mary T. | 01 FEB 1865 |
| DONELAN, Patrick H. | MYERS, Henrietta | 29 APR 1862 |
| DONELLON, James | FAY, Mary | 25 SEP 1861 |
| DONIEGAN, Cornelius | McDONALD, Rosanna | 14 APR 1864 |
| DONN, Alphonso Thomas | RAINEY, Charlotte | 04 DEC 1858 |
| DONN, Edward W. [9e] | GARDNER, Laura J. | 02 JUN 1860 |
| DONN, John C.T. | DOWDENS, Virginia | 08 OCT 1866 |
| DONN, Oliver A. | MAHORNEY, Sussie V. | 07 MAY 1863 |
| DONN, Thomas C. [11] | WEBB, Mary Ann | 17 NOV 1858 |
| DONNALLY, Thomas | FATTY, Mary | 17 JUN 1864 |
| DONNELLY, Arthur | CURTIS, Jane | 15 APR 1863 |
| DONNELLY, James | DUDLEY, Catharine | 04 NOV 1862 |
| DONNELLY, John | FITZGERALD, Johanna | 13 APR 1861 |
| DONNELLY, John | BRESNAHAN, Joanna | 28 SEP 1867 |
| DONNELLY, M. Aloysius [7b] | THOMPSON, Isabella | 14 MAR 1870 |
| DONNELLY, Peter | MURPHEY, Margaret | 16 NOV 1861 |
| DONNELLY, Peter | MURPHY, Anna | 15 MAY 1862 |
| DONNELLY, Philip | DONOHUE, Johannah | 03 APR 1869 |
| DONNELLY, Richard | CONNELLY, Ann | 01 JAN 1859 |
| DONOGHUE, Matthias | MARTIN, Mary | 29 SEP 1864 |
| DONOGHUE, Michael | CONNOLLY, Ann | 02 JAN 1863 |
| DONOGHUE, Patrick | REIDY, Johanna | 09 SEP 1868 |
| DONOGHUE, Peter | CLANSY, Margaret | 08 JAN 1863 |
| DONOGHUE, Timothy | CLAIRDY, Julia | 18 OCT 1864 |
| DONOGHUE, Timothy | NOLAN, Anna | 01 JUN 1869 |
| DONOHO, Patrick | CHRYSTAL, Ellen | 28 MAY 1864 |
| DONOHO, Redmond | THORNTON, Bridget | 22 OCT 1867 |
| DONOHO, Thomas R. | LANE, Bridget | 01 JUN 1868 |
| DONOHO, Thomas [4] | GARVEY, Jane | 08 FEB 1869 |
| DONOHO, Timothy | DORLIN, Catharine | 24 OCT 1861 |
| DONOHO, William | HURNEY, Mary | 07 SEP 1860 |
| DONOHOE, Francis | WISELY, Bridget | 10 FEB 1870 |
| DONOHOE, John | FOY, Margaret | 20 DEC 1858 |
| DONOHOE, Peter | CONNOLY, Mary | 21 JUN 1866 |
| DONOHOE, Thomas | BROWN, Johanna | 13 JUN 1864 |
| DONOHOE, Timothy | MORRISON, Ellen | 01 AUG 1864 |
| DONOHOE, Timothy | BAGHAN, Kate | 08 JUN 1867 |
| DONOHOO, Flurr | DRISCOL, Ellen | 08 MAR 1859 |
| DONOHUE, John | HOYNE, Mary | 28 MAR 1864 |
| DONOHUE, Martin | QUINN, Catherine | 31 JUL 1862 |
| DONOHUGH, Redman | MELLONEY, Margaret | 06 FEB 1860 |
| DONOVAN, David | SHIELDS, Margaret | 21 JAN 1862 |
| DONOVAN, Denis | BYRNE, Agnes | 31 MAY 1862 |
| DONOVAN, Dennis | LEE, Bridget | 17 OCT 1860 |
| DONOVAN, Dennis B.T. | GUTRIDGE, Sarah A. | 19 NOV 1862 |
| DONOVAN, Jere: | KENDRICON, Bridget K. | 20 SEP 1865 |
| DONOVAN, John | LYNCH, Mary | 19 NOV 1859 |
| DONOVAN, Michael | CREIGH, Mary | 16 FEB 1863 |
| DONOVAN, Michael | LEVIN, Catherine | 23 JUL 1863 |
| DOODY, Cornelius | O'CONNELL, Julia | 19 JAN 1864 |
| DOODY, John | CONNELL, Eliza | 27 DEC 1866 |
| DOODY, John | McCARTHY, Susan | 16 APR 1867 |
| DOOLEY, David C. | McCHESNUTT, Mary E. | 10 OCT 1860 |
| DOOLEY, Thomas | CONWAY, Catharine | 08 DEC 1859 |

| | | |
|---|---|---|
| DOOLING, Dennis | TRAMMELL, Sarah | 28 NOV 1865 |
| DORAN, James [10] * | HAYMORE, Ann | 16 JUL 1863 |
| DORAN, John | JONES, Rebecca | 03 FEB 1864 |
| DORAN, John | HEATH, Mary Ann | 03 OCT 1864 |
| DORAN, John | KANE, Ellen | 25 NOV 1864 |
| DOREN, John | BLANCHFIELD, Annie E. | 13 SEP 1862 |
| DORGERS, Charles | LOCHTERMAN, Kate | 14 OCT 1865 |
| DORMAN, A. | BUSHBY, A.V. | 03 AUG 1863 |
| DORN, Matthew | SULLIVAN, Mary | 12 NOV 1864 |
| DORNIN, Peter | WARD, Maria | 03 NOV 1858 |
| DORNSEIF, Louis | BRITNER, Louisa | 06 JUL 1864 |
| DORR, Andrew | HESSLER, Eva | 19 SEP 1862 |
| DÖRR, Conrad | SCHMIDT, Katherine | 17 OCT 1863 |
| DORRES, William C. | YOUNG, Amanda G. | 23 MAR 1868 |
| DORSETT, Charles T. | DeMAINE, Arabella | 26 AUG 1863 |
| DORSEY, Alexander [13g] | CHRISTMAS, Matilda [blk] | 08 AUG 1864 |
| DORSEY, Amos Abram | MATHEWS, Emily (blk) | 21 NOV 1867 |
| DORSEY, Charles | CLARK, Mary (blk) | 14 NOV 1867 |
| DORSEY, Charles H. | TURNER, Emily (blk) | 25 JAN 1865 |
| DORSEY, Dennis | WHITE, Fanny F. (blk) | 01 NOV 1866 |
| DORSEY, Edward | MILES, Georgiana (blk) | 04 APR 1867 |
| DORSEY, Eugene | WILLIAMS, Mary A. (blk) | 01 FEB 1864 |
| DORSEY, Francis | BROWN, Sarah (blk) | 05 JUL 1867 |
| DORSEY, Frank | JACKSON, Emma (blk) | 05 APR 1864 |
| DORSEY, George | BELT, Martha | 04 NOV 1862 |
| DORSEY, Hamilton | COLE, Elizabeth (blk) | 14 MAY 1862 |
| DORSEY, Harvey W. [11] | JAMES, Helen | 05 NOV 1868 |
| DORSEY, Henry | CHASE, Julia (blk) | 19 FEB 1867 |
| DORSEY, Henry | SHORTER, Louisa (blk) | 28 SEP 1865 |
| DORSEY, Henry | DORSEY, Malvina (blk) | 27 SEP 1866 |
| DORSEY, I.G. | MORELAND, Jane | 17 JAN 1862 |
| DORSEY, James | NEWTON, Charity (blk) | 29 AUG 1868 |
| DORSEY, James | MERRITT, Mary Frances (blk) | 21 FEB 1870 |
| DORSEY, John | HERBERT, Henrietta | 16 DEC 1864 |
| DORSEY, John | McELROY, Jane | 15 MAY 1865 |
| DORSEY, John | WASHINGTON, Emma (blk) | 27 NOV 1867 |
| DORSEY, John | COLE, Mary (blk) | 05 OCT 1869 |
| DORSEY, Josiah N. | EWELL, Georgiana | 13 DEC 1866 |
| DORSEY, L., Dr. | LINDSLEY, Ada | 28 AUG 1865 |
| DORSEY, Merritt | WHITMAN, Maria | 03 MAR 1869 |
| DORSEY, Nathan | GREEN, Jeanie (blk) | 06 MAR 1862 |
| DORSEY, Osborne | GREEN, Rachel (blk) | 25 AUG 1864 |
| DORSEY, Patrick | O'BRIEN, Sarah | 04 AUG 1862 |
| DORSEY, Samuel | SCOTT, Marion (blk) | 21 AUG 1865 |
| DORSEY, Samuel | BLACKWELL, Mary (blk) | 02 JAN 1867 |
| DORSEY, Samuel | LUCAS, Marian (blk) | 17 NOV 1869 |
| DORSEY, Stephen | FIELDS, Sarah (blk) | 29 JUN 1867 |
| DORSEY, Tighlman | EDWARDS, Mary Jane | 20 FEB 1866 |
| DORSEY, William | GROSS, Susan (blk) | 02 FEB 1865 |
| DORSEY, William B. [12s] | STONE, Margaret | 14 DEC 1859 |
| DORSEY, Wm. H. | BUCHANAN, Sarah (blk) | 24 DEC 1867 |
| DORSEY, Wm. H. | BURLEY, Barbara E. (blk) | 07 FEB 1870 |
| DORSEY, Wm. H.H. | PUMPHREY, Nettie | 10 FEB 1863 |
| DORSEY, Worthington | GODEY, Mary J. | 06 JAN 1859 |
| DORSON, John A. | WESTERN, Adelaid V. | 24 NOV 1868 |
| DOTSON, Emanuel | JORDON, Martha | 11 AUG 1864 |

| | | |
|---|---|---|
| DOUD, Patrick | SULLIVAN, Johanna | 06 JAN 1866 |
| DOUGHERTY, Cormick | DONOHOE, Catharine | 26 AUG 1865 |
| DOUGHERTY, Edward | CAESAR, Catherine | 08 AUG 1863 |
| DOUGHERTY, Edward H. | COOPER, Emily | 10 DEC 1867 |
| DOUGHERTY, George S. | SPEAKS, Louisa | 15 JUL 1869 |
| DOUGHERTY, James [12s] | DONNELLY, Ann | 06 FEB 1862 |
| DOUGHERTY, John | GILHELY, Mary | 16 MAY 1863 |
| DOUGHERTY, John | SHERLOCK, Elizabeth J. | 10 OCT 1864 |
| DOUGHERTY, Joseph | BLAINEY, Bridget | 16 JUL 1861 |
| DOUGHERTY, Patrick | HENNESSY, Bridget | 06 SEP 1862 |
| DOUGHERTY, Patrick | HELEHAN, Catharine | 16 MAR 1864 |
| DOUGHERTY, William | O'BRIEN, Anna E. | 22 NOV 1858 |
| DOUGHERTY, William | LEAHY, Julia | 05 JAN 1870 |
| DOUGHERTY, William E. | HICKEY, Carrie J. | 03 JUN 1863 |
| DOUGLAS, J.C. | FRANKLIN, M.E. | 23 JUL 1863 |
| DOUGLAS, James S. | BOWERSOF, Sarah Jane | 10 MAR 1862 |
| DOUGLAS, Martin | MITCHELL, Ellen | 29 MAR 1865 |
| DOUGLAS, Angus | RUTHERFORD, Mary | 24 JUN 1864 |
| DOUGLASS, Charles B. | TAYLOR, Mary | 04 JAN 1865 |
| DOUGLASS, Frank | MARSHALL, Fanny | 13 DEC 1860 |
| DOUGLASS, George W. | VanALLEN, Mary E. | 25 NOV 1863 |
| DOUGLASS, Henry | CHISM, Annie Elizabeth | 06 JUN 1864 |
| DOUGLASS, Henry | FORD, Hariet (blk) | 01 DEC 1868 |
| DOUGLASS, Richard | LEE, Mary Ellen (blk) | 12 OCT 1863 |
| DOUGLASS, William | FAIRFAX, Eliza (blk) | 28 FEB 1861 |
| DOUGLASS, William | HART, Mary M. | 04 AUG 1868 |
| DOUGLASS, William | McNICHELS, Mary | 09 DEC 1868 |
| DOVE, George W. | BIXLOW, Annie | 28 JUL 1863 |
| DOVE, George W. | LOWERY, Mary A. | 18 OCT 1866 |
| DOVE, Gilson J. | ADAMS, Caroline A. | 18 OCT 1858 |
| DOVE, J.S. | WITHEE, Leah | 18 SEP 1866 |
| DOVE, James | MACK, Kate | 14 APR 1866 |
| DOVE, Joseph S. | GODFREY, Lucy Ann | 23 JAN 1864 |
| DOVE, Levi | DOVE, Rebecca | 25 MAR 1863 |
| DOVE, William F. [6r] | FRYE, Susana M. | 08 FEB 1860 |
| DOVE, Wm. A. | KEMP, Charlotte R. | 08 AUG 1859 |
| DOVER, Frank | CARTER, Catherine (blk) | 03 MAR 1868 |
| DOVER, James | CATON, Julia | 17 FEB 1865 |
| DOVER, James | BURRELL, Mary Frances (blk) | 18 MAR 1868 |
| DOWBIGGIN, Thos. | GETSENDEINER, Mary E. | 13 DEC 1862 |
| DOWD, John | CRONIN, Johanna | 25 JUL 1863 |
| DOWD, Murat | MURT, Mary | 01 SEP 1865 |
| DOWDEN, Benjamin D. | BRIGHT, Margaret E. | 04 SEP 1867 |
| DOWDEN, Charles L. | FRISE, Catharine F. | 13 JAN 1866 |
| DOWELL, Charles | GRANT, Elizabeth | 01 JAN 1870 |
| DOWLING, Isaac | WHITE, Ellen | 19 AUG 1864 |
| DOWLING, John | BURK, Mary Frances | 19 JUN 1865 |
| DOWLING, Mead | CHEW, Ellen | 18 MAY 1869 |
| DOWNES, Albert | BUTLER, Eliza | 07 NOV 1868 |
| DOWNES, David | O'CONNOR, Margaret | 10 NOV 1860 |
| DOWNES, Joseph H. | WATERS, Mary A. | 12 MAY 1868 |
| DOWNES, Timothy | BYRN, Ellen | 23 APR 1859 |
| DOWNES, William | PERRY, Virginia | 08 MAY 1861 |
| DOWNEY, Horace | DRIVER, Alice Ann | 27 AUG 1868 |
| DOWNEY, Hugh | MOCKLAIR, Mary | 04 FEB 1868 |
| DOWNEY, Jeremiah | MASON, Ellen | 26 JAN 1866 |

District of Columbia Marriage Licenses, 1858-1870

| | | |
|---|---|---|
| DOWNEY, John | DOWNEY, Mary | 01 JAN 1863 |
| DOWNEY, Michael | HAYES, Julia | 13 MAY 1859 |
| DOWNEY, Patrick | MEANY, Johanna | 26 OCT 1863 |
| DOWNEY, Patrick | WALSH, Honora | 16 MAR 1864 |
| DOWNEY, Peter | GRIFFITH, Sarah E. | 30 NOV 1859 |
| DOWNEY, Thomas | BALZELL, Mary | 03 NOV 1858 |
| DOWNEY, William F. | McGRATH, Hanorah | 18 APR 1865 |
| DOWNIE, Lewis G. | DOBSON, Laura | 03 JUN 1865 |
| DOWNIE, Thomas J. | O'DONNELL, Julia A. | 06 AUG 1862 |
| DOWNING, Charles | LANGDON, Mary A. | 13 JUN 1865 |
| DOWNING, Edwin | CARTER, Mary A. | 07 MAY 1866 |
| DOWNING, George W. [6le] | WILLIAMS, Hannah | 16 MAY 1867 |
| DOWNING, George W. | WILLIAMS, Hannah | 07 MAR 1867 |
| DOWNING, John | COHNHOFF, Pauline | 08 JAN 1863 |
| DOWNING, Peter W. | BROWN, Bettie L. (blk) | 25 OCT 1864 |
| DOWNS, Alphonzo | KELLY, Rosa | 01 SEP 1866 |
| DOWNS, James H. | HARTNETT, Maggie | 10 AUG 1866 |
| DOWNS, John | GREEN, Clementine | 03 NOV 1859 |
| DOWNS, William | DIGGINS, Ann | 12 SEP 1863 |
| DOYER, John | CONNOR, Hanora | 14 FEB 1863 |
| DOYLE, David | JACKSON, Rachel | 10 SEP 1868 |
| DOYLE, Francis M. | BRANSELL, Elenore | 16 OCT 1858 |
| DOYLE, Henry L. | KELEHER, Bridget | 07 JUL 1865 |
| DOYLE, James | GOGHAN, Maria | 14 JUL 1864 |
| DOYLE, James [6m] | BRANZERR, Charlott | 13 AUG 1863 |
| DOYLE, John | REILLY, Mary | 24 AUG 1865 |
| DOYLE, John | HEDGES, Lucy | 04 SEP 1865 |
| DOYLE, Michael | HORAN, Catherine | 12 SEP 1863 |
| DOYLE, Michael | KEENAN, Mary | 02 JAN 1865 |
| DOYLE, Patrick | MURPHEY, Margaret | 26 SEP 1863 |
| DOYLE, Patrick | CASS, Elizabeth | 14 FEB 1868 |
| DOYLE, Robert E., Jr. | JOHNSON, Rebecca (blk) | 14 NOV 1868 |
| DRANE, James W. | LOWE, Emily J. | 31 OCT 1866 |
| DRANE, William | BRERETON, Eliza | 13 SEP 1859 |
| DRANEY, Felix M. | WHEELER, Saloam H. | 15 MAR 1865 |
| DRAPER, Charles S. | CORAM, Josephine | 12 OCT 1865 |
| DRAPER, Lemuel J. | MUDD, Mary E. | 17 OCT 1860 |
| DRAPER, Lemuel J. | OWEN, Mary B. | 01 FEB 1870 |
| DRAPER, Louis | COCHRAN, Ann | 30 AUG 1862 |
| DRAYTON, Charles | DETTER, Mary Ann | 11 OCT 1865 |
| DREDDEN, Gabriel | DREDDEN, Mollie (blk) | 11 DEC 1867 |
| DREDGE, James A. | QUICK, Susan | 16 APR 1868 |
| DREURY, William H. [6le] | GARTEN, Margaret J. | 18 NOV 1865 |
| DREW, William Eldred | PARKER, Harriet (blk) | 04 FEB 1864 |
| DREW, William Franklin | WALLIS, Maria Lucinda (blk) | 15 OCT 1867 |
| DREXLER, Constantine | UHLER, Mary | 14 NOV 1867 |
| DREYFUSS, Marquis | NEWMEYER, Barbet | 08 NOV 1864 |
| DRINGENBERG, John A. Lohmeyer V. | PASELA, Catharina | 08 MAY 1862 |
| DRINKHOUSE, E.J. | BARNES, Angelina | 21 APR 1869 |
| DRISCOLL, Dennis | SULLIVAN, Ellen | 12 OCT 1858 |
| DRISCOLL, Eugene | SULLIVAN, Joanna | 13 MAY 1865 |
| DRISCOLL, James | CLANSY, Bridget | 31 DEC 1862 |
| DRISCOLL, Jeremiah | CAREY, Julia | 26 APR 1865 |
| DRISCOLL, John | McCALLAN, Hanora | 08 FEB 1862 |
| DRISCOLL, Michael | DALEY, Elizabeth | 01 SEP 1862 |
| DRISH, Edwin [9n] | POWELL, Sarah Indiana | 20 DEC 1858 |

District of Columbia Marriage Licenses, 1858-1870

| | | |
|---|---|---|
| DRISKEL, Edward | QUIGLEY, Rose | 18 JUL 1864 |
| DRIVER, George | WEST, Fanny (blk) | 14 APR 1868 |
| DRIVER, Nelson C. | BEALL, Margaret A. | 05 OCT 1858 |
| DROOP, Edward | SCHMIDT, Sophia | 14 OCT 1867 |
| DROZE, Deiderick | MENSING, Christine | 24 DEC 1864 |
| DRUMMOND, John S. | HILL, Mary | 31 DEC 1867 |
| DRUMON, John | WALDRON, Annie | 04 OCT 1869 |
| DRURY, C. Walter | POOR, Teresa Virginia | 11 OCT 1859 |
| DRURY, Joseph | ARIXERSON, Annie E. | 24 NOV 1866 |
| DRURY, Robert A. | CRANNEGE, Mary Jane | 19 FEB 1866 |
| DRURY, William C. | STONE, Mary Ann | 23 MAY 1867 |
| DRURY, William S. | CHAPMAN, Margaret | 03 MAR 1860 |
| DRURY, William S. | CONNELL, Katharine | 26 AUG 1861 |
| DUBACEE, Joseph | PERRY, Kate A. | 23 JAN 1865 |
| DUBANT, Alexander | DONALDSON, Phoebe | 16 MAR 1861 |
| DUBANT, George G. | HENLEY, Louisa | 24 DEC 1864 |
| DUBANT, John | MERKINS, Mary A. | 05 JUN 1867 |
| DUBOIS, Richard C. | RICHARDSON, Ella | 07 APR 1869 |
| DUBOIS, William [6s] | TALBERT, Mary Ellen | 23 AUG 1864 |
| DUCKER, Diederich C. | BEHR, Metha Gesina | 14 JUN 1870 |
| DUCKET, Nathaniel | ANDERSON, Amelia | 16 MAY 1863 |
| DUCKET, Vincent | TAYLOR, Mary Elizabeth (blk) | 23 FEB 1866 |
| DUCKETT, Alexander | BURR, Emily (blk) | 10 OCT 1867 |
| DUCKETT, Daniel | HENSON, Lucinda (blk) | 08 NOV 1867 |
| DUCKETT, Francis | BELL, Polly (blk) | 18 JAN 1870 |
| DUCKETT, Nelson | MASON, Mary | 09 JAN 1869 |
| DUCKETT, W.G. | TABER, Carrie M. | 17 SEP 1866 |
| DUCKETT, William A. | THOMAS, Mary (blk) | 18 DEC 1862 |
| DUDLEY, Henderson | WARE, Isabella (blk) | 24 DEC 1864 |
| DUDLEY, Henry | STEWART, Sallie | 12 JUN 1860 |
| DUDLEY, John | BRANSON, Margaret (blk) | 25 JUL 1866 |
| DUDLEY, Joseph | EDELIN, Meheda Ann | 14 DEC 1863 |
| DUDLEY, Stephen A. | HOLBROOK, Anna E. | 26 JUN 1866 |
| DUDLEY, William | DOWNEY, Mary | 27 JAN 1864 |
| DUDMAN, Thomas | YOUNG, Allarey Ellen | 23 SEP 1863 |
| DUDY, William | MANNING, Mary | 25 AUG 1860 |
| DUERING, John S. | HAMILTON, Alice C. | 14 DEC 1867 |
| DUFFEY, John H. [12s] | SCHAFER, Susannah | 16 JUN 1859 |
| DUFFEY, Patrick | BERNARD, Jane | 21 JUL 1862 |
| DUFFEY, Peter J. | O'DAIE, Bridget M. | 09 NOV 1865 |
| DUFFY, Michael | WILLIAMS, Margaret Ellen | 03 JUN 1868 |
| DUFFY, Patrick | O'RORKE, Elizabeth | 05 APR 1866 |
| DUFFY, Terence A. | REDY, Margaret | 07 JUN 1866 |
| DUFFY, William H. | FRENCH, Sarah Clarinda | 08 MAY 1866 |
| DUFFY, Wm. | GODDARD, Mary Ann | 25 FEB 1868 |
| DUGAN, Daniel | COLLINS, Margaret | 19 JAN 1859 |
| DUGAN, Daniel | McINERHENY, Mary | 06 NOV 1866 |
| DUGAN, John | McCARTHY, Mary | 18 MAY 1865 |
| DUGIN, Samuel R. | WOOD, Gabrielle | 17 AUG 1865 |
| DUKE, Thomas | HIGGS, Sallie E. | 04 SEP 1867 |
| DUKEHART, Graham [6s] | HARMAN, Priscilla E. | 31 MAR 1865 |
| DUKES, Isaac P. | DAVIS, Jennie A. | 07 MAR 1868 |
| DUKES, Levin | LAMBIE, Margaret A. | 04 JAN 1860 |
| DULANEY, Bladen T. | LOVE, Jane M. | 07 APR 1859 |
| DULANEY, Charles [8] | KEESE, Dorcas Virginia [Keys] | 27 MAR 1868 |
| DULANEY, John A. | BEALL, Mary M.A. | 24 SEP 1859 |

| | | |
|---|---|---|
| DULANEY, Richard | PONEY, Laura (blk) | 19 MAR 1870 |
| DULEY, Edmund G. | MILLS, Mary F. | 13 SEP 1865 |
| DULIN, James C. | WHITE, Mary A. | 24 JAN 1862 |
| DULY, James | CONNORS, Mary | 16 APR 1863 |
| DUMAS, Austin | OWEN, Allen Elizabeth | 08 AUG 1863 |
| DUMBERTH, William A. [2] | WALKER, Lucinda D. | 16 FEB 1867 |
| DUN, Daniel | CONNOR, Catherine | 21 MAY 1870 |
| DUNAGAN, Patrick | QUILL, Mary | 25 JUN 1859 |
| DUNBAR, James K. | PERRY, Annie | 20 JAN 1864 |
| DUNBAR, Moses | GADDIS, Gracie | 03 JUN 1867 |
| DUNCAN, Cain | HOMER, Isabella | 01 OCT 1863 |
| DUNCAN, John | RUSSELL, Caroline | 27 DEC 1869 |
| DUNCAN, John G. | SHULTZ, Sophia | 31 OCT 1861 |
| DUNCASON, John M. | HARROVER, Sarah A.P. | 04 JUN 1866 |
| DUNDES, William Oswald | MARROW, Mary | 21 AUG 1865 |
| DUNDON, John | CROWLEY, Mary Ann | 28 OCT 1858 |
| DUNFORD, James | FISHER, Mary C. | 01 MAR 1862 |
| DUNGAN, Elias | McCALLAN, Bridget | 07 MAY 1861 |
| DUNGAN, John V. [1c] | DORSEY, Ellen F. | 26 APR 1862 |
| DUNHAM, Eli | HOWARD, Phebe | 05 JUL 1865 |
| DUNHAM, Martin | DESHIELD, Margaret (blk) | 27 APR 1864 |
| DUNKHOST, William H. | JACOBS, Elizabeth D. | 26 NOV 1867 |
| DUNKIN, Alison | BOWIE, Annie | 01 DEC 1868 |
| DUNLAP, A. Preston | MILLER, Eliza | 18 OCT 1864 |
| DUNLAP, Simon | MAHONEY, Fannie (blk) | 26 JUN 1866 |
| DUNLOP, David | MASON, Sophia (blk) | 02 AUG 1864 |
| DUNMORE, Henry Harrison | NELSON, Mary (blk) | 21 JUL 1869 |
| DUNMORE, John Smith | DUNMORE, Rebecca (blk) | 28 DEC 1866 |
| DUNMORE, Philip | CURRY, Ann (blk) | 08 FEB 1868 |
| DUNMORE, Solomon | BROWN, Frances (blk) | 08 MAY 1863 |
| DUNN, Dennis | MURPHEY, Julia | 01 JUN 1863 |
| DUNN, Edward | BALL, Lizzie (blk) | 01 OCT 1867 |
| DUNN, James | McCABE, Hannah | 05 NOV 1864 |
| DUNN, John | LIDEN, Bridget | 22 SEP 1864 |
| DUNN, John | DEHENER, Ellen | 21 NOV 1867 |
| DUNN, John [4] | KIPP, Malinda | 05 MAY 1870 |
| DUNN, Martin | DUNN, Catherine | 24 JAN 1868 |
| DUNN, Michael | RYAN, Joanna | 12 FEB 1863 |
| DUNN, Thomas | AIKENS, Mary Jane | 30 MAY 1859 |
| DUNN, Thomas | GREENWELL, Mary E. | 04 FEB 1864 |
| DUNN, Thomas | NEENAN, Lucy | 25 FEB 1865 |
| DUNN, Thomas | McGRATH, Kate | 25 SEP 1865 |
| DUNN, William | SINCLAIR, Harriet Lucretia | 09 JUL 1864 |
| DUNN, William E. | REAGAN, Mary | 07 JUN 1867 |
| DUNNENSFIELD, Charles J.J. | SPRING, Maggie | 30 JUN 1862 |
| DUNNICLIFF, George | SWEENY, Margaret | 04 JUN 1863 |
| DUNNINGTON, James A. | ST. JOHN, Mary E. | 05 DEC 1861 |
| DUNSTON, George E. | PRINGLE, Anginette | 30 MAR 1864 |
| DUP, Emanuel | DIEDERMAN, Bertha | 06 DEC 1865 |
| DUPEE, William S. | TATE, Courtney Ann (blk) | 15 JUN 1863 |
| duPONT, Eleuthraire Irene [of DE] [10] | HENDERSON, Charlotte Shepard | 26 OCT 1858 |
| DUPPS, Christopher | MAY, Mary | 15 JUL 1864 |
| DURDUER, Edmund | CURTAIN, Mary | 22 JUL 1862 |
| DURDY, Dennis | MOINOHAN, Margaret | 05 OCT 1863 |
| DURFEE, George W. | SMITH, Anna Xariffa | 17 JUN 1868 |
| DURHAM, George G. | ENGLISH, Catherine | 08 FEB 1860 |

| | | |
|---|---|---|
| DURHAM, Tyler V. [10] | BYANES, B. Agnes | 08 MAR 1869 |
| DURKIN, Michael | JOHNSON, Mary E. | 07 JUN 1866 |
| DUROSS, Michael J. | ASPINALL, Jane | 07 JAN 1864 |
| DUSENBURY, William B. | GLADDEN, Cornelia | 10 AUG 1864 |
| DUSHANE, Geo. W. | ROSE, Minerva A. | 13 OCT 1863 |
| DUTCH, John C. | GOODMAN, Hattie E. | 30 MAR 1868 |
| DUTCH, Thomas | WEBSTER, Eliza Ann | 06 JAN 1863 |
| DUTROW, David Edward | SIMPSON, Mary | 24 NOV 1863 |
| DUTTON, Arthur Henry | SANDS, Maria Maud | 06 JUN 1863 |
| DUTTON, Benjamin | WILLIAMS, Annie Maria (blk) | 22 JAN 1867 |
| DUTTON, John W. | LEWIS, Emma V. | 01 JUN 1869 |
| DUTY, James [9n] | ROBERTS, Emma J. Church | 15 DEC 1859 |
| DUVAL, Samuel | SWAILES, Louisa (blk) | 16 OCT 1866 |
| DUVALL, Charles H. | DAVIS, Emma | 20 OCT 1859 |
| DUVALL, Edmund B. | CATOR, Eliza A. | 02 OCT 1858 |
| DUVALL, Edmund B. | BURNS, Mary | 17 DEC 1867 |
| DUVALL, Edward S. | OSBORN, Mitta (blk) | 02 SEP 1868 |
| DUVALL, George | COLEMAN, Eliza (blk) | 18 MAY 1866 |
| DUVALL, George | SHARPER, Ida | 04 SEP 1869 |
| DUVALL, George W. | COURTNEY, Mary E. | 08 NOV 1866 |
| DUVALL, Grafton | SULLIVAN, Mary R. | 21 JUL 1864 |
| DUVALL, Ignatius | HOWARD, Jane (blk) | 26 JAN 1867 |
| DUVALL, J. William | CLARK, Lucinda | 12 JUN 1861 |
| DUVALL, James E. | ROZELL, Margaret S. | 25 MAY 1868 |
| DUVALL, James N. | GENTRY, Isabella J. | 04 SEP 1860 |
| DUVALL, John H.W. | SULLIVAN, Annie E. | 17 MAY 1866 |
| DUVALL, John W. | HOPKINS, Jane N. | 06 MAR 1862 |
| DUVALL, Leon [7a] | STOUT, Maud | 30 APR 1868 |
| DUVALL, Louis E. | GRINER, Ellen C. | 14 MAY 1867 |
| DUVALL, Marshall M. | MARSHALL, Emma Louisa | 29 SEP 1864 |
| DUVALL, Matthew E. | MACKALL, Caroline | 16 OCT 1862 |
| DUVALL, Samuel L. | BRYAN, Margaret A. | 26 APR 1864 |
| DUVALL, Thomas [6le] | MURPHY, Martha L. | 16 JAN 1866 |
| DUVALL, Wm. T.S. | STEVENS, Mary A. | 24 DEC 1862 |
| DUVE, Frederick H. | WRIGHT, Catherine | 05 JUN 1866 |
| DWYER, John | DALY, Mary | 13 MAY 1865 |
| DWYER, Levi [11] | McNAMEE, Mary Ann | 11 AUG 1865 |
| DWYER, Patrick D. | McCARTHY, Elizabeth | 03 JAN 1865 |
| DWYER, William Egleson | MUSGROVE, Rachel Deborah | 24 DEC 1866 |
| DWYRE, Anthony | LEHAY, Margaret | 16 FEB 1860 |
| DYCE, Charles | LYNN, Emily (blk) | 30 JUN 1866 |
| DYE, Amos | WHEATLEY, Susanna | 04 JAN 1862 |
| DYER, Charles [1e] | MONEY, Marthay | 27 MAR 1866 |
| DYER, Elisha | JOHNSON, Millard H. | 25 OCT 1865 |
| DYER, George H. | FENIX, Mary Ellen | 21 NOV 1865 |
| DYER, Joseph T. | HARVEY, Mary C. | 10 MAY 1869 |
| DYER, Leo | KAULENDBAUGH, Mary B. | 22 JUN 1866 |
| DYER, Thomas E. | NUTWELL, Sabra A.D. | 21 NOV 1867 |
| DYER, W.J. | SHERIDAN, Susan Cecilia | 13 JUN 1860 |
| DYER, William | WILSON, Anna K. | 28 APR 1869 |
| DYER, William B., Jr. | GRIFFIN, Anna E. | 27 NOV 1865 |
| DYLE, John D. | DORN, Bridget | 26 MAY 1863 |
| DYSER, Jacob | MOCKEBEE, Mary Virginia | 03 NOV 1860 |
| DYSON, Abraham | SMITH, Virginia (blk) | 17 DEC 1862 |
| DYSON, Abraham | GAZZAWAY, Oceana E. (blk) | 18 FEB 1868 |
| DYSON, Abraham | FIELDING, Alice (blk) | 24 FEB 1869 |

District of Columbia Marriage Licenses, 1858-1870

| | | |
|---|---|---|
| DYSON, Charles H. | BUTLER, Charlotte (blk) | 28 MAY 1867 |
| DYSON, Stephen | LEE, Treasy (blk) | 26 NOV 1862 |
| DYSON, Thomas W. | TENNEY, Rachel R. (blk) | 11 MAR 1867 |
| DYSON, William | BURKE, Jane (blk) | 17 OCT 1861 |
| DYSON, William H. | SCOTT, Sarah A. (blk) | 28 AUG 1865 |
| DYSON, William T. | BOND, Henrietta (blk) | 06 AUG 1867 |

# E

| | | |
|---|---|---|
| EACRITT, John W. | KAMMERER, Cecilia | 30 OCT 1868 |
| EADIE, William G., M.D., N.Y. | JACOBSON, Emma C. | 02 JAN 1867 |
| EAGAN, Hubert W. | WILLIAMS, Jennie E. | 19 FEB 1863 |
| EAGAN, John | WELCH, Mary | 17 OCT 1867 |
| EAGLESTON, John | TYLER, Hester Jane | 28 DEC 1869 |
| EAGLIN, Beverly | FERGUSON, Mary L. (blk) | 01 DEC 1858 |
| EALINGS, Ephraim | WILLIAMS, Mary (blk) | 24 DEC 1866 |
| EARLY, Samuel | SPEAR, Amanda E. | 13 MAR 1865 |
| EARNEST, Ulia | GROFFMAN, Augustus | 17 OCT 1868 |
| EAST, Thompson R. | DUVALL, Harriet | 22 JUL 1865 |
| EASTBORN, Isaac | WEIR, Rachel T. | 06 DEC 1866 |
| EASTEN, James | RYON, Kate | 16 APR 1864 |
| EASTERN, James R. | DOLAN, Annie | 06 JAN 1864 |
| EASTLACK, Richard N. | WILLIAMS, Charlotte F. | 19 SEP 1866 |
| EASTLAKE, Andrew W. | ANDERSON, Kate E. | 09 APR 1870 |
| EASTMAN, Albert P. | RUSSELL, Sarah N. | 24 DEC 1869 |
| EASTMAN, Hiram F. [12s] | CROOK, Martha J. | 15 JAN 1863 |
| EASTMAN, Robert L. | DORSEY, Mary A. | 30 NOV 1861 |
| EASTMAN, Thomas H. [11] | MAXWELL, Annie H. | 23 DEC 1861 |
| EASTON, John L. | CARROLL, Catherine | 10 NOV 1869 |
| EASTON, John S. | CUNNINGHAM, Sallie J. | 11 SEP 1860 |
| EATON, Alexander W. | TEACHEM, Caroline | 19 JUL 1866 |
| EATON, Henry T. | ATCHISON, Ann R. | 09 AUG 1864 |
| EATON, Henry Z. [12s] | JOHNSON, Minnie | 17 JUL 1862 |
| EATON, Walter S. | ANDREWS, Lizzie I. | 16 OCT 1869 |
| EBBS, Harry J. | ESSEX, Laura E. | 16 MAY 1863 |
| EBENBACK, John G. | EDE, Emilie | 28 JUN 1860 |
| EBER, Conrad | AIGLER, Sophia | 07 JUL 1862 |
| EBERLY, George F. | O'NIEL, Julia | 05 OCT 1863 |
| EBERT, Charles | MAEDEL, Rosalie | 07 SEP 1863 |
| EBY, James W. | DeSANNO, Eleanora | 01 MAR 1864 |
| ECKEL, Lewis | BARRETT, Margaret | 09 AUG 1865 |
| ECKELS, David H. | KEEFE, Marcella M. | 08 MAY 1868 |
| ECKERT, Adam [12s] | TOOMS, Mary Ann | 25 JUN 1862 |
| ECKERT, George | GRAULICH, Annie M. | 12 SEP 1865 |
| ECKERT, Leonhardt | GERHARDT, Elizabetha | 10 AUG 1859 |
| ECKHARDT, Nicholas | HYESETT, Mary J. | 11 JUL 1864 |
| ECKHART, Andrew | GIRSCH, Henrietta | 02 MAR 1868 |
| ECKLOFF, Christian F. | O'CONNER, Mary A. | 01 JUN 1867 |
| ECKLOFF, Joseph E. | SMITH, Catherine V. | 05 SEP 1868 |
| EDEL, Dieterick | MENTZE, Augusta | 19 OCT 1861 |
| EDELIN, Alfred [11] | BRADLEY, Sidney T. | 09 DEC 1863 |
| EDELIN, Charles A. | EDELIN, Mary E. | 03 SEP 1863 |
| EDELIN, David | SMITH, Barbara A. (blk) | 02 APR 1867 |
| EDELIN, Leonard C. | DYER, Eliza A. | 06 SEP 1858 |
| EDELIN, Leonard R. | MONTGOMERY, Catherine R. | 14 JAN 1862 |
| EDELIN, Patrick Francis | PHINRICK, Martha | 03 OCT 1867 |

| | | |
|---|---|---|
| EDELIN, Thomas J. | BARTON, Emma V. | 19 OCT 1865 |
| EDELIN, William W. | SWAIN, Julia Ann | 04 JAN 1866 |
| EDELIN, William Z. | SKIDMORE, Martha E. | 26 AUG 1869 |
| EDGERLY, Jerome | BARTLETT, Mary | 08 MAR 1869 |
| EDGERTON, Frank M. | RUMSEY, Mary A. | 05 DEC 1865 |
| EDIE, Christopher | SANDFORD, Maria A. | 06 JAN 1866 |
| EDIE, John R., Jr. [11] | McCAULEY, Julia | 17 FEB 1866 |
| EDINBURGH, William Henry | LeBARROWS, Josephine (blk) | 10 JUN 1869 |
| EDMONDS, Howard [11] | OWEN, Mary Elizabeth | 12 FEB 1866 |
| EDMONDS, Plummer A. | WATTS, Mary A. (blk) | 16 OCT 1867 |
| EDMONDSON, Henry | THOMAS, Henrietta (blk) | 26 JUN 1862 |
| EDMONSON, Aaron Joseph | TILLMAN, Elizabeth | 22 MAR 1864 |
| EDMONSON, Ephraim | BANISTER, Mary (blk) | 01 FEB 1860 |
| EDMONSON, Josiah | DOUGLAS, Mary (blk) | 02 JUL 1863 |
| EDMONSTON, Brook N. | LASHHORN, Ella V. | 02 JUL 1866 |
| EDMONSTON, Charles | REDSTREACK, Clara DeGant | 04 MAY 1868 |
| EDMONSTON, James | SINGER, Elizabeth | 29 FEB 1868 |
| EDMONSTON, Richard A. [11] | WATTS, Sarah J. | 18 NOV 1862 |
| EDMONSTON, Samuel | COLLIER, Elizabeth | 19 MAR 1867 |
| EDMONSTON, W.E. | HILLIARD, Kate S. | 10 DEC 1866 |
| EDMONSTON, William B. | HURST, Margaret A. | 18 FEB 1861 |
| EDMONSTON, William J. | JONES, Mary E. | 27 DEC 1864 |
| EDMUNDS, James | MILES, Barbara | 04 JAN 1866 |
| EDMUNDS, James | LUFF, Sarah Levinia | 19 OCT 1868 |
| EDMUNDS, Lee | RAX, Elizabeth (blk) | 10 JAN 1870 |
| EDMUNDS, Lewis | CARTER, Lucinda (blk) | 12 OCT 1869 |
| EDMUNDS, Stephen Girard | HICKS, Emily S. (blk) | 09 NOV 1865 |
| EDSON, Peter | MOORE, Frances Ann | 03 FEB 1866 |
| EDWARD, James | GRIMES, Elizabeth (blk) | 29 AUG 1868 |
| EDWARD, Jarret | WHEELER, Chloe (blk) | 08 NOV 1866 |
| EDWARDS, C. Edwin | COMPTON, A. Texas | 14 FEB 1865 |
| EDWARDS, Edward | SINK, Elizabeth | 11 OCT 1864 |
| EDWARDS, Edward | CHRISTIAN, Mary (blk) | 23 APR 1868 |
| EDWARDS, Frank W. | MORRISON, Helen F. | 06 NOV 1868 |
| EDWARDS, George T. | OSBORN, Jane A. | 28 NOV 1868 |
| EDWARDS, George W. | ATCHISON, Pauline | 06 SEP 1860 |
| EDWARDS, Henry | EDWARDS, Evelina | 24 DEC 1858 |
| EDWARDS, Henry | CLEMENTS, Frances | 02 SEP 1865 |
| EDWARDS, Henry | JOHNSON, Alice (blk) | 14 MAR 1867 |
| EDWARDS, Henry | WALLER, Hannah | 20 MAY 1869 |
| EDWARDS, Hezekiah | GREEN, Mary Eliza (blk) | 08 FEB 1866 |
| EDWARDS, James | ADAMS, Josephine (blk) | 21 NOV 1866 |
| EDWARDS, James A. | BEALE, Margaret | 10 JAN 1866 |
| EDWARDS, James Henry | JOHNSON, Alice (blk) | 18 MAR 1867 |
| EDWARDS, Nelson | BROWN, Mary S. | 24 NOV 1860 |
| EDWARDS, Robert H. | ELLIS, Lucy H. | 03 JUL 1865 |
| EDWARDS, Thomas C. | DENNISON, Lucy A. | 11 JUL 1861 |
| EDWARDS, William | HOLMES, Mary (blk) | 15 DEC 1866 |
| EDWARDS, William H. [6r] | THOMPSON, Mary L. | 26 JUN 1860 |
| EDWARDS, William H. | BAKER, Annie E. | 27 JUL 1864 |
| EDWINS, Charles C. | YOUNG, Mary L. | 10 FEB 1870 |
| EFFERSON, Tarman | CLARKE, Lucy | 29 JUN 1866 |
| EGAN, Charles | ANDERSON, Maggie | 07 JUN 1865 |
| EGAN, Charles W. | HITCHCOCK, Eunice S. | 14 MAR 1862 |
| EGAN, Charles W. | HITCHCOCK, Eunice S. | 14 NOV 1862 |
| EGAN, Eugene | HEATH, Emma Amelia | 21 NOV 1863 |

## District of Columbia Marriage Licenses, 1858-1870

| | | |
|---|---|---|
| EGAN, James R. | HOWLETT, Mary A. | 14 APR 1865 |
| EGAN, John | BABBINGTON, Joana | 04 JAN 1867 |
| EGAN, Patrick | CAMPBELL, Mary | 02 MAY 1863 |
| EGBERT, Harvey C. | YOUNG, Nelly | 26 MAY 1870 |
| EGGERS, Chas. J.F. | SWAN, Fredericka | 13 MAY 1862 |
| EGGLESTON, Virgil Silsby | BEVERIDGE, Laura Virginia | 15 OCT 1867 |
| EGLIN, Joshua | CREAMER, Lucy (blk) | 07 MAR 1866 |
| EGLIN, Robert | CARROLL, Georgiana (blk) | 02 JAN 1867 |
| EHEREST, Leon | SALVIN, Marie Barbe | 03 MAR 1863 |
| EIBEL, H. | HENRY, Kate | 29 SEP 1869 |
| EICHHOLTZ, John C. | LUGEENBEEL, Bettie C. | 09 NOV 1868 |
| EICHHOLZ, Henry | MEHRING, Dora | 06 MAY 1867 |
| EIMER, John | FAVWER, Mary | 09 OCT 1865 |
| EINAN, Mark | CURRAN, Kate | 03 AUG 1865 |
| EISENBEISS, Julius | SCHAFER, Susanna | 25 DEC 1861 |
| EISENBRAUM, Gottleib | HEIL, Elizabeth | 06 JUN 1870 |
| ELBERT, John | MITCHELL, Mary | 02 FEB 1870 |
| ELBERT, Joseph | MIDDLETON, Harriet (blk) | 09 MAY 1866 |
| ELBERT, Joseph D. | BRYAN, Josephine (blk) | 11 FEB 1870 |
| ELBERT, Melchire | SCHRODEL, Barbara | 12 MAR 1866 |
| ELBERT, Melchoir | HARDNETT, Mary | 17 AUG 1866 |
| ELBRECHT, Hermann | TIEDGEN, Marie | 01 OCT 1867 |
| ELDERKIN, William A. | GURLEY, Frances M. | 07 MAY 1861 |
| ELDRIDGE, George | McNEELY, Ann Elizth. | 01 OCT 1861 |
| ELDRIDGE, Joseph [6s] | WARD, Laura | 10 SEP 1864 |
| ELDRIDGE, Joshua H. [1c] | SIMONDS, Maggie E. | 17 DEC 1862 |
| ELDRIDGE, Watson W. | HANSELL, Reburta | 13 JUN 1867 |
| ELINE, Silverius A. | SLATFORD, Mary Jane | 27 FEB 1867 |
| ELIS, John Henry Hammon | WEBSTER, Mary Emma | 10 JAN 1867 |
| ELKIN, Abram | CALVERT, Lucy Victoria | 13 APR 1863 |
| ELKINS, Jasper | MOORE, Sarah R. | 10 FEB 1870 |
| ELLENBROOK, Henry | ARMSTRONG, Elizabeth | 29 JUN 1866 |
| ELLET, George S. | MULLEN, Bridget | 30 AUG 1860 |
| ELLIN, George T. | MURPHY, Mary H. | 11 NOV 1868 |
| ELLINGTON, Pilford | ABEL, Mary Ann (blk) | 18 JUN 1868 |
| ELLIOT, J. Henry [7b] | CHASE, Mary C. | 25 JAN 1870 |
| ELLIOT, Lewis | PAYNE, Julia | 01 JUN 1870 |
| ELLIOT, Robert K. [11] | LAKE, Emilie Theresa | 27 OCT 1866 |
| ELLIOTT, Abraham | BROWN, Mary (blk) | 22 AUG 1865 |
| ELLIOTT, Alexander, Jr. | SCAGGS, Mary L. | 08 NOV 1858 |
| ELLIOTT, Edward | SCHREAR, Jane | 25 SEP 1865 |
| ELLIOTT, Edward | LUSBY, Lucy | 10 OCT 1868 |
| ELLIOTT, J. James | WILLIAMS, Emma J. | 21 SEP 1867 |
| ELLIOTT, James W. | BLADEN, Catharine L. | 19 FEB 1861 |
| ELLIOTT, John | BATES, Mary | 11 SEP 1865 |
| ELLIOTT, John G. | BURCH, Sarah Frances | 25 NOV 1859 |
| ELLIOTT, Matthew Edwards | SHREVE, Jane Amanda | 27 SEP 1865 |
| ELLIOTT, Nelson | BERRY, Martha (blk) | 28 SEP 1863 |
| ELLIOTT, Thomas H. | BLADEN, Elizabeth Ann | 11 DEC 1866 |
| ELLIS, Archy | OSMER, Lizzie (blk) | 06 APR 1869 |
| ELLIS, Emmit [11] | BEACH, Lucinda | 27 JUN 1865 |
| ELLIS, Henry | REDDICK, Maria | 23 JAN 1869 |
| ELLIS, Henry J. | RAWLINGS, Sarah | 18 NOV 1868 |
| ELLIS, Herman L. | BRAMAR, Sarah N. (blk) | 04 MAY 1868 |
| ELLIS, James W. | DORMAN, Naomi | 08 NOV 1869 |
| ELLIS, Samuel H. [6m] | GORDON, Elizabeth A. | 16 FEB 1863 |

District of Columbia Marriage Licenses, 1858-1870

| | | |
|---|---|---|
| ELLIS, Samuel Thomas | SMITH, Leonora Amelia | 13 JAN 1864 |
| ELLIS, Theodore G. [11] | HOLMES, Angie A. | 21 FEB 1865 |
| ELLIS, Thomas | WILSON, Alice V. | 03 MAY 1869 |
| ELLIS, Thomas A. | HEALEY, Maggie | 15 NOV 1869 |
| ELLIS, William Francis | TRIVISS, Sarah Ann (blk) | 14 JAN 1868 |
| ELLIS, William L. | SAMPSON, Henrietta | 08 JUN 1870 |
| ELLIS, William M. | WATERS, Ann M. (blk) | 13 OCT 1858 |
| ELLISON, William H. | SHERWOOD, Emily | 09 FEB 1863 |
| ELLSWORTH, Edward A. (11th Inf.) | DIGGS, Catharine F. | 01 SEP 1864 |
| ELLSWORTH, George L. | ELFORT, Elizabeth Janx | 16 DEC 1867 |
| ELLSWORTH, P.C. | GREGORY, Alice | 10 FEB 1868 |
| ELM, Jacob | VOGEL, Christina | 19 JAN 1863 |
| ELMES, Webster | WHITE, Rosa E.S. | 14 JUN 1864 |
| ELMORE, Thomas | GARNER, Frances A. | 10 NOV 1862 |
| ELSCHLÄGER, Adam | RÖTH, Margaretha | 25 MAY 1863 |
| ELSWORTH, George | WALKER, Mary | 15 OCT 1861 |
| ELVERSON, James | DUVAL, Sallie R. | 02 JAN 1868 |
| ELWANGER, Frederick | STROBEL, Frodericka | 16 SEP 1858 |
| ELWOOD, Francis H. | DAWSON, Sarah E. | 24 FEB 1863 |
| ELWOOD, Francis W. | LYONS, Mary E. | 17 OCT 1863 |
| ELZY, Solomon | TURNER, Martha Ann | 24 OCT 1862 |
| EMERSON, John S. | AVERY, C.R. | 05 AUG 1863 |
| EMERSON, Robert P. | NORRIS, Lizzie | 28 NOV 1862 |
| EMERSON, William | ELLIS, Georgiana | 02 NOV 1867 |
| EMISON, Acquila [6m] | JOHNSON, Eveline | 27 APR 1863 |
| EMLEY, Fletcher J. | STOVER, Annie R. | 14 DEC 1869 |
| EMLEY, George P. | MORGAN, Matilda | 05 OCT 1865 |
| EMM, Thomas | DELANEY, Bridget | 03 SEP 1864 |
| EMMENNAN, Henry C. | LOHMILLER, Annie C. | 20 APR 1869 |
| EMMERSON, Clinton | THOMAS, Eleanor O. | 23 FEB 1863 |
| EMMERSON, James H. [6le] | CLARKE, Kate | 03 NOV 1866 |
| EMMERT, Leonard | SCHLEGEL, Catharine | 21 FEB 1862 |
| ENDERS, John | ARENZ, Mary | 13 DEC 1861 |
| ENGEL, Benjamin | PATTERSON, Mary | 23 JAN 1864 |
| ENGELS, Ewald | GREFF, Helen | 18 APR 1865 |
| ENGLAND, Charles | ARMSTRONG, Margaret | 17 DEC 1864 |
| ENGLAND, Charles E. | ANGUS, Emma S. | 21 NOV 1868 |
| ENGLAND, Edwin | HUNTER, Clara F. | 18 JUL 1865 |
| ENGLE, Christian | WAGNER, Margaretta | 05 FEB 1866 |
| ENGLE, Jacob | BINDER, Maggie | 11 JAN 1868 |
| ENGLEHART, John | ASHFORD, Sophronia | 11 JUL 1866 |
| ENGLEHART, Joseph | SAUER, Maggie | 29 APR 1868 |
| ENGLISH, Benjamin | FELTER, Jennie (blk) | 06 FEB 1866 |
| ENGLISH, Henry | SMITH, Helen Olivia | 01 JUN 1869 |
| ENGLISH, James H. | GUTHRIE, Serena | 05 JUL 1864 |
| ENGLISH, John | PHELAN, Margaret | 03 DEC 1863 |
| ENGLISH, Joseph | CANNING, Laura V. | 19 JUN 1866 |
| ENGLISH, Patrick | LONG, Eliza | 22 JUL 1862 |
| ENGLISH, Samuel T. | GREEN, Ellen | 31 JUL 1866 |
| ENGLISH, Sylvester G. | WARREN, Annie, Mrs. | 22 DEC 1863 |
| ENNIS, Gergory J. | CISSEL, Clara | 22 MAY 1865 |
| ENNIS, John | BRANSON, Mary (blk) | 22 JAN 1867 |
| ENNIS, Wm. Richard E. | BAKER, Ella | 17 SEP 1869 |
| ENOS, Ephraim | SHEPHERD, Mary | 25 FEB 1863 |
| ENSLIN, Abel | SPRINGER, Mary A. | 22 NOV 1860 |
| ENTWISTLE, Charles Isaac | DEWDNEY, Julia | 16 MAR 1868 |

| | | |
|---|---|---|
| ENTWISTLE, Isaac | SANDERSON, Phebe J. | 03 OCT 1859 |
| EPPEL, August | RUH, Amelia | 22 APR 1865 |
| EPPLER, William | MELE, Rosanna | 19 MAR 1860 |
| EPPS, Robert | TOYER, Mary Eliza (blk) | 26 NOV 1866 |
| ERB, Philip | ERBECK, Margaret | 09 AUG 1866 |
| ERBY, Jerry | SHORT, Eliza (blk) | 23 DEC 1868 |
| ERGOOD, John R. | WOODRUFF, Addie B. | 08 APR 1870 |
| ERLY, James | HILL, Amelia | 10 AUG 1865 |
| ERNER, Daniel | CONROY, Bridget | 30 NOV 1859 |
| ERNEST, Saml. T. | SHECKILLS, Elizabeth V. | 04 DEC 1858 |
| ERPENSTEIN, Adolph | WENDEL, Louise | 17 DEC 1862 |
| ERRAS, Martin | KOPPER, Margaret | 12 SEP 1864 |
| ERTMANN, Louis | DELARMAN, Lina Bruna | 25 APR 1868 |
| ERVIN, James W. | MURPHY, Emma A. | 11 NOV 1868 |
| ERVY, George | BROWN, Mary (blk) | 06 APR 1864 |
| ERWIN, Dennis | KEHOE, Elizabeth | 31 JAN 1866 |
| ESCHENBACH, Henry | FLECK, Mary | 11 SEP 1858 |
| ESELHORST, Louis | SCHREDE, Lena | 28 APR 1868 |
| ESHER, James | NELSON, Martha (blk) | 12 DEC 1865 |
| ESHER, William | BENHARDIE, Sophia | 23 MAY 1864 |
| ESKEW, John D. | McKNIGHT, Hattie M. | 02 FEB 1869 |
| ESKRIDGE, Henry [12s] | CARTER, Mary Ellen (blk) | 08 JAN 1863 |
| ESKRIDGE, Thomas | CAVENER, Mary | 07 OCT 1862 |
| ESKRIDGE, William | ANGEL, Matilda | 20 JUL 1865 |
| ESMER, Edward W.H. [4] | DANFORTH, Mattie J.P. | 08 NOV 1866 |
| ESPEY, Ferdinand | AYTON, Adaline | 06 JUL 1867 |
| ESPEY, Francis Holmead | MITCHELL, Minnie Goods | 24 NOV 1868 |
| ESPEY, Henry C. | BRIDGET, Mary E. | 13 JAN 1863 |
| ESPEY, John A.B. | AYTON, Eleanora S. | 09 DEC 1869 |
| ESPUTIA, Edward [6r] | GARDNER, Lucretia G. | 26 DEC 1860 |
| ESSEG, Ernest Gottlob | FRANK, Margaret | 24 MAY 1866 |
| ESSEX, Francis V. | CLEMENTS, Mary S.H. | 28 JAN 1864 |
| ESSEX, John T. | BAINE, Margaret A. | 02 DEC 1858 |
| ESSEX, John T.W. | POWERS, Ann Cornelia | 12 APR 1859 |
| ESSIG, John | UHLMEYER, Mary | 07 DEC 1867 |
| ESTE, George Peabody [11] | BAILEY, Emma | 03 JUN 1868 |
| ESTERHAZY, Maximillian, Count | GRIFFIN, Sallie Carroll | 04 JUN 1870 |
| ESTES, Benjamin | THOMAS, Henrietta | 26 DEC 1862 |
| EUBANK, Richard, Jr. | EUBANK, Mary C. | 22 DEC 1859 |
| EUSKO, James | DAY, Mary O. | 24 AUG 1865 |
| EUSTACE, John | EUSTACE, Sarah Frances | 21 JAN 1867 |
| EVANS, Addison | ROOT, Eloisa H. | 27 OCT 1863 |
| EVANS, Benjamin | NAILEGAN, Helen | 21 FEB 1865 |
| EVANS, Benjamin F. | TRAVERS, Kate M. | 02 NOV 1868 |
| EVANS, Charles | MADISON, Addie | 29 JUN 1864 |
| EVANS, Charles | HARRISON, America | 01 NOV 1865 |
| EVANS, Edward | JACKSON, Jane (blk) | 22 AUG 1866 |
| EVANS, Frank H. [7b] | TYLER, Emma J. | 29 MAY 1869 |
| EVANS, Frederick Augustus Adolphus | LAHAY, Elizabeth | 02 AUG 1866 |
| EVANS, Henry | JOHNSON, Caroline (blk) | 04 NOV 1858 |
| EVANS, Henry | REVEL, Margaret | 03 JAN 1865 |
| EVANS, Hezekiah | GRANT, Susan (blk) | 15 SEP 1868 |
| EVANS, John | DIXON, Fannie E. | 30 AUG 1864 |
| EVANS, John | BETTER, Emma (blk) | 22 DEC 1869 |
| EVANS, John B. | GRAY, Lucy (blk) | 25 OCT 1865 |
| EVANS, John F. | KNOTT, Emma J. | 13 FEB 1867 |

| | | |
|---|---|---|
| EVANS, John H. | CROCKETT, Triphy | 04 MAY 1867 |
| EVANS, John M. | DAVIS, Charlotte (blk) | 10 OCT 1868 |
| EVANS, Lewis | BUTCHER, Eliza | 25 NOV 1863 |
| EVANS, Nathaniel W. | TAYLOR, Sarah Jane (blk) | 10 OCT 1864 |
| EVANS, Page | CARTER, Martha | 09 DEC 1865 |
| EVANS, Phillip B. | BAKER, Abagail | 01 MAY 1862 |
| EVANS, Richard | JACKSON, Cecilia (blk) | 15 SEP 1868 |
| EVANS, Robert | SMITH, Elizabeth (blk) | 17 MAR 1864 |
| EVANS, Robert | NOWELLS, Maria | 08 NOV 1864 |
| EVANS, Robert | HAWKINS, Caroline (blk) | 12 JUN 1866 |
| EVANS, Strafford | ASHTON, Hattie | 15 OCT 1862 |
| EVANS, Thomas | ESKRIDGE, Martha Ann | 03 MAY 1864 |
| EVANS, Thomas | BONGY, Mary (blk) | 20 NOV 1866 |
| EVANS, Thomas H. | WHITE, Alice V. | 22 APR 1867 |
| EVANS, Walter H. | CLARKE, Sarah M. | 06 OCT 1864 |
| EVANS, William | HACKLEY, Martha (blk) | 04 AUG 1868 |
| EVANS, William W. | WILTBERGER, Edith M. | 12 AUG 1868 |
| EVEDEN, Peter | WEATHERS, Nettie (blk) | 03 FEB 1870 |
| EVELY, John T. [6s] | BRIGHT, Julia E. | 05 NOV 1864 |
| EVERETT, Benja. F. | ARNOLD, Catherine Virginia | 04 MAY 1859 |
| EVERETT, William W. | ARMSTRONG, Clara C. | 11 DEC 1869 |
| EVERSON, B.J. | PEDDICORD, Mary H. | 19 OCT 1866 |
| EVERSON, Mark | DEMENT, Jane W. | 14 APR 1868 |
| EVSTAPHIEVE, Alexis E. [11] * | McCORMICK, Emmeline L. | 15 FEB 1864 |
| EWALD, Henry | SHAUP, Elizabeth | 15 JAN 1862 |
| EWALD, Henry | OHL, Catharine | 15 OCT 1862 |
| EWALD, Henry | BREMER, Karoline | 10 JUL 1865 |
| EWALD, Henry | HEBBS, Anna | 23 OCT 1866 |
| EWALD, Robert | BOWMAN, Mary | 28 MAR 1863 |
| EWERS, Joseph E. | FARRAR, Elvira A. | 06 SEP 1860 |
| EXLEY, Henry | HALL, Mary J. | 14 OCT 1862 |
| EXLEY, Thomas M. | BARNHOUSE, Sarah T. | 30 MAY 1866 |
| EZEKIELS, Marcus E. | LULLEY, Lencia | 12 OCT 1867 |

# F

| | | |
|---|---|---|
| FACER, Roscoe C. [8] | HAMMOND, Lavinia | 20 MAY 1868 |
| FACEY, H.J. | LEIBIN, Amelia A. | 19 SEP 1866 |
| FAGAN, James | DALY, Honora | 28 MAY 1870 |
| FAGAN, William | TIERNAN, Bridget | 10 FEB 1868 |
| FAGG, Carter B. | JOY, Carrie E. | 15 AUG 1859 |
| FAHBUSH, Frederick | FOLEY, Mary | 15 JUN 1867 |
| FAHEY, Patrick | BALDWIN, Margaret | 02 SEP 1867 |
| FAHEY, Peter | CADEY, Mary | 05 AUG 1865 |
| FAHY, John | DONOHOE, Kate | 22 JUL 1865 |
| FAINTER, John C. | FOLEY, Bridget | 08 OCT 1863 |
| FAIR, Charles W. | POSEY, Mary Virginia | 17 DEC 1867 |
| FAIRALL, Alfred | HAYDEN, Hellen | 29 JUL 1861 |
| FAIRCHILD, Elbert W. | ISDELL, Mary E. | 30 DEC 1867 |
| FAIRCHILD, Lucius [11] | BULL, Frances | 26 APR 1864 |
| FAIRFAX, Charles | WHITE, Rachel Ann (blk) | 22 DEC 1866 |
| FAIRFAX, George D. | TAYLOR, Jane E. | 29 JUL 1868 |
| FAIRFAX, George R. | BUTLER, Elizabeth A. | 04 MAY 1870 |
| FAIRFAX, Miles | JACKSON, Harriet | 01 OCT 1866 |
| FAIRLAND, D. Remington [11] | HIGGINS, Marian K. | 15 AUG 1866 |
| FALBRYS, George | MENSING, Charlotte | 16 NOV 1861 |

District of Columbia Marriage Licenses, 1858-1870

| | | |
|---|---|---|
| FALCONER, Alfred | HENNING, Sallie Clarke | 27 JUN 1866 |
| FALCONER, George E. | CURVERWELL, Margaret R. | 16 MAY 1864 |
| FALCONER, John W. | KAIN, Matilda | 05 JUN 1866 |
| FALCONER, Richard T.J. [7a] | FLENNER, Emma E. | 18 JAN 1869 |
| FALLON, Hammond | FERGUSON, Ellen | 11 NOV 1864 |
| FALLON, Thomas J. | PERRY, Rosa C. | 01 JUL 1867 |
| FALVEY, Timothy | MORIARITY, Deborrah | 20 NOV 1867 |
| FANDT, John | STANTON, Fredericka | 10 OCT 1864 |
| FANNING, William H. | NICHOLSON, Margaret F. | 27 JUL 1863 |
| FANSEL, August | WOLLNER, Mary | 22 JUL 1867 |
| FANTNER, George W. | HARRISON, Sarah C. | 31 OCT 1861 |
| FARE, John | LYNCH, Anna F. | 09 AUG 1864 |
| FARE, John | ADAMS, Mary | 05 SEP 1867 |
| FARGUHER, James | HAYS, Hanora | 28 APR 1862 |
| FARIS, Allen | ROBERTS, Lucy | 02 APR 1866 |
| FARIS, Charles M. | ASHFORD, Emerilla | 07 SEP 1868 |
| FARIS, John Anderson | STEWART, Ary (blk) | 26 OCT 1866 |
| FARLEE, W.A. | GIVEN, Mary A. | 15 JUN 1868 |
| FARLESS, Benjamin A. | MIDDLETON, Isadore A. | 27 JUN 1865 |
| FARLEY, Peter W. | GREENE, Annie | 28 NOV 1866 |
| FARNAM, Henry S.M. | LOUGHLIN, Frances L. | 08 APR 1863 |
| FARNUM, Henry A. | BEARD, Mary L. | 26 OCT 1864 |
| FARON, George G. | RICHARDS, Amanda | 13 MAR 1867 |
| FARQUAR, Patrick | FISHER, Sarah B. | 16 JAN 1868 |
| FARQUHARSON, James Waite | PROUDFOOT, Charlotte Rhodes | 15 FEB 1864 |
| FARR, Jefferson [12s] | STEWART, Lucinda (blk) | 19 JAN 1859 |
| FARR, Joseph [12s] | BROWN, Sarah A. (col'd) | 04 OCT 1860 |
| FARRALL, Alfred F. | WOODS, Elizabeth | 15 AUG 1866 |
| FARRALL, James J. | TUOHY, Mary J. | 28 SEP 1867 |
| FARRAR, George H. [11s] | MacCARTHY, Meta Julia | 13 JUL 1869 |
| FARRAR, J.W. [4] | NICHOLS, Susan Victoria | 19 FEB 1870 |
| FARRAR, James W. [4] | FORD, Laura E. | 03 MAR 1863 |
| FARRELL, George A. | RICHARDSON, Anna L. | 19 DEC 1861 |
| FARRELL, Hugh | FEGAN, Alice | 28 OCT 1858 |
| FARRELL, John D. | McCARTHY, Mary A. | 22 NOV 1862 |
| FARRELL, Michael | MURPHY, Julia | 03 JAN 1867 |
| FARROW, Grandison | JOHNSON, Rachel (blk) | 12 JAN 1867 |
| FARWELL, Charles H. | LAHEY, Ella | 13 JUL 1864 |
| FAULKNER, Joseph | DONALDSON, Amanda E. | 14 JUN 1862 |
| FAULKNER, William | THOMPSON, Catharine | 13 SEP 1862 |
| FAULTNER, James B. | JONES, Rebecca A. | 12 SEP 1861 |
| FAUNCE, Conard [sic] | KNIGHT, Mary Susannah | 27 JUL 1869 |
| FAUNCE, George | HUGHES, Mary Ellen | 18 JUN 1859 |
| FAUNCE, Isaac | BECK, Catherine | 22 NOV 1869 |
| FAUNCE, Jacob | SELBY, Emma | 23 NOV 1865 |
| FAUNTEROY, Cornelius | CATLETT, Caroline (blk) | 17 DEC 1863 |
| FAUNTEROY, Rufus | DUNBAR, Sarah (blk) | 13 MAR 1861 |
| FAUNTLEROY, John | JACKSON, Charlotte (blk) | 06 FEB 1864 |
| FAUNTLEROY, Rufus | LEWIS, Brainer | 03 AUG 1864 |
| FAWCETT, Peter | GUNNELL, Annie (blk) | 29 DEC 1869 |
| FAWCETT, William H. | BARNES, Caroline | 09 NOV 1868 |
| FAY, Adam | KREUTER, Katharine | 22 DEC 1865 |
| FAY, Paul | SPINDLE, Anna | 12 NOV 1861 |
| FAYS, William H. | MARSH, Kate A. | 27 NOV 1865 |
| FEALY, Dennis | O'KEEFE, Elizabeth | 02 DEC 1865 |
| FEARSON, Joseph | McPHERSON, Laura A. | 29 DEC 1865 |

| | | |
|---|---|---|
| FEARSON, Samuel | FINNY, Eliza | 19 AUG 1863 |
| FEARSON, William H. | DUVALL, Julia A. (blk) | 02 DEC 1868 |
| FEAST, Samuel, Jr. | GIANNINI, Annie M.J.C. | 30 JAN 1862 |
| FEDERHOOF, Jacob C. | MEYERS, Sophia | 20 NOV 1865 |
| FEENEY, Bernard | BROWN, Ann | 09 FEB 1864 |
| FEENEY, John | McDONOUGH, Winifred | 13 JUL 1859 |
| FEENY, John | CLANSY, Bridget | 14 JUL 1865 |
| FEGAN, Thomas | TOLAND, Ann | 30 OCT 1858 |
| FEHELY, Michael | SHAUGHNESSY, Mary | 28 MAY 1866 |
| FEINOUR, Thos. E.W. | HOPKINS, Kate | 15 DEC 1863 |
| FELTY, Philip | ARBENSHINE, Kate | 20 NOV 1867 |
| FENDNER, Ferdinand | EBERTS, Sophia | 08 SEP 1862 |
| FENDNER, Wm. | LIPPOLD, Anna B. | 22 OCT 1861 |
| FENLEY, John | McCLUSKEY, Margaret | 15 NOV 1858 |
| FENNALL, Patrick | WALSH, Mary | 18 FEB 1862 |
| FENTON, Charles B. | SOUR, Barbara | 19 DEC 1866 |
| FENTON, Matthias R. | STODDARD, Elizabeth A. | 23 OCT 1860 |
| FENWICK, Francis X. | CLARK, Ann | 02 JAN 1867 |
| FENWICK, George P. | STEWART, Mary A. | 07 NOV 1866 |
| FENWICK, John T. | CARTER, Louisa S. | 01 DEC 1859 |
| FENWICK, Robert Washington | MUNSON, Annie E. | 30 MAY 1859 |
| FENWICK, William A. | HERBERT, Alice E. | 29 OCT 1867 |
| FEOGAL, Ferdinand | SUTTON, Mary Jane | 13 APR 1868 |
| FERBER, John | ENGLE, Anna Barbara | 18 JUL 1868 |
| FERGUSON, Alvin S. | STONE, Harriet V. | 13 DEC 1859 |
| FERGUSON, Andrew | BROWN, Mary E. | 08 APR 1862 |
| FERGUSON, Artless | HITT, Fanny (blk) | 15 JUL 1865 |
| FERGUSON, Benjamin S. [6s] | LEWIS, Martha E. | 12 NOV 1864 |
| FERGUSON, Charles A. | KELLY, Mary | 30 DEC 1867 |
| FERGUSON, George | LUCE, Mary A. | 05 APR 1864 |
| FERGUSON, James P. | CECIL, Mary Ellen | 25 FEB 1868 |
| FERGUSON, John F. | COLLINS, Alysha | 14 FEB 1860 |
| FERGUSON, John R. | MOFFETT, Susie R. | 18 SEP 1866 |
| FERGUSON, John T. | CARROLL, Kate | 10 JUN 1862 |
| FERGUSON, Joseph | LOMAX, Elizabeth (blk) | 16 JUL 1860 |
| FERGUSON, Peter | HARVEY, Harriet | 13 DEC 1867 |
| FERGUSON, Rezin | BALLINGER, Sarah | 21 JUN 1860 |
| FERGUSON, Stephen | CHAMBLIN, Agnes (blk) | 26 FEB 1862 |
| FERGUSON, William | GRANT, Kitty (blk) | 12 JUL 1865 |
| FERGUSON, William | WRIGHT, Elizabeth | 29 APR 1867 |
| FERNANDEZ, John M. | WORTHINGTON, Ratie K. | 22 JUL 1868 |
| FERRALL, Bernard | McCARTY, Ellen | 13 MAY 1862 |
| FERRALL, James Henry | SMITH, Lyda | 13 FEB 1862 |
| FERRAND, Simion B. | [blank], Mary Catherine | 15 SEP 1862 |
| FERRANNINI, Giovanni | GOTTI, Maria Anna | 11 SEP 1869 |
| FERREE, Newton [5] | UTERMEHLE, Rosa | 16 JUN 1869 |
| FERRELL, James | BROWN, Sarah L. | 13 JAN 1870 |
| FERRIE, James I. | LAFLIN, Abby M. | 05 DEC 1864 |
| FERRIL, Dennis | CARTER, Milly (col'd) | 18 JUN 1867 |
| FERRIS, Abraham K. | HUNT, Celestia A. | 22 APR 1867 |
| FERRIS, Gilbert J. | WATSON, Eliza E. | 02 APR 1864 |
| FERRY, James | McGEE, Mary | 26 DEC 1866 |
| FETTER, Henry | MILLER, Margaret | 01 JUL 1867 |
| FEYHL, William | MULCHY, Margaret | 15 NOV 1866 |
| FIBER, Edward | WALKER, Louisa | 30 NOV 1863 |
| FIE, Christian | KIPP, Lesaly | 13 FEB 1862 |

District of Columbia Marriage Licenses, 1858-1870

| | | |
|---|---|---|
| FIELD, Edward | YOUNG, Minna | 28 APR 1868 |
| FIELDS, Alfred | RIVERS, Sarah (blk) | 15 APR 1869 |
| FIELDS, Charles C. | WASHINGTON, Lellah R. | 12 NOV 1864 |
| FIELDS, Charles [1e] | MAGRUDER, Chloe Ann | 03 AUG 1865 |
| FIELDS, George | ROBINSON, Maria (blk) | 04 NOV 1865 |
| FIELDS, James | TAYLOR, Elizabeth (blk) | 26 NOV 1864 |
| FIELDS, James D. | PAYNE, Sarah (blk) | 24 DEC 1868 |
| FIELDS, Richard | FORTNIGHT, Harriet (blk) | 09 MAR 1865 |
| FIELDS, [torn away] | [torn away] | 30 MAY 1865 |
| FIGARO, Antonio | THRIFT, Rosa S. | 19 MAR 1869 |
| FILEY, Charles G. | STAHL, Elizabeth | 15 APR 1864 |
| FILGATE, Thomas | KELLY, Bridget | 26 APR 1865 |
| FILIUS, Jacob | LEWIS, Caroline | 29 JUL 1865 |
| FILLER, Henry [2] | MILLER, Matilda | 27 NOV 1868 |
| FILLIUS, James R. [10] | HALL, Rebekah [Virginia] | 22 SEP 1859 |
| FILLIUS, Joseph Wilbergur [6h] | SMITH, Mary Alice | 09 MAY 1868 |
| FILLMORE, George Millard | NORFLEET, Lottie A. | 25 MAY 1869 |
| FILLMORE, Horace | SPELLER, Patsey (blk) | 31 JUL 1866 |
| FILLMORE, N.E. [7b] | THOMPSON, Mary E. | 11 JAN 1870 |
| FINCH, Abraham | WELLS, Sarah Ann (blk) | 21 DEC 1866 |
| FINCKEL, Franki H. | BRADY, Charlotte | 14 OCT 1868 |
| FINCKEL, George K. | PETERS, Sophia L. | 13 MAY 1861 |
| FINDLAY, Frank S. [1e] | GARDNER, Julia A. | 26 OCT 1865 |
| FINDLEY, David L. | MINERET, Ella G. | 08 OCT 1868 |
| FINDLEY, George | PHILLPOT, Sophia | 02 SEP 1861 |
| FINDLEY, John T. | DUVAL, Mary E. | 31 MAY 1864 |
| FINDLY, James | McVEIGH, Sarah | 12 FEB 1866 |
| FINK, Battranng | PAULY, Antonio | 03 DEC 1859 |
| FINK, Caspar | DAY, Mina | 12 MAR 1861 |
| FINK, Jacob | ROEMMELE, Margaret A. | 06 JUN 1859 |
| FINK, Jacob J. [5] | CLARK, Rachel A. | 02 MAY 1870 |
| FINK, John G. | SCHUMANN, Caroline | 19 MAR 1866 |
| FINLAN, Thomas | CONNERS, Lucy | 01 AUG 1867 |
| FINLEY, John | DUDDY, Mary | 06 AUG 1860 |
| FINN, James [5] | MITCHELL, Mary | 18 MAY 1867 |
| FINNEGAN, George | McCARTHY, Mary Ellen | 12 NOV 1863 |
| FINNEGAN, Michael | DONOGHUE, Margaret | 27 OCT 1863 |
| FINNEY, Alfred | WALKER, Pamelia (blk) | 16 APR 1868 |
| FINNEY, Thomas W. | DOWNES, Julia | 16 MAR 1864 |
| FINNEY, William | GEORGE, Maria (blk) | 12 MAR 1864 |
| FINNICUM, Mark | McMASTER, Amanda | 07 JAN 1862 |
| FINNIGAN, Michael | McDONOUGH, Annie | 24 AUG 1864 |
| FINNIGHTLY, Michael | MAHONEY, Ellen | 22 FEB 1867 |
| FINNIGIN, Michael | WARD, Ann | 29 JUL 1862 |
| FINTON, John | McGARVY, Joanna | 20 JUN 1863 |
| FIRMAGE, William | AIKEN, Mary | 20 OCT 1858 |
| FIRRELL, William F. | HOOPER, Frances Odelia | 15 AUG 1859 |
| FISCHER, Andrew | BERRY, Margaret | 12 APR 1864 |
| FISCHER, Charles B. | BROWN, Mary M. (blk) | 29 OCT 1868 |
| FISCHER, Edward Theodore | GATES, Ann Eliza | 02 JUL 1860 |
| FISCHER, Frederick | STAGMULLER, Louisa | 31 MAY 1866 |
| FISCHER, John Joseph | RAUB, Paulina | 20 SEP 1859 |
| FISCHER, Philip | BARNES, Mary | 26 JAN 1863 |
| FISH, John | WATERHOLDER, Lizzie | 26 DEC 1867 |
| FISH, Willis | GENZLE, Lottie E. | 06 AUG 1866 |
| FISHER, Benjamin F. | CAUSTEN, Alice E. | 12 MAR 1864 |

| | | |
|---|---|---|
| FISHER, Daniel | HEINS, Rosa | 03 JUN 1864 |
| FISHER, David | DATCHER, Annie L. (blk) | 27 MAY 1861 |
| FISHER, George W. [1c] | STONE, Harriet A. | 26 NOV 1863 |
| FISHER, Henry | WILLIAMS, Josephine | 07 DEC 1860 |
| FISHER, Jacob | WILLIS, Margaret (blk) | 24 FEB 1864 |
| FISHER, James [12s] | MATTHEWS, Kate | 16 OCT 1862 |
| FISHER, John | CASEEN, Eliza | 18 NOV 1861 |
| FISHER, John | HAWKINS, Harriet (blk) | 20 JUL 1864 |
| FISHER, John | FINK, Kate | 01 APR 1865 |
| FISHER, John | RADCLIFF, Catharine | 12 DEC 1866 |
| FISHER, Samuel M. | BENTON, Rosetta | 22 FEB 1859 |
| FISHER, Simon | ROBB, Angela | 12 MAY 1869 |
| FISHER, Thomas | FLOOD, Ann (blk) | 02 MAY 1866 |
| FISHER, Thomas | JONES, Lavinia (blk) | 22 DEC 1868 |
| FISHER, Thomas Nelson | WOODARD, Julia Ann Eliza | 28 SEP 1867 |
| FISHER, Washington | TAYLOR, Sarah (blk) | 20 APR 1869 |
| FISHER, William | WAGNER, Kate | 26 DEC 1863 |
| FISSEL, Henry | MOORE, Sarah | 14 NOV 1863 |
| FISTER, John V. | ELMS, Lucy J. | 30 SEP 1868 |
| FITCH, Sidney A. | LUCE, Ella E. | 04 MAY 1864 |
| FITCHAN, Charles E. | KLINE, Susan | 16 MAY 1864 |
| FITCHET, William | STANNARD, Frances Ann (blk) | 25 MAY 1863 |
| FITSCH, Charles | RUEBENKAMP, Lina | 05 FEB 1862 |
| FITZ, Conrad | RESU, Fanny | 15 SEP 1864 |
| FITZGERALD, Edward | KERRON, Kate | 05 JUL 1865 |
| FITZGERALD, Eugene | CLARK, Sarah Fuller | 27 APR 1861 |
| FITZGERALD, Hobart E. Capt. [11] | HICKS, Rosa B., [Mrs.] | 20 OCT 1862 |
| FITZGERALD, James | LISTON, Bridget | 28 DEC 1869 |
| FITZGERALD, John | MURRAY, Harriet | 29 MAR 1861 |
| FITZGERALD, John R. | CONNERS, Mary | 13 JUL 1859 |
| FITZGERALD, Lawrence | O'DONNELL, Margaret | 16 FEB 1863 |
| FITZGERALD, Martin | DEE, Catherine | 02 JUL 1867 |
| FITZGERALD, Michael | OWSLEY, Bridget | 01 SEP 1859 |
| FITZGERALD, Michael | LAY, Ellen | 31 MAY 1862 |
| FITZGERALD, Michael | KANE, Ellen | 29 JAN 1863 |
| FITZGERALD, Michael | MADDEN, Annie | 25 MAY 1865 |
| FITZGERALD, Michael | O'BRIEN, Mary Ann | 22 SEP 1865 |
| FITZGERALD, Michael J. | BRANNAN, Mary Ann | 05 OCT 1858 |
| FITZGERALD, Michl. | HOLLOHAN, Mary E. | 04 MAY 1861 |
| FITZGERALD, Patrick | MULKAHA, Johanna | 11 OCT 1858 |
| FITZGERALD, Patrick | McSHAREY, Mary | 15 AUG 1859 |
| FITZGERALD, Patrick | BATTERSLY, Annie C. | 27 JAN 1864 |
| FITZGERALD, Richard | FLANIGAN, Mary Ann | 01 MAY 1863 |
| FITZGERALD, Robert | MORIARITY, Mary | 04 OCT 1867 |
| FITZGERALD, Robert | NEIL, Hanora | 17 OCT 1867 |
| FITZGERALD, Thomas | CONNER, Bridget | 17 JAN 1863 |
| FITZGERALD, Thomas | FOLEY, Mary | 18 APR 1863 |
| FITZGERALD, Thomas | RYAN, Mary | 08 JUN 1863 |
| FITZGERALD, Thomas | SHANE, Margaret | 07 JAN 1867 |
| FITZGERALD, William | MURPHY, Joanna | 11 APR 1863 |
| FITZGIBBON, Patrick | HUGHES, Johanna | 18 SEP 1865 |
| FITZHUGH, Albert W. [7b] | HYATT, Eliza J. | 19 FEB 1870 |
| FITZHUGH, George | FITZHUGH, Mary (blk) | 21 DEC 1867 |
| FITZHUGH, Gilbert | DAVIS, Adaline | 07 JAN 1864 |
| FITZHUGH, Hay Battle | ELLIOTT, Sarah (blk) | 18 APR 1866 |
| FITZHUGH, John B. | BURCH, Mary M. | 01 NOV 1864 |

District of Columbia Marriage Licenses, 1858-1870

| Groom | Bride | Date |
|---|---|---|
| FITZHUGH, Turner | MONTGOMERY, Ellen (blk) | 28 NOV 1863 |
| FITZMAURICE, Thomas | BROSNEHAN, Julia | 26 JUN 1863 |
| FITZMORRIS, Thomas | HAYS, Johanna | 18 AUG 1866 |
| FITZPATRICK, James | DARWELL, Jane | 02 SEP 1869 |
| FITZPATRICK, John | EASTON, Catherine | 07 JUL 1862 |
| FITZPATRICK, Terence | BOHLAYER, Annie Eliza | 13 JUL 1863 |
| FITZSIMMONS, Edward | TAFFE, Mary T. | 13 OCT 1865 |
| FITZUGH, Henry | MARSHALL, Chloe Ann (blk) | 21 FEB 1863 |
| FITZWILLIAM, Thomas F. [7b] | BOVEE, Lucy J. | 16 SEP 1869 |
| FIX, Francis F. (Lt. 144 Bat. V.R.) | HOPLEY, Annie | 19 SEP 1864 |
| FJORDAMN, Fleming | QUEEN, Marcy (blk) | 02 NOV 1859 |
| FLACK, John P. | WINDOM, Elizabeth C. | 23 NOV 1861 |
| FLAESCH, Charles | RELIHAN, Julia | 15 FEB 1869 |
| FLAGG, Edmund | GALLAHER, Kate A. | 18 FEB 1862 |
| FLAHERTY, Barney | CURLEY, Bridget | 20 JUL 1861 |
| FLAHERTY, Jeremiah | GRACE, Margaret | 18 JAN 1862 |
| FLAHERTY, John | KELLY, Catharine | 28 OCT 1865 |
| FLAHERTY, Patrick | FLAHERTY, Margaret | 21 MAY 1863 |
| FLAHERTY, Thomas | WEBSTER, Flora | 18 JAN 1862 |
| FLAHERTY, Thomas | GAVIN, Margaret | 15 SEP 1864 |
| FLAHETE, Michael | DRURY, Honora | 16 JAN 1864 |
| FLAMER, William J. | COOPER, Charlotte E. (blk) | 20 MAY 1869 |
| FLANAGAN, Bernard | DOLAN, Anna | 05 JUN 1860 |
| FLANAGAN, James O. | RICHTER, Barbara | 28 MAR 1861 |
| FLANAGAN, Jeremiah | KIRBY, Hannah | 02 JAN 1861 |
| FLANAGAN, John | FLAHERTY, Nora | 18 AUG 1866 |
| FLANAGAN, William | HEDIGAN, Bridget | 31 JAN 1867 |
| FLANAGEN, James J. | LUNEY, Hannah | 02 NOV 1867 |
| FLANARY, Barnard | MEAD, Ann | 09 JUN 1862 |
| FLANNAGAN, John | GRIFFIN, Mary | 17 JUL 1862 |
| FLANNAGAN, Patrick | WELCH, Catherine | 20 SEP 1859 |
| FLANNAGAN, Patrick | McLAUGHLIN, Mary | 17 APR 1863 |
| FLATHER, George W. [2] | DUTROW, R. Sophia | 01 FEB 1867 |
| FLATHER, John | GREAVES, Maria Jane | 28 JUL 1862 |
| FLATHER, John H. | WEBSTER, Martha V. | 12 MAR 1860 |
| FLAVAHN, John | KEARN, Julia | 23 SEP 1862 |
| FLEET, Robert | MINOR, Amelia (blk) | 27 JUL 1863 |
| FLEET, Robert | GREEN, Mary (blk) | 28 APR 1870 |
| FLEET, Samuel E.W. | NEALE, Lucy S. | 24 NOV 1859 |
| FLEGENSTEIN, George | SCHOLLHAUS, Eva Margaretha | 13 JUL 1859 |
| FLEISHELL, Jacob | DYSER, Anne Mary | 05 OCT 1863 |
| FLEMENTS, Charles | SEMMES, Sarah | 07 MAR 1861 |
| FLEMING, Austin | HARRIS, Grace (blk) | 14 MAY 1869 |
| FLEMING, James | WILLIAMS, Jane (blk) | 24 DEC 1868 |
| FLEMING, John E. | WISWELL, Hester | 20 OCT 1863 |
| FLEMING, Patrick | CARBERY, Ann | 04 SEP 1858 |
| FLEMING, Patrick | FOLEY, Mary | 29 DEC 1860 |
| FLEMMING, Patrick | FISHER, Eva Augusta Wilhelmina | 12 FEB 1861 |
| FLETCHER, Charles F. | KNIGHT, Jennie | 28 FEB 1865 |
| FLETCHER, Croton | BAILEY, Martha | 02 FEB 1867 |
| FLETCHER, Croton | LEACH, Alice E. | 08 AUG 1867 |
| FLETCHER, Edward T. | SEBASTIAN, Marion | 12 JUN 1865 |
| FLETCHER, Francis E. | DAVIS, Susanna | 02 JUL 1868 |
| FLETCHER, George W. | JENKINS, Adelaide | 02 AUG 1865 |
| FLETCHER, George Washington | MARSHALL, Barbara (blk) | 12 MAY 1869 |
| FLETCHER, James H. | BELL, Mariam | 04 MAR 1870 |

District of Columbia Marriage Licenses, 1858-1870

| | | |
|---|---|---|
| FLETCHER, John | MEAGHER, Bridget | 18 MAY 1867 |
| FLETCHER, John H. | ADAMS, Caroline C. | 08 DEC 1859 |
| FLETCHER, Lawrence J. | DAVIS, Mary E. (blk) | 22 AUG 1866 |
| FLETCHER, Philip Franklin | SWAN, Ann Virginia | 14 NOV 1862 |
| FLETCHER, Stephen | KERR, Lucy (blk) | 28 DEC 1863 |
| FLETCHER, Stephen | HAWKINS, Louisa (blk) | 06 APR 1865 |
| FLETCHER, William | LAUGHLIN, Susan | 17 FEB 1863 |
| FLETCHER, William | FORD, Charlotte (blk) | 24 JAN 1867 |
| FLETCHER, William | JENKINS, Maggie | 25 JAN 1870 |
| FLETCHER, William H. | DANT, Martha R. | 06 MAY 1864 |
| FLETCHER, William H. | WARD, Mary E. | 27 MAY 1868 |
| FLETCHER, William L. | JENKINS, Ann R. | 06 JUN 1860 |
| FLEURY, William B. | BAYLISS, Mary B. | 24 DEC 1868 |
| FLICK, August | WOLF, Annie | 21 JUN 1864 |
| FLIEDNER, Leo. A. | COHEN, Ellen | 27 JUL 1865 |
| FLING, John W. | WHITE, Ellen | 23 SEP 1862 |
| FLINN, Patrick | MARTIN, Emma | 10 MAY 1861 |
| FLOECKLER, Gustave | BEAVANS, Emma L. | 12 JAN 1870 |
| FLOOD, James Wm. | BARNACLO, Mary S. | 01 OCT 1866 |
| FLOOD, John | LANE, Ann | 19 NOV 1863 |
| FLOOD, Richard H. | SAUNDERS, Lizzie E. | 02 DEC 1858 |
| FLOOD, William | NOLAN, Margaret | 03 SEP 1858 |
| FLORENCE, Benj. F. | LYNN, Alice L. | 21 MAY 1866 |
| FLORENCE, Christopher | HEMMELWAY, Mary | 30 JUN 1866 |
| FLOUREY, Robert E. | SCROGGINS, Mary E. | 05 JUL 1859 |
| FLOWER, James M. [4] | CONES, Lucy L. | 03 SEP 1862 |
| FLOWERREE, John W. | BROWN, Annie E. | 09 MAR 1869 |
| FLOWERS, Alexander M. | SEMMES, Mary Ann | 30 APR 1870 |
| FLOYD, Charles M. | LAWN, Delia | 06 OCT 1864 |
| FLOYD, William | KENNEY, Catherine | 09 JAN 1869 |
| FLUGER, Gustavus | COLE, Joana | 04 OCT 1866 |
| FLYNN, Arthur | FLYNN, Catherine (dau. Cornelius) | 25 SEP 1866 |
| FLYNN, Daniel | HOGAN, Hanora | 04 MAR 1862 |
| FLYNN, David | McNAMARA, Julia | 28 JUL 1864 |
| FLYNN, James | WELCH, Delia | 12 MAR 1866 |
| FLYNN, James | LAWERCY, Kate | 21 SEP 1869 |
| FLYNN, John | McCARTY, Catherine | 01 JUN 1859 |
| FLYNN, John | HEFLYNN, Mary Ellen | 06 APR 1865 |
| FLYNN, John F. | REARDON, Julia | 22 SEP 1869 |
| FLYNN, Michael | CRIMMINS, Bridget | 14 OCT 1864 |
| FLYNN, Michael | DALTON, Ellen | 03 NOV 1864 |
| FLYNN, Michael | SULLIVAN, Ann | 06 MAY 1865 |
| FLYNN, Michael | MANNIX, Catharine | 11 NOV 1865 |
| FLYNN, Michael | McMAHON, Joanna | 10 MAY 1867 |
| FLYNN, Michael | CONNELL, Bridget | 28 FEB 1870 |
| FLYNN, Patrick | GRAHAM, Catherine | 18 JUN 1860 |
| FLYNN, Peter | BRANNAGAN, Catharine | 10 MAY 1862 |
| FLYNN, Thomas | REILY, Catherine | 10 AUG 1863 |
| FLYNN, Thomas | DOWNEY, Catharine | 19 OCT 1865 |
| FLYNN, Timothy | BRIEN, Ellen | 13 AUG 1863 |
| FLYNN, William | GRADY, Ellen | 15 JAN 1867 |
| FODER, John | ELLIOT, Cary E. | 17 APR 1860 |
| FOGARTY, Dennis | KAIN, Bridget | 20 JUN 1860 |
| FOGARTY, John | CAHIL, Johanna | 22 DEC 1864 |
| FOGARTY, William | CARROLL, Mary | 04 MAY 1863 |
| FOGEL, Jacob | FREFLERINN, Rosina | 17 JUN 1863 |

District of Columbia Marriage Licenses, 1858-1870

| | | |
|---|---|---|
| FOGG, Joseph S. | SEDRICK, Mary Virginia | 22 JUL 1867 |
| FOLEY, Bartholomew | HARRINGTON, Mary | 09 SEP 1868 |
| FOLEY, Daniel | DALTON, Ellen | 30 JAN 1866 |
| FOLEY, James | BAGLEY, Mary | 24 AUG 1861 |
| FOLEY, John | KING, Bridget | 16 FEB 1863 |
| FOLEY, John | KING, Jane | 14 FEB 1863 |
| FOLEY, John | LYNCH, Bridget | 20 APR 1864 |
| FOLEY, John | SULLIVAN, Ellen | 09 JAN 1865 |
| FOLEY, John | DONOHOO, Catharine | 12 FEB 1866 |
| FOLEY, John | O'DONNELL, Bridget | 11 APR 1866 |
| FOLEY, John | WELSH, Mary | 19 MAY 1866 |
| FOLEY, John | FITZGERALD, Margaret | 20 JUL 1868 |
| FOLEY, John J. | KNOWLES, Gertrude | 26 SEP 1868 |
| FOLEY, John P. | FITZPATRICK, Ann F. | 11 OCT 1869 |
| FOLEY, John R. | BECKENBAUGH, Clara Z. | 19 NOV 1866 |
| FOLEY, Michael | SWEENY, Johanna | 09 SEP 1865 |
| FOLEY, Patrick | SWEENY, Catherine | 15 JUL 1860 |
| FOLEY, Patrick | SULLIVAN, Mary | 05 JUL 1861 |
| FOLEY, Patrick | CRONIN, Margaret | 15 DEC 1863 |
| FOLEY, Thomas | LYNCH, Annie | 18 JUN 1860 |
| FOLK, William H. [7a] | MARSHALL, Sarah W. | 07 NOV 1866 |
| FOLKS, Thomas | FREER, Josephine | 24 DEC 1867 |
| FOLLAND, David | FISCHER, Bade | 06 APR 1864 |
| FOLLANSHEE, George | CASSIDAY, Emily | 17 JAN 1861 |
| FOLSOM, Paris H. [11] | LOWRY, Ella E. | 30 MAY 1864 |
| FOLTZ, Godfrey | WOLFE, Margaret | 04 JUN 1864 |
| FOLTZ, Henry M. | TENNISSON, Lavinia | 30 NOV 1861 |
| FOLWELL, Thomas S. | FAWSETT, Hattie | 18 FEB 1867 |
| FONDERHEIDE, Henry | VONBEITZ, Anna | 24 DEC 1863 |
| FOOT, Charles H. | LEE, Mary E. | 06 DEC 1865 |
| FOOTE, Thomas R. [13g] | STARK, Melissa G. [blk] | 11 AUG 1864 |
| FOOTE, William | MORGAN, Betsy (blk) | 17 DEC 1862 |
| FORBES, George, Senr. | FERGUSON, Mary E. | 01 FEB 1870 |
| FORCE, Moses M. | O'NEIL, Kate | 28 FEB 1865 |
| FORD, Alfred | BOONE, Rosie | 19 JUN 1869 |
| FORD, C.C. | McBRIDE, Mary E. | 29 JAN 1869 |
| FORD, C.S. | LEE, Alice | 24 JUL 1869 |
| FORD, Charles W. | BRINKLEY, Mary E. | 02 JAN 1863 |
| FORD, Columbus | HAW, Mary E. (blk) | 02 AUG 1866 |
| FORD, Edward | ADAMS, Margaret Ann | 19 OCT 1866 |
| FORD, George | BENNER, Virginia G. | 25 JUL 1863 |
| FORD, John | JOHNSON, Rose (blk) | 07 MAY 1864 |
| FORD, John | LINKUM, Louisa (blk) | 07 MAY 1864 |
| FORD, John | JACKSON, Maria (blk) | 10 AUG 1866 |
| FORD, John | LEE, Eliza (blk) | 14 AUG 1866 |
| FORD, John | WILLIAMS, Lascilla (blk) | 10 MAR 1868 |
| FORD, John | PENNY, Martha L. | 02 DEC 1869 |
| FORD, John B. | FISHER, Mary L. | 27 MAY 1865 |
| FORD, Josiah [11] | BRADFORD, Sallie | 29 DEC 1862 |
| FORD, S. Calvert, Jr. | LeCOMPTE, Anna C. | 26 NOV 1860 |
| FORD, Sylvester | JORDAN, Georgiana (blk) | 16 MAR 1868 |
| FORD, Thomas | CLAIBORNE, Mary (blk) | 26 DEC 1866 |
| FORD, Thomas | HENSON, Julia Ann Lizzie (blk) | 08 DEC 1868 |
| FORD, William | JACKSON, Lucinda (blk) | 20 DEC 1860 |
| FORD, William | KELLY, Caroline | 30 SEP 1862 |
| FORD, William | BURNS, Maria (blk) | 29 JAN 1867 |

| | | |
|---|---|---|
| FORD, William | ROBINSON, Hannah (blk) | 09 JUL 1868 |
| FORD, William | SMITH, Katie (blk) | 31 DEC 1869 |
| FORD, William T. | COOPER, Susan | 18 APR 1861 |
| FORD, Winter | NEWBY, Alice (blk) | 06 APR 1867 |
| FORD, Wm. | COLEMAN, Ellen | 27 NOV 1869 |
| FORDAN, Carl Eugene Edward | HARK, Wilhelmina Katherina Karoline | 08 JUN 1867 |
| FORDHAM, George [6le] | HUTCHERSON, Emma J. | 22 OCT 1867 |
| FOREMAN, Nicholas | HAYDEN, Helen Ann (blk) | 29 JUN 1868 |
| FOREMAN, Samuel | MERCER, Laura | 15 MAY 1866 |
| FOREN, Michael | MURT, Ellen | 24 AUG 1861 |
| FORGE, Samuel | BELL, Sarah (blk) | 19 JUN 1865 |
| FORK, Lewis F. | PETTIGREW, Grace | 27 NOV 1862 |
| FORLONG, Moses | HAYES, Margaret | 07 FEB 1861 |
| FORREST, Adolphus F. | SHEEHY, Helen | 24 AUG 1860 |
| FORREST, Adolphus R. | MULLAN, Katherine | 12 JUN 1866 |
| FORREST, Barney | CURK, Hanora | 02 MAY 1864 |
| FORREST, Calden B., Jr. [12s] | SHIELDS, Mary V. | 28 MAY 1862 |
| FORREST, Charles | LUCKY, Clarissa A. | 21 AUG 1865 |
| FORREST, D.C. | LINDSEY, C.S. | 10 JUL 1860 |
| FORREST, John | WATSON, Laura | 29 JAN 1869 |
| FORREST, John W. | DENNISON, Sarah (blk) | 27 OCT 1866 |
| FORREST, Reason | BELL, Rachel | 21 OCT 1869 |
| FORREST, Zachariah | WORSTER, M.V.A.Z. | 11 AUG 1860 |
| FORRESTER, James [10] | JARBOE, Elizabeth * | 11 FEB 1861 |
| FORSKEY, Shadrack | BARNES, Emma (blk) | 01 NOV 1869 |
| FORSYTH, Ernest E. | ADAMS, Marcie V. | 20 FEB 1865 |
| FORSYTH, George R. | HALL, Susan A. | 26 OCT 1859 |
| FORSYTH, Lewis Cass | JANVIER, Janie B. | 06 OCT 1860 |
| FORSYTHE, Edward D. [10] | BROWN, Mary C. | 04 OCT 1864 |
| FORTUNE, Reuben | LEWIS, Henrietta (blk) | 14 JUL 1865 |
| FOSKEY, George H. | CARTER, Annie M. (blk) | 07 JUL 1869 |
| FOSTER, Andrew | MAGUIRE, Minerva | 19 AUG 1863 |
| IFOSTER, Charles | BALL, Nancy (blk) | 04 APR 1865 |
| FOSTER, Connallas B. | HARDING, P.C. | 08 JUL 1867 |
| FOSTER, Edward [6le] | MIDDLETON, Eliza | 20 NOV 1866 |
| FOSTER, Edward W. | RIDDLE, Caroline M. | 31 DEC 1868 |
| FOSTER, Franklin J. | WEAVER, Elizabeth J. | 09 JUL 1866 |
| FOSTER, Frederic E. | HULL, Margaret E. | 13 NOV 1869 |
| FOSTER, George | FOSTER, Evelina (blk) | 03 JUL 1866 |
| FOSTER, Henry D., USN | CLARK, Jennie B. | 02 FEB 1864 |
| FOSTER, James A. | OWENS, Harriet A. | 03 JUN 1862 |
| FOSTER, John | GRAINER, Lena | 03 MAR 1862 |
| FOSTER, John D. | UTERNIEHLE, Mary Janet | 02 JUL 1864 |
| FOSTER, Middleton | MACK, Martha (blk) | 01 AUG 1863 |
| FOSTER, Patrick | KEHOE, Bridget | 31 OCT 1864 |
| FOSTER, Thomas | JOHNSON, Catharine (blk) | 30 MAR 1870 |
| FOSTER, William | GREEN, Sarah Jane (blk) | 23 JUL 1867 |
| FOSTER, William | SHAW, Mary | 02 JAN 1869 |
| FOTLE, George | NOA, Henrietta | 13 JUL 1865 |
| FOUKE, Isaac | BIDDLEMAN, Marian E. | 24 DEC 1864 |
| FOULKE, Charles W. | MILLS, Hannah C. | 02 AUG 1864 |
| FOUNTAIN, Benj. Franklin | REEDER, Mary Ellen (blk) | 24 DEC 1866 |
| FOUNTAIN, Felix | JOHNSON, Anna (blk) | 26 DEC 1865 |
| FOUNTAIN, Joseph | JOHNSIN. Charity (blk) | 31 AUG 1867 |
| FOUNTAIN, Thomas | SWEENY, Agnes (blk) | 21 JAN 1868 |
| FOURST, John | CHAPMAN, Annie | 15 AUG 1864 |

District of Columbia Marriage Licenses, 1858-1870

| | | |
|---|---|---|
| FOWLE, John A. | RAMSEY, Eliza B. | 26 FEB 1863 |
| FOWLER, Allen G. | BLAND, Mary E. | 27 OCT 1859 |
| FOWLER, Arthur | HOGAN, Ella A. | 22 JUN 1869 |
| FOWLER, Benjamin T. [10] | SOMERS, Margaret Ann | 02 MAY 1868 |
| FOWLER, Dewitt [6] | HARDY, Kate | 06 SEP 1869 |
| FOWLER, Edwin J. | BRITT, Elizabeth | 29 AUG 1866 |
| FOWLER, Edwin J. | BRITT, Elizabeth | 11 JUL 1868 |
| FOWLER, George Alfred [10] | WILKERSON, Rosella Edmonia | 17 FEB 1870 |
| FOWLER, Isaac | THOMMA, Mary | 20 DEC 1865 |
| FOWLER, J. Marion | BESTOR, Henrietta M. | 02 OCT 1868 |
| FOWLER, J.H. | LLOYD, Sarah Jane | 03 AUG 1868 |
| FOWLER, James D. | CONNELL, Eliza | 12 NOV 1866 |
| FOWLER, James H. | SMACK, Sarah E. | 17 APR 1865 |
| FOWLER, John R. | BRADY, Margt. E. | 21 MAR 1862 |
| FOWLER, Joseph B. [11j] | DARNALL, Mayetta B. | 28 SEP 1869 |
| FOWLER, Richard L. | DAVIS, Marian F. | 25 AUG 1865 |
| FOWLER, Samuel | BAILEY, Sarah Elizabeth | 22 JUL 1867 |
| FOWLER, Stephen | CROMPTON, Lucy | 10 FEB 1868 |
| FOWLER, Walter E. | DANFORTH, Virginia | 24 SEP 1866 |
| FOWLER, William | BRIDEWELL, Martha E. | 08 AUG 1863 |
| FOWLER, William A. | WALTZ, Barbara | 04 FEB 1861 |
| FOWLER, William Thos. | ROSE, Ann Eliza | 21 NOV 1861 |
| FOX, Albert F. [5] | KELLEY, Mary Jane | 21 JUL 1869 |
| FOX, Arthur | THOMAS, Lucinda | 14 DEC 1869 |
| FOX, Charles | BETZ, Mary | 20 JUL 1864 |
| FOX, Charles | COLEMAN, Lucinda (blk) | 12 NOV 1866 |
| FOX, George W. [6r] | SAVASTAN, Sarah [Catherine] | 03 OCT 1859 |
| FOX, John | BOYLE, Mary | 21 AUG 1868 |
| FOX, John | CONNELL, Ellen | 08 MAY 1869 |
| FOX, John W. | DICE, Amelia Elizabeth | 21 JUL 1860 |
| FOX, Martin | POWERS, Ann | 11 DEC 1865 |
| FOX, Norman | McKNIGHT, Julia T. | 25 NOV 1868 |
| FOX, Peter | QUINN, Mary | 30 SEP 1867 |
| FOX, Samuel B. [2] | EAGAN, Ella | 20 MAR 1865 |
| FOX, Thomas | CRONIN, Margaret A. | 01 SEP 1864 |
| FOY, James Madison | DENT, Elizabeth (blk) | 13 MAY 1867 |
| FRANC, Henry | ROSENTHAL, Barbette | 29 MAR 1865 |
| FRANC, Leopold | HEYN, Ida | 06 OCT 1865 |
| FRANCE, J.M.D. | SHEED, Leida R. | 11 JUL 1866 |
| FRANCE, Joseph H., Jr. | JAMES, Hannah F. | 16 OCT 1869 |
| FRANCIS, Albert A. | REED, Marion (blk) | 07 MAY 1870 |
| FRANCIS, Elias | DUNCAN, Emily (blk) | 17 MAY 1865 |
| FRANCIS, John H. | FORREST, Adelaide | 01 APR 1865 |
| FRANCIS, John P. | CLARK, Anne Howard | 30 JUL 1863 |
| FRANCISCO, Gustavus Franz | GROVER, Sarah Alice | 22 MAY 1865 |
| FRANÇOIS, Theophile | ROUX, Jennie | 06 JUN 1865 |
| FRANEY, H.B. | SMITH, Harriet M. (blk) | 16 SEP 1869 |
| FRANK, Gottlieb | EMENT, Maria | 25 APR 1860 |
| FRANK, John A. | HOPPS, Mary J. | 18 SEP 1867 |
| FRANK, Joseph | HORNBAG, Kuna | 08 MAY 1860 |
| FRANK, Joseph | CLARKE, Mary A. | 21 OCT 1861 |
| FRANK, William | SILLER, Elizabeth | 28 JAN 1862 |
| FRANKLIN, Benjamin | MAGWA, Mary | 01 AUG 1862 |
| FRANKLIN, Benjamin | DAVIS, Elizabeth | 14 NOV 1862 |
| FRANKLIN, Benjamin | McDEVITT, Jane | 16 APR 1864 |
| FRANKLIN, Fendall [12s] | EDDENS, Sarah L. | 04 OCT 1860 |

| | | |
|---|---|---|
| FRANKLIN, James | GREEN, Catherine | 09 JAN 1868 |
| FRANKLIN, James W. | JOHNSON, Anna E. (blk) | 19 JAN 1867 |
| FRANKLIN, John | TALBURT, Polly | 26 SEP 1867 |
| FRANKLIN, John | LINNEY, Margaret | 16 NOV 1867 |
| FRANKLIN, Joseph W. | CRANSTON, Mary A. | 22 NOV 1858 |
| FRANKLIN, Madison | LEWIS, Mary A. (blk) | 02 SEP 1869 |
| FRANKLIN, Richard | GAULT, Eliza (blk) | 19 NOV 1863 |
| FRANKLIN, Samuel | HILZHEIM, Rebecca | 22 SEP 1866 |
| FRANKLIN, York | RANDOLPH, Malinda (blk) | 28 JUL 1864 |
| FRANZ, John | LUTZ, Annie E. | 29 APR 1865 |
| FRANZE, Angelo V. | ROLLINGS, Annie R. | 30 AUG 1869 |
| FRANZONI, Joseph D. | PARSONS, Laura V. | 07 NOV 1862 |
| FRASCA, Robert B. | HANREHAN, Mary E. | 18 MAY 1864 |
| FRASER, Wm. | CUMMINGS, Mary | 21 JAN 1864 |
| FRAUNNCK, Jacob | PLUMMER, Mary Ann | 19 MAY 1863 |
| FRAWNER, John | SEATON, Emma | 02 DEC 1869 |
| FRAYSER, Collier C. | CROME, Margaret | 20 AUG 1860 |
| FRAZER, George | MARTIN, Mary Ann | 14 JUL 1864 |
| FRAZIER, Benjamin | WRIGHT, Mary S. | 11 MAY 1864 |
| FRAZIER, Charles Watson | SHREVE, Eugenia | 14 FEB 1868 |
| FRAZIER, Chas. Jefferson | CHILDRESS, Ann Rebecca | 04 APR 1859 |
| FRAZIER, Frederick | GIVENS, Louisa (blk) | 10 DEC 1866 |
| FRAZIER, George | TYLER, Martha (blk) | 29 DEC 1864 |
| FRAZIER, Hamilton | LEWIS, Delia [m. 2 MAR 1871] | 05 JAN 1869 |
| FRAZIER, Hercules | JOHNSON, Alexzina (blk) | 31 MAR 1859 |
| FRAZIER, James | SMITH, Eliza (blk) | 30 APR 1868 |
| FRAZIER, James | GREEN, Margaret (blk) | 15 JUL 1869 |
| FRAZIER, John | WILLIAMS, Agnes | 15 AUG 1868 |
| FRAZIER, Madison | WALKER, Ellanor (blk) | 17 JUL 1865 |
| FRAZIER, Moses | GREEN, Catherine (blk) | 24 DEC 1866 |
| FRAZIER, T. Theodore | DARNALL, M. Isadore | 19 JUN 1866 |
| FRAZIER, William | JACKSON, Martha (blk) | 23 DEC 1862 |
| FRAZIER, William | DALE, Amanda | 13 SEP 1865 |
| FREAS, E.L. | SHUGERT, Clara | 21 JUN 1866 |
| FREBER, Adam | GAMBLE, Ann | 29 AUG 1865 |
| FREBER, Adam | OWENS, Lydia | 18 APR 1867 |
| FRED, Kimith | PRICE, Mary Ellen | 20 DEC 1865 |
| FREE, Thos. | MONEY, Susan Ann | 05 JAN 1865 |
| FREEBURGER, Isaac [6m] | MARTIN, Fannie | 07 MAY 1862 |
| FREED, Michael | BROWN, Mary E. | 07 MAY 1867 |
| FREELAND, Daniel [6] | PAGET, Frances M. | 07 JAN 1869 |
| FREELAND, David | SMITH, Lydia (blk) | 18 MAR 1862 |
| FREELIN, John | HOWELL, Mary E. | 23 JAN 1869 |
| FREEMAN, Benjamin H. | EDMONSTON, Sarah (blk) | 26 OCT 1866 |
| FREEMAN, Charles | PALMER, Mary | 16 MAY 1863 |
| FREEMAN, Frank R. | BRUCE, Susan N. (blk) | 01 JUN 1864 |
| FREEMAN, Henry C. | HANKINS, Lizzie | 24 OCT 1865 |
| FREEMAN, James H. | JONES, Arietta (blk) | 05 JUL 1866 |
| FREEMAN, John | DEAKINS, Amelia | 22 NOV 1864 |
| FREEMAN, John | COLEMAN, Mary | 30 JAN 1866 |
| FREEMAN, John R. | LEWIS, Mary E. (blk) | 25 SEP 1858 |
| FREEMAN, John W. | CYRUSS, Anna | 18 DEC 1861 |
| FREEMAN, Nicholas | ROBERTSON, Betsy (blk) | 13 JUN 1867 |
| FREEMAN, William A. | WARREN, Ellen | 05 JUN 1868 |
| FREEMAN, William L. | BRENT, Emily A. (blk) | 25 FEB 1864 |
| FRENCH, Burdock | CUSTIS, Rachel (blk) | 08 JUL 1865 |

District of Columbia Marriage Licenses, 1858-1870

| | | |
|---|---|---|
| FRENCH, Charles D. | JACKEL, Matilda | 05 JUL 1859 |
| FRENCH, Evander | LANE, Sophie C. | 26 DEC 1867 |
| FRENCH, Francis O. | TUCK, Ellen M. | 28 FEB 1861 |
| FRENCH, George B. | ELLIS, Susanna | 01 MAY 1866 |
| FRENCH, George F. [12s] | HILL, Clara A. | 14 OCT 1862 |
| FRENCH, George H. | COLLIER, M. Kate | 13 MAY 1865 |
| FRENCH, James [12s] | LENNAHAM, Elizth. | 07 APR 1862 |
| FRENCH, James A. | McCOY, Susan | 29 JUN 1867 |
| FRENCH, Laurence E. | MALLOY, Josephine S. | 04 MAY 1863 |
| FRENCH, Otho [9e] | BEARDSLEY, Martha E. | 26 DEC 1860 |
| FRENCH, Samuel | LYCETT, Ellen | 06 FEB 1869 |
| FRENCH, Thomas Henry | HAGGERTY, Anne Maria | 30 SEP 1859 |
| FRENCH, William | IREWIN, Mary | 18 OCT 1866 |
| FRENCH, William T. | MILLER, Louisa A. | 15 OCT 1861 |
| FREUND, Frederick | FRIESCH, Elizabeth | 18 SEP 1862 |
| FREUND, John | RUDOLPH, Henrietta | 13 OCT 1865 |
| FREUNDT, Joseph | GUNDLING, Elizabeth | 21 NOV 1865 |
| FREY, John A. | BEACHUM, Leona V. | 07 MAR 1860 |
| FREY, John A. | DAVIS, Julia A., Mrs. | 29 JAN 1870 |
| FREY, Robert R. | STURGIS, Hannah Catherine | 16 DEC 1868 |
| FREY, [blank] | ROHRER, Mary Elizabeth | 25 JUN 1863 |
| FRICKMAN, John | SADER, Mary | 23 JUN 1864 |
| FRIDDIG, George | KRINST, Ernestine | 22 MAR 1870 |
| FRIDELL, John | HASKINS, Emma E. | 07 FEB 1868 |
| FRIDLEY, Benjamin F. | MARTIN, Mary | 09 SEP 1863 |
| FRIDLEY, W.H.H. | SADLER, Sarah A. | 09 NOV 1863 |
| FRIEBUS, J.A. Theodore | VanTYNE, Florida H. | 10 MAY 1865 |
| FRIEDRICKS, Carl A. | FALKENRICKS, Catrine W. | 14 MAY 1870 |
| FRIELL, Patrick | KILHOOLY, Mary | 30 APR 1869 |
| FRIER, Hugh | WOODS, Elizabeth | 29 MAR 1860 |
| FRIER, John J. | NORTON, Frances A.H. | 30 JAN 1865 |
| FRIETZ, Christian | KAUFMAN, Katie | 13 OCT 1869 |
| FRIGITT, Robert Eugene | THECKER, Mary Elizabeth | 08 SEP 1866 |
| FRINKS, Charles | CLEVELAND, Sarah C. | 25 APR 1865 |
| FRIPP, Joseph | HOHN, Hannah | 03 MAR 1863 |
| FRISARD, Frederick Louis | LOUMAN, Augusta | 18 JUL 1867 |
| FRISBIE, Henry | SPENCER, Caroline (blk) | 26 MAR 1868 |
| FRISBY, Thomas M. | McCARTY, Mary M. | 29 JUL 1862 |
| FRISHMUTH, Charles | MALBON, Emma Jane | 30 SEP 1863 |
| FRISTOE, Edward T. | LAUB, Julia | 02 MAR 1859 |
| FRITCH, Lawrence | BATSCHIN, Annie | 14 MAY 1869 |
| FRITZ, Frederick, Jr. | HOWARD, Margaret | 22 APR 1862 |
| FRIZZELL, William J. | MITCHELL, Louisa A. | 27 APR 1868 |
| FROMAN, August | BÖCKER, Auguste | 31 DEC 1868 |
| FROMAN, Wilson | HILL, Harriet (blk) | 16 MAR 1866 |
| FRONT ROYAL, Washington | BONZER, Rebecca (blk) | 24 AUG 1864 |
| FROST, Charles F. | DUNBAR, Sarah (blk) | 26 SEP 1867 |
| FROST, George Archibald | WISSMAN, Mary Anna | 30 SEP 1867 |
| FROST, William H. | HUGHES, Harriet Jane (blk) | 24 NOV 1862 |
| FROST, William H. | SYPHAX, Maria C. | 10 NOV 1868 |
| FROST, William S. | GLIDDEN, Nellie | 02 DEC 1864 |
| FROST, William [6m] | BOOTHE, Elizabeth | 14 JAN 1864 |
| FRY, Daniel N. [6le] | MARCHE, Adelaide S. | 28 AUG 1865 |
| FRY, Francis | BARR, Mary E. | 19 APR 1870 |
| FRY, James | SMALLWOOD, Ellen (blk) | 29 NOV 1869 |
| FRY, John | WILDMAN, Dora E. | 26 DEC 1866 |

District of Columbia Marriage Licenses, 1858-1870

| | | |
|---|---|---|
| FRY, Joseph | THORNTON, Lizzie (blk) | 26 AUG 1869 |
| FUERST, George | LYONS, Mary | 16 JUL 1866 |
| FUGITT, Chas. F. | BARRON, Laura E. | 13 FEB 1860 |
| FUGITT, Eugene | WORTHEN, Laura V. | 21 SEP 1868 |
| FUGITT, George B. [11] | BEAN, Kate | 16 APR 1868 |
| FUGITT, James A. | BEALL, Fannie | 11 AUG 1859 |
| FULLALOVE, James | STONE, Francis Ann | 22 DEC 1862 |
| FULLALOVE, Richard | PALMER, Emeline F. | 24 NOV 1858 |
| FULLALOVE, Thomas | RILEY, Ann A. | 17 JAN 1863 |
| FULLALOVE, William | WILSON, Elizabeth | 01 APR 1862 |
| FULLER, Edson Eugene | TRAVIS, Phebe Jane | 02 MAR 1869 |
| FULLER, Henry | MELLENTRE, Hannah (blk) | 02 SEP 1868 |
| FULLER, John | BAKER, Martha | 23 APR 1861 |
| FULLER, Perry [11] | REANE, Mary | 19 JUN 1865 |
| FULLER, Robert H. | BEERS, Maggie A. | 04 OCT 1866 |
| FULLER, Webster | KEITHLEY, Isabella N. | 29 SEP 1862 |
| FULLER, William H. | PETERS, Louise | 11 OCT 1862 |
| FULLMER, Joseph H. | WOOLFORD, Mary Jane | 14 DEC 1863 |
| FULTON, Charles | WILSON, Hettie (blk) | 25 DEC 1865 |
| FULTON, Henry | MEREDITH, Elizabeth | 14 DEC 1868 |
| FULTON, James Albert | FOLEY, Elizabeth | 03 MAR 1869 |
| FUNDESTEIN, Henry Philip | MOHR, Katrine | 20 DEC 1868 |
| FUNK, George | CLEAVELAND, Caroline | 30 DEC 1862 |
| FURGUSON, John H. | BECKETT, Margaret A. | 30 AUG 1866 |
| FURGUSON, Samuel | BUTLER, Ellen | 16 OCT 1862 |
| FURLONG, Daniel | BURGISS, Henrietta (blk) | 22 AUG 1863 |
| FURLONG, Josiah G. | MEEKS, Joanna | 04 FEB 1864 |
| FURY, Michael | WINGATE, Mary Jane | 16 OCT 1863 |
| FUSS, William A. | AVERY, Sallie | 18 JUL 1860 |
| FUSSELBAUGH, John S. | FORBES, Eliza J. | 28 JUL 1863 |
| FUSSELL, Jacob | KRAFFT, Caroline C. | 27 JUL 1861 |

# G

| | | |
|---|---|---|
| GABURRI, Leone | AYLWARD, Ada B. | 01 NOV 1859 |
| GADDIS, Cornelius | BROWN, Mary Jane (blk) | 20 DEC 1866 |
| GADDIS, Lemuel [10] | SPICER, Maria Leonora | 19 MAY 1859 |
| GADLEY, Daniel | JEFFERS, Martha | 14 MAY 1868 |
| GADSBY, George | HUTCHINSON, Laura Ellen (blk) | 24 MAY 1860 |
| GAEGLER, Anthony | WATTS, Martha E. | 11 OCT 1869 |
| GAEGLER, John | RAAB, Ann M.E. | 11 NOV 1869 |
| GAFFNEY, James | McFARLAND, Hannah | 08 FEB 1867 |
| GAFFNEY, Patrick | HOWARD, Jane | 24 JAN 1868 |
| GAFFNEY, Thomas | RICKARD, Mary | 08 SEP 1866 |
| GAGE, Alfred H. [11] | TILLEY, Amelia | 11 JAN 1869 |
| GAIER, Alexander A. | HAMANN, Lucinda | 05 JAN 1870 |
| GAILLARD, Eugene | FRANÇOIS, Louise C. | 22 JUL 1865 |
| GAINER, Charles | HYDE, Mary J. | 28 AUG 1865 |
| GAINES, David | BOMBREY, Sophia | 13 DEC 1869 |
| GAINES, Edmund P. [4] | HOGAN, Frances | 27 OCT 1866 |
| GAINES, Jary | ORMSBY, Sarah | 03 MAR 1863 |
| GAINES, John | CAHILL, Ellen | 06 FEB 1869 |
| GAINES, Matthew | COLEMAN, Kate | 01 NOV 1865 |
| GAINES, Spencer | JOHNSON, Ann (blk) | 09 DEC 1868 |
| GAINES, Thomas | FRY, Mary Elizabeth (blk) | 06 FEB 1865 |
| GAINES, Thomas Hicks | POWERS, Mary I. | 22 JAN 1869 |

# District of Columbia Marriage Licenses, 1858-1870

| | | |
|---|---|---|
| GAINES, William | GARRETT, Eveline (blk) | 14 DEC 1865 |
| GAINEY, Patrick | NEUEN, Catharine | 07 JUN 1862 |
| GAINOR, George | GILLIS, Mary (blk) | 11 AUG 1864 |
| GAINOR, John F. | HOLOHAN, Rose C. | 14 OCT 1858 |
| GAITHER, Eugene | PIGGOTT, Fannie E. | 20 NOV 1866 |
| GAITHER, John C. | PEARSON, Jessie M. | 27 DEC 1864 |
| GALAGHER, William J. | BROWN, Emily | 08 APR 1863 |
| GALES, Richard T. | BURROSS, Laura T. | 02 SEP 1862 |
| GALETSKI, Louis | TYSSOWSKI, Pelagia | 15 OCT 1861 |
| GALLAGER, Albert A. | KEEFER, E. Eugene | 28 APR 1863 |
| GALLAGHER, Andrew | DIXON, Elizabeth | 29 JUL 1863 |
| GALLAGHER, Charles K. | CARROLL, Alice | 16 FEB 1865 |
| GALLAGHER, Francis | BRANNAN, Elizabeth | 09 JUL 1864 |
| GALLAGHER, Hugh | MAEGHER, Ann | 25 JUN 1863 |
| GALLAGHER, James | THOMPSON, Sarah | 20 FEB 1865 |
| GALLAGHER, James [2] | TAYLOR, Comfort Elizabeth | 02 AUG 1865 |
| GALLAGHER, Michael | McCARTHY, Ellen | 03 JUL 1865 |
| GALLAHORN, James Y. | MULLEN, Gabriella | 30 NOV 1868 |
| GALLANT, William G. | O'BRIEN, Catherine H. | 10 JAN 1861 |
| GALLIGHAR, Hugh | CAREY, Mary | 26 JAN 1867 |
| GALLIHER, Bryan | DONOHOE, Mary | 14 FEB 1870 |
| GALLIHORN, George | LIMRICK, Luberta | 30 MAY 1865 |
| GALLION, John W. [2] | CAMBACH, Mary | 18 APR 1870 |
| GALLOWAY, Amos | LAMMON, Nellie | 26 OCT 1865 |
| GALLOWAY, John | BOWEN, Mary | 09 AUG 1862 |
| GALLOWAY, Joseph | HARRISON, Rachel (blk) | 03 MAY 1866 |
| GALLOWAY, William | BASH, Josephine (blk) | 01 JUL 1868 |
| GALPIN, H.M. | IRVING, Gertrude E. | 23 JUL 1864 |
| GALT, James V. | CISSEL, Emma | 24 SEP 1866 |
| GALT, Joseph L. | CUNNINGHAM, Mary J. | 30 MAY 1866 |
| GALT, William Matthew [12s] | TURNER, Hattie | 03 SEP 1861 |
| GAMBLE, Alonzo | SIMMS, Maria (blk) | 12 JUN 1869 |
| GAMBLE, James | STOUFFER, Amelia Caroline | 09 OCT 1868 |
| GAMBLE, Joseph | THOMAS, Eliza (blk) | 29 NOV 1867 |
| GAMBLE, Joseph A. | ROBERTSON, Sallie | 19 OCT 1869 |
| GAMBRAI, John | MONT, Mary A. | 24 NOV 1866 |
| GANETT, Charles E. | HODGE, Georgianna | 09 DEC 1869 |
| GANEY, Maurice | DONIVAN, Hanorah | 14 NOV 1868 |
| GANEY, Michael | CONNOR, Bridget | 08 SEP 1860 |
| GANGLOFF, George | BARCLAY, Mary Ann | 23 SEP 1865 |
| GANNON, Gilbert | CASSIDY, Jennie | 22 OCT 1864 |
| GANNON, James | McCLORY, Mary | 18 MAY 1868 |
| GANNON, Martin | BOYLE, Mary | 07 JUL 1864 |
| GANNON, Michael S. | GIBBONS, Mary | 29 JUL 1865 |
| GANS, John | KELER, Mary | 24 NOV 1862 |
| GANT, George | SHORTER, Marion | 03 MAR 1863 |
| GANT, James | JACKSON, Mary (blk) | 31 JUL 1867 |
| GANT, James E. | WARNER, Anna Rebecca (blk) | 06 MAY 1868 |
| GANT, Jerry | GANT, Hester (blk) | 05 DEC 1867 |
| GANT, John | NEAL, Margaret (blk) | 25 FEB 1868 |
| GANT, John H. | IMES, Mary (blk) | 07 JUN 1866 |
| GANT, Robert | THOMAS, Ann (blk) | 25 MAR 1865 |
| GANT, William | GANT, Lucy Ann | 22 NOV 1864 |
| GANT, William | CRACKSIR, Agnes (blk) | 06 SEP 1866 |
| GANTS, Isaac | HIGHT, Catherine | 17 JAN 1866 |
| GANTT, Alexander | HILL, Margaret (blk) | 26 JUL 1869 |

| | | |
|---|---|---|
| GANTT, Charles | LODGE, Mary Ann (blk) | 17 MAY 1859 |
| GANTT, Charles | GALLERY, Henrietta (blk) | 09 MAY 1864 |
| GANTT, Charles | MILLS, Ann (blk) | 25 JUN 1864 |
| GANTT, Edward | PRICE, Cecilia (blk) | 07 OCT 1863 |
| GANTT, Edward L. | WILLIAMS, Roberta E. | 24 JUN 1864 |
| GANTT, Elijah | BROWN, Elizabeth (blk) | 06 JUN 1866 |
| GANTT, Henry | HERBERT, Ellen (blk) | 26 MAY 1864 |
| GANTT, James | HUTCHINSON, Rachel (blk) | 15 JUN 1867 |
| GANTT, Richard | SILENCE, Josephine A. | 31 JUL 1867 |
| GANTT, Thomas | BROWN, Mary (blk) | 07 NOV 1867 |
| GANTT, William H. | BROOKS, Jane | 22 JUL 1869 |
| GAPIN, Charles C. | BLANCHFIELD, Margaret A. | 28 DEC 1863 |
| GARBERSON, John James | TAYLOR, Annie Elizabeth | 04 JAN 1864 |
| GARCEAN, Charles F. | SMALL, Eliza | 24 JUL 1867 |
| GARDETTE, Charles D. | JOHNSTON, Eulalie | 26 NOV 1866 |
| GARDINER, David | TIBBS, Mary (blk) | 24 NOV 1868 |
| GARDINER, James [10] | CHESELDINE, Alameda | 15 FEB 1866 |
| GARDINER, John W. | MANNEKY, Sarah E. | 21 JAN 1863 |
| GARDINER, Richard A. | BUCKINGHAM, Mary R. | 14 DEC 1869 |
| GARDNER, C.T. | ARNOLD, Katie | 03 NOV 1868 |
| GARDNER, Francis Harvy | HAWKINS, Evelina | 21 FEB 1865 |
| GARDNER, George [9n] | THOMAS, Rosa | 14 DEC 1858 |
| GARDNER, George C. | GARDNER, Amelia | 20 APR 1866 |
| GARDNER, Henry | ERVIN, Hannah Jane | 28 SEP 1865 |
| GARDNER, Henry | WISE, Amanda (blk) | 02 DEC 1869 |
| GARDNER, John | TAYLOR, Anne | 29 JAN 1869 |
| GARDNER, Lewis | BIGELOW, Annie | 26 JUL 1864 |
| GARDNER, William F. | HENNING, Mary J. | 14 OCT 1868 |
| GARDNER, William H. | BOUGHANAN, Carolina | 04 MAY 1865 |
| GAREY, Michael | BIERNE, Annie S.O. | 09 APR 1864 |
| GARGES, Genie | LANGLEY, Josephine N. | 18 JAN 1870 |
| GARLAND, James | LEMMON, Ellen | 21 SEP 1864 |
| GARNELL, George Henry | DICKSON, Milly (blk) | 07 JUL 1863 |
| GARNER, Alexander M. [12s] | MADDOX, Mary Ann | 08 APR 1861 |
| GARNER, Coffer | POOL, Mary Ellen | 26 DEC 1859 |
| GARNER, Granville | PAYNE, Betsy (blk) | 20 MAY 1863 |
| GARNER, Isaac | MASON, Emily (blk) | 21 DEC 1865 |
| GARNER, John F. | LOCKE, Lina E. | 07 DEC 1869 |
| GARNER, Richard | DICKSON, Mary | 15 SEP 1859 |
| GARNER, Robert | ODEN, Eliza Ann | 09 AUG 1867 |
| GARNER, William F. | HYDE, Sarah A. | 10 NOV 1869 |
| GARNETT, John Henry | STREETS, Susan (blk) | 21 OCT 1868 |
| GARNETT, Moscow | KEYS, Winney | 16 APR 1864 |
| GARNETT, Stephen [11] | HAWKINS, E.A. | 20 JUL 1863 |
| GARRETSON, P.G. | LAMB, Emma R. | 10 SEP 1866 |
| GARRETT, George T. | GAZAWAY, Hester Ann | 28 DEC 1864 |
| GARRETT, Henry J. | DERRICK, Georgine M. | 16 OCT 1860 |
| GARRETT, James | SMITH, Ann (blk) | 05 DEC 1865 |
| GARRETT, Joseph | WILSON, Fanny (blk) | 16 MAY 1868 |
| GARRETT, Peter | TWOOMEY, Ellen | 04 JUN 1864 |
| GARRETT, Simeon | CREAMER, Mary A.E. | 28 FEB 1859 |
| GARRETT, Wm. F. [6c] | HARDING, Julia A. | 29 DEC 1858 |
| GARRISON, Furman M. | LEE, Emma | 18 DEC 1867 |
| GARRISON, George H. | BECKLEY, Catharine (blk) | 16 MAY 1864 |
| GARRISON, Henry | GANT, Elizabeth (blk) | 22 AUG 1863 |
| GARRISON, J.R. | DAVIS, Jennie | 07 SEP 1869 |

# District of Columbia Marriage Licenses, 1858-1870

| | | |
|---|---|---|
| GARRISON, James [8] | JACK, Mary Ann | 08 APR 1869 |
| GARRISON, John | DEVERS, Martha | 19 JAN 1870 |
| GARRISON, Joseph | HERNONDON, Mary Elizabeth | 10 NOV 1868 |
| GARRISON, Yelverton | LENOX, Mary A. | 13 MAY 1859 |
| GARTEN, Henry D. | CURTIS, Laura | 16 DEC 1865 |
| GARTHWAIT, Jacob H. | BARNES, Margaret | 14 FEB 1863 |
| GARTLAND, Thomas | PIERCE, Susan E. | 26 JAN 1870 |
| GARTON, John | CROOKS, Mary Ann | 03 MAR 1862 |
| GARTON, Mark N. | MACKELY, Mary | 17 APR 1862 |
| GARTOPN, Mark N. | CATHERELL, Palmyra | 23 SEP 1861 |
| GARTRELL, Thomas S. | CROSS, Martha | 01 JUN 1869 |
| GARVEY, Edward | GRALISH, Ann | 07 SEP 1861 |
| GARVEY, John | GAIRN, Ann | 10 DEC 1864 |
| GARVEY, Patrick | BURKE, Mary | 13 APR 1863 |
| GARVEY, Stephen | LONG, Mary | 06 FEB 1861 |
| GARVEY, William | CARTER, Mary | 27 JUL 1861 |
| GARVIN, John | RILEY, Bridget | 23 SEP 1865 |
| GARVIS, John | KANE, Ellen | 12 OCT 1864 |
| GASCH, Richard | AMON, Rose | 13 JAN 1869 |
| GASKIN, James H.C. | HIGGINS, Sarah E. | 31 MAY 1870 |
| GASKINGS, Samuel W. | HUTCHINS, Julia A. | 27 MAR 1860 |
| GASKINS, Joseph | SHIELDS, Mary | 02 JUL 1863 |
| GASKINS, Richard S. | GASKINS, Susan | 08 SEP 1859 |
| GASKINS, Stanfield | BROWN, Mary A. (blk) | 16 MAY 1865 |
| GASKINS, William A. | WHITE, Catherine E. | 22 OCT 1863 |
| GASKINS, William H. | REMINGTON, Virginia C. | 24 NOV 1863 |
| GASLIN, Levi | CURTIS, Susan | 10 SEP 1863 |
| GASS, Henry | CEAS, Diantha E. | 04 JUN 1861 |
| GASS, James | WEST, Laura V. | 06 AUG 1866 |
| GASSAWAY, George | JOHNSON, Ann M. (blk) | 24 SEP 1864 |
| GASSAWAY, Isaac | CARTER, Terry (blk) | 01 JUN 1863 |
| GASSAWAY, Joshua | JONES, Charlotte (blk) | 12 NOV 1868 |
| GASSENHEIMER, Gustav | STRAUSS, Mena | 12 AUG 1864 |
| GATELEY, Martin | BOUGHAN, Mary | 07 OCT 1861 |
| GATELY, John | CAHILL, Margaret | 16 DEC 1864 |
| GATELY, Malachi | FLYNN, Mary | 22 MAY 1863 |
| GATES, Charles J. | HUTCHINS, Celena | 11 AUG 1859 |
| GATES, George | MARTIN, Mary Elizabeth (blk) | 21 APR 1862 |
| GATES, James L. | WILANT, Margaret J. | 21 JUN 1867 |
| GATES, John | RUMLUG, Robele | 27 APR 1859 |
| GATES, John F. | QUINN, Ellen R. | 23 NOV 1869 |
| GATES, John H. | MOORE, Lettie W. | 19 NOV 1868 |
| GATES, Richard B. | BROOKS, Olivia | 18 AUG 1863 |
| GATES, Robert | TAYLOR, Catharine (blk) | 23 JUN 1864 |
| GATES, Samuel | BELT, MAry M. | 28 DEC 1865 |
| GATES, William | BURCH, Sarah C. | 13 MAY 1863 |
| GATES, William E. | ADAMS, Anna E. | 20 JAN 1870 |
| GATES, William Theodore | DYER, Alice Rebecca | 12 JUN 1867 |
| GATEWOOD, John T. [1c] | BENJAMIN, Mary Ann | 16 FEB 1863 |
| GATEWOOD, William | GREEN, Sarah | 22 DEC 1858 |
| GATH, William | BROWNMULLER, Isabella | 01 OCT 1862 |
| GATTI, Stephen | LAVAZA, Angela | 02 JUN 1862 |
| GATTON, James | McKINNEY, Sarah | 15 AUG 1867 |
| GATTON, Robert James | LANGLEY, Margaret Ann | 28 JUN 1864 |
| GATTRELL, T. Sewall | LEAR, Estella M. | 12 OCT 1859 |
| GAULEY, Patrick | PLAYMAN, Bridget | 16 MAY 1863 |

District of Columbia Marriage Licenses, 1858-1870

| | | |
|---|---|---|
| GAUMER, Moses F. | WEAVER, Anna C. | 09 OCT 1861 |
| GAUTIER, Charles P. | BIRD, Maria Sianna | 18 FEB 1868 |
| GAVIN, John | SARSFIELD, Maria | 04 OCT 1865 |
| GAVIN, John | DALY, Maggie | 27 JUN 1867 |
| GAY, Abner | POWELLS, Hattie (blk) | 11 JUL 1868 |
| GAYER, Edward | SULLIVAN, Hanorah | 04 MAY 1859 |
| GAZAWAY, Peter | WHITE, Elizabeth (blk) | 27 JUL 1866 |
| GAZELLI, Angelo | FERRANI, Louisa | 08 JUN 1863 |
| GEATTY, William H.H. [5] | FOWBLE, Sallie A. | 04 NOV 1867 |
| GEBAUER, John | OETTLE, Juliana R. | 23 MAR 1859 |
| GEE, David | VAUGHN, Martha (blk) | 27 NOV 1867 |
| GEHRING, Charles | SHURE, Louisa | 26 JUN 1863 |
| GEIB, Adam [5] | SPEIR, Maria E. | 24 JUN 1867 |
| GEIB, John A. | WALKER, Catharine A. | 16 OCT 1861 |
| GEISENDERFER, Frederick | ENGLEHARDT, Louisa | 17 OCT 1868 |
| GEISLER, Gustav | HENNSCH, Emile | 28 SEP 1859 |
| GEISNER, Frederick | VASMERS, Gesine | 14 JUN 1865 |
| GEIST, Charles P. | BERGMANN, Henrietta | 26 DEC 1861 |
| GEISTLICH, Anton | BREDECAMP, Anna | 28 DEC 1869 |
| GENEROLDS, Resin | HULLS, Margaret (blk) | 27 JUL 1867 |
| GENSLER, Henry J. | MALONEY, Ada E. | 21 DEC 1869 |
| GENTER, Daniel | GERMANN, Catharine Susanna | 11 JUN 1864 |
| GENTNER, Daniel | BOWMAN, Rachel A. | 29 JAN 1866 |
| GENTNER, John Geo. | STUFFLE, Mary | 03 JAN 1859 |
| GENTRY, Thomas L. | BERLIN, Annie J. | 06 SEP 1864 |
| GENTY, Pierre Felix | BRUNEL, Anne | 01 NOV 1864 |
| GEORGE, Mosley | JACKSON, Matilda (blk) | 11 OCT 1865 |
| GEORGE, Samuel | GIRARD, Justine (blk) | 05 MAR 1864 |
| GERARD, Louis | PERKINS, Missouri | 07 MAY 1864 |
| GERARD, Paul | WORMLEY, Marie B. | 03 DEC 1869 |
| GERECKE, William | GUMPEL, Anna | 26 JUL 1862 |
| GERHARD, John | KUHL, Wilhelmina | 07 DEC 1869 |
| GERHARD, L. | HARRIS, C.L. | 27 AUG 1862 |
| GERMON, Andrew | GENSER, Eva | 22 MAR 1860 |
| GEROHL, Frederick | SPATES, Margaret | 08 FEB 1862 |
| GETHEN, James G. | LIPSCOMB, Clara V. | 02 OCT 1861 |
| GETT, Henry | CHITHAM, Louisa (blk) | 12 DEC 1868 |
| GETZ, August | ERDMANN, Julia | 17 FEB 1864 |
| GEYSER, John B. | TILLETT, Abbey M. | 20 DEC 1864 |
| GHEEN, B.H. | BROUGHTON, Mary A. | 12 SEP 1868 |
| GHEEN, Joseph L. [7a] | VIOLET, Emma E. | 14 JUL 1868 |
| GIBBONS, William F. | CRAYCROFT, Susan A.M.B. | 14 JAN 1863 |
| GIBBS, Andrew [11] | LANE, Fanny (blk) | 19 DEC 1865 |
| GIBBS, James A. | COGVILLE, Bettie | 18 FEB 1869 |
| GIBBS, Peyton | MARSHALL, Julia (blk) | 20 JAN 1866 |
| GIBERSON, Charles H. | HILLIARY, Susan | 25 JAN 1867 |
| GIBERSON, George W. | LIVINGGOOD, Eliza | 03 JAN 1867 |
| GIBNEY, Andrew | GARDNER, Elizabeth | 16 JAN 1870 |
| GIBSON, Augusta | MARSHALL, Catherine (blk) | 05 SEP 1861 |
| GIBSON, Charles J. | BECKETT, Kate (blk) | 02 MAR 1870 |
| GIBSON, David | RODIER, Sarah E. | 27 DEC 1864 |
| GIBSON, E.M. | THOMAS, Irene E. | 29 MAR 1869 |
| GIBSON, Edward | LUCAS, Melvina | 31 OCT 1862 |
| GIBSON, George, Capt. 11th U.S. Inf. | HUNTT, Fannie Maria | 09 NOV 1863 |
| GIBSON, George G. | BINNIX, Alpharesta | 01 SEP 1868 |
| GIBSON, George K. | GARNER, Elizabeth T. | 15 DEC 1869 |

District of Columbia Marriage Licenses, 1858-1870

| | | |
|---|---|---|
| GIBSON, Gouverneur W. | DELANEY, Martha Jane (blk | 08 AUG 1864 |
| GIBSON, Gustavus | LYLES, Louisa | 20 JUL 1865 |
| GIBSON, Hugh | SYBERT, Mary (blk) | 26 MAY 1866 |
| GIBSON, Irvin | SHEPHERD, Catherine (blk) | 02 JUL 1867 |
| GIBSON, Isaac | BANKS, Emily (blk) | 24 MAY 1866 |
| GIBSON, James [10] | TAYLOR, Mary Catherine | 14 OCT 1863 |
| GIBSON, James | O'HALLORAN, Bridget | 02 MAY 1864 |
| GIBSON, James W. | COLUMBUS, Laura M. | 16 APR 1863 |
| GIBSON, John | DORSEY, Eliza (blk) | 04 JAN 1869 |
| GIBSON, John A. | BROOKS, Catharine (blk) | 25 FEB 1862 |
| GIBSON, John C. [6s] | ROSS, Frances | 02 JUN 1864 |
| GIBSON, John H. | CROWN, Henrietta | 09 JAN 1865 |
| GIBSON, Joshua | RINNER, Elizabeth | 10 JAN 1860 |
| GIBSON, Samuel J. | JENKINS, Mary | 23 OCT 1862 |
| GIBSON, W. | RICHARDSON, Addie | 28 FEB 1868 |
| GIBSON, William | McCARRICK, Elizabeth | 30 APR 1867 |
| GIBSON, William H. | SWAYZE, Belle | 09 JAN 1866 |
| GIBSON, William J. | BURCH, Aletha V. | 25 APR 1867 |
| GIBSON, Wm. H. | CORNISH, Martha J. | 09 JUN 1864 |
| GIDDING, Henry | McDERMOTT, Bridget | 11 AUG 1862 |
| GIDDONS, George W. | STAPLETON, Margaret | 16 JUL 1866 |
| GIER, Joseph | NOLL, Kate Augusta | 14 JUN 1866 |
| GIESBAUER, John | BERGMAN, Louisa | 25 OCT 1860 |
| GIESLER, Peter | FISCHER, Mary | 14 DEC 1861 |
| GIFFORD, Anthony | WHITE, Ruth A. | 16 NOV 1864 |
| GILBERT, B.F. | BOWEN, Myra J. | 29 DEC 1865 |
| GILBERT, Charles | ANDERSON, Anna Rebecca | 17 DEC 1864 |
| GILBERT, Charles J. | DIVINE, Anna L. | 03 JUL 1862 |
| GILBERT, Edward E. | WILLETT, Margaret A. | 08 OCT 1860 |
| GILBERT, John Lewis | PARKER, Maria (blk) | 08 JUN 1869 |
| GILBERT, William Hull | STARWHITE, Julia | 03 OCT 1866 |
| GILBERT, William J. [4] | TEBBS, Laura | 21 OCT 1864 |
| GILCHRIST, Jesse | GORDIN, Betsy (blk) | 05 AUG 1869 |
| GILES, George W. [6le] | HARMAN, Margaret A. | 07 SEP 1865 |
| GILES, Joseph [Edward] [6r] | GRIFFITHS, Louisa [Ann] | 26 APR 1860 |
| GILES, Reuben | HALL, Margaret (blk) | 11 MAR 1868 |
| GILES, William | GILES, Anna (blk) | 25 NOV 1865 |
| GILES, William | CURTIS, Emily (blk) | 13 DEC 1865 |
| GILES, William | LOCKS, Margaret | 17 DEC 1867 |
| GILHAM, John | BRITT, Jenny | 05 APR 1866 |
| GILHAM, John T. | CRUTCHLEY, Annie E. | 25 NOV 1864 |
| GILHULY, Philip | McKENNA, Bridget | 27 NOV 1858 |
| GILHULY, Terence | BARTLEY, Ann | 23 JUL 1864 |
| GILISPIE, Thomas | ANDERSON, Susan A. | 26 JUN 1867 |
| GILKESON, Lewis | RUPPRECHTT, Julia | 16 APR 1866 |
| GILKEY, Aba V. | CRANSTON, Hettie | 20 APR 1869 |
| GILL, Christopher A. | KELLY, Margaret A. | 11 NOV 1858 |
| GILL, George E. | SHUNTON, Annie | 04 MAR 1868 |
| GILL, George Henry | SELECMAN, Marguarite Ann | 20 JUL 1863 |
| GILL, John F. | BRAMELL, Jane P. | 07 NOV 1860 |
| GILL, John W. | SUTTON, Sarah F. | 16 JAN 1861 |
| GILL, William [J.] [2] | RUSK, Jane | 02 JUN 1868 |
| GILLEM, Goliah | JONES, Milly (blk) | 11 MAR 1869 |
| GILLEMEYER, William J. | SMITH, Sophia | 14 FEB 1862 |
| GILLEN, George W. | NAYLOR, Josephine | 23 JUL 1862 |
| GILLEN, John | McELROY, Bridget | 06 NOV 1863 |

| | | |
|---|---|---|
| GILLESPIE, John W. | COX, Adeline S. | 22 MAR 1860 |
| GILLESPIE, Thomas | BYRNE, Elizabeth | 08 SEP 1862 |
| GILLIGAN, Andrew | BURKE, Mary Ann | 17 JUN 1864 |
| GILLIGAN, John | McCARTHY, Eliza | 07 NOV 1867 |
| GILLIGAN, John | McCAULEY, Eliza | 04 JAN 1868 |
| GILLIMON, James | CHAMWELL, Mary Virginia (blk) | 26 DEC 1867 |
| GILLIN, Patrick C. | RYAN, Kate | 23 JUN 1869 |
| GILLIS, Bosaquet W. | RADCLIFFE, Mattie E. | 20 DEC 1859 |
| GILLIS, John | HARRIS, Mary Jane (blk) | 05 MAR 1867 |
| GILLIS, William | HAYS, Nancy (blk) | 16 JAN 1865 |
| GILLISS, James [11] | STELLWAGEN, Julia | 10 OCT 1865 |
| GILLON, Patrick | BRESSNAHAN, Abbe | 13 JAN 1869 |
| GILLUM, James N. | TURNER, Ann Eliza (blk) | 08 SEP 1869 |
| GILMAN, John Richard | PRIDDY, Nannie Jane | 15 AUG 1865 |
| GILMARTIN, Daniel | KELLY, Bridget | 07 JAN 1864 |
| GILMORE, Spencer | CATTERTON, Minerva (blk) | 29 NOV 1867 |
| GILMORE, William [10] | APPLEGATE, Rebecca | 20 AUG 1867 |
| GILNECK, Walter | DIEDERICK, Doredo | 18 MAR 1864 |
| GILRON, Joseph | JONES, Mary | 22 MAR 1861 |
| GILROY, Nicholas | NOLAN, Julia | 09 NOV 1865 |
| GILULEY, John | GAFFNEY, Jane | 18 MAY 1861 |
| GINNEY, Patrick | KENNEDY, Catharine | 06 SEP 1862 |
| GIRTON, Francis M. | MORRISON, Margaret Jane | 03 APR 1866 |
| GISSEL, Benjamin [2] | RUSK, Lucy | 16 JUN 1868 |
| GIST, Henry William | ZEGOWITZ, Annie Appolline | 23 SEP 1867 |
| GITTINGS, Robert B. | MITCHELL, Mary F. | 30 APR 1867 |
| GITTINGS, Thomas D. | COVENTRY, Augusta Ellen | 26 JAN 1867 |
| GIVANDEN, Antoine Chas. | TRUMAN, Jennie | 30 DEC 1861 |
| GIVEN, George H. [10] | FURSE, Isabella T. | 10 MAY 1861 |
| GIVEN, William F. | CROGGAN, Mary A. | 01 NOV 1862 |
| GIVENS, John T. | WALTERS, Amanda C. | 06 OCT 1868 |
| GLAAK, Joseph | MEIR, Anna | 29 NOV 1858 |
| GLADMAN, Darius T. | DULEY, Mary O. | 06 FEB 1866 |
| GLADMAN, James H. | McLAUGHLIN, Mary | 08 APR 1863 |
| GLADMAN, Sylvester | TAYLOR, Anna | 19 NOV 1862 |
| GLADMON, John | MULLOY, Catharine | 04 AUG 1859 |
| GLADMON, Matthias D. | DEREAMER, Alice | 05 DEC 1860 |
| GLASCO, John T. | SCHING, Emma I. | 22 JUL 1861 |
| GLASCO, Travers [4] | LAWSON, Catherine | 13 NOV 1867 |
| GLASER, William | WITTE, Anne Maria Antonette | 14 JUL 1863 |
| GLASS, Andrew | PATTERSON, Christina | 22 APR 1869 |
| GLASS, William | SHELBY, Mary | 03 FEB 1868 |
| GLASSCOCK, Roger Chew [10] | ROBERTS, Cornelia | 10 DEC 1867 |
| GLASSPOOLE, Henry | GRANT, Mary Jane | 06 APR 1864 |
| GLAZE, Hamilton | GOLDEN, Maggie A. | 20 DEC 1865 |
| GLAZEBROOK, Thomas J. | JOYCE, Kate | 12 MAY 1865 |
| GLAZEBROOKE, Thomas J. | LANGLEY, Mary J. | 09 JUL 1859 |
| GLEASON, Albert | BROWNING, Alice E. | 01 MAR 1864 |
| GLEASON, Andrew | LYNCH, Ellen | 02 JUN 1860 |
| GLEASON, Michael | FRALEY, Mary | 08 SEP 1863 |
| GLEASON, Michael | BURGESS, Susan Matilda | 11 FEB 1867 |
| GLEESON, J.K.P., Dr. | BLOUNT, Alice K. | 02 AUG 1869 |
| GLEESON, John | CUNNINGHAM, Mary | 07 OCT 1865 |
| GLEESON, John H. | CONNER, Johanna | 13 DEC 1869 |
| GLENN, Washington D. [11] | THOMAS, Laura V. | 22 APR 1867 |
| GLENN, William | McCARTHY, Catharine | 09 OCT 1865 |

District of Columbia Marriage Licenses, 1858-1870

| | | |
|---|---|---|
| GLOCKEL, George | JOXX, Maria | 27 SEP 1866 |
| GLORY, Charles | BURCK, Catharine J. (blk) | 08 DEC 1865 |
| GLOTZBACH, Joseph P. | TASCHNER, Auguste | 26 OCT 1865 |
| GLOTZBLACK, Joseph | TOCKE, Anna | 30 MAY 1864 |
| GLOVER, Joseph | PYE, Olivia | 19 SEP 1867 |
| GLOVER, Lewis | McGRATH, Rose | 22 DEC 1863 |
| GLOVER, Thomas | BUSSEE, Julia | 09 AUG 1860 |
| GLOVER, Thos. H. | SOMERVILLE, Susan | 22 DEC 1865 |
| GLUM, Peter | MASON, Margaret | 27 DEC 1864 |
| GLUMER, Joseph | THEILER, Gertrude | 03 JAN 1860 |
| GNIDER, Thomas | KING, Martha | 30 APR 1866 |
| GOCHNAUER, P.S. | FRASIER, Catherine | 24 SEP 1868 |
| GODDALL, Richard | CRUMP, Julia (blk) | 02 JUL 1867 |
| GODDARD, Charles E. | BARR, Mary A. | 28 APR 1863 |
| GODDARD, Richard H. | HUTTON, Mary C. | 08 JUL 1868 |
| GODDARD, William | McCABE, Susan | 09 AUG 1865 |
| GODDARD, William H. | CALDEBACK, Virginia A. | 20 JUN 1859 |
| GODFREY, Charles L., Jr. [4] | PADGETT, Mary E. | 14 DEC 1868 |
| GODFREY, Edwin W. | KENNEDY, Florence | 10 MAY 1866 |
| GODFREY, Eliasaph D. | KIRKWOOD, Julia D. | 13 SEP 1866 |
| GODFREY, Frederick | CAMPBELL, Jane | 03 OCT 1862 |
| GODFREY, James H. | FARR, Ellenore | 14 APR 1866 |
| GODFREY, Joseph H. | LECKRON, Mary E. | 05 OCT 1859 |
| GODFREY, Samuel | PYLES, Mary F. | 28 MAY 1862 |
| GODFREY, William L. | REDDING, Margaret | 25 JUL 1864 |
| GOERBERT, Valtine | HATER, Mary | 01 OCT 1859 |
| GOETZ, Adolphus | MITCHELL, Susannah | 03 APR 1865 |
| GOFF, Charles | TAYLOR, Mary (blk) | 16 DEC 1867 |
| GOFF, George Washington | PAYNE, Letty (blk) | 08 SEP 1864 |
| GOFFENY, Abram | WHITLEY, Maria (blk) | 06 MAY 1869 |
| GOIN, Patrick | BRANDEN, Honora | 04 APR 1864 |
| GOINGS, Carey [7a] | CLEVELAND, Lucy Ellen | 02 JAN 1867 |
| GOINGS, Henry D. | THOMPSON, Adele Frances (blk) | 29 JUN 1863 |
| GOINGS, John H. | COGAN, Louisa | 17 DEC 1863 |
| GOINS, John G. | UPSHER, Augustine (blk) | 06 OCT 1859 |
| GOLDEN, Henry B. | JENKINS, Julia A. | 09 NOV 1864 |
| GOLDEN, Samuel | COLLINS, Anna (blk) | 20 AUG 1868 |
| GOLDEN, Samuel M. | PIERCE, Julia C. | 26 DEC 1861 |
| GOLDEN, William L. | SPELMAN, Harriet Jane | 05 SEP 1859 |
| GOLDING, Charles T. | SPRAGUE, Laura | 16 SEP 1865 |
| GOLDING, Julius | HAYS, Harriet Louisa | 15 JAN 1866 |
| GOLDSBERRY, James | MILLS, Mary | 24 MAY 1866 |
| GOLDSBERY, Henry | PHENIX, Catharine (blk) | 28 MAY 1863 |
| GOLDSBOROUGH, H.A. [11] | LESLIE, Ellen R. | 23 APR 1866 |
| GOLDSBOROUGH, James R. [11s] | WEST, Helen T. | 27 MAY 1870 |
| GOLDSBOROUGH, William | SINCLAIR, Marian Virginia | 15 SEP 1859 |
| GOLDSMITH, Edward F. | GRIFFITH, Margaret Ann | 02 JAN 1869 |
| GOLDSMITH, James A. [10] | WOOD, Drusilla A. | 02 DEC 1869 |
| GOLDSMITH, John B. | MITCHELL, Sarah Jane | 16 JUN 1863 |
| GOLEMAN, Newton | LEWIS, Mary (blk) | 22 DEC 1868 |
| GONLEY, Patrick | HARTIGAN, Mary | 05 MAY 1864 |
| GONZALES, John | CURTIS, Fanny | 27 AUG 1863 |
| GOOD, Boswell | TURNER, Mary | 23 MAR 1863 |
| GOOD, Henry T. | KEEYES, Mary G. | 12 SEP 1862 |
| GOODALL, John R. | LePETIT, Marian | 10 JAN 1866 |
| GOODALL, Thomas | PORTS, Morcilia | 22 FEB 1870 |

| | | |
|---|---|---|
| GOODCHILD, Richard | KIDWELL, Martha Ann | 16 SEP 1862 |
| GOODFELLOW, Henry, Major | BRENT, Eleanor | 26 JUN 1866 |
| GOODGER, Joseph | BAINET, Mary | 06 AUG 1860 |
| GOODHART, James | YEATLESON, Sophia | 02 DEC 1864 |
| GOODING, Edward P. [10] | BURCH, Suzy R. | 03 FEB 1868 |
| GOODING, James H. [7a] | DAVIS, Eliza A. | 28 MAY 1868 |
| GOODING, Perry | GOODING, Mary (blk) | 03 MAY 1866 |
| GOODING, Peter | FITZHUGH, Amanda M. | 07 JUN 1859 |
| GOODLOW, Armstead | JOHNSON, Agnes (blk) | 02 JUN 1866 |
| GOODMAN, Hopson C. [7b] | RAWLINGS, Carrie | 18 OCT 1869 |
| GOODMAN, James [10] | DOWNES, Martha | 04 JUN 1870 |
| GOODMAN, Jonas H. | NEWMEYER, Fannie | 31 DEC 1867 |
| GOODMAN, Patrick | RILEY, Mary | 08 JUL 1863 |
| GOODRICH, Benjamin | DAVIS, Jane | 08 NOV 1864 |
| GOODRICH, Charles W. | WASHINGTON, Alice V. (blk) | 23 MAY 1867 |
| GOODRICK, Henry H. [6s] | JACKSON, Annie Virginia | 18 AUG 1864 |
| GOODRICK, James Washington | FLEMING, Eliza Josephine | 07 JAN 1869 |
| GOODRICK, John A. | McCORMICK, Sarah J. | 11 JUN 1862 |
| GOODS, Benjamin F. [12s] | REARDON, Mildred C. | 22 APR 1861 |
| GOODSON, Samuel W. | BILLING, Mary W. | 06 SEP 1860 |
| GOODWIN, Frank | QUILL, Mary | 29 JAN 1863 |
| GOODWIN, Thomas | BROWN, Eliza (blk) | 30 JUN 1866 |
| GOODWIN, William C. | SEIKS, Susan | 31 DEC 1866 |
| GOODY, Pleasant | HESTER, Charlotte (blk) | 17 DEC 1863 |
| GOOLEY, Thomas | FLANNAGAN, Mary A. | 06 SEP 1858 |
| GOOPEY, John | JOHNSON, Martha Ann (blk) | 20 JAN 1868 |
| GOOSBY, Frank | WEEMS, Mary (blk) | 07 JUL 1868 |
| GORAM, Oscar | MUNROE, Sarah (blk) | 13 MAY 1868 |
| GORDON, Adelbert | LAWS, Elizabeth A. | 08 OCT 1868 |
| GORDON, Alfred | BOULDEN, Amonie (blk) | 25 OCT 1864 |
| GORDON, Charles | WILLIAMS, Emeline (blk) | 31 MAY 1859 |
| GORDON, Charles G. | McKELDEN, Parthenia E. | 10 OCT 1864 |
| GORDON, George | SEBREY, Julia | 08 DEC 1858 |
| GORDON, George | EMERICH, Mary A. | 28 JAN 1862 |
| GORDON, George | RIDGELEY, Mary (blk) | 22 MAY 1862 |
| GORDON, Gilbert [11] | JORDAN, Pauline | 07 OCT 1865 |
| GORDON, H. Skipwith | WHEELER, Mary T. | 08 JAN 1866 |
| GORDON, Harry | TUOHY, Mary Jane | 27 FEB 1867 |
| GORDON, James F. | HANNEGAN, Mary Jane | 28 SEP 1863 |
| GORDON, James H. | ARNOLD, Mary Jane | 26 JAN 1859 |
| GORDON, James H. | ARNOLD, Mary J. | 15 MAR 1859 |
| GORDON, Jeremiah | SHELTON, Caroline L. (blk) | 30 MAR 1867 |
| GORDON, Jesse | JACKSON, Emma (blk) | 27 FEB 1864 |
| GORDON, John | BELL, Ellen (blk) | 10 NOV 1859 |
| GORDON, John | STEWART, Annie (blk) | 14 AUG 1865 |
| GORDON, John | HOLLANDS, Jane (blk) | 16 MAY 1867 |
| GORDON, John | SILLIMAN, Margaret | 14 JUL 1868 |
| GORDON, Joseph T. [6m] | MYERS, Sallie A. | 03 MAR 1863 |
| GORDON, Lewis | FITZHUGH, Sarah (blk) | 01 DEC 1866 |
| GORDON, Malcolm B. | THOMPSON, Sarah L. | 05 APR 1866 |
| GORDON, Miles | SCOTT, Teresa (blk) | 16 JUN 1870 |
| GORDON, Shelton | JEFFERSON, Georgianna (blk) | 20 JUN 1867 |
| GORDON, Thomas | FORD, Charity (blk) | 25 JUN 1864 |
| GORDON, William S. | HOWARD, Roseanna | 07 MAY 1864 |
| GORDY, Caspar | OETZEL, Eliza | 09 AUG 1866 |
| GORE, Aaron | FISHER, Nancy (blk) | 10 AUG 1866 |

| | | |
|---|---|---|
| GORHAM, James Thomas [7b] | ROGERS, Virginia | 20 JAN 1870 |
| GORLACH, Charles | SCHOTT, Catharina | 27 SEP 1864 |
| GORMAN, Edward | MAINY, Catharine | 18 OCT 1860 |
| GORMAN, M.B. | FITZGERALD, Johanna | 21 NOV 1863 |
| GORMAN, Patrick | FLYNN, Catherine | 17 SEP 1865 |
| GORMAN, Patrick | FLYNN, Catharine | 31 JAN 1866 |
| GORMAN, Patrick F. | GERMOND, Anna M. | 07 OCT 1867 |
| GORMAN, Samuel | NEARY, Annie T. | 28 MAY 1867 |
| GORMLEY, James | SUETA, Annie | 15 JUL 1868 |
| GORRICH, Luke | KELLY, Mary | 15 JUN 1863 |
| GORSUCH, James P. [7b] | LITTLE, Susana | 12 OCT 1869 |
| GORSUCH, John Thomas [6c] | GRIFFIN, Sarah Rebecca | 14 OCT 1858 |
| GORT, Thilo | SEIDENBERG, Sophia | 31 MAY 1862 |
| GORTON, James | LEITCH, Margaret | 06 NOV 1867 |
| GORUM, Samuel | SUDDEATH, Mary E. | 09 SEP 1865 |
| GOSLIN, Thomas | NORRIS, Emma | 12 AUG 1869 |
| GOSS, Alfred F. | BAYNE, Sarah E. | 31 MAR 1862 |
| GOSS, John S. | CONNORS, Mary A. | 30 JAN 1868 |
| GOSSNER, John | MILLER, Anna E. | 28 JAN 1867 |
| GOTEHARDT, George | PFLUGER, Margaret | 22 OCT 1868 |
| GOTTHELF, Nathan | HAMMERSCHLAG, Julia | 07 AUG 1860 |
| GOTTSMAN, Charles | LOHMAN, Christina | 05 JAN 1859 |
| GOUGAR, S.N. | JACOBS, Lotta | 24 MAY 1870 |
| GOUGH, Stephen | JOHNSON, Emma | 17 DEC 1864 |
| GOULD, Charles M. | HARRIS, Mary | 02 MAR 1864 |
| GOULD, William Warren [11] | CLARK, Lillie A. | 11 JAN 1869 |
| GOULDEY, Joseph C. | BAISMEN, Flavius V. | 08 SEP 1859 |
| GOWLAND, John E. | DAMRELL, Catherine | 23 DEC 1858 |
| GRACE, James | BURKE, Catharine | 10 APR 1861 |
| GRADAY, Fountain | BROOKS, Amanda (blk) | 07 JUN 1866 |
| GRADY, Jacob | KENNEY, Elizabeth M. (blk) | 05 DEC 1867 |
| GRADY, Thomas | LYNCH, Kate | 30 JUL 1863 |
| GRADY, Thomas | SCANLIN, Joanna | 30 JUN 1866 |
| GRAFF, Charles | BENNIKE, Antonica | 19 DEC 1864 |
| GRAFF, George Usher [12s] | HAWTHORN, Mary | 02 OCT 1860 |
| GRAFF, Henry | QUINN, Mary | 06 JUL 1869 |
| GRAFTON, Benjamin F. | DORRELL, Virginia A. | 01 MAY 1868 |
| GRAHAM, Bernard | MANEY, Bridget | 19 MAY 1865 |
| GRAHAM, Christopher C. [11] | BURK, Mary E. | 11 AUG 1865 |
| GRAHAM, Henry Bomford | MOORE, Margaret | 14 APR 1860 |
| GRAHAM, James D. | LEE, Virginia | 04 JAN 1862 |
| GRAHAM, John E. | LODGE, Alice Virginia | 03 JAN 1861 |
| GRAHAM, Robert | WOOD, Elizabeth (blk) | 26 SEP 1867 |
| GRAHAM, Robert [4] | JOHNSON, Eliza (blk) | 29 AUG 1867 |
| GRAHAM, William | SNOWDEN, Mary | 16 JUL 1862 |
| GRAHAM, William | ZINNEMAN, Louisa | 05 FEB 1870 |
| GRAHAM, William H. | JOHNSON, Lavinia Virginia (blk) | 23 MAY 1863 |
| GRAHAM, William W. | JORDAN, Imogene D. | 30 APR 1866 |
| GRAHAME, John M. [7a] | CONWAY, Mary Frances | 18 FEB 1868 |
| GRALEY, Daniel | CONNOR, Julia | 28 JAN 1864 |
| GRALITZKER, Frederick | HINRIDA, Johanna Christian | 03 MAY 1869 |
| GRAMLICH, Christian F. | NESTOR, Emelia | 09 MAY 1864 |
| GRAMLICH, F.J. | CRAWFORD, S. Jennie | 02 SEP 1868 |
| GRAMM, Jonathan | WISE, Agnes | 04 MAY 1870 |
| GRAMMAR, Doctor | SETTLES, Caroline (blk) | 28 APR 1868 |
| GRAMMAR, Purnell, Dr. | SETTLES, Caroline (blk) | 07 DEC 1865 |

| | | |
|---|---|---|
| GRAMMER, George S. | BOGARDUS, Susan A. | 25 JAN 1860 |
| GRANBERY, John Cowper | MASSIE, Jane L. | 23 NOV 1858 |
| GRANDERSON, Charles | MITCHELL, Josephine (blk) | 18 MAR 1867 |
| GRANDFIELD, Richard | DAILEY, Ellen | 26 FEB 1859 |
| GRANDISON, William | JACKSON, Kate (blk) | 24 JUL 1866 |
| GRANER, George | HEILAND, Margaret | 01 DEC 1864 |
| GRANEY, Michael | CADEY, Mary | 23 OCT 1860 |
| GRANIGER, Rudolph | BURCH, Jennie | 26 DEC 1868 |
| GRANT, Albert B. | GREEN, Sarah | 10 SEP 1866 |
| GRANT, David | NUGENT, Margaret | 24 DEC 1858 |
| GRANT, Franklin | JONES, Mary (blk) | 06 MAY 1863 |
| GRANT, John | SILSBEE, Susan | 25 SEP 1863 |
| GRANT, Josiah Varden | McGUIRE, Cynthia Jane | 08 JAN 1863 |
| GRANT, Randall | CRAWFORD, Ellen (blk) | 13 DEC 1869 |
| GRANT, William J. | DOUGHERTY, Anna | 15 SEP 1862 |
| GRANTHAM, Michael | GRAY, Louisa (blk) | 29 SEP 1863 |
| GRANTLIN, William | BURRELL, Frances (blk) | 07 MAY 1870 |
| GRANTT, John W. | SMITH, Henrietta (blk) | 08 SEP 1866 |
| GRANTUN, Joseph C. | REED, Emma C. | 26 JUL 1866 |
| GRANVOGEL, John | SCHRODT, Mary Anna | 24 DEC 1862 |
| GRASER, George Lou | McWILLIAMSON, Mamie | 11 NOV 1869 |
| GRASS, Charles Henry | JOHNSON, Mary Francis Elizth. | 25 JUN 1868 |
| GRAVES, Andrew | GANT, Mary Elizth. (blk) | 04 FEB 1869 |
| GRAVES, Edward O. | ALLEN, Clara G. | 01 DEC 1868 |
| GRAVES, George | FINNIGAN, Mary | 24 JUN 1865 |
| GRAVES, John R. | POINDEXTER, Lucy Jane | 11 FEB 1870 |
| GRAVES, Julius A. | THOMAS, Lavinia | 19 MAR 1867 |
| GRAVES, Maxwell | BROWN, Sarah | 21 MAR 1865 |
| GRAVES, Porterfield | CROWN, Sarah | 17 FEB 1859 |
| GRAVES, Raymond | WARD, Mary E. | 23 DEC 1865 |
| GRAY, Alfred | EHINGER, Hattie | 12 FEB 1868 |
| GRAY, Alfred | DORSEY, Mary (blk) | 10 MAR 1868 |
| GRAY, Anthony | MAGLE, Ann | 06 DEC 1866 |
| GRAY, Benjamin | KING, Priscilla (blk) | 25 NOV 1863 |
| GRAY, Edward T. | BELL, Cornelia A. (blk) | 28 DEC 1868 |
| GRAY, Edwin F. | LONG, Mary M. | 18 APR 1867 |
| GRAY, Edwin W. [9e] | SANDERSON, Mary E.N. | 27 FEB 1862 |
| GRAY, George W. | MACON, Elizabeth | 09 APR 1868 |
| GRAY, Gilbert | SEALS, Harriet (blk) | 16 JUN 1870 |
| GRAY, H.W. | THOMAS, M.E. | 01 MAR 1861 |
| GRAY, Henry | SCOTT, Harriet (blk) | 09 MAR 1864 |
| GRAY, Henry M. | SHOWED, Elizabeth | 06 JUN 1860 |
| GRAY, Henry W. | ABBOTT, Harriet Ann | 25 MAY 1864 |
| GRAY, Ira | LOVEINGS, Mary Ann | 14 MAY 1869 |
| GRAY, Isaac | POWELL, Mary Rebecca (blk) | 25 MAY 1865 |
| GRAY, James | RUSSELL, Kate (blk) | 19 JAN 1869 |
| GRAY, John | TURNER, Sarah | 16 MAY 1864 |
| GRAY, John B. | STETTINIUS, Rose Belle | 28 JAN 1864 |
| GRAY, John W. | MORRIS, Lucinda (blk) | 07 MAY 1868 |
| GRAY, Josiah | KIDWELL, Mary Jane | 11 FEB 1860 |
| GRAY, Lloyd | GRAY, Winney (blk) | 07 JUL 1866 |
| GRAY, Randall | JONES, Susan (blk) | 21 MAR 1867 |
| GRAY, Richard | MORRISON, Matilda (blk) | 27 NOV 1869 |
| GRAY, Robert | HILL, Alsyndy | 02 APR 1859 |
| GRAY, Robert | WILSON, Rebecca (blk) | 10 AUG 1869 |
| GRAY, Thomas | TAYLOR, Adeline (blk) | 25 NOV 1862 |

| | | |
|---|---|---|
| GRAY, Thomas [10] | SHAFER, Ellen C. | 12 NOV 1866 |
| GRAY, Tobey | COLE, Sarah (blk) | 13 MAY 1867 |
| GRAY, Vincent | BELL, Mary Jane (blk) | 28 JUL 1868 |
| GRAY, Wesley | WASHINGTON, Georgiana (blk) | 03 NOV 1868 |
| GRAY, William | BOWDEN, Elvira Ann (blk) | 30 NOV 1865 |
| GRAY, William H. | BROWN, Ellen (blk) | 20 APR 1865 |
| GRAYBOW, George H. | LAUGTON, Margaret A. | 12 DEC 1862 |
| GRAYSON, George | ROBERTS, Mary (blk) | 09 APR 1867 |
| GRAYSON, Noble | FOSTER, Sarah Elizth. (blk) | 12 APR 1860 |
| GRAYSON, Patrick | KENNEDY, Ann | 16 APR 1866 |
| GRAYSON, Robert | SPRIGG, Georgiana (blk) | 05 JUN 1867 |
| GRAYSON, Walter | NELSON, Amanda (blk) | 31 JUL 1867 |
| GREASBOWER, John Andreas | KNEASS, Anna Mary | 30 DEC 1869 |
| GREASLEY, Warlow | BOOZ, Margaret | 15 JAN 1861 |
| GREELISH, Michael J. | NAYLOR, Maggie | 23 NOV 1865 |
| GREEN, Albert S. | STORY, Eliza | 11 JUL 1864 |
| GREEN, Amanuel | JOHNSON, Alice (blk) | 23 JUN 1866 |
| GREEN, Andrew | JAMES, Isabella (blk) | 26 DEC 1865 |
| GREEN, Andrew | WRIGHT, Margaret (blk) | 01 OCT 1868 |
| GREEN, Anthony | SCOTT, Isabella (blk) | 31 DEC 1868 |
| GREEN, Benjamin | LYNCH, Patience | 08 SEP 1868 |
| GREEN, C. Edwin | LAMBRIGHT, Miranda C. | 21 OCT 1859 |
| GREEN, Charles | HAMILTON, Ellen (blk) | 16 JAN 1864 |
| GREEN, Charles | BELL, Mary Ann (blk) | 18 SEP 1865 |
| GREEN, Charles | CARUSI, Julia (blk) | 21 APR 1866 |
| GREEN, Charles H. | JACKSON, Mary (blk) | 25 JUL 1868 |
| GREEN, David | WALTER, Melissa (blk) | 03 OCT 1865 |
| GREEN, David | PENDLETON, Amanda (blk) | 05 JAN 1867 |
| GREEN, David | BEALE, Ellen (blk) | 11 JUN 1868 |
| GREEN, David N. | KENGLA, Kate | 03 JUN 1862 |
| GREEN, Edward | DONOVAN, Catharine | 02 MAY 1865 |
| GREEN, Frank | HATTON, Eliza (blk) | 18 APR 1870 |
| GREEN, Gabriel H. | MORTON, Nellie (blk) | 26 JAN 1870 |
| GREEN, George | JOHNSON, Mollie (blk) | 08 DEC 1866 |
| GREEN, George | CLEVELAND, Mary Elizabeth | 13 FEB 1867 |
| GREEN, George F. | DEVEREAUX, Maria L. | 04 JUN 1860 |
| GREEN, George L. | CHEESMAN, Isabella | 15 JUL 1862 |
| GREEN, George L. | CHEESMAN, Isabella | 20 JUN 1862 |
| GREEN, George W. | JACKSON, Mary E. (blk) | 29 DEC 1864 |
| GREEN, George W. | HATTON, Sarah (blk) | 01 JUL 1867 |
| GREEN, George William | HARRIS, Mary Frances (blk) | 07 JAN 1869 |
| GREEN, Harrison | WROE, Frances (blk) | 02 JAN 1867 |
| GREEN, Henry | MORRIS, Mary Jane (col'd) | 02 JAN 1864 |
| GREEN, James | SAMSON, Julia | 23 OCT 1862 |
| GREEN, James | HOWARD, Ann D. (blk) | 24 OCT 1865 |
| GREEN, James | BOSTON, Martha E. (blk) | 31 OCT 1866 |
| GREEN, James | LOCKWOOD, Jane | 23 JAN 1867 |
| GREEN, James | GANTT, Margaret (blk) | 12 JUN 1867 |
| GREEN, James | SOPER, Mary Ann | 25 SEP 1867 |
| GREEN, James | MULLEN, Bridget | 17 JUL 1868 |
| GREEN, James | HAWKINS, Virginia (blk) | 08 DEC 1869 |
| GREEN, James Edward | ROSS, Martha | 17 MAR 1864 |
| GREEN, James Robert | DORSEY, Jane (blk) | 14 MAY 1870 |
| GREEN, Joel Cephas | WINTER, Augusta E. | 06 APR 1860 |
| GREEN, John | LAWSON, Lizzie Ann | 28 JUL 1859 |
| GREEN, John | LEE, Martha (blk) | 02 NOV 1863 |

District of Columbia Marriage Licenses, 1858-1870

| | | |
|---|---|---|
| GREEN, John A. | DUNWOOD, Mary (blk) | 20 APR 1869 |
| GREEN, John C. | CRABBS, Emma V. | 14 FEB 1866 |
| GREEN, John F. | APPEL, Celina Adala | 14 SEP 1868 |
| GREEN, John H. | GENTRY, Melzena | 15 AUG 1864 |
| GREEN, John Wesley | LEE, Mary (blk) | 16 DEC 1863 |
| GREEN, John William | WINSTON, Catherine Ann (blk) | 18 JAN 1870 |
| GREEN, Joseph | WOODWARD, Mary A. (blk) | 11 MAY 1861 |
| GREEN, Joseph | SMITH, Mary Eliza | 18 NOV 1868 |
| GREEN, Joshua J. | SMITH, Sarah Jane | 20 APR 1864 |
| GREEN, Lawrence | LANDON, Nellie (blk) | 16 JUN 1866 |
| GREEN, Mark H. | STALLINGS, Marion | 07 NOV 1864 |
| GREEN, Martin H. | DAILEY, Bridget | 30 MAR 1870 |
| GREEN, Nathan | JACKSON, Fanny (blk) | 27 NOV 1867 |
| GREEN, Nelson | LEE, Miss (blk) | 30 JAN 1868 |
| GREEN, Nelson | MULLANEY, Sidney (blk) | 26 DEC 1867 |
| GREEN, Peter | TYLER, Mary (blk) | 07 JAN 1868 |
| GREEN, Prather H. | WILLIAMS, Evelina (blk) | 24 DEC 1868 |
| GREEN, Rivon | FOSTER, Ann (blk) | 23 AUG 1864 |
| GREEN, Robert | COLBERT, Charity A. (blk) | 04 JAN 1860 |
| GREEN, Robert | STOCK, Elizabeth (blk) | 19 MAY 1864 |
| GREEN, Robert | SCOTT, Charles [sic] (blk) | 05 JUN 1866 |
| GREEN, Robert | WALLACE, Julia (blk) | 18 JUL 1868 |
| GREEN, Robert | BROOKS, Nancy (blk) | 18 AUG 1869 |
| GREEN, Robert B. | MINOR, Rosanna (blk) | 06 OCT 1864 |
| GREEN, Rudolph | HINÜBER, Minna | 16 OCT 1869 |
| GREEN, Ryburn | FOSTER, Lucy (blk) | 29 JUN 1867 |
| GREEN, Samuel | MAGRUDER, Mary (blk) | 13 AUG 1867 |
| GREEN, Taliferro | LEE, Othelia (blk) | 01 DEC 1864 |
| GREEN, Taylor | CARTER, Louisa (blk) | 05 AUG 1869 |
| GREEN, Thomas | DONALDSON, Jane (blk) | 16 MAY 1865 |
| GREEN, Thomas | SPEEDEN, Kate | 22 SEP 1866 |
| GREEN, Thomas E., Jr. | WALLER, Ella | 20 JUN 1866 |
| GREEN, Thomas H. | CROSS, Emma Elizth. | 02 JUL 1860 |
| GREEN, Wesley | HOLMES, Eliza | 08 MAR 1864 |
| GREEN, Wesley | CORBIN, Eaza (blk) | 07 OCT 1867 |
| GREEN, William | LITTLEFORD, Amanda | 01 SEP 1863 |
| GREEN, William | THOMAS, Susan (blk) | 12 MAR 1866 |
| GREEN, William | ALLEN, Annie (blk) | 11 SEP 1869 |
| GREEN, William G. | CLARK, Alice | 30 AUG 1869 |
| GREEN, Willis | BUCKNER, Maria (blk) | 06 MAR 1867 |
| GREEN, Wm. Jere | JOHNSON, Serena (blk) | 25 JUN 1868 |
| GREENFIELD, Samuel W. | YOUNG, Ann Maria | 21 APR 1860 |
| GREENLAND, Robert C. | ARTHUR, Lizzie | 13 MAR 1865 |
| GREENLEAF, Charles F., Dr. [3] | delaROCHE, Georgiana H.F. | 09 SEP 1862 |
| GREENLEAF, Edward | STEWART, Charlotte (blk) | 15 APR 1869 |
| GREENLEAF, Gazaway | HAFERMAN, Maria (blk) | 21 APR 1869 |
| GREENLOW, William P. | PERKINS, S.V.B. | 09 SEP 1858 |
| GREENSTED, Edmund | SPICE, Mary Ann | 04 JUN 1864 |
| GREENWELL, J. Robert | PERKINS, Lewellen | 02 OCT 1858 |
| GREENWELL, Jacob | GREENWELL, Elvira (blk) | 30 MAY 1866 |
| GREENWELL, James | JOY, Anna | 11 AUG 1860 |
| GREENWELL, Wm. H. | BRADLEY, Mary T. | 28 JUL 1868 |
| GREER, Chancey F. | SIMMS, Nancy | 06 AUG 1859 |
| GREER, Edward | McBRIDE, Margaret | 07 JAN 1865 |
| GREER, John R. [11] | HUMPHREY, Elizabeth | 10 OCT 1865 |
| GREER, Thomas | HUGHES, Georgeana | 10 JUL 1863 |

District of Columbia Marriage Licenses, 1858-1870

| | | |
|---|---|---|
| GREER, William | GRANAY, Mary | 09 JUN 1865 |
| GREGG, Myron E. | SMITH, Susan A. | 16 NOV 1867 |
| GREGG, Theodore | HOLD, Lydia | 25 OCT 1869 |
| GREGORI, John | BEIT, Dora | 07 FEB 1868 |
| GREGORY, Charles E. | MAURY, Alice W. | 21 NOV 1860 |
| GREGORY, Hamilton J. | DEMAIN, Marion | 21 DEC 1859 |
| GREGORY, J.W. [5] | DUTTON, Martha A. | 05 JAN 1869 |
| GREIPP, Peter Otto | DIEZ, Maria M. | 17 DEC 1863 |
| GREVEMEYER, Wm. H. [11] | McPHERSON, Bertha | 15 JUN 1866 |
| GREY, Tompkins C. | HURLEY, Julia | 24 DEC 1864 |
| GREYSON, Fount | CLARKE, Caroline | 19 MAY 1859 |
| GREYSON, Thomas W. | PADGEOT, Mary E. (blk) | 03 MAR 1864 |
| GRICE, John W. | HALL, Mary E. | 21 DEC 1863 |
| GRIFFIN, Charles G., Jr. | WATSON, Mary Jane | 11 DEC 1858 |
| GRIFFIN, Charles [4] | CARROLL, Sallie V. | 10 DEC 1861 |
| GRIFFIN, Edwin W.W. | McCUTCHEN, Carrie C. | 19 DEC 1859 |
| GRIFFIN, Francis | SLATTERY, Mary | 22 OCT 1864 |
| GRIFFIN, James | O'BYRNE, Jane | 11 JUN 1867 |
| GRIFFIN, John | CONNOR, Bridget | 04 MAY 1860 |
| GRIFFIN, John | HAGGERTY, Mary | 11 JAN 1861 |
| GRIFFIN, John | WILSON, Frances (blk) | 16 JUN 1870 |
| GRIFFIN, John C. | MEDLEY, Betsey (blk) | 14 JUL 1866 |
| GRIFFIN, Martin | FLAHERTY, Sarah | 30 JAN 1863 |
| GRIFFIN, Martin | DUNNAVIN, Ellen | 16 JAN 1864 |
| GRIFFIN, Mathew | DUKE, Ellen (blk) | 24 SEP 1867 |
| GRIFFIN, Michael | CASEY, Catherine | 04 FEB 1859 |
| GRIFFIN, Michael | GRIFFIN, Hanora | 28 fEB 1866 |
| GRIFFIN, Morris | SHEA, Eliza | 01 JUL 1865 |
| GRIFFIN, Patrick | WELSH, Bridget | 28 FEB 1865 |
| GRIFFIN, Reuben | DANDRIDGE, Patsy (blk) | 31 AUG 1864 |
| GRIFFIN, Richard | BLOW, Rosa (blk) | 20 JUL 1869 |
| GRIFFIN, Richard Thomas | JOHNSON, Julia Anna (blk) | 30 DEC 1869 |
| GRIFFIN, Robert C. [6r] | SMITH, Sarah A. | 07 APR 1859 |
| GRIFFIN, Sidney S. | EATON, Virginia A. | 23 NOV 1865 |
| GRIFFIN, Thomas | MULKERRINS, Mary | 11 JUN 1866 |
| GRIFFIN, Thomas | WELSH, Joanna | 07 JUL 1866 |
| GRIFFIN, Thomas | DAILEY, Catherine | 18 AUG 1866 |
| GRIFFIN, Thomas | O'DAY, Julia | 10 APR 1867 |
| GRIFFIN, Thos. | BARLOW, Emily (blk) | 18 OCT 1866 |
| GRIFFIN, William H. | MAGRUDER, Julia Ann | 22 JUL 1869 |
| GRIFFIN, William T. | JONES, Kate G. | 17 MAR 1859 |
| GRIFFITH, Edward Davis | SAGEE, Emily Elizabeth | 09 MAR 1867 |
| GRIFFITH, Henry C. | ROBINSON, Julia K. | 13 SEP 1859 |
| GRIFFITH, John Thos. | GATES, Sarah A. | 05 DEC 1861 |
| GRIFFITH, Michael J. | DAVIS, Frances | 30 JUN 1865 |
| GRIFFITH, Richard H. | TOWERS, Eliza P. | 19 NOV 1867 |
| GRIFFITH, Thomas [12s] | DALTON, Matilda | 18 NOV 1861 |
| GRIGG, Samuel | PARSONS, Lizzie | 01 DEC 1862 |
| GRIGGS, Abel E. | DOUGLASS, Anna V. | 23 JUN 1863 |
| GRIGGS, Clark Hunt | MORRIS, Sallie S. | 11 MAR 1867 |
| GRIGSBY, Arthur | COLES, Esther (blk) | 06 APR 1865 |
| GRIGSBY, Edward | JOHNSON, S. Ann | 17 JUL 1865 |
| GRIGSBY, Tasker M. [7a] | PURCELL, Lucy | 20 OCT 1868 |
| GRILLBORTZER, Jacob Henry | FISHER, Hannah | 01 SEP 1869 |
| GRILLET, George L. | SMITHSON, Caroline F. | 10 DEC 1868 |
| GRIMES, Alfred T. | GRIMES, Mary E. | 14 JUL 1863 |

District of Columbia Marriage Licenses, 1858-1870

| | | |
|---|---|---|
| GRIMES, Augustus | GUMP, Sarah | 16 JUN 1860 |
| GRIMES, Charles W. | CONNELL, Jennie | 28 MAR 1865 |
| GRIMES, Charles W. | BELT, Ella J. | 14 SEP 1865 |
| GRIMES, Daniel | WOOD, Lucinda (blk) | 14 APR 1870 |
| GRIMES, Debbie C. | HERMOND, Francis M. | 23 AUG 1866 |
| GRIMES, George | HENRY, Susan (blk) | 01 NOV 1866 |
| GRIMES, Harry | JOHNSON, Betsy | 24 DEC 1867 |
| GRIMES, James C. | DINGLER, Louisa | 12 MAY 1865 |
| GRIMES, John | LUCAS, Letitie (blk) | 19 DEC 1859 |
| GRIMES, John W. | ROBEY, Birdie | 26 JUL 1869 |
| GRIMES, Lewis | TAYLOR, Julia (blk) | 04 NOV 1864 |
| GRIMES, Munroe | LEE, Ann (blk) | 02 DEC 1868 |
| GRIMES, Richard F. [10] | GRIMES, Cinderalla E. | 26 DEC 1863 |
| GRIMES, Samuel | PERKINS, Henrietta | 12 MAR 1859 |
| GRIMES, Solomon | SWEENY, Anna (blk) | 06 NOV 1865 |
| GRIMES, William H. | DEVAUGHN, Elizabeth | 21 DEC 1861 |
| GRIMES, William K. | JOHNSON, E. Pauline | 16 NOV 1869 |
| GRIMES, William T. [6m] | KIDWELL, Mary E. | 16 OCT 1862 |
| GRIMES, William W. | SCOTT, Margaret (blk) | 11 FEB 1862 |
| GRIMLEY, Jacob | WILSON, Mary Jane | 07 OCT 1858 |
| GRIMM, Augustus | RISSLER, Elizabeth | 23 OCT 1862 |
| GRIMM, John | SCHWARTZ, Barbara | 02 MAY 1864 |
| GRIMSHAW, William Henry | BROOKS, Mary Frances (blk) | 26 APR 1870 |
| GRIMSLEY, Thomas | DAVIS, Rebecca | 23 OCT 1862 |
| GRINDER, Adam | BURROWS, Elizabeth | 03 JAN 1859 |
| GRINDER, George W. | VERMILLION, Sarah Jane | 10 FEB 1863 |
| GRINDER, Joseph W. | SIMPSON, Margaret | 02 NOV 1858 |
| GRINER, Edward M. | GREENWELL, Hannah E. | 20 DEC 1861 |
| GRINNELL, John | TUCKER, Sally Ann | 02 JUN 1862 |
| GRISE, George | PLUMMER, Caroline (blk) | 18 SEP 1866 |
| GRISSON, John | GINGELL, Anna O. | 20 JUL 1865 |
| GRISWELL, Charles D. | BRYAN, Alice | 29 NOV 1865 |
| GRISWOLD, William A. | BAIN, Mary A. | 11 MAR 1869 |
| GROELING, George | SEIPEL, Louise | 03 DEC 1862 |
| GROFFMAN, Augustus | EARNEST, Ulia | 17 OCT 1868 |
| GROGGIN, Edward | BROOKS, Milly (blk) | 24 AUG 1867 |
| GROMAN, Edward F. | STROWMAN, Matilda | 15 DEC 1862 |
| GRÖNER, George | ECKERT, Kate | 26 SEP 1863 |
| GROPER, William F. | NIPPER, Eleanor | 07 MAR 1862 |
| GROSBACK, John | DIETZ, Grace | 17 JUL 1865 |
| GROSEMANS, Adolph | HANSLER, Antonie | 19 MAR 1864 |
| GROSHON, Hanson | GUYTON, Georgeanna | 31 OCT 1861 |
| GROSS, Alfred G. | SKIDMORE, Emma | 07 JUL 1866 |
| GROSS, Andrew | DINICK, Mariah | 16 JUN 1863 |
| GROSS, Frederick W. | MOEWES, Mary A. | 27 JAN 1865 |
| GROSS, George | MARTH, Elizabeth | 07 DEC 1869 |
| GROSS, Henry E. | SMITH, Elizabeth | 11 SEP 1862 |
| GROSS, James | DOVER, Lucy (blk) | 16 NOV 1865 |
| GROSS, John | SUTER [Sreter], Meni | 24 AUG 1860 |
| GROSS, John | THOMAS, Henrietta (blk) | 03 APR 1868 |
| GROSS, Joseph | LEWIS, Jane (blk) | 18 SEP 1860 |
| GROSS, Robert | PROCTOR, Maria (blk) | 19 MAY 1866 |
| GROSS, Samuel | CARTWRIGHT, Susanna | 09 OCT 1861 |
| GROSS, Samuel E. [2] | MARTIN, Georgiana | 10 JUL 1868 |
| GROSS, Thomas J. | PAUL, Sarah M. | 04 JAN 1869 |
| GROSS, William | TAYLOR, Mary | 24 JAN 1870 |

District of Columbia Marriage Licenses, 1858-1870

| Groom | Bride | Date |
|---|---|---|
| GROSSMAN, Frederick | PASWA, Pauline Florentine | 06 OCT 1864 |
| GROVER, John W. | CAYWOOD, Martha Jerusha | 07 OCT 1867 |
| GROVER, William L. | MAXWELL, Jane | 08 JUL 1861 |
| GROVERMANN, Henry | SCHMITT, Dora | 04 JAN 1864 |
| GROVES, David T. | CRIDER, Laura A. | 05 DEC 1867 |
| GROVES, David T. | GOODWIN, Agnes Annie | 05 OCT 1868 |
| GROVES, Edward M. | BERRYMAN, Lucy A. | 14 JAN 1861 |
| GROVES, Eugene | KENNEDY, Margaret | 14 MAY 1863 |
| GROVES, Eugene N. | HAMAN, Hannah T. | 07 JAN 1867 |
| GROVES, James L. | WINTER, Mary E. | 01 JAN 1860 |
| GROVES, John S. | CLASK, Emily E. | 10 APR 1865 |
| GROVES, John W. | WALKER, Cecelia | 16 MAR 1861 |
| GROVES, Sargeant | McNIER, Mary Ann | 06 JAN 1859 |
| GROVES, Thomas | COOK, Nancy (blk) | 14 AUG 1867 |
| GROVES, William | DOUGHERTY, Margaretta | 08 NOV 1869 |
| GROVIER, Wm. R. [6m] | HARDING, Christiana | 20 OCT 1863 |
| GRUBB, Robert S. | WHITING, C.J. | 10 MAR 1869 |
| GRUBER, Albert | HESS, Lucinda | 04 MAY 1869 |
| GRUMBLE, John H. [6le] | WILLIAMS, Lydia C. | 20 JUN 1867 |
| GRUMBLY, John | FURGUSON, Matilda | 20 SEP 1862 |
| GRUNDEN, John C. | BROWN, Fannie | 17 JUL 1865 |
| GRUSSINGER, Charles S. | SCHMIDT, Margaret | 15 JUN 1860 |
| GRYMES, James M. | TORBUT, Mary E. Peyton | 21 DEC 1858 |
| GUDBERLET, George H. | YOST, Ferderica | 15 DEC 1868 |
| GUENTHER, Theodore | TEGLMEIER, Augusta | 16 FEB 1863 |
| GUIDICE, Edward | HÜBNER, Margaretta | 05 NOV 1864 |
| GUIN, James | BOND, Zelphy Ann | 08 APR 1863 |
| GUINEN, Patrick | CREGAN, Mary | 28 MAR 1864 |
| GUINLONG, Lawrence | RADY, Julia | 27 AUG 1861 |
| GUINN, Patrick | BRINDAN, Catherine | 12 JUL 1860 |
| GULICK, James H. | LUCKENS, Maggie E. | 27 DEC 1864 |
| GUNN, George Symington | HUNT, Elizabeth | 29 MAY 1865 |
| GUNNELL, Joseph W. | THOMPSON, Frances V. | 20 APR 1866 |
| GUNNELL, Leonard C. | RITTENHOUSE, Mamie N. | 27 OCT 1868 |
| GUNNELL, Ludwell | DIXON, Elizabeth | 25 APR 1867 |
| GUNNELL, Orlando | ADAMS, Susanna | 14 APR 1860 |
| GUNNELL, Robert | GUNNELL, Harriet (col'd) | 15 JAN 1866 |
| GUNSON, Edwin | HUTCHINSON, Margaret | 15 NOV 1865 |
| GUREX, John Thomas | PETERSON, Mary A.E. (blk) | 27 JUL 1865 |
| GURLEY, Revere W. | GURLEY, Mary C. | 03 NOV 1860 |
| GURLEY, William B. | GILMAN, Helen P. | 10 SEP 1867 |
| GURNEY, W. H. [7b] | CLEARE, Anna | 03 AUG 1869 |
| GURY, Louis C. [7b] | BUTLER, Sallie A. | 21 SEP 1869 |
| GUSHMAN, Charles W. | SWEET, Annie | 17 MAR 1864 |
| GUSS, Charles Edward | BROOKS, Isabella (blk) | 16 DEC 1868 |
| GUSTOCK, Charles F. | DeMOLL, Mary Frances Josephine | 31 OCT 1863 |
| GUTEMAN, Charles | O'DONNELL, Ellen | 11 MAY 1864 |
| GUTMAN, Emanuel | STRAUSS, Nannie | 19 SEP 1864 |
| GUTSHALL, Hezekiah | STONE, Margaret | 10 NOV 1863 |
| GUTTEKUNST, Albert | KUMNEAR, Betty | 17 JAN 1863 |
| GUTTRIDGE, James T. | SELBY, Lavinia | 15 OCT 1868 |
| GUY, George W. [7a] | REED, Mary Ann | 07 MAY 1867 |
| GUY, John F. | FORBES, Elizabeth | 10 NOV 1864 |
| GWIN, William | BUTLER, Mary L. (blk) | 17 MAY 1869 |
| GWYNN, Alfred | HOLLAND, Charlotte | 27 JUL 1869 |

District of Columbia Marriage Licenses, 1858-1870

| | | |
|---|---|---|
| GWYNN, Frank | COLE, Jane (blk) | 17 DEC 1868 |
| GWYNN, Henry | BURNS, Lucinda (blk) | 24 APR 1865 |
| GWYNN, John E. | WATTS, Mary (blk) | 03 OCT 1867 |
| GWYNNE, Carey | PRESTON, Maria O. | 16 MAR 1859 |
| GWYNNE, Henry | HAYNES, Laura Ann (blk) | 15 JUL 1865 |

# H

| | | |
|---|---|---|
| HAAS, David | OSTERBERG, Celestial V. | 23 MAR 1864 |
| HAAS, Louis | STEHLE, Frederick [sic] | 06 DEC 1859 |
| HAASE, Frederick Carlos | JOHNSON, Charlotte Victoria | 06 APR 1870 |
| HAASE, Heinrich | OPPERMANN, Johanne D. | 04 JAN 1860 |
| HABBERT, James | DOLAN, Kate | 18 MAY 1863 |
| HABBERT, Mary | O'CONNOR, Edward S. | 17 FEB 1863 |
| HABER, William | WEIBEL, Delia | 10 APR 1866 |
| HABERMAN, Charles H. | SCHEIDEGGER, Annie M. | 10 FEB 1870 |
| HABIT, John R. | SMITH, Elizabeth (blk) | 28 DEC 1866 |
| HABLE, Solomon H. | EINSTEIN, Rachel | 02 MAR 1866 |
| HACK, Frederick | HIETER, Charlotte | 18 DEC 1863 |
| HACKNEY, Zeikel | BULGER, Maria | 03 JUL 1862 |
| HADAWAY, John T. | LANE, Julia R. | 23 MAY 1868 |
| HADDAN, Josiah D.C. [9n] | WELTON, Mary Holland | 01 OCT 1858 |
| HADLEY, William M. | CHAMPION, Mary Jane | 21 JUL 1859 |
| HADLOW, Henry [7a] | HARRISON, Annie Amelia | 15 OCT 1867 |
| HAERING, David | HOESING, Elizabeth | 29 NOV 1862 |
| HAFFEKE, Charles | NOSCHEL, Louise | 23 OCT 1858 |
| HAFFY, Edward | RAGAN, Julia | 21 SEP 1863 |
| HAGAN, George W. | LACEY, Barbara E. | 21 JUL 1866 |
| HAGAN, James F. [2] | HOWARD, Fannie F. | 11 FEB 1868 |
| HAGAN, John O. | FENDALL, Mary E. | 08 MAR 1862 |
| HAGAN, Richard J. | PHILLIPS, Sarah C. | 10 DEC 1860 |
| HAGAN, William Henry | JOHNSON, Susannah (blk) | 13 JUN 1867 |
| HAGANS, Rezin | MITCHELL, Josephine | 17 NOV 1864 |
| HAGEMAN, Charles | BUNCHOFF, Elanora | 24 NOV 1860 |
| HAGEMANN, Louis | LaHAYNE, Augusta | 11 JAN 1862 |
| HAGEMANN, William | MARTZ, Ida | 21 DEC 1865 |
| HAGEN, James F. | HORTZMAN, Julia | 01 FEB 1861 |
| HAGEN, Matthew | SKULLY, Margaret | 24 MAY 1862 |
| HAGER, Frederick A. | NEWTON, Elizabeth V. | 16 JUN 1862 |
| HAGER, George W. | MOSELY, Mary V. | 10 OCT 1861 |
| HAGER, John | CLARKE, Christina | 26 OCT 1863 |
| HAGERMAN, Henry | BERGER, Doretta | 20 JAN 1865 |
| HAGERTY, Thomas | PHILLIPS, Elbertine H. | 02 NOV 1859 |
| HAGGARTY, Patrick Wm. | DEWYER, Mary Ann | 14 NOV 1860 |
| HAGGERTY, James | APPLETON, Kate | 22 OCT 1866 |
| HAGGERTY, Pat | CONNOR, Catharine | 13 MAR 1865 |
| HAGGERTY, Patrick | CONNOR, Catharine | 10 MAR 1865 |
| HAGGERTY, Timothy | PARKER, Mary C. | 29 APR 1861 |
| HAGMAN, Victor | MARTZ, Elizabeth | 30 APR 1867 |
| HAGTHROP, Robert J.B. | HARROD, Julietta S. | 18 DEC 1865 |
| HAHN, John | FAUNCE, Helen | 02 MAR 1867 |
| HAHN, William | BECKWITH, Josephine | 11 MAR 1865 |
| HAIDY, John | COXSEN, Sarah A. | 05 OCT 1858 |
| HAIGHT, Edwin R. | BULLOCK, Lucy A. | 28 OCT 1865 |
| HAIGLEY, Jos. A. | SIMONDS, Sarah | 25 OCT 1865 |
| HAILSTALK, William | ELKINS, Emeline (blk) | 27 JUL 1867 |

District of Columbia Marriage Licenses, 1858-1870

| | | |
|---|---|---|
| HAINES, David E. | WEEDEN, Lizzie | 31 DEC 1866 |
| HAINES, George J. | PRITCHARD, Mary E. | 16 JUN 1869 |
| HAINES, John P. | WHITAKER, Mary L. | 22 DEC 1863 |
| HAIR, Newton | ALLISON, Eliza A. | 29 JAN 1862 |
| HALBERT, Samuel | PEERCE, Ann J. | 13 DEC 1858 |
| HALBERT, Samuel | PEARCE, Ann J. | 04 NOV 1861 |
| HALE, George E. | SMITH, Georgiana H. | 02 FEB 1869 |
| HALE, James O. | CONKLIN, Nellie W. | 07 NOV 1863 |
| HALE, John W. | ROLLS, Josephine | 05 JUN 1869 |
| HALE, William | KNOWLES, Carrie | 05 APR 1866 |
| HALEY, Alfred G. | ISHERWOOD, Maggie | 10 DEC 1859 |
| HALEY, James W. | DeCAMP, Elizabeth Estell | 25 AUG 1864 |
| HALEY, Michael | MARTIN, Margaret | 23 AUG 1865 |
| HALEY, Patrick | McDEVITT, Rose | 22 SEP 1859 |
| HALEY, Patrick | McCARTY, Mary | 25 APR 1860 |
| HALEY, Patrick | CARROLL, Julia | 12 OCT 1863 |
| HALK, Adam | GWINLEND, Catharine | 09 OCT 1861 |
| HALL, Addison | WOODWARD, Rebecca (blk) | 14 JUL 1868 |
| HALL, Anthony | ADAMS, Courtney (blk) | 21 JAN 1863 |
| HALL, Charles | BENNETT, Elizabeth (blk) | 01 AUG 1863 |
| HALL, Columbus | CLARKE, Maria (blk) | 15 AUG 1865 |
| HALL, Columbus | WELLS, Cordelia H. | 11 NOV 1869 |
| HALL, David | GABERT, Eliza (blk) | 08 SEP 1865 |
| HALL, Francis | DICK, Joriah | 17 OCT 1860 |
| HALL, Francis T. | BOWERS, Adeline | 23 APR 1864 |
| HALL, George | LYNCH, Jemima (blk) | 04 JUN 1868 |
| HALL, George W. | MILLER, Isabella M. | 16 JUL 1864 |
| HALL, [George] W. [10] | COOK, Mary A. | 26 JUN 1865 |
| HALL, Harry | COOKE, Hannah Ann (blk) | 30 SEP 1864 |
| HALL, Harry O. | BASSETT, Emma A. | 01 JUL 1869 |
| HALL, Henry | GREEN, Martha (blk) | 09 JAN 1866 |
| HALL, Henry | CARTER, Mary | 11 MAY 1866 |
| HALL, Henry, Capt. | CARSEN, Julia E. | 01 MAY 1866 |
| HALL, Hillman A. | CARPENTER, Jennie B. | 11 APR 1866 |
| HALL, Isaac | TAYLOR, Matilda (blk) | 06 NOV 1867 |
| HALL, Isaiah | BROWN, Alethea (blk) | 10 JUN 1868 |
| HALL, James | MEGH<u>AN</u>, Catherine | 07 AUG 1867 |
| HALL, James A. | MELVIN, Virginia E. | 01 DEC 1868 |
| HALL, James E. | HALL, Mary Ann | 26 MAY 1859 |
| HALL, James H. | HODGES, Mary A. | 09 MAR 1864 |
| HALL, James Richard [4] | HOPKINS, Alice Clementine | 25 NOV 1867 |
| HALL, Jeremiah M. | THOMPSON, Frances | 11 MAR 1862 |
| HALL, John | CHEW, Jane (blk) | 09 MAY 1863 |
| HALL, John | RUSSELL, Mary (blk) | 28 DEC 1865 |
| HALL, John | MAYNARD, Fanny (blk) | 26 MAY 1866 |
| HALL, John Henry | BOSTON, Susan Ann (blk) | 24 FEB 1863 |
| HALL, John R. | HICKMAN, Sarah C. | 01 MAR 1869 |
| HALL, Joseph | RAFE, Alice (blk) | 16 MAR 1869 |
| HALL, Joseph T.H. | LEWIS, Julia A. | 08 MAY 1865 |
| HALL, Michael | CLARK, Katharine | 27 AUG 1861 |
| HALL, Nelson | SHILES, Neely (blk) | 12 DEC 1865 |
| HALL, Peter | TYLER, Anna (blk) | 09 AUG 1866 |
| HALL, Powhattan | GUNNELL, Sally E. | 09 MAR 1865 |
| HALL, Robert | MOULTON, Margaret (blk) | 06 SEP 1864 |
| HALL, Robert G. | BRISCOE, Merander James (blk) | 19 MAR 1868 |
| HALL, Thomas | RIVERS, Phyllis (blk) | 31 MAY 1866 |

## District of Columbia Marriage Licenses, 1858-1870

| | | |
|---|---|---|
| HALL, Thomas | JONES, Sarah (blk) | 17 OCT 1866 |
| HALL, Thomas A. [6le] | HAVENER, Mary [A.] | 05 DEC 1865 |
| HALL, William H. | TALBERT, Mary Elizabeth | 01 SEP 1858 |
| HALL, William I. | CUNNINGHAM, Margaret J. | 22 DEC 1864 |
| HALL, William R. | BEACH, Isabella | 10 SEP 1863 |
| HALL, William T. | ANGEL, Marion F. | 12 JAN 1864 |
| HALLACH, Ebenezer [9n] * | HOWRAN, Sarah Jane | 30 JAN 1860 |
| HALLARY, Daniel | HOLLOHAN, Abby | 03 JAN 1863 |
| HALLENBECK, Charles J. | PILLSBURY, Elvira R. | 17 JUN 1863 |
| HALLEY, Hodges | WARDER, Amelia C. | 11 AUG 1864 |
| HALLIGAN, Patrick | KILBORN, Catherine | 05 OCT 1858 |
| HALLIGAN, Peter | MULLIN, Margaret | 20 JUN 1864 |
| HALLINAN, Michael | McCARTHY, Mary | 25 FEB 1865 |
| HALLOCK, Israel | WOOD, Ida | 23 DEC 1863 |
| HALLORAN, John | DOWNEY, Mary | 01 MAR 1862 |
| HALLORAN, John | SCANLON, Ellen | 24 AUG 1864 |
| HALLOVAN, Ethan | JONES, Elizabeth (blk) | 12 OCT 1863 |
| HALLUM, John | DYER, Martha A. | 05 MAR 1869 |
| HALLY, Thomas | SHEEHY, Catharine | 11 FEB 1863 |
| HALMUTH, Voltin | HAUSMANN, Barbara | 20 FEB 1862 |
| HALNIN, Martin | GLAVIN, Catharine | 18 OCT 1864 |
| HALPIN, Cornelius | CONNOR, Winifred | 29 DEC 1859 |
| HALSEY, Norwood A. | WISE, Laura V. | 14 OCT 1863 |
| HALSTEAD, Abram | SAUNDERS, S.C. | 02 JUN 1865 |
| HAM, William | GUSTA, Mary (blk) | 11 MAY 1865 |
| HAMAHAN, Patrick | RICE, Mary A. | 17 MAY 1864 |
| HAMES, Arthur | ALLEN, Sarah (blk) | 06 OCT 1864 |
| HAMILTON, Albert | ABBOTT, Mary Ann | 27 JAN 1863 |
| HAMILTON, Albert | CARTER, Louisa (blk) | 09 JAN 1868 |
| HAMILTON, C.M. | FINLISON, Martha | 24 MAR 1869 |
| HAMILTON, Charles Henry | EDINGBURR, Mary Elizabeth (blk) | 04 SEP 1866 |
| HAMILTON, Edward | WOODWARD, Emeline (blk) | 06 JUL 1865 |
| HAMILTON, Edward | BLACKSTONE, Ellen (blk) | 06 JUL 1867 |
| HAMILTON, Edward | OTTO, Elizabeth | 13 AUG 1867 |
| HAMILTON, Edward Waters | MASON, Sarah Francis (blk) | 06 MAR 1866 |
| HAMILTON, Harrison H. | O'BRIEN, Ellen A. | 11 MAR 1867 |
| HAMILTON, Isaac W. | KENT, Minerva | 15 JUN 1863 |
| HAMILTON, James [10] | SCALA, Mary | 14 NOV 1863 |
| HAMILTON, James | WAGNER, Amelia | 18 JUL 1868 |
| HAMILTON, John | FREE, Mary E. | 27 DEC 1864 |
| HAMILTON, John | MARSHALL, Clementina | 24 JUN 1868 |
| HAMILTON, John Wm. | PERRY, Lucinda (blk) | 22 JAN 1862 |
| HAMILTON, Jonathan | JACKSON, Hester | 10 NOV 1863 |
| HAMILTON, Robert B. | KIRBY, Josephine | 24 FEB 1868 |
| HAMILTON, Samuel P. [6le] | HAMILTON, Sallie V. | 06 JUN 1866 |
| HAMILTON, Stephen N. | DRURY, Mary L.S. | 18 NOV 1862 |
| HAMILTON, William H. | KEACH, Harriet | 04 APR 1863 |
| HAMILTREE, Jere: | ARNESTY, Georgiana (blk) | 10 APR 1867 |
| HAMLINK, D.F. [1e] | LAZENBY, Nellie | 27 SEP 1865 |
| HAMMACK, John D. | GALVIN, Susan | 23 FEB 1866 |
| HAMMER, George | LONG, Mary | 26 DEC 1863 |
| HAMMER, John | O'DAY, Mary Ann | 13 JUL 1869 |
| HAMMILL, Reubin | KURTZ, Anna Maria | 06 APR 1863 |
| HAMMILL, Richard R. | SMITH, Elizabeth (blk) | 29 MAY 1865 |
| HAMMOND, Eugene Mortimer | WELSH, Minerva O. | 14 JAN 1868 |
| HAMMOND, G. Hillman | ROBINSON, M. Celia | 19 JUN 1865 |

District of Columbia Marriage Licenses, 1858-1870

| | | |
|---|---|---|
| HAMMOND, George M. | SMITH, Elizabeth | 22 MAY 1862 |
| HAMMOND, Henry | BROOKS, Jane (blk) | 25 JUN 1863 |
| HAMMOND, John E. | FRANK, Annie A. | 04 MAY 1864 |
| HAMMOND, Josephus | CLARK, Fanny (blk) | 13 SEP 1866 |
| HAMMOND, Otho | WHITE, Susan (blk) | 06 JUN 1865 |
| HAMMOND, Richard | ANTHONY, Mary R. (blk) | 07 OCT 1869 |
| HAMMOND, Theodore F. | BRADDOCK, Bettie | 19 OCT 1865 |
| HAMMOND, Wm. H. | BEALL, Elizabeth (blk) | 03 OCT 1865 |
| HAMPLETON, John | ARMSTRONG, Henrietta (blk) | 17 SEP 1867 |
| HAMPTON, Robert | CODRICK, Sallie | 30 SEP 1867 |
| HAMPTON, Thomas | KNOWLDEN, Mary A. | 17 MAY 1865 |
| HAMSLEIN, Edward | LENZ, Mary | 30 MAY 1865 |
| HANCOCK, Charles W. | MILLER, Franzelia | 15 AUG 1861 |
| HANCOCK, John T. | DUDLEY, Dorcas G. | 27 SEP 1859 |
| HANCOCK, Walter L. [6m] | WARD, Emily V. | 08 APR 1863 |
| HANDY, Calvin | STARK, Caroline V. | 04 AUG 1859 |
| HANDY, Dennis | WILSON, Fanny (blk) | 01 JUN 1864 |
| HANDY, James A. | TRIVIS, Rachel S. (blk) | 31 MAY 1869 |
| HANDY, John William | BRADY, Jemima (blk) | 05 JUL 1864 |
| HANDY, S.W.K. | VERNON, Annie E. | 09 NOV 1858 |
| HANES, John W. | MARSHONG, Elizabeth | 29 JAN 1867 |
| HANEY, Patrick | DOWD, Mary | 28 JUL 1865 |
| HANKS, Frank | THOMPSON, Margaret | 22 SEP 1862 |
| HANLIN, Anthony | COLLINS, Martha E. | 03 JUL 1865 |
| HANLON, Andrew | SHEAHAN, Mary | 05 JUL 1862 |
| HANLON, John | CAHAAN, Mary | 23 JAN 1860 |
| HANLON, John | CONNER, Jane | 19 MAY 1862 |
| HANLON, Richard | SOLON, Mary | 07 SEP 1867 |
| HANLY, Edmund [4] | SMITH, Ann L. | 28 OCT 1862 |
| HANNA, Charles W. | CRAWFORD, Kate A. | 17 MAY 1865 |
| HANNAY, John W. | BROOKS, Helen C. | 04 MAR 1867 |
| HANNON, James | KENNEDY, Jane | 21 JUL 1865 |
| HANRAHAN, Thomas | LOONEY, Margaret | 23 JAN 1866 |
| HANRIHAN, Michael | MULCAHEY, Catherine | 06 FEB 1861 |
| HANSFORD, John | TERRELL, Sallie | 04 OCT 1859 |
| HANSOM, James W. | JOHNSON, Elizabeth H. (blk) | 03 MAY 1866 |
| HANSON, Berry | WALLACE, Fanny (blk) | 31 OCT 1865 |
| HANSON, James | BROOKS, Ann (blk) | 18 MAY 1860 |
| HANSON, John H. | BEANS, Lavinia (blk) | 02 FEB 1865 |
| HANSON, Peter (by Aug. Clark) | LIBTEA, Adelaide | 04 JUN 1864 |
| HANSON, Robert E. | GREEN, Mary M. | 28 APR 1866 |
| HANSON, Stephen F. | McKENZIE, Mary | 19 JUL 1862 |
| HANSON, Thomas [7a] | STEPHENSON, Kate B. | 30 NOV 1868 |
| HANSON, William | TURNER, Eliza (blk) | 21 NOV 1867 |
| HANSSLE, Theodore | TYLER, Elizabeth | 15 MAY 1865 |
| HARBACH, John H. | LOVELL, Margaret | 06 JUL 1865 |
| HARBAUGH, Daniel | METCALF, Christiana | 06 JUL 1864 |
| HARBOUR, Joseph | WERNER, Sophia | 17 SEP 1863 |
| HARCOMB, Lucius | WALKER, Patsy (blk) | 15 MAR 1864 |
| HARD, Daniel | WYVILL, Harriet (blk) | 11 MAR 1868 |
| HARDAWAY, Tilgman | ROSS, Celia (blk) | 15 SEP 1866 |
| HARDEMAN, Henry | ALT, Barbara | 16 OCT 1869 |
| HARDEN, Elisha | SNOWDEN, Eliza (blk) | 27 JAN 1866 |
| HARDEN, James Edward | HAVEN, Delia | 23 DEC 1868 |
| HARDESTY, John R. | BECK, Rachel | 16 MAY 1868 |
| HARDESTY, John W. | MASON, Frances | 03 DEC 1866 |

| | | |
|---|---|---|
| HARDIG, George | MILLER, Mary | 27 OCT 1866 |
| HARDING, Anthony | SCOTT, Sarah | 28 JUL 1862 |
| HARDING, Josiah F. | WATT, Annie A. (blk) | 31 JUL 1866 |
| HARDING, P.C. | FOSTER, Connallas B. | 08 JUL 1867 |
| HARDING, Philip | BLAND, Mary | 13 AUG 1868 |
| HARDING, Robert | WEIFELL, Margt. | 03 SEP 1861 |
| HARDING, William H., Jr. [7b] | THOMPSON, Susan E. | 19 JAN 1870 |
| HARDMAN, Asa L. | SHEADS, Louisa Maria | 26 FEB 1866 |
| HARDON, Robert [5] | HOLLAND, Annie | 23 OCT 1868 |
| HARDTNER, Henry | LANG, Kate | 04 OCT 1865 |
| HARDY, Henry | OXLEY, Susan M. | 13 AUG 1862 |
| HARDY, Henry J. | HILTON, Sarah L. | 07 OCT 1861 |
| HARDY, John | KING, Catharine | 21 FEB 1865 |
| HARDY, William H. | BURKE, Mary Ann | 07 FEB 1859 |
| HARFORD, George T. | STICKELS, Susan | 06 AUG 1864 |
| HARGRAVE, William | MILLER, Mary | 07 DEC 1863 |
| HARGREAVE, William | BOWYER, Frances | 24 SEP 1862 |
| HARKNESS, Daniel S. | COOMBS, Mary E. | 10 OCT 1861 |
| HARKNESS, Thomas F. | HUNT, Emma J. | 12 FEB 1866 |
| HARKRICK, Joseph | BROWN, Sarah F. (blk) | 14 JUL 1864 |
| HARLAN, Burns | HONNER, Margaret | 14 JAN 1866 |
| HARLAND, George | HILL, Mary Jane (blk) | 17 SEP 1868 |
| HARLESTON, Jacob H. | FOWLER, Fanny G. | 15 JUL 1862 |
| HARLEY, Isaiah | LEOPHARD, Louisa | 28 FEB 1860 |
| HARLEY, Noah | DICKSON, Lucy Emily | 22 AUG 1867 |
| HARLING, Charles | SIMS, Matilda Wilson | 30 JAN 1862 |
| HARLOW, James [6s] | McGRATH, Rosa [M.] | 30 MAR 1865 |
| HARLOW, John | DUGAN, Rosanna | 23 MAY 1864 |
| HARLOW, Reubin | COWNE, Joanna | 03 JUN 1863 |
| HARMAN, John | WARD, Charlotte R. | 22 MAR 1866 |
| HARMAN, John M. | CANFIELD, Anna | 16 SEP 1868 |
| HARMAN, Philip George | STONE, Catharine | 26 FEB 1859 |
| HARMAN, Priscilla E. | DUKEHART, Graham [6s] | 31 MAR 1865 |
| HARN, James | COYLE, Anna | 14 DEC 1867 |
| HARNER, Edwin H. | TAYLOR, Bertie | 04 OCT 1869 |
| HARNES, Joseph | BROWN, Matilda (blk) | 08 JUL 1863 |
| HARNETT, John | READY, Eliza | 16 SEP 1865 |
| HARPER, Benjn. F. | ELLIS, Mary V. | 17 FEB 1866 |
| HARPER, George | HOPKINS, Mary Valinda (blk) | 02 APR 1866 |
| HARPER, Henry | McCOLLOF, Mary | 19 APR 1862 |
| HARPER, James | CROUGH, Ellen | 23 MAY 1859 |
| HARPER, James Grafton | SIMMONS, Indiana | 08 JAN 1864 |
| HARPER, Thomas H. | CHAUNCEY, Emma R. | 12 NOV 1862 |
| HARRAN, George H. | CLEMENTS, Martha A. | 16 NOV 1861 |
| HARRIDAY, William | FELTON, Sarah (blk) | 03 NOV 1863 |
| HARRIGAN, A.F.A. | POTTS, Ann E. | 05 JAN 1865 |
| HARRIMAN, David S. | FAY, Maggie M. | 01 JUN 1867 |
| HARRINGTON, F.H. | CALLAN, S.R. | 06 JAN 1868 |
| HARRINGTON, George | SCOTT, Mary Seaton | 29 JAN 1862 |
| HARRINGTON, John | HAGERTY, Mary | 11 JAN 1860 |
| HARRINGTON, Richard H. | MANKIN, Mary Virginia | 29 NOV 1865 |
| HARRINGTON, Stephen R. | FRANCE, Margarita B. | 13 OCT 1869 |
| HARRINGTON, Timothy | DONOHO, Ellen | 04 JUL 1863 |
| HARRINGTON, Vernon [11] | WALLACE, Julia P. | 03 APR 1862 |
| HARRINGTON, William W. | BRODERICK, Johanna | 15 DEC 1866 |
| HARRIS, Albert | BOND, Hester (blk) | 12 DEC 1866 |

District of Columbia Marriage Licenses, 1858-1870

| | | |
|---|---|---|
| HARRIS, Allen | STOKES, Ann (blk) | 13 MAY 1864 |
| HARRIS, Ambrose | TALBERT, Mary (blk) | 03 JUL 1867 |
| HARRIS, Antilochus | PLATES, Mary Ellen (blk) | 23 JUN 1863 |
| HARRIS, Benjamin | BRACKETT, Elizabeth (blk) | 22 DEC 1864 |
| HARRIS, Beverly | GALWAY, Nancy (blk) | 23 MAY 1868 |
| HARRIS, Charles | SHORTER, Mary (blk) | 03 OCT 1863 |
| HARRIS, Charles | JOHNSON, Pricey | 04 MAR 1867 |
| HARRIS, Chas. H. | SMITH, Elizabeth A. (blk) | 24 APR 1862 |
| HARRIS, Daniel | HATTON, Martha (blk) | 27 OCT 1869 |
| HARRIS, Darius | RUSSELL, Jane | 06 JAN 1868 |
| HARRIS, David W. | POSEY, Mary E. (blk) | 02 APR 1862 |
| HARRIS, David W. | SMITH, Mary Isabella Elizabeth | 21 JAN 1864 |
| HARRIS, Edwin | ALLEN, Augusta | 20 MAY 1862 |
| HARRIS, Fairfield | SEXTON, Margt. M. | 02 MAY 1862 |
| HARRIS, Francis | FILLMORE, Susan (blk) | 30 DEC 1868 |
| HARRIS, Frank | SHORTER, Martha (blk) | 16 OCT 1866 |
| HARRIS, Frank | BIRD, Rose (blk) | 29 OCT 1866 |
| HARRIS, George E. | JAMES, Catharine M. | 16 NOV 1866 |
| HARRIS, George W. | LONG, Emma Jane | 18 OCT 1864 |
| HARRIS, George W. | BONNER, Amanda (blk) | 03 AUG 1866 |
| HARRIS, George W. | SEYMOUR, Mary A.J. | 01 NOV 1858 |
| HARRIS, Harry | HAWKINS, Elizabeth | 19 FEB 1864 |
| HARRIS, Henry | COATS, Mary E. (blk) | 09 OCT 1866 |
| HARRIS, Henry | SMALLWOOD, Ann (blk) | 11 DEC 1867 |
| HARRIS, Henry G. [7a] | HAMMER, Susan E.A. | 29 MAY 1867 |
| HARRIS, Jack | ROBINSON, Fanny (blk) | 03 JUN 1865 |
| HARRIS, Jacob | PRIMROSE, Lizzie (blk) | 26 FEB 1869 |
| HARRIS, Jacob P. | BOSWELL, Margaret Helen | 11 SEP 1869 |
| HARRIS, James | VERES, Elizabeth (blk) | 07 JUN 1866 |
| HARRIS, James | COLMAN, Amanda (blk) | 21 SEP 1867 |
| HARRIS, James L. | HALL, Esther | 21 NOV 1862 |
| HARRIS, Jesse | PLUMMER, Sophia (blk) | 14 OCT 1868 |
| HARRIS, John | BELL, Nancy (blk) | 23 SEP 1861 |
| HARRIS, John | RIDEOUT, Margaret | 08 SEP 1864 |
| HARRIS, John | CARTER, Lucy | 17 MAY 1866 |
| HARRIS, John | JOHNSON, Betsey (blk) | 23 SEP 1868 |
| HARRIS, John | MASSEY, Sarah (blk) | 21 APR 1869 |
| HARRIS, John F. | CADY, Margaret | 03 NOV 1864 |
| HARRIS, John L. | BARKMAN, Alice | 23 JAN 1869 |
| HARRIS, Joseph | BUSH, Elizabeth (blk) | 02 APR 1869 |
| HARRIS, Joseph [5] | BROWN, Elizabeth (blk) | 19 FEB 1867 |
| HARRIS, Joseph C. [12c] | SHELTON, Mary | 11 MAR 1861 |
| HARRIS, Lewis | O'NEIL, Hester (blk) | 07 NOV 1865 |
| HARRIS, Lewis | BRANNON, Sallie (blk) | 03 DEC 1867 |
| HARRIS, Richard | SCHRIDER, Mary L. | 04 OCT 1862 |
| HARRIS, Richard | TURNER, Frances | 05 AUG 1867 |
| HARRIS, Robert | MOCKABEE, Rose (blk) | 01 JUN 1864 |
| HARRIS, Robert | NELSON, Jeannett L. | 18 FEB 1867 |
| HARRIS, Robert | WASHINGTON, Violet (blk) | 29 OCT 1868 |
| HARRIS, Robert C. | RILEY, Hesse | 18 APR 1864 |
| HARRIS, Robert L. | EVANS, Francis H. | 05 OCT 1858 |
| HARRIS, Samuel | TOWLES, Violet (blk) | 07 NOV 1867 |
| HARRIS, Spencer | WILSON, Mary (blk) | 20 APR 1865 |
| HARRIS, Thomas | DATCHER, Elizabeth | 01 AUG 1867 |
| HARRIS, Thomas J. | FORD, Georgiana | 04 DEC 1867 |
| HARRIS, William | COLLINS, Louisa | 12 MAY 1869 |

District of Columbia Marriage Licenses, 1858-1870

| | | |
|---|---|---|
| HARRIS, William | ALLEN, Jane (blk) | 10 JUN 1869 |
| HARRIS, William H. | CAMPBELL, Charlotte (blk) | 15 DEC 1866 |
| HARRIS, William Henry | ROBERTS, Elizabeth Ann (blk) | 03 OCT 1867 |
| HARRISON, Daniel | BUTLER, Jane (blk) | 17 APR 1866 |
| HARRISON, Daniel | COOK, Hannah | 28 DEC 1867 |
| HARRISON, Daniel C. [6h] | BAILEY, Annie | 27 MAY 1868 |
| HARRISON, Eli | BELL, Emily (blk) | 17 JUN 1867 |
| HARRISON, Henry T. | BRODERS, Laura | 25 SEP 1863 |
| HARRISON, James | MILLER, Caroline | 04 MAY 1867 |
| HARRISON, James F. | LYELL, Frances G. | 04 OCT 1860 |
| HARRISON, James T. | WILSON, Sarah | 06 DEC 1865 |
| HARRISON, James W. | READ, Laura E. | 08 SEP 1869 |
| HARRISON, John | RHODES, Sarah | 02 SEP 1862 |
| HARRISON, John | CHEW, Henrietta (blk) | 10 AUG 1866 |
| HARRISON, John W.H. | HOLT, Annie | 23 NOV 1869 |
| HARRISON, Joseph | ALLEN, Catherine | 01 AUG 1866 |
| HARRISON, Philip | DENT, Sarah K. | 13 FEB 1867 |
| HARRISON, Robert | RITTEAU, Margaret | 31 AUG 1864 |
| HARRISON, Sampson | CHESHIRE, Mary Ellen | 06 MAY 1869 |
| HARRISON, Samson | REDMAN, Virginia | 18 OCT 1866 |
| HARRISON, Samuel | TURNER, Sarah (blk) | 25 FEB 1868 |
| HARRISON, Thomas | WOODFALL, Bettie (blk) | 05 NOV 1866 |
| HARRISON, Thomas M. | CALL, Fanny A. | 24 MAY 1865 |
| HARRISON, Thos. H. | TRUMAN, Mary A. | 12 FEB 1863 |
| HARRISON, Walter | CAMPBELL, Marian (blk) | 03 NOV 1869 |
| HARRISON, William | MACKALL, Cornelia (blk) | 19 FEB 1867 |
| HARROD, Dennis B. | GREENE, Eliza Ann (blk) | 05 JUN 1867 |
| HARROD, Hilliary | JACKSON, Henrietta (blk) | 26 MAY 1868 |
| HARROD, Robert | BRISCOE, Elizabeth (blk) | 03 SEP 1863 |
| HARROD, Robert | JOHNSON, Lydia Ann (blk) | 08 OCT 1863 |
| HARROD, Samuel | WASHINGTON, Harriet E. (blk) | 02 MAY 1866 |
| HARROD, William | SMITH, Jane (blk) | 24 JAN 1861 |
| HARRODAY, Charles A. | LYLES, Mary E. (blk) | 26 FEB 1867 |
| HARROLL, Charles | MARTIN, Bridget | 31 MAR 1864 |
| HARROVER, Joseph | NELSON, Lizzie | 17 DEC 1868 |
| HARRY, George | LIJAH, Margaret | 17 AUG 1859 |
| HARRY, George W. | SHACKLEFORD, Annie C. | 25 JUN 1863 |
| HARRY, James H. | CONNER, Sarah A. | 01 OCT 1864 |
| HARRY, James H. | QUEEN, Sarah | 03 JUN 1865 |
| HARRY, Joseph W. | QUEEN, Henrietta | 23 APR 1866 |
| HARRY, Richard | WILSON, Eliza | 23 JUL 1859 |
| HART, Charles | REARDEN, Mary L. | 14 MAR 1864 |
| HART, Charles L. | FRANKS, Sarah J. | 10 AUG 1865 |
| HART, Ernst | TAYLOR, Addie | 13 FEB 1866 |
| HART, Frank | KEAFE, Annie | 27 MAR 1867 |
| HART, Henry | HAUGH, Catharine | 29 AUG 1862 |
| HART, John | RIGBY, Mary | 26 MAY 1864 |
| HART, Joseph | KENNEDY, Ellen | 05 APR 1866 |
| HART, Michael | BURLEY, Bridget T. | 02 NOV 1864 |
| HARTENSTEIN, Alven | PICKENS, Margaret | 28 SEP 1863 |
| HARTIGAN, Thomas | McNAUGHTON, Mary | 07 JAN 1865 |
| HARTLEY, Edwin D. | LYONS, Mary | 16 OCT 1865 |
| HARTLEY, Joseph H. [6m] | MORRISON, Martha J. | 03 JUL 1862 |
| HARTLEY, Joseph H. [10] | COOK, Emily | 20 DEC 1865 |
| HARTLEY, William B. | PRITCHARD, Sarah M. | 30 JAN 1866 |
| HARTMAN, Daniel | FALVEY, Margaret | 19 NOV 1862 |

District of Columbia Marriage Licenses, 1858-1870

| | | |
|---|---|---|
| HARTMANN, Frederick | MINGES, Susanna | 01 JUL 1864 |
| HARTMANN, Joseph | HERZZOG, Amelia | 02 APR 1863 |
| HARTMANN, Joseph | BOSSE, Henrietta | 30 JUN 1869 |
| HARTMEYER, Chas. | HATHMANN, Mary | 23 APR 1862 |
| HARTNETT, John C. | JAMES, Mary Ann | 25 APR 1868 |
| HARTNETT, Thomas | CAHHIL, Elizabeth | 09 JUN 1864 |
| HARTNETT, Thomas | ARMOUR, Julia (Reilly) | 05 JUL 1865 |
| HARTNETT, Timothy F. | CURTIN, Mary | 13 DEC 1862 |
| HARTONG, Sarach | MEYER, Helene | 10 JAN 1867 |
| HARTSELL, James E. | MORAN, Annie | 25 JUL 1863 |
| HARTWIG, Frederick | PRICE, Georgiana Virginia | 12 MAY 1868 |
| HARVEY, Charles G.W. | LAONHART, Annie M. | 22 FEB 1867 |
| HARVEY, George W. | EVANS, Mary Ann | 14 FEB 1860 |
| HARVEY, George W. | DUFFY, S. Kate | 20 NOV 1861 |
| HARVEY, James | GIBB, Mary Ann | 09 JAN 1863 |
| HARVEY, James W., Jr. | ELLIS, Sallie | 06 FEB 1868 |
| HARVEY, John | GRIFFIN, Ellen (blk) | 16 MAY 1867 |
| HARVEY, Joseph E. | DORSEY, Mary Elizabeth | 29 OCT 1868 |
| HARVEY, Leonard W. [6c] | JONES, Charity Ann | 02 SEP 1858 |
| HARVEY, Richard F. | REDMOND, Elizth. | 04 DEC 1861 |
| HARVEY, William G. | TAYLOR, Ellen V. | 02 JUN 1860 |
| HARVEY, William G. | TAYLOR, Ellen V. | 07 JAN 1861 |
| HARVEYCUTTER, John | McDADE, Martha | 12 MAR 1866 |
| HARWELL, Patrick | DOUGHERTY, Mary | 17 FEB 1868 |
| HARWOOD, Dwight [12s] | HINDS, Margaret A. | 01 MAR 1861 |
| HARWOOD, Franklin | HUNTER, Julia Herbert | 01 JUN 1861 |
| HASHOSS, Henry | BERKIN, Mary Ann | 11 NOV 1861 |
| HASK, Bernard | SIMON, Magdelene | 23 JAN 1861 |
| HASKE, George A. | CURTIN, Bridget | 19 NOV 1861 |
| HASKEL, Hiram M. | McDONALD, Mary | 23 JAN 1865 |
| HASKELL, F.M. | CAWOOD, Virginia | 18 JUL 1865 |
| HASKELL, Theodore J. | SPENCER, Louisa | 13 APR 1864 |
| HASKELL, Wm. P. | SWEET, Martha W. | 29 JUL 1863 |
| HASKINS, Hugh | HOAGAN, Annie | 20 MAY 1863 |
| HASKINS, Iverson | MICKINS, Susan (blk) | 02 JUL 1867 |
| HASLUP, Arthur | ANDERSON, Charlotte | 20 APR 1865 |
| HASLUP, Richard | JOHNSON, Isabella | 28 APR 1868 |
| HASLUP, Wilton Chester | ATWILL, Ella Florence | 16 SEP 1868 |
| HASSLER, Charles R. | MENSEL, Emma | 12 NOV 1861 |
| HASTINGS, Dennis | HOPKINS, Maria | 18 JUN 1866 |
| HASTINGS, John B. | CRAIG, Laura J. | 13 JUL 1865 |
| HASWELL, David B. | BOONE, Jane E. | 23 MAY 1863 |
| HATCH, Charles | McCORMICK, Mary Ann | 01 NOV 1862 |
| HATCHER, J. Thomas | PANCOAST, Sallie J. | 20 JAN 1868 |
| HATCHER, John | EVERETT, Elizabeth | 26 MAR 1862 |
| HATCHER, William | ODRICK, Sallie (blk) | 22 DEC 1869 |
| HATHAWAY, Peter | MORRIS, Maria (blk) | 05 NOV 1866 |
| HATTON, Benjamin | GANTT, Eliza | 01 MAY 1867 |
| HATTON, George W. | BECKET, Frances A. | 05 JUN 1866 |
| HATTON, Henry | YOUNG, Eliza (blk) | 20 SEP 1866 |
| HATTON, Henry | BROWN, Adaline (blk) | 28 DEC 1867 |
| HATTON, Robert | COLEMAN, Frances (blk) | 04 MAY 1863 |
| HAUBER, Laurence | GIBBONS, Mary | 22 JUL 1865 |
| HAUBER, Laurence | RUSSELL, Laura | 02 DEC 1865 |
| HAUF, John Lewis | ANCHELL, Mary Rebecca | 11 FEB 1862 |
| HAUFMAN, Sebastian | BERBERICK, Kate | 21 NOV 1865 |

| | | |
|---|---|---|
| HAUGHTON, A. Otis | TARDY, Jennie T. | 01 AUG 1868 |
| HAULENBEEK, Geo. W. | CONOVER, Susie B. | 08 OCT 1867 |
| HAUN, John I. | LEHMAN, Catherine A. | 05 NOV 1867 |
| HAUNÉ, Ernst | NAUMANN, Francisca | 15 APR 1864 |
| HAUPTMAN, George W. | BRADY, Elizabeth M. | 12 OCT 1863 |
| HAUSBARRIER, John | LIBIE, Eliza | 06 NOV 1867 |
| HAUSER, Jacob | HÖRNER, Lizzetti | 04 APR 1864 |
| HAVARD, Leopold Auguste Ferdinand | SILENCE, Susan | 20 DEC 1866 |
| HAVENER, Walter S. [10] | THOMPSON, Elizabeth A.C. | 15 AUG 1861 |
| HAVENER, Wm. [10] | THOMPSON, Ellener | 11 NOV 1867 |
| HAVENNER, Alfred | BURGESS, Margaret | 08 MAR 1859 |
| HAVERTY, Thomas | DONOGHUE, Hannah | 08 JAN 1864 |
| HAVILAND, George [1c] | TURNER, Louisa | 26 MAY 1863 |
| HAW, Jesse B. | EDWARDS, Anne | 31 DEC 1859 |
| HAWES, Charles W. | DOWNEY, Margaret | 16 AUG 1861 |
| HAWES, William | CLARKE, Virginia (blk) | 29 SEP 1863 |
| HAWKE, Charles W. | CASTEEL, Mary J. | 23 SEP 1867 |
| HAWKIN, William | WALKER, Fanny Ann (blk) | 29 MAY 1866 |
| HAWKINS, Brown | WASHINGTON, Cornelia (blk) | 20 FEB 1868 |
| HAWKINS, Caleb | McCOY, Helen (blk) | 17 AUG 1869 |
| HAWKINS, Edmund | MOORE, Jennie B. | 02 APR 1866 |
| HAWKINS, Edward | HAWKINS, Frances (blk) | 04 AUG 1865 |
| HAWKINS, Edward | RUDD, Alice | 22 SEP 1869 |
| HAWKINS, Frank | DORSEY, Jane (blk) | 09 MAR 1870 |
| HAWKINS, George | BELL, Harriet (blk) | 07 MAY 1866 |
| HAWKINS, George A. | BELL, Sarah Jane (blk) | 19 AUG 1868 |
| HAWKINS, George H. | JONES, Lizzie Virginia (blk) | 18 AUG 1862 |
| HAWKINS, George W. | DAVIS, Ellenora (blk) | 29 JUL 1861 |
| HAWKINS, Henry | POWELL, Arianna (blk) | 18 FEB 1869 |
| HAWKINS, James | BOWMAN, Amy (blk) | 03 SEP 1864 |
| HAWKINS, James | GRAY, Lucy (blk) | 19 FEB 1867 |
| HAWKINS, James L. | FLOWERS, Mary | 15 DEC 1863 |
| HAWKINS, James W. | CRAWFORD, Harriet (blk) | 22 APR 1868 |
| HAWKINS, Jefferson | JOHNSON, Lucy (blk) | 21 OCT 1867 |
| HAWKINS, John | GEEN, Isabella (blk) | 15 DEC 1866 |
| HAWKINS, John H. | BARTON, Elenora (blk) | 29 OCT 1866 |
| HAWKINS, John L. | BROWN, Fannie | 04 JAN 1864 |
| HAWKINS, John P. [4] | CRAIG, Jane B. | 09 OCT 1867 |
| HAWKINS, Miles | JACKSON, Kate (blk) | 18 JAN 1865 |
| HAWKINS, Miles | HAWKINS, Kate (blk) | 13 JUL 1865 |
| HAWKINS, Perry | SUTTON, Virginia | 12 MAY 1870 |
| HAWKINS, Robert | STEWART, Lizzie (blk) | 16 JUN 1866 |
| HAWKINS, Robert | ANDERSON, Sarah | 24 OCT 1868 |
| HAWKINS, Robert | DIXON, Mary (blk) | 17 MAY 1869 |
| HAWKINS, Thomas R. | LANDREY, Julia B. (blk) | 02 MAY 1867 |
| HAWKINS, William | LYLES, Louisa (blk) | 29 MAY 1868 |
| HAWKINS, William | JONES, Fanny (blk) | 24 FEB 1869 |
| HAWKINS, William | SMITH, Christine (blk) | 21 JUL 1869 |
| HAWKINS, Wm. S. | ALLEN, Mary Elizth. (blk) | 04 DEC 1860 |
| HAWLEY, Edward [6h] | BLAIR, Mary E. | 16 JUL 1868 |
| HAWXHURST, Job | BORDEN, Margaret D. | 14 JUN 1860 |
| HAY, James | JACKSON, Mary (blk) | 06 AUG 1860 |
| HAYCOCK, Joseph | BROWN, Sarah | 26 AUG 1869 |
| HAYDEN, Charles F. | HAYDEN, Sarah E. | 30 DEC 1864 |
| HAYDEN, George W. | PEAK, Mary A. | 01 JUL 1869 |
| HAYDEN, L.H. | ENGLISH, N.M. | 06 APR 1868 |

District of Columbia Marriage Licenses, 1858-1870

| | | |
|---|---|---|
| HAYDEN, L.H. | ENGLISH, Nellie M. | 17 JUL 1868 |
| HAYDEN, Lewis S. [11] | BULL, Kate | 26 MAR 1859 |
| HAYDEN, Michael | KELLY, Margaret | 27 NOV 1866 |
| HAYDEN, Thomas | O'KEEFE, Catherine M.J. | 11 OCT 1866 |
| HAYDEN, Zachariah | JOHNSON, Mary S. | 08 NOV 1858 |
| HAYES, Charles H. | BROWN, Margaret E. | 20 DEC 1860 |
| HAYES, Jeremiah | McGREEN, Catherine | 25 JUN 1863 |
| HAYES, John | BARRETT, Julia | 13 NOV 1861 |
| HAYES, John L. | BOYER, Mary Ellen | 26 OCT 1864 |
| HAYES, Patrick | MURPHEY, Mary | 11 MAY 1865 |
| HAYES, Thomas | BOYLE, Mary | 03 OCT 1860 |
| HAYGHE, John L., Rev. [6m] | HENNING, Mary Jane | 24 FEB 1864 |
| HAYMAN, George | JACKSON, Elizabeth (blk) | 11 JUN 1867 |
| HAYNE, John | CLARKE, Margaret | 23 APR 1859 |
| HAYNES, Charles | MOULTON, Maria L. | 24 MAR 1859 |
| HAYNES, David | HEATON, Mary A. | 03 AUG 1863 |
| HAYNES, Edwin D. | FRIZE, Martha A. | 30 JAN 1866 |
| HAYS, George W. | BROWN, Mary Ellen | 11 SEP 1862 |
| HAYS, Jacob | CHASE, Maria (blk) | 02 JAN 1865 |
| HAYS, Jacob [10] | GIBSON, Sarah Jane | 05 NOV 1867 |
| HAYS, James | HAYS, Mary | 25 NOV 1864 |
| HAYS, John N. | COATS, Louisa | 26 JUL 1859 |
| HAYS, Richard | STEWART, Nancy (blk) | 01 MAR 1870 |
| HAYS, Robert | BENNETT, Martha (blk) | 06 AUG 1860 |
| HAYS, Thomas | O'BRIEN, Julia | 25 SEP 1869 |
| HAYS, William | BIGGS, Sarah | 28 DEC 1865 |
| HAYS, William | JONES, Emily Jane | 03 JAN 1866 |
| HAYS, William | SHARPE, Mary | 18 DEC 1866 |
| HAYSON, Abraham | TINNEY, Eliza (blk) | 13 MAY 1868 |
| HAYSON, William H. | HAILSTOW, Amelia (blk) | 22 NOV 1865 |
| HAYWARD, Henderson [5] | PIGGOTT, Bertie H. | 13 AUG 1867 |
| HAYWOOD, Charles | BACON, Carrie | 17 OCT 1866 |
| HAYWOOD, Edward | DAYTON, Julia C. | 30 OCT 1862 |
| HAYWOOD, George | PAYNE, Sarah (blk) | 07 JUN 1870 |
| HAZARD, David L. | PRATHER, Josephine L. | 10 JUL 1867 |
| HAZARD, Morris | RICKCORDS, Amelia | 05 DEC 1863 |
| HAZARD, Robert R. | SANDFORD, Julia E. | 11 JUN 1864 |
| HAZARD, William H. | WADE, Ella M. | 13 APR 1868 |
| HAZARD, William K. | FARRELL, Mary | 15 DEC 1858 |
| HAZEL, Philip L. | DYER, Clara Virginia | 11 MAR 1861 |
| HAZELL, James H. | FISTER, Louisa S. | 15 DEC 1858 |
| HAZEN, A.D. | PAYNTER, Mary V. | 14 NOV 1865 |
| HAZEN, Abraham N. | CARROLL, Mary C. | 28 DEC 1867 |
| HAZEN, M.V.B. | WILLIAMS, Alice | 11 NOV 1863 |
| HAZLE, Edward | COOK, Ann Maria | 12 MAY 1863 |
| HAZLE, Edward | COOK, Ann Maria | 10 AUG 1863 |
| HAZLE, John | BARNES, Catharine | 05 AUG 1862 |
| HAZLE, Levi [6s] | COOK, Mary P. | 12 DEC 1864 |
| HAZLE, Zachariah | GRAVES, Mary Ann | 24 DEC 1858 |
| HAZLETT, Rob. C. | BARTRUFF, Mary Lee | 25 OCT 1865 |
| HEAD, George E. | BARRY, Lydia B. | 21 JAN 1865 |
| HEAD, George R. [1e] | WAUGH, Mary Lizzie | 16 JAN 1865 |
| HEAD, John W. [3] | JOHNSON, Elizabeth [Lizzie] A. | 08 FEB 1866 |
| HEAD, Montgomery W. | BALLARD, Beattrice A. | 28 AUG 1860 |
| HEADLEY, John P. | BAILEY, Harriet A. | 07 OCT 1867 |
| HEALY, Granville P. | PADGETT, Laura C. | 12 JUN 1865 |

| | | |
|---|---|---|
| HEALY, Henry G. | HICKEY, Rosalie | 27 JUN 1864 |
| HEALY, John W. | COLLIER, Carrie V. | 26 JUN 1866 |
| HEALY, M.D. | TORRENS, Anna E. | 09 AUG 1869 |
| HEALY, Matthew | MARTIN, Susan | 12 MAY 1863 |
| HEARD, M.S.V. | WILLIAMS, Josephine G. | 02 NOV 1865 |
| HEARNE, Frederick H. | McCARTHY, Bridget | 20 JUN 1864 |
| HEART, John [12s] | DONNELLY, Lydia | 07 FEB 1862 |
| HEATH, John E. | HOLLEY, Addie | 24 JAN 1863 |
| HEATLEY, James E. | WIDEMAN, Annie | 16 MAR 1870 |
| HEATLEY, William R. | MARTIN, Charlotte | 04 OCT 1864 |
| HEAVNER, Henry* | GIDDINGS, Mary | 29 NOV 1859 |
| HEBERLE, Fritz | SCHALEK, Christien | 22 OCT 1863 |
| HEBERLING, Henry | JARBOE, Margaret R. | 15 SEP 1859 |
| HEBERNEHT, Leonhard | REISS, Atilheit | 16 OCT 1861 |
| HEBNER, Martin | HARMAN, Annie | 06 MAY 1870 |
| HECK, John M. | OWENS, Martha | 04 SEP 1868 |
| HECK, William C. | DELANEY, Margt. A. | 21 OCT 1859 |
| HEDGEMAN, Albert | WARRENTON, Mary (blk) | 02 MAY 1863 |
| HEDGES, Andrew A. | HINES, Emma | 30 MAR 1866 |
| HEDGMAN, Jon | JACKSON, An (blk) | 24 AUG 1865 |
| HEDLEY, John P., Jr. | WILLIAMS, Mary V. | 23 MAY 1870 |
| HEFFERNAN, John | McCARTHY, Ellen | 28 JUL 1859 |
| HEFFNER, James E. | KING, Emma R. | 19 SEP 1867 |
| HEFLING, Westley J. | HUMPHREY, Martha Ann | 05 FEB 1859 |
| HEFTIN, William T. | SUTTON, Mary V. | 17 OCT 1868 |
| HEHL, Nicolaus | HERBERT, Louise | 10 OCT 1863 |
| HEHNE, Frederick | LENTNER, Catherine | 21 MAY 1861 |
| HEI, Charles Casper | HOHENSTEIN, Sarah | 02 APR 1863 |
| HEID, Christopher | HOPSON, Mary | 06 APR 1864 |
| HEIDER, William | HENSEL, Barbara | 19 JAN 1864 |
| HEIFERS, Henry | GAYNOR, Bridget | 30 APR 1863 |
| HEIGER, John | BUNDSCHUH, Caroline | 02 APR 1867 |
| HEIGES, David C. [11] | RAUB, Helena A. | 31 AUG 1867 |
| HEIL, John | DRUSHEIM, Catharine | 07 AUG 1865 |
| HEILMAN, Theodore | BAKER, Adelheit | 06 MAY 1864 |
| HEIM, Adam Joseph | HELLE, Mary | 03 JUL 1863 |
| HEIM, Henry | ENGLEHARD, Mary | 28 OCT 1861 |
| HEIMECKE, Charles T. | RHINEHART, Mary S. | 28 OCT 1869 |
| HEIMER, Joseph | BEAN, Sarah M. | 11 JAN 1865 |
| HEINECKE, Lewis | CULBERTSON, Mary | 25 DEC 1863 |
| HEINER, Robert G. | SLEMAKER, Helen G. | 19 JAN 1869 |
| HEINLEIN, George W. [6l] | SWEENY, Susan Jane | 19 DEC 1861 |
| HEINLEIN, Heist | BOTTAJHEMER, Babet | 27 APR 1861 |
| HEINLINE, H.D. | WEBBER, Katie F. | 04 AUG 1868 |
| HEINLUKE, Christian | RODEN, Elizabeth | 06 SEP 1861 |
| HEINOLD, Charles | WALDSHMI<u>DT</u>, Johanna | 28 JUL 1863 |
| HEINRICH, Rudolph | KUMMER, Emilie | 15 DEC 1866 |
| HEINS, Charles | SILLKINGER, Caroline | 16 JUN 1863 |
| HEINSLEY, Lawrence | JACKSON, Margaret (blk) | 13 JAN 1866 |
| HEINSON, Cato | BROWN, Hester Ann | 22 SEP 1863 |
| HEINTZEL, Edward | HETHINGER, Caroline | 30 JUL 1868 |
| HEISER, Henry | KAUFMAN, Rachel | 22 SEP 1863 |
| HEISS, John | BURKHARD, Mary | 18 MAR 1867 |
| HEISS, Louis | LUCKEI, Mary | 26 APR 1860 |
| HEITMAN, Francis B. | POORE, Mary Frances | 09 MAY 1863 |
| HEITMILLER, Alfred | ROSENTHALL, Augusta | 17 MAR 1859 |

District of Columbia Marriage Licenses, 1858-1870

| | | |
|---|---|---|
| HEITMILLER, Frederick | HESS, Mary | 12 NOV 1861 |
| HEITMULLER, Charles | SCHUBERT, Auguste | 30 AUG 1860 |
| HEITMULLER, Charles | HEITMULLER, Lena | 12 SEP 1866 |
| HELLEN, B.J., Dr. | PHILLIPS, Virginia E. | 16 SEP 1858 |
| HELLEN, Clifton [10] | DOVE, Virginia | 24 DEC 1861 |
| HELLEN, William F. | COWLES, E. Lela | 15 SEP 1869 |
| HELLER, Henry | GRAY, Ann | 23 JUN 1859 |
| HELLER, Henry | WIESER, Apolonia | 05 OCT 1865 |
| HELLIG, John | BONITZ, Emelia | 18 MAY 1863 |
| HELLMOTH, Thomas | BAUSBACH, Annie | 20 SEP 1864 |
| HELLMUTH, Stephen | BOREL, Paulina | 26 NOV 1866 |
| HELLMUTH, Valentine | OSTERMEYER, Cornelia | 25 OCT 1860 |
| HELLUMS, Edward | WATTS, Cordelia (blk) | 25 AUG 1866 |
| HELLYER, Charles | STETSON, Josephine D. | 04 DEC 1867 |
| HELMUS, William | CRAGES, Carrie | 31 DEC 1866 |
| HELMUTH, Henry | HORNER, Rosa | 03 DEC 1864 |
| HELWIG, Peter | COOK, Anna | 30 DEC 1864 |
| HEMM, Bartle | HALZFELD, Mary | 20 MAY 1869 |
| HÉNAULT, Jules S. | MEGE, Thérèse | 02 JUL 1869 |
| HENCKE, Frank | BEAN, Agatha | 09 NOV 1867 |
| HENDERSON, Alexander | HENDERSON, Susan (blk) | 26 JUN 1866 |
| HENDERSON, Charles | THOMAS, Mary E. | 02 FEB 1863 |
| HENDERSON, Charles E. | DEAN, Elizabeth | 16 OCT 1865 |
| HENDERSON, Charles W. | ROBINSON, Jennie | 13 SEP 1865 |
| HENDERSON, Daniel | SPRIGG, Mary (blk) | 05 JAN 1865 |
| HENDERSON, David | BREGGENAN, Rosa L. | 12 NOV 1861 |
| HENDERSON, George | JOHNSON, Elizabeth (blk) | 08 OCT 1864 |
| HENDERSON, George L. | VIOLETT, Georgeana | 15 JUL 1862 |
| HENDERSON, Harrison | PIERCE, Martha (blk) | 06 DEC 1866 |
| HENDERSON, Henry | SIMMS, Laura (blk) | 04 SEP 1867 |
| HENDERSON, Henry | BARNES, Catherine (blk) | 18 DEC 1867 |
| HENDERSON, John B. | FOOTE, Mary N. | 20 JUN 1868 |
| HENDERSON, John W. [6c] | AYRE, Frances A. | 28 DEC 1858 |
| HENDERSON, Lewis | NELSON, Maria (blk) | 21 FEB 1866 |
| HENDERSON, Minor | CARROLL, Ann (blk) | 01 APR 1863 |
| HENDERSON, Nathaniel | COLEMAN, Mary | 14 MAY 1866 |
| HENDERSON, Orlander G. | LANNAN, Maggie | 22 APR 1865 |
| HENDERSON, Richard | HERENS, Helen B. | 10 MAY 1859 |
| HENDERSON, Robert | TOBIAS, Elizabeth | 18 DEC 1863 |
| HENDERSON, Samuel | STOCK, Gwynnette (blk) | 15 NOV 1861 |
| HENDERSON, Simon | JOHNSON, Adeline (blk) | 19 AUG 1867 |
| HENDERSON, Walter H. | HOLBROKE, Margaret (blk) | 07 DEC 1865 |
| HENDERSON, William | MARTIN, Maryetta E. | 21 MAY 1861 |
| HENDERSON, William | WHEELER, Mary (blk) | 01 NOV 1864 |
| HENDERSON, William | WISE, Debora | 24 JUL 1865 |
| HENDERSON, William A. | ST. JOHN, Rebecca T. | 14 APR 1859 |
| HENDLEY, Basil Thos. | BUTT, Mary Verlinda | 08 DEC 1859 |
| HENDLEY, George | LYONS, Margaret | 20 AUG 1863 |
| HENDLEY, John | SHERMAN, Mary | 22 OCT 1863 |
| HENDLEY, William | BENNETT, Lela | 06 MAY 1863 |
| HENDRICK, Jacob | BRANSON, Mary Elizth. (blk) | 20 JUN 1867 |
| HENDRICK, W.O. | BOURNS, Jennie M. | 17 AUG 1865 |
| HENDRICKS, Arthur | MOORE, Ida V. | 03 MAR 1866 |
| HENDRICKS, Jeremiah | McCARTY, Ellen | 24 MAY 1862 |
| HENDRICKSON, Benjamin E. | EAYRE, Hannah H. | 10 AUG 1863 |
| HENDRICKSON, John | BARRETT, Hannah Parker | 05 FEB 1863 |

District of Columbia Marriage Licenses, 1858-1870

| | | |
|---|---|---|
| HENKLE, Conrad | WAGNER, Katherina | 18 JUL 1863 |
| HENLEY, John | KEENAN, Mary | 09 SEP 1863 |
| HENLEY, Martin | SIMPSON, Sarah L. | 14 APR 1863 |
| HENLEY, Michael | CAMPA, Ann | 22 JAN 1867 |
| HENLEY, Thomas P. | MASON, Mary E. | 25 NOV 1869 |
| HENLY, Henry Thomas | KING, Martha Ellen | 20 JAN 1869 |
| HENLY, Thomas B. | WEST, Celia | 03 MAR 1863 |
| HENNAGE, John H. | DRISH, Sarah Indiana | 10 FEB 1868 |
| HENNESSEY, Morris | McCARTHY, Bridget | 17 SEP 1864 |
| HENNESSY, Joseph | MALONEY, Ann | 23 MAR 1864 |
| HENNIG, Gustav | HARDT, Martha Elizabeth | 11 NOV 1865 |
| HENNING, Charles C. | ATCHISON, Martha A. | 11 FEB 1860 |
| HENNING, Charles C. | ATCHISON, Martha A. | 24 DEC 1861 |
| HENNING, George C. | BIRD, Maggie | 26 MAR 1861 |
| HENNING, Matthias | BUSH, Margaret | 22 JAN 1864 |
| HENNING, William H. [9n] | COLCLASER, Charlotte | 26 NOV 1858 |
| HENRICH, Rudolph | BUCKNER, Johanna | 03 MAR 1863 |
| HENRIMAN, Rudolph | DIETZ, Carolina | 18 MAR 1868 |
| HENRIQUES, S. | SCOTT, Rebecca B. | 04 SEP 1865 |
| HENRY, Albert | BURK, Ella (blk) | 21 OCT 1865 |
| HENRY, Alexander H. [12s] * | McGEFFIT, Sallie A. | 15 MAR 1859 |
| HENRY, Antle | KELLY, Hannah | 27 APR 1865 |
| HENRY, Daniel | LAGAN, Sarah | 21 JAN 1862 |
| HENRY, David | WASHINGTON, Martha | 21 JUN 1869 |
| HENRY, Frank | McELWEE, Emma | 17 FEB 1862 |
| HENRY, George W. | MORAN, Sarah E. | 26 MAR 1864 |
| HENRY, James | DUNLAP, Mary J. (blk) | 30 JUL 1863 |
| HENRY, James | TAYLOR, Mary (blk) | 05 APR 1865 |
| HENRY, James | BERRY, Martha (blk) | 19 DEC 1865 |
| HENRY, James L. [4] | KEARNEY, Kate | 07 APR 1859 |
| HENRY, John | FISHER, Henrietta | 16 OCT 1863 |
| HENRY, John F. | LEE, Emma G. | 31 DEC 1863 |
| HENRY, John W. | GROSS, Sarah Ann Elizabeth (blk) | 19 FEB 1870 |
| HENRY, Lorenzo | GASKIN, Mary (blk) | 23 OCT 1869 |
| HENRY, Robert | TERRITT, Barbara (blk) | 15 JUN 1863 |
| HENRY, William | BUTLER, Susanna (blk) | 17 DEC 1866 |
| HENSEL, John | EIDMAN, Elizabeth | 08 JAN 1862 |
| HENSELL, Harmon | ZUNHAGNER, Maria | 24 JUN 1865 |
| HENSEY, Robert A. | LINKINS, Richetta | 16 MAY 1865 |
| HENSHAW, Henry C. | WHITE, Amelia G. | 23 MAY 1865 |
| HENSLEY, H.C. | TRIMBLE, Martha | 04 DEC 1869 |
| HENSLEY, Hezekiah B. | BRODERICK, Ann | 08 FEB 1866 |
| HENSLEY, Patrick | McCARTHY, Catherine | 21 DEC 1866 |
| HENSON, Frederick | KELSEY, Catherine (blk) | 12 OCT 1868 |
| HENSON, George W. | WATKINS, Susanna (blk) | 04 DEC 1862 |
| HENSON, James Alfred | COLEMAN, Mary (blk) | 24 SEP 1868 |
| HENSON, John | SMITH, Isabella (blk) | 12 AUG 1869 |
| HENSON, John L. | SPENCER, Jane E. | 04 DEC 1868 |
| HENSON, John T. | BROWN, Mary A. (blk) | 03 DEC 1868 |
| HENSON, Sandy | WOODWARD, Hester (blk) | 07 OCT 1868 |
| HENSON, William | CAMPBELL, Amelia (blk) | 02 DEC 1858 |
| HENSON, William | LACEY, Mary F. | 20 MAY 1865 |
| HENSON, Wm. | SIMS, Louisa (blk) | 16 JAN 1864 |
| HENVIS, J. George | STAUB, Caroline D. | 18 NOV 1869 |
| HENVIS, Joseph C. | BRENT, Mattie | 14 MAY 1869 |

| | | |
|---|---|---|
| HENZ, George M. | MUSINGO, Caroline | 25 JUN 1860 |
| HEPBURN, Charles W. | ROUX, Eliza | 26 NOV 1858 |
| HEPBURN, Charles W. | ELLIOTT, Alice | 22 DEC 1863 |
| HEPBURN, John Henson | CARROLL, Charity Ann (blk) | 30 NOV 1868 |
| HEPBURN, Samuel | COOPER, Catherine (blk) | 22 DEC 1868 |
| HEPHORN, John | ALBEGIN, Mary | 12 NOV 1861 |
| HEPPEL, Charles | BOWERS, Henrietta E. | 27 DEC 1864 |
| HEPTING, Jacob | ERTEL, Annie | 26 JAN 1863 |
| HERBER, Henry | KUMEGER, Caroline Rosa | 23 MAR 1863 |
| HERBERGER, Urban | ENGLE, Louisa | 12 FEB 1866 |
| HERBERT, Andrew | BAKER, Catherine (blk) | 05 AUG 1869 |
| HERBERT, Caspar | GELLEMAN, Emile | 30 JUL 1859 |
| HERBERT, Francis | HUNTER, Sophia | 15 SEP 1859 |
| HERBERT, James | BROWN, Mary (blk) | 02 APR 1867 |
| HERBERT, James Lewis | WOOD, Maria (blk) | 10 OCT 1863 |
| HERBERT, John H. | BRUCE, Mary E. (blk) | 05 SEP 1867 |
| HERBERT, Kunhinder | RHODE, Falden | 16 JUL 1862 |
| HERBERT, Noah | SMITH, Lucinda (blk) | 11 SEP 1866 |
| HERBERT, Sidney W. | NICHOLS, Eliza E. (blk) | 09 APR 1860 |
| HERBERT, Theodore | SIMMS, Elizabeth (blk) | 28 MAR 1861 |
| HERBERT, Thomas Franklin | LORD, Mary Frances | 01 JUL 1865 |
| HERBERT, William | NELSON, Alice (blk) | 30 JUN 1866 |
| HERBERT, Willis | SMITH, Emily (col'd) | 14 MAY 1869 |
| HERCUS, George C. | TOWERS, Hannah P. | 05 FEB 1861 |
| HERDER, Henry A. | LUTHART, Dora | 28 FEB 1863 |
| HERFUPH, Theodore | WANNICK, Emily | 06 OCT 1859 |
| HERFURTH, Charles O.A. | BURKAMP, Meta | 08 OCT 1869 |
| HERGON, Remey | COLLINS, Mary Jane | 17 MAY 1865 |
| HERING, Augustus | CONRADIS, Ellen | 26 FEB 1868 |
| HERLAY, Timothy | JAY, Hanorah | 12 MAY 1859 |
| HERLEHY, Richard J. | READY, Ellen | 17 JUL 1868 |
| HERLIHY, Timothy | HOWARD, Mary | 27 DEC 1867 |
| HERMAN, Frederick | NIEVEL, Sophia | 03 SEP 1861 |
| HERMAN, Joseph P. | KING, Hannah | 29 OCT 1858 |
| HERMAN, Safer | REDDING, Emily | 14 SEP 1865 |
| HERMOND, Francis M. | GRIMES, Debbie C. | 23 AUG 1866 |
| HERN, Michael A. | ENGLISH, Catharine | 06 JUN 1865 |
| HEROLD, George W. | ROTH, Margaret A. | 02 FEB 1869 |
| HERON, Thomas | WELSH, Bridget | 13 DEC 1864 |
| HERR, Samuel | CAMPBELL, Annie R. | 13 OCT 1864 |
| HERR, William | GUNTLING, Frances P. | 17 JUL 1865 |
| HERRIMAN, Melvin H. | BOND, Martha | 02 APR 1860 |
| HERRING, William R. | KNIGHT, Mattie | 17 APR 1865 |
| HERRINGTON, Merrill | MAY, A. Elizabeth | 18 MAR 1868 |
| HERRITY, James, Junr. | FRYER, Mary | 08 FEB 1861 |
| HERRMANN, Franz | KLING, Philipine | 20 JAN 1862 |
| HERRMANN, Martin | BRADLEY, Sarah Jane | 29 MAR 1864 |
| HERRON, Francis | SHARP, Nellie | 01 SEP 1864 |
| HERRON, Patrick | MONOGUE, Ann | 15 DEC 1864 |
| HERSEY, Samuel R. | RICHARDSON, Julia N. | 30 JUL 1866 |
| HERSHEY, Andrew | HARTMAN, Fanny | 03 AUG 1869 |
| HERTZBERG, Charles O. | HONNET, Mathilde | 18 MAY 1870 |
| HESS, Frederick | NOUFSKI, Mary | 13 NOV 1866 |

| | | |
|---|---|---|
| HESS, George A. | ROBERTSON, Elizabeth Jane[3] | 22 SEP 1863 |
| HESS, Isaac, Jr. | MILLER, Mary A. | 20 SEP 1865 |
| HESS, James | SMITH, Elizabeth H. | 17 AUG 1869 |
| HESS, John | STULZ, Caroline | 06 SEP 1861 |
| HESS, John | ULSHÖFER, Philipina | 27 MAR 1862 |
| HESS, John W. | AGER, Ann V. | 19 DEC 1859 |
| HESS, Louis | WALLACE, Ella S. | 09 NOV 1865 |
| HESS, Thomas Pruett | EARGER, Alice Rebecca | 27 OCT 1862 |
| HESS, Valentine | HESS, Eliza | 11 AUG 1860 |
| HESS, William | JOST, Amelia | 21 MAR 1865 |
| HESS, William W. | SHAFFLING, Barbara | 09 APR 1869 |
| HESSBERG, Isaac | HEINE, Sarah | 05 OCT 1865 |
| HESSE, Frederick G. | SPALDING, Mary C. | 02 OCT 1861 |
| HESSLER, Andrew | DOW, Mary | 11 AUG 1866 |
| HESSLER, August [2] | MILLER, Joanna | 28 JUN 1865 |
| HESSLER, Frank J. | KELLY, Mary B. | 04 OCT 1865 |
| HESSON, Joseph | HASS, Josephine | 22 JUL 1862 |
| HESTER, James | CUMMINS, Margaret | 30 JUL 1863 |
| HETHERMAN, John | FITZ, Johanna | 29 NOV 1858 |
| HETTENGER, Charles | HEPPTING, Lehna | 28 NOV 1863 |
| HEURICH, Rudolph | BUCKNER, Johanna | 03 MAR 1863 |
| HEWETT, Robert C. | SIMPSON, Rachel M. | 05 SEP 1864 |
| HEWITT, Churchill H. | REED, Mary Virginia | 14 JAN 1869 |
| HEWITT, Wilson | YOUNG, Frances (blk) | 04 FEB 1870 |
| HEYER, Francis R. | PECK, Martinette E. | 03 SEP 1866 |
| HEYERSCH, Frederick | HEINEMANN, Maria | 16 FEB 1865 |
| HEYMAN, Robert Emil | WOLF, Margaretta Ann | 26 JAN 1865 |
| HEYMAS, John R. | RUDD, Rebecca R. | 17 JUL 1869 |
| HEYWOOD, Charles H. | WHEELER, Alice A. | 02 OCT 1869 |
| HIBBARD, Randall | MAHONEY, Margaret | 03 SEP 1864 |
| HIBBEN, George E. | BROWNE, Mary Emma | 08 MAY 1866 |
| HIBBEN, J. Henry | NICHOLLS, Louise | 07 NOV 1865 |
| HIBBS, George D.O. [12s] | CAMPBELL, Emma J. | 03 JUN 1862 |
| HIBBS, James Emery | WARDER, Marion F. | 21 NOV 1859 |
| HICKCOX, John S. | LEWIS, Mary E. | 08 APR 1863 |
| HICKERSON, John W. | HURLEY, Mary Jane | 01 JUL 1865 |
| HICKEY, Andrew | READY, Joanna | 28 DEC 1863 |
| HICKEY, Edmund P. | MacDANIEL, Fannie | 15 NOV 1869 |
| HICKEY, John | SHEA, Mary | 24 FEB 1866 |
| HICKEY, John | SHEA, Catherine | 13 NOV 1866 |
| HICKEY, Maurice | DRISCOLL, Johanna | 01 OCT 1864 |
| HICKEY, Maurice J. | RILEY, Sarah M. | 19 JUL 1864 |
| HICKEY, Patrick | MANNING, Catherine | 17 JAN 1862 |
| HICKEY, Thomas [6c] | GILL, Emily | 12 OCT 1858 |
| HICKEY, Thornton F. | CONTEY, Calista | 11 AUG 1868 |
| HICKMAN, Daniel | LOMAX, Louisa (blk) | 01 MAY 1869 |
| HICKMAN, George M. [13] | FREDMAN, Ellen F. (blk) | 17 JUN 1861 |
| HICKMAN, James A. | MESSER, Julia A. (blk) | 30 APR 1867 |
| HICKMAN, John L. | KENT, Frances (blk) | 23 MAR 1868 |
| HICKMAN, William | TURLEY, Harriot (blk) | 24 NOV 1862 |
| HICKS, Harley T. [6m] | COX, Mary C. | 16 JUL 1863 |
| HICKS, Henry | DELANEY, Matilda (blk) | 24 AUG 1865 |
| HICKS, James, Jr. | WALKER, Dorcas Virginia | 17 DEC 1860 |

[3] Note: Certificate, Rev. S. Rennick, as the marriage of these parties on 23 SEP 1863, in Georgetown.

District of Columbia Marriage Licenses, 1858-1870

| | | |
|---|---|---|
| HICKS, Jeremiah | GREEN, Louisa (blk) | 27 JUL 1864 |
| HICKS, John | GRAY, Mary (blk) | 20 MAY 1867 |
| HICKS, John T. | BIBB, Margaret F. | 12 DEC 1860 |
| HICKS, John Thomas | COONEY, Catherine | 06 OCT 1859 |
| HICKS, Thomas | BROWNLEE, Sarah | 09 JUL 1864 |
| HICKS, Thomas [6le] | WILLIAMS, Kitty (blk) | 11 JAN 1867 |
| HICKS, Thompson | WILEY, Mary Francis | 08 AUG 1867 |
| HICKS, William | AMBUSH, Sarah (blk) | 06 FEB 1862 |
| HICKS, Wm. Alexr. | BUSSART, Georgeana | 12 AUG 1862 |
| HIESTON, Robert T. | KNOWLES, Allice V. | 08 FEB 1868 |
| HIGGINS, Edwin | TYSSOWSKI, Alexandria | 31 AUG 1869 |
| HIGGINS, Francis | BEALL, M.A. | 15 APR 1862 |
| HIGGINS, Francis | O'RYAN, Jenny | 15 MAR 1864 |
| HIGGINS, Joseph | WALKER, Samuel | 02 JUL 1863 |
| HIGGINS, Mahlon J. | ROLLINGS, Dora | 05 OCT 1859 |
| HIGGINS, Martin | BYRNE, Ellen | 09 JUN 1864 |
| HIGGINS, Rezin | MATTHEWS, Eliza (blk) | 12 NOV 1861 |
| HIGGINS, William H. | STORY, Sarah H. | 20 JUN 1864 |
| HIGGINS, William S. | McALLISTER, Sarah Lewis | 24 DEC 1862 |
| HIGHLAND, Samuel | HARRISON, Rose Ann | 03 JAN 1865 |
| HILBUS, James | McCOY, Henrietta | 09 JAN 1863 |
| HILDRETH, George H. | HEWETT, Florence | 06 DEC 1862 |
| HILDRETH, George H. | HEWITT, Florence | 10 JAN 1863 |
| HILE, Henry | BETTINGER, Margaret | 14 FEB 1863 |
| HILE, John | NOLTE, Mary L. | 01 NOV 1865 |
| HILHARY, Walter | JONES, Juliette | 16 OCT 1865 |
| HILL, Alfred | LEE, Susan (blk) | 03 JAN 1866 |
| HILL, Charles S. | PHILLIPS, Fannie Eugenia | 15 MAR 1869 |
| HILL, Daniel | JOHNSON, Mary L. (blk) | 10 SEP 1868 |
| HILL, Eli | LOWNDES, Susan (blk) | 19 JUN 1866 |
| HILL, George | HENSON, Emma (blk) | 24 DEC 1866 |
| HILL, George M. | DONALDSON, Sarah E. | 18 MAY 1865 |
| HILL, George W. | LINKINS, Margaret A. | 03 JUL 1866 |
| HILL, Henry | MARSHALL, Matilda (blk) | 24 FEB 1863 |
| HILL, Henry | ALLAS, Mary (blk) | 01 JUN 1866 |
| HILL, Henry [6le] | BROWN, Anna (blk) | 27 SEP 1865 |
| HILL, J. Benjn. | BALL, Mary E. | 06 JAN 1859 |
| HILL, James | BEALL, Louisa (blk) | 24 DEC 1862 |
| HILL, James | HILL, Susan (blk) | 05 SEP 1866 |
| HILL, James | TURNER, Kate (blk) | 15 JUN 1870 |
| HILL, James B. | HILL, Mary Ann (blk) | 14 NOV 1863 |
| HILL, James H. | PALMER, Mary V. (blk) | 02 OCT 1867 |
| HILL, James W. | DEVES, Felicia A. | 29 OCT 1863 |
| HILL, Jeremiah | JOYCE, Susan (blk) | 14 MAY 1864 |
| HILL, Jerry | DUVALL, Louisa (blk) | 18 JUN 1867 |
| HILL, John | GORMON, Bridget | 04 MAY 1860 |
| HILL, John B. | WARING, Helen Anna | 19 MAY 1863 |
| HILL, John J. | KING, Mary Frances | 14 AUG 1863 |
| HILL, John J. | BROWN, Mary E. | 23 FEB 1869 |
| HILL, Lewis | PIERE, Mary (blk) | 10 MAY 1861 |
| HILL, Lewis | BECKETT, Amelia Ann (blk) | 26 MAY 1870 |
| HILL, Lloyd | OFFUTT, Rachel | 28 FEB 1860 |
| HILL, Martin | HILL, Hannah (blk) | 27 MAY 1868 |
| HILL, Michael | MAEGHER, Honora | 17 SEP 1863 |
| HILL, Nathan | KERR, Mary | 13 MAY 1865 |
| HILL, Philip, Junr. | CRAWFORD, Sarah V. | 04 OCT 1858 |

# District of Columbia Marriage Licenses, 1858-1870

| | | |
|---|---|---|
| HILL, Richard | VALENTINE, Louisa | 17 MAY 1862 |
| HILL, Richard | TAIT, Mary (blk) | 07 JAN 1864 |
| HILL, Richard | GREEN, Elizabeth (blk) | 07 APR 1868 |
| HILL, Richard A., Jr. | HAYES, Ann Eliza | 27 MAY 1861 |
| HILL, Richard J. | KIRBY, Sarah A. | 05 MAR 1860 |
| HILL, Richard Mason [4] | RAMSAY, Catherine Graham | 01 OCT 1869 |
| HILL, Rupert G. | BATEMAN, Mary E. | 02 DEC 1861 |
| HILL, Samuel | LITTLE, Mary A. | 02 DEC 1864 |
| HILL, Thomas | SMITH, Ann (blk) | 06 AUG 1866 |
| HILL, Uriah | BEACH, Mary C. | 07 JUN 1865 |
| HILL, Waverly | HURLEY, Ann (blk) | 31 MAY 1867 |
| HILL, William | WRIGHT, Maria Louise (blk) | 30 DEC 1862 |
| HILL, William | HORNER, Tulip | 02 JAN 1866 |
| HILL, William | HOWARD, Mary Jane (blk) | 27 AUG 1868 |
| HILL, William B. | BIRCH, Evelina | 01 AUG 1861 |
| HILL, William H. | HILBUS, Josephine | 24 JUL 1863 |
| HILL, William M. | MILES, Malinda (blk) | 05 JUN 1860 |
| HILL, York | LEE, Martha (blk) | 11 FEB 1864 |
| HILLARD, Nathan T. | STARBUCK, Annie C. | 28 APR 1862 |
| HILLARY, Colmore S. | WILLIAMS, Sarah W. | 06 AUG 1861 |
| HILLARY, William H. | CUSTARD, Catharine A. | 22 SEP 1858 |
| HILLE, Adolphe | REEB, Catharine | 02 OCT 1865 |
| HILLEARY, Lewis | BELT, Emeline E. (blk) | 11 OCT 1858 |
| HILLEARY, William T. [6le] | KENNARD, Margaret J.B. | 12 JUN 1867 |
| HILLERY, John | MASSEY, Mary | 24 MAY 1865 |
| HILLIARD, George | SHELL, Emma | 06 JUN 1864 |
| HILLIARD, Henry | HOODLEMEYER, Julia | 28 FEB 1860 |
| HILLIARY, Thomas E. | HOYDEN, Jennie | 21 JAN 1867 |
| HILLIARY, Walter L. [2] | GARDNER, Emma | 31 DEC 1867 |
| HILLIS, Michael | JOYCE, Ann | 31 AUG 1865 |
| HILLMAN, Andrew | ASHFORD, Sarah (blk) | 23 APR 1870 |
| HILLS, Charles | TANNENBERG, Bettie | 01 APR 1867 |
| HILLYARD, Charles | BROWN, Martha A. | 08 AUG 1863 |
| HILLYARD, Charles | HAMILTON, Harriet Ann | 27 FEB 1865 |
| HILTON, Adolphus [7a] | SUDDETH, Ann C. | 30 NOV 1867 |
| HILTON, Carbery S. [5] | CADY, Lucy E. | 27 NOV 1869 |
| HILTON, Francis [6r] | NEALE, Ellen | 18 JUL 1860 |
| HILTON, George A. | WELLS, Sarah E. | 15 JUN 1863 |
| HILTON, John A. | BERRY, Margaret | 13 MAR 1861 |
| HILTON, Joseph H. | MARDES, Alice James | 17 NOV 1868 |
| HILTON, Robert | BROWN, Lucy Mildred | 15 SEP 1868 |
| HILTZELBERGER, Charles J. | BUNYAN, Elizabeth M. | 18 SEP 1867 |
| HIMER, Louis P. | BENTZLER, Adeline | 17 JUN 1869 |
| HIMMELRICH, George Fred | HABELT, Mary | 24 JUN 1868 |
| HINDLE, Charles [5] | HOWARD, Nellie | 28 DEC 1868 |
| HINDS, Edmund | WELSH, Julia | 20 DEC 1860 |
| HINDS, Jerome J. | KAVANAUGH, Cornelia | 26 FEB 1868 |
| HINDS, Thomas | REARDON, Catherine | 08 JAN 1868 |
| HINELINE, Thos. [10] | McLEAN, Catharine | 29 SEP 1859 |
| HINES, Benjamin | MORGAN, Frances (blk) | 08 OCT 1866 |
| HINES, Chas. M. | DEVEREUX, Anna M. | 21 APR 1862 |
| HINES, Dennis | LAWLER, Maggie | 16 MAY 1870 |
| HINES, George W. | HELFISTY, Anna Piety | 24 JUL 1862 |
| HINES, Spragley | BLAGMAN, Sophia | 16 JUL 1867 |
| HINES, Thomas | MADDEN, Margaret | 02 JUN 1862 |
| HINES, Thomas | BURKE, Margaret | 25 OCT 1862 |

District of Columbia Marriage Licenses, 1858-1870

| | | |
|---|---|---|
| HINES, Thomas | MANEY, Bridget | 07 NOV 1865 |
| HINKLE, David | BALDWIN, Rowena M. | 23 APR 1861 |
| HINKLEBEIN, Joseph | GING, Ellen | 20 MAY 1862 |
| HINSCH, Albert | KILLIAN, Henrietta | 18 MAR 1865 |
| HINTON, John R. | BLAND, J. Ella | 05 FEB 1861 |
| HINTON, Thomas | MACKALL, Sarah (blk) | 11 FEB 1867 |
| HINTON, Thomas H.C. | WILSON, Rebecca P. (blk) | 30 APR 1864 |
| HINTON, Wiley | BROWN, Julia | 18 DEC 1863 |
| HINTON, William H. | ALLEN, Roxy Ann | 30 DEC 1868 |
| HIRE, Albert | BENTZLER, Mary Catherine | 18 AUG 1869 |
| HIRLIHEY, Timothy | ROCHE, Ann | 24 APR 1861 |
| HIRSCH, Benjamin | HIRSCHFIELD, Elizabeth | 28 AUG 1865 |
| HIRSCH, Jacob | LOEB, Bertha | 24 MAY 1864 |
| HIRST, Homer T. | ADAMS, S. Anne | 10 NOV 1868 |
| HIRST, John J. | BLOSSOM, Emily G. | 06 SEP 1865 |
| HIRST, Joseph | DONALDSON, Sallie F. | 21 OCT 1863 |
| HIRT, Herman | HARTMANN, Maria Anna | 06 OCT 1862 |
| HITCHCOCK, Ethan A. (Gen., USA) | NICHOLS, Martha R. | 20 APR 1868 |
| HITCHCOCK, Robert J. [6m] | TAYLOR, Jane Maria [Maria Jane] | 22 DEC 1862 |
| HITE, Andrew J. | SCOTT, Virginia | 13 NOV 1860 |
| HITE, Charles W. [11] | COURTENAY, Jessie C. | 01 MAY 1867 |
| HITS, John | FOWLE, Alice | 03 OCT 1866 |
| HITZ, Rudolph | BARNARD, Mary | 19 NOV 1864 |
| HOAG, James R. | KING, Margaret Ann | 19 AUG 1864 |
| HOAKS, Michael | MORELAND, Susannah | 13 JUN 1863 |
| HOARD, Francis | MAURICE, Jennie | 02 JUN 1864 |
| HOARD, Frank [7b] | WHITE, Millie | 15 APR 1869 |
| HOBART, William S. [11] | SANBORN, Frances L. | 05 JAN 1865 |
| HOBBS, Benjamin | SMITHSON, Rebecca V. | 11 SEP 1860 |
| HOBBS, John W. [9e] | CONNELL, Martha | 22 MAY 1860 |
| HOBBS, William J. [9n] | SHEA, Mary Jane | 19 FEB 1859 |
| HOBLITZELL, Solomon A. | FOLLIN, Ella V. | 31 MAR 1863 |
| HOBURN, Robert | SMITH, Margaret (blk) | 02 MAR 1864 |
| HOCKLEIN, Frank | ROLLATER, Maria | 01 JUN 1870 |
| HOCKMEMEYER, John | GRUDLING, Caroline | 20 JUN 1867 |
| HODGE, J. Ledyard | WILSON, Susan S. | 09 JUN 1862 |
| HODGE, Rosby | BROWN, Margaret Ann | 07 APR 1862 |
| HODGES, Benjamin* | QUEEN, Ann Eliza | 18 MAR 1859 |
| HODGES, Henry | BAILEY, Mary C. | 05 JUN 1866 |
| HODGES, William H. | WRIGHT, Sarah A. | 26 NOV 1864 |
| HODGKIN, Robert E. | THOMAS, Mary Jane | 06 AUG 1860 |
| HODGKINS, A.T. | BOHLES, E.A. | 20 JUN 1865 |
| HODGKINS, Samuel | CUDLIPP, Mary Ann | 08 FEB 1865 |
| HODGKINS, Samuel P. | JOHNSON, Susanna Ellen | 27 MAR 1860 |
| HODGMAN, Allan W. | KEENE, Ruth W. | 26 MAR 1864 |
| HODGSON, Charles H. | CONN, Emma E. | 13 AUG 1861 |
| HODGSON, John E. | WEBSTER, Lydia E. | 05 DEC 1865 |
| HOELMANN, John | WALDEMATHE, Wilhelmina | 03 APR 1860 |
| HOENS, Thomas | CAHILL, Margaret | 13 MAY 1868 |
| HOERNIG, John Charles Margaret | MAURER, Gertrude | 21 MAY 1864 |
| HOESTER, August | MAEDEL, Adelheid | 04 SEP 1866 |
| HOFER, John | SCHILDHAUER, Minna | 17 JAN 1862 |
| HOFF, Augustus W. | BARKER, Almedia J. | 23 NOV 1868 |
| HOFFEMAN, Edward Patrick | HALLORAN, Bridget | 17 JUL 1863 |
| HOFFMAN, A.M. | LATTIN, Mary E. | 10 OCT 1866 |
| HOFFMAN, August | DIETZ, Madalina | 17 JAN 1870 |

# District of Columbia Marriage Licenses, 1858-1870

| Groom | Bride | Date |
|---|---|---|
| HOFFMAN, Christopher | RUECART, Eva Margaret | 09 APR 1867 |
| HOFFMAN, George | HOFFMAN, Mary | 30 SEP 1862 |
| HOFFMAN, George | GLOVER, Eliza | 03 MAR 1863 |
| HOFFMAN, George | STROBEL, Elizabeth T. | 26 MAY 1865 |
| HOFFMAN, Herman | NORRIS, Sarah | 25 JAN 1868 |
| HOFFMAN, James | RYAN, Hannah | 28 JUN 1865 |
| HOFFMAN, John A. | MARMADUKE, Susan | 04 OCT 1865 |
| HOFFMAN, Samuel | PUSLEY, Jane | 11 APR 1859 |
| HOFFMAN, William D. | GATTON, Susan E. | 26 DEC 1868 |
| HOFFMAN, William J. [12s] | HOFFMAN, Elizabeth A. | 29 JAN 1861 |
| HOFMEISTER, George E. | SCHOTT, Martha Ann | 14 DEC 1863 |
| HOGAN, Daniel | NORRIS, Julia | 03 SEP 1864 |
| HOGAN, Dennis | McMAHON, Mary | 12 JUL 1865 |
| HOGAN, John | BABBINGTON, Hanora | 08 DEC 1860 |
| HOGAN, John | FOSTER, Rosanna | 02 JUN 1862 |
| HOGAN, John | O'SHEA, Joanna | 24 JAN 1863 |
| HOGAN, John | DAVIS, Ellen | 21 FEB 1866 |
| HOGAN, John | FITTZ, Margaret | 11 MAY 1867 |
| HOGAN, John | KELLY, Mary | 08 FEB 1869 |
| HOGAN, Martin | MURPHY, Catherine E. | 30 MAR 1866 |
| HOGE, Thomas Courtenay | BATES, Ella Virginia | 05 FEB 1866 |
| HOGUE, Andrew | O'LEARY, Margaret | 31 DEC 1862 |
| HOHLBEIN, Martin | DIESSER, Bertha | 09 MAY 1864 |
| HOHMAN, Theobold | HEILBERT, Kate | 07 OCT 1861 |
| HOHNBAUM, Fidus | FAUL, Katharine | 23 JAN 1864 |
| HOLBROOK, James M. | FINNEGAN, Maria | 02 JUL 1863 |
| HOLDEN, John | BRADY, Dephenia | 05 AUG 1859 |
| HOLFORD, William | FOSTER, Mary Ellen | 05 FEB 1866 |
| HOLIDAY, Colwell | BARTON, Mary Jane N. | 23 OCT 1868 |
| HOLLAND, Abram R. | FITZHUGH, Mary (blk) | 16 DEC 1865 |
| HOLLAND, Amos T. | WILLIAMS, Lydia E. | 03 DEC 1866 |
| HOLLAND, Edward | BUTLER, Mary (blk) | 22 MAR 1866 |
| HOLLAND, Edward | SEWELL, Amanda | 17 JAN 1870 |
| HOLLAND, George N. | WILTD, Martha M. | 07 APR 1869 |
| HOLLAND, Jacob | STROTHER, Catherine (blk) | 19 DEC 1866 |
| HOLLAND, James | FLAHERTY, Annie | 01 NOV 1861 |
| HOLLAND, James | JACKSON, Celina (col'd) | 26 MAY 1870 |
| HOLLAND, James G. | FLENNER, Margaret E. | 30 OCT 1866 |
| HOLLAND, James M. | RIDER, Ella S. | 14 AUG 1869 |
| HOLLAND, Oliver P. | STURM, Salome M. | 16 JUN 1859 |
| HOLLAND, Richard Henry | JOHNSON, Mary Ann | 13 JUN 1870 |
| HOLLAND, Thomas | BERKLEY, Sarah Ann | 13 MAY 1862 |
| HOLLAND, William | WEYMAN, Elizabeth | 13 FEB 1865 |
| HOLLARAN, Mark | McCARTY, Ellen | 04 OCT 1867 |
| HOLLE, John | SMITH, Mary | 08 FEB 1862 |
| HOLLEN, Richard | WOOD, Emeline | 07 JUL 1866 |
| HOLLIDAY, Charles | SMITH, Lucy (blk) | 02 JUN 1869 |
| HOLLIDAY, James B. | CROWN, Sarah J. | 12 DEC 1864 |
| HOLLIDAY, Nelson | STOCKTON, Amelia (blk) | 07 APR 1866 |
| HOLLIDAY, Robert | HEMSLEY, Harriet (blk) | 09 FEB 1869 |
| HOLLIDGE, Isaac S. | SPEDDEN, Annie R. | 06 OCT 1869 |
| HOLLIDGE, James B. | DEVERS, Martha A. | 02 FEB 1863 |
| HOLLIDGE, Joseph H. | BURRISS, Ruth Ann | 31 MAR 1868 |
| HOLLIN, George | MITCHELL, Frances (blk) | 05 DEC 1863 |
| HOLLINGSWORTH, John M.H. | NICHOLLS, Virginia | 20 NOV 1865 |
| HOLLINS, Spencer | COOK, Frances (blk) | 15 SEP 1865 |

District of Columbia Marriage Licenses, 1858-1870

| Groom | Bride | Date |
|---|---|---|
| HOLLISTER, Calvin R. | BARNES, Sarah Cornelia | 10 FEB 1868 |
| HOLLISTER, O.J. [5] | MATTHEWS, Carrie V. | 29 NOV 1869 |
| HOLLOHAN, Michael | SULLIVAN, Mary | 08 JUL 1867 |
| HOLLORAN, Michael | WORDIN, Ann Maria | 31 DEC 1858 |
| HOLLY, Smithy | KIMBLE, Susan (blk) | 19 NOV 1864 |
| HOLMAN, Alfred | LEE, Mary (blk) | 06 APR 1869 |
| HOLMAN, Henry | MURPHY, Ellen | 31 AUG 1867 |
| HOLMAN, Samuel | YATES, Ellen (blk) | 12 APR 1866 |
| HOLMEAD, J.E.F. | GORDON, Hannah | 14 SEP 1858 |
| HOLMES, Barnett | POLLARD, Josephine | 19 AUG 1865 |
| HOLMES, Bartlett | HOLMES, Mary (blk) | 07 DEC 1868 |
| HOLMES, Benjamin | BLACKBURN, Margaretta (blk) | 13 JAN 1870 |
| HOLMES, Claiborne | JONES, Lucy (blk) | 31 MAY 1867 |
| HOLMES, David | JOHNSON, Ellen (blk) | 13 OCT 1864 |
| HOLMES, Edward | TALIAFERRO, Hannah (blk) | 07 OCT 1867 |
| HOLMES, Edward S. | CRANE, Annie M. | 20 MAY 1867 |
| HOLMES, George | JOHNSON, Mary J. | 21 JUN 1862 |
| HOLMES, George | GOODWIN, Mary (blk) | 18 JAN 1867 |
| HOLMES, George | JENKINS, Ellen (blk) | 27 JUL 1869 |
| HOLMES, George H. | DAVIS, Barbara E. | 08 NOV 1866 |
| HOLMES, John | HEISSMANN, Miena | 24 AUG 1868 |
| HOLMES, John | TAYLOR, Amanda | 23 JUL 1866 |
| HOLMES, Joseph | JOHNSON, Ellen (blk) | 23 OCT 1867 |
| HOLMES, Lawson | YORK, Randolph (blk) | 19 OCT 1864 |
| HOLMES, Major | EDWARDS, Catherine (blk) | 01 MAR 1864 |
| HOLMES, Raleigh | HUGHES, Mary Elizabeth | 21 MAR 1866 |
| HOLMES, Ruffin | ANDERSON, Emily (blk) | 05 JAN 1870 |
| HOLMES, Samuel | MITCHELL, Caroline | 06 NOV 1867 |
| HOLMES, Solomon | TALLANT, Georgiana (blk) | 29 OCT 1866 |
| HOLMES, Washington | HARRIS, Catherine (blk) | 31 OCT 1867 |
| HOLMES, William | OVERTON, Lucy Ellen (blk) | 23 FEB 1865 |
| HOLMES, William D. | CORES, Frances (blk) | 02 DEC 1869 |
| HOLOHAN, T.R. [6h] | BATHEN, Jennie | 18 MAY 1868 |
| HOLROYD, James | PADGETT, Mary J. | 23 JAN 1860 |
| HOLSON, T.R. | PAXTON, Florida | 21 SEP 1863 |
| HOLSTEIN, Ben | MILLER, Clara E. | 14 NOV 1864 |
| HOLSTEN, Arnold | OERTEL, Anna Mary (adopted Marie Glick) | 26 OCT 1868 |
| HOLSTEN, Hermann | HEERE, Louisa | 21 JUL 1865 |
| HOLSTON, Benjamin | GRANGER, Laura | 15 OCT 1868 |
| HOLT, George | DAVIS, Aberella | 27 OCT 1864 |
| HOLT, William H. | MILLER, Catherine M. | 12 APR 1862 |
| HOLTMAN, Henry | PROTT, Catharine | 11 OCT 1862 |
| HOLTON, Seth A. | SHEDD, Margaret F. | 13 JUN 1866 |
| HOLTZMAN, John T.S. | WREN, Fannie | 11 OCT 1869 |
| HOLTZMAN, William H. | MAXWELL, Virginia | 23 JAN 1869 |
| HOLTZVILLE, Matthias | COOPER, Ellen (blk) | 02 AUG 1865 |
| HOMANN, Andreas W. | HUCKSOLL, Sophie | 18 APR 1862 |
| HOMER, Charles H. | MUDDIMAN, Carrie F. | 27 AUG 1866 |
| HOMESTON, Hubert | SMITH, Elizabeth | 03 JUL 1867 |
| HOMILLER, Charles W.[4] | HOMILLER, Catharine | 22 NOV 1864 |
| HOMILLER, Matthew | STEIN_MLE_, Rosina | 29 APR 1865 |

[4] Note pasted to register: "I make oath, that I was instructed to obatain a license for the marriage of a gentleman with a young lady of this District, ahd that I substituted, by mistake, the names of the parents of the lady, Charles H. & Catharine Homiller, instead of the name of their daughter and the gentleman in question; and the names of the parents are recordingly entered in Marriage Record, under the date of November 23 [sic], 1864. /s/ R.E. Duvall. Sworn & subscribed before me, Feby. 10, 1865, R.J. Meigs, clk."

| | | |
|---|---|---|
| HONAFINS, Cyrus | HELLMAN, Bettie | 23 SEP 1862 |
| HONEGAN, Michael | COLLINS, Margaret | 11 NOV 1862 |
| HONES, Thomas | CAHILL, Margaret | 19 OCT 1867 |
| HONESTY, David | GIBBS, Sarah Ann (blk) | 18 FEB 1867 |
| HONESTY, James | ROBINSON, Julia | 26 JAN 1867 |
| HONON, Michael | DRISCOLL, Mary T. | 29 JAN 1862 |
| HOOD, Andrew J. | RIMBY, Frances V. | 23 DEC 1869 |
| HOOE, Thomas | GRAHAM, Sarah G. (blk) | 18 DEC 1867 |
| HOOF, Lucien B. | CLAIRE, Marie | 12 APR 1869 |
| HOOFNAGLE, John Getz | MITCHELL, Eleanor C. | 17 NOV 1860 |
| HOOK, Marcus R. | LAY, Annie M. | 17 MAR 1866 |
| HOOKER, George | NEWELL, Emily E. | 28 MAR 1870 |
| HOOKER, Julius | HINDES, Sarah | 15 AUG 1865 |
| HOOKS, Charles E. [5] | BLAIR, Annie | 01 MAR 1870 |
| HOOPER, John | MAHORNEY, Emily | 23 DEC 1861 |
| HOOPER, Joseph S. | BARRIN, Julia | 04 JAN 1861 |
| HOOPER, Michael | BETZEL, Mary | 26 JAN 1870 |
| HOOPER, Thomas H. | HAEDRICK, Sarah J. | 20 JUL 1867 |
| HOOVER, Elbert C. | DONN, Martha E. | 12 JUN 1862 |
| HOOVER, Samuel S. | HAINES, Josephine | 19 JAN 1866 |
| HOOVER, Samuel S. | SEITZ, Kate V. | 18 OCT 1866 |
| HOOVER, T.Z. | HAINES, Alice S. | 15 DEC 1868 |
| HOOVER, William H.H. | LEMON, Jane McKelvie | 18 MAY 1863 |
| HOPKINS, Benjamin V. | DAVIS, Marian S. | 18 SEP 1865 |
| HOPKINS, Charles P. | REILY, Sydney J. | 20 NOV 1862 |
| HOPKINS, Charles P. | SUMMERS, Charlotte A. | 30 NOV 1864 |
| HOPKINS, Daniel W. | GARNER, Ellen Sophia | 26 SEP 1865 |
| HOPKINS, Elias | RIDDLE, Louisa | 21 MAY 1862 |
| HOPKINS, Elliot | GAHAN, Mary | 27 OCT 1858 |
| HOPKINS, Elliott | CAHILL, Mary | 18 AUG 1860 |
| HOPKINS, Frank T. | HOGG, Mary | 04 MAY 1868 |
| HOPKINS, Frank T. | HOGG, Mary | 04 MAY 1869 |
| HOPKINS, George W. | MOORE, Louisa F. | 04 DEC 1867 |
| HOPKINS, John F. | SLACK, Marcia V. | 19 APR 1861 |
| HOPKINS, John T. | HARPER, Catherine H. | 20 NOV 1862 |
| HOPKINS, Thaddeus A. | HEADLEY, Bertie | 22 DEC 1869 |
| HOPKINS, Thomas S. | EASTMAN, Carrie W. | 02 JAN 1866 |
| HOPP, Frederick | EBERBACH, Fredericka | 16 SEP 1858 |
| HOPP, Henry | VIGLE, Susan | 28 DEC 1859 |
| HOPP, Nicholas | DORSEY, Rachel (blk) | 31 DEC 1867 |
| HOPPER, Bernard W. [6r] | ROGERS, Susan V. | 15 DEC 1860 |
| HOPPER, John C. | VanOLINDA, Sarah D. | 28 JUN 1865 |
| HORN, William | SULIVAN, Mary | 01 JUL 1862 |
| HORNER, John W. | THOMAS, Maggie | 05 FEB 1866 |
| HORNER, Manlove | VINSON, Jane | 17 SEP 1863 |
| HORNING, George David | SULLIVAN, Mary | 27 MAR 1867 |
| HORNUNG, Frederick | ANSHBACH, Mary | 26 SEP 1864 |
| HORRIGAN, Dennis | KNIGHT, Jane | 04 JAN 1859 |
| HORRIGAN, John | DORSEY, Margaret | 14 FEB 1863 |
| HORSEMAN, William H. | SPILMAN, Mary Frances | 30 AUG 1859 |
| HORSMAN, Robert R. | BROWN, Mary Virginia | 19 APR 1864 |
| HORSTKAMP, John | KRAUSER, Mary E. | 03 JUL 1868 |
| HORSTKAMP, William Nicholas | DULEY, Marion Clay | 17 NOV 1863 |
| HORTON, Archibald | STONE, Jeanette | 06 MAY 1863 |
| HORTON, George | MAHALEY, Jane (blk) | 20 MAY 1869 |
| HORTON, Nathaniel G. | BAKER, Mary C. | 27 SEP 1862 |

District of Columbia Marriage Licenses, 1858-1870

| | | |
|---|---|---|
| HORTON, William E., Lt., USA | CLARKE, Josie J. | 30 SEP 1867 |
| HORTON, William S. | WARING, Helen M. | 15 OCT 1861 |
| HORWITZ, David A. | KOHN, Amelia | 09 AUG 1865 |
| HOSCH, August | KARR, Christiana | 03 SEP 1869 |
| HOSFORD, William A. | SIMPSON, Alice R. | 12 FEB 1866 |
| HOSHAL, Jesse W. | YOUNG, Mary R. | 06 OCT 1858 |
| HOSKIN, Orlando F. | TENNESON, Mary C. | 11 SEP 1867 |
| HOSMER, Charles | WASHINGTON, Mary A. | 27 AUG 1862 |
| HOSPITAL, Charles H. [1e] | GAMBLE, Elizabeth F. | 25 APR 1864 |
| HOSSEFROSS, Francis | MILON, Elizabeth | 17 MAR 1865 |
| HOTTENITZ, Louis W. | SCHALLER, Fannie | 10 MAY 1865 |
| HOUCK, Samuel D. | PITMAN, Louisa | 02 SEP 1863 |
| HOUGH, John | GRUBB, Pleasant C. | 19 SEP 1863 |
| HOUGH, Joseph | MILLER, Mary A. | 02 MAY 1865 |
| HOUGH, Joseph [7a] | ROGERS, Mary Ann | 05 NOV 1868 |
| HOUGH, Oscar R. | CREASER, Marion V. | 12 FEB 1866 |
| HOUGH, Robert B. | PAXSON, Henrietta C. | 08 MAR 1869 |
| HOUGHMAN, George | HOUGHMAN, Mary | 21 JUL 1862 |
| HOUGHTON, E.N. | GANGEWER, Josie H. | 03 APR 1867 |
| HOUPT, Charles | MITCHELL, Harriet | 31 OCT 1864 |
| HOUSE, Charles H. | TOMLIN, Sarah J. | 18 JUN 1866 |
| HOUSE, Elitha D. | CALDWELL, Jennie W. | 30 MAY 1865 |
| HOUSE, William | COURSEY, Susan (blk) | 06 JUL 1867 |
| HOUSER, James J. | LEVY, Annie | 06 JUL 1861 |
| HOUSTON, James R. | MIDDLETON, Helen | 07 JAN 1862 |
| HOUSTON, John [9e] | COLE, Annie | 07 FEB 1862 |
| HOUSTON, Stephen | CARTER, Sarah (col'd) | 23 DEC 1863 |
| HOUSTON, Thomas P., USN [12s] | POSEY, Susan | 04 APR 1859 |
| HOVEN, Michael | HINES, Catharine | 11 OCT 1869 |
| HOWARD, Alfred | NARDEN, Mary (blk) | 12 AUG 1863 |
| HOWARD, Anthony T. | PEARCE, Mary | 24 DEC 1866 |
| HOWARD, Benjamin | GAITHER, Caroline (blk) | 17 FEB 1870 |
| HOWARD, Benjamin F. | MARTIN, Annie Elizth. | 03 FEB 1860 |
| HOWARD, Bushrod Washington | HOWARD, Laura Louisa | 03 MAR 1863 |
| HOWARD, Charles | GROOMS, Hattie (blk) | 23 MAR 1869 |
| HOWARD, Charles O. | LENT, Harriet A. | 12 NOV 1862 |
| HOWARD, Dennis | MICHAEL, Ellen M. | 25 AUG 1865 |
| HOWARD, Edward | MOORE, Mary (blk) | 08 APR 1863 |
| HOWARD, Eli D. Guy | TUCKER, Ella | 25 JUN 1860 |
| HOWARD, Elias | RILEY, Mary (blk) | 30 MAY 1867 |
| HOWARD, F.A. | BURKE, Annie | 25 DEC 1862 |
| HOWARD, Floduardo W. | HENNING, Rosa | 22 OCT 1860 |
| HOWARD, Francis | KNORLEIN, Barbara Teresa | 15 SEP 1869 |
| HOWARD, Frank | DAGGS, Eliza (blk) | 01 SEP 1866 |
| HOWARD, George | SLATER, Louisa (blk) | 29 DEC 1864 |
| HOWARD, George M. [11] | TOWSON, Mary E. * | 09 MAY 1862 |
| HOWARD, George T. | COOMBS, Kate F. | 08 JUN 1869 |
| HOWARD, George W. | ADAMS, Lydia A. | 14 MAY 1863 |
| HOWARD, Henry | BOWIE, Ann Maria (blk) | 04 FEB 1864 |
| HOWARD, Henry | HOWARD, Celia | 29 JAN 1869 |
| HOWARD, Henry Peyton | DYER, Roberta | 12 APR 1869 |
| HOWARD, Horatio N. | ALLEN, Anna W. | 01 JUL 1867 |
| HOWARD, Jackson | BURKE, Ann (blk) | 31 MAR 1869 |
| HOWARD, Jacob | SIMMONS, Malinda J. | 31 JUL 1860 |
| HOWARD, James | THOMAS, Maria (blk) | 17 DEC 1868 |
| HOWARD, Jerry | DAVIS, Catharine (blk) | 07 SEP 1866 |

| | | |
|---|---|---|
| HOWARD, John C. (Balt.) | CROSS, Henrietta M. (Alex.) | 25 JUL 1863 |
| HOWARD, John E. | LOEFFLER, Louise E. | 25 FEB 1864 |
| HOWARD, John Henry | PEARSON, Ellen (blk) | 26 JUN 1865 |
| HOWARD, John L. | FAUDREE, Hardenia E. | 17 AUG 1865 |
| HOWARD, John W. | BACHE, Amelia M. | 26 JUN 1865 |
| HOWARD, Joseph | PHELPS, Ann | 27 NOV 1867 |
| HOWARD, Levi, Revd. | BROWN, May (blk) | 01 FEB 1869 |
| HOWARD, Oscar H. | BUSH, Sarah C. | 15 JAN 1861 |
| HOWARD, Pleasant | HOWARD, Cordelia Ann (blk) | 14 JAN 1864 |
| HOWARD, Pleasant | HENDERSON, Mary (blk) | 30 NOV 1866 |
| HOWARD, Presley | SNOWDEN, Anna (blk) | 09 JUN 1866 |
| HOWARD, Rudolph | ANDRE, Sarah Frances | 12 NOV 1861 |
| HOWARD, Samuel | COLLINS, Anna (blk) | 10 JUL 1865 |
| HOWARD, Thomas | FARR, Catharine (blk) | 08 JAN 1863 |
| HOWARD, Thomas | CURTIS, Minerva | 29 APR 1869 |
| HOWARD, William | DIXON, Mary Ann | 21 MAR 1860 |
| HOWARD, William | ROWLES, Indiana | 17 MAY 1870 |
| HOWARD, William H. [4] | SLEDD, Eugenia J. | 12 DEC 1860 |
| HOWARD, William McKindry | DEMENT, Ida Virginia | 18 APR 1865 |
| HOWARD, William T. | KNOTT, Jane Rebecca | 01 APR 1868 |
| HOWE, Franklin T. | GRIFFITH, Maria T. | 06 AUG 1864 |
| HOWE, George W. | TERMITT, Ellen | 13 NOV 1863 |
| HOWE, John Thomas | ROBINSON, Elizabeth A. | 26 MAY 1860 |
| HOWE, Joseph | McMAHON, Margaret | 26 OCT 1863 |
| HOWELL, Alva | BROWN, Victoria | 25 APR 1859 |
| HOWELL, George | CULL, Fannie | 14 MAY 1859 |
| HOWELL, Samuel [10] | BURROWS, Mary Rose | 03 JUN 1863 |
| HOWENSTEIN, James T. | SULLIVAN, Mary Wade | 15 JUN 1868 |
| HOWISON, Henry L. [11] | MIDDLETON, Hannah J. | 28 SEP 1865 |
| HOWLAND, Charles | KIDWELL, Anne | 12 NOV 1861 |
| HOWLAND, David | VALENTINE, Anna M. | 06 MAY 1862 |
| HOWLAND, David B. | CAVENAGH, Jane America | 12 JAN 1863 |
| HOWLE, Peter Casanove | KIECKHOEFER, Mary Louisa | 19 JAN 1859 |
| HOWLETT, J. Henry | PYEWELL, Jane E. | 07 MAY 1863 |
| HOWSON, Neils Wm. [6s] | HOLMES, Sarah | 23 JAN 1865 |
| HOXLEY, Jefferson | HARDY, Mary M. | 25 APR 1861 |
| HOY, Thomas | CLARK, Mary Elizabeth | 22 DEC 1862 |
| HOYBERGER, Martin | BENTZ, Kate | 02 JUL 1863 |
| HOYLE, James L. | CRISWELL, Annie E. | 19 NOV 1868 |
| HOYLE, Otis | GOTHE, Malvina E. | 04 APR 1866 |
| HOYT, Samuel S. | FOWLE, Emma F. | 30 APR 1864 |
| HUBBELL, August | HAINS, Henrietta S. | 06 AUG 1865 |
| HUBERT, Martin | DEURLINER, Catherine | 13 AUG 1866 |
| HUDLE, George F. | SOOPER, Eliza | 12 NOV 1863 |
| HUDNALL, Delaware | BANKS, Catharine | 03 JUN 1865 |
| HUDNELL, Don Pedro | BELL, Mary Dessirio (blk) | 30 MAY 1867 |
| HUDSON, George | GUY, Eliza J. | 30 MAR 1866 |
| HUDSON, Henry A. | DONN, Catherine | 16 DEC 1861 |
| HUDSON, James | CONNER, Catherine | 12 DEC 1863 |
| HUDSON, Richard | BURKE, E.H. | 21 JUN 1862 |
| HUDSON, Seymour M. | JONES, Mary A. | 14 JUN 1869 |
| HUDSON, William | LAWSON, Anna (blk) | 17 MAR 1866 |
| HUDSON, William | KEISER, Kate | 19 JUN 1866 |
| HUFFMAN, William | McGINTY, Mary | 02 AUG 1866 |
| HUGEL, Louis M. | BAKER, Maria L. | 28 MAY 1860 |
| HUGGINS, Elias B. | MAHER, Margaret Scott | 24 MAR 1865 |

District of Columbia Marriage Licenses, 1858-1870

| | | |
|---|---|---|
| HUGH, Henry | MAMBERG, Naitalia | 03 JUL 1861 |
| HUGHES, A.M., Jr. | SMOOT, Lizzie T. | 06 OCT 1868 |
| HUGHES, Alexander | LOGAN, Mary | 28 DEC 1864 |
| HUGHES, Alonzo | SMITH, Alice A. | 12 NOV 1861 |
| HUGHES, Arnold W. | WROE, Hellen Elizth. | 12 APR 1859 |
| HUGHES, Caleb | POWERS, Maria (blk) | 10 AUG 1866 |
| HUGHES, Carlton | ETCHINSON, Elizabeth | 01 NOV 1862 |
| HUGHES, Charles | DIXON, Maria (blk) | 20 OCT 1864 |
| HUGHES, Charles | NICHOLAS, Ella (blk) | 29 DEC 1864 |
| HUGHES, Charles L. | GOGGIN, Laura V. | 08 APR 1869 |
| HUGHES, Edward | QUIRK, Mary | 29 SEP 1859 |
| HUGHES, Edward | LORTON, Ellen | 13 JUN 1864 |
| HUGHES, Ellis | MILLER, Laura | 10 JAN 1866 |
| HUGHES, Frederick | HOVENCAMP, Sarah J. | 21 JUN 1864 |
| HUGHES, George H. | CONNELL, Jeannett | 11 FEB 1867 |
| HUGHES, James | MASON, Ida | 01 NOV 1866 |
| HUGHES, James E. | DAWSON, Jane D. | 19 SEP 1859 |
| HUGHES, John | DEVAUGHN, Mary S. | 25 FEB 1862 |
| HUGHES, John | PAYNE, Elizabeth | 09 MAY 1863 |
| HUGHES, John | RUSSELL, Ellen | 27 JUN 1863 |
| HUGHES, John O. | MASSEY, Sophia | 09 JUN 1860 |
| HUGHES, Joseph H. | SCOTT, Mary Ellen | 06 JAN 1863 |
| HUGHES, Nelson | HANES, Mary Ann (blk) | 08 OCT 1866 |
| HUGHES, Patrick | DENAAN, Bridget | 14 MAY 1864 |
| HUGHES, Philip | HOLLEY, Adelaide (blk) | 06 DEC 1859 |
| HUGHES, Richard B. [4] | DUVAL, Catharine E. | 23 JAN 1862 |
| HUGHES, Samuel | WILLIAMS, Celia (blk) | 03 MAY 1869 |
| HUGHES, Samuel Henry | EDMONSON, Emma Victoria (blk) | 16 MAR 1867 |
| HUGHES, Sandy | CARTER, Martha (blk) | 17 MAR 1868 |
| HUGHES, Thomas J. | SCRIVENER, Mary V. | 14 FEB 1870 |
| HUGHES, Wesley | BUTLER, Eliza (blk) | 28 JAN 1864 |
| HUGHES, William | HARTNETT, Ellen | 28 APR 1866 |
| HUGHES, William E. | PARIS, Jennie | 09 OCT 1869 |
| HUGHS, John | GATELY, Mary | 18 FEB 1865 |
| HUGHS, William | JIMASON, Eliza (blk) | 29 APR 1869 |
| HUHN, George | FUNK, Mary | 10 NOV 1868 |
| HUHN, Joseph | HORNING, Minne | 07 JUL 1859 |
| HUHN, Martin | BUSS, Elizabeth | 09 SEP 1858 |
| HUHN, Philip | REAVES, Margaret | 04 SEP 1860 |
| HUHN, William | SMITHSON, Mary A. | 14 JAN 1860 |
| HULINGS, Thomas M. | THOMAS, Mary B. | 23 DEC 1861 |
| HULL, Harvey | MAYHUE, Omedgia | 27 AUG 1862 |
| HULL, John | DOHERTY, Mary H. | 26 APR 1865 |
| HULL, William W. | MOREBURGER, Lucetta | 08 FEB 1865 |
| HULLINGS, William H. [7b] | THOMAS, Mary L. | 25 NOV 1869 |
| HULSE, Charles E. | TAYLOR, Margaret E. | 03 APR 1865 |
| HULSE, Charles L. | FOREMAN, Unity | 08 DEC 1863 |
| HUMASON, Stanley D. | MURRAY, Mary E. | 26 DEC 1866 |
| HUMBERG, Charles | VOHS, Mary | 15 AUG 1864 |
| HUME, Thomas L. | PICKRELL, Annie G. | 16 APR 1866 |
| HUMES, Edward | CARROLL, Elizabeth | 10 AUG 1869 |
| HUMES, George W. | DOUD, Mary | 19 JUL 1865 |
| HUMMEL, Levi | MURPHY, Georgia | 23 DEC 1869 |
| HUMPHREY, Robert T. | LANGLEY, Marion V. | 17 FEB 1863 |
| HUMPHREYS, Charles | RODGERS, Mary Etta | 23 JUL 1863 |
| HUMPHREYS, Charles | GASS, Katie P. | 04 JUN 1867 |

District of Columbia Marriage Licenses, 1858-1870

| | | |
|---|---|---|
| HUMPHREYS, Christopher | GASS, Katie P. | 29 SEP 1865 |
| HUMPHREYS, Daniel | CHEW, Clarissa A.B. (blk) | 15 MAR 1864 |
| HUMPHREYS, Edward | JACKSON, Laura Maria (blk) | 07 NOV 1866 |
| HUMPHREYS, George W. | HOLMEAD, Elizabeth A. | 08 FEB 1864 |
| HUMPHREYS, George W. | FLETCHER, Eliza J. | 23 JUN 1864 |
| HUMPHREYS, Thomas | CONNER, Rosanna M. | 02 MAR 1864 |
| HUMPHREYS, Thomas Edmund | FREDERICKS, Eliza M. | 28 JUN 1864 |
| HUMPHREYS, William | KEEYES, Selina | 19 JUN 1866 |
| HUNGERFORD, Milton | BERRYMAN, Ellen (blk) | 09 JUL 1868 |
| HUNNICUTT, Henry | PAYNE, Harriet Rebecca (blk) | 11 JUN 1868 |
| HUNNICUTT, Willis | HUNNICUTT, Milley (blk) | 23 MAR 1870 |
| HUNT, Alexander | BUTLER, Hannah (blk) | 03 AUG 1869 |
| HUNT, Charles E. | JOHNSON, Sidney T. | 01 MAR 1867 |
| HUNT, Edward A. | MURRAY, Mary | 29 MAR 1860 |
| HUNT, G.A. | CLEMENTS, Eliza | 10 MAR 1870 |
| HUNT, Henry J. [4] | CRAIG, Mary Bethune | 27 DEC 1860 |
| HUNT, Jacob (19 Ind. Vols.) | GRIGSBY, Mary J. | 12 JAN 1864 |
| HUNT, John R. [9n] | LOWE, Sarah V. | 04 OCT 1859 |
| HUNT, Richard | LUCKETT, Sarah | 05 FEB 1870 |
| HUNT, Robert | BRENDER, Elizabeth | 26 MAY 1862 |
| HUNT, Robert | ROBERTSON, Betty (blk) | 21 JUN 1864 |
| HUNT, Samuel S. | SPILLMAN, Laralia J. | 14 FEB 1866 |
| HUNT, Silas W. | POLAN, Hattie E. | 03 MAR 1870 |
| HUNT, Walter C. | VOLLBRIGHT, Louise D. | 02 SEP 1867 |
| HUNT, William | MORGAN, Annie | 18 JUN 1864 |
| HUNT, William | MAHONEY, Mary | 18 NOV 1868 |
| HUNT, William E. | SHAFER, Victorine E. | 18 MAY 1861 |
| HUNT, William G. | DUNIVAN, Sue | 04 JAN 1859 |
| HUNT, William H. [6r] | McNALLY, Amanda J. | 16 OCT 1860 |
| HUNT, William R. | PRATHER, Henrietta | 11 SEP 1860 |
| HUNTER, Alfred | FISETTE, Eloise | 26 MAY 1868 |
| HUNTER, Andrew J. | BRIDGET, Margaret N. | 02 JAN 1867 |
| HUNTER, Charles V. | BARNES, Isabella | 01 JUN 1861 |
| HUNTER, George W. | CRUMP, Elizabeth | 27 JAN 1864 |
| HUNTER, Henry Key | BIBB, Ellanor E. | 14 JUN 1867 |
| HUNTER, Jacob | RABBIT, Jennie | 29 MAY 1865 |
| HUNTER, James R. | SEARLES, Julia M. | 01 SEP 1866 |
| HUNTER, James William | DORSEY, Annie Rebecca | 28 AUG 1867 |
| HUNTER, John | BROOKE, Mollie | 23 JUN 1859 |
| HUNTER, John | HAYS, Martha (blk) | 26 NOV 1862 |
| HUNTER, John | HENDERSON, Charlotte (blk) | 11 MAR 1867 |
| HUNTER, John C. | BISCOE, Emma | 15 AUG 1865 |
| HUNTER, John W. | PRATHER, Olivia | 14 NOV 1865 |
| HUNTER, Milburn | CONNER, Elizabeth J. | 05 SEP 1865 |
| HUNTER, Robert | JONES, Louisa (blk) | 17 MAY 1865 |
| HUNTER, Robert H. | NOLAND, Mary F. | 31 OCT 1859 |
| HUNTER, Samuel | MURRAY, Catharine Lucy | 07 APR 1863 |
| HUNTER, William | RECTOR, Florence A. | 21 SEP 1864 |
| HUNTER, William F. | YOUNG, Mary A. | 16 MAR 1868 |
| HUNTER, William Milton | MARTIN, Ellen Hortense | 24 AUG 1865 |
| HUNTINGTON, George | RUSHFORD, Fanny | 24 JUN 1863 |
| HUNTON, Henry | CARTER, Mary P. | 16 AUG 1859 |
| HUNTT, Charles P. | TURPIN, Minnie J. | 22 DEC 1862 |
| HUNTT, Walter C. | O'DONNELL, Margaret F. | 13 FEB 1860 |
| HUPP, Elexius | JONES, Elizabeth | 23 FEB 1865 |
| HURD, Henry | CARTER, Catherine (blk) | 07 OCT 1869 |

District of Columbia Marriage Licenses, 1858-1870

| | | |
|---|---|---|
| HURD, John W. | SMITH, Mary A. (blk) | 24 MAY 1869 |
| HURD, Loren B. | HAZARD, Ellen Louise | 31 MAY 1867 |
| HURDEL, Charles Littleton | GARCIA, Isabella | 30 APR 1864 |
| HURDLE, Albert Dawson | METZ, Frances Rebecca | 15 JUL 1863 |
| HURDLE, Charles H. | EVANS, Teresa | 22 JUN 1860 |
| HURDLE, Charles H. [5] | MEED, Mary A. | 22 SEP 1868 |
| HURDLE, James R. | MURRAY, Catherine | 12 FEB 1862 |
| HURDLE, Thomas T. | COLLINS, Harriet A. | 25 MAR 1859 |
| HURDLE, William L. [5] | HUMPHREYS, Anna | 02 JUN 1869 |
| HURL, Marcellus | DONOVAN, Jane | 08 MAY 1861 |
| HURLEBAUS, Charles F. | CHAMBERS, Mary Ann | 18 OCT 1858 |
| HURLEY, B.F.M. | NORMENT, Ulie | 09 OCT 1867 |
| HURLEY, Daniel | HESS, Ann | 02 DEC 1867 |
| HURLEY, James | COLLINS, Hanora | 27 DEC 1867 |
| HURLEY, John | DUCKETT, Sarah | 12 MAR 1859 |
| HURLEY, John | COLLINS, Kate | 18 SEP 1860 |
| HURLEY, John | FARRELL, Mary H. | 17 FEB 1865 |
| HURLEY, Maurice | CUNNINGHAM, Anna C. | 08 JUL 1863 |
| HURLEY, W.G. | KNODEL, Frideruke | 24 MAR 1859 |
| HURLEY, William | MURPHY, Emily M. | 17 AUG 1863 |
| HURLEY, Wm. F. | MAHAGAN, Ophelia | 21 FEB 1870 |
| HURLY, William L. | KING, Mary Ann | 10 JUN 1867 |
| HURNEY, Laurence | FAHEY, Margaret | 04 APR 1863 |
| HURNEY, Michael | NOONAN, Ann | 03 FEB 1860 |
| HURRY, John H. | FRENCH, Rebecca E. | 15 FEB 1860 |
| HURST, John | KING, Lucy A. | 02 SEP 1867 |
| HURST, Lee | JONES, Lucy (blk) | 28 MAY 1866 |
| HURT, Daniel | LAMMOND, Nettie | 03 MAR 1863 |
| HURT, Henry | YOUNG, Anna | 07 SEP 1869 |
| HURT, Manfort | REEDERS, Sarah Ann | 16 NOV 1865 |
| HUSELMAN, Charles | CORNISH, Mary A. | 01 MAY 1860 |
| HUSEN, Wallace E. | RAGGERTY, Georgie L. | 19 NOV 1862 |
| HUSSY, William | RHYNE, Mary | 02 JUL 1859 |
| HUTCHINS, Benedict | GRAY, Elizabeth | 17 JAN 1861 |
| HUTCHINS, James | MORELAND, Martha | 29 APR 1859 |
| HUTCHINS, Lewis Henry | FREEMAN, Sarah Elizabeth (blk) | 05 FEB 1869 |
| HUTCHINS, Richard H. | BRADBURN, Sarah E. | 25 SEP 1867 |
| HUTCHINS, William A. [1c] | DARN, Annie A. | 22 DEC 1863 |
| HUTCHINS, William C. | HAMILTON, Josie F. | 19 NOV 1862 |
| HUTCHINS, Wm. D. | POSTON, Mary J. | 01 OCT 1861 |
| HUTCHINSON, Ananias | JOHNSON, Adaline | 07 SEP 1865 |
| HUTCHINSON, John Thomas | ROBINSON, Martha A.J. | 13 JUN 1864 |
| HUTCHINSON, Samuel | FLOOD, Eliza | 08 JUL 1868 |
| HUTCHINSON, William | BROWN, Mary Jane | 20 APR 1859 |
| HUTCHINSON, William | SPURRIER, Annie | 11 JUL 1866 |
| HUTCHINSON, William | GANT, Josephine (blk) | 15 APR 1869 |
| HUTCHINSON, William | JOHNSON, Sarah Jane (blk) | 22 MAR 1870 |
| HUTCHINSON, Zachariah | BURKE, Mary E. | 28 APR 1866 |
| HUTCHISON, Charles H. | WINDSOR, Mary | 16 JUN 1870 |
| HUTH, Ernst | BORN, Catherine | 14 JUN 1867 |
| HUTH, Frederick Gottlob | WACHEMUTH, Eliza | 28 JAN 1868 |
| HUTT, Spencer | KEY, Mary R. | 04 DEC 1865 |
| HUTTON, Archibald L. | MITCHELL, Ella A. | 03 MAR 1863 |
| HUTTON, Harry T. | LAMB, Fanny | 14 OCT 1867 |
| HUTTON, Henry | CHAMLIN, Julia (blk) | 01 MAR 1870 |
| HUTTON, James Wm. | HOWE, Mary Virginia | 08 JAN 1867 |

| | | |
|---|---|---|
| HUTTON, Richard | DAVIS, Sophia (blk) | 05 OCT 1868 |
| HUTZLER, Charles | DEMALMAR, Lina | 07 DEC 1867 |
| HUYCK, Jesse V.N. | DYER, Mary M. | 04 DEC 1865 |
| HYAM, Benjamin D. | MASI, Margaret C. | 05 JAN 1860 |
| HYATT, John | MIDDLETON, Marion | 29 JUN 1859 |
| HYDE, Francis M. | BIDWELL, Carrie D. | 27 SEP 1864 |
| HYDE, George | COOK, Elizabeth M. | 02 NOV 1864 |
| HYDE, Granville F. | TYLER, Susan | 30 JAN 1867 |
| HYDE, John L. | HOLT, Mary M. | 30 MAR 1869 |
| HYDE, Patrick | KENNY, Mary | 24 JUN 1865 |
| HYDE, Richard A. | BOSWELL, Lucy A. | 04 OCT 1859 |
| HYDE, Richard L. | BARNES, Rosella J. | 04 JUL 1867 |
| HYDE, Thomas | RITTENHOUSE, Fannie | 25 OCT 1864 |
| HYNES, John | GRIFFIN, Mary | 23 SEP 1862 |
| HYNES, Patrick | REILLY, Delia | 12 JAN 1865 |

## I

| | | |
|---|---|---|
| IDDINGS, Thomas J. | FRITZENGER, Anna Margaret | 11 JUL 1863 |
| IKLEY, Jacob L. | SHEA, Johannah | 26 MAR 1864 |
| ILLOW, Charles | MERCK, Caroline | 16 AUG 1866 |
| IMHOF, Matthias | LINDLICH, Agnes | 28 DEC 1859 |
| INARELI, Prosperi | COSTA, Angelina | 26 MAR 1864 |
| INGLE, Christopher [11] | HUTTON, Ellen [Salome] | 10 FEB 1862 |
| INGLE, Osborne, Rev. | ADDISON, Mollie M. | 10 AUG 1864 |
| INGLEHART, Andrew | BROWN, Margaret | 21 FEB 1859 |
| INGOLD, Frank D. | THOMPSON, Belle | 06 MAR 1867 |
| INGRAHAM, Samuel | KING, Martha Ann | 12 OCT 1865 |
| INGRAM, Charles N. | McGILL, Anna Louisa | 25 DEC 1865 |
| INGRAM, George | JENIFER, Cecila (blk) | 20 DEC 1865 |
| INGRAM, Thomas W. | LAWSON, Elizabeth (blk) | 14 SEP 1869 |
| INMANN, George W. | HORNBERGER, Elizabeth D. | 29 MAY 1865 |
| IRELAND, James T. | O'NEIL, Letitia | 12 MAY 1868 |
| IRELAND, Samuel | ROSS, Elizabeth | 13 JAN 1865 |
| IRICK, Daniel | BARR, Ida | 12 JUL 1869 |
| IRISH, Damion | LOSE, Elizabeth | 27 JUN 1868 |
| IRVIN, Geo. C. | CURTIS, Pamelia | 17 JAN 1866 |
| IRVIN, John Alex | HOLMES, Julia A. (blk) | 26 MAY 1868 |
| IRVIN, Thomas | LANEY, Elizabeth (blk) | 11 DEC 1862 |
| IRVINE, Alexander McLiesh | BRADY, Rose | 07 DEC 1863 |
| IRWIN, Alexander | NALLEY, Mary (blk) | 31 AUG 1869 |
| IRWIN, John | GAYNOR, Bridget | 18 JUL 1863 |
| IRWIN, John | SULLIVAN, Mary | 06 FEB 1864 |
| ISAAC, H. Clay | HUME, Mary A. | 11 DEC 1861 |
| ISAACS, George | JONES, Jennie | 31 MAY 1866 |
| ISCHMANN, Michael | SCHNEIDER, Katie | 06 OCT 1869 |
| IVERSON, William | ROSS, Maria (blk) | 14 MAY 1866 |
| IVEY, Carolina | GOLDING, Amanda (blk) | 22 JAN 1866 |
| IVEY, Charles C. | CURRAN, Georgianna | 19 JUN 1867 |
| IVY, Meredith M. | BUTLER, Julia C. | 29 JUN 1865 |

## J

| | | |
|---|---|---|
| JACCKEL, Herman P.J. | ZIRKELBACH, Caroline | 18 JUN 1864 |
| JACKSON, Allen | WHITE, Ella (blk) | 17 MAY 1869 |

District of Columbia Marriage Licenses, 1858-1870

| | | |
|---|---|---|
| JACKSON, Alonzo | OLIVER, Sophy (blk) | 08 AUG 1866 |
| JACKSON, Andrew | HUMPHREYS, Mary Ellen (blk) | 09 JUL 1863 |
| JACKSON, Andrew | STANLY, Mary Ellen (blk) | 25 DEC 1863 |
| JACKSON, Andrew | HENSON, Sarah (blk) | 20 DEC 1864 |
| JACKSON, Andrew | EDWARDS, Sally (blk) | 26 DEC 1864 |
| JACKSON, Andrew | ROGERS, Lucy Ann (blk) | 14 SEP 1865 |
| JACKSON, Andrew | BROOKS, Ellen (blk) | 03 AUG 1866 |
| JACKSON, Andrew | THOMAS, Sarah Jane (blk) | 11 APR 1868 |
| JACKSON, Andrew | RHODES, Augusta (blk) | 10 AUG 1868 |
| JACKSON, Andrew | DOWELL, Betsy (blk) | 23 DEC 1868 |
| JACKSON, Andrew | JONES, Mary Ellen | 23 DEC 1868 |
| JACKSON, Anthony | FRAZIER, Alexina (blk) | 19 DEC 1865 |
| JACKSON, Arthur | JOHNSON, Rachel | 28 JUN 1865 |
| JACKSON, Arthur | COLLIER, Nancy (blk) | 11 AUG 1866 |
| JACKSON, Basil | THOMPSON, Priscilla (blk) | 30 MAY 1867 |
| JACKSON, Benjamin | ADAMS, Elizabeth | 10 MAY 1865 |
| JACKSON, Benj. Lowndes | CANBY, Eliza | 20 FEB 1867 |
| JACKSON, Beverly | JORDAN, Margaret (blk) | 10 JUL 1866 |
| JACKSON, Charles | JACKSON, Mary Ellen | 03 NOV 1862 |
| JACKSON, Charles | BOOTHE, Virginia (blk) | 23 MAR 1864 |
| JACKSON, Charles | WIMER, Elizabeth A. | 25 MAY 1869 |
| JACKSON, Clement | JACKSON, Harriet (blk) | 16 DEC 1858 |
| JACKSON, Daniel | BROWN, Anna (blk) | 28 DEC 1864 |
| JACKSON, Daniel | BING, Frances (blk) | 29 SEP 1868 |
| JACKSON, Daniel B. | GAREY, Louisa V. | 03 MAR 1863 |
| JACKSON, Daniel T. | LOWE, Annie C. (blk) | 09 JAN 1867 |
| JACKSON, Evander J. | OMOHUNDRO, Virgin W. | 17 MAY 1860 |
| JACKSON, Fenton | BROOKS, Mary Jane (blk) | 03 MAR 1864 |
| JACKSON, Fred. R. | GIBBS, Emmie L. | 22 FEB 1865 |
| JACKSON, Frederick | BELL, Dorothea (blk) | 17 DEC 1864 |
| JACKSON, Frederick | GREEN, Ellen (blk) | 06 JUL 1867 |
| JACKSON, Frederick | PAYNE, Mary Ellen (blk) | 02 SEP 1869 |
| JACKSON, George | COLE, Susan (blk) | 03 NOV 1864 |
| JACKSON, George | DENNY, Ann (blk) | 18 NOV 1865 |
| JACKSON, George | JONES, Victoria (blk) | 24 MAY 1866 |
| JACKSON, George | JACKSON, Judy Ann (blk) | 15 JUL 1867 |
| JACKSON, George | SMITH, Lucy (blk) | 27 OCT 1868 |
| JACKSON, George H. [5] | HAYES, Helen M. | 02 MAY 1868 |
| JACKSON, Grayson | LACY, Virginia | 21 DEC 1869 |
| JACKSON, Henry | POWELL, Susan (blk) | 08 SEP 1859 |
| JACKSON, Henry | COOPER, Caroline (blk) | 23 AUG 1864 |
| JACKSON, Henry | OFFORD, Ellen (blk) | 22 OCT 1864 |
| JACKSON, Henry | FETCHEN, Susan | 05 FEB 1866 |
| JACKSON, Henry | SMITH, Maria (blk) | 10 NOV 1866 |
| JACKSON, Henry | LANGLEY, Mary (blk) | 20 SEP 1867 |
| JACKSON, Henry [not paid] | JASPER, Julia (blk) | 27 JUN 1866 |
| JACKSON, Henson | MYERS, Sarah E. | 05 APR 1870 |
| JACKSON, Herod | WILSON, Josephine (blk) | 11 NOV 1867 |
| JACKSON, Hilliary | GRAY, Sarah (blk) | 25 MAY 1869 |
| JACKSON, J.F. | KEYES, M.E. | 19 JUN 1863 |
| JACKSON, James | WILSON, Jenny (blk) | 04 AUG 1863 |
| JACKSON, James | THOMAS, Betsy (blk) | 03 DEC 1863 |
| JACKSON, James | YOUNG, Isabella (blk) | 08 OCT 1864 |
| JACKSON, James | WILLIAMS, Mary Jane (blk) | 21 AUG 1867 |
| JACKSON, James | KING, Josephine | 17 SEP 1868 |
| JACKSON, James | FORREST, Martha (blk) | 29 NOV 1869 |

District of Columbia Marriage Licenses, 1858-1870

| | | |
|---|---|---|
| JACKSON, Jerry | WASHINGTON, Ann Maria | 23 DEC 1865 |
| JACKSON, John | BRUFF, Zulima | 04 NOV 1861 |
| JACKSON, John | CARTER, Letty (blk) | 28 AUG 1862 |
| JACKSON, John | MACK, Frances (blk) | 17 SEP 1863 |
| JACKSON, John | MILTON, Mary (col'd) | 30 MAY 1864 |
| JACKSON, John | HAWKINS, Elizabeth (blk) | 28 DEC 1864 |
| JACKSON, John | WRIGHT, Mary (blk) | 04 OCT 1866 |
| JACKSON, John | GUY, Lydia (blk) | 26 DEC 1866 |
| JACKSON, John | POOLE, Teresa (blk) | 26 APR 1868 |
| JACKSON, John | SMITH, Nancy (blk) | 07 NOV 1868 |
| JACKSON, John | WILSON, Lucy (blk) | 14 DEC 1868 |
| JACKSON, John | SAVOY, Nancy (blk) | 29 DEC 1869 |
| JACKSON, John | WEBSTER, Charlotte (blk) | 10 NOV 1864 |
| JACKSON, John F. | EVANS, Hanna Ann (blk) | 27 JUL 1869 |
| JACKSON, John Henry | KEARNEY, Ellen (blk) | 17 APR 1867 |
| JACKSON, John Henry | JONES, Mary (blk) | 14 DEC 1869 |
| JACKSON, John S. [1e] | THOMAS, Margaret [Virginia] | 16 JUN 1864 |
| JACKSON, Jordan | LEWIS, Maria (blk) | 26 AUG 1865 |
| JACKSON, Joseph | JACKSON, Elizabeth | 04 JUL 1862 |
| JACKSON, Joseph | SIMMS, Letitia (blk) | 24 NOV 1862 |
| JACKSON, Joseph | FOWLER, Ada | 06 APR 1870 |
| JACKSON, Lewis | PAYNE, Mary (blk) | 06 APR 1870 |
| JACKSON, Lewis T. | BRANNUM, Mary | 03 OCT 1864 |
| JACKSON, Moses | FLEET, Kate (blk) | 28 DEC 1865 |
| JACKSON, Noah | PARKER, Ann Eliza (blk) | 16 AUG 1862 |
| JACKSON, Noah | CLARE, Easter (blk) | 04 NOV 1868 |
| JACKSON, Perry | GILDS, Mary (blk) | 06 FEB 1866 |
| JACKSON, Philip | DODSON, Harriet | 05 DEC 1867 |
| JACKSON, Philip | BROWN, Anna (blk) | 02 JUN 1869 |
| JACKSON, Presley | BOND, Mary (blk) | 13 MAY 1868 |
| JACKSON, Reuben | SCOTT, Jane (col'd) | 18 JUN 1867 |
| JACKSON, Richard | ADDISON, Amelia (blk) | 26 OCT 1867 |
| JACKSON, Richard | JOHNSON, Matilda (blk) | 18 AUG 1869 |
| JACKSON, Richard | ROBERTS, Anna (blk) | 11 DEC 1869 |
| JACKSON, Robert | LANKFORD, Margaret (blk) | 14 JUL 1863 |
| JACKSON, Robert | COLEMAN, Alice (blk) | 17 NOV 1866 |
| JACKSON, Robert | MONROE, Louisa (blk) | 18 DEC 1866 |
| JACKSON, Rubey | GREEN, Julia (blk) | 18 JUN 1866 |
| JACKSON, Samuel | MAHORNEY, Susan (blk) | 27 APR 1865 |
| JACKSON, Samuel | MASSEY, Catherine (blk) | 17 FEB 1866 |
| JACKSON, Samuel | JONES, Mary Ann (blk) | 04 AUG 1866 |
| JACKSON, Samuel | YOUNG, Sarah | 06 FEB 1868 |
| JACKSON, Sim | LIZZIE, Ann (blk) | 27 OCT 1866 |
| JACKSON, Simon | GARRETT, Adaline (blk) | 11 NOV 1869 |
| JACKSON, Squire | WALLACE, Clarissa (blk) | 06 DEC 1865 |
| JACKSON, Squire | JACKSON, Mollie (blk) | 19 MAR 1867 |
| JACKSON, Thomas | DOUGLASS, Rosina (blk) | 18 JUL 1861 |
| JACKSON, Thomas | THOMAS, Mary Jane (blk) | 28 DEC 1864 |
| JACKSON, Thomas | FRANCIS, Martha | 06 OCT 1866 |
| JACKSON, Thomas | JONES, Sylvia (blk) | 27 MAR 1867 |
| JACKSON, Thomas | HOLLING, Anna W. (blk) | 10 JUN 1869 |
| JACKSON, Thomas Elvin | RICARD, Ann Eliza | 17 JUL 1863 |
| JACKSON, Thornton A. | MERCIER, Mary E. (blk) | 11 APR 1868 |
| JACKSON, Tilghman W. | DUPPIN, Mary Jane | 15 JUN 1870 |
| JACKSON, Walter | SINGLETON, Hannah (blk) | 28 DEC 1867 |
| JACKSON, Washington | TURNER, Harriet (blk) | 17 DEC 1863 |

District of Columbia Marriage Licenses, 1858-1870

| | | |
|---|---|---|
| JACKSON, Washington | CURTIS, Margaret (blk) | 24 JUN 1869 |
| JACKSON, Wesley | SLATER, Celia | 18 JUL 1866 |
| JACKSON, William | TRIPLETT, Amelia | 27 JUN 1864 |
| JACKSON, William | LEE, Emily (blk) | 15 SEP 1866 |
| JACKSON, William | CHASE, Florence (blk) | 24 DEC 1867 |
| JACKSON, William | NORMAN, Clara (blk) | 09 APR 1870 |
| JACKSON, William Henry | ROSS, Eliza (blk) | 14 MAR 1862 |
| JACKSON, William J. | BRENT, Caroline E. (blk) | 09 OCT 1861 |
| JACKSON, Wyatt N. | ELGIN, Karen A. | 04 MAR 1867 |
| JACOB, David C. | GOETZ, Anna Mary | 04 AUG 1860 |
| JACOB, Eugene Charles | MERTENS, Clementine | 21 NOV 1863 |
| JACOB, George | LEHMAN, Sophia | 14 SEP 1858 |
| JACOB, Thomas A. | POUTCH, Emma Virginia | 28 DEC 1865 |
| JACOB, Wm. W. | WEST, Helen M. | 17 APR 1861 |
| JACOBS, A. Roszel | DAVIS, Elizabeth O'N. | 09 DEC 1862 |
| JACOBS, Bascom S. | WELLS, Rachel H. | 31 MAY 1864 |
| JACOBS, Frank | NEWTON, Sophia (blk) | 13 JUL 1863 |
| JACOBS, George | BELL, Anna Elizabeth (blk) | 11 JUL 1866 |
| JACOBS, George T. [6le] | DERR, Sarah | 14 FEB 1866 |
| JACOBS, Horace G. | SLATER, Hannah | 31 AUG 1868 |
| JACOBS, John [6le] | DIGGLE, Mary | 21 MAY 1866 |
| JACOBS, John H. | COOKSEY, Mary A. | 20 OCT 1864 |
| JACOBS, John P. | SEBASTIAN, Laura | 06 FEB 1867 |
| JACOBS, John Q. | DOHERTY, Mary | 09 MAR 1865 |
| JACOBS, Julius | KOLDITZ, Friedericka Ernestine | 06 NOV 1865 |
| JACOBS, LaFayette | CROOK, Mary | 28 JUN 1865 |
| JACOBS, Nathan | HAWKINS, Louise (blk) | 04 OCT 1866 |
| JACOBS, Oscar | ASHER, Margaret (blk) | 04 NOV 1863 |
| JACOBS, Robert Henry | WALKER, Susan E. | 24 FEB 1863 |
| JACOBSON, Jacob [12s] | HILZHEIM, Sarah | 24 JUN 1862 |
| JAMES, Andrew | JACKSON, Ellen | 04 JAN 1864 |
| JAMES, Andrew | SMITH, Lucy (blk) | 21 DEC 1866 |
| JAMES, Charles E. | HUTCHINSON, Sarah R. | 23 AUG 1864 |
| JAMES, Charles H. [10] | NAYLOR, Matilda [Verlinda] | 05 NOV 1866 |
| JAMES, Daniel Dickson | GODDARD, Annie C. | 30 SEP 1869 |
| JAMES, Francis | BEAN, Annie | 31 JAN 1866 |
| JAMES, G.S. | COOK, Louisa | 20 MAR 1860 |
| JAMES, George | WHEELER, Eliza (blk) | 14 APR 1863 |
| JAMES, Henry | CLARK, Mary (blk) | 15 OCT 1866 |
| JAMES, Henry | SNOWDEN, Lucinda (blk) | 27 FEB 1869 |
| JAMES, James Henry | MARSHALL, Lula (blk) | 26 FEB 1868 |
| JAMES, John T. | VanBOKUM, Elizabeth | 21 OCT 1869 |
| JAMES, Joseph | JOHNSON, Milly Ann (blk) | 26 AUG 1863 |
| JAMES, Joseph | BRADY, Sarah | 01 NOV 1869 |
| JAMES, Kelsey (alias Henry James) | DAVIS, Alice (blk) | 19 NOV 1864 |
| JAMES, T. Benton | BLAKELY, Eliza P. | 28 SEP 1865 |
| JAMES, William | DAVIS, Amelia (blk) | 22 SEP 1859 |
| JAMESON, John | FULLER, Kate A. | 21 JUN 1869 |
| JAMESSON, Colville A. | MILTON, Susan V. | 12 OCT 1859 |
| JAMIESSON, Colville A. | DAVIS, Chloe A. | 06 DEC 1861 |
| JANEZECK, John J. | CONWAY, Eliza | 25 JUL 1867 |
| JANNEY, George | HOOD, Rose Berta (blk) | 21 DEC 1869 |
| JANNEY, Phineas | CONNOLLY, Clara | 07 JAN 1867 |
| JANNEY, Robert | THREALKIL, Mary E. | 01 OCT 1858 |
| JANSEN, Mathias [5] | BROWN, Laura Ann | 11 DEC 1866 |
| JAQUETTE, Isaac G. | ANDERSON, Mary | 06 FEB 1867 |

| | | |
|---|---|---|
| JARBOE, Daniel W. | MARDIS, Catharine Z. | 09 MAY 1860 |
| JARBOE, Francis M. | QUEEN, Marcelena | 31 MAR 1862 |
| JARBOE, Horace [1e] | MARCEY, Olivia | 02 MAY 1866 |
| JARBOE, John S. | DUNNINGTON, Mary E. | 01 JUN 1859 |
| JARBOE, Thomas | ELLIOTT, [blank] | 15 NOV 1859 |
| JARBOW, John H. | WILLIAMS, Mary (blk) | 28 DEC 1869 |
| JARGINS, George, Jr. | OGDEN, Sarah | 23 JAN 1866 |
| JARVIS, Charles F.M. [9e] | TOWNER, Josephine | 26 APR 1860 |
| JARVIS, William B. | RILEY, Annie | 28 NOV 1862 |
| JASKINS, Isaac | WOOD, Leah (blk) | 10 JAN 1865 |
| JASPER, Edward | MARSHALL, Ellen (blk) | 14 OCT 1863 |
| JASPER, Ethan | LUCAS, Caroline (blk) | 19 MAR 1868 |
| JASPER, William | THOMAS, Elizabeth (blk) | 12 JAN 1869 |
| JAVINS, John R. | STOUT, Sarah Ann | 04 APR 1861 |
| JAVINS, John R. | RISTON, Anna | 03 JUN 1867 |
| JEFFERS, William [12s] | MILLS, Lydia | 25 FEB 1863 |
| JEFFERSON, David | JOHNSON, Susannah (blk) | 06 JUN 1870 |
| JEFFERSON, Henry | HARRIS, Judah Ann T. (blk) | 23 DEC 1865 |
| JEFFERSON, James | STEUART, Elizabeth | 11 JUL 1862 |
| JEFFERSON, Ralph | NYMAN, Emma J. | 23 JUL 1866 |
| JEFFERSON, Robert | UNDERWOOD, Cecilia (blk) | 15 AUG 1865 |
| JEFFERSON, Silas | BEVERLY, Margaret (blk) | 06 APR 1865 |
| JEFFERSON, Thaddeus | JEFFERSON, Sally (blk) | 10 JUL 1866 |
| JEFFERSON, Thomas | THORNTON, Lucy (blk) | 24 DEC 1867 |
| JEFFERSON, William C. | BEACH, Susan | 15 OCT 1862 |
| JEFFERSON, William C. | BEACH, Susan | 08 DEC 1863 |
| JEFFREYS, Lafayette | MADISON, Ann Maria | 27 SEP 1864 |
| JEMISON, John H. | WILLIAMS, Matilda (blk) | 22 DEC 1869 |
| JENEFER, John Gustavus | HARRIS, Mary Ann | 26 MAY 1868 |
| JENIFER, Charles H. | DIGGS, Leda (blk) | 04 FEB 1868 |
| JENKINS, Albert Francis | MUDD, Matilda Alice | 25 JAN 1870 |
| JENKINS, Benjamin | SMITH, Maria (blk) | 01 JAN 1863 |
| JENKINS, Charles | JENIFER, Mary (blk) | 21 FEB 1867 |
| JENKINS, Charles E. | COLLINS, Harriet | 02 MAY 1866 |
| JENKINS, Charles Henry | JOHNSON, Mary (col'd) | 22 DEC 1863 |
| JENKINS, Fleet W. | COURTNEY, Emma (blk) | 30 SEP 1869 |
| JENKINS, George | WILKINSON, Priscilla (blk) | 19 MAR 1867 |
| JENKINS, George W. | BOSTON, Lavinia | 26 JUN 1867 |
| JENKINS, Irvin | GRAY, Frances (blk) | 03 JUL 1867 |
| JENKINS, J.G. | HOWSER, Margaret E. | 26 APR 1869 |
| JENKINS, James L. | WARD, Elizabeth S. | 17 DEC 1861 |
| JENKINS, Jesse | WINEMILLER, Mary M. | 15 FEB 1866 |
| JENKINS, John | WASHINGTON, Mary | 30 SEP 1862 |
| JENKINS, John | BROOKS, Selina | 07 AUG 1867 |
| JENKINS, John H.B. | HOGG, Mary | 24 FEB 1863 |
| JENKINS, John H.B. | McNAMARA, Sarah P. | 27 OCT 1869 |
| JENKINS, Page | WARNER, Nancy (blk) | 14 SEP 1865 |
| JENKINS, Peter | WALKER, Julia | 22 JUN 1867 |
| JENKINS, Richard | JENKINS, Lucretia (blk) | 11 JUN 1866 |
| JENKINS, Richard L. | SASSER, Henrietta M. | 20 OCT 1862 |
| JENKINS, Robert | GRIFFIN, Maria (blk) | 13 MAY 1868 |
| JENKINS, Robert | BAILEY, Ella (blk) | 21 APR 1869 |
| JENKINS, William | AGER, Martha | 23 JUN 1864 |
| JENKINS, William Thos. | WATERS, Rachel (blk) | 06 AUG 1868 |
| JENKS, Winfield S. | REDWAY, Nellie M. | 07 NOV 1868 |
| JENNIFEE, Robert | WEBSTER, Elizabeth (blk) | 03 JUN 1864 |

# District of Columbia Marriage Licenses, 1858-1870

| | | |
|---|---|---|
| JENNINGS, Abram | ACCARDI, Mary | 28 MAR 1864 |
| JENNINGS, Alexander | COUNTEE, Jemima (blk) | 11 SEP 1869 |
| JENNINGS, Benjamin | JENNINGS, Julia A. | 21 NOV 1864 |
| JENNINGS, Charles | BRYAN, Emily | 15 FEB 1864 |
| JENNINGS, Charles | FORRESTER, Mary Ann (blk) | 07 MAY 1870 |
| JENNINGS, Franklin | LOGAN, Mary E. (blk) | 16 MAY 1868 |
| JENNINGS, Joseph T. | O'NEALE, Annie E. | 13 JUN 1867 |
| JENNINGS, Thomas | WRIGHT, Ellen | 30 NOV 1866 |
| JENSMER, Jeremiah, Capt. | STONE, Emma Virginia | 06 AUG 1868 |
| JENSON, Nicolay | HAWKINS, Elanora L. | 12 NOV 1860 |
| JERMAIN, Thomas J. | SHACKELFORD, Martha E. | 22 JUN 1864 |
| JESSUP, George | STARTZMAN, Sarah Ann | 04 MAR 1867 |
| JESSY, Augustus | LUCAS, Eliza | 21 JUL 1862 |
| JETT, Charles Henry | LAWS, Helen M. | 05 DEC 1866 |
| JETT, Charles T. | DETRO, Margaret S. | 13 JUN 1864 |
| JETT, Charles T. | JOHNSON, Mary E. | 14 JUN 1869 |
| JETT, Harry | WILLIAMS, Mary (blk) | 19 NOV 1864 |
| JETT, John J. [6m] | PETERS, Mary F. | 03 MAR 1863 |
| JETT, Stephen B. | NEWTON, Marietta Elizth. | 04 JAN 1860 |
| JETT, William | SMITH, Harriet (blk) | 21 DEC 1868 |
| JEWELL, Joseph | HALBERT, Margaret Ann | 10 OCT 1864 |
| JEWETT, Lewis T. | SMITH, Annie J. | 07 NOV 1864 |
| JIRDINSTON, James A.N. | BOUVET, Clarice Eugenie | 14 MAY 1863 |
| JOACKIM, Jacob H. | ANNODER, Louisa | 05 SEP 1866 |
| JOHANNSEN, Hans | WASSEROTH, Regina | 07 APR 1870 |
| JOHANSEN, H.P. Theodore | MILES, Mary | 04 AUG 1862 |
| JOHNS, J. Seton | DARRELL, Lucy M. | 19 JUN 1860 |
| JOHNS, William J. | MILLER, Mary M. | 23 APR 1863 |
| JOHNSON, Aaron | BLACKWELL, Priscilla (blk) | 15 SEP 1864 |
| JOHNSON, Abraham | BLACKWELL, Margaret (blk) | 11 JUL 1868 |
| JOHNSON, Adolphus | COOPER, Marg. Jane | 17 DEC 1861 |
| JOHNSON, Adolphus | BROWN, Harriet | 14 MAY 1870 |
| JOHNSON, Adolphus | GIBSON, Eliza (blk) | 11 JAN 1866 |
| JOHNSON, Albert | MILLER, Betty (blk) | 05 NOV 1864 |
| JOHNSON, Albert | WALKER, Elizabeth (blk) | 03 MAY 1866 |
| JOHNSON, Albert | GRAY, Ella (blk) | 22 SEP 1866 |
| JOHNSON, Albert | EDENBORO, Elizabeth (blk) | 06 DEC 1866 |
| JOHNSON, Albert | LEWIS, Fannie (blk) | 01 OCT 1868 |
| JOHNSON, Alexander | JOHNSON, Ellen (blk) | 22 OCT 1861 |
| JOHNSON, Alexander | ROSS, Elizabeth (blk) | 11 OCT 1869 |
| JOHNSON, Alexandria | SIMS, Mary E. | 22 NOV 1866 |
| JOHNSON, Alfred | SHEPHERD, Martha (blk) | 04 FEB 1867 |
| JOHNSON, Alfred | BARBOUR, Patsey (blk) | 07 JUN 1869 |
| JOHNSON, Alfred | WOOD, Anne (blk) | 21 FEB 1870 |
| JOHNSON, Allen | PEYTON, Mary | 11 OCT 1866 |
| JOHNSON, Allen | JOHNSON, Anna (blk) | 28 DEC 1869 |
| JOHNSON, Anderson | MOXLEY, Jane | 26 AUG 1865 |
| JOHNSON, Andrew | BURKE, Anna E. (blk) | 08 MAY 1867 |
| JOHNSON, Andrew | WILLIAMS, Sally (blk) | 06 JUN 1870 |
| JOHNSON, Basil | JOHNSON, Ann (blk) | 19 MAY 1866 |
| JOHNSON, Benjamin | LAMBERT, Amelia (blk) | 11 APR 1868 |
| JOHNSON, Benjamin | LOCKENS, Rachel (blk) | 02 SEP 1868 |
| JOHNSON, Benjamin F. [3] | KIRBY, Mary E. | 02 AUG 1862 |
| JOHNSON, Beverly | BROWN, Charlotte (blk) | 24 FEB 1868 |
| JOHNSON, Beverly | JOHNSON, Mary (blk) | 13 DEC 1869 |
| JOHNSON, Carter | MOORE, Jane (blk) | 05 DEC 1867 |

| | | |
|---|---|---|
| JOHNSON, Charles | ADAMS, Sarah | 10 JUN 1862 |
| JOHNSON, Charles | FOSTER, Mary | 13 DEC 1862 |
| JOHNSON, Charles | GAINES, Rebecca (blk) | 27 OCT 1863 |
| JOHNSON, Charles | MARTIN, Amelia (blk) | 21 JAN 1864 |
| JOHNSON, Charles | BROWN, Patsy (blk) | 21 APR 1864 |
| JOHNSON, Charles | ADDISON, Amelia (blk) | 03 OCT 1864 |
| JOHNSON, Charles | BUTLER, Mary (blk) | 10 MAR 1865 |
| JOHNSON, Charles | MITCHELL, Caroline (blk) | 02 JAN 1866 |
| JOHNSON, Charles | MULLIKEN, Amanda (blk) | 02 APR 1866 |
| JOHNSON, Charles | REARDON, Joanna | 30 APR 1866 |
| JOHNSON, Charles | POWELL, Fanny (blk) | 14 MAY 1867 |
| JOHNSON, Charles | NEALE, Mary Ann (blk) | 05 SEP 1867 |
| JOHNSON, Charles | TUXENT, Kate (blk) | 26 DEC 1867 |
| JOHNSON, Charles | GILLIS, Louisa (blk) | 25 FEB 1868 |
| JOHNSON, Charles | BOSS, Barbara (blk) | 04 NOV 1868 |
| JOHNSON, Charles C. | JACKSON, Olivia | 19 OCT 1866 |
| JOHNSON, Charles H. | COOMBS, Mary M. | 23 JUL 1862 |
| JOHNSON, Charles Philip [12s] | PARKER, Estelle | 15 JUN 1861 |
| JOHNSON, Cornelius | BRATTON, Ann (blk) | 07 MAR 1868 |
| JOHNSON, Dallas | LATIMER, Lettie H. | 17 AUG 1868 |
| JOHNSON, Daniel | CLARKE, Margaret | 18 FEB 1862 |
| JOHNSON, Daniel | BROOKS, Anna (blk) | 05 AUG 1869 |
| JOHNSON, David | PEYTON, Eliza Ann (blk) | 12 NOV 1868 |
| JOHNSON, David | TILLMAN, Sidney | 16 AUG 1869 |
| JOHNSON, David Lee | HOWARD, Annie (blk) | 03 OCT 1865 |
| JOHNSON, Dennis | BOWE, Maria (blk) | 16 OCT 1865 |
| JOHNSON, E.K. | WINSATT, Annie E. | 03 NOV 1868 |
| JOHNSON, Edward | COLLINS, Catherine M. | 16 MAY 1861 |
| JOHNSON, Edward | SMALLWOOD, Annie | 27 JAN 1863 |
| JOHNSON, Edward | CARTER, Zafney (blk) | 22 AUG 1866 |
| JOHNSON, Edward | BOONE, Priscilla (blk) | 01 NOV 1869 |
| JOHNSON, Edward [4] | GONSALVES, Mary E. | 25 SEP 1867 |
| JOHNSON, Edwin S. | FISHER, Roberta F. | 20 APR 1867 |
| JOHNSON, Edwin T. | REYNOLDS, Harriet Ann | 07 SEP 1863 |
| JOHNSON, Eugene | PIKE, Frances (blk) | 02 MAR 1870 |
| JOHNSON, F.J. | MYERS, M.J. | 16 FEB 1869 |
| JOHNSON, Fleming | COLEMAN, Peggy (blk) | 26 AUG 1869 |
| JOHNSON, Francis | LEWIS, Amanda | 12 AUG 1867 |
| JOHNSON, Frank | TOODLE, Ellen (blk) | 10 AUG 1865 |
| JOHNSON, Frank M. | STETSON, Ann | 24 SEP 1863 |
| JOHNSON, Franklin | LEMMON, Emma E. | 02 MAY 1865 |
| JOHNSON, Frederick | BLANCHARD, Lucy A. | 02 NOV 1865 |
| JOHNSON, Frederick | BROWN, Susan (blk) | 14 MAR 1866 |
| JOHNSON, Frederick | GRAY, Georgiana (blk) | 02 APR 1867 |
| JOHNSON, George | CARTER, Elizabeth (blk) | 24 JUN 1865 |
| JOHNSON, George | SAUNDERS, Louisa (blk) | 05 MAR 1866 |
| JOHNSON, George | CARTER, Cordelia (blk) | 30 SEP 1869 |
| JOHNSON, George | HAWKINS, Clara Ann (blk) | 02 JUN 1870 |
| JOHNSON, George D. | YOUNG, Margaret E. | 05 JUN 1867 |
| JOHNSON, George H. | MATHEWS, Rachel (blk) | 21 DEC 1863 |
| JOHNSON, Henry | WILLMOURE, Mary | 19 OCT 1863 |
| JOHNSON, Henry | THOMAS, Margaret (blk) | 11 MAY 1866 |
| JOHNSON, Henry | SMITH, Rebecca | 04 MAR 1868 |
| JOHNSON, Henry | SNOWDEN, Sarah (blk) | 29 MAY 1868 |
| JOHNSON, Henry | WATERS, Eliza (blk) | 09 SEP 1868 |
| JOHNSON, Henry | JACKSON, Ella (blk) | 20 JAN 1869 |

District of Columbia Marriage Licenses, 1858-1870

| | | |
|---|---|---|
| JOHNSON, Henry | FRANCIS, Laura (blk) | 18 AUG 1869 |
| JOHNSON, Henry | MAGRUDER, Louisa (blk) | 22 DEC 1869 |
| JOHNSON, Henry C. | ROTHWELL, Martha W. | 29 OCT 1866 |
| JOHNSON, Henry Thos. | TOPHAM, Barbara Ann (blk) | 21 DEC 1865 |
| JOHNSON, Homer A. | STRAMAEL, Mollie J. | 02 NOV 1867 |
| JOHNSON, Horace | SCOTT, Francis | 31 MAY 1867 |
| JOHNSON, Horace | COBINGTON, Anna (blk) | 11 MAY 1869 |
| JOHNSON, Howard | STANTON, Mary (blk) | 12 OCT 1865 |
| JOHNSON, Ignatius | COOPER, Sarah (blk) | 26 DEC 1865 |
| JOHNSON, Ignatius | BARNES, Mary Ellen | 07 NOV 1868 |
| JOHNSON, Isaac | NELLUMS, Virginia (blk) | 19 AUG 1868 |
| JOHNSON, Isaac, Jr. | CLARK, Elizabeth (blk) | 02 APR 1870 |
| JOHNSON, Isiah | DORSEY, Sarah A. (blk) | 24 DEC 1866 |
| JOHNSON, J. Harrison | WIMSATT, Mary J. | 19 JAN 1864 |
| JOHNSON, J. LaRae | LEAR, Bettie O'N. | 08 JUN 1863 |
| JOHNSON, J. Orville | AUSTIN, Emma | 03 NOV 1864 |
| JOHNSON, J.M. | KELEHER, Mary E. | 30 DEC 1863 |
| JOHNSON, Jacob | MARTIN, Mary | 23 JUN 1860 |
| JOHNSON, James | FRANCIS, Ivory (blk) | 10 SEP 1864 |
| JOHNSON, James | BROWN, Dorcas Ann (blk) | 29 SEP 1869 |
| JOHNSON, James H. | BROWN, Annie S. | 26 MAR 1863 |
| JOHNSON, James H. | WILKES, Maria (blk) | 22 OCT 1868 |
| JOHNSON, Jef | WILLIAMS, Harriet (blk) | 31 AUG 1867 |
| JOHNSON, Jerome F. | WOODRUFF, Eliza J. | 22 SEP 1866 |
| JOHNSON, Jerry | MACKALL, Annie (blk) | 26 AUG 1869 |
| JOHNSON, Jesse | COLE, Charlotte (blk) | 29 AUG 1868 |
| JOHNSON, John | JENKINS, Susannah | 14 NOV 1859 |
| JOHNSON, John | FOGEL, Ann | 13 DEC 1862 |
| JOHNSON, John | GOLDEN, Hannah (blk) | 11 DEC 1863 |
| JOHNSON, John | LEE, Mary (col'd) | 30 MAY 1864 |
| JOHNSON, John | JOHNSON, Sarah (blk) | 06 MAY 1865 |
| JOHNSON, John | WILLIAMS, Celestia (blk) | 14 SEP 1865 |
| JOHNSON, John | MARTIN, Barbara (blk) | 03 FEB 1866 |
| JOHNSON, John | TURNER, Louisa (blk) | 10 OCT 1866 |
| JOHNSON, John | THOMAS, Elizabeth | 09 OCT 1866 |
| JOHNSON, John | FORD, Amy | 18 JAN 1867 |
| JOHNSON, John | PLEASANTS, Mary (blk) | 02 MAY 1867 |
| JOHNSON, John | DOYLE, Bridget | 06 MAY 1867 |
| JOHNSON, John | CLINE, Mary | 17 AUG 1868 |
| JOHNSON, John | LEE, Mary (blk) | 17 DEC 1868 |
| JOHNSON, John | BALL, Susan (blk) | 07 JAN 1869 |
| JOHNSON, John | TYLER, Emeline (blk) | 15 APR 1870 |
| JOHNSON, John B. | ANDERSON, Harriet | 21 MAR 1867 |
| JOHNSON, Jno. [Benjamin] [10] | FUGETT, Josephine | 08 AUG 1861 |
| JOHNSON, John Dominick | McNAMARRA, Sarah | 13 JUN 1863 |
| JOHNSON, John F. | TIPPETT, Delia C. | 07 DEC 1869 |
| JOHNSON, John H. | ROSS, Fannie (blk) | 15 JUL 1867 |
| JOHNSON, John Henry Francis | TENNY, Sarah (blk) | 14 JAN 1864 |
| JOHNSON, John Henry | CAMPBELL, Charlotte F. (blk) | 23 DEC 1869 |
| JOHNSON, John Thos. | MILLS, Evelina | 06 JUN 1862 |
| JOHNSON, John Thos. | MOSES, Susan D. (blk) | 04 OCT 1864 |
| JOHNSON, Joseph | SMITH, Sarah (blk) | 28 DEC 1865 |
| JOHNSON, Joseph | SULLIVAN, Bettie | 02 JAN 1867 |
| JOHNSON, Joseph L. | BOARMAN, Sarah C. | 04 JUN 1867 |
| JOHNSON, Joshua | LEE, Matilda | 09 DEC 1867 |
| JOHNSON, Lafayette | DAY, Jane (blk) | 21 OCT 1867 |

154

District of Columbia Marriage Licenses, 1858-1870

| | | |
|---|---|---|
| JOHNSON, Larkin | FISHER, Emily (blk) | 05 APR 1860 |
| JOHNSON, Levi | MARTIN, Catherine | 13 NOV 1863 |
| JOHNSON, Levi | DELANY, Mary Eliza (blk) | 22 DEC 1869 |
| JOHNSON, Lewis | STRAHAN, Susan H. | 07 NOV 1859 |
| JOHNSON, Lewis | BANKS, Maria (blk) | 03 DEC 1862 |
| JOHNSON, Lewis | MASI, Matilda L. | 15 DEC 1862 |
| JOHNSON, Lewis | LEWIS, Polly (blk) | 03 JUL 1865 |
| JOHNSON, Lewis | ALEXANDER, Catharine (blk) | 09 JUN 1866 |
| JOHNSON, Lewis | DAYTON, Lucinda (blk) | 17 MAY 1870 |
| JOHNSON, Littleton | MERRICKS, Virginia (blk) | 08 AUG 1866 |
| JOHNSON, Lloyd | BELL, Elizabeth (blk) | 11 AUG 1866 |
| JOHNSON, Major | HENDERSON, Fanny (blk) | 07 MAY 1864 |
| JOHNSON, Major | CHASE, Barbary (blk) | 02 FEB 1869 |
| JOHNSON, Messias | FORTUNE, Georgianna (blk) | 08 DEC 1868 |
| JOHNSON, Moses | SCOTT, Annie (blk) | 14 NOV 1862 |
| JOHNSON, Nathan | JOHNSON, Sally (blk) | 11 NOV 1869 |
| JOHNSON, Nelson | DIGGS, Matilda (blk) | 11 MAY 1866 |
| JOHNSON, Oscar | CONNOR, Nancy (blk) | 30 MAY 1865 |
| JOHNSON, Otto | CRENER, Rosina Barbetta | 25 FEB 1869 |
| JOHNSON, Philip | BOWIE, Margaret (blk) | 13 NOV 1866 |
| JOHNSON, Pius | ANDERSON, Amelia (blk) | 05 JUN 1865 |
| JOHNSON, R. | STOWES, Mary (blk) | 11 JAN 1870 |
| JOHNSON, Randal | BAYLOR, Bettie (blk) | 28 NOV 1866 |
| JOHNSON, Richard | KING, Sarah (blk) | 11 AUG 1864 |
| JOHNSON, Richard | TAYLOR, Mary Ann (blk) | 19 OCT 1865 |
| JOHNSON, Richard | COATS, Louisa (blk) | 15 FEB 1866 |
| JOHNSON, Richard | PAYNE, Josephine (blk) | 11 NOV 1868 |
| JOHNSON, Richard | NOUNAN, Mary (blk) | 14 SEP 1869 |
| JOHNSON, Richard T. | LUSKEY, Catherine C. | 17 DEC 1863 |
| JOHNSON, Robert | DAVIS, Eliza (blk) | 23 SEP 1858 |
| JOHNSON, Robert | HOBIN, Susanna J. | 23 DEC 1859 |
| JOHNSON, Robert | GARRISON, Mary (blk) | 24 DEC 1863 |
| JOHNSON, Robert | O'CONNOR, Mary Ann | 05 MAY 1865 |
| JOHNSON, Robert | CRAWFORD, Darcus Ann (blk) | 11 APR 1866 |
| JOHNSON, Robert | BROWN, Sarah (blk) | 08 DEC 1868 |
| JOHNSON, Robert | ROLLINS, Mary (blk) | 16 DEC 1868 |
| JOHNSON, Robert | TOLLIVER, Louisa (blk) | 09 NOV 1869 |
| JOHNSON, Robert K. | SELF, Elizabeth Ann | 05 JUL 1860 |
| JOHNSON, Robert M. | MINITREE, Ann Rebecca | 05 NOV 1861 |
| JOHNSON, Samuel | BURT, Maria (blk) | 31 DEC 1861 |
| JOHNSON, Samuel | DELL, Sarah (blk) | 19 MAR 1868 |
| JOHNSON, Samuel | TILGHMAN, Sarah Jane (blk) | 10 MAR 1869 |
| JOHNSON, Samuel | JOHNSON, Anna | 28 MAY 1870 |
| JOHNSON, Scipio P. | DADE, Mary (blk) | 27 SEP 1864 |
| JOHNSON, Simeon M. | REILY, Ellen T. | 09 JUL 1861 |
| JOHNSON, Simpson | FUGITT, Sarah F. | 15 JAN 1862 |
| JOHNSON, Squire | BLAKEY, Adaline (blk) | 09 OCT 1867 |
| JOHNSON, Stephen | FORTUNE, Elea Ann (blk) | 21 APR 1864 |
| JOHNSON, T.J. | UTTERBACK, M.J. | 09 DEC 1858 |
| JOHNSON, Thomas | ADDISON, Rachel | 14 APR 1863 |
| JOHNSON, Thomas | GRIFFIN, Margaret (blk) | 13 JAN 1864 |
| JOHNSON, Thomas | JOHNSON, Agnes (blk) | 16 JUL 1864 |
| JOHNSON, Thomas | GREEN, Jennie (blk) | 10 NOV 1864 |
| JOHNSON, Thomas | HENSON, Mary (blk) | 29 AUG 1865 |
| JOHNSON, Thomas | JOHNSON, Ellen (blk) | 21 FEB 1867 |
| JOHNSON, Thomas | BETTER, Mary Jane (blk) | 04 MAY 1867 |

District of Columbia Marriage Licenses, 1858-1870

| | | |
|---|---|---|
| JOHNSON, Thomas | SHEPHERD, Henrietta | 14 MAY 1867 |
| JOHNSON, Thomas | READ, Annie E. | 26 AUG 1867 |
| JOHNSON, Thomas | HENSON, May (blk) | 30 MAY 1868 |
| JOHNSON, Thomas | ATKINS, Lucy J. | 25 NOV 1868 |
| JOHNSON, Thomas A. [12s] | MAGRUDER, Margaret (blk) | 17 MAR 1862 |
| JOHNSON, Thomas C. [10] | STEWART, Susan E. (blk) | 31 JAN 1866 |
| JOHNSON, Thomas E. | McKENNEY, Mary (blk) | 27 NOV 1861 |
| JOHNSON, Thomas E. | SMITH, Mary E. | 05 AUG 1865 |
| JOHNSON, Thomas J. | MURPHY, Sarah J. | 22 SEP 1859 |
| JOHNSON, Thomas J. | HURLEY, Bridget | 15 MAY 1965 |
| JOHNSON, Thomas R. | GALLAHER, M.S. | 31 MAY 1870 |
| JOHNSON, Thomas T. [1c] | EVANS, Emma J. | 04 JUN 1863 |
| JOHNSON, Thornton | TALIAFERRO, Sophia (blk) | 16 JAN 1866 |
| JOHNSON, Urias | FLINCHORN, Martha | 23 DEC 1864 |
| JOHNSON, Washington | WARFIELD, Hellen (blk) | 03 DEC 1868 |
| JOHNSON, Webster | JOHNSON, Margaret (blk) | 18 FEB 1869 |
| JOHNSON, Wesley | BUTLER, Jennie (blk) | 17 NOV 1865 |
| JOHNSON, William | CHAMBERLAIN, Mary E. | 01 NOV 1858 |
| JOHNSON, William | JOHNSON, Catherine (blk) | 16 MAY 1861 |
| JOHNSON, William [11] | BUTLER, Mary Jane (blk) | 15 MAY 1862 |
| JOHNSON, William | STIDMAN, Martha | 04 JAN 1864 |
| JOHNSON, William | JENNINGS, Frances (blk) | 11 FEB 1864 |
| JOHNSON, William | FOREMAN, Catharine (blk) | 06 APR 1864 |
| JOHNSON, William | BROWN, Charlotte (blk) | 27 DEC 1864 |
| JOHNSON, William | McDONALD, Mary | 29 DEC 1864 |
| JOHNSON, William | DAILEY, Mary Ann | 25 FEB 1865 |
| JOHNSON, William [10] | LITTLE, Araminta | 15 MAY 1865 |
| JOHNSON, William | GROSS, Henrietta (blk) | 17 FEB 1866 |
| JOHNSON, William | JOHNSON, Mary (blk) | 20 JUN 1866 |
| JOHNSON, William | [blank], Margaret (blk) | 20 JUN 1866 |
| JOHNSON, William | LOGAN, Mary (blk) | 25 AUG 1866 |
| JOHNSON, William | STARK, Mary (blk) | 18 JUL 1867 |
| JOHNSON, William | FILLEMORE, Louisa (blk) | 13 AUG 1867 |
| JOHNSON, William | YOUNG, Harriet Ann (blk) | 24 DEC 1867 |
| JOHNSON, William | WEST, Elizabeth (blk) | 09 JAN 1868 |
| JOHNSON, Wm. | THOMAS, Betsy | 24 JAN 1867 |
| JOHNSON, William B. | RADCLIFF, Emeline | 01 APR 1863 |
| JOHNSON, William C. | GREEN, Mary H. | 20 JAN 1868 |
| JOHNSON, William D. | BRUCE, Josephine (blk) | 29 DEC 1868 |
| JOHNSON, William F. | HARRISON, Mary R. | 06 MAY 1863 |
| JOHNSON, William H. | KELLY, Mary | 20 APR 1863 |
| JOHNSON, William H. | CARROLL, Bridget | 25 NOV 1864 |
| JOHNSON, William M. | FUGETT, Susan E. | 25 SEP 1866 |
| JOHNSON, William R. | WHITE, Anna J. | 09 MAR 1870 |
| JOHNSON, William S. | CISSEL, Georgiana | 27 OCT 1869 |
| JOHNSON, Wm. T., Rev. | WHEELER, Annie | 23 DEC 1865 |
| JOHNSON, Wyatt | JOHNSON, Mary (blk) | 29 AUG 1864 |
| JOHNSTON, George S. | LEE, Annie E. (blk) | 29 JAN 1862 |
| JOHNSTON, James H. | DIXON, Susannah (blk) | 31 AUG 1866 |
| JOHNSTON, Samuel | HUGHES, Catherine (blk) | 02 DEC 1861 |
| JONES, A.L. | BEACH, Josephine | 11 MAY 1865 |
| JONES, Addison | BRIGGS, Jane | 30 DEC 1859 |
| JONES, Albert | JONES, Emily (blk) | 18 MAY 1866 |
| JONES, Allen | HAMPTON, Lianna | 24 NOV 1866 |
| JONES, Andrew L. | PARSONS, Sarah A. | 31 DEC 1863 |
| JONES, Anthony | MITCHELL, Maria | 12 AUG 1869 |

| | | |
|---|---|---|
| JONES, Armistead | LEMON, Mary Etta (blk) | 19 MAY 1866 |
| JONES, B.R. | TALLY, Letitia | 04 OCT 1859 |
| JONES, Bazil G. | MILLS, Josephine | 23 DEC 1868 |
| JONES, Benjamin L. | WILLIAMS, Alphinia | 20 DEC 1865 |
| JONES, C.R. | SLATFORD, Mary J. | 25 FEB 1867 |
| JONES, Charles | JONES, Catherine | 15 JAN 1861 |
| JONES, Charles | HOLMES, Ann (blk) | 08 JAN 1863 |
| JONES, Charles | FLETCHER, Mary A. (blk) | 09 SEP 1865 |
| JONES, Charles | HERBERT, Julia (blk) | 04 JUN 1866 |
| JONES, Charles | ROLLINS, Eliza (blk) | 22 NOV 1866 |
| JONES, Charles L. | HARRISON, Mary E. | 13 DEC 1865 |
| JONES, Chas. T. | BACON, Olivia | 09 APR 1860 |
| JONES, Churchill | PITTS, Sarah E. | 01 APR 1861 |
| JONES, Cornelius | GATES, Elizabeth | 22 NOV 1866 |
| JONES, Daniel | SYKES, Maria (blk) | 16 APR 1868 |
| JONES, David | BIRMANN, Mary | 16 JAN 1864 |
| JONES, David | WILSON, Emma (blk) | 12 MAR 1866 |
| JONES, Edward | GORDON, Sarah (blk) | 07 SEP 1867 |
| JONES, Edward | MILLER, Maggie E. | 10 MAY 1870 |
| JONES, Edward W. | SPENCER, Ellen C. | 23 APR 1863 |
| JONES, Edwin | McGOWAN, Mary A. | 21 NOV 1859 |
| JONES, Edwin L. | ANDERSON, Hattie F. | 13 OCT 1868 |
| JONES, F. Madison | LODGE, Charlotte (blk) | 26 FEB 1862 |
| JONES, Francis | GARNER, Mary Eliza (blk) | 11 MAY 1870 |
| JONES, Frank | COOK, Rosetta (blk) | 16 NOV 1868 |
| JONES, Franklin Lewis [4] | BROOKS, Georgiana M. (blk) | 21 APR 1868 |
| JONES, Frederick | BROWN, Mary (blk) | 15 DEC 1862 |
| JONES, Frederick W. | OFFUTT, Frances M. | 15 JAN 1862 |
| JONES, George A. | TURNER, Margaret Elizth. | 19 FEB 1861 |
| JONES, George A. | IRWIN, Sarah R. | 31 AUG 1865 |
| JONES, George W. | WELLS, Jane | 11 OCT 1858 |
| JONES, H.A. | FARMER, Caroline L.V. | 21 JAN 1869 |
| JONES, Harry | JOHNSON, Martha (blk) | 10 SEP 1866 |
| JONES, Henry | GARNER, Hetty (blk) | 23 AUG 1859 |
| JONES, Henry | TRAVERS, Catherine | 03 MAR 1863 |
| JONES, Henry | WILLIAMS, Jane (blk) | 24 SEP 1866 |
| JONES, Henry A. | HOWSER, Catherine F. | 07 NOV 1863 |
| JONES, Henry C. | TAYLOR, Cora H. | 04 JAN 1859 |
| JONES, Henry C. | GUNNELL, Fannie A. | 22 AUG 1865 |
| JONES, Hiram L. | WOODRUFF, Nelia E. | 31 MAR 1868 |
| JONES, J.S. | WILEY, E.F. | 25 MAR 1868 |
| JONES, Jacob L. | DOUGLASS, Mary (blk) | 04 JUN 1866 |
| JONES, James | HINDS, Alice | 31 JUL 1861 |
| JONES, James | ATWELL, Ellen | 15 JUL 1864 |
| JONES, James | ELLIS, Jennie | 10 NOV 1864 |
| JONES, James | BROWN, Ann (blk) | 10 NOV 1864 |
| JONES, James | MILLER, Alice (blk) | 08 APR 1865 |
| JONES, James B. | RABBITT, Mary J. | 21 MAR 1861 |
| JONES, James B. | BROWN, Sarah V. | 02 SEP 1868 |
| JONES, James E. | DAVIS, Mary | 14 FEB 1867 |
| JONES, James E. | SMITH, Mary Jane | 03 JUN 1869 |
| JONES, James H. | THOMAS, Martha Catherine | 08 NOV 1860 |
| JONES, James W. | TURNER, Sarah F. | 24 JUN 1865 |
| JONES, James W. | JOHNSON, Elizabeth | 01 AUG 1867 |
| JONES, Jefferson | HALL, Ann (blk) | 01 APR 1869 |
| JONES, Jefferson | LAXLEY, Mary Jane | 02 NOV 1869 |

District of Columbia Marriage Licenses, 1858-1870

| | | |
|---|---|---|
| JONES, Jerry | FISHER, Maria (blk) | 21 JAN 1864 |
| JONES, Jesse F. | DOLIN, Mollie E. | 16 JUL 1869 |
| JONES, John | ACOMB, Fanny | 01 MAY 1862 |
| JONES, John | CARPENTER, Clarissa (blk) | 04 JAN 1865 |
| JONES, John | LEWIS, Eliza | 30 MAY 1865 |
| JONES, John | HANLEY, Julia | 12 NOV 1866 |
| JONES, John | HANLEY, Julia | 02 MAY 1867 |
| JONES, John | CURTIS, Lizzie (blk) | 16 OCT 1867 |
| JONES, John | LOMAX, Elizabeth (blk) | 09 MAR 1868 |
| JONES, John | ROBINSON, Francis (blk) | 06 AUG 1868 |
| JONES, John | LANDON, Susannah | 18 FEB 1869 |
| JONES, John | HENDERSON, Rebecca (blk) | 19 MAR 1869 |
| JONES, John | MARTIN, Ellen (blk) | 22 NOV 1869 |
| JONES, John (by J.B. Ford) | OAKES, Ellen | 09 FEB 1864 |
| JONES, John Augustus | BARNES, Mary Louisa (blk) | 13 AUG 1863 |
| JONES, John E. | MITCHELL, Marion | 27 JUN 1864 |
| JONES, John H. | HAWKINS, Anna (blk) [16 MAR 1871] | 23 APR 1870 |
| JONES, John Henry | JONES, Mary C. | 09 AUG 1864 |
| JONES, John Henry | WILLIAMS, Ann Virginia | 24 JUN 1865 |
| JONES, John Henry | COATS, Mary C. (blk) | 27 AUG 1867 |
| JONES, John L. | BLACK, Mary C. | 06 AUG 1859 |
| JONES, John R. | WHITTAKER, Mary | 12 OCT 1865 |
| JONES, John T. | WALKER, Mary E. | 01 FEB 1859 |
| JONES, John Thomas | ROCK, Elizabeth E. | 09 APR 1860 |
| JONES, John W. [6s] | BAUM, Catharine A. | 05 JUL 1864 |
| JONES, John William | BOSWORTH, Maria R. | 24 JUN 1869 |
| JONES, Joseph | PORTER, Anna | 09 AUG 1859 |
| JONES, Joseph | MITCHELL, Abbey (blk) | 29 APR 1869 |
| JONES, Joseph C. | BRANZILL, Mary Ellen | 31 MAR 1863 |
| JONES, Julius | ATKINSON, Kitty (blk) | 10 FEB 1870 |
| JONES, Lawson | GRANTLEN, Mary Ellen | 24 OCT 1867 |
| JONES, Lewis | GREEN, Mary (blk) | 08 AUG 1865 |
| JONES, Lindsay | LEE, Harriet (blk) | 12 DEC 1866 |
| JONES, Littleton | CLAIBORNE, Sarah (blk) | 26 DEC 1867 |
| JONES, Lloyd T. | MAGRUDER, Henrietta (blk) | 16 NOV 1869 |
| JONES, Louis L. | TULEY, Cecilia E. | 25 APR 1859 |
| JONES, Luke | BROWN, Rachel Ann Elizabeth (blk) | 24 SEP 1866 |
| JONES, Madison | MERRICKS, Jane Rebecca (blk) | 08 MAR 1861 |
| JONES, Major | OXLEY, Annie Redbecca (blk) | 12 AUG 1865 |
| JONES, Nelson | GRIFFIN, Jane (blk) | 12 FEB 1862 |
| JONES, Newton | WHITCOMB, Isabel | 11 FEB 1859 |
| JONES, Nicholas W. | GARRISON, Emma J. | 20 SEP 1862 |
| JONES, Parkison | ROMAN, Ophelia (blk) | 17 JAN 1860 |
| JONES, Peter | DOWD, Kate | 03 JUN 1865 |
| JONES, Philip | LYONS, Emily (blk) | 05 MAY 1870 |
| JONES, Richard | BURGISS, Emma (blk) | 01 SEP 1863 |
| JONES, Richard | WILLIAMS, Celia Ann | 18 FEB 1864 |
| JONES, Richard | CRUSER, Sarah E. (blk) | 01 MAR 1867 |
| JONES, Robert | TABBS, Catherine | 05 NOV 1868 |
| JONES, Robert | BROWN, Drucilla | 30 SEP 1869 |
| JONES, Robert | WILLIAMS, Ellen (blk) | 17 NOV 1869 |
| JONES, Robert C. | MACKENHEIMER, Georgia S. | 29 JAN 1867 |
| JONES, Robert L. | O'TOOLE, Julia | 23 AUG 1864 |
| JONES, Roger | JONES, Frederica B. | 27 DEC 1861 |
| JONES, Samuel | BARNES, Ann Perosia (blk) | 14 AUG 1868 |
| JONES, Samuel | JONES, Elizabeth (blk) | 03 OCT 1868 |

District of Columbia Marriage Licenses, 1858-1870

| | | |
|---|---|---|
| JONES, Samuel A. | CROSS, Sarah A. | 02 APR 1864 |
| JONES, Samuel H. | VENABLE, Mary | 26 NOV 1861 |
| JONES, Samuel W. | ADAMS, Louisa (blk) | 19 JUN 1861 |
| JONES, Samuel Washington | GIBBS, Elizabeth Ann | 05 OCT 1863 |
| JONES, Stephen | COGSWELL, Rebecca (blk) | 14 SEP 1865 |
| JONES, Stephen | LUCAS, Jane (blk) | 29 JAN 1868 |
| JONES, Sylvester | NOLAND, Mary C. | 08 SEP 1868 |
| JONES, Sylvester C. | NOLAND, Caroline | 08 SEP 1868 |
| JONES, Thadeus A. | MAGEE, Emily M. | 12 NOV 1860 |
| JONES, Thomas | CHEEKS, Eliza (blk) | 14 APR 1864 |
| JONES, Thomas | JOHNSON, Lucy Ann (blk) | 20 OCT 1866 |
| JONES, Thomas | GIDDINGS, Susannah | 15 DEC 1866 |
| JONES, Thomas | REDIN, Ruth | 14 JUN 1870 |
| JONES, Thomas H. | JOHNSON, Mary Eliza (blk) | 07 JUN 1860 |
| JONES, Thomas H. | CURTAIN, Catharine | 19 SEP 1865 |
| JONES, Thomas T. [10] | KIRBY, Mary | 28 SEP 1867 |
| JONES, Thornton | NEWMAN, Lucinda (blk) | 25 JUN 1868 |
| JONES, Washington | SMITH, Lucy A. (blk) | 06 MAY 1864 |
| JONES, Washington [11] | BROWN, Emma (blk) | 03 APR 1867 |
| JONES, William | DARRELL, Lucretia | 04 DEC 1861 |
| JONES, William | LOVELESS, Barbara | 12 JUN 1862 |
| JONES, William | BRIGHT, Matilda (blk) | 07 JUN 1866 |
| JONES, William | COLLINS, Elizabeth | 18 SEP 1867 |
| JONES, William | BROWN, Georgiana (blk) | 29 DEC 1869 |
| JONES, William B. | HENSON, Ellen (blk) | 15 MAY 1862 |
| JONES, William B. | TALBERT, Minta Ann Sophia | 15 APR 1863 |
| JONES, William H. [6r] | HILL, Mary J. | 21 JUN 1860 |
| JONES, William H. | BOLDEN, Lucy (blk) | 21 JAN 1863 |
| JONES, William H. | BROWN, Mary E. (blk) | 16 MAY 1867 |
| JONES, William T. | COX, Lucy A. | 10 OCT 1859 |
| JONES, William Walter | HUFFMAN, Caroline | 08 OCT 1858 |
| JONES, Wm. E. | BEHAN, Mary | 03 FEB 1866 |
| JONES, Wm. H. | ROBINSON, Mary Jane (blk) | 07 JUL 1868 |
| JONES, Wm. Henry | BUGWINE, Emily (blk) | 25 AUG 1863 |
| JONES, Wm. W. | MITCHELL, Sarah B. | 13 JAN 1870 |
| JORDAN, Alexander | BURCH, Rebecca S. | 04 MAY 1859 |
| JORDAN, Cëssalius | BEAUREGARD, Katrina | 12 DEC 1867 |
| JORDAN, Charles | TAYLOR, Lavinia (blk) | 22 OCT 1863 |
| JORDAN, Charles H. | TALBOTT, Mary F. | 10 AUG 1861 |
| JORDAN, David | CHESLEY, Mary (blk) | 11 SEP 1862 |
| JORDAN, George | JOHNSTON, Lizzie (blk) | 27 JAN 1868 |
| JORDAN, Harry [7a] | BRAUNER, Alice V. | 08 OCT 1867 |
| JORDAN, Henry | CARTER, Sarah (blk) | 27 DEC 1865 |
| JORDAN, Hilliary | BACKUS, Maria (blk) | 16 APR 1866 |
| JORDAN, Isaac | HAWKINS, Ellen (blk) | 13 DEC 1866 |
| JORDAN, James | BARRY, Mary (blk) | 22 AUG 1867 |
| JORDAN, John | HALL, Sidney (blk) | 05 NOV 1864 |
| JORDAN, Joshua | BUTLER, Catherine (blk) | 18 AUG 1869 |
| JORDAN, Luke | JAYCOCK, Catherine (blk) | 20 JUL 1867 |
| JORDAN, Sylvester | SHEPHERD, Louisa | 08 DEC 1864 |
| JORDAN, Wesley | WILSON, Susan | 26 OCT 1869 |
| JORDAN, William | DANACUR, Barbara | 31 OCT 1863 |
| JORDAN, William Pitman | TUCKER, Emily Eliza | 16 MAY 1864 |
| JOSEPH, Benjamin | RAMMERER, Kathrina | 18 MAY 1865 |
| JOSEPH, George | SIMS, Minty (blk) | 12 DEC 1868 |
| JOST, Abraham | WALTER, Kate | 07 MAY 1870 |

District of Columbia Marriage Licenses, 1858-1870

| | | |
|---|---|---|
| JOURDAN, Alexander | KIECKHOEFER, Cecilia A. | 26 JUL 1869 |
| JOY, Charles [1e] | WINGATE, Sarah Emma | 15 NOV 1865 |
| JOY, Charles H. | ADAMS, Jane | 30 NOV 1866 |
| JOY, Gilbert L. | EDMONSTON, Louisa R. (col'd) | 23 APR 1863 |
| JOY, Joseph | KOETHER, Pauline | 27 APR 1869 |
| JOY, Wm. H. | MARSHALL, Annie | 12 JAN 1867 |
| JOYCE, Daniel | CRYER, Winney (blk) | 07 APR 1862 |
| JOYCE, James W. | KIBBY, Sarah | 04 MAY 1865 |
| JOYCE, John | MULLOWAY, Ellen | 08 DEC 1865 |
| JOYCE, John L. | WARD, Mary A. | 05 FEB 1866 |
| JOYCE, Michael | O'CONNER, Catherine | 10 MAY 1859 |
| JOYCE, William | DOUGLASS, Alice | 20 APR 1866 |
| JUDGE, Jesse J. | MEREDITH, Sara E. | 05 JAN 1864 |
| JUDSON, Oliver A. [4] | BOYCE, Elizabeth | 18 APR 1866 |
| JUDSON, Robert F. | GEAGE, Elizabeth | 28 NOV 1865 |
| JUDSON, S.E. | GILL, Elizabeth M. | 03 NOV 1869 |
| JULIHN, Magnus L. | HIGDEN, Eliza Regina | 08 FEB 1864 |
| JUMP, Edward | ROGERS, Emily C. | 21 JAN 1868 |
| JÜNEMANN, William | SHEPPACH, Barbette | 30 MAY 1866 |
| JUNK, Charles | SHUMAN, Emma | 06 DEC 1858 |
| JURIX, William F. | GROSS, Susan, Mrs. | 07 OCT 1869 |
| JUST, Abraham | ERVERLING, Lena | 20 MAY 1864 |
| JUTT, Marcellus | ADAMS, Mary | 01 JUL 1869 |

## K

| | | |
|---|---|---|
| KAHLERT, Augustus | DORR, Elizabeth | 12 APR 1859 |
| KAHLERT, Herman | JENNINGS, Elizabeth | 25 NOV 1867 |
| KAHN, Moses | GRAF, Fannie | 10 APR 1867 |
| KAHN, Samuel | TURNER, Eliza (blk) | 20 OCT 1864 |
| KAIGHN, Maurice M. | TOWN, Angie L. | 07 SEP 1866 |
| KAIN, John | MAHONEY, Susan (blk) | 06 JUN 1865 |
| KAIN, Nathaniel | FLETCHER, Henny (blk) | 02 JUN 1863 |
| KAIN, Patrick | KEIGON, Mary Ann | 25 FEB 1862 |
| KAISER, Henry | SCHULTZ, Rosalina | 29 APR 1861 |
| KAISER, John | SCHNEIDER, Christine | 13 AUG 1862 |
| KAISER, John | BARTHOLOMEW, Ann Elizabeth | 28 OCT 1865 |
| KAISER, John | SNYDER, Mena | 11 AUG 1869 |
| KAISER, John H. | SCHROEDEL, Mary | 02 JUL 1863 |
| KAISER, John W. | CUNNINGHAM, Georgie | 02 MAR 1865 |
| KAN, Adam | DONOHOO, Jane | 01 JAN 1863 |
| KANE, Alfred | WILLIAMS, Carrie (blk) | 10 AUG 1869 |
| KANE, Carson [12s] | TREAKLE, Henrietta | 27 NOV 1860 |
| KANE, Carson Watson | FERGUSON, Marietta | 03 MAY 1866 |
| KANE, Dennis | SULLIVAN, Mary | 06 NOV 1865 |
| KANE, Edward | MURRAY, Mary | 14 JAN 1865 |
| KANE, James J. | SIS, Mary | 08 NOV 1869 |
| KANE, John F. | KIERNAN, Mary Ann | 27 JUN 1860 |
| KANE, John J. | EBELING, Therese | 06 JUL 1869 |
| KANE, Patrick | LYNCH, Catherine | 05 JUN 1862 |
| KANE, Patrick | LABYN, Winifred | 01 AUG 1863 |
| KANE, Thomas | DILLON, Maria | 03 JUL 1867 |
| KANE, William L. | TREXLER, Emma F. | 11 APR 1870 |
| KAILER, Henry | BAUER, Barbara | 17 MAR 1860 |
| KANNASTON, George A. | JOHNSON, Willie Ellen | 06 JAN 1864 |
| KANODE, Albert H. | FRANCE, Rebecca | 12 MAY 1863 |

District of Columbia Marriage Licenses, 1858-1870

| | | |
|---|---|---|
| KANOUSE, Ezra | FITZGERALD, Annie | 22 FEB 1865 |
| KANT, Christian Edward | WIEGMANN, Gesine Elizabeth | 15 MAY 1868 |
| KAPPOTE, Jacob | LOFMIN, Sophia | 21 DEC 1866 |
| KARBELES, Leo | MUNDHEIM, Sarah | 13 APR 1866 |
| KARNEY, Philip | ROHAN, Margaret | 29 OCT 1864 |
| KARPP, Joseph L. | WALKER, Mary L. | 14 AUG 1862 |
| KARR, Jacob | ROUTERBERG, Julia | 08 OCT 1860 |
| KARSH, Jacob | EVANS, Mary Ann | 08 FEB 1865 |
| KASE, Albert | GRAHAM, Annie E. | 17 OCT 1865 |
| KASSON, Charles D. | DRAYTON, E.J. | 01 MAY 1868 |
| KASSON, Charles D. | DRAYTON, E.J. | 28 FEB 1870 |
| KATHMAN, Clement | KRAFT, Adelaid | 04 APR 1863 |
| KATS, Gray W. | LEVINSTON, Mary E. | 26 JUL 1864 |
| KAUBER, Christian | KIEVALIER, Margaret | 13 APR 1863 |
| KAUFFMANN, Isaac | COHEN, Jeanette | 20 MAY 1859 |
| KAUFMAN, Aaron | KAUFMAN, Hanche | 31 AUG 1859 |
| KAUFMAN, Christian | SCHWARTZ, Eliza | 25 APR 1867 |
| KAUFMAN, John | NEWMAN, Augusta Louisa | 07 FEB 1862 |
| KAUFMAN, Jonas | STRAUSE, Esther | 29 DEC 1865 |
| KAUFMAN, Joseph | HEARD, Sophia | 23 JUL 1861 |
| KAUFMAN, Joseph | STERN, Rose | 29 NOV 1861 |
| KAUFMAN, Levi J. | LOWMAN, Emma | 16 OCT 1865 |
| KAUFMAN, Louis | FISHMAN, Emma | 21 MAR 1865 |
| KAUFMAN, Robert | LOUTER, Virginia | 24 SEP 1869 |
| KAUFMAN, Wolf | GANS, Rachel | 13 SEP 1867 |
| KAVANAGH, Peter | GLEESBROOK, Kate | 04 NOV 1868 |
| KAVANAUGH, James H. | SNYDER, Mary Elizabeth | 25 FEB 1865 |
| KAVANAUGH, John [2] | DOVE, Martha A. | 10 FEB 1868 |
| KAVANAUGH, John M. | COHEN, Susan M. | 12 APR 1865 |
| KAVANAUGH, Thomas | KEENAN, Bridget | 11 FEB 1860 |
| KAYSER, Christian Anton | SCHAFER, Josephine | 30 JUN 1866 |
| KAYSER, Joseph A. | LATHAM, Harriet | 15 JUL 1861 |
| KAYSER, Peter Louis | MILLER, Laura | 07 AUG 1863 |
| KEAKHAN, Alexander | STRIDER, Ann E. | 04 APR 1864 |
| KEALE, Henry C. | APPLER, Mary L. | 20 JAN 1863 |
| KEAN, Joseph | GLEAVES, Rose Ann | 20 SEP 1865 |
| KEAN, Leonard | PRECELL, Ella | 30 JAN 1868 |
| KEAN, William Horace | WROE, Adele | 13 SEP 1864 |
| KEANE, John T. | O'CONNER, Mary | 16 SEP 1865 |
| KEANE, Thomas T. | DONOVAN, Ellen | 23 MAY 1870 |
| KEARCE, Patrick | O'CONNOR, Johanna | 07 SEP 1858 |
| KEARDLEY, Jefferson | WINSTON, Harriet | 27 AUG 1864 |
| KEARN, George A. | MARTIN, Ann | 03 MAR 1863 |
| KEARNEY, James | O'REILY, Louisa | 01 SEP 1862 |
| KEARNEY, Michael | SHEA, Martha | 25 MAR 1861 |
| KEARNEY, Richard F. | CALVERT, Rose | 25 JUL 1866 |
| KEARNEY, Robert S. | THOMPSON, Ann E. | 20 SEP 1865 |
| KEARNEY, William | HENRY, Isabella | 21 JUN 1864 |
| KEARNS, John | SHEED, Susanah | 27 DEC 1860 |
| KEARNS, Matthew | FAHERTY, Mary | 13 SEP 1862 |
| KEATING, Edward | CALLAHAN, Ellen | 09 JAN 1862 |
| KEATING, Michael | CADY, Margaret | 30 JUN 1862 |
| KEAVES, James S. | DOUGHERTY, Frances Ann | 20 JUL 1864 |
| KECK, Julius N. | GODFREY, Mary M. | 28 NOV 1859 |
| KEE, Thomas [4] | SMITH, Carrie | 30 SEP 1867 |
| KEE, William | SHERMAN, Susan | 16 JUL 1864 |

District of Columbia Marriage Licenses, 1858-1870

| | | |
|---|---|---|
| KEEFE, John | BROSWHAN, Bridget | 13 AUG 1866 |
| KEEFE, Martin | DEVINE, Mary | 06 DEC 1867 |
| KEEFE, Owen | CULLAHAN, Bridget | 19 JAN 1861 |
| KEEFE, William | DEVERAUX, Mary C. | 10 APR 1866 |
| KEEFER, Philip F.H. | PAYNE, Mary E. | 19 APR 1870 |
| KEEGIN, Charles | KELLY, Bridget | 21 NOV 1866 |
| KEELER, Eben | SULLIVAN, Hanna | 30 SEP 1864 |
| KEELER, Lewis W. | FRANKLIN, Marcia T. | 20 AUG 1861 |
| KEELEY, Laurence | LAUGHLIN, Margaret | 07 JAN 1859 |
| KEELING, Charles | TILLMAN, Martha (blk) | 11 JUN 1866 |
| KEELING, Nathaniel | DICKENS, Summer (blk) | 02 APR 1869 |
| KEEN, Alexander D. | TOWNER, Kate | 14 APR 1870 |
| KEEN, George T. | McCLOSKY, Sarah E. | 24 OCT 1865 |
| KEENAN, Francis Henry | FITZGERALD, Jane | 02 AUG 1862 |
| KEENAN, John H. | COOLEY, Samuletta | 07 SEP 1863 |
| KEENAN, Michael | KAUSER, Elizabeth | 01 JUL 1863 |
| KEENAN, Michael | MALONE, Ellen | 28 SEP 1863 |
| KEENAN, Michael | O'NIEL, Ann | 30 APR 1864 |
| KEENAN, Michael | McKENNA, Margaret | 31 DEC 1867 |
| KEENAN, William | RYAN, Eliza | 02 MAY 1862 |
| KEENE, John | DODSON, Jane M. | 10 NOV 1859 |
| KEENE, John W. | DOWLING, Josephine | 26 DEC 1868 |
| KEENE, Thomas P. | NEEDHAM, Mary E. | 23 SEP 1867 |
| KEESE, Frederick | TAYLOR, Kate | 28 OCT 1869 |
| KEESE, John Henry Louis | LEHNE, Sophia Bertha | 06 JUN 1866 |
| KEEVER, Michael | RYDER, Annie | 23 JAN 1864 |
| KEFERSTEIN, Emil J. | MÖLICH, Bertha | 24 MAR 1863 |
| KEHOE, John | SUMMERS, Winney | 07 AUG 1863 |
| KEHOE, Thomas | WHELAN, Fanny | 30 NOV 1861 |
| KEILY, Timothy | McCANN, Ellen | 27 JAN 1866 |
| KEIN, Peter | MELHORN, Fredericka | 16 NOV 1861 |
| KEINSENSTEIN, Isaac | PINKNS, Johana | 20 FEB 1862 |
| KEISER, Eustice | HAGER, Mary S. | 04 APR 1863 |
| KEITHLEY, George [6le] | KEITHLEY, Ann | 28 FEB 1868 |
| KEITHLEY, John H. | BROWN, Susan | 25 OCT 1860 |
| KEITHLEY, John T. | WILKERSON, Amelia J. | 27 APR 1864 |
| KEITHLEY, Richard [6l] | MUGG, Mary Elizth. | 15 AUG 1861 |
| KEITHLY, Thomas W. | PARSONS, Miranda B. | 06 DEC 1865 |
| KELCHNER, John H. | GARNER, Martlieda E. | 11 DEC 1860 |
| KELEHER, Fergus | CLANCEY, Bridget | 17 JUN 1865 |
| KELEHER, James | LYON, Honora | 18 AUG 1868 |
| KELEHER, James T., Jr. | COLLINS, Mary M. | 04 MAY 1860 |
| KELIHER, Michael | SULLIVAN, Mary | 09 MAY 1868 |
| KELL, Robert | SURRICK, Susan | 03 MAR 1863 |
| KELLAND, Philip | MILLER, Letia | 12 MAR 1862 |
| KELLAR, Andrew J. | BIGGS, Mary A.R. | 08 NOV 1869 |
| KELLER, Charles H. | COULSON, Joanna | 01 APR 1865 |
| KELLER, Daniel S. [6le] | HEUSTIS, Martha E. | 03 MAY 1866 |
| KELLER, Henry | ENGELHAGEN, Adelheid | 19 JUL 1860 |
| KELLEY, James | BALDWIN, Mary Ann | 15 SEP 1866 |
| KELLEY, John | GAYLOR, Lizzie | 18 SEP 1863 |
| KELLEY, Thomas | JOYCE, Catherine | 13 JUL 1863 |
| KELLEY, William T. | BRINNEN, Maggie A. | 09 MAY 1866 |
| KELLOGG, George | KENNEDY, Mary | 11 APR 1863 |
| KELLY, Aaron | JOHNSON, Milly (blk) | 06 FEB 1867 |
| KELLY, Bernard | O'HARE, Margaret | 08 NOV 1862 |

District of Columbia Marriage Licenses, 1858-1870

| | | |
|---|---|---|
| KELLY, Bernard | WOODS, Rose | 11 JUL 1868 |
| KELLY, Charles H. | DAILEY, Mary | 29 APR 1865 |
| KELLY, Daniel | CURTON, Bridgett | 14 JAN 1860 |
| KELLY, Daniel | BREENIAN, Kate | 14 OCT 1865 |
| KELLY, Edward | GARRITY, Bridget | 27 SEP 1865 |
| KELLY, Francis | McNAMARA, Margaret | 27 JAN 1870 |
| KELLY, Henry | CRUMP, Annah J. | 28 APR 1868 |
| KELLY, Hubert | NAILOR, Mary | 27 NOV 1867 |
| KELLY, James | LIBBICK, Mary | 08 JUL 1864 |
| KELLY, James | JONES, Josephine | 22 APR 1865 |
| KELLY, James | FOLEY, Honora | 18 NOV 1865 |
| KELLY, James C. [8] | REEVES, Mary Jane | 11 FEB 1869 |
| KELLY, James Henry | MUNDLE, Martha (blk) | 03 JUN 1865 |
| KELLY, James J. | STALL, Amanda | 06 NOV 1865 |
| KELLY, John | GREEN, Bridget | 05 MAR 1859 |
| KELLY, John | O'BRIEN, Ellen | 22 AUG 1861 |
| KELLY, John | SHEA, Mary | 04 MAY 1863 |
| KELLY, John | DEHON, Catherine | 24 OCT 1863 |
| KELLY, John | KINNEY, Catherine | 30 DEC 1865 |
| KELLY, John | HARRIS, Matilda | 07 SEP 1866 |
| KELLY, John | NEILL, Johanna | 16 JAN 1867 |
| KELLY, John | WATERS, Rose | 31 MAR 1869 |
| KELLY, John F. | QUILL, Eliza | 25 FEB 1865 |
| KELLY, John T. | SULLIVAN, Ellen | 30 JUL 1867 |
| KELLY, Malachi J. | BALDWIN, Catharine V. | 01 SEP 1865 |
| KELLY, Martin | HENNESSY, Catherine | 17 JAN 1863 |
| KELLY, Michael | KENNEDY, Mary | 14 FEB 1863 |
| KELLY, Michael | FARRELL, Catharine | 15 APR 1865 |
| KELLY, Michael Frank | FREEMAN, Lizzie | 11 JUN 1866 |
| KELLY, Michael James | SULLIVAN, Ellen | 29 DEC 1862 |
| KELLY, Owen | WARD, Matilda | 06 OCT 1864 |
| KELLY, Paradise | MORTIMER, Carrie | 27 JUN 1868 |
| KELLY, Patrick | DAILY, Mary | 07 JAN 1864 |
| KELLY, Patrick | O'CONNOR, Kate | 23 JUN 1869 |
| KELLY, Peter J. | HARRIGON, Ellen | 13 SEP 1862 |
| KELLY, Reuben | SIMS, Martha (blk) | 28 MAR 1870 |
| KELLY, Thomas | GORMAN, Johanna | 04 OCT 1864 |
| KELLY, Thomas | KRAFT, Louisa | 02 APR 1866 |
| KELLY, Thomas | HINES, Margaret | 24 OCT 1868 |
| KELLY, Thomas C. | McPHERSON, Kate | 01 MAY 1863 |
| KELLY, Thornton | JACKSON, Charlotte (blk) | 14 MAR 1864 |
| KELLY, William | GRIFFIN, Jane | 11 FEB 1859 |
| KELLY, William | WELSH, Margaret | 07 APR 1862 |
| KELLY, William | COLLAN, Julia | 08 APR 1868 |
| KELLY, William | HEPBURN, Maria (blk) | 16 OCT 1868 |
| KELLY, William | CLARK, Elizabeth (blk) | 06 DEC 1869 |
| KELLY, William H. | GOODSON, Henrietta | 02 APR 1861 |
| KELPY, Anthony | JOY, Alberta | 24 FEB 1865 |
| KELSY, Judge | McCOY, Sallie (blk) | 15 JUN 1865 |
| KEMP, Constantine | FARROW, Bettie | 29 JUL 1868 |
| KEMP, John | FITZGERALD, Catherine | 14 NOV 1863 |
| KEMP, Samuel R. | DONOLSON, Sarah Y. | 09 AUG 1869 |
| KEMP, Solomon | LISCOMB, Matilda (blk) | 25 JUN 1867 |
| KEMP, William H. [6r] | HEFFNER, Mary E. | 26 FEB 1861 |
| KENDALL, George | BATES, Martha | 01 AUG 1867 |
| KENDRICK, George R. | GILL, Martha A. | 17 FEB 1863 |

District of Columbia Marriage Licenses, 1858-1870

| | | |
|---|---|---|
| KENDRICK, William F. | SHEY, Hannah | 06 NOV 1862 |
| KENDRICK, William T. [12s] | SEARS, Virginia C. | 18 JAN 1861 |
| KENGLA, Luis | CASSELL, Emma | 25 NOV 1863 |
| KENNALLY, John | CONNORS, Julia | 16 MAR 1867 |
| KENNAUGH, William E. | BROWN, Seraphina | 30 JUN 1868 |
| KENNEALY, John | GRANT, Bridget | 28 APR 1862 |
| KENNEDY, Barney | McANNALLY, Rose | 19 APR 1869 |
| KENNEDY, Daniel | SHEEHY, Bridget | 19 NOV 1864 |
| KENNEDY, J.C. | FERRON, Anna C. | 12 OCT 1865 |
| KENNEDY, James | FLAHERTY, Margaret | 03 FEB 1865 |
| KENNEDY, James | CONNEL, Mary | 24 APR 1865 |
| KENNEDY, John | CONNOR, Margaret | 20 DEC 1861 |
| KENNEDY, John | COLLINS, Katherine | 02 JUN 1863 |
| KENNEDY, John | HYNES, Catharine | 14 DEC 1864 |
| KENNEDY, John | SHEA, Ann | 19 NOV 1864 |
| KENNEDY, John P. | SNYDER, Sarah A. | 15 NOV 1866 |
| KENNEDY, John T. | WILSON, Louise | 04 OCT 1869 |
| KENNEDY, Landon S. | ENGLISH, Lucy A. | 26 MAY 1864 |
| KENNEDY, Thomas | MORTIMER, Elizabeth | 11 AUG 1865 |
| KENNEDY, Thomas | COTTER, Ellen M. | 13 JUL 1868 |
| KENNEDY, William | GRACE, Margaret | 09 AUG 1862 |
| KENNEDY, William | KENDRICK, Margaret | 08 JUN 1864 |
| KENNER, Henry G. | TURTON, Mary | 28 JUN 1864 |
| KENNESTON, George | JOHNSON, Willie E. | 15 OCT 1862 |
| KENNEY, Christian | RYAN, Margaret | 22 JAN 1862 |
| KENNEY, Patrick | MURPHY, Eliza | 29 AUG 1862 |
| KENNEY, Peter | HILLIARD, Catherine | 09 JAN 1862 |
| KENNEY, Robert | BEACH, Catharine | 05 SEP 1864 |
| KENNY, Patrick | McANDREWS, Kate | 23 JUN 1865 |
| KENT, Elphinston | POOL, Mary | 30 MAR 1863 |
| KENT, Frederick W. | MULLIN, Annie | 02 AUG 1865 |
| KENT, W.W.E. | JOHNSON, Jennie | 02 AUG 1865 |
| KEOGH, John | LYNCH, Mary | 17 AUG 1864 |
| KEOGH, John M. | FLYNN, Alice | 05 FEB 1864 |
| KEOUGH, Michael | GALVIN, Margaret | 04 FEB 1860 |
| KEOUGH, Thomas | GAVIN, Alice | 23 JUN 1859 |
| KEPLER, Wm. P.P. [4] | ARNOLD, Mary Elizabeth | 25 JUN 1866 |
| KEPPEL, David | CUSICK, Mary | 30 APR 1859 |
| KEPPLER, Anton | WALKER, Susanna | 18 APR 1860 |
| KEPPLER, George H. | PULLIN, Mary | 27 MAR 1860 |
| KER, Charles H. | TRIPLETT, Sarah V. | 21 DEC 1864 |
| KER, James | CHAPMAN, Rebecca B. | 29 DEC 1858 |
| KERBEY, John S. | HYATT, Kate E. | 08 JAN 1863 |
| KERDY, Jefferson | SCOTT, Mary (blk) | 23 NOV 1868 |
| KERFOOT, William Turner | CHAPIN, Ella Mosier | 19 APR 1869 |
| KERN, Charles H. | CRAMSTON, Alice | 30 MAY 1867 |
| KERN, George | MAHLER, Henge | 12 JUL 1862 |
| KERNICK, John | GRAY, Margaret | 12 SEP 1864 |
| KERNS, John R. | BEACH, Sarah A. | 25 JUN 1868 |
| KERPER, George W. | McKINNEY, Catharine | 04 MAY 1863 |
| KERR, Charles | KELLY, Kate | 19 MAY 1865 |
| KERR, Charles Goldsborough [4] | JOHNSON, Ella | 18 APR 1867 |
| KERR, Samuel | HUTCHINSON, Mary | 16 APR 1862 |
| KERR, William R. | KIERMAN, Kate | 28 DEC 1867 |
| KERSBY, Joseph | McNANA, Anna | 02 FEB 1869 |
| KERSCHER, Joseph | FOLKER, Catharine | 18 JAN 1865 |

District of Columbia Marriage Licenses, 1858-1870

| | | |
|---|---|---|
| KESLEY, William | HAIN, Amelia | 08 NOV 1869 |
| KESSLER, Albert | GUENTHER, Rose | 30 APR 1864 |
| KESSLER, George | SCHULTZ, Louisa | 12 NOV 1863 |
| KESSLER, Justus | BACKHAUSEN, Mina | 15 JUN 1863 |
| KESSLER, Paul | PAYNE, Lovina | 23 JUN 1865 |
| KETCHAM, Orlando C. | BRENNON, Annie | 15 FEB 1865 |
| KETCHAM, Orlando C. | COLLINS, Emma | 11 MAY 1869 |
| KETLAND, William | MITCHELL, Malinda | 07 JUN 1862 |
| KETTLER, Louis | KNAUST, Eliese | 21 APR 1870 |
| KETTLER, Louis | KNAUST, Eliese | 21 APR 1870 |
| KETTLER, William | FISCHER, Maria Rosina | 09 SEP 1858 |
| KETY, George Washington | TABBS, Margaret Virginia (blk) | 29 OCT 1867 |
| KEUCHEL, Anthony | BORN, Henrietta | 26 NOV 1860 |
| KEY, H.H. | TURNER, Hanna M. | 05 OCT 1867 |
| KEY, Henry | LACEY, Mary Ann (blk) | 27 FEB 1867 |
| KEY, Humphrey | FERRALL, Lucy M. | 08 APR 1861 |
| KEY, McIntyre | BURR, Mary (blk) | 28 SEP 1863 |
| KEY, Walter | BATIS, Sallie | 09 AUG 1867 |
| KEY, William | REEVES, Celia | 25 MAR 1863 |
| KEYES, Winston | PLUMMER, Fanny (blk) | 04 MAR 1870 |
| KEYS, Charles E. | GRAY, Virginia | 15 NOV 1865 |
| KEYS, Charles M. | RAY, Martha A. | 20 NOV 1863 |
| KEYS, David | BROWN, Mary (blk) | 08 AUG 1868 |
| KEYS, James B. | HOOPER, Annie L. | 25 AUG 1866 |
| KEYS, James H. | HARDIN, Sarah C. | 28 FEB 1861 |
| KEYS, John | DOYLE, Mary | 23 APR 1862 |
| KEYS, Richard | DIGGS, Nancy | 18 MAR 1870 |
| KEYSER, Benjamin M. | TODD, Esther | 21 OCT 1859 |
| KEYWORTH, Howard Q. | TOWERS, Laura Jane | 23 FEB 1869 |
| KICHER, Gotlieb | SCHMIDT, Mary | 09 JAN 1862 |
| KIDD, Robert | GOOD, Johannah (blk) | 19 SEP 1868 |
| KIDDER, Frank | MURPHY, Sarah | 27 JAN 1869 |
| KIDNEY, William | CLANCEY, Alice | 31 MAY 1860 |
| KIDWELL, Alfred | GRAY, Sarah Ellen | 13 MAR 1860 |
| KIDWELL, Allison C. [7a] | CLARKE, Annie E. | 21 MAR 1867 |
| KIDWELL, Arthur W. | KIDWELL, Frances E. | 08 MAR 1859 |
| KIDWELL, James H. | HARRISON, Jane E. | 26 APR 1859 |
| KIDWELL, James W. | WELLS, Jemima W.S. | 24 FEB 1859 |
| KIDWELL, Jeremiah L. | BARKER, Maria L. | 17 DEC 1864 |
| KIDWELL, Levi | BIGGS, Margaret A. | 21 AUG 1861 |
| KIDWELL, Richard | WELLS, Lavenia | 18 JUN 1859 |
| KIDWELL, Thomas | PARKER, Mary Francis | 14 NOV 1867 |
| KIDWELL, Thomas J. | STORM, Sarah | 02 SEP 1864 |
| KIDWELL, Thomas J. | SCOTT, Rosannah | 27 NOV 1865 |
| KIDWELL, William A. [6s] | ARNOLD, Mary | 22 SEP 1864 |
| KIDWELL, William H. | KRAFT, Louisa V. | 09 FEB 1863 |
| KIDWELL, William H. | HUTCHINSON, Sarah Jane | 21 SEP 1869 |
| KIEFER, Conrad | GERNHARD, Eliza | 30 JUN 1860 |
| KIEFER, William G. | O'NEAL, Joanna | 19 JUN 1863 |
| KIELHOLTZ, Wm. H. | HARRINGTION, Mary A.W. | 25 OCT 1859 |
| KIENTLER, Morritz | FOLY, Anna | 28 OCT 1863 |
| KIENY, Christopher | BRIGHTUPT, Agnes | 12 SEP 1865 |
| KIERNAN, Lawrence | O'RORKE, Minnie | 18 NOV 1864 |
| KIERNAN, Philip | KEARNEY, Kate | 24 DEC 1862 |
| KILBOURNE, James P. | DICKENS, Kate | 19 OCT 1863 |
| KILBY, John C. | ROACH, Mary Virginia | 10 JUN 1862 |

District of Columbia Marriage Licenses, 1858-1870

| | | |
|---|---|---|
| KILBY, Solomon R. | TYLER, Lotta | 15 JUL 1869 |
| KILCOYNE, Thomas | KANE, Ann | 10 JUN 1863 |
| KILDUFF, Thomas | DOFT, Mary C. | 02 SEP 1863 |
| KILLBRIDE, Owan | HOYNE, Maggie | 02 SEP 1867 |
| KILLEN, George | RILEY, Margaret | 26 JUL 1862 |
| KILLINGER, Philip W. | HATTER, Mary E. | 30 OCT 1858 |
| KILLMON, John M. | KIBBLE, Mary C.C. | 01 SEP 1858 |
| KILLMORE, William H. | MITCHELL, Emma R. | 07 SEP 1868 |
| KILMARTIN, Bernard | BOYLE, Mary | 22 NOV 1864 |
| KILMARTIN, Timothy | LYNCH, Bridget | 04 AUG 1866 |
| KILROY, Andrew | MAGEE, Ellen | 26 APR 1862 |
| KILROY, Peter | CONDRY, Margaret | 12 JAN 1860 |
| KIMBALL, E.S., Dr. | PEARSON, Elizabeth M. | 29 JUN 1868 |
| KIMBALL, Edward S. | ANDREWS, Louisa | 03 OCT 1864 |
| KIMBLE, John W. [6r] | LONG, Mary Ophelia | 06 MAR 1861 |
| KIMBLE, M.H. | HASLIP, L.A. | 07 JUN 1866 |
| KIMMEL, Hiram | McFAUL, Mary L. | 01 MAY 1865 |
| KIMMELL, Charles A. | COGGINS, Lydia F. | 10 OCT 1866 |
| KIMPE, Constatine | BARRY, Joanna | 04 JAN 1868 |
| KINALEY, Patrick | DOWNES, Margaret | 02 DEC 1865 |
| KINDRE, Daniel A. | ABELS, Frances | 21 FEB 1865 |
| KINDSCLUCK, Frederick | SCHMIDT, Elizabeth | 30 MAR 1863 |
| KINES, James F. | KRIER, Amanda M. | 15 MAY 1862 |
| KING, Adam | HUMBACH, Francisco | 22 SEP 1868 |
| KING, Albert | WALTER, Barbara | 21 SEP 1868 |
| KING, Alonzo H. | ELLIS, Anna M. | 22 NOV 1858 |
| KING, Andrew A. | BROWN, Louise (blk) | 21 MAR 1870 |
| KING, Benjamin | RIDGLEY, Eliza (blk) | 24 AUG 1859 |
| KING, Benjamin | SULLIVAN, Harriet F. | 19 DEC 1860 |
| KING, Charles | TUBMAN, Laura V. | 23 FEB 1864 |
| KING, Charles D. | JEFFERSON, Mary A. | 28 MAY 1868 |
| KING, Charles H. | JENKINS, Jane | 16 AUG 1864 |
| KING, Charles H. | RAGAN, Julia D. | 17 FEB 1869 |
| KING, Charles W. | COX, Emily V. | 01 SEP 1863 |
| KING, Charles W. | McCORMICK, Mary | 28 NOV 1865 |
| KING, Daniel E. | THOMPSON, Mary Ella Rose | 31 DEC 1868 |
| KING, Edgar Childs [5] | WALL, Lucinda Anna | 09 SEP 1867 |
| KING, Edmund | COX, Johanna | 07 OCT 1864 |
| KING, Edmund | ROSS, Violet (blk) | 13 JUL 1868 |
| KING, Edwin | SMITH, Nancy (blk) | 07 NOV 1868 |
| KING, Fernando | PEERCE, Martha Ann | 29 JUL 1864 |
| KING, Francis | DENNISON, Elizabeth | 13 AUG 1861 |
| KING, George E. | REYNOLDS, Marion | 19 DEC 1868 |
| KING, Henry | SICKLE, Sophia | 15 AUG 1860 |
| KING, Henry | STRAUSS, Caroline | 11 SEP 1861 |
| KING, Henry | COBB, Elizabeth (blk) | 08 JUL 1865 |
| KING, Henry | BRANSOM, Lizzie (blk) | 25 NOV 1865 |
| KING, Hiram H. | COSTAR, Mary E. | 11 JUL 1868 |
| KING, Jackson | LOVELESS, Mary E. | 21 FEB 1863 |
| KING, James | REYNOLDS, Martha (blk) | 15 NOV 1860 |
| KING, James | DOWNEY, Margaret E. | 03 JAN 1861 |
| KING, James | SEWELL, Laura Virginia | 10 SEP 1863 |
| KING, James A. [4] | DODSON, Rachel Ann | 29 JUL 1861 |
| KING, James C., Jr. | KING, Elizabeth | 19 SEP 1865 |
| KING, James H. | ESSEX, Emma | 12 AUG 1868 |
| KING, John | HUTZLER, Margaret | 16 APR 1860 |

| | | |
|---|---|---|
| KING, John | CODORA, Julia | 03 OCT 1864 |
| KING, John | WALKER, Sarah Frances (blk) | 17 SEP 1867 |
| KING, John A.B. | HOLFORD, Louisa | 29 NOV 1867 |
| KING, John F. | WILSON, Mary C.E. | 19 DEC 1862 |
| KING, John Henry | WESTERNAN, Eliza Jane | 31 DEC 1859 |
| KING, John J. | OLIVER, Mary E. | 08 FEB 1859 |
| KING, John L. | NASH, Martha R. | 09 MAR 1869 |
| KING, John Thomas | NALLEY, Mary Ann T. | 15 JUL 1862 |
| KING, John W. | PILES, Arabella | 03 SEP 1860 |
| KING, John W. | TALBERT, Susan | 07 NOV 1863 |
| KING, John W. | McDONALD, Mary E. | 30 JUN 1864 |
| KING, Joseph A. | DUNAVAN, Annie | 28 APR 1864 |
| KING, Joseph R. [10] | FALLINEON, Annie M. | 16 JUN 1868 |
| KING, Levi | WASHBURN, Emma Jane | 29 MAR 1864 |
| KING, Luke | WALKER, Emily (blk) | 24 OCT 1867 |
| KING, Marcus L. | MATHEWS, Christiana A. | 07 SEP 1868 |
| KING, Martin | ROOSE, Sarah A. | 31 MAY 1867 |
| KING, Martin D. | HALL, Mary C. | 30 NOV 1858 |
| KING, Norval W. | BOYLE, Emuella F. | 21 OCT 1867 |
| KING, Peter | HOLMES, Virginia | 03 MAR 1863 |
| KING, Ralph [3] | BRONAUGH, Mildred M. | 22 MAR 1859 |
| KING, Richard | TALBURT, Margaret R. | 06 DEC 1864 |
| KING, Richard | BROOKS, Elizabeth (blk) | 02 SEP 1869 |
| KING, Robert | WARE, Gracie (blk) | 30 DEC 1869 |
| KING, Robert H.C. | SIMMONS, Elizabeth F. | 07 JAN 1869 |
| KING, Robert J. | GALLAGHER, Kate E. | 16 MAY 1865 |
| KING, Rufus | BROWN, Susan E. | 07 MAR 1867 |
| KING, Rufus T. | POLLARD, Mary E. | 06 NOV 1869 |
| KING, Solomon | TOLIVER, Susan (blk) | 02 MAY 1870 |
| KING, Sylvester | TAYLOR, Susan | 04 DEC 1866 |
| KING, Theodore F. | SERRA, M. Isadore | 24 NOV 1868 |
| KING, Thomas | McMAHON, Bridget | 10 NOV 1865 |
| KING, Thomas | MORROW, Martha | 23 NOV 1867 |
| KING, Thomas S. | BERRY, Hester | 18 JUN 1860 |
| KING, Vincent | COOK, Mary | 25 OCT 1859 |
| KING, William | HURLEY, Anna | 01 FEB 1862 |
| KING, William | BARNES, Annie (blk) | 13 APR 1863 |
| KING, William | JACKSON, Fanny (blk) | 20 OCT 1866 |
| KING, William B. | BIGGS, Louisa | 12 JUL 1862 |
| KING, William H. | POOL, Ellen V. | 18 AUG 1868 |
| KING, William R. | WOODRUFF, Virginia S. | 29 AUG 1866 |
| KING, William W. | WEADON, Margaret E. | 30 APR 1860 |
| KING, Willis | JOHNSON, Rebecca (blk) | 02 MAY 1865 |
| KINGDON, John, Rev. | APPLER, Alverda C. | 29 MAY 1868 |
| KINGLA, Wm. F. | YEABOWER, Hellen R. | 23 NOV 1867 |
| KINGSBURY, Henry W., Lt. [11] | TAYLOR, Eva McL. | 02 DEC 1861 |
| KINGSLEY, N.R. | MANSFIELD, Margaret de | 30 MAY 1863 |
| KINKEAD, William | HARKNESS, Laura A. | 09 OCT 1866 |
| KINNAHAN, Peter | HOULEHAN, Bridget | 16 JUN 1862 |
| KINNAHAN, Peter | DONNOLLY, Margaret | 10 JUL 1862 |
| KINNESS, John | ROCK, Mary | 05 OCT 1858 |
| KINNEY, Archibald | SKIPPERS, Frances (blk) | 01 NOV 1865 |
| KINNEY, Francis | McDONNELL, Mary | 16 AUG 1866 |
| KINNEY, Johnson | MORTON, Lucy | 11 JUL 1867 |
| KINNY, Michael | DUNDEN, Mary | 16 JUN 1859 |
| KINSEY, Howard H. | PARSLEY, Margaret J. | 24 APR 1867 |

## District of Columbia Marriage Licenses, 1858-1870

| | | |
|---|---|---|
| KINSEY, John G. | PRICE, Mary A. | 22 NOV 1862 |
| KINSINGER, Louis | HARTICH, Kate | 04 OCT 1865 |
| KINSLEY, Thomas | McMAHON, Margaret | 22 FEB 1859 |
| KINSLOW, Edward T. | HAWES, Annie | 03 JUN 1868 |
| KINSLOW, James W. | FONTAIN, Lizzie | 22 DEC 1869 |
| KINSLOW, Michael | DRUMMOND, Hannah J. | 03 AUG 1865 |
| KINSLOW, Thomas | MILLER, Sarah | 22 DEC 1858 |
| KINSMAN, James M. | NORRIS, Mary A. | 14 OCT 1862 |
| KIPP, Seth W. | BREWER, Mary E. | 03 FEB 1860 |
| KIRBY, Absalom | HOGG, Sarah | 15 JUL 1862 |
| KIRBY, John E. | DUVALL, Celestia A. | 04 OCT 1869 |
| KIRBY, John N. | NULLY, Mary | 28 FEB 1859 |
| KIRBY, Thomas | MURPHY, Ellen J. | 21 FEB 1870 |
| KIRBY, Thomas L. | JACKSON, Virginia | 06 JAN 1868 |
| KIRBY, William | GAITHER, Sarah (blk) | 06 APR 1864 |
| KIRBY, William | FLYNN, Ellen | 03 OCT 1864 |
| KIRCHNER, Herman | BOUCHE, Wilhelmina S. | 12 MAR 1859 |
| KIRK, Andrew W. | REED, Alice Virginia | 04 NOV 1869 |
| KIRK, Enoch | KEMMELL, Catherine | 23 JUL 1861 |
| KIRK, Silas | PADGETT, Annie E. | 24 JAN 1861 |
| KIRK, Thomas | BROWN, Eleanor | 26 JUL 1862 |
| KIRK, Thomas D. | KNOLES, Mary Virginia | 04 JAN 1869 |
| KIRKLAND, John | JONES, Anna | 10 MAR 1865 |
| KIRKMAN, Ross | LEWIS, Betsy (blk) | 09 JAN 1868 |
| KIRKPATRICK, John | GRAY, Catherine | 13 JAN 1869 |
| KIRKPATRICK, Robert G. | FERGUSON, Mary B. | 19 APR 1864 |
| KIRKWOOD, Charles H. [6l] | HARMAN, Sarah A. | 27 AUG 1861 |
| KIRKWOOD, Samuel J. | KIRKWOOD, Marion A. | 23 JUN 1868 |
| KISNER, Henry B. | BEAN, Mary E. | 26 SEP 1867 |
| KITCHEN, Charles | MAHORNEY, Harriet Ann | 27 SEP 1859 |
| KITNER, Frederick [1c] | MOCABOY, Susan | 03 OCT 1863 |
| KITTEL, Francis | KNIGHT, Elizabeth | 08 SEP 1864 |
| KITTLER, George | SCHILLING, Christiana | 28 SEP 1866 |
| KLAKRING, Theodore | RAU, Emma Maria | 17 NOV 1860 |
| KLEINDIENST, John | KNOTE, Mary Virginia | 05 FEB 1866 |
| KLEINE, Henry | ANDRE, Annie | 02 MAY 1859 |
| KLEINFIELD, Joseph | BRADLEY, Bell | 15 MAY 1865 |
| KLEINHAUSE, George H. [6r] | COOK, Mary E. | 05 FEB 1861 |
| KLEINHENN, Luis | SCHMIDT, Augusta | 03 NOV 1865 |
| KLEINSCHMIDT, Carl, M.D. | HURDLE, Josephine | 07 JUN 1869 |
| KLEISER, John | GEIER, Josephine | 22 AUG 1865 |
| KLERLEIN, Andrew | SLATFORD, Elizabeth | 07 FEB 1866 |
| KLESATH, John | ENGEL, Mary Anna | 12 JUL 1866 |
| KLETCH, Henry | HEISE, Charlotte | 04 JUN 1861 |
| KLIEN, Peter | McCARTHY, Kate | 06 AUG 1867 |
| KLINE, B.F. [6le] | MILLER, A.M. | 28 JUL 1865 |
| KLINE, J.R. | HALEY, Jane | 08 JUL 1865 |
| KLINGLER, John George | SIMON, Johanna M. | 06 OCT 1862 |
| KLOCZEWSKI, Adrian | SMOLINSKI, Josephine Mary Ann | 21 MAY 1869 |
| KLOEBER, Charles E. | SMITH, Mary E. | 19 JAN 1863 |
| KLOZBUCHER, Joseph | GALL, Katherine | 12 AUG 1863 |
| KLUCKHUHN, Henry R. | PFEIL, Caroline | 04 JUN 1868 |
| KLUG, William | BRILLER, Mary | 03 MAR 1864 |
| KNAPP, D. Edward [5] | COUTNOR, Maggie A. | 31 OCT 1867 |
| KNAPP, Lyman E. (Maj. 17th Vt. Vol.) | SEVERANCE, Martha A. | 23 JAN 1865 |
| KNAPP, Peter | GERWIG, Louisa | 02 FEB 1867 |

District of Columbia Marriage Licenses, 1858-1870

| | | |
|---|---|---|
| KNEAL, William | JOHNSTON, Jane Ann | 25 SEP 1863 |
| KNELLER, John C. | WALKER, Sarah B. | 30 DEC 1867 |
| KNESTER, Ferdinand | REICHER, Johanna | 11 MAR 1864 |
| KNEVER, Peter H. | FINCKENSTADT, Adolphine | 26 DEC 1868 |
| KNIFESCHILD, Chas. | DETRO, Caroline | 05 MAR 1862 |
| KNIFFIN, Daniel | HUDLOE, Elizabeth | 18 MAY 1867 |
| KNIGHT, Charles A. | LEONARD, Jennie E. | 29 DEC 1862 |
| KNIGHT, Charles L. | FINNESY, Catharine | 26 MAY 1864 |
| KNIGHT, David M. | CURRAN, Catharine | 29 NOV 1864 |
| KNIGHT, Henry | GATES, Priscilla | 03 OCT 1867 |
| KNIGHT, Henry L. | MEHAN, Hanora | 23 SEP 1867 |
| KNIGHT, Jerry [6le] | GRIMES, Sarah [E.] | 18 JUN 1867 |
| KNIGHT, Zebulon | FINNE, Jane | 07 OCT 1864 |
| KNOBLOCK, William | DREAKER, Louisa | 17 OCT 1868 |
| KNOCK, Edward, alias E.K. Proctor | SMITH, [blank] | 01 OCT 1868 |
| KNOLL, Carl | HURLEY, Annie | 01 NOV 1861 |
| KNONE, John | DONOHO, Bridget | 23 OCT 1862 |
| KNOPLE, Gottlob Karl | HASENOHR, Amalie Willhelmina | 23 NOV 1863 |
| KNORL, Thomas | MINER, Catharine | 09 DEC 1869 |
| KNORR, Ernest A. | SMITH, Ellen V. | 15 JUL 1862 |
| KNORR, John M. | HAKENJOS, Barbara | 03 MAR 1866 |
| KNOST, John Charles [6le] | FRAZER, Catherine A. | 15 FEB 1867 |
| KNOTT, Charles R. | HENLY, Matilda Frances | 13 APR 1870 |
| KNOTT, Josiah H. | PICK, Sarah | 02 OCT 1858 |
| KNOTT, William | CLARKE, Louisa Virginia | 17 MAY 1862 |
| KNOUF, George | McGUIRE, Coody | 31 AUG 1867 |
| KNOWLES, Ephraim W. | LEONARD, Letitia | 25 FEB 1860 |
| KNOWLES, Leonidas | McCOOMBS, Susan G. | 13 NOV 1869 |
| KNOWLES, William | MERRICK, Jane | 27 MAY 1869 |
| KNOWLES, Wilmot | SHECKELL, Sarah E. | 27 JUN 1865 |
| KNOX, Bartholomew | WELCH, Mary | 05 DEC 1862 |
| KNOX, Benjamin | BOWMAN, Jane (blk) | 29 SEP 1865 |
| KNOX, Charles H. | QUINN, Caroline V. | 23 DEC 1864 |
| KNOXEN, Henry | PERIN, Eliza Jane | 09 APR 1863 |
| KNOXVILLE, John | CLIFF, Martha | 10 NOV 1864 |
| KOCH, Gottfried | HEIM, Josephine | 13 JUL 1865 |
| KOCH, Gustav | NOLTE, Martha | 07 NOV 1860 |
| KOCH, Gustav | NOLTE, Martha | 26 OCT 1861 |
| KOCH, Henry A. | BUERGER, Martha M. | 27 OCT 1865 |
| KOCH, Werner | BALLAUF, Adolphina | 05 FEB 1863 |
| KOCH, William | LUNTZ, Anna | 07 FEB 1862 |
| KOCK, William | CAMPLER, Agnes | 18 NOV 1862 |
| KOECHLING, Magnus | MUNCK, Amelia T. | 23 SEP 1869 |
| KOERTH, Louis | MASTERSON, Lizzie | 20 APR 1867 |
| KOFFMANN, Theodore Ludwick | KORNBACH, Maria Creszencia | 14 JAN 1863 |
| KOHL, Ferdinand H. | BURKARD, Mary Eve | 15 AUG 1862 |
| KOHL, Henry | ENGELHART, Margaret | 21 JAN 1862 |
| KOHLER, Frank | TROMPF, Annie | 28 AUG 1863 |
| KOHLER, Frederick | ANGERMANN, Matilda | 29 SEP 1868 |
| KOHR, David | ALLEN, Addie | 01 MAY 1867 |
| KOLB, Edward | WILNER, Mary | 25 SEP 1869 |
| KOLB, John G. [6m] | BLADES, Sarah C. | 09 APR 1862 |
| KOLDEWAY, Robert | HILB, Pauline | 02 MAY 1864 |
| KOLLMER, Christian Henry | OTT, Susan | 16 DEC 1859 |
| KONDRUP, John C. [10] | McCOY, Belinda | 07 JUN 1860 |
| KONUTZ, Solomon W. | MELLINGTON, Elizabeth | 10 SEP 1863 |

District of Columbia Marriage Licenses, 1858-1870

| | | |
|---|---|---|
| KOPP, Robert William Henry | TRUMPF, Rosie | 17 JUL 1869 |
| KOPPER, Henry J. [2] | WHEELER, Louisa | 15 OCT 1866 |
| KORDES, Charles | MEYER, Maria | 30 OCT 1866 |
| KOST, Alexander | FORTNER, Cecilia | 25 DEC 1862 |
| KOTTMAN, Eberhard | FRAAS, Esther | 03 JAN 1860 |
| KOTTMAN, Henry | THOMAS, Johanna | 12 MAY 1859 |
| KOUGH, Thomas | MURPHEY, Kate | 29 JAN 1861 |
| KOWALD, Adam | TRACY, Mary | 07 AUG 1866 |
| KOYNE, Timothy | McCORMICK, Bridget | 15 JUL 1865 |
| KRAENER, John Valentine | SCHULL, Louisa | 21 AUG 1865 |
| KRAEUTLER, Adolph | RÜBENKAMM, Caroline | 22 JUL 1863 |
| KRAFF, Adam | SIEVERS, Babet | 10 APR 1868 |
| KRAFFT, Lewis | CONNOWAY, Elizabeth | 11 OCT 1859 |
| KRAFT, George | RUPPERT, Agatha | 15 NOV 1858 |
| KRAFT, George M. [6s] | BAUM, Mary E. | 03 DEC 1864 |
| KRAFTT, Daniel [1e] | RABBITT, Mary C. | 02 OCT 1865 |
| KRAKE, Henry | FISCHER, Sophia | 02 NOV 1865 |
| KRAMER, Frederick | FAULWETTER, Johanna | 02 MAY 1864 |
| KRAMER, George | PROBST, Helena | 03 MAR 1863 |
| KRANCH, Ludwig Carl | CHRISTIANI, Eliza | 29 DEC 1864 |
| KRAPF, Jacob Fredk. | NAGEL, Susan | 04 NOV 1868 |
| KRASZYSKI, Maurice | MYERS, Ada F. | 31 MAR 1868 |
| KRATENBERG, Charles | RUEDEMANN, Auguste | 14 FEB 1862 |
| KRAUS, Henry | HOLSTEIN, Elizabeth | 02 AUG 1867 |
| KRAUS, John E. | FISHER, Amelia | 10 JAN 1859 |
| KRAUSE, Charles A. [5] | MAIFORTH, Helena | 16 DEC 1867 |
| KRAUSE, Charles F. | BAGGETT, Louisa | 09 FEB 1864 |
| KRAUSER, Joseph A. | POSEY, Rebecca | 08 AUG 1865 |
| KRAUSER, Joseph A. | COVERSTON, Lydia | 28 FEB 1870 |
| KREBS, John | BATES, Mary | 16 SEP 1867 |
| KREGAN, Patrick | MURTOUGH, Mary A. | 26 MAY 1865 |
| KREIFT, John | KRAEMAN, Katharine | 02 NOV 1865 |
| KREITHER, Herman | ROESER, Helena A. | 09 JAN 1867 |
| KRESS, Frederick | CUSICK, Catharine | 30 DEC 1863 |
| KRETZER, John M.C. | LAYS, Ann | 24 FEB 1862 |
| KRICHELT, William | DONNELLY, Margaret | 20 APR 1863 |
| KRICK, Joseph | HERMES, Magdalena | 17 NOV 1862 |
| KRIDER, Henry | FREUND, Johanna | 27 JUN 1860 |
| KROEHL, Julius H. | LUEBER, Sophie | 23 NOV 1858 |
| KROETER, William | AMTHOR, Hedwig | 08 OCT 1862 |
| KROHR, William | DOVE, Laura | 03 MAY 1866 |
| KRONTZ, Edward H. | LEE, Mary | 27 JUL 1863 |
| KROS, Joseph | TRALLER, Kate | 25 NOV 1865 |
| KROUHN, Charles | LIBICH, Mary | 23 APR 1864 |
| KROUSE, Christian | MONEY, Ellen | 16 FEB 1861 |
| KRULL, Anton | SCHNEIDER, Caroline | 06 APR 1867 |
| KRULL, Joseph | GLEESON, Henora | 01 NOV 1866 |
| KRZYWOSZYNSKI, Julius Constantine | FOLCH, Anne J. Intropidi | 01 DEC 1868 |
| KSCHIESCHANG, Adolph | BROWN, Elizabeth | 27 OCT 1865 |
| KUCHNEMANN, Christian | PFEIL, Anna Gertrude | 27 DEC 1862 |
| KUHL, Emil Wm. | UNKEL, Justina | 18 JUL 1868 |
| KUHN, George G. | HEITMILLER, Antonie D. | 12 MAY 1865 |
| KUHN, Gustavus | BAKER, Mary | 08 JUN 1864 |
| KUHN, Henry | ROCKANHAUSER, Lena | 11 APR 1867 |
| KUHNS, James A. | DAVIS, Julia | 02 FEB 1863 |
| KUHNS, William H. | REYNOLDS, Lottie E. | 07 SEP 1867 |

District of Columbia Marriage Licenses, 1858-1870

| | | |
|---|---|---|
| KUNNINGHAM, John | CONNELL, Margaret | 12 DEC 1860 |
| KURB, Joseph | MITCHELL, Susanna | 29 APR 1859 |
| KURL, Wilson | FELLS, Susanna (blk) | 03 OCT 1865 |
| KURTZ, Louis | BLUCHER, Eva | 02 OCT 1862 |
| KURTZ, Thomas | MORAN, Martha | 18 SEP 1858 |
| KURTZ, William D. | PACKARD, Helena | 19 NOV 1861 |
| KURZROCK, Charles | BROCKMEYER, Mina | 24 MAY 1869 |
| KUTZNER, Charles | MILLER, Amelia | 31 OCT 1862 |
| KYLE, Henry | TURNER, Emma | 16 FEB 1869 |
| KYNE, John | FOLAN, Bridget | 05 JUL 1864 |

# L

| | | |
|---|---|---|
| LABAHN, John | LOUGHLIN, Anna | 09 SEP 1868 |
| LABS, Joseph | LEE, Olivia | 21 OCT 1867 |
| LACEY, A.B.H. | DELAVERGNE, Fannie E. | 18 NOV 1868 |
| LACEY, Alfred B. [6c] | HALLEY, Angeline | 13 OCT 1858 |
| LACEY, Edward T. | TRAMMELL, Elizabeth | 06 AUG 1864 |
| LACEY, Francis E. | McGIINNEY, Annie | 02 DEC 1862 |
| LACEY, Henry | WEBSTER, Addie (blk) | 16 MAR 1865 |
| LACEY, John L. | CRIER, Jane F. | 17 MAR 1869 |
| LACEY, William | LAMBERT, Margaret | 21 NOV 1865 |
| LACKEY, Francis Edward | PATTERSON, Catherine Elizabeth F. | 05 MAR 1867 |
| LACKEY, George | WHITE, Elizabeth | 18 MAY 1866 |
| LACKEY, Milford F. | LAURENSON, Maggie | 25 OCT 1869 |
| LACKEY, William D. | MORGAN, Miranda | 07 JUL 1864 |
| LACKMANN, Tobias | SCHAFERT, Mary | 09 JAN 1863 |
| LaCROIX, Ernest | BRENNEN, Julia | 04 JUN 1864 |
| LACY, John | WILSON, Rosanna | 06 JUN 1859 |
| LACY, John | LAWS, Sallie (blk) | 22 SEP 1863 |
| LADNEY, Taltin | BOUTS, Mary (blk) | 16 JUL 1864 |
| LAEHY, Daniel | FITZGERALD, Catharine | 29 SEP 1862 |
| LaFARGE, Samuel F. | HANCOCK, Sallie | 25 JAN 1865 |
| LAFFERTY, Edward B. | HERGESHEIMER, Mary | 24 SEP 1867 |
| LAFFERTY, Robert | SEIDENSTRICKER, Mary R. | 23 OCT 1863 |
| LAFFY, Daniel | MARTIN, Ellen | 13 AUG 1867 |
| LaFLEICHE, William W. | SILVER, Amanda Jane | 31 JAN 1862 |
| LAFONTAINE, James [6r] | GRIMES, Mary Virginia | 21 FEB 1860 |
| LaFORGE, Samuel F. | HANCOCK, Ada L. | 24 DEC 1862 |
| LAGAN, John | MORGAN, Mary | 06 NOV 1858 |
| LAIRD, William, Jr. | RIDGLEY, Anna Key | 05 JUN 1866 |
| LAKE, George H. | LONGSON, Sarah F. | 01 DEC 1865 |
| LAKE, James | PRESTCUTT, Rebecca | 10 OCT 1864 |
| LAKE, Samuel M. | GREER, Marion | 19 DEC 1868 |
| LAKEMEYER, Frederick | GOLDSBOROUGH, Mary Ann | 30 NOV 1859 |
| LAKEMEYER, Frederick | RAU, Mary | 15 NOV 1861 |
| LALBONETTE, Stephen | PILLSBURY, Ann E. | 12 NOV 1866 |
| LALLOUETTE, Stephen | CUSSACK, Elizabeth | 21 JAN 1868 |
| LAMB, Anthony John [11] | HILL, Charlotte Ann | 15 DEC 1862 |
| LAMB, Charles M. | HUNTT, Mary A. | 11 MAR 1864 |
| LAMB, David | MONAGHAN, Margaret | 20 SEP 1862 |
| LAMB, Francis | RIDGELY, Annie E. | 19 JUL 1859 |
| LAMB, Nicholas | McGILL, Mary Ellen | 15 AUG 1865 |
| LAMB, William H. | FAIRFAX, Sarah F. | 03 DEC 1862 |
| LAMB, Wm. L. | HUNT, Joanna L. | 05 AUG 1868 |
| LAMBERT, David | WEST, Georgianna | 11 APR 1865 |

171

District of Columbia Marriage Licenses, 1858-1870

| | | |
|---|---|---|
| LAMBERT, Jno. D. | LETZNER, Margt. | 14 NOV 1859 |
| LAMBERT, Tallmadge A. | VanRISWICK, Ararilla | 27 APR 1870 |
| LAMBERTSON, George W. | JONES, Mary Ella | 28 OCT 1864 |
| LAMBIE, Edward L. | MASON, Johanna F. | 25 JAN 1865 |
| LAMBIE, James B. | TURTON, Mary M. | 02 SEP 1868 |
| LAMBORN, George F. | SMITH, May G. | 30 MAY 1870 |
| LAMDIN, John H. | CLAGETT, Rebecca F. | 24 MAY 1870 |
| LAMMOND, Chas. M. | DALE, Virginia M. | 16 DEC 1862 |
| LAMMOND, Peter | ELLIS, Nannie B. | 24 JUL 1861 |
| LAMON, Vincent | JACKSON, Margaret (blk) | 22 MAY 1866 |
| LAMPKIN, John | DRALEY, Mary Elizth. | 02 MAR 1863 |
| LANAHAN, William | CORCORAN, Mary | 04 FEB 1863 |
| LANAHAN, William | LOVELESS, Marien | 08 JUL 1867 |
| LANCASTER, Alexander | SISCO, Catherine Ann (blk) | 25 MAR 1869 |
| LANCASTER, Charles H. | BROOKS, Martha Ann | 13 JUN 1868 |
| LANCASTER, Emanuel F. | CHRISMAN, Mary E. | 12 SEP 1867 |
| LANCASTER, Francis M. | O'DONNOGHUE, Annie | 12 APR 1860 |
| LANCASTER, Henry | WASHINGTON, Eliza (blk) | 14 APR 1870 |
| LANCASTER, John | SMITH, Julia (blk) | 09 MAY 1867 |
| LANCASTER, John | TRUELL, Mary Ann (blk) | 04 JUN 1867 |
| LANCASTER, Theophilus | WALLACE, Beckie (blk) | 23 NOV 1865 |
| LANCASTER, Thomas | BILLAS, Catherine | 24 JUL 1862 |
| LANCASTER, Walter | AMBUSH, Jane R. (blk) | 05 APR 1859 |
| LANCASTER, William | CHASE, Emma (blk) | 19 NOV 1864 |
| LANDER, James | BROOKE, Mary P. | 25 MAR 1864 |
| LANDER, Robert Vallance | McPHERSON, Christian | 24 OCT 1865 |
| LANDGRAF, Frederick | SCHLE, Anna M. | 12 APR 1865 |
| LANDLEY, James Walter | HUMPHREYS, Delia | 07 AUG 1867 |
| LANDON, Oliver A. | CHANEY, Margaret A.R. | 28 JUL 1862 |
| LANDON, Thomas | TUCKER, Lucinda | 06 FEB 1869 |
| LANDVOIGT, Dorus W. | WEAVER, Mary Ella | 31 AUG 1865 |
| LANE, Charles | PAGE, Mary (blk) | 10 MAR 1870 |
| LANE, Eli | SMITH, Lucy (blk) | 18 NOV 1868 |
| LANE, Henry C. | LAMB, Charlotte A. | 17 OCT 1867 |
| LANE, Jeremiah | ROSS, Mary | 13 OCT 1863 |
| LANE, John | GREEN, Maria (blk) | 15 AUG 1866 |
| LANE, John | GREEN, Maria (blk) | 08 SEP 1866 |
| LANE, John W. | WASHINGTON, Harriet (blk) | 30 JAN 1863 |
| LANE, Levi Irven | BOURNE, Augusta | 09 APR 1864 |
| LANE, Patrick | KENNEDY, Margaret | 08 NOV 1860 |
| LANE, William | WILLIAMS, Mary | 21 MAR 1866 |
| LANES, Gregor | RUPERT, Walburg | 06 FEB 1863 |
| LANG, Herman F. | KARLIN, Louisa J. | 13 SEP 1865 |
| LANG, J.P. Theodore | HEITMÜLLER, Josephine M. | 26 DEC 1860 |
| LANG, John C. | DOWNS, Emma Radclyff | 06 MAY 1867 |
| LANG, John C. | SAVORCOOL, Emma | 29 JUL 1868 |
| LANG, Michael | FITZGERALD, Mary | 08 OCT 1859 |
| LANG, Patrick | McGUIRE, Margaret | 29 AUG 1859 |
| LANG, Philip | BROWNE, Columbine Augusta | 19 JUN 1869 |
| LANGDON, Chas. H. | MILLER, Sarah M. | 13 DEC 1862 |
| LANGDON, James D. | JONES, Malinda | 26 JUN 1865 |
| LANGE, Carl John Fredk. Wilh. | BRANDT, Amalie | 25 MAR 1862 |
| LANGE, Louis | RALEK, Caroline Albertini Emma | 11 JAN 1866 |
| LANGHORN, Thomas | NOA, Caroline | 28 FEB 1865 |
| LANGLEY, Benjamin F. | DOUGLASS, Isabella | 10 OCT 1863 |
| LANGLEY, Charles C. | RAY, Ann Catherine | 18 DEC 1862 |

| | | |
|---|---|---|
| LANGLEY, George S. | WILLIAMS, Anna D. | 01 MAR 1859 |
| LANGLEY, Richard | McINTIRE, Elizabeth (blk) | 03 JAN 1870 |
| LANGLEY, Richard T. | BARRETT, Mary J. | 21 JUL 1860 |
| LANGLEY, Richard T. [10] | STAPLES, Sarah | 14 AUG 1866 |
| LANGLEY, Robert [10] | BROWN, Elizabeth | 31 JUL 1863 |
| LANGLEY, Samuel G. | TILTON, Mary C. | 02 JAN 1867 |
| LANGLEY, Stephen | SMITH, Annie (blk) | 16 JUL 1868 |
| LANGLEY, William | PEGG, Rosy | 28 JAN 1869 |
| LANGRAN, William | KERVAND, Isabel | 13 APR 1868 |
| LANGSTON, George E., Jr. [12s] | DUVALL, Elizabeth | 20 JAN 1863 |
| LANGSTON, William J. | SIMONDS, Mary C. | 20 AUG 1867 |
| LANHAM, James Thomas | HUMPHREYS, Sarah Ann | 03 AUG 1864 |
| LANHAM, John W. [6r] | MILLER, Louisa | 16 JAN 1860 |
| LANHAM, John W. [6m] | MILLER, Amelia | 30 SEP 1862 |
| LANHAN, Robert | BEECH, Mary E. | 03 MAR 1868 |
| LANKAN, Augustus Leopold | BONNEMANN, Maria Elizth. | 27 OCT 1859 |
| LANNAN, John [6le] | SMITH, Sallie | 09 AUG 1867 |
| LANNON, Thomas | DUGGAN, Catherine | 09 FEB 1863 |
| LANSDALE, Asbury | JENKINS, Annie (blk) | 05 JAN 1869 |
| LANSDALE, J.W. | JOY, Mary E. | 26 OCT 1865 |
| LANSTON, Tolbert | HURDLE, Beattie | 12 DEC 1866 |
| LANTRAP, Paul Christian | AISQUITH, Delia Anna | 24 DEC 1867 |
| LAO, Thomas | MURRAY, Ellen | 08 FEB 1864 |
| LAPAN, John | O'SHAUGHENY, Catharine | 03 MAR 1863 |
| LAPOINT, Frederick | BOVAR, Agness | 16 APR 1864 |
| LaPORTE, William M. [2] | MORAN, Kate M. | 14 FEB 1870 |
| LAPORTE. Eugen[e] B. | WALKER, Emma | 21 FEB 1867 |
| LAPPERTY, John | RODIER, Mary J. | 08 MAY 1865 |
| LARCOMBE, Benj. F. | STEWART, Margt. E. | 26 JUN 1862 |
| LARCOMBE, Thomas D. | WHALEY, Laura C. | 16 FEB 1869 |
| LARKIM, Michael | HALBUS, Virginia Mary | 27 NOV 1860 |
| LARKIN, Henry | ROBINSON, Annie (blk) | 20 OCT 1866 |
| LARKIN, Patrick | McGUIRE, Elizabeth | 17 APR 1863 |
| LARKINS, Henry | THOMAS, Elizabeth (blk) | 10 JUL 1869 |
| LARNED, Benjamin F. | WILSON, Maria H. | 26 NOV 1860 |
| LARNEY, Nicholas | KING, Margaret | 11 SEP 1863 |
| LARNEY, Patrick | MULDOON, Hannah | 06 NOV 1862 |
| LARRABEE, James B. | NORFOLK, Margaret A.B. | 01 AUG 1867 |
| LARRIN, Lorenzo D. | SANDERS, Susan A. | 08 MAY 1868 |
| LARUE, Albert | PETTIBONE, Margaret E. | 23 DEC 1862 |
| LASHHORN, Jacob V. | McGONEGAL, Margaret A. | 16 APR 1866 |
| LASKEY, Robert V. | HODGES, Virginia | 18 DEC 1862 |
| LASKEY, William Wirt | TAYLOR, Mary Elizabeth | 30 JAN 1862 |
| LASSEN, John | WOODYARD, Julia (blk) | 06 DEC 1864 |
| LATCH, Edward H. | LINTON, Amanda J. | 24 DEC 1868 |
| LATHAM, Leonidas | GIBSON, Mary C. | 20 MAY 1862 |
| LATHAM, Leonidas | GIBSON, Mary | 02 MAY 1862 |
| LATHROP, Daniel W. | NIMMO, Jennie R. | 09 OCT 1869 |
| LATHROP, James R. | RICHARDSON, Mary E. | 08 OCT 1866 |
| LATHROP, Joel C. | BATES, Mary Louisa | 01 AUG 1866 |
| LATHROP, Mellen | CLARK, Mattie D. | 19 AUG 1864 |
| LATIMER, Marcus B. | LOWE, Susie B. | 11 MAY 1864 |
| LaTRUITT, Antony | DENNISON, Marion | 07 JUL 1862 |
| LATTIN, Robert P. | WILSON, Sarah | 27 MAY 1862 |
| LATZ, Henry | DREIFUS, Bertha | 06 NOV 1862 |
| LAU, Henry | HARDER, Charlotte | 06 SEP 1865 |

District of Columbia Marriage Licenses, 1858-1870

| | | |
|---|---|---|
| LAUB, Adolphus | GURHARDT, Elizabeth | 15 DEC 1862 |
| LAUBER, Philip S. | EBERBACH, M. Virginia | 27 NOV 1862 |
| LAUCK, Henry C. | McCLERY, Sidney J. | 28 JUL 1859 |
| LAUCK, William H. | HUGHES, Susan V. | 28 JUN 1869 |
| LAUER, Bernard | KREBBS, Rufina | 15 AUG 1865 |
| LAUER, David B. [1l] | KIDWELL, Catherine | 20 DEC 1865 |
| LAUER, George | KISICGA, Catharine | 13 FEB 1865 |
| LAUGHEINZ, Edward | BENZ, Cara | 22 JUL 1865 |
| LAUGHLIN, James T. | ROLLING, Kate M. | 07 OCT 1867 |
| LAURENCE, Albert T. | PIERCE, Mary C. | 30 JUN 1865 |
| LAURENCE, George L. [6r] | NALLY, Anna | 11 SEP 1860 |
| LAURENCE, John | BUTLER, Ellen (blk) | 30 AUG 1860 |
| LAURENSON, Richard S. | BROWN, Caroline E. | 08 DEC 1863 |
| LAURIE, James | SIRICH, Mary L. | 29 MAY 1867 |
| LAURIE, Lewis F.L. | MOORE, Rachel E. | 31 OCT 1867 |
| LAUTEL, Benjamin | FRIEDENBURG, Catharine | 01 NOV 1865 |
| LAUTEMANN, Henry | FISCHER, Johanna | 04 NOV 1863 |
| LAUX, Michael | WHEATLEY, Sarah (blk) | 07 JAN 1867 |
| LAUXMAN, John J. | SUMMERS, Mary B. | 04 DEC 1861 |
| LAVANCEY, Charles | WESTERMEN, Mary | 04 APR 1865 |
| LAVENDER, Robert | DAVIS, Amanda A. | 19 MAY 1864 |
| LAVEZZI, Christmas | GANDOLPHI, Teresa | 28 MAR 1864 |
| LAVEZZI, Peter | ARROTI, Kate | 25 NOV 1864 |
| LAVEZZI, Anthony | KEARNE, Hanorah | 17 MAR 1866 |
| LAVIN, Patrick | BROWNING, Mary | 22 AUG 1862 |
| LAW, George H. | SAMSON, Emily | 21 APR 1863 |
| LAW, Thomas | EDDS, Florence | 05 SEP 1863 |
| LAWLER, Bartholomew | CRAIGHAN, Mary | 20 FEB 1862 |
| LAWLER, Thomas | HANDY, Margaret | 09 FEB 1861 |
| LAWLESS, David A. | MALIHAN, Mary | 31 AUG 1865 |
| LAWN, George | MARTIN, Emma J. | 10 AUG 1861 |
| LAWRENCE, Atkins S. | GROSHON, Ella | 02 JUN 1863 |
| LAWRENCE, Centre H. [1e] | BURCH, Annie E. | 10 SEP 1866 |
| LAWRENCE, Henry C. | COOMES, Rosa | 22 JUN 1867 |
| LAWRENCE, Janie Valentine | SOUTHWORTH, Charlotte Emma | 02 MAY 1864 |
| LAWRENCE, Joseph H. [6m] | BERRY, Mary N. | 16 FEB 1863 |
| LAWRENCE, Ziebo | MILLER, Ann | 10 JUN 1865 |
| LAWS, Edwin | MATHEWS, Lydia (blk) | 26 NOV 1866 |
| LAWS, Richard | GWINN, Matilda (blk) | 15 JUN 1868 |
| LAWS, Robert S. | WILLIAMS, Patsey (blk) | 08 MAR 1866 |
| LAWS, William | MASON, Eliza (blk) | 02 FEB 1866 |
| LAWSON, Charles | BROWN, Betty (blk) | 10 NOV 1866 |
| LAWSON, Edward | BUTLER, Mary (blk) | 24 APR 1866 |
| LAWSON, Edward | TAPSCOTT, Cordelia (blk) | 24 DEC 1868 |
| LAWSON, John | WHITE, Catherine (blk) | 03 AUG 1866 |
| LAWSON, John | BOWIE, Emma (blk) | 11 JUN 1868 |
| LAWSON, Lewis | McKENNY, Julia (blk) | 16 MAY 1868 |
| LAWSON, Stanley | BENDER, Virginette M. (blk) | 22 MAR 1866 |
| LAWSON, Stephen | TAYLOR, Lucy (blk) | 07 MAR 1865 |
| LAWSON, William S. | McDANIEL, Julia | 12 SEP 1867 |
| LAWTON, Andrew | KING, Annie Augusta | 19 FEB 1862 |
| LAWTON, Edwin M. | WALSH, Sarah A. | 05 SEP 1859 |
| LAWTON, John C. | LAUB, Ellen A. | 24 NOV 1858 |
| LAY, Samuel M. | LAUGHERMAN, Caroline | 29 JUN 1865 |
| LAY, Theodore A. | SELDEN, Mary B. | 14 JUN 1870 |
| LAY, Thomas W. | ROACH, Annie E. | 04 JAN 1864 |

| | | |
|---|---|---|
| LAY, Walcott | PAGE, Martha E. | 04 AUG 1868 |
| LAYTON, Charles | McSHANE, Mary Ann | 06 JAN 1859 |
| LAZENBY, Richard | ROSS, Mary V. (blk) | 15 NOV 1866 |
| LAZENBY, Thomas T. | PEDDICORD, Romana C. | 14 OCT 1865 |
| LEA, Alexander | CARROLL, Rosena (blk) | 11 DEC 1860 |
| LEACH, Benjamin | BAYLISS, Martha Ann | 03 MAR 1862 |
| LEACH, Charles | BOSWELL, Emily R. | 01 MAR 1861 |
| LEACH, George H. | SNOOKE, Emma | 23 JUL 1864 |
| LEACH, James B. | GREEN, Louisa K. | 09 APR 1861 |
| LEACH, John | NALLS, Martha Ann | 14 AUG 1860 |
| LEACH, John | BROOKES, Mary E. | 10 SEP 1867 |
| LEACH, John, Jr. | WILSON, Sarah | 09 MAY 1859 |
| LEAHY, Michael | DRISCOLL, Catharine | 02 APR 1863 |
| LEAK, James R. | ORRIEN, Kate C. | 29 APR 1859 |
| LEAKE, Charles P. | RISTON, Aurelia F. | 16 AUG 1864 |
| LEALIGER, John | BRUCKNER, Marie | 27 JUN 1862 |
| LEAPLEY, George R. | PUMPHREY, Amanda E. | 22 FEB 1869 |
| LEAPY, John | TYE, Sarah | 25 FEB 1870 |
| LEARY, Jeremiah | HORRIGAN, Ellen | 19 SEP 1863 |
| LEARY, John | DEVLIN, Hannah | 20 JAN 1864 |
| LEARY, Paul | LONG, Margaret | 24 FEB 1862 |
| LEATHERBURY, Littleton | BROWN, Maria (blk) | 06 SEP 1866 |
| LEATHERBURY, Littleton | BROWN, Maria | 11 FEB 1867 |
| LEAYCOCK, William | O'BRIEN, Annie M. | 25 MAR 1869 |
| LECANSE, William | MINER, Charlotte | 16 DEC 1865 |
| LECHTER, Charles Henry | PAXTON, Mary Louisa | 17 JAN 1860 |
| LECHY, Thomas | DALY, Ann R. | 04 JAN 1864 |
| LECKRON, Thomas Q. | GODFREY, Mary Virginia | 20 FEB 1862 |
| LEDDON, William Joseph | DAVIS, Caroline | 03 JAN 1867 |
| LEDERER, Christian G. | ACKMAN, Anna | 15 MAY 1866 |
| LEDERER, Theophilus | MURPHEY, Mary C. | 14 AUG 1867 |
| LEDGAT, Thomas | RYAN, Bridget | 13 APR 1861 |
| LEDLEY, Daniel A.J. | GRINDALL, Harriet Amelia | 24 APR 1860 |
| LeDUC, Henry M. | WALBORN, Amelia | 07 JUL 1868 |
| LEDWITH, James | WELSH, Margaret | 16 FEB 1863 |
| LEE, Alfred | BRONAUGH, Mary (blk) | 13 FEB 1868 |
| LEE, Alfred | ROBINSON, Eliza (blk) | 28 APR 1869 |
| LEE, Chapman, Dr. | GAINOR, Martha F. | 13 JUL 1868 |
| LEE, Charles | HANSON, Lavinia (blk) | 30 JUL 1860 |
| LEE, Charles | JORDAN, Hannah (blk) | 03 JUN 1869 |
| LEE, Charles C. [7a] | JONES, Sarah | 27 NOV 1866 |
| LEE, Donald | KANE, Catharine | 27 JAN 1866 |
| LEE, Edward | HENDERSON, Mary (blk) | 06 SEP 1866 |
| LEE, Eli | JACKSON, Lucy (blk) | 06 SEP 1866 |
| LEE, Frank | TATE, Lizzie (blk) | 21 JAN 1862 |
| LEE, George | THOMAS, Mary (blk) | 28 MAR 1864 |
| LEE, George | LEE, Anna (blk) | 29 APR 1869 |
| LEE, George W. | WHITE, Ruth A. | 14 FEB 1860 |
| LEE, George W. | CHASE, Caroline (blk) | 16 MAR 1865 |
| LEE, George W. [10] | HOWARD, Alice E. (blk) | 08 MAY 1867 |
| LEE, George W. | SANDERS, Ann Elizabeth | 03 AUG 1869 |
| LEE, George W. | PALMER, Leah F. | 11 NOV 1869 |
| LEE, Henry | JACKSON, Sylvia | 01 JAN 1863 |
| LEE, Henry | DOUGLAS, Eliza Jane (blk) | 05 SEP 1865 |
| LEE, Henry H. | THOMPSON, Sarah A. | 25 JUN 1862 |
| LEE, Henry W. | CONNELL, Emily (blk) | 19 DEC 1866 |

| | | |
|---|---|---|
| LEE, Isaac | ALLEN, Matilda (blk) | 20 FEB 1869 |
| LEE, James | DOWDS, Dorah | 12 MAY 1863 |
| LEE, James | CARL, Louisa (blk) | 25 MAR 1865 |
| LEE, James C. | VERLANDER, Mary S. | 19 JUN 1865 |
| LEE, James H. | JOHNSON, Alice R. (blk) | 29 AUG 1864 |
| LEE, James N., Dr. [12s] | WATSON, Adeline | 06 JUN 1859 |
| LEE, James W. | STICKNEY, Sarah Elizabeth | 09 JAN 1865 |
| LEE, James Wesley | HAWKINS, Rebecca (bk) | 01 SEP 1868 |
| LEE, Jerome | FALCONER, Mary Almira | 15 NOV 1869 |
| LEE, John | GRICE, Ellen V. | 07 APR 1863 |
| LEE, John | BOWIE, Jane (blk) | 17 DEC 1863 |
| LEE, John | DADE, Angelina (blk) | 20 SEP 1867 |
| LEE, John F. | BELL, Maria (col'd) | 13 OCT 1864 |
| LEE, John Quincy | BROWN, Henrietta (blk) | 06 SEP 1864 |
| LEE, John W. | JACKSON, Margaret R. (blk) | 29 JAN 1863 |
| LEE, John [2] | DAVIS, George Anna | 30 SEP 1869 |
| LEE, Joseph | TRACY, Kate | 06 FEB 1865 |
| LEE, Joseph | LUCAS, Mary C. (blk) | 17 MAY 1865 |
| LEE, Lewis | CROSS, Rachel (blk) | 23 MAY 1866 |
| LEE, Michael | HINES, Margaret | 01 JAN 1864 |
| LEE, Miles | CASSERLY, Hannah | 05 JUN 1865 |
| LEE, Napoleon A. | MANSFIELD, Virginia | 06 JUN 1865 |
| LEE, Patrick | PIGGOT, Mary | 12 FEB 1863 |
| LEE, Plato | DALY, Elizabeth (blk) | 01 MAY 1862 |
| LEE, Plato T. | BURGOYNE, Charlotte (blk) | 24 OCT 1865 |
| LEE, Reverdy | GANT, Amelia (blk) | 20 JUL 1868 |
| LEE, Richard | WIGGINTON, Martha (blk) | 16 JUL 1866 |
| LEE, Richard H. | DAGENHART, Mary E. | 30 JUN 1869 |
| LEE, Robert | SANDERS, Margaret (blk) | 12 OCT 1865 |
| LEE, Robert | LEE, Matilda (blk) | 24 JAN 1868 |
| LEE, Samuel | PAYNE, Ellen Elizabeth (blk) | 27 OCT 1863 |
| LEE, Samuel | BRIDWELL, Nancy Laura Gertrude | 11 JUN 1864 |
| LEE, Spencer | LEE, Emma (blk) | 02 MAR 1868 |
| LEE, Spencer | BELL, Eliza (blk) | 06 DEC 1869 |
| LEE, Stephen P. | ADAMS, Mary V. | 13 FEB 1865 |
| LEE, Tasker | STICKNEY, Chloe (blk) | 10 MAY 1866 |
| LEE, Thomas | THORNTON, Sarah | 30 AUG 1860 |
| LEE, Thomas | MUNROE, Martha J. | 08 NOV 1860 |
| LEE, Thomas | WELSH, Mary | 17 OCT 1862 |
| LEE, Willard | GORDON, Rebecca (blk) | 26 DEC 1866 |
| LEE, William | WILSON, Josephine (blk) | 26 OCT 1860 |
| LEE, William | McMAHON, Bridget Ann | 06 SEP 1862 |
| LEE, William | SMALLWOOD, Elizabeth (blk) | 18 DEC 1862 |
| LEE, William | WHEELER, Elizabeth (blk) | 16 JUN 1863 |
| LEE, William | CARROLL, Johanna | 11 MAY 1864 |
| LEE, William | WANZER, Elizabeth (blk) | 25 OCT 1865 |
| LEE, William | STEWART, Dolly (blk) | 22 OCT 1867 |
| LEE, William | LEE, Clora (blk) | 07 OCT 1868 |
| LEE, William F. | ROSS, Martha M. (blk) | 25 JUN 1860 |
| LEE, William F. | MEADE, Sallie E. | 11 DEC 1867 |
| LEE, William F. | WHITE, Alice V. | 18 AUG 1869 |
| LEE, William H. | DAVIS, Mary Ann (blk) | 06 JUL 1865 |
| LEE, William H. | COFFEE, Alice Ann (blk) | 25 FEB 1867 |
| LEE, William Henry | BUTLER, Mary (blk) | 14 MAY 1867 |
| LEE, William J. | SINNOTT, Jennie E. | 29 NOV 1867 |
| LEE, William Perry | DOTSON, Harriet | 03 JAN 1865 |

| | | |
|---|---|---|
| LEECH, Abner Y. | FLEURY, Irene | 08 AUG 1864 |
| LEECKE, George | GAEK, Maria | 21 MAR 1864 |
| LEEHAN, Charles | CRONEN, Johanna | 10 JUL 1863 |
| LEESNETZER, Edward | LAWRENCE, Susan | 03 MAY 1864 |
| LEESNETZER, Henry J. | HOWE, Sarah E. | 10 JUN 1863 |
| LEETE, William B. | ROFF, Etta E. | 10 JAN 1867 |
| LEGARE, J. Sydney A. [4] | GREEN, Emily S. | 06 DEC 1858 |
| LEGG, James E. | TRIPLETT, Cornelia A. | 17 NOV 1868 |
| LEGGINS, Elisha | CONWAY, Lizzie (blk) | 31 MAR 1870 |
| LEHMAN, George H. | HOSEY, Elizabeth | 05 FEB 1863 |
| LEIB, Alexander R. | WOODWARD, Mary E. | 31 DEC 1862 |
| LEIFFERT, John H. | PATCH, Sarah J. | 19 NOV 1860 |
| LEIGHT, George | MILLER, Ann Virginia | 08 SEP 1864 |
| LEIKAM, John | LUBBA, Eliza | 10 AUG 1868 |
| LEIMBACH, Sebastian | BRAND, Amelia | 02 SEP 1865 |
| LEIMBACK, Henry | GODRON, Louisa | 23 JUN 1864 |
| LEIN, Godfrey | KLUMP, Julia Anna | 12 DEC 1864 |
| LEIN, Henry B. | BROWN, Mary E.M. | 06 JUL 1869 |
| LEINE, Edward | SCHERFF, Annie | 27 JUN 1864 |
| LEIR, John I. | WILLIAMS, Lucy (blk) | 06 APR 1867 |
| LEISHEAR, William M. | GRUMELL, Kate V. | 31 JUL 1867 |
| LEMBRECHT, Ferdinand | NIEBEL, Katherina | 25 MAY 1863 |
| LeMERLE, Augustus E. | MARR, M. Aretta | 14 SEP 1863 |
| LEMMON, William Lee | BREYFOGH, J.R. | 24 OCT 1864 |
| LEMMONS, Harvey | [blank] (blk) | 16 AUG 1864 |
| LEMON, Humphrey H. | DAVIS, Eliza A. | 08 OCT 1867 |
| LEMON, J.H.M. | MARKS, Mary Ann | 07 APR 1862 |
| LEMON, John H. | QUEEN, Susan (blk) | 21 MAY 1863 |
| LEMON, Thomas H. | VALIANT, Josephine J. | 15 JUN 1865 |
| LEMON, William H. [7a] | WARWICK, Arabella | 22 FEB 1868 |
| LEMOS, Charles H. | FLEET, Cora | 22 AUG 1867 |
| LEMOYNE, George S. | SMITH, Annie L. | 28 FEB 1863 |
| LENAHAN, Michael | CLANSY, Mary | 14 FEB 1865 |
| LENAHAN, Timothy | FOX, Ellen | 25 AUG 1868 |
| LENHART, Conrad | HUHN, Eugenie | 27 JUL 1864 |
| LENIHAN, Michael | DAILEY, Ellen | 07 OCT 1858 |
| LENOX, Alexander | JEFFERSON, Martha (blk) | 24 FEB 1866 |
| LENOX, David [1c] | DAWSON [Davidson], Margaret | 04 MAR 1864 |
| LENOX, James | SMALLWOOD, Anna M. | 20 JUL 1859 |
| LENTNER, Albert | CONARD, Elizabeth H. | 07 DEC 1860 |
| LENTZ, Conrad | CAMMAL, Mary | 11 JUN 1868 |
| LENZ, Henry [4] | FRASER, Julia B. | 12 JAN 1869 |
| LEONARD, Alexander B. | COLEMAN, Elizabeth | 27 JUL 1868 |
| LEONARD, Andrew | SERRO, Elenor | 23 MAY 1863 |
| LEONARD, Barney | O'NEIL, Elizabeth | 29 AUG 1868 |
| LEONARD, George W. [6m] | GENNARI, Mary Jane | 24 DEC 1863 |
| LEONARD, George W. [10] | HEAD, Lizzie | 27 NOV 1868 |
| LEONARD, H.D. | FRANKLER, Willa A. | 24 AUG 1867 |
| LEONARD, Harry | DEVRIES, Johanna | 30 SEP 1864 |
| LEONARD, Michael C. | GLUCK, Margaret | 22 JAN 1863 |
| LEONARD, Patrick | McGEE, Kate | 07 MAY 1861 |
| LePAGE, Louis C. [4] | SEDGWICK, Ellen V. | 04 JUN 1864 |
| LEPPOLD, John B. | FENDNER, Mary | 16 JUL 1859 |
| LEPREUX, Augustus | TAIT, Anne C. | 20 NOV 1860 |
| LESLIE, Hiram P. | HINTON, Mary E. | 19 MAY 1859 |
| LESTER, Joseph H. | HARRISON, Cynthia | 01 MAR 1866 |

| | | |
|---|---|---|
| LESTER, Joseph H. | YOUNG, Alice C. | 06 DEC 1869 |
| LESTER, Samuel S. | FARLEY, Annie | 10 JUN 1865 |
| LETCHER, Henry | DORSEY, Jane (blk) | 30 DEC 1868 |
| LEVENGER, Henry | BRYAND, Elizabeth A. | 29 OCT 1865 |
| LEVI, Wm. T. | NOLAN, Annie E. | 14 JAN 1868 |
| LEVICK, George D. | HALBERT, Jemima | 01 JUL 1863 |
| LEVINS, Chas. W. | FISHER, Catharine M. | 29 JAN 1863 |
| LEVINS, Christopher | HOUGHTON, Mary Ann | 24 MAY 1866 |
| LEVIS, Curtis | CLOKEY, Ann E. | 05 OCT 1863 |
| LEVRONE, David | LEVRONE, Mary | 22 APR 1865 |
| LEVY, Erastus | RUSSELL, Jennette | 30 NOV 1861 |
| LEVY, Jesse | JOHNS, Elizabeth | 24 MAY 1866 |
| LEVY, Joseph | BROWN, Sarah (blk) | 07 JUL 1866 |
| LEVY, Leopold F. | HAAS, Johanna | 12 DEC 1866 |
| LEVY, Michael | DORES, Margaret | 20 AUG 1859 |
| LEWEY, Daniel W. | BRADY, Mary | 28 JAN 1863 |
| LEWIS, Andrew | FRAZIER, Rebecca (blk) | 06 DEC 1866 |
| LEWIS, Anthony | BRYANT, Isabella (blk) | 20 MAR 1865 |
| LEWIS, Benjamin M. [9n] | DAVIS, Josephine | 06 NOV 1858 |
| LEWIS, Benjn. | FIELDS, Leanna (blk) | 23 MAY 1864 |
| LEWIS, Charles | FORD, Mary (blk) | 27 JUN 1863 |
| LEWIS, Charles A. | SMALLWOOD, Emma F. | 29 SEP 1869 |
| LEWIS, Charles E.F. | BETTERSBY, Catharine A. | 02 FEB 1865 |
| LEWIS, Charles O. | WELLS, Rebecca | 07 JAN 1861 |
| LEWIS, Christopher | STEWART, Sarah L. | 13 JAN 1868 |
| LEWIS, Christopher C. | GILES, Sarah Jane (blk) | 06 JAN 1868 |
| LEWIS, Daniel | DODSON, Delia (blk) | 19 MAY 1869 |
| LEWIS, Daniel S. | BOTTS, Isabella M. | 03 JUL 1868 |
| LEWIS, David | LANCASTER, Emily Jane (blk) | 18 FEB 1867 |
| LEWIS, David, Capt. 8th O. Inf. | McCRACKEN, Maggie | 30 MAY 1864 |
| LEWIS, David [2] | LOVELESS, Marion | 20 AUG 1868 |
| LEWIS, Dennis | WEST, Eliza (blk) | 27 DEC 1865 |
| LEWIS, Edward [12s] | OAKSHOTT, Annie | 22 JAN 1861 |
| LEWIS, Edward R. | LEWIS, Sallie S. | 03 AUG 1865 |
| LEWIS, Elam H. | GIBSON, Jessie | 06 JAN 1864 |
| LEWIS, Enoch M. | LEACH, Emily R. | 15 NOV 1866 |
| LEWIS, Eugene R. | WELLS, Martha (blk) | 02 OCT 1867 |
| LEWIS, Fielder | DIXON, Mary (blk) | 28 FEB 1866 |
| LEWIS, Fielding | GREEN, Imogine | 28 APR 1859 |
| LEWIS, George | BROWN, Catherine (col'd) | 31 DEC 1863 |
| LEWIS, George | JONES, Laura | 16 MAY 1866 |
| LEWIS, George | DELANEY, Ellen (blk) | 15 JUN 1869 |
| LEWIS, George [10] | BERKELEY, Rozela Augusta | 12 MAR 1870 |
| LEWIS, George W. | HARRIS, Catherine C. | 28 DEC 1868 |
| LEWIS, Harvey | BURGESS, Elizabeth | 18 FEB 1864 |
| LEWIS, Henry | ANDERSON, Lethe Ann | 22 DEC 1860 |
| LEWIS, Henry | TANGTANY, Margaret | 06 DEC 1861 |
| LEWIS, Ira M. | LEWIS, Elizabeth A. | 09 APR 1864 |
| LEWIS, Isaac | DAVIS, Mollie | 12 APR 1866 |
| LEWIS, James | SMITH, Anna (blk) | 28 MAR 1863 |
| LEWIS, James | COOK, Amanda | 13 JUL 1865 |
| LEWIS, James | BEVERLY, Mary (blk) | 29 AUG 1866 |
| LEWIS, James | DORNAN, Maria | 30 DEC 1867 |
| LEWIS, James E. | BROWN, Mary | 16 JUN 1870 |
| LEWIS, James H. | McINTOSH, Angeline | 02 JUN 1863 |
| LEWIS, Jerry | HURD, Mary (blk) | 15 DEC 1865 |

| | | |
|---|---|---|
| LEWIS, Jesse | JACKSON, Martha | 03 SEP 1867 |
| LEWIS, John | RICHARDSON, Emma (blk) | 18 APR 1866 |
| LEWIS, John | WOODFORK, Annie (blk) | 10 JUL 1866 |
| LEWIS, John | HOLMES, Frances (blk) | 02 DEC 1869 |
| LEWIS, John H. [12s] | FLOWEREE, Eliza E. | 24 JAN 1860 |
| LEWIS, John H. | KING, Mary Margaret | 25 SEP 1866 |
| LEWIS, Joseph | CONWAY, Priscilla (blk) | 07 MAY 1864 |
| LEWIS, Joseph | PRICE, Eliza (blk) | 28 DEC 1869 |
| LEWIS, Major | JONES, Allice (blk) | 09 JUL 1863 |
| LEWIS, Major | JOHNSON, Caroline (blk) | 29 DEC 1866 |
| LEWIS, Melvin | EDWARDS, Charlotte (blk) | 17 MAY 1870 |
| LEWIS, Nicholas P. | COOK, Eliza I. | 13 DEC 1866 |
| LEWIS, Oliver | BLAIR, Maggie A. | 25 APR 1866 |
| LEWIS, Peter [10] | MASON, Rachel E. (blk) | 05 DEC 1865 |
| LEWIS, Philip | CHAMBERLAIN, Clara | 02 JAN 1869 |
| LEWIS, Richard | SMITH, Mary Lizzie (blk) | 02 JUN 1868 |
| LEWIS, Richard C. | CUSHLY, Mary | 21 MAR 1861 |
| LEWIS, Robert | COMMODORE, Henrietta (blk) | 05 JAN 1869 |
| LEWIS, Sandford | KLOFOOT, Margaret (blk) | 04 JUN 1867 |
| LEWIS, Sanford | BLAND, Admonia Janey (blk) | 13 JAN 1870 |
| LEWIS, Silas D. | McINTOSH, Annie V. | 26 OCT 1868 |
| LEWIS, Stanford | MARSHALL, Florence (blk) | 06 MAY 1869 |
| LEWIS, Thomas [of Chicago] [10] | CLATER, Julia | 25 FEB 1864 |
| LEWIS, Thomas | McNAMEE, Mary | 03 MAY 1866 |
| LEWIS, Thomas | JOHNSON, Eliza (blk) | 30 SEP 1867 |
| LEWIS, Thomas | TUTT, Mary Frances (blk) | 28 SEP 1868 |
| LEWIS, Thomas | FOX, Hannah (blk) | 17 MAY 1870 |
| LEWIS, Thomas D. | MOORE, Annie L. | 25 OCT 1866 |
| LEWIS, Thornton | LEWIS, Dilsey (blk) | 18 JUL 1867 |
| LEWIS, Walker [12s] | BARBOUR, Virginia | 22 OCT 1860 |
| LEWIS, William | GIBBONS, Ellen | 28 MAR 1864 |
| LEWIS, William | GRAY, Susan (blk) | 12 MAY 1864 |
| LEWIS, William | SCOTT, Rose (blk) | 02 MAY 1865 |
| LEWIS, William | CARTER, Delia (blk) | 07 NOV 1865 |
| LEWIS, William | NUGENT, Martha (blk) | 11 JUL 1867 |
| LEWIS, William B. | FOLLINS, Margaret A. | 15 MAR 1860 |
| LEWIS, William Henry | DIAZO, Virginia (blk) | 04 JUN 1864 |
| LEWIS, William J. | WINSHIP, Isadora J. | 18 SEP 1866 |
| LEWIS, William J. | HALSOP, Annie M.P. | 11 FEB 1867 |
| LEWIS, William [4] | SANDFORD, Elizabeth | 25 OCT 1862 |
| LIBBEY, John E. | ORME, Emily Frances | 06 APR 1863 |
| LIBBEY, Joseph, Junr. | ORME, Mary R. | 17 DEC 1860 |
| LICKEY, George W. | BOHRER, Ellen | 05 MAY 1859 |
| LICKISS, Edwin C. | FRANKLIN, Lena | 27 MAR 1865 |
| LIDOBANSKI, John | JOYCE, Mary | 29 MAY 1863 |
| LIEKEL, Frederick | SCHMIDT, Catherine | 02 JAN 1861 |
| LIGHTELL, John [B.] [10] | NORRISS, Jane Elizth. | 14 AUG 1860 |
| LIGHTER, George W. | CROUN, Sarah E. | 29 NOV 1869 |
| LIGHTFOOT, Geo. W. | CHAMBERLAIN, Sarah | 03 AUG 1863 |
| LIGHTFOOT, John | THOMAS, Mary | 26 MAR 1870 |
| LILLARD, Howard M. | KITE, Elizabeth C. | 21 DEC 1868 |
| LINAHAN, Timothy | FOX, Ellen | 04 SEP 1868 |
| LINCKE, Gustav | WHEN, Louise | 02 JAN 1868 |
| LINCOLN, Nathan S. | RIDGATE, Margaret E. | 26 APR 1859 |
| LINCOLN, Robert T. | HARLAN, Mary | 24 SEP 1868 |
| LINCOLN, Thomas V. | DRUMMOND, Hellen C. | 11 SEP 1861 |

District of Columbia Marriage Licenses, 1858-1870

| | | |
|---|---|---|
| LINDER, Frederick [11] | TAYLOR, Sarah | 01 AUG 1865 |
| LINDIG, Adolph | STENG, Anna | 05 JUN 1861 |
| LINDIG, Ernest | NAYLOR, Elizabeth | 28 MAY 1861 |
| LINDLEY, George W. | SCHULER, Martha E. | 09 JAN 1864 |
| LINDQUIST, John | NANZ, Wilhelmina Fredericka | 06 JUL 1863 |
| LINDSAY, Thomas | CAVANAGH, Kate | 14 MAR 1866 |
| LINDSEY, Absalom | BROOKS, Malvina (blk) | 11 OCT 1869 |
| LINDSLEY, Cleland | BOWIE, Mary Auguste | 23 JAN 1865 |
| LINEHARDT, Adam | MART, Mary | 09 NOV 1858 |
| LINEHART, George | HAHN, Margaret | 16 FEB 1864 |
| LINK, Jacob | BUTTS, Sophia | 24 SEP 1859 |
| LINK, John | BERGER, Mary | 03 AUG 1865 |
| LINKINS, Henry S. | TANGLEY, Mary | 23 DEC 1862 |
| LINKINS, John F. | ATHEY, Alice Ann | 15 SEP 1865 |
| LINKINS, William | VanHORN, Margaret | 05 NOV 1861 |
| LINN, John | MOORE, Mary Ann | 02 AUG 1862 |
| LINSDEY, Warner | BROOKS, Georgiana (blk) | 11 AUG 1868 |
| LINSKEY, James | KANE, Jane | 05 SEP 1866 |
| LINTNER, John | CLEARY, Caroline | 23 JAN 1865 |
| LINTNER, William | HURDLE, Emily | 03 JAN 1865 |
| LINTON, Jerome [10] | ARNOLD, Laura V. | 31 DEC 1863 |
| LINTON, John [8] | SMILEY, Mary Ann | 22 JAN 1870 |
| LINTZ, Samuel | CAMMACK, Sarah Ann | 20 MAR 1865 |
| LION, Thomas William | WILLIAMS, Somerville | 15 DEC 1865 |
| LIPES, John | RILEY, Catherine | 18 JAN 1862 |
| LIPPERT, John Adam | SMITH, Margaret | 19 FEB 1861 |
| LIPPHERD, John F. | HOPKINS, Eldrianna A. | 19 JUN 1867 |
| LIPPOLD, John P. | ROCKAWAY, Wilhelmina | 02 NOV 1864 |
| LIPSCOMB, Jesse | GALER, Mary | 01 OCT 1861 |
| LISLES, Joseph | BROWN, Ellen | 29 MAR 1866 |
| LIST, Christian H. | BECKER, Eva E. | 14 SEP 1858 |
| LISTON, Michael | KING, Ann | 26 JUL 1860 |
| LITCHFIELD, Charles | PEERCE, Eliza | 09 DEC 1861 |
| LITCHFIELD, Edward H. | COZZENS, Martha A. | 31 DEC 1859 |
| LITCHFIELD, James A. | BURROWS, Anna | 04 APR 1865 |
| LITHGOW, George | PETTIGREW, Florence Jane | 08 DEC 1864 |
| LITSINGER, Thomas H. [6le] | DANIELS, Elizabeth A. | 06 DEC 1865 |
| LITSINGER, William D. | HAWKINS, Amelet C. | 16 MAR 1869 |
| LITTLE, Columbus M. | KELEHER, Henrietta | 21 JAN 1863 |
| LITTLE, James C. [6h] | PENN, Mary Elizabeth | 14 MAR 1868 |
| LITTLE, John | PEPPERT, Christiana | 04 DEC 1861 |
| LITTLE, John | JEFFERSON, Catharine | 18 AUG 1864 |
| LITTLE, Patrick | KANE, Ellen C. | 24 NOV 1862 |
| LITTLE, Samuel | BOYCE, Julia | 13 MAR 1867 |
| LITTLE, William M. | ANDERSON, Mary Virginia | 05 MAY 1864 |
| LITTLEFORD, John | RAWLINGS, Sarah | 24 NOV 1862 |
| LITTLETON, Thos. J. | RITTER, Elizabeth | 17 JAN 1860 |
| LITTLETON, William | HOFFMAN, Ellen | 08 DEC 1864 |
| LITZ, Balthasar | ECKSTEIN, Franciska | 21 NOV 1864 |
| LIVELY, Statia | JORDAN, Julia (blk) | 03 MAR 1862 |
| LIVERMORE, R.J. | ANTISELL, Elizabeth | 14 MAY 1868 |
| LIVERPOOL, Joseph | SOMMERVILLE, Julia (blk) | 10 JUL 1866 |
| LLOYD, Asbury | STONE, Bettie E. | 03 JUL 1865 |
| LLOYD, Joseph | CONTEE, Eliza (blk) | 04 JUN 1867 |
| LLOYD, Samuel | MARTIN, Louisa E. | 17 MAR 1864 |
| LLOYD, Samuel William | FITZGERALD, Anna | 07 MAY 1869 |

District of Columbia Marriage Licenses, 1858-1870

| | | |
|---|---|---|
| LLOYD, Wallace | GOSSOM, Martha | 01 JAN 1868 |
| LLOYD, William | GREEN, Susannah (blk) | 02 SEP 1869 |
| LLOYD, William Henry | SHEPHERD, Lucy Ann | 25 JUL 1866 |
| LOCHBEILER, Rudolph | FISHER, Mary | 04 AUG 1863 |
| LOCHBOEHLER, George P. | PFEIFER, Johanna | 19 MAY 1863 |
| LOCHBOEHLER, Joseph | EICHHORN, Margaret | 13 APR 1863 |
| LOCHBOEHLER, Nicholas | BECHTOLD, Karolina | 23 OCT 1858 |
| LOCHTER, Henry | McGARVRIN, Eliza | 28 JUL 1864 |
| LOCKE, Lloyd P. | DICE, Teany E. | 13 OCT 1868 |
| LOCKE, William | CARTER, Jennie | 10 DEC 1866 |
| LOCKE, William Q. | MILLER, Mary C. | 23 MAR 1863 |
| LOCKER, James Henry | YOUNG, Mary (blk) | 15 NOV 1865 |
| LOCKETT, William | MODIA, Anna | 27 NOV 1862 |
| LOCKHEAD, James | O'NEALE, Annie | 29 APR 1862 |
| LOCKLEY, John | CONKRON, Phoebe (blk) | 01 NOV 1866 |
| LOCKWOOD, E., Dr. | McNALL, Belva A., Mrs. | 11 MAR 1868 |
| LODGE, James | CLARKE, Martha (blk) | 02 DEC 1865 |
| LOEFFLER, Jacob | DICKEL, Helen | 03 APR 1860 |
| LOEHR, Philip | RUPRECHT, Christiana | 30 JUN 1863 |
| LOERINGS, John | DAY, Betty (blk) | 13 SEP 1867 |
| LOFTUS, Dennis | KING, Margaret | 03 MAY 1865 |
| LOFTUS, Frederick B. | FOWLER, Caroline L. | 22 DEC 1862 |
| LOGAN, Alexander | ELLIS, Emma | 29 SEP 1864 |
| LOGAN, Edward T. | SPOTTS, Margaret C. | 05 APR 1859 |
| LOGAN, James P. | CAMPBELL, Mary Elizabeth | 20 JAN 1866 |
| LOGAN, John H. | KINGSBERRY, Ellen | 31 DEC 1860 |
| LOGAN, John H. | CHATMAN, Elizabeth (blk) | 26 JAN 1870 |
| LOGAN, John J. | ROYAL, Rosetta (blk) | 03 AUG 1865 |
| LOGAN, Samual B. | THURSTON, Jeannette B. | 10 DEC 1867 |
| LOHMEYER, Albert T. | PAULY, Catherina | 15 JUL 1862 |
| LOHMEYER, Henry | PIE, Margaret | 27 SEP 1862 |
| LOMAS, John | TODTCHINSDER, Wilhelmina | 30 APR 1860 |
| LOMASNEY, Michael | ROCHE, Ellen | 08 JUN 1863 |
| LOMAX, Allen | CORBIN, Sophia (blk) | 06 DEC 1867 |
| LOMAX, Ananias William James | GADSBY, Mary (blk) | 23 APR 1870 |
| LOMAX, James | LAMBERS, Nancy (blk) | 22 DEC 1868 |
| LOMAX, James C. | JACKSON, Virginia | 04 MAR 1867 |
| LOMAX, John W. | SAMPSON, Elizabeth (blk) | 22 AUG 1866 |
| LOMAX, Lewis | BAYLOR, Lucy (blk) | 21 MAY 1870 |
| LOMAX, Richard | STUART, Minerva (blk) | 12 APR 1865 |
| LOMAX, Thomas | GUY, Ann Maria (blk) | 25 OCT 1866 |
| LOMAX, William | JACKSON, Frances (blk) | 04 JUN 1863 |
| LOMAX, William | HELMS, Louisa (blk) | 02 AUG 1866 |
| LOMAX, William | HELMS, Louisa (blk) | 31 JUL 1866 |
| LOMAX, Wm. | GREEN, Margt. (blk) | 16 OCT 1858 |
| LOMBARD, Joseph J. | POOLE, Rebecca R. | 16 FEB 1863 |
| LONDON, Daniel E. | HUFF, Mary Jane | 09 JUN 1869 |
| LONG, Aaron B. | CURREY, Catharine T. | 22 DEC 1864 |
| LONG, Christopher | BOWEN, Laura E. | 22 APR 1861 |
| LONG, Daniel | SCANLON, Catharine | 01 SEP 1862 |
| LONG, Frederick | STRICKHART, Mena | 03 OCT 1868 |
| LONG, Frederick | GOULD, Ellen | 28 DEC 1869 |
| LONG, Henry | MILLER, Susan | 18 JUL 1861 |
| LONG, Henry J.B. | BOSWELL, Mary V. | 23 APR 1867 |
| LONG, James | MAHONEY, Mary | 10 JAN 1859 |
| LONG, James | CASSADY, Julia | 19 NOV 1862 |

District of Columbia Marriage Licenses, 1858-1870

| | | |
|---|---|---|
| LONG, John | HORN, Catherine | 07 OCT 1868 |
| LONG, John H. | SHARPLEY, Mary Jane | 26 APR 1862 |
| LONG, Joseph | MORRISON, Jane (blk) | 28 DEC 1865 |
| LONG, Patrick | KELLY, Mary | 11 DEC 1858 |
| LONG, Robert Burch | SMITH, Mary A. (blk) | 13 APR 1864 |
| LONG, W.M. | FILLETT, Addie | 24 NOV 1868 |
| LONG, Walter P. | RUMSEY, Sarah C. | 14 AUG 1869 |
| LONG, William | THOMPSON, Mary F. (blk) | 14 JUL 1859 |
| LONGHERY, Edward P. | McCULLIF, Jennie | 16 FEB 1867 |
| LONGSTREET, William | KIRBY, Mary Jane | 13 AUG 1865 |
| LOOMIS, Orlando M. [7a] | WELSH, Annie M. | 13 MAY 1867 |
| LOOMIS, Simeon R. | ALTER, Mary L. | 15 FEB 1866 |
| LOONEY, William | CLINE, Bridget | 18 DEC 1865 |
| LOOPE, Eugene C. | WARREN, Marietta E. | 24 FEB 1864 |
| LOOR, John R. | COX, Julia A. | 03 JUL 1865 |
| LOPER, John A. | CRAWFORD, Elizabeth | 23 AUG 1865 |
| LORAINE, Lorenzo [Lt.] [10] | McDONALD, Fannie | 17 FEB 1862 |
| LORCH, Charles G. | SCHUBERT, Adelhied | 29 FEB 1864 |
| LORD, Benjamin F. | MYRICK, Arlitta B. | 15 FEB 1866 |
| LORD, Ebenezer | HOOVER, Indiana H. | 10 DEC 1861 |
| LORD, Edward | FOGLE, Sarah Ann | 17 APR 1862 |
| LORD, Frank P. [3] | TEMPLETON, Luanna H. | 28 MAR 1864 |
| LORD, John | PRUET, Mary | 11 JUN 1862 |
| LORD, John W. | O'BRIEN, Henrietta | 07 MAY 1866 |
| LORD, William A. | CAMP, Sarah A.R. | 30 NOV 1869 |
| LORD, William E. | CARUSI, Delphine | 25 SEP 1865 |
| LOSEKAM, Charles | WAGNER, Louisa | 15 JUN 1869 |
| LOSSEN, Peter | ROBINSON, [illegible] (blk) | 29 JUL 1864 |
| LOTHROP, John P. | YAGER, Matilda C. | 16 OCT 1867 |
| LOTTIE, Robert | LAKE, Amanda J. | 24 JAN 1862 |
| LOTZ, Thomas | HEIL, Margaret | 03 APR 1863 |
| LOTZ, Thomas | STROMAN, Anna McGregor Elizabeth | 09 SEP 1867 |
| LOUDER, Robert | COKELAND, Mary (blk) | 27 JUN 1863 |
| LOUGHRAN, John | BRODERICK, Catherine | 26 JUN 1869 |
| LOUGHRAN, Joseph F. | HILBUS, Mary Ann | 27 AUG 1867 |
| LOUHARDT, Peter | CHRISMAN, Elizebeth | 15 MAY 1860 |
| LOUIS, Max | STRAUSS, Fannie | 05 AUG 1862 |
| LOUNT, W.R. | ETCHISON, Virginia | 02 JUN 1868 |
| LOUNTS, Isaac | KING, Chloe | 13 MAY 1869 |
| LOVE, Charles K. | MAHORNEY, Isabel E. | 18 JUL 1867 |
| LOVE, Zebedee | WEST, Margaret | 12 NOV 1864 |
| LOVEJOY, Henry [11] | STEIGER, Augusta [Fern] | 06 JUN 1864 |
| LOVEJOY, J. Edward | BLAND, Rosa B. | 08 JUN 1868 |
| LOVEJOY, John S. | HERBERT, Sarah A. | 29 SEP 1862 |
| LOVELACE, Edward | PATTERSON, Sarah Ann | 27 JUL 1859 |
| LOVELESS, George H. | CAMPBELL, Mary E. | 05 FEB 1859 |
| LOVELESS, James H. | NORTON, Mary A. | 20 JAN 1862 |
| LOVING, Henry C. | GUNNELL, Marion R. | 16 APR 1860 |
| LOVING, William | SHUTTE, Bertha | 17 JAN 1868 |
| LOW, Andrew | MOXLEY, Bessie L. | 26 SEP 1859 |
| LOW, George | HOWARD, Eliza (blk) | 08 JUN 1868 |
| LOW, John E. | HEIBERGER, Emma V. | 14 JUN 1870 |
| LOWATER, Stephen L. | GATELY, Mary | 15 MAR 1864 |
| LOWBER, John | FERGUSON, Ellen A. | 10 MAR 1859 |
| LOWE, Fras. A. | MYERS, Rebecca E. | 22 JAN 1863 |
| LOWE, John | DZER, Josephine L. | 30 OCT 1867 |

District of Columbia Marriage Licenses, 1858-1870

| | | |
|---|---|---|
| LOWE, Lewis P. | ENNIS, Mary R. | 18 JUL 1868 |
| LOWE, Nathaniel | LOWE, Elethen E. | 21 JAN 1862 |
| LOWE, Walter [10] | RYAN, Susie | 11 NOV 1867 |
| LOWE, William L. | MYERS, Virginia F. | 27 DEC 1860 |
| LOWE, Zachariah | SCOTT, Cecil May | 12 JUL 1865 |
| LOWER, William | GROVES, Celia Ann | 01 MAY 1861 |
| LOWNDES, Calvin G. | SMITH, Cecelia C. | 09 OCT 1858 |
| LOWREY, Alfred | COX, Jane | 10 MAR 1870 |
| LOWREY, James H. | PARKINSON, Maria E. | 04 FEB 1869 |
| LOWREY, John H. | TARLTON, Mary E. | 01 OCT 1864 |
| LOWRY, Mason S. | COVER, Mary E. | 11 APR 1867 |
| LOWRY, William H. | BIBB, Acadia S. | 18 OCT 1865 |
| LOY, John [2] | HALL, Annie V. | 19 JUN 1867 |
| LUBER, Albert T. | CRANDLE, Mary Emma | 19 AUG 1869 |
| LUBER, George | BRANDT, Elizabeth | 30 MAY 1863 |
| LUBER, John | ENGLEHARD, Catharine | 11 FEB 1865 |
| LUBEY, Timothy | MELDON, Maria | 06 JAN 1864 |
| LUCAS, Albert | WASHINGTON, Ann (blk) | 03 DEC 1864 |
| LUCAS, Eugene I. | BAKER, Mary Susie | 25 JUL 1867 |
| LUCAS, Harvey Rollins | DAGGETT, Kate | 02 OCT 1866 |
| LUCAS, Henry | LEE, Laura (blk) | 22 DEC 1859 |
| LUCAS, James A. [6] | SMITH, Adelia | 19 OCT 1868 |
| LUCAS, James C. | JONES, Mary E. | 18 FEB 1869 |
| LUCAS, James F. | PRINTZ, Isabel V. | 17 DEC 1860 |
| LUCAS, John | GANTT, Louisa (blk) | 10 APR 1862 |
| LUCAS, John | WALLIS, Adelaid (blk) | 11 FEB 1863 |
| LUCAS, John | LONG, Ellen | 14 MAY 1863 |
| LUCAS, John | JACKSON, Annie (blk) | 08 JUN 1864 |
| LUCAS, John | SHEPHERD, Columbia (blk) | 19 FEB 1867 |
| LUCAS, Joseph F. | SULLIVAN, Mary F. | 01 SEP 1863 |
| LUCAS, Peter | HOGAN, Matilda (blk) | 10 APR 1868 |
| LUCAS, Peter | SMITH, Amanda (blk) | 16 OCT 1868 |
| LUCAS, Richard A. | ORR, Margaret | 02 SEP 1864 |
| LUCAS, Rile | CHAPMAN, Elsie | 12 APR 1869 |
| LUCAS, Samuel | BROWN, Margaret (blk) | 12 AUG 1862 |
| LUCAS, Solomon | BROWN, Dora (blk) | 23 DEC 1865 |
| LUCAS, Strother | SMITH, Caroline (blk) | 18 JAN 1865 |
| LUCAS, Theodore H. | HARMON, Ann C. | 04 DEC 1861 |
| LUCAS, William | GING, Margaret R. | 02 JUN 1859 |
| LUCAS, William | HICKMAN, Elizabeth Ann (blk) | 24 FEB 1863 |
| LUCAS, William H. | MORRIS, Julia (blk) | 05 SEP 1867 |
| LUCAS, William W. | BRANAGAN, Georgiana | 14 DEC 1863 |
| LUCE, Carlton G. | FITCH, Mary E. | 29 NOV 1867 |
| LUCÉ, John Batties | IRVIN, Constance | 21 OCT 1865 |
| LUCKENBACH, Owen A. | CROCKER, Jennie E. | 12 SEP 1864 |
| LUCKETT, George | ROBINSON, Adaline (blk) | 02 NOV 1869 |
| LUCKETT, John | WILKINS, Harriet | 26 DEC 1867 |
| LUCKETT, Marcus L. | BOSWELL, Eliza V. | 02 DEC 1867 |
| LUCKID, Samuel | BUTLER, Elizabeth (blk) | 27 NOV 1867 |
| LUDEKE, Frank J. | BARRETT, Ann E. | 11 JUL 1861 |
| LUDERS, Louis | VENABLE, Catherine, Mrs. | 21 JUL 1866 |
| LUDLOW, Daniel | DEVIS, Virginia | 10 MAY 1865 |
| LUDLOW, Levi M. [10] | STRATTON, Cynthia M. | 05 SEP 1865 |
| LUEPCKE, Edward | GRONAU, Eliza | 27 OCT 1863 |
| LUFF, John S. | COX, Eliza Ann | 11 NOV 1867 |
| LUKEI, Andrew J. | GRIMES, Indiana W. | 25 JUL 1861 |

District of Columbia Marriage Licenses, 1858-1870

| | | |
|---|---|---|
| LULAND, William R. | CULLEN, Mary Jane | 09 JAN 1864 |
| LUNCH, Andrew | WALKER, Julia E. | 23 FEB 1861 |
| LUNDY, Call | HOLLIS, Laura Annie (blk) | 14 NOV 1867 |
| LUNT, George W. | DAVIS, Mary C. | 03 APR 1865 |
| LUSBY, Charles | FISTER, Harriet | 15 FEB 1865 |
| LUSBY, Charles E. | CARROLL, Anna | 10 JAN 1862 |
| LUSBY, Cleophas B. | PHELPS, Mary F. | 25 MAY 1869 |
| LUSBY, David | TAYLOR, Margaret | 07 OCT 1861 |
| LUSBY, Edward | FISTER, Harriet A. | 06 DEC 1864 |
| LUSBY, George | RIDGEWAY, Martha Ann | 16 JAN 1867 |
| LUSBY, George W. [11s] * | EVANS, Lucinda | 24 DEC 1869 |
| LUSBY, John F. | ELLIS, Clara Jane | 27 JUN 1859 |
| LUSBY, John T. | SMITH, Rachel Mary | 11 AUG 1862 |
| LUSBY, Joseph Henry | GREEN, Lizzie Ann | 27 AUG 1867 |
| LUSBY, Robert [6r] | STAPLES, Emeline | 20 DEC 1860 |
| LUSBY, William H. | DEMENT, Jane E. | 02 OCT 1858 |
| LUSKEY, George [6le] | BOHLAYER, Margaret | 08 MAY 1867 |
| LUSKEY, John [6m] | SHECKELLS, Mary R. | 28 MAY 1862 |
| LUSKEY, John R. | STARWHITE, Mary E. | 17 AUG 1869 |
| LUSKEY, William A. [6cl] | SCOTT, Sarah F. | 09 JUN 1870 |
| LUTHER, James [1c] | STONE, Amelia | 10 FEB 1864 |
| LUTHY, Frederick E. | FAY, Celestina de | 10 NOV 1868 |
| LÜTHY, Lorenz | vonMECHOW, Ida | 05 JAN 1863 |
| LUXON, James | KNARBE, Catherine E. | 15 DEC 1864 |
| LYDDANE, Edmund | KENGLA, Maggie | 06 DEC 1869 |
| LYDDANE, John | FOX, Mary E. | 24 OCT 1866 |
| LYDEN, Valentine | REILY, Mary | 29 JAN 1862 |
| LYDON, Bartholomew | FINNEGAN, Mary | 05 DEC 1863 |
| LYDON, James | KEHOE, Ann | 30 JUL 1859 |
| LYDON, John | CLANCY, Mary | 15 DEC 1868 |
| LYDON, Michael J. | DICKENS, Agnes | 01 JAN 1866 |
| LYEN, John | SNYDER, Caroline | 18 APR 1863 |
| LYLE, John G. [4] | WEED, Lizzie B. | 05 MAY 1863 |
| LYLE, William Henry | LaVILLE, Anna | 14 JUN 1870 |
| LYLES, Edgar | BUTLER, Henrietta | 02 JUL 1860 |
| LYLES, Ferdinand | DODSON, Frances | 15 APR 1861 |
| LYLES, George | JENIFER, Lizzie (blk) | 25 APR 1862 |
| LYLES, George Washington | COKELY, Rebecca (blk) | 10 SEP 1867 |
| LYLES, Harrison, Gen. | ADAMS, Mary | 31 MAR 1865 |
| LYLES, Robert | GASSAWAY, Catharine L. | 02 FEB 1864 |
| LYLES, Silas | TOLBERT, Harriet | 16 JAN 1868 |
| LYLES, Thomas | BURL, Mary (blk) | 15 JAN 1862 |
| LYLES, Thomas C. | GODDARD, Mary A. | 28 FEB 1867 |
| LYNAM, Thomas | LUSBY, Annie L. | 27 JAN 1864 |
| LYNCH, Alpheus D. (wounded soldier) | TAYLOR, Catherine | 21 JUN 1864 |
| LYNCH, Bartholomew | LYNCH, Mary | 05 MAY 1862 |
| LYNCH, Daniel | SCANLER, Johanna | 23 JUN 1859 |
| LYNCH, Daniel | DRONAY, Mary | 30 JAN 1868 |
| LYNCH, Edmund J. | McFALL, Cecilia | 01 FEB 1864 |
| LYNCH, Edward | THOMPSON, Mary C. | 03 SEP 1867 |
| LYNCH, George J. [6le] | ROLLINS, Mary | 23 AUG 1865 |
| LYNCH, Jeremiah | SKELLY, Bridget | 22 JUN 1864 |
| LYNCH, Jeremiah | MULVIHILL, Margaret | 27 SEP 1864 |
| LYNCH, John | O'BRIEN, Margaret | 03 JUN 1859 |
| LYNCH, John | LEE, Sarah (blk) | 25 FEB 1864 |
| LYNCH, John | MULT, Ellen | 04 FEB 1864 |

| | | |
|---|---|---|
| LYNCH, John | BROWN, Margaret | 05 OCT 1866 |
| LYNCH, John | GOZLIN, Annie | 10 JUN 1869 |
| LYNCH, John D. | DOUD, Ellen | 12 MAR 1864 |
| LYNCH, John D. [10] | KILBY, Esther | 01 AUG 1866 |
| LYNCH, Matthew | MORONY, Mary | 28 FEB 1865 |
| LYNCH, Michael | CLARKE, Mary Catherine | 12 FEB 1862 |
| LYNCH, Michael | JENKINS, Cornelia T. | 26 JAN 1865 |
| LYNCH, Michael | BENNETT, Hanorah | 02 JAN 1868 |
| LYNCH, Patrick | CULL, Rose | 14 NOV 1863 |
| LYNCH, Patrick | GIBBS, Martha (blk) | 14 OCT 1869 |
| LYNCH, Thomas E. | GAINOR, Kate B. | 21 SEP 1867 |
| LYNCH, Thomas [6s] | WHITE, Sarah Elizabeth | 02 FEB 1865 |
| LYNCH, William | SULLIVAN, Mary | 13 MAY 1862 |
| LYNCH, William | KING, Elizabeth Margaret | 20 AUG 1863 |
| LYNCH, William [10] | KIRBY, Harriet | 19 JUN 1867 |
| LYNCH, William [6s] | SCHAEF [or Shafe], Eliza | 12 NOV 1864 |
| LYNN, Alfred | GENT, Rosetta | 23 DEC 1865 |
| LYNN, Alfred | GORDON, Elizabeth (blk) | 16 JAN 1868 |
| LYNN, Benjamin F. | BULLETT, Mattie | 27 MAY 1869 |
| LYNN, Henry | WILLIAMS, Mima | 26 SEP 1867 |
| LYNN, J. Shirley | DANIEL, Helen M. | 16 FEB 1870 |
| LYNN, Lycurgus F. | SELECMAN, Jane E. | 17 OCT 1859 |
| LYON, C.D. | RUTHERFORD, Mary A. | 14 JAN 1870 |
| LYON, Charles | COOMBS, Sarah F. | 16 MAR 1864 |
| LYON, J.S. [6h] | THOMPSON, Adelaide | 27 JUL 1868 |
| LYON, Jacob | BURKHARD, Clara | 11 JUL 1864 |
| LYON, John R. | JOHNSON, Barbara | 21 OCT 1863 |
| LYONS, Denis | DEAN, Mary | 22 NOV 1862 |
| LYONS, John | ELWOOD, Mary | 12 SEP 1868 |
| LYONS, John Joseph | BAKER, Julia Ellen | 22 SEP 1862 |
| LYONS, Timothy | CONACES, Joanna | 06 JAN 1863 |
| LYONS, Timothy | RONAN, Elen M. | 28 JUL 1864 |
| LYSIGHT, Austin | McINTEE, Lizzie | 12 NOV 1868 |
| LYSTER, Henry [Francis, M.D.] [4] | BRENT, Winnifred Lee | 28 JAN 1867 |
| LYTLE, Thomas | PORME, Mary Ann | 29 SEP 1862 |
| LZNOS, Thomas | COLLINS, Johanna | 24 JUN 1867 |

# M

| | | |
|---|---|---|
| MAACK, James | CURTIS, Mary | 24 DEC 1858 |
| MAACK, Wm. N.H. | REESE, Martha A. | 24 OCT 1867 |
| MAAG, Henry | BURNS, Margaret | 04 JAN 1864 |
| MABARY, William | McNELLA, Anna | 30 NOV 1861 |
| MABIE, Nelson | WASHINGTON, Lucinda (blk) | 14 MAY 1864 |
| MABREY, Franklin | ISER, Mary | 18 FEB 1865 |
| MACAULEY, William | HOGANS, Nancy | 27 SEP 1864 |
| MacBRIDE, William C. | DAVIDSON, Ellen V. | 10 OCT 1866 |
| MACDEL, Ottomar | LEYPOLT, Eliza | 26 FEB 1869 |
| MACE, Joseph | MILLER, Lizzie | 08 JUL 1869 |
| MacGILL, William W. | CORTNOR, Belle R. | 28 SEP 1859 |
| MACHAM, George | HARPER, Matilda (blk) | 23 DEC 1864 |
| MACK, Benjamin | JUDKINS, Jane | 03 FEB 1866 |
| MACK, Frederick Otto | MULLIGAN, Margaret Ann Eliza | 28 JUL 1869 |
| MACK, Leonidas G. | HILBUS, Susan E. | 15 NOV 1862 |
| MACK, Michael | DUNNAHAY, Mary | 13 MAY 1862 |
| MACK, Mike | DAVID, Nancy | 07 JUL 1865 |

| | | |
|---|---|---|
| MACK, Oscar A. | DIMICK, Catharine O. | 17 OCT 1865 |
| MACK, Philip | BROWN, Isabella | 16 JUN 1866 |
| MACK, Richard D. | GORDON, Rosanna (blk) | 16 NOV 1863 |
| MACK, Simon | GALLERY, Cornelia (blk) | 23 JUN 1869 |
| MACK, William D. | MOORE, Ella S. | 26 APR 1867 |
| MACK, William D. | MOORE, Ella S. | 08 JAN 1868 |
| MACKALL, Joseph | CROWLEY, Catherine (blk) | 17 DEC 1868 |
| MACKALL, Nathan | DAY, Lucretia (blk) | 17 OCT 1866 |
| MACKALL, Richard | BELL, Lucy (blk) | 16 OCT 1867 |
| MACKENBUR, Joseph R.C. | PHILIPS, Angeline D. | 13 FEB 1866 |
| MacKENSEY, Jefferson | SOMERVILLE, Ann Maria | 16 JUL 1862 |
| MACKEWROTH, Christopher J. [10] | HINELINE, Rose D. | 10 JUL 1865 |
| MACKEY, James P. | MULLOY, Maria | 24 JUL 1862 |
| MACKEY, John | TEIRNEY, Margaret | 22 APR 1869 |
| MACKEY, Samuel D. | DONNELLY, Ellen | 09 JUN 1870 |
| MACKEY, Thomas J. | LLOYD, Rosina | 05 MAR 1859 |
| MACKEY, Thomas, Jr. | HAMILL, Emily Louisa | 15 JUL 1867 |
| MACKIN, Charles Henry | KEELER, Grace | 01 OCT 1863 |
| MACKUBIN, Richard C. | WARING, Mary V. | 12 JUN 1860 |
| MACOMB, Oscar W. | CROWLEY, Louisa | 09 JAN 1863 |
| MACOMB, Richard A. | EVERHART, Margaret | 17 DEC 1864 |
| MACOMBER, George | GODWIN, Kate M. | 28 JUN 1866 |
| MACRAE, John H. | BEACH, Sheldena W. | 14 MAR 1861 |
| MADDEN, Samuel W. | JONES, Matilda A. (blk) | 21 FEB 1867 |
| MADDEN, Timothy | TOBIN, Ann | 31 JAN 1863 |
| MADDIN, Henry | CORNELL, Sallie A.D. | 06 JUN 1860 |
| MADDOX, Edward | CUFF, Mary Ann (blk) | 17 DEC 1866 |
| MADDOX, James L. | O'LEARY, Margaret A. | 11 FEB 1863 |
| MADDOX, John T. | JONES, Agnes | 19 DEC 1859 |
| MADDOX, John W. | GRAY, Elizabeth S. | 31 AUG 1869 |
| MADDOX, L. | SKINNER, Ann | 01 JUN 1870 |
| MADDOX, Thomas [12s] | GROVEWOOD, Margaret (blk) | 25 JAN 1859 |
| MADDOX, William | NELSON, Martha | 27 JUN 1867 |
| MADDOX, William M. | LUCAS, Maria A. (blk) | 04 NOV 1869 |
| MADERT, Jacob | MARTIN, Minna | 03 MAR 1863 |
| MADES, Charles | PORTNET, Felixine | 04 MAR 1866 |
| MADES, Charles | MILLER, Lina | 12 NOV 1867 |
| MADES, Christopher | CRAUSCAP, Amelia | 03 JAN 1863 |
| MADES, Christopher | CRONSKOPH, Catherine | 14 MAR 1866 |
| MADES, John W. [10] | PERKINS, Millison | 01 SEP 1859 |
| MADIGAN, John | MAACK, Mary | 01 AUG 1860 |
| MADIGAN, John | CULLEN, Ann | 10 FEB 1866 |
| MADIGAN, John | HART, Bridget | 04 JAN 1869 |
| MADIGAN, John | LAWLOR, Hanora | 06 JAN 1869 |
| MADIS, William | WAGNER, Francisca | 07 AUG 1863 |
| MADISON, Charles | CARDENIS, Frances (blk) | 10 FEB 1863 |
| MADISON, James G. | HOLMES, Annie Elizabeth (blk) | 08 OCT 1863 |
| MADOX, George W. | CARROLL, Sarah P. | 21 SEP 1865 |
| MAEDEL, Justus W. | STUMPF, Julia | 18 APR 1860 |
| MAFIELD, Richard | FAGAN, Christiana | 25 APR 1863 |
| MAGEE, Dennis | MULLIGAN, Susannah | 22 JUL 1859 |
| MAGEE, George W. [10] | COSTOR, Elizabeth | 31 OCT 1863 |
| MAGEE, John A. | CARBIS, Annie J. | 05 DEC 1864 |
| MAGEE, John H. | BLAKE, Julia | 15 SEP 1866 |
| MAGINLEY, Daniel | MAGUIRE, Mary C. | 09 SEP 1868 |
| MAGRATH, Edmund | RYAN, Mary | 10 DEC 1863 |

District of Columbia Marriage Licenses, 1858-1870

| | | |
|---|---|---|
| MAGRAW, Thomas | MARDEN, Mary | 29 AUG 1865 |
| MAGRUDER, Abraham | DORSEY, Mary (blk) | 30 OCT 1866 |
| MAGRUDER, Caleb C. | NALLE, Bettie R. | 30 JUN 1868 |
| MAGRUDER, Eli | JACKSON, Eliza (blk) | 16 JAN 1867 |
| MAGRUDER, Enoch | WRIGHT, Harriet (blk) | 09 NOV 1868 |
| MAGRUDER, Frank | BROOM, Ann Eliza (blk) | 13 APR 1863 |
| MAGRUDER, Frank | TURNER, Mary (blk) | 15 JAN 1866 |
| MAGRUDER, Horace | DAVIS, Lizzie (blk) | 08 JUN 1866 |
| MAGRUDER, John | JOHNSON, Sarah (blk) | 07 MAY 1866 |
| MAGRUDER, John | QUEEN, Lucretia (blk) | 08 MAR 1870 |
| MAGRUDER, John Wm. | BERRY, Sarah Jane | 28 MAY 1862 |
| MAGRUDER, Joseph | HALL, Laura (blk) | 12 SEP 1866 |
| MAGRUDER, Joseph | HARRIS, Emma (blk) | 06 DEC 1866 |
| MAGRUDER, L.G. | TIPPETT, Annie E. | 05 FEB 1863 |
| MAGRUDER, Richard A.C. | DARRELL, Virginia E. | 29 MAR 1870 |
| MAGRUDER, Samuel C. | WHITE, Emma J. | 13 DEC 1865 |
| MAGRUDER, Thomas L. | HINLY, Mary A. | 03 MAR 1863 |
| MAGRUDY, Madison M. | NORRIS, Ellen E. | 12 JAN 1864 |
| MAGUIRE, Bernard | GAFFNY, Mary | 06 SEP 1864 |
| MAHAN, James | MADDIGAN, Bridget | 01 APR 1863 |
| MAHAN, John W. | WALTERS, Julia | 28 JAN 1862 |
| MAHER, Andrew | LEAHY, Mary | 14 NOV 1867 |
| MAHER, Edward | GAFFNEY, Maria | 26 MAR 1864 |
| MAHER, George W. | RABBITT, Elizabeth F. | 09 JAN 1861 |
| MAHER, James (4th artly., C. 18) | GRADY, Ann | 23 AUG 1864 |
| MAHER, James L. | BUSHBY, Addie R. | 19 DEC 1868 |
| MAHER, Michael | McMAHON, Anna | 02 JAN 1866 |
| MAHER, Patrick | QUAID, Catharine | 02 FEB 1860 |
| MAHER, Patrick | CONLAN, Eliza | 18 APR 1863 |
| MAHLER, Victor | POTMANN, Katherine | 25 FEB 1870 |
| MAHON, Charles W. | BLADEN, Laura Meriken | 04 MAY 1864 |
| MAHON, Dennis | BROSNEHAN, Margaret | 19 MAY 1859 |
| MAHONEY, Charles | PEYTON, Jane (blk) | 11 JUN 1868 |
| MAHONEY, Cornelius | MURPHEY, Joanna | 01 SEP 1860 |
| MAHONEY, Daniel | McCARTHEY, Catherine | 25 JAN 1862 |
| MAHONEY, Daniel [2] | BECKWITH, Anna | 18 DEC 1867 |
| MAHONEY, Dennis | BUCKLEY, Margaret | 05 JAN 1867 |
| MAHONEY, J. Robert | TRAYAI, Rita | 15 FEB 1870 |
| MAHONEY, James | BOYLE, Mary | 30 JUL 1864 |
| MAHONEY, Jeremiah | READY, Mary | 16 JUN 1863 |
| MAHONEY, John | SULLIVAN, Johanna | 10 NOV 1860 |
| MAHONEY, John | SHEEHEY, Mary | 04 AUG 1864 |
| MAHONEY, John | HAINEY, Bridget | 31 MAY 1866 |
| MAHONEY, John R. | HOUSER, Deliverance Ann | 07 JAN 1865 |
| MAHONEY, John R. [6le] | PARKER, Marian | 21 JUL 1866 |
| MAHONEY, John T. | FOWLER, Elizabeth | 30 NOV 1867 |
| MAHONEY, John W. | GERMAN, Virginia | 04 APR 1867 |
| MAHONEY, Martin | McCARTHY, Ellen | 14 OCT 1865 |
| MAHONEY, Patrick | CONNOR, Mary | 05 JAN 1863 |
| MAHONEY, William L. | TOUHEY, Margaret E. | 03 SEP 1867 |
| MAHONEY, William T. | ELLIOTT, Rebecca V. | 22 MAR 1869 |
| MAHONY, James | REEDY, Elenora | 25 JUL 1863 |
| MAHONY, John B. | ALLEN, Frances R. | 30 MAY 1863 |
| MAHORNEY, James | CHAMBERLIN, Georgeana | 06 JAN 1863 |
| MAHORNEY, John J. | LONGSON, Elizabeth | 26 DEC 1859 |
| MAHORNEY, John T. | STREEKS, Elizabeth R. | 24 JUL 1861 |

District of Columbia Marriage Licenses, 1858-1870

| | | |
|---|---|---|
| MAHRER, Joseph | LUBBLE, Minnie | 26 OCT 1868 |
| MAHRLING, Philip | BOYLE, Bettie | 31 MAY 1862 |
| MAILING, Adam | RALL, Anna Maria | 13 NOV 1865 |
| MAIZ, Nicholas | ISSAMANN, Margaretta | 14 DEC 1859 |
| MAJOR, Bernard C.* | FALES, Susie L. | 05 OCT 1859 |
| MAJOR, John R. | THOMAS, Ellie | 22 APR 1863 |
| MAKIN, John | LONG, Mary | 06 MAY 1864 |
| MAKRELL, Greenbury | GAINS, Martha (blk) | 08 MAY 1862 |
| MALLABY, Thomas [11] | SMITH, Jane C. | 06 MAY 1868 |
| MALLERE, Joseph F. | COULSON, Emma Virginia | 12 JUL 1869 |
| MALLET, J. Edmond | LYONS, Mary C. | 02 SEP 1867 |
| MALLON, Michael | MINNIX, Diana | 18 AUG 1866 |
| MALLON, Thomas | CROOKE, Mary | 06 AUG 1864 |
| MALLOY, Jno. C. | HAMILTON, Eliza | 23 DEC 1865 |
| MALLOY, Patrick | MULCAHY, Ellen | 26 JAN 1865 |
| MALLOY, Samuel M. | ADAMS, Elizabeth | 18 APR 1868 |
| MALONE, Felix | MALONE, Sarah | 24 FEB 1862 |
| MALONE, John H. | HALL, Adelaide (blk) | 19 NOV 1864 |
| MALONE, Michael | CRAIGHAN, Mary | 26 OCT 1861 |
| MALONE, Nicholas | LYCETT, Joanna | 18 NOV 1865 |
| MALONE, Nicholas | LYCETT, Johanna | 27 NOV 1865 |
| MALONE, Timothy | KEALY, Mary | 08 JUN 1866 |
| MALONEY, James A. | MURRY, Lizzie Ogden | 25 JAN 1868 |
| MALONEY, John | MURPHEY, Bridget | 01 NOV 1858 |
| MALONEY, John | BALTON, Bridget | 30 APR 1859 |
| MALONEY, John | KELLY, Hanora | 31 DEC 1859 |
| MALONEY, John | RYAN, Ellen | 08 SEP 1864 |
| MALONEY, Martin L. | HICKS, Adelaide E. | 03 OCT 1865 |
| MALONEY, Michael | McCALLAN, Hanora | 29 JUL 1868 |
| MALONEY, Patrick | McVARY, Mary | 16 AUG 1860 |
| MALONEY, Patrick | FALLON, Mary | 23 SEP 1863 |
| MALONEY, Patrick | HANNAN, Hanorah | 26 JAN 1864 |
| MALONEY, Thomas | O'TOOLE, Bridget | 14 MAR 1859 |
| MALONEY, Thomas | HULLS, Martha | 13 JUN 1865 |
| MALONEY, Thomas | BURNS, Maggie | 06 JUN 1868 |
| MALOWNEY, John | KAIN, Bridget | 18 OCT 1861 |
| MALVIN, Henry | DAY, Nancy (blk) | 01 FEB 1864 |
| MALVIN, John | RICHARDS, Sarah (blk) | 17 SEP 1869 |
| MALVIN, Thornton | BRUCE, Sarah C. (blk) | 07 DEC 1858 |
| MANAHAN, Michael | CONNOR, Johanna | 10 JAN 1863 |
| MANDERS, William | McCADDIN, Annie | 27 MAY 1867 |
| MANDEVILLE, John | STEWART, Elizabeth | 19 AUG 1862 |
| MANGA, Timothy | CANOVON, Ellen | 09 OCT 1861 |
| MANGAN, Cornelius | WOODWARD, Jennie | 02 APR 1866 |
| MANGAN, Lawrance | COLLINS, Catharine | 28 SEP 1864 |
| MANGOLD, Martin | DOWNES, Christina | 15 JUN 1863 |
| MANGUM, John | CURTIN, Mary | 10 MAY 1862 |
| MANGUM, Joseph | HAZLE, Mary | 10 DEC 1861 |
| MANGUM, Luther | PURCELL, Emeline | 03 FEB 1870 |
| MANGUM, Rinaldo B.J. [6r] | SUIT, Louisa Jane | 08 SEP 1859 |
| MANGUM, William H. | WELDON, Mollie E. | 11 MAY 1863 |
| MANGUM, William Z. | ROLLINS, Sarah Jane | 26 OCT 1858 |
| MANHORN, Frederick | OSTERMAYER, Elizabeth | 20 AUG 1859 |
| MANIFIELD, George | DAVIS, Margaret | 15 MAY 1865 |
| MANION, John D. | FLANAGAN, Kate A. | 25 NOV 1867 |
| MANIX, Timothy | GIRFFY, Ellen | 05 JUL 1862 |

| | | |
|---|---|---|
| MANK, William | BIERMANN, Mary | 17 MAY 1866 |
| MANKIN, Benjamin A. [6cl] | MOORE, Fanny D.L. | 25 MAR 1870 |
| MANKINS, John O. | BAILEY, Mary V. | 20 MAY 1869 |
| MANKINS, William | FLYNN, Bridget | 30 JUL 1863 |
| MANLEY, John E. (Rev. Howlett) | CLARK, Mary E. | 28 MAR 1864 |
| MANN, Edward N. | PANCOAST, Hannah N. | 31 DEC 1864 |
| MANN, J.C. | LUCAS, Belle | 14 JUL 1864 |
| MANN, James C. | HANNAM, Ellen | 29 APR 1863 |
| MANN, John | BRICK, Catherine | 31 DEC 1868 |
| MANN, Richard | SMITH, Mary | 04 MAR 1869 |
| MANN, Robert | REYNOLDS, Emily (blk) | 03 NOV 1864 |
| MANN, William D. [Col.] [6m] | MARKS, Mary E. | 07 JAN 1864 |
| MANNCROSS, Christian | HESS, Elizabeth | 06 AUG 1862 |
| MANNER, George | LEIDECKER, Elise | 18 AUG 1865 |
| MANNING, Henry | HALLENALFOW, Catharine | 24 DEC 1862 |
| MANNING, John | MAHONEY, Margaret | 21 JUL 1866 |
| MANNING, John | TAYLOR, Mary J. | 09 AUG 1867 |
| MANNING, Michael | BARRETT, Lizzie | 24 SEP 1866 |
| MANNING, Peyton | RICHARDSON, Ella (blk) | 13 JUN 1866 |
| MANNING, Thomas | TUCKSIN, Mary Elizabeth (blk) | 25 JUN 1868 |
| MANNING, Thomas F. | DONNEGAN, Mary A. | 08 JUL 1865 |
| MANS, John | BECKER, Eliza | 29 AUG 1865 |
| MANSBACK, Levi | COHEN, Rechem | 04 FEB 1865 |
| MANSFIELD, John | SAVAN, Margaret A. | 13 OCT 1866 |
| MANSFIELD, John T. | HALES, Mary Jane | 15 SEP 1865 |
| MANSFIELD, Thomas H. | FARRELL, Frances O. | 23 NOV 1861 |
| MANSON, John G. | GUY, Indiana F. | 29 DEC 1862 |
| MANSON, Thomas | BERRY, Christiana (blk) | 15 DEC 1864 |
| MANTLY, Frank | BROWN, Elizabeth (blk) | 16 OCT 1866 |
| MANTRO, Anthony | BRAXTON, Amy (blk) | 09 JUN 1866 |
| MANTRO, Thomas | GREEN, Sarah (blk) | 21 JUL 1868 |
| MAPES, William H. | McSWEENEY, Catharine | 19 AUG 1865 |
| MARBLE, George F. | MADDOX, Martha A. | 22 NOV 1867 |
| MARCEY, John T. | PHELPS, Virginia | 19 SEP 1859 |
| MARCEY, William | BROWN, Bashby | 16 JUN 1860 |
| MARCH, John | ORTHWEIN, Catharine | 18 APR 1863 |
| MARCH, William | WEYRICH, Susannah | 02 DEC 1864 |
| MARCHAND, John A. | TODD, Mary E. | 13 OCT 1868 |
| MARCY, John | BALL, Catherine E. | 26 FEB 1859 |
| MARDEN, Sylvester | ANTHONY, Caroline | 07 FEB 1865 |
| MARDEN, Thomas S. [9n] | SMITH, Hannah A. | 11 APR 1859 |
| MAREAN, Charles F. | WEEDEN, Mary Ann | 23 FEB 1864 |
| MARFIELD, Otho L. | McMURDY, Agnes Evelina | 07 FEB 1863 |
| MARGGRAFF, Charles | ROH, Amelie | 01 OCT 1864 |
| MARIN, Don Mariano delPrada y' | ANDRADE, Dona Maria Euposia Lisbo'a | 08 APR 1863 |
| MARINI, John | GAVIN, Maria | 04 AUG 1862 |
| MARINI, Luigi Gallarati | GARNAUX, Marie | 03 OCT 1863 |
| MARION, Alfred | DEROUGES, Victorine | 13 JUL 1865 |
| MARISCAL, Ignacio | SMITH, Laura E. | 03 JUN 1867 |
| MARKHAM, George G. | DOUGLAS, Flora | 27 OCT 1868 |
| MARKHAM, Wesley | ALLEN, Lucretia (blk) | 05 SEP 1865 |
| MARKOE, Francis, Jr. | FERGUSON, Clarasa | 18 AUG 1859 |
| MARKOLF, Godfrey | DIETERICH, Rebecca | 01 APR 1869 |
| MARKRITER, John | LARMOUR, Mary A. | 11 OCT 1858 |
| MARKS, Edward W. | BUCKLEY, Mary E. | 10 OCT 1860 |
| MARKS, Samuel A.H., Jr. | SELBY, Susan F. | 24 SEP 1861 |

District of Columbia Marriage Licenses, 1858-1870

| | | |
|---|---|---|
| MARKS, William A. | ALEXANDER, Julia S. | 28 JAN 1859 |
| MARKS, William H. [10] | DAVIS, Clemenza | 14 AUG 1863 |
| MARKS, William W. | NEELY, Mary | 09 MAY 1864 |
| MARKWARD, Howard Taylor | DICE, Catherine Margaret | 22 NOV 1869 |
| MARKWARD, Thomas | JENKINS, Ella Abbie | 02 FEB 1870 |
| MARLOW, Benjamin | EDELIN, Amanda (blk) | 11 MAY 1865 |
| MARLOW, Robert H. | THELDRY, Elizabeth | 19 DEC 1861 |
| MARONEY, Thomas | CUMMINS, Margaret | 14 MAY 1866 |
| MARQUETT, Washington S. | ATCHISON, Emma P. | 18 AUG 1864 |
| MARR, James F. | ORR, Mary J. | 12 JAN 1865 |
| MARR, Samuel S. | TALBOT, Mina H. | 20 MAY 1868 |
| MARRON, William L. | WALBACH, Mary | 03 JAN 1868 |
| MARSE, Joseph | STEVENSON, Nancy (blk) | 25 AUG 1864 |
| MARSH, Daniel | GREEVES, Catherine | 30 JAN 1860 |
| MARSH, Marilla M. | BALLARD, Gabriel R. | 12 FEB 1863 |
| MARSH, Rutger B. | PEPPER, Martha | 10 JAN 1866 |
| MARSH, William P. | McKELDEN, Margaret E. | 28 NOV 1866 |
| MARSHAL, Washington | LEWIS, Sophia (blk) | 05 APR 1870 |
| MARSHALL, Alexander | GRAY, Lethe Ann (blk) | 19 JUL 1869 |
| MARSHALL, Alfred I. | BOYER, Mary Jane | 04 MAY 1866 |
| MARSHALL, Charles | JONES, Dioretta (blk) | 01 SEP 1868 |
| MARSHALL, Charles H. [7b] | DUBOIS, Eunice | 15 JUN 1870 |
| MARSHALL, Chesterfield | THOMAS, Jane E. (blk) | 12 MAR 1859 |
| MARSHALL, David | FISHER, Catherine (blk) | 21 MAY 1868 |
| MARSHALL, Edward | SHAW, Annie | 19 JAN 1863 |
| MARSHALL, Edward | TAYLOR, Margaret (blk) | 31 JUL 1867 |
| MARSHALL, Edward D. | POWELL, Eleanor A. | 04 DEC 1867 |
| MARSHALL, Francis | ROY, Julia (blk) | 26 MAY 1866 |
| MARSHALL, Francis M. | RAY, Kate | 19 NOV 1863 |
| MARSHALL, Grandison | LAWREL, Jane (blk) | 16 DEC 1865 |
| MARSHALL, Henry | WALKER, Fannie | 21 AUG 1862 |
| MARSHALL, Isaac | CONERS, Mary | 10 FEB 1865 |
| MARSHALL, Isaac | MORRIS, Laura | 03 JAN 1870 |
| MARSHALL, James | McCARTHY, Mary | 11 DEC 1861 |
| MARSHALL, John Alexander | CARTER, Mary Elizabeth | 10 APR 1867 |
| MARSHALL, Joseph | DIXON, Jane Eliza (blk) | 14 DEC 1864 |
| MARSHALL, Richard J. | FRANSZONIE, Jane V. | 18 DEC 1860 |
| MARSHALL, Sidney F. | BERRY, Julia H. | 02 MAR 1868 |
| MARSHALL, Thomas | FLETCHER, Mary (blk) | 13 DEC 1864 |
| MARSHALL, Walter S. | HUDLOE, Sarah | 26 JAN 1862 |
| MARSHALL, William | LANHAM, Mary Virginia | 23 FEB 1859 |
| MARSHALL, William | BELT, Mary Virgnia | 01 SEP 1864 |
| MARSHALL, William | SPEAKS, Caroline | 27 MAY 1869 |
| MARSHALL, Wm. H. | ROZIER, Emily (blk) | 26 MAY 1859 |
| MARSHALL, Wm. H. | NUDEN, Charity A. (blk) | 16 JAN 1860 |
| MARSHALL, William T. | KING, Sarah A. | 30 MAY 1859 |
| MARSHALL, Willis | MARSHALL, Susan (blk) | 02 DEC 1865 |
| MARSHALL, Willis G. | WILLIAMS, Mary E. | 11 DEC 1866 |
| MARSO, Michael | HARBERMEHL, Adelaide | 10 DEC 1863 |
| MARTEN, Wilhelm | WEIS, Katherine | 12 OCT 1867 |
| MARTIN, Alexander | MARTIN, Christina | 11 AUG 1865 |
| MARTIN, Andrew | O'BRIEN, Mary | 03 FEB 1862 |
| MARTIN, Augustus H. | POWELL, Kate J. | 07 DEC 1859 |
| MARTIN, Benjamin F. | CARPENTER, Augusta M. | 24 NOV 1868 |
| MARTIN, Cato | LUCAS, Fanny (blk) | 20 APR 1865 |
| MARTIN, Charles H. | NEAGHER, Caroline | 12 DEC 1861 |

| | | |
|---|---|---|
| MARTIN, D.W. [6] | SEWELL, Martha E. | 24 DEC 1868 |
| MARTIN, Edward | MURRAY, Mary E. | 08 AUG 1862 |
| MARTIN, Edward S. [10] | FILLINS, Mary E. | 27 APR 1863 |
| MARTIN, Edward Smith | AVERY, Margaret | 27 MAY 1869 |
| MARTIN, Ferdinand | LENY, Margereta | 07 APR 1860 |
| MARTIN, Francis | SCOTT, Maria | 29 JUN 1864 |
| MARTIN, Francis P. | QUERIN, Mary Jane | 27 AUG 1860 |
| MARTIN, George | BALDWIN, Elizabeth E.A. (blk) | 04 OCT 1869 |
| MARTIN, Henry | SNYDER, Mary | 07 NOV 1863 |
| MARTIN, Henry | GAMBILL, Mary (blk) | 01 FEB 1867 |
| MARTIN, Henry | FRY, Balinda | 19 MAR 1867 |
| MARTIN, Henry G.N. | DOUGLASS, Mary J. | 13 SEP 1858 |
| MARTIN, Henry L. | WASHINGTON, Lalla R. | 07 FEB 1861 |
| MARTIN, Henry W. | DICKINSON, Judith A. | 28 NOV 1867 |
| MARTIN, Herman | TAYLOR, Alice Virginia | 07 DEC 1869 |
| MARTIN, James | NEALE, Jane (blk) | 04 FEB 1862 |
| MARTIN, James | SMITH, Mary Ann | 05 FEB 1864 |
| MARTIN, James P. [11] * | BACON, Alice | 01 OCT 1864 |
| MARTIN, John | O'CONNELL, Mary Ann | 26 SEP 1868 |
| MARTIN, John L. | COLLINS, Annie | 01 JAN 1862 |
| MARTIN, Leonard | KEISER, Elizabeth | 04 AUG 1862 |
| MARTIN, Lewis G. | MONTGOMERY, Virginia | 08 MAR 1866 |
| MARTIN, Moses | BARBOUR, Ellen (blk) | 11 JUN 1862 |
| MARTIN, Richard N. | SALSBURY, Ellen E. | 24 NOV 1858 |
| MARTIN, Richard T. | HOLMEAD, Mary E. | 10 NOV 1863 |
| MARTIN, Robert L. | THOMPSON, Charlotte A. | 26 MAR 1862 |
| MARTIN, Thomas J. | FRANKLIN, Mary F. | 01 MAY 1869 |
| MARTIN, Thomas M., Rev. [3] | TEMPLETON, Emma S. | 03 JUN 1861 |
| MARTIN, Thomas T. | HAMMERSLEY, Mary V. | 27 APR 1861 |
| MARTIN, Washington | BANKS, Harriet (blk) | 17 MAR 1866 |
| MARTIN, William | DAVIS, Mary Ann | 02 DEC 1858 |
| MARTIN, William | VENIAH, Louisa (blk) | 19 AUG 1865 |
| MARTIN, William | KERR, Mary Jane | 08 OCT 1867 |
| MARTIN, William | DEENER, Annie | 23 NOV 1868 |
| MARTIN, William H. | THOMPSON, Elizabeth J. | 24 SEP 1860 |
| MARTIN, Wm. H. | SCHAFER, Josephine | 22 JAN 1861 |
| MARTIN, William J. | SMITH, Anna P. | 02 APR 1868 |
| MARTIN, Winfield S. | WALLINGSFORD, Laura V. | 24 FEB 1864 |
| MARTSH, J.F. | SWINK, Marr Susan | 03 NOV 1863 |
| MASON, Allan | FIELDS, Martha (blk) | 12 AUG 1868 |
| MASON, Andrew | JONES, Louisa (blk) | 01 MAR 1869 |
| MASON, Arthur | FISHER, Lucy (blk) | 31 OCT 1866 |
| MASON, Augustus | LYNCH, Henrietta | 26 MAR 1864 |
| MASON, Austin | WILLIVAN, Elsie (blk) | 20 JUL 1866 |
| MASON, George | COATES, Henrietta (blk) | 15 JAN 1869 |
| MASON, George | MASON, Ann (blk) | 02 MAR 1869 |
| MASON, George W. | LEE, Henrietta | 19 SEP 1864 |
| MASON, Harry | GREEN, Elizabeth | 29 OCT 1863 |
| MASON, Henry | MULLIN, Annie | 27 APR 1863 |
| MASON, Henry | HARRIS, Fannie (blk) | 07 MAY 1870 |
| MASON, James | SHEA, Julia | 02 FEB 1860 |
| MASON, James | HOLLIS, Sarah (blk) | 17 NOV 1864 |
| MASON, James H. | WOOD, Mary F. (blk) | 15 MAY 1862 |
| MASON, John B. | LOOMIS, Angeline | 06 NOV 1865 |
| MASON, John L. | POWELL, Maria | 14 JAN 1864 |
| MASON, Otis T. | HENDERSON, Sallie E. | 22 OCT 1862 |

| Groom | Bride | Date |
|---|---|---|
| MASON, Peter P. | BLADEN, Martha Ellen | 16 JAN 1860 |
| MASON, William | WEBSTER, Ellen J. | 17 AUG 1865 |
| MASON, William | JOHNSON, Fanny (blk) | 04 AUG 1866 |
| MASON, William H. | COX, Anna F. | 15 APR 1867 |
| MASS, John | BOARMAN, Eliza | 27 OCT 1869 |
| MASSEY, George | DAY, Lucy (blk) | 20 SEP 1862 |
| MASSEY, Strother | HAMPTON, Lucy (blk) | 21 JUL 1869 |
| MASTBROOKE, Henry G. | BRIDECAMP, Kate | 23 MAR 1864 |
| MASTERS, James | McCOSKER, Mary T. | 02 SEP 1864 |
| MASTERS, John | BROWN, Annie | 03 JAN 1865 |
| MASTERSON, Daniel | DOUGLASS, Maria (blk) | 04 APR 1866 |
| MASTIN, William H. | WALL, Anna Virginia | 18 OCT 1860 |
| MATHANEY, William W. | WALKER, Catharine | 03 DEC 1861 |
| MATHENY, Moses | KEYES, Emma (blk) | 21 OCT 1869 |
| MATHEWS, Alfred | NICHOLSON, Jane (blk) | 21 MAR 1870 |
| MATHEWS, Carter | SMALLWOOD, Elizabeth | 24 OCT 1866 |
| MATHEWS, Henry | SIMONS, Gracis (blk) | 26 MAR 1866 |
| MATHEWS, James | ARMS, Caroline (blk) | 07 FEB 1868 |
| MATHEWS, James | RAGAN, Mary | 13 JUN 1868 |
| MATHEWS, James | THOMAS, Catherine (blk) | 07 DEC 1868 |
| MATHEWS, James H. | CUMMINS, Caroline (blk) | 09 MAR 1870 |
| MATHEWS, John | MARLOW, Elizabeth (blk) | 02 JUL 1867 |
| MATHEWS, John | WHITELEY, Ellen | 18 FEB 1868 |
| MATHEWS, Joseph | PAYNE, Lucretia | 08 JUL 1869 |
| MATHEWS, Moses | SHAUN, Rosa (blk) | 15 JUN 1867 |
| MATHEWS, Napoleon B. | BETTER, Lucinda (blk) | 25 NOV 1869 |
| MATHEWS, Peter | FARRELL, Briget | 06 SEP 1869 |
| MATHEWS, Thornton | KNOXVILLE, Roberta (blk) | 12 JAN 1861 |
| MATHEWS, William | GRAY, Lotta (blk) | 26 MAY 1870 |
| MATHIESON, James A. | COOKE, Jessie E. | 09 OCT 1869 |
| MATHIS, George | SMITH, Anna (blk) | 26 SEP 1867 |
| MATLOCK, George S. | BEVIER, Sarah E. | 12 SEP 1867 |
| MATSON, John A. | REEDER, Elizabeth | 20 NOV 1868 |
| MATTFELDT, Gustave | KAPPEL, Julia | 09 JUL 1867 |
| MATTHAIDES, Josef | DIPPLE, Mary | 10 MAY 1865 |
| MATTHEW, David | TAYLOR, Virginia | 09 AUG 1859 |
| MATTHEW, James W. | MAHONEY, Lucinda | 23 MAY 1864 |
| MATTHEW, Thomas | FAULKNER, Mary Ellen | 14 FEB 1859 |
| MATTHEWS, Bartlett | GRIMES, Winney | 11 DEC 1865 |
| MATTHEWS, Charles | CONNOR, Mary (blk) | 24 OCT 1865 |
| MATTHEWS, Charles L. [13c] | PETERS, Orelia | 28 APR 1859 |
| MATTHEWS, Charles M. [11] | CORCORAN, Emily | 06 APR 1863 |
| MATTHEWS, George W. | CAMPBELL, Mary Jane (blk) | 26 NOV 1863 |
| MATTHEWS, George W. [7a] | GRAY, Cornelia (blk) | 01 AUG 1868 |
| MATTHEWS, H.C. | GOURLEY, Maggie | 24 FEB 1867 |
| MATTHEWS, Henry | JONES, Amelia (blk) | 12 JAN 1863 |
| MATTHEWS, Henry | WALTERS, Emma (blk) | 08 OCT 1863 |
| MATTHEWS, James | LANE, Catherine (blk) | 02 OCT 1867 |
| MATTHEWS, John | HAWKINS, Mary (blk) | 26 NOV 1850 |
| MATTHEWS, John | CURTIS, Louisa (blk) | 10 MAR 1864 |
| MATTHEWS, John Henry | HENSON, Annie (blk) | 03 OCT 1868 |
| MATTHEWS, Kellis | NELSON, Ann | 24 AUG 1863 |
| MATTHEWS, Lemuel | BROWN, Sophia A. (blk) | 31 MAY 1865 |
| MATTHEWS, Peter | HOFFMAN, Georgianna (blk) | 07 SEP 1865 |
| MATTHEWS, Wesley | HAVILAND, Caroline C. | 31 JAN 1865 |
| MATTHEWS, William | WINSLOW, Ann Eliza | 23 MAY 1867 |

| | | |
|---|---|---|
| MATTHEWS, William S. | SMOOT, Mary A. | 11 NOV 1862 |
| MATTHEWSON, William | WEBB, Bettie (blk) | 08 AUG 1863 |
| MATTHEWSON, William | YATES, Margaret | 08 AUG 1863 |
| MATTINGLY, C.A.D. | HOWARD, Eliza | 25 MAR 1868 |
| MATTINGLY, C.W. | PAYNE, Annie | 15 JUN 1869 |
| MATTINGLY, George | HARWOOD, Ella R. | 16 APR 1868 |
| MATTINGLY, Joseph | JONES, Martha | 13 APR 1863 |
| MATTINGLY, Joseph Henry | MADDOX, Mary C. | 14 APR 1862 |
| MATTINGLY, Thomas O. | ANGELL, Amanda | 30 APR 1859 |
| MATTSON, E., Lt. | GAUSE, H.R. | 30 MAY 1863 |
| MATZOULI, John | ARTH, Lehna | 17 MAY 1860 |
| MAULSBY, George [4] | LOVETT, Anna Matilda | 18 APR 1859 |
| MAURER, John | ROCH, Teresa | 11 JAN 1864 |
| MAUSS, Richard G. | MARTIN, Martha E. | 01 MAY 1866 |
| MAXFIELD, Harry | KEYS, Margaret | 01 MAY 1865 |
| MAXWELL, Albert | KNOWLES, Rebecca | 04 DEC 1867 |
| MAXWELL, Henry A. | FRENCH, Minerva | 09 MAY 1866 |
| MAXWELL, James | LAWSON, Margaret | 08 JUN 1859 |
| MAXWELL, James | CARROLL, Delia M. | 20 OCT 1863 |
| MAXWELL, James H. | HARTIGAN, Mary Josephine | 14 JUL 1863 |
| MAXWELL, John | McDERMOTT, Catherine | 19 NOV 1861 |
| MAXWELL, John M. | CROUSE, Elizabeth | 31 DEC 1858 |
| MAXWELL, Martin V. | MONSHOWER, Jennie | 02 JAN 1866 |
| MAXWELL, Wm. H.A. | COLLINS, Sarah E. | 03 OCT 1867 |
| MAY, Bernard | MALLORY, Kate | 12 JUL 1866 |
| MAY, Conrad | FREDERICK, Catharine | 28 MAY 1859 |
| MAY, Felix | LEE, Maria (blk) | 13 APR 1868 |
| MAY, Francis Russell, Jr. | MOFFETT, Susan Rebecca | 22 AUG 1863 |
| MAY, Henry | WHEELER, Ann (blk) | 04 AUG 1866 |
| MAY, Lyman B. | DeCOVER, Hellin | 03 MAR 1863 |
| MAY, Thomas O.N. | FOLK, Harriet Virginia | 03 OCT 1863 |
| MAY, William H. | TAYLOR, Emma E. | 23 OCT 1869 |
| MAYBERRY, Madison | MINOR, Betty (blk) | 10 JAN 1866 |
| MAYBERRY, William H. | FORBES, Laura A. | 19 JUL 1865 |
| MAYER, Gottlieb | RICHTER, Mary | 09 FEB 1863 |
| MAYER, Max L. | SIESFELD, Frederick | 20 AUG 1866 |
| MAYER, Sebastian | BOLAND, Maria | 20 APR 1865 |
| MAYERS, William | WILLIAMS, Kate | 06 SEP 1867 |
| MAYLERT, William S. | RILEY, Mary | 06 MAY 1868 |
| MAYN, Z.T. | PLUMMER, Octavia | 11 OCT 1869 |
| MAYNARD, Henry Greene | WHEELER, Frances (blk) | 18 DEC 1866 |
| MAYNARD, Warren | PIFER, Rachel E. | 08 OCT 1863 |
| MAYNE, Joseph N. | BROWN, Ann E. | 11 DEC 1865 |
| MAYS, Robert J. | HEGAN, Martha V. | 17 NOV 1860 |
| MAYS, Salvador | COLE, Georgianna | 18 JUL 1867 |
| MAYS, William | DADE, Adeline (blk) | 08 NOV 1866 |
| MAYSON, Austin | WILLOUGHBY, Ailsey (blk) | 13 SEP 1869 |
| MAZEL, John M. | WAYHOUSE, Birtha | 04 OCT 1869 |
| | | |
| McABE, Matthew | McINTYRE, Bridget | 25 AUG 1863 |
| McAFFERY, Joseph | WELSH, Margaret | 19 APR 1864 |
| McALEER, Philip | KELLY, Mary J. | 29 DEC 1860 |
| McALLIGATT, William | FITZGERALD, Mary | 01 JUL 1865 |
| McALLISTER, Hugh | RIEVES, Caroline | 28 APR 1859 |
| McALLISTER, Joshua B. | UTZ, Laura C. | 01 JAN 1867 |

District of Columbia Marriage Licenses, 1858-1870

| | | |
|---|---|---|
| McALLISTER, Julius S. | STALLINGS, Naremeta S. | 28 NOV 1861 |
| McALLISTER, William H. | GOOD, Mary Ann | 10 MAY 1865 |
| McALLISTER, William S. | SWAN, Mary | 24 DEC 1864 |
| McANNALLY, John T. | SCANLON, Mary | 24 JUN 1864 |
| McARDLE, Michael | FAHAY, Mary | 24 MAR 1864 |
| McAULEY, Patrick | CROSSFIELD, Maggie | 16 MAY 1870 |
| McAULIFF, David | O'DONNOGHUE, Mary | 17 NOV 1862 |
| McAULIFF, John | SULLIVAN, Margaret | 14 JUL 1866 |
| McAULIFF, W. | CADY, Ruth | 10 SEP 1863 |
| McAULIFFE, Cornelius | McKAIGE, Mary | 24 NOV 1862 |
| McAULIFFE, Denis | CONNELL, Catharine | 13 JAN 1866 |
| McBAYNE, John T. | TYLER, Cornelia | 07 JUL 1864 |
| McBEE, Charles C. | MILLER, Margaret A. | 07 JUN 1866 |
| McBEE, Charles C. | MILLER, Margaret J. | 30 MAR 1867 |
| McBERN, John | COURTNEY, Jennie | 11 SEP 1863 |
| McBRIDE, Roger | RALEY, Susan | 11 FEB 1863 |
| McBURNEY, John | BRESNAHAN, Margaret Cecilia | 16 SEP 1868 |
| McCABE, Alexander | BLOIS, Mary A. | 09 JAN 1865 |
| McCABE, Patrick | FITZPATRICK, Elizabeth | 04 JUL 1866 |
| McCAFFERTY, James E. | HILL, Julia | 25 NOV 1861 |
| McCALIGALT, Wm. | CONNER, Mary | 18 JUN 1859 |
| McCALL, Charles A., Dr. | WHITE, Delie L. | 23 JUN 1863 |
| McCALLAN, Thomas | COLLINS, Mary | 11 APR 1868 |
| McCALLISTER, W.J. | CARROLL, Jane | 07 JAN 1863 |
| McCALMAN, Donald | HALES, Nancy | 23 OCT 1869 |
| McCANE, Jacob R. [6le] | PETERS, Mahala Ellen | 26 OCT 1865 |
| McCANN, Daniel [4] | HALL, Mary | 17 SEP 1867 |
| McCANN, Louis | McCRERY, Sarah Lizzie | 06 JUL 1868 |
| McCANN, Michael | FOSTER, Jane | 06 OCT 1863 |
| McCANN, Patrick | WRIGHT, Catherine | 26 NOV 1863 |
| McCANN, Patrick | O'DAY, Hannah | 24 JAN 1865 |
| McCARDELL, Thomas F. | EVE, Alice M. | 31 AUG 1865 |
| McCARLEY, James | CARROLL, Jane | 31 MAY 1867 |
| McCARLEY, Richard | DOLING, Annie | 11 JAN 1864 |
| McCARROLL, James | KELLY, America (blk) | 17 AUG 1866 |
| McCARRON, Philip C. | MICKEY, Annie | 18 JAN 1863 |
| McCARTEN, Edward | CURTIN, Mary | 03 DEC 1867 |
| McCARTER, William | WILKINSON, Laura | 20 NOV 1869 |
| McCARTEY, Dennis | O'DAY, Catharine | 20 JUN 1863 |
| McCARTHEY, John | McLLIGOTT, Hanora | 12 OCT 1861 |
| McCARTHY, Bartholomew | DOWD, Hannah | 06 JAN 1865 |
| McCARTHY, Charles | MURPHEY, Julia | 16 AUG 1861 |
| McCARTHY, Daniel | McCARTHY, Catherine | 25 JAN 1859 |
| McCARTHY, Daniel | BUTLER, Mary | 09 JUN 1863 |
| McCARTHY, Daniel | CROWLEY, Ann | 14 OCT 1865 |
| McCARTHY, Dennis | DAILY, Catherine | 03 FEB 1866 |
| McCARTHY, Edward [12s] | SHORE, Mary Elizth. | 24 NOV 1862 |
| McCARTHY, Edward | DUNN, Ann | 10 MAY 1867 |
| McCARTHY, Florence | ASHTON, Elizabeth | 05 AUG 1865 |
| McCARTHY, Jeremiah | CROWLEY, Julia | 07 JAN 1860 |
| McCARTHY, Jeremiah | DRISCOLL, Ann O. | 09 FEB 1866 |
| McCARTHY, John | GRIMES, Susan | 22 APR 1862 |
| McCARTHY, John | MEYLER, Mary | 02 OCT 1863 |
| McCARTHY, Lawrence | SULLIVAN, Mary O. | 08 FEB 1866 |
| McCARTHY, Patrick | DIGGIN, Ellen | 12 SEP 1859 |
| McCARTHY, Patrick | MURRAY, Mary | 25 NOV 1865 |

District of Columbia Marriage Licenses, 1858-1870

| | | |
|---|---|---|
| McCARTHY, Timothy | LOWNDS, Serena | 05 FEB 1863 |
| McCARTHY, Timothy | DONOVAN, Mary | 23 FEB 1865 |
| McCARTHY, William | BROSNAN, Susan | 16 MAY 1863 |
| McCARTY, Alfred | WILLIAMS, Mary E. (blk) | 22 DEC 1868 |
| McCARTY, Chas. S. | CONNER, Ellen | 14 FEB 1860 |
| McCARTY, Daniel C. | GRIFFIN, Annie Elizabeth | 17 JAN 1867 |
| McCARTY, Dennis | CONNOR, Mary | 01 JUL 1859 |
| McCARTY, Dennis | O'DAY, Catharine | 14 FEB 1863 |
| McCARTY, John | DALEY, Johanna | 18 APR 1861 |
| McCARTY, John | CRADY, Margaret | 23 JUN 1862 |
| McCARTY, Michael | CROWLEY, Maria | 30 DEC 1861 |
| McCARTY, Timothy | PENDERGRASS, Bridget | 08 AUG 1863 |
| McCARTY, William | WOODS, Margaret | 12 FEB 1863 |
| McCATHRAN, Andrew J. | HESSTER, Mary | 27 DEC 1865 |
| McCATHRAN, Francis F. [6m] | KELLY, Mary | 29 JAN 1863 |
| McCAULEY, Charles G. [4] | COLEGATE, Elizabeth M. | 03 MAR 1863 |
| McCAULEY, Henry C. [10] | POWER, Annie E. | 22 SEP 1862 |
| McCAULEY, Patrick | HOWARD, Mary | 03 JUL 1863 |
| McCAULEY, Theodore F. | DOUGHERTY, Virginia | 14 JUN 1866 |
| McCAULEY, William | CHRISMAN, Sophia | 16 JUN 1869 |
| McCAULY, Michael | SCULLEY, Mary | 24 OCT 1866 |
| McCAY, William | SHINN, Elizebeth | 22 FEB 1859 |
| McCHESNEY, G.G. | STEWART, Carrie V. | 16 JUN 1868 |
| McCHESNEY, John D. | FULLER, Agnes | 19 MAY 1863 |
| McCHESNEY, Peter N. | MULLOY, Louisa I. | 10 DEC 1864 |
| McCLEARY, John | KING, Annie | 04 APR 1863 |
| McCLELLAN, John | LUCKETT, Margaret Ann | 16 MAY 1864 |
| McCLELLAND, George | DUGAN, Eliza | 07 OCT 1864 |
| McCLEMENT, Robert | SOMMERS, Elizabeth W. | 10 SEP 1864 |
| McCLINDER, John | EARL, Emily P. | 28 DEC 1869 |
| McCLINTOCK, John M., Jr. | FENNELLY, Martha E. | 02 JAN 1861 |
| McCLURE, Boyle Irwin | BROOKS, Julia P. | 07 APR 1864 |
| McCLURE, John H. | HAYDEN, Ann E. | 08 JUL 1864 |
| McCLURE, Walter S. | REDMOND, Kate A. | 13 JUN 1861 |
| McCOLLUM, John J. | QUEEN, Olivia M. | 17 OCT 1866 |
| McCOMAS, D. Henry (Lt., USA) | REED, Mary L. | 25 NOV 1868 |
| McCONE, William | KELLY, Emma | 28 NOV 1864 |
| McCONKLIN, Henry | ZIEGLER, Mary | 20 DEC 1865 |
| McCONNELL, Abell [4] | HORNE, Louise | 06 AUG 1866 |
| McCONNELL, George | GREENFIELD, Mary L. | 13 DEC 1864 |
| McCONNELL, Isaac | O'LEARY, Ellen | 24 FEB 1862 |
| McCONNELL, James B. | FARR, Kate | 30 SEP 1859 |
| McCONNELL, James C. | WOOLS, Anna M. | 17 MAY 1869 |
| McCONNELL, John | CAMPBELL, Elizabeth | 20 SEP 1859 |
| McCONNELL, John | CUNNINGHAM, Louisa | 18 AUG 1865 |
| McCONVEY, William J. | MONAGHAN, Ann | 14 JAN 1863 |
| McCOOE, Charles | PAGE, Laura (blk) | 13 MAY 1868 |
| McCORMICK, Alexander H. | HOWARD, Isabella | 08 FEB 1864 |
| McCORMICK, Charles | WILSON, Mary L. | 12 FEB 1866 |
| McCORMICK, Edward | GRAHAM, Mary | 28 SEP 1867 |
| McCORMICK, James | FERRALL, Mary | 04 MAR 1862 |
| McCORMICK, James W. | ALLISON, Mary E. | 13 AUG 1868 |
| McCORMICK, John | BRESNEHAN, Margaret | 08 DEC 1864 |
| McCORMICK, Michael | KAVANAH, Annie | 23 SEP 1867 |
| McCORMICK, Patrick | GOODRICH, Julia | 07 SEP 1869 |
| McCORMICK, Patrick | McALLISTER, Bridget | 28 SEP 1869 |

District of Columbia Marriage Licenses, 1858-1870

| | | |
|---|---|---|
| McCORMICK, Thomas | BETTEL, Mary Ann | 23 FEB 1865 |
| McCORMICK, Thomas | CANNON, Mary | 08 AUG 1865 |
| McCORMICK, Thomas | WALL, Elizabeth | 04 OCT 1866 |
| McCORMICK, Thomas | DONOHO, Mary | 13 JUN 1870 |
| McCORMICK, Timothy | KELLY, Bridget | 26 NOV 1864 |
| McCORMICK, William | HANDLIN, Margaret | 24 JAN 1863 |
| McCOW, William | COLLINS, Margaret | 26 DEC 1863 |
| McCOY, George | MARCERON, Delia | 18 APR 1859 |
| McCOY, J. Sigourney | SHEAFFER, Emma D. | 03 MAR 1863 |
| McCOY, James | SMITH, Martha (blk) | 25 MAY 1867 |
| McCOY, Jerry | BARTON, Martha (blk) | 01 DEC 1862 |
| McCOY, John | BAILEY, Charlotte | 15 SEP 1869 |
| McCROSSIN, Henry | ANDERSON, Mary E. | 09 DEC 1863 |
| McCUIN, William G. | BRADY, Emily E. | 27 JAN 1859 |
| McCULLEN, James | MOORE, Rachel M. | 29 APR 1861 |
| McCULLOUGH, Allen A. | WHEATLEY, Marion | 24 JUN 1869 |
| McCULLY, George | BLAND, Fanny (blk) | 10 AUG 1865 |
| McCUNE, Mathew [7a] | SIMPSON, Mary Ellen | 13 JUN 1867 |
| McCURDY, John | HERRAN, Sarah | 30 DEC 1865 |
| McCUTCHEN, John H. | DAWES, Annie E. | 28 DEC 1863 |
| McCUTCHIN, Robert | COLLINS, Martha | 13 DEC 1866 |
| McDANIEL, Enoch L. | LUCKETT, Sarah | 19 SEP 1861 |
| McDANIEL, George R. | ROBY, Sarah Ann | 06 DEC 1865 |
| McDANIEL, Humphrey C. | LEECH, Mary A. | 24 FEB 1859 |
| McDANIEL, James | DORSEY, Rebecca (blk) | 15 OCT 1866 |
| McDANIEL, John | RHODES, Margaret | 28 OCT 1862 |
| McDANIEL, John H. | COLEMAN, Catherine | 04 OCT 1859 |
| McDANIEL, William, Jr. | McGINNIS, Sarah N. | 27 SEP 1866 |
| McDERMOTT, Charles | McCLURE, Hannah | 03 AUG 1864 |
| McDERMOTT, Charles V. | PAINE, Lizzie R. | 07 OCT 1868 |
| McDERMOTT, Henry | WOODS, Mary | 25 JAN 1864 |
| McDERMOTT, James | GOLDSMITH, Margaret A. | 22 JAN 1863 |
| McDERMOTT, James | KELLY, Bessie | 09 AUG 1865 |
| McDERMOTT, Joseph A. | HANEY, Isabella A. | 12 FEB 1863 |
| McDEVITT, James A. | McDEVITT, Rebecca M.V. | 22 JAN 1862 |
| McDONALD, Baker | FERRELL, Virginia | 02 JUL 1867 |
| McDONALD, Firth Albert [7a] | McCAIN, Henrietta | 10 OCT 1866 |
| McDONALD, Henry A. | BULLOCK, Sallie A. | 07 APR 1866 |
| McDONALD, James | PRATHER, Sarah | 04 JUN 1862 |
| McDONALD, John | DOVE, Ellen | 12 JUL 1862 |
| McDONALD, John | MARYMAN, Elmira Elizth. | 13 JUN 1866 |
| McDONALD, John | KEOHAN, Ellen | 22 DEC 1869 |
| McDONALD, Lawrence | FOLEY, Hanora | 22 MAY 1868 |
| McDONALD, Philip T. | HARRISON, Anna Eliza | 25 JAN 1868 |
| McDONALD, William | BEISSER, Annie | 12 SEP 1866 |
| McDONNALL, John | CLARKE, Ann | 21 APR 1859 |
| McDONNALL, Michael | QUIGLEY, Bridget | 18 JAN 1864 |
| McDONNALL, Patrick | BUCKLEY, Mary | 13 JUL 1862 |
| McDONOUGH, Charles M. | MAGUIRE, Maria | 03 MAY 1869 |
| McDONOUGH, James W. | CARTER, Mary J. | 01 JAN 1866 |
| McDONOUGH, Leven H. | FAWLEY, Elizabeth A. | 08 OCT 1863 |
| McDONOUGH, Patrick | DONOGHUE, Bridget | 05 OCT 1861 |
| McDONOUGH, Timothy | CONNOLLY, Annie | 21 FEB 1865 |
| McDOUGH, William | McNALLY, Mary | 09 SEP 1863 |
| McDOWELL, Woodford G. | STONE, Marian L. | 12 JAN 1866 |
| McDOWNEY, Mercer | CARTER, Sarah (blk) | 13 FEB 1867 |

| | | |
|---|---|---|
| McDUELL, John L. | HUNTER, Martha A. | 26 APR 1860 |
| McELFRESH, Caleb E. | WIBER, Agnes J. | 05 SEP 1859 |
| McELFRESH, George W. | COLLINS, George Ana | 11 APR 1862 |
| McELFRESH, Zachariah | DAVIS, Mary Ellen | 27 JUN 1866 |
| McELHANEY, William | SANDERSON, Annie F. | 17 JUN 1868 |
| McELLIGOT, Richard | BROSNAN, Hannah | 09 MAY 1865 |
| McELROY, James | LEWIS, Philia (blk) | 01 FEB 1866 |
| McELROY, John | CRAIG, Margaret | 25 JUL 1863 |
| McELROY, John | ROBEY, Marcellina A.M. | 15 DEC 1864 |
| McELWEE, James | GIVEN, Jennie | 27 JAN 1864 |
| McEUEN, Charles A. | WALKER, Jennie C. | 16 APR 1870 |
| McEVOY, John | SWEENY, Mary Jane | 09 MAY 1859 |
| McFADDEN, Thomas | McDERMOTT, Lucy | 22 APR 1865 |
| McFALLS, Thaddeus B. | GOBRIGHT, Louise E. | 21 JUN 1859 |
| McFARLAN, Edwin P. | MARRIN, Annie L. | 08 FEB 1868 |
| McFARLAN, Patrick | MULQUEHAR, Sophia | 04 DEC 1861 |
| McFARLAND, C. Dodd | CHUBB, Emily W. | 30 OCT 1865 |
| McFARLAND, John M. | SLATER, Sarah J. | 16 OCT 1858 |
| McFARLAND, Joseph L. [7a] | MORTON, Arietta O. | 14 OCT 1867 |
| McFARLAND, Sidney | DADE, Mary Ellen (blk) | 18 OCT 1865 |
| McFARLANE, William J. | PERRY, Margaret | 27 JAN 1866 |
| McFARLON, Robert | VERMILLION, Susan | 20 DEC 1865 |
| McGAHEY, John | LEMMON, Mary | 31 MAY 1864 |
| McGANN, Martin | O'CONNELL, Mary | 06 MAR 1865 |
| McGARRAGHY, Peter | RADEY, Mary | 15 SEP 1864 |
| McGARVEY, Dennis | BURKE, Bridget | 13 JUN 1863 |
| McGAVEY, Thomas | GOSLIN, Ann | 02 MAR 1859 |
| McGAW, James | MURRAY, Mary | 08 JUN 1864 |
| McGEE, Edward | GODEY, Mary | 08 JAN 1866 |
| McGEE, James | CAMPBELL, Mary Ellen (blk) | 10 OCT 1864 |
| McGEE, Newton | GIVENS, Lydia (blk) | 27 AUG 1866 |
| McGEE, Patrick | O'DONNELL, Bridget | 10 SEP 1866 |
| McGILL, George Washington | HARRY, Mary Lavinia | 29 MAR 1864 |
| McGILL, James | MOCKABEE, Annie | 28 FEB 1863 |
| McGINNEY, Daniel | RAFFERTY, Margaret | 07 APR 1863 |
| McGINNIS, Nicholas | FERRIS, Jane | 17 SEP 1858 |
| McGINNTY, Niel | CODY, Bridget | 01 APR 1868 |
| McGINTERS, Henry | MOORE, Catharine | 06 APR 1863 |
| McGINTY, Neil | MORGAN, Ann | 03 SEP 1863 |
| McGIVERN, Henry | BAILEY, Marion | 03 FEB 1870 |
| McGLATHERY, Frank | GRAHAM, Jannie A. | 13 JUN 1865 |
| McGLUE, G.V. | SMITH, Victoria | 24 JUN 1859 |
| McGLUE, George T., Jr. | KELLEY, Elizabeth C. | 07 MAY 1867 |
| McGLUE, James W. | LECKRON, Laura A. | 26 MAR 1861 |
| McGOWAN, Bartholomew | CARR, Bridget | 18 MAR 1867 |
| McGOWAN, John C. | HEARN, Maggie A. | 06 MAY 1868 |
| McGOWAN, Michael A. | McGRATH, Catherine | 19 SEP 1867 |
| McGOWN, Nicholas | DUGAN, Margaret | 21 OCT 1863 |
| McGRATH, James | TWOHEY, Mary | 13 MAY 1862 |
| McGRATH, Laurence | LEAMY, Ellen | 06 SEP 1869 |
| McGRAVERY, Owen | HARTUNG, Mary | 19 AUG 1864 |
| McGRAW, James | MAHONEY, Ellen | 21 JUL 1860 |
| McGRAW, James, Jr. | REAGAN, Emma | 22 OCT 1868 |
| McGRAW, Patrick | MAGHER, Annie | 13 FEB 1867 |
| McGRAW, Thomas E. | RICHARDSON, Ella | 22 OCT 1868 |
| McGREEVY, James | GRACE, Adelaide | 24 JUL 1861 |

District of Columbia Marriage Licenses, 1858-1870

| | | |
|---|---|---|
| McGREW, John S. | ROWLAND, Pauline | 29 DEC 1866 |
| McGRUDER, Henry H. [1c] | ELLIS, Maria | 25 SEP 1863 |
| McGRUDER, Joseph E. | GREENBAY, Cinderella (blk) | 02 MAY 1866 |
| McGUGIN, Patrick | RILEY, Ann | 29 MAY 1861 |
| McGUIGAN, Alexander | GATES, Henrietta Eliza | 17 OCT 1864 |
| McGUIGUAN, Daniel | McCOLLUM, Mary | 15 AUG 1864 |
| McGUIRE, Frank | QUINN, Anna | 16 JUL 1867 |
| McGUIRE, Frederick B. | TAYLOR, Emily N. | 13 APR 1864 |
| McGUIRE, James | OUSLEY, Mary | 08 AUG 1861 |
| McGUIRE, John | KEEFE, Mary | 12 JAN 1864 |
| McGUIRE, P.H. | HIGGINS, Bettie | 19 SEP 1866 |
| McGUIRE, Peter | BOYLE, Mary | 09 APR 1863 |
| McGUIRE, Philip [12s] | MONAHAN, Margaret | 09 AUG 1861 |
| McGUIRE, Thomas | BURKE, Maria | 18 APR 1863 |
| McGUIRE, Thomas | GIBBS, Georgiana | 30 OCT 1863 |
| McGUIRE, Timothy | HOGAN, Ann | 23 JUN 1860 |
| McGURK, Charles | TINNEY, Catharine | 07 AUG 1865 |
| McGWINN, John | McGINNIS, Kate | 19 AUG 1864 |
| McHENRY, George | GIDDINGS, Ann Maria | 15 MAY 1868 |
| McHENRY, Henry | KENNEDY, Catharine | 03 DEC 1862 |
| McHUGH, Charles | McDONALD, Mary | 02 DEC 1868 |
| McILHENNY, Geo. A. | SMITH, Thysa Virginia | 04 MAY 1868 |
| McILVAIN, James C. | COLLINS, Mary | 30 APR 1864 |
| McILVAINE, John L. | SAVAGE, Caroline F. | 11 APR 1861 |
| McINTEE, James | DALY, Annie | 30 SEP 1864 |
| McINTEE, Mark | FERGUSON, Bridget | 09 JUN 1864 |
| McINTEE, Mark | DOYLE, Margaret | 30 MAR 1869 |
| McINTIRE, Charles | HENDRETTA, Margaret | 06 JUL 1868 |
| McINTIRE, R. Holden | GILLETT, Delia | 15 NOV 1869 |
| McINTOSH, David | STEVENS, Mary C. | 30 JUN 1869 |
| McINTOSH, Elijah | STEERMAN, Jane (blk) | 10 OCT 1867 |
| McINTOSH, Elmer D. | HACKNEY, Sarah | 05 DEC 1864 |
| McINTOSH, Francis | REED, Emma S. | 19 SEP 1860 |
| McINTOSH, Francis | CONNELY, Catherine | 18 JAN 1867 |
| McINTOSH, Harry J.R. | LAVEZZI, Mary L. | 25 FEB 1869 |
| McINTOSH, John [10] | MORTIMER, Matilda | 11 OCT 1862 |
| McINTOSH, Joseph | SMITH, Jane (blk) | 05 APR 1864 |
| McINTOSH, Norvell [7a] | TUCKER, Mary L. | 06 NOV 1866 |
| McINTOSH, Vernon A. | RYON, Annie | 02 MAR 1865 |
| McINTYRE, Frederick | KENNEDY, Catherine | 01 NOV 1864 |
| McINTYRE, John [10] | HINYON, Jenny Ann | 04 JUN 1863 |
| McINTYRE, John A. | BRACKETT, Lavinia | 14 JAN 1868 |
| McINTYRE, Peter | THORNE, Martha Clementina | 04 NOV 1863 |
| McINTYRE, Thomas | CHENCARY, Lizzie A. | 12 AUG 1869 |
| McINTYRE, William C. | SIMMS, Fannie | 27 DEC 1867 |
| McKAY, George F. | GELLA, Theresa | 28 MAR 1866 |
| McKAY, Jacob N. | WELSH, Mary | 30 SEP 1864 |
| McKAY, Joseph | SMITH, Rachel, Mrs. (blk) | 12 DEC 1866 |
| McKEAN, William S. | BURCH, Annie E. | 08 MAY 1869 |
| McKEE, George W. | HUNTT, Emeline | 28 APR 1864 |
| McKEE, William | COLE, Annie (blk) | 21 FEB 1865 |
| McKEEVER, Horton H. | THOM, Virginia H. | 13 FEB 1869 |
| McKEEVER, Thomas | NOONIN, Catherine | 06 NOV 1863 |
| McKELDEN, William B. | McINTOSH, Alice M. | 10 OCT 1864 |
| McKEMCE, George | McGREGOR, Jessie | 20 APR 1867 |
| McKENDREE, John | CRADOCK, Mary | 27 APR 1865 |

District of Columbia Marriage Licenses, 1858-1870

| | | |
|---|---|---|
| McKENNA, Andrew P. | GAINOR, Lucy Francis | 09 JUL 1867 |
| McKENNA, Edward T. [6le] | CROSS, Margaret Virginia | 18 JUN 1867 |
| McKENNA, Ephraim | CORBETT, Joanna | 25 NOV 1865 |
| McKENNA, Francis | KEENAN, Bridget | 07 JUL 1866 |
| McKENNA, Francis L. | BOSS, Mary E. | 10 APR 1866 |
| McKENNA, Jacob | PAYNE, Margaret | 23 JAN 1860 |
| McKENNA, James | THOMAS, Clara E. | 07 OCT 1867 |
| McKENNA, Michael | HOLLORAN, Mary | 13 APR 1866 |
| McKENNA, Stephen | MOORE, Rosa | 20 JUL 1868 |
| McKENNEY, George | SCRANDIGE, Mary | 09 DEC 1862 |
| McKENNEY, James H. | WALKER, Virginia D. | 14 MAY 1862 |
| McKENNEY, John | HART, Ellen | 05 DEC 1865 |
| McKENNEY, John D. | CROGGON, Anna | 02 NOV 1858 |
| McKENNEY, Michael | KENNEDY, Mary Agnes | 10 SEP 1864 |
| McKENZIE, Henry | CRAMPTON, Mary (blk) | 31 MAR 1870 |
| McKEON, Henry | FOSTER, Susan T. | 22 JUN 1864 |
| McKERICHER, Alexander | ROERNMELE, Frederica | 11 MAY 1866 |
| McKEWEN, William [6le] | STODDARD, Martha | 04 SEP 1866 |
| McKIBBEN, John W. | GARGES, Emily | 04 FEB 1862 |
| McKINLEY, James Edward | WHALEN, Mary Elizabeth | 08 APR 1867 |
| McKINLEY, William | SCRIVENER, Mary Susan | 14 AUG 1863 |
| McKINSEY, James | TARRY, Virginia (blk) | 11 FEB 1863 |
| McKNIGHT, John W. | SLATER, Willie | 15 AUG 1865 |
| McKRAIN, John | HILL, Alice | 30 JUL 1867 |
| McLANE, William G. | HOLROYD, Isabella V. | 28 SEP 1861 |
| McLAUGHLIN, Henry J. | KEATING, Mary C. | 23 AUG 1859 |
| McLAUGHLIN, James | WELSH, Margaret | 16 APR 1866 |
| McLAUGHLIN, James | CALDAN, Maria | 14 NOV 1868 |
| McLAUGHLIN, John | FLAHERTY, Mary | 03 MAY 1866 |
| McLAUGHLIN, Joseph | McKELEGETT, Bridget | 15 FEB 1862 |
| McLAUGHLIN, Kirk P. | FITZGERALD, Honora | 07 APR 1864 |
| McLEAN, Alfred Augustus | WHITING, Ella Louisa Magruder | 01 FEB 1864 |
| McLEAN, G.D. | BOSS, Ellen M. | 03 JUL 1865 |
| McLEAN, Henry | BROWN, Lucy | 15 DEC 1863 |
| McLEAN, John [6le] | ARMISTEAD, Jane | 03 APR 1866 |
| McLEOD, Hugh S. | ADAMS, Alice E. | 14 APR 1868 |
| McLEOD, John | SCRIVENER, Ambrosia | 06 NOV 1861 |
| McLEOD, William | BECKWITH, Jane | 24 NOV 1863 |
| McLEOD, William C. | BECKWITH, Mary J. | 20 DEC 1862 |
| McLERAN, Crawford | MARR, Sarah Josephine | 21 MAY 1861 |
| McMACKAN, Samuel S. | GOODRICK, Sarah Emma | 21 AUG 1865 |
| McMAHAN, James | HORRIGAN, Ellen | 21 MAR 1866 |
| McMAHAN, John | MARONEY, Winnie | 10 NOV 1864 |
| McMAHAN, John | SHEHAN, Kate | 02 SEP 1869 |
| McMAHON, George W. | SHANNAHAN, Mary | 04 OCT 1864 |
| McMAHON, John | McNAMARA, Mary | 27 MAY 1864 |
| McMAHON, Lawrence | BURKE, Mary | 06 FEB 1864 |
| McMAHON, Michael | MYERS, Bridget | 11 AUG 1859 |
| McMAHON, Michael | SULLIVAN, Fannie | 20 FEB 1860 |
| McMAHON, Michael | COLLISON, Mary | 02 DEC 1862 |
| McMAHON, Michael | CORBIT, Johanna | 24 JAN 1865 |
| McMAHON, Michael | McNAMARA, Jane F. | 27 MAY 1865 |
| McMAHON, Owen | SKELLY, Elizabeth A. | 23 NOV 1860 |
| McMAHON, Thomas | THORN, Eleanore | 18 JUL 1861 |
| McMAHON, William | LANGAN, Mary | 28 JAN 1870 |
| McMAKIN, Joseph | WILSON, Ellen H. | 05 JUN 1861 |

## District of Columbia Marriage Licenses, 1858-1870

| | | |
|---|---|---|
| McMANN, Thomas | EDWARDS, Julia Ann | 26 SEP 1862 |
| McMANUS, Edward P. | KING, Mary Alice | 05 OCT 1868 |
| McMANUS, Samuel | MILLER, Annie | 04 AUG 1863 |
| McMELLON, Roderick [6m] | JOSEPH, Mary | 25 JUN 1863 |
| McMENAMIN, Dominic | KELLY, Rose | 26 MAY 1864 |
| McMILLAN, James | LEONARDY, Mary D. | 01 JUN 1867 |
| McMILLAN, James [USA] [3] | RANDOLPH, Frances Jane | 29 SEP 1863 |
| McMILLAN, James E. | HALL, Emeer F. | 13 FEB 1864 |
| McMILLAN, James H. | GORMLEY, Margaret | 11 APR 1864 |
| McMILLEN, Thos. H. | GENTRY, Mary C. | 06 AUG 1866 |
| McMULLEN, Robert | MOORE, Martha E. | 06 MAR 1862 |
| McMULLIN, Levi W. | TAYLOR, Cansady W. | 03 JUL 1860 |
| McMURDY, John H. [3] | ARMSTRONG, Marion E. | 12 JUN 1866 |
| McMURRAY, Ephraim | GARTLAND, Ellen | 04 NOV 1858 |
| McMURRY, Bernard | SULLIVAN, Ellen | 22 DEC 1862 |
| McNALLY, Francis J. | BURNS, Annie S. | 07 MAY 1863 |
| McNALLY, John | MAGUIRE, Bridget | 25 OCT 1859 |
| McNALLY, Matthew [6m] | YOUNG, Jane A. | 14 MAY 1863 |
| McNAMARA, Daniel | HYDE, Margaret | 12 OCT 1867 |
| McNAMARA, Dennis J. | O'DAY, Elizabeth | 07 OCT 1869 |
| McNAMARA, James | MURRAY, Mary Cecilia | 03 JAN 1865 |
| McNAMARA, James C. | SUPPLE, Ann | 23 JUL 1860 |
| McNAMARA, John | BROESNEHAN, Ellen | 05 NOV 1869 |
| McNAMARA, Michael | RALEIGH, Mary | 17 JAN 1859 |
| McNAMARA, Patrick | HOLIN, Mary Ann | 30 SEP 1862 |
| McNAMARA, Thomas | SWEENY, Maria | 01 JUL 1865 |
| McNAMARA, William | McFADDEN, Mary Ellen | 07 MAY 1861 |
| McNAMEE, John | EATON, Bridget | 19 JUL 1862 |
| McNAMEE, Patrick | EAGAN, Bridget | 05 APR 1866 |
| McNANEY, Patrick | HANNON, Catherine | 07 DEC 1861 |
| McNANY, Thomas | CHAPMAN, Alice | 03 OCT 1860 |
| McNAROUGH, Matthew | DORSEY, Honnor | 29 AUG 1867 |
| McNAUGHTEN, David G. | HARBAUGH, Josephine D. | 24 APR 1863 |
| McNEIR, George A.R. | HENNING, Margaret Emma | 06 JUN 1864 |
| McNEIR, John H. | STAUB, Sarah Jane | 21 NOV 1859 |
| McNEIR, Jos. R. | LOWE, Priscilla | 12 OCT 1859 |
| McNELLY, Arthur [6h] | McELFRESH, Elizabeth | 10 AUG 1868 |
| McNELLY, Nicholas | PYLES, Margaret | 30 DEC 1869 |
| McNERHANEY, Francis S. | COLLINS, Mary Louisa | 19 APR 1869 |
| McNERHANEY, Thomas B. | HANLON, Mary | 19 APR 1869 |
| McNULTY, Edward | FLANAGAN, Catherine | 13 DEC 1858 |
| McNULTY, Michael | KIBBY, Amy S. | 19 SEP 1868 |
| McNULTY, Thomas | DWYER, Hanora | 15 SEP 1862 |
| McNURTNY, Patrick | O'CONER, Kittie | 08 SEP 1866 |
| McPHEETERS, William | ROGER, Elizabeth A. | 31 OCT 1867 |
| McPHERSON, John | McNIEL, Ann | 30 AUG 1860 |
| McPHERSON, John | GOODIN, Lizzie | 30 MAR 1868 |
| McPHERSON, Lewis E. | MITCHELL, Ethelda | 29 NOV 1867 |
| McQUADE, Bernard | KEECH, Elizabeth | 29 DEC 1864 |
| McQUADE, Frank Joseph | NEUMEYER, Mary Louisa | 13 NOV 1867 |
| McQUADE, Owen | CONNERS, Anna | 12 JUL 1866 |
| McQUAY, Jerry | WHITNEY, Anna | 12 SEP 1868 |
| McQUEENY, William | REARDON, Bridget | 28 SEP 1858 |
| McQUILLAN, William R. | LUNDAY, Mary Ann | 21 DEC 1864 |
| McQUINN, Charles W. | PITTS, Julia A. | 01 FEB 1860 |
| McQUINN, John S. | BOYER, Margaret | 19 APR 1864 |

District of Columbia Marriage Licenses, 1858-1870

| | | |
|---|---|---|
| McROBERTS, Charles L. | RUNDELLS, Alpha Ann | 22 MAR 1866 |
| McROBERTS, T.M. | MAURY, Ann H. | 23 APR 1866 |
| McSHEA, William | HILBUS, Sarah | 09 JAN 1860 |
| McSHEEHY, Morris P. | O'CONNOR, Nancy | 09 JAN 1862 |
| McSTAY, Patrick | CREAVAN, Catherine | 31 OCT 1863 |
| McSWEENEY, Michael J. | FARRELL, Catherine | 23 AUG 1860 |
| McUEN, Samuel | BEACHUM, Rebecca | 11 FEB 1864 |
| McVARY, James | REDINGTON, Ann | 18 OCT 1867 |
| McVEY, Thomas S. | NOBLE, R.W. | 14 DEC 1863 |
| McWADE, Robert | CHILDRESS, Laura J. | 03 JAN 1863 |
| McWILLIAMS, John | FITZPATRICK, Frances | 21 JUN 1859 |
| McWILLIAMS, John | KOCHE, Isabel | 10 OCT 1868 |
| McWILLIAMS, Thomas | MOORE, Mary | 03 APR 1860 |
| | | |
| MEAD, Henry | WARD, Bridget | 19 AUG 1861 |
| MEADE, William | RUSHMAN, Maria | 29 JUN 1865 |
| MEAGHER, Edward | FOSTER, Mary Ann | 20 FEB 1866 |
| MEAGHER, William E. | PALMER, Elizabeth Ann | 27 JAN 1864 |
| MEAGHER, William E. | PALMER, Elizabeth Ann | 01 MAR 1864 |
| MEAGLES, Michael | NOLAN, Elizabeth | 23 JUL 1865 |
| MEANY, John | GALVIN, Johanna | 25 MAR 1864 |
| MEARS, William | THOMAS, Maria (blk) | 27 JUL 1868 |
| MEATHIS, George W. | RECTOR, Nancy Ann | 15 SEP 1859 |
| MEDFELDT, Wm. | VIEGMAN, Louisa | 14 DEC 1863 |
| MEDING, John J., Jr. [4] | ROLLINS, Anna Henrietta | 08 JUL 1865 |
| MEDLAR, Frank B. | WOODWORTH, Emma S. | 14 JUN 1865 |
| MEDLER, Edward | GARDNER, Sophia | 12 OCT 1868 |
| MEDLEY, Lewis | SIMMS, Emily (blk) | 17 SEP 1867 |
| MEDLEY, Osborne | YOUNG, Cornelia (blk) | 16 SEP 1868 |
| MEEHAN, David Joseph | CRISMON, Nancy Jane | 05 AUG 1863 |
| MEEK, Sylvanus | HIGHT, Sarah | 13 NOV 1860 |
| MEEKINS, Alexander | SIMS, Emily (blk) | 17 SEP 1861 |
| MEEKS, Charles H. | MILTON, Susan F. | 26 JUN 1866 |
| MEEKS, Richard | MANEY, Annie | 21 SEP 1861 |
| MEEM, Clorevere Edwin | MOE, Mary Jane | 12 OCT 1869 |
| MEEM, George W. | GRINER, Marian | 17 AUG 1863 |
| MEEM, John T. | KING, Elizabeth | 06 JUN 1865 |
| MEEM, Peter G. [1e] | RITTER, Mary E. | 17 JAN 1865 |
| MEGILL, Edward T. | SHORTER, Elinor (blk) | 29 OCT 1866 |
| MEGINNIS, Peter | BLAKE, Bridget | 05 JAN 1861 |
| MEHAN, James | McCARTHY, Hannah | 02 MAY 1864 |
| MEHRLING, Daniel | WEBSTER, Mary Ellen | 11 APR 1860 |
| MEHRLING, John | WEBSTER, Susan | 12 NOV 1860 |
| MEICKLE, David G. | RAFFERTY, Jennie | 30 NOV 1865 |
| MEIDNER, Louis | HIRSCH, Lene | 24 DEC 1861 |
| MEIER, Anton | LEINER, Balbina | 11 APR 1864 |
| MEIER, Chas. John | WILD, Eliza Ellen | 21 DEC 1868 |
| MEIERE, Julius Ernest | BUCHANAN, Nannie | 30 MAR 1861 |
| MEISEL, Andrew | SCHAUBE, Louisa | 16 AUG 1864 |
| MEISSNER, Louis | MEILHAUN, Frances | 05 JAN 1859 |
| MELBOURNE, Charles W. | JACKSON, Annie E. | 13 APR 1865 |
| MELBURN, William | ADAMS, Helen | 26 JAN 1867 |
| MELDEN, John A. | DUFFEY, Mary A. | 09 MAR 1866 |
| MELIFF, John | DONN, Bridget | 21 MAY 1859 |
| MELLING, George | WEBSTER, Mary | 02 MAY 1867 |

# District of Columbia Marriage Licenses, 1858-1870

| | | |
|---|---|---|
| MELLINGTON, Thomas | SIMMONS, Sarah E. | 13 SEP 1865 |
| MELOY, William A. | STEUART, Emily Nourse | 15 DEC 1868 |
| MELRICK, Morris | DUNN, Mary | 27 OCT 1863 |
| MELSON, John E. | WOOD, Mary C. | 30 DEC 1865 |
| MELTON, Joseph | HALL, Charlotte (blk) | 20 OCT 1869 |
| MENBERGER, Martin | HILDENBRADT, Annie | 09 MAR 1864 |
| MENDEL, Julius | HOEFER, Dora | 27 JUL 1864 |
| MENDELL, Frederick | SCHREPPER, Elizabeth | 14 MAY 1869 |
| MENDENHALL, Washington | FERRY, Margery | 11 FEB 1864 |
| MENIFEE, Thomas [11] | POLES, Amanda (blk) | 25 OCT 1866 |
| MENKE, Isaac | DANSK, Elizabeth | 29 SEP 1866 |
| MENSEL, Charles | WÜRSCHING, Margaretha | 28 NOV 1863 |
| MENZE, Henry | VOIGT, Dora | 26 AUG 1869 |
| MERCER, Richard | WHITNEY, Alice (blk) | 03 DEC 1866 |
| MERCER, William [Van Ingen] [4] | HOGAN, Sophia L. | 13 AUG 1866 |
| MERCHANT, Silas | SHEPHERD, Anna J. | 16 JUN 1862 |
| MERCHANT, Thomas | HUDLOW, Lucretia | 12 MAY 1868 |
| MEREDITH, Charles D. | COOKE, Jeanie D. | 09 NOV 1858 |
| MEREDITH, Levi | TAYLOR, Mary E. | 07 JAN 1867 |
| MEREDITH, Philip | BARNARD, Eliza (blk) | 08 OCT 1866 |
| MERNA, Joseph | CUTHBERT, Elizabeth | 01 MAR 1862 |
| MERRIAM, Ephraim | WHITE, Helen W. | 02 MAR 1864 |
| MERRIAM, Gustavus F. | SCOTT, Mary E. | 19 SEP 1863 |
| MERRICK, Henry E. [12s] | STRATTON, Martha B. | 06 JAN 1863 |
| MERRICK, Richard T. | McGUIRE, Annie | 02 FEB 1864 |
| MERRIDY, Lewis | JOHNSON, Eliza (blk) | 10 DEC 1864 |
| MERRILL, Dwight W. [12s] | SHEPHARD, Mary | 31 JAN 1863 |
| MERRILL, Francis E. | CORSTLER, Lizzie A. | 01 APR 1867 |
| MERRILL, Henry R. | MARTIN, Mary E. | 06 SEP 1866 |
| MERRILL, James Amos | KNODE, Annie F. | 07 DEC 1863 |
| MERRILL, John H. | BEST, Margaret | 25 OCT 1865 |
| MERRILLAT, John H. [11] | BANKS, Frances L. | 27 MAY 1863 |
| MERRITT, Augustus E. | SCHALL, Annie M. | 29 SEP 1859 |
| MERRITT, Augustus E. | BRASHEARS, Josie | 22 APR 1862 |
| MERRITT, John | CAWOOD, Catharine Virginia | 07 APR 1863 |
| MERRITT, Joseph B. | THECKER, Eliza | 08 AUG 1863 |
| MERRY, Thomas H. [11] | McCUTCHINS, Emma E. | 26 DEC 1868 |
| MERRYMAN, Richard | LOCKEMAN, Margaret | 02 DEC 1867 |
| MERSEN, Isaac [7a] | TURNER, Louisa | 22 JAN 1868 |
| MERSON, Willon | JONES, Catharine | 17 JAN 1865 |
| MERTZ, Frederick M. | TURVEY, Elizabeth | 22 SEP 1864 |
| MERTZ, William | DAVISON, Martha | 13 JUN 1870 |
| MERYJO, Isaac | LANCASTER, Eliza (blk) | 11 DEC 1866 |
| MERZ, Ernest | HUGHES, Sophia Cara Wragg | 18 OCT 1862 |
| MESSER, George | PATTERSON, Hannah | 10 JAN 1866 |
| MESSER, George [8] | SCOTT, Mary | 29 SEP 1868 |
| MESSIAH, Washington | COLLIER, Martha (blk) | 28 JUN 1869 |
| METCALFE, Henry [11s] | NICHOLS, Harriet Pauline | 18 APR 1870 |
| METZ, David | LINKINS, Virginia Ellen | 06 MAY 1864 |
| METZER, James | BOWMAN, Mary L. | 24 DEC 1860 |
| METZGER, Edward | MINTER, Elizabeth | 25 JUL 1863 |
| METZGER, William A. | COOPER, Frederica | 01 AUG 1864 |
| METZLER, August | SCHEELE, Doris | 30 JUL 1866 |
| MEW, William M. | GOODRICH, Mary L. | 24 JUL 1862 |
| MEYER, Adolphus | MILLER, Sallie C. | 08 APR 1867 |
| MEYER, August | GESLER, Henrietta | 29 SEP 1862 |

District of Columbia Marriage Licenses, 1858-1870

| | | |
|---|---|---|
| MEYER, Carl | LOSSEN, Usia M. | 03 MAR 1863 |
| MEYER, Henry | ISH, Mary | 24 OCT 1859 |
| MEYER, Henry | BROWN, Caroline | 06 FEB 1862 |
| MEYER, John | WILLIAMS, Nannie | 29 DEC 1862 |
| MEYER, John | RETINGER, Rosa | 07 OCT 1865 |
| MEYER, Morius T. | CANNON, Sarah C. | 16 AUG 1862 |
| MEYER, Peter | HOGAN, Mary Ann | 30 SEP 1861 |
| MEYER, Simon | FRANK, Fanny | 28 JUL 1869 |
| MEYERS, George G. | LINDSLEY, Lucretia | 16 NOV 1869 |
| MEYERS, Wm. H. | DENNIS, Bertha S. (blk) | 22 FEB 1870 |
| MICHAELIS, Heinemann | OSTERTAG, Therese | 12 JUL 1862 |
| MICHAELS, Hiram | CORD, Sarah | 02 FEB 1869 |
| MICHAELS, Hiram | CORD, Sarah | 02 DEC 1869 |
| MICKLE, John | HENNING, Jane | 28 MAY 1866 |
| MICKUM, George G. [6r] | PARKER, Eliza J. | 14 JAN 1861 |
| MIDDLEBROOKS, William J. | HASKELL, Nancy M. | 27 APR 1865 |
| MIDDLETON, Aloysius | YOUNG, Rosana (blk) | 28 MAR 1867 |
| MIDDLETON, Benjamin F. | WARD, Sarah | 10 FEB 1869 |
| MIDDLETON, Daniel | SMITH, Kate (blk) | 28 AUG 1867 |
| MIDDLETON, Frank | BEANS, Lyly | 10 SEP 1863 |
| MIDDLETON, Jackson | WEBSTER, Harriet (blk) | 17 JUL 1865 |
| MIDDLETON, John D. | MILES, Eliza | 24 SEP 1860 |
| MIDDLETON, John F. | TEAGLE, Harriet E. (blk) | 11 MAY 1869 |
| MIDDLETON, Johnson V.D. | BARR, Helen E. | 07 MAR 1859 |
| MIDDLETON, Johnson V.D. [11] | THOMPSON, Margaret H. | 12 JUN 1865 |
| MIDDLETON, Leander B. | DANT, Annie | 08 MAY 1861 |
| MIDDLETON, R.S. | RUHLE, Mary C. | 28 OCT 1863 |
| MIDDLETON, Robert S. | TINGEY, Mary B. | 27 FEB 1862 |
| MIDDLETON, Saml. E. [11] | WASHINGTON, Sophie | 07 AUG 1861 |
| MIDDLETON, William G. | LANCASTER, Jane M. | 07 SEP 1858 |
| MIGRATH, John M. | STEVENS, Hester Emily | 01 MAR 1865 |
| MIGUERY, Frederick | MARCHAND, Catharine | 05 JUL 1862 |
| MILBURN, George | GREEN, Mary (blk) | 23 NOV 1868 |
| MILBURN, Henry | FITZHUGH, Mary Elizabeth | 23 APR 1868 |
| MILBURN, John A. | CHAPMAN, Emma F. | 07 SEP 1868 |
| MILBURN, Joseph Parker | EARL, Martha Virginia | 14 JAN 1862 |
| MILBURN, William L. | ELDRED, Catharine M. | 20 JUN 1859 |
| MILBURY, Thomas | ALLEN, Elizabeth | 23 DEC 1865 |
| MILES, Henry | YATES, Margaret (blk) | 09 MAY 1870 |
| MILES, Hiram R. [11] | FOSTER, Georgiana | 01 AUG 1868 |
| MILES, John | McDONALD, Eliza | 21 FEB 1860 |
| MILES, John | JOHNSON, Selivia | 19 NOV 1861 |
| MILES, John | PADGETT, Sarah | 15 MAY 1862 |
| MILES, John | TAYLOR, Mary Jane (blk) | 23 MAR 1865 |
| MILES, John | SPEAKS, Phebe (blk) | 27 MAY 1867 |
| MILES, John David | STEWART, Anna (blk) | 15 SEP 1868 |
| MILES, Joseph | RYAN, Ann | 08 DEC 1868 |
| MILEY, Arthur Elliott | FAIRBANK, Lizzie | 23 NOV 1868 |
| MILLAR, John W. | COX, Mary Ann | 24 SEP 1858 |
| MILLARD, Jacob | BAKER, Fanny (blk) | 07 APR 1870 |
| MILLARD, John | MILES, Jane (blk) | 08 FEB 1869 |
| MILLEDGE, John, Jr. | ROBINSON, Fanny C. | 11 JUL 1865 |
| MILLER, Adolph | GEIR, Emma | 02 NOV 1865 |
| MILLER, Anton | PETERS, Louisa | 02 FEB 1865 |
| MILLER, Charles | NALLY, Sarah | 28 APR 1860 |
| MILLER, Charles | SCHRIVER, Anne | 02 MAY 1865 |

District of Columbia Marriage Licenses, 1858-1870

| | | |
|---|---|---|
| MILLER, Charles | BLUM, Mary | 15 SEP 1866 |
| MILLER, Charles M. | FLOWERS, Lavinia | 15 SEP 1860 |
| MILLER, Conrad | BURMAN, Justine | 05 APR 1862 |
| MILLER, Cornelius F. | NAILOR, Rhoda | 28 SEP 1869 |
| MILLER, Edward [12s] | SHIPLEY, Mary M. | 11 NOV 1858 |
| MILLER, Edward | WOODWARD, Mary | 23 JUL 1866 |
| MILLER, Eleazer H. | FARNHAM, Mary | 16 MAY 1859 |
| MILLER, Frederick | HELVICH, Christine Elizabeth | 06 DEC 1866 |
| MILLER, Frederick | COYNE, Mary | 03 AUG 1868 |
| MILLER, George | HICKS, Sarah | 10 DEC 1861 |
| MILLER, George | TURNEY, Ellen | 11 APR 1863 |
| MILLER, George H. [6m] | McEVOY, Julia T. | 29 JAN 1863 |
| MILLER, George W. | EGGERS, Fredrica | 09 JUN 1865 |
| MILLER, Harrison S. | WAGNER, Mary | 16 NOV 1865 |
| MILLER, Henry | GLOVER, Sarah A. | 07 FEB 1863 |
| MILLER, Herman D. | JOYCE, Delia | 04 NOV 1865 |
| MILLER, Howard | COOGAN, Sophie Mary | 24 JAN 1866 |
| MILLER, Jacob | TECHNER, Sophia | 27 SEP 1860 |
| MILLER, Jacob | GETRIDGE, Margaret (blk) | 11 JUN 1867 |
| MILLER, Jacob | RABY, Margaret | 05 OCT 1869 |
| MILLER, Jacob F. [6le] | EDELIN, Mary F. | 01 AUG 1865 |
| MILLER, James | HUTTON, Harriet (blk) | 05 SEP 1864 |
| MILLER, James | MONTGOMERY, Mary | 04 DEC 1866 |
| MILLER, James | HOWARD, Mary (blk) | 18 JUL 1867 |
| MILLER, James S. | HARBAUGH, Ann E. | 28 APR 1863 |
| MILLER, Jerry | BAKER, Caroline (blk) | 10 NOV 1866 |
| MILLER, John | RHODES, Eliza R. | 24 JAN 1866 |
| MILLER, John | MADER, Catherine | 14 MAR 1867 |
| MILLER, John | BURRUS, Elizabeth Virginia | 15 MAR 1869 |
| MILLER, John | JOHNSON, Iowa | 11 MAY 1869 |
| MILLER, John A. | BEARDSLEY, Eliza | 13 NOV 1860 |
| MILLER, John B. | RUPPEL, Josephine | 18 SEP 1862 |
| MILLER, John B. [6] | LANGLEY, Mary | 07 JUL 1869 |
| MILLER, John F. | HART, Mary | 13 JUL 1865 |
| MILLER, John F. | CHRIST, Margaretta | 25 APR 1867 |
| MILLER, John M., Clk., D.C. [4] | WHITING, Margaret J. | 10 JUN 1863 |
| MILLER, John T. | SHEID, Catherine R. | 29 SEP 1858 |
| MILLER, John T. | CRAIG, Frances A. | 31 DEC 1869 |
| MILLER, John W. | LUBER, Anna | 10 MAY 1869 |
| MILLER, Joseph | WELLS, Louisa (lather Aschwasiden) | 21 NOV 1861 |
| MILLER, Joseph | EVANS, Mary Agnes | 02 AUG 1862 |
| MILLER, Joseph | JOHNSON, Hannah (blk) | 16 MAR 1869 |
| MILLER, Lybrun W. | KING, Jane M. | 03 MAR 1863 |
| MILLER, Marcus P. [11] | HASKIN, Catherine Sprague | 26 OCT 1863 |
| MILLER, Martin | MEDLER, Lucy (blk) | 08 FEB 1870 |
| MILLER, Milton B. | MAGEE, Hattie J. | 13 JUL 1867 |
| MILLER, Milton H. [5] | REPP, Sophia [C.] | 28 OCT 1868 |
| MILLER, Peter | ANT, Dorrity | 22 MAY 1867 |
| MILLER, Philip | SEBYERT, Vesta | 05 NOV 1866 |
| MILLER, Philip | FISHER, Fannie E. | 15 DEC 1866 |
| MILLER, Samuel | RUMAN, Sarah | 18 JUL 1865 |
| MILLER, T.W., Dr. | EDSON, A.L. | 27 FEB 1864 |
| MILLER, Thomas | JACKSON, [blank] | 04 JUL 1861 |
| MILLER, Thomas | WHITE, Caroline (blk) | 27 OCT 1865 |
| MILLER, Thomas | GRANT, Edna (blk) | 26 JUL 1866 |
| MILLER, Thomas J. | GRIFFIN, Alice H. | 30 OCT 1860 |

District of Columbia Marriage Licenses, 1858-1870

| | | |
|---|---|---|
| MILLER, Thomas L. | BRANDEBURY, Florence E. | 03 OCT 1866 |
| MILLER, Warwick W. | McPHERSON, Mary K. | 28 DEC 1869 |
| MILLER, William | BRISCOE, Elizabeth | 03 NOV 1862 |
| MILLER, William | HIEL, Sophia | 09 FEB 1869 |
| MILLER, William E. | FAWCUS, Mary A. | 16 AUG 1865 |
| MILLER, William F. | [blank],[5] Alice | 15 DEC 1864 |
| MILLER, William H. | BROWN, Ellen A. | 30 OCT 1862 |
| MILLER, William J. | JOYCE, Frances M. | 15 JAN 1867 |
| MILLER, William J. | GIBBONS, Ella C. | 02 OCT 1867 |
| MILLER, Wimar | SCHLEGEL, Barbara | 07 MAR 1861 |
| MILLS, Albert | SYDNOR, Sarah F. | 23 SEP 1863 |
| MILLS, Alexander | MILLS, Sarah Jane | 22 MAY 1869 |
| MILLS, Andrew V.D. | MORRISON, Emm T. | 05 JUN 1865 |
| MILLS, Dan | BOYD, Anna | 25 JUN 1864 |
| MILLS, Geo. W. | COLE, Emma | 09 JUN 1863 |
| MILLS, Harry | BENJAMIN, Sophronia | 16 APR 1867 |
| MILLS, Howard C. | THOMAS, Fanny, Mrs. | 13 AUG 1863 |
| MILLS, John H. [11] | BOOSE, Laura S. | 10 OCT 1861 |
| MILLS, John S. | BROWN, Hattie A. | 11 JUN 1868 |
| MILLS, Joseph | ADAMS, Manda | 05 MAY 1859 |
| MILLS, Joseph E. | HEARN, Lizzie A. | 02 APR 1870 |
| MILLS, L. Morgan | PEYTON, Laura E. | 16 DEC 1865 |
| MILLS, Myron H. | WEBB, Augusta D. | 15 JAN 1861 |
| MILLS, Samuel | FRENCH, Laura M. | 04 MAY 1860 |
| MILLS, Samuel [7b] | MURRAY, Sarah | 13 JUL 1869 |
| MILLS, Samuel C. | GOLDEN, Mary E. | 12 APR 1859 |
| MILLS, Samuel C. [11] | KNOTT, Mary A. | 30 OCT 1860 |
| MILLS, William B. | OSBORNE, Rosetta | 29 DEC 1859 |
| MILLS, William L. | NIGHTINGALE, Emily | 12 SEP 1862 |
| MILLS, William W. | LITTLE, Anna J. | 26 OCT 1859 |
| MILROY, Thomas T. | HAGHERTY, Annie | 22 OCT 1862 |
| MILSKE, Charles John | KUMHELN, Johanna Fred. Henr. Christ. | 15 JAN 1864 |
| MILSTEAD, James A. | SEARS, Mary F. | 24 JUL 1867 |
| MILSTEAD, John A. | RHODES, Ellen M. | 28 DEC 1868 |
| MINEHART, Charles | LAHAYNE, Dorothy | 21 DEC 1861 |
| MINER, George | MOCKABEE, Mary (blk) | 29 DEC 1864 |
| MINER, Henry | HALL, Harriet (blk) | 15 OCT 1866 |
| MINER, John | MATTHEWS, Matilda (blk) | 20 OCT 1868 |
| MINER, Thomas | COOK, Maria | 05 JUN 1868 |
| MINHAN, Peter | DRABAND, Kate | 04 DEC 1862 |
| MINITOR, John | HALLORAN, Johanna | 10 FEB 1860 |
| MINITOR, Thomas | LAEHY, Honora | 29 NOV 1862 |
| MINK, William | BLACK, Dorcas | 27 APR 1869 |
| MINNICH, Joseph H. [Lt.] [6le] | BUTTERBAUGH, Jennie | 19 SEP 1865 |
| MINNIS, John | BROWN, Mary J. | 01 APR 1867 |
| MINOGUE, William | REYNOLDS, Sarah Maria | 07 AUG 1863 |
| MINOR, Dabney | LEWIS, Fanny (blk) | 26 MAY 1866 |
| MINOR, Edward | WILLIS, Winnie (blk) | 09 JUN 1866 |
| MINOR, Eugene P. | MASON, Mary E. | 24 JAN 1861 |
| MINOR, Franklin | DRISCOLL, Mary | 25 AUG 1859 |
| MINOR, Henry | BEALL, Minty (blk) | 12 NOV 1864 |
| MINOR, John | SMITH, Rebecca (blk) | 14 SEP 1864 |
| MINOR, John | HOWARD, Betty (blk) | 06 MAR 1869 |
| MINOR, John Francis | ALLEN, Harriet (blk) | 23 JUN 1868 |

[5] Note: "Name forgotten."

District of Columbia Marriage Licenses, 1858-1870

| | | |
|---|---|---|
| MINOR, Olie W. | ROYSTER, Mary L. | 16 SEP 1867 |
| MINOR, Robert | STORES, Sylvia Ann | 27 AUG 1866 |
| MINOR, Thomas | HOPKINS, Betsey (blk) | 26 MAY 1866 |
| MINOR, Thomas | BROOKS, Martha (blk) | 18 JUL 1867 |
| MINOR, Thomas Overton | SPRIGG, Harriet Ann (blk) | 17 DEC 1864 |
| MINOR, Timothy | BARRY, Jane Eliza | 11 MAR 1861 |
| MINTER, Fielder | FRANCES, Mary | 11 DEC 1865 |
| MISCROL, Cary | ARMSTRONG, G.L. | 02 JAN 1865 |
| MISHLER, Jacob R. | STONE, Loretta | 05 APR 1865 |
| MITCHELL, Adam | THOMAS, Celia (blk) | 22 APR 1868 |
| MITCHELL, Andrew | SMITH, Louise (blk) | 31 MAY 1866 |
| MITCHELL, Arthur | HUTCHISON, Sarah A. | 27 NOV 1865 |
| MITCHELL, Burrill M. | TAYLOR, Ann R. | 29 APR 1869 |
| MITCHELL, David | MACKEY, Lizzie | 02 FEB 1865 |
| MITCHELL, Edward | LOWNDS, Nancy (blk) | 01 NOV 1865 |
| MITCHELL, George C.B. | FOWLER, H. Sophie | 01 NOV 1859 |
| MITCHELL, George T. | COOK, Matilda A. | 28 MAR 1861 |
| MITCHELL, Hanson | JENKINS, Martha E. (blk) | 26 JAN 1865 |
| MITCHELL, Henry | DIXON, Frances | 30 JUL 1864 |
| MITCHELL, Henry | JOHNSON, Priscilla (blk) | 21 DEC 1864 |
| MITCHELL, James | PROUT, Sarah (col'd) | 11 AUG 1863 |
| MITCHELL, James Emery [2] | BROWN, Annie S. | 24 FEB 1868 |
| MITCHELL, James J. | DERR, Maggie E. | 23 AUG 1866 |
| MITCHELL, Jerry | LEE, Martha (blk) | 04 JUN 1863 |
| MITCHELL, John | TOPPING, Caroline | 01 FEB 1870 |
| MITCHELL, John H. | HILL, Joanna | 30 MAR 1864 |
| MITCHELL, John Henry | SOMMERS, Margaret R. | 01 NOV 1862 |
| MITCHELL, John T. | TAYLOR, Carey R. | 11 DEC 1865 |
| MITCHELL, Joseph | LEWIS, Lizzie (blk) | 16 APR 1868 |
| MITCHELL, Judson | JEWELL, Anne | 03 MAR 1863 |
| MITCHELL, Lewis G. | FORD, Elizabeth (blk) | 06 APR 1866 |
| MITCHELL, Martin M. | MANNING, Mary Ann | 18 MAY 1867 |
| MITCHELL, Robert H. | MELCHER, Marcia E. | 24 OCT 1867 |
| MITCHELL, Thomas [11] | BRANNAN, Louisa F.G. | 31 MAY 1861 |
| MITCHELL, Thomas | McDONOUGH, Mary | 14 APR 1863 |
| MITCHELL, Uriah H. | RIDDLE, Rebecca | 20 JAN 1863 |
| MITCHELL, William | JACKSON, Charlotte (blk) | 05 DEC 1862 |
| MITCHELL, William C. | SHEPHARD, Jane M. | 18 JUN 1867 |
| MITTEN, James M. | O'DELL, Rachel | 29 JUN 1867 |
| MIX, Charles A. | RACKEY, Mary A. | 06 DEC 1860 |
| MIX, Edward M. | RITTER, Millie | 05 JUN 1865 |
| MOBLEY, George W. | AYTON, Elizabeth C. | 12 DEC 1860 |
| MOCKABEE, George W. [6le] | HARDIE, Fannie A. | 09 NOV 1867 |
| MOCKABEE, William | REDDICK, Charlotte (blk) | 04 AUG 1869 |
| MOCKBEE, William T. | EDMONSTON, Sallie R. | 27 MAR 1862 |
| MOCKBEE, William [6l] | NALLEY, July A. | 27 FEB 1862 |
| MOELLER, John N. | RAUCK, Louise M. | 17 MAR 1859 |
| MOESTA, Henry William | WILHELM, Leonora | 10 DEC 1864 |
| MOFFATT, James | KANE, Ann | 15 SEP 1860 |
| MOFFATT, John | CONNOR, Margaret | 16 JAN 1868 |
| MOFFETT, Benjamin F. | KELLEY, Charlotte M. | 07 MAY 1867 |
| MOHLER, Frederick | WAGLER, Mary S. | 28 SEP 1859 |
| MOHR, Jacob | BRYAN, Martha A. | 06 DEC 1864 |
| MOHR. F. | PECKDOLD, Anna | 10 JUN 1863 |
| MOLAN, Peter | WELLS, Bella | 16 JUL 1861 |
| MOLITOR, Edward | JUNG, Catharine Louisa | 30 OCT 1865 |

District of Columbia Marriage Licenses, 1858-1870

| | | |
|---|---|---|
| MOLL, William G. | DAVIS, Alberta | 16 MAY 1865 |
| MOLLER, Henry | WAGONER, Elizabeth | 11 SEP 1868 |
| MOLTON, Virginius | BRUCE, Catharine (blk) | 05 MAY 1863 |
| MONAGHAN, Patrick | HUGHES, Rose | 05 MAY 1860 |
| MONAHAN, James | BROSNAHAN, Lizzie | 17 FEB 1860 |
| MONDAY, Patrick | DULAHAN, Bridget | 14 DEC 1861 |
| MONDAY, William | THOMAS, Eliza | 12 MAY 1870 |
| MONEY, John T. | MONEY, Sarah L. | 01 MAR 1864 |
| MONEY, John [6r] | SHELTON, Susan Ann | 19 JUL 1860 |
| MONEY, Nicholas T. | ROBEY, Mary E. | 06 DEC 1858 |
| MONFORT, Robert H. | CARNELL, Maria | 25 JAN 1864 |
| MONIKHEIM, John | WAGNER, Ida | 30 JUN 1869 |
| MONKELLY, Brian | RAGAN, Jane | 01 NOV 1860 |
| MONROE, Henry | BELL, Lizzie | 16 FEB 1865 |
| MONROE, Horace R. | ROACH, Hannah | 05 OCT 1867 |
| MONROE, J. Edward | FLEMING, Emma | 20 AUG 1859 |
| MONROE, James | ROCK, Mary | 28 MAR 1864 |
| MONROE, Lawrence | DUSCHILDS, Priscilla | 09 JAN 1865 |
| MONSARD, Louis | BUTLER, Ellen (blk) | 19 JUN 1866 |
| MONTAGUE, Andrew | DOBBINS, Ula | 17 AUG 1869 |
| MONTAGUE, James | PALMER, Eliza | 26 SEP 1863 |
| MONTAGUE, James | ROBINSON, Mary Frances (blk) | 08 JAN 1867 |
| MONTAGUE, Lewis | PROCTOR, Carrie (blk) | 17 DEC 1868 |
| MONTAGUE, Peter | SYKES, Frances | 01 NOV 1858 |
| MONTAGUE, Wm. M. | YOUNG, Josephine | 10 MAR 1862 |
| MONTGOMERY, George R. | SIDEBOTTOMS, Margaret H. | 31 OCT 1864 |
| MONTGOMERY, James | JACKSON, Ann Maria (blk) | 04 JUN 1863 |
| MONTGOMERY, John | TAYLOR, Betty (blk) | 20 FEB 1868 |
| MONTGOMERY, R.H., Capt. | McKELDEN, Julia A. | 03 JAN 1870 |
| MONTGOMERY, Robert W. | McLEANY, Annie | 20 JUN 1866 |
| MONTGOMERY, Washington | WRIGHT, Fannie | 03 NOV 1862 |
| MOODY, Alexander W. | PALTELLO, Virginia A. | 18 JUN 1859 |
| MOODY, John E. | NOSAY, Sarah E. | 14 AUG 1862 |
| MOODY, William W. | MILLER, Elizabeth | 22 AUG 1866 |
| MOODY, Wm. H. | CLARK, Josephine (blk) | 30 APR 1862 |
| MOONEY, George A.C. | ELLIS, Laura A. | 01 APR 1863 |
| MOONEY, Henry | WOOD, Margaret | 14 DEC 1863 |
| MOONEY, Michael | MURPHEY, Margaret | 22 MAY 1860 |
| MOONEY, Michael | NEEDHAM, Alice | 02 APR 1864 |
| MOOR, Edwin | LYNN, Mary Mildred | 20 JAN 1863 |
| MOOR, John | KINSLEY, Maria | 04 AUG 1865 |
| MOORE, A.F. | SKINNER, Sarah R. | 07 APR 1869 |
| MOORE, Albert | COATS, Sallie (blk) | 10 NOV 1864 |
| MOORE, Alexander | BROOKS, Rachel (blk) | 27 JUN 1863 |
| MOORE, Alexander D. | DOUGLAS, Maria L. | 01 NOV 1860 |
| MOORE, Benjamin | CLARKE, Elizabeth (blk) | 29 SEP 1862 |
| MOORE, Benjamin | BATES, Martha (blk) | 27 APR 1870 |
| MOORE, Charles O. | NAYLOR, Mary A. (blk) | 14 APR 1870 |
| MOORE, Charles P. | ADAMS, Cecilia A. | 09 JUN 1862 |
| MOORE, David P. | HELMICK, Jennie B. | 05 FEB 1866 |
| MOORE, Edward L. | JENKINS, Lucinda | 06 FEB 1864 |
| MOORE, Frederick George | McGILL, Emma | 08 OCT 1863 |
| MOORE, Frederick George | MURRY, Isabel Frances | 26 MAY 1864 |
| MOORE, G. Bedell | CLEMENTS, Alice S. | 31 AUG 1864 |
| MOORE, Garrett | HICKEY, Ann | 09 JAN 1864 |
| MOORE, George | FRIZZELL, Louisa | 13 JUN 1865 |

District of Columbia Marriage Licenses, 1858-1870

| | | |
|---|---|---|
| MOORE, George | CARRICO, Sussie C. | 29 MAY 1865 |
| MOORE, George E. | LAWSON, Pattie B. | 27 MAY 1868 |
| MOORE, George H. | HAYDEN, Lizzie E. | 10 APR 1866 |
| MOORE, George M. | FRENCH, Mary L. | 18 DEC 1860 |
| MOORE, George W. | POTTS, Harriet | 31 MAR 1859 |
| MOORE, James | WELCH, Maria | 31 JUL 1863 |
| MOORE, James | MOORELL, Jane I. | 19 JUL 1865 |
| MOORE, James | TAYLOR, Sarah (blk) | 18 MAY 1866 |
| MOORE, James B. | CARROLL, Mary Ann | 04 DEC 1860 |
| MOORE, James M., USA | BOUTWELL, Rose B. | 27 AUG 1867 |
| MOORE, James M. | KEELING, Nannie P. | 01 DEC 1869 |
| MOORE, James W. | JAMES, Ellen | 05 OCT 1859 |
| MOORE, John | FITZGERALD, Catharine | 04 AUG 1865 |
| MOORE, John B. | ROLLINS, Jennie | 06 OCT 1864 |
| MOORE, John C. | GORDON, Almira E. | 11 OCT 1867 |
| MOORE, John D.W. | COLTMAN, Sarah B. | 24 NOV 1858 |
| MOORE, John F. | RIGDON, Bettie S. | 30 DEC 1862 |
| MOORE, John W. | GIBBONS, Emily Adelaide | 19 JAN 1867 |
| MOORE, John W. | MURPHY, Bridget | 15 JUN 1868 |
| MOORE, Joseph | O'MEAR, Mildred | 17 MAR 1864 |
| MOORE, Lewis | TOMPKINS, Caroline (blk) | 13 AUG 1868 |
| MOORE, Michael | PHELAN, Mary | 24 OCT 1863 |
| MOORE, Michael J. | CULLIN, Rosana | 07 APR 1860 |
| MOORE, Page | ROBINSON, Virginia | 07 AUG 1867 |
| MOORE, Robert A. | BROWN, Hannah J. | 11 JAN 1867 |
| MOORE, Ross W. | HUGHLETT, Frances A. | 01 MAY 1866 |
| MOORE, Silas H. | COOK, Annie R. | 24 OCT 1866 |
| MOORE, Temple | RIDGELEY, Ellen (blk) | 27 APR 1864 |
| MOORE, Thomas | MANGUM, Emma | 26 AUG 1869 |
| MOORE, William | BAMBERRY, Ellen | 08 NOV 1862 |
| MOORE, William | TANNER, Charlotte Ann | 23 DEC 1863 |
| MOORE, William | HUNT, Electa | 08 OCT 1864 |
| MOORE, William | MOTTO, Mary | 05 OCT 1865 |
| MOORE, William | WHIGLEY, Ann | 06 SEP 1866 |
| MOORE, William Bowen | BIDDLE, Lucy E. | 21 DEC 1869 |
| MOORE, William H. | ATKINS, Elenora (blk) | 10 SEP 1864 |
| MOORE, William H. | BURCH, Alice | 11 DEC 1868 |
| MOORE, William T. [6m] | RAMSDILL, Mary | 17 DEC 1863 |
| MOORES, Samuel S. | WILLIAMS, Emma J. | 07 JAN 1868 |
| MOOTRY, John | SINCLAIR, Ellen (blk) | 15 NOV 1866 |
| MOOY, Lewis | WILLIAND, Margaret | 03 JUN 1862 |
| MORAN, Isaiah | CARPENTER, Sallie M.J. | 12 AUG 1862 |
| MORAN, J.H. | PARKER, V.P. | 25 JUL 1859 |
| MORAN, John | LYONS, Kate | 11 SEP 1865 |
| MORAN, John Daniel | WISE, Kate | 13 APR 1868 |
| MORAN, John Edward | LOVELESS, Susan | 20 OCT 1869 |
| MORAN, John R. | KENDRICK, Araminda | 03 JUN 1867 |
| MORAN, Michael | KNIGHT, Catherine | 07 JUN 1867 |
| MORAN, Michl. F. | MURRAY, Margaret | 17 SEP 1861 |
| MORAN, Patrick | NOENN, Ann | 11 OCT 1861 |
| MORAN, Thomas M. | FOLK, Caroline M. | 03 SEP 1860 |
| MORAN, William H. | GARCIA, Kate | 25 SEP 1860 |
| MORCOE, William E. | BUSEY, Sarah E. | 19 DEC 1867 |
| MORDANT, Frank [8] | ROIX, Fannie | 15 JUN 1870 |
| MORDECAI, Alfred [11] | MAYNADIER, Sallie S. | 29 OCT 1866 |
| MOREHEAD, Washington | COOPER, Mary Ann (blk) | 19 DEC 1868 |

| | | |
|---|---|---|
| MOREHOUSE, William | PICKERILL, Jane | 23 NOV 1863 |
| MORELAND, Enoch | KING, Rachel Ann | 28 MAY 1863 |
| MORELAND, Enoch Clay | CLARK, Mary E. | 09 FEB 1867 |
| MORELAND, Jefferson R. [10] | KOLDENBACH, Elizabeth A. | 16 JUN 1864 |
| MORELAND, Thomas | JOHNSON, Rebecca | 12 FEB 1866 |
| MORELY, Dennis | SHARP, Mary Ann | 16 JUL 1867 |
| MOREY, Amos B. | ROBERTSON, Helen | 10 JAN 1867 |
| MORFITT, Henry | KING, Annie | 25 SEP 1863 |
| MORGAN, Andrew [10] | BANKS, Ellen (blk) | 09 OCT 1863 |
| MORGAN, Bernard | MAINEY, Catherine | 06 FEB 1866 |
| MORGAN, Charles H. | SHACKELFORD, Georgeana | 07 DEC 1858 |
| MORGAN, Charles O. | JONES, Sarah J. | 03 JUN 1863 |
| MORGAN, Charles W. | HOLROYD, Josephine M. | 06 JAN 1866 |
| MORGAN, Clement | GARNETT, Elizabeth (blk) | 26 MAR 1867 |
| MORGAN, Edward, Junr. | CHIPLEY, Emily O. | 15 SEP 1864 |
| MORGAN, George | SNOW, Margaret | 10 JAN 1863 |
| MORGAN, George H. [6r] | MACE, Mary V. | 02 FEB 1860 |
| MORGAN, George H. [11] | DENMEAD, Mary J. | 15 FEB 1865 |
| MORGAN, Griffith | WHITE, Eliza | 05 AUG 1868 |
| MORGAN, Henry J. [4] | HOGAN, Harriet | 01 NOV 1869 |
| MORGAN, Isaiah | SHACKLEFORD, Jane Ann | 24 DEC 1868 |
| MORGAN, James | BAGGOTT, Margaret | 30 SEP 1859 |
| MORGAN, James | CODD, Matilda | 30 JUN 1865 |
| MORGAN, John | RILEY, Bridget | 01 SEP 1869 |
| MORGAN, John T. [10] | CARROLL, Martha J. | 06 JUL 1865 |
| MORGAN, John W. | DeGRAFFT, Emma | 20 FEB 1865 |
| MORGAN, John W. | CAYWOOD, Annie | 21 JUN 1867 |
| MORGAN, Matthew | ALEXANDER, Harriet | 26 SEP 1865 |
| MORGAN, Patrick | FLANNAGAN, Mary | 09 DEC 1861 |
| MORGAN, Richard | PERRY, Rebecca (blk) | 30 OCT 1867 |
| MORGAN, Robert S. | HALPINE, Bridget | 13 JUL 1867 |
| MORGAN, St. Clair | WISE, Marcia V. | 10 JUL 1866 |
| MORGAN, William E. | GHEEN, Isabella | 26 APR 1863 |
| MORGANWEG, Henry | SCHACHT, Margaret | 02 APR 1864 |
| MORIARTY, Jeremiah | SHEA, Margaret | 18 JUN 1864 |
| MORIARTY, Michael | DIVINE, Mary | 30 JUN 1860 |
| MORIARTY, Patrick | LAHY, Catherine | 30 DEC 1868 |
| MORIARTY, Stephen | McDONALD, Catherine | 27 NOV 1863 |
| MORIARTY, Thomas | WHITE, Ellen | 23 APR 1859 |
| MORIARTY, Thomas | GARVY, Margaret | 07 JUL 1863 |
| MORKEL, George | POWERS, Kate | 06 DEC 1861 |
| MORRICE, Marcellus | BURNS, Lizzie | 05 FEB 1866 |
| MORRILL, Orrin T. | HICKS, Sarah J. | 03 JAN 1860 |
| MORRIS, Charles | BROWN, Louise (blk) | 08 MAR 1866 |
| MORRIS, Charles E. | BEACH, Eleanora | 09 OCT 1861 |
| MORRIS, Charles W. | KREAMER, Elizabeth | 02 NOV 1868 |
| MORRIS, Edward | MOORE, Annie | 26 OCT 1865 |
| MORRIS, Edward L. | RAYMOND, Emily F. | 01 NOV 1866 |
| MORRIS, George | PARKER, Louisa (blk) | 06 AUG 1861 |
| MORRIS, George W. | HARKNESS, Maggie | 11 JAN 1870 |
| MORRIS, Henry | GRADWOHL, Rosa | 05 NOV 1862 |
| MORRIS, Henry J. | DYER, Mary F. | 12 SEP 1859 |
| MORRIS, J.T. | COPELAND, Clara | 01 APR 1869 |
| MORRIS, James | McQUAY, Hannah (blk) | 03 NOV 1869 |
| MORRIS, Jeremiah | JACKSON, Letty (blk) | 03 SEP 1864 |
| MORRIS, John | McCLINTOCK, Martha E. | 04 SEP 1865 |

District of Columbia Marriage Licenses, 1858-1870

| | | |
|---|---|---|
| MORRIS, John | ARNOLD, Rosa | 10 NOV 1862 |
| MORRIS, John Edward | EDINBOROUGH, Catherine | 15 MAR 1867 |
| MORRIS, Miffley | CLARKE, Mary | 23 JAN 1864 |
| MORRIS, Thomas | MASON, Catharine (blk) | 03 MAR 1863 |
| MORRIS, Walter | POINDEXTER, Margaret A. (blk) | 11 JUL 1867 |
| MORRIS, William | EASTON, Josephine (blk) | 25 JUN 1862 |
| MORRIS, William | LUCAS, Fanny (blk) | 27 MAY 1864 |
| MORRIS, William | SENIOR, Frances (blk) | 20 DEC 1866 |
| MORRIS, William | JONES, Josiphene (blk) | 30 AUG 1867 |
| MORRIS, William W. | WILSON, Frances | 20 MAY 1861 |
| MORRISEY, Michael | McDONNOUGH, Ann | 23 JUN 1865 |
| MORRISEY, Thomas | FLYNN, Margaret | 06 JUN 1862 |
| MORRISON, Francis E. | GORDON, Georgia | 08 OCT 1863 |
| MORRISON, Isom | WOODY, Elizabeth (blk) | 27 SEP 1866 |
| MORRISON, Lindsay | FRY, Sophia | 11 FEB 1870 |
| MORRISON, Simon H. [4] | MARTIN, Clara E. | 02 JUL 1867 |
| MORRISSY, Peter | CARR, Mary | 19 NOV 1859 |
| MORROW, James | LYONS, Honora Annie | 09 JUN 1860 |
| MORSE, Archy | SHANKLAND, Winny (blk) | 02 JUN 1870 |
| MORSE, Myron | CAREY, Jane | 26 APR 1865 |
| MORSELL, Benjn. | LANCASTER, L.A. | 28 APR 1859 |
| MORTIMER, Beverly R. | DIXON, Lucinda | 14 AUG 1869 |
| MORTIMER, Henry U. | COWLEY, Delphia Ann | 18 JUL 1859 |
| MORTIMER, John | SMITH, Emily | 01 JUL 1865 |
| MORTIMER, John H. | VALK, Adaline | 25 SEP 1868 |
| MORTON, Barney | JOHNS, Maria C. | 04 SEP 1866 |
| MORTON, Benjamin | CRUMP, Caroline (blk) | 03 MAY 1866 |
| MORTON, George D. | CARROLL, Catherine (blk) | 25 NOV 1869 |
| MORTON, Henry | GIVINGS, Phoebe (blk) | 04 MAY 1865 |
| MORTON, Joseph | GORDON, Sarah | 08 JUN 1864 |
| MORTON, Nelson | BURGESS, Letta (blk) | 25 NOV 1869 |
| MORTON, Parker | LEWIS, Martha (blk) | 10 DEC 1868 |
| MORTON, Philip | BENNETT, Martha (blk) | 09 JUN 1864 |
| MORTON, Robert M. | SHANNON, Catherine, Mrs. | 14 MAY 1869 |
| MORTON, William | GREEN, Emma | 30 NOV 1864 |
| MOSEE, Richard Henry | WILKERSON, Patsey (blk) | 31 AUG 1869 |
| MOSES, Thomas F., Dr. | CRANCH, Hannah Appleton | 08 MAY 1867 |
| MOSLEY, William H. | CUNIEFF, Annie | 22 APR 1863 |
| MOSS, Crawford W. | VIE, Mary E. | 26 FEB 1861 |
| MOSS, Peter | MOORE, Mary | 19 JUL 1860 |
| MOST, William H. | SPILLMAN, Lena | 09 JUN 1870 |
| MOULDEN, A.F. | RAYMOND, E.D. | 02 DEC 1863 |
| MOULDEN, James W. [10] | WHITEMAN, Anna | 28 APR 1864 |
| MOULDEN, John A. | WATERS, Sarah | 11 AUG 1859 |
| MOULDEN, Joseph F. | TRUNDLE, Leah | 26 DEC 1861 |
| MOULDEN, Robert T. | ENGLISH, Helen | 23 JUL 1868 |
| MOULDER, Edward | HOWELL, Sarah Jane | 24 DEC 1858 |
| MOULTON, Charles H. | CUTTER, Jennie R.S. | 30 APR 1864 |
| MOULTON, Hosea B. | REESE, Annie R. | 01 OCT 1864 |
| MOWBRAY, George B. | NORRIS, Maria | 25 JUN 1867 |
| MOWNEY, Patrick | NELSON, Mary | 31 JAN 1859 |
| MOXLEY, Charles W. | THOMAS, Martha A. | 03 MAY 1865 |
| MOXLEY, John W. | HARMAN, Mary Ann | 17 JUN 1865 |
| MOYER, Augustus | FITZGERALD, Mary | 08 OCT 1864 |
| MOYER, Charles N. | CURRAN, Elizabeth | 13 MAY 1868 |
| MOZINGO, Richard | JOY, Helen | 04 APR 1865 |

District of Columbia Marriage Licenses, 1858-1870

| | | |
|---|---|---|
| MUDD, Benjamin | PLUMMER, Amelia | 16 DEC 1863 |
| MUDD, Edward [Thomas] [10] | SADLER, [Catharine Maria] | 13 SEP 1867 |
| MUDD, Emma A. | MURDOCK, Baleam | 10 NOV 1869 |
| MUDD, George P. | SHORTER, Josephine (blk) | 29 JAN 1863 |
| MUDD, Lloyd | BOOTH, Henrietta (blk) | 14 FEB 1868 |
| MUDD, Smith E. [6s] | GRINDER, Emma Virginia | 21 MAY 1864 |
| MUDDRIAN, William | PAYNE, Margaret | 17 OCT 1867 |
| MUDGETT, William H. | McDONALD, Catherine | 12 FEB 1867 |
| MUECKENBERGER, Paul J. | LANKUL, Minna | 26 MAY 1868 |
| MUELLER, F.E. | BENVER, Lisette | 31 DEC 1869 |
| MUELLER, George | BEISSER, Annie L. | 21 OCT 1868 |
| MUELLER, John | DOWNS, Isabella | 09 APR 1861 |
| MUIR, Robert D. [3] | HEPBURN, Susan S. | 17 SEP 1859 |
| MULCANY, Edward | MURRAY, Mary | 11 MAY 1868 |
| MULCARAN, Bryan | CONNOLLY, Bridget | 18 MAY 1859 |
| MULCARE, Michael | HENNESSY, Mary E. | 01 OCT 1864 |
| MULCHY, Patrick | BURKE, Anastasia | 15 FEB 1860 |
| MULDOON, David | COUSICK, Bridget | 26 FEB 1859 |
| MULHALL, William | MONAGHAN, Catherine | 21 JUL 1863 |
| MULHALL, William | ELLIS, Mary | 31 MAY 1867 |
| MULHEISER, William | KRAEMER, Louisa | 30 OCT 1867 |
| MULHOLLAND, Peter | COYLE, Bridget | 12 SEP 1866 |
| MULLABY, Charles W. | CROGHAN, Kate | 26 JUL 1869 |
| MULLANEY, Dennis | BURKE, Ellie | 03 JUN 1867 |
| MULLANY, Bryan | CULLION, Margaret | 07 MAY 1864 |
| MÜLLBACH, Christian | REINCKE, Johanne | 12 MAR 1864 |
| MULLEN, Charles | NEALE, Harriet | 08 JUN 1864 |
| MULLEN, John | KENNEDY, Mary Margaret | 01 AUG 1865 |
| MULLEN, Robert H. | MARK, Martha S. | 19 JAN 1869 |
| MULLEN, William M. | BURRISS, Ann E. | 23 JUL 1868 |
| MULLEN, William S. | GOODHUE, Sarah A. | 24 DEC 1864 |
| MÜLLER, August | MULLERY, Delia | 20 JUN 1867 |
| MÜLLER, Conrad | MILLER, Margaret | 11 JUL 1863 |
| MÜLLER, Hermann | GROSCH, Barbara | 01 MAR 1864 |
| MÜLLER, John Mike | WINGFELD, Juliana | 01 MAY 1869 |
| MÜLLER, John [1e] | STUHLMAN, Eliza | 13 JUL 1864 |
| MÜLLER, William | BRUECKER, Juliana | 02 JUL 1859 |
| MULLERS, Michael | KEELEY, Winney | 29 OCT 1864 |
| MULLIGAN, William F. | GODDARD, Sarah Ellen | 16 NOV 1865 |
| MULLIN, John | RAGAN, Sarah | 07 AUG 1867 |
| MULLIN, Timothy | DEVLIN, Mary Ann | 29 JUN 1864 |
| MULLINS, Edward, Jr. | KING, Josephine G. | 24 SEP 1866 |
| MULLOWNEY, Michael | LOUGHLIN, Elizabeth | 22 FEB 1870 |
| MULLOY, Edward | McCARRIG, Mary | 01 JAN 1861 |
| MULLOY, Edward | HIGGINS, Elizabeth | 11 JUN 1864 |
| MULLOY, George W. | HENRY, Caroline V. | 09 DEC 1867 |
| MULQUEEN, James | DONELLY, Mary | 04 OCT 1858 |
| MULQUEEN, Patrick | O'DONNELL, Bridget | 01 OCT 1858 |
| MULQUIN, Patrick | O'DONNELL, Mary | 11 JAN 1861 |
| MULRONY, Michael | FRAZIER, Mary A. | 08 JAN 1864 |
| MULROY, John | FLAHERTY, Winifred | 25 MAR 1868 |
| MUM, Nicholas | TIF, Emilie | 26 MAY 1866 |
| MUNDEL, William | HALL, Minty (blk) | 26 OCT 1867 |
| MUNDELL, Jared | FICKETT, Mary E. | 15 JUN 1861 |
| MUNDELL, Joseph | CASTELL, Mary Jane | 22 FEB 1860 |
| MUNDHEIM, Louis | FOSTER, Fannie | 24 DEC 1864 |

District of Columbia Marriage Licenses, 1858-1870

| | | |
|---|---|---|
| MUNDINE, Saunders M. | JOHNSON, Teaco Jane (blk) | 28 APR 1866 |
| MUNFORD, Thomas T. | TAYLOR, Emma | 24 APR 1866 |
| MUNGEN, Theodore | ALLEN, Kate | 28 DEC 1869 |
| MUNGER, M.J., Dr. | WILSON, Annie M. | 29 NOV 1864 |
| MUNGIVAN, Michael | KEPPLE, Bridget | 14 OCT 1861 |
| MUNROE, Frank | BROOME, Alice M. | 31 OCT 1865 |
| MUNROE, Henry | WOODLINE, Marsaline (blk) | 19 FEB 1868 |
| MUNROE, Henry | JONES, Henrietta (blk) | 16 JAN 1870 |
| MUNROE, James | HILL, Rosa (blk) | 07 FEB 1868 |
| MUNROE, Joseph | WILLIAMS, Lizzie (blk) | 03 NOV 1868 |
| MUNROE, Philip | BUCKNER, Mary (blk) | 17 DEC 1864 |
| MUNROE, Philip | JACKSON, Martha Ann (blk) | 22 MAY 1869 |
| MUNSON, Daniel A. [8] | BITTINGER, Ruhannah | 30 NOV 1868 |
| MUNSON, Lucy E. | TAYLOR, A.A.E. | 20 MAY 1868 |
| MUNSON, Myron A. | FALES, Mary Virginia | 15 JAN 1861 |
| MUNTZ, John | GRIFFIN, Mary | 01 OCT 1862 |
| MUNTZ, Thomas | LESTER, Mary | 11 APR 1863 |
| MURDOCK, Balearn | MUDD, Emma A. | 10 NOV 1869 |
| MURPHEY, Bartholomew | COLLINS, Julia | 24 SEP 1859 |
| MURPHEY, Charles M. | NEILL, Mary J. | 15 JAN 1859 |
| MURPHEY, James | BAUR, Angeline | 04 MAR 1859 |
| MURPHEY, John | CASHMON, Margaret | 26 SEP 1867 |
| MURPHEY, John H. [6l] | PEGG, Catherine V. | 21 NOV 1861 |
| MURPHEY, Michael | GARRETT, Mary A.F. | 13 JUN 1859 |
| MURPHEY, Patrick | HARRINGTON, Julia | 12 OCT 1860 |
| MURPHEY, Philip | MOORE, Lilly | 09 APR 1863 |
| MURPHEY, Thomas | GREEN, Mary Ann | 18 FEB 1863 |
| MURPHY, Cornelius | CASEY, Hanora | 06 SEP 1859 |
| MURPHY, Daniel | O'BRIEN, Ann | 10 JUL 1863 |
| MURPHY, David | LYNCH, Mary | 08 SEP 1864 |
| MURPHY, David | CONNIGAN, Mary | 23 APR 1867 |
| MURPHY, Dennis | SHEA, Mary | 19 OCT 1864 |
| MURPHY, Francis D. | ATCHINSON, Mary Ellen | 05 DEC 1867 |
| MURPHY, George | PATTERSON, Rebecca O. | 12 JAN 1865 |
| MURPHY, James | MURPHY, Jane | 17 NOV 1864 |
| MURPHY, James | CARROLL, Mary | 15 FEB 1868 |
| MURPHY, James H. | McDONALD, Rose | 20 AUG 1863 |
| MURPHY, Jeremiah | DUFFY, Ellen | 16 SEP 1862 |
| MURPHY, Jeremiah | COYLEY, Bridget | 02 AUG 1865 |
| MURPHY, Job | FERGUSON, Margaret (blk) | 22 NOV 1864 |
| MURPHY, John | ROBIN, Frances | 02 OCT 1858 |
| MURPHY, John | HOGAN, Joanna | 08 APR 1864 |
| MURPHY, John | McNAIR, Elizabeth | 14 NOV 1864 |
| MURPHY, John | GORMAN, Bridget | 08 DEC 1865 |
| MURPHY, John | CULLEN, Rose | 07 APR 1868 |
| MURPHY, John | SELVIN, Sallie (blk) | 29 OCT 1868 |
| MURPHY, John J. | SHAY, Catharine M. | 07 SEP 1866 |
| MURPHY, Lewis | MILLER, Catherine | 11 AUG 1868 |
| MURPHY, Michael | SULLIVAN, Ann | 10 OCT 1864 |
| MURPHY, Michael | MURPHY, Bridget | 23 AUG 1865 |
| MURPHY, Michael D. | BOLAND, Lizzie | 02 JUN 1868 |
| MURPHY, Morris | FALVEY, Mary Jane | 20 AUG 1864 |
| MURPHY, Nicholas | DAVIS, Frances E. | 13 NOV 1865 |
| MURPHY, Peter | O'KEEFE, Bridget | 06 NOV 1869 |
| MURPHY, Richard | MAHONEY, Bridget | 25 SEP 1865 |
| MURPHY, Thomas | HARRISON, Fanny | 21 JUN 1860 |

District of Columbia Marriage Licenses, 1858-1870

| | | |
|---|---|---|
| MURPHY, Thomas | WADE, Ann | 03 SEP 1863 |
| MURPHY, Thomas | SULLIVAN, Mary | 01 OCT 1866 |
| MURPHY, Thomas | TAYLOR, Jane | 20 AUG 1867 |
| MURPHY, Timothy | FLYNN, Mary | 24 FEB 1868 |
| MURPHY, William | O'DWYER, Honora | 08 SEP 1863 |
| MURPHY, William | GORDON, Cecilia | 24 FEB 1866 |
| MURPHY, William | RYAN, Annie | 18 FEB 1867 |
| MURPHY, William T. | HOPKINS, Mary E. | 16 JUN 1868 |
| MURRAY, Alexander | ALVY, Rebecca | 11 AUG 1859 |
| MURRAY, Alexander | McNAINY, Mary Ann | 11 AUG 1869 |
| MURRAY, Charles | JACKSON, Emma (blk) | 07 NOV 1866 |
| MURRAY, Charles E. [2] | CHAPMAN, Emma | 13 FEB 1868 |
| MURRAY, Charles H. | PADGETT, Mary | 22 MAR 1859 |
| MURRAY, George Edward | COLLINS, Susan (blk) | 14 JUN 1869 |
| MURRAY, George F. | OLMSTED, Mary L. | 11 JUN 1864 |
| MURRAY, Henry R. [6m] | WOODS, Margaret J. | 20 DEC 1862 |
| MURRAY, James A. | CORCORAN, Susan A. | 05 SEP 1865 |
| MURRAY, James H. | JOHNSON, Rebecca (blk) | 04 FEB 1864 |
| MURRAY, John | MURRAY, Catharine | 16 AUG 1862 |
| MURRAY, John | ENRIGHT, Catherine | 23 SEP 1864 |
| MURRAY, John | SCOTT, Elizabeth | 04 SEP 1868 |
| MURRAY, John A. [10] | WATSON, Margaret Ann | 26 OCT 1867 |
| MURRAY, John H. | EVERETT, Mary T. | 23 APR 1860 |
| MURRAY, John Wm. | NOLLS, Alethia | 15 OCT 1863 |
| MURRAY, Joseph C. | RILEY, Mary J. | 30 OCT 1866 |
| MURRAY, Julian J. | McLEAN, Eliza P.T. | 19 DEC 1867 |
| MURRAY, Levi | ANDERSON, Margaret A. | 24 APR 1862 |
| MURRAY, Patrick | LAUGHLIN, Mary | 09 APR 1860 |
| MURRAY, Patrick | O'DAY, Catherine | 27 SEP 1866 |
| MURRAY, Patrick J. | BAKER, Emma B. | 29 NOV 1868 |
| MURRAY, Stirling | MILLER, Anna T. | 05 NOV 1866 |
| MURRAY, William A. | SUSSEX, Louisa (blk) | 09 FEB 1864 |
| MURRAY, William R. | CREED, Mary V. | 27 MAY 1865 |
| MURRY, James G. | SWAN, Elender Sophia | 29 APR 1867 |
| MURSEN, Nathan | OWENS, Angelina | 12 FEB 1868 |
| MURT, Michael | SCALON, Johanna | 01 FEB 1866 |
| MURTAGH, William J. | LLOYD, Carrie | 18 APR 1861 |
| MURTAUGH, Jeremiah | DORSEY, Catherine | 04 FEB 1860 |
| MURTHY, Thomas | KANE, Ann | 11 NOV 1867 |
| MUSCHETT, George H. | BARNES, Eleanor A. | 28 FEB 1860 |
| MUSE, Daniel G. | WASHINGTON, Matilda (blk) | 11 AUG 1864 |
| MUSE, Frederick | ROBINSON, Rebecca (blk) | 12 NOV 1868 |
| MUSGROVE, William | BAIRD, A. Virginia | 16 MAR 1864 |
| MUSH, Hugh Washington | PENNINGTON, Lizzie M. | 25 AUG 1863 |
| MUSSER, George J. | HUTCHINSON, Sarah E. | 09 APR 1859 |
| MUSTAIN, Walker | MARSH, Elizabeth | 10 JUL 1865 |
| MUTERSBAUGH, David M. | APPLEBY, Ellen L. | 17 JAN 1863 |
| MUTH, Christian | EICHORN, Elizabeth | 05 JAN 1865 |
| MUZZY, Arthur M. | ANDREWS, Rosa May | 06 MAY 1867 |
| MYER, Ferdinand F. | OTT, Mary Virginia | 13 SEP 1858 |
| MYER, Frederick | BECKERT, Jennie | 01 SEP 1862 |
| MYERS, Abram | PARKER, Agnes | 22 OCT 1864 |
| MYERS, Albert | TURNER, Louvenia (blk) | 09 OCT 1868 |
| MYERS, Charles C. | LECKIE, Kate | 18 MAR 1864 |
| MYERS, Daniel | HICKEY, Margaret | 24 MAR 1864 |
| MYERS, Francis | CROCKER, Fanny A. | 15 JUN 1863 |

District of Columbia Marriage Licenses, 1858-1870

| | | |
|---|---|---|
| MYERS, Francis J. | CROCKER, Fannie A. | 08 MAY 1863 |
| MYERS, Frank | MARTIN, Joanna (blk) | 21 SEP 1867 |
| MYERS, Greenbury | GILBERT, Agnes (blk) | 24 OCT 1865 |
| MYERS, Harmon | JOHNSON, Emma | 11 NOV 1868 |
| MYERS, Henry Ray [11s] | GENNET, Louisa | 08 JAN 1870 |
| MYERS, Isaiah | BIRCH, Mary F. | 07 JAN 1864 |
| MYERS, James | BAILEY, Henrietta | 23 NOV 1861 |
| MYERS, Jeremiah | SMITH, Dinah | 13 JUL 1867 |
| MYERS, Jeremiah | CARTER, Gillis (blk) | 02 JAN 1869 |
| MYERS, John | MOSS, Mary Hellen | 15 FEB 1864 |
| MYERS, John | O'BRIEN, Nannie | 17 JAN 1870 |
| MYERS, John H. | HUTCHINGS, Susan A. | 12 OCT 1859 |
| MYERS, John H. | VanBURGHEN, Kate | 23 JAN 1864 |
| MYERS, John S. | REID, Catharine | 15 NOV 1864 |
| MYERS, Joseph | LEWIS, Nancy (blk) | 03 OCT 1866 |
| MYERS, Joseph P. | BRYANT, Mary M. | 06 FEB 1866 |
| MYERS, Lewis | BELL, Eliza (blk) | 19 NOV 1864 |
| MYERS, Nathaniel B. | EADY, Martha M. | 18 DEC 1865 |
| MYERS, Thomas Henry | LEACH, Mary A. | 02 NOV 1868 |
| MYERS, Thomas J. | McEVOY, Mary A. | 26 OCT 1860 |
| MYERS, William C. | DEVINE, Kattie J. | 02 NOV 1866 |
| MYERS, William F. | GRIFFIN, Mary Jane | 05 OCT 1858 |
| MYERS, William H. | THOMPSON, Salvadore (blk) | 19 NOV 1860 |
| MYERS, William H. | LIGHT, Matilda | 28 MAR 1865 |
| MYLER, William H. [10] | WAYSON, Matilda F. | 30 JUL 1866 |
| MYLES, John J. | SHIELDS, Mary | 12 NOV 1862 |
| MYRAS, John | McMAHON, Mary | 05 AUG 1859 |

# N

| | | |
|---|---|---|
| NACE, Lewis | DAVIS, Sarah F. | 23 APR 1859 |
| NACEY, Thomas | McNALLY, Catharine | 16 SEP 1864 |
| NADAB, Parker | JOHNSON, Mary Ann (blk) | 02 JAN 1867 |
| NAFF, John | OFENSTEIN, Catherine Johanna | 08 JUN 1867 |
| NAGLE, David | SULLIVAN, Johanna | 31 JAN 1868 |
| NAGLE, John | MARONEY, Bridget | 04 SEP 1862 |
| NAIRN, John W. | YOUNG, Fannie | 29 SEP 1868 |
| NAIRN, Joseph W. | FINCKEL, A.S. | 14 NOV 1860 |
| NAIRY, Laurence | MURPHY, Catherine | 22 APR 1859 |
| NAIRY, Michael | BYLOR, Catherine | 26 JAN 1869 |
| NALLS, Willis M. | EUSTACE, Martha | 25 MAR 1865 |
| NALLY, Dennis T. | WALLACE, Elizabeth | 09 JUN 1859 |
| NALLY, John B. | DAY, Emeline | 14 AUG 1861 |
| NALLY, Levi H. | CONNER, Elizabeth | 28 OCT 1867 |
| NALLY, William | BLOOMER, Louisa | 30 JUN 1859 |
| NALLY, William H. | WAGNER, Jane M. | 09 NOV 1858 |
| NALON, Patrick | MINATOR, Catharine | 22 MAY 1863 |
| NANTZ, F.G. | GIBSON, Emma L. | 28 SEP 1869 |
| NAPFEL, John | BURKHARDT, Margaretta | 19 APR 1862 |
| NARDI, Lorenzo | PERANI, Maria | 09 AUG 1864 |
| NARES, George W. | RAWLINGS, Henrietta | 13 JUN 1864 |
| NASH, John | POOLE, Margaret | 19 DEC 1862 |
| NASH, Peter | KING, Margaret | 26 FEB 1863 |
| NASON, Paul F. | McCALL, Ellen | 08 JAN 1868 |
| NASS, John Jacob | HINZEL, Carolina | 08 OCT 1858 |
| NAUMAN, Caspar | TRACY, Charlotte D. | 13 DEC 1869 |

| | | |
|---|---|---|
| NAUMAN, John | KING, Emma Louisa | 24 SEP 1868 |
| NAUMANN, Edward August | CURBY, Maria | 06 JUN 1866 |
| NAYLOR, Abner | MACKALL, Chloe | 14 FEB 1867 |
| NAYLOR, James J. [6] | MARTIN, Catherine E. | 12 NOV 1868 |
| NAYLOR, Thomas [John] [10] | NAYLOR, Lizzie [Price Smith] | 18 DEC 1866 |
| NAYLOR, William | FERGUSON, Sarah (blk) | 02 DEC 1868 |
| NAYLOR, Wm. O. | GRIMES, Henrietta | 04 MAY 1869 |
| NAZARINUS, Balthasar | CARR, Elizabeth J. | 11 JUL 1860 |
| NEAGLE, James J. | KELLER, Virginia C. | 20 FEB 1860 |
| NEALE, Benedict J. | HAMILTON, Mary H. | 06 SEP 1858 |
| NEALE, David | WILSON, Margaret (blk) | 24 JUN 1867 |
| NEALE, Francis C. | LOWENTHAWL, Carrie P. | 17 APR 1867 |
| NEALE, John | HARRISON, Susan | 15 DEC 1859 |
| NEALE, John | SHAW, Margaret | 22 SEP 1864 |
| NEALE, John | STEWART, Frances (blk) | 07 DEC 1864 |
| NEALE, John Henry | PRICE, Henrietta (blk) | 02 JAN 1866 |
| NEALIGAN, William | O'BRIEN, Mary | 02 MAY 1863 |
| NEALY, John | PLEASANT, Frances Eudora | 11 JUL 1867 |
| NEAT, Thomas B. [7a] | DONALDSON, Fannie J. | 19 NOV 1866 |
| NEBITT, John Henry | GASSAWAY, Nancy | 23 DEC 1867 |
| NEDDO, Benjamin | PERRY, Sarah | 13 SEP 1869 |
| NEEB, John | HIRSCHENHEIMER, Catherine | 16 JUL 1866 |
| NEENAN, John | KILLMARTIN, Ann | 30 JAN 1863 |
| NEILSON, George Crawford [11] | REILLY, Julia | 19 AUG 1867 |
| NELLIGAN, David | BERRY, Mary | 18 JUL 1863 |
| NELLIGAN, Patrick | SAGERSON, Mary | 27 SEP 1858 |
| NELLIGAN, Patrick | SULLIVAN, Mary | 01 MAR 1862 |
| NELLY, James C. | MEADS, Sarah Ann | 26 NOV 1860 |
| NELSON, Ack | PETERS, Ellen (blk) | 20 MAY 1868 |
| NELSON, Daniel | COOPER, Emily (blk) | 30 JUL 1864 |
| NELSON, F.M. | HAROLD, Mary Ann | 23 JUL 1860 |
| NELSON, George | MARTIN, Mary Ann | 23 SEP 1862 |
| NELSON, Harry A. | MARR, Mary V. | 14 JUN 1865 |
| NELSON, Henry | JACKSON, Mary (blk) | 01 NOV 1865 |
| NELSON, Henry S. | PAYNE, Rosa | 18 APR 1861 |
| NELSON, Isaac | TIPPETT, Jane (blk) | 07 SEP 1865 |
| NELSON, James | BUCKNER, Agnes (blk) | 03 AUG 1867 |
| NELSON, Jesse | REDMAN, Maria (blk) | 04 OCT 1866 |
| NELSON, John | MECIN, Margaret | 08 OCT 1866 |
| NELSON, Joseph | BANKS, Maria (blk) | 21 APR 1870 |
| NELSON, Martin V.B. | CONNER, Louisa Virginia | 09 DEC 1867 |
| NELSON, Reuben | THORNTON, Alverta | 27 DEC 1864 |
| NELSON, Robert N. | GASS, Mary E. | 05 MAR 1866 |
| NELSON, Samuel [10] | CRISMORE, Matilda | 17 APR 1860 |
| NELSON, Thomas J. [5] | ALEXANDER, Esther Ann | 13 FEB 1869 |
| NELSON, Walter | GALLERY, Annie (blk) | 23 JUN 1865 |
| NELSON, Washington | SEALS, Malvina (blk) | 26 SEP 1868 |
| NELSON, William | HALL, Mary (blk) | 01 APR 1863 |
| NELSON, William | SMITH, Charlotte (blk) | 22 DEC 1866 |
| NELSON, William | ROBINSON, Rose (blk) | 15 SEP 1868 |
| NELSON, William H. | WYMAN, Ellen F. | 20 JUL 1864 |
| NELSON, Yürgen | SEIP, Barbara | 05 OCT 1865 |
| NEMEGYEI, Felix Miklos de | YOUNG, Elizabeth G. | 27 AUG 1860 |
| NEPHUTH, Philip | KLEINLE, Julia | 03 DEC 1859 |
| NEPHUTH, Philip | PREINKERT, Margaret | 04 MAY 1861 |
| NESBITT, John B. | SCOLLARD, Catherine | 31 MAR 1869 |

District of Columbia Marriage Licenses, 1858-1870

| | | |
|---|---|---|
| NESMITH, Arthur S. [11] | MOULDER, Mary E. | 01 FEB 1869 |
| NESS, Samuel J. [10] | ENDERCOT, Harriet | 10 OCT 1863 |
| NETTER, Charles | MORRIS, Jane (blk) | 22 DEC 1865 |
| NEUGARTEN, Herman | LEVY, Carolina | 19 OCT 1865 |
| NEUHAUS, Jos. A.H. | ESCHERICH, Mary A. | 16 MAY 1862 |
| NEUMEYER, Henry | PAYNE, Louisa | 22 DEC 1862 |
| NEUMEYER, John | O'MARA, Margaret | 10 NOV 1862 |
| NEUMEYER, Joseph | HYATT, Ellen A. | 22 NOV 1860 |
| NEVITT, Joshua | HERBERT, Elizabeth (blk) | 19 JAN 1865 |
| NEWBOLD, Andrew | STEACOM, Annie E. | 01 DEC 1866 |
| NEWBURGH, Joseph | LOWMAN, Sophie | 15 OCT 1866 |
| NEWCOMB, Simon | HASSLER, Mary C. | 31 JUL 1863 |
| NEWELL, Charles N. | FARWELL, Marion D. | 11 JUL 1865 |
| NEWELL, George W. | WILSON, Laura L. | 23 NOV 1867 |
| NEWLY, William A. | BUCKNER, Julia A. (blk) | 16 MAY 1866 |
| NEWMAN, August | FREKIN, Ann Friederika | 02 OCT 1869 |
| NEWMAN, Edward | LUELZE, Grace (blk) | 18 JUL 1866 |
| NEWMAN, Eleazar | JONES, Elizabeth | 09 FEB 1864 |
| NEWMAN, Henry | AITCH, Ellen (blk) | 21 AUG 1865 |
| NEWMAN, Jacob | LOKEY, Sarah E. | 28 MAR 1863 |
| NEWMAN, James W. | PLATT, Mary J. | 27 DEC 1865 |
| NEWMAN, John D. | STEELE, Annie E. | 06 DEC 1860 |
| NEWMAN, Joseph | RHODES, Lizzie (blk) | 01 DEC 1869 |
| NEWMAN, Michael | BROWN, Anna J. | 09 JUL 1863 |
| NEWMAN, Thomas L. | KETCHEN, Mary E. | 13 SEP 1858 |
| NEWMEYER, Frederick | FÖLGER, Margaretta | 25 OCT 1864 |
| NEWRATH, Lewis | HENRY, Kate | 02 APR 1861 |
| NEWRO, George | DADE, Mary Nahalia | 28 NOV 1868 |
| NEWTON, Albert S. | POWER, Jessie M. | 02 JAN 1867 |
| NEWTON, Alfred | CRESTON, Rachel (blk) | 28 DEC 1868 |
| NEWTON, Anthony | SMITH, Mary (blk) | 13 NOV 1862 |
| NEWTON, Charles | MULIKEN, Sarah Jane | 16 APR 1863 |
| NEWTON, Charles | DORSEY, Mary (blk) | 16 OCT 1869 |
| NEWTON, Frank | SPARROW, Mary (blk) | 24 JUN 1868 |
| NEWTON, Frederick (by Clark) | SPENCER, Polly (blk) | 23 MAR 1864 |
| NEWTON, George W. | BING, Rosey | 04 JAN 1860 |
| NEWTON, Henry C. | GLEASON, Mary | 17 FEB 1868 |
| NEWTON, Philip | DAYTON, Anna (blk) | 12 SEP 1867 |
| NEWTON, Richard | BARKER, Matilda | 25 JUL 1862 |
| NEWTON, Robert | BOWLER, Mary V. | 29 MAY 1863 |
| NEWTON, William | FIELDS, Harriet (blk) | 20 MAR 1866 |
| NEWTON, William M. | MARTIN, Helen (blk) | 24 JUN 1868 |
| NICHLAS, Joseph O. | GRIFFETH, Lucy A.S.T. | 12 JAN 1869 |
| NICHMEYER, Christian | SHEIT, Mary | 12 JUL 1865 |
| NICHOLAS, David | HANSON, Amelia (blk) | 31 JUL 1860 |
| NICHOLAS, Wm. | FORD, Elizabeth (blk) | 24 MAR 1866 |
| NICHOLAUS, Jacob | [blank] Mary Ann | 20 APR 1861 |
| NICHOLLS, Albert | WHALEN, Anna (blk) | 11 JUN 1866 |
| NICHOLLS, Albert | WHITE, Lucinda (blk) | 21 SEP 1868 |
| NICHOLLS, Anthony B. [6le] | KING, Sarah Ann | 10 AUG 1865 |
| NICHOLLS, Edward A. | CLARKE, Ann E. | 21 NOV 1862 |
| NICHOLLS, George | JONES, Milanda (blk) | 30 MAY 1866 |
| NICHOLLS, Jared C. [9e] | WILKINSON, Sarah [E.] | 28 MAR 1861 |
| NICHOLLS, John W. | WILLIAMS, Marion Susan | 25 MAR 1863 |
| NICHOLLS, Richard | DWYER, Annie | 05 OCT 1865 |
| NICHOLLS, Thomas | TINNY, Chloe Ann (blk) | 03 APR 1866 |

| | | |
|---|---|---|
| NICHOLLS, William A. | MAY, Catharine C. (blk) | 24 MAY 1859 |
| NICHOLLS, Wm. W. | PAYNE, Ann V. | 27 JAN 1863 |
| NICHOLS, A.W. | COLLINS, Irene | 03 JUN 1865 |
| NICHOLS, Albert | BEVERLY, Betty (blk) | 07 JUN 1866 |
| NICHOLS, Frederick B. | WHITLOCK, Rachel | 09 NOV 1865 |
| NICHOLS, H. Hobart | JAY, Indiana | 29 DEC 1866 |
| NICHOLS, J.H. | ROBEY, Isabel | 12 SEP 1868 |
| NICHOLS, John R. | COSGROVE, Mary E. | 18 DEC 1865 |
| NICHOLS, Lewis | WILLIAMS, Lizzie (blk) | 11 APR 1866 |
| NICHOLS, Samuel L. | TAYLOR, Adalaide (blk) | 18 JUN 1866 |
| NICHOLSON, George N. | LANG, Anna | 13 SEP 1867 |
| NICHOLSON, George W. | FOLEY, Mary Ann | 09 MAR 1869 |
| NICHOLSON, Henry W.D. | JANVIER, Mary A. | 15 JUL 1862 |
| NICHOLSON, James | STROTHER, Lucy A. | 14 OCT 1863 |
| NICHOLSON, James W.A. [4] | MARTIN, Mary H. | 18 AUG 1862 |
| NICHOLSON, Leonard Lispenard | BRAWNER, Susie Craig | 17 FEB 1868 |
| NICHOLSON, Robert I. | GETZENDEINER, Mary E. | 22 AUG 1861 |
| NICHOLSON, Robert J. | BANKS, Sarah R. | 06 DEC 1862 |
| NICHOLSON, Walter A. | BUTLER, Mary E. | 28 OCT 1861 |
| NICHOLSON, William [1c] | BAKER, Lizzie | 13 SEP 1862 |
| NICHOLSON, William M. | BECKWITH, Jane E. | 28 AUG 1861 |
| NICKEL, August | SHUTZ, Louis | 20 APR 1867 |
| NICKELL, Frank C. | REDER, Elizabeth | 24 SEP 1863 |
| NICKENS, Amos E. | DADE, Elizabeth | 12 JUN 1867 |
| NICODEMUS, William J.L. | PETTIT, Fannie E. | 21 DEC 1864 |
| NIEDFELDER, Frederick | WOLF, Veronka | 07 DEC 1868 |
| NIEPLING, Jacob | HANSON, Elizabeth | 04 JUN 1865 |
| NIGHTINGALE, J.H. [11] | COLLINSWORTH, Julia C. | 24 JUL 1868 |
| NILAND, Dennis | NOON, Mary | 27 NOV 1863 |
| NILAND, Dennis | DORSEY, Julia | 21 APR 1859 |
| NILAND, Martin | SARSFIELD, Bridget | 01 NOV 1860 |
| NILAND, Matthias | WELSH, Sarah | 18 OCT 1869 |
| NILES, H.C. | BIELASKI, Rosa J. | 01 FEB 1866 |
| NIMBERGER, William F. | HODDINOTT, Alice V. | 30 DEC 1869 |
| NIMMO, William T. | BICKHAM, Sarah E. | 06 APR 1864 |
| NISBET, Hugh [22] | CROSSFIELD, Catherine | 04 OCT 1867 |
| NIX, Dennis | FOY, Maria | 17 OCT 1867 |
| NIX, Moses | GARNER, Mary (blk) | 13 JUL 1865 |
| NIXON, Alban H. | WITCOX, Helen M. | 02 SEP 1867 |
| NIXON, Burrell | MOORE, Martha (blk) | 05 MAR 1867 |
| NIXON, George | ANDERSON, Matilda | 20 JAN 1865 |
| NIXON, John | COFFEE, Mary (blk) | 22 NOV 1864 |
| NIXON, William | BENNETT, Penny Ann (blk) | 27 SEP 1866 |
| NOBBLE, Matthew | JENKINS, Caroline | 02 SEP 1865 |
| NOBLE, David G. | ELLIS, Alice | 26 DEC 1865 |
| NOBLE, Henry B. [11] | BIRNEY, Harriet E. | 14 OCT 1863 |
| NOBLE, Henry B., M.D. [11] | CLITCH, Henrietta | 19 SEP 1864 |
| NOERR, Martin L. | SHEDD, Frances L. | 21 JAN 1862 |
| NOERR, William B. | DUVALL, Mary V. | 11 MAY 1859 |
| NOGIER, Paul | CARROLL, Ellen | 23 AUG 1861 |
| NOKES, George T. | MUNROE, Cora (blk) | 13 APR 1870 |
| NOKES, Hanson | FERGUSON, Jane (blk) | 06 JUL 1865 |
| NOKES, John W. | NAYLOR, Georgianna C. | 18 APR 1859 |
| NOLAN, Daniel | FOLEY, Annie | 05 FEB 1859 |
| NOLAN, Edward | BYRNE, Mary | 13 JUN 1864 |
| NOLAN, Henry | RYAN, Mary | 19 AUG 1865 |

District of Columbia Marriage Licenses, 1858-1870

| | | |
|---|---|---|
| NOLAN, James | CLANSY, Sarah | 22 APR 1864 |
| NOLAN, James A. | WRYAN, Bridget | 28 JAN 1863 |
| NOLAN, Michael | SWEENEY, Mary | 10 SEP 1868 |
| NOLAN, Thomas D. | HOGAN, Anna | 13 AUG 1867 |
| NOLAND, Daniel | NOLAND, Ellen | 01 APR 1864 |
| NOLAND, George R. | HURNEY, Catharine C.A. | 08 JAN 1863 |
| NOLAND, Henry | SMITH, Margaret (blk) | 22 AUG 1863 |
| NOLAND, James | MADOX, Mary | 07 MAR 1859 |
| NOLAND, Laurence | BROSNAHAN, Mary | 27 SEP 1859 |
| NOLAND, Michael | DRISCOLL, Abagail | 03 AUG 1868 |
| NOLAND, Thomas E. | PEERCE, Maria L. | 05 FEB 1867 |
| NOLDE, Matthias | CASPARI, Christine | 21 SEP 1860 |
| NOLEN, Nicholas | SULLIVAN, Ann M. | 25 SEP 1862 |
| NOLIN, John L. | KINZER, Helen Ann | 18 SEP 1866 |
| NOLL, Henry | KRARER, Magdalena | 14 OCT 1859 |
| NOLL, Henry | RUPPERT, Catherine | 28 DEC 1861 |
| NOLLE, John | BARNS, Pricy (blk) | 26 DEC 1865 |
| NOLLS, William Henry | BROWN, Julia Ada | 07 APR 1870 |
| NOLTE, Augustus | KESSLER, Mary | 15 JUN 1864 |
| NOLTE, Christian F. | SCHRIBER, Eliza | 11 AUG 1859 |
| NOLTE, George | NOLTE, Veronica | 30 MAY 1864 |
| NOON, James | GAVIN, Maria | 22 JAN 1864 |
| NOON, Patrick | FLAHERTY, Ann | 22 JAN 1859 |
| NOONAN, James | GREELIS, Mary | 29 JAN 1867 |
| NOONAN, John | DORNAN, Ann | 07 JAN 1860 |
| NOONAN, Martin | CONNOR, Mary | 12 FEB 1863 |
| NOONAN, Matthias | GRIFFIN, Mary | 26 AUG 1859 |
| NOONAN, Matthias | KILKLINE, Bridget | 27 APR 1865 |
| NOONAN, Patrick | GRIFFIN, Bridget | 10 JUN 1863 |
| NOONAN, Patrick | SMITH, Mary | 06 OCT 1869 |
| NOONAN, T.V. | SAUTER, E.J. | 05 OCT 1863 |
| NORBECK, George W. | RUFF, Ella | 27 FEB 1868 |
| NORBECK, William | GATTENS, Ellen | 04 MAR 1867 |
| NORMAN, Alpheus J. | RAY, India | 22 MAR 1864 |
| NORMENT, Ulie | HURLEY, B.F.M. | 09 OCT 1867 |
| NORMOYLE, John | PENNYFIELD, Chloe | 22 NOV 1858 |
| NORRIS, Amos | HURD, Elizabeth (blk) | 08 APR 1869 |
| NORRIS, Florence J. | MARTIN, Emeline | 26 MAR 1861 |
| NORRIS, Frank | SMITH, Jenny (blk) | 06 AUG 1866 |
| NORRIS, George | TOPHAM, Sarah Ann (blk) | 17 OCT 1863 |
| NORRIS, James [12s] | TAYLOR, Mary F. | 21 MAR 1859 |
| NORRIS, James | AMELIA, Julia | 10 JUN 1863 |
| NORRIS, James | LONGACRE, Louisa | 12 AUG 1869 |
| NORRIS, James (Rev. Remmick) | BREWER, Alice | 24 FEB 1864 |
| NORRIS, John | PENNYFIL, Chloe Ellen | 09 OCT 1858 |
| NORRIS, John L. | CLARK, D.L. | 01 SEP 1868 |
| NORRIS, John T. [1c] | SMITH, Sarah | 07 MAR 1864 |
| NORRIS, Omer P. | PATTON, Frona | 28 OCT 1869 |
| NORRIS, Walter J. | KANE, Catherine | 26 SEP 1863 |
| NORTH, Willoughby | HUNTER, Catherine | 03 AUG 1863 |
| NORTHRUP, Henry H. | HARKNESS, Lydia B. | 10 SEP 1869 |
| NORTON, Alfred B. | ELLIS, Mary Jane | 26 OCT 1858 |
| NORTON, Andrew Ignatius | CARRICO, Helen Elizth. | 15 DEC 1860 |
| NORTON, Andrew J. | CARRICO, Hellen | 03 JAN 1860 |
| NORTON, Augustus A. | MULLOY, Lizzie | 06 APR 1866 |
| NORTON, Charles B. | PARKER, Fannie | 09 JAN 1863 |

District of Columbia Marriage Licenses, 1858-1870

| | | |
|---|---|---|
| NORTON, James | LEVINS, Catherine | 27 MAY 1868 |
| NORTON, John H. | LEACH, Louisa K. | 14 JUN 1867 |
| NORTON, John T. | GOLDSMITH, Elizabeth | 22 DEC 1863 |
| NORTON, Leonard A. | BROWN, Cornelia | 27 MAY 1868 |
| NORTON, Thomas | PAYNE, Lavinia | 21 NOV 1862 |
| NORTON, William A. | DADE, Fannie B. | 11 MAY 1867 |
| NOTT, Jacob W. | RICE, Jennie E. | 05 MAY 1862 |
| NOTTINGHAM, Julian R. | BERKLEY, Ellen M. | 26 NOV 1867 |
| NOWLAND, Thomas S. | THOMPSON, Hannah P. | 02 JUL 1864 |
| NOYES, Albert M. | ROUYARK, Hellen C. | 04 NOV 1867 |
| NOYES, Henry C. | LAUB, Clara | 16 JUL 1867 |
| NUGENT, John F. | HALL, Maria A. (blk) | 06 MAR 1867 |
| NUGENT, Meshack | DELANEY, Mary E. | 26 MAY 1863 |
| NULL, James | POWERS, Honora | 17 MAR 1864 |
| NUTHMANN, William | BROHM, Lina | 07 APR 1863 |
| NYE, John L. | DeLaMOIN, Maggie C. | 12 JUN 1865 |

## O

| | | |
|---|---|---|
| O'BEIRNE, Thomas | McLAUGHLIN, Liza | 23 FEB 1865 |
| O'BOND, John F. | MUNDY, Ellen Louisa (blk) | 20 JUN 1867 |
| O'BRIAN, John | ROURKE, Margaret | 25 OCT 1858 |
| O'BRIEN, Andrew (by Clark) | McKENLEY, Maria | 10 MAR 1864 |
| O'BRIEN, Daniel | LACEY, Ann | 20 AUG 1859 |
| O'BRIEN, Daniel | McCARTHY, Bridget | 14 OCT 1864 |
| O'BRIEN, Daniel | RAINEY, Margaret | 23 FEB 1870 |
| O'BRIEN, Dennis | MAHONEY, Ellen | 04 MAR 1862 |
| O'BRIEN, Edward | SULLIVAN, Johanna | 21 MAR 1866 |
| O'BRIEN, Edward | CALHOUNE, Margaret | 10 APR 1866 |
| O'BRIEN, Francis J. | HOOVER, Margaret A. | 10 SEP 1859 |
| O'BRIEN, James Lewis | MURRAY, Isabella Ella | 12 JUL 1869 |
| O'BRIEN, Jeremiah | McQUEY, Eliza | 16 JAN 1864 |
| O'BRIEN, Jeremiah | GALAVAN, Hanora | 18 APR 1867 |
| O'BRIEN, John | CASHMER, Catherine | 07 JAN 1861 |
| O'BRIEN, John | McCOY, Catherine | 16 JUL 1864 |
| O'BRIEN, John | DELANY, Hanorah | 25 NOV 1864 |
| O'BRIEN, John | KEENAN, Margaret | 02 MAR 1869 |
| O'BRIEN, John Edward | GARRETTSON, Ethi E. | 14 MAY 1860 |
| O'BRIEN, John H. | McCORMIC, Mary Ann | 23 JUN 1865 |
| O'BRIEN, John W. | FERRY, Sophia C. | 10 OCT 1865 |
| O'BRIEN, Kennedy | MORRISY, Ellen | 17 MAY 1859 |
| O'BRIEN, Lawrence | FALVY, Catherine | 12 OCT 1867 |
| O'BRIEN, Matthew | SCOTT, Ella V. | 09 JAN 1860 |
| O'BRIEN, Matthew | WILMOT, Catharine | 05 MAY 1864 |
| O'BRIEN, Miahcel | KENNEDY, Mary | 18 SEP 1858 |
| O'BRIEN, Michael | McLAUGHLIN, Isabella | 19 APR 1864 |
| O'BRIEN, Michael | SULLIVAN, Mary | 24 APR 1865 |
| O'BRIEN, Patrick | BOYLE, Catharine | 12 SEP 1860 |
| O'BRIEN, Patrick | DEVLIN, Sarah | 13 AUG 1863 |
| O'BRIEN, Samuel | DONOVAN, Margaret | 17 DEC 1858 |
| O'BRIEN, Thomas | TRACY, Margaret | 01 FEB 1864 |
| O'BRIEN, Thomas | BROWNING, Camilla | 14 NOV 1865 |
| O'BRIEN, William | DOWNEY, Mary | 01 OCT 1866 |
| O'BRIEN, William J. | DONALDSON, Mary L. | 07 DEC 1868 |
| O'BRIEN, William O. | McCARTHY, Kate | 08 SEP 1862 |
| O'CALLAGHAN, Edward | SUIT, Mary | 30 OCT 1868 |

District of Columbia Marriage Licenses, 1858-1870

| Groom | Bride | Date |
|---|---|---|
| O'CAREY, Cornelius | OWENS, Ellen | 30 MAY 1863 |
| O'CONNELL, Christopher | HURLEY, Ann | 24 SEP 1861 |
| O'CONNELL, J.C. | COSTELLO, Ellen Josephine | 23 JAN 1866 |
| O'CONNELL, James | PRENABLE, Mary | 05 JAN 1865 |
| O'CONNELL, James B. | FARR, Kate | 30 SEP 1859 |
| O'CONNELL, Jeremiah | SULLIVAN, Winny | 21 MAR 1862 |
| O'CONNELL, Jeremiah D. | NOONAN, Mary E. | 09 AUG 1864 |
| O'CONNELL, John | McNAMARA, Margaret | 04 FEB 1859 |
| O'CONNELL, John | NOLIN, Margaret | 09 JUN 1864 |
| O'CONNELL, Michael H. | LYDDANE, Mary G. | 28 APR 1865 |
| O'CONNELL, Thomas | HUSLEY, Ann | 20 DEC 1861 |
| O'CONNELL, Timothy | REARDON, Ellen | 30 SEP 1859 |
| O'CONNELL, Timothy | DOODY, Mary | 06 APR 1869 |
| O'CONNER, Richard A. | TAYLOR, Mary C. | 06 FEB 1862 |
| O'CONNER, Thomas | RYAN, Honora | 29 APR 1863 |
| O'CONNOR, Daniel | FLETCHER, Anne | 21 NOV 1864 |
| O'CONNOR, Dennis | GORMAN, Catharine | 28 FEB 1865 |
| O'CONNOR, Edward S. | HABBERT, Mary | 17 FEB 1863 |
| O'CONNOR, James | MURTHA, Margaret | 29 OCT 1867 |
| O'CONNOR, James | DRISCOLL, Catherine | 07 DEC 1868 |
| O'CONNOR, Jeremiah | MURPHY, Margaret | 28 NOV 1862 |
| O'CONNOR, Martin | RAINEY, Mary | 14 MAY 1864 |
| O'CONNOR, Michael | BRADLEY, Julia | 18 MAR 1865 |
| O'CONNOR, Patrick | BURKE, Margaret | 09 MAY 1861 |
| O'CONNOR, William P. | BARRETT, Johanna | 16 FEB 1860 |
| O'CONNORS, John | BARRETT, Catharine | 29 APR 1865 |
| O'DAILEY, Michael | HENNESSY, Hanora | 28 JAN 1862 |
| O'DAY, James | CONNOLLY, Ann | 03 JAN 1861 |
| O'DAY, John | SHEEHY, Mary | 03 NOV 1865 |
| O'DAY, Lawrence | KIRK, Mary | 25 NOV 1862 |
| O'DAY, Nicholas | BORLAND, Margaret | 22 SEP 1860 |
| O'DONNEGHUE, Martin | LYON, Margaret | 03 MAR 1862 |
| O'DONNELL, Francis | HALEY, Catharine | 29 APR 1863 |
| O'DONNELL, Hugh S. | BYRNES, Catharine A. | 16 JUN 1863 |
| O'DONNELL, James D. | SOUTHARD, Mary E. | 22 MAY 1862 |
| O'DONNELL, John | BERRY, Ellen | 29 JAN 1864 |
| O'DONNELL, Patrick J. | STACKE, Mary | 23 MAY 1861 |
| O'DONNELL, Thomas | O'DONNELL, Annie | 24 JUL 1860 |
| O'DONNELL, Thomas | CUNYERTY, Catherine | 04 MAR 1862 |
| O'DONNELL, William | CLANCY, Nora | 02 OCT 1862 |
| O'DONNOGHUE, Dennis | FINDLEY, Genevieve | 10 SEP 1861 |
| O'DONNOGHUE, Patrick | NORRIS, Mary | 11 JUN 1859 |
| O'DONNOUGH, John | BURNS, Hannah | 16 APR 1861 |
| O'DONOGHUE, Peter | O'DONNELL, Agnes | 15 SEP 1859 |
| O'DONOGHUE, Timothy | SHEEHY, Mary | 10 OCT 1868 |
| O'DONOHUE, Edward | FITZGERALD, Johanna | 02 SEP 1861 |
| O'DONOVAN, Timothy | FITCH, Margaret | 12 JUL 1861 |
| O'DRISCOL, Benedict J. | DALY, Elizabeth A. | 04 JUN 1866 |
| O'DWYER, John | BEAMAN, Catherine | 07 FEB 1870 |
| O'FLALLEY, Bartholomew | DULL, Mary | 08 SEP 1863 |
| O'GORMON, Francis | KELEY, Elizabeth | 30 SEP 1867 |
| O'HAGAN, James | SULLIVAN, Margaret | 30 JAN 1862 |
| O'HAGAN, Patrick | STUART, Lizzie A. | 03 AUG 1859 |
| O'HAN, Patrick | O'SHEA, Mary | 15 AUG 1866 |
| O'HARA, James | WILLIAMS, Mary | 24 JUL 1867 |
| O'HARE, Dennis | LAWTON, Ellen | 12 JUL 1860 |

| | | |
|---|---|---|
| O'HARE, George A. | BROWNE, Eva M. | 07 AUG 1866 |
| O'HARE, John | DONNELLY, Mary | 03 SEP 1869 |
| O'HARE, Martin | DESMOND, Mary | 05 MAR 1859 |
| O'HARE, Michael | GOODWIN, Mary | 27 APR 1866 |
| O'HARE, Patrick | BURKE, Julia | 06 OCT 1860 |
| O'HARE, Patrick | MORRIS, Mary | 15 JAN 1863 |
| O'HARE, William [James] [6s] | O'BARCLEY, Catharine | 26 APR 1865 |
| O'HEARN, John | BABBINGTON, Catherine | 10 NOV 1862 |
| O'HILLEARY, William | BEALL, Maria L. | 19 OCT 1858 |
| O'LAUGHLIN, John S. | OSBORNE, Mary S. | 25 JUL 1867 |
| O'LAUGHLIN, Michael | GAREY, Margaret | 04 APR 1864 |
| O'LEARY, Daniel | HANLON, Rosanna | 28 APR 1859 |
| O'LEARY, Dennis | MANGAN, Mary | 24 NOV 1858 |
| O'LEARY, Michael | McINTYRE, Anna | 08 DEC 1868 |
| O'LEARY, Patrick | MILLRICK, Margaret | 13 APR 1860 |
| O'LEARY, William | WALL, Margaret | 14 FEB 1863 |
| O'LOUGHLIN, John | KERR, Catharine | 09 MAR 1859 |
| O'MEARA, Alexander W. | PADGETT, Lizzie A. | 14 DEC 1867 |
| O'MEARA, L.L. | CROSON, Sallie C. | 15 OCT 1867 |
| O'NEAL, Israel | ENTWISLE, Amanda | 02 SEP 1863 |
| O'NEAL, Patrick | DRISCOL, Margaret | 03 JAN 1870 |
| O'NEAL, William | KINCHLOE, Bridget | 02 FEB 1866 |
| O'NEAL, William C. | HERRON, Mary Josephine | 15 JUL 1865 |
| O'NEALE, John H. | LATHAM, Ann R. | 24 OCT 1859 |
| O'NEALE, Joseph | McBRIDE, Mary A. | 16 OCT 1861 |
| O'NEALE, Peter | HOWARD, Jane | 23 MAY 1864 |
| O'NEALL, Patrick | GRIEVES, Rose | 11 MAY 1861 |
| O'NEIL, James | BURROWS, Letitia | 31 AUG 1863 |
| O'NEIL, John | COBURN, Ellen | 26 MAY 1868 |
| O'NEIL, John | COSTELLO, Mary | 20 AUG 1868 |
| O'NEIL, John | McMANUS, Jane | 23 NOV 1868 |
| O'NEIL, Thomas | KEENAN, Ellen | 02 JUN 1865 |
| O'NEIL, Thomas | MADIGAN, Norah | 09 JUL 1869 |
| O'NEIL, Timothy | BROWN, Margaret | 24 MAR 1865 |
| O'NEILL, Charles W. | CUVILLIER, Jane F. | 06 JUN 1860 |
| O'NEILL, Dennis | SULLIVAN, Margaret | 18 AUG 1859 |
| O'NEILL, Dennis | PETTIT, Katuro | 01 NOV 1866 |
| O'NEILL, Eugene | CARBERRY, Catharine | 09 AUG 1865 |
| O'NEILL, James | MUNTZ, Ann | 27 JUN 1863 |
| O'NEILL, James W. | LATHAM, Jeanette | 19 OCT 1869 |
| O'NEILL, John | WHITNEY, Georgian | 27 NOV 1866 |
| O'NEILL, John H. | OSBORN, Alice | 21 MAY 1867 |
| O'NEILL, Patrick | SHAUGHNESSY, Mary | 31 JAN 1865 |
| O'NIEL, John | CONNOR, Rose | 01 FEB 1860 |
| O'NIEL, John | ROBINSON, Ann | 09 SEP 1862 |
| O'NIEL, Patrick | BARRETT, Bridget | 15 AUG 1863 |
| O'ROURKE, John | McCARTHY, Catherine | 28 MAY 1866 |
| O'SHEA, Cornelius | McDONOUGH, Mary C. | 08 APR 1865 |
| O'SHEA, Nicholas | O'DAY, Ann | 13 MAY 1863 |
| O'SHEA, Timothy | FITZGERALD, Hanorah | 14 MAR 1859 |
| O'SULIVAN, John | FLING, Ellen | 29 SEP 1862 |
| O'SULLIVAN, Robert Aloysius | MOULDEN, Mary Cornelia | 08 FEB 1864 |
| O'TOOLE, John | LIDEN, Bridget | 02 MAR 1859 |
| O'TOOLE, Lawrence J. | VIVANS, E.A. | 13 NOV 1865 |
| O'TOOLE, Patrick | McGRATH, Maria | 06 JAN 1868 |
| OAKES, Francis J. | FLEMING, Elizabeth | 22 DEC 1865 |

# District of Columbia Marriage Licenses, 1858-1870

| | | |
|---|---|---|
| OAKES, Patrick | MULVEY, Ann | 13 OCT 1858 |
| OAKLEY, Charles | SHELTON, Frances | 12 APR 1870 |
| OAKSHOTT, Thomas H.* | CAMPBELL, Mary P. | 08 MAR 1859 |
| OAST, John J. | TERRETT, Rebecca | 14 MAY 1866 |
| OATES, Thomas | LARNEY, Lizzie | 26 SEP 1864 |
| OBER, Theodore P. | McKENZIE, Margaret E. | 18 JAN 1864 |
| ODELL, Daniel | ROBERTS, Sarah | 16 MAR 1867 |
| ODER, George B. [9n] | HARMAN, Sallie A. | 26 AUG 1859 |
| ODIN, James | WATERS, Martha (blk) | 31 AUG 1868 |
| OFELLON, Charles | BELL, Annie (blk) | 04 SEP 1867 |
| OFENSTEIN, Leopold | MULLER, Mary Elizabeth | 16 SEP 1865 |
| OFFER, Henry | SMALLWOOD, Elizabeth (blk) | 01 DEC 1863 |
| OFFERMANN, August | GREEN, Betsey | 05 MAY 1870 |
| OFFLEY, John R. [3] | MARBURY, Elizabeth | 15 OCT 1860 |
| OFFUT, Zepha. Rodolphus [6m] | PADGETT, Julia Frances | 23 SEP 1862 |
| OFFUTT, Florence J. | LYNCH, Mary A. | 18 JUN 1866 |
| OFFUTT, James E.F. | REMINGTON, Susan R. | 05 SEP 1864 |
| OFFUTT, John R. | ROBEY, Sarah Ann | 14 SEP 1859 |
| OFFUTT, Joseph C. | GOOD, Fannie M. | 23 MAY 1864 |
| OFFUTT, Lemuel | PORTER, Mary E. (blk) | 20 NOV 1862 |
| OFFUTT, William M. | TRUNDLE, Catherine V. | 06 JAN 1859 |
| OGDEN, John | McGARVEY, Ellen | 06 MAY 1863 |
| OGDEN, John | WILLIAMS, Sarah (blk) | 10 MAR 1866 |
| OGLE, Jackson | STEVENSON, Elizabeth (blk) | 22 SEP 1869 |
| OGLE, Jerry | DAVIS, Lizzie (blk) | 07 MAY 1868 |
| OGLE, Moses | JOHNSON, Virginia (blk) | 21 MAR 1867 |
| OHL, John W. | FISHER, Christina | 23 AUG 1866 |
| OHL, Martin | FRANENSCHUCH, Caroline | 01 NOV 1860 |
| OKEY, C.W. | ADAMS, Mary Blanche | 09 NOV 1867 |
| OLIFFE, Thomas | JENKINS, Jane J. | 02 JUN 1869 |
| OLIVE, Henry | KENRICK, Sarah J. | 07 MAY 1861 |
| OLIVE, Henry | BRYANT, Annie | 31 DEC 1869 |
| OLIVE, Winfield S. | ALLEN, Elizabeth A. | 14 JUL 1866 |
| OLIVER, Chesterfield | ALSOP, Virginia | 24 DEC 1866 |
| OLIVER, Elias [11] | MITCHELL, Margaret | 03 MAR 1863 |
| OLIVER, Elias | DIXON, Anna Rebecca | 30 DEC 1865 |
| OLIVER, John C. [7b] | SUTTON, Maranda E. | 12 MAY 1869 |
| OLIVER, John D. [10] | WILKINSON, Sarah Jane | 21 SEP 1863 |
| OLIVER, John N. | TOWERS, Mary E. | 20 FEB 1861 |
| OLIVER, Lewis [or Henry] L. [6s] | NAYLOR, Barbara C. | 01 SEP 1864 |
| OLIVER, Nicholas | BELL, Henrietta (blk) | 02 DEC 1862 |
| OLIVER, Theodore | WILEY, Mary C. | 10 NOV 1866 |
| OLIVER, William Alexander | CARTER, Mary Eliza (blk) | 20 AUG 1864 |
| OLIVER, William F. | CAMPBELL, Louisa E. | 20 OCT 1869 |
| OLLISTER, George | JONES, Louisa (blk) | 22 AUG 1868 |
| OLLIVE, Thomas | GREEN, Sarah | 04 NOV 1859 |
| OLLIVER, Benjamin | BAILEY, Martha | 31 MAR 1864 |
| OLMSTEAD, William S. [6r] | GATES, Mary L. | 15 AUG 1859 |
| OLSIN, Criston | TUCKER, Lucinda | 16 DEC 1865 |
| ONELY, Henry | CARTWRIGHT, Flora (blk) | 02 JUN 1868 |
| ONLY, William | JEWETT, Lucy (blk) | 29 OCT 1867 |
| OPPENHEIMER, Saml. | EHRMAN, Clara | 03 MAR 1862 |
| OPPERMAN, Uriah Louis | ANGEE, Elizabeth C. | 16 OCT 1869 |
| OPPERNAN, Charles | SCHLADER, Laura | 07 JUL 1863 |
| ORAM, John B. | HOWARD, Elizabeth J.S. | 19 SEP 1864 |
| ORME, George W. | LIBBY, Clara E. | 30 NOV 1861 |

District of Columbia Marriage Licenses, 1858-1870

| | | |
|---|---|---|
| ORME, Thomas P. [6le] | DOBBINS, Mary Ann | 30 JAN 1868 |
| ORMSBY, Dennis | McCAULY, Ellen | 27 MAY 1861 |
| ORR, Moses | LEE, Phebe (blk) | 09 JAN 1865 |
| ORR, Moses | LEE, Phebe | 06 AUG 1867 |
| ORR, Thomas | STEIN, Catharine | 23 JUN 1865 |
| ORR, William John | RUDD, Emma Frances | 17 JUL 1869 |
| ORTENSTEIN, Louis | MILLER, Nanette | 10 AUG 1868 |
| ORTH, Joseph Archibald | SCALA, Henrietta | 28 MAY 1866 |
| OSBORN, Charles | WILKERSON, Elizabeth | 20 FEB 1862 |
| OSBORN, Charles H. | THROOP, Mary G. | 17 MAY 1862 |
| OSBORN, John H. | MILLARD, Anna J. | 22 JAN 1870 |
| OSBORN, Joseph [10] | FLYNN, Ella | 21 SEP 1869 |
| OSBORN, William Henry | STEWART, Ella Annie | 16 AUG 1864 |
| OSBORNE, Charles H. [10] | GOODRICK, Mary F. | 11 JAN 1868 |
| OSBORNE, Daniel | LEWIS, Anna | 28 SEP 1867 |
| OSBORNE, Joseph | GRANGER, Jane | 08 MAR 1859 |
| OSGOOD, George F. | HENDERSON, Fanny | 28 NOV 1866 |
| OSSIRE, William H. | GREAVES, Annie A. | 01 MAY 1865 |
| OSTER, John | HESS, Mary | 07 JUL 1863 |
| OSTERHANT, Harry | RATCLIFF, Mary G. | 27 DEC 1864 |
| OSTRANDER, Peter V.L. | SLUDENY, Sharlott E. | 21 MAY 1870 |
| OSWELL, William [8] | BERRY, Susan | 30 MAR 1870 |
| OSWILL, George B. | McGRAW, Lizzie | 05 SEP 1866 |
| OTIS, George A., Dr., USA | POE, Genevieve | 14 AUG 1869 |
| OTIS, John | ROWLES, Arietta | 17 MAY 1870 |
| OTIS, Joseph | HICKS, Lizzie | 24 MAY 1869 |
| OTIS, Randall | IRONTING, Elizabeth | 02 MAY 1864 |
| OTT, Rudolph | STEINMANN, Mary | 27 AUG 1868 |
| OTTEMANN, Christian | VOGT, Rosina | 24 FEB 1868 |
| OTTERBACK, B. Louis | DAVIS, Sarah | 07 SEP 1861 |
| OTTERBACK, Philip, Junr. [10] | CROSS, Rosanna | 21 JUN 1860 |
| OTTMAN, William H. | WHITNEY, Sarah L. | 27 MAY 1862 |
| OTTO, Conrad | DRAILEY, Catharine | 04 SEP 1865 |
| OTTO, Fred Behrens | HORSMAN, Rosie | 29 JUN 1869 |
| OTZ, Kaspar | DIDERLEIN, Dorothy | 23 SEP 1867 |
| OURAND, William H.E. | BROWN, Laura V. | 01 NOV 1862 |
| OVERBY, William H. [6m] | MEAD, Emma F. | 11 DEC 1863 |
| OVERTON, William | RICHARDSON, Gracy Ann | 02 SEP 1869 |
| OWEN, Augustus A. | BALMAIN, Mary E. | 10 MAY 1861 |
| OWEN, Edward [9e] | KELLY, Ellen | 23 DEC 1861 |
| OWEN, William J. | HIGHFIELD, Lavinia D. | 12 SEP 1866 |
| OWENS, A.T. | DAVIS, Sallie A. | 21 JAN 1867 |
| OWENS, Charles A. | CREAGH, Catherine | 15 JUN 1867 |
| OWENS, Geo. W. | TENLEY, Kate A. | 23 DEC 1865 |
| OWENS, Henry | WHITAKER, Martha (blk) | 16 NOV 1865 |
| OWENS, Henry T. | TRUCKSON, Annie R. | 08 OCT 1864 |
| OWENS, James A. | KENT, Sarah F. | 12 OCT 1858 |
| OWENS, Jeff | BROWN, Sally (blk) | 11 DEC 1865 |
| OWENS, John L. [1c] | HILL, Susanna Francis | 16 OCT 1863 |
| OWENS, Marshall | McKINSEY, Martha (blk) | 12 AUG 1868 |
| OWENS, Michael B. | McMANNIVAN, Annie | 21 SEP 1863 |
| OWENS, Richard | MACKEY, Sarah Jane | 19 APR 1864 |
| OWENS, Stephen | BUTLER, Rachel Ann | 10 DEC 1868 |
| OWINGS, Thomas | CARR, Hannah (blk) | 18 NOV 1865 |
| OWSLEY, Robert | FORD, Martha (blk) | 22 MAY 1866 |
| OWSLEY, William | JOHNSON, Blanche | 19 OCT 1868 |

District of Columbia Marriage Licenses, 1858-1870

| | | |
|---|---|---|
| OXLEY, Francis M. | WELCH, Mary E. | 11 OCT 1864 |
| OXLEY, Jefferson H. | COMPTON, Alma P. | 27 JUN 1867 |
| OXLEY, William | QUEEN, Ann M. (blk) | 24 DEC 1864 |
| OYSTER, Edward W. | GAMBRILL, Mary A. | 18 AUG 1868 |

## P

| | | |
|---|---|---|
| PACE, William W. | COCKE, E. Jane | 24 JUL 1866 |
| PACH, Julius | GASSENHEIMER, Pauline | 15 APR 1866 |
| PACKARD, Benjamin F. | HUTCHINS, Mary J. | 22 SEP 1863 |
| PADDON, Geo. H. | GODDARD, Harriet C. | 25 OCT 1865 |
| PADDON, H.W. | RICHARDSON, Jane W. | 04 MAY 1869 |
| PADGETT, Benjamin T. | FRINK, Sarah L. | 13 OCT 1860 |
| PADGETT, Edward E. | MILLS, Mary E. | 06 SEP 1858 |
| PADGETT, John W. | SIMONS, Carrie | 18 DEC 1867 |
| PADGETT, Joseph Malon | HUTCHINS, Ann Arie | 30 JUN 1864 |
| PADGETT, Thomas | EDELIN, Jane | 11 FEB 1865 |
| PADGETT, Thomas [10] | ROCKETT, Mary E. | 06 SEP 1869 |
| PADGETT, William T. | FRINCKS, Merantha A. | 25 JUN 1860 |
| PADGETT, Wm. H. | BARNS, Mary E. | 15 NOV 1862 |
| PAFFENBERGER, Joseph | EMBREY, Ann | 10 NOV 1869 |
| PAGE, Ananias | BAYLEY, Harriet | 30 JUL 1862 |
| PAGE, Charles | FARMER, Harriet (blk) | 08 JUL 1865 |
| PAGE, James | TIPPETT, Virginia | 26 NOV 1862 |
| PAGE, John | HAMILTON, Ellen (blk) | 21 FEB 1863 |
| PAGE, Littleton | WEBB, Lizzie (blk) | 08 FEB 1866 |
| PAGE, Nathaniel M.T. | COX, Marianne | 02 OCT 1866 |
| PAGE, Quincy L. | DAVIDSON, Mary E. | 01 SEP 1858 |
| PAGE, William | WALTERS, Katie (blk) | 04 DEC 1866 |
| PAGGIT, John L. | PAGGIT, Susan Ann | 08 NOV 1859 |
| PAGIN, Lewis | ROLAN, Mary | 14 AUG 1862 |
| PAIN, Samuel | BATES, Mary Francis | 05 OCT 1867 |
| PAINE, Amasa Elliott [11] | RITTER, Lucy W. | 30 APR 1867 |
| PAINE, Lloyd [6c] | JEFFERSON, Georgiana | 26 NOV 1858 |
| PAINE, Rothens E. | GODDARD, Marion | 11 JAN 1864 |
| PAINS, John | WEOTEN, Frances A. (blk) | 30 OCT 1865 |
| PAINTER, James | BRENT, Catherine T. (blk) | 15 MAY 1861 |
| PALMER, A.B. | GREASON, Jennie | 01 JUN 1868 |
| PALMER, Alfred H. | MASON, Annie | 13 MAY 1865 |
| PALMER, Benjamin | GRUBB, Sarah | 18 DEC 1866 |
| PALMER, Charles | JONES, Elizabeth | 03 MAR 1863 |
| PALMER, Charles A. | DUII, Elizabeth | 05 JUL 1861 |
| PALMER, Edmund | BULGER, Johanna | 04 MAY 1865 |
| PALMER, Edward | WILSON, Catherine (blk) | 22 OCT 1868 |
| PALMER, J. William | FISHER, A. Cornelia | 04 NOV 1865 |
| PALMER, James H. | ST. JOHNS, Mary E. (blk) | 01 JUN 1864 |
| PALMER, John B. (Sgt. 2nd U.S. Arty.) | QUEEN, Sarah O. | 21 JUL 1864 |
| PALMER, John M. | RITCHIE, Eliza Jane | 01 AUG 1859 |
| PALMER, Joseph | STEELE, Mary | 09 DEC 1867 |
| PALMER, Julius A. | McCORMICK, Mary H. | 24 JUN 1863 |
| PALMER, Moses | BELL, Louisa (blk) | 17 OCT 1861 |
| PALMER, Peter | JONES, Roxanna (blk) | 13 OCT 1868 |
| PALMER, Robert | GARNER, Eliza | 21 SEP 1861 |
| PALMER, Robert | PALMER, Hester (blk) | 16 JUL 1866 |
| PALMER, Samuel Claxton | CLAXTON, Mary Susanna | 20 JAN 1864 |
| PALMER, William | WEBSTER, Mary Virginia | 07 DEC 1864 |

| | | |
|---|---|---|
| PALMER, William C. | DAVIS, Margaret R. | 07 MAR 1861 |
| PALMER, William T. | DAWSON, Margaret S. | 24 DEC 1863 |
| PALMERTON, Frederick T. | DICKEY, Mary F. | 24 MAR 1863 |
| PALMERTON, Frederick T. | COBELL, Virginia | 27 JUN 1863 |
| PANCOAST, Thompson | TAYLOR, L. Alice | 03 JUN 1870 |
| PANNELL, Otho | TILGHMAN, Francis | 27 DEC 1865 |
| PANNER, Thomas | SIMMES, Sarah E. (blk) | 15 DEC 1866 |
| PANNILL, John B. | CONWAY, Lummie Y. | 05 SEP 1867 |
| PARABLE, James E. | BARBOUR, Sylvia (blk) | 13 DEC 1866 |
| PARISH, William H. | HUGHES, Lucy A. | 05 NOV 1860 |
| PARK, James | THORP, Harriet Victorine | 17 JUN 1863 |
| PARKER, Aaron | OULD, Emeline (blk) | 14 FEB 1866 |
| PARKER, Charles | FRANCIS, Mary (blk) | 24 JUL 1863 |
| PARKER, Charles | ALEXANDER, Maria (blk) | 22 SEP 1863 |
| PARKER, Charles C. | BATES, Rachel M. | 01 NOV 1866 |
| PARKER, Charles C. | GILBERT, Elizabeth K. | 11 FEB 1869 |
| PARKER, Charles H. | SMITHLEY, Margaret A. | 16 MAR 1865 |
| PARKER, Coyle | HARRIS, Ellen (blk) | 01 SEP 1868 |
| PARKER, Daingerfield, Lt. USA [11] | NISBET, Amelia | 05 MAY 1861 |
| PARKER, Daniel A. | BENTLY, Mary A.E. (blk) | 23 JUL 1868 |
| PARKER, Edward | CARR, Emma J. | 05 OCT 1865 |
| PARKER, Edward G. | DAVIS, Eliza M. | 05 FEB 1864 |
| PARKER, Edwin T. | PILLSBURY, Elvira R. | 07 FEB 1870 |
| PARKER, Ely S., Gen. [11] | SACKETT, Minnie O. | 09 DEC 1867 |
| PARKER, Emanuel | NICKERSON, Jennie | 22 DEC 1862 |
| PARKER, George | TEAGLE, Malinda (blk) | 03 SEP 1867 |
| PARKER, George A. | WALKER, Elizabeth | 01 OCT 1859 |
| PARKER, George H. | HOBBIE, Frances P. | 20 OCT 1869 |
| PARKER, George S. [11] | NISBET, Alice | 01 NOV 1864 |
| PARKER, George S. | CARR, Sophia A. | 25 AUG 1865 |
| PARKER, George Thomas | SANDERSON, Amanda D. | 27 NOV 1865 |
| PARKER, George W. | COOPER, Mary F. | 08 NOV 1860 |
| PARKER, George W. | UMBERFIELD, Alice | 12 APR 1864 |
| PARKER, Henry | PLOWDEN, Virginia (blk) | 13 APR 1864 |
| PARKER, Henry | TAYLOR, Harriet (blk) | 18 NOV 1864 |
| PARKER, J.F. | STEVENSON, Carrie L. | 31 JAN 1866 |
| PARKER, James | WELSH, Bessy | 03 JAN 1866 |
| PARKER, John | HAWKINS, Ellen | 08 SEP 1866 |
| PARKER, John C. | FOWBLE, Mary Ellen | 25 NOV 1862 |
| PARKER, John Henry | PLUMMER, Winnie Ann | 29 MAY 1866 |
| PARKER, Lorenzo | TASKER, Jennie | 27 MAR 1866 |
| PARKER, Mathew | DOOLY, Annie E. | 01 FEB 1870 |
| PARKER, Miles | WOOD, Ellen | 04 AUG 1865 |
| PARKER, Miles | WOOD, Ellen (blk) | 08 AUG 1865 |
| PARKER, Philip | MUSE, Virginia | 26 AUG 1861 |
| PARKER, Reuben | MOSES, Amanda (blk) | 02 MAR 1870 |
| PARKER, Richard C. | MORGAN, Ellen | 31 MAR 1868 |
| PARKER, Samuel | LOMAX, Mary (blk) | 21 JUL 1863 |
| PARKER, Samuel G. | FERRALL, Bessie R. | 14 FEB 1865 |
| PARKER, Sidney | JONES, Harriet | 15 FEB 1865 |
| PARKER, Stephen | WANZER, Eleanor | 21 MAY 1863 |
| PARKER, Thomas | ADAMS, Annie (blk) | 26 JAN 1865 |
| PARKER, Thomas J. | SANDERSON, Mary | 05 OCT 1868 |
| PARKER, W.A. | MILLS, Catherine M. | 04 JAN 1862 |
| PARKER, W.H. | THOMAS, Clara E. | 26 JAN 1867 |
| PARKER, Washington | TURNER, Caroline | 30 APR 1868 |

District of Columbia Marriage Licenses, 1858-1870

| | | |
|---|---|---|
| PARKER, William | LANSDALE, Rachel M. (blk) | 23 SEP 1863 |
| PARKER, William | TILGHMAN, Barbara A. | 09 MAR 1864 |
| PARKER, William | SCARBRO, Elizabeth (blk) | 09 MAY 1866 |
| PARKER, William | MYERS, Fanny (blk) | 11 AUG 1866 |
| PARKER, William | OGLE, Adaline (blk) | 31 JUL 1867 |
| PARKER, William | CURTIS, Maria (blk) | 12 FEB 1868 |
| PARKER, William | SOMERVILLE, Lizzie (blk) | 20 MAY 1869 |
| PARKER, William | MASON, Chyndy (blk) | 09 JUN 1870 |
| PARKER, William Harrison | MILLER, Elizabeth | 22 SEP 1863 |
| PARKER, William Mellor | CLARKSON, Emily | 29 SEP 1864 |
| PARKINSON, Charles W. | THOMPSON, Sarah C. | 25 MAY 1870 |
| PARKINSON, Michael | McWILLIAM, Mary Ann | 01 SEP 1862 |
| PARKINSON, William | McCALIGATE, Mary | 25 FEB 1860 |
| PARKS, John | GANTT, Nancy | 29 DEC 1864 |
| PARKS, John | JOHNSON, Louisa (blk) | 08 AUG 1867 |
| PARKS, John [1e] | BROWN, Sadie B. | 29 NOV 1864 |
| PARKS, William | LEE, Elizabeth | 26 DEC 1867 |
| PARMELEE, Edwin E. [12s] | HINDS, Lizzie M. | 31 JAN 1863 |
| PARR, Ades C. | CHIPMAN, M.J. | 17 NOV 1868 |
| PARRINGTON, William | CARROLL, Mary Ann | 25 MAY 1865 |
| PARROTT, James T. | WHELAN, Mary | 04 NOV 1863 |
| PARRY, Alfred H. | LEE, Lucinda (blk) | 11 SEP 1866 |
| PARRY, Richard H. | ADAMS, Matilda | 28 APR 1868 |
| PARRY, Thomas H. | LEWIS, Amelia (blk) | 17 JUL 1869 |
| PARSON, John Edward | FERGUSON, Nancy (blk) | 16 SEP 1868 |
| PARSON, John T. | MORELAND, Mary E. | 02 SEP 1867 |
| PARSON, Joseph | VERMILLION, Rachel | 08 NOV 1867 |
| PARSONS, Albert N.C. | BLAIR, Elsie M. | 10 MAY 1870 |
| PARSONS, Charles D. | NEWMAN, Mary | 28 JUN 1860 |
| PARSONS, Franklin M. | PHIPPS, Jeannette | 25 APR 1870 |
| PARSONS, James L. | BRERETON, Mary | 04 NOV 1863 |
| PARSONS, William A. | WRIGHT, Annie P. | 06 JUN 1866 |
| PARTIN, Erastus H. | KITSON, Louisa | 23 NOV 1861 |
| PARTRIDGE, Benjamin F. | SHERWIN, Julia E. | 11 APR 1868 |
| PARTRIDGE, Michael J. | SHIELER, Louisa | 25 JUL 1868 |
| PARUM, Edmund | HENDERSON, Phoebe | 10 OCT 1866 |
| PASCO, George W. | COLBURN, Alice V. | 14 AUG 1867 |
| PASCO, William F. [1c] | MOCABOY, Minerva Frances | 03 OCT 1863 |
| PASCOE, Robert E. | ALLEN, Jennie | 18 MAY 1868 |
| PATCH, George B. | WALKER, Lizzie | 12 JAN 1864 |
| PATCH, John | LITTLE, Margaret Ann | 01 OCT 1858 |
| PATCH, Joseph | CRIDER, Laura | 25 APR 1860 |
| PATCHETT, Elias R. | BLADEN, Martha E. | 19 JAN 1869 |
| PATON, William | SOLON, Mary | 03 JUL 1863 |
| PATTEE, Asa F., M.D. | GUNNISON, S. Addie | 29 DEC 1864 |
| PATTEN, William | DIGGENS, Margaret | 09 SEP 1863 |
| PATTERSON, Arrington | BRIMER, Martha A. | 16 NOV 1858 |
| PATTERSON, Augustus | CHESCHER, Mary Jane | 27 JUN 1862 |
| PATTERSON, Charles | BROWN, Annie E. (blk) | 13 MAR 1867 |
| PATTERSON, George C.* | BELT, Julia B. | 10 DEC 1859 |
| PATTERSON, James | DORSEY, Elizabeth (blk) | 15 MAR 1864 |
| PATTERSON, James | WILLIAMS, Frances (blk) | 15 DEC 1866 |
| PATTERSON, James | JACKSON, Mary (blk) | 31 JUL 1869 |
| PATTERSON, James B. | BRAKELEY, Cornelia S. | 24 DEC 1867 |
| PATTERSON, John | PATTERSON, Abigail | 14 APR 1863 |
| PATTERSON, John | McLINEY, Kate | 17 AUG 1865 |

| | | |
|---|---|---|
| PATTERSON, John B. [4] | RAYBOLD, Annie E. | 07 NOV 1868 |
| PATTERSON, John H. | FLETCHER, Elizabeth (blk) | 14 AUG 1862 |
| PATTERSON, John S. [7b] | CHADWICK, Emma A. | 11 JAN 1870 |
| PATTERSON, Robert T.S. | OSBORN, Mary J. | 26 NOV 1862 |
| PATTERSON, William E. | GATES, Mary E. | 03 NOV 1866 |
| PATTERSON, William G. | BROWN, Martha | 05 MAR 1870 |
| PATTERSON, Willie C.D. | JAVINS, Mary Jennie | 12 JAN 1867 |
| PATTON, Charles L. | BUSEY, Emma | 18 OCT 1866 |
| PATTON, Lewis | BUTLER, Georgiana (blk) | 27 SEP 1866 |
| PATZE, Adolphus Henry, Dr. | TOY, Rhoda Louisa, Mrs. | 13 MAY 1867 |
| PAUL, James Albert | PAUL, Adelaide Augusta | 11 APR 1864 |
| PAUL, Joseph L. [1e] | RICARD, Mary R. | 15 SEP 1864 |
| PAUL, Thomas H. | LITTLEJOHN, Eliza S. | 02 SEP 1861 |
| PAULUS, George | LAWLOR, Anna | 10 JAN 1867 |
| PAULY, Antonio | FINK, Battranng | 03 DEC 1859 |
| PAUVRISH, John Peter | KUHNS, Emily Mary | 24 JUL 1861 |
| PAXON, John W. | PATTERSON, Laura V. | 10 APR 1865 |
| PAXSON, Fenton D. [2] | PAUL, Jane C. | 10 SEP 1867 |
| PAXTON, John S. | NEAL, Sarah E. | 02 APR 1861 |
| PAXTON, Thomas | RILEY, Hester | 21 JAN 1864 |
| PAYNE, Absalom | LEWIS, Helen (blk) | 08 AUG 1868 |
| PAYNE, Asbury R. | BURCH, Margaret Ann | 28 DEC 1868 |
| PAYNE, C.B.T. | HILL, Laura | 10 DEC 1867 |
| PAYNE, Frank | GLASCO, Harriet (blk) | 03 MAY 1866 |
| PAYNE, Franklin | WEAVER, Rachel A. | 17 MAY 1864 |
| PAYNE, George | COURSEY, Elizabeth (blk) | 20 OCT 1869 |
| PAYNE, Henry | TYSON, Anna Maria | 22 JUN 1864 |
| PAYNE, Henry | SEDGWICK, Gracie (blk) | 09 JUL 1868 |
| PAYNE, Henry | FORD, Maria (blk) | 17 DEC 1868 |
| PAYNE, Henry L. | DOWDEN, Columbia Ann | 04 APR 1870 |
| PAYNE, J.W. | HENDERSON, Estelle V. | 23 OCT 1866 |
| PAYNE, James | McCOY, Hannah (blk) | 25 FEB 1864 |
| PAYNE, James | ELLIOTT, Sarah Ann | 26 SEP 1868 |
| PAYNE, James F. | TUCKER, Mary Elizabeth | 15 OCT 1868 |
| PAYNE, John | JACKSON, Charlotte | 15 FEB 1866 |
| PAYNE, Joseph A. | DAY, Mary Ellen | 25 JUN 1869 |
| PAYNE, Melton P. | DYER, Isabel | 04 MAY 1870 |
| PAYNE, Nelson | DOUGLASS, Elizabeth (blk) | 21 JUL 1868 |
| PAYNE, Presley | HOWARD, Isabella (blk) | 09 MAY 1866 |
| PAYNE, Robert | HOWARD, Milly (blk) | 03 OCT 1867 |
| PAYNE, Stafford | RATCLIFFE, Lucinda (blk) | 09 OCT 1867 |
| PAYNE, Stafford | LEWIS, Mary Jane (blk) | 16 FEB 1870 |
| PAYNE, Theodore | RUPP, Hannah | 01 MAY 1867 |
| PAYNE, Thomas | DADE, Mary (blk) | 29 JUL 1862 |
| PAYNE, Thomas | CRAMPTON, Emeline (blk) | 11 SEP 1866 |
| PAYNE, Thomas | OSBORN, Martha (blk) | 12 FEB 1868 |
| PAYNE, William | PEARCE, Sarah | 20 JAN 1862 |
| PAYNE, William | DAVIS, Rebecca | 29 NOV 1865 |
| PAYNE, William | PAYNE, Fannie (blk) | 11 JAN 1868 |
| PAYNE, William J. | FORD, Charlotte (blk) | 11 OCT 1867 |
| PAYRON, Michael | EATON, Mary | 23 NOV 1863 |
| PEABODY, Adams | HUTCHINSON, Laura W. | 30 SEP 1863 |
| PEABODY, Charles E. | GREENBAUM, Amelia M. | 14 JUN 1864 |
| PEABODY, John J. | BALL, Mary J. | 23 MAY 1860 |
| PEACOCK, Albert | CROCKER, Amanda S. | 22 MAR 1864 |
| PEACOCK, George W. | RASH, Sarah E. | 15 JUN 1866 |

| | | |
|---|---|---|
| PEAK, Edward [6m] | ROGERS, Sarah | 20 AUG 1862 |
| PEAKE, Benj. F. | ZIMMERMAN, Mary C. | 25 APR 1870 |
| PEAKE, James B. | LUSBY, Mary E. | 20 NOV 1862 |
| PEAKE, James T. | KRANTZ, Elizabeth F. | 01 APR 1867 |
| PEAKE, Robert | BRUMMETT, Sarah | 26 JUN 1861 |
| PEALING, Charles | CUNNINGHAM, Ann | 26 JUL 1864 |
| PEARCE, Christopher G. [4] | GORDON, Virginia | 02 FEB 1863 |
| PEARSALL, Thomas C. [11] | HAZARD, Eliza A. | 21 MAR 1865 |
| PEARSON, Charles | RYAN, Ellen | 21 JAN 1859 |
| PEARSON, Edward S. | NEVERS, M. Lucy | 04 FEB 1863 |
| PEARSON, Granville L. | SLAGLE, Frances | 11 NOV 1867 |
| PEARSON, James | DAVIS, Arnette | 29 MAR 1869 |
| PEARSON, John | COLTSON, Ellen M. | 04 DEC 1865 |
| PEARSON, John A. | CROWNER, Eliza E. (blk) | 08 MAY 1862 |
| PEARSON, Joseph L. | RAINEY, Sarah A. | 30 DEC 1862 |
| PEARSON, Samuel | CASEY, Sarah (blk) | 15 SEP 1866 |
| PEARSON, William | RIZIN, Nancy Ann | 20 SEP 1858 |
| PEARSON, William | BOYLE, Susan | 06 FEB 1864 |
| PEARSON, William Hy. | BOWDEN, Eliza (blk) | 02 APR 1862 |
| PEARSON, Wilson | SHINER, Annie M. | 18 NOV 1862 |
| PEASNER, Ferdinand | SCHERRY, Mary Ann | 10 JUL 1860 |
| PEASNER, William | FAY, Jane | 30 JUL 1864 |
| PECHIN, Maurice | CROSSMAN, Kate | 11 OCT 1869 |
| PECK, Albert | FLEEMAN, Matilda S. | 02 JUL 1867 |
| PECK, Charles T. [1e] | BREMERMAN, Annie E. | 11 JUL 1866 |
| PECK, Clement A. [1e] | WARING, Anna S. | 20 APR 1864 |
| PECK, Cornelius | JOHNSON, Lilly | 25 NOV 1868 |
| PECK, Edward S. | RAYMOND, Catharine E. | 04 OCT 1865 |
| PECK, Harvey I. [7b] | PLASKET, Elizabeth | 15 SEP 1869 |
| PECK, John Jacob | HORSE, Laura | 10 FEB 1859 |
| PECK, Thomas | LUCAS, Nancy (blk) | 23 DEC 1862 |
| PECK, William N. | GREER, Mary E. | 06 SEP 1867 |
| PECK, William W. | DOUGLAS, Ann M. (blk) | 26 SEP 1861 |
| PEDDICORD, Charles | MERCER, Emma Louisa | 23 JUN 1859 |
| PEEBLES, Oscar | JONES, Mary | 08 OCT 1869 |
| PEEBLES, R.S.J., Dr. | LEE, Anna C. | 18 DEC 1865 |
| PEERCE, Ignatius H. | BUTTERBAUGH, Jennie | 18 DEC 1863 |
| PEG, Joseph H. | BURGER, Rebecca J. | 27 SEP 1862 |
| PEGG, Joseph H. | SMITH, Annie J. | 01 FEB 1866 |
| PEGG, William A. | OSBORNE, Annie | 16 DEC 1862 |
| PELBY, Forrester A. | HALL, Percy T. | 01 JUL 1863 |
| PELHAM, Burrell | TOLLIVER, Catherine (blk) | 14 OCT 1869 |
| PELHAM, Edward | THOMAS, Malinda (blk) | 24 DEC 1866 |
| PELLAM, Burd | LEWIS, Margaret (blk) | 16 JUL 1864 |
| PELT, Middleton | LOVELESS, Georgia A. | 06 OCT 1866 |
| PELTZER, Edward | COLEMAN, Louise R. | 23 JUN 1869 |
| PENDERGRAST, Michael | CUMMINS, Joanna | 09 OCT 1862 |
| PENDERGRAST, Peter | GALLAHER, Maria | 23 MAY 1861 |
| PENDLETON, Edward | JOHNSON, Ellen (blk) | 04 AUG 1859 |
| PENDLETON, Elijah | SINGLETON, Lucy (blk) | 18 FEB 1868 |
| PENDLETON, Payne | NEWTON, Mary Ann (blk) | 11 OCT 1864 |
| PENELTON, Joseph | PARKS, Annie (blk) | 04 JUN 1867 |
| PENFIELD, Luther M. | EVANS, Katie | 01 APR 1867 |
| PENN, George | DENT, Priscilla (blk) | 12 AUG 1865 |
| PENN, John | CLARK, Ann | 25 SEP 1863 |
| PENN, Joseph B. | JETT, Mary Frances | 02 NOV 1858 |

| | | |
|---|---|---|
| PENN, Mark L. | COLLINS, Sarah | 20 DEC 1861 |
| PENN, Penrose | SNOWDEN, Kate (blk) | 04 JUN 1868 |
| PENNINGTON, George W. | JENKINS, Annie | 18 JAN 1864 |
| PENNINGTON, Levi | EDMONDSON, Martha (blk) | 27 NOV 1861 |
| PENNY, James | THORNTON, Anna | 18 MAY 1863 |
| PENNY, John W. | DOUGHTY, Ann P. | 11 NOV 1863 |
| PENUTH, George W. | O'CONNER, Annie | 22 APR 1867 |
| PEPPER, Calvin | QUICK, Katharine W. | 22 DEC 1864 |
| PEPPER, John | MORRISSEY, Annie | 29 DEC 1864 |
| PEPPER, Matthew | CONNOR, Mary | 20 JAN 1859 |
| PEPPER, Patrick | DONNELLY, Rosann | 18 OCT 1861 |
| PEPPLE, Thomas B. | KELL, Sarah (blk) | 05 OCT 1865 |
| PEPPLER, Lewis D. | SUTTON, Catherine I. | 12 MAY 1870 |
| PERIN, Benjamin F. | STONELL, Harriet | 26 MAY 1863 |
| PERKINS, Charles M. | BAKER, Lucy J. | 29 JUN 1864 |
| PERKINS, Charles W. | WATERS, Julia E. | 28 JAN 1868 |
| PERKINS, Daniel[6] | DAILEY, Ann | 05 MAY 1864 |
| PERKINS, Delavan D. [4] | HARWOOD, Lizzie | 21 DEC 1864 |
| PERKINS, Duncan M. | ROWLAND, Mary E. | 30 JUL 1868 |
| PERKINS, George | MEAD, Mary E. | 03 JUN 1869 |
| PERKINS, George N. | SPEEDEN, Alice | 08 JUN 1869 |
| PERKINS, John A. | MERRILAT, Mary A. | 07 JUN 1866 |
| PERKINS, Samuel [A.] [6r] | SUIT, Martha A. | 22 NOV 1860 |
| PERKINS, Warren | CLOSE, Diana T. | 09 MAR 1870 |
| PERKINS, Warren L. | MARCEY, Jane | 28 OCT 1863 |
| PERKINS, William D. | TRACEY, Mary A. | 01 DEC 1862 |
| PERKINS, William F. [6h] | ROBEY, Sarah Jane | 13 AUG 1868 |
| PERLEMAN, Heyman | GOLDSTEIN, Sarah | 08 NOV 1865 |
| PERMILLION, John | PERMILLION, Rosetta | 29 MAR 1861 |
| PERRICKS, Thomas B. | LAWRIE, Sarah J. | 03 JUL 1866 |
| PERRIE, Enoch G. | SCAGGS, Mellie F. | 16 OCT 1858 |
| PERRIGO, Frederick [7a] | TURNER, Mary | 31 MAY 1867 |
| PERRINE, George P. | ADAMS, Annie E. | 14 SEP 1860 |
| PERRY, Asbury H. | DIXON, Rosa (blk) | 18 DEC 1862 |
| PERRY, Benjamin | BOWIE, Maria Ann (blk) | 15 DEC 1868 |
| PERRY, Hamilton | JONES, Hester Ann (blk) | 25 MAY 1867 |
| PERRY, Hanson | PERRY, Lucinda (blk) | 07 OCT 1869 |
| PERRY, John | KELSEY, Susan | 06 APR 1870 |
| PERRY, Joseph W. | MARSHALL, Cornelia Ann | 25 JUL 1867 |
| PERRY, Rezin | TAYLOR, Susan (blk) | 29 SEP 1864 |
| PERRY, Robert O. | CASH, Georgiania | 14 NOV 1866 |
| PERRY, Silas S. | BALL, Sally | 10 JUL 1863 |
| PERRYMAN, Marion W. [4] | BORIE, Victorine M. | 31 MAR 1869 |
| PERSONIUS, Martin | CONLY, Martha | 27 JUL 1865 |
| PETER, Anton | MOCKS, Ellen | 03 AUG 1866 |
| PETER, Armistead | KENNON, Martha Custis | 20 APR 1867 |
| PETERS, Charles | WILLIAMS, Julia (blk) | 02 JUL 1863 |
| PETERS, Charles | JOHNSON, Sarah (blk) | 14 OCT 1869 |
| PETERS, Charles Claus | JACOBSEN, Jenny | 19 AUG 1867 |
| PETERS, Charles F. | FRIEDEL, Kunigunde | 12 AUG 1864 |
| PETERS, Henry J. | WARNER, Alice V. | 05 APR 1866 |
| PETERS, John J. | HALL, Harriet | 02 SEP 1863 |
| PETERS, William | RANCIL, Martha | 12 FEB 1864 |
| PETERS, William B. | MAJOR, Margaret D. | 27 NOV 1860 |

---

[6] See 5 JUN 1861, license of that day ret'd. "not used..."

# District of Columbia Marriage Licenses, 1858-1870

| | | |
|---|---|---|
| PETERSEN, Rudolph Ernst | SIEVERS, Babet Mary | 04 DEC 1866 |
| PETERSON, Frederick | LYNCH, Margaret | 27 MAR 1862 |
| PETERSON, George H. [12s] | BROWN, Annie E. (blk) | 24 OCT 1861 |
| PETERSON, Henry | KENNY, Sarah | 03 SEP 1866 |
| PETERSON, Louis | KUHNS, Mary | 01 DEC 1866 |
| PETHY, George Kelly | MAHONEY, Annie Mary | 23 OCT 1865 |
| PETIT, Henry A. | GATELY, Mary | 13 APR 1867 |
| PETIT, James H. | BRYANT, Matilda | 12 SEP 1868 |
| PETROLA, Salvator | SCALA, Eliza P. | 10 NOV 1862 |
| PETTEY, George W. | ENNIS, Margaret Anna | 14 JUL 1863 |
| PETTICE, [blank] | HUMPHREYS, Louisa | 03 JAN 1870 |
| PETTIE, Arnold | ALLEN, Annie F. | 13 DEC 1864 |
| PETTIS, John | JONES, Elizabeth A. | 03 NOV 1869 |
| PETTIT, Benj. | WOOD, Hanna V. | 24 JAN 1866 |
| PETTIT, Edmund Lee | SATER, Dora Elizabeth | 23 NOV 1868 |
| PETTIT, Elias | SUTHERLAND, Aletha | 09 NOV 1858 |
| PETTIT, Hudson | CHISM, Mary W. | 12 JUL 1861 |
| PETTIT, John D. | SHYNES, Eulalia M. | 09 MAR 1866 |
| PETTIT, Joseph M. | DAVIS, Ann A. | 13 SEP 1860 |
| PETTIT, William H. | SCHRIBER, Sarah Ann | 27 DEC 1864 |
| PETTITT, Marshall [12s] | THOMPSON, Cornelia | 03 MAR 1863 |
| PEVIL, Lewis | AIRES, Prudence | 03 DEC 1867 |
| PEYTON, Anthony | HARPER, Virginia (blk) | 07 AUG 1868 |
| PEYTON, Beverly | OTTER, Mary E. (blk) | 22 JUN 1865 |
| PEYTON, Beverly | JACKSON, Winnie (blk) | 04 OCT 1865 |
| PEYTON, H.L. | KEEFE, Leonora | 04 APR 1867 |
| PEYTON, Isaac | LITTLE, Margaret | 03 JUN 1865 |
| PEYTON, Isaac | HAWKINS, Margaret Jane (blk) | 13 DEC 1866 |
| PEYTON, John | BURMBY, Virginia (blk) | 19 AUG 1863 |
| PEYTON, John | ROLAND, Sarah (blk) | 31 JAN 1865 |
| PEYTON, John | FRANKLIN, Rachel C. (blk) | 01 JUN 1867 |
| PFAFF, Frederick | FRESCEHER, Amelia | 24 MAR 1866 |
| PFAFF, Frederick Wm. | DUNICLIFF, Maggie | 25 MAR 1870 |
| PFAFFENBACH, Arnold F. | DOSUCH, Anna E. | 11 DEC 1866 |
| PFEIFFER, Donat | STROM, Augusta | 03 MAY 1866 |
| PFEIFFER, Henry H. | HERRICK, A. Virginia | 22 DEC 1864 |
| PFEIFFER, John C. | KEINLE, Barbara | 01 JUN 1867 |
| PFEIL, John K. | DIEGEBRET, Christiana | 23 MAY 1867 |
| PFEIL, Lewis | BERNHARDI, Louisa | 15 MAR 1859 |
| PFILE, John F. | TROUNECKER, Mena | 20 MAY 1864 |
| PFISTER, Gotlieb | NEWMAN, Katherine | 10 SEP 1864 |
| PFISTERER, Peter | KUHL, Justina (wid. Freidenberger) | 07 OCT 1863 |
| PFLIEGER, Chr. | SCHAFFERT, Margreth | 12 NOV 1868 |
| PFLUGER, Jacob | RAUCH, Magdalena | 18 NOV 1865 |
| PFLUGER, Jacob | HILBERT, Catherine | 26 DEC 1867 |
| PFLÜGER, John | FRITZ, Christina | 20 JUL 1863 |
| PFLUGER, John Geo. | MÜELLER, Dora | 22 AUG 1861 |
| PHELAN, Michael | O'ROURKE, Mary | 27 NOV 1862 |
| PHELAN, Nicholas | HIGGINS, Mary A. | 25 APR 1866 |
| PHELPS, John [10] | KEITHLEY, [Jane Elizabeth] | 24 OCT 1867 |
| PHELPS, John P.D. | BAYNE, Salina Catherine | 23 NOV 1868 |
| PHELPS, John T. | KING, Martha A. | 26 NOV 1867 |
| PHENY, Patrick | CLANCY, Kate | 02 SEP 1865 |
| PHIBBS, William W. | OURAND, Sarah Matilda | 06 JUL 1865 |
| PHIEL, Abraham | MORTIMER, Frances E. | 24 FEB 1866 |
| PHILIP, William H. [4] | WORTHINGTON, Eliza P. | 09 NOV 1864 |

| | | |
|---|---|---|
| PHILIPP, Louis | ZAHN, Maria Elizabeth | 08 SEP 1863 |
| PHILIPS, Charles A. | WOODWARD, Anna | 02 MAY 1860 |
| PHILIPS, William A. | HELMS, Charlotte | 28 MAR 1864 |
| PHILLIP, Patrick | SMITH, Adelaide | 05 SEP 1865 |
| PHILLIPS, Alonzo | DAWSON, Nellie (blk) | 15 MAY 1868 |
| PHILLIPS, Bartley | MOORE, Catharine | 11 OCT 1865 |
| PHILLIPS, Benjamin T. | BEALL, Marion | 25 JAN 1865 |
| PHILLIPS, George N. | SNYDER, Louisa | 10 AUG 1863 |
| PHILLIPS, James | SIMPSON, Helen B. | 01 AUG 1867 |
| PHILLIPS, James A. | NIGHTINGALE, Mary E. | 09 APR 1859 |
| PHILLIPS, James M. | BOWLES, Mary L. | 25 MAR 1859 |
| PHILLIPS, Job | CURLEY, Cornelia | 06 JUN 1863 |
| PHILLIPS, John L. | BAYLEY, Lucinda | 06 FEB 1862 |
| PHILLIPS, Joseph | KLOPFER, Martha Ellen | 19 SEP 1860 |
| PHILLIPS, Lewis H. | PHILLIPS, Mary Anna | 19 JUN 1860 |
| PHILLIPS, Martin | TREANOR, Eliza, Mrs. | 18 FEB 1867 |
| PHILLIPS, Richard | RICHARDS, Julia | 17 MAY 1860 |
| PHILLIPS, Robert H. | BERRY, Ellen M. | 02 MAR 1860 |
| PHILLIPS, Samuel A. | ERNEST, Mary E. | 04 JAN 1864 |
| PHILLIPS, Samuel D. | LEWIS, Susannah | 02 NOV 1868 |
| PHILLIPS, Seymour T. | KINSEY, Sallie | 21 NOV 1864 |
| PHILLIPS, Solomon | SHIPLEY, Ann (blk) | 19 OCT 1866 |
| PHILLIPS, William A. | SMITH, Lizzie A. | 25 APR 1865 |
| PHILLIPS, William L. | BAILEY, Hester M. | 17 FEB 1863 |
| PHILPOTT, Frederick C. | WILLISS, Blanche | 08 AUG 1864 |
| PHINNEY, Sylvanus C. | BODKIN, Elizabeth A. | 13 JAN 1864 |
| PHIPPS, John | SHILES, Caroline | 08 FEB 1869 |
| PHIPPS, John R. | BLAKE, Ella | 24 APR 1867 |
| PHIPPS, William M. [4] | HOUGH, Anna F. | 28 JUN 1869 |
| PICKELL, John H. | HENNING, Frances Adelaide | 07 MAY 1864 |
| PICKEN, Alexander | CARROLL, Mary Jane | 25 OCT 1860 |
| PICKEN, Thomas | BRANGER, Margaret | 28 JUL 1862 |
| PICKENS, Samuel | CAMERON, Louisa | 25 APR 1865 |
| PICKETT, Henry | TOLLIVER, Hellen (blk) | 26 DEC 1866 |
| PICKETT, John A. [11] | RANDOLPH, Harriet J. | 13 JUN 1860 |
| PIDCOCK, Edwin | CONNOR, Catherine | 18 NOV 1867 |
| PIELERT, John H. | GELDMACHER, Henrietta | 20 OCT 1864 |
| PIERCE, Albert | HARRIS, Clara Rebecca (blk) | 16 MAR 1867 |
| PIERCE, Alvin D. | LATIMER, Annie J. | 07 SEP 1863 |
| PIERCE, Edward W. | McGLOUGHLIN, Mollie E. | 10 MAR 1866 |
| PIERCE, Godwin | GORELL, Mary | 06 APR 1861 |
| PIERCE, Henry Hubbard | BROWN, Margaret Ellen | 29 OCT 1867 |
| PIERCE, John | VAPOR, Mary | 05 JUL 1859 |
| PIERCE, Magill | BROWN, Ellen (blk) | 30 APR 1860 |
| PIERCE, Peyton | WILLIAMS, Ann (blk) | 03 JAN 1865 |
| PIERCE, William H. | LEE, Kitty | 08 MAY 1867 |
| PIERCE, William [6s] | CORBELL, Virginia | 28 MAR 1865 |
| PIERRE, John A. | BROWN, Nannie W. (blk) | 04 MAY 1870 |
| PIERSON, James B. | THOMAS, Caroline H. | 17 FEB 1870 |
| PIERSON, Will T. | CRUTCHLEY, Emma J. | 31 DEC 1866 |
| PIERT, Thomas | SPELLING, Catharine | 01 JUL 1865 |
| PIGGOTT, Morris | READY, Mary M. | 21 DEC 1868 |
| PIGOTT, Daniel | KLINKEN, Harriet (blk) | 13 APR 1867 |
| PIGOTT, R.J. [Capt.] [3] | WESTFIELD, Sarah Caroline | 02 JAN 1864 |
| PIKE, Benjamin S. | LECKRON, Clara J. | 20 NOV 1865 |
| PIKE, William H. | KELLY, Julia | 21 FEB 1863 |

District of Columbia Marriage Licenses, 1858-1870

| | | |
|---|---|---|
| PILES, George W. | HOWARD, Mary A. | 27 AUG 1862 |
| PILKERTON, John | HILLEARY, Sarah M. | 28 NOV 1862 |
| PILKINTON, James Edwin | ADAMS, Annie Dodson | 25 OCT 1860 |
| PILLSBURY, Herber P. | MORAN, Virginia C. | 03 APR 1866 |
| PIMPER, George | KAYSER, Liezzie | 02 MAY 1868 |
| PINCKNEY, Benjamin [6le] | ADAMS, Catherine | 19 SEP 1865 |
| PINCKNEY, John | INGRAHAM, Georgianna (blk) | 23 MAY 1867 |
| PINCKNEY, John Robert | PINCKNEY, Rachel (blk) | 18 SEP 1867 |
| PINCKNEY, Robert | BROWN, Mary | 21 JAN 1865 |
| PINCKNEY, Robert | BROOKS, Laura (blk) | 11 APR 1868 |
| PINCKNEY, William Henry | LIVERY, Sarah (blk) | 21 AUG 1865 |
| PINDALL, John Henry | BUTCHER, Charlotte (blk) | 24 DEC 1867 |
| PINDLE, Charles | PINDLE, Elizabeth | 29 AUG 1865 |
| PINE, John H. | DUNN, Grace W. | 01 SEP 1868 |
| PINKERT, George | COMMODORE, Louisa (blk) | 07 SEP 1869 |
| PINKETT, Henry | HARRIS, Caroline (blk) | 29 DEC 1864 |
| PINKNEY, Francis | BOWIE, Polly (blk) | 17 MAR 1869 |
| PINN, James | WINKFIELD, Jane (blk) | 07 JUL 1868 |
| PINN, William | THOMAS, Julia | 06 OCT 1859 |
| PINN, William | CLARK, Susan (blk) | 04 NOV 1868 |
| PINN, William | CLARK, Susan (blk) | 16 SEP 1869 |
| PINNER, Willis | SEBRY, Betty (blk) | 30 MAY 1867 |
| PINNION, William | DODSON, Josephine (blk) | 24 DEC 1866 |
| PINYON, George | PINCKNEY, Harriot (blk) | 10 SEP 1866 |
| PIPITONE, Vetro | GATTO, Anna | 30 DEC 1865 |
| PIRNSTINE, Frank | CLARKE, Annie | 06 NOV 1865 |
| PITCHER, E.S. | JONES, Emeline | 22 JUN 1865 |
| PITCHLYNN, Peter P. | LOMBARDI, Caroline M. | 12 OCT 1869 |
| PITT, Albert M. | FOUNTAIN, Margaret | 06 OCT 1858 |
| PITTMAN, George W. | THOMPSON, Margaret | 20 SEP 1862 |
| PITTS, Nathaniel | WOOD, Mary | 31 DEC 1868 |
| PITTS, William | MUSE, Florida | 29 NOV 1865 |
| PIXLEY, Howell | MANGUM, Charlotte Ann | 21 FEB 1865 |
| PIZZINI, Juan A. | HICKEY, Cecelia | 23 APR 1867 |
| PLAIN, Benjamin K. | BALLENGER, Sue | 12 MAR 1869 |
| PLANCHARD, André | GALLAGHER, Kate | 15 JUN 1864 |
| PLANT, Andrew C. [4] | MORGAN, Emma F. | 19 FEB 1868 |
| PLANT, Frederick H. | DUDLEY, Drussilla R. | 29 DEC 1866 |
| PLANT, James | JURIX, Amelia (blk) | 10 DEC 1862 |
| PLANT, James W.W. | ST. CLAIR, Alice M. | 18 APR 1863 |
| PLANT, Walter S. | THOMPSON, Mollie F. | 11 AUG 1864 |
| PLANTS, George W. | JACKSON, Hattie | 18 MAR 1864 |
| PLASKETT, John [12s] | CRAWFORD, Mary | 22 DEC 1859 |
| PLATER, Sandy | DOUGLAS, Sarah (blk) | 22 JUN 1867 |
| PLATT, Amos R. [7b] | REYNOLDS, Catherine P. | 04 OCT 1869 |
| PLATT, Sherman [4] | CARPENTER, Emma C. | 25 JUN 1868 |
| PLATZ, Joseph | HAMERLING, Ann Maria | 23 AUG 1860 |
| PLATZ, Joseph | SPEER, Christina | 03 JUL 1865 |
| PLEASANT, Henrietta | LOGGANS, Jane (blk) | 30 OCT 1868 |
| PLUCKER, Daniel B. | REED, Eliza Ann | 08 DEC 1865 |
| PLUM, David | COHN, Reca | 31 DEC 1863 |
| PLUMB, Benjamin M. [11] | PARSEE, Lizzie H. | 14 JUN 1869 |
| PLUMMER, Augustus B. | O'DONALD, Josephine | 18 DEC 1866 |
| PLUMMER, Elias | PLUMMER, Rebecca (blk) | 02 DEC 1865 |
| PLUMMER, Henry V. | LOMAX, Julia (blk) | 10 JUN 1867 |
| PLUMMER, Joseph | BUTLER, Catherine (blk) | 26 DEC 1866 |

District of Columbia Marriage Licenses, 1858-1870

| | | |
|---|---|---|
| PLUMMER, Levi | PRICE, Mary (blk) | 24 AUG 1865 |
| PLUMMER, Mordecai | PRATT, Adeline | 11 FEB 1867 |
| PLUMMER, William | KEEFE, Mary | 17 AUG 1868 |
| PLUMMER, William | PARKER, Lucy (blk) | 24 DEC 1869 |
| PLUMMER, William Henry | HARDESTY, Georgiana (blk) | 11 SEP 1862 |
| PLYER, Harry G. | HOUGHTON, Ophelia E. | 04 SEP 1868 |
| POE, Toulmin A. | MAJOR, Susan | 02 APR 1866 |
| POGUE, Benjamin | POTTS, Susan | 06 AUG 1869 |
| POGUE, Joseph S. | MUIRHEAD, Isabella | 20 MAR 1865 |
| POHLERS, Augustus | VIERBUCHEN, Sophia | 04 JAN 1865 |
| POHLMANN, Michael | TRAUTNER, Maria | 28 JUL 1865 |
| POINDEXTER, James A. | MATTHEWS, Mary E. (blk) | 22 DEC 1864 |
| POIVRET, August | MICHEIL, Dorothea | 08 MAY 1862 |
| POKE, Sam'l. | MORGAN, Emma (blk) | 25 JUN 1863 |
| POLAND, John C. | PETTIT, Josephine | 07 JUN 1866 |
| POLEN, Peter | PIERCE, Mary Jane (blk) | 16 FEB 1870 |
| POLK, James | MORTON, Emily (blk) | 11 JUL 1863 |
| POLK, John H. | DANT, Eliza (blk) | 27 JUL 1865 |
| POLLAND, John | CROSS, Tansen E. | 10 APR 1860 |
| POLLARD, Benjamin | SANFORD, Mary Jane | 11 APR 1866 |
| POLLARD, Edmund P. | KENNEDY, Maria F. | 05 NOV 1868 |
| POLLARD, Edward A. [11] | BARRY, Adalaide M. | 25 APR 1859 |
| POLLARD, Phillip | RANDOM, Mary E. | 21 JUL 1863 |
| POLLARD, Samuel | GOODRICH, Mary | 15 MAY 1866 |
| POLLARD, William H. | JONES, Lucinda (blk) | 11 APR 1865 |
| POLLEN, Henry | MOXEY, Lucy Ellen | 26 MAY 1870 |
| POLLEY, John F. | GRIMES, Ella S. | 16 FEB 1866 |
| POLLOCK, Solomon | ROBINSON, Caroline (blk) | 13 JUL 1867 |
| POLLY, James | MILLER, Berti | 08 FEB 1869 |
| POLLY, Thomas | CARROLL, Mary Elizabeth | 06 FEB 1866 |
| POLONI, Pietro | CROVI, Therese | 29 DEC 1869 |
| POMEROY, John M. | CLEMENTS, Ann L. | 03 MAR 1863 |
| POMEROY, Willis B. | GUDGIN, Fanny | 05 MAR 1867 |
| POND, Frederick L. | HOLT, Anna C. | 01 OCT 1863 |
| PONY, Alexander | WILLIAMS, Martha (blk) | 24 FEB 1868 |
| POOL, David | ARMSTRONG, Mary | 13 AUG 1869 |
| POOL, James | McVAY, Annie | 24 JUL 1865 |
| POOL, John G. | WARD, Mary J. | 05 MAY 1859 |
| POOL, Lawson | JONES, Sarah C. | 15 AUG 1859 |
| POOLE, Alexander | ROBINSON, Martha (blk) | 25 JAN 1867 |
| POOLE, Alexander | PAGE, Martha Ann Maria (blk) | 06 APR 1867 |
| POOLE, Charles W. | MAHONEY, Margaret Virginia | 29 JUN 1868 |
| POOLE, Joseph L. | WENZEL, Mary C. | 11 FEB 1869 |
| POOLE, Robert H. | REYNOLDS, Annie | 17 MAY 1865 |
| POOR, [John] R. [12s] | HICKS, Virginia | 17 OCT 1860 |
| POOR, Robert | CHICK, Mary V. | 28 JUL 1868 |
| POOR, William H. | JOHNSON, Matilda J. | 11 SEP 1860 |
| POORE, Andrew Jackson | KEYHOE, Margaret E. | 28 JAN 1860 |
| POPE, Reuben | LILLY, Kate | 29 NOV 1869 |
| POPE, William H. | PUGH, Elizabeth S. | 13 NOV 1860 |
| POPHAM, John R.H. | BROWN, Kate R. | 04 DEC 1865 |
| POPKINS, Henry W. | POTTER, Sarah Ann | 08 JAN 1859 |
| POPKINS, James H. | ABBOTT, Martha E. | 22 MAY 1862 |
| POPPERS, George L. | IESELSOHN, Malchen | 11 OCT 1867 |
| POPPERS, Leon | STERNBERG, Sophia | 24 SEP 1863 |
| PORT, John | BREDERNÜTZ, Bertha | 24 DEC 1866 |

District of Columbia Marriage Licenses, 1858-1870

| | | |
|---|---|---|
| PORT, Joseph M. | CARROLL, Hercules | 29 JUL 1863 |
| PORTEOUS, Robert [11] | ZACHARY, Annie | 25 FEB 1863 |
| PORTER, Carlisle P. [4] | CAPRON, Carrie | 09 MAR 1869 |
| PORTER, Fitch J. | ELY, Susan B. | 03 DEC 1867 |
| PORTER, James S. | BURKE, Ann Virginia | 01 APR 1861 |
| PORTER, Richard A. | MILLER, Henritta | 06 DEC 1862 |
| PORTER, Thomas | CHAMBLIN, Rosa | 15 JUL 1869 |
| PORTER, William | BALTZER, Mary Jane | 11 SEP 1861 |
| PORTER, William | CUNNINGHAM, A.J. | 17 APR 1865 |
| POSEY, Charles | BAILEY, Elizabeth | 23 SEP 1862 |
| POSEY, George | LEE, Harriet (blk) | 02 SEP 1869 |
| POSEY, James H. | HURLEY, Frances E. | 10 SEP 1859 |
| POSEY, James H.H. | SHALCROSS, Louisa | 25 JAN 1860 |
| POSEY, John H. | TUCKER, Georgiana C. | 20 JUL 1867 |
| POSEY, Luther H. | STRIKER, Sarah E. | 23 NOV 1868 |
| POSEY, Samuel | CHASE, Eliza (blk) | 12 APR 1866 |
| POSS, Jacob | DODSON, Molly E. | 24 FEB 1862 |
| POST, George E. | READ, Sarah | 16 SEP 1863 |
| POSTON, James L. | HOPKINS, Mary M. | 30 APR 1861 |
| POTE, Peter R. | RAGAN, Susanna | 19 MAR 1867 |
| POTE, Philip | O'BRYAN, Margaret | 13 NOV 1865 |
| POTEET, Zephaniah | BOYLE, Emily Beale | 08 JUN 1870 |
| POTTER, George | LYLES, Ann | 10 DEC 1861 |
| POTTER, George F. [9n] | CARNE, Cecelia L. | 13 OCT 1859 |
| POTTER, John W. | COX, Almeda A. | 09 SEP 1861 |
| POTTER, John W. | COX, Almeda A. | 13 FEB 1866 |
| POTTER, Vernon, Jr. | BILLING, Amelia W. | 09 MAY 1866 |
| POTTS, Edwin C. | GABURRI, A.B. | 03 MAY 1869 |
| POTTS, Pompey | CLABOURNE, Isabella (blk) | 03 JUL 1865 |
| POTZLER, George | HAUBER, Katharina | 14 MAR 1865 |
| POULSON, George F. | KEEFE Mollie | 07 NOV 1868 |
| POULTON, William E. [11] | MILLS, Lydia E. | 20 APR 1865 |
| POWELL, Albert | HOGANS, Jane (blk) | 03 NOV 1864 |
| POWELL, Augustus I. | SOPER, Catharine R. | 22 OCT 1869 |
| POWELL, Charles Hy. | DELANEY, Mary Frances (blk) | 02 FEB 1860 |
| POWELL, Daniel | LEVI, Georgiana (blk) | 26 MAR 1866 |
| POWELL, Dennis | HAMMOND, Susan A. (blk) | 26 APR 1869 |
| POWELL, Edward | CLARKE, Virginia (blk) | 04 MAY 1864 |
| POWELL, G. Calvin | LEIGH, Annie M. | 02 DEC 1864 |
| POWELL, George | BALLENGER, Lottie | 05 FEB 1868 |
| POWELL, Henry | NELSON, Francis (blk) | 03 JUL 1866 |
| POWELL, Henry C. | CAVIS, Mary E. | 08 JUN 1869 |
| POWELL, James H. | OXLEY, Mary V. | 05 OCT 1858 |
| POWELL, John | JOHNSON, Juliana (blk) | 09 OCT 1860 |
| POWELL, John [10] | HUGHES, Mary | 29 MAY 1861 |
| POWELL, Philip | JOHNSON, Emily (blk) | 16 MAR 1869 |
| POWELL, Samuel | CALEB, Harriet (blk) | 27 SEP 1864 |
| POWELL, Samuel | DEAN, Mary (blk) | 09 NOV 1867 |
| POWELL, Wm. H. | ETCHISON, Merah | 01 DEC 1862 |
| POWELL, Zadock | BENNETT, Catherine | 20 DEC 1862 |
| POWER, James | COTTER, Ellen M. | 12 MAR 1869 |
| POWER, John A. | McDERMOTT, Harriet E. | 02 OCT 1867 |
| POWER, Thomas | SULLIVAN, Ellen | 30 APR 1859 |
| POWERS, Charles | LAHEY, Mary | 18 MAY 1865 |
| POWERS, George C. | GRANT, Carrie S. | 13 APR 1864 |
| POWERS, Jacob W. | GOODWIN, Frances E. | 26 DEC 1863 |

District of Columbia Marriage Licenses, 1858-1870

| | | |
|---|---|---|
| POWERS, John Walter | BROWN, May Frances | 15 JAN 1861 |
| POWERS, Matthew | CAHILL, Fanny | 24 MAR 1865 |
| POWERS, Nathaniel E. | BROWN, Elizabeth Q. | 23 JAN 1864 |
| POWERS, Patrick | CONNELLY, Bridget | 01 FEB 1866 |
| POWERS, Richard A. | BROWN, Mary E. | 02 JAN 1862 |
| POWERS, William | FENWICK, Emma (blk) | 09 OCT 1865 |
| PRANNER, Charles | FISCHOETTER, Margaret | 02 FEB 1865 |
| PRATHER, Albert C. | BLOYCE, Lucretia D. | 10 JUL 1862 |
| PRATHER, George W. | MADDOX, Agnes | 06 DEC 1865 |
| PRATHER, Gustavus Adolphus [10] | GRANGER, Eliz. Rebecca, Mrs. | 16 JAN 1868 |
| PRATHER, John T. | BROWN, Sarah Ann (blk) | 21 NOV 1860 |
| PRATHER, R.J. | BOWLING, Kate | 05 FEB 1869 |
| PRATT, Charles P. | BUTLER, Mary E. (blk) | 14 MAY 1868 |
| PRATT, Electus A. | NOURSE, Sarah L. | 17 SEP 1866 |
| PRATT, Fred'k. W.P. | FENCKEL, Henrietta E. | 28 FEB 1868 |
| PRATT, G. Julian | BROWN, Mary E. | 30 SEP 1865 |
| PRATT, James | WILLIAMS, Anna Eliza (blk) | 24 AUG 1868 |
| PRATT, John | WALLACE, Josephine E. | 05 JUN 1867 |
| PRATT, Jos. | THOMAS, Ellen (blk) | 25 OCT 1865 |
| PRATT, Marcellus | LAWRENCE, Martha Ann | 16 DEC 1865 |
| PRATT, Smith | MORTON, Rachel (blk) | 13 NOV 1866 |
| PREISS, Charles | MEIER, Babette | 24 OCT 1864 |
| PRENTICE, C.T.K. | THECKER, Emma A. | 04 AUG 1869 |
| PRENTISS, Charles A. | CLARK, Margaret Joanna | 03 MAY 1866 |
| PRESCOE, Samuel | WALKER, Josephine (blk) | 19 DEC 1867 |
| PRESCOTT, Benjamin [3] | TAYLOR, Catherine E. | 08 NOV 1858 |
| PRESCOTT, Wm. H. [12s] | KUGLER, Myra E. | 22 JAN 1862 |
| PRESENTIN, Ludwig V. | CRAIG, Mary E. | 16 MAY 1866 |
| PRESTON, Edmund G.W.B. | TURNER, Mary Frances | 17 SEP 1863 |
| PRESTON, George | SMEAD, Camilla A. | 25 JAN 1864 |
| PRESTON, Herbert A. | McNABB, Annie E. | 15 OCT 1869 |
| PRESTON, Robert Emmet | LASSELLE, Ellen Louise | 08 OCT 1863 |
| PREUGH, William | SNEED, Ann (blk) | 18 SEP 1865 |
| PREUSS, Peter Joachim Frederick | BOUCHER, Wilhelmina Adelia | 05 JAN 1867 |
| PRICE, A.H. | TRUSLER, Isabella M. | 17 JUL 1869 |
| PRICE, Andrew | GREEN, Catherine (blk) | 17 NOV 1863 |
| PRICE, Benjamin | THOMAS, Margaret (blk) | 21 OCT 1868 |
| PRICE, Charles | HEILBRUN, Fanny | 25 AUG 1862 |
| PRICE, Charles C. [1c] | JETT, Georgia | 03 DEC 1863 |
| PRICE, Charles C. | BEACH, Sallie J. | 11 JUL 1868 |
| PRICE, Daniel | WATKINS, Laura V. | 30 NOV 1868 |
| PRICE, Elfred | BROCKENBROUGH, Louise C. | 26 APR 1869 |
| PRICE, George A. | PHILLIPS, Margaret (blk) | 21 DEC 1869 |
| PRICE, Henry | HARRISON, Harriet (blk) | 24 MAR 1864 |
| PRICE, James B. | PRICE, Emma F. | 21 JUL 1869 |
| PRICE, James M. | RODGERS, Catherine | 01 SEP 1859 |
| PRICE, Jehu | PRITCHARD, Harriett W. | 03 MAY 1870 |
| PRICE, John | FAUNTLEROY, Ann | 05 AUG 1865 |
| PRICE, John H., Jr. [11] | BAILEY, Fannie W. | 16 FEB 1867 |
| PRICE, John Henry | DOLLY, Louisa (blk) | 22 MAY 1865 |
| PRICE, Jon P. | LEMMON, Annie R. | 02 AUG 1865 |
| PRICE, Joseph | PRICE, Daphney (blk) | 27 MAY 1868 |
| PRICE, Lewis | THOMPSON, Jane (blk) | 10 OCT 1863 |
| PRICE, Lewis B. | O'BRIEN, Mary L. | 15 NOV 1860 |
| PRICE, Marshall F. | TINGLE, C. Olivia A. | 12 JUN 1865 |
| PRICE, Maurice R. | DUNCAN, Elizabeth (blk) | 12 AUG 1867 |

District of Columbia Marriage Licenses, 1858-1870

| | | |
|---|---|---|
| PRICE, Morris | BAUM, Hannah | 03 JAN 1870 |
| PRICE, Robert | WHARTON, Evelina | 22 JAN 1866 |
| PRICE, Robert | WILLIAMS, Bettie (blk) | 26 DEC 1867 |
| PRICE, Theodore | TASKER, Lucy Ann (blk) | 09 DEC 1862 |
| PRICE, Thomas | DUNN, Bridget | 01 DEC 1865 |
| PRICE, Washington R. | GRUBB, Annie E. | 07 JUL 1869 |
| PRICE, William | WOODWARD, Hester (blk) | 20 DEC 1864 |
| PRICE, William | DUFFINS, Eliza (blk) | 28 AUG 1865 |
| PRICE, William | ROBINSON, Minna (blk) | 23 DEC 1865 |
| PRICE, William H. [12s] | MADISON, Virginia | 16 JUN 1859 |
| PRICE, William P. [6le] | WOOD, Celia | 10 OCT 1867 |
| PRICHETT, James M. | LEE, Alice | 26 DEC 1861 |
| PRIEST, Olen A. | VANNERMAN, Mary A. | 02 MAY 1864 |
| PRIGG, John Edmond | BALL, Barbara Elizabeth | 03 MAR 1863 |
| PRINDEVILLE, William | READY, Mary | 12 JAN 1869 |
| PRINDIBLAIN, Thomas | SULLIVAN, Nora | 06 MAY 1867 |
| PRINDLE, George S. | SANDERSON, Annie E. | 28 JUN 1865 |
| PRINKERT, John Frederick | SCHOLMEIR, Mary | 22 JUL 1864 |
| PRIOR, Turner | SMITH, Elizabeth | 07 AUG 1867 |
| PRITCHARD, John R. | ROGERS, Margaret | 25 JUL 1865 |
| PRITCHARD, Porter W. [10] | MULLEN, Arthelia A. | 30 OCT 1866 |
| PROBEY, Joseph A. | MOUREN, Mary B. | 22 JUN 1860 |
| PROCTER, Walter | McVEY, Mary Jane | 17 OCT 1865 |
| PROCTOR, Alexander M. | PIGGOTT, Emma Georgietta | 29 JUL 1863 |
| PROCTOR, Charles | MABURY, Mary R. | 02 NOV 1865 |
| PROCTOR, Charles W. | EVANS, Mary E. | 27 JAN 1866 |
| PROCTOR, Cornelius | JONES, Elizabeth (blk) | 08 JAN 1861 |
| PROCTOR, Franklin M. | HALL, Mary Frances | 05 JUN 1866 |
| PROCTOR, George W. | RIXON, Emily (blk) | 26 DEC 1867 |
| PROCTOR, Henry B. | COOLEY, Elmira E. | 27 SEP 1859 |
| PROCTOR, James | OSBORNE, Frances A. | 03 SEP 1864 |
| PROCTOR, John | JONES, Ann | 10 MAY 1869 |
| PROCTOR, John I. | NELSON, Adelade | 03 JUL 1860 |
| PROCTOR, Samuel | DUKEHART, Eugenia R. | 21 APR 1870 |
| PROCTOR, Samuel C. | PARKER, Pauline Matilda | 28 JUN 1869 |
| PROCTOR, Thomas | NEWBY, Agnes | 29 MAR 1866 |
| PROCTOR, William Washington | JONES, Elizabeth (blk) | 05 OCT 1867 |
| PRONTI, Annis | SACCHI, Francis | 23 MAR 1867 |
| PROSPERI, John [Francis] [10] | RAMSAY, Harriet E. | 13 APR 1863 |
| PROUT, Henry | HAWKINS, Rachel | 11 NOV 1867 |
| PROVEY, John T. | WALKER, Charlotte | 23 MAY 1864 |
| PRUCHHOLTZ, Henry | KEPHART, Christiana | 07 MAY 1861 |
| PRUETT, James Henry | STICK, Clara Victoria | 09 JUL 1868 |
| PRUETT, John M. | ESTLER, Emily F. | 20 APR 1865 |
| PRYOR, Richard S. | NOYES, Eliza B. | 31 AUG 1868 |
| PRYOR, Robert J. | SIMPSON, Alice (blk) | 06 SEP 1869 |
| PUFFER, A.E. [2] | HOWARD, Laura Va. | 28 JAN 1864 |
| PUGH, Joseph C. | MILLER, Mary | 05 SEP 1864 |
| PUGH, William G. | MORROW, Julia E. | 07 SEP 1858 |
| PUGH, York | DAVENPORT, Emily (blk) | 03 OCT 1867 |
| PULASKI, George W. | HIGGINS, Sarah | 14 JUN 1862 |
| PULASKI, William Edward | LUCAS, Alice Virginia | 27 SEP 1866 |
| PULISON, Morton | GREENFIELD, Hannah (blk) | 11 JUN 1868 |
| PULLIN, Joseph | ASHTON, Susanna | 02 MAY 1859 |
| PULLIN, William | LUCAS, Anna | 07 JUN 1860 |
| PULLISON, Beverly | BUTLER, Mary E. (blk) | 19 NOV 1862 |

| | | |
|---|---|---|
| PULMAN, Edgar J. [6s] | AUSTIN, Ellen L. | 31 OCT 1864 |
| PUMPHREY, Edward | MANNIS, Catharine | 30 JAN 1866 |
| PUMPHREY, John | WIEDEN, Betty | 07 APR 1864 |
| PUMPHREY, John G. | PEAKE, Annie E. | 19 AUG 1862 |
| PUMPHREY, John H.N. | MAYHEW, Mary Jane | 11 MAY 1866 |
| PUMPHREY, John H.N. | WILLIAMS, Anna E. | 09 NOV 1869 |
| PUMPHREY, John W., Jr. | NEWTON, Matilda | 24 FEB 1859 |
| PUMPHREY, John [Wesley] [10] | LEWIS, Mary [Catherine] | 10 MAY 1861 |
| PUMPHREY, John W. | WISE, Annie M. | 14 MAR 1865 |
| PUMPHREY, Levi | GANGHREN, Annie | 01 OCT 1862 |
| PUMPHREY, Lloyd W. | HITCHCOCK, Martha E. | 07 JAN 1862 |
| PUMPHREY, Rezin N., Jr. [6r] | MURPHY, Francis Rebecca | 27 FEB 1861 |
| PUMPHREY, Thomas B. | NELSON, Ann M. | 13 SEP 1860 |
| PURCELL, Andrew | WEST, Sarah | 24 JAN 1870 |
| PURCELL, Edward | COONEY, Ann | 27 JUL 1861 |
| PURCELL, Edward J. | NEUMEYER, Ellen | 22 FEB 1868 |
| PURCELL, Henry | DEMENT, Louisa E. | 02 DEC 1868 |
| PURCELL, James R. | BUNDICK, Virginia | 21 APR 1868 |
| PURCELL, John | NICHOLSON, Lucy | 19 APR 1864 |
| PURCELL, John | BROWN, Margaret | 26 AUG 1865 |
| PURCELL, John R. | SIMPSON, Anna L. | 18 DEC 1867 |
| PURCELY, John | ROLLINS, Sarah | 10 SEP 1859 |
| PURDY, Gilbert W. | BOWIE, Mary | 19 NOV 1861 |
| PURDY, Henry | BEHLEN, Ella | 24 FEB 1862 |
| PURDY, John | CRANE, Sarah | 31 OCT 1864 |
| PURDY, Thomas C. | STEELE, Eva A. | 27 MAR 1867 |
| PURGDORF, Augustus | ESPEY, Anne | 09 OCT 1861 |
| PURNELL, Charles J. | ROBEY, Marcelene B. | 30 SEP 1863 |
| PURSELL, James | WOOD, Maggie | 25 MAY 1870 |
| PURSELL, John | BROWN, Ellen | 26 DEC 1864 |
| PURVIS, H.C. | PADGETT, Mary C. | 22 JUN 1869 |
| PUSEY, Presley | NELSON, Patsey | 17 NOV 1866 |
| PUTNAM, John W. | CUMMINS, Cazzora V. | 01 SEP 1864 |
| PUTNAM, Julian A. [4] | HUGHES, Eliza J. | 01 APR 1862 |
| PYLES, Charles W. | BOULDING, Ann | 15 NOV 1859 |
| PYLES, Charles W. | HENLY, Lucy Ann | 08 OCT 1863 |
| PYLES, James H. [7a] | TRUCKSON, Martha | 04 OCT 1866 |
| PYLES, Samuel K. | BURT, Eliza | 07 NOV 1861 |
| PYNE, Henry [Rogers] [4] | FRAILEY, Elizabeth [Ann] | 03 AUG 1865 |
| PYON, Richard N. | SWANN, Susie E. | 16 MAR 1865 |
| PYPHER, Michael | JONES, Jane Ann | 02 NOV 1859 |
| PYWELL, William R. | SCHOFIELD, Maggie | 09 JUN 1869 |

## Q

| | | |
|---|---|---|
| QUADE, Edward | McCARTHY, Margaret | 10 DEC 1867 |
| QUAID, John D. | BROWN, Harriet E. | 20 AUG 1869 |
| QUAID, Luther M. | GIBBONS, Elizabeth E. | 28 DEC 1860 |
| QUANDER, Francis | THOMAS, Julia Ann (col'd) | 02 JUN 1870 |
| QUANDER, John P. | CASEY, Charity Ann (blk) | 26 JUN 1866 |
| QUANDER, John P. | FORD, Hannah B. (blk) | 23 FEB 1870 |
| QUANTRILL, Joseph G. [5] | THOMAS, Almira V. | 04 OCT 1869 |
| QUANTRILL, Thomas C. [5] | EDWARDS, Mary E. | 27 NOV 1869 |
| QUARLES, James | ADDISON, Theresa Ann (blk) | 13 AUG 1868 |
| QUARRELS, Benjamin | HOLMES, Mary (blk) | 24 JUN 1869 |
| QUAY, Thomas B. | HORNER, Matilda | 22 NOV 1862 |

## District of Columbia Marriage Licenses, 1858-1870

| | | |
|---|---|---|
| QUAYLE, Henry | COOK, Susan Catherine | 11 JAN 1868 |
| QUEEN, Charles Edward | HARRIS, Mary Ellen (blk) | 14 APR 1869 |
| QUEEN, Charles | CREASER, Louisa (blk) | 21 NOV 1866 |
| QUEEN, Columbus J. | NOYES, Kate E. | 22 NOV 1864 |
| QUEEN, David | WILLIAMS, Caroline (blk) | 28 MAY 1870 |
| QUEEN, Edward F. | GOODRICH, Nellie C. | 09 JAN 1861 |
| QUEEN, Frank | HEALEY, Mary Jane | 15 MAY 1865 |
| QUEEN, Samuel | RICAR, Annie | 07 JUN 1864 |
| QUEEN, Samuel | BROWN, Mary (blk) | 03 OCT 1868 |
| QUEEN, Thomas | SAVOY, Elizabeth | 26 DEC 1861 |
| QUEEN, William [12s] | JACKSON, Lydia [A.] | 28 MAY 1862 |
| QUEEN, William | SMITH, Annie M. | 28 OCT 1869 |
| QUEENAN, John | CLARKE, Bridget | 11 NOV 1858 |
| QUEENAN, Michael | MANLY, Catherine | 23 NOV 1863 |
| QUENZEL, Julius | BOETTNER, Adelheid | 19 JUL 1859 |
| QUETSCH, Henry | GRIESLER, Therese | 29 NOV 1869 |
| QUICK, John | STELLE, Susan R. | 24 DEC 1868 |
| QUICK, John H. | JONES, Jannetta | 06 FEB 1864 |
| QUIET, Solomon | HOOPER, Martha (blk) | 23 MAR 1866 |
| QUIGLEY, Hugh | GALLAGHER, Catherine | 25 MAY 1867 |
| QUIGLEY, James D. [10] | LOVE, Sarah E. | 20 JAN 1869 |
| QUIGLEY, John | DULEHENTY, Ellin | 05 JUN 1862 |
| QUIGLEY, Matthew | LANNINGHAM, Mary | 22 JAN 1866 |
| QUILL, Daniel | RICE, Rose | 25 JUL 1865 |
| QUILL, John | BIGLEY, Mary | 03 DEC 1861 |
| QUILL, Michael | CURTAIN, Johanna | 10 APR 1861 |
| QUILL, Michael | SULLIVAN, Catherine | 01 NOV 1864 |
| QUILLER, James | PRICE, Charlotte Ann (blk) | 11 NOV 1868 |
| QUILLIGAN, Patrick | MURVILLE, Bridget | 23 JUL 1862 |
| QUILTER, John | DONOVAN, Margaret | 26 JAN 1867 |
| QUIMBY, Thomas | ADAMS, Mary | 20 JUN 1865 |
| QUINLAN, Charles | O'HARA, Ann | 13 NOV 1861 |
| QUINLAN, Edward | READY, Mary | 03 APR 1866 |
| QUINLAN, Maurice M. | REDMOND, Emma F. | 03 JAN 1868 |
| QUINLAN, Michael | BRADLEY, Julia | 03 MAR 1859 |
| QUINLAN, Morris | BABBINGTON, Hannah | 25 SEP 1863 |
| QUINLON, Daniel | SHEEHY, Ellen | 29 APR 1864 |
| QUINN, Bernard | WILLIAMS, Ella | 14 OCT 1865 |
| QUINN, Daniel | HYNES, Mary | 19 AUG 1861 |
| QUINN, Edward | TRACY, Bridget | 11 JAN 1864 |
| QUINN, Edward | LOFTIS, Ellen | 01 JUL 1865 |
| QUINN, James | NEACEY, Margaret | 28 OCT 1865 |
| QUINN, John | KEOGH, Mary | 07 SEP 1864 |
| QUINN, John | BLACK, Catharine | 18 JUL 1868 |
| QUINN, Matthew | HINE, Eliza | 29 APR 1859 |
| QUINN, Peter | KEEFE, Johanna | 27 JAN 1859 |
| QUINN, Peter | CUNRAY, Bridget | 04 AUG 1865 |
| QUINN, Thomas H. [9n] | CLARKE, Virginia M. | 18 APR 1859 |
| QUINTER, Joseph R., Jr. | SIOUSSA, Clara E. | 19 APR 1869 |
| QUINTER, Thomas L. | HOLMEAD, Ada Augusta | 09 APR 1860 |
| QUIRK, James G. | STANSBURY, Jane, Mrs. | 30 JUN 1863 |
| QUIRK, Patrick | CREAGAN, Alica | 25 JUN 1860 |
| QUIRK, Thomas | RAGAN, Catharine | 06 DEC 1862 |
| QUONDER, George | CARTER, Fanny (blk) | 05 NOV 1868 |
| QUONDER, James A. | LAIR, Alcinda (blk) | 16 JAN 1868 |

District of Columbia Marriage Licenses, 1858-1870

# R

| | | |
|---|---|---|
| RAAPE, Charles [5] | HESBERGER, Eliza | 04 NOV 1869 |
| RABA, Sebastian | CRESSMAN, Elizabeth | 21 APR 1869 |
| RABBIT, Osceola [11] | LUCKET, Elizth. Ann | 02 OCT 1862 |
| RABBITT, George W. | HUNTER, Alice Jane | 05 SEP 1862 |
| RABBITT, Isaac | BALL, Maria | 20 DEC 1858 |
| RABBITT, James E. | BAKER, Emily | 18 APR 1859 |
| RABBITT, John | MOSELEY, Elizabeth | 05 DEC 1867 |
| RABBITT, William A. | DIXON, Harriet | 14 AUG 1861 |
| RACE, Wheaton H. | WOLLARD, Maria Caroline | 19 DEC 1865 |
| RACKMANN, Joseph | ORDWEEN, Eva | 09 DEC 1861 |
| RACKS, John | LAWS, Willie Ann | 30 AUG 1865 |
| RADCLIFFE, Samuel J. | RILEY, Florence C. | 28 JAN 1868 |
| RAEBURN, John S. | McKNIGHT, Amanda V. | 03 SEP 1867 |
| RAFF, Asher L. | JESSELSON, Barbara | 28 NOV 1862 |
| RAFF, Wyatt | GANTT, Maria (blk) | 23 DEC 1867 |
| RAGAN, Arsenus | THOMAS, Louisa | 09 MAY 1864 |
| RAGAN, James | RAGAN, Catherine | 07 MAR 1859 |
| RAGAN, James M. | MAACK, Margaret | 02 MAR 1859 |
| RAGAN, John | DOBBIN, Hannah | 18 JAN 1864 |
| RAGAN, John | CALLAN, Lizzie | 31 MAY 1869 |
| RAGAN, John H. | McGUIRE, Catharine | 22 JUN 1865 |
| RAGAN, Joseph H. | WORTHEN, Ellen C. | 23 OCT 1866 |
| RAGAN, Thompson | FOUNCE, Lizzie | 21 MAY 1859 |
| RAIDER, Charles | YENT, Margaretta | 01 JUN 1863 |
| RAILEY, John B. [6r] | BEEN, Margaret E. | 05 DEC 1860 |
| RAINE, Charles | JOHNSON, Sarah (blk) | 31 AUG 1864 |
| RAINEY, John | DONELAN, Bridget | 21 FEB 1860 |
| RAINEY, Saml. A. | DONN, Theodosia J. | 25 JAN 1859 |
| RAINEY, Samuel | LAUGHLIN, Catherine | 11 DEC 1867 |
| RAINS, John | YOUNG, Helen Ann (blk) | 25 AUG 1866 |
| RAINS, Rowzee | PAIGN, Rebecca | 14 MAR 1859 |
| RAISEN, William | O'TOOLE, Mary | 13 FEB 1860 |
| RALDENBACH, James H. | METHANEY, Catherine | 14 AUG 1866 |
| RALLS, C.P. | RICE, Lucy A. | 28 NOV 1865 |
| RAMBALL, Joseph C. | SULLIVAN, Margaret C. | 12 MAY 1863 |
| RAMBY, Samuel H. | ROGERSON, Sarah J. | 01 FEB 1869 |
| RAMSAY, Ezra J. | DUNCAN, Mary A. | 31 MAR 1870 |
| RAMSBURG, V.E. | ROSS, Annie C. | 09 NOV 1867 |
| RAMSBURG, Valerius A. | PAYNE, Amanda H. | 10 NOV 1862 |
| RAMSDELL, Seth B. | PHIPPS, Lucinda | 06 JUN 1863 |
| RAMSEY, William R. | STEVENS, Lucie C.M. | 24 APR 1866 |
| RAMSTELL, Peter A. | MORRIS, Clarissa | 05 APR 1865 |
| RANDALL, Daniel | MASON, Martha (blk) | 01 MAR 1869 |
| RANDALL Edward | HILL, Charlotte | 05 SEP 1865 |
| RANDALL, Henry | CAREY, Frances (blk) | 17 JAN 1865 |
| RANDALL, John | WEDGE, Margaret (blk) | 20 DEC 1866 |
| RANDALL, Joseph [1e] | ROE, Jennie E. | 20 JUN 1865 |
| RANDALL, Stephen W. | VANFLEET, Catherine | 12 APR 1859 |
| RANDALL, Walter | RIDGLEY, Ann R. | 12 SEP 1861 |
| RANDOLPH, Henry J. [9n] | WEISMAN, Ellen C. | 01 FEB 1859 |
| RANDOLPH, J. Innes | KING, Anna C. | 14 NOV 1859 |
| RANDOLPH, John | BAILEY, Mary Elizabeth (blk) | 19 AUG 1863 |
| RANDOLPH, John | TILGHMAN, Rebecca Ann (blk) | 08 OCT 1863 |
| RANDOLPH, Washington | MAIDEN, Matilda (blk) | 21 AUG 1865 |

## District of Columbia Marriage Licenses, 1858-1870

| | | |
|---|---|---|
| RANDOLPH, Willis | PHENIX, Laura | 29 SEP 1869 |
| RANFRO, George W. | WEBSTER, Mary E. | 20 SEP 1865 |
| RANIER, John | BAKEOVEN, Augustus | 03 SEP 1866 |
| RANKIN, Frederick W. [4] | BRUCE, Emmeline [C.] | 07 SEP 1869 |
| RANKIN, Robert | DIXON, Lavinia (blk) | 19 DEC 1865 |
| RANKIN, Samuel S. | ARMSTRONG, Sarah E. | 08 JUN 1864 |
| RANNEKER, Solomon | TREUMAN, Mary | 15 AUG 1863 |
| RANSDELL, George P. | HINES, Mary Elizabeth | 29 SEP 1866 |
| RANSON, William E. | BODEN, Mary C. | 19 APR 1862 |
| RATCLIFF, James A. | THOMAS, Mary C. (blk) | 28 NOV 1860 |
| RATCLIFFE, Daniel A. | BARNES, Marie A. | 06 APR 1870 |
| RATCLIFFE, James | NELAN, Annie | 15 NOV 1864 |
| RATLIFE, Joseph H. | FERGUSON, Mary A. | 04 DEC 1862 |
| RATTA, Joseph | RATTO, Rose | 29 JAN 1869 |
| RATZ, Louis | SCHMIDT, Sophia | 26 SEP 1863 |
| RAU, Gustavus L. | McDONOUGH, Elizabeth E. | 10 JUN 1863 |
| RAU, Herman A. | CRESS, Caroline | 13 APR 1866 |
| RAU, Lewis | BEITZELL, Sheba | 10 FEB 1863 |
| RAUB, George T. [11] | DESHIELL, Georgeanna L.M. | 24 OCT 1859 |
| RAUB, John P. [11] | CAYWOOD, Anna Maria | 03 OCT 1859 |
| RAUCH, Gottlieb H. | BREYER, Clinstina Susan | 15 JAN 1866 |
| RAUCH, Nicholas | BEVIG, Sophia | 11 MAY 1864 |
| RAUSCH, Henry | KEIM, Fredericka | 27 OCT 1862 |
| RAUSCHER, George | SCHEMMYER, Johanna | 13 MAY 1865 |
| RAWLET, Philip H. | WRIGHT, Rebecca | 20 DEC 1865 |
| RAWLINGS, Arthur | DYE, Patsey (blk) | 05 MAY 1865 |
| RAWLINGS, Daniel | MARDERS, Deliersa | 03 DEC 1860 |
| RAWLINGS, Francis H. | COOKSEY, Angeline R. | 22 OCT 1861 |
| RAWLINGS, J.W. | DIGGS, Millie A. | 25 MAR 1868 |
| RAWLINGS, James | BURGESS, Sarah | 07 JUL 1859 |
| RAWLINGS, Thomas | SMITH, Mary (blk) | 19 MAR 1867 |
| RAY, Basil | ALLEN, Anna | 23 MAR 1866 |
| RAY, Charles | PATTON, Milly (blk) | 25 OCT 1867 |
| RAY, Charles A. | TERRENCE, Mary C. | 30 NOV 1868 |
| RAY, Daniel | KEY, Mary Lizzie | 14 APR 1870 |
| RAY, James | CADY, Annie | 03 DEC 1869 |
| RAY, James E. | SHREVES, Gurtie E. | 14 DEC 1868 |
| RAY, John C. [7a] | McLEAN, Louisa A. | 02 JUL 1867 |
| RAY, Philip | WEITNER, Elizabeth | 07 MAY 1862 |
| RAY, Semour | GOOD, Amanda (blk) | 27 OCT 1866 |
| RAY, Theodore Curtis | PETHAN, Mary Frances (blk) | 02 MAR 1867 |
| RAY, William H. | BEAD, Anna | 10 JAN 1860 |
| RAYBOLD, Samuel Harrington [11] | HODGES, Anna Eliza [Mrs.] | 22 DEC 1866 |
| RAYHO, Joseph | HAYS, Harriet R. | 14 MAY 1866 |
| RAYMER, Henry | SCHUIER, Christine | 24 SEP 1862 |
| RAYMOND, Carrington H. [11] | GILLISS, Rebecca M. | 27 NOV 1866 |
| RAYMOND, Hyland [11] | FOSTER, Emily M. | 05 DEC 1865 |
| RAYMOND, Salathiel J. | LEWIS, Lucretia (blk) | 26 JUL 1866 |
| RAYNOR, Edward | BROUGHTON, Josephine | 28 DEC 1863 |
| RAYNOR, Smith | WHITEMORE, Sarah K. | 13 MAY 1867 |
| REA, Richard F. | SMITH, Sarah M. | 12 JUN 1865 |
| READ, Albert M. [5] | MORAN, Celia M. | 12 AUG 1867 |
| READ, James | POLLARD, Ellen | 03 MAR 1863 |
| READ, John | CLEMMENT, Otelia (blk) | 27 JUL 1865 |
| READ, N.M., Dr. | PENDLETON, Fannie R. | 09 MAY 1867 |
| READER, Thomas | CALBERT, Martha (blk) | 10 JUN 1867 |

District of Columbia Marriage Licenses, 1858-1870

| | | |
|---|---|---|
| READY, Edward | WELCH, Catharine | 13 FEB 1866 |
| READY, John | CARRIGAN, Ellen | 14 DEC 1863 |
| READY, Morris | MURPHY, Mary | 11 NOV 1865 |
| READY, Thomas | MURPHY, Honora | 12 JUN 1862 |
| REAM, Robert L., Jr. | GUY, Anna A. | 12 AUG 1868 |
| REARDEN, Francis A. | SHORTELL, Mary Ann | 01 FEB 1859 |
| REARDON, Cornelius | SULLIVAN, Ellen | 08 AUG 1864 |
| REARDON, Dennis | DONOHO, Ellen | 24 NOV 1858 |
| REARDON, J.F. | CARROLL, Jennie R. | 07 JUN 1867 |
| REARDON, James | FITZGERALD, Bridget | 08 NOV 1858 |
| REARDON, Michael | CALLAHAN, Johanna | 09 JUN 1860 |
| REARDON, Thomas | FLAHERTY, Honora | 22 DEC 1866 |
| REARICK, Peter A. | WILSON, Sarah V. | 21 FEB 1859 |
| REBEAU, Joseph | McWILLIAM, Mary | 23 DEC 1862 |
| RECTOR, Charles E. | PETERSEN, Louise | 26 MAY 1869 |
| RECTOR, Martin D. | GHEEN, Mary Etta | 15 NOV 1859 |
| RECTOR, Silas | BRISTOW, Rachel (blk) | 21 DEC 1865 |
| RECTOR, Thomas B. | WEBER, Mary L. | 04 OCT 1858 |
| RECTOR, William A. [1e] | MEANS, Sarah J. | 13 DEC 1866 |
| RECTOR, William E. [6le] | GRIFFIN, Frances E. | 05 FEB 1868 |
| RED, Edmund | PAGE, Mildred (blk) | 13 JAN 1866 |
| REDD, Henry | FOWLER, Agnes | 29 FEB 1868 |
| REDDEN, N. Stuart | REEVE, Bettie P. | 02 MAR 1869 |
| REDDEN, William | McQUEEN, Ann | 24 OCT 1859 |
| REDDER, Christian | DETRICK, Henrietta | 03 JUL 1862 |
| REDDICK, James W. | GREEN, Mary E. | 01 APR 1861 |
| REDDICK, James W. | YORK, Ellen | 22 MAR 1862 |
| REDDICK, Jesse | ROBINSON, Henrietta | 24 APR 1867 |
| REDDICK, Lewis | BUTLER, Mary Ann (blk) | 28 DEC 1868 |
| REDDICK, Stephen | SHEPHARD, Susan (blk) | 17 OCT 1863 |
| REDDISH, John Alfred | CHRISMAN, Annie | 29 DEC 1863 |
| REDFORD, Frederick P. | WREN, Eliza L. | 05 MAY 1860 |
| REDICK, Andrew | MATHEWS, Maria | 23 OCT 1868 |
| REDMAN, David | PETERS, Aggie (blk) | 18 OCT 1866 |
| REDMAN, Isaac J. | ANDERSON, Maria (blk) | 19 MAY 1870 |
| REDMILES, John | CARRICK, Annie | 21 FEB 1870 |
| REDMON, George W. | McNEE, Sarah Ellen | 13 AUG 1868 |
| REDMOND, John H. | ROLLINS, Margaret Ann | 12 AUG 1862 |
| REDMOND, Moses | NASH, Frances (blk) | 15 MAR 1866 |
| REDMOND, Nicholas | SCHAFFER, Caroline C. | 11 FEB 1863 |
| REDMOND, Philip E. | HAND, Mary Ann | 21 NOV 1861 |
| REED, Adam | GIBSON, Luellen (blk) | 16 NOV 1866 |
| REED, Daniel | AMERICA, Julia Ann (blk) | 09 JUL 1864 |
| REED, Daniel | WILLIAMS, Amanda (blk) | 05 JUL 1866 |
| REED, Elisha R. | BROWN, Isabella O. | 13 FEB 1866 |
| REED, George | HOLMES, Kesiah (blk) | 25 OCT 1866 |
| REED, George | WHITE, Julia (blk) | 31 DEC 1867 |
| REED, Harvey | PAYNE, Cecilia (blk) | 02 FEB 1865 |
| REED, Jacob | ARNOLD, Marthara | 31 JUL 1865 |
| REED, Jacob | GREEN, Harriet (blk) | 07 AUG 1866 |
| REED, James H. | CLOKEY, Emma J. | 02 JUN 1868 |
| REED, Jerome B. | COBBE, Amelia Jane | 20 DEC 1861 |
| REED, John | TINNY, Rebecca (blk) | 19 APR 1864 |
| REED, John | RIDER, Mary (blk) | 09 JUN 1864 |
| REED, John | GRAHAM, Joanna (blk) | 17 DEC 1866 |
| REED, John | WILLIAMS, Rose | 05 DEC 1867 |

District of Columbia Marriage Licenses, 1858-1870

| | | |
|---|---|---|
| REED, John James | BAXTER, Julia Ann | 22 DEC 1869 |
| REED, John T. | ROBEY, Mary V. | 03 AUG 1860 |
| REED, John W. [6r] | PORTS, Perphaney Jane | 17 JUL 1860 |
| REED, John W. | LEE, Josephine (blk) | 19 JUN 1860 |
| REED, Joseph | MANN, Ann Eliza | 14 AUG 1865 |
| REED, Joseph Henry | WALLACE, Ellen (blk) | 19 DEC 1865 |
| REED, Joseph W. | BOTELER, Rosalie T. | 25 SEP 1865 |
| REED, Joshua | BURKLEY, Catharine (blk) | 14 AUG 1865 |
| REED, Oliver H., Jr. | McCLELLAN, Isabella | 30 MAY 1860 |
| REED, Philip | BROWN, Jane (blk) | 03 JUN 1862 |
| REED, Richard | HAMILTON, Maria (blk) | 10 DEC 1858 |
| REED, Richard H.W. | HEPBURN, Ella F. | 17 DEC 1864 |
| REED, Robert | WINECOVER, Mary | 12 MAY 1863 |
| REED, Robert B. | FOWKE, Susie E. | 07 JUN 1870 |
| REED, William | WOOD, Anna | 04 APR 1860 |
| REED, Wm. B. | SCHNEIDER, Katie A. | 05 JUN 1866 |
| REED, William H. | ARNOLD, Lydia E. | 14 JUN 1860 |
| REEDER, Henderson | THOMAS, Sarah Jane (blk) | 11 JUL 1866 |
| REEDER, James | DORSEY, Emeline (blk) | 13 AUG 1868 |
| REEDER, Samuel H. | NOBLE, Mary Jane | 24 JAN 1865 |
| REEDLE, George J. | GUSSENBAYER, Barbara | 16 MAR 1864 |
| REEME, Joseph Henry | CAWOOD, Annie | 09 SEP 1864 |
| REESIDE, Francis | THOMAS, Bettie S. | 03 DEC 1861 |
| REESIDE, John | COPPAGE, Lucy | 09 FEB 1870 |
| REEVES, Charles Albert | BREAST, Susie Riley | 13 NOV 1868 |
| REEVES, Courtney [6r] | WRIGHT, Mary [Jane] | 31 MAY 1860 |
| REEVES, David C. | LEE, Carrie | 10 SEP 1863 |
| REEVES, George F. | WELLS, Emily W. | 02 APR 1868 |
| REEVES, George W. | WISEMAN, Mary A. | 13 MAY 1869 |
| REEVES, James, Jr. | EDMONDS, Harriet E. | 11 SEP 1861 |
| REEVES, John H. | BROOKES, Mary Virginia (blk) | 26 DEC 1868 |
| REEVES, Joseph C. | BREWER, Fannie R. | 30 NOV 1869 |
| REEVES, Samuel | CARROLL, Annie (blk) | 20 DEC 1866 |
| REGAN, Cornelius | DONOGHUE, Mary | 11 SEP 1863 |
| REGAN, John | McNALLY, Mary | 10 JUN 1865 |
| REGAN, Patrick | FLYNN, Catharine | 02 MAY 1863 |
| REGEN, Patrick | CAVANAUGH, Mary | 08 DEC 1866 |
| REHN, Lewis H. | STANSBURY, Sarah J.E. | 06 JAN 1859 |
| REICHHARDT, William | GURNBERLE, Sophia | 12 JAN 1860 |
| REID, James B. | HENDERSON, Kate | 26 APR 1869 |
| REID, Robert P.N. | WREN, Mary J. | 14 OCT 1868 |
| REIDEL, Henry | WOLF, Louisa | 25 MAY 1868 |
| REIDY, Daniel | CONNELL, Catherine | 23 JUN 1859 |
| REIDY, Henry | KELLY, Alice | 28 JUN 1859 |
| REIDY, Patrick | GUSSEY, Mary | 03 SEP 1863 |
| REIF, John | SHILLING, Mary | 23 OCT 1865 |
| REIGART, John M. | MIDDLETON, Frances A. | 01 MAY 1865 |
| REILLY, Dennis | KIRBY, Ellen | 15 APR 1865 |
| REILLY, Edward | MILLER, Susanna E. | 01 JUL 1862 |
| REILLY, John F. | McGRATH, Mary | 20 JAN 1868 |
| REILLY, John J. | GATES, Jane E. | 15 JUL 1862 |
| REILLY, Owen | McNAMARA, Mary | 29 JUN 1865 |
| REILLY, Philip | KELLY, Catharine | 28 NOV 1865 |
| REILY, Andrew J. | STOOPS, Cora J. | 20 JUL 1867 |
| REILY, James | BURCH, Margaret | 21 MAR 1864 |
| REILY, Lawrence | RYAN, Margaret | 28 DEC 1864 |

District of Columbia Marriage Licenses, 1858-1870

| | | |
|---|---|---|
| REILY, Patrick | GLEESEN, Ellen | 28 AUG 1861 |
| REINBURG, Lewis | WOLFE, Hannah | 06 MAR 1865 |
| REINHARDT, Caspar | ERNST, Catharine | 19 NOV 1858 |
| REINHART, John | MATHET, Catherine | 29 AUG 1863 |
| REINHOL, D.C. | BARRON, Willie F. | 12 OCT 1865 |
| REINICKER, William James | SHRYOCK, Ellen Hill | 16 MAY 1865 |
| REINMÜLLER, J. Edward | STARCK, Anna Kate | 17 MAR 1868 |
| REINTZEL, Charles H. | MOXLEY, Ann V. | 15 DEC 1858 |
| REINTZELL, James O. | CROUSE, Rosetta | 21 FEB 1868 |
| REISER, George C. | EKERT, Maria M. | 16 JAN 1860 |
| REISINGER, John Geo. | REISTER, Anna Dorothea | 05 NOV 1861 |
| REISS, Benjamin | LOWE, Adelaide K. | 28 AUG 1865 |
| REISS, John | DAIRLING, Margaret | 22 JAN 1863 |
| REITER, William E. | DAVIS, Harriet | 24 FEB 1865 |
| REITTGER, Joseph | HARK, Julia | 16 DEC 1868 |
| REMELSBECKER, Joseph | WESTON, Annie C. | 07 MAR 1865 |
| REMICK, Timothy [12s] | EVANS, Annie | 23 NOV 1858 |
| REMPP, Charles | KETTLER, Dora | 24 OCT 1867 |
| REMY, Andon | ZAGOWITZ, Clara | 14 MAY 1861 |
| RENEHAN, Francis | McCARTEN, Bridget | 30 NOV 1865 |
| RENNER, Josephus | FENTON, Anna H. | 13 JAN 1869 |
| RENOE, John H. | BRANTON, Mary | 17 JAN 1861 |
| RENTER, Philip | WOLF, Augusta | 14 DEC 1865 |
| RENTZ, Louis R. | BIERINGER, Caroline | 01 NOV 1864 |
| REORDAN, Cornelius | SHANNON, Jane | 31 MAY 1865 |
| REPP, Lewis P. [5] | MOTTER, Sophie M. | 18 MAR 1867 |
| RESHER, Elias | HAMMERSCHLACK, Sarah | 18 APR 1862 |
| RESSER, Celias | LAMPHEIMER, Caroline | 13 DEC 1867 |
| RESTERSON, George W. | SUMMERS, Margaret A. | 20 DEC 1864 |
| REVIS, Leonard | MURPHY, Alice O. | 03 SEP 1864 |
| REYNOLDS, Alexander | NUTT, Isabella (blk) | 16 DEC 1869 |
| REYNOLDS, Andrew B. | RHYON, Rebecca J. | 11 NOV 1869 |
| REYNOLDS, Chas. A. [Capt.] [10] | ROBERTS, Annie | 08 FEB 1862 |
| REYNOLDS, Charles E. | HART, Sarah | 23 FEB 1865 |
| REYNOLDS, George | WRAGG, Sarah E. | 11 SEP 1862 |
| REYNOLDS, Henry L. | HILL, Mary Wilson | 13 JUN 1859 |
| REYNOLDS, J. Mason [11] | BALL, Fannie M. | 25 MAY 1868 |
| REYNOLDS, James | DAVIS, Louise (blk) | 02 AUG 1869 |
| REYNOLDS, James | BUSEY, Anna (blk) | 15 DEC 1869 |
| REYNOLDS, John | GANT, Celia (blk) | 01 AUG 1861 |
| REYNOLDS, John T. | MARCEY, Emma | 23 DEC 1869 |
| REYNOLDS, Michael | CONNOR, Catherine | 18 AUG 1860 |
| REYNOLDS, Michael | SHIELDS, Ann | 03 NOV 1862 |
| REYNOLDS, Newton | COLLINS, Susan | 19 JUL 1862 |
| REYNOLDS, Patrick | LAND, Mary | 28 NOV 1865 |
| RHEES, Joseph | STEIN, Margaret | 17 APR 1865 |
| RHEIN, James | BAUER, Rosalie | 24 JUN 1862 |
| RHINEHART, Ferdinand | STHULMANN, Sabina | 18 APR 1867 |
| RHOADES, J.W.E. | OWENS, Sarah F. | 26 SEP 1859 |
| RHODE, Falden | HERBERT, Kunhinder | 16 JUL 1862 |
| RHODES, Edward S. | HUNTER, Mary | 05 SEP 1867 |
| RHODES, Henry | PERRY, Lizzie (blk) | 24 DEC 1867 |
| RHODES, James H. | COCKRELL, Elizabeth | 29 APR 1867 |
| RHODES, Jeremiah | JACKSON, Emma | 17 JUN 1867 |
| RHODES, Z.W. [6h] | GRIMES, Sarah E. | 30 MAY 1868 |
| RHYN, Michael Henry | LOVEJOY, Mary Frances | 15 SEP 1868 |

| | | |
|---|---|---|
| RIATHMILLER, Ignatius | SHUTT, Mary | 18 JAN 1868 |
| RICE, Edmund | SEABART, Elizabeth | 21 MAR 1868 |
| RICE, George H. | FERRY, Martha V. | 03 FEB 1870 |
| RICE, John | KROFT, Mary Magdaline | 03 JAN 1863 |
| RICE, Jonathan | DEVLIN, Annie | 24 FEB 1863 |
| RICE, Louis | FISHER, Caroline | 25 JAN 1865 |
| RICE, M.P. | GRAHAM, E.D. | 15 FEB 1865 |
| RICE, Robert | MARONEY, Catharine | 22 MAY 1862 |
| RICE, Thomas | O'BRIEN, Mary | 11 AUG 1859 |
| RICE, William C.W. | PADGETT, Martha W. | 06 MAR 1861 |
| RICH, Arby | BROOKS, Patsy (blk) | 10 MAR 1870 |
| RICH, George W. | TAYLOR, Florence | 02 JAN 1866 |
| RICH, Gilbert | MUNROE, Hester (blk) | 31 MAY 1867 |
| RICH, Hiram S. | MORTON, Ellen | 26 MAY 1864 |
| RICH, Smith P. | FORD, Drusilla V. | 21 OCT 1858 |
| RICH, Smith P. | FORD, Drusilla | 19 MAR 1862 |
| RICH, Washington | HARRISON, Letta (blk) | 12 MAY 1866 |
| RICH, William | SWEENY, Lucy | 20 DEC 1865 |
| RICH, William | CROASDALE, Belinda A. | 22 DEC 1868 |
| RICHARD, Alexander | SCOTT, Rachel | 26 NOV 1864 |
| RICHARDS, Adam | BURRIS, Ann | 31 JAN 1862 |
| RICHARDS, David | LEE, Eliza (blk) | 24 DEC 1862 |
| RICHARDS, Frank | BRYAN, Kate | 08 AUG 1863 |
| RICHARDS, George | LICH, Ruth | 19 AUG 1862 |
| RICHARDS, George F. | HORSEMAN, Catherine | 28 DEC 1858 |
| RICHARDS, George H. | RAY, Mary J. | 24 APR 1865 |
| RICHARDS, Henry | SIMS, Delala (blk) | 02 JUN 1864 |
| RICHARDS, James H. | ST. JOHN, Ellen D. | 05 JAN 1859 |
| RICHARDS, John G. | GREENWELL, Laura E. | 24 OCT 1865 |
| RICHARDS, John M. | LOCKE, Sarah | 24 JUN 1865 |
| RICHARDS, Joseph | WILLIAMS, Eliza (blk) | 16 JUN 1864 |
| RICHARDS, Rudolph | DREW, Mary Virginia | 20 NOV 1865 |
| RICHARDS, William | WAKELING, Mary M. | 28 AUG 1862 |
| RICHARDS, William | FISHER, Anna | 02 OCT 1869 |
| RICHARDS, William H. | JOHNSON, Josephine (blk) | 24 APR 1867 |
| RICHARDSON, Dudley | THOMAS, Mary Jane (blk) | 16 JUN 1970 |
| RICHARDSON, George | PETERSON, Eliza | 19 JAN 1866 |
| RICHARDSON, Henry W. | PAYNTER, Mary Frances | 31 JUL 1865 |
| RICHARDSON, Herbert | PROCTOR, Malinda (blk) | 07 DEC 1869 |
| RICHARDSON, Horace A. | MACKEY, Bridget | 29 OCT 1869 |
| RICHARDSON, Jacob Harris | BROWN, Mary Louisa (blk) | 02 APR 1866 |
| RICHARDSON, James | JOHNSON, Wilhelmina (blk) | 27 JUN 1864 |
| RICHARDSON, James Thesiger | KEIR, Caroline Frederike Bertha | 06 MAR 1869 |
| RICHARDSON, John | JENKINS, Anna (blk) | 22 JUN 1863 |
| RICHARDSON, John | BURR, Ann (blk) | 22 AUG 1867 |
| RICHARDSON, John | HALL, Adaline (blk) | 29 JUN 1869 |
| RICHARDSON, John H. | HODGES, Catherine C. | 21 FEB 1859 |
| RICHARDSON, John H. | MARSH, Victoria H. | 21 JUL 1868 |
| RICHARDSON, John [6m] | STAMP, Julia | 05 MAY 1863 |
| RICHARDSON, Loving S. | WEIMAN, Annie S. | 29 MAY 1866 |
| RICHARDSON, Richard L. | BROOKS, Louisa Jane (blk) | 03 MAR 1863 |
| RICHARDSON, William | LAUXMAN, Barbara | 03 OCT 1864 |
| RICHARDSON, William | MASON, Sarah (blk) | 06 JUL 1867 |
| RICHERSON, James H. | WRIGHT, Mary P. | 20 OCT 1858 |
| RICHEY, John W. | GARDNER, Arabella V. | 06 JAN 1864 |
| RICHMOND, George W. | SWEENY, Catherine M. | 07 FEB 1867 |

District of Columbia Marriage Licenses, 1858-1870

| | | |
|---|---|---|
| RICHTER, Ernst | BUERGER, Mary Magdalin | 16 NOV 1868 |
| RICHTER, Herman | BECKERT, Chatarina | 24 MAY 1859 |
| RICKARD, Daniel H. | CRUST, Catherine | 01 MAY 1860 |
| RICKETTS, David | ROUNTREE, Adelaide Virginia | 03 MAY 1865 |
| RICKETTS, Richard | CONNELL, Deborah M. | 26 AUG 1867 |
| RICKETTS, Robert | LITTLE, Eliza A. | 03 DEC 1867 |
| RICKETTS, Robert Henry | NALLY, Eliza Ellen | 17 OCT 1864 |
| RICKS, Samuel | JOHNSON, Fanny (blk) | 17 APR 1860 |
| RICKS, Samuel | CROCKETT, Annie (blk) | 19 JUN 1867 |
| RIDDLE, James P. | LOVELACE, Emma | 15 SEP 1869 |
| RIDEOUT, John | KING, Willie Ann (blk) | 16 FEB 1869 |
| RIDER, John | WEIGEL, Lizzie | 12 NOV 1863 |
| RIDER, John | WELSH, Catherine | 27 DEC 1866 |
| RIDER, Patrick | WARD, Mary | 02 OCT 1860 |
| RIDGATE, Thomas H. | BEARDSLEY, Marion | 11 JUN 1868 |
| RIDGE, Thomas | McDERMOTT, Margaret | 24 OCT 1862 |
| RIDGELEY, William | LEWIS, Lizzie E. (blk) | 21 AUG 1867 |
| RIDGELY, Augustus | SCOTT, Mary E. | 24 JUL 1862 |
| RIDGELY, Augustus | BALDERSTON, Lucy E. | 12 APR 1866 |
| RIDGELY, Isaiah W. | LEE, Sarah Catherine | 24 DEC 1860 |
| RIDGELY, Samuel | JOHNSON, Frances (blk) | 04 OCT 1864 |
| RIDGEWAY, Warren Edward | KNOTT, Anna Elizabeth | 15 JAN 1863 |
| RIDGLEY, William O. | HUNTER, Alice | 24 DEC 1866 |
| RIDGWAY, George W. | ANDERSON, Henrietta | 11 MAY 1869 |
| RIDGWAY, James H. | CUMBAGH, Kate, Mrs. | 16 JUL 1866 |
| RIDGWAY, Mordecai M. [4] | FUGITT, Laura Virginia | 05 OCT 1868 |
| RIDGWAY, Thomas T.W. | LOVE, Octavia J. | 11 NOV 1865 |
| RIDLEHUBER, James M. [12s] | HINDS, G.I. | 22 JAN 1861 |
| RIDY, William | POOR, Sophia Frances | 03 DEC 1863 |
| RIECKS, William H. | LEYPOLDT, Catharine | 26 NOV 1862 |
| RIEDSAMEN, Valentine | MAEDEL, Emilie | 23 MAY 1859 |
| RIEGEL, Peter | BANTER, Louisa | 28 JUL 1868 |
| RIEKER, Michael | MILLER, Margaret | 21 FEB 1866 |
| RIESSNER, John Christ. Wallgemuth | DIETRICH, Caroline Wilhelmine | 20 FEB 1868 |
| RIGGLES, Thomas | DILLON, Ann McElfish | 17 OCT 1868 |
| RIGGS, Henry | ZIMMERMAN, Elizabeth | 11 SEP 1858 |
| RIGGS, Lawrason | BRIGHT, Mary T. | 23 FEB 1859 |
| RIGGS, Myron C. [12s] | SHAW, Rebecca H. | 13 JUN 1859 |
| RIGGS, Reuben | CANBY, Martha H. | 28 JAN 1868 |
| RIGHTER, Charles | KING, Martha E. | 21 DEC 1859 |
| RIGHTER, George C. | WHITMORE, Sabella T. | 16 APR 1867 |
| RIGLEY, William | REYNOLDS, Hester (blk) | 19 NOV 1869 |
| RIGNY, Archie | COPELAND, Anna (blk) | 21 FEB 1870 |
| RIKEY, Henry | DUNDA, Mary Elizabeth | 02 JUL 1863 |
| RILEY, Benjamin F. | BRITT, Mary A. | 07 JUN 1860 |
| RILEY, Charles [4] | DARBY, Achsah Worthington | 14 DEC 1868 |
| RILEY, Gabriel | WALKER, Marietta (blk) | 30 JUL 1869 |
| RILEY, Harvy | CALVERT, Bettie | 13 MAY 1862 |
| RILEY, James E. | LEONARD, Annie M. | 11 MAY 1863 |
| RILEY, James R. | PYWELL, Alice M. | 28 NOV 1864 |
| RILEY, John | McGUIRE, Margaret | 02 OCT 1860 |
| RILEY, John | DeLAIGHY, Mary Jane | 24 SEP 1864 |
| RILEY, John | BASSETT, Mary Helen | 29 OCT 1864 |
| RILEY, John J. | COLLINS, Fannie | 28 OCT 1868 |
| RILEY, John P. | GORMAN, Rose | 27 FEB 1862 |
| RILEY, John [Capt.] [3] | GRAY, Alice H. | 05 JUN 1863 |

District of Columbia Marriage Licenses, 1858-1870

| | | |
|---|---|---|
| RILEY, Michael | RILEY, Julia | 25 JAN 1864 |
| RILEY, Peter | FARRELL, Ellen | 02 FEB 1867 |
| RILEY, Philander C. | SMITH, Virginia C. | 09 NOV 1868 |
| RILEY, Samuel S. | O'CONNOR, Bridget | 19 SEP 1865 |
| RILEY, Terrence W. | ELGIN, Emma A.S. | 01 NOV 1859 |
| RILEY, Thomas | McGEE, Mary | 07 JAN 1859 |
| RILEY, Thomas | RYAN, Bridget | 04 NOV 1861 |
| RILEY, Thomas | HAWKEY, Ann | 05 AUG 1863 |
| RILEY, Thomas | SPAULDING, Marcella | 12 DEC 1863 |
| RILEY, Thomas R. | STEPHENSON, Mary A. | 27 APR 1870 |
| RILEY, William | TURNER, Maria (blk) | 16 MAY 1866 |
| RILEY, William S. | KRAFT, Catherine | 08 JAN 1869 |
| RILEY, William T. | CURRAN, Jane | 08 MAY 1862 |
| RILLY, John | MURPHEY, Ellen | 07 NOV 1861 |
| RINE, Edmund | DELANEY, Rose | 29 NOV 1861 |
| RING, Edwin | FARRELL, Eleanor | 04 MAY 1860 |
| RINGRULER, John | SAUL, Mary Louisa | 24 MAR 1862 |
| RINING, Philip | LEMON, Emily | 18 FEB 1864 |
| RIORDAN, David | LYONS, Mary | 29 JUN 1861 |
| RIORDAN, David | CONNELL, Hanora | 25 MAY 1867 |
| RIORDAN, John | CRIPPEN, Harriet | 01 DEC 1869 |
| RIORDAN, Timothy | WHELAN, Eliza | 04 NOV 1867 |
| RIORDEN, Daniel | WALSH, Ellen | 12 MAY 1865 |
| RIOUFFE, Alexander | HANCOCK, Sallie P. | 29 JUL 1868 |
| RIPKING, Frederick | KOENIGSRENTHER, Anna | 15 APR 1864 |
| RIPLEY, John H. [11] | BROWN, Martha | 15 FEB 1865 |
| RIPPARD, William H. | QUYNN, Mary E. | 19 DEC 1864 |
| RISSO, Giambatista | RATTA, Cotiglia | 11 NOV 1864 |
| RIST, Frederick | BUSH, Sophia | 09 NOV 1864 |
| RITCHIE, Edgar | PARKER, Frances M. | 10 SEP 1861 |
| RITCHIE, John R. [2] | SKIDMORE, Mary | 29 JUN 1868 |
| RITER, Francis | FAULKNER, Angelina | 20 JUL 1861 |
| RITTENHOUSE, Miles | THOMAS, Loretta | 31 MAR 1865 |
| RITTER, Adam, Jr. | WEIST, Barbara | 20 JAN 1870 |
| RITTER, Frederic W. | COOPER, Pettie F. | 21 MAY 1866 |
| RITTER, John | SCHNEIDER, Josephina | 13 DEC 1864 |
| RITTER, John | DICKERSON, Sarah Ann | 25 APR 1865 |
| RITZ, John | MILLER, Augusta | 18 NOV 1864 |
| RITZHEIMER, Lawrence | KELLY, Susan | 31 JAN 1862 |
| RIVERS, Daniel | HUNT, Phillis Ann (blk) | 31 JUL 1863 |
| RIVERS, John L. | GESSFORD, Luvilla | 28 DEC 1868 |
| RIVES, Franklin | FREE, Jeannie M. | 20 JUL 1864 |
| RIVES, Wright | MAURY, Belle | 05 OCT 1864 |
| RIVINGTON, John S. | RAWLINGS, Emma A. | 01 AUG 1863 |
| ROACH, James | ENRIGHT, Johanna | 22 SEP 1859 |
| ROACH, James C. | SISSON, Jane R. | 12 NOV 1866 |
| ROACH, John | COSTELLO, Catharine | 08 MAY 1862 |
| ROACH, Michael | SULIVAN, Honora | 02 OCT 1868 |
| ROAKE, John E. | ROACH, Maggie | 02 AUG 1867 |
| ROANE, Nelson | SMITH, Alice (blk) | 07 SEP 1867 |
| ROANE, William Henry | MOORE, Catherine (blk) | 29 MAY 1868 |
| ROAT, George W. | SHUSTER, Mary J. | 01 APR 1865 |
| ROBB, Michael | JOHNSTON, Elizabeth A. | 09 JUL 1861 |
| ROBB, Richard | MILLER, Louisa | 04 MAR 1868 |
| ROBBINS, Christopher C. | JONES, Maria | 11 SEP 1863 |
| ROBBINS, James T. | PACKARD, Hannah | 28 SEP 1861 |

District of Columbia Marriage Licenses, 1858-1870

| | | |
|---|---|---|
| ROBBINS, Nathan H. [12s] | BURGER, Barbara E. | 09 JAN 1862 |
| ROBBINS, Thomas | HOBSON, Carrie | 30 DEC 1867 |
| ROBERSON, John L. | HODGE, Elizabeth Ann (blk) | 15 SEP 1859 |
| ROBERSON, Joseph W. [1c] | DAVIS, Julia A. | 21 OCT 1862 |
| ROBERSON, St. Vincent | WARD, Evelina (blk) | 26 DEC 1861 |
| ROBERT, Henry | SMITH, Eliza (blk) | 05 JAN 1870 |
| ROBERT, Joseph | CONNER, Mary | 09 APR 1866 |
| ROBERTS, Alexander [11] | BURMAN, Margaretta | 21 APR 1864 |
| ROBERTS, Charles M. | SWANN, Fannie A. | 05 JUN 1867 |
| ROBERTS, Erastus | BIRNEY, Rose | 05 MAY 1861 |
| ROBERTS, Erastus | BIRNEY, Rose | 05 MAY 1864 |
| ROBERTS, Henry | EDWARDS, Marion F. | 13 SEP 1859 |
| ROBERTS, Henry [11] | MAGRUDER, Victoria J. | 27 APR 1867 |
| ROBERTS, Isaac | RUSSELL, Frances (blk) | 07 MAY 1868 |
| ROBERTS, James | MUMFORD, Mary | 26 OCT 1867 |
| ROBERTS, James A. | DADE, Clara Ann | 19 JAN 1870 |
| ROBERTS, James H. | LAWRENSON, Sophia | 21 DEC 1864 |
| ROBERTS, Jesse | SHIRVING, Sarah E. | 06 MAR 1865 |
| ROBERTS, John | DeMANSFIELD, Maggie | 19 FEB 1863 |
| ROBERTS, John | WAGONER, Mary E. | 20 JUL 1865 |
| ROBERTS, John L.M. | HEATHEY, Louisa Jane | 16 JUL 1860 |
| ROBERTS, John Mc. [4] | FLEURY, Alice R. | 18 JUN 1860 |
| ROBERTS, John W. | JOHNSON, Julia A. | 04 DEC 1867 |
| ROBERTS, Joseph | McDERMOTT, Mary Ann | 15 NOV 1864 |
| ROBERTS, Joseph E. | THOMPSON, Margaret J. | 30 AUG 1862 |
| ROBERTS, Joseph M. | MARTINEZ, Margaret Mercer | 01 SEP 1869 |
| ROBERTS, Mathew | HANLEY, Mary Ann | 13 MAR 1866 |
| ROBERTS, Palmer W. [7b] | MINNICKER, Ernestine | 04 MAY 1869 |
| ROBERTS, William H. | EDWARDS, Edwardina | 09 NOV 1863 |
| ROBERTS, William H. | McLEAN, Sarah E. | 08 JUN 1867 |
| ROBERTS, William S. | OSGODBEY, Sarah L. | 07 JUL 1864 |
| ROBERTSON, Daniel | YOCUM, Margaret | 20 DEC 1866 |
| ROBERTSON, Eller | LATHAM, Malvina (blk) | 08 JUN 1864 |
| ROBERTSON, George W. | JOHN, Elizabeth | 10 JUN 1863 |
| ROBERTSON, John | DUVALL, Summerville | 12 FEB 1863 |
| ROBERTSON, John | McKERNAN, Margaret | 03 JUN 1864 |
| ROBERTSON, John | JOHNSON, Eliza | 10 MAY 1864 |
| ROBERTSON, Martin L. | GALL, Mary A. | 31 MAR 1866 |
| ROBERTSON, Robert | JOHNSON, Charity (blk) | 09 SEP 1863 |
| ROBERTSON, Robert W. | BOWEN, Elizabeth E. | 11 MAY 1861 |
| ROBERTSON, Samuel P. | WILKINS, Lizzie | 22 FEB 1859 |
| ROBERTSON, William M. | RUSSELL, Sue M. | 17 NOV 1866 |
| ROBERTSON, William M. [4] | MILLS, Charlotte J. | 01 OCT 1867 |
| ROBEY, A.V. | DeVAUGHN, Alice M. | 24 NOV 1866 |
| ROBEY, Columbus | HAUSCHMAN, Mary J. | 13 SEP 1862 |
| ROBEY, George R. [10] | ADAMS, Sarah A. | 17 FEB 1868 |
| ROBEY, Harrison | TRISCON, Mary E.P. | 08 AUG 1860 |
| ROBEY, Henry | PURSLEY, Catherine | 14 JAN 1860 |
| ROBEY, Horatio | JACOBS, Mary | 14 JUL 1859 |
| ROBEY, James M. [10] | WILLETT, Letty [of St. Mary's] | 13 APR 1863 |
| ROBEY, John E. | MANSFIELD, A.M. | 10 DEC 1868 |
| ROBEY, John Henry [12s] | ROBEY, Alexenia G.W. | 23 APR 1863 |
| ROBEY, John R. | BRADFORD, Elizabeth | 19 OCT 1863 |
| ROBEY, W.S. | BIRCH, Jeannette | 08 SEP 1869 |
| ROBIN, Chas. Lewis Joseph | DUCHEMOY, Rosamande J. | 18 OCT 1858 |
| ROBINETTE, M.B. | HERBERT, Lizzie J. | 05 AUG 1869 |

District of Columbia Marriage Licenses, 1858-1870

| | | |
|---|---|---|
| ROBINSON, Aleck | JOHNSON, Maria | 18 OCT 1866 |
| ROBINSON, Alfred | BAILEY, Sarah (blk) | 13 JAN 1869 |
| ROBINSON, Austin | FRANEY, Catherine (blk) | 24 APR 1867 |
| ROBINSON, Bushrod | MARLOW, Laura V. | 05 MAR 1862 |
| ROBINSON, Charles | MATTHEWS, Maria (blk) | 08 SEP 1863 |
| ROBINSON, Charles [10] | WILSON, Mary [Frances] | 18 NOV 1863 |
| ROBINSON, Charles | ROBINSON, Priscilla (blk) | 10 MAY 1867 |
| ROBINSON, Charles | RICE, Rebecca Jane | 06 NOV 1867 |
| ROBINSON, Charles | SMALLWOOD, Phine (blk) | 15 JUN 1870 |
| ROBINSON, Charles E. | LATCHFORD, Catherine | 05 AUG 1865 |
| ROBINSON, Charles M. | BENEDICT, Antonia H. | 21 JAN 1868 |
| ROBINSON, Charles [6r] | THOMPSON, Mary Jane | 28 JUN 1860 |
| ROBINSON, Daniel | SHORTER, Mary Ann (blk) | 16 JAN 1864 |
| ROBINSON, David S. | ROLLINS, Parthenia F. | 06 JUN 1859 |
| ROBINSON, Francis J., Jr. | RILS, Mary S. | 19 DEC 1864 |
| ROBINSON, Frank | BROWN, Sophia (blk) | 21 NOV 1867 |
| ROBINSON, Frederick | HEPBURN, Sarah L. (blk) | 03 JUN 1869 |
| ROBINSON, George | SEARS, Rosa | 11 NOV 1867 |
| ROBINSON, George | CONNOLLY, Letitia (blk) | 07 NOV 1868 |
| ROBINSON, Henry | THOMAS, Nancy (blk) | 09 APR 1864 |
| ROBINSON, Isaac | SAVOY, Fannie (blk) | 03 MAR 1864 |
| ROBINSON, James | COOPER, Mary Ann (blk) | 06 DEC 1866 |
| ROBINSON, James | POLLARD, Martha (blk) | 14 MAR 1867 |
| ROBINSON, James | BURK, Rosa (blk) | 08 DEC 1869 |
| ROBINSON, James H. | DUVAL, Barsine S. | 28 FEB 1861 |
| ROBINSON, Jesse | ROBBINS, Mary Ann | 24 DEC 1858 |
| ROBINSON, John | POWERS, Henny (blk) | 17 FEB 1862 |
| ROBINSON, John | JACKSON, Letitia (blk) | 27 JUL 1864 |
| ROBINSON, John D. | LAMBIE, Annie | 18 MAY 1865 |
| ROBINSON, John McAllen, Jr. | DUVALL, Sarah L.J. | 16 OCT 1860 |
| ROBINSON, John W. [2] | WESTERBERGER, Mary [Mrs.] | 21 AUG 1865 |
| ROBINSON, Joseph | CARTER, Fanny (blk) | 01 AUG 1864 |
| ROBINSON, Joseph [1c] | KNABE, Elizabeth | 01 MAY 1863 |
| ROBINSON, Lewis | GREEN, Harriet (blk) | 01 DEC 1866 |
| ROBINSON, Manson | DIGGS, Catherine (blk) | 03 MAR 1870 |
| ROBINSON, Mark B. | BLANCHARD, Ada D. | 27 APR 1870 |
| ROBINSON, Mitchell | BROWN, Lavinia (blk) | 27 SEP 1865 |
| ROBINSON, Moses W. | BAILEY, Ann Elizabeth | 28 OCT 1867 |
| ROBINSON, Nimrod | GADDIS, Eliza (blk) | 06 JUN 1867 |
| ROBINSON, Omanda | STEVENS, Morgan | 11 JUN 1858 |
| ROBINSON, Peter | JOHNSON, Harriet (blk) | 27 MAY 1864 |
| ROBINSON, Peter | JOHNSON, Emma (blk) | 26 DEC 1867 |
| ROBINSON, Phelan [7b] | HAMILTON, Harriet | 30 APR 1870 |
| ROBINSON, Philip | WALKER, Frances (blk) | 28 OCT 1864 |
| ROBINSON, Philip | FURLONG, Henrietta (blk) | 09 AUG 1866 |
| ROBINSON, Robert | BOSTON, Fanny (blk) | 26 MAR 1867 |
| ROBINSON, Robert B. | SUTER, Julia | 13 OCT 1869 |
| ROBINSON, Samuel W. | McGILL, Georgiana C. | 17 MAR 1864 |
| ROBINSON, Snowden W. [12s] | SMITH, Elvira E. | 06 FEB 1860 |
| ROBINSON, Spencer | BAILEY, Louisa | 13 JUN 1866 |
| ROBINSON, Strong | BRIGHTON, Susan | 31 MAY 1869 |
| ROBINSON, Thomas | BOYLEN, Catherine | 05 JAN 1861 |
| ROBINSON, Thomas | WHITE, Matilda (blk) | 28 MAY 1866 |
| ROBINSON, Thomas | DUDLEY, Priscilla (blk) | 30 NOV 1866 |
| ROBINSON, Thomas A. | HEPBURN, Elizabeth | 29 MAR 1864 |
| ROBINSON, Thomas G. [6r] | LEWIS, Sarah E. | 17 MAY 1860 |

District of Columbia Marriage Licenses, 1858-1870

| | | |
|---|---|---|
| ROBINSON, William | COOGAN, Margaret | 21 AUG 1860 |
| ROBINSON, William | NUGENT, Sarah Ann (blk) | 01 DEC 1862 |
| ROBINSON, William | BOLEN, Agnes (blk) | 09 MAY 1865 |
| ROBINSON, William | MITCHELL, Mary Ann (blk) | 12 DEC 1867 |
| ROBINSON, William | FREAM, Margaret (blk) | 22 JAN 1870 |
| ROBINSON, William S. | HAYNES, Arabella L. | 09 DEC 1869 |
| ROBISON, Charles | TENNY, Sarah (blk) | 11 FEB 1867 |
| ROBITOY, George | BEAHLEN, Emelie V. | 19 SEP 1864 |
| ROBSON, William | NEWTON, Jane (blk) | 24 JUL 1867 |
| ROBY, Berry | BURTON, Marion | 07 MAR 1864 |
| ROCH, Bernard | MEIFORT, Agnes | 28 MAR 1861 |
| ROCHE, Alexander | MEEM, Mary Clara | 09 NOV 1863 |
| ROCHE, James | DAVIDSON, Johanna E. | 03 AUG 1859 |
| ROCHE, James | HYDE, Mary | 04 APR 1863 |
| ROCHE, John | CALLAHAN, Ellen | 09 OCT 1863 |
| ROCHE, Maurice | McGEE, Annie | 03 JUL 1868 |
| ROCHE, Michael | STRIBELL, Catherine | 09 FEB 1860 |
| ROCHE, Robert F. | OSBORNE, Rose | 03 MAR 1868 |
| ROCHE, William | WREN, Catherine | 15 NOV 1858 |
| ROCHFORD, Christopher C. | ARNOLD, Annie E. | 26 FEB 1867 |
| ROCK, Joseph C. | WARING, Rose M. | 03 OCT 1866 |
| ROCK, Thomas | DUFFEY, Margaret | 20 OCT 1868 |
| ROCKAWAY, Henry | PFLUG, Louisa | 23 APR 1861 |
| ROCKE, William | WINNY, Sarah | 26 JUN 1865 |
| ROCKENHEISER, William | FRANCK, Magdelena | 28 OCT 1862 |
| ROCKER, William | DRICH, Williamina | 04 NOV 1865 |
| ROCKET, Robert W. | HEFFERN, Catherine | 17 MAR 1860 |
| ROCKETT, Edward [10] | LACEY, Jane Rebecca | 22 NOV 1859 |
| ROCKETT, Robert W. | HEFFERN, Catherine | 19 MAR 1860 |
| ROCKWELL, Charles F. [11] | HOBBIE, Ellen G. | 26 SEP 1868 |
| ROCKWELL, John E. [10] | HEROLD, Margaret C. | 07 JUL 1864 |
| ROCKWELL, Silas S. | HARKNESS, Alice J. | 15 FEB 1862 |
| RODEN, Charles | GRAYSON, Ann (blk) | 06 DEC 1866 |
| RODEN, Robert | REYNOLDS, Ellen Jane (blk) | 09 APR 1867 |
| RODERICK, Charles T. | HORN, Margaret T. | 10 OCT 1864 |
| RODEY, Martin L. | POEHLMANN, Catharine A. | 23 JUL 1864 |
| RODGERS, Arthur W. | MOWBRAY, Elizabeth S. | 05 APR 1859 |
| RODGERS, John E. | O'HARE, Annie | 16 SEP 1869 |
| RODIER, John R. | PETTY, Mary Eliza | 28 SEP 1863 |
| RODOLFF, James | STEWART, Mary C. | 24 DEC 1868 |
| ROE, David A. [6l] | SIMONDS, Maria | 14 SEP 1861 |
| ROE, Gabriel | THOMAS, Harriet (blk) | 27 SEP 1866 |
| ROE, John K. | DEGNAN, Ann | 19 MAY 1865 |
| ROEBUSH, John C. | LINCOLN, Isabella C. | 04 OCT 1860 |
| ROELKER, C.R. | PORTER, Parthenia M.T. | 31 AUG 1868 |
| ROEMER, John C. | HENRY, Catharine | 15 AUG 1865 |
| ROESEN, William | YOUNG, Maggie | 03 AUG 1868 |
| ROGERS, Abraham | ALLEN, Ellen (blk) | 17 NOV 1869 |
| ROGERS, Charles | JONES, Mary (blk) | 12 DEC 1866 |
| ROGERS, Fred. C. [1c] | SEWELL, Mary W. | 24 OCT 1862 |
| ROGERS, Geo. C.F. | DOZIER, Catherine (blk) | 30 JUN 1863 |
| ROGERS, George Reily | BROWN, Caroline | 14 APR 1865 |
| ROGERS, Henry [7a] | HUNTER, Phebe | 04 MAR 1867 |
| ROGERS, John Henry | MOORE, Lucy Jane | 03 DEC 1863 |
| ROGERS, John W. | ROBINSON, Mary Isabella | 05 FEB 1862 |
| ROGERS, Masena H. [7b] | DINKLE, Lucy V. | 14 JAN 1870 |

District of Columbia Marriage Licenses, 1858-1870

| | | |
|---|---|---|
| ROGERS, Robert | SPENCER, Catherine Ann | 14 APR 1859 |
| ROGERS, Robert | PETIT, George Anna | 23 AUG 1866 |
| ROGERS, William J. [5] | RODIER, Eloise | 07 DEC 1868 |
| ROGIER, Charles | GEGEL, Caroline | 03 NOV 1860 |
| ROHR, Frederick G. | RENST, Anna Mary | 10 JAN 1859 |
| ROHRBOUGH, William J. | WHITE, Eliza J. | 17 MAR 1870 |
| ROHRER, John E. | FREY, Theodisia | 28 NOV 1863 |
| ROHRER, Philip H. | McMANUS, Margaret | 03 OCT 1866 |
| ROHRER, William Henry | BOHRER, Fannie Maria | 05 OCT 1863 |
| ROLA, James | WALKER, Roberta (blk) | 05 JUN 1867 |
| ROLAND, Edward L. | RANDALL, Isabella | 20 MAY 1861 |
| ROLAND, George Thomas | THORNE, Martha Sarah | 01 SEP 1868 |
| ROLAND, John G. | MULLER, Fredericka | 09 JAN 1862 |
| ROLAND, William H. | CLUB, Rozelle | 03 MAR 1868 |
| ROLLER, Charles | HAWKINS, Annie P. | 26 NOV 1869 |
| ROLLINGS, James | ROLLINGS, Emily | 08 JAN 1868 |
| ROLLINGS, Philip | BROWN, Maria (blk) | 06 AUG 1869 |
| ROLLINS, Edward | COX, Elizabeth | 25 SEP 1861 |
| ROLLINS, James | HIPKINS, Margaret (blk) | 03 JUN 1864 |
| ROLLINS, James W. | CHAMBERLIN, Mary M. | 15 AUG 1861 |
| ROLLINS, John | GREEN, Elizabeth | 20 AUG 1862 |
| ROLLINS, John H. [6m] | PYLES, Alice F. | 19 JAN 1864 |
| ROLLINS, Robert B. | COX, Caroline | 05 NOV 1859 |
| ROLLINS, William | SLATFORD, Eliza | 30 MAR 1866 |
| ROLLINS, William H. | MARLL, Kate E. | 30 DEC 1867 |
| ROLLINS, Wormley A. | PORTER, Mary M. | 09 NOV 1858 |
| ROMAIN, Abraham L. | WILSON, Sarah N. | 31 AUG 1865 |
| ROMAN, Phil | STOKES, Catherine (blk) | 29 DEC 1869 |
| ROMAN, Robert S. | GOODRICK, Anna | 20 MAR 1866 |
| ROMANN, Fritz | WAGER, Joanna | 22 AUG 1865 |
| ROMBO, Frederick | BROWN, Bridget A. | 22 OCT 1863 |
| ROMELL, Benjamin | COLEMAN, Betty (blk) | 18 DEC 1867 |
| ROMER, Philip | RAUGH, Kuegundo | 12 APR 1863 |
| ROMERO, Cayetano | HAINS, Eva | 21 SEP 1869 |
| RONZ, Caspar | BEHRENS, Joanna | 11 NOV 1865 |
| ROON, Spencer | STARKE, Mary Ann | 19 AUG 1865 |
| ROONEY, Patrick | PEPPER, Mary | 12 OCT 1859 |
| ROOSA, John L. | SANDERSON, Margaret | 10 NOV 1864 |
| ROOT, Budgeman C. [11] | McINTYRE, Zelina | 21 NOV 1863 |
| ROOT, John M. | WEIGOND, Ablonia | 09 APR 1864 |
| ROOTS, Minor | GAINES, Jennie | 08 OCT 1866 |
| ROOTS, William [6s] | CHASE, Sophronia (blk) | 02 MAR 1865 |
| ROPER, Valentine | McCARTHY, Hannah | 20 APR 1870 |
| RORKE, Henry | BORRS, Anne | 25 SEP 1858 |
| RORKE, Hugh B. [12s] | FISHER, Nellie E. | 29 MAY 1862 |
| ROSANO, Mathias | MOTHERSHEAD, Isabela | 21 DEC 1859 |
| ROSCH, Francis | MEIBERT, Magdelena | 05 JUL 1862 |
| ROSE, Emanuel | BAXTER, Lethe Ann (blk) | 20 JUL 1869 |
| ROSE, Joseph B. | BORDEN, Sophia | 07 MAR 1864 |
| ROSE, Nathaniel | HARRIS, Susan (blk) | 08 JUL 1867 |
| ROSE, Reubin H. | BOOTH, Clara D. | 09 OCT 1862 |
| ROSE, William | SIMS, Mary (blk) | 25 MAR 1869 |
| ROSELLE, Dennis [12s] | CARTER, Jennie | 09 APR 1863 |
| ROSENBERG, Joseph | JOHNSON, Elizth. | 23 APR 1862 |
| ROSENBERG, Max | CHOATE, Lydia E. | 19 OCT 1863 |
| ROSENBERGER, Emanuel | HEILBRUN, Adelaide | 23 MAR 1865 |

| | | |
|---|---|---|
| ROSENBERGER, Martin | ZIESLLAR, Margaretta | 29 AUG 1862 |
| ROSENBUSCH, William | MARGRAF, Caroline | 14 SEP 1863 |
| ROSENFELDT, Louis | GRAF, Sophia | 14 JUN 1867 |
| ROSEVELT, G.W. | SEWELL, Rosa | 25 SEP 1866 |
| ROSIER, Warren | JENIFER, Sarah (blk) | 19 JUL 1867 |
| ROSS, Amos | WALKER, Susan (blk) | 21 DEC 1865 |
| ROSS, Andrew | RILEY, Mary | 17 SEP 1862 |
| ROSS, August | TWELE, Joana H.E. | 30 APR 1866 |
| ROSS, Augustus | HARRISON, Sarah (blk) | 15 SEP 1869 |
| ROSS, Benjamin S. | MAURY, Eliza | 28 OCT 1864 |
| ROSS, Berbridge | GAVITT, Elizabeth (blk) | 12 MAY 1868 |
| ROSS, Burton R. | STEHLE, Emma H. | 29 JUL 1865 |
| ROSS, Charles | LEE, Emily (blk) | 29 JUL 1869 |
| ROSS, Cornelius [11s] | DIXON, Josephine | 08 MAR 1870 |
| ROSS, Frank | BROWN, Anna (blk) | 07 JAN 1869 |
| ROSS, Frank R. | HUGHES, Annie (blk) | 14 APR 1870 |
| ROSS, George | ROSS, Ann (blk) | 12 OCT 1866 |
| ROSS, Henry | HENSON, Henrietta (blk) | 18 SEP 1866 |
| ROSS, Henry C. | EDDIE, Mary E. | 12 DEC 1866 |
| ROSS, Isaiah A. | GRAY, Emma Dodson (blk) | 10 NOV 1869 |
| ROSS, James | LARRISSY, Mary | 16 FEB 1862 |
| ROSS, James | ADAMS, Frances | 05 DEC 1862 |
| ROSS, James | BROWN, Hester Ann (blk) | 04 APR 1867 |
| ROSS, James T. | BROOKS, Jane (blk) | 07 OCT 1868 |
| ROSS, John | DYER, Nellie (blk) | 01 MAY 1865 |
| ROSS, John | BOWMAN, Lucy (blk) | 27 JUL 1865 |
| ROSS, John Edward | HARRIS, Albertha (blk) | 30 APR 1864 |
| ROSS, John M. | EKLEY, Margaret | 20 MAY 1863 |
| ROSS, John W. | RIDDLE, Catherine | 04 MAY 1867 |
| ROSS, John Wesley | MARSHALL, Martha Ellen | 12 MAY 1870 |
| ROSS, Josias | JONES, Sarah Ann (blk) | 23 DEC 1869 |
| ROSS, Julius | SHRIVER, Louisa | 07 SEP 1861 |
| ROSS, Norman N. | WELSH, Mary W. | 17 DEC 1869 |
| ROSS, Richard | BROOM, Juliet Ann (blk) | 26 DEC 1861 |
| ROSS, Richard | BLACKWELL, Virginia | 07 JAN 1864 |
| ROSS, Richard L. | MUNROE, Georgia E. | 17 JUL 1861 |
| ROSS, Theodore | SMITH, Sarah (blk) | 12 MAY 1859 |
| ROSS, Theodore | BUTLER, Margaret | 15 SEP 1869 |
| ROSS, Thomas | DODSON, Catherine | 08 JUN 1866 |
| ROSS, Wesley | RICHARDS, Mary | 31 MAY 1867 |
| ROSSER, Oliver M. | WILLIAMS, Isabel P. | 06 NOV 1866 |
| ROSSITER, James N. | CARBERY, Catherine | 02 MAR 1867 |
| ROSSITER, Lawrence | DOYLE, Julia | 22 JUL 1865 |
| ROST, Augustus | SCHULTZ, Karlina | 11 MAY 1868 |
| ROST, Frank | FIEHEGEN, Mary Louisa | 10 MAR 1860 |
| ROTH, Henry | DEIGMANN, Christiana | 04 JUN 1866 |
| ROTH, John Adam | HUBNER, Maggie | 21 MAY 1869 |
| ROTH, Philip | RHINEHART, Alwina | 23 APR 1870 |
| ROTH, Robert J. [11] | CRAWFORD, Anna S. | 31 OCT 1866 |
| ROTHCHILDS, Louis | BENSINGER, Tracy | 21 MAR 1866 |
| ROTHENY, Bowman | FARRELL, Celia | 04 MAR 1859 |
| ROTHERDALE, George | PERKINS, Marian Elizth. | 18 MAR 1868 |
| ROTHERY, Harry B. | REED, Mary C. | 10 SEP 1859 |
| ROTHERY, John [11] | BROWN, Annie | 29 APR 1865 |
| ROTHMUND, Philip | COOK, Lizzie | 18 APR 1860 |
| ROTHMUND, Philip | DUNNENBERG, Minna | 28 JUN 1869 |

District of Columbia Marriage Licenses, 1858-1870

| | | |
|---|---|---|
| ROTHSCHILD, Samuel | WALLACH, Sarah | 01 JUL 1867 |
| ROTHWELL, William | ROTHWELL, Sarah | 22 APR 1868 |
| ROUGHTON, Edwin | CROCKETT, Mary | 10 JAN 1866 |
| ROUNDS, Hudson | HILL, Sallie (blk) | 10 JAN 1866 |
| ROUNTREE, Richard R. | WELLS, Mary Ann | 28 JUN 1869 |
| ROUNTREE, William Joseph [6le] | WILLETT, Martha | 22 DEC 1866 |
| ROUSE, Joseph Thomas | POWER, Annie Camille | 15 DEC 1864 |
| ROUX, George S. | MITCHELL, Mary Elizabeth | 30 JUL 1860 |
| ROWALD, Adam | HARRINGTON, Johanna | 22 JAN 1863 |
| ROWAN, John | GODLY, Mary | 17 AUG 1864 |
| ROWE, James D. | WASHINGTON, Wilhelmina M. | 23 SEP 1863 |
| ROWELL, Charles G. | SEYMOUR, Charlotte | 09 OCT 1861 |
| ROWELL, Cromwell G. | HUBBELL, Anna | 09 OCT 1861 |
| ROWELL, Dennison P. | BRAINERD, Emma | 17 AUG 1868 |
| ROWELL, George B. | GARTRELL, Margaret J. | 18 MAR 1865 |
| ROWLAND, George | WILLING, Catharine | 05 APR 1865 |
| ROWLAND, Hugh | DONNELLY, Amelia J. | 24 OCT 1866 |
| ROWLAND, James Henry | LOVELESS, Alice J. | 15 FEB 1870 |
| ROWLAND, Thomas H. [6le] | CANNON, Frances S. | 18 NOV 1865 |
| ROWLES, Edward T. | SCRANNAGE, Elizabeth | 16 JUN 1863 |
| ROWLEY, Burnham Clinton [5] | WROE, Ida | 30 NOV 1867 |
| ROWZEE, Greenberry | HOWE, Lucinda | 03 JAN 1868 |
| ROWZEE, Samuel Lewis | RAINES, William Anna | 29 OCT 1869 |
| ROWZER, Marshal | CROSS, Elizabeth (blk) | 27 OCT 1864 |
| ROXBURY, Edward R. | SMART, Mattie W. | 03 NOV 1868 |
| ROY, Benjamin | WILKINS, Georgiana (blk) | 19 FEB 1869 |
| ROY, James | HILL, Mary (blk) | 22 DEC 1865 |
| ROY, Overton | GRIMES, Jane (blk) | 04 MAR 1867 |
| ROY, Samuel Michael [6s] | MOORE, Frances | 23 APR 1864 |
| ROY, William | HOLMES, Harriet (blk) | 10 NOV 1868 |
| ROYAL, Washington Front | BOUSER, Rebecca (blk) | 24 AUG 1864 |
| ROYCE, Frederick W. | DAVIS, Laura V. | 17 AUG 1864 |
| ROYCE, James B. | WELCH, Sarah C. | 28 APR 1866 |
| ROZELL, Endols | SEARLES, Eliza | 26 DEC 1861 |
| ROZIER, Hamilton | ROZIER, Martha (blk) | 01 NOV 1864 |
| RUCKER, Robert N. | TOLSON, Susie E. | 31 DEC 1868 |
| RUDD, Isaac | SCHWARTZ, Emma Jane | 05 JUL 1860 |
| RUDD, James N. | JEFFERSON, Laura C. | 03 NOV 1859 |
| RUDENSTEIN, Magnus F. | ENGEL, Cartriene Magretha | 26 NOV 1862 |
| RUE, Manning F. | WILLIAMS, Mary | 27 JUN 1866 |
| RUESS, Wm. A. | HAGLE, Irma C. | 22 SEP 1868 |
| RUETH, John | BUESHER, Mary | 20 JAN 1862 |
| RUFF, Henry W. | REMLEIN, Elizabeth | 17 JUL 1865 |
| RUFFIN, Cornelius | ADAMS, Annie (blk) | 19 JUL 1867 |
| RUFFIN, Henry | DAVIS, Eliza (blk) | 14 JUL 1869 |
| RUFFIN, Wm. | TWINER, Jane (blk) | 24 DEC 1867 |
| RUGER, O.J. | MORTIMER, Fannie C. | 30 APR 1859 |
| RUHLENDER, August | DELAY, Mary | 29 APR 1864 |
| RUMBLE, James | EVINS, Georgianna | 28 JUN 1865 |
| RUNNEL, Henry | WHITE, Mary (blk) | 14 JUN 1866 |
| RUPLÉ, J. George | MARTIN, Maria | 09 APR 1870 |
| RUPP, Albrecht | STOCKLEIN, Kate | 03 JUL 1866 |
| RUPP, Charles | BYRNES, Kate L. | 10 FEB 1866 |
| RUPPERT, Edward | RUPPRECHT, Maria | 24 OCT 1861 |
| RUPPERT, Ernest | OEHRING, Selma | 13 JUN 1870 |
| RUPPERT, Gustavus | HELLMUTH, Ellen | 08 APR 1863 |

| | | |
|---|---|---|
| RUPPERT, John | THOMA, Elizabeth | 10 OCT 1859 |
| RUPPERT, Matthew | RUPPEL, Elizabeth | 28 DEC 1864 |
| RUSH, John | SANDFORD, Ann | 18 OCT 1864 |
| RUSH, Noble | PULLING, Annie | 04 SEP 1866 |
| RUSK, Richard [11] | WALLACE, Margaret | 09 DEC 1864 |
| RUSS, Daniel | BECKMAN, Eliza (blk) | 05 SEP 1867 |
| RUSSEL, Michael | McNAMARRA, Hanorah | 08 JUL 1863 |
| RUSSELL, Charles | TALTY, Joanna | 23 DEC 1868 |
| RUSSELL, Charles P. | WHITMAN, Lucia | 21 APR 1870 |
| RUSSELL, Ebenezer | THOMAS, Harriet (blk) | 03 OCT 1866 |
| RUSSELL, Emanuel C. | DONNELLY, Katie | 01 OCT 1867 |
| RUSSELL, George | POWERS, Ellen | 26 NOV 1866 |
| RUSSELL, James F. | ALEXANDER, Mary Francilia | 22 JUN 1868 |
| RUSSELL, John | McPHERSON, Mary (blk) | 29 DEC 1868 |
| RUSSELL, John [6m] | BEAN, Carrie D. | 14 JUL 1862 |
| RUSSELL, John L. | DENISON, Mary L. | 02 JUL 1864 |
| RUSSELL, Josiah N. | COLLINS, Annie | 17 DEC 1868 |
| RUSSELL, Patrick | JOYCE, Lucy | 08 DEC 1868 |
| RUSSELL, Robt. | ANDERSON, Phillis (blk) | 29 FEB 1864 |
| RUSSELL, Thomas | EVANS, Frances (blk) | 16 SEP 1863 |
| RUSSELL, Thomas [11] | SERGEANT, Florence | 01 SEP 1866 |
| RUSSELL, Thornton | DIBRELL, Julia (blk) | 10 AUG 1865 |
| RUSSELL, William H. | McLAUGHLIN, Mary C. | 25 JUN 1862 |
| RUSSELL, William R. [4] | FLEURY, Pauline | 04 MAR 1867 |
| RUST, Daniel J. | PATTERSON, Margaret H. | 16 NOV 1861 |
| RUSTIN, George Washington | BECKET, Ann Maria (blk) | 05 SEP 1861 |
| RUSTON, Stephen | BUTLER, Anna Maria (blk) | 30 JUL 1860 |
| RUSTON, Stephen | CRAMPTON, Levisi (blk) | 22 DEC 1864 |
| RUTH, Dudley L. [10] | GASSAWAY, Anna L. | 26 JUL 1864 |
| RUTHERFORD, Robert G., Capt. [11] | KING, Lizzie M. | 07 APR 1866 |
| RUTLEDGE, Festus | MALONEY, Bridget | 10 JUL 1865 |
| RUTTER, Andrew L. | DULL, Emma S. | 24 OCT 1863 |
| RUTTER, John T. [7b] | MARTIN, Mary A. | 14 DEC 1869 |
| RYAN, Benjamin F. [6] | SMITH, Arabella | 22 OCT 1868 |
| RYAN, Cornelius | RAGAN, Ellen | 06 FEB 1863 |
| RYAN, Cornelius | MEHAN, Eliza | 06 OCT 1864 |
| RYAN, Cornelius | CARMODY, Ellen | 24 JUN 1869 |
| RYAN, Daniel | CLINE, Johana | 27 APR 1864 |
| RYAN, Francis | DURNAN, Mary | 04 APR 1864 |
| RYAN, George E. | BUTLER, Ellen | 07 SEP 1869 |
| RYAN, James | McNAMARA, Emma | 11 NOV 1862 |
| RYAN, James | KELLY, Eleanor | 17 FEB 1863 |
| RYAN, John | FITZGERALD, Mary Ann | 11 APR 1865 |
| RYAN, John | CARICO, Mary Ellen | 14 MAR 1867 |
| RYAN, John | COSTELLO, Berthena | 26 MAY 1868 |
| RYAN, John | BUCKLEY, Mary | 27 NOV 1868 |
| RYAN, Matthew | CALLAHAN, Mary | 30 DEC 1865 |
| RYAN, Michael | GLEASON, Ellen | 04 APR 1863 |
| RYAN, Michael W. | BARRETT, Julia | 01 AUG 1862 |
| RYAN, Patrick | DOLEN, Mary | 03 MAR 1863 |
| RYAN, Patrick A. | McNALLY, Rose | 11 APR 1863 |
| RYAN, Timothy | SCHILLS, Mary | 02 NOV 1864 |
| RYAN, William | BRESNEHAN, Mary | 24 SEP 1859 |
| RYAN, William F. | CLYNCH, Mary | 31 MAR 1864 |
| RYDER, John | NOLAN. Margaret | 30 DEC 1865 |
| RYE, John M. | BRAXTON, M.J. | 09 NOV 1869 |

District of Columbia Marriage Licenses, 1858-1870

| | | |
|---|---|---|
| RYN, John | KING, Mary | 22 JAN 1862 |
| RYNEX, Richard C. | BURNS, Amanda N. | 27 NOV 1865 |
| RYNEX, Samuel Francis | REDDICK, Adlia Frances | 13 OCT 1868 |
| RYON, John | SULLIVAN, Ann | 04 SEP 1858 |
| RYON, Robert H. | CASPARIS, Annie G. | 21 OCT 1869 |

## S

| | | |
|---|---|---|
| SABREY, E. Fugus | WALLS, Caroline Celestia | 11 NOV 1869 |
| SACHS, Robert | COHN, Rosanna | 10 DEC 1860 |
| SADDLER, John J. | MARSHAL, Virginia | 16 MAY 1867 |
| SADDLER, William H. | LUCKETT, Annie R. | 16 APR 1869 |
| SAFFELL, Richard J. | KANE, Catherine C. | 01 AUG 1868 |
| SAFFORD, Hiram S. | McPEAK, Lizzie | 31 AUG 1867 |
| SAGAR, Andrew I. | BENTLEY, Hannah J. | 07 FEB 1861 |
| SAGER, Frederick | MEISBART, Rose A. | 16 DEC 1863 |
| SAILE, Isaac D. [4] | CROSBY, Lucia R. | 27 SEP 1866 |
| ST. ALBE, Gustave, Capt. | BERAULT, Mary | 11 NOV 1864 |
| ST. CLAIR, Charles | MARTIN, Martha L. | 31 OCT 1867 |
| ST. JOHN, John | SMITH, Julia J. | 16 APR 1866 |
| ST. JOHN, William H.H. | COMPTON, Mary F. | 27 JUN 1861 |
| ST. MARIE, Henry B. | JONES, Lucinda | 03 APR 1868 |
| SALINAS, Chas. H. | ELFING, Annie E. | 13 MAR 1860 |
| SAMPLE, James A. | DEFREES, Julia M. | 14 DEC 1868 |
| SAMPSON, Alfred M. | BARR, Mary J. | 24 DEC 1864 |
| SAMPSON, Charles A. | COOMES, Alice Virginia | 03 OCT 1864 |
| SAMPSON, Columbus | FRANCIS, Rosa E. | 27 SEP 1867 |
| SAMPSON, Daniel | CARROLL, Mary | 07 JUL 1862 |
| SAMPSON, John Wesley [10] | CONNOR, Ellen | 06 JUL 1867 |
| SAMPSON, Liberty Bartlett | MOORE, Victoria M. | 26 JUN 1863 |
| SAMPSON, Thomas [6s] | WILBURN, Laura Ann | 23 MAR 1865 |
| SAMSON, James W. | LYNCH, Sarah | 21 DEC 1865 |
| SAMSON, Thomas S. | BROWN, Marian D. | 17 MAY 1870 |
| SAMUEL, John | SAMUEL, Letty (blk) | 18 DEC 1867 |
| SAMUEL, Richard | GANTT, Sarah (blk) | 07 JAN 1864 |
| SAMUELS, Richard | KING, Elizabeth (blk) | 08 DEC 1864 |
| SAMUELS, Theodore J. | SCHMIDT, Maria | 09 FEB 1863 |
| SANBORN, Francis W. | DULANEY, Catherine R. | 16 APR 1868 |
| SAND, William Otto | CORRELLE, Caroline | 18 JUL 1863 |
| SANDELL, Edward C. | DIVEN, M. Josephine | 28 OCT 1864 |
| SANDERS, Alfred | JACKSON, Ann (blk) | 12 APR 1866 |
| SANDERS, Charles | WHOODY, Ann (blk) | 27 NOV 1863 |
| SANDERS, Charles | VEIL, Maria (col'd) | 15 OCT 1867 |
| SANDERS, Cord | PETERSEN, Sophia | 31 OCT 1863 |
| SANDERS, George | JACKSON, Fanny (blk) | 28 DEC 1865 |
| SANDERS, Henry | JENKINS, Susan | 16 DEC 1858 |
| SANDERS, Henry | MILLER, Mary | 26 APR 1866 |
| SANDERS, Henson | DEAN, Louisa (blk) | 31 JUL 1867 |
| SANDERS, Richard | LEWIS, Amelia (blk) | 14 MAR 1867 |
| SANDERS, Thomas | KEYS, Alsinda | 30 JUN 1859 |
| SANDERSON, Charles T. | REIDY, Annie | 27 JUL 1864 |
| SANDERSON, Eugene | BURKS, Margaret | 30 SEP 1865 |
| SANDERSON, Harry H. | HALL, Hester | 20 JUL 1865 |
| SANDERSON, James | BATCHING, Mary | 24 AUG 1865 |
| SANDERSON, Joseph | DAVIS, Mary E. | 20 JUN 1865 |
| SANDERSON, Samuel | AUSTIN, Serena | 21 JUN 1860 |

District of Columbia Marriage Licenses, 1858-1870

| | | |
|---|---|---|
| SANDERSON, William | SANDERSON, Sarah N. | 10 JAN 1861 |
| SANDERSON, Wm. R. | FIELDS, Tellie | 28 NOV 1864 |
| SANDFORD, Benjamin | RUSSELL, Martha (blk) | 09 APR 1866 |
| SANDNER, Simon L. | KISSNER, Eliza | 21 MAY 1859 |
| SANDS, Bernard | CRANGLE, Catherine | 02 JAN 1863 |
| SANDS, Bernard | QUINN, Mary | 31 MAY 1864 |
| SANDS, Patrick | DUGGEIN, Mary | 08 AUG 1865 |
| SANDS, Thaddeus E. | BRONAUGH, Sarah Pauline | 31 MAY 1859 |
| SANFORD, Charles F. | MANAKEE, Sallie E. | 29 JAN 1868 |
| SANFORD, Daniel | GROVES, Annie | 07 AUG 1863 |
| SANFORD, Edward H. | McNABB, Mary | 23 MAR 1868 |
| SANGER, Raphael | RICHOLD, Caroline | 08 FEB 1865 |
| SANGUINETTI, Antone | CAPPELLA, Facone | 16 FEB 1863 |
| SANLON, Daniel B. | BRANDON, Ellen | 18 FEB 1860 |
| SANSBURY, Horatio | GALLAHER, Mary Alice | 10 AUG 1868 |
| SANSBURY, William | TOPHAM, Sarah | 13 FEB 1866 |
| SANTER, Michael J. | BURNS, Mary A. | 05 JUL 1865 |
| SAPLINGTON, Rowland | McLEAN, Emma (blk) | 21 JUL 1863 |
| SARDO, Albert E. | MYERS, Clara | 31 JAN 1863 |
| SARGENT, Charles | SANFORD, Rachel (blk) | 22 APR 1869 |
| SARSFIELD, Laurence | CONNOLLY, Margaret | 12 AUG 1859 |
| SARSFIELD, Lawrence | SWEENY, Ellen | 16 JUN 1866 |
| SARZENHOFEN, Clement | HERRMANN, Mary | 20 OCT 1865 |
| SATTERFIELD, Samuel Thomas [6m] | PILKERTON, Susana | 14 JAN 1863 |
| SAUFFLEY, John M. | FILLER, Sallie J. | 11 OCT 1869 |
| SAUFLEY, Benjamin F. | CRAUN, Martha Frances | 24 JAN 1870 |
| SAUL, John | McEWEN, Ann | 20 OCT 1864 |
| SAULSBURY, Francis O. | STONE, Elizabeth T. | 09 MAY 1866 |
| SAULSBURY, Hugh | LAURER, Hellen | 25 FEB 1862 |
| SAUNDERS, George | MOXLEY, Ann (blk) | 26 DEC 1864 |
| SAUNDERS, Henry | CONAWAY, Alice | 30 OCT 1867 |
| SAUNDERS, James | MORTON, Jane (blk) | 14 SEP 1864 |
| SAUNDERS, John F. | CLARK, Mary F. | 23 DEC 1867 |
| SAUNDERS, William | BROWN, Annie (blk) | 28 MAR 1863 |
| SAUTER, Caspar | BIETZ, Carolina | 30 NOV 1869 |
| SAUTER, Reinhold | RISSLER, Margaret | 23 OCT 1862 |
| SAUTER, William | MARKINS, Elizabeth M. | 29 APR 1861 |
| SAUTER, William | ELBERT, Annie M. | 08 SEP 1865 |
| SAVAGE, Richard [7b] | HALL, Ann, Mrs. | 10 SEP 1869 |
| SAVOY, Alexander | JONES, Sidney Elizth. (blk) | 03 JUL 1868 |
| SAVOY, Charles | CARTER, Eliza (blk) | 20 DEC 1866 |
| SAWYER, Babe Alexander | FORD, Lucinda Ann (blk) | 10 JUL 1867 |
| SAWYER, Jefferson [8] | COWIE, Jennie A. | 15 DEC 1869 |
| SAWYER, William | SMITH, Emily (blk) | 26 DEC 1866 |
| SAXTON, William A. | ABERCROMBIE, Sallie S. | 27 APR 1859 |
| SAXTY, Frederick | SIMONDS, Martha E. | 01 OCT 1859 |
| SAYLES, Frank | TOA, Helena | 18 MAR 1867 |
| SCALA, Francesco | IMAGNONE, Costanza | 11 OCT 1869 |
| SCALA, Francis M. | ARTH, Olivia | 13 OCT 1862 |
| SCANLAN, John | SHEHAN, Bridget | 02 DEC 1864 |
| SCANLAN, Michael | DUNN, Mary | 09 NOV 1866 |
| SCANLON, Michael | MURPHEY, Catherine | 15 JUL 1867 |
| SCANLON, Michael | HAGAN, Mary Ann | 16 JAN 1870 |
| SCHAD, George C. | SCHEPP, Frederica | 02 JUN 1870 |
| SCHADE, John M. | BARTELMAN, Atelhaid | 02 JUL 1869 |
| SCHAEFER, Frederick | FRÖSEL, Carolina | 07 NOV 1863 |

District of Columbia Marriage Licenses, 1858-1870

| | | |
|---|---|---|
| SCHAEFER, Henry | KROESCHEL, Bertha | 15 AUG 1864 |
| SCHAEFER, John | LEIBOLD, Rosine Barbara | 16 OCT 1865 |
| SCHAEFER, Peter | GOVININATER, Philiphina | 27 OCT 1864 |
| SCHAEFFER, Chas. W. | SUIT, Susanna B. | 10 NOV 1859 |
| SCHAEFFER, Samuel S. | McGLENNON, Catharine A. | 06 APR 1863 |
| SCHAFER, Frank H. | BURNS, Mary | 24 DEC 1866 |
| SCHAFER, Frederick | LEWIS, Josephine | 26 APR 1860 |
| SCHAFER, Frederick | HAGAMANN, Alwine | 03 MAR 1863 |
| SCHAFER, George M. | ARNOLD, Kate | 28 SEP 1863 |
| SCHAFER, John Casper | STEIRNACHER, Mary E. | 05 AUG 1865 |
| SCHAFER, Joseph | FRESCH, Susanna | 23 DEC 1859 |
| SCHAFER, Werner | RUBENCAMP, Anna Albertine | 28 OCT 1861 |
| SCHÄFER, George Wm. | McGRAW, Mary Ann | 01 DEC 1862 |
| SCHAFFHOLT, Joseph Anthy. | PALMER, Mary B. | 28 MAY 1861 |
| SCHAFFNER, John | MYERS, Agnes | 30 DEC 1865 |
| SCHAFHIRT, Ernst F. | BURNS, Mary C. | 23 FEB 1865 |
| SCHALCK, William F. | REMER, Louisa | 05 AUG 1863 |
| SCHALK, Frederick | BURNY, Mary | 23 DEC 1862 |
| SCHALL, Lorence | KILDER, Mary | 16 NOV 1863 |
| SCHARFFE, Gustav | BRINCKMAN, Eliza | 22 APR 1865 |
| SCHEEL, John E. | FRASER, Elizabeth S. | 23 JUN 1869 |
| SCHELHAAS, Reinhard | ERB, Catharina | 10 MAR 1859 |
| SCHELL, Charles W. | IRVIN, Mary F. | 29 DEC 1859 |
| SCHENCK, John H. [4] | DANENHOWER, Rae E. | 11 NOV 1864 |
| SCHENIG, Jon B. | GLASCO, Rachel | 12 APR 1865 |
| SCHERER, Leonhard | WAGONER, Kate | 17 JAN 1863 |
| SCHERGER, William | EWALD, Elizabeth | 01 OCT 1858 |
| SCHERIKARDI, Randolph Baldwin | UTTERBACK, Annie | 26 DEC 1868 |
| SCHERMERHORN, George | DOHERTY, Kate | 08 MAY 1866 |
| SCHERZER, John M. | DECK, Mary V. | 06 SEP 1860 |
| SCHESSLER, Martin | SCHULTZE, Juliana | 02 NOV 1858 |
| SCHIEBLER, Louis F. | ARMSTRONG, Susan | 05 DEC 1862 |
| SCHIEKEL, Heinrich | GROËN, Josepha | 28 SEP 1864 |
| SCHIEMECK, Charles F. | HARTUNG, Annie | 03 MAR 1864 |
| SCHILLING, August | RUHLAND, Maria | 03 NOV 1862 |
| SCHINDLER, August | ROBERT, Ellen | 25 JUN 1864 |
| SCHINNIGER, Gustav | OHNASH, Annie | 31 MAY 1862 |
| SCHLECHT, John | NAUMANN, Elizabeth | 01 JUL 1865 |
| SCHLEMIER, David | HESS, Ester | 02 DEC 1861 |
| SCHLEY, Eugene L. | HARDIE, Marie G. | 15 AUG 1861 |
| SCHLEY, Frederick [11] | WASHINGTON, Florence | 03 FEB 1859 |
| SCHLIEF, George | SMITH, Margaret | 08 AUG 1861 |
| SCHLOSSER, Frederick | WELSH, Cordelia | 12 JAN 1870 |
| SCHLOSSER, George | EICHELBERGER, Laura | 03 MAR 1863 |
| SCHLOSSER, George | JOHNSON, Delia | 15 OCT 1866 |
| SCHLOSSER, John | BARSACH, Elenora | 12 JUL 1866 |
| SCHLOSSER, Jost | BECKWITH, Josephine | 24 JUL 1869 |
| SCHLOSSER, Martin | BRIGHT, Catharine E. | 21 MAY 1860 |
| SCHLOSSER, William T. | PFLUEGAR, Margaret B. | 04 NOV 1867 |
| SCHLOTTERBECK, John | SCHULTZ, Mary | 30 JUN 1865 |
| SCHLÜMBACH, Frederick von | FUERLE, Celestine | 19 OCT 1861 |
| SCHLÜTER, Christopher | REESE, Louisa | 21 MAR 1867 |
| SCHLUTER, Louis | THOMPSON, Augusta | 17 AUG 1865 |
| SCHMALZEL, Leo. | UMHAN, Christina | 20 OCT 1863 |
| SCHMID, Ernst | SCHLAGEL, Franzisca | 29 DEC 1866 |
| SCHMID, Titus | BRIMO, Fredericke | 10 JUN 1867 |

## District of Columbia Marriage Licenses, 1858-1870

| | | |
|---|---|---|
| SCHMIDT, Alexander | STRASBURGER, Babet | 10 SEP 1860 |
| SCHMIDT, C.F. | HARDIG, Mary | 08 MAY 1869 |
| SCHMIDT, Charles | THOMAS, Theresa | 27 MAR 1869 |
| SCHMIDT, David | DIVINE, Mary | 16 FEB 1867 |
| SCHMIDT, Ernst Ludwig Albert | NEUMANN, Anna Ottilie | 26 AUG 1869 |
| SCHMIDT, Frederick | EICHMULLER, Anna K. | 11 FEB 1860 |
| SCHMIDT, George Henry | CASTANS, Sophia Christina C. | 27 JAN 1863 |
| SCHMIDT, Jacob | ENGLISH, Carrie F. | 02 NOV 1859 |
| SCHMIDT, John | RAAB, Louisa | 11 FEB 1864 |
| SCHMIDT, John | SHERFF, Mary | 07 APR 1865 |
| SCHMIDT, Joseph | BRILLER, Barbet | 01 NOV 1862 |
| SCHMIDT, Julius H. von | BOOTES, Elizabeth C. | 13 FEB 1860 |
| SCHMIDT, Lewis | WALTER, Mary | 25 FEB 1860 |
| SCHMITT, P.F. | FITZGERALD, M.S. | 09 MAY 1870 |
| SCHMITT, Rasnik | KLEBER, Josephine | 14 OCT 1864 |
| SCHNEIDER, David | DULAHAN, Lisie | 17 SEP 1864 |
| SCHNEIDER, George | KLINGHAMER, Louisa | 15 SEP 1864 |
| SCHNEIDER, John C. | GALLAGHER, Mary M. | 09 APR 1868 |
| SCHNEIDER, Karl | KLINGELER, Joanna | 26 OCT 1868 |
| SCHNEIDER, Yackob | EICHNER, Creyenzia | 09 JUN 1862 |
| SCHNELL, George | MILLER, Amelia | 15 OCT 1859 |
| SCHNEYDTER, George | KRAUSE, Bertha | 12 JUL 1867 |
| SCHOCK, Christian | BERNHARD, Wilhelmina | 08 JUL 1864 |
| SCHOEFFEL, George | SMITH, Elizabeth | 14 DEC 1863 |
| SCHOELER, William | GREY, Susan | 04 DEC 1862 |
| SCHÖENBORN, August Gottlieb | KLÜH, Helen | 23 APR 1861 |
| SCHOENECKER, John Wm., M.D. | KOCH, Albertine | 02 JUL 1863 |
| SCHOENI, Alfred T. | NOWLAND, Mary Virginia | 09 JUN 1870 |
| SCHOENLEBER, Paul | GIBBONS, Mary Alice | 15 DEC 1866 |
| SCHOLFIELD, George | FOX, Mary | 26 FEB 1870 |
| SCHOLFIELD, Thomas | CADY, Carrie L. | 14 APR 1864 |
| SCHOMER, G.M. | PEIFFER, Margaret | 25 JAN 1864 |
| SCHÖN, John | KRONAS, Mary | 25 MAR 1870 |
| SCHÖNBORN, Henry F. | BECKERT, Anna | 12 OCT 1858 |
| SCHOOL, John | MOLOY, Julia | 20 SEP 1858 |
| SCHRAMM, Peter | RYAN, Anna | 04 FEB 1867 |
| SCHREIBER, Richard A. | SCHMIDT, Caroline C. | 11 FEB 1862 |
| SCHREINER, John George | GERBER, Henrietta | 23 FEB 1864 |
| SCHREVE, William | HURLEY, Catharine E. | 16 JUL 1863 |
| SCHRINER, George | SCHMIDT, Annie | 16 FEB 1864 |
| SCHRIVER, Philip [11] | IRVING, Susan Elizabeth | 16 JUL 1863 |
| SCHROEDEL, Frederick | VERNSTEIN, Barbara | 25 APR 1864 |
| SCHROEDEL, George A. | KIRCHNER, Sabine | 08 AUG 1862 |
| SCHROEDER, August | HENDERSON, Altie | 22 APR 1861 |
| SCHROEDER, Charles | NOONAN, Kate | 26 SEP 1862 |
| SCHROEDER, Gottfried | RANICKER, Margaret | 12 JUN 1865 |
| SCHROTT, Henry | PAFF, Maria | 02 JUN 1870 |
| SCHUCH, John | NEIB, Emily | 31 MAY 1864 |
| SCHULER, C.F. Edwd. | CROOK, Anna E. | 10 DEC 1861 |
| SCHULTE, Harmon H. | HART, Annie | 10 OCT 1861 |
| SCHULTZ, Bartholt | HOLTZMAN, Lizzie | 29 SEP 1865 |
| SCHULTZ, Daniel | WAGNER, Mina | 13 AUG 1861 |
| SCHULTZ, Frederick | HOHENSTEIN, Mary Ann | 28 SEP 1866 |
| SCHULTZ, John | CIGYWITZ, Margaret | 16 APR 1866 |
| SCHULTZ, Rudolph | MUENNICH, Eliza | 13 AUG 1862 |
| SCHULZ, Henry | BORNEMANN, Catharine Elisa | 18 JUL 1864 |

District of Columbia Marriage Licenses, 1858-1870

| | | |
|---|---|---|
| SCHUMAKE, John | MARSHALL, Susan | 15 FEB 1870 |
| SCHUNMANN, Francis | JUNG, Augusta | 10 DEC 1867 |
| SCHUREMAN, James H.A. | JONES, Georgeanna P.C. | 19 MAR 1861 |
| SCHWAB, George J. | PLAUGHER, Barbara Ellen | 03 JUL 1862 |
| SCHWABE, John | HOPKINS, Caroline | 13 SEP 1865 |
| SCHWAMBACK, John | EINER, Catherine | 27 MAY 1862 |
| SCHWARTZ, Adam | WILHELMSEN, Caroline | 30 JUN 1862 |
| SCHWARTZ, John | BECKMAN, Lena | 18 APR 1868 |
| SCHWARTZENBERG, Henry | HILLMANN, Louisa | 08 FEB 1866 |
| SCHWARZ, Charles | HEIL, Anna | 02 JUL 1861 |
| SCHWARZ, H.M. | HAINES, Mary A. | 09 FEB 1867 |
| SCHWARZ, John | BURGHARTH, Margurete | 17 MAR 1868 |
| SCHWENK, Martin | MARTIN, Jane Frances | 09 AUG 1865 |
| SCHWENK, William [6le] | SHEPHERD, Hettie Maria | 03 APR 1867 |
| SCHWICKARD, John | McGUCKEIN, Catherine | 09 APR 1860 |
| SCHWING, Lewis | MILLER, Mary Ann Hellen | 26 OCT 1863 |
| SCHWINGEL, George | CLARK, Lucy M. | 25 AUG 1864 |
| SCHWINK, William | HURLEY, Rosa (blk) | 19 OCT 1865 |
| SCIPPACH, John G.M. | FLACK, Caroline | 10 MAR 1862 |
| SCIPPER, Lewis | DOUGLASS, Mary | 26 MAY 1866 |
| SCOFIELD, Henry | PARKHURST, Henrietta | 27 FEB 1867 |
| SCOGGIN, Philip | SCOTT, Sarah (col'd) | 28 DEC 1863 |
| SCOTT, Albert | JACKS, Rachel (blk) | 05 MAR 1869 |
| SCOTT, Anderson | MILLS, Martha (blk) | 04 JUN 1867 |
| SCOTT, Benjamin | BARNES, Annie Jane (blk) | 21 NOV 1866 |
| SCOTT, Bennett C. | SUIT, Augusta | 12 OCT 1869 |
| SCOTT, Charles R. | SIMMS, Mary M. | 11 DEC 1869 |
| SCOTT, Chester | MERCER, Indiana (blk) | 29 FEB 1868 |
| SCOTT, Davis | MAHONEY, Mary (blk) | 04 DEC 1866 |
| SCOTT, Douglass, H.M.J.A. | deBODISCO, Harriet | 28 MAY 1860 |
| SCOTT, Edward | CLARK, Lucy (blk) | 05 FEB 1867 |
| SCOTT, Edwin W. | SIMONDS, Rosanna | 02 DEC 1862 |
| SCOTT, Garland | BANKS, Juliana (blk) | 14 JUL 1865 |
| SCOTT, George | BROWN, Lucy (blk) | 11 AUG 1864 |
| SCOTT, George | JOHNSON, Charlotte (blk) | 27 DEC 1866 |
| SCOTT, Henry | FITZGERALD, Rena (blk) | 27 FEB 1864 |
| SCOTT, Henry | BINGHAM, Leanda (blk) | 14 MAR 1867 |
| SCOTT, Henry E. | PAYNE, Mary Julia | 16 JUN 1864 |
| SCOTT, Henry L. | SELF, Georgiana | 10 DEC 1868 |
| SCOTT, J.C. | WYLIE, M.F. | 23 MAY 1868 |
| SCOTT, Jacob | KEY, Harriet (blk) | 07 NOV 1868 |
| SCOTT, Jacob | CHESLEY, Julia Ann (blk) | 29 OCT 1869 |
| SCOTT, James [10] | BUMBRAY, Lavinia (blk) | 29 JAN 1864 |
| SCOTT, James H. | HARLAND, Lucinda (blk) | 28 NOV 1866 |
| SCOTT, James H. | PRUETT, Letitia | 01 MAY 1867 |
| SCOTT, James P. | McNEILL, Margery J.G. | 14 DEC 1869 |
| SCOTT, James S. | McKILDOE, Virginia | 02 OCT 1858 |
| SCOTT, Jasper | MURRAY, Mary Jane | 17 NOV 1859 |
| SCOTT, John | FORREST, Amelia Jane (col'd) | 10 NOV 1863 |
| SCOTT, John | BRADLEY, Rosetta | 18 OCT 1864 |
| SCOTT, John | SCOTT, Patsy (blk) | 23 JUN 1866 |
| SCOTT, John | LEE, Elizabeth (blk) | 17 JUL 1867 |
| SCOTT, John | GRIFFITH, Sophia, Miss (blk) | 10 JUN 1869 |
| SCOTT, John B. | DULANEY, Sarah F. | 05 NOV 1859 |
| SCOTT, John B. | HALL, Mary Jane | 30 APR 1860 |
| SCOTT, John B. [6m] | WELLS, Lucy [Isabel] | 20 OCT 1863 |

| | | |
|---|---|---|
| SCOTT, John B. | BROUGHTON, Sarah E. | 12 AUG 1867 |
| SCOTT, John F. | COBB, Emily | 30 NOV 1864 |
| SCOTT, John R. | RUNNELLS, Virginia | 05 JAN 1860 |
| SCOTT, Joseph | JAMES, Catherine (blk) | 01 OCT 1863 |
| SCOTT, Joseph | SMITH, Mary K. | 30 SEP 1869 |
| SCOTT, Lee | BURROWS, Lucinda (blk) | 01 AUG 1866 |
| SCOTT, Lorenzo | BOWMAN, Clara C.B. (blk) | 10 OCT 1868 |
| SCOTT, Noah | BOWMAN, Nancy (blk) | 03 JUN 1865 |
| SCOTT, Oliver W. | MILES, Ellen (blk) | 28 JUN 1866 |
| SCOTT, Patrick | BERRY, Susan Ann (blk) | 20 MAR 1865 |
| SCOTT, R.H. | ROBERTS, E.A., Mrs. | 22 APR 1867 |
| SCOTT, Richard | BRYAN, Mary (blk) | 29 JAN 1866 |
| SCOTT, Robert | GRANT, Betsey (blk) | 03 SEP 1863 |
| SCOTT, Robert N., Capt., USA | CASEY, Elizabeth G. | 24 NOV 1862 |
| SCOTT, Robt. H. | MARSHALL, Sarah (blk) | 29 FEB 1864 |
| SCOTT, Samuel | NELSON, Elizabeth | 15 JUN 1866 |
| SCOTT, Thomas | BROWN, Ellen | 12 MAY 1865 |
| SCOTT, Thomas | VIRGINIA, Martha (blk) | 09 DEC 1865 |
| SCOTT, Thomas | GREEN, Elizabeth (blk) | 24 SEP 1869 |
| SCOTT, Thomas W. [6le] | LIGHTELL, Mary E. | 03 JUN 1867 |
| SCOTT, Walter C. [10] | WHEATLEY, Eliza J. | 05 FEB 1867 |
| SCOTT, West | PURCELL, Margaret | 21 SEP 1858 |
| SCOTT, William | BELL, Mary | 30 APR 1860 |
| SCOTT, William | ALLEN, Ida | 24 AUG 1863 |
| SCOTT, William | CAMPBELL, Ann Virginia (blk) | 28 SEP 1863 |
| SCOTT, William | POOL, Louisa (blk) | 24 NOV 1863 |
| SCOTT, William | LINDSAY, Margaret | 23 APR 1864 |
| SCOTT, William | ADDISON, Rebella (blk) | 30 DEC 1864 |
| SCOTT, William | MORTON, Caroline (blk) | 06 JAN 1865 |
| SCOTT, William | WILLIAMS, Milly (blk) | 12 MAY 1868 |
| SCOTT, William | SUCH, Charlotte (blk) | 26 MAY 1869 |
| SCOTT, William | WILSON, Cecilia (blk) | 10 JUN 1869 |
| SCOTT, Wm. H. [10] | EDELIN, Judith Amanda | 07 NOV 1867 |
| SCOTT, William Henry | JOHNSON, Rachel (blk) | 10 OCT 1866 |
| SCOTT, William S. | SPINDLE, Elizabeth | 13 NOV 1867 |
| SCOTT, William T. | SUTLERS, Frances (blk) | 24 FEB 1866 |
| SCOTT, William T. | HARRIS, Martha (blk) | 18 SEP 1867 |
| SCOTT, Wilson | EASTIS, Caroline (blk) | 23 DEC 1864 |
| SCOTT, Winfield | COWAN, Mary E. | 03 AUG 1864 |
| SCRANAGE, William | BRAXTON, Patcy (blk) | 27 SEP 1865 |
| SCRANAGE, William | BURK, Virginia (blk) | 12 SEP 1867 |
| SCREINER, Adam | SCHMIDT, Rosina | 13 MAY 1863 |
| SCRIBER, Columbus | GIBSON, Cornelia (blk) | 20 JAN 1870 |
| SCRIVENER, Albert B. | ROBINSON, Rebecca | 30 MAY 1866 |
| SCRIVENER, Asbury [10] | JOHNSON, Julia | 29 OCT 1863 |
| SCRIVENER, Benjamin | WILKINS, Martha | 23 DEC 1862 |
| SCRIVENER, Peyton | GATTRELL, Mary C. | 27 MAY 1863 |
| SCRIVENER, William | FORBES, Rachel (blk) | 07 MAR 1867 |
| SCRIVNER, John T. | TEARNEY, Maggie | 09 OCT 1862 |
| SCROGGINS, George | HESS, Susie | 05 JAN 1867 |
| SCULLEY, Peter | BROUGHTON, Mary | 28 JAN 1865 |
| SCULLY, John | CALLAHAN, Margaret | 01 MAY 1861 |
| SEAICH, Joseph, Jr. | CHAMPION, Emma | 30 MAY 1867 |
| SEAL, William D. | BALMAIN, Annie E. | 20 MAR 1865 |
| SEALS, Charles | MONTGOMERY, Celia (blk) | 05 SEP 1866 |
| SEALS, David | WILLIAMS, Letty (blk) | 24 JUN 1859 |

District of Columbia Marriage Licenses, 1858-1870

| | | |
|---|---|---|
| SEALS, William | PARKER, Mary (blk) | 28 OCT 1867 |
| SEAMAN, William H. | SMITH, Margaret | 02 FEB 1865 |
| SEAMANS, Wilton | JONES, Sarah A. (blk) | 22 DEC 1865 |
| SEARGENT, Sylvester | CROWN, Rachel F. | 18 APR 1864 |
| SEARS, Benjamin C. [6m] | HIGGS, Leathe Ann | 15 JAN 1863 |
| SEARS, Benjamin C. | GILL, Margaret A. | 14 JUN 1870 |
| SEARS, Caleb L. | BRAMLY, Isabell | 30 JUL 1869 |
| SEARS, Clinton M. | FORTENEY, Mary E. | 05 JAN 1867 |
| SEARS, John | PIERCE, Margaret | 30 NOV 1862 |
| SEARS, John T. | LYNCH, Julia | 04 APR 1863 |
| SEARS, Richard T. | DONNAWAY, Ann Maria | 09 MAY 1865 |
| SEARS, Richard T. [6le] | GYLES, Mary E. | 31 DEC 1866 |
| SEARS, W. Leslie | ELWOOD, Ann Elizabeth | 17 JUN 1868 |
| SEATON, John Andrew | WHITING, Virginia (blk) | 23 FEB 1860 |
| SEATON, Townsend | JOHNSON, Mary P. | 08 AUG 1859 |
| SEAVA, Benjamin F. | STONE, Sallie B. | 10 AUG 1867 |
| SEAVERS, Joseph | BATEMAN, Sarah (blk) | 09 NOV 1869 |
| SEBASTIAN, Charles W. | TUTTLE, Sarah N. | 11 JUL 1864 |
| SEBASTIAN, John W. | REED, Elizth. Jane | 15 DEC 1869 |
| SEDGWICK, John W. [2] | DECKER, Sarah H. | 02 SEP 1869 |
| SEDGWICK, Walter T. | PATTERSON, Annie | 07 JAN 1870 |
| SEEBOLD, Philip D. | EAGLESTON, Maria Virginia | 30 DEC 1862 |
| SEEDERS, William | BLIGH, Kate | 13 JAN 1862 |
| SEELY, Miles H. | ROYCE, Asenath | 03 MAR 1863 |
| SEELYE, George D. | NEWTON, Annie | 01 AUG 1864 |
| SEEVERS, Georg Wilhelm August | JEAN, Caroline Charlotte | 18 NOV 1864 |
| SEEVERS, George Bailey | NOAKES, Maggie V. | 25 SEP 1866 |
| SEGAR, Travers | WOODWARD, Susan | 13 SEP 1859 |
| SEGERSON, Christopher | MULVAHAL, Mary | 06 JAN 1863 |
| SEGERSON, James | SULLIVAN, Mary | 31 AUG 1859 |
| SEILER, John A. | SOMERS, Mary M.C. | 09 FEB 1863 |
| SEILER, William J.E. | ESPEY, Laura V. | 22 JAN 1863 |
| SEITZ, James Columbus | FOSTER, Altie Hinton | 12 NOV 1866 |
| SEITZ, John A.F. | RITTER, Durette Catherine | 17 DEC 1863 |
| SEITZ, John F. | KNIGHT, Alice E. | 03 JUL 1863 |
| SELBY, Charles | BOULDING, Emma | 04 JUN 1964 |
| SELBY, John N. [6m] | NAYLOR, Dawsella V. | 24 DEC 1863 |
| SELBY, Joseph [9e] | SEABURN, Catherine Ann | 31 DEC 1861 |
| SELBY, Peter | FLEET, Oliva | 18 APR 1864 |
| SELDEN, George Henry | HALE, Judy (blk) | 24 JUN 1865 |
| SELDEN, Joseph | HAMILTON, Eliza A. (blk) | 20 DEC 1861 |
| SELDEN, Robert R. | WALKER, Augusta N. | 06 SEP 1859 |
| SELDEN, William C. | GLOVER, Angeline | 01 DEC 1862 |
| SELDNER, Louis | SELDNER, Eva | 21 JUN 1861 |
| SELECMAN, William R. | KURTZ, Henrietta C. | 12 JUL 1866 |
| SELECTMAN, Redman | COMPTON, Virginia F. | 28 MAY 1868 |
| SELECTMAN, Thomas H. | MASTON, Sarah R. | 26 MAY 1864 |
| SELFE, Stephen R. | WALKER, Julia A. | 05 NOV 1860 |
| SELLERS, Valentine W. | DEEBLE, Judie M. | 10 FEB 1866 |
| SELLING, David | BOXBAUM, Eliza | 13 FEB 1867 |
| SELLMAR, Charles | SULLIVAN, Joanna | 17 DEC 1861 |
| SELLNER, John J. | BIGGS, Mary E.R. | 01 FEB 1859 |
| SELLS, David M. | RUSSELL, Sarah E. | 02 OCT 1866 |
| SELVEY, William [6l] | SHELDON, Alice | 07 MAY 1861 |
| SELVY, Anthony | PATTERSON, Malinda (blk) | 28 JUN 1859 |
| SELVY, James | MERRITT, Emeline (blk) | 16 JAN 1865 |

| | | |
|---|---|---|
| SELZER, Philip | SIEGERT, Barbara | 21 DEC 1867 |
| SEMBLY, George | CHUT, Mary | 16 JAN 1866 |
| SENFFERT, George | CHONN, Elizabeth | 23 JUL 1861 |
| SEONSSON, William H. | BROOKS, Frances A. (blk) | 06 AUG 1868 |
| SEPHAS, James N. | MITCHELL, Mary Jane (blk) | 15 OCT 1867 |
| SERIFF, Byron [4] | FLEURY, Estelle L. | 01 DEC 1868 |
| SERRIN, David D. [2] | ELLIS, Matilda | 13 JUL 1869 |
| SERRIN, Thomas | COOK, Mary E. | 07 SEP 1869 |
| SEUERS, Stephen | LENENGS, Catherine | 23 APR 1859 |
| SEVEAR, Alexander | BUTLER, Betty Ann (blk) | 19 APR 1864 |
| SEVERSON, August | REEDER, E. | 10 FEB 1868 |
| SEWALL, Charles W. | GLASCOW, Elizabeth | 08 MAR 1864 |
| SEWALL, William [10] | STAPLES, Joanna | 22 APR 1869 |
| SEWELL, Albert | BRISCOE, Margaret (blk) | 26 DEC 1867 |
| SEWELL, Alexander | PRICE, Eliza Ann (blk) | 07 SEP 1867 |
| SEWELL, Anthony | HARRIS, Rachel (blk) | 15 NOV 1869 |
| SEWELL, Charles F. | HAWS, Abby Elizth. Ann | 20 AUG 1860 |
| SEWELL, John | LUCAS, Nancy | 25 SEP 1867 |
| SEWELL, John W. | JENKINS, Margaret A. | 20 MAR 1860 |
| SEWELL, Joseph H. | TOWNLEY, Elizabeth A. | 27 SEP 1858 |
| SEWELL, Louis | JOHNSON, Carrie | 23 DEC 1867 |
| SEWELL, Thomas J. | GRIGSBY, Sarah A. | 13 OCT 1869 |
| SEWELL, William | BLADEN, Matilda (blk) | 01 JUN 1867 |
| SEXTON, John | FOLBEY, Julia | 28 OCT 1868 |
| SEXTON, Patrick | NORMUL, Mary | 02 FEB 1869 |
| SEYBOLT, Frederick J. | INFIEF, Elizabeth C. | 12 SEP 1861 |
| SEYMOUR, Charles H. | RAYBOLD, Rebecca E. | 04 DEC 1866 |
| SEYMOUR, Charles Henry | TAFT, Deborah A.R. | 09 JUN 1862 |
| SEYMOUR, Silas H. | MORSE, Emily P. | 09 MAR 1869 |
| SHACKELFORD, John A. | WOLTZ, Mary E. | 06 DEC 1859 |
| SHADE, John | RUSS, Cecilia | 19 AUG 1863 |
| SHAFER, Daniel [7b] | BROWN, Sarah E. | 19 OCT 1869 |
| SHAFER, George | CROME, Emma | 30 NOV 1866 |
| SHAFER, John | CULLINAN, Kate | 17 DEC 1862 |
| SHAFER, John | BAWS, Johanna | 18 MAR 1867 |
| SHAFER, John [2] | HUNT, Laura | 31 AUG 1866 |
| SHAFFER, Charles G. [10] | GRAY, Mary | 02 MAY 1866 |
| SHAFFER, Michael | SMITH, Mary | 26 JUL 1865 |
| SHALEN, Philip | STRIDER, Mary C. | 25 OCT 1862 |
| SHAMBAUGH, Charles | DIVERS, Mary G. | 02 APR 1867 |
| SHAMS, Frank | REED, Mary (blk) | 19 MAR 1862 |
| SHANAHAN, Daniel | PATTERSON, Mary A. | 22 APR 1865 |
| SHANAHAN, John | WELSH, Margaret | 11 SEP 1860 |
| SHANAHAN, John | LENAHAN, Margaret | 26 DEC 1860 |
| SHANK, Henry W. | DEITRICK, Margaret | 11 DEC 1867 |
| SHANKLAND, Daniel | PAYNE, Margaret (blk) | 12 JAN 1869 |
| SHANKLIN, Alfred | JONES, Julia (blk) | 23 DEC 1869 |
| SHANKS, Charles H. | BALL, Nancy R. | 20 OCT 1863 |
| SHANKS, James R. | SEWALL, Regina | 18 APR 1867 |
| SHANNAHAN, Thomas | HANLON, Margaret | 11 FEB 1861 |
| SHANNON, Daniel | JONES, Anna F. | 04 APR 1867 |
| SHANNON, Edward | McSWEENY, Mary | 31 MAR 1865 |
| SHANNON, Edward | KENNEDY, Mary | 13 MAY 1865 |
| SHARKEY, John | DORLEY, Bessie | 13 SEP 1864 |
| SHARKEY, Peter | NAIRY, Ann | 26 MAY 1863 |
| SHARP, George C. | EDMONDS, Anna | 08 APR 1861 |

District of Columbia Marriage Licenses, 1858-1870

| | | |
|---|---|---|
| SHARP, Wm. G. [11] | McDONOUGH, Anna | 03 FEB 1865 |
| SHAUGHNESSY, Martin | KYNE, Margaret | 05 FEB 1864 |
| SHAUGHNESSY, Michael | SHEA, Mary | 19 APR 1862 |
| SHAUGNESSY, Michael | CONNOR, Mary | 15 OCT 1863 |
| SHAW, Albert | BEANS, Julia Ann | 27 JUL 1869 |
| SHAW, Alfred C. | CONWAY, Ellen C. | 15 JAN 1866 |
| SHAW, Alonzo D. | LEWIS, Sarah F. | 20 OCT 1860 |
| SHAW, Brooks | WASHINGTON, Caroline | 29 APR 1869 |
| SHAW, Charles | BRAMELL, Jane | 09 MAR 1859 |
| SHAW, George W. | COOK, Rebecca Ann | 14 DEC 1863 |
| SHAW, Granville C. | SMITH, Anna L. | 26 JUN 1863 |
| SHAW, Henry | LAMBKINS, Anna | 17 AUG 1866 |
| SHAW, Henry H. | BRAMMELL, Caroline V. | 17 NOV 1860 |
| SHAW, J. Robert | CASSELL, Mary Jane | 28 MAY 1867 |
| SHAW, James Albert | BLAIR, Jane | 12 JUL 1866 |
| SHAW, James E. [10] | JONES, Nancy E. | 29 JAN 1863 |
| SHAW, James Vila | HARRISON, Mary Jane | 12 FEB 1870 |
| SHAW, John M. | LEFTER, Sarah C. | 07 JUN 1864 |
| SHAW, John T. [1c] | BERRY, Sarah R. | 28 OCT 1862 |
| SHAW, Nicholas E. | RIDDLE, Susan M. | 06 OCT 1862 |
| SHAW, Nicholas S. | SCOTT, Mary | 08 MAY 1862 |
| SHAW, Sandy | LEE, Cariline (blk) | 03 JAN 1859 |
| SHAW, William W.F. | KENNEDY, Maggie | 30 JUN 1864 |
| SHEA, Daniel | MANSVILL, Mary | 22 MAY 1861 |
| SHEA, David | MAROONEY, Mary | 29 APR 1865 |
| SHEA, James | ENRIGHT, Margaret | 08 SEP 1861 |
| SHEA, James | BOWLER, Margaret | 27 NOV 1863 |
| SHEA, Jeremiah | CONNOR, Margaret | 03 NOV 1860 |
| SHEA, Jerry | DADY, Margaret | 11 AUG 1863 |
| SHEA, John | SEGERSON, Mary | 19 FEB 1859 |
| SHEA, John | MAHONEY, Julia | 12 AUG 1859 |
| SHEA, John | WOOD, Elizabeth | 09 JAN 1862 |
| SHEA, John | BERRINS, Bridget | 03 FEB 1863 |
| SHEA, Michael | McCARTHY, Mary | 12 MAY 1862 |
| SHEA, Thomas | COLLINS, Mary | 18 SEP 1867 |
| SHEA, Thos. J. | SWEENEY, Mary Regina | 06 OCT 1864 |
| SHEA, William | MEAGIN, Mary | 01 OCT 1862 |
| SHEA, William | SHEAHAN, Bridget | 06 FEB 1864 |
| SHEAHAN, Jeremiah | CROW, Mary | 09 AUG 1862 |
| SHEAHAN, John | RAFTER, Catharine | 27 APR 1865 |
| SHEAHAN, John | MACK, Ellen | 02 SEP 1867 |
| SHEAHAN, Michael | FULLER, Johannah | 08 OCT 1868 |
| SHEAHAN, Patrick | WARD, Kate | 02 MAY 1863 |
| SHEAHAN, Thomas | TWOOMY, Mary | 10 MAY 1864 |
| SHEAHAN, William | FOLEY, Bridget | 14 NOV 1863 |
| SHEARER, James | McGRATH, Ellenor | 12 JAN 1867 |
| SHEARMAN, William P. [11] | JAMES, Mary W. | 01 JUN 1863 |
| SHEBLE, Edgar A. | NOYES, Anna M. | 06 AUG 1866 |
| SHECKELLS, Theodore | GODDARD, Lizzie A. | 16 OCT 1865 |
| SHECKELS, James T. | KING, Elizabeth | 16 NOV 1860 |
| SHECKELS, John W. | DAVIS, Agnes N. | 05 DEC 1861 |
| SHECKELS, Theodore | TURTON, Mollie J. | 05 FEB 1861 |
| SHECKLES, Charles Theodore | CROSSING, Susannah | 26 NOV 1864 |
| SHEDD, James A. | MOORE, Emily B. | 09 OCT 1865 |
| SHEDD, William A. | WILBURN, Ann R. | 10 OCT 1859 |
| SHEED, William W. | KNIGHT, Mary | 11 DEC 1866 |

| | | |
|---|---|---|
| SHEEHAN, Andrew | GALIVAN, Bridget | 03 JUL 1863 |
| SHEEHAN, Daniel | WELSH, Catherine | 20 OCT 1866 |
| SHEEHAN, John | CREED, Mary | 29 AUG 1862 |
| SHEEHY, Abraham | PALMER, Caroline A. | 15 MAY 1865 |
| SHEEHY, Edward | GRIFFIN, Bridget | 04 MAY 1861 |
| SHEEHY, John | SULLIVAN, Winnifred | 02 AUG 1867 |
| SHEEHY, Michael | CONNELL, Ellen | 27 OCT 1865 |
| SHEEHY, Patrick | SULLIVAN, Juila | 22 NOV 1867 |
| SHEELEY, Padre | DAVIS, Theresa | 23 JAN 1862 |
| SHEEN, Corneill | LONG, Ellen | 10 OCT 1863 |
| SHEETS, John S. | HARRIS, Mary Anne | 15 NOV 1858 |
| SHEETS, William T. [7a] | BISHOP, Mary P. | 16 NOV 1868 |
| SHEFFER, Martin V.B. | GIFFORD, Naomi | 10 FEB 1864 |
| SHEHAN, Thomas | MURPHY, Alice | 01 NOV 1859 |
| SHEKELL, Edward L. | BELL, Elizabeth H. | 21 AUG 1860 |
| SHEKELL, Marinus W. | COMBS, Mary E. | 21 FEB 1860 |
| SHELDON, Albert W. | FALLON, Maggie | 02 FEB 1865 |
| SHELDON, S.A. | SANDERS, L.J. | 26 FEB 1866 |
| SHELLY, Ham | JOHNSON, Susan (blk) | 22 MAY 1866 |
| SHELLY, William [5] | RIDER, Hattie | 26 MAR 1869 |
| SHELMIRE, W. Harry | LEMON, Fannie L. | 24 APR 1869 |
| SHELTER, William | ROLLINS, George Ana | 24 MAR 1863 |
| SHELTON, Edward | WILSON, Barbara | 26 JUN 1865 |
| SHELTON, Newman | PEGG, Annie | 15 JAN 1867 |
| SHELTON, Richard T. | RANDALL, Eliza E. | 10 OCT 1866 |
| SHELTON, Thomas | BROWN, Emily | 20 SEP 1859 |
| SHELTON, William H. | SERRA, Arabella O. | 05 OCT 1869 |
| SHENAN, Patrick | FORD, Margaret | 29 JUN 1864 |
| SHEPHARD, John | PINKARD, Winnie (blk) | 06 JUL 1867 |
| SHEPHERD, Alexander | DIXON, Josephine (blk) | 05 JUL 1866 |
| SHEPHERD, Alexander R. | YOUNG, Mary G. | 28 JAN 1862 |
| SHEPHERD, Arthur | LAMBRIGHT, Emma | 22 DEC 1863 |
| SHEPHERD, George [10] | JOHNSON, Elizabeth | 24 AUG 1865 |
| SHEPHERD, Henry L. | TALLEY, Eliza M. | 15 SEP 1869 |
| SHEPHERD, John | SMITH, Ann Elizabeth | 22 OCT 1866 |
| SHEPHERD, Lewis | JOHNSON, Margaret | 11 DEC 1865 |
| SHEPHERD, Thomas M. | PAGE, Bettie E. | 20 APR 1868 |
| SHEPHERD, William | GRINNELL, Mary Jane | 06 OCT 1864 |
| SHEPHERD, William | MUNROE, Caroline (blk) | 03 NOV 1868 |
| SHEPHERD, Wilmer S. | SHEDD, Laura A. | 04 JUN 1864 |
| SHEPPARD, J. Edmund [11] | BUCKINGHAM, Martha Virginia | 15 JAN 1866 |
| SHEPPERD, Edward | COLE, Laura (blk) | 18 SEP 1865 |
| SHEPPERD, John D. [9e] | WHITACRE, Louisa | 13 NOV 1861 |
| SHEPSTON, William | CUNNINGHAM, Jane | 03 MAR 1862 |
| SHERIDAN, Francis | GRUBB, Rose E. | 30 SEP 1864 |
| SHERIDAN, Walter Alexander | BUNTON, Mary Eliza | 22 JUL 1863 |
| SHERIDAN, William | LALLY, Bridget | 26 FEB 1863 |
| SHERIER, William H. | WALKER, Martha A. | 06 OCT 1858 |
| SHERIFF, George B. | HILL, Sarah C. | 20 NOV 1858 |
| SHERIFF, Samuel | PADGETT, Maria Elizabeth | 11 SEP 1863 |
| SHERIOR, John C. | HAVENER, Catherine R. | 26 SEP 1868 |
| SHERLOCK, John | COSTELLO, Bridget | 12 NOV 1867 |
| SHERLOCK, Patrick | KYLE, Mary | 24 JAN 1863 |
| SHERMAN, Henry C. | McCONNELL, Susan | 24 SEP 1866 |
| SHERMAN, John B. (soldier) | MEIGS, Lucy | 21 JUL 1863 |
| SHERMAN, John F. | SHERWOOD, Mary C.E. | 31 MAR 1862 |

District of Columbia Marriage Licenses, 1858-1870

| | | |
|---|---|---|
| SHERMAN, John F. | WILKINSON, Agusta A. | 25 NOV 1862 |
| SHERNBACK, Henry | NOONAN, Annie | 15 AUG 1868 |
| SHERNIER, Charles | JORDAN, Louisa | 01 JUL 1863 |
| SHERRILL, Henry A. | BEMENT, Mary Louisa | 24 JAN 1867 |
| SHERRY, John William | BROWNING, Jane Ann | 19 NOV 1861 |
| SHERWOOD, Charles K. | MILLER, Sallie | 17 MAY 1866 |
| SHERWOOD, George W. | GORDON, Virginia R. | 13 MAR 1866 |
| SHERWOOD, James H. | PARKER, Mary A. | 14 FEB 1859 |
| SHERWOOD, John J. | CARLTON, Frank A. | 12 DEC 1865 |
| SHERWOOD, John L. | HORNBERGER, Mary H. | 11 MAY 1866 |
| SHERWOOD, John L. [6le] | ASH, Mary | 09 JUL 1867 |
| SHERWOOD, Robert J. | STROTHERS, Mary A. | 15 MAR 1860 |
| SHERWOOD, Silas H. | ROLLINS, Jane | 19 MAR 1861 |
| SHERWOOD, Thomas J. | ARNOLD, Maggie | 01 JUN 1868 |
| SHERWOOD, Tyler | OMAHUNDRO, Hattie E. | 26 APR 1870 |
| SHERWOOD, William A. | BLOCK, Mariana | 03 AUG 1869 |
| SHERWOOD, William Henry | BOCOLIN, Catherine | 06 JUL 1869 |
| SHEWBRIDGE, John J. | GOUMPH, Alice | 17 DEC 1861 |
| SHEWRER, Andrew | GROENER, Barbara | 14 NOV 1862 |
| SHIDY, George Washington | COOK, Jennie Eliza | 06 APR 1867 |
| SHIEHY, John | SULLIVAN, Sarah | 17 AUG 1867 |
| SHIELDS, Clarence | PLUMMER, Charlotte (blk) | 12 SEP 1867 |
| SHIELDS, Francis | GILBERT, Alice (blk) | 28 JUN 1866 |
| SHIELDS, Laurence | BARRETT, Harriet | 27 JUN 1860 |
| SHIELDS, Noah | BLACKWELL, Mary Ann | 16 NOV 1869 |
| SHIELDS, William | HENDERSON, Martha J. | 21 SEP 1860 |
| SHILLING, Anthony | BATES, Sophia | 05 MAY 1868 |
| SHINER, Annie M. | PEARSON, Wilson | 18 NOV 1862 |
| SHINER, Isaac | STEWART, Caroline M. (blk) | 18 DEC 1869 |
| SHINN, Vinicome, Dr. | ARNY, Caroline C., Mrs. | 09 NOV 1868 |
| SHIPLEY, Peter | BOONE, Mahala (blk) | 09 JUN 1869 |
| SHIPMAN, Richard | WEST, Catherine M. | 25 MAR 1869 |
| SHIPMAN, Stephen E. | SWANN, Mary E. | 30 SEP 1869 |
| SHIPP, Nelson | TUCKER, Charity (blk) | 26 MAR 1870 |
| SHIRLEY, John R. | GRAHAM, Martha L. | 29 AUG 1865 |
| SHOEMAKER, Francis D. | GARDNER, A. Catherine | 10 OCT 1863 |
| SHOEMAKER, George, Jr. [1c] | OSBORN, Mary H. | 10 OCT 1863 |
| SHOEMAKER, Jacob P. [2] | LUCAS, Mary Elizabeth [Mrs.] | 05 AUG 1865 |
| SHOEMAKER, John | CARROLL, Margaret Ann | 05 MAY 1866 |
| SHOEMAKER, Joseph | SYLENCE, Martha | 10 DEC 1861 |
| SHOEMAKER, Joseph T., Lt. | CLARKE, Sarah L. | 22 SEP 1863 |
| SHOEMAKER, Thomas F. Capt. [3] | DIXON, Laura | 06 DEC 1866 |
| SHOENHERR, William | SCHMIDT, Mary | 09 FEB 1860 |
| SHOLES, Henry D. | HUNT, Rosa D. | 09 JUN 1862 |
| SHOMBERG, John H. | YOST, Mary E. | 24 FEB 1862 |
| SHORE, John | STATEN, Margaret | 19 DEC 1867 |
| SHORES, Martin | POWELL, Malinda (blk) | 24 AUG 1865 |
| SHORT, George W. | ANKERS, Mary | 26 DEC 1868 |
| SHORTER, Charles | BUTLER, Martha (blk) | 16 MAY 1870 |
| SHORTER, Edward | POWELL, Priscilla | 01 MAY 1866 |
| SHORTER, Frederick | JOHNSON, Louisa | 30 AUG 1865 |
| SHORTER, Henry | WOOD, Lethea Ann (blk) | 12 FEB 1863 |
| SHORTER, James | CURTIS, Julia Ann | 21 MAY 1863 |
| SHORTER, Joseph | ALLEN, Josephine (blk) | 06 MAR 1865 |
| SHORTER, Richard | TUCKER, Lucinda (blk) | 22 SEP 1868 |
| SHORTRIDGE, Thomas K. | LYNN, Harriet | 06 FEB 1865 |

District of Columbia Marriage Licenses, 1858-1870

| | | |
|---|---|---|
| SHORTS, John | GASSION, Henrietta (blk) | 05 SEP 1863 |
| SHORTS, Lewis | BUTLER, Henrietta (blk) | 02 DEC 1867 |
| SHOTWELL, John W. | DUNN, Annie | 15 NOV 1864 |
| SHREEVE, John Henry | MILLER, Joanna | 11 NOV 1861 |
| SHREVE, John H. | ENGLEBRECT, Joanna | 15 NOV 1864 |
| SHREVE, Samuel R. | MALONEY, Bridget A. | 12 OCT 1868 |
| SHROEDER, Charles | COOK, Lizzie E. | 31 JAN 1862 |
| SHROSSER, John A. | BEINDER, Margaret A. (blk) | 16 MAR 1859 |
| SHRYOCK, William H. | THORN, Marah | 29 DEC 1868 |
| SHUBERT, Martin | SHRODEL, Barbara | 03 APR 1869 |
| SHUBURT, Henry | TOLT, Lana | 17 JAN 1863 |
| SHUGRUE, Timothy | DOOLING, Catharine | 30 JAN 1861 |
| SHULER, Magnus | WACHTER, Barbara | 06 FEB 1865 |
| SHUMAN, Frank | BAKER, Josephine | 30 JAN 1866 |
| SHUMWAY, Duffield | ASHTON, Annie | 19 AUG 1865 |
| SHUR, George M. | HERBERT, Augusta | 19 FEB 1864 |
| SHUSTER, H.C. | FULLER, Helen M. | 26 DEC 1865 |
| SIBEL, John | NEWMAN, Augusta | 12 APR 1870 |
| SIBLEY, Ebenezer S. | CHURCHILL, Elizabeth M. | 25 NOV 1859 |
| SIBLEY, John T. | SMALLWOOD, Sarah J. | 20 FEB 1865 |
| SIBLEY, Robert W. | REED, Angelina F. | 09 JUN 1863 |
| SIBLEY, Solomon | TAYLOR, Josephine | 19 FEB 1861 |
| SIBLEY, William J. | JACKSON, Dorothea L. | 11 MAY 1859 |
| SICK, Otto | ALDVATER, Margaret | 23 MAR 1864 |
| SIDNER, John H. | SHEPHERD, Mary E. (blk) | 27 NOV 1866 |
| SIDWELL, Alfred | ECKEL, Elizabeth Ann | 02 DEC 1864 |
| SIEBERT, Frank [7b] | DICE, Carrie | 06 MAY 1870 |
| SIEGEL, Benjamin | GLICK, Matilda | 03 MAR 1863 |
| SIEGERT, John T. | AMENT, Barbara | 11 MAR 1864 |
| SIEGNER, Charles | GECKMAN, Sophia | 26 FEB 1863 |
| SIEVERS, Henry | TRUSTHEIM, Eliza | 14 MAY 1869 |
| SIGEL, Bernard | WELSH, Margaret | 03 AUG 1863 |
| SIGNOR, William H. | HALL, Eveline V. | 20 APR 1868 |
| SIGOURNEY, Charles F. | MITCHELL, Willie | 15 NOV 1869 |
| SILENCE, John | GROVES, Caroline | 07 OCT 1862 |
| SILENCE, William H. | DESFOSSE, Susan M. | 16 SEP 1868 |
| SILER, John [9e] | TERRY, Mary A. | 03 MAR 1862 |
| SILLERS, Robert | CAHILL, Ellen | 23 JAN 1866 |
| SILSBY, Isaac | CLAXTON, Susana L. | 27 NOV 1866 |
| SILVERBERG, Bernard | HEXTER, Mary | 05 MAY 1864 |
| SILVERS, Joseph H. | MORRIS, Isabella | 24 JAN 1866 |
| SIMCESON, Peter | FLEET, Margaret | 08 SEP 1863 |
| SIMES, William | ADAMS, Emma (blk) | 21 JAN 1867 |
| SIMILOR, Andrew | TURNER, Lavinia (blk) | 06 MAY 1868 |
| SIMMONS, George | BROWN, Maria E. | 31 MAR 1866 |
| SIMMONS, George | TUNNELLY, Kate (blk) | 05 MAY 1868 |
| SIMMONS, George N. | ARMSTRONG, Mary E. | 02 FEB 1865 |
| SIMMONS, George [5] | TAYLOR, Mary [C.] | 13 JAN 1870 |
| SIMMONS, Henry S. | WERTZ, Margaretha | 29 JUN 1863 |
| SIMMONS, James | WHITAKER, Sarah (blk) | 01 FEB 1867 |
| SIMMONS, James F. | BENTON, Martha E. | 27 JUN 1860 |
| SIMMONS, James W. | BENTON, Mary A. | 09 FEB 1865 |
| SIMMONS, John | BRADY, Eveline | 08 JAN 1862 |
| SIMMONS, John | TOOTLE, Elizabeth (blk) | 04 MAY 1865 |
| SIMMONS, John B. | SHAW, Maggie A. | 08 OCT 1866 |
| SIMMONS, John E. | BEUCHLER, Mary Ann | 23 DEC 1858 |

# District of Columbia Marriage Licenses, 1858-1870

| | | |
|---|---|---|
| SIMMONS, John F. | CARROLL, Catharine | 08 FEB 1865 |
| SIMMONS, Joseph F. | HUMPHREYS, Jane | 08 SEP 1858 |
| SIMMONS, Samuel | BING, Sarah (blk) | 06 MAR 1867 |
| SIMMONS, William | NORRIS, Phillis (blk) | 27 OCT 1864 |
| SIMMONS, William | WYMAN, Elizabeth | 07 FEB 1870 |
| SIMMONS, William [7b] | SIMMS, Annie E. | 04 JAN 1870 |
| SIMMONS, William A. | CHAMBERLIN, Josephine | 05 SEP 1868 |
| SIMMONS, William Henry [2] | MOXLEY, Mary Frances | 05 AUG 1864 |
| SIMMONS, William J. | MILLS, Alice | 25 MAY 1870 |
| SIMMS, Alexander | TASCAR, Adeline (blk) | 30 JUN 1866 |
| SIMMS, Alexander | RIVERS, Mary | 09 DEC 1867 |
| SIMMS, Caleb | EVANS, Mary Ellen | 13 OCT 1863 |
| SIMMS, Charles | CURTIS, Ellen | 12 DEC 1861 |
| SIMMS, Charles N. | BURR, Mary A. | 08 FEB 1866 |
| SIMMS, Charles R. | DAVIS, Mary C. | 05 NOV 1864 |
| SIMMS, Craven | TYLER, Rosa Bell | 06 JAN 1870 |
| SIMMS, George | SIMMS, Margaret (blk) | 19 FEB 1869 |
| SIMMS, Giles G.C. | SOLLERS, Sarah E. | 09 MAY 1864 |
| SIMMS, James | LEE, Rosa (blk) | 17 MAY 1870 |
| SIMMS, James M.V. [3] | WARFIELD, Amanda | 23 AUG 1862 |
| SIMMS, Jeremiah | SUMMERVILLE, Mary M. (blk) | 19 MAY 1859 |
| SIMMS, Jeremiah | GRINNELL, Frances (blk) | 18 JUL 1861 |
| SIMMS, John | SOLOMON, Anna Rebecca (blk) | 19 NOV 1863 |
| SIMMS, John | NEALE, Miss (blk) | 31 JAN 1865 |
| SIMMS, John | MACK, Cecilia (blk) | 03 SEP 1867 |
| SIMMS, John | MAULER, Lila J. (blk) | 31 MAR 1869 |
| SIMMS, John Henry | BERRY, Mary Catherine (blk) | 20 JUL 1869 |
| SIMMS, Joseph A. | TRIPLET, Willie Ann (blk) | 05 OCT 1867 |
| SIMMS, Philip | CISSELL, Eliza Jane (blk) | 16 SEP 1869 |
| SIMMS, Richard | LEE, Rebecca (blk) | 19 SEP 1867 |
| SIMMS, Samuel | ROSS, Esther (blk) | 15 SEP 1866 |
| SIMMS, Stephen | EVANS, Minta (blk) | 11 JUL 1867 |
| SIMMS, Tyler | KERR, Hester (blk) | 09 MAR 1864 |
| SIMMS, William S. | JAVINS, Annie | 27 AUG 1869 |
| SIMMS, Wm. H. | KNODE, Helen G. | 22 JAN 1864 |
| SIMON, Benjamin | TALBURT, Maria | 31 MAY 1869 |
| SIMON, Leopold | BATTIGHEIMER, Hannah | 27 OCT 1866 |
| SIMONDS, Daniel [6m] | WATERS, Mary [Frances] | 04 APR 1862 |
| SIMONDS, Daniel G. | PIPPERT, Christinia C. | 22 AUG 1868 |
| SIMONDS, John | CARTER, Reano (blk) | 28 OCT 1865 |
| SIMONDS, John | DEMYERS, Harriet | 07 AUG 1867 |
| SIMONDS, John R. | ASH, Sarah C. | 27 OCT 1858 |
| SIMONDS, Robert | SIMONDS, Mary | 23 JUL 1863 |
| SIMONDS, Stephen [6le] | FREYER, Mary Isabel | 31 JUL 1867 |
| SIMONS, Adelbert B. | HENNESSEY, Marietta | 30 JAN 1866 |
| SIMONS, Arthur | ROBINSON, Alice | 01 JUN 1864 |
| SIMONS, George H. | MORFORD, Susan V. | 12 MAY 1865 |
| SIMONS, John Henry | BACON, Elizabeth | 14 NOV 1866 |
| SIMONS, William | HARRISON, Lucy Ann | 12 JAN 1869 |
| SIMONS, William H. | SHEREWOOD, Harriet Frances | 01 JUL 1861 |
| SIMPSON, A.J. | STAFFORD, Mary E. | 02 JUL 1867 |
| SIMPSON, Albert | VALENTINE, Catherine (blk) | 18 MAR 1868 |
| SIMPSON, David J. | HOLMES, Catharine (blk) | 17 JAN 1865 |
| SIMPSON, George | BELL, Mary | 30 OCT 1865 |
| SIMPSON, Gilbert | JENKINS, Laura Virginia | 19 MAY 1862 |
| SIMPSON, Henry T. | COX, Elizabeth E. | 11 NOV 1869 |

## District of Columbia Marriage Licenses, 1858-1870

| | | |
|---|---|---|
| SIMPSON, Jacob | BLAIN, Matilda | 24 MAR 1868 |
| SIMPSON, James H. | STEADMAN, Annie E. | 02 JAN 1864 |
| SIMPSON, James M. | LEDMAN, Cordelia | 09 APR 1866 |
| SIMPSON, James W. [10] | JONES, Anna S. | 13 JAN 1870 |
| SIMPSON, John | TAYLOR, Catherine (blk) | 09 AUG 1859 |
| SIMPSON, John H. [11] | STEELE, Fannie B. | 11 JUL 1868 |
| SIMPSON, John Thomas | DAY, Elizabeth | 01 FEB 1860 |
| SIMPSON, Judson C. [6] | BROWN, Jane Rebecca | 11 SEP 1869 |
| SIMPSON, Levi | JONES, Joanna (blk) | 13 APR 1868 |
| SIMPSON, Richard Henry | STEINER, Marietta Cathedral | 26 APR 1869 |
| SIMPSON, Thomas J. | JENKINS, Marion F. | 10 FEB 1863 |
| SIMPSON, William | AMBUSH, Martha | 09 JAN 1865 |
| SIMPSON, William | LIGHTFOOT, Lucy (blk) | 29 JUL 1868 |
| SIMPSON, William F. | INZOR, Annie E. | 01 DEC 1860 |
| SIMPSON, Wm. G. | HUMPKINS, Eliza R. | 22 JAN 1863 |
| SIMPSON, William H. | COLLINS, Mary Louisa (blk) | 10 NOV 1865 |
| SIMPSON, William J. [12s] | DEAN, Annie | 24 APR 1862 |
| SIMS, Adam | SMITH, Ellen (blk) | 11 JUL 1866 |
| SIMS, Daniel | McCOY, Letty (blk) | 24 APR 1862 |
| SIMS, Elias | JOHNSON, Henrietta (blk) | 23 OCT 1866 |
| SIMS, George | SIMS, Matilda | 29 DEC 1859 |
| SIMS, George J. | SHORTER, Elizabeth (blk) | 04 JUN 1867 |
| SIMS, George W. | MACKALL, Jane (blk) | 24 OCT 1867 |
| SIMS, Henry | SIMPSON, Sally Ann (blk) | 08 JUN 1870 |
| SIMS, John | THOMAS, Airy (blk) | 05 JAN 1867 |
| SIMS, John Lewis | WARDEN, Ann E. | 24 APR 1860 |
| SIMS, John Thomas | BUTLER, Mary Ann | 31 JUL 1865 |
| SIMS, Joseph | PLATER, Sarah | 01 JUL 1861 |
| SIMS, Paul | PARKER, Letty (blk) | 01 SEP 1866 |
| SIMS, Richard | WILLIAMS, Mary (blk) | 24 MAR 1863 |
| SIMS, Thomas W. | HALL, Mary E. | 04 FEB 1862 |
| SIMS, William | BARNES, Henrietta (blk) | 06 FEB 1864 |
| SIMS, William | GASSAWAY, Jane | 11 AUG 1868 |
| SIMS, William | MAYHEW, Rachel (blk) | 10 JUN 1869 |
| SIMS, Zachariah | FLETCHER, Mary E. (blk) | 21 DEC 1864 |
| SINCELL, William H. | PROCTOR, Mary J. | 19 JUL 1859 |
| SINCLAIR, George W. | FRYER, Annie | 29 AUG 1863 |
| SINCLAIR, John | HUFFMAN, Catherine | 04 SEP 1869 |
| SINCLAIR, John S. | WEBER, Barbara A. | 20 JAN 1870 |
| SINCLAIR, Richard E. | JIDTS, Mary Jane | 15 NOV 1860 |
| SINCLAIR, Thomas L. | HOSKIN, Kate F. | 22 APR 1861 |
| SINCLAIR, Walter J. | HERON, Ximenia E. | 14 MAR 1860 |
| SINCLAIR, William | JOHNSON, Elizabeth | 18 JUN 1863 |
| SINCLAIR, William | McDONALD, Eugenia | 09 DEC 1865 |
| SINCLAIR, Williams | SMITHING, Anna (blk) | 11 DEC 1869 |
| SINCLEAR, James M. | LATIMER, Loula | 12 DEC 1868 |
| SINGLETON, John | KELLY, Mary | 13 JAN 1863 |
| SINN, John Lewis [5] | KING, Mary Adelaid | 08 OCT 1867 |
| SINNOTT, John | HICKS, Jane E. | 03 MAR 1863 |
| SINON, Thomas | WHITE, Susan | 08 SEP 1859 |
| SINSEL, John | WEYRICH, Henrietta | 13 MAR 1862 |
| SIOUSSA, C. Maurice | DOVE, Lizzie | 20 NOV 1863 |
| SIOUSSA, Frederick | BOYD, Mary | 07 AUG 1863 |
| SIOUSSA, John Walter | LYDDANE, Gertrude | 11 NOV 1869 |
| SIPE, Edward H. | BENDER, Emma S. | 05 NOV 1864 |
| SIPES, Henry N. | POWELL, Margaret E. | 10 JUL 1860 |

District of Columbia Marriage Licenses, 1858-1870

| | | |
|---|---|---|
| SIPES, Joseph [2] | HOWARD, Mary | 23 JUN 1868 |
| SIPOS, Paul | CLANCY, Delia | 29 JUN 1869 |
| SIS, John H. | BARRETT, Kate | 24 SEP 1866 |
| SISSECOVICH, George | FLETCHER, Teresa | 07 MAY 1864 |
| SISSELL, William H. | CRAWFORD, Margaret | 08 SEP 1859 |
| SISSON, John A. | FOWKE, Lucy B. | 19 JAN 1864 |
| SITNER, Jesse | EASTON, Annie (blk) | 27 AUG 1866 |
| SITTER, Caspar August | SCHNEIDER, Mary Teresa | 11 FEB 1867 |
| SIVIERON, Etienne | GRÜNWALD, Victorine | 27 APR 1863 |
| SKERRETT, Joseph S. [Lt.] [10] | TAYLOR, Maggie L. | 13 JUN 1859 |
| SKIDMORE, Charles W. | KEYES, Sarah | 03 JAN 1865 |
| SKIDMORE, Lewis E. | MANKIN, Elizabeth | 04 SEP 1866 |
| SKIDMORE, W.S. | STARR, Eliza V. | 12 MAY 1870 |
| SKIDMORE, William R. | SANFORD, Mary E. | 18 JUL 1859 |
| SKILLMAN, Enos A. | MIDDLETON, Alice | 08 OCT 1867 |
| SKINNER, Alexander | BARKMAN, Amanda | 19 SEP 1861 |
| SKINNER, Enoch G. | GOODWIN, Rebecca M. | 31 DEC 1868 |
| SKINNER, Francis M. | TURNER, Mary E. | 04 MAY 1867 |
| SKINNER, George W. | DONALDSON, Mary R. | 04 OCT 1869 |
| SKINNER, John | BUTLER, Elizth. (blk) | 16 APR 1868 |
| SKINNER, Richard | DAVIS, Mary | 22 JUN 1867 |
| SKINNER, William | QUEEN, Ann | 06 JUL 1859 |
| SKIPPEN, Charles M. [4] | THORN, Sarah E. | 28 NOV 1868 |
| SLACK, Henry | VanHORN, Anna | 12 OCT 1864 |
| SLACK, Junius B. | WALL, Mary E. | 10 JAN 1870 |
| SLADE, Frank L. [1e] | NEILL, Susan E. | 29 JUN 1864 |
| SLADE, William Costin | LOCKE, Henrietta | 16 JUN 1869 |
| SLAGEL, Alexander G. | SHAFER, Sarah E. Wadlis | 19 NOV 1861 |
| SLAGLE, George W. | CROPLEY, Virginia | 08 OCT 1862 |
| SLATER, Charles H. | SMITH, Annie (blk) | 03 OCT 1867 |
| SLATER, Frank | ROZIER, Harriet | 30 AUG 1865 |
| SLATER, Jacob | DYER, Sarah A. | 18 NOV 1868 |
| SLATER, Jerry | BLACKSTONE, Betsy (blk) | 16 FEB 1865 |
| SLATER, John S. | FERGUSON, Mary E. | 21 SEP 1865 |
| SLATER, John S. | ROTHWELL, Annie M. | 11 OCT 1869 |
| SLATER, M.T. | PATTERSON, Annie | 02 JAN 1869 |
| SLATER, Samuel Edward [11] | McLEAN, Marian Virginia | 15 JUN 1868 |
| SLATER, Thomas | DUNNIGAN, Mary | 26 AUG 1862 |
| SLATER, William | HICKMAN, Ann Maria | 24 DEC 1863 |
| SLATOR, Jerry | JOHNSON, Louise (blk) | 01 APR 1870 |
| SLATTERY, Edmond | COLDON, Ellen | 23 JAN 1864 |
| SLATTERY, John | SHANAHAN, Sarah | 14 MAY 1867 |
| SLAUGHTER, Richard | HOLMES, Mary Jane (blk) | 19 NOV 1868 |
| SLAUGHTER, Selim | BUCKLEY, Martha E. | 10 SEP 1860 |
| SLAUGHTER, Thornton | GREEN, Frances (blk) | 08 NOV 1866 |
| SLAVEN, William Thomas | RUEHMAN, Elizabeth Ciscelia | 17 NOV 1868 |
| SLEGER, A.C. | LYNN, Virginia E. | 05 NOV 1866 |
| SLEPF, Frederick | NOLL, Madlina | 29 MAR 1864 |
| SLICK, Josiah | FERRIS, Carrie | 10 SEP 1866 |
| SLOWERS, James | WASHBURN, Ociann | 12 NOV 1862 |
| SMACKEM, John | DUFFIN, Abby (blk) | 01 FEB 1865 |
| SMACKERN, James E. | ROBINSON, Rachel (blk) | 21 SEP 1867 |
| SMALL, Thomas | LEWIS, Delia (blk) | 30 MAR 1866 |
| SMALL, William | ANDERSON, Frances M.R. | 24 MAY 1870 |
| SMALLEY, Francis | MANN, Sarah E. | 29 OCT 1863 |
| SMALLEY, Virgil E. | STEEL, Agusta F. | 18 MAR 1865 |

District of Columbia Marriage Licenses, 1858-1870

| | | |
|---|---|---|
| SMALLWOOD, Alfred | REYNOLDS, Cecila (blk) | 06 DEC 1866 |
| SMALLWOOD, Charles T. [8] | BALLARD, Mary [E.] | 03 JAN 1870 |
| SMALLWOOD, Henry | COURCEY, Jane (blk) | 24 DEC 1863 |
| SMALLWOOD, James | NORRIS, Sarah Jane (blk) | 14 NOV 1867 |
| SMALLWOOD, James | WADE, Jane (blk) | 26 DEC 1868 |
| SMALLWOOD, James B. | MORROW, Annette | 15 SEP 1859 |
| SMALLWOOD, John [6h] | FLETCHER, Ann E. | 01 JUN 1868 |
| SMALLWOOD, Joseph | GRIMES, Mary (blk) | 30 MAY 1865 |
| SMALLWOOD, Lem'l. B. | BARTLETT, Mary | 22 AUG 1861 |
| SMALLWOOD, Philip | GALWAY, Phillis (blk) | 08 NOV 1866 |
| SMALLWOOD, Robert | WORTHINGTON, Annie | 06 FEB 1865 |
| SMALLWOOD, Thomas | GILL, Anna (blk) | 08 JAN 1866 |
| SMALLWOOD, Thomas | WATERS, Nancy | 02 JUL 1866 |
| SMALLWOOD, Thomas | LEE, Eliza (blk) | 19 NOV 1868 |
| SMALLWOOD, William H. | LIGHTFOOT, Ophelia | 12 JUN 1867 |
| SMALLZEL, John S. | MYERS, Josephine A. | 12 DEC 1868 |
| SMART, Robert | HILL, Maria J. (blk) | 12 DEC 1866 |
| SMARTT, Hiram | McFARLAND, Isabella | 03 AUG 1864 |
| SMATTEN, Charles | MARSHALL, Mary (blk) | 10 JUN 1868 |
| SMILER, John | BLACK, Victoria (blk) | 08 NOV 1866 |
| SMILEY, Henry | JONES, Arena (blk) | 03 OCT 1867 |
| SMILEY, Lloyd | BUSH, Addie (blk) | 01 MAR 1864 |
| SMITH, Addison | LEE, Mary Jane (blk) | 03 OCT 1863 |
| SMITH, Addison M. [9n] | JACKSON, Sarah D. | 25 JUN 1859 |
| SMITH, Albert | STEVENS, Ailsey (blk) | 27 JAN 1866 |
| SMITH, Albert C. [10] | LITTLE, Caroline | 03 MAR 1863 |
| SMITH, Albert L. [11] | BEALL, Anna M. | 28 OCT 1865 |
| SMITH, Aleck | CARTWRIGHT, Mary Elizabeth (blk) | 22 JUN 1863 |
| SMITH, Alexander | CHAMBERS, Sarah E. (blk) | 27 APR 1867 |
| SMITH, Alexander B. | WORTHINGTON, Ella | 14 NOV 1863 |
| SMITH, Alfred | MILFORD, Dora (blk) | 20 JUL 1867 |
| SMITH, Alfred | MATHEWS, Julia (blk) | 05 FEB 1869 |
| SMITH, Alfred F. | BELT, Mary V. (blk) | 31 MAR 1869 |
| SMITH, Ambrose | LEWIS, Ann Maria (blk) | 10 JUL 1865 |
| SMITH, Andrew | RAINSBURG, Mary Louisa | 06 FEB 1865 |
| SMITH, Andrew C. | BOGGES, Frances C. | 30 OCT 1858 |
| SMITH, Augustus W. | HARDY, Henrietta E. | 20 SEP 1864 |
| SMITH, Billy | BRACE, Harriet (blk) | 07 NOV 1865 |
| SMITH, Charles | DAVIS, Mary (blk) | 17 NOV 1859 |
| SMITH, Charles | WILLEY, Mary E. | 22 OCT 1861 |
| SMITH, Charles | FLINN, Margaret | 21 AUG 1861 |
| SMITH, Charles | KIFFER, Jane | 08 SEP 1862 |
| SMITH, Charles | SCOTT, Julia (blk) | 07 NOV 1867 |
| SMITH, Charles | BARNACLE, Carrie | 03 MAY 1869 |
| SMITH, Charles | SHILES, Jane | 04 APR 1870 |
| SMITH, Charles H. | SIMS, Sarah (blk) | 02 NOV 1865 |
| SMITH, Charles H. | BRINKMAN, Caroline | 30 JUL 1867 |
| SMITH, Christian H. | BEERS, Julia | 29 JAN 1864 |
| SMITH, Curtis | GODDARD, Rebecca | 28 MAR 1865 |
| SMITH, Daniel A. | VAUGHAN, Margaret (blk) | 19 DEC 1864 |
| SMITH, David | SMITH, Alice (blk) | 23 JUN 1866 |
| SMITH, David | WILSON, Priscilla (blk) | 07 FEB 1867 |
| SMITH, Edward | MORTON, Adeline (blk) | 19 SEP 1867 |
| SMITH, Edward B. | WILLIAMSON, Ann L. | 27 SEP 1869 |
| SMITH, Edward S. [11] | ROCHE, Alice | 02 AUG 1865 |
| SMITH, Elia | ALEXANDER, Sandy | 05 JAN 1864 |

| | | |
|---|---|---|
| SMITH, Elijah H. | CONRAD, Anna M.F. | 17 JAN 1862 |
| SMITH, Emanuel | SAMPLE, Delilah | 17 DEC 1867 |
| SMITH, Erasmus D. | WHITMORE, Mary | 09 NOV 1867 |
| SMITH, F.H. [5] | BOYD, Nettie | 07 OCT 1868 |
| SMITH, Francis | SMALLWOOD, Elizabeth | 12 MAY 1863 |
| SMITH, Francis | ROTCHFORD, Georgianna | 07 DEC 1864 |
| SMITH, Frank | BENTLEY, Margaret C. | 29 MAY 1868 |
| SMITH, Frank | WILSON, Nettie | 25 JAN 1869 |
| SMITH, Frank A. | ENGLERT, Johanna M.S. | 03 MAR 1863 |
| SMITH, Frederick | WISEMULLER, Bettie | 25 FEB 1862 |
| SMITH, Frederick | HILL, Harriet (blk) | 30 MAY 1866 |
| SMITH, Gaston D. [of Gettysburg] [5] | KLINE, Ruth Anna | 26 JUN 1869 |
| SMITH, George | HOSMER, Mary | 26 OCT 1865 |
| SMITH, George | BROWN, Eliza (blk) | 14 JUN 1866 |
| SMITH, George | GREEN, Adaline (blk) | 17 MAR 1870 |
| SMITH, George A. | WILL, Mary E. | 03 OCT 1863 |
| SMITH, George L. | GLAZEBROOK, Ella C. | 17 AUG 1866 |
| SMITH, George S. [8] | TENNISON, Kate S. | 14 OCT 1869 |
| SMITH, George W. | ENDERS, Catherine | 21 JAN 1859 |
| SMITH, George W. | SMITH, Rachel M. | 26 FEB 1862 |
| SMITH, George W. | SIMS, Rebecca (blk) | 15 JUN 1863 |
| SMITH, George W. | SKINEAR, Sallie | 05 MAY 1865 |
| SMITH, George W. | JENNINGS, Lucy A.B. | 01 JUL 1865 |
| SMITH, George W. | MOCKABOY, Virginia (blk) | 09 AUG 1865 |
| SMITH, H. Clay | BOYD, Carrie A. | 21 MAR 1866 |
| SMITH, H.M. | DONALDSON, Ann Elizabeth | 14 AUG 1869 |
| SMITH, H.T. | STORY, Mollie F. | 15 FEB 1870 |
| SMITH, H.W. [11] | CLAGETT, Mary A. | 19 OCT 1867 |
| SMITH, Hampton | SMITH, Laura (blk) | 26 DEC 1866 |
| SMITH, Harrison | TAYLOR, Catherine (blk) | 20 OCT 1868 |
| SMITH, Helphestion C. | LARKIN, Penelope V. | 26 MAR 1860 |
| SMITH, Henry | BURCHE, Louisa | 12 AUG 1862 |
| SMITH, Henry | CAVANAUGH, Margaret | 09 FEB 1863 |
| SMITH, Henry | LOYLES, Mary (blk) | 11 NOV 1863 |
| SMITH, Henry | GAINES, Fanny (blk) | 08 NOV 1864 |
| SMITH, Henry | CANN, Amelia | 08 DEC 1864 |
| SMITH, Henry | PAGE, Milly (blk) | 23 DEC 1865 |
| SMITH, Henry | BONDS, Bettie (blk) | 18 OCT 1866 |
| SMITH, Henry | HOLLINS, Mary (blk) | 29 APR 1868 |
| SMITH, Henry | PRATT, Caroline (blk) | 11 AUG 1868 |
| SMITH, Henry | COOK, Joanna | 01 FEB 1869 |
| SMITH, Henry | BOWENS, Martha (blk) | 03 DEC 1869 |
| SMITH, Henry E. | SPALDING, Mary E. | 27 MAY 1870 |
| SMITH, Henry H. [1e] | HILTON, Annie | 18 NOV 1865 |
| SMITH, Henry W. [4] | McBLAIR, Virginia G. | 06 MAY 1863 |
| SMITH, Hesselius | JAMESON, J. Roberta | 15 JUN 1866 |
| SMITH, Hezekiah | DODSON, Frances (blk) | 04 JUN 1867 |
| SMITH, Hugh | PAGE, Harriet (blk) | 26 AUG 1865 |
| SMITH, Hugh K. | MOLNIEUX, Ellen L. | 25 JUN 1861 |
| SMITH, Isaac | HAMILTON, Susan E. | 30 MAR 1859 |
| SMITH, J.R. | HICKS, Sarah F. | 17 NOV 1868 |
| SMITH, Jacob | ASH, Lucy | 18 AUG 1865 |
| SMITH, Jacob F. | RIDDLE, Emma E. | 20 JUN 1860 |
| SMITH, Jacob S. | BARBER, Ella | 02 OCT 1869 |
| SMITH, James | SCOTT, Sarah (blk) | 19 MAY 1859 |
| SMITH, James | SMITH, Frances (blk) | 02 DEC 1862 |

District of Columbia Marriage Licenses, 1858-1870

| | | |
|---|---|---|
| SMITH, James | SULLIVAN, Mary | 17 JUL 1863 |
| SMITH, James | GREEN, Catherine | 29 AUG 1863 |
| SMITH, James | GASLEY, Elizabeth | 17 NOV 1863 |
| SMITH, James | CLIFFORD, Emma A. | 25 MAY 1864 |
| SMITH, James | ROBEY, Mary | 18 OCT 1864 |
| SMITH, James | GOINGS, Myra (blk) | 22 DEC 1864 |
| SMITH, James | JOHNSON, Martha (blk) | 10 APR 1866 |
| SMITH, James | HODGES, Ariana (blk) | 23 JUL 1866 |
| SMITH, James | NALLY, Margaret R. | 02 APR 1867 |
| SMITH, James | PRICE, Maria Louisa | 21 OCT 1867 |
| SMITH, James | HAWKINS, Julia | 17 JUN 1869 |
| SMITH, James A. | DAVIS, Laura V. | 17 JUN 1868 |
| SMITH, James C. | BROWN, Nettie | 06 JAN 1863 |
| SMITH, James D. [1e] | SHACKLEFORD, Isabel | 22 MAR 1866 |
| SMITH, James E. | ROCHE, Emma | 13 JAN 1863 |
| SMITH, James E. | HOPKINS, Martha | 18 OCT 1864 |
| SMITH, James G. | WADE, Olivia L. | 29 AUG 1863 |
| SMITH, James H. | KEMP, Mary V. | 03 MAR 1864 |
| SMITH, James H. | SMITH, Julia Ann (blk) | 15 JUL 1865 |
| SMITH, James Henry | COLEMAN, Mary Ann (blk) | 01 JUN 1864 |
| SMITH, James T. | MAHONEY, Mary Jane (col'd) | 28 DEC 1863 |
| SMITH, James W. | BENDER, Mary A. | 23 JUN 1868 |
| SMITH, James William Henry | DAVIS, Mary Ann (blk) | 08 DEC 1864 |
| SMITH, Jasper | KIECKHOEFER, Emily F. | 22 OCT 1866 |
| SMITH, Jedson | WILKISON, Sophia (blk) | 11 JUN 1863 |
| SMITH, Jerome | WILKISON, Sarah (blk) | 05 JUN 1863 |
| SMITH, Jesse | CARTER, Nancy (blk) | 21 MAY 1866 |
| SMITH, John | DUNN, Bridget | 08 APR 1862 |
| SMITH, John | LOVELESS, Florida | 19 JAN 1863 |
| SMITH, John | PINCKNEY, Priscilla (blk) | 05 JAN 1864 |
| SMITH, John | THORNTON, Giddy Ann (blk) | 06 JAN 1864 |
| SMITH, John | OVALL, Ann | 25 APR 1864 |
| SMITH, John | TALBURT, Elizabeth (blk) | 15 JUN 1864 |
| SMITH, John | DUCKETT, Ann (blk) | 16 AUG 1864 |
| SMITH, John | TAYLOR, Annie Elizabeth | 27 SEP 1865 |
| SMITH, John | SMITH, Elizabeth (blk) | 12 OCT 1865 |
| SMITH, John | JOHNSON, Joanna (blk) | 04 JAN 1866 |
| SMITH, John | NAMAN, Isabella | 30 AUG 1866 |
| SMITH, John | PFEIL, Augusta | 04 DEC 1867 |
| SMITH, John | COLLINS, Fanny (blk) | 08 FEB 1869 |
| SMITH, John A. | HARSHMON, Sarah S. | 15 NOV 1862 |
| SMITH, John Alexr. | RIDDELL, Louisa | 29 OCT 1861 |
| SMITH, John F. | COLCLASER, Margaret J. | 21 NOV 1861 |
| SMITH, John G. | McVEY, Louisa B. | 15 JUN 1864 |
| SMITH, John H. | ASHTON, sarah | 18 JUN 1865 |
| SMITH, John M. | CARROLL, Emily Kate | 31 MAR 1866 |
| SMITH, John W. [6le] | MARINER, Maria | 30 SEP 1865 |
| SMITH, Joseph | NOLAND, Jane | 05 OCT 1863 |
| SMITH, Joseph | McLEANEY, Annie | 15 JUL 1865 |
| SMITH, Joseph | HARREN, Eliza Ann (blk) | 30 DEC 1865 |
| SMITH, Joseph | WILSON, Henrietta | 08 AUG 1867 |
| SMITH, Joseph M. | SELBY, Margaret | 06 MAR 1869 |
| SMITH, Joseph S., Dr. | PROUT, Lizzie L. | 05 OCT 1859 |
| SMITH, Joshua | JONES, Nancy (blk) | 05 JAN 1866 |
| SMITH, Judson H. | BRUCE, Annie | 24 SEP 1861 |
| SMITH, Kendrick J. [6m] | PEABODY, Julia O. | 25 NOV 1863 |

District of Columbia Marriage Licenses, 1858-1870

| | | |
|---|---|---|
| SMITH, Lewis | NICKOLS, Caroline | 18 APR 1865 |
| SMITH, Lewis F. | LASHER, Caroline | 12 JAN 1865 |
| SMITH, Lewis M. | SHREVE, Mary G. | 06 JUN 1866 |
| SMITH, Lloyd | BARNES, Charlotte (blk) | 22 OCT 1864 |
| SMITH, Madison | COUNTEE, Julia | 06 AUG 1868 |
| SMITH, Manuel | HOWARD, Susan (blk) | 30 DEC 1869 |
| SMITH, Martin | THOHENSTEIN, Mary | 04 SEP 1863 |
| SMITH, Montgomery P. | ROSS, Mary B. | 02 SEP 1867 |
| SMITH, Moses | CARTER, Harriet (blk) | 15 AUG 1867 |
| SMITH, Moses | SMITH, Polly (blk) | 16 JUN 1868 |
| SMITH, Moses M. | FURLONG, Alexina Virginia | 29 JUN 1865 |
| SMITH, Nathaniel | HAMMOND, Emerline (blk) | 01 JAN 1861 |
| SMITH, Nelson | PURTY, Malinda | 24 MAR 1870 |
| SMITH, Newton K. | GRANT, Eliza | 04 APR 1866 |
| SMITH, Norburn | FAIRFAX, Mary | 16 DEC 1864 |
| SMITH, Odrick | SMITH, Caroline (blk) | 16 SEP 1869 |
| SMITH, Patrick | NILAND, Sarah | 19 NOV 1863 |
| SMITH, Patrick Henry | MOCKABEE, Emma Frances | 12 NOV 1864 |
| SMITH, Payne | JONES, Milly (blk) | 30 NOV 1867 |
| SMITH, Perry | POWELL, Rachel | 27 JUL 1869 |
| SMITH, Peter C. | FAUNCE, Lydia | 29 OCT 1868 |
| SMITH, Reuben | LEE, Eliza (blk) | 01 JAN 1867 |
| SMITH, Richard | BUZZEY, Lizzette | 10 OCT 1863 |
| SMITH, Richard | SELBY, Elizabeth (blk) | 30 MAR 1864 |
| SMITH, Richard | WALLINGTONN, Susan (blk) | 25 JAN 1866 |
| SMITH, Richard | DYER, Malinda (blk) | 30 JUN 1869 |
| SMITH, Richard | SPRINGSTEEL, Lottie | 07 APR 1870 |
| SMITH, Richard C. [6m] | WOOD, Frances A.E. | 09 FEB 1863 |
| SMITH, Richard G. | LUXON, Annie E. | 06 AUG 1867 |
| SMITH, Richard R. | WILLIAMS, Mary (blk) | 09 SEP 1863 |
| SMITH, Richard [6c] | KING, Rebecca Ann | 09 NOV 1858 |
| SMITH, Richard [7b] | RIDGEWAY, Harriet | 04 SEP 1869 |
| SMITH, Robert | KNOTT, Mary A. | 22 JAN 1866 |
| SMITH, Robert | FENDRICK, Mary (blk) | 21 JUN 1866 |
| SMITH, Robert | WHITE, Julia (blk) | 04 AUG 1866 |
| SMITH, Robert | QUINN, Emma | 14 JAN 1867 |
| SMITH, Robert | HAMPSHIRE, Mary (blk) | 24 JUL 1869 |
| SMITH, Robert | MILES, Nancy (blk) | 15 MAR 1870 |
| SMITH, Samuel | POWELL, Anna (blk) | 17 NOV 1864 |
| SMITH, Samuel | BANKS, Julia (blk) | 09 JAN 1865 |
| SMITH, Samuel R. | McNALLEN, Maggie | 10 OCT 1864 |
| SMITH, Sandy Alex. Burbank Stewart | GREEN, Patsy (blk) | 05 FEB 1864 |
| SMITH, Silas O. | CONNELL, Martina | 28 OCT 1864 |
| SMITH, Solomon | WASHINGTON, Martha (blk) | 18 FEB 1867 |
| SMITH, Solomon H. | GIBBONS, Mary | 20 JUL 1860 |
| SMITH, Spencer | GALLOWAY, Cheena (blk) | 19 JAN 1869 |
| SMITH, Thomas [10] | HUNTER, Mary | 27 SEP 1865 |
| SMITH, Thomas | BRYAN, Rebecca (blk) | 20 SEP 1866 |
| SMITH, Thomas C. | HAZARD, Cornelia Frances | 17 OCT 1864 |
| SMITH, Thomas H. | TINKLER, Mary A. | 20 JUN 1865 |
| SMITH, Thomas R. [13c] | YATES, Elizabeth (blk) | 14 NOV 1859 |
| SMITH, Thornton | ABBOTT, Kate | 29 DEC 1862 |
| SMITH, Toliver | WEAVER, Nora (blk) | 10 APR 1867 |
| SMITH, W. Scott | DUBANT, Annie M. | 25 FEB 1870 |
| SMITH, William | GOODRICH, Mary Ellen | 05 NOV 1861 |
| SMITH, William | SIMES, Mary Louisa | 29 APR 1863 |

District of Columbia Marriage Licenses, 1858-1870

| Groom | Bride | Date |
|---|---|---|
| SMITH, William | HARRISON, Elizabeth (blk) | 26 DEC 1863 |
| SMITH, William | SMITH, Mary (blk) | 14 JUL 1864 |
| SMITH, William | TAYLOR, Elizabeth (blk) | 13 FEB 1865 |
| SMITH, William | SHERWOOD, Annie | 15 FEB 1866 |
| SMITH, William | HALL, Jane (blk) | 15 JAN 1866 |
| SMITH, William | BIRD, Rebecca (blk) | 10 SEP 1867 |
| SMITH, William | PARKS, Martha | 17 SEP 1867 |
| SMITH, William | LEE, Agnes (blk) | 22 SEP 1868 |
| SMITH, William | CROSBY, Emeline (blk) | 24 SEP 1868 |
| SMITH, William | CAUSTEN, Mary (blk) | 22 DEC 1868 |
| SMITH, William | ROCHE, Catharine | 29 APR 1869 |
| SMITH, William | MOORE, Caroline (blk) | 24 DEC 1869 |
| SMITH, William | WILLIAMS, Mary (blk) | 02 DEC 1869 |
| SMITH, William A. | THOMPSON, Elizabeth (blk) | 14 DEC 1864 |
| SMITH, Wm. B. | YOUNG, Elizabeth | 28 AUG 1862 |
| SMITH, William Coad | VENABLE, Catherine Clay | 07 NOV 1860 |
| SMITH, William E. | SMITH, Mary | 29 NOV 1864 |
| SMITH, William H. | TUCKER, Sophia S. | 28 SEP 1859 |
| SMITH, William H. | NICHOLS, Augusta | 14 OCT 1863 |
| SMITH, William H. | SMITH, Martha J. (blk) | 29 DEC 1866 |
| SMITH, William H. | MANN, Fanny E. | 02 AUG 1869 |
| SMITH, William H.H. | ALLYN, Maria B. | 07 OCT 1865 |
| SMITH, William J. | COCHRANE, Anna Maria | 08 DEC 1864 |
| SMITH, Wm. J. | STONE, Margaret | 11 FEB 1864 |
| SMITH, William J. | KEENE, Charlotte M. | 02 JAN 1866 |
| SMITH, William M. (1st Mo. Vol. G C.) | ELLSWORTH, Margaret | 27 JUL 1864 |
| SMITH, William M. | CRUMP, Elmira (blk) | 26 JUN 1866 |
| SMITH, William R. | FAUCETT, Hannah M. | 06 AUG 1862 |
| SMITH, Wilson | DAVIS, Mary (blk) | 09 OCT 1867 |
| SMITH, Zerah A. | DONALDSON, Sarah C. | 19 NOV 1862 |
| SMITHSON, Charles F. | FERGUSON, Alice J. | 03 SEP 1862 |
| SMITHSON, Isaac | GINK, Mary Ann | 25 SEP 1862 |
| SMOOT, David | POSEY, Josephine | 16 JUN 1864 |
| SMOOT, E.D. | WANNALL, Tilly | 18 MAR 1870 |
| SMOOT, Samuel | BATES, Levisa (blk) | 17 SEP 1867 |
| SMOOT, Sellman | FLOYD, Kate | 11 SEP 1865 |
| SMOTHERS, Lemuel | DINES, Charlotte Ann (blk) | 27 APR 1864 |
| SMOTHERS, Moses | PAIN, Mary (blk) | 26 DEC 1865 |
| SMOTHERS, Thomas | HAWKINS, Margaret (blk) | 27 JAN 1868 |
| SMYLER, Lloyd | HARRIS, Anna (blk) | 04 MAY 1869 |
| SMYSER, Jacob H., Lt. | SWETT, Caroline F. | 16 MAY 1861 |
| SMYTH, Charles Frederick [10] | SWORD, Mary Elizabeth | 10 FEB 1864 |
| SMYTH, George H. | GOODRICH, Josepha F. | 10 FEB 1865 |
| SNEAD, George | MAJOR, Juliet (blk) | 15 SEP 1868 |
| SNEAD, William D. | BRANSON, Mary E. (blk) | 05 JAN 1870 |
| SNELLINGS, Beverly T. | DEMENT, Barbara | 31 AUG 1865 |
| SNELLINGS, George T. | CURTIS, Olive Smith | 07 FEB 1870 |
| SNIDER, Andrew | KNOX, Etmonia (blk) | 19 NOV 1868 |
| SNIDER, George William | BROWN, Mary Levenia | 22 FEB 1859 |
| SNIFFEN, Culver C. | JACOBI, Ada H. | 16 JUN 1866 |
| SNOOKS, Lucius | PHIPS, Cordelia | 08 NOV 1866 |
| SNOWDEN, Albert | TAYLOR, Mary (blk) | 05 DEC 1866 |
| SNOWDEN, Gurden | MUSE, Sarah (blk) | 13 MAY 1868 |
| SNOWDEN, Isaac | CASTOR, Sarah (blk) | 27 DEC 1869 |
| SNOWDEN, John | JACKSON, Anna (blk) | 13 JUN 1867 |
| SNOWDEN, John Wesley | BELL, Jane | 19 FEB 1863 |

| | | |
|---|---|---|
| SNOWDEN, Preston | AYTES, Salina (blk) | 09 NOV 1868 |
| SNOWDEN, Richard | HALL, Susan (blk) | 27 JUN 1866 |
| SNOWDEN, Spencer A. | YOUNG, Sarah (blk) | 24 MAR 1869 |
| SNOWDEN, Wesley | MASON, Eliza (blk) | 21 JUL 1869 |
| SNOWDEN, William A. | DENT, Eliza Jane | 18 NOV 1862 |
| SNYDER, Asa P. | DeQUIET, Georgiana | 14 OCT 1862 |
| SNYDER, Frederick | SIMPSON, Kate | 05 JUL 1865 |
| SNYDER, Jacob | BARRY, Virginia | 31 MAR 1859 |
| SNYDER, James A. | ELIASON, Mary | 06 MAR 1862 |
| SNYDER, John F. | PARROTT, Eliza | 29 MAY 1867 |
| SODEN, Taylor | KANE, Annie Virginia | 23 FEB 1869 |
| SOFIELD, Otis G. | KLINE, Mollie E. | 16 JUN 1864 |
| SOHL, Augustus | FLECK, Sophia | 14 MAR 1861 |
| SOHON, Gustavus | GROH, Julia | 28 APR 1863 |
| SOLLERS, John A. | SUDDATH, Casander E. | 11 FEB 1861 |
| SOLLERS, William A. | TOWNER, Cora | 31 DEC 1867 |
| SOLLEY, Thomas W. | HILLEARY, Sarah W. | 11 APR 1870 |
| SOLMONSON, Moses | BRAUNSHEIG, Theresa | 14 NOV 1864 |
| SOLMS, Joseph P. | HARRY, Margaret | 18 JAN 1865 |
| SOLOMON, Daniel G. | BURK, Mary E. (blk) | 31 MAR 1864 |
| SOLOMON, David | ADLER, Bertha | 20 NOV 1868 |
| SOLOMON, Thos. W. | SPEAKE, Emma J. | 18 JAN 1870 |
| SOMARIBA, Anthony | SULLIVAN, Margaret | 15 APR 1865 |
| SOMERS, Aaron | MILES, Martha (blk) | 01 SEP 1866 |
| SOMERS, Arthur | MARTIN, Eleanor | 01 AUG 1868 |
| SOMERS, Matthew | HARNETT, Catharine | 07 APR 1865 |
| SOMERS, Matthew | COLLINS, Margaret | 19 JAN 1866 |
| SOMERS, William H. [10] | COXSIN, Mary | 02 MAY 1868 |
| SOMERVILLE, William | MANKINS, Susan | 28 MAR 1863 |
| SOMMERS, George | OUER, Annie R. | 12 SEP 1865 |
| SOMMERS, Israel [2] | GOMPF, Mary | 22 MAY 1867 |
| SOMMERS, Philip | McAVOY, Rose | 01 SEP 1865 |
| SOMMERVILLE, Abraham | GILLISS, Ailsey (blk) | 10 SEP 1862 |
| SOMMERVILLE, Thomas | BROWN, Ellen (blk) | 02 AUG 1869 |
| SONNEBORN, Henry | BECKER, Mina | 02 SEP 1862 |
| SONNENBERG, Ernst | SELL, Fredericke | 19 JUN 1861 |
| SOONES, William | GANTT, Louisa (blk) | 13 MAR 1865 |
| SOPER, Anthony W. | WATERS, Susan Elizabeth | 11 APR 1868 |
| SOPER, Charles H. | SUPLEE, Emma | 14 DEC 1863 |
| SOPER, John H. [6l] | MURPHEY, Mary | 14 OCT 1861 |
| SOPER, John H. | SHERWOOD, Priscilla | 06 MAR 1862 |
| SORG, Joseph | WELCH, Mary | 17 SEP 1858 |
| SORREL, Thomas | COLEMAN, Ella (blk) | 22 JUN 1865 |
| SORRELL, Charles | JERMON, Mary E. | 15 JUN 1865 |
| SORRELL, James H. | MARTIN, Sarah J. | 27 APR 1870 |
| SOTER, George F. | SCHUANDER, Mary | 23 FEB 1870 |
| SOTHORON, George M. | SHERRY, Sarah L. | 01 OCT 1867 |
| SOTHORON, J.B.F. | WILLIAMS, Ann R. | 08 JUN 1864 |
| SOTHORON, John R. | SKIDMORE, Roberta | 18 OCT 1858 |
| SOUL, Charles H. [12s] | PAIGE, Mary E. | 18 APR 1863 |
| SOULÈ, J. Hartley | BAYLISS, Helen M. | 23 OCT 1867 |
| SOULES, Ezra C. | GODFREY, Eliza E. | 04 APR 1864 |
| SOULHEIM, Joseph | GOODMAN, Barbara | 07 SEP 1865 |
| SOUTHARD, Henry L. | RANEY, Mary | 06 APR 1863 |
| SOUTHARD, John T. | SUDDETH, Elizabeth | 21 JUN 1860 |
| SOUTHEY, John | COKEN, Mary | 10 OCT 1867 |

District of Columbia Marriage Licenses, 1858-1870

| | | |
|---|---|---|
| SOWER, John | SCHUBERT, Barbara | 05 JUL 1866 |
| SOWERS, William H. | GORDON, Josephine L. | 18 MAY 1870 |
| SPAID, James | McDONALD, Hanora | 03 MAR 1862 |
| SPAIN, Richard W. [12s] | HOOVER, Eliza T. | 21 DEC 1861 |
| SPALDING, Daniel | DOWNEY, Cacelia R. | 02 NOV 1858 |
| SPALDING, Enoch J. [1c] | RITTER, Helen S. | 20 AUG 1862 |
| SPALDING, John R. [9n] | CARROLL, Matilda A. | 18 OCT 1859 |
| SPALDING, Salathiel Martin | BARRETT, Emma Cornelia | 06 JUN 1864 |
| SPANGLER, Jacob W. | GREEN, Helen R. | 26 OCT 1864 |
| SPANIER, John P. | SCHWARTZ, Esther E. | 14 OCT 1862 |
| SPARKS, Frederick R. | HART, Kate | 26 SEP 1864 |
| SPARKS, Jared F. | LAWSON, Matilda A. | 04 FEB 1870 |
| SPARKS, William | SPARKS, Mary (blk) | 28 AUG 1868 |
| SPARSHOT, Charles Aldrich | EDWARDS, Emma Jane | 13 OCT 1868 |
| SPARSHOTT, Edward Henry | ELDERGRAVE, Louisa | 16 JAN 1868 |
| SPATES, Charles F. | ELLET, Mary Ann | 08 JUN 1862 |
| SPEAK, Harrison | DADE, Roberta (blk) | 21 FEB 1867 |
| SPEAKS, James | DOUGLASS, Rebecca (blk) | 18 FEB 1869 |
| SPEAKS, James H. | THOMPSON, Louisa | 21 MAR 1860 |
| SPEAKS, W.H. | HARRIS, Ann Maria (blk) | 14 APR 1869 |
| SPEAR, Hiram | PETTIGREW, Emma D. | 24 SEP 1862 |
| SPEAR, James T. | HURDLE, Alice M. | 18 JUL 1860 |
| SPEARING, Samuel J. [7b] | MURRAY, Mary H. | 15 JUN 1869 |
| SPECHT, Charles | LINK, Seraphina | 27 APR 1870 |
| SPECHT, Philip | MILLER, Mary M. | 17 DEC 1860 |
| SPECK, Richard | BENESCH, Hermine | 11 APR 1870 |
| SPEDDEN, William E. | DAVIS, Mary S. | 09 OCT 1866 |
| SPEICER, John [Henry] [10] | GADDIS, Joanna | 10 OCT 1866 |
| SPEIDEN, James F. | GORMLEY, Kate | 12 DEC 1860 |
| SPEIR, T. Hamilton | CLEPHANE, Mary A. | 22 MAY 1861 |
| SPEISS, Albert | REAGAN, Jane | 28 APR 1868 |
| SPEKES, Sandy | WILLIAMS, Octavia (blk) | 26 FEB 1867 |
| SPELLAGHN, Jeremiah | BLANCHFIELD, Mary | 02 FEB 1867 |
| SPELLERBERG, Edward | JÖHANNING, Josephine | 18 APR 1863 |
| SPELLMAN, Clement | TRIBBY, Mary E. | 26 OCT 1867 |
| SPELLMAN, Henry | DYSON, Delia (blk) | 18 FEB 1867 |
| SPENCE, Christopher | NEWELL, Catherine J. | 12 FEB 1859 |
| SPENCE, Thomas Wm. | POWELL, Annie G. | 10 OCT 1863 |
| SPENCER, Albert | TAYLOR, Delia (blk) | 03 JAN 1867 |
| SPENCER, Charles W. | MILES, Lizzie S. | 16 NOV 1858 |
| SPENCER, George | HENDERSON, Catherine O. | 30 DEC 1863 |
| SPENCER, George H. [10] | HOWARD, Catharine (blk) | 08 JUL 1865 |
| SPENCER, James | BEAVERS, Lydia A. | 28 DEC 1858 |
| SPENCER, John Henry [2] | MARTIN, Florence Virginia | 13 MAR 1865 |
| SPENCER, John T. | SMITH, Alice Virginia | 18 FEB 1869 |
| SPENCER, Munroe | JONES, Lucy (blk) | 16 OCT 1865 |
| SPENCER, Robert B. | FINCH, Mary Ann | 25 FEB 1864 |
| SPENCER, William | ANDERSON, Virginia | 20 OCT 1862 |
| SPENCER, William | HARVEY, Harriet (blk) | 29 JUN 1865 |
| SPENCER, William J. | TAYLOR, Emma B. | 12 JAN 1870 |
| SPERBER, George | GIBB, Annie | 01 JUN 1867 |
| SPERLIN, Peter | ARNOLD, Rosa | 23 DEC 1864 |
| SPICER, Erasmus | GRIMSLY, Sarah | 15 AUG 1865 |
| SPICER, Walter J. | BEAM, Margaret M. | 27 JUL 1865 |
| SPICHT, Anton | PFL_G, Kate | 21 JAN 1865 |
| SPIEARE, Frank A. | FRENCH, Harriet E. | 28 APR 1870 |

District of Columbia Marriage Licenses, 1858-1870

| | | |
|---|---|---|
| SPIELMAN, Jacob R. [8] | SHREEVE, Mary J. | 15 APR 1868 |
| SPIES, Peter | ROTH, Anna Barbara | 04 OCT 1869 |
| SPILKER, Anton Henry | GRABANKAMP, Anna Mary | 20 AUG 1864 |
| SPILLAND, Benjamin | FORD, Mary (blk) | 24 JUL 1862 |
| SPILLER, Alexander | CALVERT, Catherine (blk) | 25 SEP 1863 |
| SPILLMAN, Benjamin | TURNER, Rebecca (blk) | 19 DEC 1863 |
| SPILLMAN, James H. | RICE, Elizabeth A. | 31 MAY 1859 |
| SPILLMAN, James H. | TRIMMER, Caroline L. | 20 JAN 1869 |
| SPILMAN, John T. | COLLINS, Julia A. | 26 DEC 1861 |
| SPINNEY, Joseph S. | LODER, Emily A. | 15 MAY 1866 |
| SPONDOWITZCH, John | POSPICCHILL, Veronica | 29 JAN 1863 |
| SPONSHOLZ, John Carl Augustus | WATSON, Maria F. | 08 SEP 1864 |
| SPOTSWOOD, James M.A. | HENNING, Ariana | 27 DEC 1864 |
| SPRAGUE, Augustus M. | SIMMONS, Mary | 27 SEP 1862 |
| SPRAGUE, Lyman S. | PASQUAY, Emelie C. | 17 AUG 1867 |
| SPRAGUE, William (of R.I.) | CHASE, Kate | 12 NOV 1863 |
| SPRANDEL, Julius | HANSON, Mary | 07 SEP 1864 |
| SPREADBURY, Henry | REDDY, Elizabeth | 25 MAR 1865 |
| SPREOPER, Christian | MILLER, Catharine | 07 APR 1864 |
| SPRIGG, Daniel | THOMAS, Martha (blk) | 15 AUG 1865 |
| SPRIGG, Horace | JOHNSON, Hannah A. (blk) | 13 AUG 1862 |
| SPRIGG, Nathan | CONTEE, Maria (blk) | 28 JAN 1865 |
| SPRIGG, Thomas | TOPHAM, Caroline (blk) | 03 NOV 1864 |
| SPRIGG, Thomas | CARROLL, Julia (blk) | 30 JUN 1865 |
| SPRIGGS, Horace [12s] | BUTLER, Margaret | 16 AUG 1861 |
| SPRINGER, Edward T. [4] | GOSNELL, Anna R. | 21 MAY 1866 |
| SPRINGER, Frank A. | BATES, Anna Virginia | 02 OCT 1866 |
| SPRINGER, Thomas W. | NALLS, Mary T. | 01 OCT 1863 |
| SPRINGMAN, George A. | WINHOFER, Rosina Sophia | 30 NOV 1863 |
| SPRINGMAN, James | HENSON, Susan | 07 SEP 1865 |
| SPRINGMAN, James H. | MOORE, Joanna | 12 DEC 1863 |
| SPRINGMAN, James William | STANLEY, Bernetta | 26 MAY 1869 |
| SPRINGMAN, John Thomas | EDD, Lucinda | 09 JUL 1862 |
| SPRINGMANN, Frederick | REILY, Mary | 02 JAN 1868 |
| SPRINGSGUTH, Reynold | NIEDERHOFER, Mary | 16 JUL 1864 |
| SPROSS, A. | WEISS, Magdalene | 29 JUN 1863 |
| SPROSSER, John | BREMER, Mary | 11 APR 1859 |
| SPROUSE, William | WRIGHT, Jennie E. | 16 JAN 1868 |
| SQUIRES, Joseph C. | BROWN, Mary E. | 28 FEB 1867 |
| SQUIRES, William H. | GARNER, Mary R. | 08 JUL 1861 |
| STABLER, William H. | SULLIVAN, Ellen | 23 MAY 1865 |
| STACK, Patrick | FITZGERALD, Joanna | 18 JUL 1865 |
| STACKE, James | GARING, Mary | 14 JAN 1859 |
| STACKPOLE, Thomas | RILEY, Margaret | 30 APR 1861 |
| STAELTEL, William | MENZMAY, Frederika | 14 JUL 1859 |
| STAFFORD, Peter | MOORE, Fanny | 16 SEP 1862 |
| STAHL, Jacob | BARGAN, Julia | 02 NOV 1863 |
| STAHL, Thomas B. [6s] | FOWLER, Emma | 19 NOV 1864 |
| STAILEY, Samuel | SIPES, Margaret E. | 18 SEP 1867 |
| STALCUP, Samuel Fletcher | DEEBLE, Martha Jane | 25 JUN 1869 |
| STALLINGS, James Osceola [1e] | SHERWOOD, Jane E. | 24 APR 1865 |
| STALY, John | STONE, Eliza | 03 JUL 1861 |
| STANARD, John B. | PETER, Brittie K. | 14 OCT 1868 |
| STANFORD, William Mandeville | HANDY, Elizabeth Laurie Beck | 14 APR 1862 |
| STANHOPE, Joseph Perry [12s] | MOORE, Louisa | 08 JAN 1863 |
| STANLEY, James | CHISM, Amanda | 09 OCT 1862 |

| | | |
|---|---|---|
| STANLEY, Patrick | THOMPSON, Mary Elizth. | 01 NOV 1862 |
| STANSIL, Elijah | WILLIAMS, Emma | 30 AUG 1864 |
| STANTON, George | BROWN, Rachel (blk) | 16 NOV 1864 |
| STANTON, Harry | SHAFFER, Mary M. | 27 FEB 1865 |
| STANTON, James | KAVANAUGH, Catherine | 12 NOV 1863 |
| STANTON, John | BENJAMIN, Ann Sophia | 24 JUL 1868 |
| STANTON, Thomas J. | HOWE, Rebecca M. | 15 DEC 1868 |
| STAPLES, Robert | ROHLEDER, Frances | 22 MAR 1865 |
| STARK, Charles | WIGGINS, Mary (blk) | 02 JUL 1867 |
| STARK, Henry | GETTNER, Sophie | 01 JUL 1865 |
| STARK, William F. | HAWKINS, Annie Augusta | 08 MAY 1869 |
| STARKE, Albert | HAUF, Mary | 09 FEB 1864 |
| STARKS, Herbert | ROUNDS, Louise (blk) | 15 NOV 1866 |
| STARR, Peter | SCHLEIGH, Adelaide L. | 02 JUN 1864 |
| STAUB, John W. | RUSSELL, Jane | 12 FEB 1870 |
| STAUB, William H. | GILLIAN, Jennie | 09 SEP 1867 |
| STAUNTON, Alonzo | CLARK, Elizabeth Jane | 26 AUG 1864 |
| STEBBS, John H., Col. [11] | STRATTON, Carrie A. | 21 FEB 1866 |
| STEELE, Charles T. | POORTS, Mary Frances | 17 APR 1861 |
| STEELE, Edwin T. | BLADEN, Georgiana | 19 NOV 1863 |
| STEELE, Henry F. | STEWART, Henrietta V. | 25 NOV 1869 |
| STEELE, Jabez C. | ROOT, Clara | 07 JUN 1864 |
| STEELE, James | WASHBURN, Eunice C. | 03 JUL 1867 |
| STEELE, James R. [7a] | LEWIS, Jane L. | 11 SEP 1866 |
| STEELE, Thomas J. | TURNER, Eliza Ellen | 14 NOV 1859 |
| STEELE, Thomas M. [6h] | DAVIS, Mary H. | 20 JUL 1868 |
| STEELE, William [2] | MATTINGLY, Cornelia Jane [Clark] | 09 NOV 1867 |
| STEELE, William H. | MATTINGLY, Minerva A. | 09 MAY 1864 |
| STEELYARD, James | OWENS, Maria (blk) | 31 MAR 1870 |
| STEEN, Isaac [Capt.] [2] | HILTON, Elizabeth [Mrs.] | 04 JUL 1864 |
| STEEN, Thomas | DONNELLY, Margaret | 31 MAY 1865 |
| STEEP, Thomas M. | ORR, Mary A. | 07 JAN 1864 |
| STEER, Francis* | DOUGHERTY, Rachel Thomas | 28 NOV 1859 |
| STEEVER, Charles L. | STONE, Sarah A. | 23 APR 1868 |
| STEGALL, Henry W. | MELLEN, Alice | 23 FEB 1860 |
| STEGLICK, Charles August | McGARVEY, Julia | 07 MAY 1868 |
| STEIN, John | SIMMONS, Mary Elizabeth | 20 APR 1867 |
| STEINACKER, Franz | MINDER, Anna Maria | 31 AUG 1867 |
| STEINBERG, Adolph | GOLDMAN, Veilchen | 09 APR 1869 |
| STEINBERG, Benedict | COHN, Betty | 13 OCT 1864 |
| STEINBERGER, Charles Henry | HESS, Elizabeth | 23 JUL 1863 |
| STEINER, George | WESSELS, Rosina | 21 NOV 1865 |
| STEINER, Joseph | HARBIN, Lula | 02 OCT 1869 |
| STEINITZKI, August | WOLZ, Mary | 29 JAN 1866 |
| STEINMETZ, William George | McKELDEN, Jennie C. | 21 NOV 1864 |
| STEPHENS, Charles | WEBSTER, Frances | 08 NOV 1862 |
| STEPHENS, George | WATKINS, Rachel N. (blk) | 12 FEB 1870 |
| STEPHENS, Richard H. | GARRISON, Martha A. | 13 MAR 1860 |
| STEPHENSON, Jacob | POSEY, Elizabeth (blk) | 10 APR 1867 |
| STEPHENSON, James O. | FEENY, Sarah | 14 FEB 1862 |
| STEPHENSON, John | STEPHENSON, Jane (blk) | 11 JUN 1868 |
| STEPTOE, James W. | MICKENS, Lucy (blk) | 30 AUG 1864 |
| STERICK, Sylvester T.F. | JONES, Loulie A. | 15 DEC 1868 |
| STERLING, James T. | WEBSTER, Sallie M. | 19 JUL 1862 |
| STERLING, Jos. A. | KNOWLES, Adaline P. | 01 JUN 1866 |
| STERN, George | MICHAELS, Jeannette | 27 NOV 1869 |

District of Columbia Marriage Licenses, 1858-1870

| | | |
|---|---|---|
| STERN, John U. | LINCOLN, Josephine C. | 30 JUN 1859 |
| STERNBERG, Hezekiah | CLARK, Elizabeth E. | 14 DEC 1867 |
| STERNER, James | DECKER, Mary Rosanna | 26 OCT 1865 |
| STETLER, John K. | DUNLAP, Lydia J. | 20 JUN 1861 |
| STETTINNIS, Joseph S. | McKNEW, Maria R. | 30 JUL 1866 |
| STETSON, William Wallace | WRIGHT, Caroline Virginia | 04 JUN 1864 |
| STETSON, Wyllys S. | BATES, Mary R. | 19 MAY 1868 |
| STEUART, Alexander Sommerville | NOURSE, Emmie Josepha | 01 SEP 1860 |
| STEVEN, Henry B. | SALLE, Mary A. | 29 MAR 1861 |
| STEVENER, Henry | MILLER, Elizabeth | 27 FEB 1863 |
| STEVENS, Austin | JOHNSON, Mary C. (blk) | 14 JUL 1866 |
| STEVENS, Charles | MOLTH, Margaret | 26 JUL 1862 |
| STEVENS, Edward C. | KNIGHT, Mary L. | 04 FEB 1869 |
| STEVENS, George W. [6s] | McGARR [or Magar], Brittannia | 05 OCT 1864 |
| STEVENS, Henry Clay | RHODES, Caroline | 27 SEP 1859 |
| STEVENS, James Durell | BROWNE, Caroline Frances | 20 FEB 1865 |
| STEVENS, John T. | JONES, Catherine | 07 JAN 1864 |
| STEVENS, John W. [12s] | CAWTHORN, Rosalind M. | 25 APR 1859 |
| STEVENS, Levi | BENNETT, Vina F. | 06 APR 1868 |
| STEVENS, Morgan | ROBINSON, Omanda | 11 JUN 1858 |
| STEVENS, Samuel F. | LANCESTER, Judeth A. | 08 AUG 1861 |
| STEVENS, Thos. | WELSH, Margt. | 19 JUL 1861 |
| STEVENS, William | HARRINGTON, Mary | 10 MAY 1862 |
| STEVENS, William | RISING, Sarah Virginia | 02 NOV 1868 |
| STEVENSON, George | JACKSON, Margaret (blk) | 06 NOV 1866 |
| STEVENSON, Henry | MATTHEWS, Josephine (blk) | 11 MAR 1867 |
| STEVENSON, James H. | GRAY, Elizabeth | 21 MAY 1867 |
| STEVENSON, John Henry | JONES, Maria (blk) | 23 JUL 1868 |
| STEVENSON, Richard | BELL, Lavinia (blk) | 02 JAN 1867 |
| STEVENSON, Robert | HIESTON, Jane A. | 28 APR 1868 |
| STEVENSON, Samuel | PRATHER, Eliza (blk) | 04 DEC 1866 |
| STEVES, Morgan | ROBINSON, Amanda | 11 JUN 1859 |
| STEWARD, Charles Augustus | QUEEN, Elizabeth (blk) | 06 SEP 1869 |
| STEWARD, Henry | LYNCH, Sarah | 16 JUL 1863 |
| STEWARD, John | DEMING, Nannie (blk) | 27 MAR 1867 |
| STEWART, Alfred | HAMLIN, Susan (blk) | 30 JUL 1868 |
| STEWART, Alfred | THUSTON, Mary Ellen (blk) | 08 JUL 1869 |
| STEWART, Battle | PAYNE, Amanda (blk) | 22 MAY 1866 |
| STEWART, Benjamin | NICHOLS, Margaret (blk) | 31 AUG 1869 |
| STEWART, Charles | ADAMS, Henry Ann Davidson | 27 MAY 1859 |
| STEWART, Charles | BOICE, Nancy | 25 JUL 1861 |
| STEWART, Charles | DODSON, Harriet Ann (blk) | 13 APR 1865 |
| STEWART, Charles | JOHNSTON, Martha (blk) | 11 FEB 1867 |
| STEWART, Charles | SCHAUB, Anna B. | 03 MAR 1869 |
| STEWART, Charles H. | STEWART, Ann P. (blk) | 11 JUL 1864 |
| STEWART, Charles H. | FOLEY, Susan V. | 07 AUG 1865 |
| STEWART, Charles M. | CLARKE, Mary J. (blk) | 29 AUG 1864 |
| STEWART, Daniel | BROWN, Joanna | 23 JUL 1866 |
| STEWART, Daniel W. | HILL, Alice A. | 13 JAN 1868 |
| STEWART, David | HILL, Eliza (blk) | 24 DEC 1864 |
| STEWART, Francis [11] | BUTLER, Mary M. | 20 FEB 1864 |
| STEWART, Frank | LAVENDER, Lillie | 08 JUN 1869 |
| STEWART, Frederick | WILLIAMS, Susan (blk) | 12 NOV 1863 |
| STEWART, George | HANDY, Julia Ann (blk) | 25 FEB 1869 |
| STEWART, Henry S. | RUSSELL, Mary (blk) | 20 MAY 1869 |
| STEWART, Hilliary | DAVIS, Rose (blk) | 16 OCT 1867 |

| | | |
|---|---|---|
| STEWART, Isaac S. | KELLEHER, M.E. | 15 MAY 1862 |
| STEWART, James | FORD, Isabella | 13 SEP 1865 |
| STEWART, James E. | BERRY, Sarah Jane (blk) | 11 JUN 1866 |
| STEWART, James H. | BROOKS, Jennie | 27 FEB 1866 |
| STEWART, Jeremiah | SMITH, Nancy (blk) | 17 NOV 1868 |
| STEWART, John | CLARKE, Elizabeth (blk) | 09 JUN 1859 |
| STEWART, John | LUCAS, Louisa (blk) | 28 JUN 1860 |
| STEWART, John | FARRILL, Ann | 19 FEB 1866 |
| STEWART, John | LOMAX, Elizabeth (blk) | 31 JUL 1866 |
| STEWART, John | FIELD, Maria | 24 APR 1867 |
| STEWART, John | HANDY, Feeny (blk) | 18 JUN 1868 |
| STEWART, John | CLARK, Rachel Ann Gamble | 10 NOV 1868 |
| STEWART, John | MINKINS, Mary (blk) | 20 MAY 1869 |
| STEWART, Joseph | TURNER, Elizabeth (blk) | 21 SEP 1865 |
| STEWART, Joseph | WHITTON, Henrietta | 12 FEB 1867 |
| STEWART, Joseph B. [11] | RIDGELY, Octavia | 02 SEP 1861 |
| STEWART, Judson W. | BROWN, Rachel (blk) | 19 DEC 1860 |
| STEWART, Lamp | WEBB, Rosa (blk) | 08 DEC 1869 |
| STEWART, Lewis | OLDHAM, Malvina (blk) | 14 MAY 1866 |
| STEWART, Moses | STEWART, Maria (blk) | 29 APR 1867 |
| STEWART, Pinkney | THOMAS, Harriet Ann (blk) | 25 MAR 1865 |
| STEWART, Richard E. | BROWN, Maria (blk) | 24 JUN 1867 |
| STEWART, Robert | STEWART, Annie | 04 DEC 1860 |
| STEWART, Robert H. | GRASS, Lizzie (blk) | 05 NOV 1866 |
| STEWART, Thomas | HOLMES, Antoniette | 26 MAR 1861 |
| STEWART, Thomas W. | HOOK, Cora | 25 SEP 1866 |
| STEWART, Wallace | HAMILTON, Margaret | 17 OCT 1863 |
| STEWART, Washington | ROBISON, Mary (blk) | 13 FEB 1867 |
| STEWART, William | SAMUELS, Sarah (blk) | 03 SEP 1868 |
| STEWART, William | WILLIAMS, Lucinda (blk) | 24 DEC 1868 |
| STEWART, Wm. | MARITY, Nealy Ann | 13 JAN 1864 |
| STEWART, William A. | KELLY, Catharine M. | 12 JAN 1865 |
| STEWART, William A. | McCARTHY, Mary H. | 22 FEB 1870 |
| STEWART, William E. [9n] | RICHTER, Catherine | 24 JAN 1859 |
| STEWART, William H. | BURKS, Nina | 07 JUN 1870 |
| STEWART, Wm. H. | PERRY, Rebecca A. | 23 SEP 1868 |
| STEWART, William J.H. | FOLEY, Elizabeth | 28 OCT 1861 |
| STEWART, William James | GREENFIELD, Ann Elizabeth (blk) | 23 JUL 1863 |
| STEWART, William M. | MANN, Catharine | 04 NOV 1864 |
| STEWART, William R. | WAGNER, Louisa | 24 FEB 1862 |
| STICKELL, Harrison T. | CHAMBERLAIN, Catherine V. | 23 JUL 1866 |
| STICKNEY, George W. | GIDDINGS, Mary E. | 14 JUN 1869 |
| STICKNEY, Robert C. | HERON, Charlotte B. | 01 SEP 1869 |
| STIDHAM, James D. | WILLARD, Ellen R. | 29 MAR 1865 |
| STIER, Frederick A. | DORSEY, Anna E. | 04 JAN 1860 |
| STIER, H. Clay | CAMPBELL, Jennie L. | 28 JUN 1864 |
| STIERLIN, Charles | MOTTLEY, Jennie E. | 03 FEB 1868 |
| STILES, John [6s] | ARNOLD, Mary E. | 24 DEC 1864 |
| STILES, Samuel A. | FAY, Catharine | 25 MAR 1864 |
| STILLICH, Daniel | JOYCE, Kate (blk) | 03 APR 1867 |
| STINEMETZ, Samuel | PAYNE, Mary Elizabeth | 06 JUN 1865 |
| STINGER, John R. | CUNNINGHAM, Mary R. | 25 MAY 1865 |
| STINSING, Frederick | TILP, Rosa | 19 MAY 1862 |
| STINZING, Michael | PITZ, Caroline | 21 FEB 1868 |
| STINZING, Michael | BAKER, Margaret | 20 FEB 1869 |
| STIRRS, Edward | BALL, Julia (blk) | 12 MAY 1864 |

District of Columbia Marriage Licenses, 1858-1870

| | | |
|---|---|---|
| STIVER, Henry | FROST, Mary E. | 11 MAY 1863 |
| STOCK, Dennis | LEWIS, Sarah (blk) | 19 SEP 1866 |
| STOCKMAN, Thos. J. | MARCEY, Jennie | 01 JAN 1867 |
| STOCKTON, Charles H. | CAMERON, Lizzie J. | 15 MAR 1862 |
| STOEK, J.F. | LEAR, Sadie M. | 19 APR 1864 |
| STOHL, George | LEEF, Ellen | 11 JUN 1860 |
| STOKELY, C.H.W. | WILLIAMS, Edith E. (blk) | 26 APR 1865 |
| STOKER, Alfred | LIVERPOOL, Susan (blk) | 22 OCT 1863 |
| STOKES, Daniel | WILLIAMS, Laura (blk) | 07 NOV 1867 |
| STOKES, James | GROVES, Maria (blk) | 06 NOV 1867 |
| STOKES, John Daniel | FOX, Mary Frances (blk) | 30 OCT 1869 |
| STOKES, Robert | KING, Elizabeth | 07 AUG 1866 |
| STOKES, Robert | McDONNELL, Rose | 18 NOV 1867 |
| STOKES, Rufus B. | WALLINGSFORD, Mary E. | 03 JAN 1870 |
| STOKES, William B. | GAITHER, M. Ada | 14 NOV 1867 |
| STOLP, Gottlieb | SCHMIDT, Margaret | 13 NOV 1860 |
| STOLPP, Gottlieb | KLOPPENGER, Fredericka | 19 JUL 1865 |
| STONE, August C. | RICE, Ellen | 26 JUL 1869 |
| STONE, Brinton [11] | BOWIE, Elizabeth D. | 02 JUN 1865 |
| STONE, Charles | HUTCHISON, Elizabeth Ellen | 21 JUN 1865 |
| STONE, Geo. W. | ARRINGTON, Sarah | 11 JUL 1861 |
| STONE, James H. | GREER, Sallie S. | 13 NOV 1860 |
| STONE, Thomas | WILSON, Margaret | 07 MAR 1859 |
| STONE, Thomas | WILSON, Margaret | 30 JAN 1862 |
| STONE, Thomas A. | GOZLER, Mary Jane | 30 JUL 1866 |
| STONE, Woodford | HOFFMAN, Mary | 15 MAR 1859 |
| STONEBURNER, Christopher | STONEBURNER, Jane | 28 JUL 1862 |
| STONER, Francis E. [4] [11] | THOMPSON, Kitty B. | 10 OCT 1866 |
| STONER, Frederick A. | PEARCE, Emma E. | 15 SEP 1864 |
| STONEY, George I. | WOODS, Agnes | 08 NOV 1869 |
| STONNELL, William | LOVEJOY, Margaret | 21 MAR 1859 |
| STONNERS, Martin | COLLINS, Julia | 23 SEP 1865 |
| STOOPS, Joshua B. [6] | LANG, Jennie | 26 JUL 1869 |
| STOREY, George D. [6m] | THOMPSON, Sarah E. | 12 MAY 1862 |
| STOREY, Moorfield | CUTTS, Gertrude | 04 JAN 1870 |
| STORIN, Jerome R. | REEVES, Mary E. | 23 JUL 1861 |
| STORK, Frederick W. | MAGRUDER, Annie | 07 APR 1863 |
| STORKE, Jonannis Dent | TODD, Cecilia Ashton | 11 MAY 1867 |
| STORKS, Hiram | GRAHAM, Rachel (blk) | 25 NOV 1865 |
| STORM, Matthew | CHAPMAN, Susan | 26 MAY 1864 |
| STORRER, James L. | PASSMORE, Ester | 09 JUN 1864 |
| STORY, John Wm. [6m] | CARD, Elizabeth | 16 JAN 1864 |
| STOSCH, Ferdinand | THOMPSON, Julia S. | 16 DEC 1865 |
| STOTLAND, John C. | HAMILTON, Mary A. | 10 DEC 1862 |
| STOTT, Louis | BURGHARD, Sofi | 23 JUL 1868 |
| STOTTS, David | LEE, Ann Maria (blk) | 19 JUL 1866 |
| STOUGHTON, Harvey | FRY, Laura | 02 MAR 1868 |
| STOUT, Samuel | JAVINS, Mary A. | 15 JAN 1867 |
| STOUT, William H. | DAVIS, Rebecca | 14 MAY 1863 |
| STOUVENEL, John [Baptiste], Jr. [11] | JEWELL, Mary Ives | 24 APR 1865 |
| STOVER, George W. | LORRICK, Kate | 30 SEP 1864 |
| STOVER, William J.H. | HAMRICK, Anna Eliza | 15 SEP 1868 |
| STÖVESANDT, Charles | WENDT, Elise | 14 MAR 1862 |
| STRAHAN, James | MILLER, Mary | 02 NOV 1864 |
| STRAIGHTNER, William Perry | BAILEY, Elizabeth (blk) | 10 JAN 1866 |
| STRAIT, Newton A. | CRAMPSEY, Mary A. | 01 JUN 1867 |

## District of Columbia Marriage Licenses, 1858-1870

| | | |
|---|---|---|
| STRANBURG, Philip | FELLHEIMAR, Celia | 07 AUG 1866 |
| STRASBURGER, Henry | LISSBERGER, Matilda | 20 NOV 1865 |
| STRASBURGER, Victor | COFFMAN, Ellen | 13 AUG 1859 |
| STRASSER, John | BINDER, Mary | 30 OCT 1867 |
| STRATTON, Allen | WILKINSON, Sarah E. | 15 SEP 1864 |
| STRATTON, Charles | TALBERT, Charlissa | 08 NOV 1869 |
| STRATTON, Eugene E. | GILBERT, Beckie J. | 21 OCT 1867 |
| STRATTON, George W. | UPTON, Susan | 13 DEC 1864 |
| STRATTON, John W. | McGHEE, Louisa A. | 18 JUL 1865 |
| STRAUB, Amelius | FORSTER, Margaretha | 21 JUN 1865 |
| STRAUB, John S. | McGANN, Mary | 22 SEP 1865 |
| STRAUS, George | HUGHES, Lucy | 03 DEC 1866 |
| STRAUS, William | McCAULEY, Ellen | 18 JAN 1862 |
| STRAUSE, Frisby G.D. | DENNISON, Nannie M. | 18 MAY 1869 |
| STRAUSS, Samuel | SAMSTAG, Bertha | 13 SEP 1861 |
| STREB, Lewis | DEIST, Catharine E. | 12 JUN 1863 |
| STREB, Louis | WINTERSCH, Elizabeth | 30 MAY 1868 |
| STREET, John H. | HORSEMAN, Emily J. | 25 FEB 1862 |
| STREETER, George A. | COX, Mary V. | 25 AUG 1864 |
| STREETT, Thomas G. | WEISBACKER, Elizabeth | 13 JUL 1869 |
| STRELEIN, Charles | ZWENNER, Katharina | 22 DEC 1863 |
| STRICKHART, John Henry | MORRIS, Sarah | 24 JUL 1865 |
| STRICKLAND, William C. [6le] | STAHL, Kate A. | 28 SEP 1865 |
| STRIEBY, George | GEERY, Mary | 26 FEB 1864 |
| STRIEDER, William | WISE, Elizabeth | 03 SEP 1868 |
| STRINGFIELD, Frank M. | MUNSON, S. Agnes | 28 AUG 1862 |
| STRIPLING, Joseph W. | ALLEN, Anne (blk) | 01 MAR 1864 |
| STRIVES, Samuel | SITES, Lucinda (blk) | 20 JUL 1866 |
| STROETMAN, John W. | STEIGHAUF, Eve M. | 05 FEB 1862 |
| STROM, Andrew | KAEHLER, Auguste | 11 DEC 1865 |
| STROM, Andrew | WALKER, Sefern | 11 DEC 1865 |
| STRONG, Andrew | WALKER, Savenda | 20 OCT 1859 |
| STRONG, Richard P. [4] | SMITH, Marion B. | 06 FEB 1868 |
| STROTHER, Alexander | McDONALD, Maria | 09 FEB 1859 |
| STROTHER, Benjamim H. | McCAULEY, Frances | 11 JUN 1860 |
| STROTHER, John | SMITH, Amelia (blk) | 05 OCT 1861 |
| STRYKER, Peter A. | CARPENTER, Sarah A. | 11 MAY 1864 |
| STUART, Charles A. | PELLET, Lottie | 20 APR 1866 |
| STUART, Edwin | DOVE, Kate C. | 04 JAN 1867 |
| STÜB, Arnold | STOECKEL, Matilda | 19 JUN 1865 |
| STUCKART, George | WIND, Margaret | 10 OCT 1863 |
| STUDDS, Isaac | MUDDIMAN, Lucy E. | 26 APR 1859 |
| STUDDS, Isaac M. | MUDDEMAN, Lucy E. | 01 JUN 1859 |
| STUHLMAN, Frederick | GRESS, Auguste | 05 JUL 1864 |
| STUHLNIGER, Christian | MELHORN, Elise | 02 JUL 1863 |
| STUNDON, Daniel | O'HARA, Catherine | 01 AUG 1863 |
| STURGIS, O.T. [2] | YOUNG, Jennie | 12 OCT 1867 |
| STUVER, Aaron | SNYDER, Elizabeth | 28 MAY 1864 |
| STYLES, Augustus M. | WILLIAMS, Sarah | 28 MAY 1862 |
| STYLES, Samuel A. | FAY, Catharine | 27 FEB 1865 |
| STYLES, Thomas | YEABOWER, Annie | 21 NOV 1860 |
| SUGHRUE, John A. | MALONEY, Mary Ann | 23 JUL 1860 |
| SUGHRUE, Michael | PRENDIEHALL, Mary M. | 02 JUN 1862 |
| SUIT, Fielder B. | STONE, Josephine V. | 12 APR 1864 |
| SUIT, Grafton | SCOTT, Martha A. | 29 APR 1863 |
| SUIT, William H. | SULLIVAN, Anna E. | 17 MAY 1862 |

District of Columbia Marriage Licenses, 1858-1870

| | | |
|---|---|---|
| SULIVAN, William | FARRELL, Mary | 03 JAN 1863 |
| SULLIVAN, Andrew | TOOLE, Mary | 03 OCT 1863 |
| SULLIVAN, Daniel | BRIEN, Elizabeth | 16 AUG 1860 |
| SULLIVAN, Daniel | REIDY, Mary | 27 MAY 1861 |
| SULLIVAN, Daniel | SHEEHAN, Catherine | 09 OCT 1862 |
| SULLIVAN, Daniel | HULL, Julia A. | 08 AUG 1863 |
| SULLIVAN, Daniel | MURPHY, Ellen | 08 NOV 1864 |
| SULLIVAN, Dennis | KENNELLY, Ellen | 17 JUL 1865 |
| SULLIVAN, Edward [6m] | APPICH, Margaret | 08 MAY 1863 |
| SULLIVAN, Elijah [2] | HOLLIDAY, Martha | 04 FEB 1867 |
| SULLIVAN, Eugene | FITZMORRIS, Catharine | 01 APR 1864 |
| SULLIVAN, Eugene | CARROLL, Mary | 22 FEB 1870 |
| SULLIVAN, Eugene T. | BLOUNT, Louisa Knight | 03 APR 1865 |
| SULLIVAN, George W. | O'DWYER, Mary Ann | 10 NOV 1860 |
| SULLIVAN, Hugh | WARD, Catharine | 05 JUL 1862 |
| SULLIVAN, James | GANEY, Hannah | 12 FEB 1869 |
| SULLIVAN, Jeremiah | CASEY, Julia | 03 JAN 1863 |
| SULLIVAN, Jeremiah O. | CRIMMINGS, Ellen | 21 SEP 1863 |
| SULLIVAN, John | CRAIGH, Bridget | 01 MAR 1862 |
| SULLIVAN, John | CONNOLLY, Julia | 27 JUL 1863 |
| SULLIVAN, John J. | HARKINS, Catharine E. | 10 JUN 1865 |
| SULLIVAN, Joseph P. | BISHOP, Anna L. | 03 SEP 1867 |
| SULLIVAN, Matthew | McDONALD, Joanna | 27 MAY 1865 |
| SULLIVAN, Michael | NELSON, Hannah | 03 MAY 1860 |
| SULLIVAN, Michael | HURLEY, Annie | 16 JUN 1864 |
| SULLIVAN, Michael | MARTSH, Rose Bella | 19 MAY 1866 |
| SULLIVAN, Michael | BRESSINGHAM, Ellen | 27 OCT 1866 |
| SULLIVAN, Morris | O'BRIEN, Bridget | 15 NOV 1866 |
| SULLIVAN, Patrick | CONNOR, Ellen | 29 JUN 1859 |
| SULLIVAN, Patrick | GORDON, Mary | 14 AUG 1862 |
| SULLIVAN, Patrick | McGRATH, Mary | 31 JUL 1863 |
| SULLIVAN, Patrick | HAYS, Mary | 11 NOV 1864 |
| SULLIVAN, Patrick H. | HIGHLAND, Catharine T. | 27 DEC 1864 |
| SULLIVAN, T.M. | COLLINS, Jennie | 11 MAY 1870 |
| SULLIVAN, Thomas | FALVEY, Elizabeth | 15 DEC 1862 |
| SULLIVAN, Thomas | McDONOUGH, Bridget | 09 SEP 1864 |
| SULLIVAN, Thomas F. | BISHOP, Isabel P. | 26 AUG 1869 |
| SULLIVAN, Timothy | WELCH, Bridget | 26 SEP 1860 |
| SULLIVAN, Timothy | DONOVAN, Joanna | 26 MAY 1865 |
| SULLY, Anthony | SCHWARZENBERG, Amelia | 30 JUL 1868 |
| SULZNER, William | FOANDAN, Catharine | 14 OCT 1864 |
| SUMBREY, Samson | JOHNSON, Jane (blk) | 15 DEC 1858 |
| SUMBY, James | DUCKETT, Martha (blk) | 28 OCT 1863 |
| SUMBY, John | JONES, Eliza (blk) | 13 DEC 1865 |
| SUMMER, Samuel S., Jr. | BREHM, Fannie E. | 21 SEP 1868 |
| SUMMERS, Charles G. | QUIGLEY, Anna E. | 14 NOV 1864 |
| SUMMERS, Charles H. | CARTER, Sarah Ann (blk) | 27 MAR 1863 |
| SUMMERS, Israel | TOLAND, Sarah | 02 DEC 1858 |
| SUMMERS, James T. [6s] | KELL, Harriet Ann | 03 JAN 1865 |
| SUMMERS, Nathan R. | KING, Martha Ellen | 30 OCT 1866 |
| SUMMERS, Richard | GUNDELSHEIMER, Anna M. | 02 FEB 1863 |
| SUMMERS, Wappelo | NALLS, Frances E. | 01 APR 1861 |
| SUMMERS, William Henry | MORELAND, Ann Elizabeth | 29 OCT 1862 |
| SUMMERS, William Henry [6le] | SAUNDERSON, Mary Ellen | 19 OCT 1867 |
| SÜNNEMAN, Frederick | VIEGST, Sophia | 12 JAN 1870 |
| SUPLEE, Alfred | BUCKLEY, Josephine V. | 14 FEB 1865 |

## District of Columbia Marriage Licenses, 1858-1870

| | | |
|---|---|---|
| SUPPES, George | NEKE, Kate | 18 APR 1864 |
| SUPPLEE, George R. | COUSE, Mary C. | 30 DEC 1858 |
| SURACHO, Michael | CAZZAZA, Maria | 18 JUN 1863 |
| SURBRUG, Samuel | SHEDD, Nettie J. | 08 MAY 1866 |
| SURTON, J.H. | HAZLETT, Mary J. | 30 JUL 1869 |
| SUSSEN, Michael | CREY, Mary Ellen | 22 APR 1865 |
| SUTER, Louis P. [7a] | DAVIS, M. Sophie | 23 FEB 1867 |
| SUTHERLAND, Archwill [12s] | BOWLERSON, Elizabeth | 07 DEC 1859 |
| SUTHERLAND, George | LEE, Susan Ann (blk) | 19 APR 1870 |
| SUTHERLAND, Joseph L. | McNEAL, Frances J. | 25 APR 1865 |
| SUTPHIN, William A. | CARVER, Maria | 02 JAN 1866 |
| SUTRO, Emil | SCHUCKING, Kathinka | 22 OCT 1861 |
| SUTTON, John Aloysius | BUTLER, Annie L. (blk) | 22 NOV 1869 |
| SUTTON, John R. | CLARK, Mary | 29 FEB 1868 |
| SUTTON, T.E. | GATEWOOD, Ellen | 20 JUN 1868 |
| SUTTON, Thomas [6m] | REESE, Rebecca P. | 14 MAY 1863 |
| SWAIL, Robert | SWANN, Mary (blk) | 01 FEB 1865 |
| SWAILES, Joseph | GANT, Anna | 13 JUN 1865 |
| SWAILES, Robert | BOYD, Sarah | 08 SEP 1866 |
| SWAIN, Abram | BUTLER, Martha Ann (blk) | 02 DEC 1865 |
| SWAIN, Benedict [10] | CHENEY, M. Antonette [Mrs.] | 26 JUN 1865 |
| SWAIN, Francis G. | EMMERSON, Louisa | 24 OCT 1861 |
| SWAIN, William H. [6m] | NALLY, Georgeinna | 21 JAN 1863 |
| SWAN, William R. | GIBBINS, Sarah E. | 03 DEC 1864 |
| SWANN, John | BECKET, Elizabeth (blk) | 28 MAY 1866 |
| SWANN, John | FORREST, Rosa (blk) | 21 JUN 1866 |
| SWANN, John H. | UKERD, Martha E. (blk) | 06 DEC 1869 |
| SWANN, Josiah | DORSEY, Julia Ann (blk) | 06 APR 1868 |
| SWANN, Samuel R. | GROSS, Rosana | 14 OCT 1862 |
| SWANN, William H. | STEWART, Amelia (blk) | 31 DEC 1864 |
| SWAP, Frederick | DAVIS, Cornelia | 16 OCT 1858 |
| SWAZEY, Israel | BRANDON, Harriet | 22 OCT 1864 |
| SWEENEY, Edward | SWEENEY, Ann | 23 SEP 1859 |
| SWEENEY, Eugene | DUFFY, Bridget | 02 DEC 1868 |
| SWEENEY, Patrick | HOWLAND, Ellen | 27 OCT 1866 |
| SWEENY, Daniel | REILY, Mary | 10 APR 1865 |
| SWEENY, James | CAHILL, Mary | 14 FEB 1868 |
| SWEENY, Jeremiah | PARKER, Amelia (blk) | 01 DEC 1866 |
| SWEENY, John | VERMILLION, Sarah A. | 11 MAR 1861 |
| SWEENY, John M. | FENRICK, Elizabeth L. | 14 APR 1863 |
| SWEENY, Judson [1c] | BEYER, Victoria | 01 SEP 1863 |
| SWEENY, Michael | CONNOR, Joanna | 02 FEB 1866 |
| SWEENY, Milo | FARRELL, Ellen | 26 JUL 1866 |
| SWEENY, Richard | FERGUSON, Emma J. | 25 MAY 1869 |
| SWEENY, Roger | HAYS, Mary | 29 JAN 1864 |
| SWEENY, Timothy | SHEHAN, Mary | 17 FEB 1866 |
| SWEENY, William | HERTY, Mary Ann | 04 APR 1866 |
| SWEET, Rezin Perry | GORDON, Jane S. | 20 SEP 1864 |
| SWEET, William E. | CARPENTER, Ann E. | 28 DEC 1865 |
| SWEITZER, Adam | SMITH, Ann Maria | 19 FEB 1864 |
| SWENEY, John F. | MILLER, Louisa M.A. | 03 AUG 1859 |
| SWIFT, James A. | GARNER, Sophia | 20 DEC 1864 |
| SWIFT, John C., Jr. [10] | RIDGELY, Marie Louise | 21 FEB 1870 |
| SWIFT, William E. | JACKSON, Annie M. | 13 JAN 1865 |
| SWINDLE, John A. | HOUSE, Martha A. | 27 DEC 1864 |
| SWINEHART, George W. | DENANT, Ida V. | 21 JAN 1865 |

District of Columbia Marriage Licenses, 1858-1870

| | | |
|---|---|---|
| SWINGLE, George E. | SWINGLE, Lydia | 07 FEB 1860 |
| SWINGLE, Josiah M. | McGONNIGAL, Catherine J. | 19 MAY 1859 |
| SWINGLE, Leonard V. | STEARNS, Harriet | 15 OCT 1864 |
| SWOPE, Conrad | JACOBS, Catherine | 17 APR 1862 |
| SWORP, Frederick | BUZZARD, Kate E. | 12 JAN 1867 |
| SYFAX, Douglas | BOURBON, Malvina (blk) | 01 SEP 1863 |
| SYLVESTER, Charles E. | REED, Mary | 14 JAN 1865 |
| SYLVESTER, David M. | EBERLING, Philomena | 15 SEP 1864 |
| SYLVESTER, Henry A. | THOMPSON, Marie F. | 28 MAY 1867 |
| SYMPSON, Colman C. [7b] | WILKINS, Sophronia R. | 04 SEP 1869 |
| SYPHAX, Calvert S. | WEBSTER, Caroline C. (blk) | 05 MAY 1859 |
| SYPHAX, Charles | TAYLOR, M.L. | 02 SEP 1869 |
| SYPHAX, Cornelius | BRANHAM, Marcellina (blk) | 17 DEC 1863 |
| SYPHAX, Douglass | McKEE, Abby A.P. | 11 FEB 1867 |
| SYPHAX, William | BROWNE, Mary M. (blk) | 03 MAR 1863 |

## T

| | | |
|---|---|---|
| TABBS, America | WILLIAMS, Sarah | 20 DEC 1864 |
| TABBS, John Thos. | HOWARD, Mary Cornelia (blk) | 12 NOV 1867 |
| TABLER, Edwin Howard | BOWEN, Emma Ruth | 19 APR 1870 |
| TAFE, John A. | SULLIVAN, Anna | 03 FEB 1864 |
| TAFT, Chas. F. | WOODWARD, Sarah S.J. | 22 JUL 1861 |
| TAGGARD, Frank W. | SWIFT, Catherine A. | 11 NOV 1867 |
| TAGGART, John N. | DIVOLL, Emily | 20 MAR 1866 |
| TAHLE, Ernst A. | JACOBS, Christina | 16 OCT 1865 |
| TAIF, Andrew | DRISCOLL, Mary | 11 AUG 1865 |
| TAIT, George T. | BARNES, Ann Rebecca | 05 AUG 1862 |
| TALBERT, Charles | BROOKS, Mary (blk) | 02 NOV 1866 |
| TALBERT, George C. | GENZERODT, Annie | 28 FEB 1868 |
| TALBERT, George W. | NOKES, Mary E. | 13 JUN 1860 |
| TALBERT, James A. | HENNIGAR, Elizabeth | 11 APR 1863 |
| TALBERT, John Thos. | CHASE, Jane (blk) | 10 FEB 1862 |
| TALBERT, Sandy | SIMS, Ellen (col'd) | 15 JAN 1866 |
| TALBERT, Sidney | ALLEN, Catherine | 28 MAY 1866 |
| TALBERT, Theophilus | HUDDLESON, Harriet | 02 FEB 1863 |
| TALBERT, William S. | TALBERT, Orphelia S. | 02 MAY 1870 |
| TALBOT, Robert | LEAHY, Johanna | 02 JUL 1859 |
| TALBOT, Sampson | GASSAWAY, Sarah A. (blk) | 10 JAN 1865 |
| TALBOTT, Henry E. | FITZGERALD, Mary Ann | 06 MAR 1868 |
| TALBURT, Andrew | JACKSON, Laura (blk) | 09 AUG 1864 |
| TALBURT, Patrick | BUTLER, Harriet (blk) | 09 FEB 1869 |
| TALBURT, William H. | McKENNEY, Elizabeth E. | 10 JAN 1861 |
| TALBURT, William H. | TALBERT, Margaret V. | 27 SEP 1866 |
| TALCOTT, Allen | HALL, Mary (blk) | 26 FEB 1868 |
| TALCOTT, Charles G. | BARNARD, Theodosia L. | 18 OCT 1858 |
| TALIAFERRO, John | PETERS, Catharine | 25 AUG 1868 |
| TALIAFERRO, Sandy | BERKLEY, Anna (blk) | 18 JUN 1868 |
| TALIAFERRO, Walter | WHITAKER, Rebecca | 14 DEC 1865 |
| TALIAFERRO, Wm. A. | BOOTHE, Fanny L. (col'd) | 03 OCT 1861 |
| TALLEY, James | JOHNSON, Jane | 19 FEB 1863 |
| TALLEY, W.A. | DICKINSON, P.W. | 04 SEP 1860 |
| TALLIAFERRO, Benjamin | BEARD, Lucy (blk) | 24 FEB 1866 |
| TALLMADGE, Henry H. [5] | REISS, Lizzie | 14 NOV 1868 |
| TALLY, Sanford W. | SMITH, Mary | 26 JUN 1865 |
| TALTAVULL, James A. [10] | DOLAN, Ellen E. | 28 APR 1868 |

District of Columbia Marriage Licenses, 1858-1870

| | | |
|---|---|---|
| TALTY, John | RAWLINGS, Lizzie A. | 04 SEP 1865 |
| TALTY, Simon | KELLY, Margaret | 18 JAN 1869 |
| TANNER, Wm. G. | KEARN, Ann B. | 11 DEC 1858 |
| TAPER, Daniel | BRISCOE, Bettie | 25 NOV 1868 |
| TAPLETT, Aaron | JENKINS, Harriet (blk) | 23 MAR 1864 |
| TAPP, George | PERKINS, Elizabeth | 07 JUN 1864 |
| TAPPAN, S.F. | DANIELS, Cora L.V. | 21 APR 1869 |
| TAPPAN, William S. | RICHEY, Emma Alice | 06 JAN 1868 |
| TAPPLY, William | BIGLER, Mary | 31 OCT 1861 |
| TAPSCOE, Eduard | MASON, Ellen D. | 20 SEP 1862 |
| TARMON, Thomas L. | SHANKS, Emily A. | 01 JUN 1859 |
| TARPY, Michael | FULLER, Mary | 06 AUG 1865 |
| TASCO, Robert | JONES, Sarah (blk) | 23 APR 1866 |
| TASCOE, Charles | BROGDIN, Mary J. (blk) | 15 MAR 1859 |
| TASKER, Edward | GRAHAM, Sarah | 23 JUN 1864 |
| TASKER, J.W. | MOULDEN, Sarah E. | 04 MAY 1868 |
| TASKER, John | FORD, Mary Ann (blk) | 29 MAR 1867 |
| TASKER, Leonard | THOMAS, Emily (blk) | 10 AUG 1866 |
| TASKEY, John | GERMON, Sarah | 02 JUN 1864 |
| TASSIN, [Augustus] G. [USA] [7a] | TILLEY, Mary | 30 OCT 1867 |
| TATE, Levi L. | KINTZ, Lizzie | 21 JUL 1865 |
| TATE, Perry | TIBBINS, Sarah M. | 04 JUN 1862 |
| TATE, Robert W. | LANE, Mary B. | 02 NOV 1865 |
| TATE, William | McGUIRE, Mary Ann | 11 JUN 1870 |
| TATSAPAUGH, Richard F. [12s] | YOUNG, Susana V. [Mrs.] | 24 NOV 1862 |
| TAUBERSCHMIDT, John A. | DÖENGES, Maria | 30 SEP 1864 |
| TAUBERSCHMIDT, John George | LOHMAN, Margaretha Eva | 26 OCT 1867 |
| TAVERNS, Francis | GARRETT, Almira | 03 JUL 1866 |
| TAYLER, George A. | CATIN, Mary | 20 AUG 1861 |
| TAYLER, John | MADDOX, Barbary | 13 JUN 1861 |
| TAYLER, Stanley C. | SMITH, Mary C. | 10 OCT 1861 |
| TAYLOR, A.A.E. | MUNSON, Lucy E. | 20 MAY 1868 |
| TAYLOR, Abel Thomas | CUMMINGS, Mary | 02 JUN 1864 |
| TAYLOR, Alexander H.M. | WILLIAMS, Albertine | 08 SEP 1863 |
| TAYLOR, Alfred | FREDERICK, Mary (blk) | 21 JAN 1868 |
| TAYLOR, Andrew Jackson | BOWEN, Emma Eliza | 23 DEC 1865 |
| TAYLOR, Benjamin | GALT, Margaret (blk) | 03 MAR 1863 |
| TAYLOR, Caspey | BUTLER, Lydia (blk) | 03 JAN 1865 |
| TAYLOR, Catesby | BUCKNER, Ann (blk) | 30 JUN 1866 |
| TAYLOR, Charles | ALLISON, Elizabeth (blk) | 12 JUN 1865 |
| TAYLOR, Charles | WATSON, Mary (blk) | 29 OCT 1868 |
| TAYLOR, Charles A. | STRATTON, Mary E. | 28 DEC 1868 |
| TAYLOR, Charles M. | HOYLE, Susan Ann | 26 JUL 1867 |
| TAYLOR, Columbus | NORRIS, Laura Virginia (blk) | 28 MAR 1870 |
| TAYLOR, Cyrus H. | LOWNES, Helen M. | 01 MAY 1868 |
| TAYLOR, Edmund | SCOTT, Martha (blk) | 16 DEC 1867 |
| TAYLOR, Edom | GREEN, Frances Elizabeth (blk) | 28 DEC 1865 |
| TAYLOR, Edward | THOMPSON, Mary | 23 JAN 1865 |
| TAYLOR, Edward R. | JEFFERIES, Mary F. | 17 APR 1860 |
| TAYLOR, Elisha P. | CLEVENGER, Sarah | 10 MAY 1861 |
| TAYLOR, Frank | BEARDSLEY, Laura V. | 29 OCT 1864 |
| TAYLOR, Frank E. | WENDELL, Anna Mary | 10 DEC 1867 |
| TAYLOR, Frederick | JACKSON, Mary Ellen | 05 MAY 1870 |
| TAYLOR, George | HENSON, Julia (blk) | 23 JUL 1864 |
| TAYLOR, George | NEWTON, Mary (blk) | 13 OCT 1864 |
| TAYLOR, George | STEWART, Rosa (blk) | 08 AUG 1866 |

District of Columbia Marriage Licenses, 1858-1870

| | | |
|---|---|---|
| TAYLOR, George | TOLER, Mary (blk) | 05 APR 1867 |
| TAYLOR, George | DOVE, Louisa (blk) | 05 DEC 1867 |
| TAYLOR, George | CLAGETT, Catherine | 29 APR 1869 |
| TAYLOR, George F. | CLAGETT, Henrietta | 27 OCT 1866 |
| TAYLOR, George M. | ALBERS, Annie D. | 17 MAR 1869 |
| TAYLOR, George W. | STONE, Louisa Ellen | 22 DEC 1858 |
| TAYLOR, George W. | HART, Catherine M. | 16 SEP 1859 |
| TAYLOR, George W. | CAMERON, Lizzie | 24 SEP 1864 |
| TAYLOR, George W. | WITHEROW, Kate L. | 18 SEP 1866 |
| TAYLOR, Grafton | CARROLL, Marsilla Ann (blk) | 12 NOV 1868 |
| TAYLOR, Harrison | ROBINSON, Mary (blk) | 13 MAR 1865 |
| TAYLOR, Harry C. [11h] | McGUIRE, Mary V. | 27 OCT 1869 |
| TAYLOR, Henry | STEWART, Alexina | 02 DEC 1863 |
| TAYLOR, Henry | GARRISON, Lucy (blk) | 12 DEC 1867 |
| TAYLOR, Henry | HAWKINS, Rachel (blk) | 29 SEP 1869 |
| TAYLOR, Horace D. | DRURY, Margaret | 15 DEC 1864 |
| TAYLOR, Hunter | NEITZEY, Annie | 17 MAY 1870 |
| TAYLOR, Isaac W. | BURNS, Nancy Virginia | 30 SEP 1867 |
| TAYLOR, Jacob A. | SERRIN, Ellen Virginia | 11 JUL 1860 |
| TAYLOR, James | DAVIS, Ella S. | 19 MAR 1864 |
| TAYLOR, James | WASHINGTON, Lucy (blk) | 13 JUN 1867 |
| TAYLOR, James | LINN, Maria | 21 MAY 1867 |
| TAYLOR, James | PHILLIPS, Margaret | 24 NOV 1868 |
| TAYLOR, James T. | MITCHELL, Jennie V. | 16 OCT 1865 |
| TAYLOR, James Wm. | WILKINSON, Sidney Ann (blk) | 17 OCT 1861 |
| TAYLOR, James [6s] | THORNTON, Mary Knight | 22 DEC 1864 |
| TAYLOR, Jerome | McDONALD, Susan | 04 SEP 1860 |
| TAYLOR, John | STAPLES, Susanna | 13 FEB 1862 |
| TAYLOR, John | NUTRELL, Mary Jane | 04 SEP 1863 |
| TAYLOR, John | ROWAN, Phoebe | 12 FEB 1864 |
| TAYLOR, John | BROWN, Mary C. | 03 APR 1865 |
| TAYLOR, John | JACKSON, Eliza (blk) | 27 MAR 1865 |
| TAYLOR, John | SUMNER, Eliza (blk) | 05 SEP 1865 |
| TAYLOR, John | MITCHELL, Elizabeth | 09 APR 1866 |
| TAYLOR, John | CAMPHOR, Agnes | 15 MAY 1866 |
| TAYLOR, John | COUNTEE, Elizabeth (blk) | 25 OCT 1867 |
| TAYLOR, John | BROWN, Jennie (blk) | 03 APR 1869 |
| TAYLOR, John A. | WOOD, Matilda (blk) | 04 OCT 1862 |
| TAYLOR, John Anderson | INGRAHAM, Hannah | 07 FEB 1865 |
| TAYLOR, John H. | VanPATTEN, Henrietta A. | 13 JUL 1867 |
| TAYLOR, John Henry | WALTER, Angeline (blk) | 01 JUN 1870 |
| TAYLOR, John V., Jr. | THOMAS, Sarah L. | 03 MAY 1865 |
| TAYLOR, Joseph | BANKS, Margaret | 09 MAY 1860 |
| TAYLOR, Joseph | ROGERS, Ellen M. | 24 OCT 1860 |
| TAYLOR, Joseph | DARCEY, Martha Ann Amelia | 25 JUL 1864 |
| TAYLOR, Joseph | JOHNSON, Kitty (blk) | 02 AUG 1865 |
| TAYLOR, Joseph | DAVIS, Lizzie (blk) | 25 MAR 1870 |
| TAYLOR, Joseph H. [4] | MEIGS, Mary M. | 25 MAR 1864 |
| TAYLOR, Joseph W. [6r] | COOK, Catharine E. | 14 MAY 1860 |
| TAYLOR, Joshua | ROSS, Maria | 19 APR 1866 |
| TAYLOR, Landon | HARPER, Matilda (blk) | 14 NOV 1866 |
| TAYLOR, Lee | FULMEN, Louisa (blk) | 21 JUN 1866 |
| TAYLOR, Leroy M. | UTERMAHLE, Rose | 25 APR 1860 |
| TAYLOR, Lewis | RUSSELL, Sallie (blk) | 09 JUN 1870 |
| TAYLOR, Lucius C. | CARTER, Elizabeth | 27 JUL 1868 |
| TAYLOR, Maris | SMOOT, Kate U. | 05 DEC 1864 |

| | | |
|---|---|---|
| TAYLOR, Mark | WICKER, Elizabeth | 12 MAY 1869 |
| TAYLOR, Minor | THORNTON, Sarah Ann (blk) | 24 DEC 1867 |
| TAYLOR, Minor (blk) | CHRISTAL, Charlotte | 10 JUN 1864 |
| TAYLOR, Peter | HARRIS, Sarah Ann | 15 FEB 1868 |
| TAYLOR, Philip | FREDERICK, Jane (blk) | 10 JAN 1870 |
| TAYLOR, Richard T. | SCRIVENER, Nancy M. | 20 MAY 1863 |
| TAYLOR, Robert | LOCUST, Julia (blk) | 19 DEC 1867 |
| TAYLOR, Robert | LEWIS, Rachel (blk) | 10 AUG 1868 |
| TAYLOR, Robert E. | NASH, Mary E. | 08 MAR 1859 |
| TAYLOR, Robert E. | TAYLOR, Virginia S. | 31 OCT 1866 |
| TAYLOR, Robert T. | HOLSAPPLE, Hannah E. | 28 MAR 1861 |
| TAYLOR, S.V. | DAVIDSON, Delozier | 02 NOV 1864 |
| TAYLOR, Samuel | HOLMES, Evelina (blk) | 15 OCT 1862 |
| TAYLOR, Samuel | SCOTT, Sarah Ann (blk) | 24 DEC 1863 |
| TAYLOR, Samuel | WATKINS, Fanny (blk) | 16 JUL 1866 |
| TAYLOR, Samuel | THOMPSON, Jane M. | 25 MAR 1869 |
| TAYLOR, Samuel W. | RICHTER, Julia | 07 AUG 1860 |
| TAYLOR, Silas | BELL, Eliza (blk) | 02 APR 1866 |
| TAYLOR, Simon | BALOR, Mary (blk) | 29 DEC 1866 |
| TAYLOR, Thomas | BURNATIOUS, Hester | 29 MAR 1859 |
| TAYLOR, Thomas | CRAIG, Margaret | 08 JUL 1862 |
| TAYLOR, Wesley | HARRIS, Charlotte (blk) | 20 MAR 1865 |
| TAYLOR, William | AGERSON, Sarah | 09 FEB 1863 |
| TAYLOR, William | McARTHUR, Sarah | 05 APR 1869 |
| TAYLOR, William H.R. | TISDALE, Elizabeth W. | 13 OCT 1868 |
| TAYLOR, William Henry | CLARK, Elizabeth (blk) | 22 DEC 1864 |
| TAYLOR, William J. | GLASGOW, Rose (blk) | 18 JUN 1864 |
| TAYLOR, Wm. F. | PRITCHETT, Sarah E. | 24 DEC 1867 |
| TEARNAY, John | NOAN, Ann | 24 JAN 1861 |
| TEBBETTS, Marshall P. | NICHOLLS, Helen R. | 09 OCT 1865 |
| TEEL, William S. [4] | SIOUSSA, Isabella B. | 09 DEC 1865 |
| TEEPLE, Dewitt H. [6le] | BROWN, Mary R. | 11 APR 1867 |
| TELFER, James | ROBINSON, Mary | 12 SEP 1864 |
| TEMPLE, Benjamin F. | JONES, Mary S. | 22 AUG 1864 |
| TEMPLE, Edward [12s] | GUNTON, Mary Jane | 22 DEC 1862 |
| TEMPLE, Hamilton | MUNROE, Mary Louisa (blk) | 17 MAY 1870 |
| TEMPLETON, Henry C. | McPHERSON, Edith | 23 FEB 1870 |
| TenBROOK, Andrew | SMOOT, Emma | 30 JUN 1868 |
| TENDLEY, Peter | JACKSON, Louisa (blk) | 03 MAR 1863 |
| TenEYCK, Egbert F. | LAVERY, Anna Eliza | 27 JUL 1866 |
| TENHART, Theodore | LEADLEIN, Maria | 26 JAN 1865 |
| TENLEY, C.W. | STEWART, Maria Louisa | 19 AUG 1869 |
| TENLY, George M. | DAY, Sarah | 18 JUL 1861 |
| TENLY, William H. | MORAN, Mary E. | 08 SEP 1868 |
| TENNANT, Alexander | CLEVELAND, Eliza Matilda | 28 JAN 1868 |
| TENNANT, Andrew D. | CREIGH, Norah | 19 MAY 1863 |
| TENNANT, Nathan | GREER, Annie (blk) | 26 OCT 1864 |
| TENNENT, William R. | McCORMICK, Catherine | 06 OCT 1858 |
| TENNEY, William M. | McNAIR, Julia W. | 29 OCT 1866 |
| TENNIS, John M. | WARD, Margaret | 18 DEC 1867 |
| TENNISON, Francis | RANDALL, Frances A. | 26 APR 1859 |
| TENYSON, John | TURVEY, Julia | 25 FEB 1867 |
| TERPLINGER, George W. | JENKINS, Delia A. | 01 APR 1865 |
| TERRELL, William | STEWART, Mary | 13 MAY 1870 |
| TERRISSE, John Charles | NELSON, Mary | 25 JUL 1863 |
| TERRITT, Thomas | BONTZ, Mary C. | 25 MAY 1864 |

District of Columbia Marriage Licenses, 1858-1870

| | | |
|---|---|---|
| TERRY, Seth A. [7a] | RIGGLES, Maggie A. | 11 JUN 1867 |
| TERTON, James E. | WILSON, Mary E. | 22 MAR 1860 |
| TETLE, Albert | BRADY, Maria J. | 14 JAN 1865 |
| TEUBER, Frank | LOHMANN, Bernardine | 04 OCT 1862 |
| TEW, William E. | BUCHANAN, Maggie | 06 JUL 1868 |
| THACKRAH, Thomas | RIGGLE, Roberta | 02 NOV 1867 |
| THARP, James | CARNEY, Elizabeth | 06 MAR 1862 |
| THATCHER, Samuel M. | STEVENS, Maggie J. | 01 APR 1867 |
| THAW, Columbus | THAW, Mary Ann | 05 JUL 1865 |
| THAYER, James | SMITHSON, Elizabeth | 10 JUL 1860 |
| THAYER, James | JOHNSON, Ellen | 25 NOV 1863 |
| THAYER, James D. | JOHNSON, Ellen | 21 APR 1864 |
| THEAKER, Charles C. | GUSS, Lucinda | 11 JAN 1869 |
| THEAKER, J.C. | KELLOGG, Mary F. | 28 APR 1870 |
| THECKER, Edward | LUDEKE, Mary W. | 18 APR 1864 |
| THECKER, George W. | BURROUGHS, Annie M. | 17 FEB 1863 |
| THECKER, John | SHAW, Julia E. | 06 SEP 1864 |
| THEODORE, Henry | McNALLEY, Bessy | 02 SEP 1863 |
| THEODORE, Henry | McNALLY, Elizabeth | 16 FEB 1865 |
| THIAN, Raphael P. | RAINEY, Marguerite A. | 11 APR 1866 |
| THIEME, Charles | KASTNER, Henrietta | 19 MAY 1863 |
| THIES, John | PRIEGEL, Frieda Maria Wilhelmine | 17 MAY 1867 |
| THIES, William | UHLMANN, Anna | 08 JAN 1862 |
| THIRION, Charles | BRUNEL, Lilas | 22 NOV 1866 |
| THOBABEN, Peter | JUNG, Catharine | 07 JUN 1865 |
| THOMAS, Albert | DUCKET, Matilda (blk) | 20 JAN 1866 |
| THOMAS, Aleck | WHITNEY, Eleanora (blk) | 21 DEC 1863 |
| THOMAS, Alfred | BECKET, Sarah (blk) | 21 OCT 1864 |
| THOMAS, Andrew | THOMAS, Susan (blk) | 16 MAY 1866 |
| THOMAS, Arthur F. | BLADEN, Mary Ellen | 04 AUG 1866 |
| THOMAS, Benedict | PECK, Elizabeth | 11 DEC 1858 |
| THOMAS, Benjamin J. | PULLER, Agnes | 01 JUN 1870 |
| THOMAS, Charles | JOHNSON, Jerusha (blk) | 21 JUL 1863 |
| THOMAS, Charles | BRISCOE, Sarah | 02 MAY 1864 |
| THOMAS, Charles | DAY, Charlotta (blk) | 07 OCT 1868 |
| THOMAS, Charles | MACK, Sophia (blk) | 05 MAR 1869 |
| THOMAS, Charles W. | WHITE, Julia A. | 13 JUN 1866 |
| THOMAS, Columbus V. | BLACK, Mary E. | 09 JUL 1866 |
| THOMAS, Cylus | BREIGHT, Anna (blk) | 09 AUG 1866 |
| THOMAS, Elias, 2d | BROWN, Helen M. | 02 NOV 1869 |
| THOMAS, Emanuel | JACKSON, Amanda (blk) | 07 OCT 1869 |
| THOMAS, Evan | FOSTER, Josephine DaCosta | 25 NOV 1868 |
| THOMAS, Francis | GRIFFIN, Cassa Ann (blk) | 11 JUN 1862 |
| THOMAS, Francis | DAVIS, Amelia (blk) | 07 MAR 1867 |
| THOMAS, Gassaway | THOMAS, Mary (blk) | 11 SEP 1865 |
| THOMAS, Gassaway | SIMMONS, Mary (blk) | 16 JUL 1868 |
| THOMAS, George | BROWN, Martha Ann (blk) | 21 MAY 1863 |
| THOMAS, George | WASHINGTON, Elizabeth (blk) | 03 MAR 1864 |
| THOMAS, George | KARYS, Mary (blk) | 06 APR 1870 |
| THOMAS, George C. | RAWLING, Susan T. | 11 JUN 1866 |
| THOMAS, Geo. S. | POSEY, Josephine (blk) | 17 SEP 1860 |
| THOMAS, George W. | KING, Elizabeth R. | 14 DEC 1861 |
| THOMAS, George W. | TURNER, Jane Elizabeth | 30 OCT 1862 |
| THOMAS, George W. | TYLER, Sarah J. | 19 NOV 1863 |
| THOMAS, George W. | HUTTON, Emma V. | 28 JUN 1866 |
| THOMAS, Hardin | GALLIGAN, Mary | 16 OCT 1863 |

| | | |
|---|---|---|
| THOMAS, Henry | MOSS, Mary (blk) | 04 SEP 1863 |
| THOMAS, Henry | O'NEILL, Elizabeth (blk) | 23 FEB 1865 |
| THOMAS, Henry | BROOKS, Catherine A. (blk) | 30 DEC 1868 |
| THOMAS, Henry [C.] [11] | BRASHEARS, Irene E. | 28 JUL 1863 |
| THOMAS, J.W. | KING, Rosa | 14 APR 1866 |
| THOMAS, Jackson | HALL, Fanny (blk) | 07 AUG 1865 |
| THOMAS, Jacob | MARSHALL, Sarah (blk) | 27 APR 1865 |
| THOMAS, James | PENN, Elizabeth (col'd) | 10 FEB 1859 |
| THOMAS, James | MARTIN, Lucy (blk) | 26 NOV 1862 |
| THOMAS, James | HARRIS, Catherine (blk) | 18 JUN 1864 |
| THOMAS, James | SAVOY, Elizabeth (blk) | 25 OCT 1866 |
| THOMAS, James | THOMPSON, Mary Ann (blk) | 30 MAR 1868 |
| THOMAS, James | ADAMS, Ann Eliza (blk) | 11 JUN 1868 |
| THOMAS, James | LANGLEY, Mary E. | 24 JUL 1868 |
| THOMAS, James | WARREN, Fanny (blk) | 30 JUL 1869 |
| THOMAS, James A. | AINKRIES, Matilda | 19 OCT 1863 |
| THOMAS, James A. | SMALLWOOD, Annie | 25 MAR 1869 |
| THOMAS, James F. | JOHNSON, Mary A. | 03 DEC 1866 |
| THOMAS, James H. | BOWEN, Sarah | 23 SEP 1863 |
| THOMAS, James H. | FRAZIER, Rebecca (blk) | 07 SEP 1867 |
| THOMAS, James Henry | PERRY, Maggie (blk) | 11 JAN 1870 |
| THOMAS, James R. | LOWMAN, Elizabeth E. | 14 APR 1860 |
| THOMAS, James T. | WILLIAMS, Emeline V. | 28 JAN 1865 |
| THOMAS, Jefferson | STEVENS, Mary E. (blk) | 06 FEB 1865 |
| THOMAS, Jeremiah | CARTER, Sarah (blk) | 10 JUN 1869 |
| THOMAS, John | FONTLEROY, Henrietta (blk) | 08 AUG 1865 |
| THOMAS, John | PARKER, Susanna (blk) | 28 JUN 1866 |
| THOMAS, John | HOOD, Angeline (blk) | 29 JAN 1867 |
| THOMAS, John | BUNGY, Ann | 29 APR 1869 |
| THOMAS, John | PYE, Eliza | 17 JUN 1869 |
| THOMAS, John | SIMMS, Anna (blk) | 23 OCT 1869 |
| THOMAS, John E. | SAVOY, Martha E. | 09 MAY 1863 |
| THOMAS, John H. | BARNES, Sarah (blk) | 26 JUN 1869 |
| THOMAS, John Henry | HOWARD, Caroline (blk) | 22 SEP 1866 |
| THOMAS, John Henry | HACKETT, Mary Ann | 10 MAY 1870 |
| THOMAS, John L. | KELLY, Bridget | 26 JUL 1862 |
| THOMAS, John W. | CASEY, Mary Ellen (blk) | 06 JUN 1864 |
| THOMAS, John Wesley | CURTIS, Sarah (blk) | 08 SEP 1869 |
| THOMAS, Johnson P. [11] | MILLS, Rebecca E. | 20 AUG 1864 |
| THOMAS, Johnson P. [10] | GRINER, Sarah Josephine | 03 SEP 1866 |
| THOMAS, Josep Henry | LEE, Anna (blk) | 08 NOV 1867 |
| THOMAS, Joseph | MINGRAM, Harriet (blk) | 18 JUL 1864 |
| THOMAS, Joseph E. | HARMON, Virginia | 13 JUN 1864 |
| THOMAS, Joseph E. | ELLIN, Sallie A. | 21 JAN 1867 |
| THOMAS, Joseph E. | TAYLOR, Mary V. | 24 DEC 1867 |
| THOMAS, Joseph H. | BIRKHEAD, Anna T. | 15 NOV 1866 |
| THOMAS, Joseph M. | DOLAN, Ellen | 07 APR 1862 |
| THOMAS, Joseph R. | FOSSETT, Alice G. | 20 OCT 1866 |
| THOMAS, Lewis E. | JENKINS, Margt. E. | 02 SEP 1862 |
| THOMAS, Lloyd | EVANS, Fanny (blk) | 27 NOV 1869 |
| THOMAS, Lorenzo, Jr. | BRADLEY, Maria G. | 14 MAY 1861 |
| THOMAS, Michael | TURNER, Susan (blk) | 08 APR 1864 |
| THOMAS, Moses [7a] | STEPHENS, Rosanna | 17 OCT 1867 |
| THOMAS, Peter | ADAMS, Annie (blk) | 05 APR 1867 |
| THOMAS, Peter | GROSS, Eliza (blk) | 05 MAR 1869 |
| THOMAS, Richard | THOMAS, Mary Ann | 05 JUN 1862 |

District of Columbia Marriage Licenses, 1858-1870

| | | |
|---|---|---|
| THOMAS, Richard | FORD, Harriet (blk) | 06 DEC 1865 |
| THOMAS, Richard | BELL, Kittie | 04 SEP 1866 |
| THOMAS, Riley | BROOKE, Mary F. (blk) | 03 MAR 1863 |
| THOMAS, Robert J. | DIXON, Susan W. | 19 APR 1864 |
| THOMAS, Samuel | EDWARDS, Lavinia (blk) | 01 AUG 1866 |
| THOMAS, Samuel | NEWMAN, Mary (blk) | 26 AUG 1869 |
| THOMAS, Samuel | WHITE, Artemisia H. | 04 SEP 1869 |
| THOMAS, Samuel J. | WATERS, Sarah E. (blk) | 30 MAY 1867 |
| THOMAS, Silas | DORSEY, Mary Ellen (blk) | 24 MAR 1864 |
| THOMAS, Sylvester T. [6s] | BATHUN, Alice | 07 JUN 1864 |
| THOMAS, Tobias | JOHNSON, Martha (blk) | 31 MAR 1868 |
| THOMAS, Washington | BARNES, Harriet (blk) | 26 JUN 1862 |
| THOMAS, William | HUNT, Susan | 08 SEP 1858 |
| THOMAS, William | GLADMON, Emma | 25 APR 1861 |
| THOMAS, William | SCHULTZ, Mary Eva | 13 JUN 1864 |
| THOMAS, William | BAKER, Linda (blk) | 14 FEB 1866 |
| THOMAS, William | LANCASTER, Susan (blk) | 31 DEC 1867 |
| THOMAS, William F. | HANSON, Georgiana | 14 MAR 1859 |
| THOMAS, William H. | WILLIAMS, Catherine E. | 05 OCT 1858 |
| THOMAS, William H. | ROSS, Missie S. (blk) | 28 FEB 1860 |
| THOMAS, William H. [6s] | DAMMANS, Amelia | 14 APR 1864 |
| THOMAS, William Henry | WILLIAMS, Rena (blk) | 28 MAY 1866 |
| THOMAS, William M. | FREER, Josephine | 21 JAN 1863 |
| THOMAS, Willis | FREELAND, Margaret (blk) | 17 NOV 1864 |
| THOMPSON, Anthony | CUNNINGHAM, Eliza | 26 MAY 1859 |
| THOMPSON, Asbury N. | LOCKE, Mary Jane | 18 FEB 1862 |
| THOMPSON, Benedict, M.D. | LAWN, Alice | 21 MAY 1870 |
| THOMPSON, Benjamin F. | LARMOUR, Fannie | 13 NOV 1868 |
| THOMPSON, Christopher C. | HARRISON, Mary V. | 02 APR 1870 |
| THOMPSON, Coalman | SLACK, Josephine | 20 MAR 1862 |
| THOMPSON, Cornelius | MOXLEY, Susan | 08 AUG 1860 |
| THOMPSON, Daniel | MORTON, Martha (blk) | 17 NOV 1863 |
| THOMPSON, David | GRINNELL, Flinda (blk) | 30 JUL 1864 |
| THOMPSON, David A. | MADDOX, Louisa A. | 06 FEB 1865 |
| THOMPSON, E. | RICHARDS, Harriet | 18 OCT 1862 |
| THOMPSON, E. Herbert | WALKER, Laura | 29 JUN 1867 |
| THOMPSON, Edward | CHAPMAN, Margaret | 06 SEP 1861 |
| THOMPSON, Francis E. | BERRY, Sarah A. | 19 JAN 1860 |
| THOMPSON, Frank | HAYES, Elizabeth | 14 MAY 1869 |
| THOMPSON, Frank | ANKIT, Frances | 27 DEC 1869 |
| THOMPSON, George | REYNOLDS, Ruth Ann | 10 OCT 1859 |
| THOMPSON, George [10] | BOSWELL, Catharine | 25 APR 1863 |
| THOMPSON, George | McMULLEN, Anna Maria | 07 JAN 1864 |
| THOMPSON, George A. | FAIRFAX, Martha S. | 27 DEC 1869 |
| THOMPSON, George H. [6m] | ATCHISON, Leanah | 03 MAR 1863 |
| THOMPSON, George R. | ROBEY, Elizabeth V. | 26 SEP 1859 |
| THOMPSON, George W. [11] | MORTIMER, Joie A. | 19 MAR 1867 |
| THOMPSON, Gilbert | McNEILL, Mary F. | 24 SEP 1869 |
| THOMPSON, Goin | SEAVIS, Mary (blk) | 26 DEC 1867 |
| THOMPSON, Henry | ODRICK, Mary Frances | 02 AUG 1866 |
| THOMPSON, Henry | WILLIS, Arena (blk) | 27 DEC 1869 |
| THOMPSON, Huwalt | BRISCOE, Sarah Jane (blk) | 01 JAN 1868 |
| THOMPSON, Isaiah | KIDWELL, Octavia A. | 24 MAR 1862 |
| THOMPSON, J. Ford | GREEVES, Marion V. | 15 OCT 1860 |
| THOMPSON, James | RODEN, Mary Jane (blk) | 11 JUN 1863 |
| THOMPSON, James | DUCKET, Elizabeth (blk) | 19 OCT 1867 |

| | | |
|---|---|---|
| THOMPSON, James | RANDOLPH, Winnie (blk) | 04 DEC 1869 |
| THOMPSON, James A. | BROOKS, Jemima (blk) | 25 AUG 1865 |
| THOMPSON, James A. | WILLIAMS, Elizabeth A. | 03 OCT 1867 |
| THOMPSON, James D. | INGLEBRIGHT, Margaret V. | 14 JUN 1859 |
| THOMPSON, James G. | BROWN, Sarah | 26 JUL 1865 |
| THOMPSON, John | COMB, Isabella | 15 SEP 1863 |
| THOMPSON, John | SHECKELS, Julia | 25 FEB 1868 |
| THOMPSON, John A. | COLOMBA, Jerusha A. | 15 JUL 1863 |
| THOMPSON, John B. | GUDGIN, Mary Ann | 02 JUL 1867 |
| THOMPSON, John F. | CARROLL, Harriet (blk) | 06 JUL 1863 |
| THOMPSON, John G. | HARBAUGH, Virginia A. | 25 MAR 1865 |
| THOMPSON, John H. | JENKINS, Mary (blk) | 04 APR 1864 |
| THOMPSON, John Henry [6le] | STONE, Maria | 23 JAN 1867 |
| THOMPSON, John Henry [2] | WISE, Catherine Ann | 14 APR 1868 |
| THOMPSON, John T. | KNOTT, Laura H. | 03 OCT 1867 |
| THOMPSON, Joseph | MARTIN, Isabella | 01 JAN 1862 |
| THOMPSON, Joseph | WHEATLEY, Caroline (blk) | 04 JUN 1863 |
| THOMPSON, Joseph | BECKET, Ella (blk) | 05 AUG 1863 |
| THOMPSON, Joseph | OLIVER, Mary M. | 08 MAR 1865 |
| THOMPSON, Joseph | BOWEN, Rebecca | 24 APR 1867 |
| THOMPSON, Joseph | MAGRUDER, Roberta Bowie | 25 JAN 1870 |
| THOMPSON, Mathew | NEAL, Winnie (blk) | 24 MAR 1866 |
| THOMPSON, Moses R. | POPE, Judiah A. | 14 DEC 1867 |
| THOMPSON, Nathaniel | OLIVER, Mary V. | 09 FEB 1869 |
| THOMPSON, Nathaniel | HAMILTON, Mary C. | 20 APR 1869 |
| THOMPSON, Perry | BURGESS, Sarah (blk) | 26 DEC 1863 |
| THOMPSON, Richard | DAVIDSON, Ann Eliza | 13 MAY 1859 |
| THOMPSON, Robert G. | HILL, Mary R. | 22 MAY 1867 |
| THOMPSON, Samuel | TOLL, Elizabeth (blk) | 21 JAN 1864 |
| THOMPSON, Samuel | WALLACHER, Elizabeth | 28 JUL 1868 |
| THOMPSON, Thomas | DAVIS, Josephine C. | 16 OCT 1858 |
| THOMPSON, Thomas | BLINKO, Martha | 29 NOV 1864 |
| THOMPSON, William | CONDON, Mary | 30 DEC 1861 |
| THOMPSON, William | HASLUP, Ellen | 22 FEB 1866 |
| THOMPSON, William [1e] | DAVIS, Sarah E. | 27 OCT 1864 |
| THOMPSON, William * | NOURSE, Helen | 31 MAY 1859 |
| THOMPSON, William A. | LEE, Susan E. | 31 DEC 1864 |
| THOMPSON, William Henry | JACOBS, Emma | 01 AUG 1859 |
| THOMPSON, William N. | SELBY, Laura V. | 25 MAR 1868 |
| THOMPSON, William Nelson | PRICE, Annie | 23 MAY 1866 |
| THOMPSON, William S. | TUCKER, Annie O. | 10 NOV 1860 |
| THOMPSON, Wilson | SPOTSWORTH, Laura (blk) | 29 NOV 1866 |
| THOMPSON, Wm. | HECKLER, Emma | 31 DEC 1863 |
| THOMS, Lewis | JACKSON, Sarah (blk) | 20 JUL 1866 |
| THOMSON, Eugene Lemon | YATES, Mary Virginia | 29 JUL 1867 |
| THOMSON, Frederick Andrew | CARPENTER, Mary Louise | 01 FEB 1870 |
| THOMSON, James M. | SLYE, Mary R. | 05 SEP 1864 |
| THOREN, Henry | MINTER, Mary Louisa | 26 MAR 1869 |
| THORN, Benjamin T. | BASSETT, Eliza E. | 30 SEP 1858 |
| THORN, Clagett [10] | BARRETT, Lucy | 04 SEP 1865 |
| THORN, Joseph Lloyd | VANNEMAN, Charity Ann | 10 SEP 1859 |
| THORN, Robert | JENKINS, Olivia | 20 FEB 1868 |
| THORN, S. | WARFIELD, Harriet | 12 JUL 1866 |
| THORNBURG, Isaac N. | ROCKWELL, Ellietta T. | 30 OCT 1866 |
| THORNE, Jacob M. | ROBERTS, Mary E. | 30 JUL 1867 |
| THORNE, John H. [6le] | ROLAND, Elizabeth R. | 04 NOV 1867 |

District of Columbia Marriage Licenses, 1858-1870

| | | |
|---|---|---|
| THORNTON, Aaron | ROBINSON, Isabel (blk) | 09 JUL 1868 |
| THORNTON, Charles | WALLER, Winny (blk) | 05 JAN 1864 |
| THORNTON, Cobbin | PENDLETON, Rose | 05 MAY 1863 |
| THORNTON, Frederick | FITZGERALD, Mary | 07 NOV 1859 |
| THORNTON, George | BROWN, Ellen | 02 JUN 1866 |
| THORNTON, Henry | RUCKER, Cornelia | 09 MAR 1865 |
| THORNTON, John | RICHARDSON, Jane (blk) | 14 AUG 1865 |
| THORNTON, John | BROOKS, Mary Jane (blk) | 27 JAN 1868 |
| THORNTON, Patrick | DONOGHUE, Mary | 07 OCT 1863 |
| THORNTON, Patrick | LYDON, Mary | 30 DEC 1867 |
| THORNTON, Richard | BRADFORD, Clara (blk) | 06 DEC 1866 |
| THORNTON, Robert | MANSFIELD, Ann Maria | 19 SEP 1864 |
| THORNTON, Thomas | MOSER, Janette | 25 JAN 1862 |
| THORNTON, William | WALKER, Sarah (blk) | 14 JUL 1864 |
| THORNTON, Wilson | POWERS, Mary (blk) | 15 DEC 1866 |
| THORP, Samuel | COX, Eliza E. | 08 JUN 1863 |
| THRIFT, Elisha [10] | KNOTT, Rosie J. | 18 SEP 1865 |
| THROGMORTON, Baker | DUNLOP, Sarah (blk) | 27 APR 1865 |
| THROGMORTON, Charles | MARKHAM, Catherine (blk) | 23 NOV 1869 |
| THROOP, Ben. F. [6r] | CONNER, Annie E. | 30 JUN 1859 |
| THURBER, Harrison | HIGGINS, Winifred | 29 APR 1867 |
| THURLOW, Jesse | LAPSLEY, Catharine | 23 JAN 1866 |
| THURSTON, Randall | HALL, Josephine (blk) | 02 NOV 1869 |
| THYSON, Thomas M. | KEATING, Maggie A. | 08 NOV 1869 |
| TIBBETS, Jeremiah | TANNER, Catherine | 29 MAY 1862 |
| TIBBIS, Moses | TOLIVAR, Maria | 16 DEC 1865 |
| TIBBITTS, Chas. W. | BEZELY, Sarah | 02 MAY 1861 |
| TIBBS, Horace | SPRIGGS, Martha (blk) | 08 APR 1870 |
| TIBBS, Seymour | WILLIS, Columbia Ann (blk) | 11 JAN 1867 |
| TIDY, John B., Jr. | PHILLIPS, Emma E. | 01 NOV 1866 |
| TIERNAN, John | KELEHER, Hanah | 09 AUG 1861 |
| TIERS, E.T. | WESNER, Sarah A. | 05 JUL 1864 |
| TIGHE, Patrick | JOYCE, Catharine | 20 FEB 1864 |
| TIGNER, Ezekiel | WILLIAMS, Charlotte (blk) | 01 JUL 1868 |
| TILGHMAN, Henry | WARD, Jane (blk) | 02 DEC 1867 |
| TILGHMAN, Henry E. | HINES, Gracy (blk) | 02 OCT 1866 |
| TILGHMAN, Ignatius | LOGAN, Ailey (blk) | 06 OCT 1860 |
| TILGHMAN, John | THOMAS, Susan (blk) | 04 JAN 1864 |
| TILGHMAN, William R. | CAMPBELL, Amelia (blk) | 31 MAR 1868 |
| TILLETT, [John] R. [8] | SPITTLE, Susie F. | 06 JAN 1870 |
| TILLEY, Andrew J. [11] | BOWHAN, Ella J. | 15 AUG 1866 |
| TILLEY, Charles B. | SMITH, Mary | 10 FEB 1870 |
| TILLEY, Stephen | KILLMON, Mary J. | 30 SEP 1867 |
| TILLMAN, Addison | BLAGDEN, Julia (blk) | 06 JUN 1866 |
| TILLMAN, Andrew | TYLER, Laura (blk) | 04 OCT 1869 |
| TILLMAN, Edward | STEWART, Jane (blk) | 02 AUG 1866 |
| TILLMAN, Nace | SPEEKS, Mary | 30 DEC 1865 |
| TILLMAN, Thomas | ANDERSON, Susan | 03 JUL 1865 |
| TILLS, Ambrose | COOMBS, Harriet (blk) | 08 MAY 1866 |
| TILLS, Richard | LEE, Henrietta (blk) | 06 SEP 1865 |
| TILMAN, Isaac | DELANEY, Sidney (blk) | 24 FEB 1869 |
| TILMAN, John | GREEN, Mary (blk) | 09 JAN 1868 |
| TILMAN, Washington | TILMAN, Charlotte | 14 JAN 1865 |
| TIMMS, George F. | CATOR, Jennie E. | 30 AUG 1864 |
| TINES, James T. | JOHNSON, Victoria (blk) | 06 FEB 1864 |
| TINKER, Charles A. | SIMKINS, Lizzie A. | 10 JUN 1863 |

District of Columbia Marriage Licenses, 1858-1870

| | | |
|---|---|---|
| TINLEY, Thomas | O'TOOLE, Mary | 04 DEC 1866 |
| TINNER, John | MASON, Lucy Ann (blk) | 04 APR 1868 |
| TINNEY, W.A. | QUIRK, Margaret | 04 JAN 1869 |
| TINNY, John | TAYLOR, Josephine (blk) | 13 MAR 1865 |
| TIPPETT, Edward T. | KEITHLEY, Hester Ann | 17 AUG 1859 |
| TIPPETT, Thomas | STAINHICE, Maria E. | 27 OCT 1868 |
| TIPPETT, William C. | TURNER, Harriet Rebecca | 14 DEC 1864 |
| TIPPETT, William H. | ARNOLD, Emma | 09 OCT 1860 |
| TIPPETT, William Thomas | WATSON, Margaret V. | 08 OCT 1868 |
| TIPTON, William [5le] | TOLBERT, Margaret | 24 JUN 1867 |
| TISDEL, Willard P. | STONE, Sarah F. | 05 DEC 1865 |
| TISE, George | WALLIS, Rachel A. | 02 SEP 1868 |
| TITCOMB, William P. | UPPERMAN, Alice S. | 01 JUL 1867 |
| TITCOMBE, James | STONE, Caroline | 05 OCT 1861 |
| TITUS, Henry P. | STERLING, Hattie | 19 MAY 1864 |
| TIVANY, Feirfield | FLATHER, Martha Jane | 15 MAR 1860 |
| TOBEZISKE, Charles | GROSHARDT, Catharina | 26 JAN 1865 |
| TOBIN, Charles | BRENNAN, Catharine | 20 MAY 1864 |
| TOBIN, Edward | RUSSELL, Hannah | 30 APR 1870 |
| TOBIN, John | HARTNEDY, Helen | 09 JUL 1866 |
| TOBIN, William | HUSSEY, Ellen | 21 JAN 1865 |
| TODD, Joseph | MINOR, Sally | 23 DEC 1865 |
| TODD, Joseph | SHANE, Ellen | 21 FEB 1868 |
| TODD, Seth J. | DOVE, Georgie | 02 OCT 1865 |
| TOEL, Charles H. | BEAM, Sarah Catharine | 18 OCT 1865 |
| TOLAND, Robert | CULL, Ellen | 03 JUL 1863 |
| TOLER, Turner | JACKSON, Emily (blk) | 21 APR 1870 |
| TOLER, William J. | REESE, Martha E. | 23 JUL 1868 |
| TOLER, Wm. H. | BIAS, Sarah (blk) | 26 MAR 1863 |
| TOLIFERRO, Henry | BOWLER, Lavenia (blk) | 14 APR 1859 |
| TOLIVER, Isaac | JOHNSON, Sarah (blk) | 03 MAR 1870 |
| TOLIVER, Robert | SUTTON, Sarah (blk) | 04 SEP 1866 |
| TOLLAND, John W. | MacCOLLANS, Margaret | 26 AUG 1865 |
| TOLLIVER, Charles | DOWNES, Henrietta (blk) | 13 JUL 1868 |
| TOLLIVER, Edward | SMITH, Florence (blk) | 16 MAR 1865 |
| TOLLIVER, Ellis [11] | PAYNE, Elenora (blk) | 17 SEP 1868 |
| TOLLIVER, Frank | BANKS, Sally (blk) | 24 MAR 1869 |
| TOLLIVER, Frederick | COOK, Emily | 13 DEC 1866 |
| TOLLIVER, George | PARKER, Mary (blk) | 27 NOV 1863 |
| TOLLIVER, Henry | JACKSON, Maria (col'd) | 18 JUN 1867 |
| TOLLIVER, Robert | WASHINGTON, Matilda (blk) | 26 JAN 1867 |
| TOLSON, C.S. | BYNG, Julia A. (blk) | 22 MAY 1868 |
| TOLSON, Henson | MINOR, Louisa (blk) | 04 JAN 1868 |
| TOLSON, John | LAWRENCE, Nancy (blk) | 05 DEC 1863 |
| TOLSON, Julius Watkins [10] | MARTIN, Alice Annie | 16 DEC 1867 |
| TOLSON, Overton | GIBSON, Eveline | 23 DEC 1869 |
| TOLSON, T. Addison [10] | TURTON, [Rachel] M.A. [Mrs.] | 20 FEB 1862 |
| TOLSON, Wm. | EVY, Elizabeth | 15 DEC 1863 |
| TOMAN, Joseph | GRAY, Mary | 13 JUL 1869 |
| TOMAS, Alfred W. | McKAY, Mary | 08 JAN 1866 |
| TOMPKINS, Charles M. [Judge] [10] | RICHARDSON, Sallie R. | 03 JAN 1863 |
| TOMPKINS, Daniel S. | STETSON, Sarah W. | 11 APR 1867 |
| TOMPKINS, Julian M. | BROWN, Margaret | 31 OCT 1867 |
| TOMPKINS, Philip | COLBERT, Ellen (blk) | 04 JUN 1870 |
| TONER, James | McCANN, Annie T. | 05 APR 1864 |
| TONER, Thomas H. | MANNING, Margaret E. | 07 JUN 1860 |

District of Columbia Marriage Licenses, 1858-1870

| | | |
|---|---|---|
| TONEY, William | WOODS, Lydia (blk) | 18 OCT 1869 |
| TONKIN, John W. [2] | FINNACON, Elizabeth M. | 08 JUN 1867 |
| TONNAR, George | HAWKINS, Oliver B. | 26 APR 1866 |
| TONRY, William P. | SURRATT, Anna E. | 16 JUN 1869 |
| TOODLE, Francis | MARSHALL, Clara (blk) | 12 JUL 1864 |
| TOOMEY, Cornelius | EAGAN, Bridget | 16 APR 1863 |
| TOONE, Frederick | BARRETT, Luisa J. | 01 JUN 1867 |
| TOPHAM, Richard B. | GIBSON, Kate | 07 MAY 1869 |
| TOPLEY, Samuel | DOUGLAS, Anna A. | 26 NOV 1867 |
| TOPPIN, Gilbert | BROWN, Mary | 12 NOV 1867 |
| TOPPINS, John | McCONNELL, Rachel | 16 OCT 1862 |
| TORBERT, John P. | BRYANT, Elizabeth C. | 01 FEB 1864 |
| TORNEY, J.P. | TALBERT, Caroline M. | 02 OCT 1861 |
| TORRY, Robert E. | BALDWIN, Annie | 17 JUN 1865 |
| TOTTEN, Edward H. [4] | KINZIE, Marion | 19 FEB 1870 |
| TOUHY, Michael | GARRITY, Bridget | 07 MAR 1859 |
| TOULSON, Jesse | CLARK, Ellen (blk) | 21 SEP 1869 |
| TOUSIG, William | HAMMESCHEAG, Pauline | 22 MAR 1862 |
| TOWERS, John | KELLY, Ellen | 17 NOV 1863 |
| TOWERS, Michael | TAYLOR, Mary | 15 FEB 1870 |
| TOWLE, Samuel K. | NOYES, Isadora E. | 23 JAN 1862 |
| TOWLES, Mordecai James | KNOWLES, Addie P. | 17 DEC 1861 |
| TOWLES, Moses | GALES, Elizabeth (blk) | 03 DEC 1866 |
| TOWNLEY, Charles W. | ANDERSON, Sarah Elizabeth | 20 APR 1865 |
| TOWNSEND, Charles H. | MUNSON, Cornelia S. | 21 MAR 1866 |
| TOWNSEND, Edward C., Capt. [5] | CONNOR, Hatty E. | 21 APR 1868 |
| TOWNSEND, Hamilton | GORDON, Rebecca (blk) | 11 JUL 1866 |
| TOWNSEND, Julius L. | PRINTZ, Elizabeth | 23 APR 1867 |
| TOWNSEND, William H. | TORRISSON, Jane J. | 10 JAN 1859 |
| TOWNSEND, William T. | BOWEN, Annie M. | 29 DEC 1866 |
| TOWNSHEND, Tobias Grafton | ANNIBLE, Margaret A. | 10 OCT 1866 |
| TOWSON, Rolla | JACKSON, Ann (blk) | 02 AUG 1866 |
| TOY, John W. | GIFFORD, Louisa | 14 APR 1860 |
| TRAB, Joseph | ANDREWS, Gertrude | 11 DEC 1860 |
| TRABING, Augustus | QUIRK, Katie | 27 JUL 1867 |
| TRABUE, Peter | DAVIS, Eliza (blk) | 26 MAR 1866 |
| TRACY, Patrick | O'BRIEN, Hanora | 18 JUL 1862 |
| TRAFFORD, Edward | SHERMAN, Nelty | 13 DEC 1864 |
| TRAIL, Edward | WELLS, Mary | 13 OCT 1859 |
| TRAINER, Arthur Wolfe | KUMMER, Emilie | 04 FEB 1862 |
| TRAMELL, John | CONER, Jane | 07 MAY 1861 |
| TRAMMEL, Charles W. | DICKEY, Maria P. | 11 AUG 1863 |
| TRAMMELL, Fielder D. | WELLS, Ann E. | 15 SEP 1864 |
| TRAMMELL, George W. [12s] | TAYLOR, Martha A. | 26 NOV 1858 |
| TRAMMELL, J.E. | WARD, J.A.E., Mrs. | 23 AUG 1868 |
| TRAMMELL, Jacob | SYPHAX [Scifax], Maria (blk) | 26 JAN 1859 |
| TRAMMELL, James | STALLINGS, Mary E. | 21 NOV 1862 |
| TRAMMELL, James | WELLS, Mary Ann | 21 JAN 1864 |
| TRAMMELL, Philip | FOLLEN, Elizabeth | 12 AUG 1867 |
| TRAPP, Casper | WIPPERMAN, Mary | 19 MAY 1869 |
| TRAUTMAN, Charles Theodore | MÜMBLE, Charlotte Louisa | 15 DEC 1863 |
| TRAUXWEIN, Casper | FERGUSON, Eliza Jane | 24 SEP 1869 |
| TRAVERS, Alfred | GREEN, Melvina | 20 OCT 1866 |
| TRAVERS, Alonzo H. | McCANN, Mary Ann | 25 AUG 1869 |
| TRAVERS, Henry W. | GIBSON, Anna | 26 DEC 1865 |
| TRAVERS, John | CARTER, Mary (blk) | 14 NOV 1866 |

District of Columbia Marriage Licenses, 1858-1870

| | | |
|---|---|---|
| TRAVERS, Richard | GRAY, Emma Jane (blk) | 06 JUL 1865 |
| TRAVIS, Dandridge T. | TURNER, Lizzie | 02 MAY 1870 |
| TRAVIS, William | ANDERSON, Coatney (blk) | 09 NOV 1869 |
| TRAVIS, Wm. J. | KNOTS, Virginia Ann | 04 JUN 1865 |
| TREADWAY, William | McLAUGHLIN, Maggie | 06 NOV 1867 |
| TREBING, August | CARL, Louisa | 17 MAR 1860 |
| TRETLER, Charles E. | ROBINSON, Sallie V. | 26 NOV 1860 |
| TREW, John | MULLOY, Rose | 04 MAR 1868 |
| TRICE, Washington | HILL, Ann (blk) | 23 APR 1870 |
| TRICE, William | PENDLETON, Emily (blk) | 24 SEP 1869 |
| TRIGG, Frank | SMITH, Mary E. | 05 MAY 1870 |
| TRILLING, John | SPRENGER, Elizabeth | 13 JUN 1866 |
| TRIMBLE, Edward | BAILEY, Martha | 26 JUN 1865 |
| TRIMBLE, Joel G. | NICHOLLS, Mary H. | 02 OCT 1866 |
| TRIMBLE, John | ARNELL, Mary E. | 09 MAR 1869 |
| TRIMBLE, Mathew [4] | NAILOR, Lizzie R. | 25 NOV 1869 |
| TRIPLETT, John | JONES, Agnes (blk) | 05 NOV 1868 |
| TRIPLETT, Thomas M. | HEALY, Kate A. | 31 DEC 1867 |
| TRIPP, Henry | BANF, Anna Barbara | 01 FEB 1866 |
| TRIPPLETT, Prince A. | SMITH, Rose (blk) | 04 MAY 1869 |
| TRODDEN, Thomas J. | GLAVIN, Annie | 05 APR 1870 |
| TROLAND, Robert | COLLINS, Louisa | 14 NOV 1861 |
| TROTH, Ezra, Jr. | TEMPLE, Lydia L. | 29 MAR 1867 |
| TROTMAN, Lemuel | GROVES, Georgian (blk) | 30 AUG 1867 |
| TROUT, Jno. F. | MARSTON, Annie J. | 15 SEP 1866 |
| TROY, John | CARROLL, Margaret | 08 FEB 1864 |
| TRUE, Loring B. | HASKILL, L.P. | 07 JAN 1860 |
| TRUE, Loring Blanchard | BRADLEY, Caroline W. | 26 MAY 1863 |
| TRUEWAX, Theodore T. | BOHANIN, Lizetta | 12 OCT 1863 |
| TRUEWORTHY, B.T. | NORTON, Martha A. | 02 NOV 1867 |
| TRULL, Edward R. | DAKIN, Millie | 26 JAN 1864 |
| TRUMAN, J.C. | WALKER, Susan | 22 JUN 1863 |
| TRUMBO, Lewis W. | WROE, Mary S. | 28 DEC 1858 |
| TRUMBULL, Albert J. | KANE, Frances A. | 19 MAR 1862 |
| TRUNNEL, Joseph F. | PAXTON, Ellen Amelia | 15 JAN 1863 |
| TRUNNEL, William W. [11] | NOELL, Mary Ann | 06 FEB 1861 |
| TRUNNELL, Anthony N. | HAZLE, Harriet | 11 JUL 1859 |
| TRUNNELL, Horatio | DASEY, Catherine | 02 DEC 1861 |
| TRUNNELL, Samuel | THOMAS, Mary | 17 MAY 1865 |
| TRUNNELL, William J. | LOWE, Julia Ann | 30 JUL 1863 |
| TRUST, Edwin H. | MATTINGLY, Marian Elizabeth | 20 MAR 1865 |
| TRYAN, A. Walter | WITBECK, Annie C. | 28 AUG 1863 |
| TRYDELL, John W. | NEVILLS, Agnes | 26 DEC 1860 |
| TSCHANTZ, Christian | WITMAN, Margaret Barbara | 16 DEC 1864 |
| TUBBS, Napoleon B. | GILLAM, Lucy | 10 AUG 1866 |
| TUBBS, Smith S. | PRAISINGE, Kitty M. | 21 SEP 1865 |
| TUBMAN, John W. | CONTEE, Letty (blk) | 11 JUN 1868 |
| TUCKER, Alpheus W., Dr. | WOOD, Martha E. (blk) | 24 JAN 1867 |
| TUCKER, Beverly | SPRINAGE, Catherine (blk) | 12 FEB 1868 |
| TUCKER, Charles P. Kennedy | CALVERT, Mary | 04 MAR 1862 |
| TUCKER, George H. | DAVIS, Frances E. | 15 DEC 1868 |
| TUCKER, George P.S. | DAVISON, Annie W. | 17 NOV 1863 |
| TUCKER, George W. | GUTTRIDGE, Verina A. | 28 AUG 1860 |
| TUCKER, George Washington | RICE, Ann Maria (blk) | 17 AUG 1865 |
| TUCKER, James C. | DOWLING, Martha (blk) | 05 JUN 1867 |
| TUCKER, James H. | McELFRESH, Annie E. | 25 OCT 1866 |

District of Columbia Marriage Licenses, 1858-1870

| | | |
|---|---|---|
| TUCKER, John A. | BROWN, Mary V. | 16 NOV 1863 |
| TUCKER, John W. | TURNER, Caroline M. | 23 APR 1859 |
| TUCKER, John W. | SCHULTZ, Amelia | 15 AUG 1867 |
| TUCKER, Robert A. | WILES, Martha H. (blk) | 24 SEP 1868 |
| TUCKER, Walter S. | PAYNE, Dwana V. | 23 FEB 1865 |
| TUCKER, William | SWEENY, Louisa | 10 DEC 1863 |
| TUCKER, William E. | POWELL, Sarah S. | 29 SEP 1866 |
| TUCKER, William W. | PEDDICORD, Celinda A. | 10 SEP 1868 |
| TUDY, Henry | HENSON, Louise (blk) | 26 FEB 1869 |
| TUELL, Laurence A. | SANDERSON, Georgeanna | 15 JUN 1861 |
| TUERK, Julius G. | BEHRENS, Louisa | 15 AUG 1865 |
| TULLEY, John T. | MATHEWS, Julia A. | 23 NOV 1867 |
| TULLOCK, Thomas L. | SWAIN, Miranda | 09 JAN 1866 |
| TUNNELL, Esau | WHITE, Mary Ellen (blk) | 07 APR 1869 |
| TUNNIA, John R. | TUNNIA, Anna | 14 APR 1868 |
| TURBY, Henry | KIDWELL, Nancy Ann | 03 MAY 1869 |
| TURLEY, William | LEMO, Sarah (blk) | 30 JUN 1869 |
| TURNBURKE, James T. | O'BRIEN, Louisa | 04 FEB 1862 |
| TURNER, Albert | BALL, Sarah E. | 22 APR 1864 |
| TURNER, Alexander | EARLIE, Sallie (blk) | 02 SEP 1869 |
| TURNER, Beal | LUCKETT, Virginia Ursula | 23 NOV 1869 |
| TURNER, Benjamin | JOHNSON, Charlotte (blk) | 30 SEP 1865 |
| TURNER, Charles | HYSON, Elizabeth (blk) | 06 AUG 1868 |
| TURNER, Daniel | WASHINGTON, Martha | 07 MAR 1867 |
| TURNER, Daniel | KEY, Lucy | 08 JUL 1865 |
| TURNER, Duane | FISHER, George Ann | 23 SEP 1865 |
| TURNER, Francis | [blank], Harriet Ellen (blk) | 11 APR 1864 |
| TURNER, George | HEBUM, Alice (blk) | 17 AUG 1866 |
| TURNER, George | SIMS, Mary Lizzie (blk) | 05 AUG 1868 |
| TURNER, George W. | ALEXANDER, Mary (blk) | 07 APR 1864 |
| TURNER, Henry | COLEMAN, Agnes (blk) | 04 DEC 1866 |
| TURNER, Henry | BELL, Amanda F. | 01 MAY 1867 |
| TURNER, Henry | STURZ, Hannah (blk) | 14 OCT 1869 |
| TURNER, J. Lawrence [11] | WOODBURY, Maggie Molineux | 04 MAR 1867 |
| TURNER, James | ROBERTS, Sarah A. | 29 DEC 1866 |
| TURNER, James C. | FOWLER, Elizabeth A. | 16 DEC 1862 |
| TURNER, James Henry | SCOTT, Ann Cornelia | 21 AUG 1862 |
| TURNER, James N. | BRITWELL, Josephine | 02 AUG 1865 |
| TURNER, James O. | FOWLER, Margaret A. | 05 NOV 1862 |
| TURNER, John | DAVIS, Ellen (blk) | 27 DEC 1862 |
| TURNER, John | BROWN, Lizzie (blk) | 25 JUN 1868 |
| TURNER, John | ROSS, Georgiana | 28 SEP 1869 |
| TURNER, John F. | POSEY, Martha (blk) | 26 MAY 1865 |
| TURNER, Joseph | JOHNSON, Emma (blk) | 16 JUN 1866 |
| TURNER, Lewis | MINER, Betsy (blk) | 17 DEC 1868 |
| TURNER, Matthew H. | WONN, Susan | 29 APR 1862 |
| TURNER, Michael | LUDDY, Ellen | 22 FEB 1868 |
| TURNER, Nathan | GRIGSBY, Harriet | 25 NOV 1864 |
| TURNER, Richard | HENDERSON, Letha (blk) | 25 NOV 1867 |
| TURNER, Samuel | LLOYD, Maryland | 17 JAN 1860 |
| TURNER, Samuel | THOMAS, Caroline (blk) | 18 SEP 1868 |
| TURNER, Samuel R. [10] | WUNDERLICH, Eva Joanna | 06 MAY 1867 |
| TURNER, Samuel S. | JOHNSON, India | 01 FEB 1864 |
| TURNER, Samuel T. | HARRY, Margaret E. | 24 MAR 1864 |
| TURNER, Seth J. | RYLAND, Rebecca J. | 20 MAR 1865 |
| TURNER, Tasco | ADAMS, Sarah (blk) | 09 JUL 1860 |

| | | |
|---|---|---|
| TURNER, Thomas | OGDEN, Mary | 07 MAY 1865 |
| TURNER, Thomas [11] | OGDEN, Mary (duplicate) | 12 JAN 1866 |
| TURNER, Thomas P. | BROWN, Martha Ellen | 25 OCT 1860 |
| TURNER, Tolly | TURNER, Rose | 07 JUL 1866 |
| TURNER, William | WHEELER, Georgianna (blk) | 18 AUG 1863 |
| TURNER, William | JOHNSON, Louisa (blk) | 04 OCT 1866 |
| TURNER, William | SIMMONS, Margaret (blk) | 09 FEB 1869 |
| TURNER, William | TINNEY, Margaret (blk) | 03 SEP 1869 |
| TURNER, William H. | BIRCH, Mary P. | 24 DEC 1861 |
| TURPIN, Sterling | THOMAS, Joanna (blk) | 22 FEB 1864 |
| TURTON, George H. | OURAND, Catherine E.L. | 07 FEB 1859 |
| TURVEY, Patrick | ROBINSON, Catharine | 30 JAN 1865 |
| TUTTLE, George S. | AMEY, Ellen E. | 17 NOV 1864 |
| TUTTLE, James W. | PEYTON, Mattie | 01 JUN 1865 |
| TUTTLE, Samuel W. | ANDERN, Georgiana W. | 21 APR 1868 |
| TWINE, David | ANDERSON, Sarah (blk) | 07 APR 1863 |
| TWOMBLY, Henry H. | WARNICK, Maria L. | 02 MAY 1864 |
| TWOONEY, Michael | KALAHOR, Ellen | 09 AUG 1860 |
| TWYMAN James W. | McCUTCHEN, Maggy | 15 APR 1861 |
| TYLER, Charles | COLLINS, Martha | 12 APR 1870 |
| TYLER, Charles H. | GREENWELL, Eliza Ann | 16 DEC 1859 |
| TYLER, Charles H. | NOLAND, Virginia | 03 MAY 1866 |
| TYLER, Charles Henry | GARRISON, Eliza (blk) | 27 MAY 1868 |
| TYLER, Frank | HORIED, Frank [sic] (blk) | 27 JUL 1867 |
| TYLER, George | GRAY, Ann | 04 FEB 1864 |
| TYLER, George | HAYDEN, Mary | 07 MAY 1869 |
| TYLER, Grafton | HORTON, Virginia E. | 30 NOV 1868 |
| TYLER, Henry | BROWN, Mary Jane (blk) | 25 NOV 1863 |
| TYLER, Henry B., Jr. | EDWARDS, Mary M. | 15 FEB 1859 |
| TYLER, James | BROWN, Rachel (blk) | 28 SEP 1863 |
| TYLER, James | HOBBS, Ellen (blk) | 01 JUN 1864 |
| TYLER, John | ALLEN, Sarah Jane (blk) | 11 JUL 1865 |
| TYLER, John | HUBBARD, Sarah (blk) | 23 OCT 1869 |
| TYLER, John | WILSON, Laura (blk) | 29 DEC 1869 |
| TYLER, John C. | FULLER, Mary L. | 26 MAY 1865 |
| TYLER, John Edward [6r] | WIRT, Sarah Jane | 09 OCT 1860 |
| TYLER, Michael | MURPHEY, Franzetta | 02 JUN 1860 |
| TYLER, Nat | TYLER, Ann (blk) | 29 APR 1868 |
| TYLER, Philip | REED, Summa (blk) | 18 JUL 1867 |
| TYLER, Reuben | SIMMS, Amelia (blk) | 24 OCT 1866 |
| TYLER, Richard | BROOKS, Nannie (blk) | 07 FEB 1865 |
| TYLER, Richard | WALKER, Maria (blk) | 12 JUN 1866 |
| TYLER, Richard W. | LEARY, Eleanor | 26 FEB 1867 |
| TYLER, Robert | TASKER, Martha Ellen (blk) | 07 OCT 1869 |
| TYLER, Samuel | MASON, Annie | 09 OCT 1862 |
| TYLER, Samuel | BROOKE, Louise (blk) | 28 SEP 1869 |
| TYLER, Thomas | LEE, Nellie Ann | 03 JUN 1868 |
| TYLER, William | LEWIS, Rose (blk) | 24 JUL 1865 |
| TYLER, William | JOHNSON, Lucy Ann | 31 JAN 1866 |
| TYLER, William | TYLER, Ann (blk) | 15 FEB 1867 |
| TYLER, William [7a] | JAVEN, Frances | 23 JUL 1868 |
| TYNE, Patrick E. | KEMP, Georgiana | 15 OCT 1864 |
| TYRRELL, Michael Robert [10] | KERBY, Margaret Hunnicutt | 23 APR 1867 |
| TYSON, Custis | WRIGHT, Chaney Ann (blk) | 15 SEP 1868 |
| TYSSOWSKI, Joseph | BASSETT, Ada M. | 21 SEP 1869 |

District of Columbia Marriage Licenses, 1858-1870

## U

| | | |
|---|---|---|
| UBER, Samuel | SENKEND, Augusta | 28 JUN 1859 |
| UETRIDGE, Henderson | MACKALL, Lizzie (blk) | 24 DEC 1866 |
| UGARTE, Joseph | HAMILTON, Ellen | 09 FEB 1861 |
| UHLMANN, John | MAAS, Caroline | 02 MAR 1867 |
| ULAM, John H. [11] | HORNE, Hattie L. | 06 JUL 1865 |
| ULLMAN, Rudolph | LYDDANE, Caroline V. | 08 DEC 1864 |
| ULLMAN, Vincent | GORMAN, Joanna | 01 FEB 1869 |
| UMPLELIG, John | SCOTT, Mary Emma | 14 JUN 1861 |
| UNBERZAGT, Henry | BRODBECK, Elizabeth | 02 JAN 1865 |
| UNCLES, Isaac Henry | BROWN, Harrietta (blk) | 28 NOV 1868 |
| UNDERDUE, William | LANGFORD, Eliza (blk) | 21 AUG 1861 |
| UNDERWOOD, Alfred H. | JAMES, Marsaline (blk) | 06 DEC 1864 |
| UNDERWOOD, Bushrod | DAVIS, Susan H. | 06 JUN 1865 |
| UNDERWOOD, John | ASHBY, Virginia | 12 FEB 1868 |
| UNDERWOOD, Richard Thomas | DALDY, Frances T. | 11 JUL 1865 |
| UNDERWOOD, Stephen | BERRY, Betsy (blk) | 31 MAR 1869 |
| UNGER, Edward | McCARTHY, Jane | 07 JUL 1865 |
| UNKLE, George B. | YOUNG, Mary S. | 07 FEB 1868 |
| UPHAM, George H. | BEALL, Annie E.L. | 07 NOV 1865 |
| UPPERMAN, Edward T. | HARBAUGH, Emma F. | 05 FEB 1867 |
| UPPERMAN, Thomas H. | DODSON, Rachel | 17 OCT 1867 |
| UPSHUR, Charles | MEYER, Caroline (blk) | 07 SEP 1869 |
| UPSHUR, Francis | WALTERS, Priscilla (blk) | 28 FEB 1866 |
| UPTON, George | HARRISON, Mary F. | 04 AUG 1868 |
| UPTON, John | CODRICK, Mary | 20 JUN 1863 |
| URI, William A. | SIMONDS, Mattie | 10 JUN 1865 |
| URLAGE, Henry [11] | SHAFFORD, Mary [Mrs.] | 28 JUN 1865 |
| URQUHART, Chelsey | BUTLER, Mary (blk) | 03 DEC 1868 |
| URSPRING, Nicholas | HORN, Annie | 18 OCT 1862 |
| UTTERBACK, Ferdinand | BATON, Susan C. | 15 JAN 1863 |

## V

| | | |
|---|---|---|
| VAIL, Alfred R. | CADMUS, Annanett | 17 MAY 1862 |
| VALADON, Anatole | QUIGLEY, Maggie | 27 DEC 1865 |
| VALENCE, Charles D. | ARMSTRONG, Mary | 16 AUG 1865 |
| VALLAV, Joseph | COLD, Johanna | 08 JAN 1863 |
| VALLELY, Bernard | SHAUGHNESSY, Annie | 12 NOV 1864 |
| VanARNUM, John w. | MOULDEN, Kate | 04 OCT 1864 |
| VanBEEK, George D. [10] | SWAINE, Mary Virginia | 27 AUG 1868 |
| VanBERGEN, John | SWANN, Margaret | 24 JUN 1862 |
| VanBUREN, John H. | DOLFANCE, Mary | 06 NOV 1865 |
| VanBUREN, Martin | SPENCER, Mary (blk) | 18 MAR 1865 |
| VanBUREN, Martin | COLLINS, Julia (blk) | 17 OCT 1865 |
| VANCE, George L. | FOWLER, Elizabeth K. | 29 APR 1868 |
| VANDEMAN, Charles [6s] | JORDAN, Jane | 28 MAR 1864 |
| VANDERPOEL, John W. | CLARKE, Bessie | 15 JAN 1867 |
| VANDERPOOL, Frank [6le] | FROWIN, Maggie | 10 FEB 1868 |
| VANDEVENTER, Samuel C. | POPE, Mary Catherine | 12 MAY 1869 |
| VanDOREN, John Addison | MOFFAT, Sarah Frances | 16 DEC 1868 |
| VanDUSEN, Henry V. | FLINT, Helen H. | 25 MAR 1865 |
| VANDYKE, Howard B. [11] | WESTON, Mary E. | 08 DEC 1868 |
| VanEPPS, James | WALTER, Mary A. | 24 OCT 1863 |

District of Columbia Marriage Licenses, 1858-1870

| | | |
|---|---|---|
| VanHAVRE, Henri [11] | WEBB, Camilla H. | 14 NOV 1867 |
| VanHORN, Benj. F. | DULIN, Sarah A. | 23 JUN 1862 |
| VanHORN, John F. [10] | BEAN, Virginia E. | 17 SEP 1866 |
| VanHORN, John J. | PARKER, Martha E. | 03 MAY 1869 |
| VanLEAR, W.C. | NELSON, Anna E. | 05 FEB 1866 |
| VanMATER, J.R. | PIKE, Eva Vernon | 17 MAR 1870 |
| VanMETER, Wm. H. | HOWARD, Milly (blk) | 14 MAY 1866 |
| VANNEMAN, James | ZELL, Emma | 27 AUG 1869 |
| VANNEMAN, Robert M. | BEARD, Katie E. | 16 AUG 1869 |
| VanNESS, John C. | BARBER, Mary | 12 AUG 1863 |
| VANNUCH, Virgilio | LAVEZZI, Mary Louisa | 06 FEB 1864 |
| VanRISWICK, Aaron [6le] | BALDWIN, Sallie E. | 07 MAY 1867 |
| VanRISWICK, Leander [10] | WRIGHT, Mary E. | 20 NOV 1866 |
| VANSANT, Thomas C. | MAGILL, Isabella | 16 JUL 1868 |
| VanSCHRIVER, James | COTRELL, Mary | 27 SEP 1866 |
| VanSCIVER, Levi | BEATLY, Susan | 23 SEP 1864 |
| VANSCRIVER, Chas. | REED, Eliza | 26 JUL 1860 |
| VanSKIVER, Charles | EATHY, Marian | 12 MAY 1866 |
| VanSKIVER, Samuel | SULVIN, Mary | 01 DEC 1860 |
| VANSLIK, Edward D. [5] | DIBBLE, Jennie L. | 04 MAY 1869 |
| VanTASSEL, Elmore [6s] | CONNER, Leannah | 13 OCT 1864 |
| vanVALKENBERG, Franklin | ROWE, Margaret A. | 19 AUG 1863 |
| VanVOLKENBURG, Henry | WATT, Mary Ann | 18 OCT 1864 |
| VARELA, Alexander C. | SOUSSA, Catharine | 19 AUG 1869 |
| VARNELL, George W. | GREENWOOD, Mary A. | 09 MAR 1859 |
| VARNELL, Roasuer E. | COLLINS, Mary F. | 05 OCT 1863 |
| VARNEY, Alden M. | CUMMINGS, Mary L. | 19 AUG 1869 |
| VAUGHAN, James | DALY, Elizabeth | 10 FEB 1866 |
| VAUGHN, Frank W. | FLINT, Louie F. | 08 SEP 1869 |
| VAUX, Eathen P. | GASKINS, Margaret Ann | 19 DEC 1860 |
| VEALE, John H. | JENKINS, Ann R. | 05 AUG 1863 |
| VEDDER, Simon C. [11] | WATERS, Dollie [Edmonson] | 24 NOV 1863 |
| VEIHMYER, Daniel | KRANZ, Caroline | 18 NOV 1867 |
| VEIHRING, August | BALLOU, Therese | 15 OCT 1862 |
| VEIT, Nicholas | CHANEY, Joanna | 07 DEC 1861 |
| VEITCH, George W. | BIRCH, Margaret J. | 17 FEB 1866 |
| VEITCH, Richard A. | SHERMAN, Martha Ann | 18 MAY 1861 |
| VEITCH, Robert R. | MEAD, Catherine | 20 FEB 1868 |
| VELATI, Serafino | QUEALY, Mary | 27 DEC 1867 |
| VENABLE, George W. | ENNIS, Mary | 15 JAN 1869 |
| VERDI, Tullie Suzzara [11] | DENNY, Rebecca Adele | 09 JAN 1860 |
| VERMILLION, Asbury | BERGER, Anntoinette V. | 14 MAY 1863 |
| VERMILLION, Clinton | SWORD, Annie E. | 10 OCT 1863 |
| VERMILLION, George W. | BENSON, Catharine M. | 14 MAY 1870 |
| VERMILLION, Henry | DUNBAR, Josephine | 16 JAN 1865 |
| VERMILLION, Judson | VanHORN, Ellen | 13 SEP 1866 |
| VERNON, Charles [11] | MULREADY, Mary | 22 FEB 1864 |
| VERNON, Charles R. | KELLY, Mary E. | 18 APR 1859 |
| VERNON, Charles R. | MARTIN, Fannie | 05 JUL 1867 |
| VERNON, John | HAINEY, Janie | 02 NOV 1868 |
| VERNON, Philip Birton | STODDARD, Mary Ann | 14 DEC 1868 |
| VERNON, William R. | BELL, Virginia | 06 MAY 1867 |
| VESSELS, David | JONES, Virginia Jane (blk) | 03 JUL 1869 |
| VESSELS, Peter | MASON, Virginia | 27 NOV 1867 |
| VESSEY, Leonard [4] | TILDEN, Mary J. | 29 DEC 1868 |
| VESSEY, Thomas R. [4] | RIGGLES, Marian | 10 NOV 1859 |

District of Columbia Marriage Licenses, 1858-1870

| | | |
|---|---|---|
| VESTAL, Warner L. | YOUNG, Franc S. | 11 NOV 1865 |
| VEYER, Edward | SKARREN, Kate Louise | 03 MAR 1863 |
| VEYER, Peter | DORSEY, Julia (blk) | 21 DEC 1863 |
| VIALE, Francis Frederick | ELLMEYER, Mary Cecelia Johannah | 02 FEB 1859 |
| VIALL, J.G. | BOSWELL, Estell | 15 AUG 1865 |
| VICKERY, Charles B.[7] | REAGAN, Annie [alias Hanorah Colheen] | 07 APR 1866 |
| VIERKORN, Henry | SCHERGER, Kate | 11 DEC 1863 |
| VIGEL, Charles | YOUNG, Amanda (blk) | 28 AUG 1862 |
| VIGEL, Richard S. | JOHNSON, Martha Ellen (blk) | 03 MAR 1863 |
| VILLET, Charles B. | ROE, Fannie M. | 19 MAR 1866 |
| VINCENT, Plummer | BURGESS, Lizzie | 12 JUN 1868 |
| VINCENT, William | PRICE, Mary (blk) | 05 JUN 1867 |
| VINETTE, Emanuel | TOWERS, Annie | 03 OCT 1863 |
| VINN, Isaiah | TAYLOR, Mary (blk) | 27 APR 1868 |
| VIOLETT, Robert E. [12s] | DELPHY, Emma D. | 16 JUL 1859 |
| VISHMEYER, Jacob | FRIDLEY, Mary M. | 08 JAN 1870 |
| VISSER, Julius C. | LEVETT, Mary A.F. | 27 APR 1861 |
| VOCKÉ, George | FOLLER, Mary | 07 JUL 1865 |
| VODRAY, William | GREEN, Amelia E. (col'd) | 06 JUL 1865 |
| VOEHL, August | HENDER, Agnes Hilldegard | 11 JUL 1868 |
| VOGEL, Christina | ELM, Jacob | 19 JAN 1863 |
| VOGLE, John | WOLF, Anne | 20 MAR 1869 |
| VOGT, John L. | REH, Christina M. | 04 OCT 1861 |
| VOGT, William | KARTTER, Sophia | 28 DEC 1861 |
| VOIGHT, Christian | HUBER, Christina L. | 22 MAR 1865 |
| VOIGHT, Edward | MEYER, Teresa | 24 NOV 1865 |
| VOLKERT, Benedikt | EISENBEISS, Rosa | 09 JAN 1869 |
| VOLLAND, Conrad | AMAN, Mary | 18 JUN 1869 |
| VOLLAND, Otho | DANJAS, Elizabeth | 16 MAY 1859 |
| VOLZ, Conrad | LOMAN, Elizebeth | 27 APR 1859 |
| VonBATZ, Wilhelm Carl Ernst Freiherr | MESICK, Emily | 28 DEC 1869 |
| VonBORRIES, Otto | LIEBELT, Emma | 09 MAY 1864 |
| VonESSEN, J.P. | SHILLINGLAW, Jane | 27 SEP 1869 |
| VONIEFF, George | SENKEND, Anna | 07 JUN 1866 |
| VonOBERBECK, Gustave | GODDARD, Romaine | 11 MAR 1870 |
| VonVERSEN, Hermann | HEYSE, Ida | 19 JUL 1864 |
| VOORHEES, Joseph H. | MILLER, Eliza A. | 22 DEC 1869 |
| VORCE, Nelson | BALDWIN, Sarah A. | 08 JUL 1859 |
| VORLANDER, Isaac | GREF, Maria | 26 JAN 1869 |
| VOSE, Algernon S. | GROVER, Mary A.E. | 24 MAY 1864 |
| VOSS, Charles | GIFFEN, Jane | 19 SEP 1862 |
| VOSS, Charles | VOSS, Angeline | 04 OCT 1869 |
| VOUTÉ, Charles H. | EVANS, Minerva B. | 14 DEC 1864 |

# W

| | | |
|---|---|---|
| WACHTER, J.M. | ROGERS, Annie | 18 JAN 1870 |
| WADDY, Thomas | GREEN, Martha (blk) | 03 SEP 1868 |
| WADDY, Warner | FRAZIER, Jane (blk) | 31 MAY 1867 |

---

[7] Marriage certificate: Charles B. Vickery of Brunswick, Maine, and Mrs. Annie Reagan of New York City, N.Y., were by me joined together in holy matrimony on the 14th day of April A.D. 1866, at Washington, D.C., [signed] O.P. Pitcher, minister, in the presence of Catharine [her mark] Ferris. A note in the file, dated 17 NOV 1870, of Bath, Maine, from Mrs. Honorah Vickery, requesting that the record be changed from Annie "Ragan" to Mrs. Honorah Colheen.

District of Columbia Marriage Licenses, 1858-1870

| | | |
|---|---|---|
| WADE, Benjamin | CHRISTIAN, Eliza (blk) | 07 MAR 1867 |
| WADE, Eleazar | HALL, Mary (blk) | 16 DEC 1869 |
| WADE, Frank | BROWN, Margaret (blk) | 29 SEP 1868 |
| WADE, George T. | STONE, Margaret J. | 18 NOV 1867 |
| WADE, Henry | JAMES, Emily (blk) | 02 JUN 1866 |
| WADE, Peter B. | DODD, Virginia E. | 18 JUL 1859 |
| WADSWORTH, George A. | EVERETT, Mary | 26 SEP 1868 |
| WAFON, William | THORN, Ann Amanda | 12 JUL 1864 |
| WAGENER, David | TENNYSON, M. Lillian | 01 SEP 1866 |
| WAGGAMAN, Thomas E. | LENTHALL, Jenny | 16 JUN 1869 |
| WAGGONER, Henry | THOMAS, Mary | 20 SEP 1866 |
| WAGNER, Adam | KOLINGS, Catherine | 21 DEC 1869 |
| WAGNER, Charles H. | MORELAND, H.H. | 12 MAR 1868 |
| WAGNER, Charles K. | BECK, Margaret | 10 JUN 1862 |
| WAGNER, Francis J. | BECK, Kate | 10 JUN 1862 |
| WAGNER, George | PFEIFFER, Mathilde E.H. | 23 MAY 1868 |
| WAGNER, Henry A. [7b] | HALL, Eliza D. | 14 SEP 1869 |
| WAGNER, Jacob | WERNER, Catherine | 07 JUN 1859 |
| WAGNER, John | TAUBERSCHMIDT, Mary | 01 OCT 1859 |
| WAGNER, John | JOYCE, Frank E. | 14 MAY 1860 |
| WAGNER, John | HELD, Catharine | 11 MAY 1861 |
| WAGNER, John G. | POORTS, Ellen | 04 JUN 1859 |
| WAGNER, John T. | STANLEY, Katy | 11 MAY 1869 |
| WAGNER, Paul | MAGUIRE, Susan | 05 MAR 1869 |
| WAGNER, Robert B. | FLANIGAN, Elizabeth | 01 MAY 1867 |
| WAGNER, Rudolph | SIEBERT, Mary | 26 OCT 1863 |
| WAGNER, Valentine | KNAUF, Elizabeth | 29 JUL 1864 |
| WAGONER, George F. | WEDGER, Mary | 27 OCT 1865 |
| WAGONER, James A. | GODDARD, Charlotte E. | 10 AUG 1868 |
| WAIKINS, Benj. | BOWMAN, Louisa (blk) | 12 MAR 1864 |
| WAILES, Frederick | CHIPLEY, Mary | 29 SEP 1863 |
| WAILES, J. Newton | STANFORD, Laura V. | 26 MAR 1860 |
| WAINES, Henry | JACKSON, Harriet | 24 FEB 1864 |
| WAINRIGHT, George A. | OSGOOD, Emma | 01 OCT 1864 |
| WAISER, Charles | KNIGHT, Mary | 30 APR 1864 |
| WAKEFIELD, David | GALLERY, Willie Ann (blk) | 16 AUG 1865 |
| WAKELEE, Thomas D. [7a] | PYFER, Susan E. | 29 AUG 1866 |
| WAKENIGHT, George W. | CLARK, Catharine Virginia | 03 NOV 1865 |
| WALCH, Bartholomew | DAY, Mary O. | 28 NOV 1864 |
| WALCOTT, A.H. | CLEMENS, Cornelia | 28 DEC 1867 |
| WALCOTT, Charles W. | PETTIGREW, Harriet | 12 APR 1862 |
| WALDBURG, Lohmeyer G.A.V.D. | PAULY, Catharine | 10 JAN 1862 |
| WALDEN, Christian | PRIEST, Magrade | 12 AUG 1867 |
| WALDHEIM, Gustave Schürer | BARRY, Matilda Adelaide | 18 MAY 1865 |
| WALDO, Roswell | PAGE, Mollie S. | 11 SEP 1867 |
| WALDRON, Henry | BYRNES, Emma S. | 09 MAY 1859 |
| WALDSAUR, Frederick | HÜGLE, Theresa Virgini | 07 FEB 1866 |
| WALE, Leonhard | STROUB, Margarethe | 10 NOV 1864 |
| WALES, Frederick | CHIPLEY, Mary | 28 OCT 1863 |
| WALKER, Andrew | JOHNSON, Mary (blk) | 23 JUN 1863 |
| WALKER, Charles B. | KEYES, Ann | 28 SEP 1865 |
| WALKER, Charles E. | NORRIS, Maria F. | 12 MAY 1864 |
| WALKER, Charles H. | CREASER, Mary A. | 15 JUL 1862 |
| WALKER, Charles M. [11] | ALBRECHT, Claire | 19 JAN 1865 |
| WALKER, Christopher C. | WHALING, Cordelia | 20 DEC 1860 |
| WALKER, Cornelius | BROWN, Fanny (blk) | 12 MAR 1870 |

District of Columbia Marriage Licenses, 1858-1870

| | | |
|---|---|---|
| WALKER, Edward | SWANN, Cora | 24 AUG 1864 |
| WALKER, Elery C. | WATKINS, Harriet | 23 MAY 1867 |
| WALKER, Frank | DUVALL, Julia A. (blk) | 08 SEP 1865 |
| WALKER, George | POSEY, Maisae Ann | 24 MAR 1860 |
| WALKER, George | OSTEMEYER, Carrie | 21 AUG 1866 |
| WALKER, George L. | PAYNE, Annie R. | 02 SEP 1868 |
| WALKER, Henry | MOCKABEE, Matilda E. | 12 APR 1859 |
| WALKER, Hinckley W. | HENRY, Mary L. | 05 JUN 1862 |
| WALKER, J.C. | JONES, Margaret | 02 MAY 1859 |
| WALKER, James | BUTLER, Mary (blk) | 02 APR 1869 |
| WALKER, James Collier | PRESCOTT, Emma Elizabeth | 13 NOV 1869 |
| WALKER, James M. | BOGART, Sallie E. | 04 DEC 1869 |
| WALKER, James T. | WATKINS, Virginia G. | 22 AUG 1859 |
| WALKER, James T. | GITTINGS, Marion | 20 MAR 1860 |
| WALKER, John | GREEN, Mary (blk) | 15 DEC 1864 |
| WALKER, John | GLASGOW, Harriet (blk) | 25 OCT 1866 |
| WALKER, John R. | HARVEY, Sarah Elizabeth | 20 DEC 1862 |
| WALKER, John S. | FRANK, Kate E. | 07 OCT 1863 |
| WALKER, Joseph C. | SUMMERS, Mary E. | 26 NOV 1862 |
| WALKER, Redford W. [4] | ELLIOTT, Phebe A. | 13 JUL 1867 |
| WALKER, Reginal W. | SARTIN, Omedia | 25 APR 1859 |
| WALKER, Richard A. | ALLEN, Sophia R. | 09 JUN 1866 |
| WALKER, Robert J. [7a] | FLENNER, Susie V. | 06 NOV 1867 |
| WALKER, Rufus | PINN, Eliza (blk) | 27 JAN 1869 |
| WALKER, Samuel Henry | BOWEN, Mary E. | 20 OCT 1858 |
| WALKER, Samuel [4] | STORMENT, Catherine | 28 NOV 1868 |
| WALKER, Thomas | DORSEY, Arian (blk) | 14 FEB 1867 |
| WALKER, Thomas E. | TENLY, Lottie | 06 JUN 1868 |
| WALKER, Truman | JONES, Rachel (blk) | 22 FEB 1869 |
| WALKER, William | JOHNSON, Harriet (blk) | 13 OCT 1865 |
| WALKER, William | SMITH, Laura (blk) | 11 JAN 1866 |
| WALKER, William H. | WHEELER, Mame Virginia | 30 MAY 1863 |
| WALKER, William H. | WELFORD, Mary A. | 09 DEC 1867 |
| WALKER, William J. | ROSS, Marian E. | 14 JAN 1863 |
| WALKER, William T. | VEIRS, Ann E. | 01 MAY 1862 |
| WALKER, William T. | TRAMMEL, Margaret | 24 DEC 1868 |
| WALL, Arthur [11] | KING, Hannah | 21 AUG 1868 |
| WALL, George N. | MURRAY, Julia A. | 04 FEB 1869 |
| WALL, J.H. | CLUSKEY, Maggie | 18 APR 1870 |
| WALL, John C. | LUSBY, Fannie Adella | 16 OCT 1868 |
| WALL, Patrick | LARKIN, Mary | 15 SEP 1865 |
| WALL, Roger | LEVIN, Annie | 25 JUL 1863 |
| WALL, William | SHEA, Hannah | 14 AUG 1861 |
| WALL, William | FRANKS, Mary Jacobs | 10 JUN 1867 |
| WALL, William L. | BERRY, Mary E.B. | 02 APR 1866 |
| WALLACE, James | SCHNEIDER, Henrietta | 03 JAN 1863 |
| WALLACE, James | REIVES, Georgiana | 20 MAY 1867 |
| WALLACE, John | STAFFORD, Amanda | 25 MAY 1866 |
| WALLACE, John F. | GRIFFIN, Emma F. | 16 MAY 1870 |
| WALLACE, John W. | GRINER, Jane | 01 JUL 1864 |
| WALLACE, W.W. | ROBINSON, Isabella | 29 SEP 1869 |
| WALLACE, William Henry | ROSS, Eleanor (blk) | 07 JUN 1870 |
| WALLACH, Philip | HILZHEIM, Rachel | 20 AUG 1862 |
| WALLENUS, Francois | WARREN, Maria | 31 AUG 1865 |
| WALLER, John | HOLLORAN, Bridget | 29 OCT 1864 |
| WALLER, John R. [4] | NYE, Mary E. | 18 APR 1866 |

| | | |
|---|---|---|
| WALLER, Washington | WASHINGTON, Ellen (blk) | 03 OCT 1867 |
| WALLER, William | BRODERICK, Hannah | 18 APR 1861 |
| WALLICH, John W. | SNYDER, Mary A. | 17 FEB 1869 |
| WALLING, Isaac | DAVENPORT, Mary Emma | 14 JUN 1869 |
| WALLING, Jacob | OSBORNE, America | 04 JAN 1865 |
| WALLING, Joseph B. | CARMAN, Mary Jane | 18 JUN 1862 |
| WALLINGSFORD, Joseph O. | HOOVER, Mary E. | 27 DEC 1860 |
| WALLINGSFORD, Malcolm | STEVENS, Sallie C. | 28 MAR 1861 |
| WALLINGSFORD, William | SCRIVENER, Ella | 17 MAY 1870 |
| WALLIS, James | KING, Ann | 01 MAY 1862 |
| WALLIS, John H. | HOWARD, Hellen A. | 07 JUN 1862 |
| WALLIS, Peter | MAHONEY, Margaret (blk) | 17 OCT 1867 |
| WALLIS, William T. | HOLLIDAY, Sue B. | 10 JAN 1866 |
| WALSH, Frank S., Jr. | TALBURT, Mary A. | 11 NOV 1868 |
| WALSH, Henry B. | CARPENTER, Rose Ann | 28 OCT 1865 |
| WALSH, James W. | QUINN, Jane C. | 06 SEP 1862 |
| WALSH, John | DOWLING, Catharine | 27 FEB 1865 |
| WALSH, John [4] | REILY, Mary Ann | 08 OCT 1864 |
| WALSH, John J. | MARTYN, Elizabeth | 26 OCT 1864 |
| WALSH, John K. | IVEY, Helen L. | 01 APR 1867 |
| WALSH, Mathew | DONNELLY, Bridget | 11 MAY 1870 |
| WALSH, Mathew K. | SCANLON, Mary C. | 04 NOV 1859 |
| WALSH, Matthew K. | MEAKIN, Mary A. | 19 OCT 1861 |
| WALSH, Thomas | FLYNN, Kate | 31 JUL 1869 |
| WALSH, Thomas | SMITH, Annah | 11 OCT 1869 |
| WALSH, Timothy | NOONAN, Mary | 19 DEC 1863 |
| WALSH, William | JOYCE, Catharine | 27 AUG 1866 |
| WALSH, William | WREN, Margaret | 03 OCT 1868 |
| WALSTRUM, John F. | SMITH, Lizzie | 25 OCT 1858 |
| WALTEMEYER, Joseph R. | HARDY, Ann Rebecca | 16 JAN 1864 |
| WALTER, Charles G. | DORSEY, Mary E. | 27 APR 1869 |
| WALTER, Francis | FREEMAN, Mary Elizth. | 20 APR 1861 |
| WALTER, Frederick | HOFF, Fredricka | 18 AUG 1863 |
| WALTER, Henry Albert | ENGEL, Emma | 13 JAN 1868 |
| WALTER, Jacob | OPPENHEIMER, Gette | 28 JAN 1867 |
| WALTER, James C. [12s] | AYLOR, Annie M. | 21 DEC 1859 |
| WALTER, John | SAUTER, Wilhelmena | 09 NOV 1859 |
| WALTER, John | RIDLEY, Lenah | 16 AUG 1862 |
| WALTER, John | KEIBER, Catharine | 29 APR 1863 |
| WALTER, John | WRIGHT, Eliza (blk) | 24 JUN 1863 |
| WALTER, Nelson | DIGGS, Nancy (blk) | 09 APR 1867 |
| WALTER, Rudolph L. | LYONS, Maggie A.A. | 06 MAY 1867 |
| WALTERS, George H. | CLEMENTS, Eliza Louisa | 18 JAN 1859 |
| WALTERS, Robert | DAVIS, Lou (blk) | 13 MAY 1869 |
| WALTERS, W.S. | BRONAUGH, Fannie R. | 29 JUN 1869 |
| WALTHEN, Sil. | FLOOD, Annie (blk) | 14 MAR 1866 |
| WALTHER, Henry | UPPERMANN, Louisa | 26 JUL 1865 |
| WALTON, Moses | YOUNG, Emily (blk) | 27 JAN 1869 |
| WALTON, William B. | HARRIS, Henrietta | 30 DEC 1863 |
| WALTON, William E. | PROSPERI, Mary E. | 28 JAN 1865 |
| WALZ, John | ISEMANN, Barbara | 26 APR 1860 |
| WANDER, Hugo | CZERNY, Anna | 29 OCT 1859 |
| WANGEMANN, Ernst | MEYER, Wilhelmina | 01 JUL 1865 |
| WANSLEBAN, William | BRAFF, Lilly | 25 NOV 1868 |
| WANSOR, Thornton J. | THOMAS, Alice (blk) | 02 APR 1867 |
| WANZER, Esom | WILLIAMS, Mahala (blk) | 26 DEC 1866 |

District of Columbia Marriage Licenses, 1858-1870

| | | |
|---|---|---|
| WARD, Daniel | PARKER, Harmonia | 14 DEC 1869 |
| WARD, David | WILSON, Sarah (blk) | 07 MAR 1866 |
| WARD, Elijah J. | TUCKER, Jennie G. | 14 OCT 1862 |
| WARD, Elijah James | BEALL, Sarah Ellen | 01 DEC 1866 |
| WARD, Enoch G. | CROWN, Mary Elizabeth | 11 JUL 1863 |
| WARD, Frederick | PERRY, Martha Ann (blk) | 14 SEP 1863 |
| WARD, Frederick W. | PERRY, Martha Ann (blk) | 15 JUN 1863 |
| WARD, George | COLE, Jane (blk) | 16 JAN 1860 |
| WARD, George | SCOTT, Penelope (blk) | 04 JAN 1870 |
| WARD, Henry | BROWN, Lucinda | 14 MAY 1866 |
| WARD, Horace W. | BOUNDS, Sarah | 01 FEB 1864 |
| WARD, Horace W. [6le] | WARFIELD, Mary E. | 20 FEB 1866 |
| WARD, John | GRAY, Mary E. (blk) | 26 NOV 1861 |
| WARD, John | JONES, Camilla (blk) | 24 FEB 1863 |
| WARD, John | vonGIROLT, Carlota Wilhel. Marianna | 20 JUL 1863 |
| WARD, John | MACK, Mary | 02 JUL 1867 |
| WARD, John | FREDERICK, Amanda (blk) | 07 NOV 1867 |
| WARD, John T. | PAINE, Ann E. | 06 SEP 1860 |
| WARD, John T. | HANEY, Margaret A. | 22 NOV 1865 |
| WARD, Levin | TAYLOR, Mary | 07 NOV 1859 |
| WARD, Patrick | BARR, Catharine | 19 JUL 1865 |
| WARD, Patrick | MURPHY, Jane | 04 JAN 1869 |
| WARD, Perry | THOMAS, Kitty (blk) | 25 JUN 1866 |
| WARD, Richard | SHEPHERD, Jennie | 16 MAY 1868 |
| WARD, Robert | BOWEN, Mary F. (blk) | 25 APR 1861 |
| WARD, Robert | WELLING, Sarah (blk) | 08 DEC 1862 |
| WARD, Thomas | CAMPBELL, Henrietta (blk) | 29 SEP 1869 |
| WARD, William Edward | TUBBMAN, Mary Emma | 22 JUL 1869 |
| WARD, William H. | DAVIS, Maria E. | 03 AUG 1864 |
| WARD, William M. [6m] | BLADEN, Caroline V. | 15 APR 1862 |
| WARDELL, James | COLLINS, Sarah Jane | 14 NOV 1861 |
| WARDEMANN, Julius V. | BARNARD, Millie | 29 SEP 1864 |
| WARDER, James H. [7a] | WEAVER, Henrietta | 14 MAY 1867 |
| WARDER, John T. | HENDERSON, Emma | 25 NOV 1869 |
| WARDWELL, David K. | WEEDEN, Anna M. | 13 JUL 1864 |
| WARDWELL, Robert | BRIEN, Mary | 29 DEC 1865 |
| WARE, Battle | THOMPSON, Lucy (blk) | 23 MAR 1870 |
| WARE, Darwin E. | DICKEY, Adelaide F. | 21 MAY 1868 |
| WARE, Dudley | WALKER, Rebecca (blk) | 16 JUL 1868 |
| WARE, Henry | BURD, Mary (blk) | 25 FEB 1869 |
| WARE, Henry | BROWN, Rachel (blk) | 23 MAR 1870 |
| WARE, John Edward | SMILER, Mary Ann (blk) | 04 SEP 1866 |
| WARE, Joseph | BROWN, Maria (blk) | 23 OCT 1869 |
| WARE, Nathaniel | BERRY, Georgiana (blk) | 11 JUN 1868 |
| WARE, Walter | CARTER, Agnes (blk) | 22 JUL 1864 |
| WARE, William | SIMPSON, Alice (blk) | 08 JAN 1868 |
| WARFIELD, Alfred | DODSON, Ann Maria (blk) | 29 NOV 1860 |
| WARFIELD, Artemus | GRIFFITH, Lizzie | 15 OCT 1867 |
| WARFIELD, Augustus M. | BOTELER, Susan E. | 31 MAY 1866 |
| WARFIELD, Columbus | CURTIS, Margaret (blk) | 09 APR 1863 |
| WARFIELD, John | LANKFORD, Margaret A. (blk) | 23 JAN 1867 |
| WARFIELD, Thomas | JOHNSON, Ann (blk) | 21 APR 1862 |
| WARING, Edwin B. | GREENE, Martha J. | 02 JUN 1864 |
| WARK, Alexander | RUSSELL, Jane | 22 SEP 1862 |
| WARK, George A. | EDSON, Lavangie S. | 10 FEB 1868 |
| WARNER, David | BROWN, Mary Ellen (blk) | 25 NOV 1862 |

District of Columbia Marriage Licenses, 1858-1870

| Groom | Bride | Date |
|---|---|---|
| WARNER, David | COKE, Lavinia (blk) | 12 NOV 1868 |
| WARNER, Fred | EASTON, Laura (blk) | 30 JUN 1869 |
| WARNER, George | BARNUM, Francis L. | 31 JAN 1868 |
| WARNER, Henry | SIMS, Amanda (blk) | 22 JUL 1865 |
| WARNER, Henry | MIDDLETON, Mollie (blk) | 26 DEC 1868 |
| WARNER, John | ROBEY, Mary | 16 NOV 1861 |
| WARNER, John | CHAMBERS, Ellen | 28 SEP 1864 |
| WARNER, Joseph | BELL, Emily | 25 AUG 1868 |
| WARNER, Julian F. | PHILPOT, Mary F. | 04 MAY 1868 |
| WARNER, Robert | HEIL, Annie | 24 MAR 1862 |
| WARNER, Theodore F. | CRUIT, Alice Amelia | 10 JAN 1865 |
| WARNER, William | RODEN, Eliza (blk) | 22 APR 1868 |
| WARREN, Alexr. Overton Carr | PALMER, Anna Adeline | 12 MAR 1861 |
| WARREN, Alfred | SNOWDEN, Hannah (blk) | 10 OCT 1868 |
| WARREN, Ambrose | NELSON, Susan (blk) | 01 FEB 1867 |
| WARREN, Charles | DOVER, Jane (blk) | 22 OCT 1862 |
| WARREN, Daniel | MAHER, Mary | 30 DEC 1867 |
| WARREN, Francis | BROWN, Lucinda (blk) | 28 MAR 1866 |
| WARREN, James | PHILLIPS, Alice | 26 DEC 1865 |
| WARREN, John | COOPER, Martha | 04 APR 1866 |
| WARREN, Julius | WARREN, Charity (blk) | 06 JAN 1866 |
| WARREN, Philander R. | MONSHOWER, Ellen | 31 DEC 1863 |
| WARREN, Robert | WALKER, Sidney (blk) | 01 MAR 1870 |
| WARREN, Romulus | WARREN, Cecelia (blk) | 28 JUL 1866 |
| WARREN, Tobey | THOMAS, Mary (blk) | 01 SEP 1862 |
| WARREN, William | APPLEBY, Anna | 14 JUL 1859 |
| WARREN, William | PETERS, Martha (blk) | 26 DEC 1866 |
| WARREN, William S. | SIMMS, Eddie | 28 JAN 1861 |
| WARRICK, Richard | WAUGH, Nancy (blk) | 01 DEC 1863 |
| WARRMOND, Franz | MACK, Margaret | 01 SEP 1866 |
| WARTERS, Sandford M. [1c] | CHAMBERLAIN, Martha A. | 02 SEP 1863 |
| WARTHEN, Frank A. | McNEIL, Mary | 10 APR 1866 |
| WARWICK, James L. | KROUSE, Clara V. | 07 MAY 1861 |
| WASHBURN, Hiram S. | STONE, Charlotte R. | 23 OCT 1869 |
| WASHBURN, John J. [11] | WANTON, Hannah S. | 22 SEP 1866 |
| WASHINGTON, Albert | CLEMMONS, Mollie (blk) | 28 AUG 1866 |
| WASHINGTON, Amos | TOLBERT, Mahala (blk) | 09 AUG 1869 |
| WASHINGTON, Anthony | WARD, Martha Ann | 14 MAY 1863 |
| WASHINGTON, Anthony | HENSON, Ellen (blk) | 03 FEB 1866 |
| WASHINGTON, Arthur | BUTTON, Eliza | 03 JUL 1865 |
| WASHINGTON, Caleb | KNOX, Susan (blk) | 13 AUG 1866 |
| WASHINGTON, Charles | HALESTORK, Mary (blk) | 09 DEC 1862 |
| WASHINGTON, Charles | WILLIAMS, Emma (blk) | 06 DEC 1866 |
| WASHINGTON, Charles | NEWMAN, Agnes (blk) | 06 FEB 1868 |
| WASHINGTON, Cornelius | RUSSELL, Betsy (blk) | 23 JAN 1866 |
| WASHINGTON, Emanuel | NELSON, Mary Ann (blk) | 24 DEC 1869 |
| WASHINGTON, Fielding | VOLLINS, Lucinda (blk) | 29 MAY 1867 |
| WASHINGTON, Frank | REED, Jane (blk) | 21 MAR 1868 |
| WASHINGTON, Gabriel | RACKS, Sarah (blk) | 15 FEB 1870 |
| WASHINGTON, George | TOYER, Maria (blk) | 05 MAR 1860 |
| WASHINGTON, George | FORD, Ellen (blk) | 03 MAR 1863 |
| WASHINGTON, George | BAILEY, Rachel (blk) | 03 JUN 1863 |
| WASHINGTON, George | BRAXTON, Mahala (blk) | 28 DEC 1864 |
| WASHINGTON, George | PRATT, Jane (blk) | 20 JUN 1865 |
| WASHINGTON, George | VALENTINE, Henrietta (blk) | 15 FEB 1866 |
| WASHINGTON, George | JACKSON, Elizabeth (blk) | 10 NOV 1866 |

District of Columbia Marriage Licenses, 1858-1870

| | | |
|---|---|---|
| WASHINGTON, George | ROANE, Caroline (blk) | 26 DEC 1866 |
| WASHINGTON, George | SAUNDERS, Ann Eliza (blk) | 04 JUN 1868 |
| WASHINGTON, George | WASHINGTON, Daborey (blk) | 09 APR 1869 |
| WASHINGTON, George | MASHEY, Ange (blk) | 17 MAR 1869 |
| WASHINGTON, George | HONESTY, Ellen (blk) | 03 JUN 1869 |
| WASHINGTON, George | JOHNSON, Mary Ellen (blk) | 18 AUG 1869 |
| WASHINGTON, George | HAWKINS, Rebecca (blk) | 23 SEP 1869 |
| WASHINGTON, George | BARNES, Henrietta (blk) | 10 FEB 1870 |
| WASHINGTON, George | MODLEY, Ann Maria | 11 JUN 1870 |
| WASHINGTON, George, Rev. | BRISCOE, Nancy, Mrs. (blk) | 13 JUL 1863 |
| WASHINGTON, George W. | MAGRUDER, Louisa | 12 JUL 1864 |
| WASHINGTON, George W. | ROBINSON, Rachel (blk) | 11 MAY 1870 |
| WASHINGTON, Grigg | KEYES, Gracie (blk) | 17 OCT 1867 |
| WASHINGTON, Henry | BOMBRAY, Emily (blk) | 22 MAY 1866 |
| WASHINGTON, Henry | SMITH, Harriet (blk) | 13 OCT 1868 |
| WASHINGTON, Henry | JONES, Mahala (blk) | 12 NOV 1868 |
| WASHINGTON, Henry | MERCER, Sally (blk) | 18 DEC 1869 |
| WASHINGTON, James | JACKSON, Lavinia (blk) | 19 DEC 1866 |
| WASHINGTON, Jesse | BERRY, Lucinda (blk) | 13 APR 1867 |
| WASHINGTON, John | COUNTEE, Maria (blk) | 28 JAN 1864 |
| WASHINGTON, John | BELL, Margaret (blk) | 30 OCT 1865 |
| WASHINGTON, John | BETTER, Jane (blk) | 13 AUG 1866 |
| WASHINGTON, John | WOODFOLK, Betsey (blk) | 10 FEB 1869 |
| WASHINGTON, Joseph | SLADE, Mary Louisa | 24 MAY 1864 |
| WASHINGTON, Joshua | HOWARD, Julia (blk) | 26 AUG 1863 |
| WASHINGTON, Lewis | COOK, Mary (blk) | 15 JUL 1865 |
| WASHINGTON, Oscar | JOHNSON, Alice Virginia (blk) | 13 JUL 1863 |
| WASHINGTON, Richard | WEST, Martha (blk) | 08 NOV 1866 |
| WASHINGTON, Richard | SANDERS, Sophie (blk) | 16 SEP 1869 |
| WASHINGTON, Robert | JEFFRIES, Sylvia Ann | 28 APR 1866 |
| WASHINGTON, Samuel | JEFFERSON, Frances (blk) | 14 MAR 1867 |
| WASHINGTON, Thomas | BOSTON, Martha (blk) | 12 JUL 1859 |
| WASHINGTON, Thomas | LANCASTER, Mary (blk) | 11 JAN 1868 |
| WASHINGTON, Thomas | ADAMS, Rebecca (blk) | 27 MAY 1868 |
| WASHINGTON, Thomas F. | HARRIS, Ellen (blk) | 01 OCT 1860 |
| WASHINGTON, Warner | MOORE, Anna (blk) | 20 SEP 1866 |
| WASHINGTON, William | BELT, Anne (blk) | 02 OCT 1862 |
| WASHINGTON, William | PORTNAN, Mary (blk) | 17 MAR 1864 |
| WASHINGTON, William Henry | MERCER, Ellen (blk) | 03 DEC 1866 |
| WASSMAN, Reinhold | WENDEL, Catherine | 28 SEP 1858 |
| WATERS, Archibald | WINFIELD, Lucinda (blk) | 04 FEB 1860 |
| WATERS, Bernard | FEALEY, Hanora | 23 JUL 1864 |
| WATERS, Chas. R. | SIMPSON, Julia E. | 02 APR 1860 |
| WATERS, David | MURPHY, Sarah | 14 AUG 1862 |
| WATERS, Edward L. [7b] | CARROLL, Sarah Jane | 16 NOV 1869 |
| WATERS, Elijah D. | EWING, Merica E. | 03 MAR 1863 |
| WATERS, George | TAYLOR, Sophia | 29 JUN 1867 |
| WATERS, George | REDIN, Catherine T. | 24 OCT 1868 |
| WATERS, Henry | LEE, Eliza (blk) | 19 AUG 1863 |
| WATERS, James | RYDERS, Anna | 10 DEC 1861 |
| WATERS, James | PARKS, Elizabeth | 09 APR 1869 |
| WATERS, James A. | HIGGINS, Ruth M. | 28 NOV 1860 |
| WATERS, John | ELKINS, Mary E. | 18 NOV 1861 |
| WATERS, John | ANDERSON, Ann (blk) | 23 JUL 1862 |
| WATERS, John | WALKER, Mary (blk) | 21 DEC 1865 |
| WATERS, John | CHAPMAN, Elizabeth | 07 MAR 1867 |

| | | |
|---|---|---|
| WATERS, John A.W. | CHAMBERLIN, Margaret T. | 13 FEB 1862 |
| WATERS, John B. | DAVIS, Mary L. | 12 DEC 1860 |
| WATERS, John E. | NOLING, Mary | 03 APR 1868 |
| WATERS, John W. | SIMS, Margaret (blk) | 17 AUG 1861 |
| WATERS, John W. | PETIT, Mary Virginia | 08 JUL 1865 |
| WATERS, John W. | BALL, Sena (blk) | 06 AUG 1868 |
| WATERS, Joseph | CALBERT, Catherine (blk) | 03 DEC 1866 |
| WATERS, Mark Mabury | PEER, Emily Catherine (blk) | 16 NOV 1858 |
| WATERS, Morgan | KIRBY, Margaret J. | 17 JUL 1865 |
| WATERS, Morgan | MINITER, Maggie | 10 JUN 1870 |
| WATERS, Samuel | JONES, Martha Cornelia | 02 AUG 1864 |
| WATERS, Samuel | STEWART, Susan (blk) | 07 NOV 1867 |
| WATERS, Thomas | BROWN, Martha (blk) | 27 NOV 1861 |
| WATERS, Thomas | RIDGLEY, Ellen N. (blk) | 24 DEC 1867 |
| WATERS, Thomas | ROSS, Maria (blk) | 10 AUG 1868 |
| WATERS, W.G. | WELCH, Mollie S. | 23 JUL 1865 |
| WATERS, William | PARKER, Fanny (blk) | 18 MAY 1869 |
| WATKINS, Alexander | [illegible] | 17 AUG 1865 |
| WATKINS, Benjamin | BOWMAN, Harriet L. (blk) | 07 OCT 1868 |
| WATKINS, Greenbury M. | DUVALL, Margaret J. | 27 MAY 1867 |
| WATKINS, James | ADAMS, Gracey (blk) | 24 DEC 1864 |
| WATKINS, James | GARLAND, Henrietta (blk) | 06 NOV 1867 |
| WATKINS, James Clarence | PATTERSON, Mary Eliza | 01 APR 1869 |
| WATKINS, Jesse | DICKINSON, Mary Jane (blk) | 08 AUG 1867 |
| WATKINS, John H. | STRIEN, Sarah C. | 14 MAY 1868 |
| WATKINS, Michael | GRAYSON, Mary (blk) | 14 AUG 1867 |
| WATKINS, Nicholas | WROE, Marian J. | 13 DEC 1862 |
| WATKINS, Sephus | WILLIAMS, Mary (blk) | 19 DEC 1866 |
| WATTS, Nathaniel S. | BOYLE, Cornelia | 08 FEB 1864 |
| WATSON, Alexander | JONES, Annie | 09 SEP 1865 |
| WATSON, Alexander | JENKINS, Polly (blk) | 22 SEP 1866 |
| WATSON, Chas. F. [6r] | BOTELER, Laura V. | 21 NOV 1860 |
| WATSON, Edward D. | BURKE, Ellena | 19 SEP 1863 |
| WATSON, Henry | BANKS, Amanda (blk) | 03 JUN 1863 |
| WATSON, Henry | SHANKLAND, Julia (blk) | 10 JUL 1866 |
| WATSON, Henry C. | MELHORN, Jennie | 13 APR 1863 |
| WATSON, James | FILLMORE, Luanne (blk) | 08 JUN 1864 |
| WATSON, Jesse | BROWN, Rebecca (blk) | 16 NOV 1858 |
| WATSON, John | CONWAY, Frances Virginia (blk) | 04 JUN 1863 |
| WATSON, John Samuel | MARTIN, Marion J. | 30 JAN 1865 |
| WATSON, Joseph L. | DICKENS, Mary E. | 25 NOV 1868 |
| WATSON, Lewellen | WALKER, Mary V. | 24 NOV 1869 |
| WATSON, Martin A. | MAGRUDER, Hester A. | 01 AUG 1865 |
| WATSON, Melbone F. [Lt.] [11] | CODWISE, Mary B. * | 22 MAR 1862 |
| WATSON, Reuben | ARMSTRONG, Louisa (blk) | 11 FEB 1864 |
| WATSON, William | SIMPSON, Julia | 03 NOV 1859 |
| WATSON, William | BROWN, Mary J. | 30 AUG 1869 |
| WATSON, William A. [6r] | SMITH, Margaret F. | 04 OCT 1860 |
| WATSON, Wm. | BROWN, Mary J. | 02 NOV 1869 |
| WATTS, Basil | GRAHAM, Maria (blk) | 24 APR 1866 |
| WATTS, Henry | MERCER, Elizabeth L. | 14 AUG 1862 |
| WATTS, Henry N. | BLODGETT, Mary E. | 27 AUG 1863 |
| WATTS, James | JACKSON, Mary | 02 MAR 1863 |
| WATTS, John | LEWIS, Sarah | 08 OCT 1867 |
| WATTS, John W. | GARNER, Sarah Ann | 24 DEC 1867 |
| WATTS, Peter | MILLER, Anna | 06 JUL 1868 |

District of Columbia Marriage Licenses, 1858-1870

| | | |
|---|---|---|
| WATTS, Thomas | LEWIS, Elizabeth (blk) | 17 MAR 1864 |
| WATTS, Washington | TURNER, Harriet | 03 JUN 1865 |
| WATTS, William H. | JOHNSON, Eliza | 11 APR 1861 |
| WAUDLING, David | AXLINE, Mary A.E. | 17 OCT 1865 |
| WAUGH, James H. | MAGRUDER, Virginia (blk) | 25 OCT 1867 |
| WAUGH, John S. | KANE, Mary A. | 04 FEB 1868 |
| WAY, John [4] | RISLEY, Maria | 02 OCT 1866 |
| WAYNE, Daniel | BROOKS, Hannah (blk) | 30 SEP 1869 |
| WAYNE, William R. | LYNN, Harriet (blk) | 23 SEP 1867 |
| WAYNES, Lewis | HUBBARD, Rebbecca (blk) | 04 NOV 1863 |
| WEASNER, David H. | NICHOLSON, Josephine | 07 OCT 1859 |
| WEAVER, Andrew | THOMAS, Virginia (blk) | 08 JUL 1867 |
| WEAVER, Benjamin F. | PATTERSON, Nellie | 29 APR 1870 |
| WEAVER, Charles [1c] | McNIER, Augusta M. | 29 JAN 1863 |
| WEAVER, Charles E. | CONDICT, Eliza Stone | 03 MAR 1863 |
| WEAVER, Charles H. | SAXTY, Katie E. | 20 MAY 1865 |
| WEAVER, Charles H. | GANT, Mary Elizabeth | 23 DEC 1865 |
| WEAVER, Christian | EUSTICE, Mary | 07 NOV 1865 |
| WEAVER, Frank | MILLER, Elizabeth | 23 MAR 1870 |
| WEAVER, John T. | CRAUS, Elizabeth (blk) | 03 MAR 1863 |
| WEAVER, John W. | HAVENER, Mary E. | 11 FEB 1869 |
| WEAVER, Perry | WILSON, Eliza (blk) | 12 JUL 1865 |
| WEAVER, Richard | SHORTER, Celia (blk) | 08 JAN 1868 |
| WEAVER, Walker | BEALE, Lavinia (blk) | 30 NOV 1869 |
| WEBB, Alfred | MANNING, Charlotte | 11 JUL 1867 |
| WEBB, Charles [11] | RYAN, Sarah Ann | 23 JAN 1862 |
| WEBB, George | DOWNEY, Mary | 13 OCT 1864 |
| WEBB, J.D. | SANFORD, Mary | 02 JUL 1863 |
| WEBB, James [10] | GAYLEARD, Mary A. | 09 DEC 1861 |
| WEBB, James | SCOTT, Jane (blk) | 24 MAR 1870 |
| WEBB, James H. | PRESTON, Helen A. | 01 AUG 1868 |
| WEBB, John Converse | DUVAL, Bettie | 26 JUN 1866 |
| WEBB, Joseph [6m] | BOSWELL, Sarah Jane | 31 MAR 1863 |
| WEBB, Louis | BRANIGAN, Mary | 22 JAN 1866 |
| WEBB, Richard J. | LOVEJOY, Rebecca C. | 04 JAN 1859 |
| WEBB, Strother | CHURCHWILLE, Milly (blk) | 10 APR 1866 |
| WEBB, Thomas | WALTERS, Maria (blk) | 19 AUG 1867 |
| WEBB, William J. | NELSON, Maggie A. | 09 MAY 1865 |
| WEBBER, A. Harry | FARLAY, Kate F. | 01 MAY 1865 |
| WEBBER, Christopher | BOWER, Sarah J. | 14 OCT 1862 |
| WEBBER, John | LYNN, Isabella | 15 NOV 1868 |
| WEBEL, Charles | WEBER, Lizzie | 19 AUG 1861 |
| WEBER, Charles | LYNCH, Ann | 29 JUN 1861 |
| WEBER, Enos | WEITZBACHER, Frances | 18 FEB 1863 |
| WEBER, Fredk. W. [10] | MULLIGAN, Mary Ann | 25 JAN 1867 |
| WEBER, Henry | WENZEL, Gustina | 18 MAY 1865 |
| WEBER, Philip | MATTERN, Elizabeth | 19 JUN 1865 |
| WEBER, Philip Henry | LYNN, Eliza Jane | 13 NOV 1863 |
| WEBER, William | SCHNEIDER, Lizzi | 20 JAN 1862 |
| WEBSTER, Amos, Junr. | WILSON, Adelia S. | 21 JAN 1863 |
| WEBSTER, Andrew | BROOMFIELD, Georgianna (blk) | 03 JUL 1867 |
| WEBSTER, Charles | EDMONDS, Fannie (blk) | 20 JUN 1868 |
| WEBSTER, D. | SCHNEIDER, Emily A. | 01 OCT 1864 |
| WEBSTER, Daniel | BECKETT, Ellen (blk) | 04 JUN 1863 |
| WEBSTER, Daniel | CHISLEY, Louisa (blk) | 26 DEC 1866 |
| WEBSTER, Daniel | JORDAN, Theresa | 25 APR 1870 |

District of Columbia Marriage Licenses, 1858-1870

| | | |
|---|---|---|
| WEBSTER, David | GIBSON, Rosa (blk) | 09 JUN 1866 |
| WEBSTER, David | FORD, Mary Susan (blk) | 12 SEP 1868 |
| WEBSTER, Elial [10] | DUCKET, Caroline Eliz'th. | 04 JUN 1865 |
| WEBSTER, George | SNIER, Margaret | 11 MAR 1862 |
| WEBSTER, George | PRICE, Eliza | 16 JAN 1866 |
| WEBSTER, Isaac | PRINCE, Martha (blk) | 09 JUN 1868 |
| WEBSTER, John L. | PESTERIDGE, Sarah | 23 SEP 1867 |
| WEBSTER, John T. | MORRISON, Mary Elizabeth | 01 SEP 1864 |
| WEBSTER, Rosier | SMITH, Laura | 03 FEB 1870 |
| WEBSTER, T. Edward | BOHLAYER, Sarah Ann | 22 FEB 1864 |
| WEBSTER, Thomas S. | GODDARD, Catherine F. | 05 FEB 1861 |
| WEBSTER, William | WEAVER, Caroline (blk) | 26 FEB 1866 |
| WEBSTER, William | HALL, Etta Jane (blk) | 21 JAN 1867 |
| WEBSTER, William | REORDAN, Mary | 24 JAN 1868 |
| WEBSTER, William W. | WORTHING, Hellen B. | 08 JAN 1863 |
| WEBSTER, William [5] | EVANS, Augusta J. | 28 NOV 1868 |
| WEBSTER, Wilson | HUNLEY, Fannie (blk) | 17 AUG 1867 |
| WECKER, John | COOK, Mary | 07 AUG 1865 |
| WEDDERBURN, George C. | LAURENCE, Virginia M. | 25 APR 1861 |
| WEDDING, John William [10] | KING, Georgianna | 20 JAN 1864 |
| WEDLOCK, John | SMITH, Mary Ann (blk) | 06 OCT 1866 |
| WEED, J. Lesley | REYNOLDS, Maggie E. | 17 JUL 1865 |
| WEEDEN, Levin | MALOY, Lindea | 21 NOV 1866 |
| WEEDON, Lewis C. | JARBOE, Elizabeth R. | 18 SEP 1868 |
| WEEKS, David S. | RICE, Emma Skelly | 14 NOV 1864 |
| WEEKS, George Washington | PHILLIPS, Ellen Ann (blk) | 16 AUG 1860 |
| WEEMS, Henry | BROWN, Ellen (blk) | 13 JUN 1867 |
| WEEMS, Isaiah | HOLLAND, Christiana (blk) | 17 MAY 1866 |
| WEEMS, John | NICKENS, Nancy (blk) | 07 MAY 1868 |
| WEEMS, John | THOMAS, Elizabeth (blk) | 14 MAY 1868 |
| WEGGEMAN, Francis H. | LETON, Clara A. | 09 JAN 1869 |
| WEHRHEIM, Philip | HÖB, Mary | 14 OCT 1864 |
| WEIBERSAHR, Frederick | MILLER, Margaret | 07 JUL 1865 |
| WEIDEMAN, John | SCHWINGHAMMER, Maria M. | 05 MAR 1869 |
| WEIGLE, John J. | KRAFT, Louisa D. | 03 AUG 1869 |
| WEIL, Christian | BURKAN, Margreth | 21 DEC 1864 |
| WEIL, Jacob | DREIFUS, Rigge | 13 MAY 1865 |
| WEIL, John | SONNENBORN, Mina Rebecca | 15 JUL 1868 |
| WEILD, Samuel | KAUFMAN, Sarah | 16 MAY 1862 |
| WEILER, Ferdinand | WAUGH, Martha E. | 10 JUL 1867 |
| WEILL, Charles | FUCHS, Fanny | 06 APR 1869 |
| WEINANDT, George | HARDMAN, Rabarbara | 16 SEP 1863 |
| WEINBERGER, John A. | LAURY, Virginia | 10 NOV 1862 |
| WEIR, Richard | THRUSH, Mary A. | 08 MAY 1865 |
| WEISBROD, Henry | MÜLLER, Mina P. | 24 NOV 1862 |
| WEISEL, Christian A. | BUERGER, J.S. | 05 JUL 1865 |
| WEISEL, Daniel | WATERS, Isabel | 20 JAN 1868 |
| WEISER, Gottlieb | RIPPLE, Dorothy | 20 DEC 1865 |
| WEISGER, Frank | RUPP, Rosina | 06 FEB 1864 |
| WEISIGER, Ryland R. | ABBOTT, Mary M. | 07 JUN 1859 |
| WEISIGER, Thomas C. | O'DELL, Sue B. Suttle | 11 DEC 1860 |
| WEISSENFELD, Max | MURPHEY, Amanda D. | 04 NOV 1862 |
| WEISSINGER, Lewis | WAGNER, Louisa | 15 AUG 1862 |
| WEITNER, William | CLEMISON, Sarah J. | 25 JAN 1864 |
| WEITZELL, Frederick M. | BROGAN, Frances | 29 SEP 1864 |
| WELBY, Alfred B. | WRIGHTSON, Hester R. | 01 MAR 1860 |

District of Columbia Marriage Licenses, 1858-1870

| | | |
|---|---|---|
| WELCH, Alonzo T. [11] | HEPBURN, Maria O. | 23 JUL 1866 |
| WELCH, Edward P. | CONNOLLY, Mary Jane | 02 DEC 1863 |
| WELCH, George M. | BAYLEY, Mary Elizabeth | 18 AUG 1869 |
| WELCH, Henry | VEASEY, Martha E. (blk) | 26 DEC 1867 |
| WELCH, James H. | LAMB, Lollie | 25 JUL 1866 |
| WELCH, John | THORNTON, Margaret | 12 JUL 1865 |
| WELCH, Michael | O'DAY, Delia | 03 JAN 1870 |
| WELCH, Mollie S. | WATERS, W.G. | 23 JUL 1865 |
| WELCH, Patrick | FITZGERALD, Ellen | 13 FEB 1866 |
| WELCH, Patrick | LAUGHLIN, Annie | 11 JAN 1867 |
| WELCH, Paul | PAYNE, Maria (blk) | 09 JUL 1868 |
| WELCH, Philemon H. | CROGGON, Elizabeth V. | 10 FEB 1866 |
| WELCH, Treuman Smith | DOUGLAS, Catherine Elizabeth | 17 JUL 1863 |
| WELCH, William | JONES, Harriet Frances | 24 MAR 1862 |
| WELCH, William | O'DONNELL, Bridget | 21 NOV 1863 |
| WELCH, William | HUNTER, Nancy (blk) | 25 APR 1868 |
| WELDON, William Henry | MATTHEWS, Lizzie | 02 MAR 1867 |
| WELLER, Edwin A. | DOWNING, Sarah L. | 12 MAR 1860 |
| WELLER, Henry | WADSCHMIDT, Eliza | 08 SEP 1862 |
| WELLS, Daniel James | THECKER, Sarah Amanda | 05 JUN 1867 |
| WELLS, Edward | SHUGARS, Margaret (blk) | 27 FEB 1867 |
| WELLS, George | RANDAL, Rachel (blk) | 16 OCT 1866 |
| WELLS, George H. | PADDON, Henrietta | 12 JAN 1863 |
| WELLS, Hamilton | WISE, Anna (blk) | 19 MAR 1868 |
| WELLS, John | RUSSELL, Eliza Ann | 11 SEP 1861 |
| WELLS, John | WILLIAMS, Rosa (blk) | 02 AUG 1866 |
| WELLS, Robert | FINLEY, Ruth Ann (blk) | 06 AUG 1866 |
| WELLS, Samuel | VAUGHN, Esther Ann (blk) | 02 AUG 1865 |
| WELLS, Solomon | ANADALE, Charlotte | 10 JUL 1862 |
| WELLS, Thos. C. | CLARK, Maria C. | 10 NOV 1859 |
| WELLYAMS, James A.W. | BEERMAN, Emily | 02 DEC 1861 |
| WELMOTT, Joel | SARGENT, Mary C. | 20 DEC 1862 |
| WELSH, Daniel | HAVERTY, Julia | 09 OCT 1863 |
| WELSH, Garrett | BROWN, Joanna | 18 MAY 1863 |
| WELSH, Henry W. | ESCUDERO, Phillipine Mary | 17 JUL 1868 |
| WELSH, James | FITZPATRICK, Margaret | 14 JUN 1859 |
| WELSH, John E. | BALINGER, Mary E. | 19 NOV 1859 |
| WELSH, John E. | BALENGER, Mary E. | 26 MAR 1860 |
| WELSH, Joseph | BANE, Catharine | 11 APR 1863 |
| WELSH, Michael | SYPES, Mary Jane | 30 JUL 1859 |
| WELSH, Michael | FLANNAGAN, Margaret | 11 SEP 1862 |
| WELSH, Michael | SLATTERY, Margaret | 29 AUG 1862 |
| WELSH, Michael | GRACE, Margaret | 17 MAR 1864 |
| WELSH, Patrick | MADDEN, Ann | 07 OCT 1861 |
| WELSH, Patrick | EASTY, Mary | 10 AUG 1865 |
| WELSH, Thomas | FORD, Bridget | 07 OCT 1865 |
| WELSH, Thomas H. | FENTON, Annie | 31 JUL 1865 |
| WELSH, William H. | MARTIN, Georgiana | 13 JUN 1864 |
| WEMYSS, Alexr. W. | KANE, Hanora | 20 SEP 1861 |
| WENBAN, William | BLYTH, Ellen S. | 11 MAY 1868 |
| WENDELL, J.A. Theodore | HALE, Anna Maria | 02 FEB 1869 |
| WENDERLING, George | KÖRBER, Sophia | 25 MAY 1864 |
| WENER, Charles | YOUNG, Margaret | 31 MAR 1864 |
| WENNER, Louis | CRAF, Dorothy | 16 FEB 1863 |
| WENTWORTH, Conrad | CISSELL, Lizzie | 10 OCT 1861 |
| WENTWORTH, Conrad | CECIL, Kate | 15 APR 1864 |

| | | |
|---|---|---|
| WENZEL, John | FULMORE, Mary | 12 DEC 1861 |
| WENZEL, John | SCHURTZ, Elizabeth | 10 DEC 1868 |
| WERNER, Chas. F. Wm. Fernando | vanWURKEL, Lizzie W. | 06 NOV 1862 |
| WERNER, Robert | NOLTE, Martha | 07 OCT 1861 |
| WERST, John | KANFELT, Emilie | 25 MAY 1865 |
| WERTENBAKER, Woodward E. [12s] | WROE, Lizzie | 27 JUL 1861 |
| WESCHKE, Charles | GIESEKE, Chalarina | 05 JAN 1867 |
| WESCHLER, Adam | HOWELL, Maggie | 11 JAN 1870 |
| WESLEY, John | CARROLL, Hannah (blk) | 22 FEB 1867 |
| WESLEY, John | BURNETT, Angeline (blk) | 12 MAR 1868 |
| WESLEY, William | ROSS, Louisa | 17 JUN 1863 |
| WEST, Alonzo S. | HALLEY, Bettie V. | 01 NOV 1866 |
| WEST, Benjamin S. [7a] | ASHBY, Catherine | 04 NOV 1868 |
| WEST, Charles | SIMPSON, Eliza Ann (blk) | 13 OCT 1864 |
| WEST, Clement L. | ADDISON, Sallie C. | 08 DEC 1860 |
| WEST, Clement T. | PHENIX, Jane (blk) | 03 MAR 1869 |
| WEST, Cornelius | HENSON, Jane (blk) | 17 OCT 1865 |
| WEST, David P. | HESS, Amelia Martha | 16 JAN 1867 |
| WEST, Edmund | JONES, Mary (blk) | 11 MAY 1869 |
| WEST, Frank | JONES, Mary Jane (blk) | 06 JUN 1865 |
| WEST, George N. | STEWART, Lizzie L. | 04 OCT 1869 |
| WEST, Henry | WATSON, Anna (blk) | 30 SEP 1867 |
| WEST, James W. | DOVE, Catherine Ann | 26 OCT 1869 |
| WEST, Jeremiah | ARNOLD, Jane (blk) | 14 OCT 1869 |
| WEST, John | BOWIE, Elizabeth (blk) | 14 APR 1864 |
| WEST, John Thomas | CASSELL, Mary Elizabeth | 17 MAY 1860 |
| WEST, Laurence | MARSHALL, Rachael A.C. | 03 JUL 1862 |
| WEST, Lewis | ROSS, Harriet (blk) | 21 DEC 1865 |
| WEST, Lewis R. | THOMAS, Clarissa (blk) | 14 OCT 1867 |
| WEST, Louis | CHURCH, Martha E. (blk) | 28 JUL 1862 |
| WEST, Richard | WELLS, Eliza (blk) | 30 OCT 1869 |
| WEST, Richard | CARROLL, Mary (blk) | 16 FEB 1870 |
| WEST, Theodore Spencer | LANCASTER, Mary Vandalia | 12 DEC 1864 |
| WEST, Tobias | BROWN, Emma Jane (blk) | 06 JUL 1864 |
| WEST, Vinson | SMITH, Mary Ann (blk) | 10 DEC 1864 |
| WEST, William Henry | BOWIE, Kate (blk) | 11 JUN 1867 |
| WEST, William Thos. | HENDLEY, Sarah Virginia | 08 DEC 1859 |
| WESTERBERGER, John A. [1c] | JONES, Mary Ann | 09 NOV 1863 |
| WESTERMAYER, John | METZCELLER, Babette | 09 SEP 1864 |
| WESTFALLS, Charles | KRAIDER, Elizabeth D. | 04 JAN 1865 |
| WESTON, Joseph P. | SCHOOL, Helen Agnes | 19 APR 1869 |
| WESTWOOD, William P. | FERGUSON, Elizabeth A. | 01 JUL 1862 |
| WETHERALL, John W. | STEVENS, Elizabeth N. | 06 JAN 1862 |
| WETHERILT, William | CECIL, Margaret N. | 09 FEB 1864 |
| WETSELL, John Joseph | WALKER, Susanna | 14 JAN 1862 |
| WETZEL, Henry | YERBY, Cynthia Jane | 11 APR 1863 |
| WETZEL, Philip | BEHRENS, Henrietta M. | 21 NOV 1862 |
| WETZELL, Frederick | SHOEMAKER, Margaret Ann | 08 DEC 1859 |
| WETZERICK, George F. | TRUNNELL, Ida E. | 28 MAR 1864 |
| WEY, Chapman | HICKS, Joanna (blk) | 21 DEC 1865 |
| WEY, George | HAMILTON, Lizzie (blk) | 08 MAY 1867 |
| WEYGANT, W.E. | GREER, M.E. | 27 SEP 1869 |
| WEYN, Max | RAFF, Mary | 08 FEB 1862 |
| WHALEN, Charles | CARTER, Mary | 17 MAY 1860 |
| WHALEN, Dennis | HANLAN, Mary | 10 DEC 1864 |
| WHALEN, Henry | GRIMES, Elizabeth | 19 OCT 1859 |

District of Columbia Marriage Licenses, 1858-1870

| | | |
|---|---|---|
| WHALEN, James | CHAMBERLAIN, Mary M. | 10 FEB 1859 |
| WHALEN, John | DUFFY, Catharine | 13 JAN 1865 |
| WHALEN, Thomas | PENDERGRAST, Mary | 19 FEB 1862 |
| WHALEN, William | McNERHANEY, Catharine | 11 APR 1861 |
| WHALEY, James | DRISCOLL, Margaret | 05 APR 1870 |
| WHALEY, Robert | BANKS, Eliza (blk) | 03 DEC 1864 |
| WHALING, John | ARRINGTON, Catherine | 14 AUG 1861 |
| WHARTON, John S. | WHARTON, Ella D. | 19 JUL 1859 |
| WHEAT, Joseph F. | DUNNINGTON, Bettie C. | 21 MAR 1868 |
| WHEATLEY, James | BENTON, Catherine | 01 FEB 1866 |
| WHEATLEY, James F. | GRIMES, Mary E. | 09 OCT 1866 |
| WHEATLEY, James P. | GOLDSMITH, Mary V. | 15 JAN 1863 |
| WHEATLEY, Joseph | ROSS, Mary (blk) | 08 DEC 1866 |
| WHEATLEY, Thomas H. | OXLEY, Sophia | 23 APR 1867 |
| WHEATLEY, William G. | MELSON, Mary T. | 07 OCT 1861 |
| WHEATLEY, William G. | MELSON, Mary T. | 25 JAN 1862 |
| WHEATON, Frank, Maj. Gen. [4] | MILLER, Maria B. | 12 JAN 1867 |
| WHEATON, James H. | ROBERTS, Margaret Ann | 30 OCT 1865 |
| WHEEDEN, Thomas J. | HANNA, Annie M. | 11 JUL 1865 |
| WHEELER, Charles | SMITH, Mary (blk) | 09 NOV 1868 |
| WHEELER, Charles H. | WRENN, Hellen A. | 09 JUN 1860 |
| WHEELER, Edmund G. | MURRAY, Sarah A. | 04 FEB 1864 |
| WHEELER, George H. | McEWEN, Lois H. | 25 JUN 1866 |
| WHEELER, John | GREEN, Sarah (blk) | 23 NOV 1869 |
| WHEELER, John B. | CHEDAL, Mary E. | 01 NOV 1859 |
| WHEELER, John B. | JONES, Annie M. | 02 JAN 1867 |
| WHEELER, John W. | HORE, Mary Ellen | 10 MAY 1865 |
| WHEELER, Joseph | RAMSAY, Margaret A. | 16 MAY 1862 |
| WHEELER, Philip | BROWN, Sarah M. | 12 AUG 1867 |
| WHEELER, Samuel | MATHEWS, Catherine (blk) | 09 APR 1867 |
| WHEELER, Thomas C. | CHEW, Anna M. | 27 JUN 1859 |
| WHEELER, William | COOPER, Maria (blk) | 21 MAY 1868 |
| WHEELING, Wm. | BUHENEY, Johanna C. | 18 DEC 1863 |
| WHEELER, William H. | FOSTER, Adeline (blk) | 16 APR 1868 |
| WHEELER, William T. | MYERS, Margaret | 30 SEP 1869 |
| WHEELOCK, Alphonso M. | CLEMENTS, Mary F. | 12 JUN 1869 |
| WHEELOCK, William W. | ROACH, Annie R. | 14 MAR 1864 |
| WHEELWRIGHT, Frederick D. | HUNGERFORD, Eleanor | 04 DEC 1858 |
| WHELAN, Alexander | FITZPATRICK, Norah | 13 JAN 1870 |
| WHELAN, John | COLLINS, Hanora | 20 FEB 1868 |
| WHELAN, Pearce | WELSH, Eliza | 11 NOV 1862 |
| WHELAN, William | POTIS, Fannie | 22 OCT 1868 |
| WHETZELL, Samuel | THOMPSON, Mary C. | 17 JUL 1869 |
| WHIP, Robert | MOORE, Sarah Jane (blk) | 04 MAY 1865 |
| WHIPPLE, Charles M. | CAYWOOD, Sarah J. | 14 DEC 1864 |
| WHITAKER, Edward W. | DAVIS, Theodosia | 07 JUN 1865 |
| WHITAKER, Gilbert | TURNER, Saviny | 07 SEP 1859 |
| WHITAKER, Jesse H. | PREVOST, Eleanor A. | 13 JUN 1868 |
| WHITCOMB, Gustavus A. [4] | WILSON, Mary V. | 01 JUN 1867 |
| WHITCOMB, William H. | NEALE, Susan V. | 26 JAN 1864 |
| WHITE, Alfred P. | GRIMES, Helen M. | 03 AUG 1864 |
| WHITE, Alge | SIMS, Josephine (blk) | 29 AUG 1867 |
| WHITE, Arthur | RICKS, Elizabeth (blk) | 18 FEB 1867 |
| WHITE, Boswell | FOSKEY, Clarissa (blk) | 11 NOV 1863 |
| WHITE, Charles | HENDERSON, Mary Ann | 29 OCT 1863 |
| WHITE, Charles [11] | MILLS, Mary Jane Roberts | 23 DEC 1865 |

District of Columbia Marriage Licenses, 1858-1870

| | | |
|---|---|---|
| WHITE, Charles | GRIFFIN, Fanny | 17 JUL 1867 |
| WHITE, Charles | HOWARD, Lucy (blk) | 29 JUN 1867 |
| WHITE, Charles | GREENLEAF, Catherine (blk) | 19 MAY 1870 |
| WHITE, Charles Henry | CLAIBOURN, Mary Jane (blk) | 18 JUN 1866 |
| WHITE, Emanuel | KANE, Lucy (blk) | 31 AUG 1865 |
| WHITE, Frederick | HOLKER, Mary | 02 AUG 1864 |
| WHITE, George | HARRIS, Marion A. | 05 OCT 1858 |
| WHITE, George A. | WILLIAMS, Amelia (blk) | 12 JUL 1869 |
| WHITE, George W. | ROWLES, Jane Isabella | 22 JUN 1863 |
| WHITE, George W. (Vt.) | SHERMAN, Amanda M. (Vt.) | 18 SEP 1863 |
| WHITE, Harry | BROWN, Clara (blk) | 27 MAR 1868 |
| WHITE, Henry | COX, Mary Ellen (blk) | 20 MAY 1864 |
| WHITE, Hollis [11] | SYKES, Agnes H. | 20 JUL 1864 |
| WHITE, Horace A. | ROWELL, Harriet M. | 24 SEP 1864 |
| WHITE, Isaac | JOHNSON, Caroline (blk) | 20 JUN 1864 |
| WHITE, Isaac | BRUCE, Eliza (blk) | 09 NOV 1865 |
| WHITE, Jackson | DEVAUGHN, Judy | 26 DEC 1865 |
| WHITE, James W. | WALKER, Ella | 30 AUG 1860 |
| WHITE, James W. [7b] | HALLOCK, Marion V. | 06 MAY 1869 |
| WHITE, John | KNOX, Ellen | 21 JUN 1860 |
| WHITE, John | McFOULAND, Emily | 29 OCT 1863 |
| WHITE, John | CARTER, Amanda (blk) | 12 NOV 1866 |
| WHITE, John | BRADY, Jemima | 21 AUG 1865 |
| WHITE, John | BREWER, Martha (blk) | 18 SEP 1868 |
| WHITE, John D. | LONG, Catherine | 21 OCT 1867 |
| WHITE, John L. | SHAFFER, Catharine | 21 SEP 1864 |
| WHITE, Jonah H. | HAYS, Mary Ann | 11 JAN 1867 |
| WHITE, Joseph | TILLMAN, Eliza Ann (blk) | 21 NOV 1863 |
| WHITE, Joseph W. | STUART, Julia W. | 26 OCT 1869 |
| WHITE, Lawrence B. | TALIAFERRO, Eliza | 06 JUL 1860 |
| WHITE, Lewis | ROBINSON, Martha (blk) | 26 MAR 1870 |
| WHITE, Lewis C. | YOUNT, Susan | 21 NOV 1868 |
| WHITE, Matthew | McPHERSON, Emily Jane (blk) | 17 AUG 1868 |
| WHITE, Michael | QUINLON, Mary | 30 JAN 1864 |
| WHITE, Mills | SCOTT, Nancy (blk) | 13 DEC 1864 |
| WHITE, Nicholas | SMITH, Margaret | 22 JUL 1865 |
| WHITE, Oliver L. | MEACHAM, Polly E. | 07 JAN 1865 |
| WHITE, Patrick | O'BRIEN, Mary Ann | 24 JAN 1859 |
| WHITE, Peter | GRAY, Julia (blk) | 20 DEC 1864 |
| WHITE, Peter B. | JOHNSON, Ellen (blk) | 24 SEP 1863 |
| WHITE, Philip | SCOTT, Martha (blk) | 31 DEC 1867 |
| WHITE, Robert | THOMAS, Lucy (blk) | 31 MAY 1865 |
| WHITE, Robert H. [10] | PERRY, Mary Ann | 05 FEB 1870 |
| WHITE, Samuel | BUMREY, Rosa (blk) | 11 MAY 1870 |
| WHITE, Samuel S. | PURCELL, Julia A. | 03 JUL 1866 |
| WHITE, Samuel W. | SLEIGH, Jemima | 26 JUL 1866 |
| WHITE, Simon | WHITE, Catherine (blk) | 15 FEB 1869 |
| WHITE, Spencer | BOSWELL, Martha (blk) | 14 JUN 1869 |
| WHITE, Thomas | POTTER, Rosa | 28 OCT 1863 |
| WHITE, Thomas | HAILEY, Bridget | 28 APR 1866 |
| WHITE, Thos. P. | HAYDEN, Mary A.C. | 15 MAY 1862 |
| WHITE, Walker | OSBORN, Harriet (blk) | 30 MAY 1867 |
| WHITE, William Christian | WATKINS, Ruth Annie | 21 AUG 1865 |
| WHITE, William H. | KUHL, Margaret | 27 MAY 1865 |
| WHITE, William H. | CONSTABLE, Cinderella | 11 MAY 1866 |
| WHITE, William L. [6l] | LYON, Mary C. | 28 MAY 1861 |

District of Columbia Marriage Licenses, 1858-1870

| | | |
|---|---|---|
| WHITE, William Washington | WILKERSON, Margaret (blk) | 27 JUN 1863 |
| WHITEHEAD, Alfred E. | CROSS, Sarah | 07 SEP 1865 |
| WHITEHEAD, Joel H. [6s] | TAYLOR, Laura V. | 20 JUN 1864 |
| WHITEHEAD, William | WETSELL, Francetta | 06 SEP 1865 |
| WHITELEY, Lambert A. | BRADFORD, Clara Bel | 09 JAN 1866 |
| WHITELEY, Marsland | McGRAW, Ellen | 25 SEP 1865 |
| WHITELY, William H., M.D. | WÜRDEMANN, Alice | 12 FEB 1867 |
| WHITESELL, Daniel A. | EDWARDS, Mary Caroline | 18 NOV 1865 |
| WHITESIDE, A.S. | BEVIER, Katie E. | 18 AUG 1866 |
| WHITFIELD, Henry | ROBINSON, Catherine (blk) | 19 SEP 1867 |
| WHITING, George B. | LYONS, Annie N. | 08 OCT 1866 |
| WHITING, Harlow H. [4] | MILLER, Joanna E. | 20 SEP 1864 |
| WHITING, Harry Carlyle [11] | EVELETH, Sarah Maynadier | 17 JUN 1865 |
| WHITLER, Randolph | BERRY, Elizabeth (blk) | 12 MAY 1863 |
| WHITLEY, Alexander | WASHINGTON, Lizzie (blk) | 23 JUN 1864 |
| WHITLEY, Andrew | ALEXANDER, Catherine (blk) | 27 MAR 1868 |
| WHITLOCK, Abraham | KRESLOWSKI, Sarah | 30 SEP 1869 |
| WHITLOW, John H. | NEALE, Sarah (blk) | 24 NOV 1858 |
| WHITLY, Mercer | PAGE, Dolly (blk) | 28 DEC 1865 |
| WHITMORE, Joseph | CARR, Mary | 31 JUL 1863 |
| WHITMORE, William | LEEK, Kesiah | 16 FEB 1865 |
| WHITMORE, William H. | BEAGLE, Elizabeth | 07 OCT 1858 |
| WHITMORE, Willis G. | BELL, Kate | 04 MAR 1864 |
| WHITNALL, Asa M. | GUTRICK, Julia E. | 24 JUL 1862 |
| WHITNEY, Charles S. | BARBER, Susan | 13 SEP 1862 |
| WHITNEY, Horace A. | MOORE, Laura A. | 31 AUG 1868 |
| WHITNEY, Joseph | WILSON, Mary Ann | 23 JUN 1868 |
| WHITNEY, Joseph N. [11] | BURROUGHS, Charlotte S., Mrs. | 09 NOV 1865 |
| WHITNEY, William H. | McGOWAN, Alberta S. | 14 SEP 1869 |
| WHITON, Edward | WALKER, Patsy (blk) | 29 DEC 1864 |
| WHITTINGTON, George W. | PREUSS, Barbara C. | 08 MAY 1865 |
| WHITTINGTON, Jefferson | MILLS, Margaret (blk) | 23 SEP 1869 |
| WHITTLESEY, William G. [12s] | HOUSTON, Sallie H. | 06 JUN 1860 |
| WHITTY, Edward | GALLAGHER, Elizabeth | 16 MAY 1862 |
| WHITTY, Robert | O'BRIEN, Mary | 27 APR 1859 |
| WHITWELL, John C. | MILLER, Margaret L. | 10 FEB 1868 |
| WHONOHAN, Patrick T. | RONAN, Bridget | 22 FEB 1865 |
| WHONOHAN, Robert | SCANLON, Ellen | 21 SEP 1861 |
| WIBBROSKI, Vicenti | ULBRIGHT, Cimlin | 20 JAN 1868 |
| WICKHAM, Horace | EVANS, Catharine | 15 APR 1864 |
| WICKS, George W. | LAYTON, Winney (blk) | 08 MAR 1865 |
| WIDINEIRE, John D. | ROGERS, Hanna | 22 DEC 1864 |
| WIDMAYER, Christian | BETTS, Catherine | 19 APR 1862 |
| WIDMAYER, William G. | GUNSER, Catharine F. | 11 JUL 1868 |
| WIDSTRAND, Chas. T. | THAYER, Adelaide E. | 28 JAN 1867 |
| WIEDERSHEIM, John Andrew [5] | SCHNEIDER, Louisa Henrietta | 05 DEC 1867 |
| WIEGAND, John C. | LUDIG, Fredericka | 28 OCT 1863 |
| WIENHOLZ, Frank | BIVENGER, Mina | 26 FEB 1863 |
| WIESER, Lewis | AILER, Sophia | 27 FEB 1867 |
| WIESNER, Charles | WILLARD, Mary Teresa | 11 MAY 1863 |
| WIGERTON, John | QUEEN, Virginia (blk) | 03 MAY 1866 |
| WIGGINS, Horace | BLAND, Victoria (blk) | 09 OCT 1866 |
| WIGGINS, William H. | PARISH, Virginia A. | 24 JUL 1867 |
| WIGGINTIN, Henry | NUGENT, Rebecca (blk) | 25 NOV 1869 |
| WIGHTMAN, John | FLETCHER, Martha V. | 02 AUG 1867 |
| WILBER, Emery A. | BARNES, Elizabeth A. | 30 JUL 1867 |

District of Columbia Marriage Licenses, 1858-1870

| | | |
|---|---|---|
| WILBORN, William H. [6s] | PYLES, Martha A. | 03 JAN 1865 |
| WILBURN, George W. | GIFFIN, Mary A. | 02 JUL 1867 |
| WILCOX, Chas. F. | DUVALL, Susan R. | 09 FEB 1865 |
| WILCOXEN, George | McDONNELL, Mary | 04 MAY 1863 |
| WILCOXEN, Nathan T. [7a] | BROWN, Ann Elizabeth | 23 AUG 1866 |
| WILD, George [of Martinsburg] [5] | AVERY, Ida Mary | 02 JAN 1869 |
| WILD, John F. | ANDERSON, Sarah E. | 27 JUL 1867 |
| WILDER, William W. [11] | GALE, Annie | 05 NOV 1864 |
| WILEY, Edward | HICKS, Frances | 15 MAR 1866 |
| WILEY, Isaac | WINTERS, Lucy (blk) | 11 FEB 1869 |
| WILEY, James F. (sailor) [6m] | BROWN, Mary E. | 20 JUL 1863 |
| WILEY, John T. | HOWARD, Frances Anne | 17 MAR 1865 |
| WILEY, Nelson | LAWSON, Lizzie (blk) | 21 MAY 1866 |
| WILFORD, Henry C. | O'NEIL, Sarah | 20 AUG 1868 |
| WILFRED, George R. | WARRING, Marshall Sallie | 22 NOV 1865 |
| WILHAN, Joseph | MYERS, Maria | 19 MAY 1869 |
| WILIAMS, Henry Charles | EGAND, Elizabeth | 15 MAY 1865 |
| WILIAMS, William M. | CARTER, Martha (blk) | 30 OCT 1862 |
| WILKE, William F. | HOLLIES, Mary Elizabeth | 02 SEP 1864 |
| WILKERSON, John A. [6h] | WILKERSON, Alice | 04 APR 1868 |
| WILKERSON, John H. [6h] | LANGLEY, Margaret | 28 AUG 1868 |
| WILKERSON, Samuel | POWERS, Amanda M. | 28 JAN 1863 |
| WILKERSON, William | COLE, Mary Ann | 18 APR 1864 |
| WILKERSON, Wm. | THOMAS, Harriet (blk) | 25 MAR 1862 |
| WILKEY, Benjamin J. | WINN, Mary | 02 AUG 1865 |
| WILKINS, Charles A. | REINHARD, Clemmie | 08 SEP 1866 |
| WILKINS, Melville | CONWAY, Deborah (blk) | 20 FEB 1868 |
| WILKINS, Samuel A. | BRADLEY, Martha A. | 08 JUL 1865 |
| WILKINSON, John | TOPPIN, Virginia (blk) | 29 OCT 1868 |
| WILKINSON, John F.N. | BELL, Rachel Ann (blk) | 05 OCT 1868 |
| WILKINSON, Joseph | McNANNEY, [blank] | 02 JUN 1866 |
| WILKINSON, Josiah | GOODWIN, Margaret J. | 14 APR 1868 |
| WILKINSON, N.W. | SANDS, Emma R. | 22 DEC 1869 |
| WILKINSON, Richard | BOYLE, Catherine | 07 OCT 1868 |
| WILKINSON, Robert H. | SIMPSON, Cornelia B. (blk) | 20 APR 1865 |
| WILKINSON, Samuel D. | CROWDER, Mary L. | 27 NOV 1866 |
| WILKINSON, Walter S. | MORGAN, Mary M. | 08 AUG 1861 |
| WILKINSON, William | STEWART, Rosetta (blk) | 06 MAY 1869 |
| WILKISON, Lewis L. | WARING, Mary E. | 05 JUN 1869 |
| WILL, Joseph B. | WARREN, Mary E. | 28 FEB 1863 |
| WILLARD, Joseph C. | FORD, Antonia | 10 MAR 1864 |
| WILLCOX, Edward J. | POCHON, Sophia, Mrs. | 13 AUG 1868 |
| WILLENBÜCHER, Eugene | HAMMERSCHLAG, Harriet | 26 OCT 1863 |
| WILLETT, Charles W. | HICKS, Mary Jane | 08 FEB 1865 |
| WILLETT, John A. [6] | MARTIN, Sallie | 10 AUG 1869 |
| WILLEY, Charles | GREER, Caroline | 08 NOV 1865 |
| WILLHOMS, Thomas | SMOLINSKA, Honorine Maudd | 16 OCT 1865 |
| WILLIAM, Samuel H. | FISHER, Emily M. | 26 JUN 1860 |
| WILLIAMS, Abraham | COOK, Ann Matilda | 18 JUL 1867 |
| WILLIAMS, Allmon | LEWIS, Annie | 19 MAR 1864 |
| WILLIAMS, Andrew | LEMONS, Julia (blk) | 15 JUL 1868 |
| WILLIAMS, Andrew E. | HARRINGTON, Henrietta (blk) | 03 DEC 1867 |
| WILLIAMS, Archibald | JOHNSON, Ellen (blk) | 14 JAN 1862 |
| WILLIAMS, Arthur | PRIGGIN, Marguerita | 13 DEC 1861 |
| WILLIAMS, Arthur | MITCHELL, Mary | 28 JUN 1864 |
| WILLIAMS, Arthur | THOMAS, Mary (blk) | 30 MAR 1866 |

District of Columbia Marriage Licenses, 1858-1870

| | | |
|---|---|---|
| WILLIAMS, Arthur T. | CONAWAY, Kitty (blk) | 05 JUL 1866 |
| WILLIAMS, Augustus | GLOVER, Ella H. | 22 SEP 1862 |
| WILLIAMS, Benjamin | REDMAN, Emeline (blk) | 05 NOV 1868 |
| WILLIAMS, Benjamin F. | RICHARDSON, Mary A. | 26 APR 1869 |
| WILLIAMS, Charles | BECKWID, Louisa (blk) | 09 AUG 1860 |
| WILLIAMS, Charles | BAHANS, Hannah | 21 AUG 1860 |
| WILLIAMS, Charles | LARKINS, Emily Elizth. | 27 JAN 1862 |
| WILLIAMS, Charles | WALKER, Mary (blk) | 09 MAR 1864 |
| WILLIAMS, Charles | CARROLL, Maria (blk) | 10 JUL 1866 |
| WILLIAMS, Charles | VOGLE, Dolly | 09 MAY 1867 |
| WILLIAMS, Charles | WILLIAMS, Martha Ellen | 12 JAN 1870 |
| WILLIAMS, Charles | HOLMES, Mary (blk) | 21 MAY 1870 |
| WILLIAMS, Charles F., Lt. | FAGUE, Josie B. | 13 NOV 1865 |
| WILLIAMS, Charles H. | WEBSTER, Lucy (blk) | 07 APR 1869 |
| WILLIAMS, Charles L. | RYAN, Josephine | 12 AUG 1861 |
| WILLIAMS, Charles Thomas | HALL, Almira Jane (blk) | 24 MAR 1864 |
| WILLIAMS, Charles W. | SALMONS, Alice H. | 09 APR 1869 |
| WILLIAMS, Daniel | BALL, Elizabeth (blk) | 19 JUL 1864 |
| WILLIAMS, Daniel | VAUGHN, Maria | 30 DEC 1865 |
| WILLIAMS, Daniel | HYSON, Elizabeth (blk) | 13 OCT 1869 |
| WILLIAMS, Daniel A. | WIGGINTON, Frances Ann (blk) | 08 DEC 1866 |
| WILLIAMS, David H. | MEADER, Catharine | 27 AUG 1862 |
| WILLIAMS, DeWit C. | UMBERFIELD, Alice | 06 JAN 1869 |
| WILLIAMS, Edgar | HAMMOND, Catherine (blk) | 10 MAY 1866 |
| WILLIAMS, Edward [10] | WILLIAMS, Ann Elizabeth | 03 JUN 1865 |
| WILLIAMS, Edward | MYERS, Mary E. (blk) | 10 JAN 1862 |
| WILLIAMS, Edward C. | JOHNS, Annie (blk) | 15 OCT 1864 |
| WILLIAMS, Edward T. | HOPEWELL, Fannie (blk) | 30 SEP 1867 |
| WILLIAMS, Ephraim | SKIPWORTH, Patsy (blk) | 27 MAR 1867 |
| WILLIAMS, Fielder | ELMORE, Elizabeth F. | 06 FEB 1863 |
| WILLIAMS, Francis Xavier | MANSFIELD, Annie | 24 DEC 1863 |
| WILLIAMS, Frank C. | DALY, Ellen | 17 JUN 1864 |
| WILLIAMS, Frank C. | DALY, Ellen | 16 MAR 1865 |
| WILLIAMS, Frank H. | FLEMING, Mollie A. | 29 SEP 1866 |
| WILLIAMS, George [12s] | JONES, Sarah E. | 12 MAR 1861 |
| WILLIAMS, George | HOWARD, Mary J. (blk) | 15 AUG 1861 |
| WILLIAMS, George | CURTIS, Susan (blk) | 25 JUN 1863 |
| WILLIAMS, George | WASHINGTON, Christiana (blk) | 23 JUL 1863 |
| WILLIAMS, George | STEWART, Margaret (blk) | 11 AUG 1864 |
| WILLIAMS, George | WILLIAMS, Lucy | 30 NOV 1865 |
| WILLIAMS, George | WILLIAMS, Leona (blk) | 08 DEC 1865 |
| WILLIAMS, George | GETZ, Anna (blk) | 07 AUG 1866 |
| WILLIAMS, George | THOMAS, Rachel (blk) | 06 OCT 1866 |
| WILLIAMS, George W. | DOWNING, Caroline (blk) | 18 MAY 1867 |
| WILLIAMS, Granville Hisler | HARRISON, Sarah Helena | 26 AUG 1868 |
| WILLIAMS, Guilford | MARCHAEL, Martha E. | 14 JUN 1862 |
| WILLIAMS, Harrison C. | PREALL, Mattie | 06 JAN 1870 |
| WILLIAMS, Harrison Clay | CROWN, Leah Jane | 12 DEC 1863 |
| WILLIAMS, Henry | DOUGLASS, Lavinia (blk) | 21 FEB 1861 |
| WILLIAMS, Henry | BERKLEY, Jane (blk) | 23 SEP 1862 |
| WILLIAMS, Henry | JOHNSON, Emeline (col'd) | 22 DEC 1863 |
| WILLIAMS, Henry | WARTERS, Priscilla (blk) | 27 APR 1864 |
| WILLIAMS, Henry | STAUNER, Malvina (blk) | 22 OCT 1864 |
| WILLIAMS, Henry | DYER, Catharine | 09 NOV 1865 |
| WILLIAMS, Henry | TAYLOR, Mary | 06 JAN 1868 |
| WILLIAMS, Henry | BURNS, Susan (blk) [22 NOV 1870] | 28 JAN 1868 |

| | | |
|---|---|---|
| WILLIAMS, Henry | HILL, Mahala (blk) | 21 DEC 1868 |
| WILLIAMS, Henry | CHISLER, Sarah (blk) | 08 DEC 1868 |
| WILLIAMS, Hilliard | PAYNE, Mahala (blk) | 05 DEC 1865 |
| WILLIAMS, Holand C. | MAGILL, Frances R. | 24 SEP 1867 |
| WILLIAMS, Horace | WASHINGTON, Mary (blk) | 04 SEP 1866 |
| WILLIAMS, Howard | WILLIAMS, Jennie | 20 MAR 1865 |
| WILLIAMS, Irving | DOUGLAS, Nancy (blk) | 18 MAR 1865 |
| WILLIAMS, Isaac | MAGRUDER, Mary Ann | 20 DEC 1860 |
| WILLIAMS, Isaac | BROWN, Berija (blk) | 18 MAY 1867 |
| WILLIAMS, J. Hamilton | SPALDING, Mary E. | 24 OCT 1860 |
| WILLIAMS, James | ARNOLD, Elvia Ann | 13 MAY 1862 |
| WILLIAMS, James | ROWSER, Alice (blk) | 13 JUL 1864 |
| WILLIAMS, James | SMITH, E. Augusta | 17 NOV 1865 |
| WILLIAMS, James | GREGORY, Violet Mc. | 29 JAN 1866 |
| WILLIAMS, James | LACEY, Mary Ann (blk) | 16 FEB 1869 |
| WILLIAMS, James E. | BOWMAN, Emma J. | 10 DEC 1859 |
| WILLIAMS, James H. | SIMS, Ann Eliza (blk) | 07 FEB 1862 |
| WILLIAMS, James M. | BRAWNER, Mary E. | 27 JAN 1868 |
| WILLIAMS, James S. | MILLER, Alice D. | 27 JUN 1867 |
| WILLIAMS, John | COLLINS, Catherine | 21 APR 1860 |
| WILLIAMS, John | PRINCE, Mary Louisa | 06 APR 1865 |
| WILLIAMS, John | HOWARD, Jane (blk) | 07 JUL 1865 |
| WILLIAMS, John | BLUE, Frances | 11 SEP 1865 |
| WILLIAMS, John | HAMERSON, Mary Louisa (blk) | 13 DEC 1866 |
| WILLIAMS, John | BUDD, Martha (blk) | 01 MAY 1867 |
| WILLIAMS, John | WEST, Tena (blk) | 11 FEB 1868 |
| WILLIAMS, John | HUGHES, Jennie (blk) | 06 MAR 1868 |
| WILLIAMS, John | WAIL, Barbara | 14 MAY 1869 |
| WILLIAMS, John | PAYNE, Maria (blk) | 12 MAY 1870 |
| WILLIAMS, John [6s] | BROWN, Emma (blk) | 03 NOV 1864 |
| WILLIAMS, John A., Jr. | FORD, Ann Maria | 27 SEP 1859 |
| WILLIAMS, John Benson | ATKINSON, Mary E. | 08 FEB 1862 |
| WILLIAMS, John H. | SMILER, Helen E.H. (blk) | 04 NOV 1862 |
| WILLIAMS, John H. | WHITE, Sarah | 04 FEB 1865 |
| WILLIAMS, John H. | KNEW, Delia Ann | 13 MAY 1867 |
| WILLIAMS, John Henry | TRIPPETT, Annie E. | 16 NOV 1865 |
| WILLIAMS, John Stewart | WILLIAMS, Delia Ann (blk) | 22 OCT 1868 |
| WILLIAMS, John T. | JONES, Mary A. | 27 MAY 1869 |
| WILLIAMS, John V. | WELHOF, Annie | 16 AUG 1865 |
| WILLIAMS, John W. [11] | O'DELL, Sarah C. | 09 AUG 1862 |
| WILLIAMS, Joseph | CARPENTER, Sophia (blk) | 31 MAR 1860 |
| WILLIAMS, Joseph | GRINER, Ellen Maria | 09 APR 1863 |
| WILLIAMS, Joseph B. | HANDLEY, Mary T. | 24 DEC 1868 |
| WILLIAMS, Joseph N. | NUGENT, Emma Jane | 03 MAY 1869 |
| WILLIAMS, Lang | BUTLER, Sarah Ann (blk) | 31 OCT 1866 |
| WILLIAMS, Lewis | BELL, Martha A.E. (blk) | 24 SEP 1862 |
| WILLIAMS, Lewis | ROBINSON, Cecilia | 19 MAY 1870 |
| WILLIAMS, Ludwell | LITTON, Caroline | 23 APR 1869 |
| WILLIAMS, Lyman | PAGE, Mina (blk) | 08 NOV 1869 |
| WILLIAMS, Marshall | CAMPBELL, Mary (col'd) | 01 JUN 1870 |
| WILLIAMS, Osborne | JOHNSON, Martha (blk) | 03 AUG 1865 |
| WILLIAMS, Otho | ROBINSON, Virginia (blk) | 21 NOV 1867 |
| WILLIAMS, Ottaway | BOND, Martha | 19 APR 1869 |
| WILLIAMS, Parker | BELL, Amanda | 11 SEP 1865 |
| WILLIAMS, Pelham [Rev.] [11] | GUNNELL, Helen M. | 06 AUG 1861 |
| WILLIAMS, Peter | BOOTH, Louisa (blk) | 31 DEC 1868 |

District of Columbia Marriage Licenses, 1858-1870

| | | |
|---|---|---|
| WILLIAMS, Phillip | WHITE, Susan (blk) | 06 JAN 1870 |
| WILLIAMS, Pleasant | MELTON, Mary Jane (blk) | 13 AUG 1868 |
| WILLIAMS, Richard | JOHNSON, Anna (blk) | 15 DEC 1866 |
| WILLIAMS, Richard | SHAW, J.H. | 05 FEB 1867 |
| WILLIAMS, Robert | JETT, Mary | 09 JUN 1862 |
| WILLIAMS, Robert | MUNROE, Elizabeth (blk) | 05 OCT 1865 |
| WILLIAMS, Robert A. | BARRY, Cynthia | 02 NOV 1869 |
| WILLIAMS, Robert E. | ALLEN, Maria L. | 30 AUG 1869 |
| WILLIAMS, Robt. | DOUGLAS, Adele | 23 JAN 1866 |
| WILLIAMS, Samuel | KING, Harriet (blk) | 12 APR 1859 |
| WILLIAMS, Samuel | SMITSON, Eliza Ann | 17 APR 1860 |
| WILLIAMS, Samuel F. | BELT, Mary Ellen (blk) | 13 SEP 1865 |
| WILLIAMS, Sandy | FIELDS, Harriet (blk) | 03 OCT 1865 |
| WILLIAMS, Silas | HILL, Betsy (blk) | 28 FEB 1863 |
| WILLIAMS, Theodore | PARKER, Mary (col'd) | 04 JAN 1864 |
| WILLIAMS, Thomas | BROWN, Eliza (blk) | 25 NOV 1863 |
| WILLIAMS, Thomas | GORDON, Sophia (blk) | 07 DEC 1863 |
| WILLIAMS, Thomas | ALLEN, Tabitha (blk) | 12 OCT 1868 |
| WILLIAMS, Thomas | CLARK, Susan (blk) | 01 OCT 1868 |
| WILLIAMS, Thomas | CHASE, Sarah (blk) | 24 JUN 1868 |
| WILLIAMS, Walker | KENNEDY, Mary Ann | 22 JUL 1869 |
| WILLIAMS, Walter B. | GITTINGS, Clara V. | 25 NOV 1867 |
| WILLIAMS, Walter W. | BRADLEY, Alice | 24 FEB 1859 |
| WILLIAMS, William | HAYES, Annie | 17 MAY 1862 |
| WILLIAMS, William | JOVAN, Sophia (blk) | 03 JUL 1862 |
| WILLIAMS, William | CLARKE, Annie | 14 DEC 1863 |
| WILLIAMS, William | DULANEY, Caroline (blk) | 08 MAY 1869 |
| WILLIAMS, William H. | PARTELLO, Flora | 17 DEC 1866 |
| WILLIAMS, William M. | FRYE, Ella M. | 13 MAY 1861 |
| WILLIAMS, William W. | HARROW, Nellie | 18 DEC 1866 |
| WILLIAMS, Willis | SCOTT, Harriet (blk) | 26 MAY 1866 |
| WILLIAMS, Wilson | RICHARDS, Miranda (blk) | 17 OCT 1868 |
| WILLIAMS, Wm. H.H. | METER, Mary E. | 08 MAY 1866 |
| WILLIAMSON, Daniel | DAINTY, Emeline | 05 NOV 1862 |
| WILLIAMSON, Edward | GEOGHAN, Henrietta | 16 OCT 1867 |
| WILLIAMSON, James | TAYLOR, Bettie A. | 19 SEP 1867 |
| WILLIAMSON, James | McGOWAN, Mary | 02 JAN 1868 |
| WILLIAMSON, John | METCALF, Margaret | 24 AUG 1864 |
| WILLIAMSON, John [1c] | DAVIS, Cynthia | 23 SEP 1863 |
| WILLIAMSON, Joseph B. | BOTELER, Jeminia E. | 24 JAN 1861 |
| WILLIAMSON, Thomas | PETTIT, Roxy Ann | 13 JAN 1859 |
| WILLIAMSON, Thos., USN [11] | PRICE, Julia | 30 NOV 1861 |
| WILLIAMSON, William B. | CASWELL, Gertrude | 30 MAY 1867 |
| WILLIS, Abner | GRAVES, Caroline (blk) | 23 FEB 1867 |
| WILLIS, Dennis | CARTER, Sarah | 11 DEC 1865 |
| WILLIS, Dock | PARKER, Julia (blk) | 05 SEP 1866 |
| WILLIS, Edward | WASHINGTON, Rose (blk) | 23 DEC 1865 |
| WILLIS, James | WAGNER, Margaret (blk) | 01 JAN 1863 |
| WILLIS, James | WROE, Maria (blk) | 04 DEC 1867 |
| WILLIS, John | SHREVE, Mary Catherine | 18 OCT 1860 |
| WILLIS, John | DULANEY, Josephine | 08 NOV 1862 |
| WILLIS, John | SEARL, Emma (blk) | 21 JAN 1864 |
| WILLIS, Joseph | LECKIE, Susan (blk) | 16 MAR 1864 |
| WILLIS, Montello | SMITH, Amanda | 22 DEC 1866 |
| WILLIS, Rajah | CHIZLEY, Lizzie (blk) | 18 DEC 1866 |
| WILLIS, Robert | JACKSON, Julia (blk) | 16 NOV 1864 |

| | | |
|---|---|---|
| WILLIS, Samuel | SCHRINAGE, Mary (blk) | 02 JAN 1866 |
| WILLIS, Squire | GREEN, Mandy (blk) | 24 DEC 1866 |
| WILLISON, Eli | HARDEST, Rachael Elisabeth | 19 NOV 1863 |
| WILLISS, Joseph | LANE, Susannah | 15 AUG 1864 |
| WILLISTON, Edward B. | MOORE, Beatrice | 20 JAN 1868 |
| WILLMOTT, Joshua | ALEXANDER, Catharine | 04 JAN 1865 |
| WILLNER, H.R.J. Franz | MULLIGAN, F. Marian | 07 NOV 1861 |
| WILLNER, William | PFEIL, Louisa | 06 FEB 1868 |
| WILLS, Grayson | TINKER, Rachel A. (blk) | 15 SEP 1865 |
| WILLS, James | NEAL, Maria (blk) | 20 JUL 1869 |
| WILLS, John | SHERIER, Elizabeth | 10 MAY 1861 |
| WILLS, William | HAYSON, Margaret (blk) | 20 DEC 1866 |
| WILLSE, Peter | THOMAS, Emma | 16 MAR 1865 |
| WILLSEY, John W. | CUTLER, Catherine Jane | 01 OCT 1863 |
| WILLSEY, Theodore F. | BRADDOCK, Mary | 10 AUG 1865 |
| WILLSON, John B. | McDOWELL, Jennie | 09 OCT 1866 |
| WILMAN, Lewis | HORSEMAN, Jane | 05 DEC 1867 |
| WILMARTH, James G. [11] | COBURN, Caroline A. | 20 MAY 1863 |
| WILMS, Peter P. | HERZINGER, Lena | 13 NOV 1866 |
| WILSON, A.M. | TIBBITT, Ella | 14 NOV 1865 |
| WILSON, Andrew | McGUIRE, Bridget | 26 OCT 1858 |
| WILSON, Andrew [6r] | PELKERTON, Mary [Jane] | 07 JUL 1859 |
| WILSON, Archibald | BRIEN, Margaret | 20 SEP 1859 |
| WILSON, Arthur | SHREVE, Annie B. | 08 DEC 1868 |
| WILSON, Benjamin | JOHNSON, Marshy (blk) | 12 MAY 1869 |
| WILSON, C. Irving | HOUSTON, Gertrude L. | 17 JAN 1866 |
| WILSON, Christopher C. | O'NEIL, Elizabeth | 15 AUG 1861 |
| WILSON, Clement | SLATER, Eliza (blk) | 17 JAN 1861 |
| WILSON, Columbus | JONES, Cornelia (blk) | 20 OCT 1863 |
| WILSON, Cornelius | JOHNSON, Sarah Elizth. (blk) | 10 DEC 1869 |
| WILSON, Daniel | JOHNSON, Sarah (blk) | 13 AUG 1868 |
| WILSON, Edlot | HUTCHISON, Ann E. | 04 APR 1860 |
| WILSON, Edwin A. | HANNON, Cynthie C. | 13 JUL 1864 |
| WILSON, Edwin C. | HARDESTY, Mary E. | 26 APR 1867 |
| WILSON, Fenton Mercer | HONESTY, Lavinia (blk) | 09 DEC 1862 |
| WILSON, Francis Asbury | PAYNE, Virginia Wicks | 02 DEC 1867 |
| WILSON, Frank B. | DAVIS, Marion V. | 18 JUN 1867 |
| WILSON, Geo. T. | PURYEAR, S. Josephine | 18 DEC 1860 |
| WILSON, George | JARBOE, Sarah Jane | 05 NOV 1861 |
| WILSON, George B. | SCAGGS, Martha R. | 20 APR 1863 |
| WILSON, George S. [12s] | PARKINSON, Arispa | 04 OCT 1861 |
| WILSON, Gilbert P. [7b] | BARTON, Gertrude I. | 16 DEC 1869 |
| WILSON, Harrison [1c] | BURNES, Mary Isabella | 27 JAN 1863 |
| WILSON, Harry B. | DODD, Mary A. | 07 AUG 1866 |
| WILSON, Henry | WILLIAMS, Cecilia (blk) | 09 MAR 1864 |
| WILSON, Henry | SIMS, Mary (blk) | 04 OCT 1865 |
| WILSON, Henry | TYLER, Ann (blk) | 29 OCT 1868 |
| WILSON, Henry C. | WHITWORTH, Elizabeth | 06 OCT 1860 |
| WILSON, Henry C. | WADDY, Letty (blk) | 23 DEC 1865 |
| WILSON, Horace | CARR, Louisa (blk) | 12 AUG 1863 |
| WILSON, Isaiah | LANCASTER, Emma J. (blk) | 30 MAR 1865 |
| WILSON, Isaiah | HOPKINS, Helen (blk) | 08 MAR 1866 |
| WILSON, James | SMITH, Henrietta (blk) | 06 MAY 1864 |
| WILSON, James | JACKSON, Adeline (blk) | 28 DEC 1868 |
| WILSON, James [6c] | SCOTT, Rachel P. | 15 DEC 1858 |
| WILSON, James W. | READEY, Ellen | 21 JUL 1863 |

District of Columbia Marriage Licenses, 1858-1870

| | | |
|---|---|---|
| WILSON, James W. | BAGGETT, Annie E. | 12 APR 1870 |
| WILSON, Jefferson | DADE, Josephine (blk) | 16 JUN 1870 |
| WILSON, Jeffrey | SMITH, Rebecca Ann (blk) | 09 MAY 1865 |
| WILSON, Jeremiah | TURNER, Elizabeth (blk) | 21 AUG 1863 |
| WILSON, Jeremiah D. | BROWN, Hattie | 19 AUG 1865 |
| WILSON, Jesse Cook | DORSEY, Alcinda Rilla (blk) | 09 DEC 1863 |
| WILSON, John | LAWTON, Margaret | 17 AUG 1859 |
| WILSON, John | BELL, Mary | 11 JUN 1860 |
| WILSON, John | JACKSON, Sarah Ann (blk) | 23 MAR 1864 |
| WILSON, John | LEE, Julia (blk) | 29 APR 1865 |
| WILSON, John | RILEY, Ellen | 15 DEC 1866 |
| WILSON, John | BROOKS, Josephine (blk) | 17 NOV 1868 |
| WILSON, John B. [4] | HEILEMAN, Celestine Huger | 07 JUN 1859 |
| WILSON, John G. [4] | MORGAN, Sarah E. | 19 FEB 1868 |
| WILSON, John H. | ADAMS, Anna (blk) | 14 APR 1866 |
| WILSON, John M. [11] | WALLER, Augusta B. | 04 NOV 1861 |
| WILSON, John P. | JACOBS, Kate Adelaide | 10 DEC 1864 |
| WILSON, John V. [7a] | RAY, M. Ida | 30 AUG 1866 |
| WILSON, John Wesley [10] | BROWN, Margaret Jane (blk) | 24 JUN 1863 |
| WILSON, John Wesley | GAITHER, Eliza Jane (blk) | 04 APR 1864 |
| WILSON, Joseph S. | CARR, Julie A. | 10 MAY 1859 |
| WILSON, Lawrence | ABBOTT, Mary L. | 03 MAY 1870 |
| WILSON, Leander G. | MILES, Amanda R. | 15 SEP 1859 |
| WILSON, Lewis | SMITH, Annie (blk) | 23 APR 1863 |
| WILSON, Lewis | HILL, Celia (blk) | 14 NOV 1867 |
| WILSON, Louis C. | KENT, Louisa E. | 17 SEP 1864 |
| WILSON, Marcellus | CARVER, Amelia | 12 MAY 1862 |
| WILSON, Mark | LEWIS, Betty (blk) | 18 JUL 1867 |
| WILSON, Mason | HEATLEY, Mary E. | 29 NOV 1867 |
| WILSON, McKenzie | CARTER, Dradie D. (col'd) | 31 AUG 1868 |
| WILSON, Michael | KEONEY, Martha | 03 JAN 1867 |
| WILSON, Nathaniel [11] | HUTTON, Annie E. | 05 OCT 1863 |
| WILSON, Ned | WILSON, Nancey (blk) | 02 NOV 1868 |
| WILSON, Norval | HARRIS, Sarah E.D. | 08 JAN 1870 |
| WILSON, Orrsy | WARD, Margaret (blk) | 28 DEC 1868 |
| WILSON, Patrick | GRIFFITH, Thema Ann (blk) | 28 OCT 1867 |
| WILSON, Perry | WOOD, Minta (blk) | 27 JUL 1868 |
| WILSON, Robert | KITTINGER, Ann Eliza | 24 DEC 1864 |
| WILSON, Robert A. | HANAHAN, Margaret | 05 OCT 1864 |
| WILSON, Robert Butler | HUGUELY, Addie Emmett | 06 APR 1864 |
| WILSON, Samuel | WILSON, Catherine (blk) | 07 JUL 1866 |
| WILSON, Thomas | CARUTHERS, Susan C. | 31 JAN 1862 |
| WILSON, Thomas | VERMILLION, Sarah | 04 JAN 1866 |
| WILSON, W.V.S. | STEWART, Mary C. | 06 SEP 1866 |
| WILSON, William | WAILES, Lucy | 31 MAR 1864 |
| WILSON, William | MERCER, Margaret | 09 MAY 1866 |
| WILSON, William | WHITNEY, Mildred (blk) | 24 DEC 1868 |
| WILSON, William | BROWN, Jane (blk) | 08 SEP 1869 |
| WILSON, William A. | GILL, Mary | 13 APR 1863 |
| WILSON, William A. | SERPELL, Florence H. | 18 JUL 1867 |
| WILSON, William Grantt | STAHL, Mary E. | 04 APR 1865 |
| WILSON, William M. | RIGGLES, Catharine V. | 13 JUL 1864 |
| WILSON, William W. | LAMBERT, Jeannette E. | 05 MAY 1868 |
| WILSON, Wm. Hy. | NELSON, Martha Ann (blk) | 24 AUG 1864 |
| WILSON, Zachariah G. [11] | NORTON, Mary E. | 10 OCT 1865 |
| WILTON, Charles | MOORE, Elizabeth | 13 JUL 1863 |

District of Columbia Marriage Licenses, 1858-1870

| | | |
|---|---|---|
| WIMER, James B. | MOLAN, Mary | 08 DEC 1866 |
| WINCKLEMAN, Columbus | SWIFT, Elizabeth | 25 MAR 1864 |
| WINDHAM, James A. | NICHOLLS, Eveline | 06 NOV 1867 |
| WINDHOLZ, Louis | HOUSEWRIGHT, Margaretta | 10 OCT 1864 |
| WINDHURST, George | CLUB, Susanna | 01 NOV 1865 |
| WINDSBECKER, Julius | SUMMERS, M.F. | 06 JUL 1864 |
| WINDSOR, Sampson | GOBLE, Frances | 11 MAY 1868 |
| WINDSOR, Thos. John | WATERS, Alisa | 05 AUG 1869 |
| WINDUS, Caspar | HILDEBRAND, Martha | 16 OCT 1866 |
| WINEBERGER, William C. | BERLIN, Caroline | 05 OCT 1863 |
| WINEMULLER, John C. | COOK, Mary A.V. | 29 MAR 1860 |
| WINFIELD, Arsemias A. | LONGSTREET, Augusta | 21 JAN 1869 |
| WINFIELD, Henderson | MOORE, Martha Ann (blk) | 27 FEB 1869 |
| WINFIELD, Jacob H. | TOWNSEND, Juliet E. | 30 APR 1868 |
| WINFIELD, Joseph | KENNEDY, Kate | 08 FEB 1865 |
| WINFIELD, Peyton | MASON, Lucinda (blk) | 27 FEB 1866 |
| WINFIELD, Robert | LAWSON, Charity (blk) | 04 FEB 1869 |
| WINFIELD, Thomas S. | BAILEY, Mary E. | 17 SEP 1860 |
| WINGATE, A. LaRue | PARKER, S.G. | 08 NOV 1865 |
| WINGATE, James E. | BRAY, Ann Salome | 11 JAN 1870 |
| WINGFIELD, Charles W. | WINGFIELD, Harriet J. (blk) | 11 JUL 1865 |
| WINGFIELD, Philip | MONROE, Mary (blk) | 15 OCT 1867 |
| WINGFIELD, Robert | SIDNER, Sarah (blk) | 01 OCT 1863 |
| WINKEL, John | SPANENPERYER, Laura C. | 08 JAN 1859 |
| WINKFIELD, A.W. | HOLLEY, Carrie M. | 25 NOV 1863 |
| WINKFIELD, John | GOLDEN, Mary | 15 MAR 1869 |
| WINKLE, James R. | DANDERSON, Martha V. | 17 JAN 1861 |
| WINKLER, William | MEADOWS, Fannie | 23 DEC 1858 |
| WINN, Charles | WOODS, Mary | 07 MAR 1864 |
| WINN, Edward | WILLIAMS, Mary | 30 SEP 1864 |
| WINNEMORE, Isaac J. | JULLIEN, Adelaide | 03 NOV 1866 |
| WINSLOW, Benjamin Franklin | MIDDLETON, Mary Patton | 30 DEC 1867 |
| WINSLOW, Henry | BRACKIS, Margaret (blk) | 14 MAR 1865 |
| WINSLOW, Solomon | BROWN, Matilda | 23 OCT 1866 |
| WINSLOW, William Randolph [11] | EVELETH, Catharine P.S. | 01 JUL 1865 |
| WINSTON, Curtis | OWENS, Mary Ella (blk) | 09 NOV 1868 |
| WINSTON, Isaiah | HILL, Jane (blk) | 17 SEP 1868 |
| WINSTON, Jefferson | THOMPSON, Jane (blk) | 06 MAY 1865 |
| WINSTON, Rice | PAYNE, Celia (blk) | 23 MAY 1868 |
| WINTER, Charles | MALOWNEY, Delia | 30 JUN 1862 |
| WINTER, Charles E. | GARRATT, Sarah E. | 13 DEC 1869 |
| WINTER, James | TESKEY, Mary Ann | 03 MAY 1864 |
| WINTER, John E. | MURRAY, Joanna A. | 11 APR 1862 |
| WINTER, John T. | HIRST, Allie R. | 20 OCT 1869 |
| WINTERHALTER, John B. | SCHMITT, Elizabeth | 01 OCT 1864 |
| WINTERMITZ, William | WHITFIELD, Sophia | 04 JAN 1865 |
| WINTERS, Adam C. | KENADEY, Mary Ann | 23 FEB 1866 |
| WINTERS, Douglas | WARD, Louisa (blk) | 21 DEC 1866 |
| WINTERS, Francis | McGRATH, Mary Ann | 19 AUG 1865 |
| WINTERS, George M. | TUNNIA, Margaret (blk) | 15 JUN 1868 |
| WINTERS, Henry S. | MILLS, Ida | 24 DEC 1867 |
| WINTERS, James W. | BOSTON, Sarah (blk) | 18 OCT 1866 |
| WINTERS, Richard | WEST, Henrietta (blk) | 30 JUN 1866 |
| WIRT, R.W. | CLARKE, Kate E. | 10 DEC 1867 |
| WIRT, William | SELBY, Priscilla (blk) | 02 OCT 1862 |
| WIRT, William | PENDLETON, Sophia (blk) | 19 JUN 1867 |

District of Columbia Marriage Licenses, 1858-1870

| | | |
|---|---|---|
| WIRT, William Wall | DOUGLAS, Catharine Louisa | 26 JUN 1861 |
| WIRTH, Sebastian | MERTEL, Margaretha | 23 JUN 1864 |
| WISE, Abil | WINS, Margaret | 01 NOV 1865 |
| WISE, Dennis | THOMAS, Emma (blk) | 03 DEC 1868 |
| WISE, George W. [10] | LANGLEY, Mary F. | 25 JAN 1869 |
| WISE, Jerome | KELLY, Sallie A. | 04 OCT 1866 |
| WISE, Joel | CUMMINS, Mary Jane | 19 OCT 1858 |
| WISE, John | COOLIDGE, Ellen (blk) | 14 SEP 1868 |
| WISE, John H. | ECKLOFF, Sarah E. | 13 MAY 1867 |
| WISE, William | BOWMAN, Sophronia (blk) | 29 JAN 1867 |
| WISE, William D. | WILLARD, Fanny | 10 DEC 1867 |
| WISMAN, Andrew | BAKERGELLAG, Margaret | 20 NOV 1867 |
| WISNER, George W. [6m] | MUNJOY, Virginia | 12 JAN 1863 |
| WISNER, James W. | HARLAN, Maria | 01 SEP 1869 |
| WISSNER, Henry B. | VOLK, Anna | 13 JUN 1861 |
| WISWALL, Joseph C. | CARTER, Florence E. | 29 MAY 1865 |
| WITHEL, Charles E. [2] | KAYSER, Alberta | 26 OCT 1864 |
| WITHERS, James | PINN, Ann Maria (blk) | 05 AUG 1863 |
| WITHERS, James O. | FOSTER, Emma G. | 26 JAN 1864 |
| WITHERS, Thomas T. | BARKMAN, Mary Virginia | 19 JAN 1867 |
| WITHERS, William | GOURLEY, Jennie | 25 APR 1865 |
| WITMER, Calvin | McNEILL, Margaret E.B. | 20 AUG 1867 |
| WITZ, Frederick | LOENTHAL, Louisa | 20 JUN 1865 |
| WOELLMER, Frederick A. | PETERS, Caroline | 26 AUG 1863 |
| WOGAN, James P. | POWELL, Ella G. | 08 SEP 1865 |
| WOLCOT, James M. [9c] | BEALL, Henrietta E. | 07 DEC 1861 |
| WOLF, Harry | HOLLAK, Betsy | 10 MAR 1870 |
| WOLF, Rudolph | CASSIDY, Catherine | 19 FEB 1870 |
| WOLFE, August | WELSH, Catharine | 27 JAN 1864 |
| WOLFE, Charles | MACKEY, Sarah | 09 APR 1864 |
| WOLFE, Frank | MAGRUDER, Maria C. | 18 JAN 1865 |
| WOLFE, John C. | BROMLEY, Eliza J. | 06 FEB 1866 |
| WOLFE, Thomas | KENNEDY, Bridget | 14 FEB 1859 |
| WOLFRAN, Charles H. | BUERGER, Clara J. | 14 MAY 1862 |
| WOLFSHEIMER, Nathan | SCHOOLHER, Bawael | 24 MAY 1861 |
| WOLHAUPTER, D.P. | POWELL, S.A. | 08 OCT 1864 |
| WOLLARD, Charles F. | STONE, Mary Catherine | 11 NOV 1868 |
| WOLLARD, James F. | VENABLE, Matilda P. | 05 MAY 1860 |
| WOLLARD, James F. | GITTINGS, Laura E. | 20 AUG 1863 |
| WOLLARD, James F. | STINEMETZ, Mary E. | 19 JUL 1869 |
| WOLTGE, John F. [1c] | GAUER, Catrina Friederika | 28 NOV 1862 |
| WOLTZ, George W. | SMITH, Laura A. | 07 NOV 1866 |
| WONDERLY, Harry | ABBOTT, Serena W. | 23 MAY 1868 |
| WONN, Alfred [6s] | WOODWARD, Annie M. | 16 MAR 1865 |
| WONN, William | COVERSTONE, Matilda | 06 DEC 1864 |
| WONNERSLEY, Wm. H. | McGLUE, Esther | 29 OCT 1866 |
| WOOD, Alfred [7a] | MOULTON, Nellie M. (blk) | 03 NOV 1868 |
| WOOD, Burrill | KELLEY, Ellen (blk) | 06 APR 1868 |
| WOOD, Charles H. | CHAMPEON, Elizabeth | 02 OCT 1862 |
| WOOD, Chauncey Q. | YEO, Pamelia J. | 26 JUL 1864 |
| WOOD, David | STEWART, Emily J. (blk) | 13 DEC 1865 |
| WOOD, Edward | HAILSTOCK, Julia (blk) | 25 JUN 1867 |
| WOOD, Francis | HOUGHTON, Margaret Emma | 02 APR 1867 |
| WOOD, Francis | SMITH, Jane (blk) | 19 SEP 1867 |
| WOOD, Francis M. | RYE, Eliza Ann | 16 SEP 1858 |
| WOOD, Frank | SMITH, Nelly (blk) | 03 JUN 1864 |

## District of Columbia Marriage Licenses, 1858-1870

| Groom | Bride | Date |
|---|---|---|
| WOOD, Frank | LANEY, Mary (blk) | 25 JUN 1866 |
| WOOD, George J. Pettingill [8] | HUNTT, Harriet [A.] | 02 SEP 1869 |
| WOOD, George W. | NALLY, Maria | 24 NOV 1858 |
| WOOD, Henry | DOYLE, Margaret Ann | 30 MAY 1860 |
| WOOD, Horatio N. | CLARKE, Mary O. | 23 SEP 1867 |
| WOOD, Isaac | BROWN, Leathe (blk) | 07 MAR 1867 |
| WOOD, J.W. | BLACKFORD, Kate | 29 MAR 1864 |
| WOOD, James | HARRIS, Margaret Ann (blk) | 26 FEB 1866 |
| WOOD, James | BURGES, Mary Jane (blk) | 18 OCT 1867 |
| WOOD, James F. | PRICE, Marietta | 21 JUL 1868 |
| WOOD, John | GREENWILL, Georgian (blk) | 23 APR 1866 |
| WOOD, John | TURNER, Amanda (blk) | 24 MAR 1870 |
| WOOD, Lemuel W. | THOMAS, Mary R. | 22 JUL 1862 |
| WOOD, Matthew | SPINDLE, Mary Catherine | 13 AUG 1863 |
| WOOD, Nelson | MARTIN, Lucinda (blk) | 12 JAN 1865 |
| WOOD, Phineas F. | CLEMENTS, Mary E. | 29 JAN 1861 |
| WOOD, Richard | HOWELL, Mary Ann | 17 NOV 1863 |
| WOOD, Richard | STANT, Mary | 01 JUL 1869 |
| WOOD, Robert | GOOD, Ann | 03 MAY 1866 |
| WOOD, Robert M. [11s] | EASTON, Flora (blk) | 23 JUN 1869 |
| WOOD, Sidney | JORDAN, Mary (blk) | 11 SEP 1869 |
| WOOD, Thomas | PARKHURST, Sarah L. | 16 AUG 1864 |
| WOOD, Thomas | RODEN, Anna (blk) | 12 JAN 1869 |
| WOOD, Thomas C. | PEMBERTON, Ella F. | 06 JAN 1868 |
| WOOD, Ulra D. [6s] | REILLY, Lodiema | 25 JAN 1865 |
| WOOD, William | REMELEY, Catherine | 16 JUL 1866 |
| WOOD, William Bradley | BROWN, Elizabeth Adelle (blk) | 01 OCT 1860 |
| WOODARD, John | CLAGETT, Ann Maria (blk) | 27 SEP 1866 |
| WOODEY, John William | OLDS, Frances E. | 19 SEP 1867 |
| WOODFIELD, Henry B. | WOODFIELD, Mary E. | 23 FEB 1870 |
| WOODFORK, John | BURK, Hattie (blk) | 11 SEP 1869 |
| WOODRUFF, Carle A. | UPPERMAN, Emma | 30 JUN 1865 |
| WOODRUFF, Edmund W. | DENNISON, Frances A. | 04 SEP 1865 |
| WOODRUFF, George | MAJOR, Mary Emma | 08 JUN 1868 |
| WOODS, Alexander M. | RITTENHOUSE, Mary D. | 06 NOV 1860 |
| WOODS, Andrew | TRIPLETT, Sarah F. | 15 JUL 1865 |
| WOODS, Bernard | MATTHEWS, Mary | 31 DEC 1863 |
| WOODS, James | GILHULY, Honer | 14 JUN 1866 |
| WOODS, James | GILHULY, Anna | 04 JUL 1867 |
| WOODS, John F. | GRAY, Ellen | 14 MAY 1868 |
| WOODS, Moses | NUTTE, Martha | 09 FEB 1865 |
| WOODS, Owen | LUNNEY, Ann | 03 JUN 1868 |
| WOODS, Robert | LOWRY, Julia (blk) | 18 DEC 1866 |
| WOODS, Russell B. | RUDD, Alpha Virginia | 14 JUN 1865 |
| WOODS, Samuel | LEE, Isabella | 13 AUG 1868 |
| WOODS, William L. | HUNT, Josephine S. | 04 NOV 1863 |
| WOODSTON, Moses | JACKSON, Anna (blk) | 10 SEP 1868 |
| WOODWARD, Abraham G. | ANDERSON, Martha A. | 07 DEC 1861 |
| WOODWARD, Bennett | POSEY, Emily (blk) | 13 JUN 1867 |
| WOODWARD, Daniel D. | ANDERSON, Mary V. | 02 JAN 1868 |
| WOODWARD, Elon A. | COUTNER, Josephine T. | 16 DEC 1864 |
| WOODWARD, Gilbert M. | PARKER, Ella R. | 21 OCT 1864 |
| WOODWARD, J. Bingham | APPEL, Annie E. | 22 JUN 1868 |
| WOODWARD, James | KING, Sarah | 18 JUN 1863 |
| WOODWARD, John | CLARK, Jennie (blk) | 16 FEB 1865 |
| WOODWARD, John | CHAPPEL, Sarah (blk) | 05 OCT 1869 |

District of Columbia Marriage Licenses, 1858-1870

| | | |
|---|---|---|
| WOODWARD, John H. | JONES, Mary Elizabeth | 07 JAN 1865 |
| WOODWARD, Joseph | SAMUELS, Rebecca (blk) | 11 JAN 1865 |
| WOODWARD, Joseph H. | BARRY, Rachel | 11 OCT 1858 |
| WOODWARD, Joseph J. | WENDELL, Blanche | 09 FEB 1870 |
| WOODWARD, Mark R. | PURSEL, Martha J. | 01 OCT 1864 |
| WOODWARD, Oscar D. | FLYNN, Eliza | 22 DEC 1869 |
| WOODY, William H. | HARRINGTON, Catherine | 06 OCT 1869 |
| WOOLDRIDGE, George | HARBAUGH, Julia A. | 04 NOV 1861 |
| WOOLFORD, Richard D. | JONES, Mary Jane | 03 JAN 1866 |
| WOOLLEY, George A. | SPAULDING, Betsey L. | 03 JUL 1868 |
| WOOTEN, Baker | HARRIS, Millie (blk) | 14 JUL 1865 |
| WOOTEN, Edwin H. [11] | WAIGHT, Mary H. | 21 FEB 1867 |
| WOOZR, Stephen | SMITH, Josephine (blk) | 17 JAN 1865 |
| WORDEN, Charles H. | HALLER, Sophia Ann | 07 JUL 1864 |
| WORMLEY, Gerrett S. | BRENT, Amelia E. (blk) | 14 AUG 1866 |
| WORMLEY, J.T., Dr. | RINGGOLD, Mary A.A. (blk) | 05 MAR 1870 |
| WORMLEY, James T. | SLADE, Josephine | 07 JUN 1865 |
| WORMLEY, John H. | WATSON, Anna (blk) | 16 JUN 1870 |
| WORMLEY, William H.A. | SLADE, Rachel J. | 24 SEP 1862 |
| WORMLEY, William H.A. | SHADD, Addie E. | 24 JUL 1867 |
| WORTH, Algernon S. | TORBERT, Bettie B. | 10 MAY 1869 |
| WORTH, William | HINES, Rebecca A. | 23 DEC 1862 |
| WORTHAM, Ennis | BANKS, Sarah (blk) | 30 AUG 1864 |
| WORTHING, Francis [10] | BATEMAN, Ann R. | 19 NOV 1858 |
| WORTHINGTON, Augustus S. | BABCOCK, Clara J. | 14 JAN 1869 |
| WORTHINGTON, Joseph S. | ANDREWS, Sarah E. | 13 JAN 1868 |
| WORTHINGTON, Landon W. | MAXWELL, Priscilla | 01 FEB 1860 |
| WORTHINGTON, William | BOWIE, Sarah L. | 11 OCT 1860 |
| WOSTER, M.J. | FOX, Arianna | 15 DEC 1859 |
| WREN, Lawrence | COLLINS, Margaret | 02 FEB 1866 |
| WRENN, John T. | WRENN, Bettie L. | 20 DEC 1861 |
| WRENN, John W. | PAYNE, Lucy S. | 18 MAY 1863 |
| WRIGHT, Alpheus S. | HOBBS, Sarah E. | 26 JUL 1867 |
| WRIGHT, Charles | GANTT, Ann | 15 MAR 1865 |
| WRIGHT, Charles H. | GATES, Elizabeth C. | 30 OCT 1862 |
| WRIGHT, Charles T. | WEBSTER, Mary A.E. | 17 DEC 1863 |
| WRIGHT, David | HOWELL, Mary (blk) | 28 AUG 1865 |
| WRIGHT, Edward S. | DIVINE, Mary A. | 24 DEC 1860 |
| WRIGHT, Elias | JOHNSON, Sarah (blk) | 06 MAR 1869 |
| WRIGHT, Francis | GENARD, Kate | 01 JAN 1867 |
| WRIGHT, Frederick | RUPPEL, Anna Kate | 11 APR 1866 |
| WRIGHT, George | TOWNER, Victoria | 25 MAY 1867 |
| WRIGHT, Irvin B. | PARTRIDGE, Minnie | 02 AUG 1866 |
| WRIGHT, J.L. | SUMMERS, M.E. | 11 MAY 1870 |
| WRIGHT, James | CLADABUCK, Julia | 18 FEB 1865 |
| WRIGHT, James | BALL, Eliza (blk) | 12 JUL 1867 |
| WRIGHT, John | HICKEY, Margaret | 20 JAN 1863 |
| WRIGHT, John | SHERMAN, Hanorah | 16 FEB 1863 |
| WRIGHT, John | RICHARDSON, Harriet (blk) | 10 MAR 1865 |
| WRIGHT, John J. | CALLAHAN, Johanna | 14 FEB 1867 |
| WRIGHT, Joseph | CLINTON, Jane (blk) | 20 JUL 1863 |
| WRIGHT, Joseph M. | POOR, Lottie | 17 DEC 1868 |
| WRIGHT, Lewis | BURCH, Margaret | 06 JUL 1865 |
| WRIGHT, Lewis W. | DISHMAN, Mollie F. | 12 OCT 1864 |
| WRIGHT, Luther E. | COLEMAN, Susan W. | 28 NOV 1859 |
| WRIGHT, Richard T. | PALMER, Mary L. | 01 SEP 1860 |

## District of Columbia Marriage Licenses, 1858-1870

| | | |
|---|---|---|
| WRIGHT, Samuel H. [10] | WILEY, Ada B. | 13 MAR 1866 |
| WRIGHT, Thomas | DOUGLASS, Rachel (blk) | 09 AUG 1866 |
| WRIGHT, Thomas | JACKSON, Anna (blk) | 18 JUN 1869 |
| WRIGHT, Thomas H. | CLARK, Ellen R. | 14 MAY 1867 |
| WRIGHT, William | CASPER, Rosa | 20 MAY 1859 |
| WRIGHT, William | DAVIS, Julia (blk) | 08 NOV 1861 |
| WRIGHT, William | KEANON, Tracy | 07 OCT 1866 |
| WRIGHT, William | SEARLE, Annie (blk) | 10 NOV 1869 |
| WRIGHT, William | RHODES, Louisa (blk) | 06 JAN 1870 |
| WRIGHT, William M. | SCHOOLCRAFT, Alice A. | 27 MAR 1866 |
| WRISLEY, Silas Pond [11] | BLANCHARD, Frances | 01 SEP 1868 |
| WRONE, John | GRAY, Lizzie (blk) | 04 NOV 1869 |
| WUNDER, Paulus | WUNDER, Anna | 04 MAR 1859 |
| WUNDERLY, Edward | SULLIVAN, Annie | 03 AUG 1867 |
| WURDEMAN, Ferdinand H. | MURRAY, Ann, Mrs. | 02 NOV 1866 |
| WURTENBERG, Louis | GANZ, Johanna | 13 FEB 1864 |
| WURTZ, Charles | WEISS, Ann | 18 JUN 1862 |
| WURTZ, Henry | CLARKE, Augusta H. | 22 APR 1861 |
| WÜSTEFELD, August (Hanover) | POOLE, Emma C. (Va.) | 03 AUG 1863 |
| WYANT, Edward P. | SMITH, Amanda | 25 JUL 1860 |
| WYATT, Charles A. | DAVIS, Elizabeth | 18 SEP 1862 |
| WYCH, Thomas P. | PATTERSON, Jane | 04 DEC 1863 |
| WYGATT, James J. | STROUD, Mary R. | 09 JAN 1867 |
| WYLIE, Henry J. [6le] | MARKS, Julia A. | 24 MAR 1866 |
| WYMAN, Charles T., Jr. [4] | NOURSE, Charlotte E. | 29 OCT 1866 |
| WYMAN, Hanibal G. | WYMAN, Malvina F. | 24 NOV 1860 |
| WYMAN, John F., Jr. [4] | MOREHEAD, Hester A. | 31 DEC 1866 |
| WYMAN, Smith | LUCAS, Eliza (blk) | 29 JUN 1863 |
| WYNKOOP, B.J. | OSBORN, Martha E. | 10 MAR 1866 |
| WYNN, Joseph F. | SWAGART, Margaret V. | 29 MAY 1867 |
| WYNNE, Peter | RYAN, Mary | 03 NOV 1867 |
| WYNNE, Thomas | HOULIHAN, Bridget | 17 SEP 1863 |
| WYUN, Ralph | DADE, Ellen (blk) | 28 NOV 1866 |
| WYVILL, Walter D. | ACKER, Henrietta L. | 18 NOV 1861 |

## X

| | | |
|---|---|---|
| XANDER, Christian | BLUME, Caroline | 20 DEC 1864 |
| XELOWSKI, Henry W. | TYSSOWSKI, Henrietta W. | 29 OCT 1861 |

## Y

| | | |
|---|---|---|
| YAGER, Charles | DESSING, Mary | 27 DEC 1864 |
| YARNELL, Eugene B. | BORTELL, Priscilla A. | 22 APR 1867 |
| YARNELL, Eugene B. | RAY, Anna | 23 MAY 1870 |
| YATES, Alexander | DEMAINE, Laura | 27 APR 1863 |
| YATES, Charles A. | GROSHON, Missouri | 02 OCT 1860 |
| YATES, E. Laffant | TILLY, Harriet H. | 29 APR 1861 |
| YATES, George W. | LYBRAND, Mary T. | 13 NOV 1869 |
| YATES, Gideon D. | NORRIS, Virginia Cooper | 24 MAR 1866 |
| YATES, Henry C. [11] | SHIELDS, Elizabeth C.D. | 13 MAR 1867 |
| YATES, William | WILSON, Jennie | 03 NOV 1869 |
| YEABOWER, George | O'REILLY, Kathleen L. | 27 JUL 1868 |
| YEAGER, William Henry | CARTER, Charity (blk) | 17 MAR 1869 |

District of Columbia Marriage Licenses, 1858-1870

| | | |
|---|---|---|
| YEATMAN, Robert H. | SIMPSON, Mollie O. | 02 DEC 1861 |
| YEATMAN, Samuel M. | HALL, Anne V. | 13 APR 1869 |
| YEATS, Jackson | LEE, Louisa | 19 DEC 1861 |
| YEATS, Matthew | DAVIS, Martha (blk) | 08 DEC 1864 |
| YECKEL, John | HANBURY, Margaret E. | 25 JUL 1866 |
| YELVERTON, Jacob | LUDLOW, Idyllia | 02 NOV 1858 |
| YENNE, Henry | SAUER, Ann Elizabeth | 20 APR 1867 |
| YEWELL, John W. | OSBORNE, Mary E. | 27 NOV 1861 |
| YOACHIM, John C. | KAUFMAN, Sophia | 10 MAY 1860 |
| YODER, Charles T. | WARDER, Anna E. | 25 MAR 1867 |
| YOHE, Charles A. | STEINER, Bettie | 27 DEC 1862 |
| YORK, Henry | SCHMIDT, Anna | 14 AUG 1866 |
| YORK, Walter | PAYNE, Mary Lena | 22 JUL 1862 |
| YOST, Henry | BRAND, Catherine | 24 FEB 1862 |
| YOST, Lewis Henry | HINEMAN, Arynthia Catherine | 07 NOV 1859 |
| YOST, Robert V. | OGDEN, Lizzie F. | 25 NOV 1868 |
| YOUNG, Aaron | CRYER, Emily | 02 JUL 1866 |
| YOUNG, Alexander | TYLER, Lucy (blk) | 30 MAY 1868 |
| YOUNG, Benjamin W. | HAWES, Viola M. | 09 AUG 1864 |
| YOUNG, Charles | DYNES, Mary Jane | 08 OCT 1864 |
| YOUNG, Clinton | DIGGS, Eliza Jane (blk) | 27 MAR 1868 |
| YOUNG, Clinton | DIGGS, Eliza Jane (blk) | 16 NOV 1869 |
| YOUNG, Daniel | BUTLER, Matilda A. (blk) | 05 SEP 1867 |
| YOUNG, Daniel | JONES, Sarah (blk) | 18 DEC 1867 |
| YOUNG, Daniel | GROSS, Eliza (blk) | 19 OCT 1868 |
| YOUNG, David | BROWN, Mary J. (blk) | 25 AUG 1869 |
| YOUNG, Edmund K. | KNEASS, Kate | 16 DEC 1861 |
| YOUNG, Edward L. | BUTT, Sarah E. | 18 OCT 1869 |
| YOUNG, Edward O. | JOHNSON, Josephine (blk) | 30 NOV 1869 |
| YOUNG, Francis | O'HERRON, Annie | 22 APR 1863 |
| YOUNG, Francis A. | HARRISON, Mary O. | 12 MAR 1866 |
| YOUNG, Frank | JOHNSON, Mary (blk) | 23 NOV 1867 |
| YOUNG, Frank | DUVALL, Mary | 29 JAN 1868 |
| YOUNG, George L. | QUEEN, Mary Jane (blk) | 29 JUL 1868 |
| YOUNG, George W. [1e] | DAWSON, Mary I. | 06 APR 1864 |
| YOUNG, George W. [6s] | CARROLL, Jennie | 20 APR 1865 |
| YOUNG, H.C. | COLEMAN, Jane | 08 SEP 1863 |
| YOUNG, Henry | WILLIS, Lizzie (blk) | 03 JUL 1866 |
| YOUNG, Henry | MITCHELL, Emily (blk) | 07 JAN 1869 |
| YOUNG, Henry | BUTLER, Mary F. (blk) | 09 AUG 1869 |
| YOUNG, Howard H. | DARRELL, Florence E. | 11 JUN 1859 |
| YOUNG, Isaac | TURNER, Lucy (blk) | 05 NOV 1868 |
| YOUNG, James | CARROLL, Malinda (blk) | 20 DEC 1865 |
| YOUNG, James | BROOKE, Jennie (blk) | 23 OCT 1867 |
| YOUNG, James | MARSHALL, Margaret (blk) | 27 DEC 1867 |
| YOUNG, John | DYSON, Jane (blk) | 19 SEP 1867 |
| YOUNG, John | LURCH, Elizabeth | 18 APR 1868 |
| YOUNG, John | THOMAS, Louisa (blk) | 25 NOV 1869 |
| YOUNG, John A. [10] | RAY, Mary Jane | 18 FEB 1868 |
| YOUNG, John M. | HOWARD, Mary E. | 17 MAY 1859 |
| YOUNG, John Russell | FITZPATRICK, Rosa | 17 OCT 1864 |
| YOUNG, John T. | INGERSOLL, Sallie T. | 30 DEC 1861 |
| YOUNG, John Thomas | BROWN, Rebecca Frances | 08 DEC 1859 |
| YOUNG, John W. | DORSEY, Emily (blk) | 28 OCT 1863 |
| YOUNG, Joseph H. | HANSON, Mary E. | 31 AUG 1864 |
| YOUNG, Lewis H. | STANHOPE, Fannie Louisa | 02 JUN 1860 |

District of Columbia Marriage Licenses, 1858-1870

| | | |
|---|---|---|
| YOUNG, Patrick | GREENHOUGH, Amanda (blk) | 26 JUN 1865 |
| YOUNG, Peter | MATHEWS, Susan (blk) | 20 JUN 1866 |
| YOUNG, Peter | HOLMES, Betty (blk) | 15 JUN 1867 |
| YOUNG, Robert | WALKER, Ann | 06 JUN 1864 |
| YOUNG, Robert | DAVIDSON, Rosannah | 25 FEB 1865 |
| YOUNG, Robert H. | MINNIS, Susan Ann (blk) | 24 JUN 1868 |
| YOUNG, Robt. H. | MINNIS, Susan Ann (blk) | 27 JUL 1868 |
| YOUNG, Terence | COUGHLIN, Mary | 29 SEP 1869 |
| YOUNG, Thomas | TAYLOR, Susan | 12 JUL 1867 |
| YOUNG, Thomas E. | OTTERBACK, Emma J. | 18 MAY 1864 |
| YOUNG, William | RITCHIE, M.A. | 10 FEB 1862 |
| YOUNG, William | MARTIAN, Magtalena | 05 OCT 1863 |
| YOUNG, William | BARNES, Mary (blk) | 14 JAN 1864 |
| YOUNG, William | LOMAX, Fanny (blk) | 05 SEP 1865 |
| YOUNG, William | HOWARD, Frances (blk) | 22 MAY 1866 |
| YOUNG, William | THOMPSON, Elizabeth (blk) | 26 MAR 1867 |
| YOUNG, William | DYSON, Jane (blk) | 19 SEP 1867 |
| YOUNG, William, Dr. [4] | HAWLEY, Wilhelmina | 03 APR 1861 |
| YOUNG, William E. | EDELEN, Sarah | 29 DEC 1864 |
| YOUNG, William H. | WILLIAMS, Maria J. (blk) | 04 DEC 1867 |
| YOUNG, William Henry | HENSON, Mary Ellen (blk) | 14 SEP 1869 |
| YOUNG, Willis [17 AUG 1863] | ORANGE, Margaret (blk) | 29 JUN 1863 |
| YOUNG, Willis | GREENWELL, Charlotte (blk) | 29 JUN 1863 |
| YOUNG, Wm. | MEYER, Bird | 18 MAY 1865 |
| YOUNGER, Edward L. | MASON, Mary C. (blk) | 16 OCT 1866 |
| YOUNGS, Elphonso | WOODRUFF, Amelia L. | 08 JUN 1867 |
| YOUNGS, Theophilus P. [2] | MILLER, Mary J.C. | 11 JAN 1866 |
| YOUR, Jeremiah | MILES, Eliza (blk) | 26 NOV 1866 |

# Z

| | | |
|---|---|---|
| ZACKARIE, George J. | BURNES, Ann | 10 SEP 1861 |
| ZAIRS, Charles | DOWNES, Mary | 13 MAR 1860 |
| ZANE, Edmund P. | LOUGHBOROUGH, Mary Louisa | 22 APR 1867 |
| ZANNER, William | WEST, Maria | 24 APR 1865 |
| ZANSENZE, Marco | MÜNDELL, Margaritha | 06 DEC 1865 |
| ZARONI, Pietro | HUHN, Virginia | 13 JUL 1865 |
| ZEGOWIETZ, Joseph | SCHWARZ, Veronica | 09 APR 1863 |
| ZEGOWITZ, George | OBERST, Rosina | 17 DEC 1867 |
| ZEITLER, Edward | HOFFMAN, Isabella | 02 MAY 1866 |
| ZELL, Henry | CANAVAN, Mary | 04 FEB 1862 |
| ZELLA, John | HAMER, Fannie | 04 MAR 1868 |
| ZELLINSKY, Charles L.H. | WAGLER, Hellen Virginia | 14 AUG 1865 |
| ZERGA, Dominiko | LEVERONE, A. Maria | 29 MAR 1864 |
| ZERGA, Giovanni Mana | CASSASSA, Vittoria | 10 FEB 1870 |
| ZETSMAN, August Theodore [11] | STEVENS, Mary Olivia | 22 DEC 1869 |
| ZIERMIEKE, John | SCOTT, Jane | 25 MAR 1865 |
| ZIMMERMAN, Alfred | WEYRECH, Mary E. | 12 JUL 1866 |
| ZIMMERMAN, Archibald M. | FLEMING, Eliza T. | 03 DEC 1867 |
| ZIMMERMAN, August | BROOKMEYER, Elenora | 17 JAN 1868 |
| ZIMMERMAN, Christian | VOLZ, Louisa | 27 DEC 1861 |
| ZIMMERMAN, Franklin | DANA, Barbara | 01 AUG 1860 |
| ZIMMERMAN, Henry M. | SIMMONS, Fanny | 29 OCT 1867 |
| ZIMMERMAN, William D. | MILLS, Missouri | 10 JAN 1870 |
| ZIMMERMAN, William H. | BAKER, Elizabeth | 11 JUL 1865 |
| ZIRWES, John | WELLER, Anna | 28 MAY 1866 |

District of Columbia Marriage Licenses, 1858-1870

| | | |
|---|---|---|
| ZUCK, David | BANNISTER, Margaret A. | 06 FEB 1864 |
| ZUSCHNITT, Frederick | HEYRICH, Kate | 27 JUL 1869 |
| ZWERZIG, William | MEYERS, Wilhelmina | 23 DEC 1861 |

## INCOMPLETE RECORDS

| | | |
|---|---|---|
| [blank] | NOLAN, Margaret | 15 JAN 1867 |
| [blank] | CORNWELL, Mary | 29 JUN 1863 |
| [blank], Charles | COLEMAN, Teresa | 03 DEC 1862 |
| [blank], Charles | ROTH, Magdalena | 27 DEC 1869 |
| [blank], Peter | FISCHER, Sophia | 27 AUG 1864 |
| [illegible], Alfred | WADDY, Susan (blk) | 08 JUL 1865 |
| [torn away], Robert B. | [torn away] | 24 MAY 1865 |

—A—

ABBOTT
 Harriet Ann, 115
 Kate, 272
 Martha E., 233
 Mary Ann, 123
 Mary L., 320
 Mary M., 309
 Rebecca Jane, 7
 Serena W., 322
ABEL
 Mary Ann (blk), 90
ABELL
 Virginia, 5
ABELS
 Frances, 166
ABERCROMBIE
 Sallie S., 255
ACCARDI
 Mary, 152
ACKER
 Henrietta L., 325
ACKMAN
 Anna, 175
ACOMB
 Fanny, 158
ACTON
 Elizabeth, 29
 Isabella, 66
ADAIR
 Maggie, 24
ADAM
 Catharine, 7
ADAMS
 Alice E., 199
 Ann Eliza (blk), 289
 Anna (blk), 320
 Anna E., 108
 Annie (blk), 225, 252, 289
 Annie Dodson, 232
 Annie E., 229
 Caroline (blk), 33
 Caroline A., 83
 Caroline C., 99
 Catherine, 232

Cecelia A., 15
Cecilia A., 207
Courtney (blk), 122
Elizabeth, 148, 188
Emma (blk), 265
Frances, 251
Gracey (blk), 307
Helen, 201
Henrietta, 8
Henry Ann
 Davidson, 278
Hester A., 61
Jane, 160
Josephine (blk), 89
Julia (blk), 25
Louisa (blk), 159
Lucinda (blk), 51
Lydia A., 142
Manda, 205
Marcie V., 101
Margaret, 12, 78, 100
Margaret A., 78
Margaret Ann, 100
Martha C., 50
Mary, 10, 30, 32, 34, 58, 94, 160, 176, 184, 222, 238
Mary (blk), 32, 34, 58
Mary Blanche, 222
Mary Emma, 10
Mary V., 176
Matilda, 226
Rebecca (blk), 306
S. Anne, 138
Sarah, 35, 63, 153, 247, 296
Sarah (blk), 35, 296
Sarah A., 247
Sarah E., 63
Susanna, 120
ADAMSON
 Ellen, 2
ADDISON
 Amelia (blk), 149, 153

Jennie (blk), 5
Mollie M., 147
Rachel, 155
Rebella (blk), 259
Sallie C., 311
Theresa Ann (blk), 237
ADELLA
 Rosanna, 75
ADKINSON
 Mary, 48
ADLER
 Bertha, 274
AGER
 Ann V., 135
 Clarence Louisa, 49
 Josepha H., 10
 Martha, 151
AGERSON
 Sarah, 287
AHERN
 Catherine, 62
AIGLER
 Sophia, 88
AIKEN
 Mary, 96
AIKENS
 Mary Jane, 86
AILER
 Sophia, 314
AINKRIES
 Matilda, 289
AIRES
 Prudence, 230
AISQUITH
 Delia Anna, 173
AITCH
 Ellen (blk), 216
AKERS
 Elizabeth, 3
ALBEGIN
 Mary, 134
ALBERS
 Annie D., 286
ALBRECHT
 Claire, 301
ALBRITTON
 Jane, 70

District of Columbia Marriage Licenses, 1858-1870

ALDVATER
  Margaret, 265
ALEXANDER
  Annie (blk), 42
  Catharine, 155, 319
  Catharine (blk), 155
  Catherine (blk), 314
  Catherine
    Mariamne, 24
  Esther Ann, 215
  Harriet, 209
  Julia (blk), 11
  Julia S., 190
  Maria, 72, 225
  Maria (blk), 225
  Mary (blk), 296
  Mary Francilia, 253
  Sandy, 3, 269
  Sarah (blk), 35
ALLAS
  Mary (blk), 136
ALLEN
  Addie, 169
  Alma L., 44
  Amanda, 19
  Anna, 142, 240
  Anna W., 142
  Anne (blk), 281
  Annie (blk), 117
  Annie F., 230
  Augusta, 126
  Catherine, 127, 284
  Clara G., 115
  Elizabeth, 203, 222
  Elizabeth A., 222
  Ellen (blk), 249
  Frances R., 187
  Harriet (blk), 205
  Ida, 259
  Jane (blk), 127
  Jennie, 226
  Josephine (blk), 264
  Kate, 212
  Lucretia (blk), 189
  Margaret, 31, 60
  Margaret (blk), 31
  Maria L., 318
  Mary (blk), 36, 46

  Mary Elizth. (blk), 129
  Matilda (blk), 176
  Ophelia, 12
  Roxy Ann, 138
  Sarah (blk), 123
  Sarah Jane (blk), 297
  Sophia R., 302
  Tabitha (blk), 318
  Virginia Elizabeth (blk), 53
ALLENBAUGH
  Mary Jane, 66
ALLISON
  Eliza A., 122
  Elizabeth (blk), 285
  Elizabeth D., 47
  Mary E., 195
ALLOWAY
  Jennie, 2
ALLYN
  Maggie, 42
  Maria B., 273
ALOWAY
  Mary Ellen, 15
ALSOP
  Virginia, 222
ALT
  Barbara, 124
ALTEMUS
  Charlotte P., 28
ALTER
  Mary L., 31, 182
ALTSCHU
  Elizabeth E., 4
ALVY
  Rebecca, 213
AMAN
  Mary, 300
AMBROSE
  Michael, viii
AMBROSUS
  Elizabeth, 32
AMBUSH
  Charity (blk), 72
  Eliza (blk), 12
  Elizabeth (blk), 51
  Jane R. (blk), 172

  Martha, 267
  Sarah (blk), 136
AMELIA
  Julia, 218
AMENT
  Barbara, 265
AMERICA
  Jane Elizabeth, 50
  Julia Ann (blk), 241
AMEY
  Ellen E., 297
AMON
  Rose, 108
AMTHOR
  Hedwig, 170
ANADALE
  Charlotte, 310
ANCHELL
  Mary Rebecca, 128
ANDERN
  Georgiana W., 297
ANDERSON
  Amelia, 85, 155
  Amelia (blk), 155
  Ann (blk), 306
  Anna (blk), 78
  Anna Dora (blk), 56
  Anna Rebecca, 110
  Betty (blk), 33
  Charlotte, 128
  Coatney (blk), 295
  Eliza (blk), 45
  Elizabeth (blk), 35
  Ella, 21
  Emily (blk), 140
  Emma, 44
  Frances M.R., 268
  Harriet, 154
  Hattie F., 157
  Henrietta, 41, 245
  Henrietta (blk), 41
  Hetty, 36
  Jane (blk), 34
  Kate E., 88
  Lethe Ann, 178
  · Maggie, 89
  Margaret A., 213
  Maria (blk), 241
  Martha A., 323

ANDERSON
  Martha Ann (blk), 55
  Martha E. (blk), 57
  Mary, 49, 150, 180, 196, 323
  Mary (blk), 49
  Mary E., 196
  Mary V., 323
  Mary Virginia, 180
  Matilda, 217
  Phillis (blk), 253
  Sarah, 129, 294, 297, 315
  Sarah (blk), 297
  Sarah E., 315
  Sarah Elizabeth, 294
  Susan, 110, 292
  Susan A., 110
  Virginia, 275
ANDRADE
  Dona Maria Euposia Lisbo'a, 189
ANDRE
  Annie, 168
  Sarah Frances, 143
ANDREWS
  Eugenia N., 72
  Gertrude, 294
  Lizzie I., 88
  Louisa, 166
  Rosa May, 213
  Sarah E., 324
ANGEE
  Elizabeth C., 222
ANGEL
  Laura V., 59
  Margaret, 44
  Marion F., 123
  Martha E., 17
  Matilda, 92
ANGELL
  Amanda, 193
ANGERMANN
  Matilda, 169
ANGUS
  Emma S., 91
ANKERS
  Mary, 264

ANKIT
  Frances, 290
ANNIBLE
  Margaret A., 294
ANNODER
  Louisa, 152
ANSHBACH
  Mary, 141
ANT
  Dorrity, 204
ANTHONY
  Caroline, 189
  Frances Ida, 58
  Mary R. (blk), 124
ANTISELL
  Elizabeth, 180
  Margaret Euphrasia, 67
APPEL
  Annie E., 323
  Celina Adala, 117
APPERSON
  Ann E., 73
APPICH
  Margaret, 282
APPLEBY
  Anna, 305
  Ellen L., 213
  Sallie M., 11
APPLEGATE
  Rebecca, 111
APPLER
  Alverda C., 167
  Mary L., 161
APPLETON
  Kate, 121
ARBENSHINE
  Kate, 95
ARCHER
  Maria, 30
  Mary H., 47
  Sarah, 65
  Susanna, 11
ARENZ
  Mary, 91
ARIXERSON
  Annie E., 85
ARMISTEAD
  Jane, 199

ARMOUR
  Julia (Reilly), 128
ARMS
  Caroline (blk), 192
ARMSTEAD
  Mary (blk), 79
ARMSTRONG
  Clara C., 93
  Elizabeth, 90
  Frances (blk), 40
  G.L., 6, 206
  Henrietta (blk), 124
  Jane, 53
  Louisa (blk), 307
  Margaret, 41, 91
  Margaret (blk), 41
  Marion E., 200
  Mary, 233, 265, 298
  Mary E., 265
  Sarah E., 240
  Susan, 256
ARNELL
  Mary E., 295
ARNESTY
  Georgiana (blk), 123
ARNOLD
  Annie E., 249
  Catherine V., 93
  Elvia Ann, 317
  Emma, 293
  Jane (blk), 311
  Kate, 256
  Katie, 107
  Laura V., 180
  Lydia E., 242
  Maggie, 264
  Marthara, 241
  Mary, 113, 164, 165, 279
  Mary E., 279
  Mary Elizabeth, 164
  Mary J., 113
  Mary Jane, 113
  Rosa, 210, 275
ARNY
  Caroline C., 264
ARRINGTON
  Catherine, 312
  Sarah, 280

ARROTI
  Kate, 174
ARTH
  Lehna, 193
  Margaret, 52
  Olivia, 255
ARTHUR
  Lizzie, 117
ASH
  Lucy, 270
  Mary, 264
  Sarah C., viii, 266
ASHBY
  Catherine, 311
  Virginia, 298
  Wilhelmina, 39
ASHER
  Margaret (blk), 150
ASHFORD
  Emerilla, 94
  Sarah (blk), 137
  Sophronia, 91
ASHTON
  Annie, 265
  Elizabeth, 194
  Fanny (blk), 45
  Hattie, 93
  Mary Eliz. (blk), 32
  sarah, 271
  Susanna, 236
ASPINALL
  Jane, 87
ATCHINSON
  Mary, 42, 212
  Mary Ellen, 212
ATCHISON
  Ann R., 88
  Elizabeth, 75
  Emma P., 190
  Leanah, 290
  Martha A., 133
  Mary H., 61
  Pauline, 89
ATHEY
  Alice Ann, 180
ATKINS
  Elenora (blk), 208
  Lucy J., 156
ATKINSON
  Kitty (blk), 158
  Mary E., 317
ATLEE
  Fanny Yorke, 9
ATOCHA
  Carmen, 72
  Zoe, 5
ATWELL
  Ellen, 157
ATWILL
  Ella Florence, 128
AUGUSTA
  Elizabeth (blk), 40
  Mary M. (blk), 50
AUSTIN
  Adeline, 20
  Ellen L., 237
  Emma, 154
  Serena, 254
AVERY
  Arabell E., 14
  C.R., 91
  Ida Mary, 315
  Margaret, 191
  Sallie, 105
AXLINE
  Mary A.E., 308
AYER
  Julia, 8
AYLOR
  Annie M., 303
AYLWARD
  Ada B., 105
AYRE
  Frances A., 132
AYRES
  Caroline (blk), 13
AYTES
  Salina (blk), 274
AYTON
  Adaline, 92
  Eleanora S., 92
  Elizabeth C., 206
  Ginnie, 44

—B—

BABB
  Sarah E., 62

BABBINGTON
  Catherine, 221
  Hannah, 238
  Hanora, 139
  Joana, 90
  Joanna, 70
BABCOCK
  Clara J., 324
BABER
  Charlotte (blk), 21
BACHE
  Amelia M., 143
BACHING
  Laura, 78
BACKHAUSEN
  Mina, 165
BACKUS
  Gracie (blk), 1
  Maria (blk), 159
BACON
  Alice, 191
  Carrie, 130
  Cornelia M.A.V., 66
  Elizabeth, 10, 266
  Elizabeth C., 10
  Lizzie, 33
  Louisa H., 75
  Mary, 65
  Olivia, 157
BADEN
  Eliza Elizabeth, 26
BAGGETT
  Annie E., 320
  Louisa, 170
BAGGOTT
  Margaret, 209
BAGHAN
  Kate, 81
BAGLEY
  Mary, 100
BAHANS
  Hannah, 316
BAILEY
  Ann Elizabeth, 248
  Annie, 127
  Charlotte, 196
  Elizabeth, 234, 280
  Elizabeth (blk), 280
  Ella (blk), 151

BAILEY
 Ellen F., 28
 Emma, 92
 Fannie W., 235
 Harriet A., 130
 Henrietta, 214
 Hester M., 231
 Jane Elizabeth, 5
 Louisa, 248
 Lucy C., 2
 Marion, 197
 Martha, 98, 222, 295
 Mary, 34, 138, 189, 239, 321
 Mary C., 138
 Mary E., 321
 Mary Elizabeth (blk), 239
 Mary V., 189
 Rachel (blk), 305
 Sarah (blk), 248
 Sarah Elizabeth, 102
BAILOR
 Martha Ellen (blk), 9
BAILY
 Louisa H. (blk), 46
 Margaret (blk), 18
BAIN
 Mary A., 119
BAINE
 Margaret A., 92
BAINET
 Mary, 113
BAIRD
 A. Virginia, 213
 Margaret P., 52
BAISMEN
 Flavius V., 114
BAKEOVEN
 Augustus, 240
BAKER
 Abagail, 93
 Adelheit, 131
 Anna C.C., 29
 Annie E., 89
 Caroline (blk), 204
 Catharine C., 58
 Catherine (blk), 134
 Christiann, 24
 Elisa H., 2
 Elizabeth, 24, 327
 Elizabeth, 24
 Ella, 91
 Emily, 239
 Emma B., 213
 Evea Anna, 75
 Fanny (blk), 203
 Josephine, 265
 Julia Ellen, 185
 Linda (blk), 290
 Lizzie, 217
 Lucy J., 229
 Margaret, 279
 Maria L., 143
 Martha, 105
 Mary, 141, 170, 183
 Mary C., 141
 Mary Susie, 183
 Nellie (blk), 79
 Patience (blk), 11
BAKERGELLAG
 Margaret, 322
BALDERSON
 Frances A., 59
BALDERSTON
 Lucy E., 245
BALDWIN
 Annie, 294
 Catharine V., 163
 Elizabeth E.A. (blk), 191
 Flora J., 74
 Margaret, 93
 Mary Ann, 162
 Mary Flora, 62
 Rowena M., 138
 Sallie E., 299
 Sarah A., 300
BALENGER
 Mary E., 310
BALINGER
 Mary E., 310
BALL
 Ann E., 19
 Ann Maria (blk), 72
 Barbara Elizabeth, 236
 Catherine E., 189
 Eliza (blk), 324
 Elizabeth (blk), 316
 Fannie M., 243
 Joann Ellen, 28
 Josephine C., 11
 Julia (blk), 279
 Kate, 46
 Lizzie (blk), 86
 Margaret (blk), 39
 Maria, 239
 Mary E., 136
 Mary J., 227
 Nancy (blk), 101
 Nancy R., 261
 Sally, 229
 Sarah E., 296
 Sena (blk), 307
 Susan (blk), 154
BALLARD
 Beattrice A., 130
 Gabriel R., 10, 190
 Mary E., 269
BALLAUF
 Adolphina, 169
BALLENGER
 Lottie, 234
 Sue, 232
BALLINGER
 Sarah, 95
BALLOU
 Therese, 299
BALMAIN
 Annie E., 259
 Mary E., 223
BALOR
 Mary (blk), 287
BALTON
 Bridget, 188
BALTZER
 Mary Jane, 234
BALZELL
 Mary, 84
BAMBERRY
 Ellen, 208
BAMPF
 Catharina, 2

333

BANE
  Catharine, 310
BANF
  Anna Barbara, 295
BANGS
  Irene M., 69
  Lucy A., 21
BANISTER
  Mary (blk), 89
BANKS
  Amanda (blk), 307
  Catharine, 143
  Eliza (blk), 312
  Ellen (blk), 209
  Emily (blk), 110
  Frances L., 202
  Harriet (blk), 191
  Henritta (blk), 11
  Julia (blk), 272
  Juliana (blk), 258
  Margaret, 286
  Maria (blk), 155, 215
  Melvina (blk), 11
  Sally (blk), 293
  Sarah (blk), 324
  Sarah R., 217
  Susan (blk), 11
BANNISTER
  Margaret A., 328
  Mary E., 68
BANTER
  Louisa, 245
BANTLIN
  Louisa (blk), 9
BARBER
  Ella, 270
  Mary, 16, 299
  Mary A., 16
  Susan, 314
BARBOUR
  Ellen (blk), 191
  Isabella, 79
  Patsey (blk), 152
  Sylvia (blk), 225
  Virginia, 179
BARCLAY
  Jane L., 1
  Mary Ann, 106

BARGAN
  Julia, 276
BARGER
  Mary Ann, 5
BARGY
  Hannah Johnson, 55
BARICKMAN
  Mary Ann, 30
BARKER
  Almedia J., 138
  Catherine W., 12
  Lucinda (blk), 20
  Maria L., 165
  Mary V., 11
  Matilda, 216
  Sarah J., 21
BARKMAN
  Alice, 126
  Amanda, 268
  Mary Virginia, 322
BARLOW
  Emily (blk), 118
BARNACLE
  Carrie, 269
  Emma E., 32
BARNACLO
  Mary S., 99
BARNARD
  Eliza (blk), 202
  Mary, 138
  Millie, 304
  S.L., 29
  Theodosia L., 284
BARNES
  Angelina, 84
  Ann M., 41
  Ann Perosia (blk), 158
  Ann Rebecca, 284
  Annie (blk), 167, 258
  Caroline, 94
  Catharine, 130
  Catherine (blk), 132
  Charlotte (blk), 272
  Eleanor A., 213
  Eliza (blk), 4
  Elizabeth, 80, 314
  Elizabeth A., 314

  Emma (blk), 101
  Frances Virginia, 53
  GeorgeAnn (blk), 52
  Harriet (blk), 290
  Henrietta, 48, 267, 306
  Henrietta (blk), 267, 306
  Isabella, 145
  Julia (blk), 69
  Louisa, 63
  Margaret, 16, 108
  Marie A., 240
  Martha (blk), 43
  Martha E., 27
  Mary, 58, 96, 154, 158, 327
  Mary (blk), 327
  Mary Ellen, 154
  Mary Louisa (blk), 158
  Mary V., 58
  Rosella J., 147
  Sarah, 10, 73, 140, 289
  Sarah (blk), 289
  Sarah Cornelia, 140
  Sarah Jane, 73
BARNEY
  Julia, 14
BARNHOUSE
  Sarah T., 93
BARNS
  Helen M., 45
  Mary E., 224
  Pricy (blk), 218
  Winnie F. (blk), 40
BARNSLEY
  Annie F., 10
BARNUM
  Francis L., 305
BARON
  Ella (blk), 33
BARR
  Catharine, 304
  Helen E., 203
  Ida, 147
  Laura Virginia, 76
  Margaret E., 6

BARR
  Mary A., 112
  Mary E., 104
  Mary J., 254
BARRETT
  Ann E., 183
  Bridget, 221
  Catharine, 220
  Ellen, 15
  Emma Cornelia, 275
  Hannah Parker, 132
  Harriet, 264
  Johanna, 220
  Julia, 130, 253
  Kate, 268
  Lizzie, 189
  Lucy, 291
  Luisa J., 294
  Margaret, 88
  Mary, 69, 173
  Mary J., 173
BARRIN
  Julia, 141
BARRIS
  Elizabeth, 3
BARRON
  Laura E., 105
  Willie F., 243
BARROWS
  Elizabeth R., 63
BARRY
  Adalaide M., 233
  Cynthia, 62, 318
  Jane Eliza, 206
  Joanna, 166
  Lucinda, 14
  Lydia B., 130
  Mary (blk), 159
  Matilda Adelaide, 301
  Rachel, 324
  Rosina, 9
  Virginia, 274
BARSACH
  Elenora, 256
BARTELMAN
  Atelhaid, 255
BARTHOLMAI
  Julia, 21

BARTHOLOMEW
  Ann Elizabeth, 160
BARTHOLOW
  Mattie E., 4
BARTLETT
  Elizabeth J., 76
  Kate F., 1
  Mary, 89, 269
BARTLEY
  Ann, 110
BARTON
  Charlotte E., 75
  Elenora (blk), 129
  Emma V., 89
  Gertrude I., 319
  Martha (blk), 196
  Mary Jane N., 139
BARTRUFF
  Mary Lee, 130
BASH
  Josephine (blk), 106
BASSETT
  Ada M., 297
  Eliza E., 291
  Emma A., 122
  Mary A., 40
  Mary Helen, 245
BASSY
  Fanny (blk), 14
BATCHING
  Anna, 69
  Mary, 254
BATEMAN
  Ann R., 324
  Harriet A., 63
  Mary E., 137
  Sallie L., 20
  Sarah (blk), 260
BATES
  Anna Virginia, 276
  Ella Virginia, 139
  Levisa (blk), 273
  Martha, 163, 207
  Martha (blk), 207
  Mary, 90, 170, 173, 224, 278
  Mary Francis, 224
  Mary Louisa, 173
  Mary R., 278

  Rachel M., 225
  Sophia, 264
BATHEN
  Jennie, 140
BATHUN
  Alice, 290
BATIS
  Sallie, 165
BATON
  Susan C., 298
BATSCHIN
  Annie, 104
BATTERSLY
  Annie C., 97
BATTIGHEIMER
  Hannah, 266
BAUER
  Amelia, 15
  Barbara, 160
  Rosalie, 243
  Wilhelmina, 7
BAUM
  Catharine A., 158
  Hannah, 236
  Mary E., 170
BAUMAN
  Elizabeth Caroline, 19
BAUR
  Angeline, 212
BAUSBACH
  Annie, 132
BAWS
  Johanna, 261
BAXTER
  Julia Ann, 242
  Lethe Ann (blk), 250
BAYLEY
  Harriet, 224
  Lucinda, 231
  Mary Elizabeth, 310
BAYLISS
  Emma, 49
  Helen M., 274
  Martha Ann, 175
  Mary B., 99
  Trace C., 71

BAYLOR
  Bettie (blk), 155
  Evelina (blk), 22
  Lucy (blk), 181
  Lydia (blk), 77
  Maria (blk), 69
  Octavia (blk), 15
BAYLUM
  Mary (blk), 77
BAYNE
  Salina Cath., 230
  Sarah E., 114
BAYNERD
  Lydea, 79
BEACH
  Catharine, 164
  Eleanora, 209
  Isabella, 123
  Jane C., 43
  Josephine, 156
  Lucinda, 74, 90
  Mary C., 137
  Mary E., 68
  Sallie J., 235
  Sarah A., 164
  Sheldena W., 186
  Susan, 9, 151
  Susanna, 9
BEACHAM
  Josephine M., 63
  Mary (blk), 74
BEACHUM
  Leona V., 104
  Rebecca, 201
BEAD
  Anna, 240
BEAGLE
  Elizabeth, 314
BEAHLEN
  Emelie V., 249
BEALE
  Ellen (blk), 116
  Lavinia (blk), 308
  Margaret, 89
BEALL
  Anna M., 269
  Annetta Josephine, 76
  Annie E.L., 298

Elizabeth (blk), 124
Fannie, 105
Henrietta E., 322
Josephine A., 53
Louisa (blk), 136
M.A., 136
Margaret A., 85
Maria L., 221
Marion, 231
Mary M.A., 85
Minty (blk), 205
Sarah Ellen, 304
BEAM
  Margaret M., 275
  Sarah Catharine, 293
BEAMAN
  Catherine, 220
BEAN
  Agatha, 132
  Ann (blk), 47
  Annie, 150
  Carrie D., 253
  Eliza, 7
  Kate, 105
  Margaret Ellen, 57
  Mary E., 168
  Mary J., 6
  Sarah E., 26
  Sarah M., 131
  Virginia E., 299
  Winnie (blk), 41
BEANS
  Julia Ann, 262
  Kitty, 16
  Lavinia (blk), 124
  Lyly, 203
BEARD
  Katie E., 299
  Lucy (blk), 284
  Mary E., 43
  Mary L., 94
BEARDSLEY
  Eliza, 204
  Laura V., 285
  Marion, 245
  Martha E., 74, 104
BEATLY
  Susan, 299

BEAUREGARD
  Katrina, 159
BEAVANS
  Emma L., 99
BEAVERS
  Lydia A., 275
  Martha R., 41
BECHTOLD
  Karolina, 181
BECK
  Catherine, 94
  Henrietta, 17
  Kate, 301
  Margaret, 301
  Rachel, 124
BECKENBAUGH
  Clara Z., 100
BECKER
  Eliza, 189
  Eva E., 180
  Mina, 274
BECKERT
  Anna, 257
  Chatarina, 245
  Jennie, 213
BECKET
  Ann Maria (blk), 253
  Elizabeth (blk), 283
  Ella (blk), 291
  Frances A., 128
  Jane Bayliss, 54
  Sarah (blk), 288
BECKETT
  Amelia Ann (blk), 136
  Ellen (blk), 308
  Kate (blk), 109
  Margaret A., 105
BECKLEY
  Catharine (blk), 107
BECKMAN
  Eliza (blk), 253
  Lena, 258
BECKWID
  Louisa (blk), 316
BECKWITH
  Anna, 187
  Jane, 199, 217

BECKWITH
  Jane E., 217
  Josephine, 121, 256
  Malinda Ann, 40
  Mary J., 199
BEECH
  Mary E., 173
BEEDLE
  Emma, 37
BEEN
  Margaret E., 239
BEERMAN
  Emily, 310
BEERS
  Julia, 269
  Maggie A., 105
BEHAN
  Mary, 159
BEHLEN
  Ella, 237
BEHR
  Metha Gesina, 85
BEHREND
  Caroline, 13
BEHRENS
  Emma, 6
  Henrietta M., 311
  Joanna, 250
  Louisa, 296
BEICHERT
  Kathe, 23
BEINDER
  Margaret A. (blk), 265
BEISSER
  Annie, 196, 211
  Annie L., 211
BEIT
  Dora, 118
BEITZELL
  Sheba, 240
BEKERSCHMIDT
  Anna, 21
BELFILS
  Virginia, 30
BELFOUR
  Caroline (col'd), 79
BELL
  Amanda, 296, 317

Amanda F., 296
Amelia A., 9
Ann Maria (blk), 5
Anna Elizabeth
  (blk), 150
Anne (blk), 33
Annie (blk), 222
Cornelia A. (blk), 115
Dorothea (blk), 148
Eliza, 35, 155, 176, 214, 263, 287
Eliza (blk), 176, 214, 287
Elizabeth (blk), 155
Elizabeth H., 263
Ellen (blk), 113
Emily, 127, 305
Emily (blk), 127
Harriet (blk), 129
Henrietta (blk), 222
Jane, 273
Kate, 314
Kittie, 290
Lavinia (blk), 278
Lizzie, 207
Louisa (blk), 27, 57, 224
Lucy (blk), 186
Margaret (blk), 306
Maria, 74, 98, 176
Maria (col'd), 176
Mariam, 98
Martha A.E. (blk), 317
Mary, 116, 143, 259, 266, 320
Mary Ann (blk), 116
Mary D. (blk), 143
Mary Jane (blk), 116
Nancy (blk), 36, 126
Polly (blk), 85
Rachel, 68, 101, 315
Rachel Ann, 68, 315
Rachel Ann (blk), 315
Sarah (blk), 101
Sarah Jane (blk), 129

Sidney L., 7
Virginia, 299
BELT
  Anne (blk), 306
  Catharine A., 8
  Ella J., 119
  Emeline E. (blk), 137
  Julia B., 226
  Martha, 82
  Mary Ellen (blk), 318
  MAry M., 108
  Mary V. (blk), 269
  Mary Virgnia, 190
  Nellie (blk), 9
BEMENT
  Mary Louisa, 264
BEMIS
  Sylvia S., 22
BENDER
  Emma S., 267
  Mary A., 271
  Virginette M. (blk), 174
BENEDICT
  Antonia H., 248
BENESCH
  Hermine, 275
BENHARDIE
  Sophia, 92
BENJAMIN
  A.A., 14
  Ann Sophia, 277
  Mary Ann, 108
  Rachel I., 58
  Rebecca L., 35
  Sophronia, 205
BENKHERT
  Julia, 41
BENNER
  Virginia G., 100
BENNET
  Sarah A., 68
BENNETT
  Catherine, 234
  Elizabeth (blk), 122
  Hanorah, 185
  Lela, 132

337

BENNETT
- Martha (blk), 130, 210
- Penny Ann (blk), 217
- Vina F., 278

BENNIKE
- Antonica, 114

BENSINGER
- Tracy, 251

BENSON
- Catharine M., 299
- Harriet, 43
- Ida A., 44

BENTLEY
- Hannah J., 254
- Margaret C., 270

BENTLY
- Mary A.E. (blk), 225

BENTON
- Catherine, 312
- Martha Ann, 1
- Martha E., 265
- Mary A., 265
- Rosetta, 97

BENTZ
- Kate, 143

BENTZLER
- Adeline, 137
- Mary Catherine, 138

BENVER
- Lisette, 211

BENZ
- Cara, 174

BERAULT
- Mary, 254

BERBERICK
- Kate, 128

BERCHARD
- Mary A., 5

BERGER
- Anntoinette V., 299
- Doretta, 121
- Mary, 180

BERGMAN
- Charlotte, 24
- Louisa, 110

BERGMANN
- Henrietta, 109
- Mary, 24
- Minna, 6

BERKELEY
- Rozela Augusta, 178

BERKER
- Clarinda, 9

BERKIN
- Mary Ann, 128

BERKLEY
- Anna (blk), 284
- Ellen M., 219
- Jane (blk), 316
- Mary Jane (blk), 53
- Sarah Ann, 139

BERLIN
- Annie J., 109
- Caroline, 321
- Emma C., 1

BERNARD
- Jane, 21, 85
- Laura, 16

BERNHARD
- Catherine, 6
- Wilhelmina, 257

BERNHARDI
- Louisa, 230

BERRINS
- Bridget, 262

BERRY
- Amelia O., 20
- Betsy (blk), 298
- Christiana (blk), 189
- Elizabeth (blk), 314
- Ellen, 220, 231
- Ellen M., 231
- Georgiana (blk), 304
- Hester, 167
- Julia H., 190
- Lucinda (blk), 306
- Lucy (blk), 20
- Margaret, 96, 137
- Martha (blk), 90, 133
- Mary, 2, 35, 174, 215, 266, 302
- Mary Catharine (blk), 35
- Mary Catherine (blk), 266
- Mary E.B., 302
- Mary Ellen (blk), 2
- Mary N., 174
- Rose (blk), 59
- Sarah A., 290
- Sarah Jane, 187, 279
- Sarah Jane (blk), 279
- Sarah M., 33
- Sarah R., 262
- Susan, 223, 259
- Susan Ann (blk), 259

BERRYMAN
- Bemy (blk), 50
- Ellen (blk), 145
- Lucy A., 120

BEST
- Ellen S., 32
- Margaret, 202

BESTOR
- Henrietta M., 102

BETTEL
- Mary Ann, 196

BETTER
- Emma (blk), 92
- Jane (blk), 306
- Lucinda (blk), 192
- Mary J. (blk), 18
- Mary Jane (blk), 155

BETTERSBY
- Catharine A., 178

BETTINGER
- Margaret, 136

BETTS
- Catherine, 314
- Harriet C., 28
- Nancy (blk), 39

BETZ
- Mary, 102

BETZEL
- Mary, 141

BEUCHLER
- Mary Ann, 265

BEVANS
- Belinda, 21
- Margaret V., 30

BEVEL
  Eliza (blk), 38
BEVERIDGE
  Laura Virginia, 90
BEVERLY
  Betty (blk), 217
  Margaret (blk), 151
  Mary (blk), 178
BEVIER
  Katie E., 314
  Sarah E., 192
BEVIG
  Sophia, 240
BEYER
  Victoria, 283
BEZELY
  Sarah, 292
BIALEY
  Henrietta W., 60
BIAS
  Sarah (blk), 293
BIBB
  Acadia S., 183
  Ellanor E., 145
  Margaret F., 136
BICKHAM
  Sarah E., 217
BIDDLE
  Lucy E., 208
BIDDLEMAN
  Marian E., 101
BIDWELL
  Carrie D., 147
BIELASKI
  Rosa J., 217
BIERINGER
  Caroline, 243
BIERMANN
  Mary, 189
BIERNE
  Annie S.O., 107
BIERS
  Margaretta A., 9
BIETZ
  Carolina, 255
BIGELOW
  Annie, 107

BIGGS
  Louisa, 167
  Margaret A., 165
  Mary A.R., 162
  Mary E.R., 260
  Sarah, 130
  Simphronia, 3
BIGLER
  Mary, 285
BIGLEY
  Mary, 238
BILLAS
  Catherine, 172
BILLING
  Amelia W., 234
  Mary W., 113
BINDER
  Maggie, 91
  Mary, 281
BING
  Frances (blk), 148
  Rosey, 216
  Sarah (blk), 266
BINGHAM
  Leanda (blk), 258
BINNIX
  Alpharesta, 109
BIRCH
  Evelina, 137
  Jeannette, 247
  Margaret J., 299
  Mary F., 214
  Mary P., 297
BIRD
  Elizabeth, 22
  Maggie, 133
  Maria Sianna, 109
  Rebecca (blk), 273
  Rose (blk), 126
BIRKHEAD
  Anna T., 289
BIRMANN
  Mary, 157
BIRNEY
  Harriet E., 217
  Rose, 247
BIRNIE
  Hessie H.N., 12

BISCOE
  Emma, 145
BISHOP
  Ada E., 57
  Anna L., 282
  Annie, 49
  Isabel P., 282
  Mary P., 263
BITTINGER
  Ruhannah, 212
BIVENGER
  Mina, 314
BIXLOW
  Annie, 83
BLACK
  Catharine, 238
  Dorcas, 205
  Jenny (blk), 21
  Mary, 24, 158, 288
  Mary C., 158
  Mary E., 288
  Victoria (blk), 269
BLACKBURN
  Margaretta (blk), 140
BLACKFORD
  Kate, 323
BLACKMAN
  Frances, 4
BLACKSTONE
  Betsy (blk), 268
  Ellen (blk), 123
  Julia Adaline, 48
BLACKWELL
  Laura (blk), 29
  Margaret (blk), 152
  Mary (blk), 82
  Mary Ann, 264
  Priscilla (blk), 152
  Virginia, 251
BLADEN
  Adaline V., 7
  Caroline V., 304
  Catharine L., 90
  Elizabeth Ann, 90
  Georgiana, 277
  Laura Meriken, 187
  Martha E., 226
  Martha Ellen, 192

District of Columbia Marriage Licenses, 1858-1870

BLADEN
  Mary Ellen, 288
  Matilda (blk), 261
  Sarah E., 74
BLADES
  Sarah C., 169
BLAGDEN
  Julia (blk), 292
BLAGMAN
  Sophia, 137
BLAIN
  Matilda, 267
BLAINEY
  Bridget, 83
BLAIR
  Annie, 141
  Elizabeth, 59
  Elsie M., 226
  Jane, 262
  Maggie A., 179
  Mary E., 129
BLAKE
  Bridget, 201
  Ella, 231
  Julia, 186
BLAKELY
  Eliza P., 150
BLAKENEY
  Mary Elizabeth, 4
  Sarah E., 80
BLAKEY
  Adaline (blk), 155
BLANCHARD
  Ada D., 248
  Frances, 325
  Lucy A., 153
BLANCHFIELD
  Annie E., 82
  Margaret A., 107
  Mary, 275
BLAND
  Admonia Janey (blk), 179
  Denizar Ann, 75
  Fanny (blk), 196
  J. Ella, 138
  Mary, 102, 125
  Mary E., 102
  Rosa B., 182

  Victoria (blk), 314
BLIGH
  Kate, 260
BLINKO
  Martha, 291
BLOCK
  Mariana, 264
BLODGETT
  Mary E., 307
BLOIS
  Mary A., 194
BLOOMER
  Louisa, 214
BLOSSOM
  Emily G., 138
BLOUNT
  Alice K., 111
  Louisa Knight, 282
  Mary B., 25
BLOW
  Rosa (blk), 118
BLOYCE
  Lucretia D., 235
BLUCHER
  Eva, 171
BLÜCHER
  Louisa, 75
BLUE
  Frances, 317
BLUM
  Mary, 204
BLUME
  Caroline, 325
BLYTH
  Ellen S., 310
BOARMAN
  Annie, 1
  Eliza, 192
  Sarah C., 154
BOCK
  Mary Ann, 17
BÖCKER
  Auguste, 104
BOCOLIN
  Catherine, 264
BODEN
  Mary C., 240
BODKIN
  Elizabeth A., 231

BOETTNER
  Adelheid, 238
BOGAN
  Leanna, 68
BOGARDUS
  Susan A., 115
BOGART
  Sallie E., 302
BOGGES
  Frances C., 269
BOGGS
  Catherine Stewart, 20
BOGLE
  Mary, 40
  Ottaway (blk), 53
BOHANIN
  Lizetta, 295
BOHLAYER
  Annie Eliza, 98
  Catharine Virginia, 14
  Margaret, 184
  Sarah Ann, 309
BOHLE
  Eliza Anne, 50
BOHLES
  E.A., 138
BOHRER
  Ellen, 179
  Fannie Maria, 250
BOICE
  Nancy, 278
BOLAND
  Lizzie, 212
  Maria, 193
  Mary, 40
BOLDEN
  Lucy (blk), 159
BOLEN
  Agnes (blk), 249
BOMBRAY
  Emily (blk), 306
BOMBREY
  Sophia, 105
BOND
  Eleanor E., 18
  Henrietta (blk), 88
  Hester (blk), 125

BOND
　Jane (blk), 56
　Martha, 134, 317
　Mary (blk), 149
　Mary Eliza, 5
　Zelphy Ann, 120
BONDS
　Bettie (blk), 270
　Mary (blk), 57
BONGY
　Mary (blk), 93
BONITZ
　Emelia, 132
BONNEMANN
　Maria Elizth., 173
BONNER
　Amanda (blk), 126
BONTZ
　Mary C., 287
BONZER
　Rebecca (blk), 104
BOONE
　Jane E., 128
　Lizzie, 11
　Mahala (blk), 264
　Priscilla (blk), 153
　Rosie, 100
BOOSE
　Laura S., 205
BOOTES
　Elizabeth C., 257
BOOTH
　Clara D., 250
　Henrietta (blk), 211
　Louisa (blk), 317
　Mary Ann, 69
BOOTHE
　Elizabeth, 104
　Fanny L. (col'd), 284
　Virginia (blk), 148
BOOZ
　Margaret, 116
BORDEN
　Margaret D., 129
　Sophia, 250
BOREL
　Paulina, 132
BORIE
　Victorine M., 229

BORLAND
　Margaret, 220
BORN
　Catherine, 146
　Henrietta, 165
BORNEMANN
　Catharine Elisa, 257
BORRS
　Anne, 250
BORTELL
　Priscilla A., 325
BOSS
　Barbara (blk), 153
　Edna J., 71
　Ellen M., 199
　Mary E., 199
BOSSE
　Henrietta, 128
BOSTON
　Fanny (blk), 248
　Lavinia, 151
　Martha (blk), 10, 306
　Martha E. (blk), 116
　Sarah (blk), 321
　Susan A. (blk), 122
BOSWELL
　Catharine, 290
　Eliza V., 183
　Emily R., 175
　Estell, 300
　Louisa, 26
　Lucy A., 147
　Margaret Helen, 126
　Martha (blk), 313
　Mary S., 70
　Mary V., 181
　Sarah Jane, 308
BOSWORTH
　Maria R., 158
BOTELER
　Jeminia E., 318
　Laura V., 307
　Rosalie T., 242
　Susan E., 304
BOTTAJHEMER
　Babet, 131
BOTTLEMY
　Kate, 4

BOTTS
　Isabella M., 178
　Lucinda (blk), 57
　Mary (blk), 21
　Rosalie, 14
BOUCHE
　Wilhelmina S., 168
BOUCHER
　Margaretta, 45
　Wilhelmina A., 235
BOUGHAN
　Mary, 108
BOUGHANAN
　Carolina, 107
BOULDEN
　Amonie (blk), 113
BOULDING
　Ann, 237
　Emma, 260
BOUNDS
　Sarah, 304
BOURBON
　Malvina (blk), 284
BOURNE
　Augusta, 172
BOURNS
　Jennie M., 132
BOUSER
　Rebecca (blk), 252
BOUTS
　Mary (blk), 171
BOUTWELL
　Rose B., 208
BOUVET
　Clarice Eugenie, 152
BOVAR
　Agness, 173
BOVEE
　Lucy J., 98
BOWDEN
　Ann Maria, 51
　Eliza (blk), 228
　Ellen, 70
　Elvira A. (blk), 116
　Mary E. (blk), 75
BOWE
　Maria (blk), 153
BOWEN
　Annie M., 294

BOWEN
　Elizabeth E., 247
　Emma Eliza, 285
　Emma Ruth, 284
　Henrietta (blk), 79
　Hester (blk), 67
　Joanna, 46
　Josephine (blk), 55
　Laura E., 181
　Mary, 106, 302, 304
　Mary E., 302
　Mary F. (blk), 304
　Myra J., 110
　Rebecca, 291
　Sarah, 289
BOWENS
　Martha (blk), 270
BOWER
　Sarah J., 308
BOWERS
　Adeline, 122
　Henrietta E., 134
BOWERSOF
　Sarah Jane, 83
BOWHAN
　Ella J., 292
BOWIE
　Ann Maria (blk), 142
　Annie, 86
　Clarissa (blk), 45
　Elizabeth (blk), 311
　Elizabeth D., 280
　Emma (blk), 174
　Henrietta (blk), 44
　Jane (blk), 176
　Kate (blk), 311
　Lotte E., 3
　Margaret (blk), 155
　Maria Ann (blk), 229
　Mary, 180, 237
　Mary Auguste, 180
　Polly (blk), 232
　Sarah L., 324
BOWLER
　Lavenia (blk), 293
　Margaret, 262
　Mary V., 216

BOWLERSON
　Elizabeth, 283
BOWLES
　Caroline (blk), 70
　Mary L., 231
BOWLING
　Kate, 235
BOWMAN
　Amy (blk), 129
　Clara C.B. (blk), 259
　Emma J., 317
　Harriet L. (blk), 307
　Jane (blk), 169
　Louisa, 80, 301
　Louisa (blk), 301
　Lucy (blk), 251
　Mary, 93, 202
　Mary L., 202
　Nancy (blk), 259
　Rachel A., 52, 109
　Rachel A. (blk), 52
　Sophronia (blk), 322
　Susan E., 44
BOWSER
　Margaret (blk), 72
BOWYER
　Frances, 125
BOXBAUM
　Eliza, 260
BOYCE
　Elizabeth, 58, 160
　Emma, 23
　Julia, 180
BOYD
　Anna, 205
　Carrie A., 270
　Emma D., 4
　Georgiana (blk), 51
　Mary, 267
　Nettie, 270
　Sarah, 283
BOYER
　Christiana, 13
　Kitty, 42
　Margaret, 200
　Mary Ellen, 130
　Mary Jane, 190

BOYLE
　Bettie, 188
　Catharine, 219
　Catherine, 315
　Cornelia, 307
　Elizabeth, 1
　Ellen, 63
　Emily Beale, 234
　Emuella F., 167
　Julia, 78
　Laura A., 5
　Mary, 102, 106, 130, 166, 187, 198
　Susan, 228
BOYLEN
　Catherine, 248
BRACE
　Harriet (blk), 269
BRACKETT
　Elizabeth (blk), 126
　Lavinia, 198
BRACKIS
　Margaret (blk), 321
BRADBURN
　Sarah E., 146
BRADDOCK
　Bettie, 124
　Mary, 319
BRADFORD
　Clara (blk), 292
　Clara Bel, 314
　Elizabeth, 247
　Elmira, 67
　Sallie, 100
BRADLEY
　Alice, 318
　Bell, 168
　Caroline W., 295
　Julia, 220, 238
　Lucinda (blk), 28
　Maria G., 289
　Martha A., 315
　Mary T., 117
　Rose A., 52
　Rosetta, 258
　Sarah Jane, 134
　Sidney T., 88

District of Columbia Marriage Licenses, 1858-1870

BRADLY
  Polly (blk), 50
BRADSHAW
  Mary (blk), 55
BRADY
  Charlotte, 96
  Dephenia, 139
  Elizabeth M., 129
  Ellen, 26
  Emily E., 196
  Eveline, 265
  Jemima, 124, 313
  Jemima (blk), 124
  Margt. E., 102
  Maria J., 288
  Mary, 60, 178
  Mollie, 49
  Rose, 147
  Sarah, 150
BRAFF
  Lilly, 303
BRAIN
  Amanda, 74
BRAINERD
  Emma, 252
BRAKELEY
  Cornelia S., 226
BRAMAR
  Sarah N. (blk), 90
BRAMELL
  Jane, 110, 262
  Jane P., 110
BRAMLEE
  Helen, 45
BRAMLY
  Isabell, 260
BRAMMELL
  Caroline V., 262
  Mary Maria, 56
BRANAGAN
  Georgiana, 183
BRAND
  Amelia, 177
  Catherine, 326
BRANDEBURY
  Florence E., 205
BRANDEN
  Honora, 112

BRANDON
  Ellen, 255
  Harriet, 283
BRANDT
  Amalie, 172
  Elizabeth, 183
BRANEMAN
  Mary, 16
BRANGER
  Margaret, 231
BRANHAM
  Marcellina (blk), 284
BRANIGAN
  Mary, 308
BRANNAGAN
  Catharine, 99
BRANNAN
  Elizabeth, 106
  Louisa F.G., 206
  Mary Ann, 97
BRANNER
  Frances C., 80
BRANNON
  Sallie (blk), 126
BRANNUM
  Mary, 149
BRANSELL
  Elenore, 84
BRANSOM
  Lizzie (blk), 166
  Susan H., 46
BRANSON
  Margaret (blk), 85
  Mary (blk), 91
  Mary E. (blk), 132, 273
  Sallie A., 64
BRANTON
  Mary, 243
BRANZERR
  Charlott, 84
BRANZILL
  Mary Ellen, 158
BRASHEARS
  Flowilly (blk), 51
  Irene E., 289
  Josie, 202
  Susan (blk), 38

BRASNAHAN
  Margaret, 70
BRATTON
  Ann (blk), 153
BRAUMEN
  Adelaide, 63
BRAUNER
  Alice V., 159
BRAUNSHEIG
  Theresa, 274
BRAWNER
  Mary E., 317
  Susie Craig, 217
BRAXTON
  Amy (blk), 189
  M.J., 253
  Mahala (blk), 305
  Patcy (blk), 259
BRAY
  Ann Salome, 321
BREASHEAR
  Sarah, 35
BREAST
  Susie Riley, 242
BRECHT
  Sophia, 39
BRECKENRIDGE
  E. (blk), 30, 62
BREDECAMP
  Anna, 109
  Sarah, 41
BREDERNÜTZ
  Bertha, 233
BREENIAN
  Kate, 163
BREGGENAN
  Rosa L., 132
BREHM
  Fannie E., 282
BREIGHT
  Anna (blk), 288
BREMER
  Karoline, 93
  Mary, 276
BREMERMAN
  Annie E., 228
BREMMERMAN
  Lottie A., 71

# District of Columbia Marriage Licenses, 1858-1870

BRENDEL
 Pauline, 7
BRENDER
 Elizabeth, 145
BRENNAN
 Catharine, 293
 Honora, 11
BRENNEN
 Julia, 171
BRENNON
 Annie, 165
BRENT
 Amelia E. (blk), 324
 Caroline (blk), 150
 Catherine T. (blk), 224
 Eleanor, 113
 Emily A. (blk), 103
 Mary L. (blk), 44
 Mattie, 133
 Winnifred Lee, 185
BRERETON
 Eliza, 84
 Mary, 226
BRESNAHAN
 Catharine, 76
 Joanna, 81
 Margaret C., 194
BRESNEHAN
 Margaret, 195
 Mary, 253
BRESSINGHAM
 Ellen, 282
BRESSNAHAN
 Abbe, 111
BRESTE
 Mary F., 62
BRETT
 Martha, 38
BREWER
 Alice, 218
 Amanda V., 12
 Fannie R., 242
 Louisa E., 16
 Martha (blk), 313
 Mary B., 7
 Mary E., 168
BREYER
 Clinstina Susan, 240

BREYFOGH
 J.R., 177
BRIAN
 Jane, 2
BRICE
 Anna R., 51
BRICK
 Catherine, 189
BRIDECAMP
 Kate, 192
BRIDEWELL
 Martha E., 102
BRIDGET
 Margaret N., 145
 Mary E., 92
BRIDWELL
 Nancy L. G., 176
BRIEN
 Elizabeth, 67, 282
 Ellen, 99, 123, 163
 Margaret, 184, 319
 Mary, 97, 190, 215, 235, 244, 304, 313, 314
BRIGGS
 Cecilia (blk), 31
 Jane, 156
 Margaret (blk), 9
BRIGHT
 Catharine E., 256
 Julia E., 93
 Margaret E., 83
 Mary T., 245
 Matilda (blk), 159
BRIGHTON
 Susan, 248
BRIGHTUPT
 Agnes, 165
BRILLER
 Barbet, 257
 Mary, 168
BRILY
 Bridget, 30
BRIMER
 Martha A., 226
BRIMO
 Fredericke, 256
BRINCKMAN
 Eliza, 256

BRINDAN
 Catherine, 120
BRINKLEY
 Mary E., 100
BRINKMAN
 Caroline, 269
BRINNEN
 Maggie A., 162
BRISCOE
 Bettie, 285
 Elizabeth, 127, 205
 Elizabeth (blk), 127
 Margaret (blk), 261
 Martha A., 12
 Merander James (blk), 122
 Nancy, 306
 Sarah, 288, 290
 Sarah J. (blk), 290
BRISTOW
 Rachel (blk), 241
BRITNER
 Louisa, 82
BRITT
 Elizabeth, 102
 Jenny, 110
 Mary A., 245
BRITWELL
 Josephine, 296
BROADBACK
 Mary Ann, 9
BROADBENT
 Jane, 13
BROCKENBROUGH
 Louise C., 235
BROCKMEYER
 Mina, 171
BROCKWAY
 Louisa A., 12
BRODBECK
 Elizabeth, 298
BRODEN
 Mary, 22
BRODERICK
 Ann, 133
 Catherine, 182
 Hannah, 303
 Johanna, 125
 Margaret, 44

BRODERS
 Laura, 127
BRODHEAD
 Eliza, 2
BROESNEHAN
 Ellen, 200
BROGAN
 Frances, 309
BROGDIN
 Mary J. (blk), 285
BROHM
 Lina, 219
BROKAW
 Frances, 32
BROMLEY
 Eliza J., 322
BRONAUGH
 Fannie R., 303
 Mary (blk), 175
 Mildred M., 167
 Sarah Pauline, 255
BRÖND
 Christina, 77
BROOKE
 Jennie (blk), 326
 Louise (blk), 297
 Mary A., 80
 Mary F. (blk), 290
 Mary P., 172
 Mollie, 145
 Nannie E., 71
BROOKER
 Mildred A. (blk), 59
BROOKES
 Mary E., 175
 Mary V. (blk), 242
BROOKMEYER
 Elenora, 327
BROOKS
 Amanda (blk), 114
 Ann (blk), 124
 Anna (blk), 153
 Catharine (blk), 110
 Catherine A. (blk), 289
 Elizabeth (blk), 17, 167
 Ellen (blk), 148

Frances A. (blk), 261
Georgiana (blk), 157, 180
Gracey (blk), 23
Hannah (blk), 4, 308
Helen C., 124
Henrietta (blk), 66
Isabella (blk), 120
Jane, 107, 124, 251
Jane (blk), 124, 251
Jemima (blk), 291
Jennie, 279
Josephine (blk), 320
Julia P., 195
Laura (blk), 232
Louisa Jane (blk), 244
Malvina (blk), 180
Margaret (blk), 22, 25
Maria (blk), 29
Martha (blk), 206
Martha Ann, 172
Mary (blk), 55, 284
Mary A. (blk), 34
Mary F. (blk), 119
Mary Jane (blk), 148, 292
Millie (blk), 45, 66
Milly (blk), 119
Nancy (blk), 117
Nannie (blk), 297
Olivia, 108
Patsy (blk), 244
Rachel (blk), 207
Sarah (blk), 35
Sarah Ann (blk), 22
Selina, 151
Susan (blk), 7
BROOM
 Ann Eliza (blk), 187
 Juliet Ann (blk), 251
 Laura (blk), 32
BROOME
 Alice M., 212
BROOMFIELD
 Georgianna (blk), 308

BROSNAHAN
 Lizzie, 207
 Mary, 58, 63, 218
 Mary A., 58
BROSNAN
 Bettie J., 31
 Hannah, 197
 Susan, 195
BROSNEHAN
 Bridget, 64
 Julia, 98
 Margaret, 187
BROSWHAN
 Bridget, 162
BROUGHTON
 Josephine, 240
 Mary, 109, 259
 Mary A., 109
 Sarah E., 259
BROWDER
 Ellen, 2
BROWN
 Adaline (blk), 128
 Admonia (blk), 35
 Alethea (blk), 122
 Amanda (blk), 59
 Ann, 54, 95, 99, 136, 148, 149, 154, 157, 192, 193, 206, 216, 226, 230, 251, 255, 315
 Ann (blk), 54, 157
 Ann E., 193
 Ann Elizabeth, 315
 Anna (blk), 136, 148, 149, 251
 Anna J., 216
 Annie, 99, 154, 192, 206, 226, 230, 251, 255
 Annie (blk), 255
 Annie E., 99, 226, 230
 Annie E. (blk), 226, 230
 Annie S., 154, 206
 Bashby, 189
 Berija (blk), 317

**BROWN**
Betsey, 11
Bettie L. (blk), 84
Betty, 75, 174
Betty (blk), 174
Bridget A., 250
Caroline, 17, 18, 41, 174, 203, 249
Caroline (blk), 17, 41
Caroline E., 174
Catharine (blk), 16
Catherine (col'd), 178
Charlotte (blk), 152, 156
Charotte A. (blk), 33
Clara (blk), 313
Cornelia, 7, 219
Diana (blk), 36
Dora (blk), 183
Dorcas A. (blk), 154
Drucilla, 158
Drusilla (blk), 18
Eleanor, 168
Eliza (blk), 23, 32, 113, 270, 318
Elizabeth, 48, 77, 107, 126, 170, 173, 189, 235, 323
Elizabeth (blk), 48, 77, 107, 126, 189
Elizabeth Adelle (blk), 323
Elizabeth Q., 235
Ellen, 10, 33, 116, 180, 205, 231, 237, 259, 274, 292, 309
Ellen (blk), 10, 33, 116, 231, 274, 309
Ellen A., 205
Elvira (blk), 35
Emily, 106, 263
Emma (blk), 159, 317
Emma Jane (blk), 311
Fannie, 120, 129
Fanny (blk), 301
Fanny A., 49
Frances (blk), 86
Georgiana (blk), 159
Hannah J., 208
Harriet, 14, 41, 152, 237, 298
Harriet Ann, 14
Harriet E., 237
Harriet Ellen (blk), 41
Harrietta (blk), 298
Hattie, 205, 320
Hattie A., 205
Helen A., 18
Helen M., 288
Henrietta (blk), 176
Henrietta Ann, 23
Hester Ann, 131, 251
Hester Ann (blk), 251
Isabella, 186, 241
Isabella O., 241
Jane, 10, 27, 29, 35, 242, 267, 320
Jane (blk), 27, 35, 242, 320
Jane Rebecca, 267
Jemima P., 10
Jennie (blk), 286
Joanna, 29, 278, 310
Johanna, 81
Josephine (blk), 50
Julia, 138, 218
Julia Ada, 218
Kate R., 233
Laura (blk), 35
Laura Ann, 150
Laura V., 223
Lavinia (blk), 248
Leathe (blk), 323
Lillie V., 10
Lizzie (blk), 296
Louisa (blk), 28
Louise (blk), 166, 209
Lucinda, 304, 305
Lucinda (blk), 305
Lucy, 34, 137, 199, 258
Lucy (blk), 34, 258
Lucy Mildred, 137
Lydia (blk), 48
Margaret, 130, 138, 147, 183, 185, 221, 231, 237, 293, 301, 320
Margaret (blk), 183, 301
Margaret Ann, 138
Margaret E., 130
Margaret Ellen, 231
Margaret Jane (blk), 320
Maria, 58, 175, 250, 254, 265, 279, 304
Maria (blk), 175, 250, 279, 304
Maria E., 265
Marian D., 254
Martha, 17, 63, 137, 227, 246, 288, 297, 307
Martha (blk), 17, 307
Martha A., 137
Martha A. (blk), 288
Martha Ellen, 297
Martha M. (blk), 63
Martha V., 63
Martha Virginia, 63
Mary, 17, 21, 36, 51, 53, 57, 64, 71, 89, 90, 92, 95, 96, 101, 103, 105, 107, 108, 130, 133, 134, 136, 141, 146, 157, 159, 165, 177, 178, 205, 232, 235, 238, 244, 273, 276, 286, 287, 294, 296, 297, 304, 307, 315, 326

BROWN
  Mary (blk), 17, 64,
    90, 92, 107, 134,
    157, 165, 238
  Mary A. (blk), 36,
    108, 133
  Mary Ann, 21, 57
  Mary Ann (blk), 57
  Mary C., 101, 286
  Mary E., 51, 53, 95,
    103, 130, 136, 159,
    177, 235, 276, 304,
    315
  Mary E. (blk), 51,
    159, 304
  Mary E.M., 177
  Mary J., 205, 307,
    326
  Mary J. (blk), 326
  Mary Jane, 51, 105,
    146, 297
  Mary Jane (blk), 51,
    105, 297
  Mary L., 273
  Mary L. (blk), 244
  Mary M. (blk), 96
  Mary R., 287
  Mary S., 89
  Mary V., 296
  Mary Virginia, 141
  Matilda, 31, 125, 321
  Matilda (blk), 31,
    125
  Mattie (blk), 74
  Mattie L., 49
  May (blk), 143
  May Frances, 235
  Nancy, 52
  Nannie (blk), 231
  Nettie, 271
  Patsy (blk), 153
  Rachel (blk), 158,
    277, 279, 297, 304
  Rebecca (blk), 307
  Rebecca F., 326
  Rhoda, 27
  Rosey (blk), 21
  Sadie B., 226
  Sallie (blk), 5
  Sally (blk), 223
  Sarah, 17, 42, 57, 82,
    94, 95, 115, 125,
    129, 155, 157, 178,
    235, 261, 291, 312
  Sarah (blk), 57, 82,
    155, 178
  Sarah A. (blk), 42
  Sarah A. (col'd), 94
  Sarah A.L.V., 17
  Sarah A. (blk), 235
  Sarah E., 261
  Sarah F. (blk), 125
  Sarah L., 95
  Sarah M., 312
  Sarah V., 157
  Seraphina, 164
  Sophia (blk), 248
  Sophia A. (blk), 192
  Susan, 40, 61, 153,
    162, 167
  Susan (blk), 61, 153
  Susan A., 40
  Susan E., 167
  Sydney A. (blk), 22
  Victoria, 143
BROWNE
  Caroline F., 278
  Columbine A., 172
  Eva M., 221
  Mary Emma, 135
  Mary M. (blk), 284
BROWNING
  Alice E., 111
  Camilla, 219
  Jane Ann, 264
  Mary, 174
BROWNLEE
  Dianah, 73
  Lizzie, 35
  Sarah, 136
BROWNMULLER
  Isabella, 108
BRUCE
  Annie, 271
  Catharine (blk), 207
  Eliza (blk), 313
  Ella A., 56
  Emmeline, 240
  Josephine (blk), 156
  Margaret A., 7
  Maria L. (blk), 5
  Mary C., 46
  Mary E. (blk), 134
  Sarah C. (blk), 188
  Susan N. (blk), 103
BRUCKNER
  Marie, 175
BRUECKER
  Juliana, 211
BRUFF
  Zulima, 149
BRUMBACK
  Barbara Ann, 74
BRUMFIELD
  Mary L., 38
BRUMMETT
  Sarah, 228
BRUNEL
  Anne, 109
  Lilas, 288
BRYAN
  Alice, 119
  Ann Elizabeth, 38
  Edna, 55
  Emily, 152
  Josephine (blk), 90
  Kate, 244
  Margaret A., 87
  Martha A., 206
  Mary (blk), 259
  Rebecca (blk), 272
  Sarah Jeannette, 41
  Sluday, 62
BRYAND
  Elizabeth A., 178
BRYANT
  Annie, 222
  Elizabeth C., 294
  Isabella (blk), 178
  Mary M., 214
  Matilda, 230
BRYDEE
  Josephine (blk), 25
BRYSON
  Elizabeth, 43
BUB
  Susanne Ann, 52

BUCHANAN
 Alice (blk), 74
 Maggie, 288
 Nannie, 201
 Sarah (blk), 82
BUCKEY
 Jane C., 35
BUCKINGHAM
 Martha V., 263
 Mary R., 107
BUCKLEY
 Ellen, 17
 Hannah, 71
 Josephine, 19, 282
 Josephine V., 282
 Julia A., 78
 Margaret, 187
 Martha E., 268
 Mary, 189, 196, 253
 Mary E., 189
BUCKNER
 Agnes (blk), 215
 Ann (blk), 285
 Delphia (blk), 21
 Johanna, 133, 135
 Julia A. (blk), 216
 Maria (blk), 117
 Mary (blk), 212
BUDD
 Martha (blk), 317
 Mary, 31
BUERGER
 Clara J., 322
 J.S., 309
 Martha M., 169
 Mary Magdalin, 245
BUESHER
 Mary, 252
BUGWINE
 Emily (blk), 159
BUHENEY
 Johanna C., 312
BULGER
 Johanna, 224
 Maria, 121
BULL
 Anna, 50
 Frances, 93
 Kate, 130

BULLETT
 Mattie, 185
BULLOCK
 Lucy A., 121
 Sallie A., 196
BULLOCKS
 Mary (blk), 73
BUMBRAY
 Fanny (blk), 46
 Lavinia (blk), 258
BUMBREY
 Lucy (blk), 38
BUMERY
 Henrietta, 27
BUMREY
 Rosa (blk), 313
BUNCHOFF
 Elanora, 121
BUNDICK
 Virginia, 237
BUNDSCHUH
 Caroline, 131
BUNDY
 July (blk), 56
BUNGY
 Ann, 289
BUNTON
 Mary Eliza, 263
BUNYAN
 Elizabeth M., 137
BURBON
 Rachel, 74
BURCH
 Adaline, 19
 Aletha V., 110
 Alice, 208
 Amanda E., 58
 Annie E., 174, 198
 Jennie, 115
 Margaret, 227, 242, 324
 Margaret Ann, 227
 Mary M., 97
 Polina, 59
 Rebecca S., 159
 Sarah C., 108
 Sarah Frances, 90
 Suzy R., 113

BURCHE
 Louisa, 270
BURCK
 Catharine J. (blk), 112
BURD
 Mary (blk), 304
BURGER
 Barbara E., 247
 Rebecca J., 228
BURGES
 Mary Jane (blk), 323
BURGESS
 Elizabeth, 178
 Emma, 46
 Laura, 57, 72
 Laura (blk), 57
 Letta (blk), 210
 Lizzie, 300
 Margaret, 129
 Mary, 58
 Salina M., 12
 Sarah, 240, 291
 Sarah (blk), 291
 Susan Matilda, 111
BURGHARD
 Sofi, 280
BURGHARTH
 Margurete, 258
BURGISS
 Emma (blk), 158
 Henrietta (blk), 105
BURGOYNE
 Charlotte (blk), 176
BURK
 Eliza (blk), 68
 Ella (blk), 133
 Hattie (blk), 323
 Mary E., 114, 274
 Mary E. (blk), 274
 Mary Frances, 83
 Mary T., 64
 Rosa (blk), 248
 Virginia (blk), 259
BURKAMP
 Meta, 134
BURKAN
 Margreth, 309

BURKARD
  Mary Eve, 169
BURKE
  Anastasia, 211
  Ann (blk), 142
  Ann Virginia, 234
  Anna E. (blk), 152
  Annie, 142
  Bridget, 197
  Catharine, 114
  Catherine, 10
  E.H., 143
  Ellena, 307
  Ellie, 211
  Jane (blk), 88
  Johanna, 31
  Julia, 221
  Lucy J., 12
  Margaret, 137, 220
  Maria, 198
  Mary, 18, 19, 54,
    60, 108, 111, 125,
    146, 199
  Mary Ann, 19, 111,
    125
  Mary Ann (blk), 19
  Mary E., 146
  Mary J., 18
BURKHARD
  Clara, 185
  Mary, 131
BURKHARDT
  Elizabeth, 71
  Margaretta, 214
BURKLEY
  Catharine (blk), 242
BURKS
  Margaret, 254
  Nina, 279
BURL
  Mary (blk), 184
BURLEY
  Barbara E. (blk), 82
  Bridget T., 127
BURMAN
  Justine, 204
  Margaretta, 247
BURMBY
  Virginia (blk), 230

BURNARD
  Milley (blk), 3
BURNATIOUS
  Hester, 287
BURNES
  Ann, 327
  Martha E., 72
  Mary Isabella, 319
BURNETT
  Angeline (blk), 311
BURNS
  Amanda N., 254
  Annie S., 200
  Eveline, 58
  Hanna, 13, 220
  Hannah, 220
  Lizzie, 209
  Lucinda (blk), 121
  Maggie, 188
  Margaret, 185
  Maria (blk), 100
  Mary, 87, 255, 256
  Mary A., 255
  Mary C., 256
  Nancy Virginia, 286
  Susan (blk), 316
BURNY
  Mary, 256
BURR
  Ann (blk), 244
  Emily (blk), 85
  Maria L., 21
  Mary (blk), 165
  Mary A., 266
  Rebecca (blk), 40
BURRELL
  Frances (blk), 115
  Mary Frances (blk),
    83
BURRIKER
  Martha, 9
BURRIS
  Ann, 244
BURRISS
  Ann E., 211
  Mary Ellen, 67
  Ruth Ann, 139
BURRITT
  Mary J., 4

BURROSS
  Laura T., 106
BURROUGHS
  A.E.G., 65
  Annie M., 288
  Catharine H., 6
  Catharine R.A.W.,
    58
  Charlotte S., 314
  Martha E., 7
  Sallie R., 9
BURROWES
  Sarah (blk), 18
BURROWS
  Anna, 180
  Elizabeth, 119
  Letitia, 221
  Lucinda (blk), 259
  Mary Rose, 143
  Mary V., 34
BURRUS
  Elizabeth V., 204
  Maggie A., 58
BURT
  Eliza, 237
  Maria (blk), 155
BURTON
  Katie, 41
  Marion, 249
  Narcissus H. (blk),
    16
BUSEY
  Anna (blk), 243
  Emma, 227
  Sarah E., 208
BUSH
  Addie (blk), 269
  Anna, 24
  Annie, 25
  Cecilia A. (blk), 57
  Elizabeth (blk), 126
  Margaret, 133
  Sarah C., 143
  Sophia, 246
BUSHBY
  A.V., 82
  Addie R., 187
  Emina, 38
  Mary E., 15

349

BUSS
  Elizabeth, 144
BUSSART
  Georgeana, 136
BUSSEE
  Julia, 112
BUSTER
  Mildred, 25
BUTCHER
  Charlotte (blk), 232
  Eliza, 93
BUTHMANN
  Adeline E., 43
BUTLER
  Agnes (blk), 56
  Anna M. (blk), 253
  Annie L. (blk), 283
  Betty Ann (blk), 261
  Cassy (blk), 79
  Catherine (blk), 159, 232
  Charlotte (blk), 88
  Cornelia (blk), 70
  Eliza, 28, 34, 83, 93, 144, 183
  Eliza (blk), 28, 34, 144
  Elizabeth (blk), 183
  Elizabeth A., 93
  Elizth. (blk), 268
  Ellen, 105, 174, 207, 253
  Ellen (blk), 174, 207
  Fanny, 75
  Frances, 22, 73
  Frances E., 22
  Francis (blk), 62
  Georgiana (blk), 227
  Hannah (blk), 145
  Harriet (blk), 284
  Helen M., 23
  Henrietta, 5, 184, 265
  Henrietta (blk), 5, 265
  Isabella, 7
  Jane (blk), 26, 27, 127
  Jennie (blk), 156
  Julia C., 147
  Louisa (blk), 26
  Lydia (blk), 285
  M., 30
  Margaret, 251, 276
  Martha (blk), 1, 264
  Martha Ann (blk), 283
  Mary, 120, 139, 153, 156, 174, 176, 194, 217, 235, 236, 241, 267, 278, 302, 326
  Mary (blk), 139, 153, 174, 176, 302
  Mary Ann, 241, 267
  Mary Ann (blk), 241
  Mary E., 217, 235, 236
  Mary E. (blk), 235, 236
  Mary F. (blk), 326
  Mary Jane (blk), 156
  Mary L. (blk), 120
  Mary M., 278
  Matilda A. (blk), 326
  Rachel Ann, 223
  Rebecca (blk), 65
  Sallie A., 120
  Sarah Ann (blk), 317
  Susan (blk), 21
  Susanna (blk), 133
  Virginia, 28, 54
  Virginia (blk), 54
BUTT
  Mary Verlinda, 132
  Sarah E., 326
BUTTERBALL
  Emily A., 23
BUTTERBAUGH
  Jennie, 205, 228
BUTTON
  Eliza, 305
BUTTS
  Sophia, 180
BUZZARD
  Kate E., 284
BUZZEY
  Lizzette, 272
BYANES
  B. Agnes, 87
BYLOR
  Catherine, 214
BYNG
  Julia A. (blk), 293
BYRN
  Ellen, 83
BYRNE
  Agnes, 81
  Annie, 50
  Catherine, 54
  Elizabeth, 111
  Ellen, 136
  Lizzie C., 2
  Marion H., 12
  Mary, 217
BYRNES
  Catharine A., 220
  Emma S., 301
  Kate L., 252

—C—

CADEY
  Mary, 93, 115
CADLE
  Mary A., 39
CADMUS
  Annanett, 298
CADY
  Annie, 240
  Carrie L., 257
  Lucy E., 137
  Margaret, 126, 161
  Ruth, 194
CAESAR
  Catherine, 83
CAHAAN
  Mary, 124
CAHHIL
  Elizabeth, 128
CAHIL
  Johanna, 99

CAHILL
  Ellen, 105, 265
  Fanny, 235
  Margaret, 64, 108,
    138, 141
  Mary, 141, 283
CAIN
  Bridget, 43
CALBERT
  Catherine (blk), 307
  Martha (blk), 240
CALDAN
  Maria, 199
CALDEBACK
  Virginia A., 112
CALDWELL
  Catharine, 73
  Jennie W., 142
CALEB
  Harriet (blk), 234
CALHOUNE
  Margaret, 219
CALL
  Fanny A., 127
CALLAGHAN
  Joahanna, 44
CALLAHAN
  Ellen, 161, 249
  Johanna, 241, 324
  Margaret, 259
  Mary, 253
CALLAN
  Alice M.A., 2
  Florence E., 48
  Lizzie, 239
  Mary A., 61
  S.R., 125
CALLENDER
  Catherine, 48
CALVERT
  Alice, 25
  Bettie, 245
  Catherine (blk), 276
  Lucy Victoria, 90
  Martin (blk), 3
  Mary, 44, 295
  Mary Ann (blk), 44
  Rose, 161

CAMARON
  Susan (blk), 57
CAMBACH
  Mary, 106
CAMBRIL
  Edie (blk), 32
CAMERON
  Bella, 67
  Lizzie, 280, 286
  Lizzie J., 280
  Louisa, 231
  Lucy (blk), 33
  Mary (blk), 51
CAMMACK
  Elphine, 21
  Sarah Ann, 180
CAMMAL
  Mary, 177
CAMP
  Sarah A.R., 182
CAMPA
  Ann, 133
CAMPBELL
  Ada B., 76
  Alice G., 55
  Amelia (blk), 133, 292
  Ann Virginia (blk), 259
  Annie R., 134
  Bridget, 10
  Caroline, 28
  Charlotte (blk), 127
  Charlotte F. (blk), 154
  Chlora Ann, 74
  Eliza (blk), 65
  Elizabeth, 195
  Emma J., 135
  Hannah (blk), 8
  Henrietta (blk), 304
  Jane, 112
  Jennie L., 279
  Laura A. (blk), 22
  Louisa (blk), 47
  Louisa E., 222
  Marian (blk), 127

  Mary, 11, 25, 62,
    90, 181, 182, 192,
    197, 222, 317
  Mary (blk), 11, 25
  Mary (col'd), 317
  Mary E., 182
  Mary Elizabeth, 181
  Mary Ellen (blk), 197
  Mary J., 62
  Mary Jane (blk), 192
  Mary P., 222
  Susan (blk), 66
CAMPHOR
  Agnes, 286
CAMPLER
  Agnes, 169
CANAVAN
  Mary, 327
CANBY
  Eliza, 148
  Martha H., 245
CANFIELD
  Anna, 125
CANN
  Amelia, 270
CANNING
  Laura V., 91
CANNON
  Frances S., 252
  Mary, 196
  Sarah C., 203
CANOVON
  Ellen, 188
CAPPELLA
  Facone, 255
CAPRON
  Carrie, 234
CARBERRY
  Catharine, 221
CARBERY
  Ann, 98
  Catherine, 251
CARBIS
  Annie J., 186
CARD
  Elizabeth, 280
CARDENIS
  Frances (blk), 186

## District of Columbia Marriage Licenses, 1858-1870

CAREY
  Frances (blk), 239
  Jane, 210
  Julia, 84
  Martha, 77
  Mary, 46, 65, 106
CARICO
  Mary Ellen, 253
CARL
  Louisa, 176, 295
  Louisa (blk), 176
CARLTON
  Frank A., 264
CARMAN
  Mary Jane, 303
CARMODY
  Ellen, 253
CARNE
  Cecelia L., 234
CARNELL
  Maria, 207
CARNEY
  Elizabeth, 288
  Margaret, 53
CARPENTER
  Ann E., 283
  Augusta M., 190
  Charlotte (blk), 52
  Clarissa (blk), 158
  E. Virginia, 66
  Emma C., 232
  Jennie B., 122
  Mary, 36, 291
  Mary Louise, 291
  Rose Ann, 303
  Sallie M.J., 208
  Sarah A., 281
  Sophia (blk), 317
CARR
  Amanda Jane (blk), 78
  Bridget, 197
  Elizabeth J., 215
  Emma F., 22
  Emma J., 225
  Hannah (blk), 223
  Julie A., 320
  Louisa (blk), 319
  Lucinda, 48
  Martha A., 27
  Mary, 29, 74, 210, 314
  Mary Ann, 74
  Mary Jane, 29
  Sophia A., 225
CARRICK
  Annie, 241
  Eliza, 46
CARRICO
  Helen Elizth., 218
  Hellen, 218
  Sussie C., 208
CARRIE
  Cecilia Ardell, 10
CARRIER
  Amanda D., 51
CARRIGAN
  Ellen, 241
CARRINGTON
  Jane (blk), 52
CARROLL
  Alice, 106
  Alida, 35
  Ann (blk), 132
  Anna, 184
  Anne (blk), 46
  Annie (blk), 242
  Bridget, 156
  Catharine, 266
  Catherine, 88, 210
  Catherine (blk), 210
  Charity Ann (blk), 134
  Delia M., 193
  Elizabeth, 144
  Ellen, 31, 217
  Emily Kate, 271
  Georgiana (blk), 90
  Hannah (blk), 311
  Hannah M., 12
  Harriet (blk), 291
  Hercules, 46, 234
  Jane, 64, 194
  Jane A., 64
  Jennie, 241, 326
  Jennie R., 241
  Johanna, 176
  Julia, 122, 276
  Julia (blk), 276
  Kate, 95
  Malinda (blk), 326
  Margaret, 264, 295
  Margaret Ann, 264
  Maria (blk), 316
  Marsilla Ann (blk), 286
  Martha J., 209
  Mary, 31, 99, 130, 208, 212, 226, 231, 233, 254, 282, 311
  Mary (blk), 311
  Mary Ann, 208, 226
  Mary C., 130
  Mary Elizabeth, 233
  Mary Ellen, 31
  Mary Jane, 231
  Matilda A., 275
  Nancy (blk), 11
  Rosena (blk), 175
  Sallie V., 118
  Sarah A., 22
  Sarah Jane, 306
  Sarah P., 186
CARSEN
  Julia E., 122
CARTER
  Agnes (blk), 304
  Amanda (blk), 313
  Annie (blk), 10
  Annie M. (blk), 101
  Caroline (blk), 63
  Catherine, 49, 83, 145
  Catherine (blk), 83, 145
  Charity (blk), 325
  Cordelia (blk), 153
  Delia (blk), 179
  Delphi (blk), 47
  Dradie D. (col'd), 320
  Eliza (blk), 255
  Elizabeth, 153, 286
  Elizabeth (blk), 153
  Emily, 55

**CARTER**
Fanny (blk), 238, 248
Florence E., 322
Gillis (blk), 214
Harriet (blk), 272
Jennie, 181, 250
Laura V., 47
Letty (blk), 149
Lizzie (blk), 3
Louisa (blk), 18, 117, 123
Louisa S., 95
Lucinda (blk), 89
Lucy, 126
Margaret, 30
Martha, 93, 144, 315
Martha (blk), 144, 315
Mary, 43, 58, 84, 92, 108, 122, 145, 190, 196, 222, 294, 311
Mary (blk), 58, 294
Mary A., 84
Mary Ann (col'd), 43
Mary E. (blk), 222
Mary Elizabeth, 190
Mary Ellen (blk), 92
Mary J., 196
Mary P., 145
Milly (col'd), 95
Nancy (blk), 21, 271
Rachel (blk), 48
Reano (blk), 266
Rosa Ann (blk), 26
Rose, 77
Rosina (blk), 6
Sarah, 71, 142, 159, 196, 282, 289, 318
Sarah (blk), 159, 196, 289
Sarah (col'd), 142
Sarah A. (blk), 282
Sophia (blk), 6
Terry (blk), 108
Zafney (blk), 153
**CARTRIGHT**
Mary E. (blk), 56

**CARTWRIGHT**
Flora (blk), 222
Mahala (blk), 35
Mary E. (blk), 269
Susanna, 119
**CARUSI**
Delphine, 182
Julia (blk), 116
**CARUTHERS**
Susan C., 320
**CARVER**
Alice, 79
Amelia, 320
Maria, 283
**CASALEGE**
Maria Julia, 79
**CASCORRO**
Mary, 44
**CASEEN**
Eliza, 97
**CASEY**
Bridget A., 35
Caroline (blk), 22
Catherine, 118
Charity A. (blk), 237
Elizabeth G., 259
Hanora, 212
Julia, 282
Mary E. (blk), 289
Sarah (blk), 228
**CASH**
Georgiania, 229
**CASHMER**
Catherine, 219
**CASHMON**
Margaret, 212
**CASPARI**
Christine, 218
**CASPARIS**
Annie G., 254
**CASPER**
Mary Rose, 20
Rosa, 325
**CASS**
Elizabeth, 84
**CASSADY**
Julia, 181
Louisa, 29

**CASSASSA**
Vittoria, 327
**CASSEDY**
Mary, 68
**CASSELL**
Emma, 164
Mary Elizabeth, 311
Mary Jane, 262
**CASSERLY**
Hannah, 176
**CASSIDAY**
Emily, 100
**CASSIDY**
Catherine, 322
Jennie, 106
**CASTANS**
Sophia C. C., 257
**CASTEEL**
Mary J., 129
**CASTELL**
Mary Jane, 211
**CASTOR**
Sarah (blk), 273
**CASWELL**
Gertrude, 318
**CATEN**
Alice, 46
**CATHALL**
Emma R., 10
**CATHERELL**
Palmyra, 108
**CATIN**
Mary, 285
**CATLETT**
Caroline (blk), 94
**CATON**
Julia, 9, 83
Julia Ann, 9
Margaret, 23
**CATOR**
Eliza A., 87
Jennie E., 292
**CATTERTON**
Minerva (blk), 111
**CAUSINE**
Margaret, 58
**CAUSTEN**
Alice E., 96
Mary (blk), 273

CAVANAGH
  Kate, 180
  Maria, 45
CAVANAUGH
  Margaret, 270
  Mary, 242
CAVENAGH
  Jane America, 143
CAVENER
  Mary, 92
CAVIS
  Mary E., 234
CAWOOD
  Annie, 242
  Catharine V., 202
  Elizabeth J., 67
  Virginia, 128
CAWTHORN
  Rosalind M., 278
CAYWOOD
  Anna Maria, 240
  Annie, 209
  Charlotte E., 63
  Martha Jerusha, 120
  Sarah J., 312
CAZZAZA
  Maria, 283
CEAS
  Diantha E., 108
CECIL
  Dora, 37
  Kate, 310
  Margaret N., 311
  Mary Ellen, 95
CHADWICK
  Emma A., 227
CHAMBERLAIN
  Catherine V., 279
  Clara, 179
  Martha A., 305
  Mary E., 156
  Mary M., 312
  Sarah, 179
  Virginia, 69
CHAMBERLIN
  Georgeana, 187
  Georgette A., 50
  Josephine, 266
  Margaret T., 307

Mary E., 61
Mary M., 250
CHAMBERS
  Agnes, 15
  Ann, 33
  Ellen, 305
  Hannah M., 63
  Mary Ann, 146
  Sarah E. (blk), 269
CHAMBLIN
  Agnes (blk), 95
  Rosa, 234
CHAMICK
  Matilda P., 61
CHAMLIN
  Julia (blk), 146
CHAMPEON
  Elizabeth, 322
CHAMPION
  Elizth., 66
  Emma, 259
  Mary Jane, 121
CHAMWELL
  Mary V. (blk), 111
CHANDLER
  Caroline, 45
CHANEY
  Ellen A., 7
  Joanna, 299
  Margaret A.R., 172
CHAPIN
  Ella Mosier, 164
CHAPMAN
  Alice, 200
  Ann, 20, 101
  Annie, 101
  Elizabeth, 306
  Elsie, 183
  Emma, 203, 213
  Emma F., 203
  Margaret, 85, 290
  Rebecca B., 164
  Susan, 280
CHAPPEL
  Sarah (blk), 323
CHARETTE
  Rosalie, 15
CHASE
  Barbary (blk), 155

Caroline (blk), 175
Eliza (blk), 234
Emma (blk), 172
Florence (blk), 150
Harriet (blk), 18
Jane (blk), 284
Julia (blk), 82
Kate, 276
Lizzie H., 75
Maria (blk), 130
Mary, 2, 79, 90
Mary (blk), 2
Mary C., 90
Sarah (blk), 318
Sarah Ann (blk), 60
Sophronia (blk), 250
CHATMAN
  Elizabeth (blk), 181
CHAUNCEY
  Emma R., 125
  Margaret Ann, 39
CHEDAL
  Mary E., 312
CHEEKS
  Eliza (blk), 159
CHEESMAN
  Isabella, 116
CHENCARY
  Lizzie A., 198
CHENEY
  M. Antonette, 283
CHERRAY
  Elizabeth, 5
CHESCHER
  Mary Jane, 226
CHESELDINE
  Alameda, 107
CHESHIRE
  Mary Ellen, 127
CHESLEY
  Julia Ann (blk), 258
  Mary (blk), 159
CHEW
  Anna M., 312
  Clarissa (blk), 145
  Ellen, 83
  Henrietta (blk), 127
  Jane (blk), 122
  Louisa (blk), 36

CHICK
　Georgia, 49
　Mary V., 233
CHILDRESS
　Ann Rebecca, 103
　Laura J., 201
CHILDS
　Adeline (blk), 51
　Almina, 22
　Margaret A., 51
CHINN
　Hannah (blk), 39
CHIPLEY
　Emily O., 209
　Mary, 301
CHIPMAN
　M.J., 51, 226
CHISLER
　Sarah (blk), 317
CHISLEY
　Louisa (blk), 308
CHISM
　Amanda, 276
　Annie Elizabeth, 83
　Mary W., 230
　Susanna, 13
CHITHAM
　Louisa (blk), 109
CHIZLEY
　Lizzie (blk), 318
CHOATE
　Lydia E., 250
CHONN
　Elizabeth, 261
CHRISMAN
　Annie, 241
　Elizebeth, 182
　Mary E., 172
　Sophia, 195
CHRIST
　Margaretta, 204
CHRISTAL
　Charlotte, 287
CHRISTIAN
　Eliza (blk), 301
　Mary (blk), 89
CHRISTIANI
　Eliza, 170

CHRISTIE
　Sarah C., 45
CHRISTMAS
　Matilda (blk), 82
CHRYSTAL
　Ellen, 81
CHUBB
　Emily W., 197
CHURCH
　Frances, 8
　Martha E. (blk), 311
　Victoria, 27
CHURCHILL
　Elizabeth M., 265
CHURCHWILLE
　Milly (blk), 308
CHUT
　Mary, 261
CIGYWITZ
　Margaret, 257
CISSEL
　Clara, 91
　Emma, 106
　Georgiana, 156
CISSELL
　Eliza Jane (blk), 266
　Lizzie, 310
CISSON
　Lucretia, 51
CLABOURNE
　Isabella (blk), 234
CLADABUCK
　Julia, 324
CLAGETT
　Ann Maria (blk), 323
　Catherine, 286
　Eliza, 3
　Henrietta, 286
　Mary A., 270
　Rebecca F., 172
　Ruth, 2
CLAIBORNE
　Mary (blk), 100
　Sarah (blk), 158
CLAIBOURN
　Mary Jane (blk), 313
CLAIRDY
　Julia, 81

CLAIRE
　Marie, 141
CLANCEY
　Alice, 165
　Bridget, 162
CLANCY
　Delia, 268
　Kate, 230
　Margaret, 67
　Mary, 184
　Nora, 220
CLANSY
　Bridget, 84, 95
　Margaret, 43, 81
　Mary, 177
　Sarah, 218
CLARE
　Easter (blk), 149
　Jane, 38
CLARK
　Alice, 117
　Ann, 34, 65, 95, 102, 228
　Anna, 34
　Anne Howard, 102
　Annie E., 65
　Catharine V., 301
　D.L., 218
　Elizabeth (blk), 154, 163, 287
　Elizabeth E., 278
　Elizabeth Jane, 277
　Ellen (blk), 4, 294
　Ellen R., 325
　Fannie (blk), 47
　Fanny (blk), 124
　Jennie (blk), 323
　Jennie B., 101
　Josephine (blk), 207
　Katharine, 122
　Lillie A., 114
　Lucinda, 87
　Lucy (blk), 258
　Lucy M., 258
　Maggie A., 74
　Margaret Joanna, 235
　Maria C., 310

District of Columbia Marriage Licenses, 1858-1870

CLARK
  Mary, 55, 67, 82,
    143, 150, 189,
    209, 255, 283
  Mary (blk), 55, 82,
    150
  Mary E., 189, 209
  Mary Elizabeth, 143
  Mary F., 255
  Mattie D., 173
  Minty, 36
  Rachel A., 96, 279
  Rittle E., 48
  Sarah Fuller, 97
  Susan (blk), 232, 318
CLARKE
  Adeline (blk), 3
  Ann, 14, 53, 165,
    196, 216, 232, 318
  Ann E., 216
  Ann Rebecca, 53
  Annie, 165, 232,
    318
  Annie E., 165
  Augusta H., 325
  Bessie, 298
  Bridget, 238
  Caroline, 118
  Christina, 121
  Elizabeth (blk), 207,
    279
  Ellen M., 78
  Josie J., 142
  Julia, 45
  Kate, 91, 321
  Kate E., 321
  Leonora, 37
  Louisa (blk), 32
  Louisa Virginia, 169
  Lucy, 89
  Margaret, 130, 153
  Maria (blk), 122
  Martha (blk), 181
  Mary, 102, 185,
    210, 278, 323
  Mary A., 102
  Mary Catherine, 185
  Mary J. (blk), 278
  Mary O., 323

  Sarah L., 264
  Sarah M., 93
  Virginia (blk), 129,
    234
  Virginia M., 238
CLARKSON
  Emily, 226
CLASK
  Emily E., 120
CLATER
  Julia, 179
CLAUSON
  Anna M., 18
CLAXTON
  Mary Susanna, 224
  Sarah L., 38
  Susana L., 265
CLEARE
  Anna, 120
CLEARY
  Caroline, 180
  Mary, 42
CLEAVELAND
  Caroline, 105
CLEMENS
  Cornelia, 301
CLEMENTS
  Alice S., 207
  Alice Virginia, 70
  Ann L., 233
  Annie, 19
  Annie E., 59
  C.A. Lavina, 58
  E.C. Mills, 22
  Eliza, 41, 145, 303
  Eliza Louisa, 303
  Elizabeth Ann, 41
  Emily (blk), 55
  Frances, 89
  Harriet K., 1
  Martha A., 125
  Mary E., 66, 323
  Mary Ellen, 52
  Mary F., 312
  Mary Jane, 16, 59
  Mary S.H., 92
CLEMISON
  Sarah J., 309

CLEMMENT
  Otelia (blk), 240
CLEMMONS
  Mollie (blk), 305
CLEPHANE
  Mary A., 275
CLEVELAND
  Eliza Matilda, 287
  Lucy Ellen, 112
  Mary Elizabeth, 116
  Sarah C., 104
CLEVENGER
  Sarah, 285
CLIFF
  Martha, 169
CLIFFORD
  Emma A., 271
CLINE
  Annie Rebecca, 68
  Bridget, 182
  Johana, 253
  Mary, 154
CLINTON
  Jane (blk), 324
CLITCH
  Henrietta, 217
CLOKEY
  Ann E., 178
  Emma J., 241
CLOSE
  Diana T., 229
CLOUGH
  Catherine, 40
CLOWSER
  Margaret, 39
CLUB
  Rozelle, 250
  Susanna, 321
CLUBB
  Sarah Ann, 15
CLUSKEY
  Maggie, 302
CLYNCH
  Mary, 253
COATES
  Henrietta (blk), 191
  Lizzie (blk), 10

COATS
  Louisa, 130, 155
  Louisa (blk), 155
  Mary C. (blk), 158
  Mary E. (blk), 126
  Sallie (blk), 207
COBB
  Elizabeth (blk), 166
  Emily, 259
COBBE
  Amelia Jane, 241
COBELL
  Virginia, 225
COBINGTON
  Anna (blk), 154
COBURN
  Caroline A., 319
  Catharine, 19
  Ellen, 221
COCHRAN
  Ann, 84
COCHRANE
  Anna Maria, 273
COCKE
  E. Jane, 224
COCKRELL
  Elizabeth, 243
  Julia F., 71
  Sarah E., 62
CODD
  Matilda, 209
CODORA
  Julia, 167
CODRICK
  Mary, 298
  Sallie, 124
CODWISE
  Mary B., 307
CODY
  Bridget, 197
COFFEE
  Alice Ann (blk), 176
  Catharine, 39
  Lizzie, 79
  Mary (blk), 217
  Sally, 47
COFFMAN
  Ellen, 281

COGAN
  Louisa, 112
COGGINS
  Lydia F., 166
COGSWELL
  Annie, 58
  Rebecca (blk), 159
COGVILLE
  Bettie, 109
COHAN
  Margaret, 56
COHEN
  Ellen, 99
  Jeanette, 161
  Mary, 78
  Rechem, 189
  Sallie E., 70
  Susan M., 161
COHILL
  Mary E., 3
COHN
  Betty, 277
  Reca, 232
  Rosanna, 254
COHNHOFF
  Pauline, 84
COHOE
  Sarah Elizabeth, 6
COKE
  Lavinia (blk), 305
COKELAND
  Mary (blk), 182
COKELEY
  Magline, 72
COKELY
  Rebecca (blk), 184
COKEN
  Mary, 274
COLBERT
  Charity A. (blk), 117
  Ellen (blk), 293
  Ophelia (blk), 78
COLBURN
  Alice V., 226
COLBY
  Laura M., 45
COLCLASER
  Barbara C., 55
  Charlotte, 133

  Margaret J., 271
COLD
  Johanna, 298
COLDON
  Ellen, 268
COLE
  Annie, 142, 198
  Annie (blk), 198
  Barbara (blk), 56
  Charlotte (blk), 154
  Elizabeth (blk), 82
  Emma, 205
  Fannie T., 65
  Georgianna, 193
  Jane (blk), 121, 304
  Joana, 99
  Josephine (blk), 3
  Laura (blk), 263
  Margaret (blk), 18
  Margaret Ann, 59
  Mary (blk), 32, 82
  Mary Ann, 315
  Mary F., 67
  Sarah (blk), 116
  Susan (blk), 148
  Virginia, 61
COLEGATE
  Elizabeth M., 195
COLEHOUSE
  Virginia Ann, 13
COLEMAN
  Agnes (blk), 296
  Alice (blk), 149
  Amy (blk), 62
  Betsey (blk), 57
  Betty (blk), 6, 15, 250
  Catherine, 196
  Eliza (blk), 87
  Elizabeth, 177
  Ella (blk), 274
  Ellen, 101
  Frances (blk), 128
  Jane, 326
  Julia A. (blk), 17
  Kate, 105
  Laura (blk), 5
  Louise R., 228
  Lucinda, 57, 102

COLEMAN
 Lucinda (blk), 102
 Margaret, 46
 Mary, 64, 103, 132, 133, 271
 Mary (blk), 133
 Mary Ann (blk), 271
 Peggy (blk), 153
 Sally, 62
 Susan W., 324
 Teresa, 328
COLES
 Esther (blk), 118
COLHEEN
 Honorah, 300
COLISON
 Mary Jane, 21
COLKIN
 Laura S., 53
COLLAN
 Julia, 163
COLLIER
 Carrie V., 131
 Elizabeth, 89
 M. Kate, 104
 Martha (blk), 202
 Nancy (blk), 148
COLLINS
 Alysha, 95
 Ann, 28, 112, 143, 191, 253
 Anna (blk), 112, 143
 Annie, 191, 253
 Catharine, 44, 188
 Catherine, 153, 317
 Catherine M., 153
 Elizabeth, 159
 Ellen, 23
 Emma, 165
 Fannie, 245
 Fanny (blk), 271
 George Ana, 197
 Hanora, 146, 312
 Harriet, 146, 151
 Harriet A., 146
 Irene, 217
 Jennie, 282
 Johanna, 185

Julia, 212, 276, 280, 298
 Julia (blk), 298
 Julia A., 276
 Kate, 64, 146
 Katherine, 164
 Laura V., 34
 Louisa, 126, 295
 Margaret, 9, 48, 85, 141, 196, 274, 324
 Margaret (blk), 48
 Maria (blk), 41
 Martha, 124, 196, 297
 Martha E., 124
 Mary, 12, 17, 26, 134, 162, 194, 198, 200, 262, 267, 299
 Mary Ann, 26
 Mary E., 12
 Mary F., 299
 Mary J. (blk), 17
 Mary Jane, 134
 Mary L., 200, 267
 Mary L. (blk), 267
 Mary M., 162
 Sarah, 193, 229, 304
 Sarah E., 193
 Sarah Jane, 304
 Sealeaner, 37
 Susan, 213, 243
 Susan (blk), 213
 Tamar, 32
COLLINSWORTH
 Julia C., 217
COLLISON
 Mary, 199
COLMAN
 Amanda (blk), 126
COLMUS
 Mary A., 30
COLOMBA
 Jerusha A., 291
COLTMAN
 Sarah B., 208
COLTSON
 Ellen M., 228
COLUMBUS
 Laura M., 110

COLVIN
 Pfelenia C.C., 59
COMB
 Isabella, 291
COMBS
 Mary E., 47, 263
COMMENS
 Mary F. (blk), 47
COMMODORE
 Henrietta (blk), 179
 Louisa (blk), 232
COMPTON
 A. Texas, 89
 Alma P., 224
 Jeannette D., 75
 Linda, 76
 Mary F., 254
 Virginia F., 260
CONACES
 Joanna, 185
CONARD
 Elizabeth H., 177
CONAWAY
 Alice, 255
 Kitty (blk), 316
CONDICT
 Eliza Stone, 308
CONDON
 Mary, 291
CONDRY
 Margaret, 166
CONER
 Jane, 294
CONERS
 Mary, 190
CONES
 Lucy L., 99
CONIA
 Johanna, 62
CONKLIN
 Nellie W., 122
CONKRON
 Phoebe (blk), 181
CONLAN
 Eliza, 187
 Maggie, 64
CONLAY
 Margaret, 44

CONLON
  Catharine, 1
  Catherine, 58
  Ellen, 63
CONLY
  Martha, 229
CONN
  Emma E., 138
CONNEL
  Mary, 164
CONNELL
  Annie, 54
  Bridget, 99
  Catharine, 194
  Catherine, 242
  Deborah M., 245
  Eliza, 81, 102
  Ellen, 102, 263
  Emily (blk), 175
  Hanora, 246
  Jeannett, 144
  Jennie, 119
  Julia, 23, 81
  Katharine, 85
  Margaret, 60, 171
  Martha, 138
  Martina, 272
  Mary, 59, 69, 191, 197
  Sarah E., 62
CONNELLY
  Ann, 81
  Bridget, 235
  Catherine, 49
  Sally, 1
CONNELY
  Catherine, 198
CONNER
  Annie E., 292
  Bridget, 97
  Catherine, 17, 24, 143, 160
  Elizabeth, 34, 145, 214
  Elizabeth A., 34
  Elizabeth J., 145
  Ellen, 195
  Jane, 124
  Johanna, 111

Leannah, 299
Louisa Virginia, 215
Mary, 70, 88, 161, 194, 247
Rosanna M., 145
Sarah, 35, 127
Sarah A., 127
Susan (blk), 35
CONNERS
  Anna, 200
  Lucy, 96
  Mary, 97
CONNIGAN
  Mary, 212
CONNOLL
  Kathleen, 45
CONNOLLY
  Ann, 81, 196, 220
  Annie, 196
  Bridget, 211
  Clara, 150
  Julia, 282
  Letitia (blk), 248
  Margaret, 23, 71, 255
  Mary E., 63
  Mary Jane, 310
CONNOLY
  Mary, 81
CONNOR
  Annie (blk), 37
  Bridget, 25, 106, 118, 246
  Catharine, 63, 121
  Catherine, 61, 86, 231, 243
  Catherine E., 61
  Ellen, 8, 13, 254, 282
  Hanora, 84
  Hatty E., 294
  Joanna, 43, 283
  Johanna, 46, 63, 161, 188
  Julia, 114
  Kate, 48, 163
  Margaret, 27, 83, 164, 206, 262

Mary, 23, 30, 57, 155, 187, 192, 195, 218, 229, 262
Mary (blk), 192
Nancy (blk), 155
Rose, 221
Winifred, 123
CONNORS
  Hanora, 53
  Julia, 164
  Mary, 38, 86, 114
  Mary A., 114
CONNOWAY
  Elizabeth, 170
CONOVER
  Susie B., 129
CONOWAY
  Margaret (blk), 27
CONRAD
  Anna M.F., 270
CONRADIS
  Ellen, 134
CONREY
  Mary, 69
CONROY
  Bridget, 92
CONSTABLE
  Cinderella, 313
  Margaret, 38
CONTEE
  Catherine (blk), 78
  Eliza (blk), 180
  Elizabeth, 37
  Letty (blk), 295
  Maria (blk), 276
  Martha, 46
CONTEY
  Calista, 135
CONWAY
  Amelia E. (blk), 10
  Catharine, 81
  Deborah (blk), 315
  Eliza, 150
  Ellen C., 262
  Frances Virginia (blk), 307
  Lizzie (blk), 177
  Lummie Y., 225

359

District of Columbia Marriage Licenses, 1858-1870

CONWAY
  Mary Frances, 114
  Priscilla (blk), 179
  Susan (blk), 16
COOGAN
  Margaret, 249
  Sophie Mary, 204
COOK
  Amanda, 178
  Ann E., 61
  Ann Maria, 130
  Ann Matilda, 315
  Anna, 132
  Annie R., 208
  Catharine (blk), 1
  Catharine E., 286
  Eliza I., 179
  Elizabeth, 59, 147
  Elizabeth M., 147
  Emily, 127, 293
  Frances (blk), 139
  Hannah, 127
  Harriet Ann, 78
  Jennie Eliza, 264
  Joanna, 270
  Julia, 35
  Lizzie, 251, 265
  Lizzie E., 265
  Louisa, 150
  Margaret (blk), 38
  Margt. H., 41
  Maria, 205
  Martha E., 77
  Mary, 6, 27, 56, 71,
    122, 130, 167,
    168, 261, 306,
    309, 321
  Mary (blk), 306
  Mary A., 122, 321
  Mary A.V., 321
  Mary Ann, 6
  Mary E., 168, 261
  Mary Jane, 27
  Mary P., 130
  Mary V., 71
  Matilda A., 206
  Nancy (blk), 120
  Rebecca (blk), 65
  Rebecca Ann, 262

  Rosetta (blk), 157
  Sarah (blk), 61
  Susan C., 238
COOKE
  Hannah (blk), 122
  Jeanie D., 202
  Jessie E., 192
  John B., viii
COOKSEY
  Angeline R., 240
  Mary A., 150
COOLEY
  Elmira E., 236
  Samuletta, 162
COOLIDGE
  Ellen (blk), 322
COOMBS
  Annie, 54
  Elizabeth, 78
  Harriet (blk), 292
  Kate F., 142
  Mary, 20, 125, 153
  Mary E., 125
  Mary M., 153
  Sarah F., 185
COOMES
  Alice Virginia, 254
  Rosa, 174
COONEY
  Ann, 237
  Catherine, 136
COOPER
  Caroline (blk), 148
  Catherine (blk), 134
  Charlotte E. (blk), 98
  Ellen (blk), 140
  Emily, 83, 215
  Emily (blk), 215
  Frederica, 202
  Maggie, 12
  Marg. Jane, 152
  Maria (blk), 312
  Martha, 305
  Mary Ann (blk),
    208, 248
  Mary F., 225
  Pettie F., 246
  Sarah (blk), 154
  Susan, 101

  W., 30, 62
COOVER
  Elizth. V., 19
COPELAIN
  Emma, 61
COPELAND
  Anna (blk), 245
  Clara, 209
  Maggie (blk), 78
COPPAGE
  Lucy, 242
COQUILLARD
  Helen, 57
CORAM
  Josephine, 84
CORBELL
  Virginia, 231
CORBETT
  Joanna, 199
CORBIN
  Ann Eliza (blk), 73
  Eaza (blk), 117
  Louisa (blk), 21
  Sophia (blk), 181
CORBIT
  Johanna, 199
CORCORAN
  Emily, 192
  Louise Morris, 69
  Mary, 172
  Susan A., 213
CORD
  Sarah, 203
CORES
  Frances (blk), 140
CORNELL
  Maria, 54
  Sallie A.D., 186
CORNEY
  Martha, 74
CORNISH
  Martha J., 110
  Mary A., 146
CORNWELL
  Mary, 328
CORRELLE
  Caroline, 254
CORSTLER
  Lizzie A., 202

CORTNOR
  Belle R., 185
COSBY
  Maria (blk), 18
COSGROVE
  Jane, 44
  Mary E., 217
COST
  Sarah E., 43
COSTA
  Angelina, 147
COSTAR
  Mary E., 166
COSTELLO
  Berthena, 253
  Bridget, 263
  Catharine, 246
  Ellen, 8, 63, 220
  Ellen Josephine, 220
  Louisa Brenta, 80
  Mary, 221
COSTOR
  Elizabeth, 186
COTRELL
  Mary, 299
COTTER
  Alice, 44
  Ellen M., 164, 234
COUGHLAN
  Anna Stacia, 22
COUGHLIN
  Mary, 327
COULSON
  Emma Virginia, 188
  Joanna, 162
COUNTEE
  Celia (blk), 73
  Elizabeth (blk), 286
  Ellen (blk), 19
  Fanny (blk), 28
  Jemima (blk), 152
  Julia, 272
  Maria (blk), 306
COUNTESS
  Oceana, 1
COURBY
  Mary, 64
COURCEY
  Jane (blk), 269

COURSEY
  Elizabeth (blk), 227
  Susan (blk), 142
COURTENAY
  Jessie C., 138
COURTNEY
  Catherine, 69
  Emma (blk), 151
  Jennie, 194
  Mary E., 87
COUSE
  Mary C., 283
COUSICK
  Bridget, 211
COUTNER
  Josephine T., 323
COUTNOR
  Maggie A., 168
COVENTRY
  Augusta Ellen, 111
COVER
  Mary E., 183
COVERSTON
  Lydia, 170
COVERSTONE
  Matilda, 322
COWAN
  Mary E., 259
COWGY
  Henny (blk), 60
COWIE
  Jennie A., 255
COWLES
  E. Lela, 132
COWLEY
  Delphia Ann, 210
COWNE
  Joanna, 125
COX
  Addie S., 67
  Adeline S., 111
  Almeda A., 234
  Ann Elizabeth, 75
  Anna F., 192
  Arabella, 64
  Caroline, 250
  Eliza Ann, 183
  Eliza E., 292
  Elizabeth, 250, 266

Elizabeth E., 266
Emily V., 166
Jane, 183
Johanna, 166
Julia A., 182
Lizzie (blk), 78
Lucy A., 159
Marianne, 224
Mary Ann, 203
Mary C., 135
Mary E., 5
Mary Ellen (blk), 313
Mary V., 281
Sarah (blk), 34
Susanna, 10
COXSEN
  Sarah A., 121
COXSIN
  Mary, 274
COY
  Bridget, 59
COYLE
  Anna, 125
  Bridget, 211
  Ellen, 75
  Mary Ann, 53
COYLEY
  Bridget, 212
COYNE
  Mary, 204
COZZENS
  Martha A., 180
CRABBS
  Emma V., 117
CRACKNELL
  Coralie A., 6
CRACKSIR
  Agnes (blk), 106
CRADOCK
  Mary, 198
CRADY
  Margaret, 195
CRAF
  Dorothy, 310
CRAGES
  Carrie, 132
CRAHEN
  Bridget, 69

District of Columbia Marriage Licenses, 1858-1870

CRAIG
  Catharine E., 37
  Frances A., 204
  Jane B., 129
  Laura J., 128
  Margaret, 197, 287
  Martha E., 73
  Mary Bethune, 145
  Mary E., 235
CRAIGH
  Bridget, 282
CRAIGHAN
  Mary, 174, 188
CRAMPSEY
  Mary A., 280
CRAMPTON
  Emeline (blk), 227
  Levisi (blk), 253
  Mary (blk), 199
CRAMSTON
  Alice, 164
CRANAGE
  Rosina, 45
CRANCH
  Hannah Appleton, 210
CRANDLE
  Mary Emma, 183
CRANE
  Annie M., 140
  Sarah, 237
CRANGLE
  Catherine, 255
CRANNEGE
  Mary Jane, 85
CRANSTON
  Hettie, 110
  Mary A., 103
CRANWELL
  Harriet, 15
CRAUN
  Martha Frances, 255
CRAUS
  Elizabeth (blk), 308
CRAUSCAP
  Amelia, 186
CRAWFORD
  Anna S., 251
  Charlotte, 62
  Darcus Ann (blk), 155
  Eliza Susanna, 15
  Elizabeth, 182
  Ellen (blk), 115
  Emily, 30
  Emma J., 24
  Fannie (blk), 17
  Harriet (blk), 129
  Henrietta (blk), 57
  Isabel, 41
  Kate A., 124
  Louisa (blk), 2
  Louisa C.C. (blk), 42
  Margaret, 268
  Mary, 47, 232
  Mary Eliza, 47
  S. Jennie, 114
  Sarah V., 136
CRAWLEY
  Clara (blk), 59
  Jane (blk), 54
CRAYCROFT
  Susan A.M.B., 109
CREAGAN
  Alica, 238
CREAGH
  Catherine, 223
CREAMER
  Lucy (blk), 90
  Margaret, 5
  Mary A.E., 107
CREASER
  Louisa (blk), 238
  Marion V., 142
  Mary A., 301
CREAVAN
  Catherine, 201
CREED
  Mary, 213, 263
  Mary V., 213
CREGAN
  Mary, 120
CREIGH
  Mary, 81
  Norah, 287
CREIGHTON
  Annie E., 61
  Emilie, 28
  Emily R., 63
CRENER
  Rosina Barbetta, 155
CRESHAW
  Alice, 21
CRESS
  Caroline, 240
CRESSMAN
  Elizabeth, 239
CRESTON
  Rachel (blk), 216
CREY
  Mary Ellen, 283
CRIDER
  Laura, 120, 226
  Laura A., 120
CRIER
  Jane F., 171
  Sarah V., 10
CRIMMINGS
  Ellen, 282
CRIMMINS
  Bridget, 99
CRIPPEN
  Harriet, 246
  Victoria, 59
CRISMON
  Nancy Jane, 201
CRISMORE
  Matilda, 215
CRISWELL
  Annie E., 143
CROASDALE
  Belinda A., 244
CROCKER
  Amanda S., 227
  Fannie A., 214
  Fanny A., 213
  Jennie E., 183
CROCKET
  Eliza, 66
CROCKETT
  Annie (blk), 245
  Mary, 252
  Triphy, 93
CROEKEN
  Kate Virginia, 69

CROGGAN
  Mary A., 111
CROGGON
  Anna, 199
  Elizabeth V., 310
  Mary, 64
CROGHAN
  Kate, 211
CROKE
  Margaret, 29
CROME
  Emma, 261
  Henritta, 41
  Margaret, 103
CROMPTON
  Lucy, 102
CROMWELL
  Hattie A., 20
CRONEN
  Johanna, 177
CRONIKEN
  Mary, 4
CRONIN
  Johanna, 83
  Margaret, 100, 102
  Margaret A., 102
  Mary, 81
CRONSKOPH
  Catherine, 186
CROOK
  Anna E., 257
  Martha J., 88
  Mary, 150
CROOKE
  Mary, 188
CROOKS
  Emeline, 66
  Mary Ann, 108
CROPLEY
  Virginia, 268
CROSBY
  Emeline (blk), 273
  Lucia R., 254
CROSON
  Sallie C., 221
CROSS
  Elizabeth, 8, 252
  Elizabeth (blk), 252
  Emma Elizth., 117

  Fannie V., 1
  Hannah E., 62
  Henrietta M.
    (Alex.), 143
  Jane (blk), 17
  Joanna, 46
  Margaret V., 199
  Martha, 108
  Mary C., 51
  Mary E., 64
  Rachel (blk), 176
  Rosanna, 223
  Sarah, 51, 159, 314
  Sarah A., 159
  Tansen E., 233
CROSSFIELD
  Catherine, 217
  Maggie, 194
CROSSING
  Susannah, 262
CROSSMAN
  Kate, 228
CROSSON
  Mollie E., 8
CROUCH
  Jane S., 37
CROUDEN
  Martha (blk), 50
CROUGH
  Ellen, 125
CROUN
  Sarah E., 179
CROUSE
  Elizabeth, 193
  Rosetta, 243
CROVI
  Therese, 233
CROW
  Mary, 262
  Rachel (blk), 33
CROWDER
  Mary L., 315
CROWDY
  Mary Ann (blk), 36
CROWELL
  Maria B., 69
CROWLEY
  Ann, 194
  Bridget, 30

  Catherine, 56, 186
  Catherine (blk), 186
  Julia, 69, 194
  Louisa, 186
  Margaret, 61
  Maria, 195
  Mary Ann, 86
CROWLY
  Louisa, 29
CROWN
  Ann Amelia, 68
  Henrietta, 110
  Leah Jane, 316
  Margaret S., 3
  Mary Elizabeth, 304
  Rachel F., 260
  Sarah, 115, 139
  Sarah J., 139
CROWNER
  Eliza E. (blk), 228
CROZIER
  Virginia H., 69
CRUIT
  Alice Amelia, 305
CRUMP
  Annah J., 163
  Caroline (blk), 210
  Elizabeth, 145
  Elmira (blk), 273
  Julia (blk), 112
CRUSER
  Sarah E. (blk), 158
CRUST
  Catherine, 245
CRUTCHER
  Maria L. J., 6
CRUTCHLEY
  Annie E., 110
  Emma J., 231
CRYER
  Emily, 326
  Mary A. (blk), 74
  Winney (blk), 160
CUDLIPP
  Mary Ann, 138
CUFF
  Mary Ann (blk), 186
CULBERTSON
  Mary, 131

CULL
  Ellen, 293
  Fannie, 143
  Rose, 185
  Sarah, 43
CULLAHAN
  Bridget, 162
CULLAN
  Mary, 40
CULLEN
  Ann, 186
  Elizabeth, 75
  Mary Jane, 184
  Rose, 212
CULLIN
  Margaret T., 77
  Rosana, 208
CULLINAN
  Jane, 5
  Kate, 261
  Mary, 68
CULLION
  Margaret, 211
CUMBAGH
  Kate, 245
CUMBERLAND
  Emma I., 55
  Marian E., 56
CUMINSKY
  Hannah, 61
CUMMINGS
  Amanda, 64
  Laura C., 29
  Mary, 16, 103, 285, 299
  Mary F. (blk), 16
  Mary L., 299
CUMMINS
  Caroline (blk), 192
  Cazzora V., 237
  Joanna, 228
  Margaret, 135, 190
  Mary Jane, 322
CUNDIFF
  Virginia, 68
CUNIEFF
  Annie, 210
CUNIO
  Maria, 18

CUNNINGHAM
  A.J., 234
  Agnes L., 44
  Ann, 146, 228
  Anna C., 146
  Eliza, 290
  Esther A., 72
  Georgie, 160
  Jane, 263
  Louisa, 195
  Margaret J., 123
  Mary, 79, 106, 111, 279
  Mary J., 106
  Mary R., 279
  Sallie J., 88
  Sarah J., 49
  T.R., 68
CUNRAY
  Bridget, 238
CUNYERTY
  Catherine, 220
CURBY
  Maria, 215
CURK
  Hanora, 101
CURLEY
  Bridget, 98
  Cornelia, 231
CURRAN
  Catharine, 169
  Elizabeth, 210
  Georgianna, 147
  Jane, 246
  Julia A., 3
  Kate, 90
CURREY
  Catharine T., 181
CURRY
  Ann (blk), 86
  Anna, 63
CURTAIN
  Catharine, 159
  Johanna, 238
  Mary, 86
CURTIN
  Ann, 13
  Bridget, 128
  Ellin, 61

Mary, 2, 128, 188, 194
CURTIS
  Elizabeth Ann (blk), 35
  Ellen, 266
  Emily (blk), 110
  Fanny, 112
  Jane, 81
  Josephine (blk), 53
  Julia Ann, 264
  Laura, 108
  Lizzie (blk), 158
  Louisa (blk), 192
  Margaret (blk), 150, 304
  Maria (blk), 226
  Mary, 42, 185
  Minerva, 143
  Olive Smith, 273
  Pamelia, 147
  Rachel Ann (blk), 26
  Sallie (blk), 65
  Sarah (blk), 42, 289
  Susan, 108, 316
  Susan (blk), 316
CURTON
  Bridgett, 163
CURVERWELL
  Margaret R., 94
CUSHAN
  Ellen, 2
CUSHLY
  Mary, 179
CUSICK
  Catharine, 170
  Mary, 164
CUSSACK
  Elizabeth, 171
CUSTARD
  Catharine A., 137
CUSTIS
  Rachel (blk), 103
  Rose (blk), 46
CUTHBERT
  Elizabeth, 202
CUTLER
  Catherine Jane, 319

CUTTER
  Jennie R.S., 210
CUTTS
  Gertrude, 280
CUVILLIER
  Jane F., 221
CYRUSS
  Anna, 103
CZERNY
  Anna, 303

—D—

DACEY
  Honora, 48
DADE
  Adeline (blk), 193
  Angelina (blk), 176
  Clara Ann, 247
  Cornelia (blk), 39
  Elizabeth, 217
  Ellen (blk), 325
  Fannie B., 219
  Josephine (blk), 320
  Mary (blk), 155, 227
  Mary E. (blk), 197
  Mary Nahalia, 216
  Roberta (blk), 275
DADEY
  Mary, 48
DADY
  Margaret, 262
DAGENHART
  Mary E., 176
DAGGETT
  Kate, 183
DAGGS
  Eliza (blk), 142
DAILEY
  Ann, 229
  Bridget, 117
  Catherine, 67, 118
  Ellen, 115, 177
  Mary, 156, 163
  Mary Ann, 156
DAILY
  Catherine, 194
  Eliza, 73
  Mary, 58, 163

DAINTY
  Emeline, 318
DAIRLING
  Margaret, 243
DAKER
  Mary Rosannah, 75
DAKIN
  Millie, 295
DALDY
  Frances T., 298
DALE
  Amanda, 103
  Virginia M., 172
DALEY
  Elizabeth, 84
  Johanna, 195
  Mary, 55
DALLAHUNT
  Margaret, 27
DALTON
  Ellen, 99, 100
  Matilda, 118
DALY
  Ann R., 175
  Annie, 198
  Elizabeth, 176, 220, 299
  Elizabeth (blk), 176
  Ellen, 316
  Honora, 93
  Maggie, 109
  Mary, 87
DAMMANS
  Amelia, 290
DAMRELL
  Catherine, 114
DANA
  Barbara, 327
  Jennie, 38
DANACUR
  Barbara, 159
DANCE
  Mary, 52
DANDERSON
  Martha V., 321
DANDRIDGE
  Patsy (blk), 118
DANENHOWER
  Rae E., 256

DANFORD
  Martha M., 40
DANFORTH
  Mattie J.P., 92
  Virginia, 102
DANGERFIELD
  Caroline, 3
DANIEL
  Helen M., 185
  Mary Maack, 47
DANIELS
  Cora L.V., 285
  Elizabeth A., 180
DANJAS
  Elizabeth, 300
DANSEY
  Sarah Ellen, 76
DANSK
  Elizabeth, 202
DANT
  Annie, 203
  Eliza (blk), 233
  Martha R., 99
  Nora, 42
DARBY
  Achsah Worthington, 245
DARCEY
  Margaret, 72
  Martha Ann Amelia, 286
DARN
  Annie A., 146
DARNALL
  M. Isadore, 103
  Mayetta B., 102
DARRELL
  Florence E., 326
  Lucretia, 159
  Lucy M., 152
  Virginia E., 187
DARWELL
  Jane, 98
DASEY
  Catherine, 295
  Ellen, 70
DATCHER
  Annie L. (blk), 97
  Elizabeth, 126

**DAVENPORT**
 Eliza (blk), 72
 Emily (blk), 236
 Mary Emma, 303
**DAVID**
 Mena, 31
 Nancy, 185
**DAVIDSON**
 Ann Eliza, 291
 Delozier, 72, 287
 Ellen V., 185
 Johanna E., 249
 Maria L., 28
 Mary E., 224
 Rosannah, 327
 Susanna, 71
**DAVIES**
 Mary Virginia, 20
**DAVINE**
 Maggie T., 9
**DAVIS**
 Aberella, 140
 Abigal E., 3
 Adaline, 97
 Agnes N., 262
 Alberta, 207
 Alice (blk), 150
 Amanda A., 174
 Amelia, 71, 150, 288
 Amelia (blk), 150, 288
 Ann, 18, 19, 23, 45, 230
 Ann A., 230
 Anna, 23
 Annie (blk), 45
 Annie M., 18
 Arnette, 228
 Barbara E., 140
 Caroline, 175
 Catharine (blk), 142
 Catherine, 43
 Charlotte (blk), 93
 Chloe A., 150
 Clemenza, 190
 Cornelia, 283
 Cynthia, 318
 Eliza (blk), 155, 252, 294
 Eliza A., 113, 177

 Eliza M., 225
 Elizabeth, 36, 54, 102, 150, 325
 Elizabeth Emma, 36
 Elizabeth O'N., 150
 Ella S., 286
 Ellen, 24, 129, 139, 296
 Ellen (blk), 296
 Ellen Seville, 24
 Ellenora (blk), 129
 Emma, 87
 Fannie, 7
 Frances, 9, 21, 118, 212, 295
 Frances (blk), 9
 Frances E., 212, 295
 George Anna, 176
 Harriet, 243
 Hassie, 78
 Hester (blk), 46
 Jane, 15, 64, 113
 Jane (blk), 64
 Jane V., 15
 Jennie, 85, 107
 Jennie A., 85
 Josephine, 178, 291
 Josephine C., 291
 Julia, 104, 170, 247, 325
 Julia (blk), 325
 Julia A., 104, 247
 Laura V., 252, 271
 Lizzie (blk), 187, 222, 286
 Lizzie A., 49
 Lou (blk), 303
 Louisa (blk), 66
 Louise (blk), 243
 Lucy, 10
 M. Sophie, 283
 Mardie, 72
 Margaret, 8, 188, 225
 Margaret Ann, 8
 Margaret R., 225
 Maria E., 304
 Marian F., 102
 Marian S., 141

 Marion V., 319
 Martha (blk), 326
 Mary, 12, 34, 49, 73, 76, 99, 157, 176, 184, 191, 197, 254, 266, 268, 269, 271, 273, 275, 277, 307
 Mary (blk), 269, 273
 Mary Ann, 176, 191, 271
 Mary Ann (blk), 176, 271
 Mary C., 184, 266
 Mary E., 12, 34, 73, 99, 254
 Mary E. (blk), 99
 Mary E.A., 34
 Mary Ellen, 197
 Mary H., 277
 Mary L., 307
 Mary S., 76, 275
 Mary V., 49
 Mollie, 178
 Rebecca, 119, 227, 280
 Rose (blk), 278
 Sallie A., 223
 Sally, 46
 Sarah, 60, 214, 223, 291
 Sarah E., 60, 291
 Sarah F., 214
 Sophia (blk), 147
 Susan H., 298
 Susanna, 98
 Theodosia, 312
 Theresa, 263
**DAVISON**
 Annie W., 295
 Martha, 202
 Sarah Ann, 5
**DAWES**
 Annie E., 196
**DAWSON**
 Jane D., 144
 Margaret, 177, 225
 Maria (blk), 42

DAWSON
  Mary I., 326
  Nellie (blk), 231
  Sarah E., 91
DAY
  Bettie (blk), 44
  Betty (blk), 181
  Caroline E., 5
  Celia (blk), 31
  Charlotta (blk), 288
  Elizabeth, 200, 267
  Emeline, 214
  Frances V. (blk), 51
  Jane (blk), 154
  Lucretia (blk), 186
  Lucy (blk), 192
  Mary Ellen, 227
  Mary O., 92, 301
  Mina, 96
  Nancy (blk), 188
  Sarah, 287
DAYTON
  Anna (blk), 216
  Julia C., 130
  Kate, 10
  Lucinda (blk), 155
DEAGLE
  Sarah, 27
DEAKINS
  Amelia, 103
DEAN
  Annie, 267
  Elizabeth, 77, 132
  Julia, 23
  Louisa, 64, 254
  Louisa (blk), 254
  Mary, 185, 234
  Mary (blk), 234
  Sarah, 58
DEANE
  Mary A., 10
deBODISCO
  Harriet, 258
DeCAMP
  Elizabeth Estell, 122
DECK
  Mary V., 256
DECKER
  Mary E., 33

Mary Rosanna, 278
Sarah H., 260
DeCOSTA
  Catherine (blk), 31
DeCOVER
  Hellin, 193
DEE
  Cado, 78
  Catherine, 97
DEEBLE
  Judie M., 260
  Martha Jane, 276
DEENER
  Annie, 191
DEFREES
  Julia M., 254
DEGGES
  Mollie V., 25
DEGILE
  Louise Marie, 69
DEGNAN
  Ann, 249
DeGRAFFT
  Emma, 209
DEHENER
  Ellen, 86
DEHON
  Catherine, 163
DEIGMANN
  Christiana, 251
DEIST
  Catharine E., 281
DEITRICK
  Margaret, 261
DEITZ
  Gertrude, 29
DeJARDINS
  Marie Anastasie, 46
DeLAIGHY
  Mary Jane, 245
DeLaMOIN
  Maggie C., 219
DELANEY
  Bridget, 91
  Ellen (blk), 178
  Frances (blk), 17
  Margt. A., 131
  Martha J. (blk, 110
  Mary Anne, 48

Mary E., 219
Mary F. (blk), 234
Matilda (blk), 135
Rose, 246
Sidney (blk), 292
DELANY
  Catherine (blk), 25
  Hanorah, 219
  Mary E. (blk), 155
DELARMAN
  Lina Bruna, 92
delaROCHE
  Georgiana H.F., 117
DELAVERGNE
  Fannie E., 171
DELAY
  Martha E., 12
  Mary, 252
DELEVI
  Julia, 70
DELL
  Elizabeth S., 30
  Sarah (blk), 155
DELPHY
  Emma D., 300
DEMAIN
  Marion, 118
  Mary H., 31
DeMAINE
  Arabella, 82
  Laura, 325
DEMALMAR
  Lina, 147
DeMANSFIELD
  Maggie, 247
DeMARQUE
  Mary, 5
DEMENT
  Barbara, 273
  Ida Virginia, 143
  Jane E., 184
  Jane Elizabeth, 24
  Jane W., 93
  Louisa E., 237
  Virginia, 6
DEMENTT
  Susan A., 50
DEMING
  Nannie (blk), 278

DeMOLL
  Mary Frances
    Josephine, 120
DEMOLLE
  Charlotte, 67
DEMOND
  Harriet, 43
DEMPSTER
  Eunice A., 54
DEMSEY
  Annie, 77
DEMYERS
  Harriet, 266
DENAAN
  Bridget, 144
DENANT
  Ida V., 283
DeNEAL
  Mary E., 1
DENHAM
  Caroline A., 45
DENISON
  Mary L., 253
DENMARK
  Rachel Ann, 26
DENMEAD
  Mary J., 209
DENNIS
  Bertha S. (blk), 203
  Henrietta B., 19
DENNISON
  Elizabeth, 166
  Elmonia, 5
  Frances A., 323
  Lucy A., 89
  Marion, 173
  Nannie M., 281
  Sarah (blk), 101
DENNO
  Josephine, 76
DENNY
  Ann (blk), 148
  Catharine, 76
  Rebecca Adele, 299
DENT
  Eliza Jane, 274
  Elizabeth (blk), 76, 102
  Priscilla (blk), 228

Sarah K., 127
Susana (blk), 17
DeQUIET
  Georgiana, 274
DEREAMER
  Alice, 111
DEROUGES
  Victorine, 189
DERR
  Maggie E., 206
  Sarah, 150
DERRICK
  Georgine M., 107
DeSANNO
  Eleanora, 88
deSAVAGNE
  Sophie Favaiger, 69
DESFOSSE
  Susan M., 265
DESHIELD
  Margaret (blk), 86
DESHIELL
  Georgeanna L.M., 240
DESMOND
  Mary, 221
DESPAR
  Fanny (blk), 77
DESSING
  Mary, 325
DETRICK
  Henrietta, 241
DETRO
  Caroline, 169
  Margaret S., 152
DETTER
  Mary Ann, 84
DEURLINER
  Catherine, 143
DeVAUGHAN
  Emma R., 77
DEVAUGHN
  Alice M., 247
  Elizabeth, 119
  Judy, 313
  Landonia, 3
  Mary S., 144
DEVERAUX
  Mary C., 162

DEVEREAUX
  Maria L., 116
DEVEREUX
  Anna M., 137
DEVERS
  Martha, 108, 139
  Martha A., 139
DEVES
  Felicia A., 136
DEVINE
  Kattie J., 214
  Margaret, 70
  Mary, 162
DEVIS
  Virginia, 183
DEVLIN
  Annie, 244
  Hannah, 175
  Mary Ann, 211
  Sarah, 41, 219
  Sarah Ann, 41
DEVRIES
  Johanna, 177
DEWDNEY
  Julia, 91
DEWEES
  Mary Amelia, 24
DEWYER
  Mary Ann, 121
DIAZO
  Virginia (blk), 179
DIBBLE
  Jennie L., 299
DIBRELL
  Julia (blk), 253
DICE
  Amelia Elizabeth, 102
  Carrie, 265
  Catherine Margaret, 190
  Dora, 22
  Teany E., 181
DICK
  Joriah, 122
  Lavinia (blk), 39
  Rutha, 21
DICKEL
  Helen, 181

DICKENS
  Agnes, 184
  Kate, 165
  Mary E., 307
  Summer (blk), 162
DICKENSON
  Ellen, 66
DICKERSON
  Sarah Ann, 246
DICKEY
  Adelaide F., 304
  Maria P., 294
  Mary F., 225
DICKINSON
  Judith A., 191
  Mary Jane (blk), 307
  P.W., 284
DICKSON
  Harriett A., 33
  Lucy Emily, 125
  Mary, 107
  Milly (blk), 107
DIDERLEIN
  Dorothy, 223
DIEDERICK
  Doredo, 111
DIEDERMAN
  Bertha, 86
DIEGEBRET
  Christiana, 230
DIESSER
  Bertha, 139
DIETENCH
  Gottdilde Catharina, 14
DIETERICH
  Rebecca, 189
DIETRICH
  Caroline Wilhelmine, 245
DIETZ
  Carolina, 133
  Grace, 119
  Madalina, 138
DIEZ
  Maria M., 118
DIGGENS
  Margaret, 226
DIGGES
  Fanny (blk), 18
  Henrietta (blk), 57
  Mary S., 27
  Matilda (blk), 36
DIGGIN
  Ellen, 194
DIGGINS
  Ann, 84
  Margaret, 60
DIGGLE
  Mary, 150
DIGGS
  Catharine F., 91
  Catherine (blk), 4, 248
  Eliza Jane (blk), 326
  Leda (blk), 151
  Maria (blk), 55
  Mary (blk), 77
  Matilda (blk), 155
  Millie A., 240
  Nancy, 165, 303
  Nancy (blk), 303
  Sophia, 14
  Susan, 74
DIGNAN
  Bridget, 5
DIGNO
  Sarah, 62
DILLON
  Ann McElfish, 245
  Kate J., 13
  Margaret, 13
  Maria, 160
DIMICK
  Catharine O., 186
DIMMOCK
  Cora, 46
DINAWOOD
  Louisa (blk), 56
DINES
  Charlotte Ann (blk), 273
DINGLER
  Louisa, 119
DINICK
  Mariah, 119
DINKLE
  Lucy V., 249

DIPPLE
  Mary, 192
DISHMAN
  Mollie F., 324
DIVEN
  M. Josephine, 254
DIVERS
  Mary G., 261
DIVINE
  Anna L., 110
  Louisa A., 60
  Mary, 209, 257, 324
  Mary A., 324
DIVOLL
  Emily, 284
DIXON
  Ann (blk), 79
  Anna Rebecca, 222
  Cornelia, 1
  Elizabeth, 6, 106, 120
  Emily, 68
  Fannie E., 92
  Frances, 206
  Harriet, 239
  Jane Eliza (blk), 190
  Josephine, 251, 263
  Josephine (blk), 263
  Laura, 264
  Lavinia (blk), 240
  Lucinda, 210
  Maria (blk), 144
  Mary (blk), 35, 129, 178
  Mary Ann, 143
  Rosa (blk), 229
  Susan W., 290
  Susannah (blk), 156
DOBBIN
  Hannah, 239
DOBBINS
  Mary Ann, 223
  Ula, 207
DOBBS
  Alice J., 71
DOBSON
  Laura, 84
  Winnie (blk), 70
DOCKET
  Julia, 7

DODD
  Mary A., 319
  Virginia E., 301
DODENHOFF
  Nannie J., 38
DODGE
  Elizabeth, 16, 51
  Mary Elizabeth, 41
DODSON
  Ann M. (blk), 304
  Catherine, 251
  Delia (blk), 178
  Frances, 184, 270
  Frances (blk), 270
  Georgiana (blk), 56
  Harriet, 80, 149, 278
  Harriet Ann (blk), 80, 278
  Jane M., 162
  Josephine (blk), 232
  Julia, 80
  Molly E., 234
  Rachel, 166, 298
  Rachel Ann, 166
DÖENGES
  Maria, 285
DOFT
  Mary C., 166
DOHERTY
  Kate, 256
  Mary, 144, 150
  Mary H., 144
DOLAN
  Anna, 98
  Annie, 61, 88
  Annie F., 61
  Ellen, 284, 289
  Ellen E., 284
  Kate, 44, 121
DOLEN
  Mary, 253
DOLFANCE
  Mary, 298
DOLIN
  Mollie E., 158
DOLING
  Annie, 194
DÖLL
  Eliza, 78

DOLLY
  Louisa (blk), 235
DOMLESS
  Emma, 36
DOMLISS
  Anna (blk), 62
DONAHO
  Ella, 30
DONAHUE
  Joanna, 77
DONALDSON
  Amanda E., 94
  Ann Elizabeth, 270
  Fannie J., 215
  Jane (blk), 117
  Mary L., 219
  Mary R., 268
  Phoebe, 85
  Roberta, 1
  Sallie F., 138
  Sarah C., 273
  Sarah E., 136
DONELAN
  Bridget, 239
DONELLY
  Mary, 211
DONIVAN
  Hanorah, 106
DONN
  Bridget, 201
  Catherine, 143
  Martha E., 141
  Rosa A., 42
  Theodosia J., 239
DONNAWAY
  Ann Maria, 260
DONNEGAN
  Mary A., 189
DONNELLY
  Amelia J., 252
  Ann, 83
  Bridget, 303
  Catherine, 67
  Ellen, 186
  Katie, 253
  Leddy, 13
  Lydia, 131
  Margaret, 170, 277
  Mary, 221

  Rosann, 229
DONNOGHUE
  Mary, 60, 194
DONNOLLY
  Margaret, 167
DONOGHUE
  Bridget, 196
  Hannah, 129
  Margaret, 96
  Mary, 52, 70, 242, 292
  Sarah A., 44
DONOHO
  Bridget, 169
  Catharine, 73
  Catherine, 77
  Ellen, 125, 241
  Mary, 196
DONOHOE
  Catharine, 83
  Kate, 93
  Mary, 106
DONOHOO
  Catharine, 100
  Jane, 160
DONOHUE
  Johannah, 81
DONOLSON
  Sarah Y., 163
DONOVAN
  Catharine, 16, 116
  Ellen, 161
  Jane, 146
  Joanna, 282
  Margaret, 219, 238
  Mary, 195
DONOVEN
  Johanna, 70
DOODY
  Mary, 220
DOOLING
  Catharine, 265
DOOLY
  Annie E., 225
DORAN
  Bridget, 68
DOREMUS
  Mary E., 49
DORES
  Margaret, 178

DOREY
  Annie (blk), 59
DORLEY
  Bessie, 261
DORLIN
  Catharine, 81
DORMAN
  Lottie, 52
  Naomi, 90
DORN
  Bridget, 87
DORNAN
  Ann, 218
  Maria, 178
DORR
  Elizabeth, 160
DORRELL
  Virginia A., 114
DORSEY
  Alcinda Rilla (blk), 320
  Anna E., 279
  Annie (blk), 31
  Annie Rebecca, 145
  Arian (blk), 302
  Ariana, 16
  Catherine, 60, 213
  Deborah (blk), 3
  Eliza (blk), 110
  Elizabeth (blk), 226
  Ellen F., 86
  Emeline (blk), 242
  Emily (blk), 326
  Fannie E., 16
  Honnor, 200
  Jane (blk), 116, 129, 178
  Julia, 217, 283, 300
  Julia (blk), 300
  Julia Ann (blk), 283
  Kate (blk), 39
  Lucretia (blk), 77
  Malvina (blk), 82
  Margaret, 141
  Mary (blk), 115, 187, 216
  Mary A., 88
  Mary E., 303
  Mary Elizabeth, 128
  Mary E. (blk), 290
  Mary I., 15
  Phoebe (blk), 51
  Rachel (blk), 141
  Rebecca (blk), 196
  Sarah A. (blk), 154
  Sophia, 50
DORSY
  Bridget, 52
DOSUCH
  Anna E., 230
DOTSON
  Harriet, 176
DOUD
  Ellen, 185
  Mary, 144
DOUGHADAY
  Sarah Jane, 33
DOUGHERTY
  Anna, 115
  Frances Ann, 161
  Margaretta, 120
  Mary, 128
  Rachel Thomas, 277
  Virginia, 195
DOUGHTY
  Ann P., 229
  Julia, 2
DOUGLAS
  Adele, 318
  Ann M. (blk), 228
  Anna A., 294
  Catharine L., 322
  Catherine E., 310
  Eliza Jane (blk), 175
  Flora, 189
  Margaretta M. (blk), 66
  Maria L., 207
  Marion P., 37
  Mary (blk), 89
  Nancy (blk), 317
  Sarah (blk), 232
DOUGLASS
  Alice, 160
  Ann (blk), 18
  Anna V., 118
  Elizabeth (blk), 227
  Isabella, 172
  Lavinia (blk), 316
  Margaret Ann, 59
  Maria (blk), 192
  Mary, 157, 191, 258
  Mary (blk), 157
  Mary J., 191
  Rachel (blk), 325
  Rebecca (blk), 275
  Rosina (blk), 149
  Zelia, 41
DOVE
  Amand, 71
  Caroline A., 2
  Caroline A. (blk), 2
  Catherine Ann, 311
  Eliza J., 26
  Ellen, 196
  Georgie, 293
  Kate C., 281
  Laura, 170
  Lizzie, 267
  Louisa (blk), 286
  Martha A., 161
  Mary A., 24
  Rebecca, 83
  Sarah E., 55
  Virginia, 132
DOVER
  Jane (blk), 305
  Lucy (blk), 119
  Marion, 19
  Sallie (blk), 13
  Wealthy Ann, 55
DOW
  Belle, 3
  Helen M., 65
  Julia A., 4
  Mary, 135
DOWD
  Hannah, 194
  Kate, 158
  Mary, 124
DOWDEN
  Columbia Ann, 227
DOWDENS
  Virginia, 81
DOWDS
  Dorah, 176

371

District of Columbia Marriage Licenses, 1858-1870

DOWELL
  Betsy (blk), 148
DOWLING
  Catharine, 303
  Josephine, 162
  Martha (blk), 295
DOWNELY
  Mary, 39
DOWNES
  Christina, 188
  Elizabeth, 62
  Henrietta (blk), 293
  Julia, 96
  Margaret, 166
  Martha, 113
  Mary, 327
DOWNEY
  Cacelia R., 275
  Catharine, 99
  Margaret, 129, 166
  Margaret E., 166
  Mary, 84, 85, 123, 219, 308
DOWNING
  Caroline (blk), 316
  Cordelia, 76
  Mary Ann, 41
  Sarah L., 310
DOWNS
  Alice, 60
  Emma Radclyff, 172
  Isabella, 211
  Mary Elizabeth, 40
DOYLE
  Bridget, 46, 154
  Hannah (blk), 76
  Julia, 251
  Margaret, 198, 323
  Margaret Ann, 323
  Mary, 60, 165
DOZIER
  Catherine (blk), 249
DRABAND
  Kate, 205
DRAILEY
  Catharine, 223
DRAKE
  Jane, 69

DRALEY
  Mary Elizth., 172
DRANE
  Kate, 40
DRAPER
  Fannie, 31
DRAYTON
  Annie R., 36
  E.J., 161
DREAKER
  Louisa, 169
DREDDEN
  Mollie (blk), 84
DREIER
  Eliza, 17
DREIFUS
  Bertha, 173
  Rigge, 309
DREW
  Mary Virginia, 244
  Willie B., 27
DRICH
  Williamina, 249
DRISCOL
  Ellen, 81
  Margaret, 221
DRISCOLL
  Abagail, 218
  Ann O., 194
  Catharine, 175
  Catherine, 220
  Joanna, 70
  Johanna, 43, 135
  Johannah, 43
  Margaret, 31, 312
  Mary, 27, 141, 205, 284
  Mary C., 27
  Mary T., 141
DRISH
  Sarah Indiana, 133
DRIVER
  Alice Ann, 83
DRONAY
  Mary, 184
DRUMMON
  Sarah C., 28
DRUMMOND
  Hannah J., 168

  Hellen C., 179
DRURY
  Annie, 43
  Honora, 98
  Margaret, 286
  Mary L.S., 123
DRUSHEIM
  Catharine, 131
DUBANT
  Annie M., 272
DUBOIS
  Eunice, 190
DUCHEMOY
  Rosamande J., 247
DUCKET
  Caroline Eliz'th., 309
  Elizabeth (blk), 290
  Matilda (blk), 288
DUCKETT
  Alice, 28
  Ann (blk), 271
  Margarett Ann (blk), 33
  Martha (blk), 282
  Sarah, 32, 146
  Sarah (blk), 32
DUDDY
  Mary, 96
DUDLEY
  Catharine, 81
  Dorcas G., 124
  Drussilla R., 232
  Priscilla (blk), 248
DUFFEY
  Margaret, 249
  Mary A., 201
DUFFIN
  Abby (blk), 268
DUFFINS
  Eliza (blk), 236
DUFFY
  Bridget, 283
  Catharine, 312
  Catherine, 68
  Ellen, 212
  S. Kate, 128
DUFOUR
  Hevila R., 56

DUGAN
  Eliza, 195
  Margaret, 24, 197
  Rosanna, 125
DUGGAN
  Catherine, 173
DUGGEIN
  Mary, 255
DUII
  Elizabeth, 224
DUKE
  Annie M., 4
  Ellen (blk), 118
DUKEHART
  Eugenia R., 236
  Graham, 85, 125
DUKES
  Margaret A., 59
DULAHAN
  Bridget, 207
  Lisie, 257
DULANEY
  Caroline (blk), 318
  Catherine R., 254
  Josephine, 318
  Sarah F., 258
DULEHENTY
  Ellin, 238
DULEY
  Marion Clay, 141
  Mary O., 111
DULIN
  Sarah A., 299
DULL
  Emma S., 253
  Mary, 220
DUMMEL
  Cecilia, 1
DUMPHY
  Catharine, 65
DUNAVAN
  Annie, 167
DUNBAR
  Isabella K., 66
  Josephine, 299
  Sarah (blk), 94, 104
DUNCAN
  Elizabeth (blk), 235
  Emily (blk), 102

Mary A., 239
Mary P., 28
DUNDA
  Emma, 19
  Mary Elizabeth, 245
DUNDEN
  Mary, 167
DUNICLIFF
  Maggie, 230
DUNIVAN
  Sue, 145
DUNLAP
  Lydia J., 278
  Mary J. (blk), 133
DUNLOP
  Margaret L., 64
  Sarah (blk), 292
DUNMORE
  Rebecca (blk), 86
DUNN
  Ann, 32, 194, 265
  Ann (blk), 32
  Annie, 265
  Bridget, 236, 271
  Catherine, 86
  Grace W., 232
  Johanna, 73
  Mary, 33, 202, 255
DUNNAHAY
  Mary, 185
DUNNAVIN
  Ellen, 118
DUNNENBERG
  Minna, 251
DUNNIGAN
  Mary, 268
DUNNINGTON
  Bettie C., 312
  Mary E., 151
DUNWOOD
  Mary (blk), 117
DUPPIN
  Mary Jane, 149
DURKIN
  Maria, 76
DURNAN
  Mary, 253
DUSCHILDS
  Priscilla, 207

DUST
  Rachel Ann, 33
DUTROW
  R. Sophia, 98
  Sarah Catherine, 75
DUTTON
  Martha A., 118
DUVAL
  Barsine S., 248
  Bettie, 308
  Catharine E., 144
  Mary E., 96
  Sallie R., 91
DUVALL
  Annie E., 34
  Celestia A., 168
  Dora E., 69
  Elizabeth, 74, 173
  Elizabeth Catherine, 74
  Harriet, 88
  Julia A. (blk), 95, 302
  Louisa (blk), 136
  Lucy A., 20
  Margaret B., 47
  Margaret J., 307
  Mary, 20, 217, 326
  Mary Jane, 20
  Mary V., 217
  Mollie, 30
  R. E., 140f
  Sarah L.J., 248
  Summerville, 247
  Susan R., 315
DWYER
  Annie, 216
  Hanora, 200
DYE
  Patsey (blk), 240
DYER
  Alice Rebecca, 108
  Ann O., 46
  Catharine, 316
  Clara Virginia, 130
  Eliza A., 88
  Isabel, 227
  Josephine, 68
  Malinda (blk), 272

DYER
  Martha A., 123
  Mary F., 209
  Mary M., 147
  Nellie (blk), 251
  Roberta, 142
  Sarah A., 268
DYNES
  Mary Jane, 326
DYSER
  Anne Mary, 98
DYSON
  Delia (blk), 275
  Emeline, 15
  Jane (blk), 326, 327
  Lucinda (blk), 36
  Margaret (blk), 71
DZER
  Josephine L., 182

—E—

EADY
  Martha M., 214
EAGAN
  Bridget, 200, 294
  Ella, 102
EAGLESTON
  Maria Virginia, 260
EARGER
  Alice Rebecca, 135
EARL
  Emily P., 195
  Martha V., 203
EARLIE
  Sallie (blk), 296
EARNEST
  Ulia, 88, 119
EASTER
  Harriet (blk), 16
EASTIS
  Caroline (blk), 259
EASTMAN
  Carrie W., 141
EASTON
  Annie (blk), 268
  Catherine, 98
  Flora (blk), 323
  Josephine (blk), 210

  Laura (blk), 305
  Matilda (blk), 54
  Nellie (blk), 77
  Sophie, 53
EASTY
  Mary, 310
EATHY
  Marian, 299
EATON
  Bridget, 200
  Margaret L., 37
  Mary, 227
  Virginia A., 118
EAYRE
  Hannah H., 132
EBELING
  Therese, 160
EBERBACH
  Fredericka, 141
  M. Virginia, 174
EBERLE
  Sarah, 23
EBERLING
  Madeline, 20
  Philomena, 284
EBERTS
  Sophia, 95
ECK
  Annie, 72
ECKEL
  Elizabeth Ann, 265
ECKERT
  Kate, 119
ECKLOFF
  Sarah E., 322
ECKSTEIN
  Franciska, 180
ECKTON
  Mary E., 5
EDD
  Lucinda, 276
EDDENS
  Sarah L., 102
EDDIE
  Mary E., 251
EDDS
  Florence, 174
EDE
  Emilie, 88

EDELEN
  Sarah, 327
EDELIN
  Amanda (blk), 190
  Eleanor C., 31
  Frances H., 2
  Jane, 224
  Judith Amanda, 259
  Mary E., 88
  Mary F., 204
  Meheda Ann, 85
EDENBORO
  Elizabeth (blk), 152
EDINBOROUGH
  Catherine, 210
EDINGBURR
  Mary Elizabeth
    (blk), 123
EDMONDS
  Anna, 261
  Fannie (blk), 308
  Harriet E., 242
EDMONDSON
  Martha (blk), 229
EDMONSON
  Emma Victoria
    (blk), 144
EDMONSTON
  Emma, 52
  Louisa R. (col'd),
    160
  Mary E., 41
  Sallie R., 206
  Sarah (blk), 103
EDSON
  A.L., 204
  Lavangie S., 304
EDWARDS
  Anne, 129
  Catherine (blk), 140
  Charlotte (blk), 179
  Edwardina, 247
  Emma, 74, 275
  Emma Jane, 275
  Evelina, 89
  Jennett, 7
  Johnana P., 50
  Julia Ann, 200
  Lavinia (blk), 290

EDWARDS
  Margaret S., 40
  Marion F., 247
  Mary Caroline, 314
  Mary E., 237
  Mary Jane, 82
  Mary M., 297
  Rosa C., 53
  Sally (blk), 148
  Sarah M., 74
  Susan E., 76
EFFRINGER
  Anna, 12
EFFUTTS
  Elizabeth Ellen, 45
EGAN
  Margaret, 63
EGAND
  Elizabeth, 315
EGGERS
  Fredrica, 204
EHINGER
  Hattie, 115
EHRMAN
  Clara, 222
EICHELBERGER
  Laura, 256
EICHHORN
  Margaret, 181
EICHMULLER
  Anna K., 257
EICHNER
  Creyenzia, 257
EICHORN
  Elizabeth, 213
EIDMAN
  Elizabeth, 133
EIFERT
  Elizabeth, 6
EINER
  Catherine, 258
EINSTEIN
  Rachel, 121
EISENBEISS
  Rosa, 300
EKERT
  Maria M., 243
EKLEY
  Margaret, 251

ELBERT
  Annie M., 255
ELD
  Julia A., 15
ELDERGRAVE
  Louisa, 275
ELDRED
  Catharine M., 203
  Emma L., 37
ELFING
  Annie E., 254
ELFORT
  Elizabeth Janx, 91
ELGIN
  Emma A.S., 246
  Karen A., 150
ELIASON
  Mary, 274
ELKINS
  Edinborough, 36
  Emeline (blk), 121
  Mary E., 306
ELLET
  Mary Ann, 275
ELLIN
  Sallie A., 289
  Sallie Ann, 1
ELLIOT
  Cary E., 99
  Sarah A., 53
ELLIOTT
  [blank], 151
  Alice, 134
  Mary E., 29, 71
  Mary R., 10
  Phebe A., 302
  Rebecca V., 187
  Sarah (blk), 97
  Sarah Ann, 227
ELLIS
  Alice, 217
  Anna M., 166
  Clara Jane, 184
  Emma, 181
  Georgiana, 91
  Hannah A., 4
  Jennie, 157
  Laura A., 207
  Laura V., 11

  Lucy H., 89
  Maria, 198
  Mary, 125, 211, 218
  Mary Jane, 218
  Mary V., 125
  Matilda, 261
  Nannie B., 172
  Sallie, 128
  Susanna, 104
ELLISS
  Elizabeth, 40
ELLMEYER
  Mary C. ., 300
ELLMORE
  Juli, 44
ELLS
  Frances (blk), 42
ELLSWORTH
  Margaret, 273
ELM
  Jacob, 91, 300
ELMORE
  Elizabeth F., 316
ELMS
  Lucy J., 97
  Susan, 73
ELRICKS
  Eliza, 24
ELWOOD
  Ann Elizabeth, 260
  Mary, 185
ELY
  Susan B., 234
ELZY
  Sarah, 20
EMBREY
  Ann, 224
EMENT
  Maria, 102
EMERICH
  Mary A., 113
EMERSON
  Hester A., 77
EMMEL
  Rachel L., 36
EMMERSON
  Emma D., 23
  Louisa, 283
  Martha (blk), 42

EMMERT
  Wilhelmina, 79
ENDERCOT
  Harriet, 216
ENDERS
  Catherine, 270
ENGEL
  Cartriene Magretha, 252
  Emma, 303
  Mary Anna, 168
ENGELHAGEN
  Adelheid, 162
ENGELHART
  Margaret, 169
ENGLAND
  Emily (blk), 64
  Lydia C., 25
ENGLE
  Anna Barbara, 95
  Louisa, 134
  Mary, 22, 24
ENGLEBRECT
  Joanna, 265
ENGLEBRIGHT
  Amanda E., 28
ENGLEHARD
  Catharine, 183
  Mary, 131
ENGLEHARDT
  Louisa, 109
ENGLERT
  Johanna M.S., 270
ENGLISH
  Carrie F., 257
  Catharine, 134
  Catherine, 86
  Helen, 210
  Lucy A., 164
  N.M., 129
  Nellie M., 130
ENNES
  Estelle M., 11
ENNESS
  Cornelia, 51
ENNIS
  Ann (blk), 42
  Catharine, 8
  Margaret Anna, 230

Mary, 183, 299
Mary R., 183
ENRIGHT
  Catherine, 213
  Hanora, 64
  Johanna, 246
  Margaret, 38, 46, 262
ENTWISLE
  Alina, 37
  Amanda, 221
ENTWISTLE
  Elizabeth E., 1
EPPERSON
  Mary (blk), 45
ERB
  Caroline Josephine, 37
  Catharina, 256
ERBECK
  Margaret, 92
ERCKMAN
  Eva, 2
ERDMANN
  Julia, 109
ERNEST
  Alice Virginia, 77
  Mary E., 231
ERNST
  Catharine, 243
ERTEL
  Annie, 134
ERVERLING
  Lena, 160
ERVIN
  Hannah Jane, 107
ESCHERICH
  Mary A., 216
ESCHHOLTZ
  Fannie G., 19
ESCUDERO
  Phillipine Mary, 310
ESKRIDGE
  Martha Ann, 93
ESLIN
  Cornelia A., 60
  Harriet E., 55
ESPEY
  Anne, 237

Laura V., 260
Maggie, 38
ESSELBURGGE
  Wilhelmina, 29
ESSEX
  Alice V., 51
  Emma, 166
  Hattie, 25
  Laura E., 88
ESTLER
  Emily F., 236
ETCHINSON
  Elizabeth, 144
ETCHISON
  Alice, 29
  Merah, 234
  Virginia, 182
EUBANK
  Mary C., 92
EUSTACE
  Martha, 214
  Sarah Frances, 92
EUSTICE
  Mary, 308
EVANS
  Annie, 243
  Augusta J., 309
  Catharine, 314
  Emily E., 33
  Emma J., 156
  Evanina F., 18
  Fanny (blk), 289
  Frances (blk), 253
  Francis H., 126
  Hanna A. (blk), 149
  Jane, 37
  Katie, 228
  Laura B., 63
  Lucinda, 184
  Mary Agnes, 204
  Mary Ann, 128, 161
  Mary E., 236
  Mary Ellen, 266
  Minerva B., 300
  Minta (blk), 266
  Sallie P., 38
  Sarah M., 5
  Sarah R., 7
  Teresa, 146

EVE
Alice M., 194
EVELETH
Catharine P.S., 321
Sarah Maynadier, 314
EVERETT
Elizabeth, 128
Mary, 58, 213, 301
Mary H., 58
Mary T., 213
EVERHART
Margaret, 186
EVERITT
Elizabeth, 75
EVERTS
Eloise M., 26
EVINS
Georgianna, 252
EVY
Elizabeth, 293
EWALD
Elizabeth, 256
EWELL
Annie (blk), 32
Georgiana, 82
EWING
Merica E., 306
EZEKIAL
Josephine G., 29

—F—

FAEYNE
Catherine, 65
FAGAN
Annie, 8
Christiana, 186
Fanny, 16
FAGUE
Josie B., 316
FAHAY
Mary, 194
FAHERTY
Mary, 161
FAHEY
Margaret, 146
FAIRBANK
Lizzie, 203

FAIRFAX
Eliza (blk), 83
Martha S., 290
Mary, 23, 272
Mary (blk), 23
Sarah Ann (blk), 7
Sarah F., 171
FALCONER
Mary Almira, 176
FALES
Mary Virginia, 212
Susie L., 188
FALKENRICKS
Catrine W., 104
FALLINEON
Annie M., 167
FALLON
Maggie, 263
Mary, 188
FALVEY
Elizabeth, 282
Ellen, 63
Lizzie, 33
Margaret, 127
Mary Jane, 212
FALVY
Catherine, 219
FANTROY
Elizabeth, 57
FARLAY
Kate F., 308
FARLEY
Annie, 178
FARMAN
Delia (blk), 70
FARMER
Caroline L.V., 157
Harriet (blk), 224
Rebecca (blk), 35
FARNHAM
Carrie, 69
Mary, 204
FARR
Catharine (blk), 143
Ellenore, 112
Kate, 195, 220
FARRAR
Anne E., 31
Elvira A., 93

FARRELL
Briget, 192
Catharine, 163
Catherine, 2, 201
Celia, 251
Eleanor, 246
Ellen, 246, 283
Frances O., 189
Mary, 130, 146, 282
Mary H., 146
FARRILL
Ann, 279
FARROW
Bettie, 163
FARWELL
Marion D., 216
FATELY
Catherine C. (blk), 29
FATIO
Florence A., 11
Ida deM., 42
FATTY
Mary, 81
FAUCETT
Hannah M., 273
FAUDREE
Hardenia E., 143
FAUL
Katharine, 139
FAULCONER
Annie Letitia, 17
FAULKNER
Angelina, 246
Maria L., 18
Mary Ellen, 192
FAULWETTER
Johanna, 170
FAUNCE
Helen, 121
Lydia, 272
Mary Ellen, 36
FAUNTLEROY
Ann, 235
FAVWER
Mary, 90
FAWCUS
Mary A., 205
FAWLEY
Elizabeth A., 196

FAWSETT
  Hattie, 100
FAY
  Catharine, 279, 281
  Celestina de, 184
  Jane, 228
  Louisa, 8
  Maggie M., 125
  Mary, 81
FEALEY
  Hanora, 306
FEDRICK
  Emma (blk), 3
FEENY
  Sarah, 277
FEGAN
  Alice, 94
FELLHEIMAR
  Celia, 281
FELLS
  Susanna (blk), 171
FELTER
  Jennie (blk), 91
FELTON
  Sarah (blk), 125
FENCKEL
  Henrietta E., 235
FENDALL
  Mary E., 121
FENDNER
  Mary, 177
FENDRICK
  Mary (blk), 272
FENIX
  Mary Ellen, 87
FENNELLY
  Martha E., 195
FENNESY
  Mary Jane, 50
FENRICK
  Elizabeth L., 283
FENTON
  Anna H., 243
  Annie, 310
FENWICK
  Emma (blk), 235
  Maria M., 40
  Sarah C., 65

FERGURSON
  Caroline, 59
  Clarasa, 189
FERGUSON
  Alice J., 273
  Bridget, 198
  Eliza Jane, 294
  Elizabeth A., 311
  Ellen, 94, 182
  Ellen A., 182
  Emily D., 5
  Emma J., 283
  Jane (blk), 217
  Louisa M. (blk), 40
  Margaret (blk), 212
  Marietta, 160
  Mary A., 240
  Mary B., 168
  Mary E., 61, 100, 268
  Mary E. (blk), 61
  Mary Frances, 35
  Mary L. (blk), 88
  Nancy (blk), 226
  Sarah (blk), 215
FERNEY
  Mary E., 26
FERRALL
  Bessie R., 225
  Lucy M., 165
  Mary, 195
FERRANI
  Louisa, 109
FERRELL
  Virginia, 196
FERRIS
  Carrie, 268
  Catherine, 300f
  Jane, 197
FERRON
  Anna C., 164
FERRY
  Margery, 202
  Martha V., 244
  Sophia C., 219
FETCHEN
  Susan, 148
FETLER
  Margaret, 76

FICKETT
  Mary E., 211
FIEHEGEN
  Mary Louisa, 251
FIELD
  Maria, 279
FIELDING
  Alice (blk), 87
FIELDS
  Harriet (blk), 216, 318
  Leanna (blk), 178
  Martha (blk), 191
  Mary (blk), 47
  Nellie (blk), 63
  Sarah (blk), 82
  Tellie, 255
FILLEMORE
  Louisa (blk), 156
FILLER
  Sallie J., 255
FILLETT
  Addie, 182
FILLINS
  Mary E., 191
FILLMORE
  Luanne (blk), 307
  Susan (blk), 126
FINCH
  Mary Ann, 275
FINCKEL
  A.S., 214
FINCKENSTADT
  Adolphine, 169
FINDLEY
  Genevieve, 220
FINK
  Battranng, 96, 227
  Kate, 97
  Lizzie S., 67
FINLEY
  Ruth Ann (blk), 310
FINLISON
  Martha, 123
FINN
  Kate, 48
  Lizzie, 64
FINNACON
  Elizabeth M., 294

FINNE
  Jane, 169
FINNEGAN
  Maria, 139
  Mary, 184
FINNESY
  Catharine, 169
FINNIGAN
  Mary, 115
FINNY
  Eliza, 95
FISCHER
  Bade, 100
  Johanna, 174
  Maria Rosina, 165
  Mary, 110
  Sophia, 170, 328
FISCHOETTER
  Margaret, 235
FISETTE
  Eloise, 145
FISHER
  A. Cornelia, 224
  Amelia, 170
  Anna, 47, 244
  Annie, 35
  Caroline, 244
  Catharine M., 178
  Catherine (blk), 190
  Christina, 222
  E.E., 78
  Elizth. E., 78
  Emily (blk), 155
  Emily M., 315
  Eva Augusta
    Wilhelmina, 98
  Fannie E., 204
  George Ann, 296
  Hannah, 118
  Henrietta, 133
  Lucy (blk), 191
  Maria (blk), 158
  Mary, 20, 86, 100,
    181
  Mary C., 86
  Mary E., 20
  Mary L., 100
  Nancy (blk), 113
  Nellie E., 250

  Roberta F., 153
  Sarah B., 94
FISHMAN
  Emma, 161
FISTER
  Harriet, 184
  Harriet A., 184
  Louisa S., 130
FITCH
  Margaret, 220
  Mary E., 183
FITTZ
  Margaret, 139
FITZ
  Johanna, 135
FITZCHEW
  Mary (blk), 27
FITZGERALD
  Alice, 42
  Anna, 180
  Annie, 161
  Bridget, 241
  Catharine, 171, 208
  Catherine, 163
  Ellen, 37, 310
  Hanorah, 221
  Honora, 33, 199
  Jane, 162
  Joanna, 276
  Johanna, 59, 81,
    114, 220
  Kate, 48
  M.S., 257
  Margaret, 49, 100
  Maria, 42
  Mary, 35, 63, 172,
    193, 210, 253,
    284, 292
  Mary Ann, 253, 284
  Reine (blk), 7
  Rena (blk), 258
FITZHUGH
  Amanda M., 113
  Helen S., 38
  Mary (blk), 97, 139
  Mary Elizabeth, 203
  Sarah (blk), 54, 113
FITZMORRIS
  Catharine, 282

FITZPATRICK
  Ann F., 100
  Elizabeth, 194
  Frances, 201
  Joanna F., 31
  Margaret, 310
  Norah, 312
  Rosa, 326
FLACK
  Caroline, 258
  Mary, 25
FLAHERTY
  Ann, 139, 218
  Annie, 139
  Honora, 241
  Margaret, 98, 164
  Mary, 199
  Nora, 98
  Sarah, 118
  Winifred, 211
FLANAGAN
  Catherine, 200
  Kate A., 188
FLANIGAN
  Catharine, 60
  Elizabeth, 301
  Mary Ann, 97
FLANNAGAN
  Margaret, 310
  Mary, 113, 209
  Mary A., 113
FLASHMAN
  Barbara, 20
FLATHER
  Martha Jane, 293
FLATTERMAN
  Berthina, 8
FLECK
  Mary, 92
  Sophia, 274
FLEEMAN
  Matilda S., 228
FLEET
  Annette (blk), 32
  Cora, 177
  Kate (blk), 149
  Margaret, 265
  Oliva, 260

FLEMING
  Eliza Josephine, 113
  Eliza T., 327
  Elizabeth, 221
  Emma, 207
  Mary, 60
  Mollie A., 316
FLENNER
  Emma E., 94
  Margaret E., 139
  Susie V., 302
FLETCHER
  Ann E., 269
  Anne, 220
  Eliza J., 145
  Eliza Jane, 36
  Elizabeth (blk), 227
  Ellenora (blk), 67
  Emily (blk), 41
  Henny (blk), 160
  Martha V., 314
  Mary (blk), 51, 190
  Mary A. (blk), 157
  Mary E. (blk), 64, 267
  Sophia (blk), 52
  Teresa, 268
FLEURY
  Alice R., 247
  Estelle L., 261
  Irene, 177
  Pauline, 253
  Seraphine, 9
FLINCHORN
  Martha, 156
FLING
  Ellen, 221
FLINN
  Margaret, 58, 269
FLINT
  Helen H., 298
  Isabella (blk), 48
  Louie F., 299
  Rosina, 26
FLOOD
  Ann (blk), 97
  Annie (blk), 303
  Eliza, 146
  Mary Jane (blk), 7

FLOWEREE
  Eliza E., 179
FLOWERS
  Jane L., 76
  Lavinia, 204
  Mary, 129
FLOYD
  Kate, 273
FLYNN
  Alice, 164
  Bridget, 189
  Catharine, 114, 242
  Catherine, 99, 114
  Catherine, 99
  Eliza, 60, 324
  Ella, 223
  Ellen, 66, 168
  Ellen H., 66
  Hannah, 58
  Kate, 303
  Margaret, 75, 210
  Mary, 59, 108, 213
FOANDAN
  Catharine, 282
FOCACHY
  Theresia, 51
FOGEL
  Ann, 154
FOGLE
  Sarah Ann, 182
FOLAN
  Bridget, 171
FOLBEY
  Julia, 261
FOLCH
  Anne J. Intropidi, 170
FOLEY
  Annie, 217
  Bridget, 62, 93, 262
  Catharine, 55
  Elizabeth, 105, 279
  Hanora, 196
  Honora, 163
  Mary, 62, 93, 97, 98, 217
  Mary A., 62
  Mary Ann, 217
  Susan V., 278

FÖLGER
  Margaretta, 216
FOLK
  Caroline M., 208
  Harriet Virginia, 193
FOLKER
  Catharine, 164
FOLLEN
  Elizabeth, 294
FOLLER
  Mary, 300
FOLLIN
  Ella V., 138
FOLLINS
  Margaret A., 179
FOLTZ
  Amelia, 11
FOLY
  Anna, 165
FONTAIN
  Lizzie, 168
FONTANA
  Charrisia Maria, 76
  Josephine, 3
FONTLEROY
  Henrietta (blk), 289
FOOTE
  Augusta, 7
  Mary N., 132
FORBES
  Eliza J., 105
  Elizabeth, 120
  Laura A., 193
  Mary E. (blk), 9
  Rachel (blk), 259
FORD
  Amy, 154
  Ann Maria, 317
  Antonia, 315
  Bridget, 310
  Catharine, 74, 77
  Catharine E., 77
  Catherine E., 77
  Charity (blk), 113
  Charlotte (blk), 99, 227
  Drusilla, 244
  Drusilla V., 244

FORD
  Elizabeth (blk), 206, 216
  Elizth. Ward, 5
  Ellen (blk), 305
  Georgiana, 126
  Hannah (blk), 237
  Hariet (blk), 83
  Harriet (blk), 290
  Isabella, 279
  Josephine (blk), 54
  Laura E., 94
  Lucinda (blk), 255
  Margaret, 263
  Maria (blk), 227
  Martha (blk), 223
  Mary (blk), 178, 276
  Mary Ann, 47, 285
  Mary Ann (blk), 285
  Mary E., 51
  Mary S. (blk), 309
  Sarah E. (blk), 54
  Sophia (blk), 42
FOREMAN
  Catharine (blk), 156
  Unity, 144
FORRELL
  Annie, 26
FORREST
  Adelaide, 102
  Alethea (blk), 2
  Amelia J. (col'd), 258
  Martha (blk), 148
  Rosa (blk), 283
FORRESTER
  Mary Ann (blk), 152
FORSTER
  Margaretha, 281
FORSYTH
  Elizabeth, 8
  Margaret C., 4
  Mary R., 44
FORTENEY
  Mary E., 260
FORTNER
  Cecilia, 170
  Lavinia, 22
FORTNIGHT
  Harriet (blk), 96

FORTUNE
  Elea Ann (blk), 155
  Georgianna (blk), 155
  Susan, 21
FORWARD
  Laura P., 52
FOSKEY
  Clarissa (blk), 312
FOSSETT
  Alice G., 289
  Emma F., 31
  Harriet, 20
FOSTER
  Adeline (blk), 312
  Altie Hinton, 260
  Ann (blk), 117
  Connallas B., 101, 125
  Emily M., 240
  Emma G., 322
  Evelina (blk), 101
  Fannie, 211
  Georgiana, 203
  Jane, 194
  Josephine DaC., 288
  Lucy (blk), 117
  Mary, 39, 139, 153, 201
  Mary Ann, 201
  Mary Ellen, 139
  Mary G. (blk), 39
  Rosanna, 139
  Sarah Elizth. (blk), 116
  Susan T., 199
FOUNCE
  Lizzie, 239
FOUNTAIN
  Margaret, 232
  Mary Jane, 48
FOWBLE
  Mary Ellen, 225
  Sallie A., 109
FOWKE
  Lucy B., 268
  Susie E., 242
FOWLE
  Alice, 138
  Emma F., 143

FOWLER
  Ada, 149
  Agnes, 241
  Caroline L., 181
  Elizabeth, 45, 187, 296, 298
  Elizabeth A., 296
  Elizabeth K., 298
  Ella C., 72
  Emma, 276
  Fanny G., 125
  H. Sophie, 206
  Margaret A., 296
  Maria L., 23
  Mary, 16, 32, 67
  Mary E., 67
  Mary Frances, 16
  Rutha A., 24
  Willie E., 62
FOX
  Annie, 22
  Arianna, 324
  Ellen, 177, 179
  Fanny, 22
  Hannah (blk), 179
  Lucind (blk), 67
  Mary, 61, 184, 257, 280
  Mary (blk), 61
  Mary E., 184
  Mary Frances (blk), 280
  Rebecca (blk), 33
FOY
  Margaret, 81
  Maria, 217
FRAAS
  Esther, 170
FRAILER
  Catherine, 77
FRAILEY
  Elizabeth, 237
FRALEY
  Mary, 111
FRANCE
  Margarita B., 125
  Rebecca, 160
FRANCES
  Mary, 206

FRANCIS
  Ivory (blk), 154
  Laura (blk), 154
  Martha, 149
  Mary, 13, 225
  Mary (blk), 225
  Rosa E., 254
FRANCK
  Magdelena, 249
FRANÇOIS
  Louise C., 105
FRANENSCHUCH
  Caroline, 222
FRANEY
  Catherine (blk), 248
FRANK
  Alice V., 20
  Annie A., 124
  Fanny, 203
  Kate E., 302
  Louisa, 80
  Margaret, 92
FRANKLER
  Willa A., 177
FRANKLIN
  Ada, 29
  Lena, 179
  M.E., 83
  Marcia T., 162
  Mary F., 191
  Rachel C. (blk), 230
  Sarah P., 6
FRANKS
  Mary Jacobs, 302
  Sarah J., 127
FRANSZONIE
  Jane V., 190
FRANTUM
  Barbara Ellen, 12
FRANZ
  Frederika, 23
FRANZONI
  B., 9
FRASER
  Elizabeth S., 256
  Julia B., 177
FRASHER
  Angella C. (blk), 79

FRASIER
  Catherine, 112
FRAULY
  Mary, 48
FRAYNE
  Julia, 63
FRAZER
  Catherine A., 169
FRAZIER
  Alexina (blk), 148
  Jane (blk), 300
  Jane Ann, 41
  Mary A., 211
  Rebecca (blk), 178, 289
  Sarah, 53, 58
  Sarah Jane (blk), 58
FREAM
  Margaret (blk), 249
FREDERICK
  Amanda (blk), 304
  Catharine, 193
  Jane (blk), 287
  Mary (blk), 285
FREDERICKS
  Eliza M., 145
FREDMAN
  Ellen F. (blk), 135
FREE
  Jeannie M., 246
  Mary E., 123
FREELAND
  Dorcas (blk), 48
  Jane, 20
  Margaret (blk), 290
FREEMAN
  Elizabeth (blk), 47
  Lizzie, 163
  Mary Elizth., 303
  Rebecca (blk), 79
  Sarah E. (blk), 146
FREER
  Josephine, 100, 290
FREFLERINN
  Rosina, 99
FREKIN
  Ann Friederika, 216
FREMIN
  Mary L., 78

FRENCH
  Harriet E., 275
  Laura M., 205
  Mary L., 208
  Minerva, 193
  Olivia, 5
  Rebecca E., 146
  Sarah Clarinda, 85
FRESCEHER
  Amelia, 230
FRESCH
  Susanna, 256
FREUND
  Johanna, 170
FREY
  Emma L., 8
  Theodisia, 250
FREYER
  Mary Isabel, 266
FRIDLEY
  Mary M., 300
FRIDLY
  Jane Ann, 76
FRIEDE
  Sophia, 4
FRIEDEL
  Kunigunde, 229
FRIEDENBURG
  Catharine, 174
FRIES
  Barbara A., 12
  Henrietta, 55
  Regena, 41
FRIESCH
  Elizabeth, 104
FRIK
  Mary, 2
FRINCKS
  Merantha A., 224
FRINDE
  Mary Jane, 19
FRINK
  Sarah L., 224
FRISBIL
  Henrietta (blk), 35
FRISE
  Catharine F., 83
FRITZ
  Christina, 230

FRITZENGER
  Anna Margaret, 147
FRIZE
  Martha A., 130
FRIZZELL
  Louisa, 207
  Mary Alice, 41
FROEDE
  Emilie, 39
FRÖSEL
  Carolina, 255
FROST
  Lizzie A., 43
  Mary E., 280
FROWIN
  Maggie, 298
FRY
  Balinda, 191
  Laura, 280
  Magdalena, 20
  Mary E. (blk), 105
  Sophia, 52, 210
FRYE
  Amanda M., 43
  Ella M., 318
  Susana M., 83
FRYER
  Annie, 267
  Mary, 134
FUCHS
  Fanny, 309
  Harriet, 32
  Josaphona, 20
FUERLE
  Celestine, 256
FUGAL
  Jane, 23
FUGETT
  Josephine, 154
  Susan E., 156
FUGITT
  Laura Virginia, 245
  Sarah F., 155
FULLER
  Agnes, 195
  Helen M., 265
  Johannah, 262
  Kate A., 150
  Mary, 71, 285, 297

Mary L., 297
FULMEN
  Louisa (blk), 286
FULMORE
  Mary, 311
FUNK
  Annie, 78
  Mary, 144
FURGUSON
  Matilda, 120
FURLONG
  Alexina V., 272
  Henrietta (blk), 248
FURSE
  Isabella T., 111

—G—

GAA
  Louisa, 71
GABERT
  Eliza (blk), 122
GABURRI
  A.B., 234
GADDIS
  Eliza (blk), 248
  Gracie, 86
  Joanna, 275
GADSBY
  Mary (blk), 181
GAEK
  Maria, 177
GAFFNEY
  Jane, 111
  Maria, 187
GAFFNY
  Mary, 187
GAHAN
  Mary, 141
GAINES
  Ellen (blk), 61
  Fanny (blk). 270
  Jennie, 250
  Louisa (blk), 33
  Rebecca (blk), 153
GAINEY
  Honora, 30
GAINOR
  Kate B., 185

Lucy Francis, 199
Martha F., 175
GAINS
  Martha (blk), 188
GAIRN
  Ann, 108
GAITHER
  Caroline (blk), 142
  Eliza Jane (blk), 320
  M. Ada, 280
  Sarah (blk), 168
GALAVAN
  Hanora, 219
GALE
  Annie, 315
GALER
  Mary, 180
GALES
  Elizabeth (blk), 294
  Matilda (blk), 28
GALIVAN
  Bridget, 263
GALL
  Katherine, 168
  Mary A., 247
GALLAGHER
  Catherine, 238
  Elizabeth, 314
  Johanna, 79
  Kate, 167, 232
  Kate E., 167
  Mary M., 257
  Sarah Jane, 68
GALLAHER
  Kate A., 98
  M.S., 156
  Maria, 228
  Mary Alice, 255
GALLERY
  Annie (blk), 215
  Cornelia (blk), 186
  Henrietta (blk), 107
  Willie A. (blk), 301
GALLIGAN
  Mary, 288
GALLOWAY
  Cheena (blk), 272
  Henrietta (blk), 4
  Jamima L., 63

GALT
  Margaret (blk), 285
GALVIN
  Johanna, 65, 201
  Margaret, 164
  Susan, 123
GALWAY
  Nancy (blk), 126
  Phillis (blk), 269
GAMBILL
  Mary (blk), 191
GAMBLE
  Ann, 103
  Elizabeth F., 142
GAMBRILL
  Mary A., 224
GANDOLPHI
  Teresa, 174
GANEY
  Hannah, 282
GANGEWER
  Josie H., 142
GANGHREN
  Annie, 237
GANLY
  Mary, 30
GANNON
  Catharine C., 29
GANS
  Rachel, 161
GANT
  Amelia (blk), 176
  Anna, 283
  Celia (blk), 243
  Elizabeth (blk), 107
  Hester (blk), 106
  Josephine (blk), 146
  Lucy Ann, 106
  Maria (blk), 77
  Mary Elizabeth, 308
  Mary Elizth. (blk), 115
GANTT
  Airy (blk), 52
  Ann, 324
  Eliza, 51, 128
  Eliza (blk), 51
  Jane (blk), 77

Louisa (blk), 183, 274
  Margaret (blk), 116
  Maria (blk), 239
  Nancy, 226
  Sarah (blk), 254
GANZ
  Johanna, 325
GARACTY
  Margaret, 64
GARCIA
  Isabella, 146
  Kate, 208
GARDINER
  Annie M., 67
GARDNER
  A. Catherine, 264
  Amelia, 107
  Arabella V., 244
  Caroline, 20
  Elizabeth, 109
  Ellen (blk), 52
  Emma, 137
  Julia A., 96
  Laura J., 81
  Lucretia G., 92
  Rachel Ann, 17
  Ruth Ann, 2
  Sophia, 201
GAREY
  Louisa V., 148
  Margaret, 221
GARGES
  Emily, 199
GARING
  Mary, 276
GARLAND
  Henrietta (blk), 307
GARNAUX
  Marie, 189
GARNER
  Annie D., 67
  Caroline (blk), 36
  Eliza, 17, 38, 109, 224
  Eliza R., 17
  Elizabeth F., 38
  Elizabeth T., 109
  Ellen Sophia, 141

Frances A., 91
  Hetty (blk), 157
  Lucretia A., 62
  Martlieda E., 162
  Mary (blk), 217
  Mary Eliza (blk), 157
  Mary R., 276
  Sarah Ann, 307
  Sophia, 283
GARNET
  Biddy (blk), 22
  Sarah, 32
GARNETT
  Elizabeth (blk), 209
GARRATT
  Sarah E., 321
GARRET
  Georgietta, 4
GARRETT
  Adaline (blk), 149
  Almira, 285
  Caroline E. (blk), 33
  Elizabeth F. (blk), 69
  Eveline (blk), 106
  Mary A.F., 212
GARRETTSON
  Ethi E., 219
GARRISON
  Eliza (blk), 297
  Emma J., 158
  Lucy (blk), 286
  Martha A., 277
  Mary (blk), 155
GARRITY
  Bridget, 163, 294
GARTEN
  Margaret J., 84
GARTH
  Sarah C., 29
GARTLAND
  Ellen, 200
GARTRELL
  Margaret J., 252
  Mary Kate, 49
GARVEY
  Jane, 81
GARVIN
  Mary, 59, 63

GARVY
  Margaret, 209
GASKIN
  Lucinda (blk), 80
  Mary (blk), 133
GASKINS
  Margaret Ann, 299
  Susan, 108
GASLEY
  Elizabeth, 271
GASS
  Katie P., 144, 145
  Mary E., 215
GASSAWAY
  Anna L., 253
  Catharine L., 184
  Catherine L. (blk), 17
  Charlotte (blk), 52
  Jane, 267
  Lethea (blk), 36
  Nancy, 35, 215
  Nancy (blk), 35
  Sarah A. (blk), 284
GASSENHEIMER
  Pauline, 224
GASSION
  Henrietta (blk), 265
GASTING
  Elizabeth (blk), 58
GATCHEL
  Melissa C., 61
GATELY
  Mary, 144, 182, 230
GATERS
  Sinah (blk), 27
GATES
  Ann Eliza, 96
  Elizabeth, 157, 324
  Elizabeth C., 324
  Henrietta Eliza, 198
  Jane E., 242
  Mary C., 77
  Mary E., 227
  Mary Ellen, 76
  Mary L., 222
  Priscilla, 169
  Salie M., 28
  Sarah A., 118

GATEWOOD
  Ellen, 283
  Frances, 8
  Mary J., 51
GATLEY
  Sarah, 31
GATTENS
  Ellen, 218
GATTO
  Anna, 232
  Maggie, 25
GATTON
  Susan E., 139
GATTRELL
  Mary C., 259
GAUBERT
  Mary, 49
  Sarah A., 24
GAUER
  Catrina F., 322
GAUGHAN
  Jennie, 69
GAULT
  Eliza (blk), 103
GAUSE
  H.R., 193
GAVIN
  Alice, 164
  Margaret, 98
  Maria, 189, 218
GAVIT
  Josephine O., 23
GAVITT
  Elizabeth (blk), 251
GAYLEARD
  Mary A., 308
GAYLOR
  Lizzie, 162
GAYNOR
  Bridget, 131, 147
GAZAWAY
  Hester Ann, 107
GAZZAWAY
  Oceana E. (blk), 87
GEAGE
  Elizabeth, 160
GECKMAN
  Sophia, 265

GEEN
  Isabella (blk), 129
GEERY
  Mary, 281
GEGEL
  Caroline, 250
GEIER
  Josephine, 168
GEIG
  Elizabeth, 69
GEIR
  Emma, 203
GELDMACHER
  Henrietta, 231
GELLA
  Theresa, 198
GELLEMAN
  Emile, 134
GENARD
  Kate, 324
GENNARI
  Mary Jane, 177
GENNET
  Louisa, 214
GENSER
  Eva, 109
GENSLER
  Mary, 20
GENT
  Rosetta, 185
GENTRY
  Isabella J., 87
  Mary C., 200
  Melzena, 117
GENZERODT
  Annie, 284
GENZLE
  Lottie E., 96
GEOGHAN
  Henrietta, 318
GEORGE
  Maria (blk), 96
GERBER
  Elizabeth, 19
  Henrietta, 257
GERHARDT
  Elizabetha, 88

District of Columbia Marriage Licenses, 1858-1870

GERMAN
  Lula Virginia, 55
  Virginia, 187
GERMANN
  Catharine S., 109
GERMON
  Sarah, 285
GERMOND
  Anna M., 114
GERNHARD
  Eliza, 165
GERNHART
  Catherine, 10
GERWIG
  Louisa, 168
GESLER
  Henrietta, 202
GESSFORD
  Luvilla, 246
GETHEN
  Clara V., 49
GETRIDGE
  Margaret (blk), 204
GETSENDEINER
  Mary E., 83
GETTNER
  Sophie, 277
GETZ
  Anna (blk), 316
GETZENDANER
  Catherine, 66
GETZENDEINER
  Mary E., 217
GHEEN
  Isabella, 209
  Margaret, 38
  Mary Etta, 241
GIANNINI
  Annie M.J.C., 95
GIBB
  Annie, 275
  Mary Ann, 128
GIBBINS
  Sarah E., 283
GIBBONS
  Anna, 55
  Elizabeth E., 237
  Ella C., 205
  Ellen, 179

  Emily Adelaide, 208
  Lizzie, 45
  Mary, 106, 128, 257, 272
  Mary Alice, 257
GIBBS
  Elizabeth Ann, 159
  Emmie L., 148
  Georgiana, 198
  Martha (blk), 185
  Mary Ann, 2
  Sarah A. (blk), 141
GIBSON
  Anna, 294
  Catherine A., 38
  Cornelia (blk), 10, 259
  Eliza (blk), 79, 152
  Elizabeth, 68
  Emma L., 214
  Eveline, 293
  Jessie, 178
  Julia, 26
  Kate, 294
  Luellen (blk), 241
  Mary, 36, 173
  Mary C., 173
  Mary E., 36
  Rebecca, 17
  Rosa (blk), 309
  Sarah Jane, 130
GIDDINGS
  Ann Maria, 198
  Elizabeth O., 62
  Mary, 61, 131, 279
  Mary E., 279
  Mary Ellen, 61
  Susannah, 159
GIDEON
  Susie, 59
GIESEKE
  Chalarina, 311
GIFFEN
  Jane, 300
GIFFIN
  Mary A., 315
GIFFORD
  Louisa, 294
  Naomi, 263

GILBERT
  Agnes (blk), 214
  Alice (blk), 264
  Beckie J., 281
  Elizabeth K., 225
  Lizzie, 36
  Sarah M., 25
  Sarah R., 24
GILDS
  Mary (blk), 149
GILES
  Anna (blk), 110
  Ellen (blk), 36
  Margaret (blk), 63
  Sarah J. (blk), 178
GILHELY
  Mary, 83
GILHULY
  Anna, 323
  Honer, 323
GILL
  Anna (blk), 269
  Elizabeth M., 160
  Ellen, 72
  Emily, 135
  Margaret A., 260
  Martha A., 163
  Mary, 320
  Rachel Ann, 13
GILLAM
  Lucy, 295
  Sarah, 31
GILLETT
  Delia, 198
  Mary Louise, 25
GILLIAN
  Jennie, 277
GILLIS
  Louisa (blk), 153
  Mary (blk), 106
GILLISS
  Ailsey (blk), 274
  Rebecca M., 240
GILMAN
  Helen P., 120
GILMORE
  Nellie J., 80

District of Columbia Marriage Licenses, 1858-1870

GING
 Ellen, 138
 Margaret R., 183
GINGELL
 Anna O., 119
GINK
 Mary Ann, 273
GIRAND
 Maria, 76
GIRARD
 Justine (blk), 109
GIRFFY
 Ellen, 188
GIRSCH
 Henrietta, 88
GITTINGS
 Clara V., 318
 Laura E., 322
 Marion, 302
GIVEN
 Jennie, 197
 Mary A., 94
GIVENS
 Louisa (blk), 103
 Lydia (blk), 197
GIVINGS
 Phoebe (blk), 210
GLADDEN
 Alice, 12
 Cornelia, 87
GLADMON
 Emma, 290
GLASCO
 Ellen, 60
 Harriet (blk), 227
 Rachel, 256
GLASCOW
 Elizabeth, 50, 261
GLASGO
 Margaret, 56
GLASGOW
 Birdie (blk), 13
 Harriet (blk), 302
 Rose (blk), 287
GLASSGOW
 Mary Caroline, 21
GLASTER
 Elizabeth (blk), 51

GLAVIN
 Annie, 295
 Catharine, 123
GLAZEBROOK
 Ella C., 270
GLEASON
 Annie, 59
 Ellen, 253
 Mary, 216
GLEAVES
 Rose Ann, 161
GLEESBROOK
 Kate, 161
GLEESEN
 Ellen, 243
GLEESON
 Henora, 170
GLICK
 Matilda, 265
GLIDDEN
 Nellie, 104
GLOVER
 Angeline, 260
 Eliza, 139
 Ella H., 316
 Sarah A., 204
GLUCK
 Margaret, 177
GOBLE
 Frances, 321
GOBRIGHT
 Louise E., 197
GODDARD
 Annie C., 150
 Catherine F., 309
 Charlotte E., 301
 Harriet C., 224
 Lizzie A., 262
 Marion, 224
 Mary A., 184
 Mary Ann, 85
 Rebecca, 269
 Romaine, 300
 Sarah E., 46
 Sarah Ellen, 211
GODEY
 Mary, 82, 197
 Mary J., 82

GODFREY
 Eliza E., 274
 Lucy Ann, 83
 Margaret, 13
 Mary Annie, 34
 Mary M., 161
 Mary Virginia, 175
GODLY
 Mary, 252
GODRON
 Louisa, 177
GODWIN
 Kate M., 186
GOETZ
 Anna Mary, 150
GOGGIN
 Laura V., 144
GOGHAN
 Maria, 84
GOINGS
 Adda (blk), 8
 Jane E., 68
 Malinda (blk), 79
 Myra (blk), 271
GOLDEN
 Catherine A., 47
 Hannah (blk), 154
 Maggie A., 111
 Mary, 73, 205, 321
 Mary A., 73
 Mary E., 205
GOLDING
 Amanda (blk), 147
GOLDMAN
 Amanda, 29
 Veilchen, 277
GOLDSBOROUGH
 Mary Ann, 171
GOLDSMITH
 Elizabeth, 219
 Margaret A., 196
 Mary V., 312
GOLDSTEIN
 Sarah, 229
GOMPF
 Mary, 274
GONSALES
 Martha J., 1

387

GONSALVES
  Mary E., 153
GONZALES
  Ettie A., 53
GOOD
  Amanda (blk), 240
  Ann, 323
  Fannie M., 222
  Johannah (blk), 165
  Mary Ann, 194
  Mary J., 27
  Sallie Jane, 75
GOODHUE
  Sarah A., 211
GOODIN
  Lizzie, 200
GOODING
  Mary (blk), 113
GOODMAN
  Barbara, 274
  Hattie E., 87
  Sarah L., 58
GOODRICH
  Jane R., 31
  Josepha F., 273
  Julia, 195
  Mary, 202, 233, 272
  Mary Ellen, 272
  Mary L., 202
  Nellie C., 238
GOODRICK
  Anna, 250
  Mary A., 52
  Mary F., 223
  Sarah Emma, 199
GOODRICKS
  Laura, 79
GOODSON
  Henrietta, 163
GOODWIN
  Agnes Annie, 120
  Frances E., 234
  Margaret J., 315
  Mary, 140, 221
  Mary (blk), 140
  Rebecca M., 268
GOODYEAR
  Mary Virginia, 28

GOODYER
  Augusta S., 58
GORDIN
  Betsy (blk), 110
GORDON
  Almira E., 208
  Caroline (blk), 22
  Cecilia, 213
  Elizabeth (blk), 185
  Elizabeth A., 90
  Florida, 48
  Georgia, 210
  Hannah, 140
  Jane S., 283
  Josephine L., 275
  Mary, 38, 282
  Mary Ann (blk), 38
  Rebecca (blk), 176, 294
  Rosanna (blk), 186
  Sarah, 157, 210
  Sarah (blk), 157
  Sophia (blk), 318
  Virginia, 228, 264
  Virginia R., 264
GORELL
  Mary, viii, 231
GORMAN
  Bridget, 212
  Catharine, 220
  Joanna, 298
  Johanna, 163
  Rose, 245
GORMLEY
  Kate, 275
  Margaret, 200
GORMON
  Bridget, 136
GOSLIN
  Ann, 197
GOSNELL
  Anna R., 276
GOSSOM
  Martha, 181
GOSZLER
  Sarah, 34
GOTHE
  Malvina E., 143

GOTTI
  Maria Anna, 95
GOULD
  Ellen, 181
  Mary F., 50
GOULEY
  Anna, 61
GOUMPH
  Alice, 264
GOURLEY
  Jennie, 322
  Maggie, 192
GOVER
  Eliza A., 80
GOVININATER
  Philiphina, 256
GOZLER
  Mary Jane, 280
GOZLIN
  Annie, 185
GRABANKAMP
  Anna Mary, 276
GRACE
  Adelaide, 197
  Catharine, 68
  Margaret, 98, 164, 310
  Mary, 48
GRADWOHL
  Rosa, 209
GRADY
  Ann, 187
  Ellen, 99
  Hanora, 70
  Mary Ann, 39
GRAF
  Fannie, 160
  Sophia, 251
GRAHAM
  Ann (blk), 66
  Annie E., 161
  Catherine, 76, 99
  Catherine L., 76
  E.D., 244
  Jannie A., 197
  Joanna (blk), 241
  Maria (blk), 307
  Martha (blk), 40
  Martha L., 264

GRAHAM
  Mary, 34, 195
  Rachel (blk), 280
  Sarah, 141, 285
  Sarah G. (blk), 141
GRAINER
  Lena, 101
GRALISH
  Ann, 108
GRANAY
  Mary, 118
GRANGER
  Eliz. Rebecca, 235
  Jane, 223
  Laura, 140
GRANT
  Alice H., 76
  Betsey (blk), 259
  Bridget, 164
  Carrie S., 234
  Edna (blk), 204
  Eliza, 83, 272
  Elizabeth, 83
  Ellen (blk), 32
  Kitty (blk), 95
  Mary Jane, 111
  Susan, 29, 92
  Susan (blk), 92
GRANTLEN
  Mary Ellen, 158
GRASS
  Lizzie (blk), 279
GRAULICH
  Annie M., 88
GRAVES
  Caroline (blk), 318
  Mary Ann, 130
GRAY
  Abby, 70
  Alice H., 245
  Ann, 73, 132, 297
  Anne Emma, 73
  Catherine, 168
  Charlotte, 23
  Charlotte (blk), 23
  Cornelia (blk), 192
  Eliza (blk), 16, 74
  Elizabeth, 146, 186, 278

  Elizabeth S., 186
  Ella (blk), 152
  Ellen, 323
  Emma D. (blk), 251
  Emma J. (blk), 295
  Frances (blk), 151
  Georgiana (blk), 153
  Jane E., 3
  Julia (blk), 313
  Kate M., 71
  Lethe Ann (blk), 190
  Lizzie (blk), 325
  Lotta (blk), 192
  Louisa (blk), 115
  Lucy (blk), 92, 129
  Margaret, 164
  Mary, 1, 42, 136, 261, 293, 304
  Mary (blk), 42, 136
  Mary E. (blk), 1, 304
  Sarah (blk), 148
  Sarah Ellen, 165
  Susan (blk), 179
  Virginia, 165
  Winney (blk), 115
GRAYSON
  Ann (blk), 249
  Eliza Ann (blk), 12
  Emma J. (blk), 72
  Lavinia (blk), 32
  Mary (blk), 307
  Sarah C., 1
GREASON
  Jennie, 224
GREAVES
  Annie A., 223
  Margaret, 39
  Maria Jane, 98
GREELIS
  Mary, 218
GREEN
  Adaline (blk), 270
  Adolphina, 11
  Amelia E. (col'd), 300
  Anna (blk), 2
  Betsey, 222

  Bridget, 163
  Catherine, 103, 235, 271
  Catherine (blk), 103, 235
  Clementine, 84
  Eliza (blk), 4, 23
  Elizabeth, 4, 44, 137, 191, 250, 259
  Elizabeth (blk), 4, 137, 259
  Ellen, 91, 148
  Ellen (blk), 148
  Emily S., 177
  Emma, 210
  Frances (blk), 268
  Frances A., 67
  Frances Elizabeth (blk), 285
  Harriet (blk), 241, 248
  Helen R., 275
  Imogine, 178
  Jane (blk), 14
  Jeanie (blk), 82
  Jennie (blk), 155
  Julia (blk), 149
  Lizzie Ann, 184
  Louisa (blk), 136
  Louisa K., 175
  Mandy (blk), 319
  Margaret (blk), 103
  Margt. (blk), 181
  Maria (blk), 172
  Martha (blk), 122, 300
  Mary (blk), 98, 158, 203, 292, 302
  Mary A., 38
  Mary Ann, 33, 212
  Mary E., 241
  Mary Eliza (blk), 89
  Mary H., 156
  Mary J., 62
  Mary M., 124
  Melvina, 294
  Patsy (blk), 272
  Rachel (blk), 82

GREEN
  Rebecca, 10
  Sadie A. (blk), 70
  Sarah, 49, 51, 101,
    108, 115, 189,
    222, 312
  Sarah (blk), 51, 189,
    312
  Sarah E., 49
  Sarah Jane (blk),
    101
  Susannah (blk), 181
GREENBAUM
  Amelia M., 227
GREENBAY
  Cinderella (blk), 198
GREENE
  Annie, 94
  Eliza Ann (blk), 127
  Martha J., 304
  Mary (blk), 71
GREENFIELD
  Ann Elizabeth (blk),
    279
  Catherine, 31
  Elizabeth (blk), 48
  Hannah (blk), 236
  Mary L., 195
GREENHOUGH
  Amanda (blk), 327
GREENLEAF
  Catherine (blk), 313
GREENWELL
  Alice, 62
  Charlotte (blk), 327
  Eliza Ann, 297
  Elvira (blk), 117
  Hannah E., 119
  Kate A., 40
  Laura E., 244
  Mary E., 86
  Sarah, 25
GREENWILL
  Georgian (blk), 323
GREENWOOD
  Eliza V., 1
  Mary A., 299
GREER
  Annie (blk), 287

  Caroline, 315
  M.E., 311
  Marion, 171
  Mary E., 228
  Sallie S., 280
GREEVES
  Catherine, 190
  Marion V., 290
GREF
  Maria, 300
GREFF
  Helen, 91
GREGG
  Laura V., 56
GREGORY
  Alice, 91
  Eliza A., 68
  Violet Mc., 317
GRENDLE
  Mary E., 20
GRESS
  Auguste, 281
GREY
  Susan, 257
GRICE
  Ellen V., 176
GRIESLER
  Therese, 238
GRIEVES
  Rose, 221
GRIFFETH
  Lucy A.S.T., 216
GRIFFIN
  Alice H., 204
  Ann, 43, 87, 195
  Anna E., 87
  Annie Elizabeth,
    195
  Bridget, 218, 263
  Cassa Ann (blk),
    288
  Catharine (blk), 70
  Eliza E., 39
  Ellen (blk), 128
  Emma F., 302
  Fanny, 313
  Frances E., 241
  Hanora, 118
  Jane, 158, 163

  Jane (blk), 158
  Jeannie, 20
  Margaret (blk), 155
  Maria (blk), 151
  Mary, 34, 69, 70,
    98, 147, 212, 214,
    218
  Mary Jane, 214
  Sallie Carroll, 92
  Sarah Rebecca, 114
GRIFFITH
  Alice, 45, 54
  Alice C., 45
  Lizzie, 304
  Margaret Ann, 112
  Maria T., 143
  Sarah E., 54, 84
  Sophia, 258
  Thema Ann (blk),
    320
GRIFFITHS
  Louisa, 110
GRIGSBY
  Harriet, 296
  Mary J., 145
  Sarah A., 261
GRILLBORTZER
  Christiana, 15
GRIMES
  Ada, 9
  Ann A. Needen, 45
  Cinderalla E., 119
  Debbie C., 119, 134
  Elizabeth, 89, 311
  Elizabeth (blk), 89
  Ella S., 233
  Helen M., 312
  Henrietta, 215
  Indiana W., 183
  Jane (blk), 252
  Lizzie S., 5
  Mary (blk), 269
  Mary E., 118, 312
  Mary Ellen, 75
  Mary Virginia, 171
  Rebecca, 56
  Sarah E., 169, 243
  Susan, 194
  Winney, 192

GRIMSLY
  Sarah, 275
GRINDALL
  Harriet Amelia, 175
  Juliana (blk), 7
GRINDELL
  Racheal R., 77
GRINDER
  Emma Virginia, 211
GRINER
  Ellen C., 87
  Ellen Maria, 317
  Jane, 302
  Marian, 201
  Sarah Josephine, 289
GRINNELL
  Flinda (blk), 290
  Frances (blk), 266
  Mary Jane, 263
GROËN
  Josepha, 256
GROENER
  Barbara, 264
GROFFMAN
  Augustus, 88, 119
GROGAN
  Bridget, 42
GROH
  Julia, 274
GRONARD
  Ellen C., 59
GRONAU
  Eliza, 183
GROOMS
  Hattie (blk), 142
GROSCH
  Barbara, 211
GROSHARDT
  Catharina, 293
GROSHON
  Ella, 174
  Missouri, 325
GROSS
  Eliza (blk), 18, 289, 326
  Henrietta (blk), 156
  Maria (blk), 35
  Rosana, 283
  Sarah Ann Elizabeth (blk), 133
  Susan, 82, 160
  Susan (blk), 82
GROVE
  Just, 10
  Maria (blk), 15
GROVER
  Mary A.E., 300
  Sarah Alice, 102
  Sarah E., 42
GROVES
  Annie, 255
  Caroline, 265
  Celia Ann, 183
  Georgian (blk), 295
  Maria (blk), 280
GROVEWOOD
  Margaret (blk), 186
GRUBB
  Annie E., 236
  Eliza A., 68
  Louisa, 25
  Pleasant C., 142
  Rose E., 263
  Sarah, 224
GRUDLING
  Caroline, 138
GRUMELL
  Kate V., 177
GRÜNWALD
  Victorine, 268
GUDGIN
  Fanny, 233
  Mary Ann, 291
GUENTHER
  Rose, 165
GUMP
  Sarah, 119
GUMPEL
  Anna, 109
GUNDELSHEIMER
  Anna M., 282
GUNDLING
  Elizabeth, 104
GUNNEL
  Paulina (blk), 5
GUNNELL
  Annie (blk), 94
  Fannie A., 157
  Gertrude, 38
  Harriet (col'd), 120
  Helen M., 317
  Marion R., 182
  May, 28
  Sally E., 122
GUNNISON
  S. Addie, 226
GUNSER
  Catharine F., 314
GUNTLING
  Frances P., 134
GUNTON
  Mary Jane, 287
GURHARDT
  Elizabeth, 174
GURLEY
  Frances M., 90
  Mary C., 120
GURNBERLE
  Sophia, 242
GUSS
  Lucinda, 288
GUSSENBAYER
  Barbara, 242
GUSSEY
  Mary, 242
GUSTA
  Mary (blk), 123
GUTHRIDGE
  Mary V. (blk), 67
GUTHRIE
  Serena, 91
GUTRICK
  Julia E., 314
GUTRIDGE
  Sarah A., 81
GUTTRIDGE
  Verina A., 295
GUY
  Alto V., 64
  Ann Maria (blk), 181
  Anna A., 241
  Eliza J., 143
  Indiana F., 189
  Lydia (blk), 149
  Sarah, 21

District of Columbia Marriage Licenses, 1858-1870

GUYNON
  Julia, 23
GUYTON
  Georgeanna, 119
GWINLEND
  Catharine, 122
GWINN
  Matilda (blk), 174
GYLES
  Mary E., 260

—H—

HAAS
  Johanna, 178
  Louisa, 21
HABBERT
  Mary, 121, 220
HABELT
  Mary, 137
HACKETT
  Mary Ann, 289
HACKLEY
  Martha (blk), 93
  Susan F., 28
HACKNEY
  Sarah, 198
HAEDRICK
  Sarah J., 141
HAFERMAN
  Maria (blk), 117
HAGAMANN
  Alwine, 256
HAGAN
  Elizabeth (blk), 42
  L.A., 77
  Mary Ann, 255
  Sarah Ann, 45
HAGARTY
  Anna E., 41
HAGER
  Mary S., 162
HAGERTY
  Mary, 46, 125
HAGGERTY
  Anne Maria, 104
  Mary, 118
HAGGISON
  Caroline (blk), 12

HAGHERTY
  Annie, 205
HAGLE
  Irma C., 252
HAHN
  Margaret, 180
  Mary Elizabeth, 7
HAILEY
  Bridget, 313
HAILSTOCK
  Julia (blk), 322
HAILSTOW
  Amelia (blk), 130
HAIN
  Amelia, 165
HAINES
  Alice S., 141
  Ellen (blk), 27
  Josephine, 141
  Mary A., 258
HAINEY
  Bridget, 187
  Janie, 299
HAINS
  Eva, 250
  Henrietta S., 143
HAISLIP
  Catharine S., 26
HAKENJOS
  Barbara, 169
HALBERT
  Jemima, 178
  Margaret Ann, 152
HALBUS
  Virginia Mary, 173
HALE
  Anna Maria, 310
  Judy (blk), 260
HALES
  Mary Jane, 189
  Nancy, 194
HALESTORK
  Mary (blk), 305
HALEY
  Catharine, 220
  Jane, 168
HALL
  Adaline (blk), 244
  Adelaide (blk), 188

  Almira Jane (blk),
    316
  Ann, 157, 183, 255,
    326
  Ann (blk), 157
  Anne V., 326
  Annie V., 183
  Augusta (blk), 25
  Caroline (blk), 41
  Caroline V., 66
  Catharine, 1, 15
  Catharine (blk), 1
  Charlotte (blk), 202
  Eliza D., 301
  Elizabeth, 42
  Ellen E., 69
  Emeer F., 200
  Esther, 126
  Etta Jane (blk), 309
  Eveline V., 265
  Fanny (blk), 289
  Harriet, 205, 229
  Harriet (blk), 205
  Hester, 254
  Jane (blk), 273
  Jane C., 26
  Josephine (blk), 292
  Josephine S., 36
  Laura (blk), 187
  Margaret (blk), 110
  Maria A. (blk), 219
  Mary, 69, 93, 118,
    122, 167, 194,
    215, 236, 258,
    267, 284, 301
  Mary (blk), 215,
    284, 301
  Mary Ann, 122
  Mary C., 167
  Mary E., 118, 267
  Mary Frances, 236
  Mary J., 93
  Mary Jane, 258
  Mercy, 62
  Minty (blk), 211
  Nancy (blk), 77
  Nellie Maud, 53
  Percy T., 228
  Rebecca, 18, 75

# District of Columbia Marriage Licenses, 1858-1870

HALL
  Rebecca (blk), 18
  Rebekah, 96
  Rosa E., 10
  Sallie, 73
  Sarah E. (blk), 41
  Sidney (blk), 159
  Susan (blk), 274
  Susan A., 101
  Thirza Virginia, 71
HALLENALFOW
  Catharine, 189
HALLER
  Sophia Ann, 324
HALLEY
  Angeline, 171
  Bettie V., 311
  Sarah E., 67
HALLIGER
  Louisa (blk), 69
HALLOCK
  Marion V., 313
HALLORAN
  Bridget, 110, 138
  Johanna, 205
  Mary, 61
HALPINE
  Bridget, 209
HALSOP
  Annie M.P., 179
HALZFELD
  Mary, 132
HAMAN
  Hannah T., 120
HAMANN
  Lucinda, 105
HAMER
  Fannie, 327
HAMERLING
  Ann Maria, 232
HAMERSON
  Mary Louisa (blk), 317
HAMILL
  Emily Louisa, 186
HAMILTON
  Alice C., 85
  Ann Rebecca, 68
  Edwardanna, 43
  Eliza, 188, 260
  Eliza A. (blk), 260
  Ellen, 116, 224, 298
  Ellen (blk), 116, 224
  Emeline (blk), 34
  Harriet, 137, 248
  Harriet Ann, 137
  Josie F., 146
  Julia N., 55
  Lizzie (blk), 311
  Margaret, 6, 279
  Maria (blk), 33, 242
  Mary A., 280
  Mary C., 291
  Mary H., 215
  Sallie V., 123
  Sarah (blk), 61
  Susan E., 270
HAMLIN
  Amanda M., 17
  Susan (blk), 278
HAMMELL
  Margaret, 6
HAMMER
  Susan E.A., 126
HAMMERSCHLACK
  Sarah, 243
HAMMERSCHLAG
  Harriet, 315
  Julia, 114
HAMMERSLEY
  Mary V., 191
HAMMERSLY
  Catharine, 15
HAMMESCHEAG
  Pauline, 294
HAMMOND
  Amelia, 23
  Catherine (blk), 316
  Emerline (blk), 272
  Lavinia, 93
  Susan A. (blk), 234
HAMMONDS
  Susan (blk), 14
HAMPSHIRE
  Mary (blk), 272
HAMPTON
  Lianna, 156
  Lucy (blk), 192

HAMRICK
  Anna Eliza, 280
HANADY
  Mary (blk), 29
HANAHAN
  Margaret, 320
HANBURY
  Margaret E., 326
HANCOCK
  Ada L., 171
  Eva Drusilla, 24
  Martha A., 75
  Sallie, 171, 246
  Sallie P., 246
HAND
  Mary Ann, 241
HANDLEY
  Ellen, 46
  Mary T., 317
HANDLIN
  Margaret, 196
HANDY
  Elizabeth L., 276
  Feeny (blk), 279
  Julia Ann (blk), 278
  Margaret, 174
  Sciota C., 4
  Shepherd H., 8
HANES
  Mary Ann (blk), 144
HANEY
  Isabella A., 196
  Margaret A., 304
HANFORD
  Mary A., 54
HANKINS
  Lizzie, 103
HANLAN
  Mary, 311
HANLEY
  Julia, 158
  Mary Ann, 247
HANLIN
  Ella, 41
HANLON
  Margaret, 261
  Mary, 200
  Rosanna, 221

District of Columbia Marriage Licenses, 1858-1870

HANNA
  Annie M., 312
HANNAM
  Ellen, 189
HANNAN
  Hanorah, 188
HANNEGAN
  Mary Jane, 113
HANNEN
  Catherine, 9
HANNON
  Catherine, 200
  Cynthie C., 319
HANNY
  A.E., 76
HANREHAN
  Mary E., 103
HANRIHAN
  Mary Ann, 64
HANSELL
  Reburta, 90
HANSLER
  Antonie, 119
HANSON
  Amelia (blk), 216
  Elizabeth, 217
  Georgiana, 290
  Lavinia (blk), 175
  Mary, 276, 326
  Mary E., 326
  W. Maria, 30
HAPP
  Catherine E., 24
HARBAUGH
  Ann E., 204
  Emma F., 298
  Josephine D., 200
  Julia A., 324
  Virginia A., 291
HARBERMEHL
  Adelaide, 190
HARBIN
  Lula, 277
HARDEN
  Catharine A., 39
HARDER
  Charlotte, 173
HARDEST
  Rachael E., 319

HARDESTY
  Georgiana (blk), 233
  Mary E., 319
HARDIE
  Fannie A., 206
  Marie G., 256
HARDIG
  Mary, 257
HARDIN
  Sarah C., 165
HARDING
  Christiana, 120
  Eliza, 15
  Henrietta, 10
  Julia A., 107
  P.C., 101, 125
HARDMAN
  Rabarbara, 309
HARDNETT
  Mary, 90
HARDT
  Martha E., 133
HARDY
  Ann Rebecca, 303
  Henrietta E., 269
  Kate, 102
  Mary M., 143
HARK
  Julia, 243
  Wilhelmina Katherina
  Karoline, 101
HARKINS
  Catharine E., 282
  Ellen, 60
  Margaret, 14
HARKNESS
  Alice J., 249
  Emma E., 71
  Laura A., 167
  Lydia B., 218
  Maggie, 209
  Mary V., 1
HARLAN
  Josephine, 8
  Maria, 322
  Mary, 179
HARLAND
  Lucinda (blk), 258

HARMAN
  Annie, 131
  Margaret A., 110
  Mary Ann, 210
  Priscilla E., 85, 125
  Sallie A., 222
  Sarah A., 168
HARMON
  Ann C., 183
  Catherine, 37
  Mary (blk), 56
  Virginia, 289
HARNER
  Sarah R., 21
HARNETT
  Catharine, 274
HAROLD
  Mary Ann, 215
HARP
  Margaret, 54
HARPER
  Catherine H., 141
  Eliza (blk), 48
  Ellen (blk), 35
  Julia, 6
  Martha, 17
  Mary, 60
  Matilda (blk), 185, 286
  Virginia (blk), 230
HARREN
  Eliza Ann (blk), 271
HARRIGON
  Ellen, 163
HARRINGTION
  Mary A.W., 165
HARRINGTON
  Catherine, 27, 324
  Henrietta (blk), 315
  Johanna, 252
  Julia, 212
  Mary, 100, 278
HARRIS
  Albertha (blk), 251
  Ann C., 59
  Ann Maria (blk), 275
  Anna (blk), 76, 273
  Annie (blk), 64

HARRIS
Bettie, 21
C.L., 109
Caroline (blk), 232
Catharine, 4
Catherine (blk), 140, 289
Catherine C., 178
Charlotte (blk), 287
Clara R. (blk), 231
Eliza (blk), 4, 27, 71
Ellen (blk), 74, 225, 306
Emma (blk), 187
Fannie (blk), 191
Grace (blk), 98
Henrietta, 303
Judah A. (blk), 151
Julia (blk), 34
Lizzie (blk), 27
Maisie Ann (blk), 26
Margaret Ann (blk), 323
Marion A., 313
Martha (blk), 259
Mary, 32, 33, 111, 114, 116, 151, 238, 263
Mary Ann, 32, 151, 263
Mary Anne, 263
Mary E. (blk), 33, 238
Mary Frances (blk), 116
Mary Jane (blk), 111
Matilda, 37, 163
Millie (blk), 324
Rachel (blk), 261
Sarah Ann, 287
Sarah E.D., 320
Susan (blk), 250
HARRISON
Alice, 52
America, 92
Anna Eliza, 196
Annie Amelia, 121
Cynthia, 20, 177
Cynthia A., 20

Elizabeth (blk), 31, 273
Ella, 19
Fanny, 212
Harriet (blk), 235
Jane E., 165
Letta (blk), 244
Lucy Ann, 47, 266
Lucy Ann (blk), 47
Margaret E., 49
Marion, 13
Martha, 16
Mary E., 157
Mary F., 298
Mary Jane, 262
Mary O., 326
Mary R., 156
Mary V., 290
Patience A., 47
Rachel (blk), 106
Rose Ann, 136
Sarah (blk), 251
Sarah C., 94
Sarah Helena, 316
Susan, 215
HARROD
Julietta S., 121
Martha Ellen (blk), 53
Mary G., 38
HARROVER
Georgianna, 64
Sarah A.P., 86
HARROW
Nellie, 318
HARRY
Emily M., 71
Kate, 54
Margaret, 274, 296
Margaret E., 296
Mary Lavinia, 197
Sarah I., 75
HARSCH
Catharine, 1
HARSHMON
Sarah S., 271
HARSTKAMP
Mary E., 39

HART
Annie, 257
Bridget, 186
Caroline, 17
Catherine M., 286
Ellen, 199
Kate, 275
Mary, 83, 204
Mary M., 83
Sarah, 243
HARTICH
Kate, 168
HARTIGAN
Ellen, 66
Mary, 112, 193
Mary Josephine, 193
HARTLEY
Martha F., 56
HARTMAN
Fanny, 134
HARTMANN
Louisa, 75
Maria Anna, 138
HARTNEDY
Helen, 293
HARTNET
Annie, 58
HARTNETT
Ellen, 144
Maggie, 84
Margaret, 38
HARTONSTEIN
Mary, 2
HARTUNG
Annie, 256
Mary, 197
HARVEY
Agatha Elizth., 74
Fannie M., 64
Harriet, 95, 275
Harriet (blk), 275
Mary C., 87
Sarah Elizabeth, 302
HARWOOD
Ella R., 193
Lizzie, 229
Sally A., 8
HASENOHR
Amalie W., 169

HASKELL
  Nancy M., 203
HASKILL
  L.P., 295
HASKIN
  Catherine S., 204
HASKINS
  Emma E., 104
HASLETT
  Annie B., 31
HASLIP
  L.A., 166
HASLUP
  Ellen, 291
HASS
  Josephine, 135
HASSEL
  Anna M., 31
HASSLER
  Mary C., 216
HASTUP
  Kate B., 12
HATER
  Mary, 112
HATEWILL
  Margaret, 68
HATHAWAY
  Mary, 34
HATHMANN
  Mary, 128
HATTER
  Mary E., 166
HATTON
  Eliza (blk), 116
  Martha (blk), 126
  Phebe E., 1
  Sarah (blk), 116
HAUBER
  Katharina, 234
HAUF
  Mary, 277
HAUGH
  Catharine, 127
HAUPTMAN
  Helen C., 46
HAUSCHMAN
  Mary J., 247
HAUSMANN
  Barbara, 123

HAUSTINE
  Sophie, 78
HAVEN
  Delia, 124
HAVENER
  Catherine R., 263
  Mary, 123
  Mary E., 308
  Sarah A.S., 50
HAVERTY
  Julia, 310
HAVILAND
  Caroline C., 192
HAVRESS
  Mary, 65
HAW
  Mary E. (blk), 100
HAWES
  Annie, 168
  Viola M., 326
HAWKEY
  Ann, 246
HAWKINS
  Amelet C., 180
  Ann C. (blk), 51
  Anna (blk), 158
  Annie Augusta, 277
  Annie P., 250
  Caroline (blk), 93
  Catherine, 23
  Clara Ann (blk), 153
  E.A., 107
  Elanora L., 152
  Eliza (blk), 72
  Elizabeth, 126, 149
  Elizabeth (blk), 149
  Ellen, 159, 225
  Ellen (blk), 159
  Evelina, 107
  Frances (blk), 129
  Harriet (blk), 97
  Julia, 271
  Kate (blk), 129
  Lizzie, 48
  Louisa (blk), 99
  Louise (blk), 150
  Margaret (blk), 273
  Margaret Jane (blk), 230

Mary (blk), 192
Mary Catherine
  (blk), 51
Oliver B., 294
Rachel, 236, 286
Rachel (blk), 286
Rebecca (bk), 176
Rebecca (blk), 306
Susan (blk), 69
Virginia (blk), 64, 116
HAWLEY
  A.S., 43
  Wilhelmina, 327
HAWS
  Abby Elizth. Ann, 261
HAWTHORN
  Mary, 114
HAYDEN
  Ann E., 195
  Helen Ann (blk), 101
  Hellen, 93
  Lizzie E., 208
  Mary, 70, 297, 313
  Mary A.C., 313
  Mary Ann, 70
  Sarah E., 129
HAYES
  Ann Eliza, 137
  Annie, 318
  Elizabeth, 290
  Helen M., 148
  Julia, 84
  Margaret, 101
  Matilda Ann (blk), 45
HAYMORE
  Ann, 82
HAYNES
  Arabella L., 249
  Laura Ann (blk), 121
HAYS
  Annie (blk), 61
  Frances M., 74
  Hanora, 94
  Harriet Louisa, 112

HAYS
　Harriet R., 240
　Johanna, 98
　Maria T., 30
　Martha (blk), 145
　Mary, 58, 130, 282, 283, 313
　Mary Ann, 313
　Nancy (blk), 111
HAYSON
　Margaret (blk), 319
HAZARD
　Cornelia Frances, 272
　Eliza A., 228
　Ellen Louise, 146
　Helen H., 28
HAZLE
　Harriet, 295
　Mary, 188
HAZLETT
　Mary J., 283
HEAD
　Lizzie, 177
HEADLEY
　Bertie, 141
HEALEY
　Maggie, 91
　Mary Jane, 238
HEALY
　Elizabeth, 1
　Kate A., 295
　Mary, 30
HEARD
　Sophia, 161
HEARN
　Lizzie A., 205
　Maggie A., 197
HEATH
　Emma Amelia, 89
　Mary Ann, 82
HEATHEY
　Louisa Jane, 247
HEATLEY
　Mary E., 320
HEATON
　Mary A., 130
HEBBS
　Anna, 93

HEBUM
　Alice (blk), 296
HECKLER
　Emma, 291
HEDDEN
　Charlotte R., 28
HEDGEMAN
　Catherine (blk), 47
　Lucy (blk), 36
HEDGES
　Lucy, 84
HEDIGAN
　Bridget, 98
HEERE
　Louisa, 140
HEFFEL
　Mary A., 18
HEFFERN
　Catherine, 249
HEFFNER
　Mary E., 163
HEFLYNN
　Mary Ellen, 99
HEGAN
　Martha V., 193
HEIBERGER
　Emma V., 182
HEIDER
　Mary, 75
HEIGGINS
　Mary, 9
HEIL
　Anna, 258
　Annie, 305
　Elizabeth, 90
　Margaret, 182
HEILAND
　Margaret, 115
HEILBERT
　Kate, 139
HEILBRUN
　Adelaide, 250
　Fanny, 235
HEILEMAN
　Celestine H., 320
HEILMAN
　Bauliene, 38
HEIM
　Josephine, 169

HEIMHOFER
　Walburger, 77
HEINACKE
　Sarah E., 12
HEINE
　Sarah, 135
HEINEMANN
　Maria, 135
HEINS
　Rosa, 97
HEISE
　Charlotte, 168
HEISSMANN
　Miena, 140
HEITMILLER
　Antonie D., 170
　Lizzie, 2
HEITMULLER
　Lena, 132
HEITMÜLLER
　Josephine M., 172
HELD
　Catharine, 301
HELEHAN
　Catharine, 83
HELFISTY
　Anna Piety, 137
HELLE
　Mary, 131
HELLMAN
　Bettie, 141
HELLMUTH
　Ellen, 252
HELMICK
　Jennie B., 207
　Susie E., 38
HELMS
　Charlotte, 231
　Louisa (blk), 181
HELVICH
　Christine Elizabeth, 204
HEMMELWAY
　Mary, 99
HEMSLEY
　Harriet (blk), 139
HENDER
　Agnes Hilldegard, 300

HENDERSON
  Altie, 257
  Catherine O., 275
  Charlotte (blk), 145
  Charlotte S., 86
  Emma, 304
  Estelle V., 227
  Fanny, 73, 155, 223
  Fanny (blk), 155
  Kate, 242
  Letha (blk), 296
  Martha J., 55, 264
  Mary (blk), 143, 175
  Mary Ann, 312
  Phoebe, 226
  Rebecca (blk), 158
  Roberta, 20
  Sallie E., 191
  Susan (blk), 132
HENDLEY
  Sarah Virginia, 311
HENDRETTA
  Margaret, 198
HENKE
  Karolina, 26
HENLEY
  Louisa, 85
HENLY
  Lucy Ann, 237
  Mary Ellen, 65
  Matilda Frances, 169
HENNESSEY
  Marietta, 266
HENNESSY
  Bridget, 83
  Catherine, 163
  Hanora, 220
  Mary E., 211
HENNIGAR
  Elizabeth, 284
HENNING
  Alice C., 73
  Ariana, 276
  Elizth. Virginia, 74
  Frances Adelaide, 231
  Jane, 203
  Margaret E., 200

Mary J., 107
Mary Jane, 130
Rosa, 142
Sallie Clarke, 94
HENNSCH
  Emile, 109
HENRY
  Caroline V., 211
  Catharine, 249
  Ellen (blk), 75
  Isabella, 161
  Kate, 90, 216
  Lucy C., 61
  Mary (blk), 45
  Mary L., 302
  Mary S., 26
  Sallie C., 73
  Susan (blk), 119
HENSEL
  Barbara, 131
HENSHAW
  Ella P., 44
HENSON
  Annie (blk), 192
  Eliza (blk), 73
  Elizabeth (blk), 48
  Ellen (blk), 159, 305
  Emma (blk), 136
  Eveline (blk), 65
  Henrietta (blk), 251
  Jane (blk), 311
  Julia (blk), 285
  Julia Ann Lizzie (blk), 100
  Louise (blk), 296
  Lucinda (blk), 85
  Mary (blk), 155
  Mary Ann (blk), 79
  Mary Ellen (blk), 327
  May (blk), 156
  Sarah (blk), 148
  Susan, 37, 41, 276
  Susan (blk), 37, 41
HEPBURN
  Eliza (blk), 28
  Elizabeth, 248
  Ella F., 242
  Maria (blk), 163

Maria A., 3
Maria O., 310
Mary M., 19
Sarah L. (blk), 248
Susan S., 211
HEPPTING
  Lehna, 135
HERBERT
  Alice E., 95
  Augusta, 265
  Caroline (col'd), 40
  Elizabeth (blk), 216
  Ellen (blk), 107
  Henrietta, 82
  Julia (blk), 157
  Kunhinder, 134, 243
  Lena (blk), 72
  Lizzie G., 39
  Lizzie J., 247
  Louise, 131
  Martha (blk), 47
  Mary C. (blk), 20
  Rebecca (blk), 34
  Sarah A., 182
HERBY
  Louisa (blk), 17
HERENS
  Helen B., 132
HERGESHEIMER
  Mary, 171
HERLIHY
  Mary, 30
HERMES
  Magdalena, 170
HERMOND
  Catherine, 38
  Francis M., 119, 134
HERNONDON
  Mary Elizabeth, 108
HEROLD
  Margaret C., 249
HERON
  Charlotte B., 279
  Ximenia E., 267
HERRAN
  Sarah, 196
HERRICK
  A. Virginia, 230
  M.E., 53

District of Columbia Marriage Licenses, 1858-1870

HERRMANN
 Mary, 255
HERRON
 Mary Josephine, 221
HERTY
 Mary Ann, 283
HERTZING
 Magadelana, 71
HERZINGER
 Lena, 319
HERZZOG
 Amelia, 128
HESBERGER
 Eliza, 239
HESS
 Amelia Martha, 311
 Ann, 146
 Caroline, 34
 Eliza, 135, 189, 277
 Elizabeth, 189, 277
 Ester, 256
 Lucinda, 120
 Mary, 132, 223
 Susie, 259
HESSEMER
 Abbie J., 29
HESSLER
 Eva, 82
HESSTER
 Mary, 195
HESTER
 Charlotte (blk), 113
HETHINGER
 Caroline, 131
HEUSTIS
 Martha E., 162
HEVERN
 Mary Jane (blk), 18
HEWETT
 Florence, 136
HEWITT
 Florence, 136
HEXTER
 Elizabeth, 15
 Mary, 265
HEYN
 Ida, 102
HEYRICH
 Kate, 328

HEYSE
 Ida, 300
HICKEY
 Ann, 207
 Carrie J., 83
 Cecelia, 232
 Margaret, 13, 213, 324
 Rosalie, 131
HICKHOCK
 Louisa, 2
HICKMAN
 Ann Maria, 268
 Elizabeth Ann (blk), 183
 Sarah C., 122
HICKS
 Adelaide E., 188
 Charlotte (blk), 51
 Elizabeth E. (blk), 58
 Emily S. (blk), 89
 Frances, 315
 Jane E., 267
 Joanna (blk), 311
 Lizzie, 223
 Martha, 15, 43
 Mary (blk), 26
 Mary Jane, 315
 Rebecca A., 23
 Rosa B., 97
 Sarah, 204, 209, 270
 Sarah F., 270
 Sarah J., 209
 Virginia, 233
HIEL
 Sophia, 205
HIESTON
 Jane A., 278
HIETER
 Charlotte, 121
HIGDEN
 Eliza Regina, 160
HIGDON
 Mary Ann, 50
HIGGINS
 Bettie, 198
 Elizabeth, 211
 Ellen, 24

 Marian K., 93
 Mary (blk), 47
 Mary A., 230
 Ruth M., 306
 Sarah, 108, 236
 Sarah E., 108
 Winifred, 292
HIGGS
 Leathe Ann, 260
 Sallie E., 85
HIGHFIELD
 Lavinia D., 223
HIGHLAND
 Catharine T., 282
HIGHT
 Catherine, 106
 Sarah, 201
HILB
 Pauline, 169
HILBERT
 Catherine, 230
HILBRUSH
 Mary E., 49
HILBUS
 Josephine, 137
 Mary Ann, 182
 Sarah, 201
 Susan E., 185
HILDEBRAND
 Martha, 321
HILDENBRADT
 Annie, 202
HILL
 Alice, 199, 278
 Alice A., 278
 Alsyndy, 115
 Amelia, 92
 Ann (blk), 295
 Betsy (blk), 318
 Celia (blk), 320
 Charlotte, 171, 239
 Charlotte Ann, 171
 Clara A., 104
 Eliza (blk), 278
 Elizabeth, 7, 80
 Elizabeth (blk), 80
 Emma G., 49
 Fanny (blk), 32
 Francis (blk), 50

399

HILL
 Hannah (blk), 136
 Harriet (blk), 104,
  270
 Helen, 32
 Isabella (blk), 12
 Jane (blk), 321
 Joanna, 206
 Johanna, 45
 Julia, 194
 Laura, 227
 Mahala (blk), 317
 Margaret (blk), 106
 Maria J. (blk), 269
 Mary, 18, 85, 125,
  136, 159, 243,
  252, 291
 Mary (blk), 252
 Mary, 18
 Mary Ann (blk), 136
 Mary J., 159
 Mary Jane (blk), 125
 Mary R., 291
 Mary Wilson, 243
 Rosa (blk), 212
 Sallie (blk), 252
 Sarah A., 23
 Sarah C., 263
 Susan (blk), 136
 Susanna Francis,
  223
HILLEARY
 Sarah Ann, 41
 Sarah M., 232
 Sarah W., 274
HILLER
 Louisa, 34
HILLERY
 Emmeline (blk), 51
HILLIARD
 Catherine, 164
 Kate S., 89
HILLIARY
 Susan, 109
HILLMANN
 Louisa, 258
HILTON
 Annie, 270
 Elizabeth, 277

Martha A., 47
Sarah L., 125
HILZHEIM
 Rachel, 302
 Rebecca, 103
 Sarah, 150
HINDES
 Sarah, 141
HINDS
 Alice, 157
 Anna, 52
 Bridget, 65
 Catharine, 30
 G.I., 245
 Lizzie M., 226
 Margaret A., 128
HINE
 Eliza, 238
 Mary, 38
HINELINE
 Rose D., 186
HINEMAN
 Arynthia Catherine,
  326
HINES
 Catharine, 142
 Emma, 131
 Gracy (blk), 292
 Margaret, 163, 176
 Mary, 60, 240
 Mary Elizabeth, 240
 Rebecca A., 324
HINLY
 Mary A., 187
HINRIDA
 Johanna CHristian,
  114
HINSON
 Anna (blk), 66
 Lucinda, 37
HINTON
 Jennie, 44
 Mary E., 177
HINÜBER
 Minna, 117
HINYON
 Jenny Ann, 198
HINZEL
 Carolina, 214

HIPKINS
 Margaret (blk), 250
HIRBITZ
 Sophie, 6
HIRSCH
 Lene, 201
HIRSCHENHEIMER
 Catherine, 215
HIRSCHFIELD
 Elizabeth, 138
HIRST
 Allie R., 321
HIRT
 Regina Barbara, 26
HITCHCOCK
 Eunice S., 89
 Martha E., 237
HITT
 Fanny (blk), 95
HOAGAN
 Annie, 128
HOAGLAND
 Annie M., 1
HÖB
 Mary, 309
HOBBIE
 Ellen G., 249
 Frances P., 225
HOBBS
 Ellen (blk), 297
 Margaret Ann (blk),
  50
 Sarah E., 324
HOBIN
 Susanna J., 155
HOBSON
 Carrie, 247
HOCH
 Katherina Jacobina,
  78
HODDINOTT
 Alice V., 217
HODGE
 Elizabaeth, 62
 Elizabeth Ann (blk),
  247
 Georgianna, 106
 Mary Louise, 42

HODGES
 Anna Eliza, 240
 Ariana (blk), 271
 Catherine C., 244
 Mary A., 122
 Mary E., 62
 Virginia, 55, 173
HODGSON
 Christiana A., 10
 Martha E., 53
HOEFER
 Dora, 202
HOESING
 Elizabeth, 121
HOFF
 Fredricka, 303
HOFFMAN
 Elizabeth A., 139
 Ellen, 180
 Georgianna (blk), 192
 Isabella, 327
 Mary, 43, 45, 139, 280
 Mary Jane, 45
HOFFMANN
 Eliza, 77
HOFLER
 Virginia A., 67
HOGAN
 Ann, 198, 218
 Anna, 218
 Ella A., 102
 Frances, 105
 Hanora, 99
 Harriet, 209
 Joanna, 212
 Mary Ann, 203
 Matilda (blk), 183
 Sophia L., 202
HOGANS
 Jane (blk), 234
 Nancy, 185
HOGE
 Roberta V., 66
HOGG
 Mary, 141, 151
 Sarah, 168

HOHENSTEIN
 Mary Ann, 257
 Sarah, 131
HOHLSCHUH
 Katherine, 78
HOHN
 Hannah, 104
HOLBROKE
 Margaret (blk), 132
HOLBROOK
 Anna E., 85
HOLD
 Lydia, 118
HOLDEN
 Bridget, 39
HOLDSWORTH
 Sarah E., 68
HOLFORD
 Louisa, 167
HOLIN
 Mary Ann, 200
HOLKER
 Mary, 313
HOLLAK
 Betsy, 322
HOLLAND
 Annie, 125
 Bridget, 35
 Charlotte, 120
 Christiana (blk), 309
 Harriet Ann (blk), 78
 Johanna, 79
 Kate, 60
 Sarah, 64
HOLLANDS
 Jane (blk), 113
HOLLEY
 Addie, 131
 Adelaide (blk), 144
 Carrie M., 321
HOLLIDAY
 Emiline (blk), 32
 Martha, 282
 Sue B., 303
HOLLIES
 Mary Elizabeth, 315
HOLLING
 Anna W. (blk), 149

HOLLINGSWORTH
 Hester Frances, 11
HOLLINS
 Mary (blk), 270
HOLLIS
 Laura A. (blk), 184
 Sarah (blk), 191
HOLLISTER
 Mary D., 7
HOLLOHAN
 Abby, 123
 Mary E., 97
HOLLORAN
 Bridget, 13, 302
 Mary, 199
HOLMAN
 Margaret, 37
HOLMEAD
 Ada Augusta, 238
 Elizabeth A., 145
 Mary E., 191
HOLMES
 Angie A., 91
 Ann (blk), 157
 Annie E. (blk), 186
 Antoniette, 279
 Bettie (blk), 18
 Betty (blk), 327
 Catharine (blk), 266
 Eliza, 117
 Evelina (blk), 287
 Frances (blk), 179
 Harriet (blk), 252
 Julia A. (blk), 147
 Kesiah (blk), 241
 Mary (blk), 89, 140, 237, 316
 Mary Jane (blk), 268
 Sarah, 143
 Susan C., 20
 Virginia, 167
HOLOHAN
 Rose C., 106
HOLORAN
 Mary Ann, 30
HOLROYD
 Isabella V., 199
 Josephine M., 209
 Sarah E., 31

HOLSAPPLE
  Hannah E., 287
HOLSTEIN
  Bettie T., 68
  Elizabeth, 170
HOLT
  Anna C., 233
  Annie, 127
  Henrietta J., 22
  Mary M., 147
HOLTER
  Kate A., 55
HOLTZMAN
  Lizzie, 257
HOMER
  Isabella, 86
HOMILLER
  Catharine, 140
  Isadora, 49
HONESTY
  Ellen (blk), 306
  Harriet E. (blk), 46
  Lavinia (blk), 319
  Maria L. (blk), 34
  Mary (blk), 44
HONNER
  Margaret, 125
HONNET
  Mathilde, 134
HOOD
  Angeline (blk), 289
  Rose Berta (blk), 150
HOODLEMEYER
  Julia, 137
HOOE
  Catherine (blk), 55
  Mary F., 9
HOOK
  Cora, 279
HOOKER
  Anna Eliza, 47
HOOPER
  Annie L., 165
  Frances Odelia, 96
  Martha (blk), 238
HOOVER
  Eliza T., 275
  Indiana H., 182

Margaret A., 219
Mary E., 303
HOPEWELL
  Fannie (blk), 316
HOPKINS
  Abbie Louise, 14
  Alice C., 122
  Annie Sophia, 70
  Betsey (blk), 206
  Caroline, 258
  Eldrianna A., 180
  Helen (blk), 319
  Jane N., 87
  Kate, 95
  Maria, 128
  Martha, 271
  Mary E., 43, 213
  Mary M., 234
  Mary V. (blk), 125
HOPLEY
  Annie, 98
HOPPS
  Mary J., 102
HOPSON
  Mary, 131
HORAN
  Catherine, 84
  Kate, 70
HORE
  Mary Ellen, 312
HORIED
  Frank (blk), 297
HORN
  Annie, 298
  Catherine, 182
  Margaret T., 249
HORNBAG
  Kuna, 102
HORNBERGER
  Elizabeth D., 147
  Mary H., 264
HORNE
  Hattie L., 298
  Louise, 195
HORNER
  Anna M., 73
  Matilda, 237
  Rosa, 132
  Tulip, 137

HÖRNER
  Lizzetti, 129
HORNING
  Minne, 144
HORRIGAN
  Ellen, 175, 199
  Margaret, 44
HORSE
  Laura, 228
HORSEMAN
  Catherine, 244
  Emily J., 281
  Jane, 319
HORSMAN
  Rosie, 223
HORTON
  Mary, 10
  Virginia E., 297
HORTZMAN
  Julia, 121
HOSEY
  Elizabeth, 177
HOSKIN
  Kate F., 267
HOSKINS
  Susan, 49
HOSMER
  Mary, 270
HOST
  Ann Madora, 80
HOTTENFELLER
  Ellen, 23
HOUGH
  Anna F., 231
  Elmira, 78
HOUGHMAN
  Mary, 142
HOUGHTILLING
  Ida, 19
HOUGHTON
  Margaret Emma, 322
  Mary Ann, 178
  Ophelia E., 233
HOULEHAN
  Bridget, 167
HOULIHAN
  Bridget, 325

HOUSE
  Annie S., 48
  Martha A., 283
HOUSER
  Deliverance Ann, 187
HOUSEWRIGHT
  Margaretta, 321
HOUSTON
  Gertrude L., 319
  Sallie H., 314
HOVENCAMP
  Sarah J., 144
HOWARD
  Alice E. (blk), 175
  Ann D. (blk), 116
  Ann O., 76
  Annie (blk), 153
  Betty (blk), 205
  Caroline (blk), 289
  Catharine (blk), 275
  Celia, 142
  Charity, 63
  Cordelia Ann (blk), 143
  Eliza, 182, 193, 222
  Eliza (blk), 182
  Elizabeth J.S., 222
  Ellen, 51
  Emma, 71
  Fannie F., 121
  Frances (blk), 327
  Frances Anne, 315
  Hellen A., 303
  Henrietta, 13
  Isabella, 195, 227
  Isabella (blk), 227
  Jane, 35, 69, 87, 105, 221, 317
  Jane (blk), 35, 87, 317
  Julia (blk), 306
  Julia, 47
  Kattie (blk), 41
  Laura Louisa, 142
  Laura Va., 236
  Louisa, 54
  Lucy (blk), 313
  Margaret, 104
  Mary, 15, 77, 134, 137, 195, 204, 232, 268, 284, 316, 326
  Mary (blk), 77, 204
  Mary A., 232
  Mary C. (blk), 284
  Mary E., 326
  Mary J. (blk), 316
  Mary Jane (blk), 137
  Mary V., 15
  Milly (blk), 227, 299
  Miranda (blk), 53
  Nellie, 137
  Phebe, 86
  Roseanna, 113
  Susan (blk), 59, 272
  Susannah (blk), 48
HOWE
  Lucinda, 252
  Mary Virginia, 146
  Rebecca M., 277
  Sarah E., 177
HOWELL
  Emily, 25
  Maggie, 311
  Mary (blk), 324
  Mary Ann, 323
  Mary E., 103
  Sarah Jane, 210
HOWISON
  Lucretia, 12
HOWLAND
  Ellen, 283
HOWLE
  Mary E., 70
HOWLETT
  Mary, 44, 90
  Mary A., 90
HOWRAN
  Sarah Jane, 123
HOWSE
  Sarah S., 67
HOWSER
  Catherine F., 157
  Margaret E., 151
HOYDEN
  Jennie, 137
HOYLE
  Susan Ann, 285
HOYNE
  Maggie, 166
  Mary, 81
HUBBARD
  Mary, 67
  Rebecca (blk), 308
  Sarah (blk), 297
HUBBELL
  Anna, 252
HUBER
  Christina L., 300
HUBNER
  Maggie, 251
HÜBNER
  Margaretta, 120
HUCKSOLL
  Sophie, 140
HUDDLESON
  Harriet, 284
HUDGINS
  Susan, 41
HUDLOE
  Elizabeth, 169
  Sarah, 190
HUDLOW
  Lucretia, 202
HUDSON
  Elizabeth, 28
HUESTIS
  Almira L., 24
HUFF
  Mary Jane, 181
HUFFMAN
  Caroline, 159
  Catherine, 267
HUGHES
  Annie (blk), 251
  Catherine (blk), 156
  Cordelia, 34
  Eliza J., 237
  Ellen, 77
  Georgeana, 117
  Harriet J. (blk), 104
  Jennie (blk), 317
  Johanna, 97
  Lucy, 225, 281
  Lucy A., 225

HUGHES
  Mary, 56, 94, 140, 234
  Mary E. (blk), 56
  Mary Elizabeth, 140
  Mary Ellen, 94
  Mollie J., 57
  Rebecca, 72
  Rose, 207
  Sophia C.W., 202
  Susan V., 174
HUGHLETT
  Frances A., 208
HÜGLE
  Theresa Virgini, 301
HUGUELY
  Addie Emmett, 320
HUHN
  Eugenie, 177
  Rosina, 24
  Virginia, 327
HULL
  Julia A., 282
  Margaret E., 101
HULLS
  Margaret (blk), 109
  Martha, 188
HUMBACH
  Francisco, 166
HUME
  Ella A., 70
  Mary A., 147
HUMPHREY
  Elizabeth, 117
  Martha Ann, 131
HUMPHREYS
  Anna, 146
  Caroline, 24
  Delia, 172
  Jane, 266
  Louisa, 230
  Mary A.E. (blk), 46
  Mary Ellen (blk), 148
  Sarah Ann, 173
HUMPHRIES
  Annie, 11
HUMPKINS
  Eliza R., 267

HUNGERFORD
  Eleanor, 312
HUNLEY
  Fannie (blk), 309
HUNNICUTT
  Milley (blk), 145
HUNT
  Celestia A., 95
  Electa, 208
  Elizabeth, 120
  Emma J., 125
  Joanna, 25, 171
  Joanna L., 171
  Josephine S., 323
  Laura, 261
  Mary E., 74
  Phillis A. (blk), 246
  Rosa D., 264
  Sarah, 45
  Susan, 290
HUNTER
  Alice, 239, 245
  Alice Jane, 239
  Anna R., 62
  Catherine, 218
  Clara F., 91
  Elizabeth, 70
  Hariett A., 17
  Isabel L., 45
  Julia Herbert, 128
  Lucinder, 60
  M. Alice, 57
  Margaret, 61
  Maria, 15
  Martha, 72, 197
  Martha A., 197
  Mary, 243, 272
  Nancy (blk), 310
  Phebe, 249
  Sophia, 134
HUNTINGTON
  Elizabeth A., 71
  Susan, 13
HUNTT
  Emeline, 198
  Fannie Maria, 109
  Harriet, 323
  Mary, 68, 171
  Mary A., 171

HURD
  Elizabeth (blk), 218
  Mary (blk), 178
HURDLE
  Alice M., 275
  Beattie, 173
  Emily, 180
  Fannie E., 76
  Josephine, 168
  Lavinia E., 9
  Marian M., 53
  Martha D., 53
  Mary E., 58
HURLEY
  Ann, 137, 167, 169, 220, 282
  Ann (blk), 137
  Anna, 167
  Annie, 169, 282
  B.F.M., 146, 218
  Bridget, 156
  Catharine E., 257
  Frances E., 234
  Jane, 43
  Julia, 60, 118
  Margaret, 57
  Mary, 70, 135
  Mary Jane, 135
  Rosa (blk), 258
  Susan, 48
HURLY
  Margaret G., 51
HURNEY
  Ann, 60
  Catharine C.A., 218
  Mary, 81
HURST
  Margaret A., 89
  Mary, 15
HURT
  Louisa, 59
HUSER
  Celia, 75
HUSLEY
  Ann, 220
HUSSEY
  Ellen, 293
HUTCHERSON
  Emma J., 101

HUTCHESON
  Mary E., 31
HUTCHINGS
  Susan A., 214
HUTCHINS
  Ann Arie, 224
  Celena, 108
  Julia A., 108
  Laura V., 58
  Mary J., 224
HUTCHINSON
  Emma, 19
  Laura E. (blk), 105
  Laura W., 227
  Margaret, 120
  Mary, 9, 164
  Mary J., 9
  Rachel (blk), 107
  Sarah E., 213
  Sarah Jane, 165
  Sarah R., 150
HUTCHISON
  Ann E., 319
  Elizabeth Ellen, 280
  Sarah A., 206
HUTTON
  Annie E., 320
  Ellen Salome, 147
  Emma V., 288
  Harriet (blk), 204
  Mary C., 112
HUTZLER
  Margaret, 166
HYATT
  Eliza J., 97
  Ellen A., 216
  Emma S., 38
  Kate E., 164
HYDE
  Catharine E., 50
  Margaret, 200
  Mary, 105, 249
  Mary J., 105
  Sarah A., 107
  Virginia, 51
HYESETT
  Mary J., 88

HYNES
  Catharine, 164
  Mary, 238
HYSON
  Elizabeth (blk), 296, 316

—I—

IESELSOHN
  Malchen, 233
IGNORANT
  Mary (blk), 79
IGO
  Margaret, 49
IMAGNONE
  Costanza, 255
IMES
  Mary (blk), 106
INFIEF
  Elizabeth C., 261
INGERSOLL
  Alice C., 49
  Georgie, 76
  Sallie T., 326
INGLEBRIGHT
  Margaret V., 291
INGRAHAM
  Georgianna (blk), 232
  Hannah, 286
INZOR
  Annie E., 267
IREWIN
  Mary, 104
IRONTING
  Elizabeth, 223
IRVIN
  Constance, 183
  Mary F., 256
IRVING
  Elizabeth, 38
  Gertrude E., 106
  Sarah, 50
  Susan Elizabeth, 257
IRWIN
  Sarah R., 157

ISAACS
  Rebecca, 16
ISDELL
  Mary E., 93
ISEMANN
  Barbara, 303
ISER
  Mary, 185
ISH
  Mary, 203
ISHERWOOD
  Maggie, 122
ISSAMANN
  Margaretta, 188
IVEY
  Helen L., 303

—J—

JACK
  Ella G., 11
  Mary Ann, 108
JACKEL
  Matilda, 104
JACKS
  Rachel (blk), 258
JACKSON
  [blank], 204
  Adeline (blk), 319
  Alice, 8
  Amanda (blk), 288
  Amelia (blk), 4
  An (blk), 131
  Ann (blk), 78, 254, 294
  Ann Maria (blk), 207
  Anna (blk), 50, 57, 273, 323, 325
  Annie (blk), 28, 183
  Annie E., 201
  Annie M., 283
  Annie Virginia, 113
  Catherine, 5
  Cecilia (blk), 34, 93
  Celina (col'd), 139
  Charlotte, 94, 163, 206, 227

JACKSON
　Charlotte (blk), 94,
　　163, 206
　Dorothea L., 265
　Eliza (blk), 17, 19,
　　31, 187, 286
　Eliza Ann (blk), 18
　Elizabeth, 14, 40,
　　44, 130, 149, 305
　Elizabeth (blk), 14,
　　40, 44, 130, 305
　Ella (blk), 153
　Ellen, 150
　Emily (blk), 293
　Emma, 82, 113, 213,
　　243
　Emma (blk), 82,
　　113, 213
　Esther, 14
　Fanny (blk), 117,
　　167, 254
　Frances (blk), 181
　Hannah (blk), 33
　Harriet, 93, 148, 301
　Harriet (blk), 148
　Harrison (blk), 76
　Hattie, 232
　Henrietta (blk), 127
　Hester, 123
　Jane (blk), 92
　Judy Ann (blk), 148
　Julia (blk), 1, 318
　Kate (blk), 115, 129
　Laura (blk), 45, 284
　Laura Maria (blk),
　　145
　Lavinia (blk), 306
　Letitia (blk), 248
　Letty (blk), 209
　Louisa (blk), 72,
　　287
　Lucinda (blk), 100
　Lucy, 2, 57, 79, 175
　Lucy (blk), 2, 175
　Lucy Ann (blk), 57
　Lydia A., 238
　Margaret (blk), 12,
　　17, 131, 172, 278
　Margaret R. (blk),
　　176
　Maria, 1, 100, 293
　Maria (blk), 100
　Maria (col'd), 293
　Martha, 38, 103,
　　179, 212
　Martha (blk), 38,
　　103
　Martha A. (blk), 212
　Mary, 12, 30, 37,
　　48, 61, 65, 106,
　　116, 129, 148,
　　215, 226, 285,
　　307
　Mary (blk), 30, 48,
　　65, 106, 116, 129,
　　215, 226
　Mary A. (blk), 61
　Mary E. (blk), 116
　Mary Ella (blk), 61
　Mary Ellen, 148,
　　285
　Mary R., 12
　Matilda, 57, 109
　Matilda (blk), 109
　Mollie (blk), 149
　Olivia, 57, 153
　Phidelia (blk), 32
　Rachel, 44, 84
　Rachel (blk), 44
　Rose (blk), 27
　Rosetta (blk), 57
　Sarah (blk), 52, 291
　Sarah Ann (blk),
　　320
　Sarah D., 269
　Sophie D., 12
　Susan (blk), 39, 55
　Sylvia, 40, 175
　Virginia, 168, 181
　Winnie (blk), 230
JACOBI
　Ada H., 273
JACOBS
　Caroline E., 78
　Catherine, 284
　Christina, 284
　Elizabeth D., 86
　Emma, 291
　Harriet C., 20
　Kate Adelaide, 320
　Lotta, 114
　Mary, 247
　Sarah V., 10
　Sidney (blk), 53
JACOBSEN
　Jenny, 229
JACOBSON
　Emma C., 88
JACOBUS
　Sarah L., 28
JAGER
　Emily, 53
JAMES
　Catharine M., 126
　Catherine (blk), 259
　Cecelia M., 16
　Ellen, 208
　Emily (blk), 301
　Hannah F., 102
　Helen, 82
　Isabella (blk), 116
　Jennie, 8
　Laura, 27
　Marsaline (blk), 298
　Mary Ann, 128
　Mary W., 262
　Sarah E., 75
JAMESON
　J. Roberta, 270
JANNEY
　Eliza Ann, 11
JANVIER
　Janie B., 101
　Mary A., 217
JARBOE
　Elizabeth, 101
　Elizabeth R., 309
　Margaret R., 131
　Mary H., 6
　Sarah Jane, 319
JASPER
　Henrietta (blk), 42
　Julia (blk), 148
JAVEN
　Frances, 297

**JAVINS**
 Annie, 266
 Mary A., 280
 Mary Jennie, 227
**JAY**
 Hanorah, 134
 Indiana, 217
 Virginia, 19
**JAYCOCK**
 Catherine (blk), 159
**JEAN**
 Caroline C., 260
**JEFFERIES**
 Mary F., 285
**JEFFERS**
 Martha, 105
**JEFFERSON**
 Catharine, 180
 Chloe (blk), 14
 Frances (blk), 306
 Georgiana, 224
 Georgianna (blk), 113
 Laura C., 252
 Martha (blk), 177
 Mary A., 166
 Sally (blk), 151
**JEFFRIES**
 Sylvia Ann, 306
**JENIFER**
 Cecila (blk), 147
 Charlotte (blk), 41
 Elizabeth (blk), 47
 Lizzie (blk), 184
 Martha (blk), 17
 Mary (blk), 151
 Sarah (blk), 52, 251
**JENKINS**
 Adelaide, 98
 Ann R., 99, 299
 Anna (blk), 244
 Annie, 173, 229
 Annie (blk), 173
 Caroline, 217
 Cornelia T., 185
 Delia A., 287
 Ella Abbie, 190
 Ellen (blk), 140
 Harriet (blk), 285
 Jane, 166, 222
 Jane J., 222
 Julia A., 112
 Laura Virginia, 266
 Lucinda, 207
 Lucretia (blk), 151
 Lydia, 24
 Maggie, 99
 Margaret, 32, 56, 261
 Margaret A., 261
 Margaret E., 32
 Margt. E., 289
 Marion F., 267
 Martha E. (blk), 206
 Mary, 77, 80, 110, 291
 Mary (blk), 291
 Mary F., 80
 Mary J., 77
 Olivia, 291
 Polly (blk), 307
 Sarah M., 79
 Susan, 154, 254
 Susannah, 154
**JENNEY**
 Sophia S., 51
**JENNINGS**
 Elizabeth, 160
 Florence (blk), 31
 Frances (blk), 156
 Julia A., 152
 Lucy A.B., 270
 Willie Ann, 26
**JERMON**
 Mary E., 274
**JESSELSON**
 Barbara, 239
**JETT**
 Georgia, 235
 Mary, 228, 318
 Mary Frances, 228
**JEWELL**
 Anne, 206
 Mary Ives, 280
**JEWETT**
 Lucy (blk), 222
**JIDTS**
 Mary Jane, 267
**JIMASON**
 Eliza (blk), 144
**JOACHIM**
 Anna M., 45
**JOCKEL**
 Catherine, 7
**JÖHANNING**
 Josephine, 275
**JOHN**
 Elizabeth, 247
**JOHNS**
 Annie (blk), 316
 Elizabeth, 178
 Maria C., 210
**JOHNSIN**
 Charity (blk), 101
**JOHNSON**
 Adaline, 146
 Adeline (blk), 132
 Agnes (blk), 113, 155
 Airy (blk), 16
 Alexzina (blk), 103
 Alice (blk), 37, 89, 116
 Alice R. (blk), 176
 Alice Virginia (blk), 306
 Almira (blk), 78
 Amanda (blk), 24
 America J., 8
 Ann (blk), 105, 152, 304
 Ann M. (blk), 108
 Anna, 17, 74, 101, 103, 152, 155, 318
 Anna (blk), 17, 74, 101, 152, 318
 Anna E. (blk), 103
 Annie (blk), 35
 Annie E., 3
 Barbara, 185
 Betsey (blk), 126
 Betsy, 119
 Blanche, 223
 Caroline (blk), 92, 179, 313
 Carrie, 261

JOHNSON
Catharine (blk), 101
Catherine (blk), 156
Charity (blk), 247
Charlotte (blk), 258, 296
Charlotte Victoria, 121
Delia, 256
E. Pauline, 119
Elia (blk), 51
Eliza, 20, 22, 114, 124, 130, 132, 157, 179, 202, 247, 263, 267, 308
Eliza (blk), 22, 114, 179, 202
Elizabeth, 124, 130, 132, 157, 263, 267
Elizabeth (blk), 132
Elizabeth Lizzie A., 130
Elizabeth H. (blk), 124
Elizth., 250
Ella, 164
Ellen, 62, 140, 152, 155, 228, 288, 313, 315
Ellen (blk), 62, 140, 152, 155, 228, 313, 315
Emeline (blk), 80
Emeline (col'd), 316
Emily (blk), 65, 234
Emma, 114, 214, 248, 296
Emma (blk), 248, 296
Eveline, 91
Fanny (blk), 34, 192, 245
Frances (blk), 245
Hannah, 6, 48, 50, 204, 276
Hannah (blk), 6, 48, 204

Hannah A. (blk), 276
Harriet (blk), 248, 302
Henrietta (blk), 267
Huldah P., 3
India, 296
Iowa, 204
Isabell (blk), 57
Isabella, 21, 128
Jane, 282, 284
Jane (blk), 282
Jeannette, 60
Jennie, 23, 24, 164
Jennie (blk), 23, 24
Jerusha (blk), 288
Joanna (blk), 271
Josephine, 62, 74, 244, 326
Josephine (blk), 244, 326
Josephine Arnice Charlotte, 74
Julia, 74, 118, 234, 247, 259
Julia A., 247
Julia Anna (blk), 118
Juliana (blk), 234
Kate, 73
Kitty (blk), 286
Lavinia (blk), 5
Lavinia Virginia (blk), 114
Lethe (blk), 54
Levian (blk), 16
Lilly, 228
Lizzie (blk), 69
Louisa, 44, 226, 264, 297
Louisa (blk), 226, 297
Louise (blk), 268
Lucinda (blk), 22
Lucy (blk), 129
Lucy Ann, 20, 159, 297
Lucy Ann (blk), 159

Lydia Ann (blk), 127
Madora Ellen, 2
Malvina, 41
Margaret, 51, 156, 263
Margaret (blk), 156
Margaret Ann, 51
Maria, 1, 25, 40, 248
Maria (blk), 1, 40
Maria Jane (blk), 25
Marshy (blk), 319
Martha (blk), 44, 157, 271, 290, 317
Martha Ann (blk), 113
Martha Ellen (blk), 300
Martha Virginia (blk), 39
Mary, 22, 26, 41, 50, 68, 71, 87, 115, 130, 136, 139, 140, 151, 152, 156, 159, 214, 260, 278, 289, 301, 306, 326
Mary (blk), 22, 50, 71, 152, 156, 301, 326
Mary (col'd), 151
Mary A., 289
Mary Ann, 139, 214
Mary Ann (blk), 214
Mary C. (blk), 278
Mary C. (col'd), 68
Mary E., 26, 87, 152
Mary Eliza (blk), 159
Mary Ellen (blk), 306
Mary Francis Elizth., 115
Mary G. (blk), 41
Mary J., 140
Mary L. (blk), 136

JOHNSON
  Mary P., 260
  Mary S., 130
  Matilda (blk), 69, 149
  Matilda J., 233
  Mattie, 43
  Millard H., 87
  Milly (blk), 162
  Milly Ann (blk), 150
  Minnie, 88
  Miranda (blk), 9
  Mollie (blk), 116
  Myra (blk), 79
  Nancy (blk), 47
  Nellie (blk), 50
  Patsey (blk), 22
  Polly, 26
  Pricey, 126
  Priscilla (blk), 206
  Priscilla Ann (blk), 78
  Rachel, 94, 148, 259
  Rachel (blk), 94, 259
  Rebecca, 84, 167, 209, 213
  Rebecca (blk), 84, 167, 213
  Rose (blk), 100
  S. Ann, 118
  Sallie F., 30
  Sally (blk), 155
  Sarah (blk), 154, 187, 229, 239, 293, 319, 324
  Sarah Ann, 46
  Sarah Elizabeth, 50
  Sarah Elizth. (blk), 319
  Sarah Jane (blk), 146
  Selivia, 203
  Serena (blk), 117
  Sidney T., 145
  Susan (blk), 263
  Susanna Ellen, 138
  Susannah (blk), 121, 151
  Teaco Jane (blk), 212
  Victoria (blk), 292
  Virginia (blk), 222
  Wilhelmina (blk), 244
  Willie E., 164
  Willie Ellen, 160
JOHNSTON
  Elizabeth A., 246
  Emeline (blk), 30
  Eulalie, 107
  Jane Ann, 169
  Lizzie (blk), 159
  Martha (blk), 278
  Virginia, 38
JONES
  Agnes, 186, 295
  Agnes (blk), 295
  Alice J., 66
  Allice (blk), 179
  Amelia (blk), 192
  Ann, 1, 48, 49, 74, 168, 236, 261, 267, 307, 312
  Ann (blk), 49, 74
  Ann Maria, 48
  Anna, 1, 168, 261, 267
  Anna F., 261
  Anna L., 1
  Anna S., 267
  Annie, 307, 312
  Annie M., 312
  Arena (blk), 269
  Arietta (blk), 103
  Camilla (blk), 304
  Caroline, 3, 28, 35
  Caroline (blk), 3
  Caroline V., 28
  Catharine, 28, 202
  Catherine, 32, 157, 278
  Catherine S., 32
  Charity Ann, 128
  Charlotte (blk), 31, 108
  Cornelia (blk), 319
  Cornelia E., 16
  Dioretta (blk), 190
  E.M.F., 48
  Eliza (blk), 282
  Elizabeth, 6, 25, 47, 76, 123, 145, 158, 216, 224, 230, 236
  Elizabeth (blk), 47, 76, 123, 158, 236
  Elizabeth A., 230
  Elizabeth Frances, 6
  Emeline, 232
  Emily, 47, 130, 156
  Emily (blk), 156
  Emily Jane, 130
  Emma A., 17
  Fannie L., 50
  Fanny (blk), 129
  Frederica B., 158
  Georgeanna P.C., 258
  Hannah (blk), 73
  Harriet, 6, 225, 310
  Harriet Ann, 6
  Harriet Frances, 310
  Henrietta (blk), 212
  Hester Ann (blk), 229
  Hester E., 45
  Jane Ann, 237
  Jannetta, 238
  Jennie, 147
  Joanna (blk), 267
  Josephine, 163
  Josiphene (blk), 210
  Julia (blk), 261
  Juliette, 136
  Kate G., 118
  Laura, 31, 178
  Laura J., 31
  Laurelia (blk), 33
  Lavinia (blk), 97
  Lizzie Virginia (blk), 129
  Louisa (blk), 145, 191, 222
  Loulie A., 277
  Lucinda, 233, 254
  Lucinda (blk), 233

JONES
Lucy (blk), 140, 146, 275
Maggie R., 71
Mahala (blk), 306
Malinda, 172
Margaret, 67, 302
Maria, 4, 246, 278
Maria (blk), 278
Marion H., 5
Martha, 193, 307
Martha Cornelia, 307
Mary, 5, 6, 10, 12, 30, 60, 89, 111, 115, 143, 148, 149, 158, 172, 183, 228, 249, 287, 311, 317, 324
Mary (blk), 115, 149, 249, 311
Mary A., 60, 143, 317
Mary Ann, 10, 149, 311
Mary Ann (blk), 149
Mary C., 158
Mary E., 89, 183
Mary Elizabeth, 324
Mary Ella, 172
Mary Ellen, 5, 30, 148
Mary Ellen (blk), 5, 30
Mary Jane, 30, 311, 324
Mary Jane (blk), 311
Mary S., 287
Matilda A. (blk), 186
Milanda (blk), 216
Milly (blk), 110, 272
Nancy (blk), 271
Nancy E., 53, 262
Rachel (blk), 302
Rebecca, 66, 82, 94
Rebecca A., 94
Robina W., 22
Rosa (blk), 47
Roxanna (blk), 224
Sarah, 67, 123, 175, 209, 233, 251, 260, 285, 316, 326
Sarah (blk), 123, 285, 326
Sarah A. (blk), 260
Sarah Ann (blk), 251
Sarah C., 233
Sarah E., 316
Sarah J., 209
Sarah Jane (blk), 67
Sidney Elizth. (blk), 255
Susan (blk), 13, 115
Sylvia (blk), 149
Victoria (blk), 148
Virginia Jane (blk), 299
Winney, 22, 65
Winney (blk), 65
JORDAN
Delilah, 4
Georgiana (blk), 100
Hannah (blk), 175
Imogene D., 114
Jane, 298
Julia (blk), 180
Louisa, 264
Margaret (blk), 148
Maria, 48
Mary (blk), 323
Pauline, 113
Theresa, 308
JORDON
Martha, 82
JOSEPH
Hannah T., 41
Mary, 200
JOSSLYN
Sarah, 41
JOST
Amelia, 135
JOVAN
Sophia (blk), 318

JOXX
Maria, 112
JOY
Alberta, 163
Ann, 65, 117
Anna, 117
Carrie E., 93
Helen, 210
Jane E., 43
Mary E., 173
JOYCE
Ann, 137
Catharine, 44, 292, 303
Catherine, 162
Delia, 204
Frances M., 205
Frank E., 301
Hannah, 60
Josephine A., 8
Kate, 111, 279
Kate (blk), 279
Lucy, 253
Margaret I., 70
Mary, 63, 179
Susan (blk), 136
JUDKINS
Jane, 185
JUGH
Frances, 32
JULLIEN
Adelaide, 321
JUNG
Augusta, 258
Catharine, 206, 288
Catharine Louisa, 206
JUNIPER
Caroline (blk), 47
Margaret (blk), 66
JURIX
Amelia (blk), 232
Georgiana (blk), 27

—K—

KAEHLER
Auguste, 281

KAHL
  Margaret E., 29
KAIN
  Bridget, 99, 188
  Matilda, 94
KAISER
  Caroline Virginia, 52
KALAHOR
  Ellen, 297
KAMMERER
  Cecilia, 88
KANE
  Ann, 166, 206, 213, 274
  Annie Virginia, 274
  Catharine, 77, 175
  Catherine, 218, 254
  Catherine C., 254
  Eliza, 37
  Ellen, 82, 97, 108, 180
  Ellen C., 180
  Frances A., 295
  Hanora, 310
  Jane, 180
  Lucy (blk), 313
  Margaret, 70
  Mary, 9, 308
  Mary A., 308
  Treacy, 72
KANFELT
  Emilie, 311
KAPPEL
  Julia, 192
KARLIN
  Louisa J., 172
KARPP
  Mary L., 4
KARR
  Christiana, 142
KARTTER
  Sophia, 300
KARYS
  Mary (blk), 288
KASTNER
  Henrietta, 288
KATTENER
  Rachel, 79

KAUFMAN
  Amelia R., 66
  Hanche, 161
  Katie, 104
  Rachel, 131
  S.C., 75
  Sarah, 309
  Sophia, 326
KAULENDBAUGH
  Mary B., 87
KAUSER
  Elizabeth, 162
KAVANAH
  Annie, 195
KAVANAUGH
  Catherine, 277
  Cornelia, 137
KAYSER
  Alberta, 322
  Liezzie, 232
KAYWOOD
  Elizabeth, 29
KEACH
  Harriet, 123
KEAFE
  Annie, 127
KEALIN
  Catharine, 9
KEALY
  Bridget, 68
  Mary, 188
KEANON
  Tracy, 325
KEARN
  Ann B., 285
  Julia, 98
KEARNE
  Hanorah, 174
KEARNEY
  Ellen (blk), 149
  Jane, 71
  Kate, 133, 165
  Margaret, 69
KEARNS
  Bridget, 49
KEATING
  Annorah Rosilla, 38
  Maggie A., 292
  Mary C., 199

KEECH
  Elizabeth, 200
KEEFE
  Johanna, 238
  Kate, 44
  Leonora, 230
  Marcella M., 88
  Mary, 198, 233
KEEFER
  E. Eugene, 106
KEELER
  Grace, 186
KEELEY
  Winney, 211
KEELING
  Fannie, 37
  Nannie P., 208
KEELY
  Hellen, 2
KEENAN
  Bridget, 161, 199
  Ellen, 221
  Margaret, 219
  Mary, 24, 84, 133
  Mary Jane, 24
KEENE
  Charlotte M., 273
  Ruth W., 138
KEENT
  Lucy (blk), 26
KEESE
  Charlotte D., 29
  Dorcas Virginia, 85
KEEYES
  Mary G., 112
  Selina, 145
KEHOE
  Ann, 184
  Bridget, 101
  Elizabeth, 92
  Georgiana, 45
KEIBER
  Catharine, 303
KEIGON
  Mary Ann, 160
KEIM
  Fredericka, 240
KEIN
  Alcyndia Ann, 23

KEINLE
 Barbara, 230
KEIR
 Caroline F.B., 244
KEISER
 Elizabeth, 191
 Kate, 143
KEITHLEY
 Ann, 162
 Hester Ann, 293
 Isabella N., 105
 Jane Elizabeth, 230
KELCHER
 Hanoragh, 60
KELEHER
 Bridget, 84
 Hanah, 292
 Henrietta, 180
 Mary E., 154
 Sarah, 3
KELER
 Mary, 106
KELEY
 Elizabeth, 220
KELL
 Harriet Ann, 282
 Sarah (blk), 229
KELLEHER
 M.E., 279
 Mary, 41
KELLER
 Elizabeth, 14
 Louisa, 44
 Virginia C., 215
KELLEY
 Cecilia (blk), 47
 Charlotte M., 206
 Elizabeth C., 197
 Ellen (blk), 322
 Mary Jane, 102
KELLIGAN
 Ellen, 23
KELLOGG
 Mary F., 288
KELLY
 Alice, 242
 America (blk), 194
 Bessie, 196
 Bridget, 57, 96, 111, 162, 196, 289
 Caroline, 72, 100
 Caroline T., 72
 Catharine, 98, 242, 279
 Catharine M., 279
 Eleanor, 253
 Ellen, 23, 223, 294
 Emma, 195
 Hannah, 133
 Hanora, 188
 Julia, 231
 Kate, 164
 Margaret, 58, 110, 130, 285
 Margaret A., 110
 Mary, 18, 74, 79, 80, 95, 114, 135, 139, 156, 182, 193, 195, 267, 299
 Mary A.V., 79
 Mary B., 135
 Mary E., 18, 74, 299
 Mary J., 193
 Rosa, 84
 Rose, 200
 Sallie A., 322
 Susan, 246
KELSEY
 Catherine (blk), 133
 Susan, 229
KEMAN
 Sarah Jane, 26
KEMMELL
 Catherine, 168
KEMP
 Charlotte R., 83
 Georgiana, 297
 Mary V., 271
KENADEY
 Mary Ann, 321
KENDALL
 Marian, 9
KENDRICK
 Araminda, 208
 Margaret, 164
KENDRICON
 Bridget K., 81
KENGLA
 Kate, 116
 Maggie, 184
KENNALLY
 Mary, 60
KENNARD
 Agnes M., 64
 Margaret J.B., 137
KENNAWAY
 Agnes, 70
KENNEDY
 Ann, 21, 26, 116
 Anna (blk), 26
 Annie E., 21
 Bridget, 21, 322
 Catharine, 111, 198
 Catherine, 198
 Eliza, 46
 Ellen, 25, 67, 127
 Florence, 112
 Jane, 124
 Kate, 321
 Maggie, 262
 Margaret, 120, 172
 Maria F., 233
 Mary, 24, 162, 163, 199, 211, 219, 261, 318
 Mary Agnes, 199
 Mary Ann, 318
 Mary Jane, 24
 Mary Margaret, 211
KENNELLY
 Ellen, 282
KENNER
 Julia Ann (blk), 54
KENNEY
 Ane, 40
 Catherine, 99
 Elizabeth M. (blk), 114
KENNON
 Martha Custis, 229
KENNY
 Mary, 147
 Sarah, 230
KENRICK
 Sarah J., 222

District of Columbia Marriage Licenses, 1858-1870

KENT
  Frances (blk), 135
  Louisa E., 320
  Lucy (blk), 52
  Minerva, 123
  Sarah F., 223
KEOGH
  Mary, 238
KEOHAN
  Ellen, 196
KEONEY
  Martha, 320
KEPHART
  Christiana, 236
KEPPLE
  Bridget, 212
KERBY
  Margaret Hunnicutt, 297
KERR
  Catharine, 221
  Hester (blk), 266
  L.M., 49
  Lucy (blk), 99
  Mary, 62, 136, 191
  Mary Jane, 191
  Sarah Ann, 80
KERRON
  Kate, 97
KERSHAW
  Alice, 21
KERVAND
  Isabel, 173
KERVIN
  Mary, 59
KESSLER
  Mary, 218
KETCHEN
  Mary E., 216
KETCHENS
  Sarah, 27
KETTLER
  Dora, 243
  Mary E., 58
KEY
  Harriet (blk), 258
  Lucy, 296
  Mary Lizzie, 240
  Mary R., 146

KEYES
  Ann, 301
  Emma (blk), 192
  Gracie (blk), 306
  M.E., 148
  Sarah, 268
KEYHOE
  Margaret E., 233
KEYS
  Alsinda, 254
  Margaret, 193
  Mary A., 75
  Nancy, 73
  Winney, 107
KHARN
  Christine, 1
KIBBLE
  Henrietta, 65
  Mary C.C., 166
KIBBY
  Amy S., 200
  Sarah, 160
KIDWELL
  Anne, 143
  Catherine, 174
  Frances C., 16
  Frances E., 165
  Martha Ann, 113
  Mary E., 119
  Mary Jane, 115
  Nancy Ann, 296
  Octavia A., 290
  Sarah E., 67
KIEBER
  Frances, 41
KIECKHOEFER
  Cecilia A., 160
  Emily F., 271
  Mary Louisa, 143
KIEFER
  Christiana K., 75
KIERMAN
  Kate, 164
KIERNAN
  Mary Ann, 160
KIEVALIER
  Margaret, 161
KIFFER
  Jane, 269

KILBORN
  Catherine, 123
KILBY
  Esther, 185
KILDER
  Mary, 256
KILDUFF
  Mary, 6
KILEY
  Margaret, 68
KILHOOLY
  Mary, 104
KILKLINE
  Bridget, 218
KILLBRIGHT
  Sarah E., 15
KILLIAN
  Henrietta, 138
KILLMAN
  Annie S., 16
KILLMARTIN
  Ann, 215
KILLMON
  Mary J., 292
KIMBLE
  Adeline, 33
  Susan (blk), 140
KINCH
  Angella H., 19
KINCHLOE
  Bridget, 221
  Mary A.L., 52
KING
  Amanda L., 16
  Ann, 27, 43, 174, 180, 195, 209, 239, 303
  Ann E., 43
  Anna, 27, 239
  Anna C., 239
  Annie, 174, 195, 209
  Annie Augusta, 174
  Bridget, 100
  Caroline, 67
  Catharine, 125
  Catherine, 31
  Chloe, 182

413

KING
  Elizabeth, 166, 185,
    201, 254, 262, 280,
    288
  Elizabeth (blk), 254
  Elizabeth M., 185
  Elizabeth R., 288
  Emma Louisa, 215
  Emma R., 131
  Georgianna, 309
  Hannah, 134, 302
  Harriet (blk), 318
  Jane, 61, 100, 204
  Jane Eliza, 61
  Jane M., 204
  Josephine, 148, 211
  Josephine G., 211
  Julia Ann, 16
  Lizzie M., 253
  Lucy A., 146
  Margaret, 138, 173,
    181, 214
  Margaret Ann, 138
  Martha, 112, 133,
    147, 230, 245, 282
  Martha A., 230
  Martha Ann, 147
  Martha E., 245
  Martha Ellen, 133, 282
  Mary, 34, 47, 50, 55,
    58, 62, 63, 136, 146,
    179, 200, 254, 267
  Mary (col'd), 34
  Mary Adelaid, 267
  Mary Alice, 200
  Mary Ann, 146
  Mary Catherine, 47
  Mary E., 63
  Mary Elizabeth, 55
  Mary Ellender, 62
  Mary Frances, 136
  Mary Jane, 50
  Mary Margaret, 179
  Olivia J., 53
  Priscilla (blk), 115
  Rachel Ann, 209
  Rebecca Ann, 272
  Rosa, 289
  Sarah, 155, 190,
    216, 323
  Sarah (blk), 155
  Sarah A., 190, 216
  Sylvia L., 23
  Teresa (blk), 50
  Virginia, 73
  Willie A. (blk), 245
KINGSBERRY
  Ellen, 181
KINNEY
  Catherine, 163
KINSEY
  Sallie, 231
KINSLEY
  Maria, 207
KINTZ
  Lizzie, 285
KINZER
  Helen Ann, 218
KINZIE
  Marion, 294
KIPP
  Lesaly, 95
  Malinda, 86
KIRBY
  Ellen, 242
  Hannah, 98
  Hanorah, 72
  Harriet, 185
  Josephine, 123
  Margaret J., 307
  Mary, 152, 159, 182
  Mary E., 152
  Mary Jane, 182
  Sarah A., 137
KIRCHNER
  Sabine, 257
KIRK
  Mary, 220
KIRKWOOD
  Julia D., 112
  Marion A., 168
KIRVAN
  Cordelia, 72
KISICGA
  Catharine, 174
KISSNER
  Eliza, 255
KITE
  Elizabeth C., 179
KITSON
  Louisa, 226
KITTINGER
  Ann Eliza, 320
KLEBER
  Josephine, 257
KLEINLE
  Julia, 215
KLINE
  Mollie E., 274
  Ruth Anna, 270
  Susan, 97
KLING
  Philipine, 134
KLINGELER
  Joanna, 257
KLINGHAMER
  Louisa, 257
KLINKEN
  Harriet (blk), 231
KLINKER
  Mary E., 24
KLINTENCE
  Mary S., 19
KLOCKE
  Ann, 37
KLOFOOT
  Margaret (blk), 179
KLOPFER
  Martha Ellen, 231
  Rachel A., 6
KLOPPENGER
  Fredericka, 280
KLÜH
  Gertruth, 8
  Helen, 257
KLUMP
  Julia Anna, 177
KNABE
  Elizabeth, 248
KNARBE
  Catherine E., 184
KNAUF
  Elizabeth, 301
KNAUST
  Eliese, 165

KNEASS
  Anna Mary, 116
  Kate, 326
KNEW
  Delia Ann, 317
KNIGHT
  Alice E., 260
  Catherine, 208
  Elizabeth, 168
  Jane, 141
  Jennie, 98
  Mary, 94, 262, 278, 301
  Mary L., 278
  Mary Susannah, 94
  Mattie, 134
  Virginia E., 37
KNODE
  Amanda H., 41
  Annie F., 202
  Helen G., 266
KNODEL
  Frideruke, 146
KNOLES
  Mary Virginia, 168
KNOPF
  Amelia, 11
KNORLEIN
  Barbara Teresa, 142
KNOTE
  Mary Virginia, 168
KNOTS
  Virginia Ann, 295
KNOTT
  Anna Elizabeth, 245
  Emma J., 92
  Jane Rebecca, 143
  Laura H., 291
  Mary A., 205, 272
  Rosie J., 292
KNOWLAND
  Catherine, 9
KNOWLDEN
  Mary A., 124
KNOWLES
  Adaline P., 277
  Addie P., 294
  Allice V., 136
  Carrie, 122

  Gertrude, 100
  Rebecca, 193
KNOX
  Elizabeth, 80
  Ellen, 313
  Etmonia (blk), 273
  Susan (blk), 305
KNOXVILLE
  Roberta (blk), 192
KOCH
  Albertine, 257
  Augusta, 38
KOCHE
  Isabel, 201
KOENIGSRENTHER
  Anna, 246
KOETHER
  Pauline, 160
KOHN
  Amelia, 142
KOLB
  Emma, 4
  Sarah, 73
KOLDENBACH
  Elizabeth A., 209
KOLDITZ
  Friedericka E., 150
KOLINGS
  Catherine, 301
KOONS
  Agnes, 6
KOPPER
  Margaret, 92
KÖRBER
  Sophia, 310
KORFF
  Virginia, 37
KORNBACH
  Maria C., 169
KORNER
  Rosa, 17
KÖRNER
  Louise, 24
KOUGH
  Sarah, 18
KRAEMAN
  Katharine, 170
KRAEMER
  Louisa, 211

KRAFFT
  Ann Maria, 27
  Caroline C., 105
KRAFT
  Adelaid, 161
  Catherine, 246
  Louisa, 163, 165, 309
  Louisa D., 309
  Louisa V., 165
KRAIDER
  Elizabeth D., 311
KRANTZ
  Elizabeth F., 228
KRANZ
  Caroline, 299
KRARER
  Magdalena, 218
KRAUS
  Lizzie, 7
KRAUSE
  Bertha, 257
KRAUSER
  Mary E., 141
KRAUTER
  Caroline, 38
KREAMER
  Alice, 66
  Elizabeth, 209
KREBBS
  Rufina, 174
KREGER
  Christiana, 19
KRESLOWSKI
  Sarah, 314
KRETZER
  Anna, 18
KREUTER
  Katharine, 94
KRIER
  Amanda M., 166
KRINST
  Ernestine, 104
KROESCHEL
  Bertha, 256
KROFT
  Mary M., 244
KRONAS
  Mary, 257

District of Columbia Marriage Licenses, 1858-1870

KRONISE
  Catharine, 6
KROUSE
  Clara V., 305
  Margaret R., 4
KUGLER
  Myra E., 235
KUHL
  Justina, 230
  Margaret, 313
  Wilhelmina, 109
KUHNS
  Emily Mary, 227
  Mary, 230
  Susana, 15
KUMEGER
  Caroline Rosa, 134
KUMHELN
  Johanna Fred. Henr. Christ., 205
KUMMER
  Emilie, 131, 294
KUMNEAR
  Betty, 120
KUNATH
  Caroline, 29
KURTZ
  Anna Maria, 123
  Henrietta C., 260
KYLE
  Mary, 263
KYNE
  Margaret, 262

— L —

LABYN
  Winifred, 160
LACEY
  Amelia (blk), 56
  Ann, 219
  Barbara E., 121
  Jane Rebecca, 249
  Mary Ann (blk), 165, 317
  Mary F., 133
LACY
  Lizzie, 22
  Virginia, 148

LADAMEIL
  Mary Lucinda, 5
LAEHY
  Honora, 205
LAFFERTY
  Alice, 80
  Sarah Ann, 40
LAFLIN
  Abby M., 95
LAGAN
  Sarah, 133
LAHAY
  Elizabeth, 92
LaHAYNE
  Augusta, 121
  Dorothy, 205
LAHEY
  Ella, 94
  Mary, 234
LAHY
  Catherine, 209
LAIR
  Alcinda (blk), 238
LAKE
  Amanda J., 182
  Emilie Theresa, 90
LALLY
  Bridget, 263
LAMB
  Charlotte A., 172
  Emma R., 107
  Fanny, 146
  Lollie, 310
  Martha, 79
LAMBERS
  Nancy (blk), 181
LAMBERT
  Amelia (blk), 152
  Jeannette E., 320
  Margaret, 171
LAMBIE
  Annie, 248
  Margaret A., 85
LAMBKINS
  Anna, 262
LAMBRIGHT
  Emma, 263
  Miranda C., 116

LAMMON
  Nellie, 106
LAMMOND
  Nettie, 146
LAMPHEIMER
  Caroline, 243
LAMPKINS
  Sina, 35
LANCASTER
  Eliza (blk), 202
  Elizabeth A. (blk), 42
  Emily J. (blk), 178
  Emma J. (blk), 319
  Frances (blk), 17
  Jane M., 203
  L.A., 210
  Mary (blk), 306
  Mary Vandalia, 311
  Susan (blk), 290
LANCESTER
  Judeth A., 278
LAND
  Mary, 243
LANDES
  Susan (blk), 6
LANDON
  Nellie (blk), 117
  Susannah, 158
LANDREY
  Julia B. (blk), 129
LANE
  Ann, 25, 99
  Anna, 25
  Bridget, 81
  Catherine (blk), 192
  Fanny (blk), 73, 109
  Julia R., 121
  Margaret (blk), 2
  Mary B., 285
  Sophie C., 104
  Susannah, 319
LANEY
  Elizabeth (blk), 147
  Louisa (blk), 35
  Mary (blk), 323
LANG
  Anna, 217
  Jennie, 280
  Kate, 125

LANGAN
  Mary, 199
LANGDON
  Mary A., 84
LANGE
  Martha E., 25
LANGFORD
  Eliza (blk), 298
LANGLEY
  Josephine N., 107
  Margaret, 108, 315
  Margaret Ann, 108
  Marion V., 144
  Mary, 111, 148,
    204, 289, 322
  Mary (blk), 148
  Mary E., 289
  Mary F., 322
  Mary J., 111
LANHAM
  Mary Virginia, 190
LANKFORD
  Margaret (blk), 149
  Margaret A. (blk),
    304
LANKUL
  Minna, 211
LANNAN
  Maggie, 132
LANNINGHAM
  Mary, 238
LANSDALE
  Rachel M. (blk), 226
LAONHART
  Annie M., 128
LAPSLEY
  Catharine, 292
LARKIN
  Mary, 302
  Penelope V., 270
LARKINS
  Emily Elizth., 316
LARMAN
  Elizabeth, 11
LARMOUR
  Fannie, 290
  Mary A., 189
LARNEY
  Lizzie, 222

LARRIMOUR
  Polly (blk), 57
LARRISSY
  Mary, 251
LASALLE
  Louisa P., 5
LASHER
  Caroline, 272
LASHHORN
  Ella V., 89
LASSELLE
  Ellen Louise, 235
LATCHFORD
  Catherine, 248
LATHAM
  Alice, 52
  Ann R., 221
  Harriet, 161
  Jeanette, 221
  Malvina (blk), 247
LATIMER
  Annie J., 231
  Lettie H., 153
  Loula, 267
LATTIN
  Mary E., 138
LAUB
  Clara, 219
  Ellen A., 174
  Julia, 104
LAUCK
  E. Serena, 66
LAUGHERMAN
  Caroline, 174
LAUGHLIN
  Annie, 310
  Catherine, 239
  Margaret, 162
  Mary, 213
  Susan, 99
LAUGTON
  Margaret A., 116
LAURENCE
  Virginia M., 309
LAURENSON
  Maggie, 171
LAURER
  Hellen, 255

LAURY
  Virginia, 309
LAUXMAN
  Barbara, 244
LAVAZA
  Angela, 108
LAVENDER
  Lillie, 278
LAVERY
  Anna Eliza, 287
LAVEZZI
  Mary L., 198
  Mary Louisa, 299
LaVILLE
  Anna, 184
LAWERCY
  Kate, 99
LAWLER
  Anna, 37
  Maggie, 137
  Margaret, 15
  Mary, 48
LAWLOR
  Anna, 227
  Hanora, 186
LAWN
  Alice, 290
  Delia, 99
LAWREL
  Jane (blk), 190
LAWRENCE
  Cecilia (blk), 43
  Martha Ann, 235
  Nancy (blk), 293
  Rebecca (blk), 61
  Susan, 177
LAWRENSON
  Sophia, 247
LAWRIE
  Sarah J., 229
LAWS
  Elizabeth A., 113
  Helen M., 152
  Sallie (blk), 171
  Willie Ann, 239
LAWSON
  Anna (blk), 143
  Catherine, 111
  Charity (blk), 321

417

LAWSON
  Elizabeth (blk), 147
  Lizzie (blk), 315
  Lizzie Ann, 116
  Margaret, 193
  Matilda A., 275
  Pattie B., 208
LAWTON
  Catharine, 63
  Ellen, 220
  Margaret, 320
LAXLEY
  Mary Jane, 157
LAY
  Annie M., 141
  Ellen, 97
LAYS
  Ann, 170
LAYTON
  Winney (blk), 314
LAZENBY
  Nellie, 123
LAZIER
  Ellen, 59
LEACH
  Alice E., 98
  Emily R., 178
  Louisa K., 219
  Margaret H., 36
  Mary A., 214
LEADLEIN
  Maria, 287
LEAHY
  Johanna, 284
  Julia, 83
  Mary, 187
LEAKE
  Aurelia, 21
LEAMY
  Ellen, 197
LEAR
  Bettie O'N., 154
  Estella M., 108
  Sadie M., 280
LEARY
  Eleanor, 297
  Mary, 13, 56
  Mary C., 56

LeBARROWS
  Josephine (blk), 89
LECKIE
  Kate, 213
  Susan (blk), 318
LECKRON
  Clara J., 231
  Laura A., 197
  Mary E., 112
LeCOMPTE
  Anna C., 100
LEDMAN
  Cordelia, 267
LEDNER
  Ellen, 54
LEDWITH
  Catherine, 10
LEE
  Adele (blk), 17
  Agnes (blk), 273
  Alice, 100, 236
  Ann (blk), 119
  Ann Maria (blk), 280
  Anna (blk), 175, 289
  Anna C., 228
  Annie E. (blk), 156
  Betsey (blk), 12
  Bridget, 81
  Cariline (blk), 262
  Caroline (blk), 5
  Carrie, 242
  Chloe (blk), 47
  Clora (blk), 176
  Cornelia (blk), 35
  Eliza, 7, 17, 23, 32, 52, 100, 226, 244, 258, 269, 272, 306
  Eliza (blk), 7, 32, 100, 244, 269, 272, 306
  Elizabeth, 17, 52, 226, 258
  Elizabeth (blk), 17, 52, 258
  Ellin (blk), 12
  Emily (blk), 2, 150, 251
  Emma, 107, 133, 176
  Emma (blk), 176

  Emma G., 133
  Fanny (blk), 18
  Harriet (blk), 158, 234
  Harriett A. (blk), 66
  Henrietta, 191, 292
  Henrietta (blk), 292
  Isabella, 323
  Jane (blk), 32
  Josephine (blk), 242
  Julia (blk), 38, 320
  Kitty, 231
  Laura (blk), 183
  Louisa, 2, 50, 326
  Louisa (blk), 2
  Louisa (col'd), 50
  Louise (blk), 67
  Lucinda (blk), 226
  Lucinda E. (blk), 36
  Maria (blk), 193
  Maria L. (blk), 65
  Martha (blk), 116, 137
  Mary, 53, 83, 100, 117, 140, 154, 170, 269
  Mary (blk), 117, 140, 154
  Mary (col'd), 154
  Mary E., 53, 100
  Mary Ellen (blk), 83
  Mary Jane (blk), 269
  Matilda, 51, 154, 176
  Matilda (blk), 176
  Matilda Jane, 51
  Miss (blk), 117
  Nannie (blk), 42
  Nellie Ann, 297
  Olivia, 171
  Othelia (blk), 117
  Phebe, 223
  Phebe (blk), 223
  Rebecca (blk), 266
  Rosa (blk), 266
  Sarah (blk), 184
  Sarah Catherine, 245
  Sarah E., 36
  Susan (blk), 28, 136

LEE
  Susan Ann (blk), 283
  Susan E., 291
  Treasy (blk), 88
  Virginia, 114
LEECH
  Mary A., 196
LEEF
  Ellen, 280
LEEK
  Kesiah, 314
LEFTER
  Sarah C., 262
LEHAY
  Margaret, 87
LEHMAN
  Catherine A., 129
  Sophia, 150
LEHNE
  Sophia Bertha, 162
LEIB
  Emma J., 52
LEIBIN
  Amelia A., 93
LEIBOLD
  Rosine Barbara, 256
LEIDECKER
  Elise, 189
LEIGH
  Annie M., 234
LEIMBACH
  Mary L., 29
LEINER
  Balbina, 201
LEITCH
  Margaret, 114
LEMMON
  Annie R., 235
  Ellen, 107
  Emma E., 153
  Mary, 197
LEMMONS
  Martha (blk), 53
LEMO
  Sarah (blk), 296
LEMON
  Emily, 246
  Fannie L., 263
  Frances (blk), 27
  Jane McKelvie, 141
  Mary Etta (blk), 157
  Mary V., 17
LEMONS
  Julia (blk), 315
LENAHAN
  Margaret, 261
LENDON
  Kate, 15
LENEHEN
  Margaret, 43
LENENGS
  Catherine, 261
LENNAHAM
  Elizth., 104
LENOIR
  Louisa, 7
LENOX
  Mary A., 108
LENT
  Harriet A., 142
LENTHALL
  Jenny, 301
LENTNER
  Catherine, 131
LENY
  Margereta, 191
LENZ
  Mary, 124
LEONARD
  Ann, 70, 245
  Annie M., 245
  Jennie E., 169
  Letitia, 169
LEONARDY
  Mary D., 200
LEOPHARD
  Louisa, 125
LePATCH
  Lizzie, 34
LePETIT
  Marian, 112
LESLIE
  Ellen R., 112
LESTER
  Mary, 212
LETON
  Clara A., 309
LETTON
  Laura D., 13
LETZNER
  Margt., 172
LEVEQUE
  Margarite A., 50
LEVERONE
  A. Maria, 327
LEVETT
  Mary A.F., 300
LEVI
  Georgiana (blk), 234
LEVIN
  Annie, 302
  Catherine, 81
LEVINS
  Catherine, 219
LEVINSTON
  Mary E., 161
LEVRONE
  Mary, 178
LEVY
  Annie, 142
  Carolina, 216
LEWIS
  Amanda, 153
  Amelia (blk), 226, 254
  Ann (blk), 13
  Ann M. (blk), 269
  Anna, 223
  Annie, 315
  Betsy (blk), 168
  Betty (blk), 320
  Brainer, 94
  Caroline, 1, 96
  Cassy (blk), 11
  Delia (blk), 268
  Delia, 103
  Dilsey (blk), 179
  Eliza, 158, 178, 308
  Elizabeth (blk), 308
  Elizabeth A., 178
  Elizabeth (blk), 42
  Ella (blk), 25
  Ellen (blk), 11
  Emily, 81
  Emma (blk), 67
  Emma C., 51

District of Columbia Marriage Licenses, 1858-1870

LEWIS
Emma V., 87
Fannie (blk), 152
Fanny (blk), 205
Georgiana, 32, 54
Georgiana (blk), 54
Harriet, 77
Helen (blk), 227
Henrietta (blk), 101
Jane (blk), 119
Jane L., 277
Josephine, 256
Julia A., 122
Katherine C., 47
Lizzie (blk), 206
Lizzie E. (blk), 245
Lizzie S., 62
Lucinda, 62
Lucretia (blk), 240
Margaret (blk), 228
Maria (blk), 149
Martha (blk), 210
Martha E., 95
Mary (blk), 80, 112
Mary Catherine, 237
Mary A. (blk), 103
Mary E., 66, 103, 135
Mary E. (blk), 66, 103
Mary Etta, 23
Mary Jane (blk), 227
Nancy (blk), 214
Philia (blk), 197
Polly (blk), 155
Rachel (blk), 287
Rose (blk), 297
Sallie S., 178
Sarah, 248, 262, 280, 307
Sarah (blk), 280
Sarah E., 248
Sarah F., 262
Sophia (blk), 190
Susannah, 231
LEYDEN
Bridget, 60
LEYPOLDT
Catharine, 245

LEYPOLT
Eliza, 185
LIBBICK
Mary, 163
LIBBY
Clara E., 222
LIBICH
Mary, 170
LIBIE
Eliza, 129
LIBTEA
Adelaide, 124
LICH
Ruth, 244
LIDEN
Bridget, 86, 221
LIEBELT
Emma, 300
LIGHT
Matilda, 214
LIGHTELL
Mary E., 259
LIGHTFOOT
Lucy (blk), 267
Ophelia, 269
LIJAH
Margaret, 127
LILLY
Kate, 233
LIMRICK
Luberta, 106
LINCOLN
Elizabeth (blk), 8
Isabella C., 249
Josephine C., 278
LINDLICH
Agnes, 147
LINDSAY
Emma, 9
Helen, 15
Margaret, 259
LINDSEY
C.S., 101
LINDSLEY
Ada, 82
Lucretia, 203
LINK
Seraphina, 275

LINKINS
Margaret A., 136
Richetta, 133
Virginia Ellen, 202
LINKUM
Louisa (blk), 100
LINN
Maria, 286
LINNEY
Margaret, 103
LINTHICUM
Maria E., 10
Mary Kate, 76
LINTNER
Mary, 19
LINTON
Amanda J., 173
LINZ
Anna, 56
LIPPOLD
Anna B., 95
LIPSCOMB
Clara V., 109
LISCOMB
Matilda (blk), 163
LISLE
Josephine, 77
LISSBERGER
Matilda, 281
LISTON
Bridget, 97
LITTLE
Anna J., 205
Annie E., 16
Araminta, 37, 156
Caroline, 269
Eliza A., 245
Emily F., 59
Finnella Maury, 3
Julia A., 40
Margaret, 226, 230
Margaret Ann, 226
Mary A., 137
Mary Jane (blk), 58
Sarah F., 10
Susana, 114
LITTLEFORD
Amanda, 117

LITTLEJOHN
  Eliza S., 227
LITTON
  Caroline, 317
  Harriet Josephine, 68
LITZ
  Frances P., 75
LIVERPOOL
  Sophia (blk), 78
  Susan (blk), 280
LIVERY
  Sarah (blk), 232
LIVINGGOOD
  Eliza, 109
LIZZIE
  Ann (blk), 149
LLOYD
  Carrie, 213
  Jane Maria, 3
  Mary Elizabeth, 30
  Maryland, 296
  Nellie E., 68
  Rosalie, 28
  Rosina, 186
  Sarah Jane, 102
LÖB
  Yette, 56
LOBER
  Ellen (col'd), 33
LOCHTERMAN
  Kate, 82
LOCKE
  Florella E., 55
  Henrietta, 268
  Lina E., 107
  Mary Jane, 290
  Sarah, 244
LOCKEMAN
  Margaret, 202
LOCKENS
  Rachel (blk), 152
LOCKER
  Martha (blk), 20
LOCKINS
  Maria, 18
LOCKS
  Margaret, 110

LOCKWOOD
  Emily (blk), 31
  Jane, 116
LOCUST
  Julia (blk), 287
LODER
  Emily A., 276
LODGE
  Alice Virginia, 114
  Charlotte (blk), 157
  Mary Ann (blk), 107
LOEB
  Bertha, 138
LOEFFLER
  Louise E., 143
LOENTHAL
  Louisa, 322
LOEWEL
  Ottilie, 25
LOEWENTHAL
  Betsy, 56
LOFMIN
  Sophia, 161
LOFTIS
  Ellen, 238
LOGAN
  Ailey (blk), 292
  Mary, 144, 152, 156
  Mary (blk), 156
  Mary E. (blk), 152
LOGGANS
  Jane (blk), 232
LOHMAN
  Christina, 114
  Margaretha Eva, 285
LOHMANN
  Bernardine, 288
LOHMILLER
  Annie C., 91
LOHNESS
  Alice A., 14
LOKEY
  Sarah E., 216
LOMAN
  Elizebeth, 300
LOMAX
  Elizabeth (blk), 95, 158, 279
  Fanny (blk), 327

Julia (blk), 232
Louisa (blk), 135
Lucy (blk), 57
Martha, 15, 78
Martha S., 15
Mary (blk), 225
LOMBARDI
  Caroline M., 232
LOND
  Fannie L.W., 10
LONG
  Catherine, 313
  Eliza, 91
  Ellen, 183, 263
  Emma Jane, 126
  Margaret, 175
  Mary, 108, 115, 123, 166, 188
  Mary M., 115
  Mary Ophelia, 166
LONGACRE
  Louisa, 218
LONGSON
  Elizabeth, 187
  Sarah F., 171
LONGSTREET
  Augusta, 321
LOOMIS
  Angeline, 191
LOONEY
  Margaret, 124
LORD
  Mary Frances, 134
LORRICK
  Kate, 280
LORTON
  Ellen, 144
LOSE
  Elizabeth, 147
LOSSEN
  Usia M., 203
LOUGHBOROUGH
  Mary Louisa, 327
LOUGHLIN
  Anna, 171
  Elizabeth, 211
  Frances L., 94
LOUIS
  Mary Emeline, 5

# District of Columbia Marriage Licenses, 1858-1870

LOUMAN
  Augusta, 104
LOUTER
  Virginia, 161
LOVE
  Jane M., 85
  Octavia J., 245
  Sarah E., 238
LOVEINGS
  Mary Ann, 115
LOVEJOY
  Margaret, 280
  Mary Frances, 243
  Rebecca C., 308
LOVELACE
  Emma, 245
LOVELESS
  Alice J., 252
  Barbara, 159
  Eliza J., 47
  Florida, 271
  Georgia A., 228
  Jane C., 73
  Marien, 172
  Marion, 178
  Mary E., 166
  Susan, 208
LOVELL
  Margaret, 124
LOVETT
  Anna Matilda, 193
LOW
  Harriet Ann (blk), 40
  Phoebe Ann, 37
LOWE
  Adelaide K., 243
  Annie C. (blk), 148
  Elethen E., 183
  Emily J., 84
  Julia Ann, 295
  Priscilla, 200
  Sarah V., 145
  Susie B., 173
LOWENTHAWL
  Carrie P., 215
LOWERY
  Mary A., 83

LOWMAN
  Elizabeth E., 289
  Emma, 161
  Sophie, 216
LOWNDES
  Nancy (blk), 78
  Susan (blk), 136
LOWNDS
  Nancy (blk), 206
  Serena, 195
LOWNES
  Helen M., 285
LOWRY
  Ella E., 100
  Julia (blk), 323
  Sarah, 65
LOYLES
  Mary (blk), 270
LUBBA
  Eliza, 177
LUBBLE
  Minnie, 188
LUBER
  Anna, 204
LUCAS
  Alice Virginia, 236
  Anna, 236
  Belle, 189
  Caroline (blk), 151
  Eliza, 152, 325
  Eliza (blk), 325
  Fanny (blk), 190, 210
  Francis (blk), 80
  Jane (blk), 159
  Josephine (blk), 37
  Letitie (blk), 119
  Louisa (blk), 279
  Margaret (blk), 48
  Maria A. (blk), 186
  Marian (blk), 82
  Mary Ann (blk), 2
  Mary C. (blk), 176
  Mary Elizabeth, 264
  Melvina, 109
  Nancy, 228, 261
  Nancy (blk), 228
LUCE
  Ella E., 97
  Mary A., 95

LUCHESSI
  Josephine, 43
LUCK
  Eliza, 62
LUCKEI
  Mary, 131
LUCKENS
  Maggie E., 120
LUCKET
  Elizth. Ann, 239
LUCKETT
  Annie R., 254
  Margaret Ann, 195
  Sarah, 145, 196
  Virginia Ursula, 296
LUCKY
  Clarissa A., 101
LUDDY
  Ellen, 296
LUDEKE
  Annie, 23
  Mary W., 288
LUDIG
  Fredericka, 314
LUDLOW
  Idyllia, 326
LUEBER
  Sophie, 170
LUELZE
  Grace (blk), 216
LUFF
  Sarah Levinia, 89
LUGEENBEEL
  Bettie C., 90
LULLEY
  Lencia, 93
LUMSDEN
  Sarah (blk), 26
LUNAHER
  Barbar L., 36
LUNDAY
  Mary Ann, 200
LUNDY
  Susan (blk), 62
LUNEY
  Hannah, 98
LUNKIN
  Mary Jane (blk), 73

LUNNEY
　Ann, 323
LUNTZ
　Anna, 169
LURCH
　Elizabeth, 326
LUSBY
　Annie L., 184
　Cordelia, 33
　Elizabeth, 49
　Fannie Adella, 302
　Lucy, 90
　Mary E., 228
LUSKEY
　Catherine C., 155
LUTHART
　Dora, 134
LUTZ
　Annie E., 103
LUTZENBERG
　Caroline, 41
LUXEN
　Sarah D., 38
LUXON
　Annie E., 272
LYBRAND
　Mary T., 325
LYCETT
　Ellen, 104
　Joanna, 188
　Johanna, 188
LYDDANE
　Caroline V., 298
　Gertrude, 267
　Mary G., 220
LYDON
　Mary, 292
LYELL
　Frances G., 127
LYLES
　Amelia (blk), 10
　Ann, 234
　Biney Smith, 75
　Elizabeth (blk), 79
　Laura (blk), 9
　Louisa, 110, 129
　Louisa (blk), 129
　Mary E. (blk), 127

LYNCH
　Ann, 94, 100, 308
　Anna F., 94
　Annie, 100
　Bridget, 6, 43, 59,
　　100, 166
　Bridget Catherine, 6
　Catherine, 160
　Elizabeth, 31
　Ellen, 111
　Henrietta, 191
　Jemima (blk), 122
　Julia, 260
　Kate, 25, 114
　Margaret, 230
　Mary, 4, 47, 68, 81,
　　164, 184, 212,
　　222
　Mary A., 222
　Mary Ann, 4
　Patience, 116
　Sarah, 254, 278
LYNN
　Alice L., 99
　Eliza Jane, 308
　Emily (blk), 87
　Harriet, 264, 308
　Harriet (blk), 308
　Isabella, 308
　Mary, 72, 207
　Mary Mildred, 207
　Virginia E., 268
LYON
　Honora, 162
　Margaret, 220
　Mary C., 313
LYONS
　Anna, 35
　Annie N., 314
　Emily (blk), 158
　Honora Annie, 210
　Kate, 208
　Maggie A.A., 303
　Margaret, 69, 132
　Mary, 91, 105, 127,
　　188, 246
　Mary C., 188
　Mary E., 91

—M—

MAACK
　Margaret, 239
　Mary, 2, 186
MAAS
　Caroline, 298
MABURY
　Mary R., 236
MacCARTHY
　Meta Julia, 94
MacCOLLANS
　Margaret, 293
MacDANIEL
　Fannie, 135
MACE
　Mary V., 209
MACHAMARA
　Mary, 31
MACK
　Cecilia (blk), 266
　Elizabeth (blk), 32
　Ellen, 262
　Frances (blk), 149
　Kate, 83
　Margaret, 305
　Martha (blk), 101
　Mary, 304
　Sophia (blk), 288
MACKALL
　Annie (blk), 154
　Caroline, 87
　Chloe, 215
　Cornelia (blk), 127
　Isabella (blk), 76
　Jane (blk), 267
　Lizzie (blk), 298
　Sarah (blk), 138
MACKELY
　Mary, 108
MACKENHEIMER
　Georgia S., 158
MACKEY
　Bridget, 244
　Lizzie, 206
　Sarah, 223, 322
　Sarah Jane, 223
MacLELLAN
　Carrie V., 52

MACON
 Elizabeth, 115
MADDEN
 Ann, 97, 310
 Annie, 97
 Catharine, 45
 Margaret, 43, 137
 Mary, 19, 75
MADDIGAN
 Bridget, 187
MADDOCKS
 Josephine, 73
MADDOX
 Agnes, 235
 Barbary, 285
 Jane (blk), 1
 Louisa A., 290
 Martha A., 189
 Mary Ann, 107
 Mary C., 193
MADER
 Catherine, 204
MADIGAN
 Ann, 39
 Norah, 221
MADISON
 Addie, 92
 Ann Maria, 151
 Virginia, 236
MADOX
 Mary, 218
MAEDEL
 Adelheide, 138
 Emilie, 245
 Rosalie, 88
MAEGHER
 Ann, 106
 Honora, 136
MAFFIS
 Ellen (blk), 23
MAGBYRN
 Mary, 29
MAGEE
 Ellen, 166
 Emily M., 159
 Hattie J., 204
MAGHER
 Annie, 197

MAGILL
 Frances R., 317
 Isabella, 299
MAGIRR
 Margaret, 31
MAGLE
 Ann, 115
MAGRAW
 Margaret, 45
MAGRUDER
 Annie, 280
 Chloe Ann, 96
 Ellen, 37
 Henrietta (blk), 158
 Hester A., 307
 Hester Ann, 18
 Julia (blk), 79
 Julia Ann, 118
 Louisa, 154, 306
 Louisa (blk), 154
 Margaret (blk), 156
 Maria C., 322
 Mary (blk), 117
 Mary Ann, 317
 Nelie, 27
 Roberta Bowie, 291
 Victoria J., 247
 Virginia (blk), 308
MAGUIRE
 Bridget, 200
 Maria, 196
 Mary C., 186
 Minerva, 101
 Susan, 301
MAGWA
 Mary, 102
MAHAGAN
 Ophelia, 146
MAHALEY
 Jane (blk), 141
MAHER
 Margaret Scott, 143
 Mary, 305
 Winifred, 25
MAHLER
 Henge, 164
MAHONEY
 Annie Mary, 230
 Bridget, 79, 212

 Elizabeth (blk), 72
 Ellen, 12, 96, 197, 219
 Fannie (blk), 86
 Julia, 262
 Lucinda, 192
 Margaret, 135, 189, 233, 303
 Margaret (blk), 303
 Margaret Virginia, 233
 Mary, 145, 181, 258, 271
 Mary (blk), 258
 Mary Jane (col'd), 271
 Susan (blk), 160
MAHORNEY
 Emily, 141
 Harriet Ann, 168
 Isabel E., 182
 Mary E., 67
 Sarah C., 43
 Susan (blk), 149
 Sussie V., 81
MAIDEN
 Matilda (blk), 239
MAIFORTH
 Helena, 170
MAINEY
 Catherine, 209
MAINY
 Catharine, 114
MAJOR
 Juliet (blk), 273
 Margaret D., 229
 Mary Emma, 323
 Sarah (blk), 39
 Susan, 233
MALBON
 Emma Jane, 104
MALIGAN
 Mary, 58
MALIHAN
 Mary, 174
MALLEY
 Alice, 54
MALLON
 Ann, 54

MALLORY
  Kate, 193
MALLOY
  Josephine S., 104
  Mary M., 65
MALONE
  Ellen, 63, 162
  Margaret, 44
  Sarah, 36, 188
  Sarah E., 36
MALONEY
  Ada E., 109
  Ann, 133
  Bridget, 253, 265
  Bridget A., 265
  Eliza, 39
  Johana, 64
  Mary, 2, 13, 57, 281
  Mary Ann, 281
  Mary Ellen, 13
MALONY
  Margaret, 69
MALOWNEY
  Delia, 321
MALOY
  Lindea, 309
MAMBERG
  Naitalia, 144
MANAKEE
  Sallie E., 255
MANEY
  Annie, 201
  Bridget, 114, 138
MANGAN
  Mary, 221
MANGHAR
  Bridget, 44
MANGUM
  Charlotte Ann, 232
  Emma, 208
  Martha N., 76
  Mary A., 77
  Mary Ann, 78
MANKIN
  Deborah C., 32
  Elizabeth, 268
  Mary E., 14
  Mary Virginia, 125

MANKINS
  Susan, 274
MANLY
  Catherine, 238
  Ellen, 35
MANN
  Ann Eliza, 242
  Catharine, 279
  Fanny E., 273
  Hannah F., 23
  Sarah, 49, 268
  Sarah E., 268
MANNEKY
  Sarah E., 107
MANNING
  Catherine, 135
  Charlotte, 308
  Margaret E., 293
  Mary, 85, 206
  Mary Ann, 206
MANNIS
  Catherine, 237
MANNIX
  Catharine, 99
MANSFIELD
  A.M., 247
  Ann Maria, 292
  Annie, 316
  Margaret de, 167
  Virginia, 176
MANSVILL
  Mary, 262
MANUETT
  Mary V., 66
MARANVILL
  Ellen, 60
MARBURY
  Anna, 72
  Elizabeth, 222
MARCELLUS
  Emily, 26
MARCERON
  Delia, 196
MARCEY
  Emma, 243
  Jane, 229
  Jennie, 280
  Olivia, 151

MARCHAEL
  Martha E., 316
MARCHAND
  Catharine, 203
MARCHE
  Adelaide S., 104
MARCY
  Mary, 48
MARDEN
  Mary, 187
MARDERS
  Deliersa, 240
MARDES
  Alice James, 137
MARDIS
  Catharine Z., 151
MARGRAF
  Caroline, 251
MARINER
  Maria, 271
MARITY
  Nealy Ann, 279
MARK
  Martha S., 211
MARKEY
  Annie, 14
MARKHAM
  Catherine (blk), 292
MARKINS
  Elizabeth M., 255
MARKS
  Josie R., 79
  Julia A., 325
  Mary Ann, 177
  Mary E., 189
MARLL
  Kate E., 250
MARLOW
  Elizabeth (blk), 192
  Laura V., 248
  Lydia (blk), 47
  Margaret (col'd), 69
  Sarah (blk), 37
MARMADUKE
  Susan, 139
MARONEY
  Bridget, 214
  Catharine, 60, 244
  Winnie, 199

### District of Columbia Marriage Licenses, 1858-1870

MAROONEY
  Bridget R., 45
  Catherine, 61
  Mary, 262
MARR
  M. Aretta, 177
  Mary V., 215
  Sarah J., 199
MARRIN
  Annie L., 197
MARROW
  Mary, 86
MARS
  Adaline (blk), 18
MARSH
  Elizabeth, 213
  Kate A., 94
  Marilla M., 10, 190
  Victoria H., 244
MARSHAL
  Virginia, 254
MARSHALL
  Anna, 25
  Annie, 160
  Barbara (blk), 98
  Catherine (blk), 109
  Chloe Ann (blk), 98
  Christiana (blk), 31
  Clara (blk), 294
  Clementina, 123
  Cornelia Ann, 229
  Delia Ann (blk), 36
  Eliza (blk), 25, 29
  Ellen (blk), 151
  Emma Louisa, 87
  Fanny, 83
  Florence (blk), 179
  Josephine (blk), 22
  Julia (blk), 109
  Lula (blk), 150
  Margaret (blk), 326
  Martha Ellen, 251
  Mary, 14, 45, 79, 269
  Mary (blk), 269
  Mary Jamison, 45
  Mary V. (blk), 79
  Matilda (blk), 136
  Rachael A.C., 311
  Sarah (blk), 259, 289

  Sarah W., 100
  Susan, 190, 258
  Susan (blk), 190
MARSHONG
  Elizabeth, 124
MARSTON
  Annie J., 295
  Mary S., viii
MART
  Mary, 180
MARTH
  Elizabeth, 119
MARTIAN
  Magtalena, 327
MARTIN
  Alice Annie, 293
  Amelia (blk), 153
  Ann, 142, 161
  Annie Elizth., 142
  Barbara (blk), 154
  Bridget, 13, 127
  Carrie L., 33
  Catherine, 155, 215
  Catherine E., 215
  Charlotte, 131
  Christina, 190
  Clara E., 210
  Eleanor, 274
  Ellen, 145, 158, 171
  Ellen, 158
  Ellen Hortense, 145
  Emeline, 218
  Emma, 99, 174
  Emma J., 174
  Fannie, 103, 299
  Florence V., 275
  Georgiana, 119, 310
  Hannah M., 21
  Harriet (blk), 7
  Helen (blk), 216
  Isabella, 291
  Jane Frances, 258
  Joanna (blk), 214
  Josephine R., 47
  Louisa, 69, 180
  Louisa E., 180
  Lucinda (blk), 78, 323
  Lucy (blk), 289
  Margaret, 20, 122

  Margaret B., 20
  Maria, 252
  Marion J., 307
  Martha E., 193
  Martha L., 254
  Mary, 31, 44, 57, 58,
    60, 74, 78, 80, 81,
    103, 104, 108, 132,
    154, 202, 215, 217,
    253
  Mary (blk), 57
  Mary A., 31, 253
  Mary Alice, 74
  Mary Ann, 103, 215
  Mary C. (blk), 78
  Mary E., 60, 80, 202
  Mary E. (blk), 108
  Mary H., 217
  Mary J., 80
  Maryetta E., 132
  Millie (blk), 32
  Minna, 186
  Phebe (blk), 53
  Sallie, 76, 315
  Sallie A., 76
  Sarah J., 274
  Susan, 131
  Valinda F., 74
MARTINEZ
  Margaret M., 247
MARTSH
  Rose Bella, 282
MARTYN
  Elizabeth, 303
MARTZ
  Elizabeth, 121
  Ida, 121
MARX
  Caroline, 59
MARYMAN
  Elmira Elizth., 196
MASHEY
  Ange (blk), 306
MASI
  Caroline R., 75
  Margaret C., 147
  Matilda L., 155

MASON
  Ann (blk), 191
  Ann Rebecca, 55
  Annie, 224, 297
  Catharine (blk), 65, 210
  Catherine, 70
  Chyndy (blk), 226
  Eliza (blk), 174, 274
  Ellen, 83, 285
  Ellen D., 285
  Emily (blk), 107
  Frances, 124
  Ida, 144
  Johanna F., 172
  Kitty (blk), 35
  Lucinda (blk), 321
  Lucy Ann (blk), 293
  Margaret, 112
  Martha (blk), 239
  Mary, 47, 85, 133, 205, 327
  Mary C. (blk), 327
  Mary E., 133, 205
  Mary Nicholas, 47
  Rachel E. (blk), 179
  Sally M., 19
  Sarah (blk), 244
  Sarah F. (blk), 123
  Sophia (blk), 86
  Virginia, 299
MASSEY
  Catherine (blk), 149
  Mary, 137
  Sarah (blk), 126
  Sophia, 144
MASSIE
  Jane L., 115
MASTERS
  Emma, 46
MASTERSON
  Lizzie, 169
MASTON
  Sarah R., 260
MATHET
  Catherine, 243
MATHEWS
  Catherine (blk), 312
  Christiana A., 167
  Cordelia, 42
  Emily (blk), 35, 82
  Julia (blk), 269
  Julia A., 296
  Lydia (blk), 174
  Maggie (blk), 61
  Maria, 241
  Martha, 27
  Rachel (blk), 153
  Susan (blk), 327
  Victoria, 70
MATHISON
  Sarah A., 39
MATLOCK
  Emma, 14
MATTERN
  Elizabeth, 308
MATTHEWS
  Ann V. (blk), 42
  Carrie V., 140
  Eliza (blk), 136
  Elizabeth, 57
  Josephine (blk), 278
  Kate, 97
  Laura, 45
  Lizzie, 310
  Margaret (blk), 33
  Maria (blk), 248
  Mary, 36, 233, 323
  Mary E. (blk), 233
  Mary W., 36
  Matilda (blk), 205
  Sarah (blk), 69
MATTHIESON
  Mary E., 56
MATTINGLY
  Cornelia Jane, 277
  Julia Francis, 23
  Julia Jane, 53
  Marian E., 295
  Minerva A., 277
MAULER
  Lila J. (blk), 266
MAURER
  Gertrude, 138
MAURICE
  Jennie, 138
MAURY
  Alice W., 118
  Ann H., 201
  Belle, 246
  Eliza, 251
MAXWELL
  Annie H., 88
  Jane, 120
  Priscilla, 324
  Virginia, 140
MAY
  A. Elizabeth, 134
  Catharine (blk), 217
  Elizabeth, 41
  Mary, 86
MAYHEW
  Mary Jane, 237
  Rachel (blk), 267
MAYHUE
  Omedgia, 144
MAYNADIER
  Margaret F., 10
  Sallie S., 208
MAYNARD
  Fanny (blk), 122
McALLISTER
  Bridget, 195
  Sarah Lewis, 136
McANDREWS
  Kate, 164
McANNALLY
  Rose, 164
McARTHUR
  Sarah, 287
McAULIFFE
  Margaret, 29
McAVOY
  Rose, 274
McBLAIR
  Virginia G., 270
McBRIDE
  Margaret, 117
  Mary A., 221
  Mary E., 100
  Sarah Jane, 39
McCABE
  Hannah, 86
  Susan, 112
McCADDIN
  Annie, 188

McCAFFRY
　Mary, 55, 68
　Mary Louisa S., 68
McCAIN
　Henrietta, 196
McCALIGATE
　Mary, 226
McCALL
　Ellen, 214
McCALLAN
　Bridget, 86
　Hanora, 84, 188
McCANN
　Annie, 40, 293
　Annie T., 293
　Ellen, 162
　Mary Ann, 294
McCARDDEN
　Maggie F., 79
McCARRICK
　Elizabeth, 110
McCARRIG
　Mary, 211
McCARTEN
　Bridget, 243
McCARTHEY
　Catherine, 187
McCARTHY
　Bridget, 131, 133, 219
　Catharine, 111
　Catherine, 133, 194, 221
　Eliza, 87, 111
　Elizabeth, 87
　Ellen, 106, 131, 187
　Hannah, 64, 201, 250
　Jane, 298
　Julia, 54
　Kate, 168, 219
　Margaret, 237
　Mary, 49, 85, 94, 96, 123, 190, 262, 279
　Mary A., 94
　Mary Ellen, 96
　Mary H., 279
　Susan, 81

McCARTIN
　Mary Ann, 52
McCARTON
　Ann, 71
McCARTY
　Catherine, 99
　Ellen, 95, 132, 139
　Hanora, 29
　Mary, 16, 104, 122
　Mary M., 104
McCAULEY
　Eliza, 61, 111
　Elizabeth, 61
　Ellen, 281
　Frances, 281
　Julia, 89
　Mary Ann, 50
McCAULY
　Ellen, 223
　Kate, 59
McCHESNUTT
　Mary E., 81
McCLELLAN
　Isabella, 242
McCLERY
　Sidney J., 174
McCLINTOCK
　Martha E., 209
McCLORY
　Mary, 106
McCLOSKY
　Sarah E., 162
McCLURE
　Hannah, 196
McCLUSKEY
　Margaret, 95
McCOLLOF
　Mary, 125
McCOLLUM
　Mary, 198
McCONNELL
　Mary C., 51
　Rachel, 294
　Susan, 263
McCOOMBS
　Susan G., 169
McCORMIC
　Mary Ann, 219

McCORMICK
　Ann, 70
　Bridget, 170
　Catherine, 287
　Emmeline L., 93
　Mary, 128, 166, 224
　Mary Ann, 128
　Mary H., 224
　Sarah J., 113
McCORRIGAN
　Mary, 56
McCOSKER
　Mary T., 192
McCOY
　Anna, 39
　Belinda, 169
　Catherine, 219
　Emily (blk), 53
　Hannah (blk), 227
　Helen (blk), 129
　Henrietta, 136
　Letty (blk), 267
　Sallie (blk), 163
　Susan, 104
McCRACKEN
　Maggie, 178
McCRERY
　Sarah Lizzie, 194
McCUEN
　Julia, 13
McCULLIF
　Jennie, 182
McCULLOUGH
　Hester G., 70
McCUTCHEN
　Carrie C., 118
　Maggy, 297
McCUTCHINS
　Emma E., 202
McDADE
　Martha, 128
McDANIEL
　Julia, 174
　Sarah, 15
McDANIELS
　Annie, 9
McDERMOTT
　Bridget, 110
　Catherine, 193

McDERMOTT
Cecelia, 43
Ellen, 58
Harriet E., 234
Lucy, 197
Margaret, 245
Mary Ann, 247
Mary Francis, 42
McDEVITT
Emma, 77
Hannah, 45
Jane, 102
Rebecca M.V., 196
Rose, 122
McDONALD
Catherine, 209, 211
Elichea, 49
Eliza, 203
Eugenia, 267
Fannie, 182
Hanora, 275
Joanna, 282
Julia J., 55
Maria, 281
Mary, 70, 128, 156, 167, 198
Mary E., 167
Rosanna, 50, 81
Rose, 212
Susan, 286
McDONNEL
Maria, 6
McDONNELL
Mary, 167, 315
Rose, 280
Sallie V., 14
McDONNOUGH
Ann, 210
McDONOLD
Isabel, 13
McDONOUGH
Anna, 262
Annie, 96
Bridget, 282
Elizabeth E., 240
Mary, 206, 221
Mary C., 221
Winifred, 95

McDOWELL
Jennie, 319
McELFRESH
Annie E., 295
Elizabeth, 200
McELROY
Bridget, 110
Jane, 82
McELWEE
Emma, 133
McENERY
Mary, 78
McEVOY
Julia T., 204
Mary A., 214
Rose, 57
McEWEN
Ann, 255
Lois H., 312
McFADDEN
Mary Ellen, 200
McFALL
Cecilia, 184
McFARLAND
Catharine, 23
Hannah, 105
Isabella, 269
McFARLIN
Jane VanDelia, 49
McFAUL
Mary L., 166
McFEE
Annie, 60
McFOULAND
Emily, 313
McGANN
Mary, 281
McGARITY
Catherine, 46
McGARR
Brittannia, 278
McGARVEY
Catherine, 35
Ellen, 222
Julia, 277
Mary, 54
McGARVRIN
Eliza, 181

McGARVY
Joanna, 96
McGEE
Annie, 249
Kate, 177
Mary, 95, 246
McGEFFIT
Sallie A., 133
McGEORGE
Sarah A., 50
McGHEE
Louisa A., 281
McGIINNEY
Annie, 171
McGILL
Anna Louisa, 147
Emma, 207
Georgiana C., 248
Julia, 80
Mary Ellen, 171
McGINNIS
Catherine, 75
Kate, 198
Sarah N., 196
McGINTY
Mary, 143
McGLENNON
Catharine A., 256
McGLOUGHLIN
Mollie E., 231
McGLUE
Esther, 322
McGONEGAL
Margaret A., 173
McGONNIGAL
Catherine J., 284
McGOWAN
Alberta S., 314
Mary, 157, 318
McGRATH
Catherine, 197
Ellenor, 262
Hanorah, 84
Kate, 86
Maria, 221
Mary, 242, 282, 321
Mary Ann, 321
Rosa M., 125
Rose, 112

McGRAW
  Annie, 58
  Ellen, 314
  Lizzie, 223
  Mary A., 67
  Mary Ann, 256
McGREEN
  Catherine, 130
McGREGOR
  Jessie, 198
McGUCKEIN
  Catherine, 258
McGUIRE
  Ann, 59, 68, 202
  Annie, 202
  Bridget, 319
  Catharine, 37, 239
  Coody, 169
  Cynthia Jane, 115
  Elizabeth, 173
  Margaret, 172, 245
  Mary A., 18
  Mary Ann, 285
  Mary V., 286
McGWINN
  Hanora, 20
McHUNE
  Anna, 70
McINERHENY
  Mary, 85
McINTEE
  Lizzie, 185
McINTIRE
  Elizabeth (blk), 173
McINTOSH
  Alice M., 198
  Angeline, 178
  Annie V., 179
McINTYRE
  Anna, 221
  Bridget, 193
  Laura E., 10
  Margaret, 43
  Zelina, 250
McKAIGE
  Mary, 194
McKANAN
  Catherine, 56

McKAY
  Mary, 293
McKEE
  Abby A.P., 284
  Bridget, 58
McKELDEN
  Jennie C., 277
  Julia A., 207
  Margaret E., 190
  Parthenia E., 113
  Susan J., 21
McKELEGETT
  Bridget, 199
McKENLEY
  Maria, 219
McKENNA
  Bridget, 110
  Margaret, 162
  Susan, 25
McKENNEY
  Elizabeth E., 284
  Mary (blk), 156
McKENNY
  Julia (blk), 174
McKENZIE
  Margaret E., 222
  Mary, 124
McKERNAN
  Margaret, 247
McKILDOE
  Virginia, 258
McKIN
  Kate, 66
McKINLEY
  Mollie, 27
McKINNEY
  Catharine, 164
  Sarah, 23, 108
  Sarah (blk), 23
McKINSEY
  Martha (blk), 223
McKINSTRY
  Calista A., 21
McKNEW
  Maria R., 278
McKNIGHT
  Amanda V., 239
  Hattie M., 92
  Julia T., 102

McLAUGHLIN
  Isabella, 219
  Liza, 219
  Maggie, 295
  Mary, 71, 98, 111, 253
  Mary C., 253
  Rebecca C., 39
McLEAN
  Catharine, 137
  Eliza P.T., 213
  Emma (blk), 255
  Louisa A., 240
  Marian V., 268
  Mary Louisa, 68
  Sarah E., 247
McLEANEY
  Annie, 271
McLEANY
  Annie, 207
McLEOD
  Mary Helen, 40
McLINEY
  Kate, 226
McLLIGOTT
  Hanora, 194
McMAHAN
  Mary, 67
McMAHON
  Anna, 187
  Bridget, 167, 176
  Bridget Ann, 176
  Joanna, 99
  Margaret, 143, 168
  Mary, 9, 139, 214
McMANN
  Margaret, 70
McMANNIVAN
  Annie, 223
McMANUS
  Jane, 221
  Margaret, 250
McMASTER
  Amanda, 96
McMEEKIN
  Jane, 60
McMULLEN
  Anna Maria, 290

McMUN
  Jane, 45
McMURDY
  Agnes Evelina, 189
McNABB
  Annie E., 235
  Mary, 255
McNAINY
  Mary Ann, 213
McNAIR
  Annie Stuart, 64
  Elizabeth, 212
  Julia W., 287
McNALL
  Belva A., 181
McNALLEN
  Maggie, 272
McNALLEY
  Bessy, 288
McNALLY
  Amanda J., 145
  Catharine, 214
  Elizabeth, 288
  Mary, 196, 242
  Rose, 253
McNAMARA
  Bridget, 58
  Emma, 253
  Jane F., 199
  Johana, 66
  Julia, 99
  Margaret, 29, 163, 220
  Mary, 58, 68, 199, 242
  Sarah P., 151
McNAMARRA
  Hanorah, 253
  Sarah, 154
McNAMEE
  Mary, 87, 179
  Mary Ann, 87
McNANA
  Anna, 164
McNANNEY
  [blank], 315
McNAUGHTON
  M.E., 76
  Mary, 127

McNAULTY
  Margaret, 30
McNEAL
  Frances J., 283
McNEE
  Sarah Ellen, 241
McNEELY
  Ann Elizth., 90
McNEIL
  Mary, 305
McNEILL
  Margaret E.B., 322
  Margery J.G., 258
  Marion W., 70
  Mary F., 290
McNELLA
  Anna, 185
McNERHANEY
  Catharine, 312
McNERHY
  Catherine, 28
McNICHELS
  Mary, 83
McNICKLE
  Selecia, 60
McNIEL
  Ann, 200
McNIER
  Augusta M., 308
  Mary Ann, 120
McPEAK
  Lizzie, 254
McPHERSON
  Ann M. (blk), 25
  Bertha, 118
  Christian, 172
  Edith, 287
  Emily J. (blk), 313
  Julia (blk), 42
  Kate, 163
  Laura A., 94
  Mary (blk), 253
  Mary K., 205
McQUAY
  Hannah (blk), 209
McQUE
  Mary, 28
McQUEEN
  Ann, 241

McQUEY
  Eliza, 219
McREA
  Sarah V., 79
McSHANE
  Mary Ann, 175
McSHAREY
  Mary, 97
McSWEENEY
  Catharine, 189
McSWEENY
  Margaret E., 44
  Mary, 261
McVARRY
  Bridget, 80
McVARY
  Mary, 188
McVAY
  Annie, 233
McVEIGH
  Sarah, 96
McVEY
  Louisa B., 271
  Mary Jane, 236
McWILLIAM
  Mary, 226, 241
  Mary Ann, 226
McWILLIAMSON
  Mamie, 115
MEACHAM
  Polly E., 313
MEACHEN
  Sylla (blk), 55
MEAD
  Ann, 98
  Catherine, 299
  Emma F., 223
  Mary E., 229
MEADE
  Sallie E., 176
MEADER
  Adelaide, 17
  Catharine, 316
MEADOWS
  Fannie, 321
MEADS
  Sarah Ann, 215
MEAGHER
  Bridget, 99

MEAGIN
  Mary, 262
MEAKIN
  Mary A., 303
MEANS
  Sarah J., 241
MEANY
  Johanna, 84
MECHAN
  Mary, 39
MECIN
  Margaret, 215
MECKES
  Louisa, 11
MEDLER
  Lucy (blk), 204
MEDLEY
  Betsey (blk), 118
MEECHAN
  Emma, 19
MEED
  Mary A., 146
MEEKINS
  Rachel A. (blk), 78
MEEKS
  Joanna, 105
MEEM
  Ann America, 75
  Mary Clara, 249
MEGE
  Thérèse, 132
MEGHAN
  Catherine, 122
MEHAN
  Eliza, 253
  Hanora, 169
MEHRING
  Dora, 90
MEIBERT
  Magdelena, 250
MEIER
  Babette, 235
MEIFORT
  Agnes, 249
MEIGS
  Lucy, 263
  Maria (blk), 57
  Mary M., 286
  R. J., 140f

MEILHAUN
  Frances, 201
MEINIKLEIM
  Barbara, 55
MEIR
  Anna, 111
MEISBART
  Rose A., 254
MEISCH
  Rosina, 33
MELCHER
  Marcia E., 206
MELDON
  Maria, 183
MELE
  Rosanna, 92
MELHORN
  Cornelia, 66
  Elise, 281
  Fredericka, 162
  Jennie, 307
  Joanne, 15
MELLEN
  Alice, 277
MELLENTRE
  Hannah (blk), 105
MELLINGTON
  Elizabeth, 169
MELLONEY
  Margaret, 81
MELSON
  Mary T., 312
MELTON
  Mary Jane (blk), 318
MELVIN
  Virginia E., 122
MENSEL
  Emma, 128
MENSING
  Charlotte, 93
  Christine, 85
MENTZE
  Augusta, 88
MENZE
  Lotte, 19
MENZMAY
  Frederika, 276
MERCER
  Elizabeth L., 307

  Ellen (blk), 306
  Emma Louisa, 228
  Indiana (blk), 258
  Julia, 34
  Laura, 101
  Margaret, 320
  Sally (blk), 306
MERCIER
  Mary E. (blk), 149
MERCK
  Caroline, 147
MERCURY
  Lucy A. (blk), 37
MEREDITH
  Elizabeth, 105
  Sara E., 160
MERKINS
  Mary A., 85
MERRICK
  Jane, 169
MERRICKS
  Jane R. (blk), 158
  Virginia (blk), 155
MERRILAT
  Mary A., 229
MERRITT
  Eliza, 58
  Emeline (blk), 260
  Mary Frances (blk), 82
  Mary Jane (blk), 31
MERTEL
  Margaretha, 322
MERTENS
  Clementine, 150
MESICK
  Emily, 300
MESSER
  Julia A. (blk), 135
METCALF
  Christiana, 124
  Margaret, 318
METER
  Mary E., 318
METHANEY
  Catherine, 239
METZ
  Frances R., 146

METZCELLER
  Babette, 311
MEURER
  Laura W., 55
MEYER
  Bird, 327
  Caroline (blk), 298
  Helene, 128
  Maria, 170
  Teresa, 300
  Wilhelmina, 303
MEYERS
  Margaret, 24
  Sophia, 95
  Wilhelmina, 328
MEYLER
  Mary, 194
MICHAEL
  Ellen M., 142
MICHAELS
  Jeannette, 277
MICHEIL
  Dorothea, 233
MICHEL
  Mary Louisa, 21
MICKENS
  Lucy (blk), 277
MICKEY
  Annie, 194
MICKINS
  Susan (blk), 128
MIDDLETON
  Alice, 268
  Catherine (blk), 53
  Eliza, 101
  Frances A., 242
  Hannah J., 143
  Harriet (blk), 90
  Helen, 142
  Isadore A., 94
  Marion, 147
  Mary Patton, 321
  Mary T., 15
  Mollie (blk), 305
  Susan R., 6
MILBURN
  Margt. A., 4
MILES
  Amanda R., 320

Barbara, 89
Eliza, 203, 327
Eliza (blk), 327
Ellen (blk), 259
Frances, 6
Georgiana (blk), 82
Jane (blk), 203
Lizzie S., 275
Malinda (blk), 137
Maria (blk), 48
Martha (blk), 274
Mary, 51, 152
Mary J., 51
Nancy (blk), 272
Sarah J., 39
MILFORD
  Dora (blk), 269
MILLARD
  Anna J., 223
MILLER
  A.M., 168
  Alice (blk), 157
  Alice D., 317
  Almyra, 39
  Amelia, 171, 173, 257
  Ann, 7, 114, 174, 177, 200, 213, 307
  Ann Virginia, 177
  Anna, 114, 213, 307
  Anna E., 114
  Anna T., 213
  Annie, 7, 200
  Augusta, 246
  Berti, 233
  Betty (blk), 152
  Bridget, 43
  Caroline, 127
  Catharine, 276
  Catherine, 77, 140, 212
  Catherine M., 140
  Charlotte (blk), 15
  Clara E., 140
  Eliza, 52, 86, 207, 226, 278, 300, 308
  Eliza A., 300

Elizabeth, 52, 207, 226, 278, 308
Franzelia, 124
Helen A., 38
Henritta, 234
Isabella M., 122
Joanna, 135, 265, 314
Joanna E., 314
Julia A., 74
Laura, 144, 161
Letia, 162
Lina, 186
Lizzie, 65, 185
Louisa, 76, 104, 173, 246, 283
Louisa A., 104
Louisa M.A., 283
Lucinda C., 39
Maggie, 23, 38, 157
Maggie D., 23
Maggie E., 157
Margaret, 12, 27, 95, 194, 211, 245, 309, 314
Margaret A., 194
Margaret J., 194
Margaret L., 314
Margaret R., 12
Maria B., 312
Mary, 16, 21, 26, 42, 66, 71, 75, 125, 135, 142, 152, 181, 236, 254, 258, 275, 280, 327
Mary A., 135, 142
Mary Ann, 16, 42, 71, 258
Mary Ann Hellen, 258
Mary C., 181
Mary E. (blk), 66
Mary J., 26, 327
Mary J.C., 327
Mary L., 21
Mary M., 152, 275
Matilda, 96
Nanette, 223

MILLER
  Pauline, 16
  Sallie, 202, 264
  Sallie C., 202
  Sarah, 168, 172
  Sarah M., 172
  Susan, 181, 242
  Susanna E., 242
MILLRICK
  Margaret, 221
MILLS
  Alice, 266
  Ann (blk), 107
  Catherine M., 225
  Charlotte J., 247
  Evelina, 154
  Hannah C., 101
  Ida, 321
  Josephine, 157
  Lucinda, 33
  Lydia, 151, 234
  Lydia E., 234
  Margaret (blk), 314
  Maria, 56
  Martha (blk), 258
  Mary, 15, 86, 112, 224, 312
  Mary E., 224
  Mary F., 15, 86
  Mary J. R., 312
  Missouri, 327
  Rebecca E., 289
  Sarah Jane, 205
MILON
  Elizabeth, 142
MILTON
  Mary (col'd), 149
  Susan F., 201
  Susan V., 150
MINATOR
  Catharine, 214
MINDER
  Anna Maria, 277
MINER
  Betsy (blk), 296
  Catharine, 169
  Charlotte, 175
  Mary Margaret (blk), 42

MINERET
  Ella G., 96
MINGES
  Susanna, 128
MINGRAM
  Harriet (blk), 289
MINITER
  Maggie, 307
MINITREE
  Ann Rebecca, 155
MINKINS
  Mary (blk), 279
MINN
  Genevive M., 58
MINNEX
  Margaret, 46
MINNICE
  Jennie, 73
MINNICKER
  Ernestine, 247
MINNIS
  Susan A. (blk), 327
MINNIX
  Diana, 188
MINOR
  Amelia (blk), 98
  Betty (blk), 193
  Louisa (blk), 293
  Rosanna (blk), 117
  Sally, 293
MINT
  Ann, 58
MINTER
  Elizabeth, 202
  Mary Louisa, 291
MISCROL
  Cary, 6, 206
MITCHELL
  Abbey (blk), 158
  Annie, 61, 74
  Annie (blk), 74
  Caroline, 140, 153
  Caroline (blk), 153
  Catherine (blk), 18
  Eleanor C., 141
  Elizabeth, 286
  Ella A., 146
  Ellen, 83
  Emily (blk), 326

  Emma R., 166
  Ethelda, 200
  Frances (blk), 139
  Harriet, 142
  Jane, 67
  Jennie V., 286
  Josephine, 115, 121
  Josephine (blk), 115
  Julia, 65
  Louisa (blk), 47
  Louisa A., 104
  Maggie, 56
  Malinda, 165
  Margaret, 20, 222
  Maria, 156
  Marion, 158
  Martha, 15
  Mary, 1, 7, 90, 96, 111, 249, 252, 261, 315
  Mary Ann (blk), 249
  Mary E., 7
  Mary Elizabeth, 252
  Mary Ella (blk), 1
  Mary F., 111
  Mary Jane (blk), 261
  Minnie Goods, 92
  Sarah B., 159
  Sarah Jane, 112
  Susan R., 21
  Susanna, 112, 171
  Susannah, 112
  Willie, 265
MOCABOY
  Minerva F., 226
  Susan, 168
MOCK
  Eliza D., 33
MOCKABEE
  Annie, 197
  Emma Frances, 272
  Harriet (blk), 11
  Mary (blk), 205
  Mary W., 71
  Matilda E., 302
  Rose (blk), 126
MOCKABOY
  Virginia (blk), 270

MOCKEBEE
  Mary Virginia, 87
MOCKLAIR
  Mary, 83
MOCKS
  Ellen, 229
MOCLEAR
  Kate, 28
MODIA
  Anna, 181
MODLEY
  Ann Maria, 306
MODOCK
  Lizzie (blk), 66
MOE
  Mary Jane, 201
MOELER
  Eliza, 72
MOEWES
  Mary A., 119
MOFFAT
  Sarah Frances, 298
MOFFETT
  Susan Rebecca, 193
  Susie R., 95
MOHLER
  Christina, 6
MOHR
  Katrine, 105
MOINOHAN
  Margaret, 86
MOLAN
  Mary, 321
MÖLICH
  Bertha, 162
MOLNIEUX
  Ellen L., 270
MOLOY
  Julia, 257
MOLTH
  Margaret, 278
MONAGHAN
  Ann, 195
  Catherine, 211
  Margaret, 171
MONAHAN
  Margaret, 198
MONEY
  Ellen, 170

Marthay, 87
  Sarah L., 207
  Susan Ann, 103
MONOGUE
  Ann, 134
MONOQUE
  Mary, 29
MONROE
  Jane, 79
  Louisa (blk), 42, 149
  Mary (blk), 321
MONSHOWER
  Ellen, 305
  Fannie, 25
  Jennie, 193
MONT
  Mary A., 106
MONTGOMERY
  Catherine R., 88
  Celia (blk), 259
  Ellen (blk), 98
  Emily, 50
  Margaret (blk), 47
  Mary, 204
  Sarah A., 62
  Virginia, 191
MONTOVERDE
  Mary, 49
MOORE
  Alabama J., 80
  Alice, 21
  Anna (blk), 306
  Annie, 59, 179, 209
  Annie A., 59
  Annie L., 179
  Beatrice, 319
  Caroline (blk), 273
  Catharine, 197, 231
  Catherine (blk), 246
  Catherine F., 45
  Elizabeth, 1, 320
  Elizabeth J., 1
  Ella S., 186
  Ellen, 28
  Emily B., 262
  Eveline, 78
  Fanny, 189, 276
  Fanny D.L., 189

  Frances, 89, 252
  Frances Ann, 89
  Ida V., 132
  Jane (blk), 152
  Jane Margaret, 57
  Jennie B., 129
  Joanna, 276
  Laura A., 314
  Laurinda (blk), 73
  Lettie W., 108
  Lilly, 212
  Louisa, 141, 276
  Louisa F., 141
  Lucinda (blk), 67
  Lucy Jane, 249
  Margaret, 1, 114
  Margaret L., 1
  Martha (blk), 217
  Martha A. (blk), 321
  Martha E., 200
  Mary, 42, 142, 180, 201, 210
  Mary (blk), 142
  Mary Ann, 180
  Mary V., 42
  Rachel E., 174
  Rachel M., 196
  Rosa, 199
  Sarah, 90, 97, 312
  Sarah J. (blk), 312
  Sarah R., 90
  Victoria M., 254
MOORELL
  Jane I., 208
MORAN
  Annie, 128
  Celia M., 240
  Emma J., 54
  Kate M., 173
  Margaret, 62
  Martha, 171
  Mary, 8, 11, 63, 287
  Mary C., 11
  Mary E., 287
  Mary M., 8
  Sarah E., 133
  Virginia C., 232
MOREBURGER
  Lucetta, 144

District of Columbia Marriage Licenses, 1858-1870

MOREHEAD
  Hester A., 325
MORELAND
  Alice (blk), 76
  Ann Elizabeth, 282
  Anna, 59
  H.H., 301
  Jane, 82
  Martha, 146
  Mary E., 226
  Susannah, 138
MORFIT
  Ann, 76
MORFORD
  Susan V., 266
MORGAN
  Ann, 35, 40, 145, 197
  Anna, 35, 40
  Anna C., 40
  Annie, 145
  Betsy (blk), 100
  Bridget, 74
  Ellen, 225
  Emma (blk), 233
  Emma F., 232
  Frances (blk), 137
  Mary, 30, 70, 171, 315
  Mary M., 315
  Matilda, 91
  Miranda, 171
  Sarah E., 320
MORIARITY
  Deborrah, 94
  Mary, 97
MORIARTY
  Mary, 58
MORICE
  Sarah E., 76
MORONY
  Mary, 185
MORRIS
  Amanda W., 78
  Clarissa, 239
  Harriet Elizabeth (blk), 73
  Isabella, 265
  Jane (blk), 216

  Julia (blk), 33, 183
  Laura, 190
  Lucinda (blk), 115
  Maria (blk), 128
  Martha (blk), 54
  Mary, 116, 221
  Mary J. (col'd), 116
  Sallie S., 118
  Sarah, 281
MORRISON
  Anna, 77
  Ellen, 81
  Emm T., 205
  Helen F., 89
  Jane (blk), 182
  Margaret Jane, 111
  Martha J., 127
  Mary Elizabeth, 309
  Matilda (blk), 115
MORRISSEY
  Annie, 229
MORRISY
  Ellen, 219
MORROW
  Annette, 269
  Julia E., 236
  Martha, 167
MORSE
  Emily P., 261
MORTIMER
  Carrie, 163
  Elizabeth, 164
  Fannie C., 252
  Frances E., 230
  Joie A., 290
  Matilda, 198
MORTON
  Adeline (blk), 269
  Arietta O., 197
  Caroline (blk), 259
  Ellen, 244
  Emily (blk), 233
  Jane (blk), 255
  Lucy, 167
  Martha (blk), 290
  Mary (blk), 6
  Nellie (blk), 116
  Rachel (blk), 235

MOSELEY
  Elizabeth, 239
  Mollie A., 37
MOSELY
  Mary V., 121
MOSER
  Janette, 292
MOSES
  Amanda (blk), 225
  Susan D. (blk), 154
MOSS
  Mary (blk), 289
  Mary Hellen, 214
  Nancy, 13
  Susan, 35
MOTHERSHEAD
  Isabela, 250
  Julia M., 40
  Julia Mary, 62
MOTTER
  Sophie M., 243
MOTTLEY
  Jennie E., 279
MOTTO
  Mary, 208
MOULDEN
  Kate, 298
  Mary Cornelia, 221
  Sarah E., 285
MOULDER
  Mary E., 216
MOULTON
  Margaret (blk), 122
  Maria L., 130
  Nellie M. (blk), 322
MOUREN
  Mary B., 236
MOWBRAY
  Elizabeth S., 249
MOXEY
  Lucy Ellen, 233
MOXLEY
  Ann (blk), 255
  Ann V., 243
  Bessie L., 182
  Jane, 152
  Mary Frances, 266
  Mary T., 76
  Susan, 290

MOYER
  Amanda, 52
MUDD
  Emma A., 211, 212
  Issabella, 62
  Mary E., 84
  Matilda Alice, 151
MUDDEMAN
  Lucy E., 281
MUDDIMAN
  Carrie F., 140
  Lucy E., 281
MÜELLER
  Dora, 230
MUENNICH
  Eliza, 257
MUGG
  Mary Elizth., 162
MUIRHEAD
  Isabella, 233
MULANY
  Hannah, 45
MULCAHEY
  Catherine, 124
MULCAHY
  Ellen, 188
MULCHY
  Margaret, 95
MULDOON
  Hannah, 173
MULIKEN
  Sarah Jane, 216
MULKAHA
  Johanna, 97
MULKERRINS
  Mary, 118
MULLAN
  Katherine, 101
MULLANEY
  Sidney (blk), 117
MULLARNY
  Bridget, 46
MULLEN
  Arthelia A., 236
  Bridget, 90, 116
  Gabriella, 106
  Mary E., 63
MULLER
  Fredericka, 250
  Mary Elizabeth, 222
MÜLLER
  Mina P., 309
MULLERY
  Delia, 211
MULLIGAN
  F. Marian, 319
  Margaret, 5, 185
  Mary Ann, 308
  Susannah, 186
MULLIKEN
  Amanda (blk), 153
  Mary F., 23
MULLIN
  Annie, 164, 191
  Catherine, 62
  Margaret, 123
  Mary (blk), 24
  Sallie E., 32
MULLOWAY
  Ellen, 160
MULLOWNEY
  Mary, 60
MULLOY
  Catharine, 111
  Elizabeth, 34, 53
  Elizabeth (blk), 53
  Lizzie, 218
  Louisa I., 195
  Maria, 186
  Rose, 295
MULQUEHAR
  Sophia, 197
MULREADY
  Mary, 299
MULROY
  Bridget, 49
MULT
  Ellen, 184
MULVAHAL
  Mary, 260
MULVEY
  Ann, 222
MULVIHILL
  Margaret, 184
MÜMBLE
  Charlotte L., 294
MUMENTHALER
  Louisa, 56
MUMFORD
  Mary, 247
MUNCK
  Amelia T., 169
MUNDELL
  Margaret R., 11
MÜNDELL
  Margaritha, 327
MUNDHEIM
  Sarah, 161
MUNDLE
  Martha (blk), 163
MUNDY
  Ellen Louisa (blk), 219
MUNGAN
  Maggie, 30
MUNJOY
  Virginia, 322
MUNROE
  Caroline (blk), 263
  Cora (blk), 217
  Elizabeth (blk), 318
  Georgia E., 251
  Hester (blk), 244
  Martha J., 176
  Mary Louisa (blk), 287
  Sarah (blk), 113
MUNSON
  Annie E., 95
  Cornelia S., 294
  Lucy E., 212, 285
  S. Agnes, 281
MUNTZ
  Ann, 221
MURDOCK
  Baleam, 211, 212
MURLOCK
  Emma, 17
MURPHEY
  Amanda D., 309
  Bridget, 188
  Catherine, 255
  Ellen, 246
  Franzetta, 297
  Joanna, 187
  Julia, 86, 194
  Kate, 170

District of Columbia Marriage Licenses, 1858-1870

MURPHEY
  Margaret, 77, 81,
    84, 207
  Mary, 70, 130, 175,
    274
  Mary C., 175
MURPHY
  Alice, 243, 263
  Alice O., 243
  Anna, 81
  Bridget, 208, 212
  Catharine, 57
  Catherine, 9, 139,
    214
  Catherine E., 139
  Eliza, 164
  Ellen, 36, 49, 62,
    140, 168, 282
  Ellen J., 168
  Emily M., 146
  Emma A., 92
  Francis Rebecca,
    237
  Georgia, 144
  Honora, 241
  Jane, 212, 304
  Joanna, 97
  Johanna, 4, 43
  Julia, 3, 94
  Julia Ann, 3
  Kate P., 51
  Lizzie A., 67
  Margaret, 29, 220
  Martha L., 87
  Mary, 22, 29, 57,
    58, 66, 67, 68, 74,
    79, 90, 241
  Mary (blk), 79
  Mary A., 74
  Mary Ellen, 58
  Mary H., 90
  Mary Jane, 66
  Mary M., 29
  Sarah, 48, 156, 165,
    306
  Sarah J., 156
MURRAY
  Ann, 51, 325
  Anna (blk), 51
  Catharine, 145, 213
  Catharine Lucy, 145
  Catherine, 146
  Ellen, 173
  Harriet, 97
  Isabella Ella, 219
  Joanna A., 321
  Julia A., 302
  Margaret, 10, 49,
    208
  Margaret A., 10
  Mary, 13, 35, 144,
    145, 160, 191,
    194, 197, 200,
    211, 258, 275
  Mary Ann, 35
  Mary Cecilia, 200
  Mary E., 144, 191
  Mary H., 275
  Mary Jane, 258
  Mildred, 21
  Sarah, 205, 312
  Sarah A., 312
MURRONEY
  Mary, 39
MURROONEY
  Margaret, 13
MURRY
  Isabel Frances, 207
  Lizzie Ogden, 188
MURT
  Catharine, 45
  Ellen, 101
  Mary, 83
MURTH
  Kate, 71
MURTHA
  Margaret, 220
MURTHY
  Annie, 66
MURTOUGH
  Mary A., 170
MURVILLE
  Bridget, 238
MUSE
  Florida, 232
  Lucind (blk), 76
  Sarah (blk), 273
  Virginia, 225

MUSGRIFF
  Augusta, 74
MUSGROVE
  Rachel Deborah, 87
MUSINGO
  Caroline, 134
MYER
  Mary, 20
MYERS
  Ada F., 170
  Agnes, 256
  Amelia, 4
  Bridget, 199
  Clara, 255
  Eliza V., 49
  Emma J., 20
  Emma S., 61
  Fanny (blk), 226
  Henrietta, 81
  Josephine A., 269
  Julia F., 34
  M.J., 153
  Margaret, 312
  Maria, 315
  Martha (blk), 31
  Mary, 65, 72, 80,
    316
  Mary E., 80, 316
  Mary E. (blk), 316
  Nannie, 45
  Rebecca E., 182
  Rosa, 39
  Sallie A., 113
  Sarah E., 148
  Tacy Virginia, 21
  Virginia C., 32
  Virginia F., 183
MYRICK
  Arlitta B., 182

—N—

NAGEL
  Susan, 170
NAILEGAN
  Helen, 92
NAILOR
  Lizzie R., 295
  Malvinia, 26

NAILOR
  Marion F., 53
  Mary, 163
  Rhoda, 204
NAIRY
  Ann, 261
NALIGAN
  Mary, 13
NALLE
  Bettie R., 187
  Mary D., 18
NALLEY
  Eliza Jane, 63
  Harriet Louisa, 36
  July A., 206
  Mary (blk), 147
  Mary Ann T., 167
NALLS
  Frances E., 282
  Martha Ann, 175
  Mary E., 65
  Mary T., 276
NALLY
  Anna, 174
  Eliza A., 64
  Eliza Ellen, 245
  Elizabeth R., 20
  Georgeinna, 283
  Margaret R., 271
  Maria, 323
  Mary Catherine, 13
  Mary E., 24
  Sarah, 203
NAMAN
  Isabella, 271
NAMRELLE
  Blanche, 79
NANZ
  Frederika, 20
  Wilhelmina Fredericka, 180
NARDEN
  Mary (blk), 142
NASH
  Amelia (blk), 67
  Ellen, 66
  Frances (blk), 241
  Maria (blk), 77
  Martha R., 167

Mary E., 287
Sally, 11
NAUMANN
  Elizabeth, 256
  Francisca, 129
NAYLOR
  Barbara C., 222
  Dawsella V., 260
  Elizabeth, 180
  Georgianna C., 217
  Henrietta M., 31
  Josephine, 110
  Lizzie, 215
  Maggie, 116
  Mary A. (blk), 207
  Matilda Verlinda, 150
  Rachel Elizabeth, 6
  Sarah E., 5
NEACEY
  Margaret, 238
NEAGHER
  Caroline, 190
NEAL
  Margaret (blk), 106
  Maria (blk), 319
  Sarah E., 227
  Winnie (blk), 291
NEALE
  Elizabeth A., 3
  Ellen, 137
  Flora (blk), 47
  Frances (blk), 61
  Glorvina A., 5
  Harriet, 211
  Henrietta, 56
  Indiana, 72
  Jane (blk), 191
  Lucinda (blk), 34
  Lucy S., 98
  Margaret (blk), 70
  Mary (blk), 58
  Mary Adelia T., 15
  Mary Ann (blk), 153
  Miss (blk), 266
  Sarah (blk), 314
  Susan V., 312
NEARY
  Annie T., 114

NEEDHAM
  Alice, 207
  Mary E., 162
NEELY
  Mary, 190
NEENAN
  Lucy, 86
NEIB
  Emily, 257
NEIL
  Hanora, 97
NEILL
  Johanna, 163
  Mary J., 212
  Sue E., 68
  Susan E., 268
NEITZEY
  Annie, 286
NEKE
  Kate, 283
NELAN
  Annie, 240
NELLUMS
  Virginia (blk), 154
NELSON
  Adelade, 236
  Alice (blk), 134
  Amanda (blk), 10, 116
  Ann, 192, 237, 299
  Ann M., 237
  Anna E., 299
  Caroline (blk), 53
  Elizabeth, 259
  Francis (blk), 234
  Hannah, 282
  Jeannett L., 126
  Lizzie, 127
  Maggie A., 308
  Margaret Ann (blk), 11
  Maria (blk), 132
  Martha, 92, 186, 320
  Martha (blk), 92
  Martha Ann (blk), 320
  Mary, 17, 48, 71, 86, 210, 287, 305

439

District of Columbia Marriage Licenses, 1858-1870

NELSON
  Mary (blk), 17, 48, 86
  Mary Ann (blk), 305
  Mary Frances, 71
  Patsey, 237
  Susan (blk), 305
NESTOR
  Emelia, 114
NETTER
  Ellen (blk), 58
NEUEN
  Catharine, 106
NEUMANN
  Anna Ottilie, 257
NEUMEYER
  Ellen, 237
  Mary Louisa, 200
NEVERS
  M. Lucy, 228
NEVILLE
  Ellen, 66
NEVILLS
  Agnes, 295
NEWBY
  Agnes, 236
  Alice (blk), 101
NEWCOMB
  C. Virginia, 44
NEWELL
  Catherine J., 275
  Emily E., 141
NEWHOUSE
  Virginia M., 4
NEWMAN
  Agnes (blk), 305
  Augusta, 161, 265
  Augusta Louisa, 161
  Elizabeth, 40
  Katherine, 230
  Louisa, 1
  Lucinda (blk), 159
  Mary, 38, 226, 290
  Mary (blk), 38, 290
NEWMEYER
  Barbet, 84
  Fannie, 113
NEWMYER
  Jenny, 43

NEWN
  Barbara, 5
NEWTON
  Annie, 260
  Charity (blk), 82
  Elizabeth V., 121
  Jane (blk), 249
  Marietta Elizth., 152
  Mary (blk), 285
  Mary Ann (blk), 228
  Matilda, 237
  Sophia (blk), 150
NICHOLAS
  Ella (blk), 144
NICHOLLS
  Eveline, 321
  Helen R., 287
  Louise, 135
  Mary H., 295
  Virginia, 139
NICHOLS
  Augusta, 273
  Eliza E. (blk), 134
  Georgianna (blk), 20
  Harriet Pauline, 202
  Margaret (blk), 278
  Martha R., 138
  Susan Victoria, 94
NICHOLSON
  Elizabeth, 40
  Jane (blk), 192
  Josephine, 308
  Lucy, 237
  Margaret F., 94
  Sarah F., 20
NICKENS
  Jane (blk), 3
  Nancy (blk), 309
NICKERSON
  Jennie, 225
NICKOLS
  Caroline, 272
NIE
  Rachael K., 73
NIEBEL
  Katherina, 177
NIECA
  Louisa, 51

NIEDERHOFER
  Mary, 276
NIEVEL
  Sophia, 134
NIGHTENGALE
  Arminta, 65
NIGHTINGALE
  Emily, 205
  Mary E., 231
NILAND
  Bridget, 67
  Sarah, 272
NIMMO
  Jennie R., 173
NIPPER
  Eleanor, 119
NISBET
  Alice, 225
  Amelia, 225
NOA
  Caroline, 172
  Henrietta, 101
NOAKES
  Maggie V., 260
NOAN
  Ann, 287
NOBLE
  Alice, 54
  Mary Jane, 242
  R.W., 201
NOELL
  Mary Ann, 295
NOENN
  Ann, 208
NOKES
  Mary E., viii, 284
NOLAN
  Anna, 81
  Annie E., 178
  Elizabeth, 201
  Harriet L., 50
  Julia, 111
  Margaret, 99, 253, 328
  Mary, 65
  Sarah, 52
NOLAND
  Caroline, 159
  Catherine, 68

NOLAND
  Ellen, 218
  Fannie F., 24
  Jane, 271
  Mary C., 159
  Mary F., 145
  Virginia, 297
NOLEN
  Ann Rachel, 6
NOLIN
  Margaret, 220
NOLING
  Mary, 307
NOLL
  Kate Augusta, 110
  Madlina, 268
NOLLS
  Alethia, 213
NOLTE
  Martha, 169, 311
  Mary L., 136
  Veronica, 218
NOLTEN
  Mary, 32
NOON
  Mary, 217
NOONAN
  Ann, 146, 264
  Annie, 264
  Kate, 257
  Mary, 220, 303
  Mary E., 220
NOONIN
  Catherine, 198
NORFLEET
  Lottie A., 96
NORFOLK
  Margaret A.B., 173
NORMAN
  Clara (blk), 150
NORMENT
  Ulie, 146, 218
NORMUL
  Mary, 261
NORRIS
  Anne (blk), 17
  Ellen E., 187
  Emma, 114
  Julia, 139

  Laura V. (blk), 285
  Lidia, 46
  Lizzie, 91
  Louisa M., 36
  Maria, 210, 301
  Maria F., 301
  Mary, 68, 168, 220
  Mary A., 168
  Phillis (blk), 266
  Rachel Ann, 72
  Sarah, 139, 269
  Sarah Jane (blk), 269
  Virginia Cooper, 325
NORRISS
  Jane Elizth., 179
NORTON
  Catharine, 3
  Cornelia, 34
  Frances A.H., 104
  Laura V., 66
  Martha A., 295
  Mary, 29, 47, 182, 320
  Mary (blk), 47
  Mary A., 182
  Mary E., 320
NOSAY
  Mary, 37
  Sarah E., 207
NOSCHEL
  Louise, 121
NOTBAUM
  Emma, 59
NOTHEY
  Eliza, 44
NOUFSKI
  Mary, 134
NOUNAN
  Mary (blk), 155
NOURSE
  Annie W., 80
  Charlotte E., 325
  Emmie Josepha, 278
  Helen, 291
  Sarah L., 235
NOWELLS
  Maria, 93

NOWLAND
  Mary Virginia, 257
NOYES
  Anna M., 262
  Eliza B., 236
  Isadora E., 294
  Kate E., 238
NUDEN
  Charity A. (blk), 190
NUGENT
  Emma Jane, 317
  Margaret, 115
  Martha (blk), 179
  Rebecca (blk), 314
  Sarah Ann (blk), 249
NULLY
  Mary, 168
NUTRELL
  Mary Jane, 286
NUTT
  Isabella (blk), 243
NUTTE
  Martha, 323
NUTWELL
  Sabra A.D., 87
  Sophia Fannie, 79
NYE
  Mary E., 302
NYMAN
  Emma J., 151

—O—

O'BARCLEY
  Catharine, 221
O'BRIAN
  Ellen, 9
O'BRIEN
  Ann, 75, 83, 175, 212
  Anna E., 83
  Annie M., 175
  Bridget, 282
  Catharine, 68
  Catherine H., 106
  Elizabeth Ann, 67
  Ellen, 123, 163
  Ellen A., 123

O'BRIEN
  Endora, 66
  Hanora, 294
  Henrietta, 182
  Johana, 46
  Julia, 130
  Louisa, 296
  Margaret, 184
  Mary, 97, 190, 215, 235, 244, 313, 314
  Mary Ann, 97, 313
  Mary L., 235
  Nannie, 214
  Rebecca, 80
  Sarah, 82
O'BRYAN
  Margaret, 234
O'BYRNE
  Jane, 118
O'CALLAGHAN
  Catherine, 69
O'CONER
  Kittie, 200
O'CONNELL
  Julia, 81
  Mary, 69, 191, 197
  Mary Ann, 191
O'CONNER
  Annie, 229
  Catharine, 48
  Catherine, 17, 24, 160
  Margaret, 44
  Mary, 88, 161
  Mary A., 88
O'CONNOR
  Bridget, 246
  Catharine, 63
  Edward S., 121, 220
  Johanna, 46, 63, 161
  Kate, 163
  Margaret, 27, 83
  Mary Ann, 155
  Nancy, 201
O'DAIE
  Bridget M., 85
O'DAY
  Ann, 221
  Catharine, 13, 194, 195
  Catherine, 213
  Delia, 310
  Elizabeth, 200
  Hannah, 194
  Julia, 118
  Mary, 56, 123
  Mary Ann, 123
O'DELL
  Rachel, 206
  Sarah C., 317
  Sue B. Suttle, 309
O'DONALD
  Josephine, 232
O'DONNELL
  Agnes, 220
  Annie, 220
  Bridget, 100, 197, 211, 310
  Ellen, 120
  Julia A., 84
  Margaret, 97, 145
  Margaret F., 145
  Mary, 61, 211
O'DONNOGHUE
  Annie, 172
  Mary, 194
O'DONOGHUE
  Eleanor, 55
O'DWYER
  Honora, 213
  Mary Ann, 282
O'FLYNN
  Mary V., 59
O'HALLORAN
  Bridget, 110
O'HARA
  Ann, 238
  Catherine, 281
O'HARE
  Annie, 249
  Eliza, 38
  Margaret, 162
O'HEARN
  Margaret, 72
O'HERRON
  Annie, 326
O'KEEFE
  Bridget, 212
  Catherine M.J., 130
  Elizabeth, 94
O'LEARY
  Ellen, 44, 195
  Margaret, 139, 186
  Margaret A., 186
O'MARA
  Margaret, 216
O'MEAR
  Mildred, 208
O'MERA
  Annie, 66
O'NEAL
  Ann Maria, 26
  Joanna, 165
O'NEALE
  Anna E., 35
  Annie, 152, 181
  Annie E., 152
O'NEIL
  Bridget, 43
  Elizabeth, 177, 319
  Hester (blk), 126
  Kate, 100
  Letitia, 147
  Mary Elizabeth, 3
  Sarah, 315
O'NEILL
  Ann M., 8
  Catherine, 43
  Elizabeth (blk), 289
O'NIEL
  Ann, 162
  Julia, 88
  Mary, 6
O'REILLY
  Kathleen L., 325
O'REILY
  Louisa, 161
O'RORKE
  Elizabeth, 85
  Minnie, 165
O'ROURKE
  Catherine, 60
  Mary, 230
O'RYAN
  Jenny, 136

## District of Columbia Marriage Licenses, 1858-1870

O'SHAUGHENY
  Catharine, 173
O'SHEA
  Abbey, 14
  Joanna, 139
  Mary, 220
O'SULLIVAN
  Margaret, 42
O'TOOLE
  Bridget, 188
  Fanny, 64
  Julia, 158
  Mary, 239, 293
OAKES
  Ellen, 158
OAKSHOTT
  Annie, 178
OATES
  Sarah, viii
OBERST
  Rosina, 327
ODEN
  Eliza Ann, 107
ODRICK
  Mary Frances, 290
  Sallie (blk), 128
OEHRING
  Selma, 252
OERTEL
  Anna Mary (adopted Marie Glick), 140
OETTLE
  Juliana R., 109
OETZEL
  Eliza, 113
OFENSTEIN
  Catherine Johanna, 214
OFERMAN
  Eliza, 2
OFFORD
  Ellen (blk), 148
OFFUTT
  Eugenia E., 38
  Frances M., 157
  Rachel, 136
  Sarah R., 40
OGDEN
  Lizzie F., 326

Mary, 297
Rebecca M., 21
Sarah, 151
OGLE
  Adaline (blk), 226
  Rachel (blk), 46
OHL
  Catharine, 93
OHNASH
  Annie, 256
OLDHAM
  Malvina (blk), 279
OLDS
  Frances E., 323
OLIVER
  Catherine, 24
  Martha, 11
  Mary E., 167
  Mary M., 291
  Mary V., 291
  Sophy (blk), 148
OLLIVER
  Annie, 34
OLMSTED
  Mary L., 213
OMAHUNDRO
  Hattie E., 264
OMOHUNDRO
  Virgin W., 148
OPPENHEIMER
  Gette, 303
OPPERMANN
  Johanne D., 121
ORANGE
  Margaret (blk), 327
ORDWEEN
  Eva, 239
ORME
  Anna, 78
  Emily Frances, 179
  Mary R., 179
ORMSBEE
  Delphine, 25
ORMSBY
  Sarah, 105
ORR
  Margaret, 183
  Mary A., 277
  Mary J., 190

Rebecca (blk), 39
ORRIEN
  Kate C., 175
ORRISON
  Jennie, 43
ORSSCESER
  Kate, 16
ORTHWEIN
  Catharine, 189
OSBORN
  Alice, 66, 221
  Alice M., 66
  Harriet (blk), 313
  Jane (blk), 18
  Jane A., 89
  Martha (blk), 227
  Martha E., 325
  Mary H., 264
  Mary J., 227
  Mitta (blk), 87
  Victoria A., 40
OSBORNE
  America, 303
  Annie, 228
  Frances A., 236
  Mary E., 326
  Mary S., 221
  Rose, 205, 249
  Rosetta, 205
OSGODBEY
  Sarah L., 247
OSGOOD
  Emma, 301
OSMER
  Lizzie (blk), 90
OSMUN
  Elsie B., 4
OSTEMEYER
  Carrie, 302
OSTERBERG
  Celestial V., 121
OSTERMAYER
  Elizabeth, 188
OSTERMEYER
  Cornelia, 132
OSTERTAG
  Therese, 203
OSTHAUS
  Mary M., 21

OTT
　Mary Virginia, 213
　Susan, 169
OTTER
　Mary E. (blk), 230
OTTERBACK
　Emma J., 327
OTTO
　Elizabeth, 123
OUER
　Annie R., 274
OULD
　Carrie S., 29
　Emeline (blk), 225
OURAND
　Catherine E.L., 297
　Sarah Matilda, 230
OUSLEY
　Margaret, 5
　Mary, 198
OVALL
　Ann, 271
OVER
　Caroline, 3
　Mary E. (blk), 8
OVERTON
　Lucy Ellen (blk), 140
OWEN
　Allen Elizabeth, 86
　Mary B., 84
　Mary Elizabeth, 89
　Mary Jane, 48
OWENS
　Angelina, 213
　Elizabeth (blk), 11
　Ellen, 220
　Harriet A., 101
　Lydia, 103
　Maria (blk), 277
　Martha, 131
　Mary E. (blk), 39
　Mary Ella (blk), 321
　Rose E., 43
　Sarah F., 243
　Seleah, 64
　Susan Ann, 63
OWSLEY
　Bridget, 97

OXLEY
　Annie Redbecca (blk), 158
　Mary V., 234
　Sophia, 312
　Susan M., 125
OYSTER
　Ann Louisa, 27
　Mary C., 12

—P—

PACKARD
　Hannah, 246
　Helena, 171
PADDON
　Henrietta, 310
PADGEOT
　Mary E. (blk), 118
PADGETT
　Annie E., 168
　Elizabeth A., 7
　Julia Frances, 222
　Laura C., 130
　Lizzie A., 221
　Maria Elizabeth, 263
　Martha W., 244
　Mary, 112, 140, 213, 237
　Mary C., 237
　Mary E., 112
　Mary J., 140
　Sarah, 55, 203
　Sarah A. (blk), 55
PAFF
　Maria, 257
PAGE
　Bettie E., 263
　Dolly (blk), 314
　Emmelyn Webster, 9
　Evelin (blk), 38
　Harriet (blk), 270
　Laura (blk), 195
　Martha Ann Maria (blk), 233
　Martha B., 72
　Martha E., 175

　Mary (blk), 172
　Mildred (blk), 241
　Milly (blk), 270
　Mina (blk), 317
　Mollie S., 301
　Sarah, 43
PAGENKOFF
　Albertine, 1
PAGET
　Frances M., 103
PAGGETT
　Sarah E., 72
PAGGIT
　Susan Ann, 224
PAIGE
　Mary E., 274
PAIGN
　Rebecca, 239
PAIN
　Mary (blk), 273
PAINE
　Ann E., 304
　Ann M., 16
　Cecelia (blk), 59
　Lizzie R., 196
　Mary D., 9
PALMER
　Anna Adeline, 305
　Balinda, 12
　Caroline A., 263
　Eliza, 65, 201, 207
　Elizabeth Ann, 201
　Elizabeth Ella, 65
　Emeline F., 105
　Hester (blk), 224
　Leah F., 175
　Mary, 103, 136, 256, 324
　Mary B., 256
　Mary L., 324
　Mary V. (blk), 136
　Priscilla, 14
　Sarah Jane, 13
PALTELLO
　Virginia A., 207
PANCOAST
　Hannah N., 189
　Sallie J., 128

PANGSLEY
  Lizzie, 21
PARDEE
  Lavina, 37
PARIS
  Jennie, 144
PARISH
  Sarah H., 62
  Virginia A., 314
PARKER
  Agnes, 213
  Amelia (blk), 283
  Ann Eliza (blk), 149
  Ann V., 15, 35
  Annie (blk), 73
  Caroline, 73, 77
  Caroline (blk), 73
  Eliza J., 203
  Ella R., 323
  Estelle, 153
  Fannie, 218
  Fanny (blk), 307
  Frances M., 246
  Harmonia, 304
  Harriet, 31, 55, 84
  Harriet (blk), 31, 84
  Jane, 44, 63
  Jane (blk), 44
  Julia (blk), 318
  Letty (blk), 267
  Louisa (blk), 209
  Lucy (blk), 233
  Margaret (blk), 52
  Maria (blk), 110
  Marian, 187
  Martha, 67, 299
  Martha E., 299
  Mary (blk), 260, 293
  Mary (col'd), 318
  Mary A., 61, 264
  Mary C., 121
  Mary E. (blk), 41
  Mary Elizabeth, 26
  Mary Francis, 165
  Pauline Matilda, 236
  Rebecca J., 6
  Rebecca W., 61
  S.G., 321
  Sarah (blk), 45
  Sophronia, 26
  Susan Ann (blk), 13
  Susanna (blk), 289
  V.P., 208
  Zora, 68
PARKHURST
  Annie T., 44
  Henrietta, 258
  Sarah L., 323
PARKINSON
  Arispa, 319
  Maria E., 183
PARKS
  Annie (blk), 228
  Elizabeth, 306
  Martha, 273
PARR
  Ades C., 51, 226
PARRIS
  Susan (blk), 3
PARROTT
  Eliza, 274
PARSEE
  Lizzie H., 232
PARSLEY
  Margaret J., 167
  Sarah, 61
PARSONS
  Laura V., 103
  Lizzie, 118
  Miranda B., 162
  Sarah Louisa, 28
  Sarah A., 156
PARTELLO
  Eliza A., 64
  Flora, 318
  Kate, 62
PARTRIDGE
  Minnie, 324
PASELA
  Catharina, 84
PASQUAY
  Emelie C., 276
PASSMORE
  Ester, 280
PASTORFIELD
  Martha A., 75
PASWA
  Pauline F., 120
PATCH
  Sarah J., 177
PATTERSON
  Abigal, 226
  Annie, 260, 268
  Bettie C., 36
  Catherine E. F., 171
  Christina, 111
  Hannah, 202
  Harriet (blk), 73
  Jane, 325
  Laura V., 227
  Malinda (blk), 260
  Margaret H., 253
  Mary, 49, 80, 91, 261, 307
  Mary A., 261
  Mary E., 49
  Mary Eliza, 307
  Mary Jane, 80
  Nellie, 308
  Rebecca O., 212
  Sarah Ann, 182
PATTIENT
  Eliza, 25
PATTISON
  Margaret, 75
PATTON
  Frona, 218
  Milly (blk), 240
PAUL
  Adelaide A., 227
  Jane C., 227
  Sarah M., 119
PAULINE
  Eleanor, 14
PAULY
  Antonio, 96, 227
  Catharine, 301
  Catherina, 181
PAXON
  Ann E., 49
PAXSON
  Henrietta C., 142
PAXTON
  Ellen Amelia, 295
  Florida, 140
  Mary, 67, 175
  Mary Louisa, 175

PAYNE
 Ada, 79
 Amanda (blk), 278
 Amanda H., 239
 Ann V., 217
 Anna, 54
 Annie, 193, 302
 Annie R., 302
 Betsy (blk), 107
 Catharine, 23
 Catherine J., 31
 Cecilia (blk), 241
 Celia (blk), 321
 Dwana V., 296
 Elenora (blk), 293
 Elizabeth, 144
 Ellen Elizabeth
  (blk), 176
 Fannie (blk), 227
 Harriet Rebecca
  (blk), 145
 Henrietta, 77
 Jane (blk), 64
 Josephine (blk), 155
 Julia, 90
 Laura, 38
 Lavinia, 219
 Letty (blk), 112
 Louisa, 216
 Lovina, 165
 Lucretia, 192
 Lucy (blk), 15
 Lucy S., 324
 Mahala (blk), 317
 Margaret, 2, 199,
  211, 261
 Margaret (blk), 261
 Maria (blk), 310,
  317
 Martha, 4, 57
 Martha (blk), 57
 Mary (blk), 53, 149
 Mary Catharine, 51
 Mary E., 162
 Mary Elizabeth, 279
 Mary Ellen (blk),
  148
 Mary Emma, 43
 Mary Julia, 258

 Mary Lena, 326
 Matilda (blk), 29
 Rosa, 215
 Sarah (blk), 96, 130
 Susan (blk), 72
 Virginia Wicks, 319
PAYNTER
 Mary Frances, 244
 Mary V., 130
PEABODY
 Julia O., 271
PEAK
 Mary A., 129
PEAKE
 Annie E., 237
PEARCE
 Ann J., 122
 Emma E., 280
 Mary, 142
 Sarah, 227
PEARSON
 Elizabeth M., 166
 Ellen (blk), 143
 Jessie M., 106
 Mary (blk), 37
 Wilson, 228, 264
PEASE
 Ellen W., 42
PECK
 Elizabeth, 288
 Martinette E., 135
PECKDOLD
 Anna, 206
PEDDICORD
 Celinda A., 296
 Mary H., 93
 Romana C., 175
PEER
 Emily C. (blk), 307
PEERCE
 Ann J., 122
 Eliza, 180
 Maria L., 218
 Martha Ann, 166
PEGG
 Annie, 263
 Catherine V., 212
 Mary E., 39
 Rosy, 173

PEIFFER
 Margaret, 257
PELKERTON
 Mary Jane, 319
PELLET
 Lottie, 281
PEMBERTON
 Ella F., 323
PENDERGAST
 Bridget, 39
PENDERGRASS
 Bridget, 195
PENDERGRAST
 Mary, 312
PENDLETON
 Amanda (blk), 116
 Elizabeth, 25
 Emily (blk), 295
 Fannie R., 240
 Rose, 71, 292
 Rose B., 71
 Sophia (blk), 321
PENN
 Amelia (blk), 79
 Elizabeth (col'd),
  289
 Mary Elizabeth, 180
PENNINGTON
 Lizzie M., 213
PENNY
 Martha L., 100
PENNYBACHER
 Mary V., 77
PENNYFIELD
 Chloe, 218
PENNYFIL
 Chloe Ellen, 218
PEPPER
 Henrietta, 50
 Martha, 190
 Mary, 250
PEPPERT
 Christiana, 180
PERANI
 Maria, 214
PERES
 Caroline M., 26
PERIN
 Eliza Jane, 169

PERKINS
  Elizabeth, 285
  Fannie M., 44
  Hallie B., 65
  Henrietta, 119
  Lewellen, 117
  Marian Elizth., 251
  Millison, 186
  Missouri, 109
  S.V.B., 117
PERMILLION
  Rosetta, 229
PERRY
  Annie, 86
  Elizabeth, 5
  Emma, 56
  Kate A., 85
  Lizzie (blk), 243
  Lucinda (blk), 123, 229
  M. Fannie, 56
  M.J.M., 40
  Maggie (blk), 289
  Margaret, 197
  Martha Ann (blk), 304
  Mary Ann, 313
  Rebecca (blk), 209
  Rebecca A., 279
  Rosa C., 94
  Sarah, 215
  Virginia, 83
PESTERIDGE
  Sarah, 309
PESTRIDGE
  Selena (blk), 39
PETER
  Brittie K., 276
PETERS
  Aggie (blk), 241
  Annie (blk), 28
  Caroline, 322
  Catharine, 284
  Ellen (blk), 215
  Louisa, 70, 203
  Louisa (blk), 70
  Louise, 105
  Mahala Ellen, 194
  Martha (blk), 305
  Mary A. (blk), 40
  Mary F., 152
  Orelia, 192
  Sophia L., 96
PETERSEN
  Louise, 241
  Sophia, 254
PETERSON
  Eliza, 67, 244
  Elizabeth (col'd), 67
  Mary A.E. (blk), 120
PETHAN
  Mary F. (blk), 240
PETIT
  George Anna, 250
  Mary Virginia, 307
PETSCH
  Caroline H., 42
PETTIBONE
  Margaret E., 173
  Rosalia H., 75
PETTIGREW
  Emma D., 275
  Florence Jane, 180
  Grace, 101
  Harriet, 301
PETTIT
  Fannie E., 217
  Josephine, 233
  Katuro, 221
  Lucinda V., 49
  Mary Frances, 73
  Roxy Ann, 318
PETTY
  Mary E., 47
  Mary Eliza, 249
  Sallie M., 72
PEYTON
  Eliza Ann (blk), 153
  Jane (blk), 187
  Laura E., 205
  Laura M., 76
  Mary, 80, 152
  Mary (blk), 80
  Mattie, 297
  Rachel (blk), 1
PFEIFER
  Johanna, 181
PFEIFFER
  Mathilde E.H., 301
PFEIL
  Anna Gertrude, 170
  Augusta, 271
  Caroline, 168
  Louisa, 319
PFISTER
  Maria, 50
PFL_G
  Kate, 275
PFLUEGAR
  Margaret B., 256
PFLUG
  Louisa, 249
PFLUGER
  Margaret, 114
PHELAN
  Margaret, 91
  Mary, 208
PHELPS
  Ann, 143
  Mariam, 75
  Mary F., 184
  Virginia, 189
PHENIX
  Catharine (blk), 112
  Jane (blk), 311
  Laura, 240
PHILIPS
  Angeline D., 186
PHILLIPS
  Alice, 305
  Elbertine H., 121
  Elizabeth, 5
  Ellen Ann (blk), 309
  Emma E., 292
  Fannie Eugenia, 136
  Margaret, 235, 286
  Margaret (blk), 235
  Mary Anna, 231
  Sarah C., 121
  Virginia E., 132
PHILLPOT
  Sophia, 96
PHILPOT
  Mary F., 305
PHINRICK
  Martha, 88

District of Columbia Marriage Licenses, 1858-1870

PHIPPS
  Jeannette, 226
  Lucinda, 239
PHIPS
  Cordelia, 273
PHOENIX
  Annie (blk), 51
PICK
  Sarah, 169
PICKEN
  Eliza, 2
PICKENS
  Margaret, 127
PICKERILL
  Jane, 209
PICKRELL
  Annie G., 144
PIE
  Margaret, 181
  Mary, 74
PIERCE
  Godum, viii
  Julia C., 112
  Margaret, 260
  Martha (blk), 132
  Martha O., 27
  Mary C., 174
  Mary Jane (blk), 233
  Susan E., 108
PIERE
  Mary (blk), 136
PIFER
  Rachel E., 193
PIGGOT
  Mary, 176
PIGGOTT
  Bertie H., 130
  Emma G., 236
  Fannie E., 106
  Isabella Marcy, 6
PIKE
  Eva Vernon, 299
  Frances (blk), 153
PILES
  Arabella, 167
PILKERTON
  Susana, 255
PILLSBURY
  Ann E., 171

  Elvira R., 123, 225
  Frances T., 22
PINCKNEY
  Harriet, 2
  Harriot (blk), 232
  Priscilla (blk), 271
  Rachel (blk), 232
PINDLE
  Elizabeth, 232
PINKARD
  Winnie (blk), 263
PINKNEY
  Mary (blk), 49
PINKNS
  Johana, 162
PINN
  Ann Maria (blk), 322
  Eliza (blk), 302
PIPER
  Matilda (blk), 3
PIPPERT
  Christinia C., 266
PITCHER
  O.P., 300f
PITMAN
  Louisa, 142
PITTS
  Caroline (blk), 11
  Julia A., 200
  Sarah E., 157
PITZ
  Caroline, 279
PLANT
  Georgie A., 19
  Indiana, 64
PLASKET
  Elizabeth, 228
PLATER
  Sarah, 267
PLATES
  Mary Ellen (blk), 126
PLATT
  Mary J., 216
PLAUGHER
  Barbara Ellen, 258
PLAYMAN
  Bridget, 108

PLEASANT
  Frances Eudora, 215
PLEASANTS
  Mary (blk), 154
PLOWDEN
  Virginia (blk), 225
PLUMMER
  Amelia, 211
  Caroline (blk), 119
  Charlotte (blk), 264
  Elizabeth (blk), 17
  Fanny (blk), 165
  Josephine A., 73
  Mary Ann, 103
  Octavia, 193
  Rebecca (blk), 232
  Sophia (blk), 126
  Winnie Ann, 225
POCHON
  Sophia, 315
POE
  Genevieve, 223
POEHLMANN
  Catharine A., 249
POINDEXTER
  Lucy Jane, 115
  Margaret A. (blk), 210
POLAN
  Hattie E., 145
POLES
  Amanda (blk), 202
POLK
  Patsy (blk), 51
POLKINHORN
  Caroline, 15
POLLARD
  Ellen, 240
  Josephine, 140
  Martha (blk), 248
  Mary E., 167
  Mary L., 18
PONEY
  Laura (blk), 86
POOL
  Annie E., 22
  Ellen V., 167
  Louisa (blk), 259
  Mary, 24, 107, 164

448

POOL
  Mary Ellen, 107
  Mary James, 24
POOLE
  Emma C. (Va.), 325
  Julia E., 10
  Lydia A., 4
  Margaret, 214
  Rebecca R., 181
  Teresa (blk), 149
POOR
  Lottie, 324
  Sophia Frances, 245
  Teresa Virginia, 85
POORE
  Mary Frances, 131
POORTS
  Ellen, 301
  Mary Frances, 277
POPE
  Jane E., 64
  Judiah A., 291
  Mary Catherine, 298
PORME
  Mary Ann, 185
PORT
  Josephine M., 46
PORTELLO
  Flora, 52
PORTER
  Anna, 158
  Julia Ann, 64
  Laura A., 12
  Mary (blk), 6
  Mary E. (blk), 222
  Mary M., 250
  Parthenia M.T., 249
  Sarah, 54
PORTNAN
  Mary (blk), 306
PORTNET
  Felixine, 186
PORTS
  Frances D.M., 38
  Morcilia, 112
  Perphaney Jane, 242
POSEY
  Elizabeth (blk), 277
  Emily (blk), 323

Josephine, 273, 288
Josephine (blk), 288
Maisae Ann, 302
Martha (blk), 296
Mary E. (blk), 126
Mary M., 15
Mary Virginia, 93
Rebecca, 170
Susan, 142
POSKER
  Cora (blk), 14
POSPICCHILL
  Veronica, 276
POSTON
  Mary J., 146
POTIS
  Fannie, 312
POTMANN
  Katherine, 187
POTTER
  Hannah, 53
  Rosa, 313
  Sarah Ann, 233
POTTS
  Ann E., 125
  Harriet, 208
  Susan, 233
POUTCH
  Emma Virginia, 150
POWELL
  Anna (blk), 272
  Annie G., 275
  Arianna (blk), 129
  Eleanor A., 190
  Ella G., 322
  Fanny (blk), 153
  Kate J., 190
  Malinda (blk), 264
  Margaret E., 267
  Maria, 191
  Mary R. (blk), 115
  Priscilla, 264
  Rachel, 272
  Rebecca (blk), 36
  S.A., 322
  Sarah Indiana, 84
  Sarah S., 296
  Susan, 70, 148
  Susan (blk), 148

POWELLS
  Hattie (blk), 109
POWER
  Annie Camille, 252
  Annie E., 195
  Cassie (blk), 40
  Jessie M., 216
  Mary, 17, 68
  Mary C., 68
POWERS
  Amanda M., 315
  Ann, 92, 102
  Ann Cornelia, 92
  Ellen, 63, 253
  Henny (blk), 248
  Honora, 219
  Kate, 209
  Maria (blk), 144
  Mary (blk), 292
  Mary I., 105
PRAISINGE
  Kitty M., 295
PRATER
  Jane (blk), 2
PRATHER
  Adda L., 27
  Eliza (blk), 278
  Henrietta, 145
  Josephine L., 130
  Laura V., 51
  Marion, 41
  Olivia, 145
  Sarah, 196
  Susan E., 26
PRATT
  Adeline, 233
  Caroline (blk), 270
  Jane (blk), 305
PREALL
  Mattie, 316
PRECELL
  Ella, 161
PREDAGAM
  Catharine, 6
PREINKERT
  Margaret, 215
PRENABLE
  Mary, 220

449

District of Columbia Marriage Licenses, 1858-1870

PRENDIEHALL
  Mary M., 281
PRENOT
  Rose, 14
PRESCOTT
  Emma E., 302
PRESTCUTT
  Rebecca, 171
PRESTON
  Helen A., 308
  Maria O., 121
PRETTYMAN
  Mary Julia, 27
PREUSS
  Barbara C., 314
  Emma, 29
PREVOST
  Eleanor A., 312
PRICE
  Annie, 291
  Cecilia (blk), 107
  Charlotte A. (blk), 238
  Daphney (blk), 235
  Eliza, 179, 261, 309
  Eliza (blk), 179
  Eliza Ann (blk), 261
  Emma F., 235
  Georgiana V., 128
  Henrietta (blk), 215
  Ida, 34
  Julia, 318
  Maria Louisa, 271
  Marietta, 323
  Mary, 11, 103, 168, 233, 300
  Mary (blk), 233, 300
  Mary A., 168
  Mary Ellen, 103
PRIDDY
  Nannie Jane, 111
PRIEGEL
  Frieda M. W., 288
PRIEST
  Magrade, 301
PRIGGIN
  Marguerita, 315
PRIMAS
  Sophia (blk), 21

PRIMROSE
  Lizzie (blk), 126
PRINCE
  Martha (blk), 309
  Mary Louisa, 317
PRINGLE
  Anginette, 86
PRINTER
  Mary, 54
PRINTZ
  Elizabeth, 294
  Isabel V., 183
PRIOR
  Julia (blk), 16
PRITCHARD
  Bertha E., 4
  Harriett W., 235
  Mary E., 122
  Sarah M., 127
PRITCHETT
  Sarah E., 287
PROBST
  Helena, 170
PROCTOR
  Carrie (blk), 14, 207
  Jane (blk), 18
  Malinda (blk), 244
  Maria (blk), 27, 119
  Mary J., 267
  Mary R. (blk), 7
  Rose V., 33
  Sarah C. (blk), 78
PROPELTON
  Catharine, 47
PROSPERA
  Annie Maria, 66
PROSPERI
  Mary E., 303
PROTT
  Catharine, 140
PROUDFOOT
  Charlotte R., 94
PROUT
  Lizzie L., 271
  Sarah (col'd), 206
PRUET
  Mary, 182
PRUETT
  Letitia, 258

PRYOR
  Barbary (blk), 59
  Jeremiah P. (blk), 43
  Sarah Ann, 32
PUE
  Rebecca D., 65
PUGH
  Elizabeth S., 233
PULLEN
  Martha A., 28
PULLER
  Agnes, 288
PULLIN
  Mary, 164
PULLING
  Annie, 253
  Sarah H., 7
  Susannah M., 24
PUMPHREY
  Amanda E., 175
  Catherine S., 16
  Dorcas A. (blk), 61
  Elizabeth, 17
  Frances, 29
  Mary E.S., 27
  Nettie, 82
PURCELL
  Emeline, 188
  Julia A., 313
  Lucy, 118
  Margaret, 259
  Mary F., 55
PURDY
  Susan, 14
PURKS
  Anna F., 2
PURSEL
  Martha J., 324
PURSLEY
  Catherine, 247
PURTY
  Malinda, 272
PURYEAR
  S. Josephine, 319
PUSLEY
  Jane, 139
PYE
  Eliza, 289
  Olivia, 112

PYEWELL
  Jane E., 143
PYFER
  Susan E., 301
PYLES
  Alice F., 250
  Margaret, 200
  Martha A., 315
  Mary F., 112
  Sarah Ellen, 21
PYWELL
  Alice M., 245

—Q—

QUAID
  Catharine, 187
QUALLS
  Annie E., 32
QUEALY
  Mary, 299
QUEEN
  Adeline (blk), 73
  Ann, 138, 224, 268
  Ann Eliza, 138
  Ann M. (blk), 224
  Elizabeth (blk), 278
  Harriet (blk), 60
  Henrietta, 127
  Lucinda J. (blk), 12
  Lucretia (blk), 187
  Marcelena, 151
  Marcy (blk), 98
  Martha (blk), 61
  Mary (blk), 18
  Mary E. (blk), 57
  Mary Jane (blk), 326
  Olivia M., 195
  Sarah, 7, 127, 224
  Sarah E., 7
  Sarah O., 224
  Susan (blk), 177
  Treacy, 72
  Virginia (blk), 314
QUERIN
  Mary Jane, 191
QUICK
  Katharine W., 229
  Matilda C., 26

  Susan, 84
QUIGLEY
  Anna E., 282
  Anna Maria, 77
  Bridget, 14, 196
  Maggie, 298
  Mary E., 73
  Rose, 85
QUILL
  Eliza, 163
  Ellen, 60, 63
  Joanna, 33
  Mary, 60, 86, 113
QUINLAN
  Mary, 39
QUINLON
  Mary, 313
QUINN
  Anna, 198
  Caroline V., 169
  Catherine, 81
  Ellen R., 108
  Emma, 272
  Isabella, 25
  Jane C., 303
  Mary, 102, 114, 255
QUIRK
  Katie, 294
  Margaret, 293
  Mary, 144
QUYNN
  Mary E., 246

—R—

RAAB
  Ann M.E., 105
  Louisa, 257
RABBIT
  Jennie, 145
RABBITT
  Beckie, 8
  Elizabeth F., 187
  Mary C., 170
  Mary J., 157
RABY
  Margaret, 204
RACKEY
  Mary A., 206

RACKS
  Elizabeth, 40
  Sarah (blk), 305
RADCLIFF
  Catharine, 97
  Emeline, 156
RADCLIFFE
  Ada B., 54
  Mattie E., 111
RADEY
  Mary, 197
RADY
  Julia, 120
RAFE
  Alice (blk), 122
RAFF
  Mary, 311
RAFFERTY
  Jennie, 201
  Margaret, 197
RAFTER
  Catharine, 262
RAGAN
  Catharine, 238
  Catherine, 239
  Ellen, 59, 253
  Jane, 207
  Johanna, 65
  Julia, 121, 166
  Julia D., 166
  Kate M., 52
  Mary, viii, 48, 192
  Sarah, 211
  Susanna, 234
  Victoria, 24
RAGGERTY
  Georgie L., 146
RAHM
  Vorona, 14
RAINES
  William Anna, 252
RAINEY
  Charlotte, 81
  Margaret, 219
  Marguerite A., 288
  Mary, 220
  Sarah A., 228
RAINGER
  Sarah Elizabeth, 60

RAINSBURG
  Mary Louisa, 269
RALEIGH
  Mary, 200
RALEK
  Caroline A.E., 172
RALEY
  Mary Jane, 13
  Susan, 194
RALL
  Anna Maria, 188
RALPH
  Sena, 73
RAMMERER
  Kathrina, 159
RAMSAY
  Catherine Graham, 137
  Harriet E., 236
  Margaret A., 312
  Marion, 69
RAMSDILL
  Mary, 208
RAMSEY
  Eliza B., 102
RANCIL
  Martha, 229
RANDAL
  Rachel (blk), 310
RANDALL
  Eliza E., 263
  Frances A., 287
  Isabella, 250
  Malvina, 54
  Mary, 26
RANDOLPH
  Bettie Gibbon, 44
  Frances Jane, 200
  Harriet J., 231
  Jane (blk), 56
  Malinda (blk), 103
  Mary G., 16
  Winnie (blk), 291
RANDOM
  Mary E., 233
RANEY
  Mary, 274
RANICKER
  Margaret, 257

RASH
  Sarah E., 227
RATCLIFF
  Mary G., 223
RATCLIFFE
  Elizabeth, 57
  Emma Irene, 48
  Lucinda (blk), 227
  Roberta L., 26
RATTA
  Cotiglia, 246
RATTO
  Rose, 240
RAU
  Emma Maria, 168
  Mary, 171
RAUB
  Helena A., 131
  Paulina, 96
RAUCH
  Magdalena, 230
RAUCK
  Louise M., 206
RAUGH
  Kuegundo, 250
RAWLING
  Susan T., 288
RAWLINGS
  Carrie, 113
  Emma A., 246
  Henrietta, 214
  Lizzie A., 285
  Malina, 79
  Malvina, 79
  Sarah, 90, 180
RAX
  Elizabeth (blk), 89
RAY
  Ann Catherine, 172
  Anna, 325
  India, 218
  Kate, 190
  M. Ida, 320
  Martha A., 165
  Mary J., 244
  Mary Jane, 326
RAYBOLD
  Annie E., 227
  Rebecca E., 261

RAYMOND
  Catharine E., 228
  E.D., 210
  Emily F., 209
RAYNOR
  Anne L., 74
  Josephine, 40
READ
  Annie E., 156
  Laura E., 127
  Mary Jane, 4
  Sarah, 234
READEY
  Ellen, 319
READY
  Catharine, 60
  Eliza, 125
  Ellen, 60, 134
  Joanna, 135
  Margaret, 80
  Mary, 187, 231, 236, 238
  Mary M., 231
REAGAN
  Annie, 300
  Emma, 197
  Jane, 275
  Mary, 86
REALS
  Anna, 53
REANE
  Mary, 105
REARDEN
  Mary L., 127
REARDON
  Bridget, 200
  Catherine, 137
  Ellen, 220
  Joanna, 153
  Julia, 99
  Mildred C., 113
REAURA
  Lavinia G., 60
REAVER
  Carrie, 30
REAVES
  Margaret, 144
RECKER
  Frederica Louisa, 9

District of Columbia Marriage Licenses, 1858-1870

RECTOR
  Florence A., 145
  Nancy Ann, 201
RED
  Betsey (blk), 31
REDDICK
  Adlia Frances, 254
  Charlotte (blk), 206
  Maria, 90
  Maude A., 76
REDDING
  Emily, 134
  Margaret, 112
REDDY
  Elizabeth, 276
REDER
  Elizabeth, 217
REDIN
  Catherine T., 306
  Ruth, 159
REDINGTON
  Ann, 201
REDMAN
  Emeline (blk), 316
  Maria (blk), 215
  Virginia, 127
REDMOND
  Elizth., 128
  Emma F., 238
  Kate A., 195
REDSTREACK
  Clara DeGant, 89
REDWAY
  Nellie M., 151
REDY
  Margaret, 85
REEB
  Catharine, 137
REED
  Alice Virginia, 168
  Angelina F., 265
  Cilia (blk), 57
  Eliza, 72, 232, 299
  Eliza Ann, 232
  Elizth. Jane, 260
  Emma C., 115
  Emma L., 55
  Emma S., 198
  Jane (blk), 305
  Jennie (col'd), 41
  Margaret E., 71
  Marion (blk), 102
  Mary, 53, 120, 135,
    195, 251, 261, 284
  Mary (blk), 261
  Mary Ann, 53, 120
  Mary C., 251
  Mary L., 195
  Mary Virginia, 135
  Summa (blk), 297
REEDER
  E., 261
  Elizabeth, 192
  Mary E. (blk), 101
  Sarah C., 67
REEDERS
  Sarah Ann, 146
REEDY
  Elenora, 187
REESE
  Annie R., 210
  Caroline, 25
  Louisa, 256
  Martha A., 185
  Martha E., 293
  Mary E., 34
  Rebecca P., 283
REEVE
  Bettie P., 241
  Sarah E., 73
REEVES
  Carrie E., 54
  Celia, 165
  Martha J., 72
  Mary E., 280
  Mary Jane, 163
  Sallie, 44
REH
  Christina M., 300
REHBERGER
  Agnes, 20
REICHER
  Johanna, 169
REID
  Catharine, 214
REIDY
  Annie, 254
  Barbara, 7
  Ellen, 64
  Johanna, 81
  Mary, 282
REILLEY
  Margaret, 7
REILLY
  Delia, 147
  Julia, 215
  Lodiema, 323
  Mary, 84
REILY
  Catherine, 99
  Ellen T., 155
  Mary, 184, 276,
    283, 303
  Mary Ann, 303
  Sydney J., 141
REINCKE
  Johanne, 211
REINHARD
  Clemmie, 315
  Minnie, 22
REISS
  Atilheit, 131
  Lizzie, 284
REISTER
  Anna Dorothea, 243
REITER
  Louise, 79
REIVES
  Georgiana, 302
RELIHAN
  Julia, 98
REMELEY
  Catherine, 323
REMER
  Louisa, 256
REMINGTON
  Anne, 34
  Susan R., 222
  Virginia C., 108
REMLEIN
  Elizabeth, 252
RENNER
  Cornelia, 8
RENNICK
  S., 135f
RENNEY
  Julia Olivia, 8

District of Columbia Marriage Licenses, 1858-1870

RENST
  Anna Mary, 250
REORDAN
  Mary, 309
REPP
  Sophia C., 204
RESU
  Fanny, 97
RETINGER
  Rosa, 203
REVEL
  Margaret, 92
REYNOLDS
  Annie, 233
  Catherine P., 232
  Cecila (blk), 269
  Charlotte (blk), 5
  Elizabeth Belt, 12
  Ellen, 74, 249
  Ellen Jane (blk), 249
  Emily (blk), 189
  Harriet Ann, 153
  Hattie C., 8
  Hester (blk), 245
  Jane P., 37
  Lottie E., 170
  Louisa Ann, 37
  Maggie E., 309
  Marion, 166
  Martha (blk), 166
  Mary (blk), 63
  Ruth Ann, 290
  Sarah Maria, 205
  Sophronia E., 72
RHEA
  Harriet Virginia, 13
  Mary (blk), 26
RHEINHARDT
  Lizzie, 18
RHINEHART
  Alwina, 251
  Mary S., 131
RHODE
  Falden, 134, 243
RHODES
  Augusta (blk), 148
  Caroline, 278
  Eliza R., 204
  Ellen M., 205
  Lizzie (blk), 216
  Louisa (blk), 325
  Margaret, 196
  Mary E. (blk), 46
  Mary H., 79
  Sarah, 127
RHULE
  Mary A., 77
RHUMSEIR
  Louisa, 33
RHYNE
  Mary, 146
RHYON
  Rebecca J., 243
RICAR
  Annie, 238
RICARD
  Ann Eliza, 149
  Mary R., 227
  Sarah Elizabeth, 58
RICARDE
  Clara, 71
RICE
  Ann M. (blk), 295
  Elizabeth A., 276
  Ellen, 280
  Emma Skelly, 309
  Jennie E., 219
  Lucy A., 239
  Mary A., 123
  Mary E., 3
  Rebecca Jane, 248
  Rose, 238
RICH
  Eliza (blk), 30
  Frances (blk), 69
  Mary Frances, 16
RICHARDS
  Amanda, 94
  Fannie R., 76
  Harriet, 290
  Julia, 231
  Mary, 251
  Miranda (blk), 318
  Sarah (blk), 188
RICHARDSON
  Addie, 110
  Alice (blk), 37
  Anna L., 94
  Clarissa A. (blk), 40
  Ella, 85, 189, 197
  Ella (blk), 189
  Emma, 30, 179
  Emma (blk), 179
  Gracy Ann, 223
  Harriet (blk), 324
  Jane (blk), 292
  Jane W., 224
  Julia N., 134
  Margaret K., 61
  Maria (blk), 71
  Mary A., 316
  Mary E., 173
  Matilda B., 26
  Sallie R., 293
  Virginia A., 36
RICHEY
  Emma Alice, 285
  Jane Elizabeth, 57
RICHOLD
  Caroline, 255
RICHTER
  Barbara, 98
  Catherine, 279
  Julia, 287
  Mary, 193
RICKARD
  Mary, 105
RICKCORDS
  Amelia, 130
RICKERS
  Mary, 24
RICKETTS
  Addie, 16
RICKS
  Elizabeth (blk), 312
RIDDELL
  Louisa, 271
RIDDLE
  Caroline M., 101
  Catherine, 251
  Emma E., 270
  Florence, 14
  Louisa, 141
  Rebecca, 206
  Susan M., 262
RIDEOUT
  Margaret, 126

RIDER
  Ella S., 139
  Hattie, 263
  Mary (blk), 241
RIDGATE
  Margaret E., 179
RIDGELEY
  Ellen (blk), 208
  Mary (blk), 113
RIDGELY
  Annie E., 171
  Katie, 12
  Marie Louise, 283
  Octavia, 279
RIDGEWAY
  Harriet, 272
  Martha Ann, 184
RIDGLEY
  Ann R., 239
  Anna Key, 171
  Eliza (blk), 166
  Ellen N. (blk), 307
RIDGWAY
  Emma, 55
RIDLEY
  Lenah, 303
RIESSNER
  Margaretha, 57
RIEVES
  Caroline, 193
RIGBY
  Mary, 127
RIGDON
  Bettie S., 208
RIGGINS
  Betsey (blk), 54
RIGGLE
  Roberta, 288
RIGGLES
  Catharine V., 320
  M.C., 52
  Maggie A., 288
  Marian, 299
RIGGS
  Maria (blk), 42
RIGNER
  Hester, 73
RIGNEY
  Catherine, 28

RIGSBY
  Mary, 1
RILEY
  Ann, 105, 151, 198
  Ann A., 105
  Annie, 151
  Bridget, 108, 209
  Catharine, 28
  Catherine, 180
  Ellen, 320
  Florence C., 239
  Hesse, 126
  Hester, 227
  Julia, 246
  Margaret, 166, 276
  Mary, 28, 113, 142,
    193, 213, 251
  Mary (blk), 142
  Mary Ann, 28
  Mary J., 213
  Sarah, 60, 135
  Sarah M., 135
  Susan, 11
RILS
  Mary S., 248
RIMBEL
  Ernestine, 54
RIMBY
  Frances V., 141
RINGGOLD
  Mary A. (blk), 324
RINNER
  Elizabeth, 110
RIORDAN
  Jennie C., 15
RIPPLE
  Dorothy, 309
RISING
  Sarah Virginia, 278
RISLEY
  Maria, 308
RISON
  Mary Ann, 9
RISSLER
  Elizabeth, 119
  Margaret, 255
RISTON
  Anna, 151
  Aurelia F., 175

RITCHIE
  Eliza Jane, 224
  Liberta E., 27
  M.A., 327
RITLEY
  Ellen F., 20
RITTEAU
  Margaret, 127
RITTENHOUSE
  Clementina C., 52
  Fannie, 147
  Mamie N., 120
  Mary D., 323
RITTER
  Durette C., 260
  Elizabeth, 180
  Helen S., 275
  Lucy W., 224
  Mary E., 201
  Mary Fannie, 22
  Millie, 206
RITZ
  Stephana, 56
RIVERS
  Mary, 266
  Phyllis (blk), 122
  Sarah (blk), 96
RIXON
  Emily (blk), 236
RIZIN
  Nancy Ann, 228
ROACH
  Annie E., 174
  Annie R., 312
  Elizabeth, 44
  Hannah, 207
  Maggie, 246
  Mary Virginia, 165
  Virginia H., 45
ROAN
  Nellie (blk), 15
ROANE
  Caroline (blk), 306
ROBB
  Angela, 97
ROBBINS
  Julia, 57
  Mary Ann, 248
  Sarah, 80

ROBERT
  Ellen, 256
ROBERTS
  Anna (blk), 149
  Annie, 243
  Caroline J., 20
  Cornelia, 111
  E.A., 259
  Elizabeth, 74, 127
  Elizabeth (blk), 127
  Emma J. Church, 87
  Lucy, 94
  Margaret Ann, 312
  Mary (blk), 116
  Mary E., 291
  Sarah, 222, 296
  Sarah A., 296
  Sue B., 61
ROBERTSON
  Betsy (blk), 103
  Betty (blk), 145
  Helen, 209
  Margaret Ann, 47
  Sallie, 106
ROBESON
  Jane (blk), 69
ROBEY
  Alexenia G.W., 247
  Annie, 38
  Birdie, 119
  Edwardina, 9
  Elizabeth V., 290
  Harriet, 53
  Isabel, 217
  Marcelene B., 237
  Marcellina A.M., 197
  Mary, 207, 242, 271, 305
  Mary E., 207
  Mary V., 242
  Sarah Ann, 222
  Sarah Jane, 229
  Sianna, 14
ROBIN
  Frances, 212
ROBINSON
  [illegible] (blk), 182
  Adaline (blk), 183

Agnes (blk), 23
Alice, 266
Amanda, 278
Ann, 31, 32, 73, 173, 221
Ann (blk), 32
Ann Maria (blk), 73
Anna, 31
Annie (blk), 173
Caroline (blk), 9, 233
Catharine, 297
Catherine (blk), 314
Cecilia, 317
Celia (blk), 4
Eliza (blk), 175
Elizabeth (blk), 55
Elizabeth A., 143
Fanny (blk), 126
Fanny C., 203
Francis (blk), 158
Hannah (blk), 101
Henrietta, 241
Isabel (blk), 292
Isabella, 302
Jennie, 132
Julia, 118, 141
Julia K., 118
Kate, 20
Louisa (blk), 33
M. Celia, 123
Margaret, 64
Maria (blk), 96
Martha (blk), 233, 313
Martha A.J., 146
Mary, 53, 71, 159, 207, 249, 286, 287
Mary (blk), 53, 286
Mary Elizabeth, 71
Mary F. (blk), 207
Mary Isabella, 249
Mary Jane (blk), 159
Matilda (blk), 17
Minna (blk), 236
Omanda, 248, 278
Priscilla (blk), 248
Rachel (blk), 268, 306

Rebecca, 213, 259
Rebecca (blk), 213
Rose (blk), 215
Sallie V., 295
Sarah B.E., 49
Sidney A.G., 26
Virginia, 208, 317
Virginia (blk), 317
ROBISON
  Ellen (blk), 19
  Mary (blk), 279
ROBY
  Sarah Ann, 196
ROCH
  Teresa, 193
ROCHE
  Alice, 269
  Ann, 138
  Catharine, 273
  Ellen, 31, 181
  Emma, 271
  Hannah, 14
ROCK
  Elizabeth E., 158
  Mary, 167, 207
ROCKANHAUSER
  Lena, 170
ROCKAWAY
  Wilhelmina, 180
ROCKETT
  Mary E., 224
ROCKFELLER
  Eve Ann, 65
ROCKWELL
  Ellietta T., 291
RODBIRD
  Jane Catharine, 66
  Ruth A., 25
RODD
  Sarah, 8
RODEN
  Anna (blk), 323
  Eliza (blk), 305
  Elizabeth, 131
  Mary Jane (blk), 290
RODES
  J. Cyntha V., 57
  Lucy (blk), 18

RODGERS
  Catherine, 235
  Mary Etta, 144
RODIE
  Annie E., 14
RODIER
  Alice Virginia, 67
  Eloise, 250
  Mary J., 173
  Sarah E., 109
ROE
  Fannie M., 300
  Jennie E., 239
ROEMMELE
  Margaret A., 96
ROERNMELE
  Frederica, 199
ROESER
  Helena A., 170
ROFF
  Etta E., 177
ROGER
  Elizabeth A., 200
ROGERS
  Annie, 300
  Ellen M., 286
  Emily C., 160
  Hanna, 314
  Lucy Ann (blk), 148
  Margaret, 236
  Mary Ann, 142
  Millie A., 69
  Sarah, 228
  Susan V., 141
  Virginia, 114
ROGERSON
  Sarah J., 239
ROH
  Amelie, 189
ROHAN
  Margaret, 161
ROHLEDER
  Frances, 277
ROHRER
  Mary Elizabeth, 104
ROIX
  Fannie, 208
ROLAN
  Mary, 224

ROLAND
  Elizabeth R., 291
  Sarah (blk), 230
ROLLATER
  Maria, 138
ROLLET
  Mary F., 76
ROLLING
  Kate M., 174
ROLLINGS
  Annie R., 103
  Dora, 136
  Emily, 250
ROLLINS
  Anna Henrietta, 201
  Eliza (blk), 157
  Fannie, 54
  George Ana, 263
  Jane, 264
  Jennie, 208
  Margaret Ann, 241
  Mary, 155, 184
  Mary (blk), 155
  Parthenia F., 248
  Sarah, 188, 237
  Sarah Jane, 188
ROLLS
  Josephine, 122
ROMAN
  Ophelia (blk), 158
  Sarah (blk), 74
RONAN
  Bridget, 314
  Elen M., 185
RONEY
  Elizabeth R., 57
ROOSE
  Sarah A., 167
ROOT
  Clara, 277
  Eloisa H., 92
ROPER
  Octavia, 42
ROSA
  Dolcini, 3
ROSE
  Ann Eliza, 102
  Jane E., 43
  Minerva A., 87

  Nettie F., 12
  Susannah, 49
ROSENTHAL
  Barbette, 102
ROSENTHALL
  Augusta, 131
  Bertha, 30
ROSS
  Ann (blk), 251
  Annie C., 239
  Celia (blk), 124
  Eleanor (blk), 302
  Eliza (blk), 150
  Elizabeth, 69, 147, 152
  Elizabeth (blk), 69, 152
  Emma (blk), 54
  Esther (blk), 266
  Fannie (blk), 154
  Frances, 110
  Georgiana, 296
  Harriet (blk), 311
  Louisa, 311
  Lucretia (blk), 74
  Marcellina, 38
  Maria, 35, 147, 286, 302, 307
  Maria (blk), 35, 147, 307
  Marian E., 302
  Martha, 116, 176
  Martha M. (blk), 176
  Mary, 25, 172, 175, 272, 312
  Mary (blk), 25, 312
  Mary B., 272
  Mary V. (blk), 175
  Missie S. (blk), 290
  Rose (blk), 44
  Sophia (blk), 25
  Violet (blk), 166
ROSSON
  Mary, 25
ROTCHFORD
  Georgianna, 270

District of Columbia Marriage Licenses, 1858-1870

ROTH
  Anna Barbara, 276
  Catherine, 30
  Magdalena, 328
  Margaret A., 134
RÖTH
  Margaretha, 91
ROTHWELL
  Annie M., 268
  Martha W., 154
  Sarah, 252
ROUNDS
  Louise (blk), 277
ROUNTREE
  Adelaide V., 245
ROURKE
  Julia, 44
  Margaret, 219
ROUTERBERG
  Julia, 161
ROUX
  Eliza, 134
  Jennie, 102
ROUYARK
  Hellen C., 219
ROVER
  Catherine, 59
ROWAN
  Margaret, 49
  Phoebe, 286
ROWE
  Margaret A., 299
ROWELL
  Harriet M., 313
ROWLAND
  Mary E., 229
  Pauline, 198
ROWLES
  Arietta, 223
  Indiana, 143
  Jane Isabella, 313
ROWSER
  Alice (blk), 317
ROY
  Julia (blk), 190
  Maria (blk), 37
  Rebecca (blk), 42
ROYAL
  Rosetta (blk), 181

ROYCE
  Asenath, 260
ROYSTER
  Mary L., 206
ROZELL
  Margaret S., 87
ROZIER
  Emily (blk), 190
  Harriet, 268
  Martha (blk), 252
RUBENCAMP
  Anna Albertine, 256
RÜBENKAMM
  Caroline, 170
RUCKER
  Cornelia, 9, 292
  Cornelia (blk), 9
RUDD
  Alice, 129
  Alpha Virginia, 323
  Emma Frances, 223
  Rebecca R., 135
  Sarah, 16
RUDOLPH
  Henrietta, 104
RUEBENKAMP
  Lina, 97
RUECART
  Eva Margaret, 139
RUEDEMANN
  Auguste, 170
RUEHMAN
  Elizabeth C., 268
RUFF
  Ella, 218
  Virginia M., 73
RUH
  Amelia, 92
RUHLAND
  Maria, 256
RUHLE
  Mary C., 203
RUMAN
  Sarah, 204
RUMLUG
  Robele, 108
RUMSEY
  Mary A., 89
  Sarah C., 182

RUNDELLS
  Alpha Ann, 201
RUNDLE
  Annie, 21
RUNNELLS
  Catharine (blk), 65
  Virginia, 259
RUPERT
  Walburg, 172
RUPP
  Caroline E., 36
  Hannah, 227
  Rosina, 309
RUPPEL
  Anna Kate, 324
  Elizabeth, 253
  Josephine, 204
RUPPERT
  Agatha, 170
  Catherine, 218
  Lizzie, 24
RUPPRECHT
  Maria, 252
RUPPRECHTT
  Julia, 110
RUPRECHT
  Christiana, 181
RUSHFORD
  Fanny, 145
RUSHMAN
  Maria, 201
RUSHMOND
  Fanny, 12
RUSK
  Jane, 110
  Lucy, 111
RUSS
  Cecilia, 261
RUSSEL
  Kate, 13
RUSSELL
  Betsy (blk), 305
  Caroline, 86
  Celia A., 3
  Eliza Ann, 310
  Ellen, 144
  Frances (blk), 247
  Hannah, 293
  Jane, 126, 277, 304

RUSSELL
  Jennette, 178
  Kate (blk), 115
  Laura, 128
  Martha (blk), 255
  Mary (blk), 122, 278
  Sallie (blk), 286
  Sarah, 32, 88, 260
  Sarah E., 260
  Sarah N., 88
  Sue M., 247
RUSTIN
  Annie (blk), 47
  Sarah Ann (blk), 36
RUTHERFORD
  Jane, 30
  Mary, 83, 185
  Mary A., 185
RYAN
  Ann, 4, 203, 213, 257
  Anna, 257
  Anne, 4
  Annie, 213
  Bridget, 36, 175, 246
  Catharine, 48
  Eliza, 162
  Ellen, 28, 52, 60, 188, 228
  Emma L., 37
  Hannah, 139
  Honora, 220
  Joanna, 86
  Josephine, 316
  Kate, 111
  Margaret, 60, 164, 242
  Mary, 48, 59, 81, 97, 186, 217, 325
  Mary T., 81
  Penelope, 29
  Sarah Ann, 308
  Susie, 183
RYDER
  Annie, 162
RYDERS
  Anna, 306
RYE
  Eliza Ann, 322

RYLAND
  Mary, 68
  Rebecca J., 296
RYON
  Annie, 198
  Elizabeth M., 63
  Kate, 88

—S—

SACCHI
  Francis, 236
SACK
  C. Sophie, 24
SACKETT
  Minnie O., 225
SADER
  Mary, 104
SADLER
  Catharine Maria, 211
  Ann Elizabeth, 60
  Sarah A., 104
SAGE
  Agnes Virginia, 44
  Caroline, 40
  Clara A., 49
  Fannie W., 44
SAGEE
  Emily Elizabeth, 118
SAGERSON
  Mary, 215
SALBIER
  Emma, 2
SALE
  Sarah A., 3
SALLE
  Mary A., 278
SALMONS
  Alice H., 316
SALSBURY
  Ellen E., 191
SALVIN
  Marie Barbe, 90
SALZMAN
  Barbara, 15
SAMMONS
  Elizabeth (blk), 62

SAMPLE
  Delilah, 270
SAMPSON
  Elizabeth (blk), 181
  Henrietta, 91
SAMSON
  Emily, 174
  Julia, 116
SAMSTAG
  Bertha, 281
SAMUEL
  Letty (blk), 254
SAMUELS
  Rebecca (blk), 324
  Sarah (blk), 279
SANBORN
  Frances L., 138
SANDERS
  Ann Elizabeth, 175
  Elizabeth, 24
  L.J., 263
  Louisa (blk), 3
  Margaret (blk), 176
  Sophie (blk), 306
  Susan A., 57, 173
SANDERSON
  Amanda D., 225
  Annie E., 236
  Annie F., 197
  Georgeanna, 296
  Margaret, 250
  Mary, 115, 225
  Mary E.N., 115
  Phebe J., 92
  Saddie P., 1
  Sarah N., 255
SANDFORD
  Ann, 253
  Elizabeth, 179
  Julia E., 130
  Maria A., 89
SANDS
  Emma R., 315
  Maria Maud, 87
SANFORD
  Mary, 3, 233, 268, 308
  Mary E., 268
  Mary Ella, 3

SANFORD
  Mary Jane, 233
  Rachel (blk), 255
SANGER
  Fannie, 13
SANLEY
  Jane (blk), 48
SARGENT
  Mary C., 310
SARSFIELD
  Bridget, 217
  Maria, 109
SARTIN
  Omedia, 302
SASSER
  Henrietta M., 151
  Mary C., 22
SATER
  Dora Elizabeth, 230
SAUDER
  Johanna, 29
SAUER
  Ann Elizabeth, 326
  Maggie, 91
SAUL
  Mary Louisa, 246
SAUNDERS
  Ann E. (blk), 34, 306
  Lizzie E., 99
  Louisa (blk), 153
  Rachel (blk), 28
  S.C., 123
SAUNDERSON
  Mary Ellen, 282
SAUTER
  E.J., 218
  Wilhelmena, 303
SAVAGE
  Alice (col'd), 33
  Caroline F., 198
  Mary E., 11
  Sarah E., 8
SAVAN
  Margaret A., 189
SAVASTAN
  Sarah Catherine, 102
SAVORCOOL
  Emma, 172

SAVOY
  Elizabeth, 238, 289
  Elizabeth (blk), 289
  Fannie (blk), 248
  Martha E., 289
  Nancy (blk), 149
SAWYER
  Louie, 45
SAXTY
  Katie E., 308
SAYRE
  Josephine, 72
SCAGGS
  Caroline V., 41
  Martha R., 319
  Mary L., 90
  Mellie F., 229
SCALA
  Eliza P., 230
  Henrietta, 223
  Mary, 123
SCALON
  Johanna, 213
SCANLER
  Johanna, 184
SCANLIN
  Joanna, 114
SCANLON
  Catharine, 181
  Ellen, 123, 314
  Mary, 194, 303
  Mary C., 303
SCARBRO
  Elizabeth (blk), 226
SCHACHT
  Margaret, 209
SCHAEF
  Eliza, 185
SCHAEFER
  Martha, 17
SCHAFER
  Josephine, 161, 191
  Susanna, 85, 90
  Susannah, 85
SCHAFERT
  Mary, 171
SCHAFFER
  Caroline C., 241
  Christina B., 24

SCHAFFERT
  Margreth, 230
SCHALEK
  Christien, 131
SCHALL
  Annie M., 202
SCHALLER
  Fannie, 142
SCHAUB
  Anna B., 278
SCHAUBE
  Louisa, 201
SCHEELE
  Doris, 202
SCHEIDEGGER
  Annie M., 121
SCHEMMYER
  Johanna, 240
SCHEPP
  Frederica, 255
SCHERFF
  Annie, 177
SCHERGER
  Kate, 300
SCHERRY
  Julia A., 6
  Mary Ann, 228
SCHESINGER
  Leana, 42
SCHILDHAUER
  Minna, 138
SCHILLING
  Christiana, 168
SCHILLS
  Mary, 253
SCHING
  Emma I., 111
SCHLADER
  Laura, 222
SCHLAGEL
  Franzisca, 256
SCHLE
  Anna M., 172
SCHLEGEL
  Barbara, 205
  Catharine, 91
  Maria, 22
SCHLEIGH
  Adelaide L., 277

SCHLOUGH
  Sabina C., 22
SCHMIDT
  Anna, 326
  Annie, 257
  Augusta, 168
  Caroline C., 257
  Catherine, 179
  Elizabeth, 166
  Katherine, 82
  Margaret, 120, 280
  Maria, 254
  Mary, 165, 264
  Rosina, 259
  Sophia, 85, 240
SCHMITT
  Barbara, 15
  Dora, 120
  Elizabeth, 321
SCHNEIDER
  Auguste, 21
  Caroline, 170
  Christine, 160
  Emily A., 308
  Henrietta, 302
  Josephina, 246
  Katie, 147, 242
  Katie A., 242
  Lizzi, 308
  Louisa H., 314
  Mary Teresa, 268
SCHOCHT
  Dorah, 27
SCHOENHOF
  Sarah, 64
SCHOFIELD
  Maggie, 237
SCHOLLHAUS
  Eva Margaretha, 98
SCHOLMEIR
  Mary, 236
SCHOOL
  Helen Agnes, 311
SCHOOLCRAFT
  Alice A., 325
SCHOOLHER
  Bawael, 322
SCHOTT
  Catharina, 114

  Martha Ann, 139
SCHREAR
  Jane, 90
SCHREDE
  Lena, 92
SCHREPPER
  Elizabeth, 202
SCHRIBER
  Eliza, 218
  Sarah Ann, 230
SCHRIDER
  Mary L., 126
SCHRIER
  Annie, 42
SCHRINAGE
  Mary (blk), 319
SCHRIVER
  Anne, 203
SCHRODEL
  Barbara, 90
SCHRODT
  Mary Anna, 115
SCHROEDEL
  Mary, 160
SCHUANDER
  Mary, 274
SCHUBERT
  Adelhied, 182
  Auguste, 132
  Barbara, 275
SCHUCKING
  Kathinka, 283
SCHUCKLER
  Mary C., 4
SCHUH
  Minnie, 16
SCHUHKNECHT
  Selma Hermine, 6
SCHUIER
  Christine, 240
SCHULER
  Martha E., 180
SCHULL
  Louisa, 170
SCHULTZ
  Amelia, 296
  Karlina, 251
  Louisa, 165
  Mary, 256, 290

  Mary Eva, 290
  Rosalina, 160
SCHULTZE
  Juliana, 256
SCHUMANN
  Caroline, 96
SCHURTZ
  Elizabeth, 311
SCHWARTZ
  Barbara, 119
  Eliza, 161
  Emma Jane, 252
  Esther E., 275
SCHWARTZE
  Emma G., 52
SCHWARZ
  Veronica, 327
SCHWARZENBERG
  Amelia, 282
SCHWERKE
  Louisa, 2
SCHWINGHAMMER
  Maria M., 309
SCHWINN
  Maria, 51
SCHWORZ
  Helen, 37
SCOLLARD
  Catherine, 215
SCOTLAND
  Margaret (blk), 27
SCOTT
  Adelaide V., 48
  America V., 71
  Ann Cornelia, 296
  Anna E., 55
  Annie (blk), 155
  Catherine, 41
  Cecil May, 183
  Cecilia, 3
  Charles (blk), 117
  Cora L.V., 71
  Elizabeth, 213
  Ella V., 219
  Ellen, 36
  Francis, 154
  Harriet (blk), 115, 318
  Isabella (blk), 116

District of Columbia Marriage Licenses, 1858-1870

SCOTT
 Jane, 149, 308, 327
 Jane (blk), 308
 Jane (col'd), 149
 Jennie C., 37
 Julia (blk), 269
 Lucy A., 23
 Margaret (blk), 119
 Maria, 191
 Marion (blk), 82
 Martha (blk), 285, 313
 Martha A., 281
 Mary, 14, 25, 54, 74, 125, 144, 164, 202, 245, 262, 298
 Mary (blk), 25, 54, 164
 Mary A. (blk), 74
 Mary E., 202, 245
 Mary Ellen, 144
 Mary Emma, 298
 Mary Jane, 14
 Mary Seaton, 125
 Nancy (blk), 313
 Patsy (blk), 258
 Penelope (blk), 304
 Rachel, 244, 319
 Rachel P., 319
 Rebecca B., 133
 Rosannah, 165
 Rose (blk), 179
 Sarah, 17, 88, 125, 184, 258, 270, 287
 Sarah (blk), 270
 Sarah (col'd), 258
 Sarah A. (blk), 88
 Sarah Ann (blk), 287
 Sarah Elizabeth (blk), 17
 Sarah F., 184
 Teresa (blk), 113
 Virginia, 138
SCRANDIGE
 Mary, 199
SCRANNAGE
 Elizabeth, 252

SCRIVENER
 Ambrosia, 199
 Anna, 7
 Elizabeth A., 80
 Elizabeth Ann, 75
 Ella, 303
 Martha, 68
 Mary Susan, 199
 Mary V., 62, 144
 Nancy M., 287
SCROGGINS
 Mary E., 99
SCULLEY
 Mary, 195
SEABART
 Elizabeth, 244
SEABURN
 Catherine Ann, 260
 Mary, 54
SEABURY
 Eliza M., 24
SEALS
 Harriet (blk), 115
 Malvina (blk), 215
SEARL
 Emma (blk), 318
SEARLE
 Annie (blk), 325
SEARLES
 Eliza, 252
 Julia M., 145
SEARS
 Mary F., 205
 Rosa, 248
 Virginia C., 164
SEATON
 Emma, 103
SEAVIS
 Mary (blk), 290
SEBASTIAN
 Laura, 150
 Marion, 98
SEBREY
 Julia, 113
SEBRY
 Betty (blk), 232
SEBYERT
 Vesta, 204

SEDDEN
 Eliza, 9
SEDGWICK
 Ellen V., 177
 Gracie (blk), 227
 Virginia (blk), 34
SEDRICK
 Mary Virginia, 100
SEGERSON
 Mary, 262
SEIBEL
 Gertrude E., 29
SEIBERT
 Malvina E., 14
SEIDENBERG
 Sophia, 114
SEIDENSTRICKER
 Mary R., 171
SEIDLER
 Wilhelmina, 30
SEIFFERT
 Margaret J., 31
SEIKS
 Susan, 113
SEIP
 Barbara, 215
SEIPEL
 Louise, 119
SEITZ
 Kate V., 141
 Sophia A., 2
SELBY
 Elizabeth (blk), 272
 Emma, 94
 Laura V., 291
 Lavinia, 120
 Margaret, 271
 Martha J., 28
 Mary, 22
 Priscilla (blk), 321
 Susan F., 189
SELDEN
 Eliza (blk), 26
 Emily M. (blk), 65
 Laura, 1
 Mary B., 174
SELDNER
 Eva, 260

SELECMAN
  Jane E., 185
  Marguarite A., 110
  Virginia, 35
SELEE
  Mary L., 19
SELF
  Elizabeth Ann, 155
  Georgiana, 258
SELL
  Fredericke, 274
SELLA
  Elizabeth, 77
SELMAN
  Anna (blk), 32
SELVIN
  Sallie (blk), 212
SEMMES
  Ada, 54
  Mary Ann, 99
  Sarah, 98
SEMTER
  Catherine, 28
SENIOR
  Frances (blk), 210
SENKEND
  Anna, 300
  Augusta, 298
SERGEANT
  Catharine E., 20
  Florence, 253
SERPELL
  Florence H., 320
SERRA
  Arabella O., 263
  M. Isadore, 167
SERRIN
  Ellen Virginia, 286
SERRO
  Elenor, 177
SESSFORD
  Caroline K., 70
  Jeannie E., 16
SESTER
  Sophia (blk), 36
SETTLES
  Caroline (blk), 14, 114

SEVERANCE
  Martha A., 168
SEWALL
  Elizabeth, 72
  Jane A., 7
  Regina, 261
SEWELL
  Amanda, 139
  Laura Virginia, 166
  Martha E., 191
  Mary W., 249
  Rosa, 251
  Ruth Anna, 54
SEXTON
  Annie, 50
  Margt. M., 126
SEYMOUR
  Charlotte, 252
  Florence, 15
  Mary A.J., 126
SHACKELFORD
  Georgeana, 209
  Martha E., 152
SHACKLEFORD
  Annie C., 127
  Isabel, 271
  Jane Ann, 209
  Sucillia, 45
SHADD
  Addie E., 324
SHAFER
  Ellen C., 116
  Johanna, 61
  Sarah E. W., 268
  Victorine E., 145
SHAFFER
  Catharine, 313
  Mary M., 277
SHAFFLING
  Barbara, 135
SHAFFORD
  Mary, 298
SHALCROSS
  Louisa, 234
SHANAHAN
  Catherine, 4
  Margaret, 40
  Sarah, 268

SHANE
  Agnes, 30
  Ellen, 293
  Margaret, 97
SHANK
  Viola Jane, 16
SHANKLAND
  Julia (blk), 307
  Winny (blk), 210
SHANKLIN
  Susan, 32
SHANKS
  Emily A., 285
SHANNAHAN
  Mary, 199
SHANNON
  Catherine, 210
  Jane, 243
  Margaret, 39
SHARESWOOD
  Mary E., 57
SHARP
  Mary Ann, 209
  Nellie, 134
  Sophia (blk), 79
SHARPE
  Abby Jane (blk), 69
  Mary, 130
SHARPER
  Ida, 87
SHARPLEY
  Mary Jane, 182
SHAUGHNESSY
  Annie, 298
  Mary, 95, 221
SHAUN
  Rosa (blk), 192
SHAUNESSY
  Mary, 70
SHAUP
  Elizabeth, 93
SHAW
  Annie, 2, 190
  Annie (blk), 2
  Emma V., 19
  Frances Cornelia, 73
  J.H., 318
  Jane Susan, 71
  Julia E., 288

District of Columbia Marriage Licenses, 1858-1870

SHAW
  Maggie A., 265
  Margaret, 215
  Mary, 36, 101
  Mary (blk), 36
  Rebecca H., 245
SHAWS
  Elizabeth (blk), 57
SHAY
  Catharine M., 212
SHEA
  Ann, 164
  Bridget, 68
  Catherine, 135
  Eliza, 118
  Hannah, 302
  Johannah, 147
  Julia, 78, 191
  Margaret, 60, 209
  Martha, 161
  Mary, 135, 138,
    163, 212, 220,
    262
  Mary Jane, 138
SHEAD
  Mary Ann (blk), 34
SHEADS
  Louisa Maria, 125
SHEAFFER
  Emma D., 196
SHEAHAN
  Bridget, 72, 262
  Catherine, 33
  Margaret, 54
  Mary, 9, 124
SHEARER
  Amanda C., 53
SHECKELL
  Sarah E., 169
SHECKELLS
  Elizabeth, 41
  Martha, 33
  Mary R., 184
SHECKELS
  Julia, 291
SHECKILLS
  Elizabeth V., 92
SHEDD
  Alice J., 19

Frances L., 217
Laura A., 263
Margaret F., 140
Nettie J., 283
Susie L., 24
SHEED
  Leida R., 102
  Susanah, 161
SHEEHAN
  Catherine, 282
  Mary, 52
SHEEHEY
  Mary, 187
SHEEHY
  Bridget, 164
  Catharine, 123
  Ellen, 238
  Helen, 101
  Mary, 220
SHEETS
  Elizabeth A., 50
SHEHAN
  Bridget, 255
  Kate, 199
  Mary, 283
SHEID
  Catherine R., 204
SHEIT
  Mary, 216
SHEKELL
  Margaret E., 76
SHELBY
  Mary, 111
SHELDON
  Alice, 260
SHELL
  Emma, 137
SHELTER
  Mildred (blk), 80
SHELTON
  Caroline (blk), 113
  Frances, 222
  Mary, 126
  Rebecca (blk), 18
  Susan Ann, 207
SHENNESSY
  Margaret, 80
SHEPHARD
  Jane M., 206

Mary, 202
Susan (blk), 241
SHEPHERD
  Ann (blk), 47
  Anna J., 202
  Caroline (blk), 6
  Catherine (blk), 110
  Columbia (blk), 183
  Henrietta, 156
  Hettie Maria, 258
  Jennie, 304
  Louisa, 159
  Lucy Ann, 181
  Martha (blk), 152
  Mary, 91, 265
  Mary E. (blk), 265
SHEPPACH
  Barbette, 160
SHEREWOOD
  Harriet Frances, 266
SHERFF
  Mary, 257
SHERIDAN
  Rose, 29
  Susan Cecilia, 87
SHERIER
  Elizabeth, 319
SHERLOCK
  Elizabeth J., 83
SHERMAN
  Amanda M., 313
  Eunice R., 47
  Hanorah, 324
  Martha Ann, 299
  Mary, 3, 39, 132
  Mary C., 3
  Nelty, 294
  Susan, 161
SHERRIER
  Emile Elizabeth, 21
SHERRY
  Catharine, 28
  Sarah L., 274
SHERWIN
  Julia E., 226
SHERWOOD
  Annie, 273
  Emily, 91
  Jane E., 276

SHERWOOD
  Kate A., 36
  Mary C.E., 263
  Priscilla, 274
  Rosa A., 46
SHEY
  Hannah, 164
SHIED
  Mary C., 28
SHIELDS
  Ann, 243
  Elizabeth C.D., 325
  Margaret, 81
  Mary, 101, 108, 214
  Mary V., 101
  Sarah E., 8
SHIELER
  Louisa, 226
SHILES
  Caroline, 231
  Jane, 269
  Maria (blk), 52
  Neely (blk), 122
SHILLING
  Mary, 242
SHILLINGLAW
  Jane, 300
SHINER
  Annie M., 228, 264
SHINN
  Elizebeth, 195
SHIPLEY
  Ann (blk), 231
  Mary (blk), 11
  Mary M., 204
SHIRLEY
  Virginia, 14
SHIRVING
  Sarah E., 247
SHOEMAKER
  Margaret Ann, 311
SHOOTER
  Sally (blk), 32
SHORE
  Mary Elizth., 194
SHORT
  Eliza (blk), 92
SHORTELL
  Mary Ann, 241

SHORTER
  Annie M. (blk), 9
  Celia (blk), 308
  Elinor (blk), 201
  Elizabeth (blk), 267
  Josephine (blk), 211
  Laura Jane, 53
  Lizzie (blk), 47
  Louisa (blk), 82
  Marion, 106
  Martha (blk), 126
  Mary (blk), 126
  Mary Ann (blk), 248
SHOTROW
  Mahala Jane, 10
SHOWED
  Elizabeth, 115
SHOWELL
  L.M., 21
SHREEVE
  Mary J., 276
  Susan S., 67
SHREVE
  Annie B., 319
  Eugenia, 103
  Jane Amanda, 90
  Mary Catherine, 318
  Mary G., 272
SHREVES
  Gurtie E., 240
SHRIVER
  Louisa, 251
SHRODEL
  Barbara, 265
SHRYOCK
  Ellen Hill, 243
  Narcissa A., 28
SHUGARS
  Margaret (blk), 310
SHUGERT
  Clara, 103
SHULTZ
  Eliza, 13
  Sophia, 86
SHUMAN
  Emma, 160
SHUNTON
  Annie, 110

SHURE
  Louisa, 109
SHUSTER
  Mary J., 246
SHUTT
  Mary, 244
SHUTTE
  Bertha, 182
SHUTZ
  Louis, 217
SHYNES
  Eulalia M., 230
SHYROCK
  Maggie, 24
SIBLEY
  Elizabeth, 65
SICKEL
  Caroline, 46
SICKLE
  Sophia, 166
SIDEBOTTOMS
  Margaret H., 207
SIDNER
  Sarah (blk), 321
SIDNEY
  Catharine, 14
SIEBERT
  Mary, 301
SIEBOLD
  Jane, 7
SIEGERT
  Barbara, 261
SIESFELD
  Frederick, 193
SIEVERS
  Babet, 170, 230
  Babet Mary, 230
SIGH
  Betsy (blk), 5
SILENA
  Martha V., 51
SILENCE
  Josephine A., 107
  Regenda, 37
  Susan, 129
SILK
  Caroline, 61
SILLER
  Elizabeth, 102

SILLIMAN
  Margaret, 113
SILLKINGER
  Caroline, 131
SILSBEE
  Susan, 115
SILVER
  Amanda Jane, 171
SIMAKER
  Barbara, 35
SIMES
  Mary Louisa, 272
SIMKINS
  Lizzie A., 292
SIMMAKA
  Mary, 12
SIMMES
  Sarah E. (blk), 225
SIMMONS
  Elizabeth F., 167
  Fanny, 327
  Indiana, 125
  Louisa, 49
  Malinda J., 142
  Margaret (blk), 297
  Mary, 33, 276, 277, 288
  Mary (blk), 288
  Mary E., 33
  Mary Elizabeth, 277
  Sarah E., 202
SIMMS
  Amelia (blk), 297
  Anna (blk), 289
  Annie E., 266
  Charlotte (blk), 37
  Eddie, 305
  Elizabeth (blk), 134
  Emily (blk), 201
  Fannie, 198
  Laura (blk), 132
  Letitia (blk), 149
  Margaret (blk), 266
  Maria (blk), 106
  Martha, 13
  Mary M., 258
  Nancy, 117
  Rebecca, 14
  Sarah (blk), 80

SIMON
  Johanna M., 168
  Kate, 69
  Magdelene, 128
SIMONDS
  Georgiana (blk), 65
  John R., viii
  Maggie E., 90
  Maria, 249
  Martha E., 255
  Mary, 173, 266
  Mary C., 173
  Mattie, 298
  Rosanna, 258
  Sarah, 121
SIMONS
  Carrie, 224
  Gracis (blk), 192
SIMPSON
  Alice (blk), 236, 304
  Alice R., 142
  Ann Jane, 42
  Anna L., 237
  Caroline Roberta, 64
  Carrie (blk), 27
  Cornelia B. (blk), 315
  Eliza Ann (blk), 311
  Helen B., 231
  Julia, 306, 307
  Julia E., 306
  Kate, 274
  Lavinia C., 69
  Margaret, 23, 119
  Margaret A., 23
  Mary, 64, 87, 196
  Mary Ellen, 196
  Mary F., 64
  Mollie O., 326
  Rachel M., 135
  Roberta, 64
  Sally Ann (blk), 267
  Sarah L., 133
  Winnie (blk), 69
SIMS
  Amanda (blk), 305
  Ann Eliza (blk), 317
  Delala (blk), 244
  Ellen (col'd), 284

Emily (blk), 201
Josephine (blk), 312
Louisa (blk), 133
Margaret (blk), 307
Martha (blk), 163
Mary (blk), 250, 319
Mary E., 152
Mary L. (blk), 296
Matilda, 79, 125, 267
Matilda (blk), 79
Matilda Wilson, 125
Minty (blk), 159
Rebecca (blk), 270
Rosa (blk), 66
Sarah (blk), 269
SINCLAIR
  Ellen (blk), 208
  Harriet Lucretia, 86
  Marian V., 112
SINGER
  Elizabeth, 89
SINGLETON
  Hannah (blk), 149
  Lucy (blk), 228
SINK
  Elizabeth, 89
SINNOTT
  Jennie E., 176
SIOUSSA
  Clara E., 238
  Isabella B., 287
  Lottie R., 44
SIPES
  Margaret E., 276
  Philippine, 7
SIPPLE
  Mary A., 75
SIRICH
  Mary L., 174
SIRLY
  Sarah Louisa, 19
SIS
  Mary, 160
SISCO
  Catherine (blk), 172
SISSON
  Jane R., 246
SITES
  Lucinda (blk), 281

SKARREN
  Kate Louise, 300
SKELLY
  Bridget, 184
  Elizabeth A., 199
SKIDMORE
  Emma, 119
  Henrietta, 14
  Martha E., 89
  Mary, 246
  Roberta, 274
SKILES
  Fannie, 74
SKILLEN
  Mary, 45
SKINEAR
  Sallie, 270
SKINNER
  Ann, 186
  Sarah F., 1
  Sarah R., 207
SKIPPERS
  Frances (blk), 167
SKIPWORTH
  Patsy (blk), 316
SKULLY
  Margaret, 121
SLACK
  Josephine, 290
  Marcia V., 141
SLADE
  Josephine, 324
  Mary Louisa, 306
  Rachel J., 324
SLAGLE
  Frances, 228
SLATER
  Celia, 150
  Eliza (blk), 319
  Hannah, 150
  Louisa (blk), 142
  Margaert (blk), 60
  Mary, 79
  Sarah J., 197
  Willie, 199
SLATFORD
  Eliza, 168, 250
  Elizabeth, 168
  Mary J., 157

Mary Jane, 90
SLATTERY
  Ellen, 39
  Johana, 60
  Margaret, 310
  Mary, 118
SLAVEN
  Martha C., 21
SLEDD
  Eugenia J., 143
SLEIGH
  Jemima, 313
SLEMAKER
  Helen G., 131
SLOAN
  Mary, 42
SLUDENY
  Sharlott E., 223
SLUSHER
  Elizabeth C., 7
SLYE
  Mary R., 291
SMACK
  Sarah E., 102
SMALL
  Eliza, 107
  Grace, 20
SMALLWOOD
  Ann (blk), 126
  Anna, 14, 177
  Anna M., 177
  Annie, 25, 153, 289
  Annie (blk), 25
  Elizabeth, 54, 176, 192, 222, 270
  Elizabeth (blk), 54, 176, 222
  Ellen (blk), 104
  Emma F., 178
  Henrietta, 62
  Phine (blk), 248
  Rosetta, 73
  Sarah J., 265
  Treecy, 31
SMART
  Emma, 72
  Mattie W., 252
SMEAD
  Camilla A., 235

SMILER
  Helen (blk), 317
  Margaret, 4
  Mary Ann (blk), 304
SMILEY
  Mary Ann, 180
SMILY
  Susan, 8
SMITH
  [blank], 169
  Adaline (blk), 72
  Adelaide, 231
  Adelia, 183
  Alice (blk), 246, 269
  Alice A., 144
  Alice Virginia, 275
  Amanda, 183, 318, 325
  Amanda (blk), 183
  Amelia (blk), 281
  Ann (blk), 107, 137
  Ann Elizabeth, 263
  Ann L., 124
  Ann Maria, 283
  Anna (blk), 178, 192
  Anna L., 262
  Anna P., 191
  Anna Xariffa, 86
  Annah, 303
  Annie (blk), 173, 268, 320
  Annie A., 33
  Annie Elizabeth, 7
  Annie J., 152, 228
  Annie L., 177
  Annie M., 238
  Annie Virginia, 4
  Arabella, 253
  Barbara A. (blk), 88
  Caroline, 26, 183, 272
  Caroline (blk), 183, 272
  Carrie, 161
  Catherine, 59, 88
  Catherine V., 88
  Cecelia C., 183
  Charlotte (blk), 215
  Christine (blk), 129

SMITH
  Dinah, 214
  E. Augusta, 317
  Elia, 3, 269
  Eliza (blk), 103, 247
  Elizabeth, 93, 119,
    121, 123, 124,
    126, 135, 140,
    236, 257, 271
  Elizabeth (blk), 93,
    121, 123, 271
  Elizabeth A. (blk),
    126
  Elizabeth H., 135
  Ella B., 79
  Ellen (blk), 267
  Ellen V., 169
  Elvira E., 248
  Emily, 63, 134, 210,
    255
  Emily (blk), 255
  Emily (col'd), 134
  Fannie (blk), 70
  Florence (blk), 293
  Florida, 24
  Frances (blk), 67,
    270
  Georgiana H., 122
  Hannah A., 189
  Harriet (blk), 152,
    306
  Harriet M. (blk), 102
  Helen Olivia, 91
  Hellen, 72
  Henrietta (blk), 115,
    319
  Isabella (blk), 133
  Jane (blk), 127, 198,
    322
  Jane C., 188
  Jenny (blk), 218
  Jessy, 10
  Josephine (blk), 324
  Judy (blk), 45
  Julia (blk), 5, 172
  Julia A., 8, 13
  Julia Ann (blk), 271
  Julia J., 254
  Kate (blk), 203
  Kathrine R., 13
  Katie (blk), 101
  Laura, 189, 270,
    302, 309, 322
  Laura (blk), 270,
    302
  Laura A., 322
  Laura E., 189
  Leonora Amelia, 91
  Lizzie, 22, 45, 57,
    231, 303
  Lizzie (blk), 22, 45,
    57
  Lizzie A., 231
  Louise (blk), 65,
    206
  Lucinda (blk), 134
  Lucy (blk), 47, 139,
    148, 150, 172
  Lucy A. (blk), 159
  Lyda, 95
  Lydia (blk), 103
  Margaret, 30, 138,
    180, 218, 256,
    260, 307, 313
  Margaret (blk), 138,
    218
  Margaret F., 307
  Maria (blk), 148,
    151
  Marion B., 281
  Martha (blk), 196
  Martha J. (blk), 273
  Mary, 8, 16, 19, 29,
    32, 38, 39, 41, 48,
    51, 61, 68, 78, 96,
    117, 126, 139,
    146, 156, 157,
    168, 179, 182,
    189, 191, 216,
    218, 240, 259,
    261, 273, 284,
    285, 292, 295,
    309, 311, 312
  Mary (blk), 48, 216,
    240, 273, 312
  Mary A. (blk), 146,
    182
  Mary Alice, 96
  Mary Ann, 16, 191,
    309, 311
  Mary Ann (blk),
    309, 311
  Mary C., 38, 285
  Mary E., 8, 19, 32,
    51, 68, 78, 156,
    168, 295
  Mary E. (blk), 8, 32,
    51, 78
  Mary Eliza, 41, 117
  Mary Elizabeth, 41
  Mary Ellen (blk), 29
  Mary Isabella
    Elizabeth, 126
  Mary Jane, 157
  Mary K., 259
  Mary Lizzie (blk),
    179
  Mary T. (blk), 19
  May G., 172
  Milly (blk), 74
  Nancy (blk), 149,
    166, 279
  Nelly (blk), 322
  Polly (blk), 272
  Rachel, 184, 198,
    270
  Rachel M., 270
  Rachel Mary, 184
  Rebecca, 153, 205,
    320
  Rebecca (blk), 205
  Rebecca Ann (blk),
    320
  Rose (blk), 295
  Sallie, 30, 173
  Sallie A., 30
  Sarah, 26, 33, 46,
    65, 117, 118, 154,
    218, 240, 251
  Sarah (blk), 33, 65,
    154, 251
  Sarah A., 118
  Sarah J., 46
  Sarah Jane, 117
  Sarah M., 240
  Sarah V., 26
  Sophia, 110

SMITH
  Susan A., 118
  Thysa Virginia, 198
  Victoria, 197
  Virginia (blk), 87
  Virginia C., 246
SMITHING
  Anna (blk), 267
SMITHLEY
  Margaret A., 225
SMITHSON
  Caroline F., 118
  Elizabeth, 288
  Mary A., 144
  Mary Ellen, 63
  Rebecca V., 138
SMITSON
  Eliza Ann, 318
SMOLINSKA
  Honorine M., 315
SMOLINSKI
  Josephine, 168
SMOOT
  Ann Virginia, 57
  Charity (blk), 11
  Emma, 287
  Kate U., 286
  Lizzie T., 144
  Mary A., 193
  Winnie (blk), 65
SMOTHERS
  Annie F. (blk), 66
SNEED
  Ann (blk), 235
SNIER
  Margaret, 309
SNIFFIN
  Susan A., 46
SNOOKE
  Emma, 175
SNOW
  Jane, 59
  Margaret, 209
SNOWDEN
  Anna (blk), 143
  Eliza (blk), 124
  Hannah (blk), 305
  Jane (blk), 11
  Kate (blk), 229

Lucinda (blk), 150
Mary, 114
Sarah (blk), 153
SNYDER
  Caroline, 184
  Elizabeth, 281
  Louisa, 231
  Lucinda, 30
  Margaret Ann, 75
  Mary, 161, 191, 303
  Mary A., 303
  Mary Elizabeth, 161
  Mena, 160
  Sarah A., 164
  Sophia C., 34
SOLDSBERRY
  Ellen, 7
SOLLERS
  Sarah E., 266
SOLOMON
  Anna R. (blk), 266
  Ellen (blk), 76
  Nannie, 64
  Rosa, 19
  Sarah (blk), 55
SOLON
  Mary, 124, 226
SOMERS
  Margaret Ann, 102
  Mary M.C., 260
SOMERVILLE
  Ann Maria, 186
  Lizzie (blk), 226
  Susan, 112
SOMMERS
  Elizabeth W., 195
  Margaret R., 206
SOMMERVILLE
  Julia (blk), 180
SONNENBORN
  Mina Rebecca, 309
SOOPER
  Eliza, 143
SOPER
  Catharine R., 234
  Mary Ann, 116
SORRELL
  Mary (blk), 25

SOTHORON
  Roberta, 64
SOUDER
  Tenie, 71
SOUR
  Barbara, 95
SOUSSA
  Catharine, 299
SOUTHARD
  Mary E., 220
SOUTHWORTH
  Charlotte E., 174
SPAIT
  Annie, 19
SPALDING
  Mary C., 135
  Mary E., 270, 317
SPANENPERYER
  Laura C., 321
SPARKS
  Mary (blk), 275
SPARROW
  Maria, 8
  Mary (blk), 216
SPATES
  Margaret, 109
  Mollie R., 32
SPAULDING
  Betsey L., 324
  Marcella, 246
SPEAKE
  Emma J., 274
  Susanna Virginia, 5
SPEAKS
  Caroline, 190
  Louisa, 83
  Phebe (blk), 203
  Winnie Ann, 17
SPEAR
  Amanda E., 88
  Sarah E., 56
SPEDDEN
  Annie R., 139
SPEEDEN
  Alice, 229
  Kate, 117
SPEEKS
  Mary, 292

SPEER
  Christina, 232
SPEIR
  Maria E., 109
SPELLER
  Patsey (blk), 96
SPELLING
  Catharine, 231
SPELMAN
  Ann Maria, 55
  Harriet Jane, 112
SPENCER
  Caroline (blk), 104
  Catherine Ann, 250
  Ellen C., 157
  Emma, 62
  Harriet V., 10
  Jane E., 133
  Louisa, 128
  Maria (blk), 9
  Mary, 74, 298
  Mary (blk), 298
  Polly (blk), 216
  Sarah (blk), 27
SPICE
  Mary Ann, 117
SPICER
  Maria Leonora, 105
SPIGNALL
  Mary, 6
SPILLMAN
  Frances M., 35
  Laralia J., 145
  Lena, 210
SPILMAN
  Mary Frances, 141
SPINDLE
  Anna, 94
  Elizabeth, 259
  Mary Catherine, 323
SPITTLE
  Landonia C., 67
  Susie F., 292
SPOTSWOOD
  Fanny (blk), 37
  Hannah (blk), 61
SPOTSWORTH
  Laura (blk), 291

SPOTTS
  Margaret C., 181
SPRAGUE
  Laura, 112
SPRENGER
  Elizabeth, 295
SPRIGG
  Georgiana (blk), 116
  Harriet Ann (blk), 206
  Mary (blk), 132
SPRIGGS
  Martha (blk), 292
  Rachel, 35
SPRINAGE
  Catherine (blk), 295
SPRING
  Maggie, 86
SPRINGER
  Martha, 33
  Mary, 78, 91
  Mary A., 91
SPRINGSTEEL
  Lottie, 272
SPROUT
  Celestia (col'd), 77
SPURLOCK
  Mahala (blk), 32
SPURRIER
  Annie, 146
ST. CLAIR
  Alice M., 232
  Maggie L., 1
ST. JOHN
  Ellen D., 244
  Mary E., 86
  Rebecca T., 132
ST. JOHNS
  Mary E. (blk), 224
STACKE
  Mary, 220
STAFFEL
  Catarina, 34
STAFFORD
  Amanda, 302
  Mary E., 266
STAGMULLER
  Louisa, 96

STAHL
  Elizabeth, 96
  Josephine, 37
  Kate A., 281
  Mary E., 320
STAINHICE
  Maria E., 293
STALCUP
  Jane A., 40
STALER
  Jennie, 8
STALL
  Amanda, 163
STALLINGS
  Marion, 117
  Martha E., 75
  Mary E., 56, 294
  Naremeta S., 194
STALLINS
  Martha, 75
STAMP
  Julia, 244
STANBURY
  Emeline (blk), 50
STANDFORD
  Fanny, 48
STANFORD
  Laura V., 301
STANHOPE
  Fannie Louisa, 326
STANLEY
  Bernetta, 276
  Katy, 301
  Sarah H., 38
STANLY
  Mary E. (blk), 148
STANNARD
  Frances A. (blk), 97
STANSBURY
  Eliza, 36
  Jane, 238
  Mary Jane, 71
  Sarah J.E., 242
STANT
  Mary, 323
STANTON
  Fredericka, 94
  Mary (blk), 154

STAPLES
  Emeline, 184
  Joanna, 261
  Sarah, 19, 173
  Sarah (blk), 19
  Susanna, 286
STAPLETON
  Margaret, 110
STARBUCK
  Annie C., 137
STARCK
  Anna Kate, 243
STARK
  Caroline V., 124
  Mary (blk), 156
  Melissa G. (blk), 100
STARKE
  Mary Ann, 250
STARR
  Eliza V., 268
  Florida L., 33
STARTZMAN
  Sarah Ann, 152
STARWHITE
  Julia, 110
  Mary E., 184
STARWIGHT
  Elizabeth, 66
STATEN
  Margaret, 264
  Sarah, 80
STAUB
  Caroline D., 133
  Sarah Jane, 200
STAUGHAN
  John, viii
STAUNER
  Malvina (blk), 316
STEACOM
  Annie E., 216
STEADMAN
  Annie E., 267
STEARNS
  Harriet, 284
STEEL
  Agusta F., 268
  Susan V., 62

STEELE
  Annie E., 216
  Emma E., 74
  Eva A., 237
  Fannie B., 267
  Fannie H., 37
  Georgiana, 27
  Lizzie, 64
  Mary, 224
STEERMAN
  Jane (blk), 198
STEGNER
  Elmira, 25
STEHLE
  Emma H., 251
  Frederick, 121
  Lina, 19
STEIGER
  Augusta, 182
STEIGHAUF
  Eve M., 281
STEIN
  Catharine, 223
  Margaret, 243
STEINBRENNER
  Eva Mary, 78
STEINER
  Bettie, 326
  Marietta C., 267
STEINMANN
  Mary, 223
STEINMLE
  Rosina, 140
STEIRERNAGEL
  Mari, 17
STEIRNACHER
  Mary E., 256
STELLE
  Adelaide H., 57
  Susan R., 238
STELLWAGEN
  Julia, 111
STENG
  Anna, 180
STEPHENS
  Eliza Jane, 16
  Rosanna, 289
STEPHENSON
  Jane (blk), 277

  Kate B., 124
  Mary A., 246
  Mary G., 52
STERLING
  Hattie, 293
STERN
  Rose, 161
STERNBERG
  Sophia, 233
STETSON
  Ann, 153
  Josephine D., 132
  Sarah W., 293
STETTINIUS
  Rose Belle, 115
STEUART
  Elizabeth, 151
  Emily Nourse, 202
STEVENS
  Ailsey (blk), 269
  Elizabeth N., 311
  Emma F., 3
  Hester Emily, 203
  Kate M., 21
  Lizzie M., 13
  Lucie C.M., 239
  Maggie J., 288
  Mary A., 87
  Mary C., 198
  Mary E. (blk), 289
  Mary Olivia, 327
  Mary R., 11
  Morgan, 248, 278
  Sallie C., 303
STEVENSON
  Ann, 50
  Carrie L., 225
  Elizabeth (blk), 222
  Luvenia, 14
  Matilda (blk), 11
  Nancy (blk), 190
STEVER
  Elizabeth A., 4
STEWART
  Alexina, 55, 286
  Amelia (blk), 283
  America (blk), 53
  Ann E. (blk), 76
  Ann P. (blk), 278

STEWART
  Anna (blk), 203
  Anna H., 42
  Annie, 113, 279
  Annie (blk), 113
  Ary (blk), 94
  Caroline M. (blk), 264
  Carrie V., 195
  Cary Ann, 40
  Charlotte (blk), 117
  Dolly (blk), 176
  Eliza, 69, 73, 188
  Elizabeth, 73, 188
  Ella Annie, 223
  Ella R., 63
  Ellen S. (blk), 47
  Emily J. (blk), 322
  Emma, 70
  Frances (blk), 215
  Henrietta V., 277
  Jane (blk), 292
  Josephine B., 64
  Julia A., 31
  Lizzie (blk), 129
  Lizzie L., 311
  Lucinda (blk), 94
  Margaret (blk), 316
  Margt. E., 173
  Maria (blk), 279
  Maria Louisa, 287
  Marietta, 68
  Martha Ann, 45
  Mary, 49, 73, 95, 249, 287, 320
  Mary A., 95
  Mary C., 49, 73, 249, 320
  Nancy (blk), 25, 130
  Rosa (blk), 285
  Rosetta (blk), 315
  Sallie, 85
  Sarah L., 178
  Susan (blk), 307
  Susan E. (blk), 156
STHULMANN
  Sabina, 243
STICK
  Clara Victoria, 236

STICKELS
  Susan, 125
STICKNEY
  Chloe (blk), 176
  Sarah Elizabeth, 176
STIDMAN
  Martha, 156
STIEFLER
  Margaret, 39
STILLINGS
  [blank], 80
STINEMETZ
  Mary E., 322
STINGEL
  Lena, 29
STINSON
  Mary, 22
STOCK
  Elizabeth (blk), 117
  Gwynnette (blk), 132
STOCKLEIN
  Kate, 252
STOCKTON
  Amelia (blk), 139
STODDARD
  Elizabeth A., 95
  Martha, 199
  Mary Ann, 299
STOECKEL
  Matilda, 281
STOFFEL
  Mary U., 20
STOKES
  Ann (blk), 126
  Catherine (blk), 250
STONE
  Alice, 2
  Amelia, 184
  Bettie E., 180
  Caroline, 293
  Catharine, 125
  Charlotte R., 305
  Eliza, 8, 255, 276
  Elizabeth, 8, 255
  Elizabeth T., 255
  Emma C., 23
  Emma Virginia, 152
  Frances, 58

Francis Ann, 105
Harriet A., 97
Harriet V., 95
Jeanette, 141
Josephine V., 281
Loretta, 206
Louisa Ellen, 286
Margaret, 82, 120, 273, 301
Margaret J., 301
Maria, 196, 291
Marian L., 196
Martha H. (blk), 7
Mary Ann, 85
Mary Catherine, 322
Sallie B., 260
Sarah A., 277
Sarah F., 293
STONEBURNER
  Jane, 280
STONELL
  Harriet, 229
STOOPS
  Cora J., 242
STORES
  Sylvia Ann, 206
STORM
  Sarah, 165
STORMENT
  Catherine, 302
STORY
  Eliza, 116
  Mollie F., 270
  Sarah H., 136
STOTT
  Jennie, 14
STOUFFER
  Amelia Caroline, 106
STOUT
  Maud, 87
  Sarah Ann, 151
STOVER
  Annie R., 91
  Sarah M., 3
STOWES
  Mary (blk), 155
STRAHAN
  Susan H., 155

STRAMAEL
　Mollie J., 154
STRANG
　Mollie J., 6
STRASBURGER
　Babet, 257
STRATTON
　Calista G., 38
　Carrie A., 277
　Cynthia M., 183
　Martha B., 202
　Mary E., 285
　Sarah, 14
STRAUSE
　Esther, 161
STRAUSS
　Caroline, 166
　Fannie, 182
　Mena, 108
　Nannie, 120
STREEKS
　Elizabeth R., 187
STREETS
　Susan (blk), 107
STRIBELL
　Catherine, 249
STRICKHART
　Mena, 181
STRIDER
　Ann E., 161
　Mary C., 261
STRIEN
　Sarah C., 307
STRIKER
　Sarah E., 234
STROBEL
　Elizabeth T., 139
　Frodericka, 91
STROEBEL
　Elizabeth D., 50
STROHL
　Catharine, 27
STROM
　Augusta, 230
STROMAN
　Anna McGregor
　Elizabeth, 182
STRONG
　Amanda, 14

　Regina, 38
STROSSNER
　Mary, 14
STROTHER
　Catherine (blk), 139
　Lucy A., 217
STROTHERS
　Mary A., 264
STROUB
　Margarethe, 301
STROUD
　Mary R., 325
STROWMAN
　Matilda, 119
STUART
　Bettie A., 56
　Julia W., 313
　Lizzie A., 220
　Minerva (blk), 181
STUDDS
　Emma, 67
STUFFLE
　Mary, 109
STUHLMAN
　Eliza, 211
STULZ
　Caroline, 135
STUMPF
　Julia, 186
STURGIS
　Hannah Catherine, 104
STURM
　Salome M., 139
STURZ
　Hannah (blk), 296
SUCH
　Charlotte (blk), 259
SUDDATH
　Casander E., 274
SUDDEATH
　Mary E., 114
SUDDETH
　Ann C., 137
　Elizabeth, 274
SUETA
　Annie, 114
SUISKIND
　Mary Ann, 23

SUIT
　Augusta, 258
　Louisa Jane, 188
　Martha A., 229
　Mary, 13, 44, 219
　Mary Amanda, 13
　Susanna B., 256
SULIVAN
　Honora, 246
　Mary, 141
SULLIVAN
　Ann, 67, 87, 99,
　　212, 218, 254,
　　281, 284, 325
　Ann M., 218
　Anna, 67, 281, 284
　Anna E., 281
　Annie, 87, 325
　Annie E., 87
　Bettie, 154
　Catherine, 238
　Ellen, 46, 58, 66, 84,
　　100, 163, 200,
　　234, 241, 276
　Fannie, 199
　Hanna, 162
　Hanorah, 109
　Harriet F., 166
　Ida, 10
　Joanna, 75, 84, 260
　Johanna, 13, 70, 83,
　　187, 214, 219
　Juila, 263
　Julia, 75
　Margaret, 42, 60,
　　194, 220, 221,
　　239, 274
　Margaret C., 239
　Mary, 59, 68, 74,
　　79, 82, 87, 100,
　　140, 141, 143,
　　147, 160, 162,
　　183, 185, 194,
　　213, 215, 219,
　　260, 271
　Mary F., 183
　Mary O., 194
　Mary R., 87
　Mary Wade, 143

SULLIVAN
  Nora, 236
  Sarah, 264
  Winnifred, 263
  Winny, 220
SULVIN
  Mary, 299
SUMBY
  Mary A. (blk), 20
SUMMERS
  Charlotte A., 141
  Elizth. F., 38
  M.E., 324
  M.F., 321
  Margaret A., 243
  Martha E., 80
  Mary B., 174
  Mary E., 302
  Winifred, 46
  Winney, 162
SUMMERVILLE
  Mary M. (blk), 266
SUMNER
  Eliza (blk), 286
SUPLEE
  Emma, 274
SUPPLE
  Ann, 200
SURMIHL
  Jane, 34
SURRATT
  Anna E., 294
SURRICK
  Susan, 162
SUSSEX
  Louisa (blk), 213
SUTER
  Julia, 248
SUTER
  Meni, 119
SUTHERLAND
  Aletha, 230
SUTLERS
  Frances (blk), 259
SUTTON
  Annie R., 53
  Catherine I., 229
  Maranda E., 222
  Mary Jane, 95

Mary V., 131
Sarah (blk), 293
Sarah F., 110
Virginia, 71, 129
SWAGART
  Margaret V., 325
SWAILES
  Louisa (blk), 87
SWAIN
  Julia Ann, 89
  Mary E., 8
  Mary Louisa, 36
  Miranda, 296
SWAINE
  Mary Virginia, 298
  Minnie A., 75
SWALES
  Nancy, 27
SWALIES
  Anna (blk), 59
SWAN
  Ann Virginia, 99
  Elender Sophia, 213
  Fredericka, 90
  Mary, 194
SWANAGIN
  Laura (blk), 69
SWANIGAN
  Martha (blk), 23
SWANN
  Anna, 46
  Cora, 302
  Fannie A., 247
  Georgiana (blk), 32
  Julia, 22
  Margaret, 298
  Mary (blk), 283
  Mary E., 264
  Susie E., 237
SWANSBERRY
  Amelia, 53
SWAYZE
  Belle, 110
SWEENEY
  Ann, 283
  Bettie, 13
  Mary, 218, 262
  Mary Regina, 262

SWEENY
  Agnes (blk), 101
  Anna (blk), 119
  Catherine, 100, 244
  Catherine M., 244
  Ellen, 255
  Johanna, 100
  Louisa, 296
  Lucy, 244
  Margaret, 61, 86
  Maria, 200
  Mary, 44, 45, 197
  Mary Ann, 45
  Mary Jane, 197
  Rosetta, 75
  Susan Jane, 131
SWEET
  Annie, 120
  Martha W., 128
SWETT
  Caroline F., 273
SWIFT
  Catherine A., 284
  Elizabeth, 321
  Sarah (blk), 50
SWINGLE
  Lydia, 284
SWINK
  Marr Susan, 191
SWITZER
  Elvira, 59
SWOARD
  George Emma, 65
SWORD
  Annie E., 299
  Mary Elizabeth, 273
SYBERT
  Mary (blk), 110
SYBOTT
  Eliza (blk), 8
SYDNOR
  Sarah F., 205
SYKES
  Agnes H., 313
  Frances, 207
  Maria (blk), 157
SYLENCE
  Martha, 264

SYPES
  Mary Jane, 310
SYPHAX
  Maria C., 104
SYPHAX
  Maria (blk), 294
SYPHERD
  Molly, 4

—T—

TABBS
  Catherine, 158
  Margaret Virginia (blk), 165
TABER
  Carrie M., 85
TADLE
  Harriet (blk), 61
TAFFE
  Mary T., 98
TAFT
  Deborah A.R., 261
TAIT
  Anne C., 177
  Mary (blk), 137
  Mary Ann (blk), 7
TAITE
  Jane, 59
TALBERT
  Caroline M., 294
  Charlissa, 281
  George W., viii
  Jane, 28
  Jennie, 61
  Mary (blk), 126
  Mary Elizabeth, 123
  Mary Ellen, 85
  Minta Ann S., 159
  Orphelia S., 284
  Susan, 167
TALBOT
  Mina H., 190
TALBOTT
  Mary F., 159
TALBURT
  Elizabeth (blk), 271
  Margaret R., 167
  Margaret V., 284

Maria, 266
Mary A., 303
Polly, 103
TALIAFERRO
  Beattie, 62
  Eliza, 313
  Hannah (blk), 140
  Sophia (blk), 156
TALLANT
  Georgiana (blk), 140
TALLEY
  Ann Eliza, 79
  Eliza M., 263
TALLY
  Letitia, 157
TALTAVULL
  Catherine, 67
TALTY
  Joanna, 253
TANGLEY
  Mary, 180
TANGTANY
  Margaret, 178
TANNENBERG
  Bettie, 137
TANNER
  Catherine, 292
  Charlotte Ann, 208
  Esther, 26
TANWEL
  Mary, 16
TAPSCOTT
  Cordelia (blk), 174
TARDY
  Jennie T., 129
TARLTON
  Mary E., 183
TARMAN
  Laura V., 8
TARRY
  Virginia (blk), 199
TASCAR
  Adeline (blk), 266
TASCHNER
  Auguste, 112
TASCOE
  Ellen (blk), 27
TASKER
  Jennie, 225

Lucy Ann (blk), 236
Martha, 61, 297
Martha E. (blk), 297
TATE
  Ann (blk), 43
  Courtney A. (blk), 86
  Lizzie (blk), 175
TATSAPAUGH
  Julia, 13
TATTERSON
  Malissa, 56
TAUBERSCHMIDT
  Mary, 301
TAYLER
  Belle, 53
TAYLOR
  A.A.E., 212, 285
  Adalaide (blk), 217
  Addie, 127
  Adeline (blk), 115
  Alice Virginia, 191
  Alvira V., 26
  Amanda, 30, 140
  Amanda J., 30
  Ann R., 206
  Anna, 111
  Anne, 107
  Annie, 68, 76, 107, 271
  Annie E., 68, 107, 271
  Barbara A., 21
  Bertie, 125
  Bettie A., 318
  Betty (blk), 207
  Cansady W., 200
  Carey R., 206
  Caroline M., 54
  Catharine (blk), 108
  Catherine, 8, 184, 235, 267, 270
  Catherine (blk), 267, 270
  Catherine E., 235
  Catherine J., 8
  Comfort E., 106
  Cora H., 157
  Delia (blk), 275

475

TAYLOR
  Eliza J., 11
  Elizabeth (blk), 96, 273
  Ellen (blk), 18
  Ellen V., 128
  Emily N., 198
  Emma, 193, 212, 275
  Emma B., 275
  Emma E., 193
  Eva McL., 167
  Florence, 244
  Hannah (blk), 12
  Harriet (blk), 225
  Helen J.W., 55
  Isabella, 26
  Jane, 12, 46, 93, 138, 213
  Jane (blk), 46
  Jane E., 93
  Jane L. (blk), 12
  Jane Maria, 138
  Jennie, 78
  Josephine, 265, 293
  Josephine (blk), 293
  Julia (blk), 119
  Kate, 162
  L. Alice, 225
  Laura V., 314
  Lavinia (blk), 159
  Lucinda (blk), 80
  Lucy (blk), 174
  M.L., 284
  Maggie L., 268
  Margaret, 3, 144, 184, 190
  Margaret (blk), 190
  Margaret E., 144
  Margaret E., 3
  Maria (blk), 5
  Martha, 4, 46, 294
  Martha A., 4, 294
  Mary, 8, 11, 16, 51, 67, 79, 83, 85, 110, 112, 119, 133, 155, 173, 189, 202, 203, 218, 220, 265, 273, 289, 294, 300, 304, 316
  Mary (blk), 16, 79, 112, 133, 273, 300
  Mary C., 265
  Mary A., 67
  Mary Ann (blk), 155
  Mary C., 220
  Mary Catherine, 110
  Mary E., 11, 85, 173, 202
  Mary E. (blk), 85
  Mary F., 218
  Mary J., 189
  Mary Jane (blk), 203
  Mary V., 289
  Matilda (blk), 122
  Nellie (blk), 79
  S.V., 72, 287
  Sallie Ann (blk), 57
  Sallie C., 32
  Sarah, 93, 97, 180, 208
  Sarah (blk), 97, 208
  Sarah Jane (blk), 93
  Sophia, 306
  Susan, 167, 229, 327
  Susan (blk), 229
  Virginia, 192, 287
  Virginia S., 287
TEACHEM
  Caroline, 88
TEACHUM
  Susie, 41
TEAGLE
  Harriet E. (blk), 203
  Malinda (blk), 225
TEARNEY
  Maggie, 259
TEBBS
  Laura, 110
TECHNER
  Sophia, 204
TEEBOW
  Mary Ann, 55
TEGLMEIER
  Augusta, 120
TEIRNEY
  Margaret, 186
TEMPLE
  Lydia L., 295
TEMPLETON
  Emma S., 191
  Luanna H., 182
TENLEY
  Kate A., 223
TENLY
  Lottie, 302
TENNANT
  Caroline, 65
TENNESON
  Mary C., 142
TENNEY
  Rachel R. (blk), 88
TENNISON
  Kate S., 270
TENNISSON
  Lavinia, 100
TENNY
  Sarah (blk), 154, 249
TENNYSON
  M. Lillian, 301
TERMITT
  Ellen, 143
TERRELL
  Sallie, 124
TERRENCE
  Mary C., 240
TERRETT
  Rebecca, 222
TERRITT
  Barbara (blk), 133
TERRY
  Mary A., 265
TESKEY
  Mary Ann, 321
TEWS
  Elizabeth (blk), 42
THAW
  Mary Ann, 288
THAYER
  Adelaide E., 314
THECKER
  Eliza, 202
  Emma A., 235
  Mary Elizabeth, 104
  Sarah Amanda, 310
THEILER
  Gertrude, 112

THELDRY
   Elizabeth, 190
THOHENSTEIN
   Mary, 272
THOM
   Virginia H., 198
THOMA
   Elizabeth, 253
   Josephine, 40
THOMAS
   Airy (blk), 267
   Alice (blk), 303
   Almira V., 237
   Ann (blk), 31, 33, 47, 106
   Ann Amelia (col'd), 36
   Betsy, 148, 156
   Betsy (blk), 148
   Bettie S., 242
   Caroline (blk), 296
   Caroline H., 231
   Catherine (blk), 31, 192
   Celia (blk), 206
   Clara E., 199, 225
   Clarissa (blk), 311
   Eleanor O., 91
   Eliza, 17, 106, 151, 154, 173, 207, 309
   Eliza (blk), 17, 106
   Elizabeth, 151, 154, 173, 309
   Elizabeth (blk), 151, 173, 309
   Ellen (blk), 235
   Ellen E., 11
   Ellie, 188
   Emily (blk), 285
   Emma, 12, 319, 322
   Emma (blk), 322
   Emma J., 12
   Fanny, 205
   Harriet (blk), 249, 253, 315
   Harriet Ann (blk), 279
   Henrietta, 89, 92, 119
   Henrietta (blk), 89, 119
   Irene E., 109
   Jane E. (blk), 190
   Joanna (blk), 297
   Johanna, 170
   Julia, 232, 237
   Julia Ann (col'd), 237
   Kitty (blk), 304
   Laura V., 111
   Lavinia, 115
   Lizzie, 39
   Loretta, 246
   Louisa, 239, 326
   Louisa (blk), 326
   Lucinda, 22, 102
   Lucinda (blk), 22
   Lucy (blk), 313
   M.E., 115
   Maggie, 141
   Malinda (blk), 228
   Margaret (blk), 153, 235
   Margaret V. 149
   Maria (blk), 142, 201
   Martha (blk), 18, 276
   Martha A., 210
   Martha C., 157
   Mary, 58, 85, 132, 138, 144, 149, 175, 179, 240, 244, 288, 289, 295, 301, 305, 315, 323
   Mary (blk), 85, 175, 288, 305, 315
   Mary Ann, 289
   Mary B., 144
   Mary C. (blk), 240
   Mary E., 132
   Mary Jane, 138, 149, 244
   Mary Jane (blk), 149, 244
   Mary L., 144
   Mary Lucinda, 58
   Mary R., 323
   Nancy (blk), 248
   Rachel (blk), 316
   Rosa, 107
   Sarah Elizabeth, 80
   Sarah Jane (blk), 148, 242
   Sarah L., 286
   Sophia (blk), 73
   Susan (blk), 117, 288, 292
   Theresa, 257
   Virginia (blk), 308
THOMMA
   Mary, 102
THOMPSON
   A. Eliza, 38
   Addie Cecelia, 18
   Adelaide, 185
   Adele F. (blk), 112
   Amelia (blk), 25
   Ann E., 161
   Ann Eliza, 22
   Annie (blk), 35
   Annie E., 11
   Annie L., 20
   Augusta, 256
   Belle, 147
   Catharine, 94
   Charlotte A., 191
   Clara (blk), 50
   Cornelia, 230
   Elizabeth, 13, 129, 191, 273, 327
   Elizabeth (blk), 273, 327
   Elizabeth A.C., 129
   Elizabeth J., 191
   Ellen A., 59, 63
   Ellen Ann, 33
   Ellener, 129
   Emily, 80
   Frances, 120, 122
   Frances V., 120
   Hannah P., 219
   Isabella, 81
   Jane (blk), 235, 321
   Jane M., 287
   Julia P., 26
   Julia S., 280
   Kitty B., 280
   Laura J.C., 28

THOMPSON
  Louisa, 275
  Lucy (blk), 304
  Margaret, 32, 124,
    203, 232, 247
  Margaret E., 32
  Margaret H., 203
  Margaret J., 247
  Marie F., 284
  Mary, 36, 89, 96,
    166, 182, 184, 248,
    277, 285, 289, 312
  Mary Ann (blk), 289
  Mary C., 184, 312
  Mary E., 36, 96
  Mary Elizth., 277
  Mary Ella Rose, 166
  Mary F. (blk), 182
  Mary Jane, 248
  Mary L., 89
  Mollie F., 232
  Priscilla (blk), 148
  Salvadore (blk), 214
  Sarah, 2, 60, 106,
    113, 175, 226, 280
  Sarah A., 175
  Sarah C., 226
  Sarah E., 2, 60, 280
  Sarah E.M., 60
  Sarah L., 113
  Susan E., 125
THOMSON
  Lucinda, 74
THORN
  Ann Amanda, 301
  Eleanore, 199
  Marah, 265
  Mary Elizabeth, 10
  Sarah E., 268
THORNE
  Martha C., 198
  Martha Sarah, 250
THORNTON
  Alverta, 215
  Anna, 229
  Bridget, 81
  Giddy (blk), 271
  Hagar (blk), 40
  Lizzie (blk), 105

  Lucy (blk), 151
  Margaret, 310
  Mary (blk), 37
  Mary Knight, 286
  Sarah, 176, 287
  Sarah A. (blk), 287
THORP
  Harriet V., 225
THREALKIL
  Mary E., 150
THRIFT
  Rosa S., 96
THROOP
  Mary G., 223
THRUSH
  Mary A., 309
THURSTIN
  Harriet, 7
THURSTON
  Jeannette B., 181
THUSTON
  Mary E. (blk), 278
TIBBINS
  Sarah M., 285
TIBBITT
  Ella, 319
TIBBLES
  Mary L. (blk), 19
TIBBS
  Albert (blk), 66
  Mary (blk), 107
TIEDGEN
  Marie, 90
TIERNAN
  Bridget, 93
TIF
  Emilie, 211
TIGHE
  Margaret, 64
TILDEN
  Mary J., 299
TILGHMAN
  Barbara A., 226
  Frances (blk), 3
  Francis, 225
  Rebecca (blk), 239
  Sarah J. (blk), 155
TILLETT
  Abbey M., 109

TILLEY
  Amelia, 105
  Mary, 285
TILLMAN
  Eliza Ann (blk), 313
  Elizabeth, 89
  Martha (blk), 162
  Sidney, 153
TILLY
  Harriet H., 325
TILMAN
  Charlotte, 292
TILMON
  Rosetta (blk), 52
TILP
  Rosa, 279
TILTON
  Mary C., 173
TINGEY
  Mary B., 203
TINGLE
  C. Olivia A., 235
TINKER
  Rachel A. (blk), 319
TINKLER
  Mary A., 272
TINNEY
  Catharine, 198
  Eliza (blk), 130
  Margaret (blk), 297
  Sarah (col'd), 50
TINNY
  Chloe A. (blk), 216
  Rebecca (blk), 241
TIPPETT
  Annie E., 187
  Delia C., 154
  Jane (blk), 215
  Lizzie J., 62
  Virginia, 224
TISDALE
  Charlotte L., 10
  Elizabeth W., 287
TOA
  Helena, 255
TOBIAS
  Elizabeth, 132
  Mary Ann, 68

TOBIN
　Ann, 186
TOCKE
　Anna, 112
TODD
　Cecilia Ashton, 280
　Esther, 165
　Mary E., 189
TODTCHINSDER
　Wilhelmina, 181
TOLAND
　Ann, 95
　Sarah, 282
TOLBERT
　Harriet, 184
　Mahala (blk), 305
　Margaret, 293
TOLER
　Mary (blk), 286
TOLIVAR
　Maria, 292
TOLIVER
　Susan (blk), 167
TOLL
　Elizabeth (blk), 291
TOLLIVER
　Catherine (blk), 228
　Hellen (blk), 231
　Louisa (blk), 155
　Nancy, 30
TOLOVER
　Mary (blk), 57
TOLSON
　Susie E., 252
TOLT
　Lana, 265
TOMA
　Josephine Mary, 40
TOMLIN
　Sarah J., 142
TOMLINSON
　M. Jane, 12
TOMPKINS
　Caroline (blk), 208
TONNET
　Louise, 29
TONNETT
　Louisa, 63

TOODLE
　Ellen (blk), 153
　Nancy (blk), 50
TOOLE
　Mary, 239, 282, 293
TOOMS
　Mary Ann, 88
TOOTLE
　Elizabeth (blk), 265
TOPHAM
　Barbara Ann (blk), 154
　Caroline (blk), 276
　Sarah, 218, 255
　Sarah Ann (blk), 218
TOPPIN
　Virginia (blk), 315
TOPPING
　Caroline, 206
TORBERT
　Bettie B., 324
TORBUT
　Mary E. Peyton, 120
TORRENS
　Anna E., 131
TORRISSON
　Jane J., 294
TOUHEY
　Margaret E., 187
TOULSON
　Sarah Jane (blk), 55
TOWERS
　Annie, 300
　Bettie G., 16
　Eliza P., 118
　Ellie, 39
　Hannah P., 134
　Laura Jane, 165
　Mary E., 222
TOWLES
　Violet (blk), 126
TOWN
　Angie L., 160
TOWNER
　Cora, 274
　Josephine, 151
　Kate, 162
　Victoria, 324

TOWNLEY
　Elizabeth A., 261
TOWNSEND
　Juliet E., 321
　Sophia (blk), 78
TOWSON
　Mary E., 142
TOY
　Rhoda Louisa, 227
TOYER
　Maria (blk), 305
　Mary Eliza (blk), 92
TRACEY
　Mary A., 229
TRACY
　Bridget, 238
　Charlotte D., 214
　Kate, 176
　Margaret, 219
　Mary, 170
TRALLER
　Kate, 170
TRAMMEL
　Margaret, 302
TRAMMELL
　Elizabeth, 171
　Jane A., 63
　Sarah, 82
TRAUTNER
　Maria, 233
TRAVERS
　Catherine, 157
　Kate M., 92
TRAVIS
　Phebe Jane, 105
TRAYAI
　Rita, 187
TREADWAY
　Ella A., 14
　Frances A., 54
TREAKLE
　Henrietta, 160
　Mary Jane, 40
TREANOR
　Eliza, 231
TREFETHERN
　Sarah J.S., 7
TREUMAN
　Mary, 240

District of Columbia Marriage Licenses, 1858-1870

TREXLER
　Emma F., 160
TRIBBY
　Mary E., 275
TRIMBLE
　Martha, 133
TRIMMER
　Caroline L., 276
TRIPLET
　Willie Ann (blk), 266
TRIPLETT
　Amelia, 150
　Cornelia A., 177
　Sarah F., 323
　Sarah V., 164
TRIPPETT
　Annie E., 317
TRISCON
　Mary E.P., 247
TRIVIS
　Rachel S. (blk), 124
TRIVISS
　Sarah Ann (blk), 91
TROMPF
　Annie, 169
TROOK
　Amanda S., 26
TROUNECKER
　Mena, 230
TROXELL
　Julia S., 72
TRUAX
　Margaret (blk), 27
TRUCKSON
　Annie R., 223
　Martha, 237
TRUELL
　Mary Ann (blk), 172
TRUMAN
　Jennie, 111
　Mary A., 127
TRUMBULL
　Harriet S., 37
TRUMPF
　Rosie, 170
TRUNDLE
　Catherine V., 222
　Leah, 210

TRUNNELL
　Anna M., 35
　Ellen G., 16
　Ida E., 311
　Mary A., 56
TRUSLER
　Isabella M., 235
TRUSTHEIM
　Eliza, 265
TRUSTY
　Annie, 9
TUBBMAN
　Mary Emma, 304
TUBMAN
　Laura V., 166
TUCK
　Ellen M., 104
TUCKER
　Annie O., 291
　Charity (blk), 264
　Dorcas A., 29
　Drusie M., 19
　Ella, 142
　Ellen B., 8
　Emily Eliza, 159
　Georgiana C., 234
　Jennie G., 304
　Laura Virginia, 34
　Lucinda, 172, 222, 264
　Lucinda (blk), 264
　M.J., 16
　Maria E., 39
　Mary Elizabeth, 227
　Mary L., 198
　Sally Ann, 119
　Sophia S., 273
TUCKSIN
　Mary Elizabeth (blk), 189
TUDEN
　Eliza (blk), 62
TULEY
　Cecilia E., 158
TUNNELLY
　Kate (blk), 265
TUNNIA
　Anna, 296
　Margaret (blk), 321

TUOHY
　Mary J., 94
　Mary Jane, 113
TURKENTON
　Ann Jane, 52
TURLEY
　Harriot (blk), 135
TURNER
　Adeline, 32
　Amanda (blk), 323
　Ann Eliza (blk), 111
　Caroline, 225, 296
　Caroline M., 296
　Cecilia A. (blk), 56
　Celia (blk), 66
　Christina, 4
　Eliza (blk), 31, 124, 160
　Eliza Ellen, 277
　Elizabeth (blk), 279, 320
　Emily (blk), 82
　Emma, 171
　Frances, 126
　Hanna M., 165
　Hannah (blk), 48
　Harriet, 46, 149, 293, 308
　Harriet (blk), 46, 149
　Harriet Rebecca, 293
　Hattie, 106
　Jane (blk), 6
　Jane Elizabeth, 288
　Kate (blk), 136
　Lavinia (blk), 265
　Lizzie, 295
　Louisa, 129, 154, 202
　Louisa (blk), 154
　Louvenia (blk), 213
　Lucretia, 63
　Lucy (blk), 326
　Marceline (blk), 27
　Margaret, 20, 157
　Margaret Elizth., 157
　Maria (blk), 246

480

TURNER
  Martha Ann, 91
  Mary, 4, 32, 112,
    187, 229, 235, 268
  Mary (blk), 32, 187
  Mary E., 268
  Mary Frances, 235
  Mary L. (blk), 4
  Rebecca (blk), 276
  Sarah, 16, 115, 127,
    157
  Sarah (blk), 127
  Sarah F., 157
  Sarah Rebecca, 16
  Saviny, 312
  Susan (blk), 289
TURNEY
  Ellen, 204
TURPIN
  Minnie J., 145
  Sarah A., 39
TURTON
  M.A., 293
  Mary, 164, 172
  Mary M., 172
  Mollie J., 262
  Rachel, 293
TURVEY
  Elizabeth, 202
  Julia, 287
TUTT
  Mary F. (blk), 179
TUTTLE
  Sarah N., 260
TUXENT
  Kate (blk), 153
TWELE
  Joana H.E., 251
TWINE
  Ann, 56
TWINER
  Jane (blk), 252
TWOHEY
  Mary, 197
TWOOMEY
  Ellen, 107
TWOOMY
  Catharine, 30
  Mary, 262

TYE
  Sarah, 175
TYLER
  Ann (blk), 297, 319
  Anna (blk), 122
  Annie Catherine, 18
  Cornelia, 194
  Elizabeth, 124
  Emeline (blk), 154
  Emma J., 92
  Hester (blk), 36
  Hester Jane, 88
  Kitty, 51
  Laura (blk), 292
  Lotta, 166
  Lucy (blk), 326
  Martha (blk), 103
  Mary, 4, 17, 22, 49,
    117
  Mary (blk), 4, 22, 117
  Mary A., 49
  Nancy (blk), 41
  Rachel, 50
  Rosa Bell, 266
  Sarah E., 43
  Sarah J., 288
  Susan, 55, 147
  Susan (blk), 55
TYSER
  Laura Virginia, 25
TYSON
  Anna Maria, 227
TYSSOWSKI
  Alexandria, 136
  Henrietta W., 325
  Pelagia, 106

—U—

UHLER
  Mary, 84
UHLMANN
  Anna, 288
UHLMEYER
  Mary, 92
UKERD
  Martha E. (blk), 283
ULBRIGHT
  Cimlin, 314

ULSHÖFER
  Philipina, 135
UMBERFIELD
  Alice, 225, 316
UMBRIDGE
  Regina V., 8
UMHAN
  Christina, 256
UNDERWOOD
  Cecilia (blk), 151
  Ella, 1
UNKEL
  Justina, 170
UPHAM
  Abby G., 54
UPPERMAN
  Alice S., 293
  Emma, 323
UPPERMANN
  Louisa, 303
UPSHER
  Augustine (blk), 112
  Ellen (blk), 30
UPTON
  Sarah, 56
  Susan, 281
UTERMAHLE
  Rose, 286
UTERMEHLE
  Rosa, 95
UTERNIEHLE
  Mary Janet, 101
UTTERBACK
  Annie, 256
  M.J., 155
UTZ
  Laura C., 193

—V—

VALENTINE
  Anna M., 143
  Catherine (blk), 266
  Henrietta (blk), 305
  Louisa, 137
VALIANT
  Josephine J., 177
VALK
  Adaline, 210

District of Columbia Marriage Licenses, 1858-1870

VanALLEN
  Mary E., 83
VanBOKUM
  Elizabeth, 150
VanBURGHEN
  Kate, 214
VanBUSKIRK
  Mary, 8
VanBUSSUM
  Hannah, 51
VanDOREN
  Jane Elizabeth, 28
VANFLEET
  Catherine, 239
VanHOLT
  Mary Cordelia, 53
VanHORN
  Anna, 268
  Ellen, 299
  Margaret, 180
  Martha W., 30
VANNEMAN
  Charity Ann, 291
VANNERMAN
  Mary A., 236
VanOLINDA
  Sarah D., 141
VanPATTEN
  Henrietta A., 286
VanRISWICK
  Ararilla, 172
VanTYNE
  Florida H., 104
  Mary A., 9
vanWURKEL
  Lizzie W., 311
VAPOR
  Mary, 231
VASMERS
  Gesine, 109
VAUGHAN
  Margaret (blk), 269
VAUGHN
  Esther Ann (blk), 310
  Maria, 316
  Martha (blk), 109
VAUX
  Sylvia, 28

VEAK
  Emma, 2
VEASEY
  Martha E. (blk), 310
VEIL
  Maria (col'd), 254
VEIRS
  Ann E., 302
VENABLE
  Catherine, 183, 273
  Catherine Clay, 273
  Margaret, 63
  Mary, 48, 159
  Matilda P., 322
VENIAH
  Louisa (blk), 191
VERES
  Elizabeth (blk), 126
VERLANDER
  Mary S., 176
VERMILLION
  Dorcas A.C., 5
  Louisa J., 55
  Rachel, 226
  Sarah, 53, 119, 283, 320
  Sarah A., 283
  Sarah Jane, 119
  Susan, 197
VERNON
  Annie E., 124
  Julia E., 9
  Madeline, 77
VERNSTEIN
  Barbara, 257
VICKERY
  Honorah, 300f
VICKERS
  Mary E., 70
VIE
  Mary E., 210
VIEGMAN
  Louisa, 201
VIEGST
  Sophia, 282
VIERBUCHEN
  Sophia, 233
VIERS
  Kate, 68

VIGLE
  Susan, 141
VINSON
  Jane, 141
  Martha Jane, 14
VIOLET
  Emma E., 109
VIOLETT
  Georgeana, 132
VIRGINIA
  Martha (blk), 259
VIVANS
  E.A., 221
VOEHL
  Elise, 80
VOGEL
  Christina, 91, 300
VOGELESANG
  Anna E., 19
VOGELSBERGER
  Amelia, 77
VOGLE
  Dolly, 316
VOGT
  Rosina, 223
VOHS
  Mary, 144
VOIGT
  Dora, 202
VOLANDT
  Augusta F., 50
VOLK
  Anna, 322
VOLLAND
  Caroline, 74
VOLLBRIGHT
  Louise D., 145
VOLLINS
  Lucinda (blk), 305
VOLZ
  Louisa, 327
VONBEITZ
  Anna, 100
vonGIROLT
  Carlota Wilhel. Marianna, 304
VonKAMECKE
  Elizabeth, 9

482

vonMECHOW
  Ida, 184
VOSS
  Angeline, 300
  Louisa A., 30
  Martha Ann (blk), 2
VOWELL
  Hattie N., 66

—W—

WACHEMUTH
  Eliza, 146
WACHTER
  Barbara, 265
WADDY
  Letty (blk), 319
  Susan (blk), 328
WADE
  Ann, 213
  Ella M., 130
  Jane (blk), 269
  Olivia L., 271
  Sarah F., 11
WADSCHMIDT
  Eliza, 310
WAGER
  Joanna, 250
WAGLER
  Hellen Virginia, 327
  Mary S., 206
WAGNER
  Amelia, 123
  Francisca, 186
  Helen V., 71
  Ida, 207
  Jane M., 214
  Kate, 97
  Katherina, 133
  Louisa, 182, 279, 309
  Margaret, 52, 91, 318
  Margaret (blk), 318
  Margaretta, 91
  Mary, 204
  Mina, 257
WAGONER
  Elizabeth, 207

  Kate, 256
  Mary E., 247
WAHL
  Anna E., 70
WAIGHT
  Mary H., 324
WAIL
  Barbara, 317
WAILES
  Lucy, 320
WAKELING
  Mary M., 244
WALBACH
  Mary, 190
WALBORN
  Amelia, 175
WALDEMATHE
  Wilhelmina, 138
WALDEN
  Ann, 34
  Helen, 56
WALDRON
  Annie, 85
WALDSHMIDT
  Johanna, 131
WALINGSFORD
  Alice, 27
WALKER
  Ann, 54, 66, 327
  Anna, 54, 66
  Anna (blk), 66
  Augusta N., 260
  Belle, 13
  Catharine, 109, 192
  Catharine A., 109
  Cecelia, 120
  Charlotte, 236
  Dorcas Virginia, 135
  Elizabeth, 152, 225
  Elizabeth (blk), 152
  Ella, 103, 313
  Ellanor (blk), 103
  Emily (blk), 167
  Emma, 173
  Fannie, 190
  Fanny A. (blk), 129
  Frances (blk), 248
  Jennie C., 197

  Jettie, 6
  Josephine (blk), 235
  Julia, 151, 184, 260
  Julia A., 260
  Julia E., 184
  Laura, 290
  Lizzie, 226
  Louisa, 95
  Lucinda D., 86
  Mahalia (blk), 1
  Maria (blk), 297
  Marietta (blk), 245
  Martha (blk), 80
  Martha A., 263
  Mary, 10, 39, 91, 158, 161, 306, 307, 316
  Mary (blk), 306, 316
  Mary E., 10, 158
  Mary L., 161
  Mary V., 307
  Pamelia (blk), 96
  Patsy (blk), 124, 314
  Rebecca (blk), 304
  Roberta (blk), 250
  Samuel, 136, 302
  Sarah (blk), 292
  Sarah B., 169
  Sarah Frances (blk), 167
  Savenda, 281
  Sefern, 281
  Sidney (blk), 305
  Susan, 150, 164, 251, 295, 311
  Susan (blk), 251
  Susan E., 150
  Susanna, 164, 311
  Virginia D., 199
WALL
  Anna Virginia, 192
  Elizabeth, 196
  Helen, 65
  Lucinda Anna, 166
  Margaret, 221
  Mary, 3, 68, 268
  Mary Ann, 3
  Mary E., 268

District of Columbia Marriage Licenses, 1858-1870

WALLACE
  Ann, 28
  Beckie (blk), 172
  Clarissa (blk), 149
  Elizabeth, 214
  Ella S., 135
  Ellen (blk), 242
  Fanny (blk), 124
  Josephine E., 235
  Julia (blk), 117
  Julia P., 125
  Margaret, 253
  Mary, 76, 78
  Mary H., 78
  Susan (blk), 70
WALLACH
  Sarah, 252
WALLACHER
  Elizabeth, 291
WALLER
  Augusta B., 320
  Ella, 117
  Hannah, 89
  Winny (blk), 292
WALLINGSFORD
  Laura V., 191
  Mary E., 280
WALLINGTONN
  Susan (blk), 272
WALLIS
  Adelaid (blk), 183
  Maria Lucinda (blk), 84
  Rachel A., 293
WALLS
  Caroline Celestia, 254
WALSH
  Annie, 39
  Ellen, 246
  Honora, 84
  Jane, 28
  Kate J., 59
  Mary, 95
  Sarah A., 174
WALTER
  Angeline (blk), 286
  Barbara, 166
  Kate, 159
  Magdalina M., 19
  Mary, 257, 298
  Mary A., 298
  Melissa (blk), 116
  Rosanna (blk), 71
WALTERS
  Amanda C., 111
  Catharine, 30
  Emma (blk), 192
  Julia, 187
  Katie (blk), 224
  Maria (blk), 308
  Priscilla (blk), 298
WALTHAN
  Martha A., 29
WALTZ
  Barbara, 102
WALZ
  Catherine, 15
WANNALL
  Tilly, 273
WANNICK
  Emily, 134
WANTON
  Hannah S., 305
WANZER
  Eleanor, 225
  Elizabeth (blk), 176
WARD
  Amanda (blk), 18
  Ann, 96
  Bridget, 201
  Catharine, 282
  Charlotte R., 125
  Cornelia (blk), 25
  Elizabeth, 22, 151
  Elizabeth S., 151
  Emily V., 124
  Evelina (blk), 247
  Isabella, 37
  J.A.E., 294
  Jane (blk), 292
  Kate, 262
  Laura, 90
  Louisa (blk), 50, 321
  Margaret, 287, 320
  Margaret (blk), 320
  Maria, 82
  Martha Ann, 305
  Mary, 19, 99, 115, 160, 233, 245
  Mary A., 160
  Mary E., 99, 115
  Mary J., 233
  Matilda, 163
  Sarah, 203
WARDEN
  Ann E., 267
  Margaret Elizth., 76
WARDER
  Amelia C., 123
  Anna E., 326
  Marion F., 135
WARE
  Gracie (blk), 167
  Isabella (blk), 69, 85
  Julia (blk), 53
WARFIELD
  Amanda, 266
  Ellen A., 65
  Harriet, 291
  Hellen (blk), 156
  Mary E., 304
WARING
  Anna S., 228
  Celestia, 49
  Helen Anna, 136
  Helen M., 142
  Mary E., 315
  Mary V., 186
  Rose M., 249
WARMBOLD
  Mary, 37
WARNER
  Alice V., 229
  Anna R. (blk), 106
  Annie M. (blk), 34
  Ellenora (blk), 5
  Fannie E., 55
  Jane Elizth. (blk), 71
  Margaret A.E., 72
  Nancy (blk), 151
  Sarah Jane, 62
WARNICK
  Maria L., 297
WARNZER
  Mary, 5

### WARREN
Annie, 91
Cecelia (blk), 305
Charity (blk), 305
Ellen, 103
Fanny (blk), 289
Maria, 302
Marietta E., 182
Mary E., 315
Minerva Ann (blk), 31
Susan (blk), 34
### WARRENTON
Mary (blk), 131
### WARRING
Marshall Sallie, 315
### WARTERS
Priscilla (blk), 316
### WARTHEN
Mary H., 8
### WARWICK
Arabella, 177
### WASHBURN
Emma Jane, 167
Eunice C., 277
Ociann, 268
### WASHEMUTH
Caroline L., 15
### WASHINGTON
Alice (blk), 9
Alice V. (blk), 113
Ann (blk), 183
Ann Maria, 149
Anna L., 72
Caroline, 262
Catherine (blk), 80
Christiana (blk), 316
Cornelia (blk), 129
Daborey (blk), 306
Eliza (blk), 172
Elizabeth (blk), 288
Ellen (blk), 303
Emily (blk), 22
Emma (blk), 82
Florence, 256
Georgiana (blk), 116
Harriet (blk), 172
Harriet E. (blk), 127
Lalla R., 191

Lellah R., 96
Lizzie (blk), 314
Lucinda (blk), 185
Lucy (blk), 286
Maria (blk), 42
Maria Ann, 7
Martha, 53, 61, 133, 272, 296
Martha (blk), 53, 61, 272
Mary, 142, 151, 317
Mary (blk), 317
Mary A., 142
Matilda (blk), 213, 293
Nancy (blk), 56
Rose (blk), 7, 30, 318
Ruthie (blk), 42
Sarah (blk), 21, 78
Sophie, 203
Violet (blk), 126
Wilhelmina M., 252
### WASSEROTH
Regina, 152
### WATERHOLDER
Lizzie, 96
### WATERS
Alisa, 321
Ann M. (blk), 91
Dollie Edmonson, 299
Eliza (blk), 153
Isabel, 309
Julia E., 229
Martha (blk), 222
Mary Frances, 266
Mary A., 83
Mary E. (blk), 34
Nancy, 269
Polly (blk), 52
Rachel (blk), 151
Rose, 163
Sallie (blk), 42
Sarah, 210, 290
Sarah E. (blk), 290
Susan Elizabeth, 274
W.G., 307, 310

### WATKINS
Euphemia, 69
Fanny (blk), 287
Harriet, 302
Laura V., 235
Rachel N. (blk), 277
Ruth Annie, 313
Susanna (blk), 133
Virginia G., 302
### WATSON
Adeline, 176
Alice (blk), 36
Anna (blk), 311, 324
Catharine, 57
Eliza E., 95
Laura, 101
Margaret Ann, 213
Margaret V., 293
Maria F., 276
Maria L., 11
Martha Rebecca, 49
Mary (blk), 285
Mary Jane, 118
Sarah (blk), 80
### WATT
Annie A. (blk), 125
Mary Ann, 299
### WATTS
Cordelia (blk), 132
Lena (blk), 64
Martha E., 105
Mary (blk), 121
Mary A. (blk), 89
Sarah J., 89
### WAUGH
Helen (blk), 72
Martha E., 309
Mary Lizzie, 130
Nancy (blk), 305
### WAYHOUSE
Birtha, 193
### WAYSON
Matilda F., 214
### WEADERMAN
Martha, 61
### WEADON
Margaret E., 167
### WEAKLEY
Sarah, 15

WEATHERELL
  Augusta, 64
WEATHERS
  Nettie (blk), 93
WEAVER
  Amelia, 18
  Anna C., 109
  Caroline (blk), 309
  Elizabeth, 71, 101
  Elizabeth J., 101
  Henrietta, 304
  Ida Elizabeth, 26
  Mary Ella, 172
  Nora (blk), 272
  Rachel A., 227
  Sarah Jane, 4
WEBB
  Augusta D., 205
  Bettie (blk), 193
  Camilla H., 299
  Jennie Eunice, 41
  Julia (blk), 33
  Lizzie (blk), 224
  Mary Ann, 81
  Rosa (blk), 279
WEBBER
  Katie F., 131
WEBER
  Barbara A., 267
  Lizzie, 308
  Mary L., 241
WEBSTER
  Addie (blk), 171
  Caroline C. (blk), 284
  Charlotte (blk), 149
  Eliza Ann, 87
  Elizabeth (blk), 40, 151
  Ellen J., 192
  Flora, 98
  Frances, 277
  Harriet (blk), 203
  Lucy (blk), 316
  Lucy F., 80
  Lydia E., 138
  Martha, 72, 98
  Martha V., 98
  Mary, 90, 201, 224, 240, 324
  Mary A.E., 324
  Mary E., 240
  Mary Ellen, 201
  Mary Emma, 90
  Mary Virginia, 224
  Minnie, 33
  Sallie M., 277
  Sarah Frances, 36
  Susan, 201
WEDGE
  Margaret (blk), 239
WEDGER
  Mary, 301
WEED
  Lizzie B., 184
WEEDEN
  Anna M., 304
  Lizzie, 122
  Mary Ann, 189
WEEDON
  Martha, 40
WEEKS
  Ann Rebecca (blk), 2
WEEMS
  Mary (blk), 113
WEIBEL
  Delia, 121
WEIFELL
  Margt., 125
WEIGEL
  Lizzie, 245
WEIGOND
  Ablonia, 250
WEIMAN
  Annie S., 244
WEIR
  Rachel T., 88
WEIS
  Katherine, 190
WEISBACKER
  Elizabeth, 281
WEISMAN
  Ellen C., 239
WEISS
  Ann, 325
  Magdalene, 276
WEIST
  Barbara, 246
WEITNER
  Elizabeth, 240
WEITZBACHER
  Frances, 308
WELCH
  Bridget, 282
  Catharine, 241
  Catherine, 98
  Delia, 99
  Maria, 208
  Mary, 88, 169, 224, 274
  Mary E., 224
  Mollie S., 307, 310
  Sarah C., 252
  Susan T., 22
WELDEN
  Lizzie (blk), 25
WELDON
  Mary, 22
  Mollie E., 188
WELFORD
  Mary A., 302
WELHOF
  Annie, 317
WELLER
  Anna, 327
WELLING
  Sarah (blk), 304
WELLS
  Ann E., 294
  Bella, 206
  Cordelia H., 122
  Eliza (blk), 311
  Emily W., 242
  Jane, 157
  Jemima W.S., 165
  Lavenia, 165
  Louisa, 204
  Lucy Isabel, 258
  Martha (blk), 178
  Mary, 49, 252, 294
  Mary Ann, 252, 294
  Mary F., 49
  Rachel H., 150
  Rebecca, 178
  Sarah Ann (blk), 96

WELLS
 Sarah E., 137
 Sarah H., 76
 Susana, 19
WELSH
 Ann, 13, 29, 182
 Annie M., 182
 Bessy, 225
 Bridget, 118, 134
 Catharine, 322
 Catherine, 7, 245, 263
 Cordelia, 256
 Eliza, 312
 Ellen, 29, 30
 Joanna, 118
 Julia, 137
 Margaret, 78, 163, 175, 193, 199, 261, 265
 Margt., 278
 Mary, 59, 75, 100, 176, 198, 251
 Mary W., 251
 Minerva O., 123
 Sarah, 217
WELTON
 Mary Holland, 121
WENDEL
 Catherine, 306
 Louise, 92
WENDELL
 Anna Mary, 285
 Blanche, 324
WENDT
 Elise, 280
WENZEL
 Gustina, 308
 Mary C., 233
WEOTEN
 Frances A. (blk), 224
WERDEN
 Emily R., 71
WERNER
 Catherine, 301
 Sophia, 124
WERTZ
 Margaretha, 265

WESEN
 Susan, 23
WESER
 Mary, 17
WESNER
 Sarah A., 292
WESSELS
 Rosina, 277
WEST
 Catherine M., 264
 Celia, 133
 Eliza (blk), 178
 Elizabeth (blk), 156
 Ella, 40
 Fanny (blk), 85
 Frances, 45
 Georgianna, 171
 Helen M., 150
 Helen T., 112
 Henrietta (blk), 321
 Laura V., 108
 Margaret, 182
 Maria, 327
 Martha (blk), 2, 306
 Rebecca (blk), 27
 Sarah, 237
 Tena (blk), 317
WESTEN
 Emma L., 67
WESTERBERGER
 Mary, 248
WESTERFIELD
 Ida E.M., 1
WESTERMEN
 Mary, 174
WESTERN
 Adelaid V., 82
 Sarah, 73
WESTERNAN
 Eliza Jane, 167
WESTFIELD
 Sarah Caroline, 231
WESTON
 Annie C., 243
 Laura, 21
 Mary E., 298
 Sarah A., 43
WESTWOOD
 Eliza C., 46

WETSELL
 Francetta, 314
WETTEMANN
 Josephine, 12
WETZEL
 Maria (blk), 55
WETZELL
 Henrietta, 49
WEYMAN
 Elizabeth, 139
WEYRECH
 Mary E., 327
WEYRICH
 Henrietta, 267
 Susannah, 189
WHALEN
 Anna (blk), 216
 Mary Elizabeth, 199
WHALEY
 Laura C., 173
WHALING
 Cordelia, 301
WHARTON
 Ella D., 312
 Evelina, 236
WHEAT
 Charlotte, 10
WHEATLEY
 Caroline (blk), 291
 Eliza J., 259
 Georgiana, 11
 Marion, 196
 Sarah, 8, 174
 Sarah (blk), 174
 Susanna, 87
WHEELER
 Alice A., 135
 Ann (blk), 193
 Annie, 156
 Chloe (blk), 89
 Eliza (blk), 150
 Elizabeth (blk), 176
 Frances (blk), 193
 Georgianna (blk), 297
 Louisa, 170
 Mame Virginia, 302
 Mary (blk), 132
 Mary A., 52

WHEELER
  Mary E., 5
  Mary T., 113
  Saloam H., 84
  Sarah (blk), 20
WHELAN
  Eliza, 246
  Fanny, 162
  Mary, 226
WHEN
  Louise, 179
WHIGGINS
  Sarah (blk), 34
WHIGLEY
  Ann, 208
WHINUM
  Maria Louisa (blk), 65
WHITACRE
  Louisa, 263
WHITAKER
  Martha (blk), 223
  Mary L., 122
  Rebecca, 284
  Sarah, 22, 265
  Sarah (blk), 265
WHITCOMB
  Isabel, 158
WHITE
  Alice, 59, 93, 176
  Alice V., 93, 176
  Amelia F., 10
  Amelia G., 133
  Ann E., 74
  Anna J., 156
  Artemisia H., 290
  Caroline, 66, 204
  Caroline (blk), 204
  Catherine (blk), 174, 313
  Catherine E., 108
  Delie L., 194
  Eliza, 109, 171, 209, 250
  Eliza J., 250
  Elizabeth, 109, 171
  Elizabeth (blk), 109
  Ella (blk), 147
  Ellen, 83, 99, 209

Emma J., 187
Fanny F. (blk), 82
Helen W., 202
Hester (blk), 6
Hildah, 55
Jane (blk), 11
Julia (blk), 241, 272
Julia A., 288
Lizzie (blk), 11
Lucinda (blk), 216
Martha E., 76
Mary, 65, 86, 252, 296
Mary (blk), 252
Mary A., 86
Mary Ellen (blk), 296
Matilda, 11, 248
Matilda (blk), 248
Millie, 138
Rachel Ann (blk), 93
Rosa E.S., 91
Ruth A., 110, 175
Sarah, 9, 36, 185, 317
Sarah A., 9
Sarah Elizabeth, 185
Susan, 50, 124, 267, 318
Susan (blk), 50, 124, 318
WHITELEY
  Ellen, 192
WHITELY
  Anna J. (blk), 73
WHITEMAN
  Anna, 210
WHITEMORE
  Mary E., 80
  Sarah K., 240
WHITFIELD
  Sophia, 321
WHITING
  C.J., 120
  Ella Louisa Magruder, 199
  Margaret J., 204
  Mary E., 10, 40

Mary E. (blk), 10
Mattie Kennon, 52
Virginia (blk), 260
WHITLEY
  Maria (blk), 112
WHITLOCK
  Rachel, 217
WHITLY
  Susan (blk), 25
WHITMAN
  Lucia, 253
  Maria, 82
WHITMORE
  Mary, 270
  Rachel, 77
  Sabella T., 245
WHITNEY
  Alice (blk), 202
  Anna, 200
  Eleanora (blk), 288
  Eliza S., 58
  Georgian, 221
  Mildred (blk), 320
  Sarah L., 223
  Susan E., 52
WHITON
  Sarah (blk), 78
WHITTAKER
  Mary, 158
WHITTON
  Henrietta, 279
WHITWORTH
  Elizabeth, 319
WHITZELL
  Mary, 66
WHOODY
  Ann (blk), 254
WHYTE
  Laura A., 30
WIBER
  Agnes J., 197
WICKER
  Elizabeth, 287
WIDDECOMB
  Catherine M., 24
WIDEMAN
  Annie, 131
WIEDEN
  Betty, 237

WIEGMANN
  Caroline A., 14
  Gesine E., 161
WIELAND
  Dorothea, 25
WIERE
  Sarah, 18
WIESER
  Apolonia, 132
WIGGINS
  Mary (blk), 277
WIGGINTON
  Frances (blk), 316
  Martha (blk), 176
WILANT
  Margaret J., 108
WILBURN
  Ann R., 262
  Laura Ann, 254
WILCOXEN
  Martha Ann, 19
WILD
  Eliza Ellen, 201
WILDMAN
  Dora E., 104
WILES
  Martha H. (blk), 296
WILEY
  Ada B., 325
  E.F., 157
  Martha, 34
  Mary C., 222
  Mary Francis, 136
  Susan, 34
WILHELM
  Leonora, 206
WILHELMSEN
  Caroline, 258
WILKERSON
  Alice, 315
  Amelia J., 162
  Elizabeth, 223
  Margaret (blk), 314
  Maria, 54
  Mary Jane (blk), 37
  Patsey (blk), 210
  Rosella E., 102
WILKES
  Maria (blk), 154

WILKINS
  Georgiana (blk), 252
  Harriet, 183
  Lizzie, 247
  Martha, 23, 259
  Martha L. (blk), 23
  Mary E., 63
  Sophronia R., 284
WILKINSON
  Agusta A., 264
  Amanda (blk), 17
  Laura, 194
  Lucinda A. (blk), 27
  Mary L., 13
  Priscilla (blk), 151
  Sarah E., 216
  Sarah A., 14
  Sarah E., 281
  Sarah Jane, 222
  Sidney A. (blk), 286
  Sophia (blk), 32
WILKISON
  Sarah (blk), 271
  Sophia (blk), 271
WILL
  Mary E., 270
WILLARD
  Ellen R., 279
  Fanny, 322
  Mary Teresa, 314
WILLETT
  Letty, 247
  Margaret A., 110
  Martha, 252
  Sallie, 65
WILLEY
  Mary E., 269
WILLIAM
  Annie Elizabeth, 49
  Bell (blk), 19
WILLIAMS
  Agnes, 103
  Albertine, 285
  Alice, 43, 130
  Alice (blk), 43
  Alphinia, 157
  Amanda (blk), 241
  Amelia (blk), 313
  Ann (blk), 231

  Ann Elizabeth, 316
  Ann R., 274
  Ann Virginia, 158
  Anna D., 173
  Anna E., 237
  Anna E. (blk), 235
  Anna M. (blk), 56
  Annie (blk), 48
  Annie M. (blk), 87
  Bettie (blk), 236
  Caroline (blk), 238
  Carrie (blk), 160
  Carrie A., 68
  Catharine B., 12
  Catherine (blk), 53
  Catherine E., 290
  Cecilia (blk), 319
  Celestia (blk), 154
  Celia (blk), 144
  Celia Ann, 158
  Charity (blk), 26
  Charlotte (blk), 292
  Charlotte F., 88
  Christy A. (blk), 18
  Clara (blk), 16
  Cordelia (blk), 11
  Delia Ann (blk), 317
  Edith E. (blk), 280
  Eliza (blk), 244
  Eliza E., 22
  Elizabeth A., 291
  Ella, 238
  Ellen (blk), 158
  Emeline (blk), 113
  Emeline V., 289
  Emma, 74, 90, 208,
    277, 305
  Emma (blk), 305
  Emma J., 90, 208
  Emma T., 74
  Evelina (blk), 117
  Fannie, 69
  Frances (blk), 226
  Frances C., 39
  Hannah, 84
  Harriet (blk), 154
  Harriet A., 7
  Isabel P., 251
  Jane, 42, 46, 98, 157

WILLIAMS
Jane (blk), 42, 98, 157
Jennie, 88, 317
Jennie E., 88
Josephine, 30, 97, 131
Josephine (blk), 30
Josephine G., 131
Julia (blk), 229
Kate, 193
Kitty (blk), 136
Lascilla (blk), 100
Laura (blk), 280
Leathy (blk), 14
Leona (blk), 316
Letty (blk), 259
Lizzie (blk), 212, 217
Lucinda (blk), 279
Lucy, 55, 177, 316
Lucy (blk), 55, 177
Lydia (blk), 56
Lydia C., 120
Lydia E., 139
Mahala (blk), 303
Margaret E., 19
Margaret Ellen, 85
Maria (blk), 48
Maria J. (blk), 327
Marion Susan, 216
Martha (blk), 78, 233
Martha Ellen, 316
Mary, 22, 46, 55, 62, 82, 88, 131, 148, 151, 152, 172, 190, 195, 220, 252, 267, 272, 273, 307, 321
Mary (blk), 55, 62, 88, 151, 152, 267, 272, 273, 307
Mary A. (blk), 22, 46, 82
Mary E., 190, 195
Mary E. (blk), 195
Mary Jane (blk), 148
Mary V., 131
Matilda (blk), 151

Milly (blk), 259
Mima, 185
Nannie, 11, 203
Octavia (blk), 275
Olivia A., 70
Patsey (blk), 174
Rachel (blk), 79
Rena (blk), 290
Rhoda O'Neal, 64
Roberta (blk), 42
Roberta E., 107
Roberta V., 77
Rosa (blk), 310
Rose, 4, 241
Rose (blk), 4
Sally (blk), 152
Sarah, 18, 24, 40, 137, 222, 281, 284
Sarah (blk), 24, 222
Sarah (col'd), 18
Sarah Virginia, 40
Sarah W., 137
Seldra (blk), 56
Somerville, 180
Susan (blk), 278
Susanna (blk), 41
Violet A., 1
Virginia E., 18
WILLIAMSON
Ann L., 269
Harriet E., 43
Lizzie R., 23
WILLIAND
Margaret, 208
WILLIKIN
Clarissa (blk), 32
WILLING
Catharine, 252
WILLIS
Arena (blk), 290
Columbia (blk), 292
Lizzie (blk), 326
Margaret (blk), 97
Martha, 45
Winnie (blk), 205
WILLISS
Blanche, 231

WILLIVAN
Elsie (blk), 191
WILLMOURE
Mary, 153
WILLNER
Margaret A.H., 5
WILLOUGHBY
Ailsey (blk), 193
WILLS
Mary, 10
Sarah A.T., 61
WILMORE
Delia (blk), 47
WILMOT
Catharine, 219
WILNER
Mary, 169
WILSON
Adelia S., 308
Alice V., 91
Ann, 26, 28, 87, 212
Anna (blk), 26
Anna K., 87
Annie M., 212
Barbara, 263
Catherine (blk), 224, 320
Cecilia (blk), 259
Eliza, 105, 127, 308
Eliza (blk), 308
Elizabeth, 105
Ellen H., 199
Emma (blk), 157
Fanny (blk), 107, 124
Frances, 118, 210
Frances (blk), 118
Georgiana (blk), 33
Harriet (blk), 52
Henrietta, 271
Hettie (blk), 105
Jane, 18, 58
Jennie, 325
Jenny (blk), 148
Josephine, 50, 148, 176
Josephine (blk), 148, 176
Laura (blk), 56, 297

District of Columbia Marriage Licenses, 1858-1870

WILSON
  Laura L., 216
  Louise, 164
  Lucinda, 12
  Lucy (blk), 149
  Margaret, 4, 215, 280
  Margaret (blk), 215
  Margaret McA., 4
  Maria H., 173
  Marion, 15, 30
  Marion Virginia, 30
  Mary (blk), 63, 126
  Mary Frances, 248
  Mary Ann, 314
  Mary C.E., 167
  Mary E., 56, 288
  Mary Jane, 119
  Mary L., 195
  Mary V., 312
  Nancey (blk), 320
  Nettie, 270
  Olivia H. (blk), 63
  Penelope, 36
  Priscilla (blk), 269
  Rachel (blk), 23
  Rebecca (blk), 115, 138
  Rosanna, 171
  Sarah, 20, 127, 173, 175, 241, 250, 304
  Sarah (blk), 304
  Sarah E., 20
  Sarah N., 250
  Sarah V., 241
  Susan, 138, 159
  Susan S., 138
  Virginia, 3
WILTBERGER
  Edith M., 93
WILTD
  Martha M., 139
WIMER
  Elizabeth A., 148
WIMMERSBERGER
  Johanna B., 15
WIMSATT
  Mary J., 154
  Mary Lodaisca, 22

WINCHESTER
  W. W., 6f
WIND
  Margaret, 281
WINDOM
  Elizabeth C., 98
WINDSOR
  Catherine, 15
  Frances Ann, 71
  Mary, 146
WINECOVER
  Mary, 242
WINEMILLER
  Mary M., 151
WINFIELD
  Lucinda (blk), 306
  Susan V. (blk), 17
WINGATE
  Mary Jane, 105
  Sarah Emma, 160
WINGFELD
  Juliana, 211
WINGFIELD
  Elizabeth (blk), 10
  Harriet J. (blk), 321
  Henrietta C., 75
WINHOFER
  Rosina Sophia, 276
WINKFIELD
  Jane (blk), 232
WINN
  Christina W., 53
  Mary, 315
WINNY
  Sarah, 249
WINS
  Margaret, 322
WINSATT
  Annie E., 153
WINSHIP
  Isadora J., 179
WINSLEY
  Mary (blk), 7
WINSLOW
  Ann Eliza, 192
WINSTANDLEY
  Rebecca, 1
WINSTON
  Catherine (blk), 117

  Harriet, 161
WINTER
  Augusta E., 116
  Mary E., 120
WINTERS
  Carrie S., 6
  Emma, 5
  Lucy (blk), 315
WINTERSCH
  Elizabeth, 281
WIPPERMAN
  Mary, 294
WIRT
  Airey E., 50
  Sarah Jane, 297
WISE
  Agnes, 114
  Amanda (blk), 107
  Anna (blk), 310
  Annie M., 237
  Catherine Ann, 291
  Debora, 132
  Elizabeth, 281
  Kate, 208
  Laura V., 123
  Loucinda (blk), 17
  Marcia V., 209
  Mary A., 12
  Mary Ann, 33
  Mary L., 74
WISEBECKER
  Elizabeth, 73
WISELY
  Bridget, 81
WISEMAN
  Mary A., 242
WISEMULLER
  Bettie, 270
WISSMAN
  Mary Anna, 104
WISWELL
  Hester, 98
WITBECK
  Annie C., 295
WITCOX
  Helen M., 217
WITHEE
  Leah, 83

District of Columbia Marriage Licenses, 1858-1870

WITHEROW
  Kate L., 286
WITHERS
  Rosa Lee, 1
WITMAN
  Margaret Barbara, 295
WITTE
  Anne Maria Antonette, 111
WOLF
  Anne, 300
  Annie, 99
  Augusta, 243
  Louisa, 242
  Margaretta Ann, 135
  Mary Dorcas, 19
  Veronka, 217
WOLFE
  Eliza H., 38
  Hannah, 243
  Margaret, 100
  Mary Emma, 65
WOLFF
  Bertha, 46
WOLFORD
  Elizabeth, 77
WOLLARD
  Lizzie, 34
  Maria Caroline, 239
WOLLNER
  Mary, 94
WOLPHE
  Cécile Augustine, 50
WOLTZ
  Mary E., 261
WOLZ
  Mary, 277
WONN
  Susan, 296
WOOD
  Agnes (blk), 42
  Anna, 77, 242
  Anna (blk), 77
  Anne (blk), 152
  Blandina D., 27
  Celia, 236
  Drusilla A., 112

  Elizabeth, 9, 114, 262
  Elizabeth (blk), 9, 114
  Ellen, 225
  Ellen (blk), 225
  Emeline, 139
  Frances A.E., 272
  Gabrielle, 85
  Hanna V., 230
  Harriet (blk), 41
  Ida, 123
  Leah (blk), 151
  Lethea Ann (blk), 264
  Lucinda (blk), 119
  Maggie, 237
  Margaret, 207
  Margy (blk), 2
  Maria (blk), 134
  Martha E. (blk), 295
  Mary, 16, 191, 202, 232
  Mary C., 202
  Mary F. (blk), 191
  Mary Porter, 16
  Matilda (blk), 286
  Minta (blk), 320
WOODARD
  Julia Ann Eliza, 97
WOODBECK
  Maria, 29
WOODBON
  Frances, 24
WOODBURY
  Maggie Molineux, 296
WOODFALL
  Bettie (blk), 127
WOODFIELD
  Mary E., 323
WOODFOLK
  Betsey (blk), 306
WOODFORK
  Annie (blk), 179
WOODLINE
  Marsaline (blk), 212
WOODMAN
  Creecy (blk), 63

WOODRIDGE
  Sarah Jane (blk), 80
WOODRUFF
  Addie B., 92
  Amelia L., 327
  C. Elise, 73
  Eliza J., 154
  Nelia E., 157
  Virginia S., 167
WOODS
  Agnes, 280
  Annie, 80
  Elizabeth, 94, 104
  Ellen, 19
  Lydia (blk), 294
  Margaret, 195, 213
  Margaret J., 213
  Mary, 196, 321
  Rose, 163
WOODWARD
  Anna, 231
  Annie M., 322
  Elizabeth (blk), 16
  Emeline (blk), 123
  Fannie, 52
  Hester (blk), 133, 236
  Jennie, 188
  Mary, 117, 177, 204
  Mary A. (blk), 117
  Mary E., 177
  Rebecca (blk), 122
  Sarah S.J., 284
  Susan, 260
WOODWORTH
  Emma S., 201
WOODY
  Elizabeth (blk), 210
WOODYARD
  Julia (blk), 173
WOODYWARD
  Virginia, 31
WOOLFORD
  Emily, viii
  Mary Jane, 105
WOOLLS
  Anna Maria, 3
WOOLS
  Anna M., 195
  Lizzie, 3

WORDIN
  Ann Maria, 140
WORLING
  Julia, 3
WORMLEY
  Maria Louisa, 59
  Marie B., 109
WORSTER
  M.V.A.Z., 101
WORTH
  Josephine, 76
WORTHEN
  Ellen C., 239
  Laura V., 105
WORTHING
  Hellen B., 309
WORTHINGTON
  Annie, 269
  Eliza P., 230
  Ella, 269
  Frances Ann, 19
  Margaret Anna, 48
  Ratie K., 95
  Rebecca M., 49
WRAGG
  Sarah E., 243
WREN
  Catherine, 249
  Eliza L., 241
  Fannie, 140
  Margaret, 303
  Mary J., 242
WRENN
  Bettie L., 324
  Hellen A., 312
WRIGHT
  Annie P., 226
  Caroline Virginia, 278
  Catherine, 87, 194
  Chaney Ann (blk), 297
  Eliza (blk), 303
  Elizabeth, 12, 15, 95
  Elizabeth A.F., 12, 15
  Ellen, 152
  Fannie, 207
  Harriet (blk), 187
  Jennie E., 276
  Josephine, 78
  Kate (blk), 35
  Laura C., 19
  Louisa, 80
  Margaret (blk), 116
  Maria Louisa, 80
  Maria Louise (blk), 137
  Marthetta (blk), 33
  Mary (blk), 40, 149
  Mary Jane, 242
  Mary E., 299
  Mary P., 244
  Mary S., 103
  Rebecca, 240
  Sarah A., 138
  Sarah E., 42
  Susanna Emily, 77
WRIGHTSON
  Hester R., 309
WROE
  Adele, 161
  Frances (blk), 116
  Hellen Elizth., 144
  Ida, 252
  Lizzie, 311
  Maria (blk), 318
  Marian J., 307
  Mary S., 295
WRYAN
  Bridget, 218
WRYNN
  Bridget, 12
WULFORT
  Maria, 78
WUNDER
  Anna, 325
WUNDERLICH
  Eva Joanna, 296
WÜRDEMANN
  Alice, 314
WÜRSCHING
  Margaretha, 202
WYLAND
  Mary, 72
WYLIE
  M.F., 258
WYMAN
  Elizabeth, 266
  Ellen F., 215
  Malvina F., 325
WYNN
  Caroline, 36
WYVILL
  Harriet (blk), 124

—Y—

YAGER
  Matilda C., 182
YATES
  Annie M., 9
  Elizabeth (blk), 272
  Ellen (blk), 51, 140
  Julia E. (blk), 54
  Margaret, 193, 203
  Margaret (blk), 203
  Mary Virginia, 291
YEABOWER
  Annie, 281
  Hellen R., 167
YEAGER
  Catherine E., 34
YEATLESON
  Sophia, 113
YEATMAN
  Anna R., 24
YENT
  Margaretta, 239
YEO
  Pamelia J., 322
YERBY
  Cynthia Jane, 311
  Fannie J., 32
YOCHON
  Margaret, 65
YOCUM
  Margaret, 247
YORK
  Ellen, 241
  Randolph (blk), 140
YOST
  Ferderica, 120
  Mary D., 17
  Mary E., 264

YOUNG
  Alice C., 178
  Allarey Ellen, 85
  Amanda, 5, 82, 300
  Amanda (blk), 300
  Amanda G., 82
  Amazi B., vii
  Ann Maria, 117
  Anna, 146
  B. Addie, 65
  Bettie (blk), 18
  C. Alice, 16
  Carrie H., 79
  Cornelia (blk), 201
  Eliza (blk), 128
  Elizabeth, 215, 273
  Elizabeth G., 215
  Emily (blk), 303
  Emma Jane (blk), 36
  Fannie, 214
  Franc S., 300
  Frances (blk), 135
  Harriet (blk), 22
  Harriet A. (blk), 156
  Helen A. (blk), 239
  Isabella (blk), 56, 148
  Jane A., 200
  Jennie, 281
  Josephine, 207
  Maggie, 249
  Margaret, 153, 310
  Margaret E., 153
  Mary (blk), 27, 181
  Mary A., 145
  Mary B., 76
  Mary Cecilia, 72
  Mary G., 263
  Mary L., 89
  Mary P., 71
  Mary R., 142
  Mary S., 298
  Minna, 96
  Nelly, 34, 90
  Nelly (blk), 34
  Rosana (blk), 203
  Sarah, 41, 149, 274
  Sarah (blk), 274
  Sarah E. (blk), 41
  Susana V., 285
  Virginia (blk), 3
YOUNGER
  Mary, 75
  Pauline (blk), 24
YOUNT
  Susan, 313

—Z—

ZACHARY
  Annie, 234
  E.G., 15
ZAGOWITZ
  Clara, 243
ZAHN
  Maria Elizabeth, 231
ZANDER
  Magdalena, 78
ZEFONT
  Elizabeth, 45
ZEGOWITZ
  Annie Appolline, 111
ZEIR
  Mary Catherine, 80
ZEKIEL
  Adaline, 29
ZELL
  Emma, 299
  Mary, 46
ZIEGLER
  Mary, 195
ZIESLLAR
  Margaretta, 251
ZIMMERMAN
  Dora E., 4
  Elizabeth, 245
  Mary C., 228
ZINNEMAN
  Louisa, 114
ZIRKELBACH
  Caroline, 147
ZIRKLE
  Jennie M., 18
ZUNHAGNER
  Maria, 133

ZWENNER
  Katharina, 281

Other Heritage Books by Wesley E. Pippenger:

*Alexandria (Arlington) County, Virginia Death Records, 1853–1896*

*Alexandria City and Arlington County, Virginia Records Index: Vol. 1*

*Alexandria City and Arlington County, Virginia Records Index: Vol. 2*

*Alexandria County, Virginia Marriage Records, 1853–1895*

*Alexandria Virginia Marriage Index, January 10, 1893 to August 31, 1905*

*Alexandria, Virginia Marriages, 1870–1892*

*Alexandria, Virginia Town Lots, 1749–1801
Together with the Proceedings of the Board of Trustees, 1749–1780*

*Alexandria, Virginia Wills, Administrations and Guardianships, 1786–1800*

*Alexandria, Virginia 1808 Census (Wards 1, 2, 3, and 4)*

*Alexandria, Virginia Death Records, 1863–1896*

*Alexandria, Virginia Hustings Court Orders, Volume 1, 1780–1787*

*Connections and Separations: Divorce, Name Change and Other
Genealogical Tidbits from the Acts of the Virginia General Assembly*

Daily National Intelligencer *Index to Deaths, 1855–1870*

Daily National Intelligencer, *Washington, District of Columbia
Marriages and Deaths Notices (January 1, 1851 to December 30, 1854)*

*Dead People on the Move: Reconstruction of the Georgetown Presbyterian
Burying Ground, Holmead's (Western) Burying Ground, and
Other Removals in the District of Columbia*

*Death Notices from Richmond, Virginia Newspapers, 1841–1853*

*District of Columbia Ancestors, A Guide to Records of the District of Columbia*

*District of Columbia Death Records: August 1, 1874–July 31, 1879*

*District of Columbia Foreign Deaths, 1888–1923*

*District of Columbia Guardianship Index, 1802–1928*

*District of Columbia Interments (Index to Deaths)
January 1, 1855 to July 31, 1874*

*District of Columbia Marriage Licenses, Register 1: 1811–1858*

*District of Columbia Marriage Licenses, Register 2: 1858–1870*

*District of Columbia Marriage Records Index
June 28, 1877 to October 19, 1885: Marriage Record Books 11 to 20*
Wesley E. Pippenger and Dorothy S. Provine

*District of Columbia Marriage Records Index
October 20, 1885 to January 20, 1892: Marriage Record Books 21 to 30*

*District of Columbia Marriage Records Index
January 20, 1892 to August 30, 1896: Marriage Record Books 31 to 40*

*District of Columbia Marriage Records Index
August 31, 1896 to December 17, 1900: Marriage Record Books 41 to 65*

*District of Columbia Probate Records, 1801–1852*

*District of Columbia: Original Land Owners, 1791–1800*

*Early Church Records of Alexandria City and Fairfax County, Virginia*

*Georgetown, District of Columbia 1850 Federal Population Census (Schedule I) and 1853 Directory of Residents of Georgetown*

*Georgetown, District of Columbia Marriage and Death Notices, 1801–1838*

*Husbands and Wives Associated with Early Alexandria, Virginia (and the Surrounding Area), 3rd Edition, Revised*

*Index to District of Columbia Estates, 1801–1929*

*Index to District of Columbia Land Records, 1792–1817*

*Index to Virginia Estates, 1800–1865 Volumes 4, 5 and 6*

*John Alexander, a Northern Neck Proprietor, His Family, Friends and Kin*

*Legislative Petitions of Alexandria, 1778–1861*

*Pippenger and Pittenger Families*

*Proceedings of the Orphan's Court, Washington County, District of Columbia, 1801–1808*

*The Georgetown Courier Marriage and Death Notices: Georgetown, District of Columbia, November 18, 1865 to May 6, 1876*

*The Georgetown Directory for the Year 1830: to which is appended, a Short Description of the Churches, Public Institutions, and the Original Charter of Georgetown, and Extracts of the Laws Pertaining to the Chesapeake and Ohio Canal Company*

The Virginia Gazette and Alexandria Advertiser:
*Volume 1, September 3, 1789 to November 11, 1790*

The Virginia Journal and Alexandria Advertiser:
*Volume I (February 5, 1784 to January 27, 1785)*

*Volume II (February 3, 1785 to January 26, 1786)*

*Volume III (March 2, 1786 to January 25, 1787)*

*Volume IV (February 8, 1787 to May 21, 1789)*

*The Washington and Georgetown Directory of 1853*

*Tombstone Inscriptions of Alexandria, Volumes 1–4*

www.ingramcontent.com/pod-product-compliance
Lightning Source LLC
Chambersburg PA
CBHW071932240426
43668CB00038B/1248